Welcome to

Social Gerontology: A Multidisiplinary Perspective

with Research Navigator™

This text is accompanied by a manual that will help you do outside reading and research in the field of social gerontology.

To gain access to Research Navigator™, go to **www.researchnavigator.com** and log in using the passcode you'll find on the inside front cover of your *Research Navigator Guide*™.

Research Navigator™ includes three databases of dependable source material to get your research process started.

EBSCO's ContentSelect Academic Journal Database. EBSCO's ContentSelect Academic Journal Database contains scholarly, peer-reviewed journals. These published articles provide you with a specialized knowledge and information about your research topic. Academic journal articles adhere to strict scientific guidelines for methodology and theoretical grounding. The information obtained in these individual articles is more scientific than information you would find in a popular magazine, in a newspaper article, or on a Web page.

The New York Times **Search by Subject Archive.** Newspapers are considered periodicals because they are issued in regular installments (i.e., daily, weekly, or monthly) and provide contemporary information. Information in periodicals—journals, magazines, and newspapers—may be useful, or even critical, for finding up-to-date material or information to support specific aspects of your topic. Research Navigator™ gives you access to a one-year, "search by subject" archive of articles from one of the world's leading newspapers—*The New York Times*.

"Best of the Web" Link Library. Link Library, the third database included on Research Navigator™, is a collection of Web links, organized by academic subject and key terms. Searching on your key terms will provide you with a list of five to seven editorially reviewed Web sites that offer educationally relevant and reliable content. The Web links in Link Library are monitored and updated each week, reducing your incidence of finding "dead" links.

In addition, Research Navigator™ includes extensive online content detailing the steps in the research process, including:

- Starting the Research Process
- Finding and Evaluating Sources
- Citing Sources
- Internet Research
- Using Your Library
- Starting to Write

For more information on how to use Research Navigator™ go to
www.ablongman.com/aboutrn.com.

SEVENTH EDITION

SOCIAL GERONTOLOGY

A MULTIDISCIPLINARY PERSPECTIVE

Nancy R. Hooyman

University of Washington

H. Asuman Kiyak

University of Washington

Boston   New York   San Francisco
Mexico City   Montreal   Toronto   London   Madrid   Munich   Paris
Hong Kong   Singapore   Tokyo   Cape Town   Sydney

Senior Editor: Jeff Lasser
Associate Developmental Editor: Andrea Christie
Senior Marketing Manager: Krista Groshong
Editorial Production Service: Tom Conville Publishing Services, LLC
Manufacturing Buyer: JoAnne Sweeney
Cover Administrator: Linda Knowles
Electronic Composition: Omegatype Typography, Inc.

For related titles and support materials, visit our online catalog at www.ablongman.com.

Between the time Website information is gathered and then published, some sites may have closed. Also, the transcription of URLs can result in unintentional typographical errors. The publisher would appreciate being notified of any problems with URLs so that they may be corrected in subsequent editions.

Library of Congress Cataloging-in-Publication Data

Hooyman, Nancy R.
    Social gerontology : a multidisciplinary perspective / Nancy R. Hooyman, H. Asuman Kiyak.—7th ed.
        p.   cm.
    Rev. ed. of: Social gerontology. 6th ed. c2002.
    Includes bibliographical references and index.
    ISBN 0-205-44611-6
    1. Gerontology. 2. Aging. 3. Aged—United States. I. Kiyak, H. Asuman.
II. Hooyman, Nancy R. Social gerontology. III. Research navigator. IV. Title.

HQ1061.S583 2005
305.26—dc22
                                                            2004043694

Printed in the United States of America

10 9 8 7 6 5   09 08 07 06

Photo Credits
Photo credits may be found on page 665, which should be considered an extension of the copyright page.

In memory of my son, Chris, and my husband, Gene, and in celebration of my children, Kevin and Mani

—NRH

In fond memory of my parents, Yahya and Leman Kiyak; with love and gratitude to Lara and Joe

—HAK

CONTENTS

chapter **2** Historical and Cross-Cultural Issues in Aging   45

part **two**
The Biological and Physiological Context of Social Aging   65

chapter **3** The Social Consequences of Physical Aging   68 chapter **4** Managing Chronic Diseases and Promoting Well-Being in Old Age **109**

chapter 7 Love, Intimacy, and Sexuality
in Old Age   252

c h a p t e r **10** Opportunities and Stress
of Informal Caregiving   349

chapter **13** Death, Dying, Bereavement,
and Widowhood   **480**

part **five**

The Societal Context of Aging   587

PREFACE

Aging is a complex and fascinating process, one that we will all experience. It is complex because of its many facets—physiological, emotional, cognitive, economic, and interpersonal—that influence our social functioning and well-being. It is a fascinating process because these changes will occur differently in each one of us. There is considerable truth to the statement that, as we grow older, we become more unlike each other.

Aging is also a process that attracts the attention of the media, politicians, business and industry, and the general public, largely because we live in a rapidly aging society. Changes in the numbers and proportion of older people in our population have numerous implications for societal structures, including the family, health and social services, long-term care, pension and retirement practices, political processes, recreational services, and housing. In addition, these changes are of growing concern because of the problems of poverty, inadequate housing, and chronic disease faced by some older people—particularly women, ethnic minorities, the oldest-old, and those living alone. Public officials as well as individuals in the private sector are faced with the challenge of planning for a future when there will be more people over age 65 than ever before.

These changes have also meant that most colleges and universities now offer courses in *gerontology,* the study of aging. The goal of many of these courses is to prepare students to understand the process of aging and the diversity among older people and to work effectively with older adults. These programs also attempt to enhance students' personal understanding of their own and others' aging. Frequently, students take such a course simply to meet a requirement, not realizing how relevant the aging process is to their own lives. Thus, instructors are often faced with the need to help students see the connection between learning about aging and understanding their own behavior, the behavior of their relatives, and often the behavior of their clients.

This book grew out of our experiences in teaching gerontology courses to undergraduate students. In doing so, we were unable to locate a textbook that conveyed the excitement and relevance of understanding the aging process or one that adequately addressed the biological, physiological, psychological, and social aspects of aging. For years, we were frustrated by the lack of a text that was comprehensive, thorough, and current in its review of the rapidly growing research on older adults. As a sociologist/social worker and a psychologist, we have been committed to developing a text that could be useful to a wide range of disciplines, including nursing, social work, sociology, psychology, health education, and the allied health professions. We also created a text that has been found to be useful both to undergraduate and graduate students.

Aims and Focus

The primary focus of this book is *social* gerontology. As the title implies, however, our goal is to present the diversities of the aging experience and the older population in a multidisciplinary manner. It is our premise that an examination of the social lives of older people requires a basic understanding of the historical, cultural, biological, physiological, psychological, and social contexts of aging. It is important to understand the changes that occur within the aging individual, how these changes influence interactions with social and physical environments, and how the older person is, in turn, affected by such interactions. Throughout this book, the impact of these dynamic interactions between older people and their environments on their quality of life is a unifying theme.

Social gerontology encompasses a wide range of topics with exciting research in so many domains. This book does not cover all these areas, but rather highlights major research findings that illuminate the processes of aging. Through such factual information, we intend to dispel some of the myths and negative attitudes about aging. We also hope to encourage the reader to pursue this field, both academically and for the personal rewards that come from gaining insight into older people's lives. Because the field is so complex and rapidly changing, more recent research findings may appear to contradict earlier studies. We have attempted to be thorough in presenting a multiplicity of theoretical perspectives and empirical data to ensure that the reader has as full and accurate a picture of the field as possible. Because the field—and especially policies and programs—are changing so rapidly, some current revisions will inevitably be out-of-date by the time the text is published. Nevertheless, we have tried to include up-to-date content throughout.

Features

This book begins by reviewing major demographic, historical, and cross-cultural changes, and their implications for the development of the field of social gerontology, as well as methods used to study aging and older people. We then turn to the major biological and physiological changes that affect older people's daily functioning, as well as their risk of chronic diseases and consequent utilization of health and long-term care services. The third section considers psychological changes, particularly in learning and memory, personality, mental health,

and sexuality. Given our emphasis on how such physical and psychological changes affect the social aspects of aging, the fourth section examines social theories of aging, the social context of the family, friends, and other multigenerational supports, new living arrangements, productivity in the later years, and the conditions under which people die. Throughout the book, the differential effects that these changes have on women and ethnic minorities are identified, with two chapters focusing specifically on such differences as well as their strength and resilience. We conclude by turning to the larger context of social, health, and long-term care policies. To highlight the application of research findings to everyday situations, each chapter integrates discussions of both the policy and practice implications of the aging process and career opportunities as well as some predictions for what future cohorts of elders will experience. Vignettes of older people in different situations, Points to Ponder, and summary charts attempt to bring to life many of the concepts discussed in these chapters.

New to This Edition

The positive responses of faculty and students to the first six editions suggest that we have been successful in achieving our goals for this book. Based on feedback from faculty who have used the text in different colleges across the United States, the seventh edition builds on and expands many of the changes made in the sixth edition. The book is designed to be completed in a 16-week semester, but readers can proceed at a faster pace through the chapters and select only the chapters most relevant to their focus of study. Themes that underlie each chapter are the interaction of the person and environment and of the biological, psychological, and social aspects of aging, active aging and resilience, and quality of life, all within a life span perspective. The epilogue has been eliminated. Instead, most chapters include a section on Implications for the

Future and career opportunities. New research findings are presented on extending both years and quality of life, enhancing active aging, and maintaining productivity (e.g., contributing to society in a wide range of ways) through both paid and unpaid activities. Critiques of these concepts are also discussed. Recent developments on early diagnosis and treatment of dementia and depression are reviewed. The chapters on caregiving and informal supports have been rewritten to expand content on the gains as well as the burdens of caregiving, elder mistreatment, the multigenerational family, and the role of underpaid direct care workers in long-term care. The importance of health promotion has been expanded. Both the resilience and the problems faced by older women and elders of color are emphasized. Given the dramatically changing political arena, the chapters on social, health, and long-term care policies have been rewritten to reflect contemporary policy debates such as privatization of Social Security and the Medicare prescription drug law that was passed in 2003, to address the need for home and community-based alternatives to institutionalization, including the use of technology to support aging in place, and to take account of the increasing diversity of the older population.

Each chapter begins with clearly "bulleted" points to be covered in the chapter. The glossary has been reduced in length, while more resources, especially internet resources, have been added at the end of each chapter. These resources are described more fully in the companion website for this text: www.ablongman.com/hooyman.

Social Gerontology with Research Navigator™ adds a new feature to the seventh edition. This is the use of "ContentSelect," a rich and readily accessible database of contemporary publications in the scientific and popular literature. The articles selected for you to review in that database are related to topics covered in corresponding chapters; they are designed to integrate the content of this book with resources of Research Navigator™. By answering questions raised at the end of each topic in the Research Navigator™ booklet linked to the

seventh edition, you will learn more about the current debates and discussions surrounding many of the topics in each chapter. Instructions are available online at www.researchnavigator.com, and in the Research Navigator™ booklet.

Annenberg/CPB Telecourse

Social Gerontology is being offered as part of the Annenberg/CPB college-level telecourse *Growing Old in a New Age,* broadcast on PBS.

Growing Old in a New Age is a thirteen-part public television series and college-level course that provides an understanding of the processes of aging, of old age as a stage of life, and of the impact of aging on society. The course responds to the demographic wave that is sweeping our nation and our world, exploring questions about what roles people will play in their eighth, ninth, and tenth decades, and how institutions may evolve to address their needs. *Growing Old in a New Age* also offers opportunities for the student and viewer to examine personal attitudes toward aging and older people. Material contributed by outstanding social scientists, medical professionals, and clinicians provides a multidisciplinary, multicultural approach. Extensive interviews with older people themselves support this cross-cultural and comprehensive introduction to gerontology.

In addition to *Social Gerontology,* a student *Telecourse Study Guide* is available for purchase from Allyn and Bacon. *A Telecourse Faculty Guide* is available without charge from Allyn and Bacon to those who license the telecourse. The programs may be purchsed on videocassettes by calling the Annenberg/CPB Collection at 1-800-LEARNER. Off-air taping licenses may be acquired from either the Annenberg CPB Collection or the PBS Adult Learning Service. Colleges and universities may licence the use of *Growing Old in a New Age* as a telecourse for college credit through the PBS Adult Learning Service (1-800-257-2578; in Virginia, 1-703-739-5363).

A Note on Terminology

As with most other disciplines, the field of gerontology is constantly evolving and recognizing the problem of language that makes sweeping generalizations or has negative connotations. The commonly used terms "elderly," "the old," and "old people" have come to be associated with negative images of the older population. For this reason, we have chosen the terms "older adults," "older persons," and "elders" throughout this textbook. These terms parallel those of younger person/adult. The term "elder," used widely among Native Americans, typically conveys respect and honor. Another change in terminology is our use of the word "Latino" in place of "Hispanic" wherever appropriate. This is because a growing number of scholars in this community have suggested that "Hispanic" has been associated with colonialism and the conquest of Spanish-speaking people in the Americas. Except where dictated by publications such as reports of the U.S. Census Bureau (where "Hispanic" is the standard term), we have chosen to refer to older adults from Spanish-speaking origins as "Latinos" and "Latinas."

Acknowledgments

We are grateful to the many people who have contributed significantly to the successful completion of the seventh edition of *Social Gerontology*. In particular, we thank Emily Gaynor and Alison Beck for library research and help with preparing the new Research Navigator™; Justin Yeates for preparing PowerPoint charts and graphs; and Shayna Esteban and Elise De Gooyer for assistance with references. Their willingness to do whatever tasks necessary was a tremendous support. We also thank our many colleagues around the United States who have given us valuable feedback about the seventh edition: Dwight L. Adams, University of Utah, Weber State University, Salt Lake Community College, and Columbia College; M. Jocelyn Armstrong, University of Illinois at Urbana-Champaign; Michael Cheang, University of Hawaii at Manoa; Paul K. Dezendorf, Winthrop University; Gloria Fennell, University of Wisconsin-Eau Claire; W. Edward Folts, Appalachian State University; Judith E. Gallagher, University of Pittsburgh; Christina S. McCrae, University of Florida; Jo Ann O'Quin, University of Mississippi; Debra Secord, Coastline College; Sharon Hines Smith, Rutgers University; Shirley K. Sorenson, Des Moines Area Community College; and M. Jean Turner, University of Arkansas. Our families have been a mainstay of support throughout the preparation of all editions of this book, and we take this opportunity to express our gratitude to all of them.

ABOUT THE AUTHORS

Nancy R. Hooyman   Nancy R. Hooyman is professor and dean emeritus at the School of Social Work at the University of Washington in Seattle. Her Ph.D. is in sociology and social work from the University of Michigan. She is nationally recognized for her scholarship in aging, issues related to family caregiving, gender inequities in caregiving, and feminist social work practice. In addition to this textbook, Dr. Hooyman is the coauthor of *Taking Care of Aging Family Members* and *Feminist Perspectives on Family Care: Policies for Gender Justice* and has edited *Feminist Social Work Practice in Clinical Settings*. She is currently coauthoring a book, *Grieving Well Through Loss*. She has published over 100 articles and chapters related to gerontology and women's issues. Her research interests are in family caregiving of persons with chronic disabilities, feminist practice models, and older women's issues. She is Principal Investigator of the John A. Hartford Geriatric Education in Social Work Program and actively involved with the four other Hartford Geriatric Social Work Initiatives. She is a Fellow in the Gerontological Society of America, and, in 1998, she received the Career Achievement Award from the Association for Gerontology in Social Work Education.

H. Asuman Kiyak   H. Asuman Kiyak is Director of the Institute on Aging, professor in the School of Dentistry, and adjunct professor in the Departments of Architecture and Psychology at the University of Washington. She obtained her Ph.D. in psychology at Wayne State University. Professor Kiyak has been the recipient of major research grants from NIH, CDC, AOA, and private foundations in the areas of health promotion and health service utilization by older adults, and in person–environment adaptation to Alzheimer's disease by patients and their caregivers. She has published over 120 articles and 35 chapters in these areas and is known nationally and internationally for her research on geriatric dental care and the application of psychological theory to health promotion. In 2000 she received the Distinguished Scientist Award from the International Association for Dental Research, and has served as president of the Geriatric Oral Research and Behavioral Sciences and Health Services Research Groups of IADR. She is currently Principal Investigator of the first clinical trial in geriatric dentistry funded by the National Institute of Dental and Craniofacial Research, a community-based intergenerational health promotion grant from the CDC, and collaborating with Intel to test new technologies for older adults with dementia. In 2003 she was named Distinguished Professor of Geriatrics at UCLA, and received the Teaching Excellence Award from the University of Washington Educational Outreach division. Professor Kiyak is a Fellow in the Gerontological Society of America.

part One

Toward Understanding Aging

From the perspective of youth and middle age, old age seems a remote and, to some, an undesirable period of life. Throughout history, humans have tried to prolong youth and to delay aging. The attempts to discover a substance to rejuvenate the body and mind have driven explorers to far corners of the globe and have inspired alchemists and scientists to search for ways to restore youth and extend life. Indeed, the discovery of Florida by Ponce de Leon in 1513 was an accident, as he searched for a fountain in Bimini whose waters were rumored to bring back one's youth. Medieval Latin alchemists believed that eating gold could add years to life and spent many years trying to produce a digestible form of gold. In the seventeenth century, a popular belief was that smelling fresh earth each morning could prolong one's youth. The theme of prolonging or restoring youth is evident today in advertisements for skin creams, soaps, vitamins, and certain foods; in the popularity of cosmetic surgery; in books and movies that feature attractive, youthful-looking older characters; and even in medical research that is testing technological methods to replace depleted hormones in older people in an attempt to rejuvenate aging skin and physical and sexual functioning. One organization, by its name, reveals its bias that aging is a disease or process that can be fought or prevented. The International Academy of

The Field of Social Gerontology

Anti-Aging Medicine actually promotes preventive and naturopathic medicine, but its name suggests a more negative view of aging than does its goal.

All these concerns point to underlying fears of aging. Many of our concerns and fears arise from misconceptions about what happens to our bodies, our minds, our status in society, and our social lives as we reach our 70s, 80s, and beyond. They arise, in part, from negative attitudes toward older people within our own culture. These attitudes are sometimes identified as manifestations of **ageism,** a term that was coined by Robert Butler, the first Director of the National Institute on Aging, to describe stereotypes about

Most people are unprepared for the physical and cognitive signs of aging. As Leo Tolstoy noted, "Old age is the most unexpected of all things that happen to a man."

old age. As is true for sexism and racism, ageism attributes certain characteristics to all members of a group solely because of a characteristic they share—in this case, their age. In fact, ageism is one prejudice that we are all likely to encounter sooner or later, regardless of our gender, ethnic minority status, social class, or sexual orientation. A frequent result of ageism is discriminatory behavior against the target group (i.e., older persons). For example, some aging advocates have argued that older, experienced workers are encouraged to retire early because of stereotypes about older people's abilities and productivity. Instead, advocates suggest that employers should consider each worker's skills and experience when organizational restructuring requires layoffs.

To distinguish the realities of aging from the social stereotypes surrounding this process requires an understanding of the "normal" changes that can be expected in the aging body, in mental and emotional functioning, and in social interactions and status. Aging can then be understood as a phase of growth and development—a universal biological phenomenon. Accordingly, the normal processes due to age alone need to be differentiated from pathological changes or disease. As life expectancy increases, as the older proportion of our population grows, and as more of us can look forward to becoming older ourselves, concerns and questions about the aging process continue to attract widespread public and professional attention.

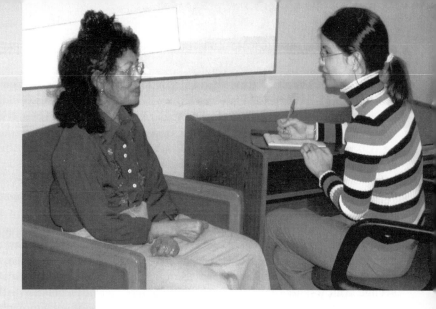

1

The Growth of Social Gerontology

The Field of Gerontology

The growing interest in understanding the process of aging has given rise to the multidisciplinary field of **gerontology,** the study of the biological, psychological, and social aspects of aging. Gerontologists include researchers and practitioners in such diverse fields as biology, medicine, nursing, dentistry, physical and occupational therapy, psychology, psychiatry, sociology, economics, political science, pharmacy and social work. These individuals are concerned with many aspects of aging, from studying and describing the cellular processes involved to seeking ways to improve the quality of life for older people. **Geriatrics** focuses on how to prevent or manage the diseases of aging. Geriatrics has become a specialty in medicine, nursing, and dentistry, and is receiving more attention with the increase in the number of older people who have long-term health problems.

Gerontologists view aging in terms of four distinct processes that are examined throughout this book:

- *Chronological aging* is the definition of aging on the basis of a person's years from birth. Thus, a 75-year-old is chronologically older than a 45-year-old. Chronological age is not necessarily related to a person's biological or physical age, nor to his or her psychological or social age, as we will emphasize throughout this book. For example, we may remark that someone "looks younger (or older)" or "acts younger (or older)" than her or his age. This implies that the individual's *biological* or *psychological* or *social age* is incongruent with the *chronological age*.
- *Biological aging* refers to the physical changes that reduce the efficiency of organ systems, such as the lungs, heart, and circulatory system. A major cause of biological aging is the decline in the number of cell replications as an organism becomes chronologically older. Another factor is the loss of certain types of cells that do not replicate. This type of aging can be determined by measuring the efficiency and functional abilities of an individual's organ systems, as well as physical activity levels. Indeed, some have referred to this as *functional aging* (Hayflick, 1996).
- *Psychological aging* includes the changes that occur in sensory and perceptual processes, mental functioning (e.g., memory, learning, and intelligence), adaptive capacity, and personality. Thus, an individual who is intellectually active and adapts well to new situations can be considered psychologically young.
- *Social aging* refers to an individual's changing roles and relationships with family and friends, in both paid and unpaid productive roles, and within organizations such as religious and political groups. As people age chronologically, biologically, and psychologically, their social roles and relationships also alter. The social context, which can vary considerably for different people, determines the meaning of aging for an individual and

whether the aging experience will be primarily negative or positive.

Social gerontologists study the impact of changes on both older people and social structures. They also study social attitudes toward aging and the effects of these attitudes on older adults. For example, as a society, we have tended to undervalue older people and to assume that most of them are less intelligent than younger people; that they are unemployable, nonproductive, uninterested in interacting with younger people, forgetful, and asexual. As a result, they have been limited in their access to activities such as jobs in high-tech fields. The research reviewed throughout this book demonstrates that these stereotypes are not true for the great majority of older adults and that many continue to participate actively in society.

With the rapid growth in the number and diversity of older persons, societal myths and stereotypes are increasingly being challenged. The public has become more aware of older citizens' strengths and contributions. Accordingly, the status of older people and the way they are viewed by other segments of the U.S. population are changing. Contemporary advertising, for example, reflects the changing status of older people from a group that is viewed as weak, ill, and poor to one perceived as politically and economically powerful and, therefore, a growing market.

As older people have become more politically active and as age-based advocacy groups have emerged, they have influenced not only public perceptions, but also policies and programs such as Social Security and Medicare. In the past 50 years, organized groups of older people have helped make changes in retirement and pension policies, housing options, health and long-term care policy, education, and other services. As described in Chapter 12, age-based advocacy is being replaced by cross-generational collaboration today.

Equally significant in this area of study are the social and health problems that continue to affect a large percentage of older people. Even though older adults today are financially better off than they were 50 years ago, slightly less than 11 percent still fall below the U.S. government's official poverty line. Poverty is an even greater problem for women, older people of color, those living alone, and the oldest of the old. Although less than 5 percent of the older population resides in nursing homes at any given time, the number who will require long-term care at some point in their lives is increasing. Growing percentages of older people in the community face chronic diseases that may limit their daily activities. At the same time, however, health and long-term care costs have escalated. In general, older people pay a higher proportion of their income for health and long-term care than they have at any time in the past, and often lack access to publicly supported home- and community-based services. Therefore, many gerontologists are also concerned with developing public policy and practice interventions to address these problems.

Social Gerontology

The purpose of this book is to introduce you to *social gerontology.* This term was first used by Clark Tibbitts in 1954 to describe the area of gerontology that is concerned with the impact of social and sociocultural conditions on the process of aging and with the social consequences of this process. This field has grown as we have recognized the extent to which aging differs across cultures and societies.

Social gerontologists are interested in how the older population and the diversity of aging experiences both affect and are affected by the social structure. As discussed later in this chapter, older people are now the fastest-growing population segment in the United States. This fact has far-reaching social implications for health and long-term care, the workplace, pension and retirement practices, community facilities, and patterns of government spending. Already, it has led to new specialties in health care and long-term care; the growth of specialized services such as assisted living and adult day health programs; and a leisure industry aimed at the older population. Changes in the sociopolitical structure, in turn, affect characteristics of the older population. For example, the greater availability of secondary and higher education, health promotion programs, and employment-based pensions offers hope that future generations of older people will be better educated, healthier, and economically more secure than the current generation.

What Is Aging?

Contrary to the messages on birthday cards, aging does not start at age 40 or 65. Even though we are less conscious of age-related changes in earlier stages of our lives, we are all aging from the moment of birth. In fact, **aging** in general refers to changes that take place in the organism throughout the life span—good, bad and neutral. Younger stages are referred to as *development* or *maturation,* because the individual develops and matures, both socially and physically, from birth through adolescence. After age 30, additional changes occur that reflect normal declines in all organ systems. This is called **senescence.** Senescence happens gradually throughout the body, ultimately reducing the viability of different bodily systems and increasing their vulnerability to disease. This is the final stage in the development of an organism (International Longevity Center, 1999).

Our place in the social structure also changes throughout our life span. Every society is *age-graded;* that is, it assigns different roles, expectations, opportunities, status, and constraints to people of different ages. For example, there are common societal expectations about the appropriate age to attend school, begin work, have children, and retire—even though many people deviate from these expectations, and some of these

POINTS TO PONDER

For each age group below, think of one activity or event that you think is typical for that age. These might include marriage, attending school, learning to ride a bike. Then think of an activity or event that is not so typical:

	TYPICAL	ATYPICAL
Toddler (ages 2–4)		
Child (ages 4–12)		
Young adult (ages 18–24)		
Old person (age 65+)		

expectations change over time. To call someone a *toddler, child, young adult,* or an *old person* is to imply a full range of social characteristics. As we age, we pass through a sequence of defined stages, each with its own social norms and characteristics. In sum, age is a social construct with social meanings and social implications.

The specific effects of age grading, or age stratification, vary across different cultures and historical time periods. A primitive society, for instance, has very different expectations associated with stages of childhood, adolescence, and old age from our contemporary American cultures. Even within our own culture, those who are old today have different experiences of aging than previous or future groups of older people. The term **cohort** is used to describe groups of people who were born at approximately the same time and therefore share many common experiences. For example, current cohorts of older persons experienced the Great Depression, World War II, and the Korean War. These experiences have shaped their lives. Its members include large numbers of immigrants who came to the United States in the first third of the twentieth century, and many who have grown up in rural areas. Their average levels of education are lower than those of later generations. Such factors set today's older population apart from other cohorts and must be taken into account in any studies of the aging process.

The Older Population Is Diverse

Throughout this book, we will refer to the phenomenon of aging and the population of older people. These terms are based, to some extent, on chronological criteria, but, more importantly, on individual differences in functional age. In fact, each of us differs somewhat in the way we define old age. You may know an 80-year-old who seems youthful and a 50-year-old whom you consider old. Older people also define themselves differently. Some individuals, even in their eighties, do not want to associate with "those old people," whereas others readily join age-based organizations and are proud of the years they have lived. There are significant differences among the "young-old" (ages 65–74), the "old-old" (ages 75–84), and the "oldest-old" (ages 85 and over) (Riley & Riley, 1986). In addition, intragenerational diversity exists even within these divisions.

Older people vary greatly in their health status, their productive activities, and their family situations. Some are still employed full- or part-time; most are retired. Most are healthy; some are frail, confused, or homebound. Most still live in a house or apartment; a small percentage are in nursing homes. Some receive large incomes from pensions and investments; most depend primarily on Social Security and have little discretionary income. Most men over age 65 are married, whereas women are more likely to become widowed and live alone as they age. For all these reasons, we cannot consider the social aspects of aging without also assessing the impact of individual variables such as physiological changes, health status, psychological well-being, socioeconomic class, gender, and ethnic minority status. Recognizing this, many chapters in this book focus on biological, physiological, health, psychological, gender, and ethnic minority characteristics of older persons that influence their social functioning and active aging.

It is likewise impossible to define aging only in chronological terms, since chronological age only partially reflects the biological, psychological, and sociological processes that define life stages. Although the terms *elders, elderly,* and *older persons*

POINTS TO PONDER

Discuss with friends and family some common terms used to describe older adults, such as "elderly," "old folks," and "elders." What images of aging and older people do these terms convey?

are often used to mean those over 65 years in chronological age, this book is based on the principle that aging is a complex process that involves many different factors and is unique to each individual. Rather than chronological age, the more important distinction may be functional ability—that is, the ability to perform activities of daily living that require cognitive and physical well-being.

An Active Aging Framework

The concept of "active aging" is an important new perspective in gerontology. It is defined by the World Health Organization as "the process of optimizing opportunities for health, participation, and security in order to enhance quality of life as people age" (WHO, 2002). This concept focuses on

improving quality of life for all people, including those who are frail, disabled, or require some assistance with daily activities. "Active aging" is consistent with the growing emphasis on independence and autonomy with aging, regardless of physical and mental decline, which benefits both the individual and society. Such a definition also shifts our thinking of old age as a time of passivity to one of continued participation in the family, community, workplace, and religious and political life. It serves as a useful framework for this textbook as we address the growing number of studies that support the importance of active aging for physical, psychological, and social well-being in the later years.

Consistent with the approach underlying this book, the active aging perspective implies that aging is a lifelong process. As a result, people's lifestyles, socioeconomic status, health care, and intellectual and social activities in their youth and middle years determine the quality of their lives in their later years. This is also an important assumption of other models of active aging that we will introduce later in this book, including the concepts of "resilient," "successful," "robust," and "productive" aging. Accordingly, the determinants of active aging, as shown in Figure 1.1, include

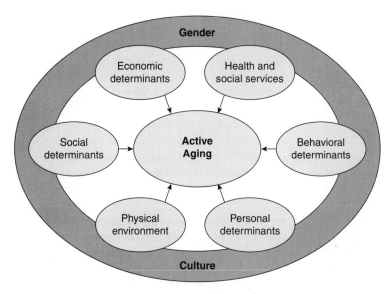

FIGURE 1.1   The Determinants of Active Aging
SOURCE: World Health Organization, *Active ageing: A policy framework* (WHO: 2002).

individual behavior, personal characteristics, the physical and social environment (e.g., family, friends, and informal and formal support systems), economic security, and access to and use of health and social services. This model also places great importance on cultural and gender variables that influence opportunities for active aging, such as discrimination as well as educational and employment opportunities across the life span. This perspective thus suggests that inequities that limit opportunities earlier in the life cycle generally persist in old age (Stoller and Gibson, 2000).

A Person–Environment Perspective on Social Gerontology

Consistent with the perspective of the interaction of physiological, psychological, and social changes with aging, this textbook will approach topics in social gerontology from a person–environment perspective. A **person–environment perspective** suggests that the environment is not a static backdrop but changes continually as the older person takes from it what he or she needs, controls what can be manipulated, and adjusts to conditions that cannot be changed. Adaptation thus implies a dual process in which the individual adjusts to some characteristics of the social and physical environment (e.g., completing the numerous forms required by Medicare), and brings about changes in others (e.g., lobbying to expand Medicare benefits to cover prescription drugs).

Environmental Press

The **competence model** is one useful way to view the dynamic interactions between the person's physical and psychological characteristics and the social and physical environment (Lawton and Nahemow, 1973; Lawton, 1989; Parmelee and Lawton, 1990). *Environment* in this model, which is shown in Figure 1.2, may refer to the larger society, the community, the neighborhood, or the

home. **Environmental press** is defined as the demands that social and physical environments make on the individual to adapt, respond, or change. The environmental press model can be approached from a variety of disciplinary perspectives. A concept fundamental to social work, for example, is that of human behavior and the environment, and the need to develop practice and policy interventions that achieve a better fit between the person and his or her social environment. Health care providers are increasingly aware of the necessity to take account of social and physical environmental factors (e.g., family caregiver and living situation) in their assessments of health problems.

Architects and advocates for persons with disabilities are developing ways to make physical environments more accessible. Psychologists are interested in how physical and social environments may be modified to maximize the older person's ability to learn new tasks and perform familiar ones such as driving, taking tests, and self-care. Sociologists study ways that the macroenvironment (larger political and economic structures) affects and is affected by an individual's interactions with it. Because the concepts of this model are so basic to understanding the position of older people and to developing ways to improve the quality of their lives, such environmental interactions are referred to throughout this text.

The environmental press in such settings can range from minimal to quite high. For example, often very little environmental press is present in an institutional setting where an individual is not responsible for self-care, such as personal grooming and housekeeping, and has few resources to stimulate the senses or challenge the mind. Other environments can create a great deal of press—for example, a multigenerational household in which the older person plays a pivotal role. Living in a familiar setting with few visitors generates low levels of environmental press. An increase in the number of people sharing the living arrangement or a move to a new home increases the environmental demands. As the demands change, the in-

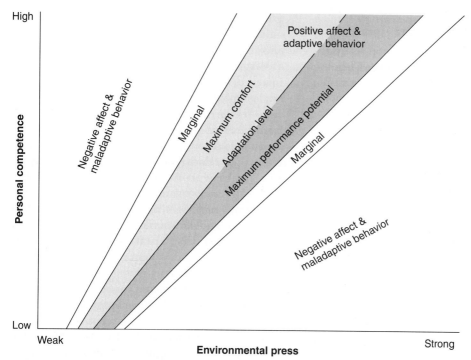

FIGURE 1.2   Diagrammatic Representation of the Behavioral and Affective Outcomes of Person–Environment Transactions

SOURCE: M. P. Lawton and L. Nahemow, Ecology and the aging process. In C. Eisdorfer and M. P. Lawton (Eds.), *Psychology of adult development and aging* (Washington, D.C.: American Psychological Association, 1973). p. 661. Copyright 1973 by the American Psychological Association. Reprinted by permission of the author and publisher.

dividual must adapt to the changes in order to maintain one's sense of competence.

Individuals perform at their maximum level when the environmental press slightly exceeds the level at which they adapt. In other words, the environment challenges them to test their limits but does not overwhelm them. If the level of environmental demand becomes too high, the individual experiences excessive stress or overload. When the environmental press is far below the individual's adaptation level, sensory deprivation, boredom, learned helplessness, and dependence on others may result. However, a situation of mild to moderate stress, just below the person's adaptation level, results in maximum comfort. It is important to challenge the individual in this situation as

well, to prevent a decline to boredom and inadequate stimulation. In either situation—too much or too little environmental press—the person or the environment must change, if the individual's adaptive capacity is to be restored and quality of life enhanced.

Individual competence is another concept central to this model. This is defined by Lawton and Nahemow (1973) as the theoretical upper limit of an individual's abilities to function in the areas of health, social behavior, and cognition. Some of the capacities needed to adapt to environmental press include good health, effective problem-solving and learning skills, job performance, and the ability to manage the basic activities of daily living such as dressing, grooming, and cooking (Parmelee and Lawton, 1990). As suggested by the model in Figure 1.2, the higher a person's competence, the higher the levels of environmental press that can be tolerated. Thus, an older person with multiple physical disabilities and chronic illnesses has reduced physical competence, which may limit the level of social and physical demands with which he or she can cope.

Environmental Interventions

The competence model has numerous implications for identifying interventions to enhance the quality of older adults' lives. Most services for older people are oriented toward minimizing environmental demands and increasing supports. These services may focus on changing the physical or the social environment, or both. Physical environmental modifications, such as ramps and handrails, and community services, such as Meals-on-Wheels and escort vans, are relatively simple ways to reestablish the older person's level of adaptation and to ease the burdens of daily coping. Such arrangements are undoubtedly essential to the well-being of some older people who require supports in the form of environmental adaptations or occasional assistance from family and paid caregivers to enhance their independence. For example, many older people with chronic conditions are able to remain in their own homes because of environmental modifications such as emergency systems that allow them to call for help, vans equipped for wheelchairs, computers that aid them with communication, and medication reminders.

POINTS TO PONDER

Think about your own home. In what ways would it create high environmental press for an older person with multiple health problems? How could you change it to make it more congruent with the older user's level of personal competence, in order to help him or her achieve positive affect and adaptive behavior?

Other examples of both environmental and individual interventions to enhance older people's choices are considered throughout this text.

A fine line exists, however, between minimizing excessive environmental press and creating an environment that is not stimulating or is "too easy" to navigate. Well-intentioned families, for example, may do too much for the older person, assuming responsibility for daily activities, so that their older relative no longer has to exert any effort and may no longer feel he or she is a contributing family member. Likewise, professionals and family members may try to shield the older person from experiencing too many changes. For example, they may presume that an older person is too set in her or his ways to adjust to sharing a residence, thereby denying the person the opportunity to learn about and make an independent decision on home-sharing options. Well-intentioned nursing home staff may not challenge residents to perform such daily tasks as getting out of bed or going to the dining hall. Protective efforts such as these can remove necessary levels of environmental press, with the result that the person's social, psychological, and physical levels of functioning may decline. Understimulating conditions, then, can be as negative in their effects on older people as those in which there is excessive environmental press.

Organization of the Text

This book is divided into five parts:

- Part One is a general introduction to the field of social gerontology and the demographics of an aging society, and includes a brief history of the field, the growth of the older population, a discussion of research methods and designs, and descriptions of aging in other historical periods and cultures.
- Part Two addresses the physiological changes that influence social aging. It begins with a review of normal age-related changes in the body's major

organ systems, including changes in the sensory system and their social/environmental effects. It also discusses the chronic diseases that occur most frequently among older people, how these diseases can be managed, factors that influence health care behavior (e.g., when and why older people are likely to seek professional care), and health promotion programs aimed at improving physical, psychological, and social functioning among older people.

- In Part Three, we move to the psychological context of aging; this includes normal and disease-related changes in cognitive functioning (learning, intelligence, and memory), theories of personality development and coping styles, mental health issues, and the use of mental health services, as well as love, intimacy, and sexuality in the later years.

- Part Four explores the social issues of aging, beginning with a discussion of current social theories of aging, the importance of family, friends, and neighbors for elders, informal caregiving of older adults, and how the array of housing arrangements for older adults affects their social interactions and sense of competence. Issues related to productivity, employment, retirement, and income are next explored, followed by a review of unpaid productive roles in the community, educational and religious institutions, and politics. This part concludes with topics related to death, dying, and widowhood. The last two chapters of Part Four present both the challenges and strengths of older ethnic minorities and women.

- Part Five goes beyond the individual's social context to address societal perspectives, particularly social, health, and long-term care policy issues and contemporary policy debates.

Each part begins with an introduction to the key issues of aging that are discussed in that section. In order to emphasize the variations in physiological, psychological, social, and societal aspects of aging, vignettes of older people representing these differences are presented. Throughout each chapter, the diversity of the older population and of the aging process itself is high-lighted in terms of chronological age, gender, culture, ethnic minority status, and sexual orientation. Where appropriate, the dynamic interaction between older people and their environment is emphasized. How age-related changes are measured and methods for improving measurement in this field are also discussed.

We encourage you to read the facts and examples in the boxed material, which illustrate some of the key concepts discussed in the chapters. At the end of each chapter you will find a brief description of emerging trends, possible future directions relevant to that topic and implications for careers in gerontology. These projections are based on population trends and biological, social, and psychological research that allows us to glean some ideas of what aging will be like by the middle of the twenty-first century. A new feature of the seventh edition is the use of "ContentSelect," a rich and readily accessible database of publications in the scientific and popular literature. Questions in the accompanying booklet explore in greater detail some of the controversies and concerns in the field of aging. By using Content Select to answer the questions, you learn more about these topics as you search for the articles cited in the questions. Each chapter concludes with a glossary of key terms that have been introduced as well as Web-based and print resources.

Why Study Aging?

As you begin this text, you may find it useful to think about your own motivations for learning about older adults and the aging process. You may be in a required course, questioning its relevance, and approaching this text as something you must read to satisfy requirements. Or you may have personal reasons for wishing to learn about aging. You may be concerned about your own age-related changes, wondering whether reduced energy or alterations in physical features are inevitable with age. After all, since middle and old age together encompass a longer time span than any other stage of our lives, it is important that we understand and prepare for these years. Perhaps you are looking forward to the freedom made possible by retirement and the "empty nest." Through increased knowledge about the aging process, you may be hoping to make decisions that can enhance your own positive adaptation to aging and old age. Or perhaps you are interested in assisting aging relatives, friends, and neighbors, wanting to know what can be done to help them maintain their independence, what housing options exist for them, and how you can improve your caregiving abilities.

Learning about aging not only gives us insight into our own interpersonal relationships, self-esteem, competence, and meaningful activities as we grow older; it also helps us comprehend the aging process of our parents, grandparents, clients, patients, and friends. It is important to recognize that change and growth take place throughout the life course, and that the concerns of older people are not distinct from those of the young, but represent a continuation of earlier life periods. Such understanding can improve our effectiveness in communicating with relatives, friends, or professionals. In addition, such knowledge can help change any assumptions or stereotypes we may hold about behavior appropriate to various ages.

Perhaps you wish to work professionally with older people, but are unsure how your interests can fit in with the needs of the older population. Career, opportunities, and needs in gerontology are discussed throughout this book. If you are already working with older people, you may genuinely enjoy your work, but you may be concerned about the social and economic problems facing some older adults and thus feel a responsibility to change these negative social conditions. As a professional or future professional working with older people, you are probably eager to learn more about policy and practice issues that can enhance their quality of life and life satisfaction.

Regardless of your motivations for reading this text, chances are that, like most Americans,

you have some misconceptions about older people and the aging process. As products of our youth-oriented society, we have all sensed the pervasiveness of negative attitudes about aging, although our own personal experiences with older people may counter many stereotypes and myths. By studying aging and older people, you will not only become more aware of the older population's competence in many areas, but also be able to differentiate the normal changes that are associated with the aging process from pathological or disease-related changes. Such an understanding may serve to reduce some of your own fears about aging, as well as positively affect your professional and personal interactions with older people.

Our challenge as educators and authors is to present you with the facts and the concepts that will give you a more accurate picture of the experience of aging in U.S. society. We also want to convey to you the excitement and importance of learning about the field of aging. We hope that by the time you have completed this text, you will have acquired information that strengthens positive attitudes toward living and working with older people and toward your own experience of aging. First, we will turn to the demographic changes that are resulting in the largest population of people aged 65 and older in history, not just in the United States, but also throughout the world.

Growth of the Older Population

The growing size of the older population is the single most important factor affecting current interest in the field of gerontology. In 1900, people over 65 accounted for approximately 4 percent of the United States population—less than one in twenty-five. Today, slightly more than 100 years later, this segment of our population has grown to 35 million, or 12.4 percent of the United States (U.S. Administration on Aging, 2002). This represents a twelve-fold increase in the older population during this period, compared with a threefold increase in the population under age 65. Population growth for this age group declined slightly between 1990 and 2000 because of the low birthrates experienced in the United States during the Great Depression (1929–1935). After 2010, however, as the baby boom generation begins to reach old age, the population over 65 will again increase significantly. Thus, demographers predict that by 2030 the population aged 65 and older may be as high as 70.3 million, representing a 100 percent increase over 30 years, compared with a 30 percent growth in the total population.*

Changes in Life Expectancy

Why have these changes in the older population occurred? Chiefly because people are living longer. In 1900, the average **life expectancy** at birth in the United States (i.e., the average length of time one could expect to live if one were born that year) was 47 years. At that time, there were approximately 772,000 people between the ages of 75 and 84 in the United States, and only 123,000 aged 85 and older. In 2000 there were over 4.2 million in the oldest group. The average life expectancy is now much longer. Females born in 2000 can expect to reach age 79.5, and men, age 74.1 (U.S. Census Bureau, 2001b). About four out of five individuals can now expect to reach age 65, at which point there is a better than 50 percent chance of living past age 80.

According to the Census Bureau, life expectancy at birth is expected to increase from the current 76.9 years to 77.6 in 2005 and to 82.6 in 2050. Sex differences in life expectancy have declined since 1980, when females born that year could expect to live 7.4 years more than men; in 2000 the difference was only 5.4 years. Projec-

tions by the Census Bureau assume a fairly constant 5- to 6-year difference in life expectancy well into the future. Therefore, females born in 2005 are expected to reach age 81; males in that birth cohort will reach age 74. Even in the year 2050, however, male life expectancy will be less than 80 years, whereas women will achieve 84.3 years (U.S. Census Bureau, 2001b). Of course, these projections do not take into account potentially new diseases that could differentially increase mortality risks for men and women. For example, if AIDS continues to be a fatal disease that infects younger men more than women, there could be a much greater sex differential in life expectancy. On the other hand, death rates due to hypertension and stroke have already started to decline because of lifestyle changes. Since both conditions are somewhat more likely to affect men, these factors may narrow the sex differential and increase life expectancy even more for both men and women. Nevertheless, the trend illustrated in Figure 1.3, where women outnumber men at every age after 55, will continue well into this century.

Most of the gains in life expectancy have occurred in the younger ages. For example, during the period from 1900 to 2000, the average life expectancy at birth increased from 47 years to 77 years. Although less dramatic, gains in life expectancy beyond age 65 during this same period have also occurred, from about 12.3 to 17.9 years between 1900 and 2000. Gender differences are particularly striking; older men can expect to live 16.3 years, and women 19.2 years, after age 65. The gains that occurred in the early years of life are largely attributable to the eradication in the prior century of many diseases that caused high infant and childhood mortality. On the other hand, increases in survival beyond age 65 may increase significantly in future cohorts, when heart disease and cancer become more chronic and less fatal diseases in adulthood. Already there has been an acceleration of years gained. Between 1900 and 1960 only 2.4 years were gained beyond age 65, while the gain since 1960 has been 3.7 years.

---

*Estimates by the Urban Institute and the Census Bureau range from a low of 64.3 million to 70.3 million (National Academy, 1999).

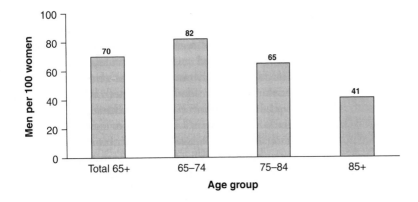

FIGURE 1.3 **Number of Men per 100 Women by Age: 2000**
SOURCE: U.S. Census Bureau, 2001b.

This shift results mostly from advances in medicine. A hundred years ago, adults generally died from acute diseases, with influenza and pneumonia the principal killers. Few people survived these diseases long enough to need care for chronic or long-term conditions. Today, death from acute diseases is rare. Maternal, infant, and early childhood death rates have also declined considerably. The result is a growing number of people who survive to old age, often with one or more health problems requiring long-term care. The evidence from epidemiological studies suggests that older Americans are receiving better health care than their counterparts in other developed countries. As a result, white Americans at age 80 have a greater life expectancy (women = 9.1 years, men = 7 years) than 80-year-olds in Sweden, Japan, France, and England, even though life expectancy at birth is higher in Sweden and Japan (Manton and Vaupel, 1995).

Maximum Life Span

It is important to distinguish life expectancy from **maximum life span.** While life expectancy is a probability estimate based on environmental conditions such as disease and health care, as described previously, maximum life span is the maximum number of years a given species could expect to live if environmental hazards were eliminated. There appears to be a maximum biologi-

cally determined life span for cells that comprise the organism, so that even with the elimination of all diseases, we could not expect to live much beyond 120 years. For these reasons, more and more persons will expect to live longer, but the maximum number of years they can expect to live will not be increased in the foreseeable future unless, of course, some extraordinary and unanticipated biological discoveries occur. Research on some biological factors that may increase longevity for future cohorts is discussed in Chapter 3.

Perhaps the most important goal of health planners and practitioners should be to approach a rectangular survival curve, that is, the "ideal curve." As seen in the survival curve in Figure 1.4, developments in medicine, public hygiene, and health have already increased the percentage of people surviving into the later years. The ideal situation is one where all people would survive to the maximum life span, creating a "rectangular curve." The survival curves of developed countries serve as a model for developing countries; that is, about 50 percent of all babies born today in developed countries will reach age 80, or two-thirds of the maximum life span of 120 years (Hayflick, 1996). We are approaching this ideal curve, but it will not be achieved until the diseases of youth and middle age—including cancer, heart disease, diabetes, and kidney diseases—can be totally prevented or at least managed as chronic conditions.

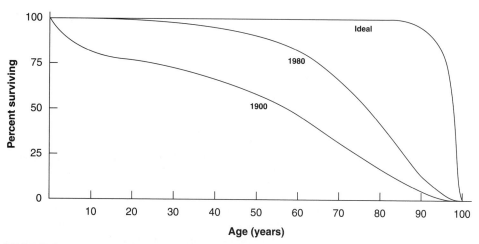

FIGURE 1.4 **Increasing Rectangularization of the Survival Curve**
SOURCE: Adapted from L. Hayflick, The cell biology of human aging. *Scientific American,* 1980, *242,* p. 60, by permission of the publisher.

MORE FORMER U.S. PRESIDENTS AND FIRST LADIES ARE ALIVE TODAY

One example of the increasing likelihood of survival beyond age 65 is the current number of U.S. presidents who are still alive. In 2003, six were still alive, from Ronald Reagan at age 92 to Gerald Ford at 89, George Bush and Jimmy Carter at age 78, Bill Clinton and George H. Bush at age 57. This was not the case at any other point in U.S. history. As an illustration of greater longevity among women beyond age 65, in 2003 there were seven surviving former first ladies.

Picture taken during a dinner in honor of the 200th Anniversary of the White House in 2000. Photo courtesy Associated Press (AP).

The Oldest-Old

Ages 85 and Older

The population aged 85 and older, also referred to as the "oldest-old," has grown more rapidly than any other age group in our country. In 2000, of the 35 million persons aged 65 and over in the United States:

- Twelve million or 35.3 percent were age 75 to 84.
- More than 12 percent were age 85 and over (U.S. Bureau of the Census, 2001b).

Since World War II, mortality rates in adulthood have declined significantly, resulting in an un-precedented number of people who are reaching advanced old age and who are most likely to re-quire long-term care.

- The oldest-old population of Americans has increased by a factor of 23.
- The old-old (ages 75–84) have increased twelvefold.
- The young-old (ages 65–74) increased eight-fold.

Those over age 85 have increased by more than 300 percent from 1960 to 2000, to 4.2 million. As Table 1.1 illustrates, the oldest-old population has

WHO ARE THE OLDEST-OLD?

- Not surprisingly, the great majority are women (70 percent).
- Their educational level is lower than for those aged 65 to 74 (8.6 years vs. 12.1 in 1990),
- Most are widowed, divorced, or never married (77.2 percent vs. 62 percent).
- Their mean personal income is lower than for young-old cohorts,
- A high proportion live below or near poverty (19 percent of married persons 85 and older were classified as poor or near poor in 1998, com-pared with 11 percent of their counterparts aged 65–69) (SSA.gov/policy/pubs, 2000).
- The current cohort of oldest-old includes 15 percent who are foreign born. Many immigrated from Italy, Poland, Russia, and other European countries in the early 1900s, while others are later immigrants from China, Japan, the Philip-pines, Vietnam, and Mexico. The usual problems of aging may be exacerbated for these non-native speakers of English as they try to commu-nicate with health care providers. Misdiagnosis of physical, psychological, and cognitive dis-orders may occur in such cases.

grown much more rapidly than other segments of the United States. In just ten years their numbers grew at a rate more than 20 times that of 15- to 44-year-olds and more than three times that of the total population aged 65 and older. This does not mean that their absolute numbers are higher than the younger groups in Table 1.1, but that their rate of increase is much faster. Demographers project this age group to number 8.9 million by 2030, more than twice their current number. However, these projections vary depending on assumptions about changes in chronic disease morbidity and mortality rates (U.S. Administration on Aging, 2002), as we will see in Chapter 4. They are ex-pected to reach 8.9 million in 2030, although pro-jections vary depending on predictions about changes in chronic disease morbidity and mortal-ity rates (U.S. Administration on Aging, 2002).

TABLE 1.1   **Population Increase per Age Group: United States (in millions)**

YEAR	AGE		
	15–44	65+	85+
1960		16.6	0.9
1990	118	31.1	3.02
2000	120	35.0	4.2
Increase (1990–2000)	1.7%	12.5%	39%

SOURCE: U.S. Census Bureau, 2001b.

This tremendous growth in the oldest-old will take place *before* the influx of baby boomers reaches old age, because this latter group will not begin to turn age 85 until after 2030. The baby boom generation is generally defined as those born between 1946 and 1964, and currently numbers 69 million. By the year 2050, when the survivors of this generation are age 85 and older, they are expected to number 19 million, or 5 percent of the total U.S. population (U.S. Census Bureau, 2001b). This represents a 500 percent increase within 60 years. The impact of such a surge in the oldest-old on the demand for health services, especially hospitals and long-term care settings, will be dramatic.

It is also important to consider the distribution of selected age groups now and in the future. The young-old (ages 65–74) currently represent almost 53 percent of the older population; those over 85 make up 12 percent. In contrast, the corresponding proportions in 2050 are projected to be 44 percent young-old and 23 percent oldest-old (see Figure 1.5).

Because they are more likely to have multiple health problems that often result in physical frailty, and because up to 50 percent of the oldest-old may have some form of cognitive impairment, this group is disproportionately represented in institutional settings such as nursing homes, assisted living, and hospitals (Carr, Goate, Phil, and Morris, 1997). Almost 20 percent live in a long-term care setting, and they make up more than 50 percent of the population of nursing homes (U.S. Census Bureau, 2001b). However, the incidence of institutionalization among African Americans aged 85 and older is only about half this rate (12 percent). The oldest-old blacks are far more likely to be living with relatives other than a spouse (40 percent). Very few of the oldest-old (regardless of ethnic minority status) live with a spouse, compared with 55 percent of all people over age 65 (U.S. Administration on Aging, 2002). Although functional health is more impaired in the oldest-old, a major study of Medicare expenditures during the last year of life showed that medical costs were not higher for this age group. The researchers compared Medicare expenditures during the last year of life for people aged 85 and over versus those who died at ages 65 to 74. They found that the charges to Medicare for the former group were 60 to 70 percent lower than the average charges for the latter group, regardless of gender and ethnicity.

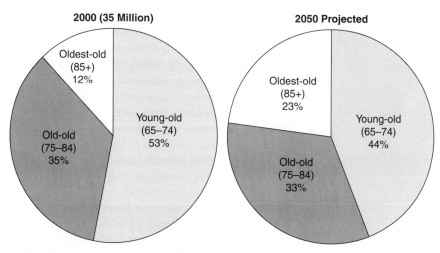

FIGURE 1.5 **Percentage of Older Americans by Age Group**
SOURCE: U.S. Census Bureau, 2001b.

These findings reflect the shorter hospitalizations and less aggressive terminal health care received by the oldest-old (Levinsky, Yu, Ash, Moskowitz, Gazelle, Saynina, and Emanuel, 2001). These costs may be even lower for future cohorts of the oldest-old, who are likely to be healthier and more active than today's population.

Centenarians

Projections by the U.S. Census Bureau also suggest a substantial increase in the population of centenarians, people age 100 or older. In 2000, more than 50,000 Americans had reached this milestone, a 35 percent increase since 1990. Baby boomers are expected to survive to age 100 at rates never before achieved; one in 26 Americans can expect to live to be 100 by 2025, compared with only 1 in 500 in 2000 (U.S. Administration on Aging, 2002).

As more Americans become centenarians, there is growing interest in their genetics and the lifestyle that may have influenced their longevity.

MANY CENTENARIANS ARE ACTIVE IN THEIR COMMUNITIES

In one assisted-living facility, two centenarians are active participants in that community. They join in most of the social activities, enjoy local outings, and have numerous friends who visit them. They regularly go to the exercise room after dinner, pedaling on stationary bikes while reading or watching the news.

Data from the Georgia Centenarian Study support other findings of greater survival among women, as well as race crossover effects in advanced old age. In this follow-up of 137 people aged 100 at entry into the study, African American women survived longest beyond age 100. On average, they survived twice as many months as white men, who lived the shortest time beyond 100. White women had the next best survival rates, and lived slightly longer than African American men (Poon et al., 2000).

The New England Centenarian Study points to genetic factors that determine how well the older person copes with disease (Perls, 1995; Perls and Silver, 1999; Perls and Wood, 1996). As shown in Figure 1.6, the model proposed by this study suggests that the oldest-old are hardy because they have a higher threshold for disease and show slower rates of disease progression than their peers who develop chronic diseases at a younger age and die earlier. Perls and colleagues illustrate this hypothesis with the case of a 103-year-old man who displayed few symptoms of Alzheimer's disease; however, at autopsy this man's brain had a high number of neurofibrillary tangles, which are a hallmark of this disease. The likelihood of a genetic advantage is also supported by the finding that male siblings of centenarians are 17 times as likely as the general population, and female siblings eight times as likely to survive to age 100 (Perls et al., 1998).

Older men who survive to age 90, in particular, represent the hardiest segment of their birth

---

LIVING AND DYING AT AGE 100

Bob Hope, labeled by the American media as "the quintessentially American entertainer" and the "greatest entertainer of the 20th century," turned 100 on May 29, 2003. He was honored by television, radio, and print stories for his contributions to the evolution of standup comedy, but more substantively for his dedication to America's armed forces through his USO-sponsored tours in World War II, Korea, Vietnam, and the 1991 Persian Gulf War. Because of his role as an American icon, 35 states declared his birthday "Bob Hope Day" and a famous street intersection in Los Angeles at Hollywood and Vine was named "Bob Hope Square." Only 2 months later, on July 28, 2003, Hope died of pneumonia. Although his eyesight and hearing had failed, his family reported that he was alert and aware of world events until his death. Comedian George Burns, a contemporary of Hope's, also died shortly after his 100th birthday, in 1996.

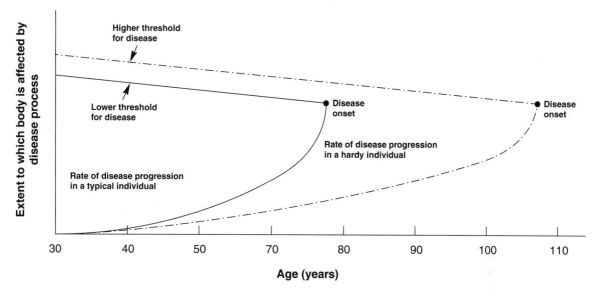

FIGURE 1.6   **Response to Chronic Disease among Elders Who Survive to Age 100 versus Nonsurvivors**
SOURCE: Adapted from Perls, 1995.

cohort. Between ages 65 and 89, women score higher on tests of cognitive function. However, after age 90, men perform far better on these tests. Even at age 80, 44 percent of men were found to be robust and independent, compared with 28 percent of women. Contrary to the prior belief prevalent in gerontology that dementia is a concomitant of advanced age, it appears that as many as 30 percent of centenarians have no memory problems, 20 percent have some, and 50 percent have serious problems. In one study of 69 centenarians who were tested for dementia, none of these robust elders showed significant levels of dementia, either in their neuropsychological testing or in the neuropathological studies of their brains (Samuelsson et al., 1997; Silver et al., 1998; Suzman, Willis, and Manton, 1992). Indeed, other researchers who have studied dementia in older adults have suggested that the genetic mutations most closely associated with Alzheimer's disease are not present in the oldest-old. Environmental factors that emerge much later in life appear to cause dementia in these survivors (Kaye, 1997).

Further evidence for the robustness of centenarians comes from the New England Centenarian Study and a similar assessment of centenarians in Sweden (Samuelsson et al., 1997). Of the 79 people who were age 100 or older in the former study, all lived independently into their early 90s and, on average, took only one medication. In the Swedish Centenarian Study, among 143 respondents:

- Fifty-two percent were able to perform their activities of daily living with little or no assistance.
- Thirty-nine percent had a disorder of the circulatory system.
- Eighty percent had problems with vision and hearing.
- Twenty-seven percent had some signs of dementia and all performed worse on a test of cognitive function (memory and attention) than 70- to 80-year-olds.

Centenarians appear to be healthy for a longer period of time, although almost 50 percent live in nursing homes, compared with 25 percent of all persons aged 85 and older (U.S. Census Bureau, 1999).

Population Pyramids

The increase in longevity is partly responsible for an unusually rapid rise in the *median age* of the U.S. population—from 28 in 1970 to 36 in 2000—meaning that half the population was older than 36 and half younger in 2000. From a historical perspective, an 8-year increase in the median age over a 30-year period is a noteworthy demographic event. The other key factors contributing to this rise include a dramatic decline in the birth rate after the mid-1960s, high birthrates in the periods from 1890 to 1915 and just after World War II (these baby boomers are now all older than the median), and the large number of immigrants before the 1920s.

As stated earlier in this chapter, the baby boom generation (currently aged 40 to 58) will dominate the age distribution in the United States in the next three decades. In fact, between 2010 and 2030, they will form the "senior boom" and swell the ranks of the 65-plus generation to the point that one in five Americans will be old. The projected growth in the older population will increase the median age of the U.S. population from 36 in 2000 to age 38 by 2015. If current fertility and immigration levels remain stable, the only age groups to experience significant growth in the next century will be those older than 55 (U.S. Census Bureau, 1999).

One of the most dramatic examples of the changing age distribution of the American population is the shift in the proportion of older adults in relation to the proportion of young persons, as illustrated in Figure 1.7. In 1900, when approximately 4 percent of the population was age 65 and over, young persons aged 0 to 17 years made up 40 percent of the population. By 1994, reduced birthrates in the 1970s and 1980s had resulted in a decrease of young persons to 25 percent of the population. The U.S. Census Bureau predicts that, by 2030, the proportion of young and old persons will be almost equal, with those aged 0 to 17 forming 22 percent of the population and older adults forming 21 percent. Indeed, in 1990 the proportion of people under age 14 was the same as those aged 60 or older (U.S. Census Bureau, 1993). After 2030 the death rate will be greater than the birthrate because baby boomers will be in the oldest cohorts.

The *population pyramid* is one way of illustrating the changing proportions of young and old persons in the population. Figure 1.8 contrasts the population pyramids for the years 2000, 2025, and 2050. Each horizontal bar in these pyramids represents a 10-year *birth cohort* (i.e., people born within the same 10-year period). By comparing these bars, we can determine the relative proportion of each birth cohort. As you can see in the first graph, the distribution of the

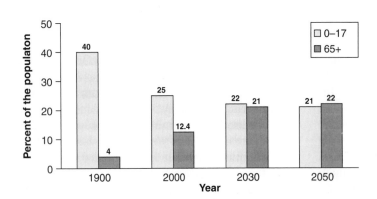

FIGURE 1.7   **Actual and Projected Distribution of Children and Older Adults in the Population: 1900–2050**
SOURCE: U.S. Census Bureau, Projections of the population of the United States, by age, sex, and race: 1983–2080. *Current Population Reports,* Series P-25-1104, 1993, and Census Bureau, 2001b.

(NP-P2) Projected Resident Population of the United States as of July 1, 2000, Middle Series

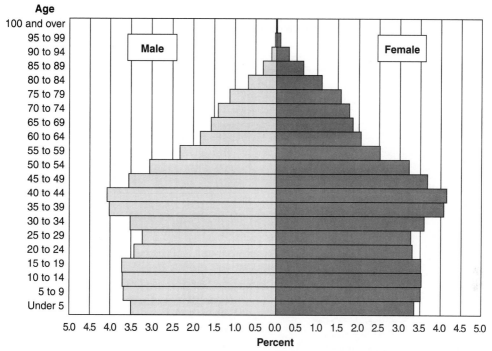

(NP-P3) Projected Resident Population of the United States as of July 1, 2025, Middle Series

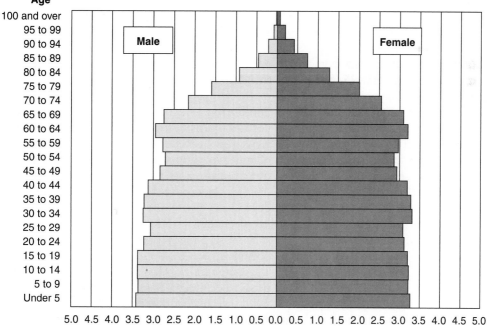

FIGURE 1.8 Projected Resident Populations of the United States for 2000, 2025, and 2050

SOURCE: National Projections Program, Population Division, U.S. Census Bureau, Washington, DC 20233

(continued)

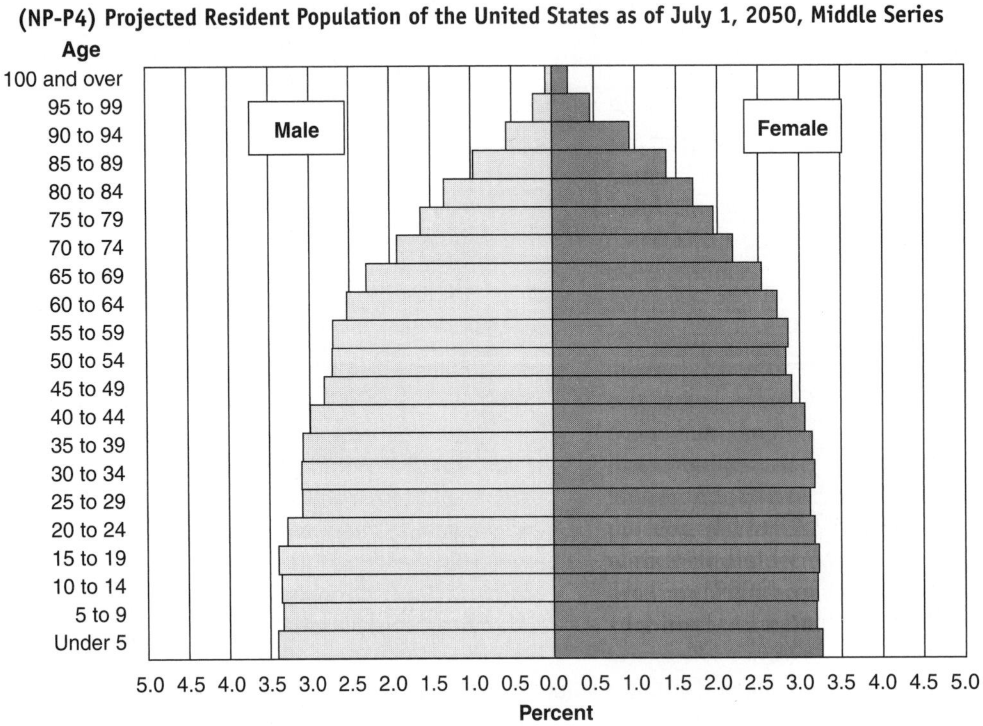

(NP-P4) Projected Resident Population of the United States as of July 1, 2050, Middle Series

FIGURE 1.8   **(Continued)**

population in 2000 had already moved from a true pyramid to one with a bulge in the 35- to 54-year-old group; this represents the population of baby boomers. This pyramid grows more column-like over the years, as shown in the other two graphs. These changes reflect the aging of the baby boomers (note the "pig in a python" phenomenon as this group moves up the age ladder), combined with declining birth rates and reduced death rates for older cohorts.

Dependency Ratios

One aspect of the changing age distribution in our population that has raised public concern is the so-called *dependency ratio*, or "elderly support ra-

tio." The way this ratio has generally been used is to indicate the relationship between the proportion of the population that is employed (defined as "productive" members of society) and the proportion that is not in the workforce (and is thus viewed as "dependent"). This rough estimate is obtained by comparing the percent of the population aged 18 to 64 (the working years) to the proportion under age 18 (yielding the childhood dependency ratio) and over 65 (yielding the old-age dependency ratio). This ratio has increased steadily, such that proportionately fewer employed persons appear to support older persons today. In 1910, the ratio was less than .10 (i.e., ten working people per older person), compared with .19 in 2000 (i.e., five working people per older person). Assuming that the lower birth rate continues, this trend will be apparent in the early part of this century, as the baby boom cohort reaches old age. By the year 2020, a ratio of .28 (or fewer than four working people per retired person) is expected (U.S. Administration on Aging, 2002). These changes since 1960, along with projections through 2050, are illustrated in Figure 1.9.

Such a crude measure of dependency rates is problematic, however. Many younger and older persons are actually in the labor force and not dependent, while many people of labor-force age may not be employed. Another flaw is that dependency ratios do not take account of the labor-force participation rates of different groups; for example, the rates of women aged 16 and older are expected to increase in this century, while those of men are projected to remain steady. When these variations are taken into account, the total dependency ratio in the year 2050 will remain lower than recent historical levels, even though it increases as the population ages. Moreover, despite population aging, those under the age of 16 will continue to constitute the largest "dependent" group into this century. Therefore, we need to be cautious when policy makers pre-dict "burdens" on the younger population and blame rising costs of public pension programs primarily on the changing dependency ratio (National Academy, 1999; Quinn, 1996).

Population Trends

In addition to the proportional growth of the older population in general, other demographic trends are of interest to gerontologists. These include statistics related to the social, ethnic, racial, gender, and geographic distribution of older populations. In this section, we will review some of these trends, beginning with the demographics of ethnic minorities in the United States.

Ethnic Minorities

Because of lifelong socioeconomic inequities in access to health care and preventive health services, elders of color have a lower life expectancy than

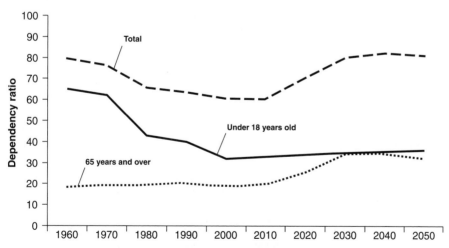

FIGURE 1.9   **Number of Dependents per 100 Persons Aged 18–64 Years: Estimates and Projections 1960–2050**
SOURCE: U.S. Census Bureau, International Data Base, Census 2000 Summary File 1.

whites. For example, in 1998, life expectancy at birth was 80 years for white females and 74.8 for African American females. White males could expect to live 74.5 years, compared with 67.6 years for their black counterparts. Nevertheless, the greatest improvement in life expectancy between 1997 and 1998 occurred for the latter group, an increase of 0.4 years. White males showed no change in life expectancy during that same period (U.S. Bureau of the Census, 2000).

Today, ethnic minorities comprise 16.4 percent of the population over age 65 (8 percent African American, 5.6 percent Latino, 2.4 percent, Asian or Pacific Islander, and less than 1 percent American Indian); they include a smaller proportion of older people and a larger proportion of younger adults than the white population. In 2000, 14.4 percent of whites, but only 8.1 percent of African Americans and 4.9 percent of Latinos were age 65 and over. The difference results primarily from the higher fertility and mortality rates among the nonwhite population under age 65 than among the white population under 65. Census figures in 2000 suggest that the proportion of older persons will increase at a

higher rate for the nonwhite population than for the white population. This is partly because of the large percent of children in these groups, who, unlike their parents and especially their grandparents, are expected to reach old age (U.S. Administration on Aging, 2002). Figures 1.10 and 1.11 illustrate these differential patterns of growth. A more detailed description of ethnic minority elders is provided in Chapter 14.

Geographic Distribution

Demographic information on the location of older populations is important for a variety of reasons. For example, the differing needs of rural and urban older people may affect service delivery and local government policy decisions. Statistical information on older populations state-to-state is necessary in planning for the distribution of federal funds. A comparison of demographic patterns in different nations and cultures may provide insights into various aspects of the aging process. The following are some of the most salient statistics on the geographic dis-

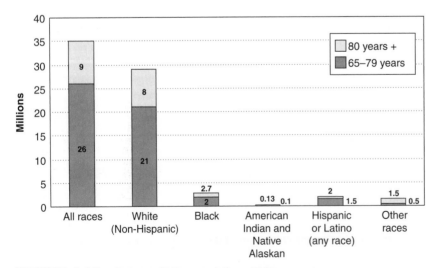

FIGURE 1.10 **Persons 65 Years and Over: 2000**
SOURCE: U.S. Bureau of the Census, 2001b.

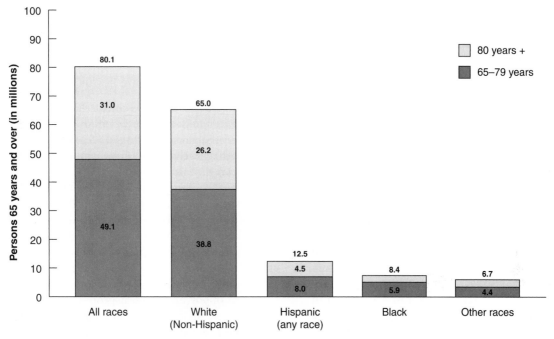

FIGURE 1.11   **Persons 65 Years and Over: 2050 (projected numbers in millions)**
Hispanics are also included in racial group totals.
SOURCE: U.S. Bureau of the Census, Middle Series Projections (1993).

tribution of older adults today. The implications of these changes will be considered in later chapters, including their impact on living arrangements, social, health and long-term care policies, and cross-cultural issues.

Although older adults live in every state and region of the United States and represent 12.4 percent of the total U.S. population, they are not evenly distributed:

- The Northeast continues to be the region with the oldest population; those over age 65 represent 13.8 percent of its population.
- The western states have approximately 11 percent elders.
- In the Midwest, and the South, the proportion of older adults declined between 1990 and 2000, from 13 percent to 12.8 percent, and from 12.6 percent to 12.4 percent, respectively (U.S. Administration on Aging, 2002).

About 52 percent of all persons 65 and older lived in nine states in 2000:

- California (3.6 million older residents)
- Florida (2.8 million)
- New York (2.5 million)

POINTS TO PONDER

The majority of older people, 77 percent in 1998, lived in metropolitan areas. About 28 percent lived in cities, 49 percent in suburbs, and 23 percent in rural areas. Despite their low distribution in rural communities, older adults make up a greater percentage of rural populations than in the general population: 15 percent of all rural residents vs. 13 percent of the total U.S. population (AARP, 2000). What do you think accounts for this higher proportion of elders in rural communities?

- Pennsylvania and Texas (about 2 million in each)
- Ohio, Illinois, Michigan, and New Jersey (over 1 million each)

This does not necessarily mean that all these states have a higher *proportion* of older Americans than the national average, but their absolute numbers are large. Some states have a much higher proportion of residents over 65 than the national average. For example, in 2000 they represented:

- 17.6 percent of the population in Florida.
- almost 16 percent in Pennsylvania.
- approximately 15 percent in West Virginia, Iowa, North Dakota, South Dakota, and Rhode Island.

In contrast, elders represented just 5.7 percent of the population of Alaska and 8.5 percent of the population of Utah (U.S. Administration on Aging, 2002).

Because of these disparate proportions of older adults in their states' population, it is not surprising that Florida has the highest median age in the United States (37.6 years), and Utah the lowest (26.8 years). In some cases, such as that of Florida, migration of retired persons to the state explains the increase, whereas in others, such as West Virginia and South Dakota, migration of younger persons out of the state leaves a greater proportion of older people. More than 20 percent of some rural counties in these states are over age 65. Other states may simply reflect the generalized "graying of America." These regional differences are expected to continue in this century.

Residential relocation is relatively rare for older people in the United States. In a typical year, less than 5 percent of people aged 65 and older move, compared with 18 percent of people under age 65 (U.S. Administration on Aging, 2002). The movement that occurs tends to be within the same region of the country and the same types of environment; that is, people over age 65 generally move from one metropolitan area to another or from one rural community to another. These trends and their implications for well-being in the later years are described further in Chapter 11.

Educational and Economic Status

In 1960, less than 20 percent of the population over age 65 had finished high school. By 2001, 70 percent of the new cohort aged 65 and older had completed high school and 17 percent held a bachelor's degree or more, with only slight gender differences. However, racial and generational differences are striking. Among whites who were age 65 and older in 2001, 74 percent had completed high school, compared with 51 percent of African Americans and 35 percent of Latinos in this age group (U.S. Administration on Aging, 2002). Because of historical patterns of discrimination in educational opportunities, a disproportionate ratio of older persons of color today have less than a high school education. Because educational level is so closely associated with economic well-being, these ethnic differences have a major impact on poverty levels of persons of color across the life span and particularly in old age. Other implications of these gaps in educational attainment are discussed further in Chapter 14.

Not surprisingly, people aged 65 to 69 are more educated today than the old-old and oldest-old. Two-thirds of the former (67 percent) have at least a high school education, compared with 52 percent of their older peers. For this reason, the median educational level today is 12.1 years for the young-old, 10.5 years for the old-old, and 8.6 years for the oldest-old (age 85+). Women in all older cohorts of whites and African Americans (but not Latinos) are more likely than men to have completed high school. The situation shifts for college education. Because of cultural values in previous generations, fewer white women age 65 and older have college degrees than do white men. Among African Americans the pattern is mixed; for those 70 and older, more black women than men have completed college while for the 65- to 69-year-olds, fewer have completed college (U.S.

Bureau of the Census, 1998a). It is noteworthy that an even greater proportion of people over 25 today (75 percent) have at least a high school education. This suggests that future generations of older people will be better educated—many with college degrees—than their grandparents are today. The implications of this shift for political activism, employment, and the nature of productive roles are explored in later chapters.

The 2000 Census showed a slight increase in the proportion of older people in the labor force. Comprising 3.0 percent of the U.S. labor force, 17.7 percent of men and 9.7 percent of women aged 65 and older reported working full-time outside the home. Many older adults prefer to work part-time, but are unable to find such jobs. This is an option for 54 percent of older people (48 percent of men and 62 percent of women) employed in a part-time or temporary capacity (U.S. Administration on Aging, 2002).

Social Security remains the major source of income for many older Americans; in 2000 only 23 percent said that their primary source was earnings from employment and about 18 percent from private pensions. In fact, increases in Social Security benefits along with annual cost-of-living adjustments are major factors underlying the improved economic status of the older population. Currently, about 10.4 percent of older people subsist on incomes below the poverty level, compared to 35 percent in the late 1950s, and equal to the poverty rate of Americans aged 18 to 64. Another 6.3 percent of older Americans are classified as "near-poor," with income levels between poverty and 125 percent of the poverty level (U.S. Administration on Aging, 2002). The improved economic status of the older population as a whole masks the growing rates of poverty among older women, elders of color, the oldest-old, and those living alone. Older women in 2000 were almost twice as likely to be poor as men (about 13 percent vs. 7.0 percent). Older African Americans and Latinos are far more likely to be poor than whites, although their situation has improved (26 and 22 percent vs. 8.2 percent for whites). Poverty

is higher among elders in central cities (12.8 percent) and in rural communities (12.2 percent). The combination of ethnicity and marital status displays even more disparities; for example, in 2001 the median income for a non-Latino white household headed by someone 65 and older was $24,114, compared with $16,761 for older African American households and $16,870 for older Latino households (U.S. Census Bureau, 2001b). The current and projected economic status of the older population is discussed in detail in Chapters 12, 13, and 14.

Worldwide Trends

All world regions are experiencing an increase in the absolute and relative size of their older populations. The number of persons age 65 or older in the world is expected to increase from an estimated 420 million in 2000 to 761 million in 2025. This will result in a world population in which one out of every seven people will be 65 years of age or older by the year 2025 (U.S. Census Bureau, 2001a). As seen in the projections for population growth in the United States, the global age distribution will change from a pyramid to a cylindrical form (Figure 1.12). This is due to a reduction in fertility rates worldwide, even in the less developed countries of Africa and South America. It is estimated that 120 countries will reach total fertility rates below replacement levels (i.e., 2.1 children per woman) by 2025, compared to 22 countries in 1975 and 70 in 2000 (WHO, 2002).

The current numbers and expected growth of the older population differ substantially between the industrialized and developing countries. Currently 60 percent of older adults live in developing countries, which may increase to 75 percent by 2020. For example, in 2000 the population aged 65 and older for most Western European countries was estimated to be greater than 15 percent:

- Italy currently has the highest proportion of elders in the world (18.1 percent).

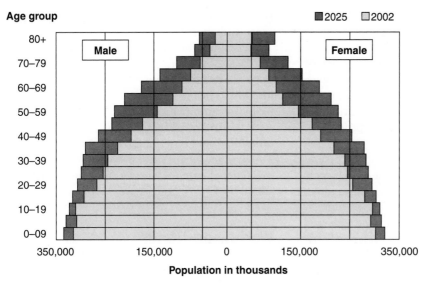

FIGURE 1.12   **Global Population Pyramid in 2002 and 2025**
SOURCE: World Health Organization, *Active ageing: A policy framework*. WHO, 2002.

- Greece and Sweden each have 17.3 percent.
- Japan has 17 percent (U.S. Census Bureau, 2001a).

A major reason for such large proportions is increased life expectancy beyond age 65 in developed countries, as illustrated by trends in the United States and Japan (Figure 1.13). In less than 30 years, both countries have made great strides in keeping people alive into advanced old age. In par-

ticular, Japanese men and women have gained considerable advantage since 1970—almost 5 years for men and an additional 7 years for women (U.S. Census Bureau, 2001a). In contrast, Sub-Saharan Africa and South Asia each counted only 3 percent of their population aged 65 or over. The median age of these regions also varies:

- The median age is 23.5 worldwide.
- It is 37 in Western Europe.

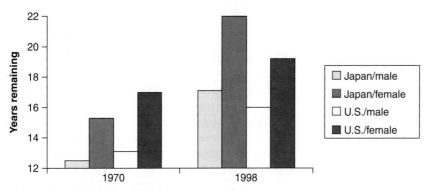

FIGURE 1.13   **Life Expectancy at Age 65: United States and Japan**
SOURCE: U.S. Census Bureau, 2000a.

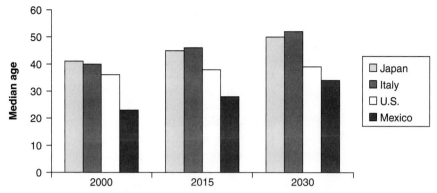

FIGURE 1.14 **Median Age: 2000 versus 2015 versus 2030**
SOURCE: U.S. Census Bureau, 2001a.

- It is 32 in the United States.
- It is 20 in Latin America.

In Africa, with continued high fertility and high mortality rates, the median age will remain around 20 in the year 2020, while that of other countries will rise (U.S. Bureau of the Census, 2001a). Figure 1.14 shows this projected increase in the median age of three developed countries and for Mexico. In less than 30 years, the median age in Italy, the "oldest" country, will be 52, followed closely by Japan at 50. Even Mexico's median age is expected to increase significantly, from the current 23 to 34 by 2030. The United States will show a much smaller increase, from a median age of 36 currently to 39 in 2030. This is due primarily to higher birthrates in the United States compared to these other countries (U.S. Census Bureau, 2001a).

At the same time, the less developed regions of the world expect to show a nearly fivefold increase in their oldest population, from 3.8 percent in 1975 to 17 percent in 2075. An even greater rise in the proportion of the old-old (ages 75–84) and oldest-old (85+) is expected in these countries, from the current 0.5 percent to 3.5 percent in 2075. Reasons for this increase in developing countries include:

- improved sanitation
- medical care

- immunizations
- better nutrition

By the year 2025, only 30 percent of the world's older adults are expected to reside in industrialized nations, while 70 percent will live in developing countries. Unfortunately, this rapid growth in their

JAPAN'S AGING CRISIS

Japan is experiencing the most rapid rate of population aging in the world. In 1970, 7 percent of its population was 65 or older, but this has increased to 17 percent in 2000. This group will comprise 26 percent of Japan's population by 2020. Even more striking is the prediction that 7.2 percent will be age 80 and older in 2020, compared with 4.1 percent in the United States (U.S. Census Bureau, 1996). By 2050, Japan is expected to have one million people aged 100 and older. Nevertheless, there is great resistance by politicians and society in general to immigration, which could increase the number of young workers contributing to the economic support of retirees in Japan. Reports by the United Nations and demographers project a need for 13 million to 17 million new immigrants by 2050 in order to prevent the collapse of Japan's pension system. Yet, in the past 25 years only one million foreigners have been accepted as immigrants in this insular country (*New York Times,* July 24, 2003).

THE CRISIS IN EUROPE'S PENSION SYSTEMS

Pension programs in European nations have already started to feel the pinch of a growing population of retirees. The average portion of gross domestic product spent on pensions is 10 percent for the European Union; in Italy it is 14 percent. It will most likely rise in Italy if the current law that allows retirement at age 57 persists. Some regional government workers in Italy can retire even earlier; in Sicily, for example, male government workers can retire after 25 years on the job and women after 20 years. While other European countries like France and Germany are enacting legislation to require 40 years of employment or extending the retirement age to 67, efforts by the Italian government to protect its pension system by changing retirement laws have met with fierce resistance from labor unions.

population of older people has not led to policy and social planning in developing countries. While industrialized countries like France took more than 100 years to double their population of elders, it will take China only 27 years to reach this level. Such an increase requires government planning, but few developing countries have been able to focus on this coming crisis (Kalache and Keller, 2000). It is also important to note that the less developed regions of the world are currently coping with the tremendous impact of high fertility rates. Even with the continued high infant mortality rates in these countries, children under 15 represent 37 percent of the population in less developed regions, compared with 22 percent in more developed regions (United Nations, 2001).

As noted above, the improved life expectancy in industrial nations, which has increased by 6 years for men and 8.5 years for women since 1953, has resulted in a dramatic increase in the older population. The rate has grown more rapidly over the past 20 years, with a significant impact on the availability of workers to support retired persons. If current retirement patterns continue, the dependency ratio for older retired persons will drop from 3.5 workers to support one

retiree in 1990 to about 2 in 2030 in the industrialized countries of Europe. In Japan, the pyramid will become even more rectangular, with a decline from 4 to 2 workers in the next 30 years. In contrast, the ratio in the United States will drop from the current 5 workers to 3 during this same period. These changes will place tremendous demands on the social security systems, government-subsidized health care, and pension programs of these nations. They may need to develop incentives for later retirement, which may be difficult, considering the trend toward early retirement in most industrial nations. It may also be necessary for developed countries to permit more immigration of young workers from the developing world and to provide training in the technology required by these countries. However, this is a controversial proposal for countries where immigrants often are not easily assimilated because of languages, religions, and cultures divergent from those of the host country, as noted in the prior discussion of Japan.

Other countries are implementing new programs for elder care. With a growing population of people over 65, combined with fewer children to care for them, China has increased its publicly funded housing for childless elders. A private residential care facility industry is also emerging in response to the anticipated 16 percent older population by 2030. In Singapore a more radical approach to caring for a growing older population has emerged. In 1997 the government opened a special court where older persons can bring legal claims against their children for not providing assistance in their old age.

INTERNATIONAL COMPARISONS

The United States has a lower healthy life expectancy than countries such as Japan, Australia, Sweden, France, and Italy. Japan's advantage in healthy life expectancy has been attributed to lower rates of smoking and heart disease among older cohorts (AARP, 2000).

Impact of Demographic Trends in the United States

As discussed later in this book, the growth of older populations has wide-ranging implications. The impact of demographic changes in the United States is most striking in terms of federal spending. The growth in numbers and proportions of older people has already placed pressures on our health, long-term care, and social service systems, as discussed in Chapters 16 and 17. Although some expenditures are directly related to the high cost of health care, the increase in life expectancy also has changed people's expectations about the quality of life in late adulthood. Increasingly in our society, those facing retirement anticipate living 20 to 30 years in relatively good health, with adequate retirement incomes. When these expectations are not met, because of catastrophic medical costs, widowhood, or a retirement income eroded by inflation, older adults may not be prepared to manage a change in their lifestyles. For other segments of the older population, particularly women and elders of color, old age may represent a continuation of a lifetime of poverty or near-poverty. Fortunately, for most older people, the problems associated with old age, particularly chronic illness and the attendant costs, are forestalled until their 70s and 80s. Nevertheless, rapid growth in numbers of frail elders, the majority of whom are women, may severely strain the health and income systems designed to provide resources in old age.

Longevity in Health or Disease?

Future cohorts of older people may be healthier and more independent well into their eighties and nineties. A strong argument was put forth to this effect by Fries (1980, 1990), who suggests that more people will achieve the maximum life span in future years because of healthier lifestyles and better health care during their youth and mid-dle years. Furthermore, Fries argues that future cohorts will have fewer debilitating illnesses and will, in fact, experience a phenomenon he labelled **compression of morbidity** (i.e., experiencing only a few years of major illness in very old age). The concept of "compressed morbidity" implies that premature death is minimized, because disease and functional decline are compressed into a brief period of 3 to 5 years before death. As a result, people die a "natural death" from the failure of multiple organ systems, not because of disease per se (Hazzard, 2001). These older adults of the future may therefore expect to die a "natural death," or death due to the natural wearing out of all organ systems by approximately age 100. If this process does occur, it will have a significant impact on both the type of health and long-term care services needed by future generations of older people and their ability to experience productive aging. Long-term care needs may be reduced, with more subacute care facilities and short-term home health services required.

Indeed, some evidence from a review of large national health surveys indicates that the older population today is generally healthier than previous cohorts. An analysis of two large longitudinal health surveys—the Longitudinal Study on Aging and the National Health Interview Survey (NHIS)—from 1982 through 1993 for respondents who were age 70 and older in each year, reveals that rates of disability are declining or stabilizing. At the same time, recovery from acute disabilities (e.g., due to falls) is improving. This may be due to more aggressive rehabilitation efforts for older adults in recent years and is consistent with the findings of another analysis of national health surveys. In a comparison of responses to the National Long-term Care Survey from 1982 through 1999, there was a notable decline in disability rates, from 26 percent in 1982 to 20 percent in 1996 (Manton and Gu, 2001). This means that future generations of the oldest-old may have lower health care expenditures and less reliance on long-term care services.

The concept of **active versus dependent life expectancy** (Katz et al., 1983) is useful in this context. Katz and others distinguish between merely living a long life and living a healthy old age. This is consistent with the concept of maintaining active aging. Instead of death, they define the endpoint of "active" life expectancy as the loss of independence or the need to rely on others for most activities of daily living. Life expectancy has increased beyond age 65, but about a third of the years lived will be in a dependent state (WHO, 2002). For example:

- A 65-year-old woman today has approximately 19.2 years remaining, 13.2 in active life expectancy, 6 in dependency.
- A 65-year-old man can look forward to living 16 more years, about one-third of these in a dependent state.

Not surprisingly, differences in life conditions of older persons with inadequate income and those above the median income have led to the conclusion that active life expectancy differs by 1 to 2.5 years between the poor and nonpoor. This may result in a growing bimodal distribution of older people remaining healthier and free of disease (as predicted by Fries), and another, probably larger distribution of older adults surviving diseases that would have been fatal years ago, but living with "battle scars." This latter group may be the segment of the population that is distorting projections for compressed morbidity; as we have seen in the reviews of NHIS findings, this latter group also appears to be increasing in size. These are most likely the elders who will require long-term care in the future.

How Aging and Older Adults Are Studied

You are undoubtedly aware that more researchers are studying older people and the process of aging now than in the past. Some of the concerns that have motivated this increasing professional interest in the field have probably influenced your own decision to study gerontology. In this section we turn to the question of how the older population is studied: What are the particular challenges of social gerontological research, and how are they addressed? Methods of conducting research in this field are described. The net effect of this information is to give you a basic orientation to the field of aging, how it has developed, and methods of studying the older population.

Development of the Field

Although the scientific study of social gerontology is relatively recent, it has its roots in biological studies of the aging processes and in the psychology of human development. Biologists have long explored the reasons for aging in living organisms. Several key publications and research studies are milestones in the history of the field.

One of the first textbooks on aging, *The History of Life and Death*, was written in the thirteenth century by Roger Bacon. With great foresight, Bacon suggested that life expectancy could be extended if health practices, such as personal and public hygiene, were improved. The first scientist to explain aging as a developmental process, rather than as stagnation or deterioration, was a nineteenth-century Belgian mathematician–statistician named Adolph Quetelet. His interest in age and creative achievement preceded the study of these issues by social scientists by 100 years. His training in the field of statistics also led him to consider the problems of **cross-sectional research**—that is, the collection of data on people of different ages at one time, instead of **longitudinal research,** the study of the same person over a period of months or years. These problems are examined in greater detail in the next section of this chapter.

One of the first laboratory studies of aging was undertaken in the 1920s by the Russian physiologist Ivan Pavlov. Pavlov is best known for his research with animals, which has provided the foundation for stimulus-response theories of behavior. Recognizing that the ability of older animals to learn and distinguish a response differed from that of younger animals, Pavlov explored the reasons for these differences in animal brains. The work of Raymond Pearl and colleagues in the 1920s established the insect *Drosophila* (or fruit fly) as an ideal animal model for studying biological aging and longevity. During this era, in 1922, American psychologist G. Stanley Hall published one of the first books on the social–psychological aspects of aging in the United States. Titled *Senescence, the Last Half of Life,* it remains a landmark text in social gerontology because it provided the experimental framework for examining changes in cognitive processes and social and personality functions.

Historical Forces of the Late Nineteenth and Early Twentieth Centuries

Two important forces led to the expansion of research in social gerontology in the late nineteenth and early twentieth centuries:

- the growth of the population over age 65 (as described earlier)
- the emergence of retirement policies

Changes in policies toward older adults were first evident in many European countries (e.g., Germany) where age-based social services and health insurance programs were developed. In contrast, these changes did not occur in the United States until the 1930s. In 1900, the focus on economic growth and the immediate problems of establishing workers' rights and child welfare laws took precedence over improving the welfare of older people. The prevailing belief in this country had been that families should be responsible for their aging members.

However, the Great Depression of the 1930s brought to policy makers the stark realization that families struck by unemployment and homelessness could not be responsible for their elders. The older segments of society suffered a disproportionate share of the economic blight of the Depression. New concern for the needs of the aging population was exemplified by the Social Security system, established in 1935 to help people maintain a minimal level of economic security after retirement. Early work in social gerontology dealt largely with social and economic problems of aging. For example, E. V. Cowdry's *Problems of Ageing,* published in 1939, focused on society's treatment of older people and their particular needs. It amazes us today that the second edition of Cowdry's book, published in 1942, contained all the research knowledge available on aging at that time!

Formal Development of the Field

As society grew more aware of issues facing the older population, the formal study of aging emerged in the 1940s. In 1945, the Gerontological Society of America (GSA) was founded, bringing together the small group of researchers and practitioners who were interested in gerontology and geriatrics at that time. Gerontology became a division of the American Psychological Association in 1945 and, later, of the American Sociological Association.

The *Journal of Gerontology,* which the GSA began publishing in 1946, served as the first vehicle for transmitting new knowledge in this growing field. In 1988 it became two journals, *The Journals of Gerontology* composed of *Psychological Sciences and Social Sciences,* and *Biological Sciences and Medical Sciences,* which reflect the growth of

---

THE GERONTOLOGICAL SOCIETY OF AMERICA

Today, the GSA has over 5000 members. It is the major professional association for people in diverse disciplines focused on research in aging. The GSA's mission is "to add life to years, not just years to life." This emphasizes the goal of most gerontologists—to enhance quality of life in the later years, not just to extend it.

gerontology. Today numerous others are devoted to the study of aging and to the concerns of those who work with older people. An indicator of the knowledge explosion in the field is that the literature on aging published between 1950 and 1960 equaled that of the previous 115 years (Birren and Clayton, 1975). An effort to compile a bibliography of biomedical and social research from 1954 to 1974 produced 50,000 titles (Woodruff, 1975). Today, the burgeoning periodicals in diverse disciplines focused on gerontology have resulted in an exponential growth of research publications in this field. Gerontology has become increasingly more interdisciplinary; that is, specialists in diverse areas of the basic, clinical, behavioral, and social sciences are working together on research projects focused on specific aspects of aging (Birren, 1996).

Major Research Centers Founded

Research in gerontology assumed greater significance after these developments, and an interest in the social factors associated with aging grew in the late 1950s and early 1960s. In 1946, a national gerontology research center, headed by the late Nathan Shock, a leader in geriatric medicine, was established at Baltimore City Hospital by the National Institutes of Health. This federally funded research center undertook several studies of physiological aspects of aging, using a cross-sectional approach.

In 1958, Dr. Shock and his colleagues began a longitudinal study of physiological changes in healthy, middle-aged and older men living in the community, by testing them every two years on numerous physiological parameters. They later started to examine the cognitive, personality, and social–psychological characteristics of these men. Much later, in 1978, older women were included in their samples. Known as the **Baltimore Longitudinal Studies of Aging,** these assessments of changes associated with healthy aging are still continuing, now under the direction of the National Institute on Aging. More than 2200 volunteers, men and women, aged 20 to 90, have participated or are currently participating in this ongoing study of the basic processes of aging. On average, these volunteers remain in the study for 13 years. More recently, ethnic minorities have been recruited as subjects; 13 percent are African Americans, mostly in the younger cohorts. The results of this ongoing research effort continue to provide valuable information about normal age-related changes in physiological and psychological functions. As more persons of color in this longitudinal study grow older, they will provide valuable insights into the process of normal, age-related changes versus disease in these populations.

Concurrently with the Baltimore Longitudinal Studies, several university-based centers were developed to study the aging process and the needs of older adults. One of the first, the Duke University Center on Aging, was founded in 1955 by one of the pioneers in gerontology, Ewald Busse. This center focused initially on physiological aging and on mental health, but has also examined many social aspects of aging.

The University of Chicago, under Robert Havighurst's direction, developed the first research center devoted exclusively to the social aspects of aging. The Kansas City studies of adult development, discussed in Chapters 6 and 8, represent the first major social–psychological studies of adult development, and were conducted by researchers from the Chicago center. Research and training centers on aging have since evolved at many other universities, generally stimulated by government sponsorship of gerontological research through the National Institute on Aging (established in 1974), the National Institute of Mental Health (which established its center for studies of the mental health of the aging in 1976), and the Administration on Aging (established in 1965).

Research Methods

Before examining the issues and areas of special concern to social gerontologists, we first consider the ways in which such information about the aging process is gathered. The topic of research methodologies in gerontology may seem an advanced one to introduce in a basic text, but in fact, it is essential to understanding the meaning and validity of information presented throughout this book.

The study of aging presents particular conceptual and methodological difficulties. A major one is how research is designed and data interpreted regarding age changes. A point that complicates research in aging and also produces some misleading interpretations of data is how to distinguish *age changes* from *age differences*. This differentiation is necessary if we are to understand the process of aging and the conditions under which age differences occur. If we wish to determine what changes or effects are experienced as an individual moves from middle age to old age and to advanced old age, we must examine the same individual over a period of years, or at least months. In order to understand age changes, longitudinal research is necessary—that is, the repeated measurement of the same person over a specified period of time.

Unfortunately, the time and cost of such studies prevent many researchers from undertaking longitudinal research. Instead, much of the research in this field focuses on age differences, by comparing people of different chronological ages at the same measurement period. These studies, cross-sectional in nature, are the most common ones in gerontology.

The unique problems inherent in how gerontological research is designed and how data are interpreted are evident in the following question: Given that aging in humans is a complex process that proceeds quite differently among individuals in varied geographic, cultural, and historical settings, and that it occurs over a time span as long as 100 to 120 years, how does one study it? Obviously, scientists cannot follow successive generations—or even a single generation of subjects—throughout their life span. Nor can they be expected to address the entire range of variables that affect aging—including lifestyle, social class, cultural beliefs, gender, ethnic minority status, public policies, and so on—in a single study.

The Age/Period/Cohort Problem

The problem in each case is that of distinguishing *age differences* (ways that one generation differs from another) from *age changes* (ways that people normally change over time). This has been referred to as the "age/period/cohort" problem. (The word *cohort*, you will recall, refers to those people born at roughly the same time. *Period,* or time of measurement effect, refers to the impact of the specific historical period involved.) The concept of cohort is an important one in gerontology because historical events differentiate one generation from another in attitudes and behaviors. People in the same cohort are likely to be more similar to each other than to people in other cohorts because of comparable social forces acting on them during a given era.

Cross-Sectional Studies

As noted earlier, the most common approach to studying aging is cross-sectional; that is, researchers compare a number of subjects of different ages on the same characteristics in order to

Many older adults participate in research that could benefit others.

determine age-related differences. One reason that cross-sectional studies are frequently used is that, compared to other designs, data can be readily gathered. Some examples might include a comparison of the lung capacity of men aged 30 with those who are aged 40, 50, 60, 70, and 80, or a study comparing church attendance by American adults under age 65 with those over age 65. The average differences among different age groups in each study might suggest conclusions about the changes that come with age.

The danger with such cross-sectional studies is that these differences might not be due to the process of aging, but rather to particular cultural and historical conditions that shaped each group of subjects being studied. For example, a higher rate of church attendance among today's older adults than among younger adults probably reflects a change in social attitudes toward attending church, as opposed to an increased need for spiritual and religious life as one grows older.

Even in studies of biological factors, such as lung capacity, many intervening variables may threaten the validity of comparative results. In this case, they include the effects of exercise, smoking, and other lifestyle factors, genetic inheritance, and exposure to pollution (this, in turn, might be a product of work environments and social class) on relevant outcome variables.

The major limitation of cross-sectional studies occurs when differences among younger and older respondents are erroneously attributed to growing old; for example, some researchers have found that the older the respondent, the lower his or her score on intelligence tests. As a result, cognitive abilities have been misinterpreted as declining with age. In fact, such differences may be due to the lower educational levels and higher test anxiety of this cohort of older adults compared to younger adults, not to age. This is an example of *confounding*, or a joint effect of two variables on an outcome of interest. In this case, age effects are confounded by the impact of cohort differences. Because many issues in social gerontology center on distinguishing age from cohort effects, a num-

ber of research designs have emerged that attempt to do this. They include "longitudinal" and "sequential" designs.

Longitudinal Studies: Design and Limitations

Longitudinal designs permit inferences about *age changes*. They eliminate cohort effects by studying the same people over time. Each row in Table 1.2 represents a separate longitudinal study in which a given cohort (e.g., A, B, or C) is measured once every 10 years. Despite the advantages of longitudinal designs over the cross-sectional approach, they still have limitations. First, the longitudinal method does not allow a distinction between age and time of testing. Second, it cannot separate the effects of events extraneous to the study that influence people's responses in a particular measurement period.

Another problem with longitudinal studies is the potential for practice effects. This is a partic-

TABLE 1.2   Alternative Research Designs in Aging

COHORT BORN IN	TIME OF MEASUREMENT			
	1970	1980	1990	2000
1920	A_1	A_2		
1930		B_1	B_2	
1940		C_1	C_2	C_3
1950				D_4

Cross-sectional: Cohorts A, B, and C are measured in 1980. *Longitudinal:* Cohort A is measured in 1970 and 1980; or Cohort B is measured in 1980 and 1990; or Cohort C is measured in 1980, 1990, and 2000. *Cohort-sequential:* Cohort A is measured in 1970 and 1980; Cohort B is measured in 1980 and 1990. *Time-sequential:* Cohorts B and C are measured in 1980; Cohorts C and D are measured in 2000. *Cross-sequential:* Cohorts B and C are both measured in 1980 and 1990.

SOURCE: Adapted from K. W. Schaie (Ed.), *Longitudinal studies of adult psychological development* (New York: Guilford Press, 1983).

AN EXAMPLE OF MISINTERPRETING LONGITUDINAL DATA

Imagine a study that attempted to determine attitudes about retirement. If a sample of 55-year-old workers had been interviewed in 1980, before mandatory retirement was changed to age 70, and again in 1990, after mandatory retirement was eliminated, it would be difficult to determine whether the changes in the workers' attitudes toward retirement occurred because of their increased age and proximity to retirement, or because of the modifications in retirement laws during this period.

ular concern in studies that administer aptitude or knowledge tests, where repeated measurement with the same test improves the test-taker's performance because of familiarity or practice. For example, a psychologist who is interested in age-related changes in intelligence could expect to obtain improvements in people's scores if the same test is administered several times, with a brief interval (e.g., less than one year) between tests. In such cases, it is difficult to relate the changes to maturation unless the tests can be varied or parallel forms of the same tests can be used.

Longitudinal studies also present the problem of *attrition,* or dropout. Individuals in experimental studies and respondents in surveys that are administered repeatedly may drop out for many reasons—death, illness, loss of interest, or frustration with poor performance. To the extent that people who drop out are not different from the original sample in terms of demographic characteristics, health status, and intelligence, the researcher can still generalize from the results obtained with the remaining sample. However, more often it is the case that dropouts differ significantly from those who stay until the end. As we shall see in Chapter 5, those who drop out of longitudinal studies of intelligence are more likely:

- to be in poorer health,
- to score lower on intelligence tests, and
- to be more socially isolated.

In contrast, older participants who remain in a longitudinal study are generally:

- more educated,
- healthier, and
- motivated.

This is known as the problem of *selective dropout.* While many researchers have pointed to the potential bias introduced by selective dropout, others have suggested that the results of such longitudinal data provide a positive developmental image about aging (Cooney, Schaie, and Willis, 1988; Schaie, 1996).

Sequential Designs

Some alternative research designs have emerged in response to the problems of cross-sectional and longitudinal methods. One is the category of **sequential research designs** (Schaie, 1967, 1973, 1977, 1983). They combine the strengths of cross-sectional and longitudinal research designs. These include the cohort-sequential, time-sequential, and cross-sequential methods, which are illustrated in Table 1.2.

A *cohort-sequential* design is an extension of the longitudinal design, whereby two or more

EXAMPLE OF A COHORT-SEQUENTIAL DESIGN

An investigator may wish to compare changing attitudes toward federal aging policies among the cohort born in 1930 and the cohort born in 1940 and follow each one for 10 years, from 1980 to 1990 for the first cohort, and from 1990 to 2000 for the second. This approach is useful for many social gerontological studies in which age and cohort must be distinguished. However, it still does not separate the effects of cohort from historical effects or time of measurement. As a result, historical events that occurred just before one cohort entered a study (in this case, the Great Depression), but later than another cohort entered, may influence each cohort's attitude scores differently.

EXAMPLE OF A TIME-SEQUENTIAL DESIGN

A group of 70-year-olds and a group of 60-year-olds might be compared on their attitudes toward religious activities in 1990. The latter group then could be compared with a new group of 60-year-olds in 2000. This would give some information on how people approaching old age at two different historical periods view the role of religion in their lives.

EXAMPLE OF A CROSS-SEQUENTIAL DESIGN

A researcher interested in examining the effects of cohort and historical factors on attitudes toward federal aging policy might compare two groups: people who were age 40 and 50 in 1990, and the same people in 2000 when they are age 50 and 60, respectively. This would permit the assessment of cohort and historical factors concurrently, with one providing information on changes from age 40 to 50, and the other representing changes from age 50 to 60.

---

cohorts are followed for a period of time, so that measurements are taken of different cohorts at the same ages, but at different points in time.

The *time-sequential* design is useful for distinguishing between age and time of measurement or historical factors. It can be used to determine if changes obtained are due to aging or to historical factors. The researcher using this design would compare two or more cross-sectional samples at two or more measurement periods. Time-sequential designs do not prevent the confounding of age and cohort effects, but it is acceptable to use this method where one would not expect age differences to be confused with cohort differences.

The third technique proposed by Schaie (1983) is the *cross-sequential* design, which combines cross-sectional and longitudinal designs. This approach is an improvement over both the traditional cross-sectional and longitudinal designs, but it still confounds age and time of measurement effects. These three sequential designs are becoming more widely used by gerontological researchers, especially in studies of intelligence. Table 1.3 summarizes potential confounding effects in each of these methods.

Despite the growth of new research methods, much of social gerontology is based on cross-sectional studies. For this reason, it is important to read carefully the description of a study and its results in order to make accurate inferences about age changes as opposed to age differences, and to determine whether the differences found between groups of different ages are due to cohort effects or to the true effects of aging.

TABLE 1.3   Potential Confounding Effects in Developmental Studies

	CONFOUNDING EFFECT		
DESIGN	AGE × COHORT CONFOUNDED	AGE × TIME OF MEASUREMENT CONFOUNDED	COHORT × TIME OF MEASUREMENT CONFOUNDED
Cross-sectional	Yes	No	No
Longitudinal	No	Yes	No
Cohort-sequential	No	No	Yes
Time-sequential	Yes	No	No
Cross-sequential	No	Yes	No

SOURCE: Adapted from M. F. Elias, P. K. Elias, and J. W. Elias, *Basic processes in adult developmental psychology* (St. Louis: C. V. Mosby, 1977).

Problems with Representative Samples of Older Persons in Research

Accurate sampling can be difficult with older populations. If the sample is not representative, the results are of questionable validity. However, comprehensive lists of older people are not readily available. Membership lists from organizations such as AARP tend to overrepresent those who are healthy, white, and financially secure. Studies in institutions, such as nursing homes and adult day centers, tend to overrepresent those with chronic impairments. Because whites represent almost 84 percent of the population over age 65 today, it is not surprising that they are more readily available for research.

Reaching older persons of color through organizational lists can be especially difficult. More effective means of recruiting these groups include the active participation of community leaders such as ministers and respected elders in churches attended by the population of interest. The problem of ensuring diverse samples of research participants is compounded by the mistrust toward research among many elders of color. Many African Americans, in particular, remember the unethical practices of the Tuskegee Syphilis Study in the early twentieth century and are reluctant to participate in research today, despite significant improvements in the ethics of human research. Researchers must be sensitive to these issues when attempting to recruit elders of color into research projects. For example, older African Americans:

- prefer to participate in social science studies more than in clinical research.
- may need transportation to the research site.
- feel more comfortable when African Americans are represented on the research staff (Burnette, 1998).

Such disproportionate focus on whites and lack of data on ethnic minorities has slowed the development of gerontological theories that consider the impact of race, ethnicity, and culture on the aging process. Yet, even as researchers and

POINTS TO PONDER

Think about some studies that are reported in newspapers, such as surveys of voter preferences. In the 2000 presidential election, several national polls reported the likelihood of "older voters" choosing one candidate or another. Did these surveys reflect the diversity among older voters, or put them into a monolithic block that distinguished them from another diverse group, "middle-class voters"?

funding agencies emphasize the need to include more people of color in all types of research, multiple confounding factors must be considered. For example, Latino elders represent U.S.-born as well as immigrant populations who have come here from countries as diverse as Mexico, Cuba, and Argentina. Therefore, any research that includes ethnic minorities must distinguish among subgroups by language, place of birth, and religion, not just the broader categories of Latino, African American, and Asian. It is not necessary to include all possible subgroups of a particular ethnic minority population in a given study. However, it behooves the researcher to state clearly who is represented, in order to assure appropriate generalizability of the findings.

The problem of *measurement equivalence* in gerontological research is compounded when the sample includes elders of color. As will be discussed in Chapters 5 and 6, many tests of intelligence, memory, and personality traits were originally developed for testing younger populations. As a result, they may not be appropriate for older cohorts whose educational level is generally lower and whose educational and cultural experiences as children differed widely from newer cohorts. In order to achieve equivalence of tests and measures for diverse age groups, gerontologists have spent many years testing the *validity* of existing measures for this population—modifying them and developing new tests as needed. Similar work with elders of color has not been undertaken as extensively. Although there has been some work to assure linguistic equivalence, researchers have not spent as much time on testing the *conceptual equivalence* of these measures (i.e., that people of different ethnic backgrounds see the same meaning or concepts underlying a particular test). If we are to understand ethnic differences in aging, it is important to use valid measures that mean the same thing to all groups participating in research.

The problem of *selective survival* affects most studies of older people. Over time, the birth cohort loses members, so that those who remain are not necessarily representative of all members of the original group. Those who survive, for example, probably were healthiest at birth, and maintained their good health throughout their lives—all variables that tend to be associated with higher socioeconomic status.

Even when an adequate sample is located, older respondents may vary in their memories or attention spans; such variations can interfere with conducting interviews or tests. Ethical issues and unique difficulties arise in interviewing frail elders, yet there are no ethical guidelines specifically aimed at research with older adults. The issue of informed consent becomes meaningless when dealing with a confused or a severely medically compromised older person. In such cases, family members or guardians must take an active role in judging the risks and benefits of research for frail older persons. An additional problem is that studies of the old-old may be influenced by **terminal drop,** a decline in some tests of intelligence shortly before death (Botwinick, 1984; White and Cunningham, 1988). Since death becomes increasingly likely with age, terminal drop will manifest as a gradual decline in performance test scores with age in cross-sectional designs. In longitudinal studies, this problem may result in an overestimation of performance abilities in the later years because those who survive are likely to represent the physically and cognitively most capable older individual (Schaie, 1996). This problem is explored further in Chapter 5.

Further refinement of research methodologies is a challenging task for social gerontologists. As progress is made in this area, the quality of data with which to study aging will continually improve.

Summary and Implications for the Future

A primary reason for the growing interest in gerontology is the increase in the population over age 65. This growth results from a reduction in infant and child mortality and improved treatment of acute diseases of childhood and adulthood, which in turn increases the proportion of people living to age 65 and beyond. In the United States, average life expectancy from birth has increased from 47 years in 1900 to 77 in 2000, with women continuing to outlive men. The growth in the population over age 85 has been most dramatic, reflecting major achievements in disease prevention and health care since the turn of the twentieth century. More recently, there has been increased attention on centenarians. Those who live to be 100 and older may have a biological advantage over their peers who die at a younger age. Studies have found greater tolerance to stress and fewer chronic illnesses in centenarians. Elders of color in the United States and older persons in developing nations are less likely to live beyond age 65 than whites and those in industrialized nations, but population projections anticipate a much higher rate of growth for these groups in the next 20 years.

The growth in the numbers and proportions of older people, especially the oldest-old, requires that both public and private policies affecting employment and retirement, health and long-term care, and social services be modified to meet the needs and improve the quality of life of those who are living longer. Fundamental issues need to be resolved about who will receive what societal resources and what roles private and public sectors will play in sharing responsibilities of elder care.

In many industrialized countries, controversial questions of immigration policy need to be addressed as birthrates decline dramatically among native-born citizens.

Gerontology is growing as a field of study since early philosophers and scientists first explored the reasons for changes experienced with advancing age. Roger Bacon in the thirteenth century, Adolph Quetelet in the early nineteenth century, Botkin in the late nineteenth century, and Ivan Pavlov and G. Stanley Hall in the early twentieth century made pioneering contributions to this field. During the early 1900s, in Europe and the United States, the impact of an increasing aging population on social and health resources began to be felt. Social gerontological research has expanded since the 1940s, paralleling the rapid growth of the older population and its needs.

The growing older population and associated social concerns have stimulated great interest in gerontological research. However, existing research methodologies are limited in their ability to distinguish the process of aging per se from cohort, time, and measurement effects. Cross-sectional research designs are most often used in this field, but these can provide information only on age differences, not on age changes. Longitudinal designs are necessary for understanding age changes, but they suffer from the possibility of subject attrition and the effects of measuring the same individual numerous times. Newer methods in social gerontology, known as cohort-sequential, time-sequential, and cross-sequential designs, test multiple cohorts or age groups over time. They also are limited by possible confounding effects, but represent considerable improvement over traditional research designs.

Because research methods in gerontology have improved, today there is a better understanding of many aspects of aging. Research findings to date provide the empirical background for the theories and topics to be covered in the remaining chapters. Despite the recent explosion of knowledge in gerontology, there are many gaps in what is known about older people and the aging process. The problem is particularly acute in our understanding of aging among ethnic minority populations. Throughout the text, we will call attention to areas in which additional research is needed.

GLOSSARY

active aging a new model of viewing aging as a positive experience of continued growth and participation in family, community, and societal activities, regardless of physical and cognitive decline

active versus dependent life expectancy a way of describing expected length of life, the term *active* denoting a manner of living that is relatively healthy and independent in contrast to being *dependent* on help from others

ageism attitudes, beliefs, and conceptions of the nature and characteristics of older persons that are prejudicial, distorting their actual characteristics, abilities, etc.

aging changes that occur to an organism during its life span, from development to maturation to senescence

Baltimore Longitudinal Studies of Aging a federally funded longitudinal study that has examined physiological, cognitive, and personality changes in healthy, middle-aged and older men since 1958, and in women since 1978

cohort a group of people of the same generation sharing a statistical trait such as age, ethnicity, or socioeconomic status (for example, all African American women between the ages of 60 and 65 in 1999)

competence model a conception or description of the way persons perform, focusing on their abilities vis-á-vis the demands of the environment

compression of morbidity given a certain length of life, a term referring to relatively long periods of healthy, active, high-quality existence and relatively short periods of illness and dependency in the last few years of life

cross-sectional research research that examines or compares characteristics of people at a given point in time and attempts to identify factors associated with contrasting characteristics of different groupings of people

environmental press   features of the social, technological, natural environment that place demands on people

geriatrics   clinical study and treatment of older people and the diseases that affect them

gerontology   the field of study that focuses on understanding the biological, psychological, social, and political factors that influence older people's lives

life expectancy   the average length of time persons, defined by age, sex, ethnic group, and socioeconomic status in a given society, are expected to live

longitudinal research   research that follows the same individual, over time, to measure change in specific variables

maximum life span   biologically programmed maximum number of years that each species can expect to live

person–environment (P–E) perspective   a model for understanding the behavior of people based on the idea that persons are affected by personal characteristics, such as health, attitudes, and beliefs, as they interact with and are affected by the characteristics of the cultural, social, political, and economic environment

sequential research designs   research designs that combine features of cross-sectional and longitudinal research designs to overcome some of the problems encountered in using those designs

RESOURCES

See the companion Website for this text at <www .ablongman.com/hooyman> for information about the following:

- ACTION—Older Americans Volunteer Programs
- AoA—Administration on Aging
- Alliance for Aging Research
- American Federation for Aging Research
- Gerontological Society of America
- MedWeb: Geriatrics
- National Institute on Aging (NIA)

REFERENCES

AARP. *Global Aging Report.* 2000, *5,* 4–5.

Birren, J. E. History of gerontology. In J. E. Birren (Ed.), *Encyclopedia of gerontology,* Vol. 1. San Diego: Academic Press, 1996.

Birren, J. E., and Clayton, V. History of gerontology. In D. S. Woodruff and J. E. Birren (Eds.), *Aging: Scientific perspectives and social issues.* New York: Van Nostrand, 1975.

Botwinick, J. *Cognitive processes in maturity and old age* (3rd ed.). New York: Springer, 1984.

Burnette, D. Conceptual and methodological considerations in research with non-white ethnic elders. *Journal of Social Service Research,* 1998, *23,* 71–91.

Carr, D. B., Goate, A., Phil, D., and Morris, J. C. Current concepts in the pathogenesis of Alzheimer's disease. *American Journal of Medicine,* 1997, *103,* 3S–10S.

Cooney, T. M., Schaie, K. W., and Willis, S. L. The relationship between prior functioning on cognitive and personality dimensions and subject attrition in longitudinal research. *Journals of Gerontology,* 1988, *43,* P12–17.

Fries, J. F. Aging, natural death, and the compression of morbidity. *New England Journal of Medicine,* 1980, *303,* 130–135.

Fries, J. F. The compression of morbidity: Near or far? *Milbank Quarterly,* 1990, *67,* 208–232.

Fries, J. F., and Crapo, L. M. *Vitality and aging.* San Francisco: W. H. Freeman, 1981.

Hayflick, L. *How and why we age* (2nd ed.). New York: Ballantine Books, 1996.

Hazzard, W. R. Aging, health, longevity, and the promise of biomedical research. In E. J. Masoro and S. N. Austad (Eds.), *Handbook of the biology of aging* (5th ed.). San Diego: Academic Press, 2001.

International Longevity Center–USA. *The aging factor in health and disease.* (Report of an interdisciplinary workshop). New York: The Center, 1999.

Kalache, A., and Keller, I. The graying world: A challenge for the 21st century. *Science Progress,* 2000, *83,* 33–54.

Katz, S., Branch, L. G., Branson, M. H., Papsidero, J. A., Beck, J. C., and Greer, D. S. Active life expectancy. *New England Journal of Medicine,* 1983, *309,* 1218–1224.

Kaye, J. A. Oldest-old healthy brain function. *Archives of Neurology,* 1997, *54,* 1217–1221.

Lawton, M. P. Behavior-relevant ecological factors. In K. W. Schaie and C. Scholar (Eds.). *Social structure and aging: Psychological processes.* Hillsdale, NJ: Erlbaum, 1989.

Lawton, M. P., and Nahemow, L. Ecology and the aging process. In C. Eisdorfer and M. P. Lawton (Eds.), *Pychology of adult development and aging.* Washington, DC: American Psychological Association, 1973.

Levinsky, N. G., Yu, W., Ash, A., Moskowitz, M., Gazelle, G., Saynina, O., and Emanuel, E. J. Influence of age on Medicare expenditures and medical care in the last year of life. *Journal of the American Medical Association (JAMA),* 2001, *286,* 1349–1355.

Manton, K. G., and Gu, X. L. Changes in the prevalence of chronic disability in U.S. black and non-black population above age 65 from 1982 to 1999. *Proceedings of the National Academy of Sciences,* Online article #1522, May 8, 2001.

National Academy on an Aging Society. *Demography is not destiny.* Washington, DC: Gerontological Society of America, 1999.

New York Times. Insular Japan needs, but resists immigration. July 24, 2003, A1–A3.

Parmelee, P. A., and Lawton, M. P. The design of special environments for the aged. In J. E. Birren and K. W. Schaie (Eds.), *Handbook of the psychology of aging* (3rd ed.). San Diego: Academic Press, 1990.

Perls, T. T. The oldest old. *Scientific American,* 1995, 70–75.

Perls, T. T., Alpert, L., Wagner, G. G., Vijg, J., and Kruglyak, L. Siblings of centenarians live longer. *Lancet,* 1998, *351,* 1560–1565.

Perls, T. T. and Silver, M. H. *Living to 100: Lessons in living to your maximum potential at any age.* New York: Basic Books, 1999.

Perls, T. T., and Wood, E. R. Acute care costs of the oldest old: They cost less, their care intensity is less, and they go to nonteaching hospitals. *Archives of Internal Medicine,* 1996, *156,* 754–760.

Poon, L. W., Johnson, M. A., Davey, A., Dawson, D. V., Siegler, I. C., and Martin, P. Psychosocial predictors of survival among centenarians. In P. Martin, A. Rott, B. Hagberg, and K. Mongan (Eds), *Centenarians.* New York: Springer Publishing, 2000.

Quinn, J. *Entitlements and the federal budget: Securing our future.* Washington, DC: National Academy on Aging, 1996.

Riley, M. W., and Riley, J. Longevity and social structure: The potential of the added years. In A. Pifer and L. Bronte (Eds.), *Our aging society: Paradox and promise.* New York: W.W. Norton, 1986.

Samuelsson, S. M., Baur, B., Hagberg, B., Samuelsson, G., Norbeck, B., Brun, A., Gustafson, L., and Risberg, J. The Swedish Centenarian Study: A multidisciplinary study of five consecutive cohorts at the age of 100. *International Journal of Aging and Human Development,* 1997, *45,* 223–253.

Schaie, K. W. Age changes and age differences. *The Gerontologist,* 1967, *7,* 128–132.

Schaie, K. W. *Intellectual development in adulthood.* Cambridge: Cambridge University Press, 1996.

Schaie, K. W. (Ed.), *Longitudinal studies of adult psychological development.* New York: Guilford Press, 1983.

Schaie, K. W. Methodological problems in descriptive developmental research on adulthood and aging. In J. R. Nesselroade and H. W. Reese (Eds.), *Lifespan developmental psychology: Methodological issues.* New York: Academic Press, 1973.

Schaie, K. W. Quasi-experimental research designs in the psychology of aging. In J. E. Birren and K. W. Schaie (Eds.), *Handbook of the psychology of aging.* New York: Van Nostrand Reinhold, 1977.

Silver, M. H., Newell, K., Hyman, B., Growdon, J., Hedley, E. T., and Perls, T. Unraveling the mystery of cognitive changes in old age. *International Psychogeriatrics,* 1998, *10,* 25–41.

Stoller, E., and Gibson, R. C. *Worlds of difference: Inequalities in the aging experience.* Thousand Oaks, CA: Pine Forge Press, 2000.

Suzman, R. M., Willis, D. P., and Manton, K. G. (Eds.), *The oldest old.* New York: Oxford University Press, 1992.

U.S. Administration on Aging. *A profile of older Americans.* Washington, DC: 2002.

U.S. Census Bureau. *An aging world: 2001.* http://www.census.gov/prod/2001 pubs/p95-01-1.pdf, 2001a.

U.S. Census Bureau. Centenarians in the United States. *Current Population Reports,* P23, No. 199RV, 1999.

U.S. Census Bureau. Educational attainment in the U.S.: March 1998. *Current Population Reports,* P20, No. 513, 1998a.

U.S. Census Bureau. *Global Aging into the 21st Century.* Washington, DC: U.S. Department of Commerce, 1996.

U.S. Census Bureau. Projections of the population of the United States, by age, sex, and race: 1983–2080. *Current Population Reports,* Series P25, No. 1104, 1993.

U.S. Census Bureau. Life expectancy at birth: United States 1940, 1950, 1960, 1970, and 1998. *National Vital Statistics Reports,* 48, No. 11, 2000.

U.S. Census Bureau. *The 65 years and over population: 2000.* C2KBR/01-10. Washington, DC: October 2001b.

United Nations. *World population prospects: The 2000 revision.* New York: U.N. Publications, 2001.

White, N., and Cunningham, W. R. Is terminal drop pervasive or specific? *Journals of Gerontology,* 1988, *44,* S141–144.

Woodruff, D. Introduction: Multidisciplinary perspectives of aging. In D. Woodruff and J. Birren (Eds.), *Aging: Scientific perspectives and social issues.* New York: Van Nostrand, 1975.

World Health Organization (WHO). *Active Ageing: A Policy Framework.* Geneva, Switzerland: WHO, 2002.

chapter

2

Historical and Cross-Cultural Issues in Aging

This chapter includes both historical and cross-cultural views related to

- The role of older people in stable, preliterate, or primitive societies
- Elders in some non-western cultures
- Changes in the social roles of older persons
- Societal norms regarding aging
- Older adults' expectations of society
- Contrasting perspectives regarding the impact of modernization on the relationship between older persons and the larger society

The experience of aging is dramatically different from earlier historical periods. The social and economic roles of older persons, their interactions with families and the larger social system where they live are in many ways profoundly different today from previous generations. Until relatively recently, only a minority of people lived long enough to be considered old. As the number of older people has grown and as social values have changed, the authority and power of older adults in society have also shifted.

The experiences of older adults differ cross-culturally as well as historically. That is, in addition to historical changes, significant cultural variations affect the social position of older persons. Perhaps the greatest differences in the status of older adults are between traditional societies and those of the modernized world, with its rapidly changing values and norms. Examining the different ways that other societies, both historical and contemporary, have dealt with issues affecting their elders can shed light on the process of aging in our society. The emergence of "comparative sociocultural gerontology" or an "anthropology of aging" has served to refute some of the myths of the "good old days" presumed to exist in historical times and in contemporary nonindustrial societies. It begins to differentiate what aspects of aging are universal or biological as opposed to which factors are largely shaped by the sociocultural system (Sokolovsky, 1997; Infeld, 2002).

Understanding how aging in contemporary American society differs from that experienced elsewhere, and which factors are socioculturally determined, can also suggest strategies for improving environments in which to grow old. Within the constraints of this one chapter, we can only glance at a few other cultures. For a more complete view, we urge you to turn to the available literature on the anthropology of aging, including the *Journal of Cross-Cultural Gerontology*. While this chapter explores aging cross-culturally and historically, Chapter 14 focuses on the cultural diversity represented by older ethnic minorities, including recent refugees and immigrants, within contemporary American society.

Old Age Historically

Old Age in Ancient Cultures

Although our knowledge of aging in prehistoric and primitive societies is limited, we know that people of advanced age were rare, with most dying before the age of 35. Nevertheless, there were always a few people perceived to be old, although they were probably chronologically relatively young, since maturity and death came quickly in the lives of people struggling to survive in harsh environments. Those few elders were treated with respect, in a manner that reflected a sense of sacred obligation. During ceremonial occasions, elders were seated in positions of high honor and served as the clan's memory. The belief that an

> **EXAMPLES OF DEATH-HASTENING BEHAVIOR IN HISTORICAL PERIODS**
>
> In some rural areas of ancient Japan, older people were carried into the mountains and left there to die. It was not unusual for aged Eskimos to walk off into the snow when famine and disease placed great burdens on the tribe. In other cases, Eskimo families moved to other areas and left their frail elders behind.

older person was a mediator between this world and the next gave added prestige to elders by conferring on them the role of witch doctors or priests.

Even though positive attitudes toward the young-old were widespread, nonsupportive or death-hastening behavior was shown toward those who survived beyond an "intact" stage of life. This stage of old-old age was often referred to as the "sleeping period." No longer able to contribute to the common welfare and look after themselves, older people were then viewed as useless, "overaged," or "already dead," and were sometimes treated brutally. Those who outlived their usefulness were a heavy burden in societies that existed close to the edge of subsistence, particularly those in harsh climates with little agriculture, or with no system of **social stratification** (Barker, 1997; Glascock, 1997).

The practice of **geronticide** or **senecide**—the deliberate destruction of older community members—was viewed as functional and, for many traditional societies, was often performed with great reverence or ceremony. In a minority of primitive tribes, the frail were killed outright; in most, they

> **GERONTICIDE WITH REVERENCE**
>
> Ritual sacrifice was used to kill the oldest members perceived to be a burden among the Ojibwa Indians of Lake Winnipeg and the Siriono of the Bolivian rain forest.

were abandoned, neglected, or encouraged to commit suicide, and the burial place was often converted into an ancestral shrine. Consistent with the coexistence of positive attitudes toward the old along with their nonsupportive treatment, geronticide in many societies often occurred under the older person's direction and by a close relative, usually a son. Examples of geronticide, abandonment, and forsaking support to the oldest-old were reported in remote cultures as recently as the twentieth century (Glascock, 1997).

Old Age in Greek and Roman Cultures

In Greek and Roman classical cultures, 80 percent of the population perished before reaching the stage of life that we now consider to be middle age. Nevertheless, our chronological conception of age, with *old* defined as age 65 and over, began during this period. Age implied power in the ancient cities, which were ruled by councils of elders who derived their authority from their years. Within the family, the eldest male's authority was nearly absolute, and the young were dependent on the old by custom and by law. However, only the elite members of society, not the peasants, benefited from the respect accorded age by the community.

Some idea of the changing status of older people in ancient Greek society can be obtained by analyzing how old and young were depicted in Greek tragedy. In her book, *Time in Greek Tragedy*, de Romilly (1968) points to an evolution

AGING IN GREEK MYTHOLOGY

In the myth of Eos and Tithonus, Eos (or Aurora), the goddess of dawn, fell in love with Tithonus, a mortal. She prevailed on Zeus to grant him immortality but forgot to ask that he remain eternally young like her. She left him when he became very old and frail, and eventually turned him into a grasshopper. Presumably this was a better fate for the ancient Greeks and Romans than remaining a feeble old man.

of views about age from Aeschylus in the late sixth and early fifth centuries B.C., to Euripides in the mid- to late fifth century B.C. For Aeschylus, age brought with it wisdom, especially about justice and prudence. Although he refers to the destructive influences of age, particularly loss of physical strength, Aeschylus insists that such physical decline has no impact on the older person's mind or spirit. In contrast, Sophocles' tragedies, which were written during the middle of the fifth century, depict old age as distasteful, a time of decline in physical and mental functioning. For Sophocles, youth is the only period of life characterized by true happiness. Later, in Euripides' plays, older people are both wise and weak. Older characters of Euripides long for eternal youth; old age is described as miserable, bitter, and painful. The shift from Aeschylus' admiration of old age to the exaltation of youth and denigration of old age by Sophocles and Euripides may be a reflection of the growth of democracy in fifth-century Greece (and, consequently, a growing belief in social equality) as well as of the heroism of young men in the wars of that era.

This coincided with the Classical period, when beauty, youth, and strength were idealized in the visual arts. Greek mythology also depicts the old as tyrannical and wicked, the ultimate enemy in many myths. The gift of immortality was cherished only if it meant rejuvenation or eternal youth. Greek and later Roman mythology contrasted the eternal youthfulness of the gods with the gradual deterioration of mortals. Many philosophers and physicians in ancient Greece, such as Plato, Aristotle and Galen, sought to explain the meaning of old age, the place of elders in the social order, and how to maintain health as the body aged. Human development was described by Hippocratic writers as being divided into four stages, although Aristotle suggested three stages of youth, a fourth stage that he labeled the "prime of life," and old age (Warren, 2002). These stages are in some ways precursors to the developmental phases proposed by modern psychologists, as described in Chapter 6.

Old Age in Medieval Europe

Little is known about the role of older people during the medieval period, except that life expectancy was even shorter than in the Greek and Roman eras. To a large extent, increasing urbanization and related problems of sanitation and disease were responsible for the high death rates before people reached old age. Nevertheless, older people were more likely than the young to survive the Black Plague and other epidemics, creating a disproportionate population of elders and arousing bitterness among the young.

The nobility lived longer than the common people during the Middle Ages, largely because of better standards of living. Furthermore, the general populace was more likely to die of war or the numerous diseases that plagued this era. The nobility had the freedom to flee such conditions. For the small proportion of poor people who did manage to survive, old age was a cruel period of life.

To the extent that the prevailing attitudes toward older persons in that historical period can be inferred from art, one would have to conclude that old age was depicted as ugly, weak, and deceptive. During the Renaissance, artists and poets reestablished links with Classical Greece, contrasting the beauty of youth with the unattractiveness and weakness they, like the ancient Greeks, saw in old age. Many of Shakespeare's plays, including *Hamlet, Othello,* and *As You Like It,* portray a contrast between the vitality and energy of youth versus the weakness and immobility of old age.

Nevertheless, discussions prevailed on how to avoid deterioration in old age. One of the first "handbooks on aging" was written by Arnaldus of Villa Nova in 1290, who recommended "moderation in all things" as well as maintaining cleanliness of the body and one's home (Warren, 2002).

Old Age in Colonial America

In seventeenth- and eighteenth-century America, old age was treated with deference and respect, in part because it was so rare. This attitude has been described as one of veneration, an emotion closer to awe than affection and a form of worship deeply embedded in the Judeo-Christian ethic of early America. The Puritans, for example, viewed old age as a sign of God's favor and assumed that youth would inevitably defer to age. Old men occupied the highest public offices, as well as positions of authority within the family, until they died; fathers waited until their sixties before giving their land to the eldest son. Church seats were given to the old. The primary basis of the power enjoyed by older people in colonial times was their control of property, especially productive farmland. In this agricultural society, such control amounted to the ability to dominate all key institutions—the family, the church, the economy, and the polity.

Even though the oldest members of society were exalted by law and custom in colonial times, they received little affection or love from younger people; in fact, most were kept at an emotional distance. In reserving power and prestige for older persons, society in many ways created this separation between young and old. Elders frequently complained that they had lived to become

---

SHAKESPEARE'S VIEW OF AGING

In Shakespeare's play, *As You Like It,* youth evolves from an impulsive boy to soldier, to the fifth age "full of wise saws and modern instances." The sixth age is depicted as weak, with "his big manly voice, turning again toward childish treble." The seventh and final stage "is second childishness and mere oblivion, sans teeth, sans eyes, sans taste, sans everything." Thus, Shakespeare's view of old age is that of decline and uselessness; this may reflect the attitude of sixteenth-century Europe that the old were a burden to a community struggling with food shortages and high death rates among its infants and young soldiers. Perhaps most striking is Shakespeare's attribution of wisdom and perspective to middle age, in contrast to the beliefs of pre-Classical and Hellenistic Greek playwrights and philosophers that old age is the time of greatest wisdom.

strangers in their communities. Old age was not a time of serenity, but rather anxiety about adequately fulfilling social obligations and keeping faith with God (Achenbaum, 1996).

This pattern persisted until about 1770, when attitudes toward the older population began to change and the relative status of youth was elevated. Indications of this change included:

- Church-seating arrangements that had favored the old were abolished.
- The first mandatory retirement laws for legislators were passed.
- The eldest son no longer automatically inherited the family property.
- New fashions were introduced that flattered youth—a change from the white wigs and broadwaisted coats that favored older men.
- New words appeared that negatively portrayed elders, such as *codger* and *fuddy-duddy*.
- Family portraits of all members were placed on the same horizontal plane rather than positioning the oldest male members to stand over women and children (Fischer, 1978).

A major demographic change occurred in approximately 1810, when the median age began to rise, creating a greater percentage of the population older than the typical "old" age of 40 or 50. This was due primarily to a declining birth rate, not a falling death rate. After 1810, the median age advanced at a constant annual rate, approximately 0.4 percent per year, until about 1950 (Fischer, 1978); this has been attributed to reductions in the impact of diseases. A dramatic change was that parents began to live beyond the period of their children's dependency, for the first time in history experiencing relatively good health at the time their children left the family home.

The Effects of Modernization

As the foregoing historical examples suggest, definitions of old age—as well as the authority exercised

Older people in Asian cultures enjoy teaching traditional arts to younger generations.

by older people—largely rested on the material and political resources controlled by older members of society. These resources include:

- traditional skills and knowledge
- security bestowed by property rights
- civil and political power
- food for communal sharing
- information control
- general welfare from routine services performed by older people such as child care

Within the constraints set by the social environment and its ideology, older people's social rank was generally determined by the balance between the cost of maintaining them and the societal contributions they were perceived to make. As age became a less important criterion for determining access to and control of valued resources, older members of society lost some of their status and authority.

A number of explanations have been advanced for the declining status of the old in our society. **Modernization theory** is a major explanation. One of the first comparative analyses that raised this issue was reported by Leo Simmons in

The Role of the Aged in Primitive Society (1945). He noted that the status of older persons, as reflected in their resources and the honor bestowed upon them, varied inversely with the degree of technology, social and economic diversity, and occupational specialization (or modernization) in a given society. As society becomes more modernized, according to this theory, older people lose political and social power, influence, and leadership. These social changes also may lead to disengagement of aging persons from community life. In addition, younger and older generations become increasingly separated socially, morally, and intellectually. Youth is glorified as the embodiment of progress and achievement, as well as the means by which society can attain such progress. Modernization theory has been advanced primarily by Cowgill (1974a, 1974b, 1986), and is defined by Cowgill (1974a) as:

> The transformation of a total society from a relatively rural way of life based on animate power, limited technology, relatively undifferentiated institutions, parochial and traditional outlook and values, toward a predominantly urban way of life, based on inanimate sources of power, highly differentiated institutions, matched by segmented individual roles, and a cosmopolitan outlook which emphasizes efficiency and progress (p. 127).

The characteristics of modernization that contribute to lower status for older people were identified by Cowgill as:

- health technology
- scientific technology as applied in economic production and distribution
- urbanization
- literacy and mass education

According to Cowgill, the application of *health technology* reduced infant mortality and maternal deaths, and prolonged adult life, thereby increasing the number of older persons. With more older people in the labor market, competition between generations for jobs intensified, and retirement developed as a means of forcing older people out of the labor market.

Scientific technology creates new jobs primarily for the young, with older workers more likely to remain in traditional occupations that become obsolete. The rapid development of industries that rely on high technology today and the gap between generations in the use of computers illustrate this phenomenon. Unable to perform the socially valued role of contributors to the workforce, many older workers feel marginalized and alienated.

In the early stages of modernization, when the society is relatively rural, young people are attracted to urban areas, whereas older parents and grandparents remain on the family farm or in rural communities. The resulting residential segregation of the generations has a dramatic impact on family interactions. The geographical and occupational mobility of the young, in turn, leads to increased social distance between generations and to a reduced status of the old.

Finally, modernization is characterized by efforts to promote *literacy and education,* which

---

ROLE CHANGES AND OLDER WOMEN

Evidence of international differences in adaptation to role loss is reflected in suicide rates among older women. Although the rate among women in the United States *drops* from 11.6 per 100,000 among those aged 40 to 50 to 6.6 per 100,000 among women over 65, the suicide rate *increases* dramatically in Japan, tripling from 11.6 to 39.3 per 100,000. In Taiwan there is also a striking increase, from 10.4 to 34.6 per 100,000 in this same age range (Hu, 1995). In general, women aged 75 and older have higher suicide rates than their counterparts in English-speaking countries. Suicide rates for men aged 75 and older are higher than for any other age group in Asian countries, especially in rural China and Singapore, less so in Japan (Pritchard and Baldwin, 2002).

tend to be targeted toward the young. As younger generations acquire more education than their parents, they begin to occupy higher-status positions. Intellectual and moral differences between the generations increase, with older members of society experiencing reduced leadership roles and influence (Cowgill, 1974a, 1974b).

Some social historians have criticized modernization theory, arguing that it idealizes the past and ignores the fact that older people in many preindustrial societies were treated harshly and at the whim of younger family members (Albert and Cattell, 1994; Kertzer and Laslett, 1994). However, there is considerable empirical support for this theory. For example, rapid urbanization in many developing countries has dislodged the tradition of family support for many older people. Modern migration programs in India, while providing resources for young and old, have resulted in younger people obtaining more education and creating a sense of superiority over their illiterate elders. Rapid urbanization has left almost 30 percent of old people in rural areas in India without family nearby to care for them (Dandekar, 1996; Vincentnathan and Vincentnathan, 1994). Meanwhile, families who eke out a meager living in urban areas have little with which to assist their elders who live with them. In the economically more successful countries of East Asia, such as Japan and Taiwan, older people have benefited from improvements in health care, income, and longer life expectancy, but at the cost of power and prestige that was accorded previous generations of older adults (Silverman, Hecht, and McMillin, 2000).

Occupation and education appear to have a reversed J-shaped relationship to modernization. In the early phases of rapid social change (illustrated by nations such as Turkey and the Philippines), the occupational and educational status of older adults shows a decline, but then later improves (exemplified by New Zealand, Canada, and the United States). This suggests that, as societies move beyond an initial state of rapid modernization, status differences between generations decrease and the relative status of older people may rise, particularly when reinforced by social policies such as Social Security, which have helped to improve older adults' financial status. Societies in advanced stages of modernization may become more aware of the older population's devalued status. Through public education, social policies, and the media, they then attempt to create more opportunities for and positive images of older people. This has already begun in the United States, in part because of the aging of the baby boomers, who have the political clout and resources to change popular stereotypes of aging. Advertising and television programs increasingly portray older persons as vital, active, and involved.

Alternatives to Modernization Theory

More recent analyses of older people's status in nonindustrial societies have found that conditions for high status did not always apply. For example, differences often existed between the prestige of the old and the way they were actually treated; over 60 percent of the 41 nonindustrial societies examined by Glascock (1997) had some form of nonsupportive treatment (ranging from insults to killing) for the old, even though older members were also respected in many of these cultures. Death-hastening activities are often justified by claims that they are directed toward elders who are no longer active and productive and are a liability to society and their families. Most societies have some norms of favorable treatment toward their elders, but considerable variability exists in practice. For example, filial piety in China and Taiwan was not always manifest, but was affected by family resources and the number of living children (Ikels, 1997). The coexistence of high status and bad treatment in many traditional societies can be partially explained in terms of differential behavior toward the young-old versus old-old, noted in our earlier discussion of traditional societies that abandoned or murdered their frail elders.

Class and gender differences also come into play. For instance, the norms of filial piety were more often practiced by wealthy families in traditional rural China. Despite the Confucian reverence for age, older people in lower-class families had fewer resources to give them status. The importance of women's household responsibilities throughout life may explain their relatively higher status in old age than men's (Cool and McCabe, 1987).

Turning to contemporary China, there has been a major transformation of life for older people on the mainland. The "political economy" has had an impact on elders' status as government policies have been altered. For example, women have benefited from changes such as not having to submit to arranged marriages or having their feet bound. Their work opportunities have expanded by opening up more jobs to women. National social insurance also benefits older Chinese citizens. But not all changes have had positive effects. Rules limiting family size and the breaking up of communes have had negative consequences for the childless older population in particular. Both the Chinese government and entrepreneurs have begun to build group housing for childless elders. These effects are expected to continue as future cohorts of older people contend with fewer children to care for them in times of need. These changes will also reduce multigenerational living arrangements in China (Ikels, 1997).

Another alternative to modernization theory is that the development of state or nation represented a shift in older people's roles (Dickerson-Putnam, 1994; Fry, 1996). With the movement from kin-based societies to modern states and capitalist economies in the nineteenth century, labor became a commodity that was sold in exchange for economic security rather than for the security of an extended family. Such marketplace exchanges also created competition between old and young for jobs; this led to the emergence of retirement laws in nineteenth-century Europe that served to formally remove older people from competition for jobs and increase opportunities for the young. The emergence of social security programs in capitalist economies was intended to provide a safety net for retired people that could reduce their dependence on kin and prevent the older person from reentering the job market (Achenbaum, 1996).

Ideal of Equality versus Status of Age in America

In his classic historical analysis, Fischer (1978) formulated reasons other than modernization for explaining changes between generations in American society. He argues that these changes cannot be attributed to modernization, because the decline in elders' status occurred before industrialization and urbanization. He also contends that the increase in numbers of older people does not fully explain the shifts in attitudes toward the old. Instead, he suggests that the emphasis on youthfulness that characterizes our society can be partially attributed to our cultural values of liberty and equality. Both of these values run counter to a hierarchy of authority based on age.

According to Fischer, the elevated status of older persons in earlier historical periods gradually became supplanted in the late eighteenth and early nineteenth centuries by an emerging ideal of age equality. The fundamental change was caused by the social and intellectual forces unleashed by revolutions in America and France. The spirit of equality was dramatically expressed in public fetes borrowed from the French Revolution, where a symbolic harmony of youth and age was celebrated in elaborate rituals of young and old exchanging food.

However, although our society's ideology was egalitarian, economic inequalities actually grew in the nineteenth century. For example, economic status became the basis of seating arrangements in public meetings. Individualistic pursuits of wealth created countervailing forces to a sense of community that had previously been founded on the power of elders. Thus, the age equality that had initially replaced veneration of elders was later supplanted by a celebration of youthfulness and a derogation of age. Inequalities based on age reemerged, but this time to the advantage of youth. Growing contempt toward older people in the mid-1800s is vividly illustrated by Thoreau's (1856) conclusion, "Age is no better, hardly so well qualified for an instructor of youth, for it has not profited as much as it has lost." Heroes and legends centered on younger men, such as Daniel Boone. Social trends in the early twentieth century, such as the development of retirement policies, mass education, and residential segregation of generations, furthered perceptions of older people as useless, with the cult of youth reaching its peak in the 1960s. A common expression of the time was "Don't trust anyone over age 30!" One irony was that as the economic and social conditions of many older adults declined, their ties of family affection, especially between grandparents and grandchildren, often grew stronger. In addition, adult children assumed responsibility for the care of their parents, who were living longer than at any other time in history.

Other Perspectives on Historical Change

Historians and gerontologists have questioned whether a critical turning point in age relations

Even the oldest-old have important roles in most Asian families.

occurred between 1770 and 1830 (Achenbaum, 1996). Achenbaum, for example, has taken a position somewhere between Fischer's view and modernization theory regarding the change in status of older adults in the United States. He has identified social trends similar to those documented by Fischer, stating that prior to the middle of the nineteenth century, elders were venerated because of their experiences and were actively involved in socially useful roles. A decline in their status, Achenbaum asserts, occurred during the post–Civil War era. The growing emphasis on efficiency and impersonality in bureaucracies, along with increased misperceptions about senility, furthered a perception of old age as obsolescence. Both Fischer and Achenbaum suggest that it is not possible to establish a firm relationship between modernization and older people's status; rather, they maintain that Americans have always been ambivalent about old age. Shifting beliefs and values are viewed as more salient in accounting for loss in status than are changes in the economic and political structures that occurred with modernization.

These contrasting perspectives of social gerontologists and anthropologists suggest that there is not a simple "before and after" relationship in the meaning and significance of old age between preindustrial and modern societies (Achenbaum, 1996). People in preindustrial societies who, by reason of social class, lacked property and power undoubtedly suffered from loss of status, regardless of their age. For such persons, modernization brought less improvement in status than for older people who were better educated and of higher socioeconomic background. Such inequities continue to be problematic, particularly among persons of color within our society. Cultural gerontologists have emphasized that modernization is not a linear process, but proceeds at different rates and through varied stages, each of which may have a different impact on older people's status (Fry, 1996).

In addition, cross-cultural evidence shows that cultural values can mitigate many of the negative effects of modernization on older people.

This is illustrated in modern, industrialized, and urban Japanese society. Confucian values of filial piety and ancestor worship have helped to maintain older persons' relatively high status and integration in family life, as well as their leadership in national politics. Traditional values of reciprocity and lifelong indebtedness to one's parents are a major reason for continued three-generational households in Japan, with 54 percent of older adults in metropolitan areas living with an adult child. Nevertheless, fewer Japanese elders live with their children today than in the past—55 percent in 1995 versus 90 percent in 1960 (Akiyama, Antonucci, and Campbell, 1997; Kinsella and Velkoff, 2001; Maeda, 1998).

Filial piety also plays a dominant role in family attitudes and government policies regarding care for aging parents in Korea, where the number of people 65 and older has increased threefold in 25 years. Surveys of young Koreans reveal that more than 90 percent believe that adult children must care for their older parents, and in fact 90 percent of older adults cite family as their primary source of support. These values are supported by the high proportion of people aged 65 and older—65 percent—who live with their adult children, even in urbanized areas like Seoul (Kim, 1998; Levande, Herrick, and Sung, 2000; Sung, 1998, 2000, 2001). In particular, daughters-in-law are expected to provide most of the day-to-day care for their aging parents-in-law. The government of Korea promotes family-based caregiving by sponsoring a "Respect for Elders Day" and a "Respect for Elders Week," as well as prizes to honor outstanding examples of filial piety. These initiatives help reduce Koreans' expectations from the government, although changing demographics today have placed a greater burden on families, with average family size down to 3.0 and with 46 percent of all married women in Korea working outside the home.

Other Asian countries where filial piety has been maintained, despite changing work and family patterns, are Singapore, Thailand, and the Philippines, where 91 percent, 69 percent, and 67 percent of women 60 and older, respectively, live with their children (Kinsella and Velkoff, 2001). The importance of filial piety—a sense of reverence and deference toward elders—supersedes modern social demands in these Asian countries.

Political ideology may also be an intervening variable. This is illustrated by the effect of Communist party policies in Maoist China, which at first villified older people but eventually sought them to work with the young to promote the Cultural Revolution. Despite their emphasis on collectivization, the Communist leaders did not provide a comprehensive welfare program for older people, especially those in rural China. Families were expected to provide care for their elders, except for those who were childless in their old age. However, as modernization and especially urbanization continued in China after the 1950s, societal views of and governmental benefits to older persons improved (Ikels, 1997).

In sum, the effects of modernization historically do not appear to be uniform or unidirectional. As shown in the next section, many contemporary cultures are still struggling to define meaningful roles for their rapidly increasing populations of older people. Changing values and declining resources result in conflicting attitudes toward their older members in many transitional societies.

THE UNDERPINNINGS OF FILIAL PIETY IN ASIAN CULTURE

In his writings, Confucius emphasized that young people should respect, not just provide care for, their elders:

> Filial piety today is taken to mean providing nourishment for parents, but dogs and horses are provided with nourishment. If it is not done with reverence for parents, what is the difference between men and animals?

SOURCE: From *Analects*, Book 2, Chapter 7, quoted in Sung, 2000.

A Cross-Cultural View of Old Age in Contemporary Societies

As we have discussed, every society defines people as old on some basis, whether chronological, functional, or generational, and assigns that group a particular set of rights, privileges, and duties that differ from those of its younger members. For example, older persons in our society today qualify for Social Security and Medicare on the basis of their age. In some religious groups, only the oldest members are permitted to perform the most sacred rituals. Societies generally distinguish two, sometimes three, classes of elders:

- those who are no longer fully productive economically, but are physically and mentally able to attend to their daily needs.
- those who are totally dependent, who require custodial care, and who are regarded as social burdens and thus may be negatively treated.
- those who continue to participate actively in the economy of the social system, through farming or self-employment, care of grandchildren, or household maintenance, while younger adults work outside the home.

Consistent with social exchange theory discussed in Chapter 8, older people who can no longer work but who control resources essential to fulfill the needs of younger group members generally offset the societal costs incurred in maintaining them. In some social systems, political, judicial, or ritual power and privileges are vested in older people as a group, and this serves to mediate social costs. For instance, in societies such as those of East Africa, politically powerful positions are automatically assigned to men who reach a certain age (Keith, 1990). In other societies, the old do not inherently have privileges, but gain power as individuals, often through diplomatic skills and contacts with powerful others. The following examples from other cultures illustrate the balance between the costs and contributions made by older adults:

- Older Sherpas in Nepal today must cope with the indirect effects of modernization. Job opportunities for young adults in Darjeeling and other parts of India have increased in recent years, as young men have found jobs as porters for climbers in the Himalayas. As a result, adult children are not available or interested in living with their aging parents, resulting in many older adults who live alone and express a sense of abandonment (Goldstein and Beall, 2002).
- In Australia, the traditional respect accorded to older people in the Aborigine culture has resulted in a valuable role for older women. In one Aborigine community in central Australia, a group of women, all over age 70, have formed a night patrol that intervenes to stop rowdy parties and disco activity that result in excessive drinking and violence. These peacekeepers receive more cooperation from the young perpetrators than do police, and community leaders report a decline in assaults and arrests for drunken behavior over the past ten years since this group began its work (AARP, 2000).
- Older women play a valuable role in Zulu culture. Their pensions are a steady source of family income, and grandmothers provide an important caregiving function. Despite their contributions, these older women reported feeling that younger Zulus did not respect them. Grandchildren reported a schism between their new values of individualism and traditional tribal values of kinship held by their grandmothers (AARP, 1999).

TRADITIONAL EXTENDED HOUSEHOLDS IN CHINA

The position of the aging father in the Chinese family depends almost entirely on the political and economic power he wields. Elders in wealthy Chinese households and those with substantial pensions to contribute to family expenses enjoy higher status within the family and are better able to control the lives of their adult children than those in poor households.

In other cultures, respect toward intact elders may be promoted, but a subtle acceptance of benign neglect may result in the demise of older persons who are physically and/or cognitively impaired. An ethnographic analysis of Niue, an independent Polynesian island, revealed significant discrepancies between the status of older people who were in good health and had important social and political functions, and those who were too frail to care for themselves. Although medical services are free on Niue, families and neighbors did not summon visiting doctors and public health nurses, even for infected sores, painful joints, and other treatable conditions in these frail elders. The basic needs of cognitively impaired elders were even more frequently ignored. This may stem from values of reciprocity. Like other societies where reciprocity is crucial for intergenerational exchanges, the frail elders of Niue can no longer contribute to the group's well-being. Therefore, such neglect may be seen as a way of merely hastening the inevitable death of these weaker members of that society (Barker, 1997; Glascock, 1997).

Importance of Social Position and the Control of Property

Consistent with social exchange theory, control of property is a means to achieve power in most societies. In both past and present times, older people have used their rights over property to guarantee their security by compelling others to support them or to provide them with goods and services. For example, among the Etal Islanders in Micronesia, the old try to keep enough property to ensure continued care by younger members who hope to inherit it (Nason, 1981). In the Gwembe Tonga tribe in Zambia, males were formerly able to secure their positions by accumulating land and livestock. As their lineage land became covered by water, however, forced relocation cost many older people their exclusive control of property, and the old became dependent on sons and nephews, who acquired better land at the time of flooding (Colson and Scudder, 1981). In other societies, the leadership of males derives from their positions within the family.

Substantial class differences exist in elders' power in many countries. In addition, the extended family structure confers status on older members, even in the face of modernization. As economic resources decline and class differences disappear in such traditional cultures as China, with increasing modernization, filial piety may become undermined. For example, the growing pressures of limited housing and low income in China appear to be having a negative effect on younger generations' attitudes toward old people. In such instances, increased provision of public housing, health care, old-age pension plans, and policies that support family care of elders may serve to reduce tensions between generations. Some demographers have suggested that the improving health and financial status of older populations have resulted in more older adults choosing to live independently. In contrast to this concept of a normative trend toward individualism in traditional societies, other demographers have found that increases in older persons' income or that of their adult children do not result in significant changes in traditional family structures and the value of family interdependence (Cameron, 2000; Kinsella and Velkoff, 2001).

Older persons from traditional cultures who immigrate to Western countries face even more problems adjusting to the loss of power. In the past 30 years, waves of Indochinese refugees have come to the United States from countries experiencing political strife and unrest. Older relatives who arrived with younger family members have had more difficulties in adapting to American culture. Property and other resources in their native lands that afforded them importance and power have been stripped from them. Being in the United States has brought them a different life than the one they might have expected for their later years. These older refugees do not have the ability to provide material goods, land, or other financial support, which has traditionally given them status (Yee, 1997). Accordingly, traditional power has been eroded as families have started new lives in this culture. Indeed, financial self-sufficiency is a major determinant of adjustment to life in the United States among older Indochinese refugees, regardless of education, gender, and English proficiency. Refugees from Russia and other countries of the former Soviet Union are also struggling with the adjustment to their loss of status in their host country.

When older adults immigrate to the United States, it is often to join younger family members who moved here previously. They usually help their adult children in family-owned businesses and as caregivers for grandchildren. Many of these older immigrants lack economic and educational resources and are not proficient in English, thereby making acculturation more difficult. For all these reasons, immigrant elders are more likely than their U.S.-born counterparts to live in multigenerational households (Angel et al., 1999; Wilmoth, 2001; Wilmoth, DeJong, and Himes, 1997). In an analysis of U.S. census data on almost 64,000 older immigrants, Wilmoth (2001) compared the living arrangements of Latino (mostly Cuban and Mexican), Asian (mostly from China or Southeast Asia), and non-Hispanic white (mostly from Europe) immigrants. Significant differences emerged across immigrant groups, with the highest rates of independent living among white, Japanese, and Cuban immigrants. Living in another family member's home was more common among other Asian groups and elders from Mexico, especially among those who were unmarried, with lower incomes and less than a college education, and those with a physical disability. Therefore, immigration by people aged 60 and older may reduce their independence and personal control.

Knowledge as a Source of Power

Control over knowledge, especially ritual and religious knowledge, is another source of power. The aged Shaman is an example, revered in many societies for knowledge or wisdom. The importance of older members of society in maintaining cultural values is illustrated in India, where traditional Hindu law prescribes a four-stage life cycle for high-caste men: student, householder, ascetic, and mendicant. In the last two stages, older religious men are expected to renounce worldly attachments to seek enlightenment in isolated retreats. This practice ensures that the pursuit of the highest form of knowledge is limited to older men of higher castes (Sokolovsky, 1997).

Knowledge as the basis of older people's power has been challenged as traditional societies become more urbanized or assimilated into the majority culture. Over the course of the twentieth century, American Indian elders lost their roles as mentors and counselors to younger tribal members. Their knowledge of tribal customs and stories, agricultural skills, and folk medicine was no longer valued as family structures changed and people migrated away from the reservation (Baldridge, 2001).

Among some cultural groups, however, including many American Indian tribes, a revival of interest and pride in native identity and religion has occurred, thus raising the esteem of elders who possess ritual knowledge. For example, they are the only ones who know the words and steps for many traditional songs and dances. Knowledge of the group's culture, particularly its arts and handicrafts, native songs and epics, has enhanced the

---

GAINS AND LOSSES WITH INCREASED WORK ROLES

Women in Ganga in Papua New Guinea have assumed a larger role in local coffee production. However, these changes in their work lives have affected their traditional control over the rituals of education and initiation for younger girls. This was once an important part of their knowledge base and power. What was previously provided by a group of older women is now acted out by a young girl's closest relatives. Consequently the power base of older women in shaping the lives of young women has eroded (Dickerson-Putnam, 1994).

social status of older persons in these societies; furthermore, the traditions of reverence for old age and wisdom remain strong, overriding the impact of modernization on older people's roles. The timing of such a revival is critical, however. A similar revival among Plains Indians did not have comparable positive consequences for the tribe's older members who were no longer expert in traditional ways (Keith, 1990).

The growing desire for ethnic or tribal identity among many Native Americans, which has led to a conscious restoration of old forms, illustrates that modernization does not automatically erode the status of the elders. Similarly, the search for one's heritage or roots has led to increased contacts between younger generations seeking this information from older persons who often are a great repository of family histories.

Indeed, modernization has not resulted in the disintegration of extended families in most non-Western societies, including the rapidly developing Asian and Third World countries. Extended families in rural Thailand have adapted to the need for adult children to migrate to the cities for jobs by creating "skip-generation households," where grandparents remain in their rural homes, caring for grandchildren, while their adult children work in urban settings. This reciprocal dependency has also proved useful for many Asians and Eastern European refugee families in the United States where grandparents have immigrated with their adult children to provide regular child care to grandchildren in the extended family. At the same time, however, immigration by older people for the sake of their children and grandchildren can severely disrupt their lives and psychological well-being at a time when their own health may be declining (Dossa, 1999; Ikels, 1998; Pang, 1998).

In some countries, societal changes have placed unexpected burdens on elders. Older people in many African countries face multiple challenges created by major sociodemographic shifts, poverty, and the AIDS epidemic. Although much smaller in proportion than in other regions of the world, people aged 60 and older make up a growing share of the population in most African countries, from 6.8 percent in South Africa to 4.3 percent in Zimbabwe. Most still reside in rural areas, but a growing number in countries like Kenya and South Africa live in urban settings. With increasing migration of younger family members to urban centers, older adults in rural parts of Africa cannot rely on family caregivers. In fact, many provide a critical role as caregivers to grandchildren left behind by parents who seek employment in distant cities. In recent years, this responsibility has been compounded by the growing number of AIDS orphans, especially in sub-Saharan Africa. Of the 2.5 million deaths due to AIDS worldwide in 1998, two million occurred in sub-Saharan Africa. Given that the population aged 15 to 49 has been hardest hit by AIDS, older adults are often left to care for their grandchildren as well as extended family members. In most cases, they receive very little government support for their surrogate parenting. To make matters worse, most African countries provide little if any social security or pension benefits for their older citizens (Darkwa and Mazibuko, 2002; Kinsella and Ferreira, 1997; UNAIDS, 2000).

The way that older people react to change can serve to maintain or improve their position. Among the Sherpa in Tibet, for example, as younger sons move away from the community, and are not available to share households and care for the old, the old resist the traditional division of

---

POINTS TO PONDER

Think about immigrant and refugee groups in the United States. In what ways are elders in such families involved or not involved in the lives of their children and grandchildren? What impact do a common language and shared cultural values have on their interactions? To what extent have cultural differences created family conflicts and reduced the status of elders?

Older grandparents in rural China serve a vital role as full-time caregivers for their grandchildren.

property and tend to keep the younger sons' shares for themselves. Sherpa elders are also becoming proponents of birth control; since they cannot count on sons to take care of them as they wish, they prefer to share their property among fewer children, keeping more for themselves (Keith, 1990).

Effects of Culture and Modernization: The Case of Japan

In other situations, the buffering effects of culture on modernization are less distinct. For example, the issue of modernization and aging in contemporary Japan is particularly complex. Older adults traditionally have had high status and prestige. Values adopted from Confucianism are viewed as linking the old to a family system that emphasizes filial devotion, in which the dependence of elders in this "second privileged period"

is accepted (Ogawa and Retherford, 1993). This perspective has been criticized, however, as being based on cultural values and census figures that reflect intergenerational harmony rather than systematic anthropological or social research (Sokolovsky, 1997).

Indeed, the rapid demographic shifts in Japan that have made it one of the world's oldest populations (as described in Chapter 1) and the growth in the numbers of employed women (41 percent currently) have altered traditional conceptions of old age and reduced the positive influences of cultural values on intergenerational relations. For instance, the modernization of Japanese society has resulted in increased economic demands on the nuclear family. This is compounded by the fact that the unprecedented numbers of older people in Japan today have increased the societal costs of maintaining older members, and have created dilemmas for younger family members who are responsible for their support.

The majority of middle-aged persons in Japan still believe that care of older parents is the children's responsibility. Indeed, negligence toward one's parents is a source of great public shame in Japan. Society also assumes responsibility for the care of Japan's elders; all those over 70 receive free basic medical services, which is often viewed as a model by other Asian countries. The Japanese government provides incentives for home care by families; they can receive subsidies to remodel their homes in order to accommodate joint households as well as a tax credit for providing elder parent care (Maeda and Shimizu, 1992). For these reasons, the proportion of older parents living in multigenerational households is higher than in any other industrialized nation. In 1995, 55 percent of people over age 65 lived with their children and grandchildren, but this is a decline from 1985, when 69 percent of older households were multigenerational. Meanwhile, the number of households consisting only of the older couple has grown. In 1995 they made up 26 percent of older households, compared with 19 percent in 1985 (Jenike, 1997; Kinsella and Velkoff, 2001).

The number of nursing homes and long-stay hospitals in Japan has also grown, but more options are needed. These trends suggest that traditional customs of caring for aging parents in adult children's homes are slowly changing. The percentage of parents living with children has declined, due to urbanization, industrialization, the growing number of employed women, and the declining number of children since 1950. Urban–rural differences in family expectations are demonstrated by the fact that 25 percent of people age 75 and older in Tokyo live alone, compared with 15 percent in rural regions. Despite the growth of long-term care facilities, institutionalization in any form is still viewed as abandonment by many older people. As a result, most elder care still takes place in private homes.

Middle-aged women are the primary caregivers to Japanese elders, as in most other countries. As more older adults live longer, they may increasingly require goods and services at the perceived expense of younger members and may place even greater demands on middle-aged women in Japanese society. With the increased proportion of educated, professional women and newer cohorts influenced more by Western values than by Confucianism, many women do not want to leave their jobs to become caregivers to their parents or parents-in-law. Because of public concerns about long-term care needs for its growing population of oldest-old, the Japanese Diet passed the Public Long Term Care Insurance Act in 1997 (Maeda, 1998). This national policy guarantees comprehensive long-term care for all Japanese persons aged 65 or older, and for those aged 40 to 64 who may require long-term care. Funding is provided by a combination of mandatory insurance premiums paid by older persons (estimated to be approximately equivalent to $19 per month in 2000 and $27 in 2010) and taxes that will be paid to federal, prefecture, and municipal governments. Users of this service also must co-pay 10 percent of all incurred expenses.

This bold new legislation in Japan was implemented in 2000, but its impact has not yet been determined. The current shortage of long-term care options needs to be addressed to fully implement this program. Nevertheless, if it succeeds, this universal long-term care program is expected to relieve somewhat the burden on Japanese families and hospitals, where most long-term care occurs. The program is being watched closely by policy makers in other developed countries to see if it can serve as a model for caring for their increasing populations of oldest-old.

Summary and Implications for the Future

These brief examples from diverse cultures around the world illustrate how each society responds to its aging members within the constraints set by both the natural environment and the larger human environment of social and technological change. A basic principle governing the status of older adults appears to be the effort to achieve a balance between older people's contributions to the society and the costs of supporting them. As will be discussed in detail in Chapter 10, however, the family plays an important role in supporting the old in most societies. Historical and cross-cultural evidence also suggests that maximum social participation of older adults in society results in greater acceptance and respect of elders by the young in most cultures.

The extent to which older citizens are engaged in society appears to vary with the nature of their power resources, such as their material possessions, knowledge, and social authority. In most of their exchanges, older people seek to maintain reciprocity and to be active independent agents in the management of their own lives. That is, they prefer to give money, time, or other resources in exchange for services or materials. This theoretical perspective, described as social exchange theory in Chapter 8, suggests that modern society should seek ways to increase older people's exchange resources so that they are valued by society. For example, maximizing the social value and productivity of the old in our society might include retraining older adults, developing innovative educational programs for older learners (see Chapter 5), and creating opportunities for part-time employment (see Chapter 12).

Control of resources as a basis for social interactions between members of a society is important throughout the life cycle. However, it becomes even more crucial in old age, because retirement generally results in a decline in one's level of control over material and social resources. As their physical strength diminishes and their social world correspondingly shrinks, many older people face the challenge of altering their environments and using their capacities in ways that will help them to maintain reciprocal exchanges and to protect their competence and independence. This may be an even greater problem for older refugees who may still have full physical and cognitive functions, but have lost material resources in their homeland that would have given them power and prestige. Older people who immigrate to the United States often do so to be with their adult children and generally help with child care or the family business. Although this may represent a reciprocal exchange, immigration in the later years can also deprive elders of their independence and opportunities for active aging. These attempts to maintain control over one's environment in the face of changing personal capacities and resources are consistent with the person–environment model presented in Chapter 1. This issue will be discussed in detail in subsequent chapters on biological, psychological, and social changes with aging.

The growth of Japan's older population, combined with the effects of modernization and economic demands on the nuclear family, has resulted in major legislation to support long-term care for frail Japanese elders. Efforts to provide options in long-term care for U.S. elders are described in Chapters 11 and 17. The dearth of information on cross-cultural issues in gerontology suggests a need for more anthropologists to direct their research toward comparing culture and countries in how the aging process and elders are viewed in different settings.

GLOSSARY

filial piety   a sense of reverence and deference to elders that encourages care for one's aging family members.

geronticide (or senecide)   inducing the death of old persons, as practiced in some ancient cultures

modernization theory   advances in technology, applied sciences, urbanization, and literacy which, in this context, are related to a decline in the status of older people

social stratification   divisions among people (e.g., by age, ethnic group) for purposes of maintaining distinctions between different strata by significant characteristics of those strata

REFERENCES

AARP. Adapting to a new social order. *Global aging report*, 1999, 4, 6

AARP. *Global aging report*, 2000, 5, 5.

Achenbaum, W. A. Historical perspectives on aging. In R. H. Binstock and L. K., George (Eds.), *Handbook of aging and the social sciences* (4th ed.). San Diego: Academic Press, 1996.

Akiyama, H., Antonucci, T. C., and Campbell, R. Exchange and reciprocity among two generations of Japanese and American women. In J. Sokolovsky (Ed.), *The cultural context of aging* (3rd ed.). Westport, CT: Bergin and Garvey, 1997.

Albert, S. M., and Cattell, M. G. *Old age in global perspective*. New York: G. K. Hall and Co., 1994.

Angel, J. L., Angel, R. J., Lee, G. Y., and Markides, K. S. Age at migration and family dependency among older Mexican immigrants: Recent evidence from the Mexican American EPESE. *The Gerontologist*, 1999, 39, 59–65.

Baldridge, D. Indian elders: Family traditions in crisis. *American Behavioral Scientist*, 2001, 44, 1515–1527.

Barker, J. C. Between humans and ghosts: The decrepit elderly in a Polynesian society. In J. Sokolovsky (Ed.), *The cultural context of aging*. Westport, CT: Bergin and Garvey, 1997.

Cameron, L. The residency decision of elderly Indonesians: A nested logit analysis. *Demography*, 2000, 37, 17–27.

Colson, E., and Scudder, T. Old age in Gwemba District, Zambia. In P. Amoss and S. Harrell (Eds.), *Other ways of growing old*. Stanford, CA: Stanford University Press, 1981.

Cool, L., and McCabe, J. The "scheming hag" and the "dear old thing." The anthropology of aging women. In J. Sokolovsky (Ed.), *Growing old in different cultures*. Acton, MA: Copley, 1987.

Cowgill, D. Aging and modernization: A revision of the theory. In J. F. Gubrium (Ed.), *Late life communities and environmental policy*. Springfield, IL: Charles C. Thomas, 1974a.

Cowgill, D. *Aging around the world*. Belmont, CA: Wadsworth, 1986.

Cowgill, D. The aging of populations and societies. In F. Eisele (Ed.), *Political consequences of aging. The annals of the American Academy of Political and Social Science*, 1974b, *415*, 1–18.

Dandekar, K. *The elderly in India*. Thousand Oaks, CA: Sage, 1996.

Darkwa, O. K., and Mazibuko, F. N. M. Population aging and its impact on elderly welfare in Africa. *International Journal of Aging and Human Development*, 2002, *54*, 107–123.

de Romilly, J. *Time in Greek tragedy*. Ithaca, NY: Cornell University Press, 1968.

Dickerson-Putnam, J. Old women at the top: An exploration of age stratification among Bena Bena women. *Journal of Cross-Cultural Gerontology*, 1994, *9*, 193–205.

Dossa, P. A. Re-imagining aging lives: Ethnographic narratives of Muslim women in diaspora. *Journal of Cross-Cultural Gerontology*, 1999, *14*, 245–272.

Fischer, D. H. *Growing old in America*. Oxford: Oxford University Press, 1978.

Fry, C. L. Age, aging, and culture. In R. H. Binstock and L. K. George (Eds.), *Handbook of aging and the social sciences* (4th ed.). San Diego: Academic Press, 1996.

Glascock, A. P. When is killing acceptable: The moral dilemma surrounding assisted suicide in America and other societies. In J. Sokolovsky (Ed.), *The cultural context of aging* (3rd ed.). Westport, CT: Bergin and Garvey, 1997.

Goldstein, M. C., and Beall, C. M. Modernization and aging in the third and fourth world: Views from the rural hinterland in Nepal. In D. L. Infeld (Ed.), *Disciplinary approaches to aging: Anthropology of aging* (Vol. 4). New York: Routledge, 2002.

Hu, Y. H. Elderly suicide risk in family context: A critique of the Asian family care model. *Journal of Cross-Cultural Gerontology*, 1995, *10*, 199–217.

Ikels, C. Aging, In C. Loue (Ed.), *Handbook of immigrant health*. New York: Plenum Press, 1998.

Ikels, C. Long-term care and the disabled elderly in urban China. In J. Sokolovsky (Ed.), *The cultural context of aging* (3rd ed.). Westport, CT: Bergin and Garvey, 1997.

Ikels, C., and Beall, C. M. Age, aging and anthropology. In R. H. Binstock and L. K. George (Eds.), *Handbook of aging and the social sciences* (5th ed.). San Diego: Academic Press, 2001.

Infeld, D. L. (Ed.). *Disciplinary approaches to aging: Anthropology of aging* (Vol. 4). New York: Routledge, 2002.

Jenike, B. R. Gender and duty in Japan's aged society: The experience of family caregivers. In J. Sokolovsky (Ed.), *The cultural context of aging* (3rd ed.). Westport, CT: Bergin and Garvey, 1997.

Keith, J. Age in social and cultural context: Anthropological perspectives. In R. Binstock and L. George (Eds.), *Handbook of aging and the social sciences* (3rd ed.). New York: Academic Press, 1990.

Kertzer, D., and Laslett, P. (Eds.). *Demography, society and old age*. Berkeley: University of California Press, 1994.

Kim, K. H. A study of determinants of elderly people's coresidence living patterns. *Journal of the Korea Gerontological Society*, 1998, *18*, 107–122.

Kinsella, K., and Ferreira, M. *International brief: Aging trends in South Africa*. Washington, DC: U.S. Department of Commerce, Economics and Statistics Administration, IB/92–2, 1997.

Kinsella, K., and Velkoff, V. A. *An aging world: 2001*. Washington, DC: U.S. Dept. of Health and Human Services: National Institutes of Health/National Institute on Aging, 2001.

Levande, D. I., Herrick, J. M., and Sung, K. T. Eldercare in the United States and South Korea. *Journal of Family Issues*, 2000, *21*, 632–651.

Maeda, D. Recent policy of long term care in Japan. Paper presented at meetings of the American Public Health Association. Washington DC: November, 1998.

Nason, J. D. Respected elder or old person: Aging in a Micronesian community. In P. Amoss and S. Harrell (Eds.), *Other ways of growing old*. Stanford, CA: Stanford University Press, 1981.

Ogawa, N., and Retherford, R. Care of the elderly in Japan: Changing norms and expectations. *Journal of Marriage and the Family,* 1993, *55,* 585–597.

Pang, K. Y. C. Symptoms of depression in elderly Korean immigrants: Narration and the healing process. *Culture, Medicine and Psychiatry,* 1998, *22,* 93–122.

Pritchard, C., and Baldwin, D. S. Elderly suicide rates in Asian and English-speaking countries. *Acta Psychiatrica Scandinavica,* 2002, *105,* 271–275.

Silverman, P., Hecht, L., and McMillin, J. D. Modeling life satisfaction among the aged: A comparison of Chinese and Americans. *Journal of Cross-Cultural Gerontology,* 2000, *15,* 289–305.

Simmons, L. W. *The role of the aged in primitive society.* New Haven, CT: Yale University Press, 1945.

Sokolovsky, J. (Ed.) *The cultural context of aging* (3rd ed.). Westport, CT: Bergin and Garvey, 1997.

Sung, K. T. An exploration of actions of filial piety. *Journal of Aging Studies,* 1998, *12,* 369–386.

Sung, K. T. Family support for the elderly in Korea: Continuity, change, future directions and cross-cultural concerns. *Journal of Aging and Social Policy,* 2001, *12,* 65–77.

Sung, K. T. Respect for elders: Myths and realities in East Asia. *Journal of Aging and Identity,* 2000, *5,* 197–205.

Thoreau, H. D. *Walden.* New York: New American Library, 1856, Chapter 1, p. 8.

United Nations AIDS Programme (UNAIDS). *HIV/AIDS in Africa: Fact sheet.* http://www.unaids.org, 2000.

Vincentnathan, S. G., and Vincentnathan, L. Equality and hierarchy in untouchable intergenerational relations and conflict resolutions. *Journal of Cross-Cultural Gerontology,* 1994, *9,* 1–19.

Warren, C. A. B. Aging and identity in premodern times. In D. L. Infeld (Ed.), *Disciplinary approaches to aging: Anthropology of aging* (Vol. 4). New York: Routledge, 2002.

Wilmoth, J. M. Living arrangements among older immigrants in the United States. *The Gerontologist,* 2001, *41,* 228–238.

Wilmoth, J. M., DeJong, G. F., and Himes, C. L. Immigrant and non-immigrant living arrangements among America's white, Hispanic, and Asian elderly population. International *Journal of Sociology and Social Policy,* 1997, *17,* 57–82.

Yee, B. W. K., The social and cultural context of adaptive aging by Southeast Asian elders. In J. Sokolovsky (Ed.), *The cultural context of aging* (3rd ed.). Westport, CT: Bergin and Garvey, 1997.

part two

The Biological and Physiological Context of Social Aging

If we are to understand how older people differ from younger age groups, and why the field of gerontology has evolved as a separate discipline, we must first review the *normal* changes in biological and physiological structures as well as diseases that impair these systems and affect the day-to-day functioning of older persons. Part Two provides this necessary background.

• Chapter 3 describes normal changes in major organ systems and how they influence older persons' ability to perform activities of daily living and to interact with their social and physical environments. This area of research has received considerable attention as scientists have explored the basic processes of aging. Numerous theories have emerged to explain observable changes such as wrinkles, gray hair, stooped shoulders, and slower response time, as well as changes in other biological functions that can only be inferred from tests of physiologic function. These include changes in the heart, lungs, kidneys, and bones. There are many normal changes in these organ systems within the same person that do not imply disease, but in fact may slow down the older adult. Furthermore, significant differences have been observed among people and among organ systems within the same person in the degree of change experienced. The effects of health promoting behaviors, such as vigorous exercise and an active lifestyle, on the extent of physical aging are discussed.

• Chapter 3 also highlights some of the exciting new discoveries in biological research that show the potential of modifying cellular processes and using human growth hormones to slow down aging and even increase the maximum life span of humans. Some of the debates surrounding potential ways to extend cell life and cell regeneration are also presented in Chapter 3.

• Age-related changes in the five major senses are also discussed in Chapter 3. Because sensory functions are so critical for our daily interactions with our social and physical environments, and because many of the normal declines observed in sensory systems are a model of changes throughout the body, it is useful to focus on each sensory system and its role in linking individuals with their environments. Recommendations are made for modifying the environment and for communicating with older people who are experiencing significant declines in vision, hearing, taste, smell, touch, and kinesthetic functioning.

• Chapter 4 focuses on secondary aging—diseases of the organ systems described in Chapter 3, and how these diseases can affect active aging. Acute and chronic diseases are differentiated, and the impact of these diseases on the demand for health and social services among different segments of the older population is presented. The growing problem of AIDS among older persons and implications for long-term care are discussed in this chapter. Recent research findings on the risks and benefits of hormone replacement therapy for postmenopausal women are also discussed.

• Because automobile accidents among older people often result from psychomotor changes associated with aging, methods to reduce auto fatalities through new programs in driver training and through better environmental design are considered. Differences across states in licensing older drivers are examined in Chapter 4.

• Chapter 4 also provides some striking statistics on older people's use of health services, barriers to their use, and recommendations for enhancing appropriate utilization of culturally appropriate services. Most existing medical, dental, and mental health services do not adequately address the special needs of the older population, especially those with low income and less education or who have been historically disadvantaged. As a result, older people who could benefit most from the services fail to use them.

• Health promotion has proved successful in maintaining and even improving older people's health in many areas, including exercise, prevention of falls and osteoporosis, and nutrition. Chapter 4 describes some of these programs and the research evidence for the benefits of health promotion.

Throughout Part Two, the tremendous variations in how people age physically are emphasized. Because of lifestyle, environmental, and genetic factors, some people will show dramatic declines in all their organ systems at a relatively early age. Most older people, however, will experience slower rates of decline and at different levels across the organ systems. For example, some people may suffer from chronic heart disease, yet at the same time maintain strong bones and muscle strength. In contrast, others may require medications for painful osteoarthritis, even as their heart and lungs remain in excellent condition. The following vignettes illustrate these variations.

A HEALTHY OLDER PERSON

Mrs. Hill is an 80-year-old widow and retired librarian. She has been slightly deaf all her life, has some recent loss of vision, and has high blood pressure that is managed by regular use of antihypertensive medications. Despite her minor physical limitations, Mrs. Hill is able to volunteer at the local library, where she spends two afternoons each week reading new books to children aged 4–6. She can still drive, but prefers walking to most places, so she can get her exercise. Active in the local senior center, she was one of the first participants in a health promotion project for older adults. Now she helps teach an exercise class at the center three times a week. She rarely visits the doctor except for a semiannual checkup and medication review. Mrs. Hill admits that she has less energy than in her middle years, but for the most part, she accepts these changes and adjusts her physical activities accordingly. Her son-in-law has made some minor modifications in her home, especially in the height and location of kitchen shelves, so that her daily routines do not place her at risk for a fall or tire her out too much. Friends and relatives are frequently telling her how she does not look her age; she, in turn, becomes impatient with older people who stay home all the time, watch TV, and complain. She is usually optimistic about her situation, and believes that each person can control how well or poorly he or she faces old age.

AN OLDER PERSON WITH CHRONIC ILLNESS

Mr. Jones, age 70, had a stroke at age 65 and is paralyzed on his left side, so he is unable to walk. The stroke has also left him with slightly slurred speech and some personality changes. His wife states that he is not the kind, gentle man she used to know. He has to be lifted from bed to chair and recently became incontinent. His wife first tried to care for him at home, but after he became incontinent, she felt she could no longer handle the responsibility and made the difficult decision to move him to a nearby nursing home. Both Mr. and Mrs. Jones are having difficulty adjusting to the nursing home placement. Since Mr. Jones remains mentally alert and aware of all the changes he has been experiencing, he continually expresses his frustration with his physical limitations and with his forced retirement and reduced income. Their children live in another state and have been unable to help their mother with the daily care or the financial burden of the nursing home. As their financial resources dwindle, Mr. and Mrs. Jones are facing the need to apply for Medicaid to cover nursing home costs. Mr. Jones starts to cry easily, sobbing that he is losing control of his life and that his life was never meant to be like this. Mrs. Jones feels angry that her caregiving efforts have not been appreciated and that her husband is so difficult.

These two vignettes point to the complexity of physiological aging. Chronological age is often a poor predictor of health and functional status, as illustrated by Mrs. Hill's excellent functional and emotional health and Mr. Jones's situation of physical dependency, even though he is 10 years younger than Mrs. Hill. As noted above, Part Two describes these variations in normal physiological aging. It contrasts these with changes due to disease, and presents factors that influence functional status in the later years.

chapter

3

The Social Consequences
of Physical Aging

This chapter includes

- Major theories of biological aging
- Research on reversing the effects of biological aging
- Effects of aging on body composition
- Aging in different organ systems and the impact of these changes on normal functions
- The implications of these changes for older people's functions and ability to interact with their social and physical environments
- Ways in which the environment can be modified to help accommodate the biological changes experienced by most older people

For most people, aging is defined primarily by its visible signs—graying hair, balding among some men, sagging and wrinkled skin, stooped shoulders, and a slower walk or shuffling gait. Although these are the most visible signs of old age among humans, there are numerous other changes that occur in our internal organs—the heart, lungs, kidneys, stomach, bladder, and central nervous system. These changes are not as easy to detect because they are not visible. In fact, x-rays and computer-assisted images of organ systems are not very useful for showing most changes that take place. It is primarily by measuring the **functional capacity** of these systems (i.e., the performance capacity of the heart, lungs, kidneys, and other organs) that their relative efficiency across the life span can be determined. This chapter describes normal changes that all of us experience in our biological systems as we age. In the next chapter, the diseases of aging that may impair organ functions more than would be expected from normal aging are discussed.

68

As noted in Chapter 1, biological aging, or **senescence,** is defined as the normal process of changes over time in the body and its components. It is a gradual process common to all living organisms that eventually affects an individual's functioning vis-à-vis the environment but does not necessarily result in disease or death. It is not, in itself, a disease. But aging and disease are often linked in most people's minds, since declines in organ capacity and internal protective mechanisms do make us more vulnerable to sickness. Because certain diseases such as Alzheimer's, arthritis, and heart conditions have a higher incidence with age, we may erroneously equate age with disease. However, a more accurate conception of the aging process is a gradual accumulation of irreversible functional losses to which the average person tries to accommodate in some socially acceptable manner. As discussed in Chapter 1, people can continue to maintain an active lifestyle as they experience age-related changes in their biological and physiological systems. In order to achieve active aging, people may alter their physical and social environments by reducing the demands placed on their remaining functional capacity (e.g., relocating to a one-story home or apartment to avoid stairs, driving only during the day, avoiding crowds). This is consistent with the person–environment model of aging; as their physical competence declines, older people may simplify their physical environment to reestablish homeostasis or their comfort zone.

Individual differences are evident in the rate and severity of physical changes, as illustrated by the vignettes of Mrs. Hill and Mr. Jones. Not all people show the same degree of change in any given organ system, nor do all the systems decline at the same rate and at the same time. Individual aging depends largely on genetic inheritance, nutrition and diet, physical activity, and environment. Thus, while one 78-year-old feels "old" because of aches and pains due to arthritis but uses her excellent cognitive skills at work every day, another 78-year-old may retain her physical ability but be institutionalized due to advanced dementia. One way of understanding these variations in biological aging is to examine the major theories that have been advanced to explain the changes in all living organisms over time.

Biological Theories of Aging

Popular culture, as reflected in books and magazines, is full of stories about "anti-aging hormones," "fighting aging," and "preventing death." The problem with these optimistic projections is that no single scientific theory has yet been able to explain what causes aging and death. Without a clear understanding of this process, it is impossible to prevent, fight, or certainly to stop this normal mechanisim of all living organisms.

The process of aging is complex and multidimensional, involving significant loss and decline in some physiological functions, and minimal change in others. Scientists have long attempted to find the causes for this process. A theme of some theories is that aging is a process that is programmed into the genetic structure of each species. Other theories state that aging represents an accumulation of stimuli from the environment that produce stress on the organism. Any theory of aging must be based on the scientific method, using systematic tests of hypotheses and empirical observations. It is generally agreed that biological theories must meet four requirements to be viable:

1. The process must be universal; that is, all members of a species must experience the phenomenon.
2. The process must be deleterious, or result in physiological decline.
3. The process must be progressive, that is, losses must be gradual over time.
4. Finally, the losses must be intrinsic, that is, they cannot be corrected by the organism.

These guidelines are helpful for excluding biological phenomena that are different from aging per se. For example, they help to distinguish disease from normal aging. While diseases are often deleterious, progressive, and intrinsic, they are not universal (e.g., not all older adults will develop arthritis or Alzheimer's disease). Each of the following theories meets these criteria, although the evidence to support them is not always clear. Even though these theories help our understanding of aging, none of them is totally adequate for explaining what *causes* aging. The theories that will be discussed in this section are based on extensive research with animals or humans:

- Wear and tear
- Autoimmune
- Cross-linkage
- Free radical
- Cellular aging

The **wear and tear theory** suggests that, like a machine, the organism simply wears out over time (Wilson, 1974). In this model, aging is a preprogrammed process; that is, each species has a biological clock that determines its maximum life span and the rate at which each organ system will deteriorate. For example, fruit flies (drosophilae) have a natural life span of a few hours, butterflies a few weeks, dogs up to 20 years, and humans about 120 years. This process is compounded by the effects of environmental stress on the organism (e.g., nutritional deficiencies). Cells continually wear out, and existing cells cannot repair damaged components within themselves. This is particularly true in tissues that are located in the striated skeletal and heart muscle and throughout the nervous system; these tissues are composed of cells that cannot undergo cell division. As we will see later, these systems are most likely to experience significant decline in their ability to function effectively with age.

One of the earliest theories of biological aging, the **autoimmune theory,** proposes that aging is a function of the body's immune system becoming defective over time and attacking not just foreign proteins, bacteria, and viruses, but also producing antibodies against itself. Older people become more susceptible to infections. This ex-

planation of the immune system is consistent with the process of many diseases that increase with age, such as cancer, diabetes, and rheumatoid arthritis (Finch, 1990). Nevertheless, this theory does not explain why the immune system becomes defective with age; only the effects of this change are described. For example, the thymus gland, which controls production of disease-fighting white blood cells, shrinks with aging, but the *reasons* for both this reduction in size and why more older people do not suffer from autoimmune diseases are unclear.

The **cross-linkage theory** (Bjorksten, 1974) focuses on the changes in the protein called *collagen* with age. Collagen is an important connective tissue found in most organ systems; indeed, about one-third of all the protein in our body is collagen. As a person ages, there are clearly observable changes in collagen, for instance, wrinkling of the skin. These changes lead to a loss of elasticity in blood vessels, muscle tissue, skin, the lens of the eye and other organs, and to slower wound healing. Another visible effect of changes in collagen is that the nose and ears tend to increase in size. From this theoretical perspective, collagen changes are due to the binding of essential molecules in the cells through the accumulation of cross-linking compounds, which in turn slows the process of normal cell functions and shows signs of aging. These cross-links are necessary to join together the parallel molecules of collagen. However, in older animals and humans these links increase, making the tissue less pliable and rigid, as seen in wrinkled skin.

An extension of cross-linkage theory is the **free radical theory** of aging (Finch 1990; Harman, 1956, 1993). Free radicals are highly reactive molecules that break off in cells and possess an unpaired electron. They are produced normally by the use of oxygen within the cell but are multiplied by smoking, exposure to ultraviolet radiation, and psychological stress. They interact with other cell molecules and may cause DNA mutations, cross-linking of connective tissue, changes in protein behavior, and other damage. Such reactions continue until one free radical pairs with another or meets an *antioxidant*. These are chemical inhibitors that can safely absorb the extra electron and prevent oxygen from combining with susceptible molecules to form free radicals. It has been proposed that the ingestion of antioxidants such as vitamins E and C, beta carotene, and selenium can inhibit free radical damage; this can then slow the aging process by delaying the loss of immune function and reducing the incidence of many diseases associated with aging (Beckman and Ames, 1998; Grune and Davies, 2001).

Nevertheless, it appears that free radicals are not totally destroyed. Those that survive in the organism damage the proteins needed to make cells in the body by interacting with the oxygen used to produce protein. As a result, free radicals may destroy the fragile process of building cells and the DNA strands that transmit messages of genes. Some have argued that this continuous pounding by dangerous oxidants wears away the organism over time, not just by interfering with cell-building but also by requiring antioxidants to be ever-vigilant. This damage to cell tissue by free radicals has been implicated in normal aging, as well as in the development of some cancers, heart disease, Alzheimer's disease, and Parkinson's disease.

Molecular biologists have explored this theory further by splicing genes to measure the cumulative effects of free radicals in cells, with the goal of developing ways to counter these effects. It may be that synthetic antioxidants can be developed and administered to older people as the body's natural supply is depleted. Animal studies have shown dramatic enhancements of memory and physical activity with high doses of antioxidants. For example, two drugs containing the enzymes superoxide dismutase and catabase (known to have antioxidant properties) have been found to extend the lifespan of worms by more than 50 percent. These drugs may also be effective in reducing the damage caused by strokes or Parkinson's disease (Melov et al., 2000). Until research with mice supports the promising results emerging

from worm studies, it is difficult to predict whether humans will experience similar benefits. It may be that the free radical theory holds the greatest promise for slowing the aging process in the future. However, while increasing the intake of antioxidants may eventually result in more people achieving their *life expectancy,* there is no evidence that the *maximum life span* of 120 years would increase (Hayflick, 1996). Indeed, there is little support for the positive impact of increasing antioxidant defenses (Grune and Davies, 2001).

The **cellular aging theory** suggests that aging occurs as cells slow their number of replications. Hayflick and Moorehead (1961) first reported that cells grown in culture (i.e., in controlled laboratory environments) undergo a finite number of replications, approaching 50 doublings. Cells from older subjects replicate even fewer times, as do cells derived from individuals with progeria and Werner syndrome—both rare genetic anomalies in which aging is accelerated and death may occur by age 15 to 20 in the former and by 40 to 50 in the latter condition. It appears that cells are programmed to follow a biological clock and stop replicating after a given number of times. The number of divisions a normal cell undergoes depends on the specific cell type. As the number of replications decreases, telomeres show a consistent shortening effect (Hornsby, 2001). In addition, proponents of this theory point out that each cell has a given level of DNA that is eventually depleted. This in turn reduces the production of RNA, which is essential for producing enzymes necessary for cellular functioning. Hence, the loss of DNA and subsequent reduction of RNA eventually result in cell death (Goldstein and Reis, 1984).

Of all the theories of physiological aging, cellular aging appears to explain best what is going on. The role of cell replication, RNA production, and telomere shortening in aging is widely accepted in the scientific community. It should not be assumed, however, that the step from understanding to reversing the process of aging will be achieved soon. It is often erroneously assumed that scientific discoveries of the *cause* of a particular physiological process or disease can immediately lead to *changing* or reversing that condition. Unfortunately, that step is a difficult one to make, as evidenced by progress in cancer research. Scientists have long observed the structural changes in cancer cells, but the reasons for these changes are far from being understood. Without a clear understanding of *why* a particular biological process takes place, it is impossible to move toward reversing that process. However, some hope is offered by recent scientific research that successfully forced cells to produce **telomerase,** the enzyme responsible for rebuilding telomeres and in this manner continued cell replication. The reverse process may be effective in preventing the rapid proliferation of cancer cells, which do not show any limits on replication. Researchers have recently found methods of inhibiting or blocking the production of this enzyme (Bodner et al., 1998). There is growing evidence that significant shortening of telomeres may play a role in some diseases, such as ulcerative colitis, cirrhosis of the liver, and colon cancer (Eastwood, 1995; Kinouchi et al., 1998; Rudolph et al., 2000). By controlling the biological mechanisms that cause telomeres to shorten, researchers may eventually reduce the prevalence of these diseases.

Can Aging Be Reversed or Delayed?

Growth Hormones

Genetic researchers have made great strides in the past 30 years in their understanding of the aging process. Indeed, contrary to our long-held assumptions about aging, many scientists have become convinced that aging is *reversible*. New research on telomeres is one example of this development. Another approach is the possibility of introducing new hormones into the body to replace the depleted hormones in genes that serve as chemical messengers. Researchers at the National Institute on Aging, Veterans Administration cen-

> **POINTS TO PONDER**
>
> How would you feel if the aging process could be reversed? What might happen to society if more people could achieve the maximum life span of 120 years? What are some of the ethical and resource allocation issues raised by scientific efforts to reverse or slow the aging process?

ters, and universities around the country are testing the effects of injecting growth hormones into aging animals and humans. So far, many startling discoveries have been made, such as increased lean muscle mass and vertebral bone density, and reduced fat levels. These changes in turn have led to increased activity and vigor. While these effects are short-lived, it may not be long before a human growth hormone is marketed that can safely be administered on a regular basis, like daily doses of vitamins.

One promising compound that is being tested by U.S. and French researchers is the hormone dehydroepiandrosterone, or DHEA. This hormone is secreted by the adrenal glands, and the body converts it into testosterone and estrogen. Production of DHEA increases from age 7 to 30, when it stabilizes, then begins to decline. By the age of 80, the body has less than 5 percent of the level of DHEA it produced in its peak. Animal studies have shown that administering DHEA to adult mice results in increased activity levels and learning speed. Human studies are just beginning. Preliminary studies in which DHEA was given orally have shown improved sleep, greater energy, increased sexual activity, and greater tolerance of stress. It may also increase production of an insulin-like growth factor that stimulates cell growth and cell division. The effects were sustained up to three months in these studies (Morales et al., 1995). Research evidence is currently not sufficient to recommend the regular, long-term use of DHEA. Side effects in these short-term studies included liver problems, growth of facial hair in women, and enlarged prostate and breasts among some men, especially at higher doses. Those effects may be due to DHEA's stimulation of testosterone and estrogen. While these and other experiments with growth hormones and other compounds are still in their infancy, they offer promise of active aging (described in Chapter 1) for future cohorts of older adults. That is, they may not add years to the human life span, but will more likely add life to the years available to each individual.

Caloric Restriction

Several studies using animal models (mice, fruit flies, fish) have demonstrated that reducing caloric intake by 50 to 70 percent increased the life span of experimental animals by as much as 30 to 50 percent, because it appears to slow down the aging process. Dietary restriction did not, however, include limiting nutrients in these studies. Caloric restriction that was accomplished mostly through reducing fat intake has been found to be most successful in extending the life of experimental animals without causing malnutrition. Yet, it is evident from these studies that restriction of fat, protein, or carbohydrate intake alone is not sufficient; total caloric intake must also be reduced. Nor have the same benefits been found from merely increasing the intake of antioxidants or specific vitamins. The benefits of caloric restriction are greatest when it is initiated soon after birth; however, even when mice were placed on such diets in early middle age, their maximum life span increased by 10 to 20 percent (Weindruch, 1996). In fact, caloric restriction has even been found to extend the reproductive capacity of female mice (McShane, Wilson, and Wise, 1999).

Until the results of longitudinal studies with primates are available, these conclusions are not generalizable to humans. The first such major study with primates is an ongoing one by researchers at the Baltimore Longitudinal Studies Gerontology Research Center (Lane et al., 1997, 2002; Roth, Ingram and Lane, 2001; Weed et al., 1997). This study has examined the effects of

STEM CELL RESEARCH

Advances in stem cell research were recognized as the "scientific breakthrough of the year" in 1999 by the journal *Science*. This is because of significant advances in guiding such cells into becoming organ-specific tissues. Nevertheless, this new technology, even more than other emerging areas of genetic research, is fraught with ethical dilemmas. In order to obtain human embryonic stem cells by current methods, it is necessary to use human embryos. Such embryos are often derived from aborted fetuses, so this has stirred debate among people opposed to abortion. Indeed, in 1995, Congress banned the National Institutes of Health (NIH) from funding research using human stem cells. Researchers in private biotech firms that do not receive government funding continued their work in this area. In 2000, the NIH issued new rules that federally funded researchers could use stem cells derived from frozen embryos that are due to be discarded by fertility clinics. These rules were accompanied by strict guidelines on how embryonic cells are to be harvested. This makes them valuable for replacing cells in diseased or dead tissues as in Parkinson's disease, Alzheimer's disease, or strokes. Ethical concerns regarding the harvesting of stem cells from embryonic tissue may be alleviated in the future as research with adult stem cells finds ways of differentiating them into organ-specific tissues as successfully as embryonic cells (Bloom, 1999).

feeding rhesus monkeys 30 percent less than their normal caloric intake. After 6 years on this diet, these monkeys showed higher activity levels, lower body temperature, less body fat, lower fasting glucose and insulin levels, and a slower decline in DHEA levels produced by the adrenal glands than an age-matched control group of monkeys that were fed freely, with no caloric restrictions.

These results provide the first evidence in primates that caloric restriction may have anti-aging effects by slowing down metabolism, thereby reducing the number of free radicals created in the organism. Lower caloric intake may also maintain the production of adrenal steroids such as DHEA without artificially replacing them. Caloric restriction also reduces the growth of tumors, delays kidney dysfunction, decreases loss of muscle mass, and slows other age-related changes ordinarily found in these animals. It delays the onset of autoimmune disease, hypertension, type II diabetes, cataracts, glaucoma, and cancers in these animals, and appears to improve immune response and wound healing. These studies offer further support that caloric restriction may be useful for humans in improving their active life expectancy (Li and Wolf, 1997; Masoro, 2001).

Antiaging Compounds

Recent studies have found that living organisms produce specific enzymes that can be boosted to survive the damage caused by stressors such as ionizing radiation, and can delay cell death. Although this research has focused on simple organisms such as yeast, fruit flies, and worms (specifically the nematode *Caenorhabditis elegans*, or *C. elegans*), the findings provide evidence that cellular enzymes can be boosted by compounds such as *resveratrol* (Howitz et al., 2003). Resveratrol is a type of polyphenol, a chemical that is found in red wine and seems to be responsible for the preventive benefits observed in red wine against heart disease. In laboratory studies, Howitz and colleagues found that adding these enzyme boosters to yeast cells increased their life span by 70 percent. These findings may eventually lead to important discoveries that can slow the aging process in humans, but it will require many more years of research to move beyond single cell and simple organisms to complex mammals.

Researchers at the National Institute on Aging (NIA) Baltimore Longitudinal Studies have also been searching for a medication that can alter cellular metabolism to mimic the effects of caloric restriction. One such compound is 2-deoxy-D-glucose (2DG), that has been found to reduce insulin levels in the blood and slow tumor growth in rodents. This compound causes cells to produce smaller amounts of glucose's byproducts

in the same way as caloric restriction, and in turn slow the formation of free radicals. Research with mice has demonstrated significant benefits in reducing blood glucose, body temperature, and in reducing damage to nerve cells. However, the NIA researchers have also found that 2DG can have toxic effects in higher doses or when used for prolonged periods. This may limit its application to primates, but these findings may open the door to testing other compounds that can mimic caloric restriction (Lane et al., 2002).

Research on Physiological Changes with Age

It is difficult to distinguish normal, age-related changes in many human functions from changes that are secondary to disease or other factors. Until the late 1950s, much of our knowledge about aging came from cross-sectional comparisons of healthy young persons with institutionalized or community-dwelling older populations who had multiple chronic diseases. These comparisons led to the not-surprising conclusion that the organ systems of older persons function less efficiently than those of younger persons.

Since the 1950s, a series of longitudinal studies have been undertaken with healthy younger

---

ANTI-AGING AS BIG BUSINESS

The promise of extending the human life span beyond the currently accepted 120 years has spawned many new biotech companies, whose primary goal is to find the ultimate "antiaging pill." By late 2003, there were at least a dozen biotechnology companies conducting research on antiaging chemicals. The names of the leading companies in this field reflect their corporate mission and include Elixir, LifeGen, Longevity, Chronogen, GeroTech, Jevenon, and Rejuvenon.

New York Times, September 21, 2003, Sect. 3, pp. 1, 10.

and middle-aged persons to determine changes in various physiological parameters. The first of these studies began in 1958 at the Gerontology Research Center in Baltimore, as described in Chapter 1 (Shock, 1962). The initial sample of 600 healthy males between the ages of 20 and 96 was expanded in 1978 to include females. Today, many of the people in the original sample are still participating in the study. Another longitudinal study began in 1955 at Duke University's Center for the Study of Aging, with a sample composed entirely of older adults. Some of these individuals were followed every two years for more than 20 years (Palmore, 1974, 1985). Many other researchers around the country are now examining physiological functions longitudinally. The information in this chapter is derived from their work.

Aging in Body Composition

In this section, we will review *normal* changes in the human body, both visible and invisible. These include changes in:

- muscle mass, fat tissue, and water (body composition)
- skin
- hair

CHANGES IN BODY COMPOSITION Although individuals vary greatly in body weight and composition, the proportion of body weight contributed by water generally declines for both men and women: on the average, from 60 percent to 54 percent in men, and from 52 percent to 46 percent in women (Blumberg, 1996). Lean body mass in muscle tissue is lost, whereas the proportion of fat increases (see Figure 3.1). This decline in muscle mass and increase in fat is known as "sarcopenia." Because of an increase in fibrous material, muscle tissue loses its elasticity and flexibility. After age 50, the number of muscle fibers steadily decreases; muscle mass declines by 40 percent between ages 30 and 80 (Kohrt and Holloszy, 1995). However, as described in Chapter 4 and illustrated by master athletes, older people who maintain a vigorous exercise program can prevent a significant loss of

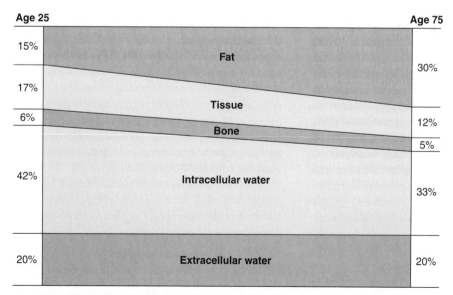

FIGURE 3.1   **Distribution of Major Body Components**
SOURCE: Reprinted with permission from the American Geriatrics Society. Speculations on vascular changes with age, by R. J. Goldman (*Journal of the American Geriatrics Society,* Vol. 18, p. 766, 1970).

muscle tone. The loss of muscle mass and water, and increase in fat tissue, all have a significant effect on older adults' ability to metabolize many medications. Some medications are processed by muscle tissue, some in fat, and some in water throughout the human body. With the changes in body composition described here, these medications may remain in fat tissue longer than needed, or may be too concentrated relative to the available water and muscle volume.

These changes also are associated with weight alterations, from increased weight for some people in the middle years, until the later years when there is a tendency toward lower weight and lower calorie intake. This is why we rarely see people in their eighties and nineties who are obese. The balance of sodium and potassium also changes, with the ratio of sodium increasing by 20 percent from age 30 to 70. Changes in body composition also have implications for the diets of older people; although older adults generally need fewer total calories per day than active younger people, they need to consume a higher proportion of protein, calcium, and vitamin D (Blumberg, 1996). However, many older individuals do not change their diet during the later years unless advised specifically by a physician. Others, especially those living alone, eat poorly balanced meals.

CHANGES IN THE SKIN   As stated at the beginning of this chapter, changes in the appearance and texture of skin and hair are often the most visible signs of aging. These also tend to have deleterious consequences on how older people view themselves and are perceived by others. The human skin is unique among that of all other mammals in that it is exposed directly to the elements, with no protective fur or feathers to shield it from the direct effects of sunlight. In fact, ultraviolet light from the sun, which damages the elastic fibers beneath the skin's surface, is probably most directly responsible for the wrinkled, dried, and tougher texture of older people's skin, known as photoaging or extrinsic aging. Indeed, UV radiation may be the main culprit in skin aging. Human skin cells collected from exposed parts of the body grow much more slowly than skin from areas protected by the sun (e.g., underarms). This is evident when one compares the appearance of the skin of two 75-year-olds: one a retired farmer who has worked under the sun most of his life, the other a retired office worker who has spent most of his years indoors. The farmer generally will have more wrinkles; darker pigmentation known as **melanin,** which has been produced by the body to protect it from ultraviolet rays; and drier skin with a leathery texture. He is also more likely to have so-called *age spots* or *liver spots*—harmless from a health standpoint but of concern sometimes for their appearance. As one might expect, people who spend most of their lives in sunny climates are more prone to these changes. Concern about the negative consequences of extensive exposure to the sun is more prevalent today.

Besides these environmental factors, the human body itself is responsible for some of the changes in the skin with age. The outermost layer of skin, the epidermis, constantly replenishes itself by shedding dead cells and replacing them with new cells. As the person gets older, the process of cell replacement is slowed, up to 50 percent between ages 30 and 70. More importantly, the connective tissue that makes up the second layer of skin, the *dermis,* thins because the number of dermal cells diminishes and makes it less elastic with age. This results in reduced elasticity and thickness of the outer skin layer, longer time required for the skin to spring back into shape, and increased sagging and wrinkling. Sometimes women in their twenties and thirties may experience these problems earlier than men. This is because women tend to have less oil in the sebaceous glands. However, the process of skin aging varies widely, depending on the relative amount of oil in the glands, exposure to the sun, and heredity. Despite its changing appearance, the skin can still perform its protective function throughout old age.

Wound healing is also slower in older persons. Thus, people over age 65 require more time than those under age 35 to form blisters as a means of closing a wound, and more time to form new epithelial tissue to replace blistered skin.

The sebaceous and sweat glands, located in the dermis, generally deteriorate with age. Changes also occur in the deepest, or *subcutaneous,* skin layers, which tend to lose fat and water. The changes in subcutaneous skin are compounded by a reduction in the skin's blood circulation, which can damage the effectiveness of the skin's temperature regulatory mechanism and make older people more sensitive to hot and cold temperatures. As a result, older persons' comfort zone for ambient temperature is generally three to five degrees warmer than that for younger persons. It also takes longer for an older person to adjust after being exposed to either hot or cold extreme temperatures. This leaves the older individual much more vulnerable to **hypothermia** (low body temperature, sometimes resulting in brain damage and death) and **hyperthermia** (heat stroke), as evidenced by reports of increased accidental deaths among older adults during periods of extremely cold winter weather and during prolonged heat spells. For example, the long heat wave in Europe during August 2003 claimed over 10,000 lives in France alone, most of whom were older people who lacked adequate ventilation in their homes and apartments (*New York Times,* August 24, 2003). To prevent hypothermia, it is recommended that indoor temperatures be set above 68°F during winter months in older people's homes, and that humidity be minimized. Some older people who are concerned about conserving energy and money may not maintain this temperature and may set their thermostats below 68°F, especially at night (Macey, 1989; Macey and Schneider, 1993).

CHANGES IN THE HAIR   As we age, the appearance and texture of our hair changes. Hair is thickest in early adulthood and decreases by as much as 20 percent in diameter by age 70. This is why so many older people appear to have fine, limp-looking hair. This change is compounded by the increased loss of hair with age. Although up to 60 strands of hair are lost daily during youth and early adulthood, the hair is replaced regularly through the action of estrogen and testosterone. As we age, however, more hairs are lost than replaced, especially in men. Some men experience rapid hair loss, leading to a receding hairline or even complete baldness by their mid-forties. Some older women also find their hair thins so much that they cannot hide bald spots. Reasons for the observed variation in hair loss are not clear, but genetic factors appear to play a role.

Gray hair is a result of loss of pigment in the hair follicles. As we age, less pigment is produced at the roots. Eventually all the hair becomes colorless, or white in appearance. The gray color of some people's hair is an intermediate stage of pigment loss. In fact, some people may never experience a total loss of pigment production, but will live into an advanced old age with relatively dark hair. Others may experience graying in their twenties. In our society, graying of hair tends to have more stigma associated with it for women than for men, and women are more likely to tint or color their hair.

Changes in Organ Systems

Although some change occurs with age in all organ systems, this chapter focuses on changes in the:

- musculoskeletal and kinesthetic system
- respiratory system
- cardiovascular system
- urinary system
- gastrointestinal system
- endocrine system
- nervous system

CHANGES IN THE MUSCULOSKELETAL AND KINES-THETIC SYSTEM   Stature or height declines an average of 3 inches with age, although the total loss varies across individuals and between men and women. Indeed, the Baltimore Longitudinal Studies found that a gradual reduction in height begins around age 30, about 1/16 inch per year on average. We reach our maximum size and strength at about age 25, after which our cells decrease steadily in number and size. This decline occurs in both the trunk and the extremities, and may be attributable to the loss of bone mineral. This loss of bone mineral density is, in turn, attributed to a decline in estrogen levels with menopause in women. A decline in testosterone may explain the similar but less dramatic loss of bone mineral in older men (Rudman et al., 1991). The spine becomes more curved, and discs in the vertebrae become compacted. Such loss of height is intensified for individuals with **osteoporosis,** a disease that makes the bones less dense, more porous, and hence more prone to fractures following even a minor stress. For older people who have no natural teeth remaining, it is not unusual to lose a considerable

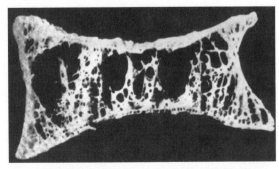

With osteoporosis, both trabecular and cortical bones become more brittle and lace-like.

volume of bone in the jaw or alveolar bone. This results in a poor fit of dentures and a painful feeling when chewing or biting with dentures. The loss of bone mass characteristic of osteoporosis is *not* a normal process of aging, but a disease that occurs more frequently among older women, as discussed in Chapters 4 and 15.

Another normal change with aging is that shoulder width decreases as a result of bone loss, weakened muscles, and loss of elasticity in the ligaments. Crush fractures of the spine cause the vertebrae to collapse, such that over time, some older people (especially women) appear to be stoop-shouldered or hunched—a condition known as **kyphosis.** Stiffness in the joints is also characteristic of old age; this occurs because cartilage between the joints wears thin and fluid that lubricates them decreases. Strength and stamina also decline with aging. Maximum strength at age 70 has been found to be 65 to 85 percent of the maximum capacity of a 25-year-old. This drops to 50 percent by age 80, although older persons who maintain an active physical fitness program show much less decline in strength. Grip strength declines by 50 percent in men between age 30 and 75, and to a lesser degree in women.

The **kinesthetic system** lets an individual know his or her position in space; adjustments in body position become known through kinesthetic cues. Because of age-related changes in the central nervous system, which controls the kinesthetic mechanism, as well as in muscles, older people demonstrate a decreased ability to orient their bodies in space and to detect externally induced changes in body position. Other physiological and disease-related changes, such as damage to the inner ear, may exacerbate this problem. Comparisons of old and young subjects find that older persons need more external cues to orient themselves in space, and can be incorrect by 5 to 20 degrees in estimating their position. If both visual and surface cues of position are lost, older people experience postural sway or inability to maintain a vertical stance (Teasdale, Stelmach, and Breunig, 1991).

INCONGRUENCE BETWEEN THE ENVIRONMENT AND OLDER ADULTS' MOTOR FUNCTIONING AND BALANCE

Mrs. Guitierrez, age 83, lives alone and is determined to be as independent as possible. Her neighbors watch carefully, however, when she goes out to walk her small dog. She shuffles, moves very slowly, and often has to stop and grab hold of something to avoid falling. When her son and daughter-in-law visit, they shudder when she climbs on a stool to reach a can or bottle on the upper cabinet shelves. Her son has tried to make her home safer, by moving the food to lower shelves, putting grab bars in the bathroom, and removing throw rugs. These changes are necessary to accommodate normal age-related changes in her kinesthetic and motor functioning.

Not surprisingly, these changes in motor functioning and in the kinesthetic system result in greater caution among older persons, who then tend to take slower, shuffling, and more deliberate steps. Older people are more likely to seek external spatial cues and supports while walking. As a result, they are less likely to go outside in inclement weather for fear of slipping or falling. Some may complain of dizziness and vertigo. These normal, age-related changes combine with the problems of slower reaction time, muscle weakness, and reduced visual acuity to make it far more likely for older people to fall and injure themselves. However, attempts to improve balance through general and aerobic exercise, alternative approaches such as Tai Chi, and systematic programs to increase visual cues are successful in enhancing the postural stability of healthy older persons (Hu and Woollacott, 1994). Other advantages of exercise programs for older adults are discussed in Chapter 4.

CHANGES IN THE SENSE OF TOUCH   *Somesthetic,* or touch, sensitivity also deteriorates with age. This is partially due to changes in the skin and to age-related loss in the number of nerve endings. Reduced touch sensitivity is especially prevalent in the fingertips, palms, and lower extremities. Age differences in touch sensitivity of the fingertips are much more dramatic than in the forearm. Using two-point discrimination tests (i.e., the minimum distance at which the subject detects the two points of a caliper), researchers have found that older persons need two to four times the separation of two points that younger persons do. This has significant implications for daily tasks that require sensitivity of the fingertips, such as selecting medications from a pillbox (Stevens, 1992).

Pain perception is an important aspect of touch sensitivity. Older adults are less able to discriminate among levels of painful stimuli than younger persons. One reason for this may be that nerve cells in the skin become less efficient with age. As a result, burns are often more serious in older people because they do not respond to the heated object or flame until it is too late.

The distinction between pain perception and pain behavior is a critical one. Tolerance for pain is a subjective experience, which may be related to cultural, gender, and personality factors. In older people, increased complaints of pain may be a function of depression and psychosomatic needs. On the other hand, some people may attempt to minimize their pain by not reporting above-threshold levels of unpleasant stimuli. This is consistent with a frequently observed attitude among many older adults that pain, illness, and discomfort are necessary corollaries of aging. In fact, most older adults probably underreport actual pain experienced. For example, an older person may not report symptoms of a heart attack unless

POINTS TO PONDER

Look around your own home, or your parents' home. What physicial factors can you identify that would be a problem if you were an 80-year-old woman living there? Think about lighting, stairs, floor, cabinets, and so on. What changes could make the home more congruent with an older person's needs?

or until it is severe. This has significant implications for health-seeking behaviors, as described in Chapter 4.

CHANGES IN THE RESPIRATORY SYSTEM Almost every organ system shows some decline in **functional** (or **reserve**) **capacity** with age, as illustrated by several physiological indices in Figure 3.2. It is important to keep in mind that this graph is based on *cross-sectional* data collected from healthy men in these age groups; results from the Baltimore Longitudinal Studies of Aging show more variability when longitudinal data for each cohort are examined. On average, many organ systems show a functional decline of about one percent per year after age 30. Complex functions that require the

integration of multiple systems experience the most rapid decline. For example, maximum breathing capacity—which requires coordination of the respiratory, nervous, and muscular systems—is greatly decreased. Accordingly, normal changes in the respiratory and cardiovascular system become most evident with age. These changes are responsible for an individual's declining ability to maintain physical activity for long periods and the increasing tendency to fatigue easily. With aging, the muscles that operate the lungs lose elasticity so that respiratory efficiency is reduced. Gradual declines in organ function are caused by increasing rates of cell loss and inability of tissues to repair themselves with aging, resulting in impaired replication and reserve capacity of the or-

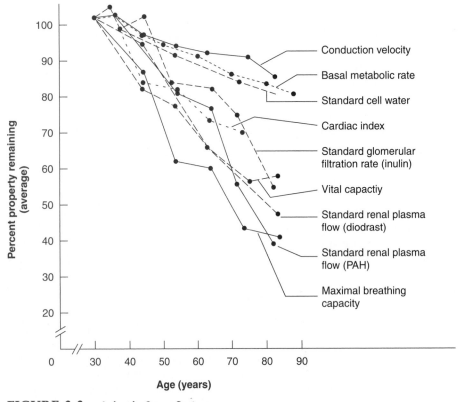

FIGURE 3.2 **Aging in Organ Systems**
SOURCE: N. W. Shock, The physiology of aging. *Scientific American,* 1962, *206,* 110.

gan. Indeed, this loss of reserve capacity with aging may be responsible for some diseases associated with aging (Hornsby, 2001).

Vital capacity, or the maximum amount of oxygen that can be brought into the lungs with a deep breath, declines. In fact, the average decline for men is estimated to be 50 percent between ages 25 and 70, or a decline from 6 quarts of air to 3 quarts. Breathing may become more difficult after exercise, such as climbing up several flights of stairs, but it does not necessarily impair the older person's daily functions. It may simply mean that the person has to move more slowly or rest on the stairway landing. However, the rate of decline in vital capacity is slower in physically active men, such as athletes, than in sedentary healthy men. A longitudinal study that followed well-trained endurance athletes (average age 62 at baseline) and a control group of sedentary men (average age 61 at baseline) over 8 years suggests that aging per se plays only a small role in the decline of the respiratory system:

- Maximum volume of oxygen declined in master athletes by 5.5 percent.
- Maximum volume of oxygen declined in sedentary men by 12 percent (Rogers et al., 1990).

Of all the organ systems, the respiratory system suffers the most punishment from environmental pollutants and infections. This makes it difficult to distinguish normal, age-related changes from pathological or environmentally induced diseases. **Cilia,** which are hairlike structures in the airways, are reduced in number and less effective in removing foreign matter, which diminishes the amount of oxygen available. This decline, combined with reduced muscle strength in the chest that impairs cough efficiency, makes older adults more susceptible to chronic bronchitis, emphysema, and pneumonia. Older people can avoid serious loss of lung function by remaining active, pacing their tasks, taking part in activities that do not demand too much exertion, and avoiding

strenuous activity on days when the air quality is poor.

CARDIOVASCULAR CHANGES AND THE EFFECTS OF EXERCISE   Structural changes in the heart and blood vessels include a reduction in bulk, a replacement of heart muscle with fat, a loss of elastic tissue, and an increase in collagen. Within the muscle fibers, an age pigment composed of fat and protein, known as *lipofuscin,* may take up 5 to 10 percent of the fiber structure (Pearson and Shaw, 1982). These changes produce a loss of elasticity in the arteries, weakened vessel walls, and **varicosities,** or an abnormal swelling in veins that are under high pressure (e.g., in the legs). In addition to loss of elasticity, the arterial and vessel walls become increasingly lined with lipids (fats), creating the condition of **atherosclerosis,** which makes it more difficult for blood to be pumped through the vessels and arteries. This buildup of fats and lipids occurs to some extent with normal aging, but it is exacerbated in some individuals whose diet includes large quantities of saturated fats. Such

Walking provides many physical and emotional benefits.

HOW TO CALCULATE MAXIMUM ACHIEVABLE HEART RATE

The maximum heart rate achievable by sustained exercise is directly associated with age. An easy way to calculate this is: 220 minus age in years. For example:

- For a 25-year-old, 220–25 = 195 beats per minute
- For a 70-year-old, 220–70 = 150 beats per minute

lifestyle risk factors for heart disease are reviewed in Chapter 4.

Blood pressure is expressed as the ratio of **systolic** to **diastolic pressure.** The former refers to the level of blood pressure (in mm.) during the contraction phase (systole), whereas the latter refers to the stage when the chambers of the heart are filling with blood. For example, a blood pressure of 120/80 indicates that the pressure created by

the heart to expel blood can raise a column of mercury 120 mm. During diastole, in this example, the pressure produced by blood rushing into the heart chambers can raise a column of mercury 80 mm. In normal aging (i.e., no signs of cardiovascular disease), systolic blood pressure increases somewhat, but the diastolic blood pressure does not (see Figure 3.3). As with changes in the heart, extreme elevation of blood pressure is not normal and is associated with diet, obesity, and lifestyle, all of which have cumulative effects over the years. The harmful effects of abnormally high or low blood pressure are examined in Chapter 4.

However, heart rate varies across individuals, remaining relatively high in physically active older persons. Resting heart rates also decrease with aging, although physically well-conditioned older people tend to have heart rates more similar to the average younger person.

These changes in the heart and lungs cause them to be less efficient in utilizing oxygen. This, in turn, reduces an individual's capacity to main-

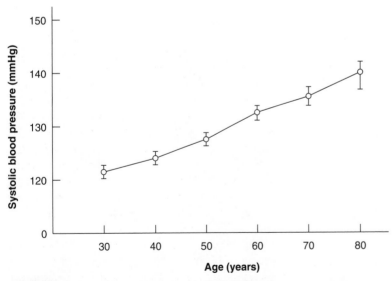

FIGURE 3.3   Effect of Age on Systolic Blood Pressure

SOURCE: J. D. Tobin, Physiological indices of aging. In D. Danon, N. W. Shock, and M. Marois (Eds.), *Aging: A challenge in science and society,* Vol. 1 (New York: Oxford University Press, 1981).

AN OLDER ADULT CAN IMPROVE CARDIOVASCULAR FUNCTION

Mrs. Carson had gained weight after retiring at age 66. She was never very interested in exercise. However, a medical checkup at age 68 revealed high LDL and total cholesterol, as well as marginally high blood pressure. She began an exercise program of walking 30 minutes, five times weekly, and cut down her intake of red meat. After 6 months she had lost 10 pounds, her blood lipids were in the normal range, and her blood pressure was 120/70, ideal for a woman her age.

tain physical activity for long periods. Nevertheless, physical training for older persons can significantly reduce blood pressure and increase their aerobic capacity (Vincent et al., 2002). Studies of master athletes show that physical training results in a greater volume of oxygen, more lean body weight, lower levels of low density lipoprotein (LDL) cholesterol, also known as "bad cholesterol," and higher levels of high density lipoprotein (HDL), or good cholesterol, than is found in sedentary older persons (Yataco et al., 1997). However, these levels in master athletes are worse than in younger athletes, underscoring the reality that normal changes in the body's physiology and its operation cannot be eliminated completely. For example, world-class sprinters are generally in their late teens or early 20s, but marathon winners are normally in their late 20s or early 30s, since strength and neuromuscular coordination peak earlier than stamina. After age 30, running speed declines by a few percent each year (Hayflick, 1996).

Nevertheless, moderate exercise, such as a brisk walk three to four times per week, appears to slow down these age-related changes. Researchers have found a significant increase in aerobic capacity, as measured by maximum volume of oxygen intake, among older persons after 24 weeks of low-intensity or high-intensity training (e.g., walking vs. jogging for 30 minutes). Both low and high

intensity resulted in improved aerobic capacity (Vincent et al., 2002). However, high-intensity training can also result in more orthopedic injuries than low-intensity training. For this reason, given that both high- and low-intensity training are effective for improving aerobic capacity, walking may be the best exercise for many older adults. However, exercise may not be sufficient for reducing LDL cholesterol levels in the blood, which has been associated with heart disease. Instead, reduced intake of animal fats, tropical oils, and refined carbohydrates appears to be essential for lowering these elements in the blood. Although there are limitations, such findings justify optimism that physical health can be considerably improved through lifestyle changes, even after age 65. Aerobic exercise and a healthy lifestyle can significantly increase active life expectancy by postponing and shortening the period of morbidity (e.g., days of sickness) that one can expect in the later years. The significance of certain lifestyle habits for maintaining good health in old age is discussed further in Chapter 4.

CHANGES IN THE URINARY SYSTEM Both kidney and bladder functions change with age. The kidneys play an important role in regulating the body's internal chemistry by filtering blood and urine through an extraordinary system of tubes and capillaries, known as glomeruli. As blood passes through these filters, it is cleaned, and the necessary balance of ions and minerals is restored. In the process, urea (e.g., water and waste materials) is collected and passed through the ureter and the bladder, where it is excreted in the form of urine. With age, the kidneys decrease in volume and weight, and the total number of glomeruli correspondingly decreases by 30 percent from age 30 to age 65. As a result, **renal function,** defined by the rate at which blood is filtered through the kidneys, declines by up to 50 percent with age. These changes have significant implications for an older person's tolerance for certain medications such as penicillin, tetracycline, digoxin, and others that are cleared by glomerular filtration. These drugs

> **OLDER WOMAN WITH BLADDER CONTROL PROBLEMS**
>
> Mrs. RedHorse, age 75, has experienced increasing problems with urinary incontinence, especially since she began using diuretics for her high blood pressure. This has forced her to curtail many of her favorite activities, such as her daily walks with her dog, overnight visits to her daughter's home, and her afternoon tea breaks. She feels frustrated and embarrassed to talk with her physician or daughter about this problem.

remain active longer in an older person's system and may be more potent, indicating a need to reduce drug dosage and frequency of administration.

The kidneys also lose their capacity to absorb glucose, as well as their concentrating and diluting ability. This contributes to increased problems with dehydration and hyponatremia (i.e., a loss of salt in the blood). Of all organ systems, renal function deteriorates most dramatically with age, irrespective of disease.

Compounding this problem, bladder function also deteriorates with age. The capacity of the bladder may be reduced by as much as 50 percent in some persons older than age 65. At the same time, however, the sensation of needing to empty the bladder is delayed. The latter condition may be more a function of central nervous system dysfunction than changes in the bladder. As a result, **urinary incontinence** is common in older adults. As many as 30 percent of older people living in the community and at least 50 percent of those in nursing homes suffer from difficulties with bladder control. The problem may be made worse by a stroke, dementia, or other diseases associated with the nervous system, such as Parkinson's (Thom and Brown, 1998).

Because of these changes in the kidney and the bladder, older people may be more sensitive to the effects of alcohol and caffeine. Both of these substances inhibit the production of a hormone that regulates urine production. Ordinarily, this

hormone, known as antidiuretic hormone (ADH), signals to the kidneys when to produce urine in order to keep the body's chemistry balanced. When it is temporarily inhibited by the consumption of alcohol, coffee, or tea, the kidneys no longer receive messages and, as a result, produce urine constantly. This, in turn, dehydrates the body. It appears that ADH production is slowed with aging, so substances that inhibit its production increase the load on the kidneys and the bladder. These changes can force older people to avoid social outings, even a trip to the grocery store, out of fear that they may not have access to a bathroom. Possible treatments for urinary incontinence, as well as ways that older people can alter their daily habits to accommodate bladder problems, are discussed more fully in Chapter 4.

CHANGES IN THE GASTROINTESTINAL SYSTEM   The gastrointestinal system includes the esophagus, stomach, intestines, colon, liver, and biliary tract. Although the esophagus does not show age-related changes in appearance, some functions do change. These may include a decrease in contraction of the muscles and more time for the cardiac sphincter (a valvelike structure that allows food to pass into the stomach) to open, thus taking more time for food to be transmitted to the stomach. The result of these changes may be a sensation of being full before having consumed a complete meal. This in turn may reduce the pleasure a person derives from eating, and result in inadequate nutrient intake. This sensation also explains why older people may appear to eat such small quantities of food at mealtimes.

Secretion of digestive juices in the stomach apparently diminishes after age 50, especially among men. As a result, older people are more likely to experience the condition of **atrophic gastritis,** or a chronic inflammation of the stomach lining. Gastric ulcers are more likely to occur in middle age than in old age, but older people are at greater risk for colon and stomach cancer. Because of this risk, older people who complain of gastrointestinal discomfort should be urged to seek medical attention for the problem, instead of relying on home remedies or over-the-counter medications.

As with many other organs in the human body, the small and large intestines decrease in weight after age 40. There are also functional changes in the small intestine, where the number of enzymes is reduced, and simple sugars are absorbed more slowly, resulting in diminished efficiency with age. The smooth muscle content and muscle tone in the wall of the colon also decrease. Anatomical changes in the large intestine are associated with the increased incidence of chronic constipation in older persons.

Behavioral factors are probably more critical than organic causes of constipation, however, as discussed in Chapter 4. Spasms of the lower intestinal tract are an example of the interaction of physiological with behavioral factors. Although they may occur at any age, such spasms are more common among older persons. These spasms are a form of functional disorder—that is, a condition without any organic basis, often due to psychological factors. Many gastrointestinal conditions that afflict older people are unrelated to the anatomical changes described previously. Nevertheless, they are very real problems to an older person who experiences them. For these reasons, many physicians routinely do a complete checkup of the gastrointestinal system in their patients age 50 and older, every 2 to 3 years.

The liver also grows smaller with age, by about 20 percent, although this does not appear to have much influence on its functions. However, there is a deterioration in the ability to process medications that are dependent on liver function. Jaundice occurs more frequently in older people, and may be due to changes in the liver or to the obstruction of bile in the gall bladder. In addition, high alcohol consumption may put excessive strain on the older person's liver.

CHANGES IN THE ENDOCRINE SYSTEM   The endocrine system is made up of cells and tissues that produce a variety of hormones. One of the most obvious age-related changes in the endocrine system is **menopause,** resulting in a reduced production of two important hormones in women—**estrogen** and progesterone. Many other hormones besides estrogen and progesterone appear to decline with aging. These include **testosterone,** thyroid, growth hormones, and insulin. Changes in insulin levels with aging may affect the older person's ability to metabolize **glucose** in the diet efficiently, resulting in high blood sugar levels. It is unclear if the changes in hormone production are a cause or an effect of aging. Nevertheless, much of the research aimed at reversing or delaying aging has focused on replacing other hormones whose levels decline with aging. Some support for this is found in animal studies; for example, by stimulating the hypothalamus in the brain (which produces growth hormones) of old female rats, researchers have stimulated the development of eggs and increased the synthesis of protein in these animals. Thyroid hormones administered to old rats have been found to increase the size of the thyroid and the efficiency of their immune systems (Hayflick, 1996).

CHANGES IN THE IMMUNE SYSTEM   There are many complex changes in the immune system with aging. The concept of *"immunosenescence"* implies that aging results in a significant decline in the immune system, increasing the older person's susceptibility to infectious disease and risk of death. However, recent research findings contradict the prevailing wisdom that the aging process always results in deterioration or immunodeficiency (i.e., an inadequate response to infectious organisms). Studies of centenarians show highly effective immune responses when compared to some young-old persons (Cossarizza et al., 1997; Effros, 2001; Franceschi et al., 1995; Solana, 2003). Nevertheless, the fact that most deaths in people age 80 and older are caused by infections implicates failure of the immune system in these cases. This may be because of lower production of T-cells, B-cells, and lymphocytes with aging. Declines in these critical cells for creating antibodies to infectious organisms are aggravated by a decline in CD3, CD4, CD8, and CD28 molecules that are critical as a secondary activator signal for T-cells.

The variation across organ systems in cellular composition is noteworthy. Although healthy adults show declines in the production of these cells in blood, T-cells in the tonsil and spleen actually *increase* with age. Based on studies of old and young mice, aging appears to cause a qualitative change in immune responses. The quantity of antibody production may be high but it is activated more slowly and less efficiently in older animals. Age-related changes in some physiological processes, such as a decline in lipid metabolism and pulmonary function, reduced acid secretion in the gut, and reductions in sex hormones may all influence immune function. Altered immune function has been linked to some diseases of aging, including prostate and skin cancers as well as cardiovascular disease.

CHANGES IN THE NERVOUS SYSTEM   The brain is composed of billions of neurons, or nerve cells, and billions of glial cells that support these. We lose some of both types of cells as we grow older. Neuronal loss begins at age 30, well before the period termed *old*. It is compounded by alcohol consumption, cigarette smoking, and breathing polluted air. The frontal cortex experiences a greater loss of cells than other parts of the brain. A moderate degree of neuronal loss does not create a major decline in brain function, however. In fact, contrary to popular belief, we can function with fewer neurons than we have, so their loss is not the reason for mild forgetfulness in old age. Even in the case of Alzheimer's disease and other **dementias,** severe loss of neurons may be less significant than changes in brain tissue, blood flow, and receptor organs (Thomas et al., 1996).

Other aging-related changes in the brain include a reduction in its weight by 10 percent, an accumulation of lipofuscin (i.e., an age pigment composed of fat and protein), and slower transmission of information from one neuron to another. The reduction in brain mass occurs in all species, and is probably due to loss of fluids. The gradual buildup of lipofuscin, which has a yellowish color, causes the outer cortex of the brain to take on a yellow-beige color with age. As with the moderate loss of neurons, these changes do not appear to alter brain function in old age. That is, difficulties in solving problems or remembering dates and names cannot be attributed to these slight changes in the size and appearance of the brain. Indeed, research comparing age-related changes in brain structures of healthy men and women shows that men experience greater loss of cerebrospinal fluid volume, but this does not translate to any greater or less change in memory or learning among men with normal aging (Coffey et al., 1998).

Age-related changes in neurotransmitters and in the structure of the synapse (the junction between any two neurons) are shown to impair cognitive and motor function. Electroencephalograms, or readings of the electrical activity of the brain, show a slower response in older brains than in the young. These changes may be at least partially responsible for the increase in reaction time with age. The Baltimore Longitudinal Studies of Aging (BLSA) found that reaction time slows by as much as 20 percent between age 20 and age 60 (Hayflick, 1996). Other hypotheses include neuronal loss and reduced blood flow; however, available data are inconclusive. Reaction time is a complex product of multiple factors, primarily the speed of conduction and motor function, both of which are slowed by the increased time needed to transmit messages at the synapses.

The reduced speed with which the nervous system can process information or send signals for action is a fairly widespread problem, even in middle age when people begin to notice lagging reflexes and reaction time. As a result, such tasks as responding to a telephone or doorbell, crossing the street, completing a paper and pencil test, or deciding among several alternatives generally take longer for older people than for the young. Most people adjust to these changes by modifying their physical environment or personal habits, such as taking more time to do a task and avoiding rush situations; for example:

- leaving the house one hour before an appointment instead of the usual 15 minutes
- shopping for groceries during times when stores are not crowded
- shopping in smaller stores
- avoiding freeway driving

Such adaptations are perhaps most pronounced in the tasks associated with driving. The older driver tends to be more cautious, to slow down well in advance of a traffic signal, to stay in the slower lane, and to avoid freeways during rush hour. Many choose to drive larger cars that can survive collisions better than compact cars. Despite this increased cautiousness, accident rates are high among older drivers, as discussed in the next chapter.

Changes in the central nervous system that accompany aging also affect the senses of hearing, taste, smell, and touch. Despite these changes, intellectual and motor function do not appear to deteriorate significantly with age. The brain has tremendous reserve capacity that takes over as losses begin. It is only when neuronal loss, inadequate function of neurotransmitters, and other structural changes are severe that the older person experiences significant loss of function. The changes in the brain that appear to be associated with Alzheimer's disease are discussed in Chapter 6.

Changes in Sleep Patterns with Aging

One of the most common complaints of older people is that they can no longer sleep well, with up to 40 percent of older persons in community surveys complaining of sleep problems. These complaints have a basis in biological changes that occur with aging. Results of laboratory studies of sleep–wake patterns of adults have consistently revealed age-related changes in electroencephalogram (EEG) patterns, sleep stages, and circadian

rhythms (Vitiello, 1996). Sleep progresses over five stages:

- non-REM sleep; i.e., no rapid eye movements during sleep (stages 1–4)
- REM (rapid eye movement) sleep (stage 5)

Sleep stages occur in a linear pattern from stage 1 through stage 4, then REM sleep in stage 5. Stage 4 is when deep sleep takes place. Each cycle is repeated four or five times through the night. Brain wave activity differs in a characteristic pattern for each stage.

Many of these brain waves slow down with aging, and the length of time in each stage changes. In particular, lab tests have shown a decline in total sleep time in stages 3, 4, and 5, and sleep is lighter. Older people have shorter cycles from stages 1 to 4 and REM sleep, with the latter stage occurring earlier in the cycle. During these stages, older people, more so than the young, are easily awakened, apparently by environmental stimuli that would not disturb a younger person (Vitiello and Prinz, 1991).

Changes in circadian rhythms, or the individual's cycle of sleeping and waking within a 24-hour period, are characterized by a movement from a two-phase pattern of sleep (awake during the day, asleep during the night) to a multiphasic

---

TIPS FOR IMPROVING SLEEP

Sleep disturbances can be alleviated by improving one's **sleep hygiene.** These include:

- increasing physical exercise
- increasing exposure to natural light during the days
- reducing the intake of caffeine and other medications
- avoiding napping during the day
- improving the sleeping environment (e.g., a quieter bedroom with heavy curtains to block out the light, because exposure to light can change circadian rhythms) (Vitiello, 1996)

rhythm that is more common in infants—daytime napping and shorter sleep cycles at night. These changes may be associated with changes in core body temperatures in older people, as discussed earlier in this chapter.

The older person may compensate by taking more daytime naps, which can lead to further disruptions in night sleep. More often, older people who report sleep disturbances to their primary physician are prescribed sleeping pills (sedative-hypnotic medications); this age group represents the highest users of such medications, receiving almost one-half of all sedative-hypnotic drugs prescribed. Yet medications do not necessarily improve their sleep patterns, especially if used long-term (Ohayon and Caulet, 1995; Vitiello, 1996). Many hypnotics used to treat sleep disorders can produce a paradoxical effect by resulting in insomnia if used for a long time.

It is important to emphasize that a true sleep disturbance is one that interferes with daytime activities. Researchers who have examined older people with sleep complaints have found that chronic diseases, psychiatric disorders, and alcohol and prescription drug use are more likely to cause disturbed sleep in this population than aging per se. Research by Vitiello, Moe and Prinz (2002) found that only 3.2 percent of one community-dwelling sample of older people and 1.4 percent of another could be classified as experiencing a significant sleep disorder, after excluding all persons who had medical or psychiatric conditions that could affect sleep. An even larger study of almost 12,000 people (ages 15+) in Canada found that increased age was not significantly related to insomnia, but life stress, smoking, low education and income, multiple health problems, and activity limitations were all associated with insomnia at any age (Sutton, Moldofsky, and Badley, 2001). There are a few true *disorders of sleep* that can occur with aging; these include respiratory problems, **sleep apnea,** which is defined as a 5- to 10-second cessation of breathing, and **nocturnal myoclonus** or *restless leg syndrome (RLS),* which is a neuromuscular dis-

turbance affecting the legs during sleep. Generally these conditions are treated with medications. Sleep disturbance in older persons with dementia is not uncommon, and can disrupt both the patient's and caregiver's quality of life. This often leads to premature institutionalization of elders with dementia. For these reasons, many families seek medical help for the patient's insomnia, resulting in the use of sedative-hypnotic medications that can further aggravate the sleep disturbance. It is important to try nonpharmacological therapies along with behavioral and environmental interventions (e.g., preventing daytime napping, keeping the patient physically active during the day) to treat sleep problems in dementia patients. Medications should not be the treatment of first choice for this population (McCurry et al., 2000; Vitiello and Borson, 2001).

Sleep disorders in older persons should be treated because in some cases they can increase the risk of mortality. A large study of community-dwelling older adults found that daytime sleepiness was associated with increased death rates in men and women (1.40 times the rate for men with normal sleep, 2.12 times the rate for women with normal sleep). Frequent awakenings or early morning awakenings had no discernible effect on mortality (Newman et al., 2000).

Changes in Sensory Functions

Our ability to see, hear, touch, taste, and smell has a profound influence on our interactions with our social and physical environments. Given the importance of our sensory functions for social interactions, and the gradual decline in our sensory abilities with aging, it is critical that we understand these changes and how they can influence our social capabilities as we age. A popular belief is that, as we get older, we cannot see, hear, touch, taste, or smell as well as we did when we were younger. This appears to be true. The decline in all our sensory receptors with aging is normal; in fact, it begins relatively early. We reach our optimum

POINTS TO PONDER

Think about the wine taster who, in old age, may still be considered the master of his trade, performing a job that requires excellent taste discrimination. Perfume developers also attain their expertise over many years. What other jobs require intrinsic sensory abilities as well as skills that take years to master?

capacities in our twenties, maintain this peak for a few years, and gradually experience a decline, with a more rapid rate of decline after the ages of 45 to 55. Having said this, we should note that there is tremendous diversity among individuals in the rate and severity of sensory decline, as illustrated earlier by Mrs. Hill and Mr. Jones. Some older persons may have better visual acuity than most 25-year-olds; many 75-year-olds can hear better than most younger persons. Although age per se does not determine deterioration in sensory functioning, it is clear that many internal changes do occur. The older person who has better visual or hearing acuity than a 25-year-old probably had even better sensory capacities in the earlier years. It is important to focus on *intraindividual* changes with age, not *interindividual* differences, when studying sensory and perceptual functions. Unfortunately, most of the research on sensory changes with age is cross-sectional—that is, based on comparing different persons who are older and younger. For this reason, the reader needs to be aware that there are tremendous individual differences in how much and how severely sensory functions deteriorate with age.

Changes in different senses also vary within the same individual. Thus, the person who experiences an early and severe decline in hearing acuity may not have any deterioration in visual functioning. Some sensory functions, such as hearing, may show an early decline, yet others, such as taste and touch, change little until well into advanced old age. Over time, however, sensory changes affect an older person's social functions.

Because these changes are usually gradual, people adapt and compensate by using other, still-intact sensory systems. For example, they may compensate by:

- standing closer to objects and persons in order to hear or see
- using nonverbal cues such as touch and different body orientations
- utilizing external devices such as bifocals or hearing aids

To the extent that people can make their environment conform to their changing needs, sensory decline need not be incapacitating. It becomes much more difficult for individuals to use compensatory mechanisms if the environment does not allow for modification to suit individual needs, if the decline in any one system is severe, or if several sensory systems deteriorate at the same time. Such problems are more likely to occur in advanced old age. There is considerable evidence that, with normal aging, a decline occurs in all sensory systems. That

DISTINCTIONS IN TERMINOLOGY RELATED TO SENSORY FUNCTIONS

- *Sensation* is the process of taking in information through the sense organs.
- *Perception* is a higher function in which the information received through the senses is processed in the brain.
- *Sensory threshold* is the minimum intensity of a stimulus that a person requires in order to detect the stimulus. This differs for each sensory system.
- *Recognition threshold* is the intensity of a stimulus needed in order for an individual to identify or recognize it. As might be expected, a greater intensity of a stimulus is necessary to recognize than to detect it.
- *Sensory discrimination* is defined as the minimum difference necessary between two or more stimuli in order for a person to distinguish between them.

is, sensory and recognition thresholds increase, and discrimination between multiple stimuli demands greater distinctions between them.

Changes in Vision

Vision problems increase with age; when we compare 55- to 64-year-olds with those over age 85, the rate of visual impairments increases fourfold from 55 per 1000 people to 225 per 1000 (Bognoli and Hodos, 1991). As a result, older adults are more likely to experience problems with daily tasks that require good visual skills, such as reading small print or signs on moving vehicles, threading a needle, or adapting to sudden changes in light level. In addition, visual impairments can cause significant problems with activities of daily living and increase the risk of falls and fractures (Desai et al., 2001).

EFFECTS OF STRUCTURAL CHANGES IN THE EYE Most age-related problems in vision are attributable to changes in parts of the eye (see Figure 3.4). However, these problems are aggravated by changes in the central nervous system that block the transmission of stimuli from the sensory organs.

Changes in the visual pathways of the brain and in the visual cortex may be a possible source of some of the alterations that take place in visual sensation and perception with age. The parts of the eye that show the greatest age-related changes are:

- the cornea
- the pupil
- rods and cones in the retina
- the lens

The cornea is usually the first part of the eye to be affected by age-related changes. The surface of the cornea thickens with aging, and the blood vessels become more prominent. The smooth, rounded surface of the cornea becomes flatter and less smooth, and may take on an irregular shape. The older person's eye appears to lose its luster and is less translucent than it was in youth. In some cases, a fatty yellow ring, known as the *arcus senilis*, may form around the cornea. This is not a sign of impending vision loss; in fact, it has no impact on vision. It is sometimes associated with increased lipid deposits in the blood vessels.

At its optimal functioning, the pupil is sensitive to light levels in the environment, widening in

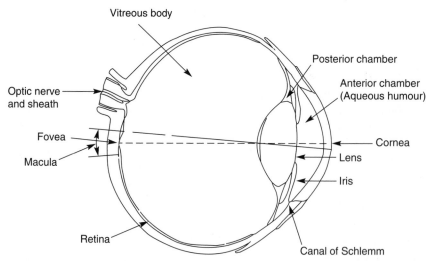

FIGURE 3.4 **The Eye**

PROBLEMS WITH RESTAURANT ENVIRONMENTS

Many older people may feel frustrated when they go to a special restaurant for an evening dinner, only to find that the tables are lit by candles. This makes it difficult to read the menu, to see the way to the table, and even to have eye contact with companions. Family and friends may be frustrated in such situations if they do not understand that the older person's complaints about the restaurant stem from these changes in vision, not from a lack of appreciation for their efforts. Some older people cope with these problems by avoiding such restaurants altogether or going there only during daylight hours.

It is important for restaurant owners to provide good lighting at each table and write their menus in large, legible print against a white background. In response to the growing number of baby boomers who are experiencing problems of visual accommodation, some restaurants have begun to stock reading glasses with different levels of magnification to lend to their customers!

response to low light levels and contracting when light levels are high. With aging, the pupil appears to become smaller and more fixed in size. The maximum opening of the pupil is reduced in old age, commonly to about two-thirds its original maximum. That is, the older person's pupil is less able to respond to low light levels by dilating or opening to the extent needed. The eye also responds more slowly to changes in light conditions. This problem is compounded by a slower shift from cones to rods under low-light conditions. As a result, the older person may have considerable difficulty functioning in low-light situations, or in adjusting to significant changes in ambient light. In fact, older people may need three times more light than younger persons to function effectively; for example, highway signs must be 65 to 75 percent closer than for younger drivers to be readable at night. These changes may also reduce the older person's ability to discern images in conditions of poor light contrast (e.g., driving at twilight or under foggy or rainy conditions), and to

detect details in moving objects. Even among healthy older persons who are still driving, age-related visual changes may significantly alter their abilities under marginal conditions. For example, a survey of participants aged 22 to 92 in the Baltimore Longitudinal Studies (described in Chapter 1) revealed that age was highly correlated with reports of problems with:

- sudden merging of other vehicles
- judging their own and other vehicles' speed
- driving under glare and hazy conditions
- reading street signs while driving (Kline et al., 1992)

For these reasons, older people may choose to avoid such activities, especially driving among fast-moving traffic on freeways at night when bright headlights create glare against asphalt surfaces, and in rain. Although this is a safe method of coping with age-related difficulties in low-light situations, older people must be encouraged to maintain their activity level and not become isolated because of declines in visual function. In such instances, families and professionals may have to encourage older people to use other forms of transportation, such as buses and taxis, thereby avoiding the problem of too little environmental stimulation relative to the person's competence.

PROBLEMS RELATED TO OXYGEN AND FLUID LEVELS
Problems in rod and cone function may be related to a reduced supply of oxygen to the retina. This may be due to a deficiency of vitamin A. However, there is little research evidence to suggest that increased intake of vitamin A in old age can improve visual functioning under low-light conditions.

As stated earlier, two fluid-filled chambers are in the eye: *aqueous humour* fills the anterior or front portion of the eye, and *vitreous humour* is found in the posterior chamber, behind the lens. The *aqueous humour* drains through the canal of Schlemm. In the disease state known as **glaucoma,** drainage is less efficient, or excess production of the aqueous humour occurs and causes pressure on the optic nerve. Glaucoma occurs more frequently after middle age and can be managed with regular medications if it is caught early. Unfortunately, it is an insidious disease that progresses slowly and may not be detected until it is more advanced. More severe cases may require surgery or, more recently, the use of laser treatment. In its later stages, glaucoma may result in tunnel vision, which is a gradual narrowing of an individual's field of vision, such that peripheral vision is lost and the individual can focus only in the center. Untreated glaucoma is the second leading cause of blindness in the United States (Braille Institute, 2004), and increases in frequency with age. Among African Americans, glaucoma is the leading cause of blindness. It is more prevalent and more difficult to treat in African Americans, with rates of 15 percent versus 7 percent in whites aged 70 and older (Desai et al., 2001).

EFFECTS OF AGING ON THE LENS   Perhaps the greatest age-related changes in the eye occur in the lens. In fact, the lens is a model system for studying aging because it contains some of the oldest cells in the body, formed during the earliest stages of the embryo's development. Furthermore, the lens is a relatively simple structure biochemically; all of its cells are of the same type, composed of protein.

Collagen is the primary protein in the lens, and makes up 70 to 80 percent of the total tissue composition of the entire body. As it ages, collagen thickens and hardens. This change in collagen makes the lens less elastic, thereby reducing its ability to change form (i.e., from rounded to elongated and flat) as it focuses from near to far. Muscles that help stretch the lens also deteriorate with age, thereby compounding the problem of changing the shape of the lens. This process, known as **accommodation,** begins to deteriorate in middle age and is manifested in increasing problems with close vision. By the time many people reach their forties and fifties, they need to hold their reading material at arm's length. As a result, many turn to reading glasses or bifocals.

By age 60, accommodative ability is significantly deteriorated. Decrements in accommodation may cause difficulties for the older person when shifting from near to far vision; for example, when looking across a room, walking up or down stairs, reading and glancing up, and writing notes while looking up at a blackboard or a lecturer. The hardening of the lens due to changes in collagen tissue does not occur uniformly. Rather, there is differential hardening, with some surfaces allowing more light to enter than others. This results in uneven refraction of light through the lens and onto the retina. When combined with the poor refraction of light through the uneven, flattened surface of the cornea, extreme sensitivity to glare often results. This problem becomes particularly acute in environments with a single source of light aimed at a shiny surface, such as a large window at the end of a long, dark corridor with highly polished floors, occasional streetlights on a rain-slicked highway, or a bright, single, overhead incandescent light shining on a linoleum floor. These conditions may contribute to older people's greater caution and anxiety while driving or walking.

From childhood through early adulthood, the lens is a transparent system through which light can easily enter. With normal aging, the lens becomes more opaque, and less light passes through (especially shorter wavelengths of light); these changes compound the problems of poor vision in low light that were described earlier. Some older persons experience a more severe opacification (clouding of the lens) to the point that the lens prevents light from entering. This condition, known as a **cataract,** is the fourth leading cause of blindness in the United States and the primary cause of blindness worldwide (Sperduto, 1994, Braille Institute, 2004). Symptoms of cataracts include:

- cloudy or fuzzy vision
- double vision
- problems with glare from bright light
- problems with color discrimination

> **SUGGESTIONS FOR IMPROVING PERSON–ENVIRONMENT FIT FOR PEOPLE EXPERIENCING CHANGES IN THEIR VISION**
>
> - Use widely contrasting colors on opposite ends of the color spectrum, such as red and yellow, green and orange.
> - Define edges and corners such as stairs, walls, and doors clearly with color or texture.
> - Avoid using blue and green together to define adjoining spaces, such as stairs and stair landings, floors and ramps, and curbs and curbcuts, especially where the junction represents different levels.
> - Avoid shiny floor and wall surfaces that can cause glare.
> - Avoid placing a single, large window at the end of a long, dark corridor.

Researchers in the Framingham eye study have examined the incidence of cataracts, that is, the development of the condition in the same individual over a number of years. In a reexamination of survivors of the original Framingham eye study 13.6 years later, the incidence rate was 50 percent for people aged 55 to 59 at the beginning of the study. It jumped to 80 percent for older adults who had been age 70 to 74 at the start (Milton and Sperduto, 1991). Its prevalence increases tenfold between ages 52 and 85. There is strong evidence for a relationship between the development of cataracts with age and the lack of antioxidants such as vitamins A, C, and E (Jacques, Chylack, and Taylor, 1994; Seddon et al., 1994b).

A cataract may occur in any part of the lens—in the center, the peripheral regions, or scattered throughout. If the lens becomes totally opaque, cataract surgery may be required to extract the lens. It carries relatively little risk, even for very old persons, and can significantly enhance quality of life. Indeed, this is the most common surgical procedure performed on people over age 65, with about 1.5 million extractions performed per year, usually as an outpatient procedure. A lens implant in place of the extracted lens capsule is the most common treatment. Almost half of these 85 years and older in a U.S. survey reported that they had undergone cataract surgery, compared with about 20 percent at age 70 to 74. Older women were more likely to report having had cataract surgery than their male counterparts (Desai et al., 2001). When the older person first obtains a replacement lens, it takes some time to adjust to performing daily activities. Patients who receive a lens implant show improvement not just in visual function, but also in objective assessments of activities of daily living and manual function within a few months.

In addition to getting harder and more opaque, the lens becomes yellower with age, especially after age 60. The increasingly more opaque and yellowing lens acts as a filter to screen out wavelengths of light, thus reducing the individual's color sensitivity and ability to discriminate among colors that are close together in the blue-green range. Older people may have problems selecting clothing in this color range, sometimes resulting in poorly coordinated outfits. Deterioration in color discrimination may also be due to age-related changes in the visual and neural pathways.

OTHER CHANGES IN VISION *Depth and distance perception* also deteriorate with aging, because of a loss of convergence of images formed in the two eyes. This is caused by differential rates of hardening and opacification in the two lenses, uneven refraction of light onto the retina, and reduced visual acuity in aging eyes. As a result, there is a rapid decline after age 75 in the ability to judge distances and depths, particularly in low-light situations and in the absence of orienting cues, such as stairs with no color distinctions at the edges and pedestrian ramps or curb cuts with varying slopes.

Another age-related change is narrower peripheral vision (the ability to see on either side without moving the eyes or the head). This problem becomes particularly acute when driving; for example, an older person may not see cars approaching from the left or right at an intersection. Illumination levels also affect older people's ability to read text written in small font (i.e., less than 12 point), and with low contrast between text and background. When 80-year-olds were compared with 30-year-olds, low levels of illumination (10 lux*) caused the former to make twice as many errors as the latter, even with high contrast between figure and ground. However, at the highest illumination levels (1000 lux), older adults benefited from high contrast and performed as well as young adults. Unfortunately, most homes and offices do not provide such high lighting levels (Steenbekkers, 1998; Fozard and Gordon-Salant, 2001).

Some older persons experiencing **age-related macular degeneration (AMD)** lose acuity in the center of their visual field. The macula is that point in the retina with the best visual acuity, especially for seeing fine detail. Macular degeneration is the leading cause of blindness in American adults (Braille Institute, 2004). It occurs if the macula receives less oxygen than it needs, resulting in destruction of the existing nerve endings. The incidence of macular degeneration increases with age, even more dramatically than cataracts. About 6 million Americans, mostly over age 65, have this condition. Rates of AMD increase dramatically with age, from 18 percent among those aged 70 to 74 to 47 percent among people 85 and older (Desai et al., 2001). The condition is more common in older women and in white elders than in men and African Americans. There is evidence for both a genetic basis and environmental risk factors, such as a lack of antioxidants for age-related macular degeneration. Researchers are searching for the specific genes responsible for AMD, with the goal of developing early detection and prevention programs. By studying a large family with a history of AMD, geneticists have

identified *HEMICENTIN-1* as the gene where a mutation occurs in people with AMD. Future research will lead to animal models where the mutation can be created and treated, with the eventual goal of modifying the gene in humans before it manifests as AMD (Schultz et al., 2003). Studies that have supplemented older people's diets with carotenoid-rich foods or used zinc supplements have found positive effects on visual activity of AMD patients (Allikmets et al., 1997; Blumberg, 1996; Seddon et al., 1994a).

The early stages of macular degeneration may begin with a loss of detail vision; then central vision gradually becomes worse. Total blindness rarely occurs, but reading and driving may become impossible. Older persons with this condition may compensate by using their remaining peripheral vision. They may then appear to be looking at the shoulder of someone they are addressing, but actually be relying on peripheral vision to see the person's face. Laser treatment in the early stages of this disease is effective, but it carries a risk of burning away the center of the retina entirely. A new form of therapy combines a light-activated drug treatment (Visudyne) with a low-power laser light to activate the drug. This procedure is effective in destroying the abnormal blood vessels and scar tissue in the eye without damaging the retina. Although macular degeneration cannot be cured, this new treatment can slow retinal damage and improve central vision.

Some older people, most often postmenopausal women, experience reduced secretion of tears. They may complain of "dry eyes" that cause irritation and discomfort. Unfortunately, this condition has no known cure, but it does not cause blindness and can be managed with artificial tears to prevent redness and irritation. Artificial tears can be purchased at most drugstores.

The muscles that support the eyes, similar to those in other parts of the body, deteriorate with age. In particular, two key muscles atrophy. These are the elevator muscles, which move the eyeball up and down within its socket, and the ciliary muscle, which aids the lens in changing its shape.

---

*Lux is a unit of measurement for illumination, referring to the amount of light received by a surface at a distance of one meter from a light source.

DIAGNOSING MACULAR DEGENERATION

Mr. Lopez noticed over the past 5 years that objects appear blurry when he looks directly at them, but sharper as he glances more peripherally. He finally went for an eye exam after experiencing more problems with driving. The ophthalmologist diagnosed macular degeneration and was able to treat it with Visudyne. Mr. Lopez can now drive safely again and continue to play bridge and participate in other activities.

Deterioration of the elevator muscles results in a reduced range of upward gaze. This may cause problems with reading overhead signs and seeing objects that are placed above eye level, such as on high kitchen shelves.

Assisting Adaptation and Quality of Life through Environmental Modifications

As suggested above, many older adults report significant impairments in their activities of daily living, including reading small print, adjusting to dimly lit environments, tracking moving targets, and locating a sign in a cluttered background. This may mean that an older person feels compelled to give up valued social activities. To maintain person–environment congruence and psychological well-being, an aging person should be encouraged to maintain social contacts, even if new activities must be substituted for old. Family and friends also can help by improving the physical environment, such as replacing existing lightbulbs with higher wattage, fluorescent lighting with color correction, and three-way bulbs, moving low tables and footstools outside the traffic flow, and putting large-print labels on prescription bottles, spices, and cooking supplies. Older people can also take advantage of:

- large-print newspapers and books
- audiotapes of books that are available in community libraries

- playing cards with large letters
- larger fonts on flat-screen computer monitors that are designed to reduce glare

Local agencies serving the visually impaired often provide low-vision aids at minimal cost. These include:

- needle threaders for sewing
- templates for rotary telephones, irons, and other appliances
- large-print phone books, clocks, and calendars
- magnifying glasses for situations where large-print substitutes are unavailable

Other environmental modifications may be more costly or require the use of a professional architect. Families and designers can help make the home and work environment safer by:

- placing contrasting color strips on stairs, especially on carpeted or slippery linoleum stairs, to aid the older person's depth perception
- color and light coding of ramps and other changes in elevation
- clearly marking changes in floor surfaces such as door sills
- increasing the number of light sources
- installing nonslip and nonglossy floor coverings
- using a flat paint instead of glossy finishes to reduce the problem of glare on walls
- installing venetian and vertical blinds to control glare throughout the day
- using indirect or task lighting (e.g., reading lamps, countertop lamps) rather than ceiling fixtures
- adding dimmer switches

Age-related vision changes need not disadvantage people if they can be encouraged to adapt their activities and environment to fit their level of visual functioning and their needs. An older adult who is having difficulty adjusting to vision-related losses may initially resist such modifications. One way to address this resistance is to involve the older person in decisions about such changes.

Changes in Hearing

In terms of survival, vision and hearing are perhaps our most critical links to the world. Although vision is important for negotiating the physical environment, hearing is vital for communication. Because hearing is closely associated with speech, its loss disrupts a person's understanding of others and even the recognition of one's own speech. An older person who is experiencing hearing loss learns to make changes in behavior and social interactions, so as to reduce the detrimental social impact of hearing loss. Many younger hearing-impaired persons learn sign language or lip reading. But these are complex skills requiring extensive training and practice, and are less likely to be learned by older adults.

THE ANATOMY AND PHYSIOLOGY OF THE EAR   It is useful to review the anatomy of the ear in order to understand where and how auditory function deteriorates with age. The auditory system has three components, as illustrated in Figure 3.5. The outer ear begins at the pinna, the visible portion that is identified as the ear. The auditory canal is also part of the outer ear. Note the shape of the pinna and

POINTS TO PONDER

Consider some ways in which we rely on our hearing ability in everyday life: in conversations with family, friends, and coworkers; in localizing the sound of approaching vehicles as we cross the street or drive; and in interpreting other people's emotions through their tone of voice and use of language. How does a person function if these abilities gradually deteriorate?

auditory canal; it is a most efficient design for localizing sounds.

The eardrum, or tympanic membrane, is a thin membrane that separates the outer ear from the middle ear. This membrane is sensitive to air pressure of varying degrees and vibrates in response to a range of loud and soft sounds. Three bones, or *ossicles,* that transfer sound waves to the inner ear are located in the middle ear (the *malleus, incus,* and *stapes*).

These very finely positioned and interrelated bones carry sound vibrations from the middle ear to the **inner ear**—that snail-shaped circular structure called the cochlea. Amplified sounds are con-

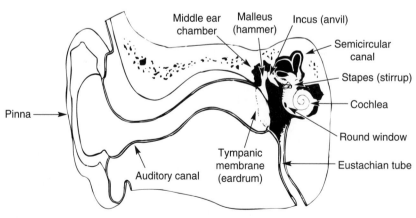

FIGURE 3.5   **The Ear**

verted in the cochlea to nerve impulses. These are then sent through the internal auditory canal and the cochlear nerve to the brain, where they are translated into meaningful sounds. The cochlea is a fluid-filled chamber with thousands of hair cells that vibrate two parallel membranes to move sound waves. The vibration of these hair cells is one of several factors involved in perceiving the pitch (or frequency) and loudness (intensity) of a sound.

AGE-RELATED CHANGES   The pinna appears somewhat elongated and rigid in some older adults. These changes in the outer ear, however, have no impact on hearing acuity. The supporting walls of the external auditory canals also deteriorate with age, as is true for many muscular structures. Arthritic conditions may affect the joints between the malleus and stapes, making it more difficult for these bones to perform their vibratory function. **Otosclerosis** is a condition in which the stapes becomes fixed and cannot vibrate. It is most likely to affect older persons.

The greatest decline with age occurs in the cochlea, where structural changes result in **presbycusis,** or age-related hearing loss. Changes in auditory thresholds can be detected by age 30 or even younger, but the degeneration of hair cells and membranes in the cochlea is not observed until much later. Age-related declines in the middle ear include:

- atrophy of hair cells
- vascular changes
- changes in the cochlear duct
- loss of auditory neurons
- deterioration of neural pathways between the ear and brain (Rees, 2000)

Tests of pure-tone thresholds (i.e., the level at which a tone of a single frequency can be detected) have revealed a steady decline over 15 years. Changes in the high-frequency range are about 1 dB per year. In the range of speech, changes are

slow until age 60, then accelerate to a rate of 1.3 dB per year after age 80 (Brant and Fozard, 1990). About one-third of the population age 70 and older in the United States is estimated to have some loss of hearing, increasing to 50 percent among those aged 85 and older. Rates are higher among white men (61 percent) than any other group at age 85 and older. Thirteen percent suffer from advanced presbycusis. Again, age differences are dramatic; 17 percent of people 85 and older were deaf in 1995, compared with 5 percent of those aged 70 to 74 (Desai et al., 2001; National Academy, 1999).

As with studies regarding visual changes, researchers suggest that age-related changes in the brain are primarily responsible for the deterioration in auditory functioning. These may include cellular deterioration and vascular changes in the major auditory pathways to the brain. However, aging and disease-related pathological changes can damage the auditory system itself. Together with exposure to environmental noise over a lifetime, these factors can cause presbycusis.

Tinnitus, a high-pitched "ringing," is another problem that affects hearing in old age. It may occur bilaterally or in one ear only. The incidence increases threefold between youth and middle age, and fourfold between youth and old age, and may be aggravated by other types of hearing loss (Rosenhall and Karlsson, 1991). Tinnitus may be related to occupational noise exposure; for example, men with tinnitus have been found to have 20 to 30 years of exposure to noisy work environments. It cannot be cured, but people suffering from tinnitus can generally learn to manage it or try alternative approaches such as acupuncture (Micozzi, 1997).

In contrast to visual changes, hearing loss appears to be significantly affected by environmental causes. People who have been exposed to high-volume and high-frequency noise throughout their lives (e.g., urban dwellers and factory workers) experience more hearing decrements in old age than do those from rural, low-noise environments. Over the last three decades, hearing loss among

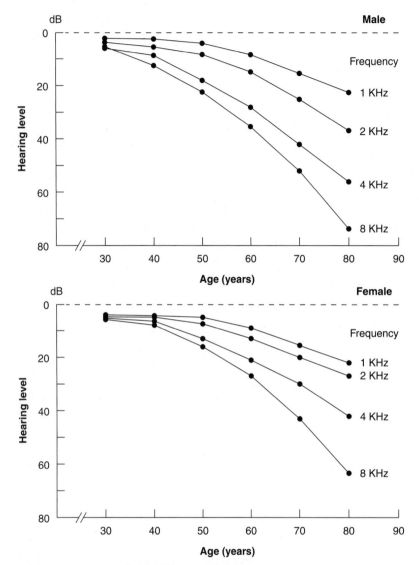

FIGURE 3.6 **Gender Differences in Hearing Thresholds**
SOURCE: Ordy, J. M., Brizzee, K. R., Beavers, T., and Medart, P. Age differences in the functional and structural organization of the auditory system in man. In J. M. Ordy and K. R. Brizzee (Eds.), *Sensory systems and communication in the elderly* (New York: Raven Press, 1979), p. 156. Reprinted with permission of the author and publisher.

people age 18 to 44 has increased significantly. This means that future cohorts will include more elders with hearing loss that was environmentally induced during their youth (Wallhagen et al., 1997). As shown in Figure 3.6, women generally show less decline than men; about 61 percent of people with hearing loss are men. Gender differences in hearing loss occur across the life span:

- 3 percent of men versus 2 percent of women at ages 18 to 44
- 8 percent versus 3 percent at ages 45 to 64
- 19 percent versus 10 percent among those 65 and older (National Academy, 1999)

It is interesting to speculate why these sex differences appear. Are they due to variations in noise exposure or to hormonal differences? The fact that severe hearing loss is found only in some women suggests that the former hypothesis may be more likely.

COMPENSATION AND ADAPTATION   Hearing loss can be of several types, involving limited volume and range or distortion of sounds perceived. Regardless of type, however, hearing loss results in some incongruence between the person and his or her environment. Older persons who have lost hearing acuity in the range of speech (250–3000 Hz) have particular difficulties distinguishing the sibilants or high-frequency consonants such as *z, s, sh, f, p, k, t,* and *g*. Their speech comprehension deteriorates as a result, which may be the first sign of hearing loss. In contrast, low-frequency hearing loss has minimal impact on speech comprehension. As Figure 3.6 illustrates, higher-frequency sounds can be heard better by raising the intensity. The recognition of consonants (*p, t, k, b, d, g*) can be increased by 50 to 90 percent among older persons simply by raising their intensity.

Thus, an individual may compensate by raising the volume of the TV and radio, moving closer to the TV, or listening to other types of music made by lower-pitched instruments such as an organ. When this occurs, it is imperative to determine whether a hearing loss exists, to identify the cause, and to fit the individual with an appropriate hearing aid, if possible. The older design of hearing aids, using analog technology, merely increases the volume of sound. A major difficulty with some hearing aids is that the volume of background noise is raised, in addition to the sound that the user of the device is trying to hear. This

> **RELUCTANCE TO USE HEARING AIDS**
>
> The social stigma associated with wearing a hearing aid is greater than with wearing glasses. These are undoubtedly some of the reasons why only about one-third of older people with hearing loss use them. Nevertheless, after President Clinton was fitted with a new digital hearing aid in 1997, while he was still in office, there was a dramatic increase in the number of hearing aids sold. Sales jumped by 25 percent between 1996 and 1997; many of these were baby boomers like President Clinton who purchased a hearing aid for the first time (National Academy, 1999).

may compensate for loss of higher-frequency sounds, but cannot completely obliterate the problem of presbycusis. In fact, hearing aids often result in such major adaptation problems that older persons stop wearing them after several months.

Fortunately, developments in hearing aid technology are resulting in digital hearing aids with tiny computer chips that filter sounds to match each user's hearing loss profile, without amplifying background noises. These newer designs also are less obtrusive and fit well inside the ear. However, they can cost about twice as much as conventional hearing aids and are not covered by Medicare or by most private health insurance plans.

Other means of compensating for hearing loss are to design environments that dampen background noises or to select such settings for communicating with older persons. Sound levels should not exceed 80 decibels. Soundproof rooms, while costly, are beneficial, particularly if housing for older people is built on busy streets or near freeways. Offices of health professionals should have at least one quiet area without the distraction of background noises. Older people can also benefit from new designs in telephones with volume adjusters and lights that blink when the phone rings.

When conversing with people who are experiencing age-related hearing loss, the following hints can help both younger and older persons enjoy their communication:

- Face an older person directly and maintain eye contact.
- Sit somewhat close and at eye level with the older person.
- Do not cover the face with hands or objects when speaking.
- Speak slowly and clearly, but without exaggerating speech.
- Do not shout.
- Avoid distracting background noises by selecting a quiet, relaxing place away from other people, machines, and traffic sounds.
- Speak in a lower, but not monotonic, tone of voice.
- Repeat key points in different ways.
- If specific information is to be transmitted (e.g., how to take medications), structure the message in a clear, systematic manner (Kiyak, 1996).

Helping older people with hearing impairment compensate for this loss is essential to avoid harmful effects on interpersonal relationships and self-esteem. For some older adults, increasing levels of hearing impairment can disrupt functional abilities, resulting in social withdrawal and even clinical depression (Strawbridge et al., 2000; Wallhagen, Strawbridge, and Kaplan, 1996). One of the most frustrating experiences is the simultaneous deterioration of both hearing and vision. Although it is relatively rare for both functions to decline significantly with age, family, friends, and professionals must be especially sensitive to the communication techniques suggested earlier. For example, when talking with an older person who is impaired in both hearing and vision, touching a hand, arm, or shoulder may aid communication.

Changes in Taste and Smell

Although older people may complain that food does not taste as good as it once did, these complaints are probably not due to an age-associated generalized loss of taste sensitivity. It was once thought that age brought dramatic decreases in the number of taste buds on the tongue, that this loss of receptor elements led to functional loss that was experienced as a dulling of taste sensation, and that these changes accounted for older people's reduced enjoyment of food (Mistretta, 1984). Subsequent studies, however, have challenged each link in this chain of reasoning.

Early research on taste anatomy reported taste-bud loss (Arey, Tremaine, and Monzingo, 1935), but subsequent studies have shown that the number of taste buds does not decline with age (Miller, 1988). Early studies of taste function found large age-related changes in taste thresholds (Murphy, 1979). However, subsequent studies found much smaller declines and concluded that threshold loss almost never involves more than one of the four basic taste qualities (Cowart, 1989).

The notion that various functions decline differentially has replaced the belief that older people experience a generalized taste loss. The research task now is to specify *which* aspects of taste function remain intact and which decline with normal aging or disease. Although the taste

Cooking with spices can enhance olfactory and taste sensitivity.

function of older people does not undergo a general decline in strength, it demonstrates specific changes. For example, although the relationship between taste intensity and stimulus strength is age-stable, judgments of taste intensity become less reliable with age. Older adults have more difficulty than younger people in discriminating between varying intensities of a flavor (e.g., tested by increasing the level of bitterness in coffee, saltiness of food), but such discrimination occurs less often with a stimulus that differs in its sweetness. These differences have been observed across age groups, from teens to people in their 80s. It is also important to note that in studies where the average taste performance of the older individuals is poorer, some perform as well as, or better than, many younger persons.

Appreciation of food does not depend on taste alone. The sense of smell clearly is involved. We have all experienced changes in the way food "tastes" while ill with a head cold and a stuffy nose. These changes suggest that sensitivity to airborne stimuli plays a key role in the perception of foods. Older people perceive airborne stimuli as less intense than younger persons, and do less well on odor identification. External factors such as smoking and medications contribute to these differences, but even after accounting for these factors, age differences are dominant (Ship and Weiffenbach, 1993; Tuorila, Niskanen, and Maunuksela, 2001). When parallel assessments are made in the same subject, age-related declines for smell are greater than for taste. This suggests that one way to increase older people's enjoyment of eating is to provide them with enhanced food odors. Classes in cooking with herbs and spices can be valuable for older people who are experiencing changes in their taste and olfactory abilities. These activities can also help older people in sharpening their sensitivity to tastes and odors, improve the palatability and intake of food, increase salivary flow and immunity, and ultimately enhance their quality of life (Schiffman and Graham, 2000).

Implications for the Future

As the twenty-first century unfolds, new discoveries in genetics, pharmacology, biomedical technology, and surgical techniques hold great possibilities for enhancing the quality of life and extending the human life span. Today scientists can already place embryonic stem cells in culture at an early stage, and watch them maintain telomerase activity and indefinite replication. In the future they will be able to transplant stem cells to human organs in a successful attempt to reverse the decline or disease processes in these organs (Carpenter et al., 1999; Hornsby, 1999).

Someday people will know their predisposition to genetically linked conditions such as Huntington's disease. The long-term impact of caloric restriction and the use of enzyme boosters and antioxidants throughout adulthood on pathogenic conditions in old age as well as folic acid on atherosclerosis and heart disease will become clearer. We will also learn the long-term effects of pharmacological and exercise interventions to prevent insulin resistance and coronary artery disease, osteopenia, and functional decline. In many ways, biological aging in the twenty-first century will move away from the treatment of disease and genetic disorders to their prevention. Trends in microbiological research suggest that an important focus will be on ways to extend the average life span while at the same time maintaining quality of life.

Summary

As shown by this review of physiological systems, the aging process is gradual, beginning in some organ systems as early as the twenties and thirties, and progressing more rapidly after age 70, or even 80, in others. Even with 50 percent deterioration in many organ systems, an individual can still function adequately. The ability of human beings to compensate for age-related changes attests to their significant amount of excess reserve capacity. In most instances, the normal physical changes of aging need not diminish a person's quality of life if person–environment congruence can be maintained. Since many of the decrements are gradual and slight, older people can learn to modify their activities to adapt to their environments—for example, by pacing the amount of physical exertion throughout the day. Family members and professionals can be supportive by encouraging modifications in the home, such as minimizing the use of stairs, moving the focus of the older person's daily activities to the main floor of the home, and reinforcing the older person's efforts to cope creatively with common physical changes.

The rate and severity of decline in various organ systems vary substantially, with the greatest deterioration in functions that require coordination among multiple systems, muscles, and nerves. Similarly, wide variations across individuals in the aging process spring from differences in heredity, diet, exercise, and living conditions. Many of the physiological functions that were once assumed to deteriorate and to be irreversible with normal aging are being reevaluated by researchers in basic and clinical physiology as well as by health educators. Examples of master athletes who continue their swimming, running, and other competitive physical activities throughout life show that age-related declines are not always dramatic. Even people who begin a regular exercise program late in life have experienced significant improvements in their heart and lung capacity. The role of preventive maintenance and health promotion in the aging process is discussed in Chapter 4.

Sleep patterns change with normal aging. Lab studies reveal changes in EEG patterns, sleep stages, and circadian rhythms with advancing years. However, recent studies demonstrate that true sleep disturbances are associated with physical and psychiatric disorders and the medications used to treat these conditions, and are not due to aging per se. Sedative-hypnotic drugs are widely used by older people who complain of sleep disturbance. However, improving sleep hygiene by increasing physical exercise, reducing the intake of alcohol, caffeine, and some medications, and improving the sleep environment are generally more effective methods than sleeping pills for long-term use. This is particularly true for older persons with dementia. Medications are useful only in the case of true sleep disorders, such as sleep apnea and twitching legs during sleep.

Changes in sensory function with age do not occur at a consistent rate in all senses and for all people. Some people show rapid declines in vision while maintaining their hearing and other sensory abilities. Others experience an early deterioration in olfactory sensation, but not in other areas. All of us experience some loss in these functions with age, but interindividual differences are quite pronounced. Normal age-related declines in vision reduce the ability to respond to differing light levels; to function in low-light situations; to see in places with high levels of glare; to discern color tones, especially in the green-blue-violet range; and to judge distances and depth. Peripheral vision becomes somewhat narrowed with age, as does upward and downward gaze. Older people have more diseases of the eye, including glaucoma, cataracts, and macular degeneration; if these diseases are not treated, blindness can result. Visual impairments generally result in more problems with activities of daily living than do hearing impairments. Therefore, older persons who experience significant declines in visual function with age should be encouraged to maintain former levels of activity, either by adapting the environment to fit changing needs or by substituting new activities for those that have become more difficult. Unfortunately, some older people prefer to withdraw from previous activities, thereby becoming more isolated and at risk of depression and declining quality of life.

Decline in auditory function generally starts earlier than visual problems, and affects more people. Significant impairments in speech comprehension often result. Although hearing aids can frequently improve hearing in the speech range by raising the intensity of speech that is in the high-frequency range, many older people feel uncomfortable and even stigmatized when using them. Hence, the solutions to communicating with hearing-impaired older people may lie mostly in the environment, not within older persons themselves. These include changes in communication styles, such as speaking directly at an older person in a clear voice, but not shouting; speaking in a lower tone; repeating key points; and sitting closer to a hearing-impaired person. Environmental aids such as soundproof or quiet rooms and modified telephones can also be invaluable for older people who are experiencing significant hearing declines.

Although many older people complain that food does not taste as good as it once did, changes with age in taste acuity are minimal. The decline in olfactory receptors with age is more significant than in taste receptors, and may be responsible for the perception of reduced taste acuity. These changes are more pronounced in people who smoke or drink heavily, but the use of medications has only modest effects. There is less change in people who have sharpened their taste and olfactory sensitivity, such as professional winemakers and perfumers. This pattern suggests that older people should be encouraged to participate in activities that enhance their taste and olfactory functions.

As we learn more from studies of normal physiological changes with aging, reports that once appeared definitive are found to be less so, and a complete understanding of some areas is shown to be lacking. This is particularly true in the areas of taste, smell, and pain perception. Research is needed to distinguish normal changes in these areas from those that are related to disease, and those that can be prevented. Longitudinal research would help to answer many of these questions. Finally, research that examines the impact of sensory deterioration on the older person's interactions with the environment is also needed.

GLOSSARY

accommodation ability of the lens of the eye to change shape from rounded to flat, in order to see objects that are closer or farther from the lens

age-related macular degeneration (AMD) loss of vision in the center of the visual field caused by insufficient oxygen reaching the macula

antiaging medicine a new field of biological research aimed at slowing or reversing biological aging

atherosclerosis accumulation of fats in the arteries and veins, blocking circulation of the blood

atrophic gastritis chronic inflammation of the stomach lining

autoimmune theory of aging the hypothesis that aging is a function of the body's immune system becoming defective, producing antibodies against itself

cataract clouding of the lens of the eye, reducing sight and sometimes leading to blindness; requires surgical extraction of the lens

cellular aging theory the hypothesis that aging occurs as cells slow their number of replications, based on the observation that cells grown in controlled laboratory environments are able to replicate only a finite number of times

cross-linkage theory the hypothesis that aging is a function of the reduction of collagen with age, causing loss of elasticity in most organ systems

dementia diminished ability to remember, make accurate judgments, etc.

diastolic blood pressure the level of blood pressure during the time that chambers of the heart are filling with blood

estrogen a female sex hormone that declines significantly with aging; can be replaced alone (ERT) or in combination with progesterone, another female sex hormone (HRT)

free radical theory a special case of the cross-linkage theory of aging that posits that free radicals, highly reactive molecules, may produce DNA mutations

functional (or reserve) capacity the ability of a given organ to perform its normal function, compared with its function under conditions of illness, disability, and aging

glaucoma   a disease in which there is insufficient drainage or excessive production of aqueous humor, the fluid in the front portion of the eye

hyperthermia   body temperatures several degrees above normal for prolonged periods

hypothermia   body temperatures several degrees below normal for prolonged periods

kinesthetic system   the body system that signals one's position in space

kyphosis   stoop-shouldered or hunched condition caused by collapsed vertebrae as bone mass is lost

master athletes   individuals who have continued to participate in competitive, aerobic exercise into the later years

melanin   skin pigmentation

menopause   one event during the climacteric in a woman's life when there is a gradual cessation of the menstrual cycle, which is related to the loss of ovarian function; considered to have occurred after 12 consecutive months without a menstrual period

neurons   nerve cells in the brain

nocturnal myoclonus   a neuromuscular disturbance affecting the legs during sleep

orthopedic injuries   injuries to the bones, muscles, and joints

osteoporosis   a dramatic loss in calcium and bone mass resulting in increased brittleness of the bones and increased risk of fracture, more frequently found in white, small-stature women

presbycusis   age-related hearing loss

renal function   kidney function, defined by the rate at which blood is filtered through the kidneys

senescence   biological aging, i.e., the gradual accumulation of irreversible functional losses to which the average person tries to accommodate in some socially acceptable way

sleep apnea   five- to 10-second cessation of breathing, which disturbs sleep in some older persons

sleep hygiene   behaviors associated with sleep, e.g., location, lighting, regular vs. irregular bedtime, use of drugs that promote or hinder sleep

systolic blood pressure   the level of blood pressure during the contraction phase of the heart

telomerase   the enzyme responsible for rebuilding telomeres

telomerase inhibitors   chemicals produced by the organism that block the production of telomerase

telomeres   excess DNA at ends of each chromosome, lost as cells replicate

testosterone   a male sex hormone

tinnitus   high-pitched ringing in the ear

urinary incontinence   diminished ability to retain urine; loss of bladder control

varicosities   abnormal swelling in the veins, especially the legs

vital capacity   the maximum volume of oxygen intake through the lungs with a single breath

wear and tear theory   one of the biological theories of aging; states that aging occurs because of the system simply wearing out over time

RESOURCES

See the companion Website for this text at <www .ablongman.com/hooyman> for information about the following:

- AARP Andrus Foundation publication, "Lighting the Way" (2002)
- American Foundation for the Blind, Unit on Aging
- American Printing House for the Blind
- American Speech-Language Hearing Association
- Better Hearing Institute
- International Hearing Aid Helpline of the International Hearing Society
- International Longevity Center
- Library of Congress, Blind and Physically Handicapped Division
- National Association for Continence
- Self-Help for Hard of Hearing People (SHHH)

REFERENCES

Allikmets, R., Shroyer, N. F., Singh, N., Seddon, J. M., and Lewis, R. A. Mutation of the Stargardt disease gene (ABCR) in age-related macular degeneration. *Science*, 1997, *277*, 1805–1807.

Arey, L., Tremaine, M., and Monzingo, F. The numerical and topographical relations of taste buds to human circumvallate papillae throughout the life span. *Anatomical Record*, 1935, *64*, 9–25.

Beckman, K. B., and Ames, B. N. The free radical theory of aging matures. *Physiological Reviews*, 1998, *78*, 547–581.

Bjorksten, J. Crosslinkage and the aging process. In M. Rockstein, M. L. Sussman, and J. Chesky (Eds.), *Theoretical aspects of aging*. New York: Academic Press, 1974.

Bloom, F. Breakthroughs. *Science*, 1999, 286, 2267.

Blumberg, J. B. Status and functional impact of nutrition in older adults. In E. L. Schneider and J. W. Rowe (Eds.), *Handbook of the biology of aging* (4th ed.). New York: Van Nostrand, 1996.

Bodner, A. G., Ouelette, M., Frolkis, M., Holt, S. E., Chiu, C. P., Morin, G. B., Harley, C. B., Shay, J. W., Lichtsteiner, S., and Wright, W. E. Extension of life-span by introduction of telomerase into normal human cells. *Science*, 1998, *279*, 349–352.

Bognoli, P., and Hodos, W. *The changing visual system: Maturation and aging in the central nervous system.* New York: Plenum Press, 1991.

Braille Institute. Statistics on sight loss. http://www.brailleinstitute.org/Education-Statistics.html, 2004.

Brant, L. J., and Fozard, J. Age changes in pure-tone hearing thresholds in a longitudinal study of normal human aging. *Journal of the Acoustical Society of America*, 1990, *88*, 813–820.

Carpenter, M. K., Cui, X., Hu, Z. Y., Jackson, J., Sherman, S., Seiger, A., and Wahlberg, L. U. In vitro expansion of a multipotent population of human neural progenitor cells. *Experimental Neurology*, 1999, *158*, 265–278.

Coffey, C. E., Lucke, J. F., Saxton, J. A., Ratcliff, G., Unitas, L. J., Billig, B., and Bryan, R. N. Sex differences in brain aging. *Archives of Neurology*, 1998, *55*, 169–179.

Cossarizza, A., Ortolani, C., Monti, D., and Franceschi, C. Cytometric analysis of immunosenescence. *Cytometry*, 1997, *27*, 297–313.

Cowart, B. J. Relationships between taste and smell across the life span. In C. Murphy, W. S. Cain, and D. M. Hegsted (Eds.), Nutrition and the chemical senses in aging: Recent advances and current research needs. *Annals of the New York Academy of Sciences*. New York: New York Academy of Sciences, 1989.

Desai, M., Pratt, L. A., Lentzner, H., and Robinson, K. N. Trends in vision and hearing among older Americans. *Aging Trends*, 2001, *2*, Hyattsville, MD: National Center for Health Statistics.

Eastwood, G. L. A review of gastrointestinal epithelial renewal and its relevance to the development of adenocarcinomas of the gastrointestinal tract. *Journal of Clinical Gastroenterology*, 1995, *21*, 1–11.

Effros, R. B. Immune system activity. In E. J. Masoro and S. N. Austad (Eds.), *Handbook of the biology of aging* (5th ed.). San Diego: Academic Press, 2001.

Finch, C. E. *Longevity, senescence and the genome.* Chicago: University of Chicago Press, 1990.

Fozard, J. L., and Gordon-Salant, S. Changes in vision and hearing with aging. In J. E. Birren and K. W. Schaie (Eds.), *Handbook of the psychology of aging* (5th ed.). San Diego: Academic Press, 2001.

Franceschi, C., Monti, D., Sansoni, P., and Cossarizza, A. The immunology of exceptional individuals: The lesson of centenarians. *Immunology Today*, 1995, *16*, 12–16.

Goldstein, S., and Reis, R. J. S. Genetic modifications during cellular aging. *Molecular and Cellular Biochemical*, 1984, *64*, 15–30.

Grune, T., and Davies, K. J. A. Oxidative processes in aging. In E. J. Masoro and S. N. Austad (Eds.), *Handbook of the biology of aging* (5th ed.). San Diego: Academic Press, 2001.

Harman, D. Aging: A theory based on free radical and radiation chemistry. *Journal of Gerontology*, 1956, *2*, 298–300.

Harman, D. Free radical involvement in aging: Pathophysiology and therapeutic implications. *Drugs and Aging*, 1993, *3*, 60–80.

Hayflick, L. *How and why we age.* New York: Ballantine Books, 1996.

Hayflick, L., and Moorehead, P. S. The serial cultivation of human diploid cell strains. *Experimental Cell Research*, 1961, *25*, 285–621.

Hornsby, P. J. Cell proliferation in mammalian aging. In E. J. Masoro and S. N. Austad (Eds.), *Handbook of the biology of aging* (5th ed.). San Diego: Academic Press, 2001.

Hornsby, P. J. The new science and medicine of cell transplantation. *American Society for Experimental Microbiology News,* 1999, *65,* 208–214.

Howitz, K. T., Bitterman, K. J., Cohen, H. Y., Lamming, D. W., Lavu, S., Wood-Zipkin, R. E., Chung, P., Kisielewski, A., Zhang, L. L., Scherer, B., and Sinclair, D. Small molecule activators of sirtuins extend *Saccharomyces cerevisiae* lifespan. *Nature,* 2003, *425,* 191–196.

Hu, M. H., and Woollacott, M. H. Multisensory training of standing balance in older adults. *Journals of Gerontology,* 1994, *49,* M52–M71.

Jacques, P. F., Chylack, L. T., and Taylor, A. Relationships between natural antioxidants and cataract formation. In B. Frei (Ed.), *Natural antioxidants in human health and disease.* San Diego: Academic Press, 1994.

Kinouchi, Y., Hiwatashi, N., Chida, M., Nagashima, F., Takagi, S., Maekawa, H., and Toyota, T. Telomere shortening in the colonic mucosa of patients with ulcerative colitis. *Journal of Gastroenterology,* 1998, *33,* 343–348.

Kiyak, H. A. Communication in the practitioner-aged patient relationship. In P. Holm-Pedersen and H. Loe (Eds.), *Textbook of geriatric dentistry* (2nd ed.). Copenhagen: Munksgaard, 1996.

Kline, D. W., Kline, T. J. B., Fozard, J. L., Kosnik, W., Schieber, F., and Sekuler, R. Vision, aging, and driving: The problems of older drivers. *Journals of Gerontology,* 1992, *47,* M27–34.

Kohrt, W. M., and Holloszy, J. O. Loss of skeletal mass with aging: Effect on glucose tolerance. *Journals of Gerontology: Biological and Medical Sciences,* 1995, *50,* 68–72.

Lane, M. A., Ingram, D. K., Ball, S. S., and Roth, G. S. Dehydroepiandrosterone sulfate: A biomarker of primate aging slowed by calorie restriction. *Journal of Clinical Endocrinology and Metabolism,* 1997, *82,* 2093–2096.

Lane, M. A., Ingram, D. K., and Roth, G. S. The serious search for an anti-aging pill. *Scientific American,* 2002, *287,* 36–41.

Li, Y., and Wolf, N. S. Effects of age and long-term caloric restriction on the aqueous collecting channel in the mouse eye. *Journal of Glaucoma,* 1997, *6,* 18–22.

Macey, S. M. Hypothermia and energy conservation: A tradeoff for elderly persons? *International Journal of Aging and Human Development,* 1989, *29,* 151–161.

Macey, S. M., and Schneider, D. Deaths from excessive heat and excessive cold among the elderly. *The Gerontologist,* 1993, *33,* 497–500.

Masoro, E. J. Dietary restriction: An experimental approach to the study of the biology of aging. In E. J. Masoro and S. N. Austad (Eds.), *Handbook of the biology of aging* (5th ed.). San Diego: Academic Press, 2001.

McCurry, S. M., Reynolds, F., Ancoli-Israel, S., Teri, L., and Vitiello, M. V. Treatment of sleep disturbance in Alzheimer's disease. *Sleep Medicine Reviews,* 2000, *4,* 603–628.

McShane, T. M., Wilson, M. E., and Wise, P. M. Effects of lifelong moderate caloric restriction. *Journals of Gerontology: Biological Sciences,* 1999, *54A,* B14–B21.

Melov, S., Ravenscroft, J., Malik, S., Gill, M. S., Walker, D. W., Clayton, P. E., Wallace, D.C., et al. Extension of life-span with superoxide dismutase/catalase mimetics. *Science,* 2000, *287,* 1567–1569.

Micozzi, M. Exploring alternative health approaches for elders. *Aging Today,* 1997, *18,* 9–12.

Miller, I. J. Human taste bud density across adult age groups. *Journals of Gerontology,* 1988, *43,* B26–30.

Milton, R. C., and Sperduto, R. D. Incidence of age-related cataract: 13.6 year follow-up in the Framingham eye study. *Investigations in Ophthalmic Vision Science,* 1991, *32,* 1243–1250.

Mistretta, C. M. Aging effects on anatomy and neurophysiology of taste and smell. *Gerodontology,* 1984, *3,* 131–136.

Morales, A. J., Nolan, J. J., Nelson, J. C., and Yen, S. S. Effects of replacement dose of dehydroepiandrosterone in men and women of advancing age. *Journal of Clinical Endocrinology and Metabolism,* 1995, *80,* 2799.

Murphy, C. The effect of age on taste sensitivity. In S. Han and D. Coons (Eds.), *Special senses in aging.* Ann Arbor: Institute of Gerontology, University of Michigan, 1979.

National Academy on an Aging Society. *Hearing loss,* 1999, 2.

New York Times. In France, nothing gets in the way of vacation. August 24, 2003, p. 5.

Newman, A. B., Spiekerman, C. F., Enright, P., Lefkowitz, D., Manolio, T., Reynolds, C. F., and

Robbins, J. Daytime sleepiness predicts mortality and CVD in older adults. *Journal of the American Geriatrics Society,* 2000, *48,* 115–123.

Nordin, S., Razani, L. J., Markison, S., and Murphy, C. Age-associated increases in intensity discrimination for taste. *Experimental Aging Research,* 2003, *29,* 371–386.

Ohayan, M. M., and Caulet, M. Insomnia and psychotropic drug consumption. *Progress in Neuropsychopharmacology, Biology and Psychiatry,* 1995, *19,* 421–431.

Palmore, E. (Ed.). *Normal aging II: Reports from the Duke Longitudinal Study,* 1970–1973. Durham, NC: Duke University Press, 1974.

Palmore, E. (Ed.). *Normal aging III: Reports from the Duke Longitudinal Study.* Durham, NC: Duke University Press, 1985.

Pearson, D., and Shaw, S. *Life extension.* New York: Warner Books, 1982.

Rees, T. Health promotion for older adults: Age-related hearing loss. *Northwest Geriatric Education Center Curriculum Modules,* Seattle: University of Washington NWGEC, 2000.

Rogers, M. A., Hagberg, J. M., Martin, W. H., Ehsani, A. A., and Holloszy, J. O. Decline in VO2 max with aging in master athletes and sedentary men. *Journal of Applied Physiology,* 1990, *68,* 2195–2199.

Rosenhall, U., and Karlsson, A. K. Tinnitus in old age. *Scandinavian Audiology,* 1991, *20,* 165–171.

Roth, G. S., Ingram, D. K., and Lane, M. A. Caloric restriction in primates and relevance to humans. *Annals of the New York Academy of Sciences,* 2001, *928,* 305–315.

Rudman, D., Drinka, P. J., Wilson, C. R., Mattson, D. E., Scherman, F., Cuisinier, M. C., and Schultz, S. Relations of endogenous anabolic hormones and physical activity to bone mineral density in elderly men. *Clinical Endocrinology,* 1991, *40,* 653–661.

Rudolph, K. L., Chang, S., Millard, M., Schreiber-Agus, N., and DePinho, R. A. Inhibition of experimental liver cirrhosis in mice by telomerase gene delivery. *Science,* 2000, *287,* 1253–1258.

Schiffman, S. S., and Graham, B. G. Taste and smell perception affect appetite and immunity in the elderly. *European Journal of Clinical Nutrition,* 2000, *54,* S54–S63.

Schultz, D. W., Klein, M. L., Humbert, A. J., Luzier, C. W., Persun, V., et al. Analysis of the ARMD1 locus: Evidence that a mutation in *HEMICENTIN-1* is associated with age-related macular degeneration in a large family. *Human Molecular Genetics,* 2003, http://hmg.oupjournals.org/content/abstract/ddg348v1.

Seddon, J. M., Ajani, U. A., Sperduto, R. D., Hiller, R., Blair, H. N., and Burton, T. C. Dietary carotenoids, vitamins A, C, and E, and advanced age-related macular degeneration. *Journal of the American Medical Association,* 1994a, *272,* 1413–1420.

Seddon, J. M., Christen, W. G., Manson, J. E., Lamotte, F. S., Glynn, R. J., Buring, J. E., and Hennekens, C. H. The use of vitamin supplements and the risk of cataract among U.S. male physicians. *American Journal of Public Health,* 1994b, *84,* 788–792.

Ship, J. A., and Weiffenbach, J. M. Age, gender, medical treatment, and medication effects on smell identification. *Journals of Gerontology,* 1993, *48,* M26–M32.

Shock, N. W. The physiology of aging. *Scientific American,* 1962, *206,* 100–110.

Solana, R. Immunosenescence in centenarians and the old-old. Symposium presented at the International Association of Gerontology, Barcelona, July 2003.

Sperduto, R. D. Age-related cataracts: Scope of problem and prospects for prevention. *Preventive Medicine,* 1994, *23,* 735–739.

Steenbekkers, L. P. A. Visual contrast sensitivity. In L. P. A. Steenbekkers and C. E. M. van Beijsterveldt (Eds.), *Design-relevant characteristics of ageing users.* Delft, The Netherlands: Delft University of Technology Press, 1998.

Stevens, J. C. Aging and spatial acuity of touch. *Journals of Gerontology,* 1992, *47,* B35–40.

Strawbridge, W. J., Wallhagen, M. I., Shema, S. J., and Kaplan, G. A. Negative consequences of hearing impairment in old age: A longitudinal analysis. *The Gerontologist,* 2000, *40,* 320–326.

Sutton, D. A., Moldofsky, H., and Badley, E. M. Insomnia and health problems in Canadians. *Sleep,* 2001, *24,* 665–670.

Teasdale, N., Stelmach, G. E., and Breunig, A. Postural sway characteristics of the elderly under normal and altered visual and support surface conditions. *Journals of Gerontology,* 1991, *46,* B238–B244.

Thom, D. H., and Brown, J. S. Reproductive and hormonal risk factors for urinary incontinence in later life: A review of the clinical and epidemiological literature. *Journal of the American Geriatrics Society,* 1998, *46,* 1411–1417.

Thomas, T., Thomas, G., McLendon, C., Sutton, T., and Mullan, M. Beta-amyloid-mediated vasoactivity and vascular endothelial damage. *Nature,* 1996, *380,* 168–171.

Tuorila, H., Niskanen, N., and Maunuksela, E. Perception and pleasantness of a food with varying odor among the elderly and young. *Journal of Nutrition, Health and Aging,* 2001, *5,* 266–268.

Vincent, K. R., Braith, R. W., Feldman, R. A., Kallas, H. E., Lowenthal, D. T. Improved cardiorespiratory endurance following 6 months of resistance exercise in elderly men and women. *Archives of Internal Medicine,* 2002, *162,* 673–678.

Vitiello, M. V. Sleep disorders and aging. *Current Opinions in Psychiatry,* 1996, *9,* 284–289.

Vitiello, M. V., and Borson, S. Sleep disturbances in patients with Alzheimer's disease. *CNS Drugs,* 2001, *15,* 777–796.

Vitiello, M. V., Moe, K. E., and Prinz, P. N. Sleep complaints cosegregate with illness in older adults. *Journal of Psychosomatic Research,* 2002, *53,* 555–559.

Vitiello, M. V., and Prinz, P. N. Sleep and sleep disorders in normal aging. In M. J. Thorpy (Ed.), *Handbook of sleep disorders.* New York: Marcell Decker, 1991.

Wallhagen, M. I., Strawbridge, W. J., Cohen, R. D., and Kaplan, G. A. An increasing prevalence of hearing impairment and associated risk factors over three decades of the Alameda County Study. *American Journal of Public Health,* 1997, *87,* 440–442.

Wallhagen, M. I., Strawbridge, W. J., and Kaplan, G. A. Six year impact of hearing impairment on psychosocial and physiologic functioning. *Nurse Practitioner,* 1996, *21,* 11–14.

Weed, J. L., Lane, M. A., Roth, G. S., Speer, D. L., and Ingram, D. K. Activity measures in rhesus monkeys on long-term calorie restriction. *Physiology and Behavior,* 1997, *62,* 97–103.

Weindruch, R. Caloric restriction and aging. *Scientific American,* 1996, *274,* 46–52.

Wilson, D. L. The programmed theory of aging. In M. Rockstein, M. L. Sussman, and J. Chesky (Eds.), *Theoretical aspects of aging.* New York: Academic Press, 1974.

Yamauchi, Y., Endo, S., and Yoshimura, I. A new whole mouth gustatory test procedure: Effects of aging, gender, and smoking. *Acta Otolaryngologica Supplement,* 2002, *546,* 49–59.

Yataco, A. R., Busby-Whitehead, J., Drinkwater, D. T., and Katzel, L. I. Relationship of body composition and cardiovascular fitness to lipoprotein lipid profiles in master athletes and sedentary men. *Aging,* 1997, *9,* 88–94.

4

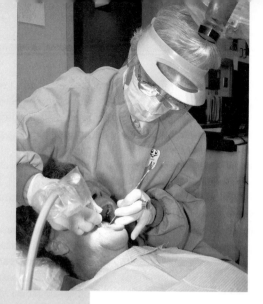

Managing Chronic Diseases and Promoting Well-Being in Old Age

No aspect of old age is more alarming to many of us than the thought of losing our health. Our fears center not only on the pain and inconvenience of illness, but also on its social-psychological consequences, such as loss of personal autonomy and economic security. Poor health, more than other changes commonly associated with aging, can reduce a person's competence in dealing with his or her environment.

Defining Health

Most people would agree that good health is something more than merely the absence of disease or infirmity. As defined by the World Health Organization, health is a state of complete physical, mental, and social well-being. Thus, health implies an interaction and integration of body, mind, and spirit, a perspective that is reflected in the growth of health promotion programs and alternative medicine.

As used by health care workers and researchers, the term **health status** refers to: (1) the presence or absence of disease, and (2) the degree of disability in an individual's level of functioning. Thus, activities that older people can do, or think they can do, are useful indicators of both how healthy they are and the services and environmental changes needed in order to cope with their impairments. Older people's ability to function independently at home is of primary concern. The concept of *activities of daily living (ADL)* is described in the box on the next page.

The World Health Organization defines **disability** as impairments in the ability to complete

multiple daily tasks. Slightly more than 20 percent of older people are estimated to have a mild degree of disability in their ADL, but only about 4 percent are severely disabled. The more disabled older population is limited in their amounts and types of major activities and mobility, such as eating, dressing, bathing, or toiletry, and requires the assistance of family or paid caregivers. The extent of disabilities and need for help in personal care activities increase with age and differ by gender, as shown in Figure 4.1.

Women aged 90 and older are twice as likely to be disabled and to require assistance than those aged 70 to 74. Men are less likely to have ADL limitations in both age groups and show a smaller increase in disability with age. For example, 24 percent of noninstitutionalized men over age 70 report ADL limitations, compared with 32 per-

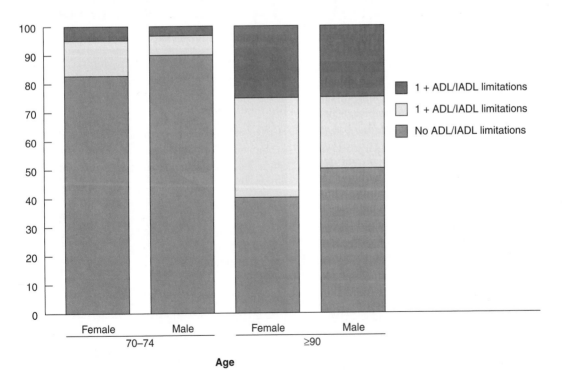

FIGURE 4.1 Comparing ADL and IADL Limitations among Men and Women, Young-Old and Oldest-Old

SOURCE: National Center for Health Statistics, 1997.

ASSESSING FUNCTIONAL HEALTH

The most commonly used measure of *functional health,* termed the **activities of daily living (ADL),** summarizes an individual's ability to perform basic, personal care tasks such as:

- bathing
- dressing
- using the toilet, eating
- getting in or out of a bed or chair
- caring for a bowel-control device
- walking (the most common ADL limitation for older adults)

Instrumental activities of daily living (IADL) summarize an individual's ability to perform more complex, multidimensional activities and interact with the environment:

- home management
- managing money
- meal preparation
- making a phone call
- grocery shopping (the most common IADL problem)

cent of women (NCHS, 2000a). This may be because men who survive to 70, and especially to age 90, have a genetic advantage and are hardier than men who die of similar conditions earlier in life.

In 2000, approximately 10 million persons 65 years or older needed some assistance to remain in the community (including 10.5 percent of those aged 65–79 and 51 percent of those over age 85). This figure is expected to reach 15 million by the year 2020 and 21 million by 2030. Another way to describe these projections is to state that 30 percent of persons over age 65 will have activity limitations that require some assistance by 2030. About 20 percent of this group will have severe limitations in ADL (National Academy, 2000a; U.S. Administration on Aging, 2000). The implications of this growth for long-term care are described in Chapter 11.

Frailty is one way of describing such severe limitations in ADL. More specifically, frailty includes problems with walking speed, declining activity levels, weak grip strength, and chronic exhaustion. These characteristics often result in hospitalization, institutionalization, and falls (Fried et al., 2001).

Quality of Life in Health and Illness

As noted in Chapter 1, the concept of active aging implies that aging need not be a time of decline or dependency. Even those who experience chronic diseases can maintain some degree of independence and avoid disability. As we will illustrate in this chapter, social and health behaviors throughout life, such as diet, smoking, alcohol consumption, and physical activity, as well as the physical environment where we live and work, all play a role in the development and progress of chronic diseases. To the extent that people practice health promotion and an active lifestyle in their younger years, many chronic conditions can be prevented, while others can be managed so they do not result in a severe disability that prevents active aging (Kalache and Kickbusch, 1997). Indeed, disability rates among older adults have declined noticeably over the past two decades as the concept of active aging has been adopted more widely. Not only are people living longer, but they are more likely to manage their chronic conditions without resulting in frailty or physical disability. National surveys have found a decline in the proportion of people aged 70 and older who reported problems with daily activities in 1995 compared to their counterparts in 1984. In particular, fewer women reported problems with walking (18 vs. 21 percent), bending over (16 percent in 1995 vs. 20 percent in 1984), and climbing stairs (12 vs. 16 percent) (NCHS, 2000). Limitations in other areas such as shopping have declined even more dramatically so that only half the people age 65 and older reported problems with shopping in 1999 compared to 1984. Disability rates have declined in all age groups over 65 (AARP, 2003).

Nevertheless, chronic illnesses often accompany old age, and societal values affect our attitudes toward loss of health. The importance placed by our culture on being independent and highly active may underlie our relative inability to accept illness graciously. Such values may also partially explain why healthy older people often do not want to share housing or recreational activities with those who have mental or physical disabilities.

A reliable evaluation of health takes into account not only a physician's assessment of a patient's physical condition, but also the older person's self-perceptions, observable behavior, and life circumstances. **Quality of life** may be defined as this combination of an individual's functional health, feelings of competence, independence in ADL, and satisfaction with one's social circumstances. Most older people appear to adjust their perceptions of their health in response to the aging process. In a 1999 national health survey, 42 percent of respondents aged 65 to 74 rated their health as excellent or very good, compared with 31 percent of those aged 85 and older. Even institutionalized older persons tend to rate their health positively (Merck Institute, 2002). Older people who must take multiple medications, who are experiencing chronic pain, or who have financial and ADL limitations are more likely to report lower quality of life.

**WHY OLDER ADULTS RATE
THEIR HEALTH POSITIVELY**

- perceived comparison with peers
- sense of accomplishment from having survived to old age
- perception of competence to meet environmental demands
- a broad definition of quality of life to include social and economic factors

---

On the other hand, those who have recently had a successful medical or surgical intervention to *alleviate* the symptoms of their chronic conditions are more likely to report improved quality of life. It is noteworthy that physicians rate the quality of life of older persons with diabetes, arthritis, or even ischemic heart disease lower than do these elders themselves. This may indicate greater adaptation to disabling conditions among patients than physicians expect, or may suggest that medical professionals' definitions of quality of life are more constrained by health factors than are patients' own perceptions. The concept of resilience, described in Chapters 1 and 6, may also help explain the generally positive evaluations of their health by older adults with disabilities.

Social and psychological factors also influence people's assessments of their physical well-being. An older person's position in the social structure, for example—whether one is male or female, black or white, high or low income—affects perceptions of health. Health self-ratings as good or excellent have been found among:

- more than 72 percent of white persons age 65
- only 52 percent of older African Americans
- less than 50 percent of older Latinos (NCHS, 1999).

African Americans are least likely to report their health as excellent: 26 percent of those aged 65 to 74 compared to 42 percent of all ethnic groups in this age group (NCHS, 2003). Self-ratings of health as poor are found in:

- only about 5.4 percent of persons aged 65 and older with incomes over $35,000
- 14 percent of their peers who have incomes less than $10,000

In general, older women do not rate their health more poorly than men, even though they have more chronic diseases and are more likely to live in long-term care facilities (NCHS, 1999).

Perceptions of good health tend to be associated with other measures of well-being, particu-

POINTS TO PONDER

Think about your own health perceptions. To what extent do you compare your health to others of your age or gender? How does your ability to perform various ADLs affect your health perceptions? How does your day-to-day health affect your overall quality of life?

larly life satisfaction. Older persons who view themselves as reasonably healthy tend to be happier, more satisfied, more involved in social activities, and less tense and lonely. In turn, lower life satisfaction is associated with lower levels of self-perceived health. It has also been found that self-ratings of health are correlated with mortality. That is, older people who report poorer health, especially poorer functional abilities, are more likely to die in the next 3 years than those who perceive their functional health to be good (Bernard et al., 1997).

Chronic and Acute Diseases

As noted in Chapter 3, the risk of disease and impairment increases with age; however, the extreme variability in older people's health status, as illustrated by Mrs. Hill and Mr. Jones in the vignettes in the introduction to Part Two, shows that poor health is not necessarily a concomitant of aging. The incidence of acute or temporary conditions, such as infections or the common cold, decreases with age. Those **acute conditions** that occur, however, are more debilitating and require more care, especially for older women:

* The average number of days of restricted activity due to acute conditions is nearly three times greater for people age 65 and over than it is for those 17–44 years old.
* Older people report, on average, 33 days per year of restricted activity days, of which 14 are spent in bed (NCHS, 2003).

An older person who gets a cold, for example, faces a greater risk of pneumonia or bronchitis because of changes in organ systems (described in Chapter 3) that reduce his or her resistance and recuperative capacities. Thus, older people are more likely to suffer restrictions on their social activities as a result of temporary health problems.

In some cases, an acute condition that merely inconveniences a younger person may result in death for an older person. For example, respiratory infection rates are similar in young and old people, but people aged 65 and older account for 89 percent of all deaths due to pneumonia and influenza (CDC, 1995). This is why it is important for older people to be vaccinated against pneumonia and influenza. These vaccines can reduce the risk of pneumonia by 67 percent and of flu by 50 percent among older people, can save medical costs and increase days of healthy living. Yet surveys reveal that less than 50 percent obtain a pneumococcal vaccination and only 63 percent receive annual vaccines against influenza. Rates are lower for African Americans and Latinos than for whites: 36 percent, 35 percent, and 57 percent, respectively, received flu vaccines in

ETHNIC AND RACIAL DIFFERENCES IN CHRONIC DISEASES

Among those 70 and older:

* African American and Latino elders are more likely to suffer from diabetes than non-Latino whites.
* Diabetes is twice as common among women of color as in white women.
* Hypertension is 1.5 times more likely in African Americans than in whites.
* Rates of stroke are also higher among the former groups, but only when comparing black vs. white women.
* In contrast, white men age 70 and older are more likely to report heart disease than their Latino or African American counterparts (NCHS, 1999).

1999 (CDC, 2003c). Changes in Medicare to cover the full cost of vaccinations may increase these rates.

Older people are much more likely than the young to suffer from **chronic conditions.** Chronic health conditions are:

- long-term (more than three months)
- often permanent, leaving a residual disability that may require long-term management or care rather than a cure

More than 80 percent of persons age 70 and over have at least one chronic condition, with multiple health problems being common in older adults (NCHS, 1999). Chronic problems are often accompanied by continuous pain and/or distress. At the very least, the individual is inconvenienced by the need to monitor health and daily activities, although ADL may not always be limited. National surveys have found that almost 40 percent of older persons with chronic diseases report limitations in their ability to perform basic ADLs (NCHS, 1999).

Although one can live a satisfying life with multiple chronic conditions, these diseases may influence the decision to continue working or to retire. An analysis of recently retired older adults' responses in the 1994–1996 National Health Interview Survey (NHIS) revealed that the majority of people age 51 to 61 who had retired cited chronic health problems as the reason. This varied by type of disease:

- 76 percent of those with heart disease
- 62 percent with orthopedic impairments
- 61 percent with arthritis

Many of these mature but not older adults have converted to part-time work; as a result, their median income is lower on retirement than for their healthier peers, as discussed more fully in Chapter 12 (National Academy, 2000a).

Although the nature and the severity of any chronic condition vary with the individual, most older persons are capable of carrying out their normal daily routines. Only about 2 percent of those age 65 and over are confined to bed by their chronic illness or disability, and most older people with chronic conditions are not dependent on others for managing their daily routines. On the other hand, the small percentage who do need assistance with care have placed enormous pressures on formal health and long-term care services as well as on informal caregivers, as discussed in Chapters 10 and 17.

The most frequently reported chronic conditions causing limitation of activity in persons age 65 and over are shown in Figure 4.2. Arthritis, hypertension, and heart disease are the leading chronic diseases, but older women are less likely to suffer from heart disease (although their rates of heart disease are increasing dramatically and approximating rates for men) and more likely to report arthritis and diabetes than older men. The most common heart condition for both men and women is ischemic heart disease.

Not surprisingly, most chronic conditions increase in prevalence with age (NCHS, 2003). For example, people age 65 and over are twice as likely to suffer from arthritis as those age 45 to 64. Other conditions, such as heart disease and diabetes, show lower rates in the oldest-old, probably because of the higher mortality associated with these diseases.

Disabling chronic illnesses tend to occur earlier among African Americans, Latinos, and American Indians than among whites. These conditions result in higher rates of hospitalization, longer hospital stays, and a shorter life expectancy. Therefore, it is not surprising that older persons of color with chronic conditions are more likely to describe their health as fair or poor than whites with the same conditions, as shown in Figure 4.3 (National Academy, 1999a; NCHS, 2000a). Poorer self-assessments of health and lower life expectancies are explained as products of discriminatory policies, whereby nonwhites have lower incomes and inadequate nutrition throughout their lives. An additional factor is that

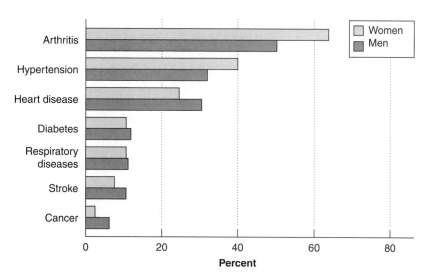

FIGURE 4.2   Percent of Persons 70 Years and Older Who Reported Selected Chronic Conditions by Gender: United States, 1995

SOURCE: NCHS, 1999.

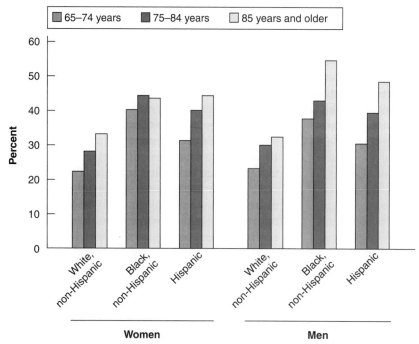

FIGURE 4.3   Fair or Poor Health among Noninstitutionalized Persons 65 and Older, by Age, Gender, Race, and Hispanic Origin: United States, 1994–1996

SOURCE: NCHS, 1999.

elders of color, because of their cultural values and negative experiences with formal services, may be less likely to utilize the health care system. The effects of ethnic minority status on the incidence and treatment of chronic conditions are further discussed in Chapter 14.

Co-morbidity, or the problem of coping with two or more chronic conditions, is more common in older women than in men. Researchers have found that, among women aged 65 and older, 50 percent have at least two chronic diseases. One-fourth of older women report three or more such conditions. Older women of color, especially in the lower socioeconomic range, have a higher prevalence of chronic illness, functional limits on their ADLs, and disability. Because of their greater likelihood of coping with multiple chronic conditions, the old-old report more problems in performing ADLs. At age 65 to 74, 34 percent report significant ADL limitations, compared with 45 percent of people 75 and older (Clancey and Bierman, 2000; National Academy, 1999a; Smith and Kingston, 1997).

Interactive Effects

Even though the majority of chronic conditions are not severely limiting, they can nevertheless make life difficult and lower older people's resistance to other illnesses. As noted earlier, the functional limits imposed by a chronic illness interact with the social limits set by others' perceptions of the illness to influence an older person's daily functioning. Therefore, it is important to look beyond the statistics on the frequency of chronic conditions to the nature of chronic illnesses, the interaction of physical changes with emotional and sociocultural factors, and the physiological differences between younger and older people.

Certain types of chronic diseases (e.g., cancer, anemia, and toxic conditions) may be related to older people's declining **immunity,** that is, reduced resistance to environmental carcinogens, viruses, and bacteria. The accumulation of long-term, degenerative diseases may mean that a chronic condition, such as bronchitis, can have different and more negative complications than the same disease would have in a younger person. With reduced resistance to physical stress, an older individual may be less able to respond to treatment for any acute disease, such as a cold or flu, than a younger person would. The cumulative effect of chronic illness and an acute condition may become the crisis point at which the older person becomes dependent on others for care. The impact of any chronic condition appears to be mediated by the physiological changes that occur with age, the sociocultural context, and the person's mental and emotional outlook.

In sum, disabling health changes occur at different rates in different individuals and are not inevitable with age. We turn now to an examination of the chronic conditions that are the most common causes of death in older people.

Causes of Death in Later Years

Heart disease, cancer, and strokes accounted for 60 percent of all deaths among people over age 65 and older in 2000 (Merck Institute, 2002). Even though there have been rapid declines over the past 30 years, heart disease remains the major cause of death among both men and women. It is the number-one risk factor among adults age 65 and over, killing almost twice as many people as do all forms of cancer combined, and accounting for 20 percent of adult disabilities. Heart disease accounts for 18 percent of hospital admissions, and over 45 percent of deaths that occur among older people, with the highest rates among the oldest-old. Although death rates from cancer continue to rise among older cohorts, they have shown some decline in younger populations. Even if cancer were eliminated as a cause of death, this would only extend the average life span by less than 2 years at age 65. Eliminating deaths due to major cardiovascular diseases, however, would add an average of 14 years to life expectancy at age 65. The benefits of eliminating cardiovascular diseases would be especially significant for older white

HEART DISEASE AS A CHRONIC CONDITION

The dramatic decline in deaths due to heart attacks and strokes in the United States became front-page news in the *New York Times* in 2003: "The stereotypical heart attack patient is no longer a man in his 50s who suddenly falls dead. Instead, the typical patient is a man or woman of 70 or older who survives." The article addressed the growing challenge of maintaining heart attack survivors who must cope with chronic heart disease, including congestive heart failure that can impair functional health.

SOURCE: *New York Times*, January 19, 2003, pp. 1, 16.

women (17.4 years) and nonwhite women (22 years). This would also lead to a sharp increase in the proportion of older persons in the total population (Hayflick, 1996). Declines in death rates since 1981, from 2600 to less than 2000 in 2000 may explain the growing survival rates of people beyond age 65. Meanwhile, stroke has been decreasing as a leading cause of death among the oldest-old; it is the third leading cause for women over age 65 but fourth for men, slightly less than chronic obstructive pulmonary diseases (COPD) such as asthma and emphysema. Dramatic differences in rates of death due to the three primary causes of death are found across ethnic groups and gender. As Figure 4.4 demonstrates for 55- to 64-year-olds, African American men are at highest risk for death due to heart disease and cerebrovascular accidents (CVAs). Among women, African Americans are more likely than any other ethnic group to die of heart disease and CVAs, but have about the same death rates as Latina women for cancer. Lower death rates among whites are attributable to greater health care access that allows early detection and management of these conditions so they become chronic diseases among whites rather than causing death. Likewise, Asian American adults are more likely to survive strokes and cancer because these conditions are detected earlier than among African

Americans, Latinos, and American Indians, while Asian Americans have the lowest incidence of heart diseases (NCHS, 2003a). For older African American and Latina women, diabetes is the fourth major cause of death. It accounts for more than twice the rate of deaths as COPD, which is sixth in this population group (NCHS, 2003b).

Nevertheless, educational achievement moderates the effect of ethnicity on chronic disease and disability, especially among older women. While African American women who have completed 0 to 8 years of school can expect 18.4 years of unhealthy life, their counterparts with 13 or more years of school can expect 12.9 years. Among white women the difference is 17.5 versus 11.8 years of unhealthy life, respectively. Differences between more and less educated men are less dramatic; African Americans with 0 to 8 years of education can expect 13.4 years of unhealthy life versus 9.0 for those with 13 or more years of education. Comparable patterns for white men have been reported: 14.1 versus 10.0 years. Thus, education benefits people into old age, especially women, by enhancing their awareness of and access to preventive health services (Crimmins and Saito, 2001).

Men have higher rates of heart disease and cancer than women. In fact, gender differences in mortality are due mainly to the greater incidence of the principal fatal chronic diseases among men. However, women experience more nonfatal chronic conditions, including arthritis, incontinence, osteoarthritis, osteoporosis, and cataracts, than do men. These diseases are less likely to result in death than cancer and heart disease, but they may lead to nearly as many days spent in bed. In other words, older women are more likely to be bothered by chronic conditions, many of which can cause functional disability and impair their quality of life. However, they are less likely to face life-threatening diseases than are older men.

When examining rates of chronic diseases among low-income and ethnic minority elders, a life span perspective highlights the interplay among generational influences and economic and

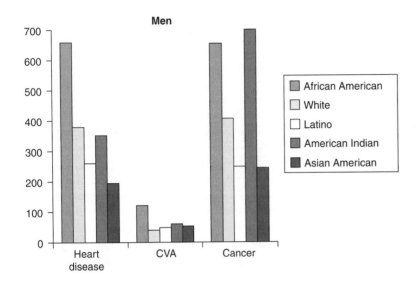

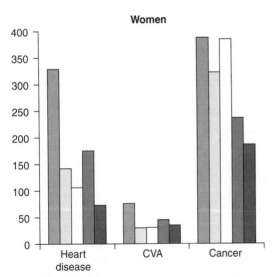

FIGURE 4.4 Death Rates for Selected Diseases at Age 55 to 64 (per 100,000)

SOURCE: NCHS, 2003b.

health inequalities. For example, in both developing and developed countries, chronic diseases are linked to poor health and lower levels of quality of life. Poor people of all ages face an increased risk of health problems and disabilities. Although the likelihood of chronic illness increases with age, research increasingly shows that the origins of risk for chronic health conditions begin in early childhood or earlier (World Health Organization, 2002). Existing research demonstrates the intergenerational transmission of specific health-risk behaviors and lifestyles, including eating behaviors, depression, and family functioning processes (Baker, Whisman, and Brownell, 2000; Jacob and

Johnson, 2001; Lawson and Brossart, 2001; Wickrama et al., 1999). Furthermore, risk continues to be influenced by factors such as socioeconomic status and life experiences across the life span. For example, childhood conditions explain a substantial portion of the difference in men's moretality by race, operating indirectly through adult socioeconomic achievement, not lifestyle factors (Warner and Hayward, 2002). Alternatively, increases in socioeconomic status are related to people living longer and healthier lives (Lynch et al., 2000). Thus, any analysis of chronic conditions in old age needs to consider the role of racial, gender, and socioecoomic inequities across the life span.

Common Chronic Conditions

Heart Disease and the Cardiovascular System

Heart disease is a condition in which blood to the heart is deficient because of a narrowing or constricting of the cardiac vessels that supply it. This narrowing may be due to **atherosclerosis,*** in which fatty deposits (plaque formation) begin early in life and accumulate to reduce the size of the passageway of the large arteries. People in industrialized nations have higher levels of atherosclerosis, but the extent to which this is due to lifestyle factors is unknown.

---

*The terms *atherosclerosis* and **arteriosclerosis** are often used interchangeably, causing confusion regarding their distinction. Arteriosclerosis, a generic term, sometimes called hardening of the arteries, refers to the loss of elasticity of the arterial walls. This condition occurs in all populations, and can contribute to reduced blood flow to an area. In atherosclerosis, the passageway of the large arteries narrows as a result of the development of plaques on their interior walls; atherosclerosis has been found to be age-related and of higher incidence in industrialized populations. Arteriosclerosis and atherosclerosis can be superimposed, but there is not a causative relationship between the degree of atherosclerosis and the loss of elasticity (arteriosclerosis).

> **HEALTH AND BEHAVIORAL FACTORS THAT INCREASE THE RISK OF ATHEROSCLEROSIS**
>
> - hypertension or high blood pressure
> - elevated blood lipids (resulting from a dietary intake of animal products high in cholesterol)
> - cigarette smoking
> - diabetes mellitus
> - obesity
> - inactivity
> - stress
> - family history of heart attack

As the reduced blood flow caused by atherosclerosis becomes significant, angina pectoris may result. The symptoms of angina are shortness of breath and pain from beneath the breastbone, in the neck, and down the left arm. For older individuals, these symptoms may be absent or may be confused with signs of other disorders, such as indigestion or gallbladder diseases. Treatment includes rest and nitroglycerine, which serves to dilate the blood vessels.

If deficient blood supply to the heart persists, heart tissue will die, producing a dead area known as an *infarct*. In other words, coronary artery disease can lead to a myocardial infarction, or heart attack. **Acute myocardial infarction** results from blockage of an artery supplying blood to a portion of the heart muscle. The extent of heart tissue involved determines the severity of the episode. Heart attacks may be more difficult to diagnose in older people, since their symptoms are often different from those in younger victims. These include:

- a generalized state of weakness
- dizziness
- confusion
- shortness of breath

These are different from the chest and back pain or numbness in the arms that characterizes heart attacks in younger people. Symptoms in older people may also merge with other problems, so

PREVENTIVE MEASURES TO REDUCE CARDIOVASCULAR RISK

- weight control
- daily physical activity
- treatment of diabetes
- reduced intake of salt and saturated fats
- increased intake of fruits and vegetables (rich in magnesium)
- fruits rich in potassium (e.g., bananas, oranges)
- foods high in calcium
- avoidance of cigarette smoking
- avoidance of excessive alcohol intake

that a heart attack may not be reported or treated until it is too late for effective help. Although women are far less likely to have heart attacks than men prior to menopause, their rates increase after age 65.

The term *congestive heart failure,* or heart failure, indicates a set of symptoms related to the impaired pumping performance of the heart, so that one or more chambers of the heart do not empty adequately during the heart's contractions. Heart failure does not mean that the heart has stopped beating. But decreased pumping efficiency results in shortness of breath, reduced blood flow to vital body parts (including the kidneys), and a greater volume of blood accumulating in the body tissues, causing edema (swelling). Treatment involves drugs, dietary modifications (e.g., salt reduction), and rest.

Most cardiovascular problems can be treated with diet, exercise, and medications. They should not prevent older people from carrying out most ADLs. Nevertheless, about 50 percent of older adults with heart diseases report limitations in their ADLs, compared with 26 percent of their aged peers who do not have this condition (National Academy, 2000a). Preventive steps are most important. For example, *hypertension,* or high blood pressure, has been found to be the major risk factor in the development of cardiovascular

complications and can be affected by preventive actions, as illustrated in the box below. As shown in Figure 4.2, the risk of hypertension is greater for women than men after age 65 (NCHS, 1999). This may partially explain why the incidence of coronary heart disease and strokes increases with age among women, although women with these conditions, on average, live longer than men.

The rates of *hypertension* are significantly higher among African Americans than whites (58.7 percent vs. 44 percent, respectively), but whether this difference is due to lifestyle or genetic factors is unclear. Significant increases in blood pressure should never be considered normal. In some isolated primitive populations, a rise in pressure with age does not occur. Although genetic factors may come into play, this difference suggests that individuals can make lifestyle changes that may reduce their vulnerability to high blood pressure (Merck Institute, 2002).

Most people can control their hypertension by improving these health habits, although some must also use antihypertensive medications (National Heart, Lung, and Blood Institute, 1997). Older adults who have been prescribed an antihypertensive must continue using it consistently and correctly. Because hypertension is not easily recognized by laypersons, they may stop taking their medications if symptoms such as dizziness and headaches disappear. Some older adults discontinue their antihypertensive medications be-

COMMONLY PRESCRIBED CLASSES OF MEDICATIONS TO CONTROL HYPERTENSION

- *diuretics* (also known as "water pills"), which reduce excess water
- *beta blockers,* which reduce heart rate
- *ACE inhibitors,* which block an enzyme that constricts blood vessels
- *calcium channel blockers,* which work by preventing calcium from causing muscle contractions in the heart and inside blood vessels

cause they cannot afford the cost. This can lead to significant elevations in blood pressure as well as a stroke or aneurysms.

Another cardiovascular problem, which is less frequently addressed than hypertension, is *hypotension,* or low blood pressure. Yet hypotension, characterized by dizziness and faintness from exertion after a period of inactivity and frequently related to anemia, is actually very common among older adults. Problems with hypotension may be more pronounced after sitting or lying down for a long time (postural hypotension) or suddenly standing, after which a person may appear to lose balance and sway. Hypotension is not in itself dangerous, but can increase the risk of falls. Older people who have a history of low blood pressure or who are taking some types of antihypertensive medications need to move more carefully.

Strokes and Other Cerebrovascular Problems

We have seen how heart tissue can be denied adequate nourishment because of changes in the blood vessels that supply it. Similarly, arteriosclerotic and atherosclerotic changes in blood vessels that serve the brain can reduce its nourishment and result in the disruption of blood flow to brain tissue and malfunction or death of brain cells. This impaired brain tissue circulation is called *cerebrovascular disease.* When a portion of the brain is completely denied blood, a cerebrovascular accident (CVA), or stroke, occurs. The severity of the stroke depends on the particular areas as well as the total amount of brain tissue involved. Many older adults who have heart problems also are at risk for cerebrovascular disease.

CVAs represent the fourth leading cause of death following accidents. Of the 200,000 deaths from strokes each year, 80 percent occur among persons aged 65 and over (NCHS, 2003). African American elders and men in general are at greater risk of dying from strokes than whites or other minority groups. The rate of CVA incidents increases from 10.3 at age 65 to 74 to 30 at age 85

and older. The young-old stroke victim is twice as likely as the oldest-old to be discharged to home after recovery (63 percent and 32 percent respectively). Conversely, the oldest-old stroke victim is twice as likely to die as the young-old (12.5 percent and 6.4 percent, respectively) (CDC, 2003a).

Atherosclerotic changes, in which fatty deposits gradually obstruct an artery in the brain or neck, are a common underlying condition. The most frequent cause of strokes in older persons is a *cerebral thrombosis,* a blood clot that either diminishes or closes off the blood flow in an artery of the brain or neck. Another cause of stroke is cerebral hemorrhage, in which a weak spot in a blood vessel of the brain bursts. This is less common in older adults, although more likely to cause death when it does occur. The risk of stroke appears to be related to social and personal factors, most prominently hypertension, but also:

- age
- previous lifestyle
- diet
- exercise patterns

Regular, sustained exercise and low-fat diets are associated with the reduction of fatty particles that clog the bloodstream. The use of such over-the-counter drugs as aspirin and warfarin in preventing blood clots also reduces the risk of strokes. Indeed, the death rate from strokes has dropped by 40 percent in the last 20 years, especially among the older population, because of these preventive measures and improved and immediate treatment (Gorelick, Shanmugam, and Pajeau, 1996). The area of the brain that is damaged by a stroke dictates which body functions may be affected. These include:

- *aphasia,* or inability of the stroke victim to speak or understand speech if the speech center of the brain dies
- *hemiplegia,* or paralysis of one side of the body

- *heminanopsia,* or blindness in half of the victim's visual field

The treatment for strokes is similar to that for heart attacks and hypertension: modulated activity and supervised schedules of exercise and drugs. The FDA has approved new drugs to dissolve blood clots within three hours of the stroke. However, many victims do not receive this treatment because it generally takes longer than three hours to reach a diagnosis of the stroke and the location of the clot. An alternative method is to deliver the clot-dissolving drug directly with a long, fine tube through the artery; this can be effective within six hours after symptoms begin. These new techniques offer great hope for patients and their families, but do not entirely prevent the neurological losses caused by a stroke.

Stroke victims often require physical, occupational, and speech therapy, and their recovery process can be slow, frustrating, and emotionally draining for the victim and family. It is important to assess carefully the effects of a stroke and determine what functions can be retrained (Gresham, Duncan, and Stason, 1995). Newer, more aggressive and immediate rehabilitation methods are effective in reducing the rates of residual impairments following a stroke. Within a year, about 50 percent have regained most of their motor function, but more people report residual nonmotor impairments such as problems with vision, speech, and loss of balance (Ferrucci et al., 1995).

Rehabilitation must address not only physical conditions, but also the psychosocial needs for support and respite of stroke patients and their families. The recognition of this wider range of rehabilitation has led to the creation of stroke support groups in many communities.

Cancer

Among those 65 years old and over, about 25 percent of deaths are due to cancer, especially cancers of the stomach, lungs, intestines, and pancreas. In fact, these malignancies in old age are the lead-ing cause of death among women 65 to 74, and roughly equal to heart disease among men. Fifty percent of all cancer occurs and is diagnosed after age 65. Cancer of the bowel is the most common malignancy in those age 70 and over, and is second to lung cancer in cancer-related deaths. Lung cancer has its highest incidence in men age 65 and over, but appears to be associated more with smoking than with age. Cancer of the colon is more common in women, whereas colorectal cancer is more frequent in men. Men over age 65, especially African American men, are at greatest risk for prostate cancer. Women also face increasing risks of breast and cervical cancers with age (NCHS, 1999). Both the incidence and mortality rates due to cervical and breast cancer are greater in older African American women than in older white women, primarily because of lower use of cancer screening services. However, when screenings are done regularly and the time between screening and diagnosis is minimized, both groups experience a similarly favorable prognosis (American Cancer Society, 2001; Dignam, 2000; Woolam, 2000). The greater risk of cancer with age may be due to a number of factors:

- the effects of a slow-acting carcinogen
- prolonged development time necessary for growth to be observable
- extended preexposure time
- failing immune capacity that is characteristic of increased age

Some cancers that have a high prevalence in the middle years and again in old age may have a different etiology. For example, breast cancer in premenopausal women appears to have a genetic basis and is related to family history, while that in postmenopausal women may have external or environmental causes. Certain dietary and lifestyle factors may also be related to cancer in older people. Diagnosing cancer in old age is often more difficult than at earlier life stages, because of the existence of other chronic diseases and because symptoms of cancer, such as weight loss, weakness, or fatigue, may be inaccurately attributed to aging, depression, or dementia. In addition, the current older generation's fear of cancer may be so great that they do not seek medical help to address their suspicions and fears. Nevertheless, many older adults today are cancer survivors and report this as a chronic condition. Because of ethnic differences in screening and early diagnosis, described previously, cancer is more likely to be a chronic disease in whites aged 70 and older (21 percent) than among Latinos (10.5 percent) and African Americans (9.1 percent) (Merck Institute, 2002).

Gentle massage can relieve the pain of arthritis.

Arthritis

Although not a leading cause of death, arthritis is the most common chronic condition affecting older people and is a major cause of limited activity. In fact, the great majority of persons over age 70 are estimated to have some physical evidence of arthritis; 58 percent today report this problem, compared with 55 percent in 1984 (Merck Institute, 2002). Because arthritis is so common and the symptoms are so closely identified with the normal aging process, older people may accept arthritis as inevitable. If so, they may fail to seek treatment or to learn strategies to reduce pain and support their independent functioning. Although many treatments are used to control arthritic symptoms, little is known about ways to postpone or eliminate these disorders.

Arthritis is not a single entity, but includes over 100 different conditions of inflammations and degenerative changes of bones and joints. **Rheumatoid arthritis,** a chronic inflammation of the membranes lining joints and tendons, is characterized by pain, swelling, bone dislocation, and limited range of motion. It afflicts two to three times more women than men and can cause severe crippling. Rheumatoid arthritis is not associated with aging per se; many young people also have this condition, with initial symptoms most commonly appearing between 20 and 50 years of age.

Rheumatoid arthritis is characterized by acute episodes followed by periods of relative in-

activity. Its cause is unknown; treatment includes a combination of rest, exercise, and use of aspirin, which provides relief from pain, fever, and inflammation. Use of other antiinflammatory agents, antimalarials, and corticosteroids, as well as surgical procedures to repair joints and correct various deformities, are effective for some people. There are extensive new developments in drug therapy for rheumatoid arthritis.

Osteoarthritis, which is presumed to be a universal corollary of aging, is a gradual degeneration of the joints that are most subject to stress—those of the hands, knees, hips, and shoulders. Pain and disfigurement in the fingers are manifestations of osteoarthritis, but are generally not disabling. Osteoarthritis of the lower limbs,

---

SYMPTOMS OF RHEUMATOID ARTHRITIS

- malaise
- fatigue
- loss of weight
- fever
- joint pain
- redness
- swelling
- stiffness affecting many joints

however, can limit mobility. Heredity as well as environmental or lifestyle factors are identified as causes of osteoarthritis, particularly:

- obesity
- occupational stresses
- wear and tear on the joints

Some progress has been made in minimizing inflammation and pain through the use of several types of therapy. A natural supplement (chondroitin sulfate, or CS) has been shown to be effective in managing the pain associated with osteoarthritis without significant side effects (Leeb et al., 2000). Unfortunately, however, none of these techniques can reverse or cure the disease.

Even on "good days" when pain subsides, an older arthritic may live with the fear of the inevitable "bad day" and may structure daily activities to avoid pain. Each day may seem to consist of a succession of obstacles, from getting out of bed and fastening clothing to opening packages, dialing the phone, and handling dishes for meals. Concentrating on coping with one obstacle after another in the completion of tasks can be exhausting, even when minimal physical exertion is involved in each task.

An estimated 50 percent of adults aged 70 and older who have arthritis need help with ADL, compared with 23 percent of their peers without arthritis. Not surprisingly, the former group uses health services (physicians, hospitals, medications, nursing homes) and social services at a higher rate than the latter. Because of the constant pain and discomfort experienced by elders with arthritis, it is highly correlated with self-reports of poor health. Among people in their 60s, correlates of poor subjective health include:

- arthritis
- poor vision
- few social resources

Among people in their 80s, subjective reports of poor health are associated with:

THERAPIES FOR OSTEOARTHRITIS

- anti-inflammatory drugs
- steroids
- mild exercise
- heat and cold
- reduction of strain on weight-bearing joints through weight loss and the use of weight-bearing appliances
- surgical procedures that restore function to the hips and knees

---

- arthritis
- heart disease
- low education
- poor mental health (Quinn et al., 1999)

It is important to note that arthritis is the only variable that appears as an important component of subjective health for both age groups.

The prime danger for people with arthritis is reducing their physical activity in response to pain. Movement stimulates the secretion of synovial fluid, the substance that lubricates the surfaces between joints and increases blood flow to joint areas. Movement also tones the muscles that hold joints in place and that shield joints from excessive stress. When someone tries to avoid pain by sitting still as much as possible, the losses in lubricating fluid and muscular protection make movement still more painful. Eventually, the muscles surrounding immobilized areas lose their flexibility, and affected joints freeze into rigid positions called **contractures.** For these reasons, older people need to be encouraged to maintain physical activity in spite of pain. The adage "use it or lose it" has special meaning to a person with arthritis.

The pervasive and unpredictable nature of the pain of arthritis can also result in frustration and depression. A program to teach African American elders about managing their arthritis pain resulted in fewer symptoms of depression up to two years later than in elders who received no training (Phillips, 2000). Conversely, treating depression can reduce symptoms associated with arthritis. In a study testing antidepressant medications and psychotherapy with depressed older adults, 56 percent reported arthritis as a coexisting medical condition. Elders in the treatment group experienced a significant reduction in pain intensity and interference with ADL due to arthritis, compared with those not receiving any treatment. They also gave higher subjective ratings of health and quality of life. These indirect benefits of treating depression illustrate the importance of psychological factors in a systemic condition like arthritis (Lin et al., 2003).

The environment may need to be restructured in these cases, so that a person with arthritis is able to walk around and keep up with daily activities, but is not burdened by extreme press or demands. For example, a smaller home on one level can reduce the environmental press. Despite the relatively low cost of physically modifying private homes, this is not widely done. A national survey revealed that only 17 percent of women and 12 percent of men aged 70 and older have installed railings; 13 percent and 11 percent, respectively, have installed ramps in their homes. Even the most frequently reported home modification—bathroom bars and shower seats—had been installed by only 43 percent of women and 36 percent of men (National Academy, 2000a).

Osteoporosis

The human body is constantly forming and losing bone through the metabolism of calcium. As noted in Chapter 3, osteoporosis involves a more dramatic loss in bone mass. The increased brittleness of the bones associated with this condition can result in diminished height, slumped posture, backache, and a reduction in the structural strength of bones, making them susceptible to fracture. Compressed or collapsed vertebrae are the major cause of kyphosis, or "dowager's hump," the stooped look that many of us associate with aging.

Osteoporosis apparently starts well before old age (perhaps as young as age 35) and is more than

four times more common in women than in men. Caucasian and Asian American women are more likely to develop it than African American women; estimates are that 20 percent of white and Asian women age 50 and older have this condition, compared with 5 percent of African American and 10 percent of Latina women (NIA, 2001). The causes of osteoporosis are unclear, although several risk factors have been suggested:

- small stature and low body weight
- loss of calcium and estrogen in menopausal women
- a sedentary lifestyle
- cigarette smoking
- excessive alcohol and caffeine consumption
- long-term dieting or fasting
- inadequate fluoride intake

Even severe osteoporosis does not inevitably limit elders' independence.

> **RISK FACTORS FOR HIP FRACTURES AMONG WHITE WOMEN WITH OSTEOPOROSIS**
>
> - age (especially over 70)
> - family history of hip fractures
> - low body weight
> - use of medications that affect balance
> - not using estrogen
> - disabilities or weakness of the lower extremities
> - stiffness affecting many joints (LaCroix, 1997)

- genetic factors that determine bone density
- family history of a hip fracture in a close relative (e.g., mother or sister)

The primary risk posed by osteoporosis is a fracture of the neck of the femur, or thigh. Many of the falls and associated hip fractures of old age actually represent an osteoporotic femoral neck that broke from bearing weight, causing the individual to fall. Osteoporosis and its less serious counterpart, **osteopenia** (a significant loss of calcium and reduced bone density but without the risk of fractures), together affect about 25 million Americans, 80 percent of whom are women. Osteoporosis results in 1.5 million fractures per year; one in two women will have an osteoporosis-related fracture in their lifetime. Increases in life expectancy are expected to double the number of hip fractures within the next 50 years (Compston and Rosen, 1997). The most common sites of fractures are:

- 47 percent vertebrae
- 20 percent hip
- 17 percent wrist
- 16 percent other sites (NIH, 2003).

Many older people have undiagnosed osteoporosis, often showing no symptoms until a fall or fracture occurs. Typically, no immediate precipitating event can be identified as the cause of the fracture. Some 20 percent of white women experience fractures by age 65, increasing to more than 30 percent by age 90. Although both men and women lose bone mass with aging, men rarely develop symptomatic osteoporosis before age 70. White men are far less likely than white women to experience hip fractures; African American men and women have even lower rates of fractures than white men.

Hip fractures are of concern because of their impact on morbidity and mortality; about 24 percent die within a year after a hip fracture (NIH, 2003). Even when the older person does not die from a hip fracture, falls that result in hip fractures can cause long-term disability and are responsible for more days of restricted activity than any other health problem. Six months after a hip fracture, only about 15 percent of other people can walk across a room on their own (NIH, 2003). The costs to society are also high because of hospitalizations and long-term care. With the growth of the older population, it is predicted that more than $40 billion will be spent over the next 10 years to care for women in the United States who sustain a fracture (Rosen, 1996).

Not all falls and fractures among older people result from osteoporosis, however. Cardiovascular disease underlies approximately 50 percent of them. Others are due to a decline in postural control, produced by impairments of the senses and the central nervous system, changes previously discussed in Chapter 3. Table 4.1 lists some of these risk factors.

PREVENTING OSTEOPOROSIS: THE CASE FOR AND AGAINST ESTROGEN   In the years immediately following menopause, the rate of bone loss can be as high as 5 percent, compared to a normal rate of 1 or 2 percent. For women entering menopause, reduced estrogen—not calcium—is the primary cause of bone loss in the first 5 years after menopause. The goal in treating osteoporosis is to prevent further bone loss. Hormone replacement therapy (HRT), combining estrogen with progestin, or using estrogen alone (ERT), has been used for many years to prevent osteoporosis and bone fractures. HRT can decrease the risk of hip

TABLE 4.1   Risk Factors for Falls

RISK FACTOR	RELATIVE RISK**	
	FOR WOMEN	FOR MEN
Body mass index* less than 23.1 (i.e., a thin frame)	2.0	1.5
Daily alcohol consumption per day greater than 27 grams	2.9	1.9
No load-bearing exercise	2.0	3.4
No vigorous exercise in young adulthood	7.2	2.4
Two or more falls in past 12 months	3.0	3.4
History of stroke	3.8	3.6
Cigarette smoker (current or past)	1.5	not tested
Regularly uses sedatives	2.5	3.0
Regularly uses thyroid drugs	7.1	11.8

*Body mass index (BMI) is calculated by dividing weight (in kilograms) by height (in meters) squared: kg/m^2. To calculate your own BMI, check the Website: www.nhlbi.nih.gov/guidelines/obesity/bmi_tbl.htm.

**Increased risk relative to elders without these conditions

SOURCE: Lau et al., 2001.

fractures by 25 to 50 percent, and of spinal crush fractures by 50 to 75 percent. Since estrogen blocks the process of bone reabsorption, it can help the bones absorb dietary calcium and thereby increase bone mineral density (BMD) 3 to 5 percent in the first year. However, the effects may not be permanent, and benefits may be lost after discontinuing HRT.

Recent findings from the Women's Health Initiative (WHI) have raised serious questions about the benefits versus risks of HRT. As part of this large (more than 100,000 women age 65 and older) national randomized controlled trial of exercise, diet, and hormone replacement therapy for preventing osteoporosis, heart disease, and cancer, one arm of the study tested the effects of a combined estrogen with progesterone intervention (HRT) against a placebo pill. Women enrolled in this arm did not know which drug they were using. Although the study was designed to measure health outcomes after 8.5 years of HRT or placebo use, it was stopped in 2002 after 5.6 years. This was because the research team found no benefits of HRT on their primary outcomes, and in fact showed that HRT had several adverse

effects. The relative risk of coronary heart disease, breast cancer, and stroke was *higher* among women in the HRT group compared to those in the placebo condition, although this translated to a slightly higher absolute risk (i.e., number of women who actually developed these conditions). It should be noted that women using HRT were at much *lower* relative risk of developing colorectal cancer and hip fractures. These relative and absolute risks are shown in Table 4.2 (WHI, 2002).

On the basis of these unexpected findings, the WHI researchers do not recommend using HRT to prevent chronic diseases, especially coronary heart disease. In early 2004, the WHI director instructed all participants in the estrogen-only arm of this clinical trial to stop using their pills. After 7 years, women using estrogen had a higher incidence of strokes than women on a placebo. No differences were found in heart disease incidence, or in breast cancer. However, ERT did reduce the risk of hip fractures (NIH, 2004). Women coping with menopausal symptoms and attempting to prevent osteoporosis need to weigh the risks and benefits of HRT and ERT for their own health profile. Table 4.3 summarizes these findings.

TABLE 4.2 **Risks and Benefits of HRT for Some Diseases**

COMPARED TO PLACEBO	RELATIVE RISK	ABSOLUTE RISK
Blood clot	111% increase	18 more cases per 10,000 women
Stroke	41% increase	8 more cases
Heart attack	29% increase	7 more cases
Breast cancer	26% increase	8 more cases
Colon cancer	37% *decrease*	6 fewer cases
Hip fractures	33% *decrease*	5 fewer cases

SOURCE: WHI, 2002

TABLE 4.3 **Risks and Benefits of HRT**

ADVANTAGES	DISADVANTAGES
Combined HRT • can reduce risk of osteoporosis and hip fractures • can relieve hot flashes and night sweats • can relieve vaginal dryness • can improve cholesterol levels • can reduce risk of colon cancer	Combined HRT • can increase risk of blood clots • can increase heart attack and stroke risk • can increase risk of breast cancer • may contribute to gallbladder disease (pill form only) Estrogen only • may increase risk of endometrial cancer

SOURCES: NIA, 2001; WHI, 2002.

For women who cannot or choose not to use ERT or HRT, and because of their potential risks, new drugs have been approved by the Food and Drug Administration (FDA). Some of these have been found to slow the rate of bone loss and prevent vertebral fractures. However, none of these medications eliminates the need for increased intake of calcium and Vitamin D among older women. Combinations of fluoride and calcium treatments are also given, but may have negative side effects of gastrointestinal and rheumatic complaints. Researchers are also testing the effectiveness of phytoestrogenic or "natural" estrogens that are found in some foods such as wild yams.

Scientists are working on new forms of estrogen that will have the benefits of current forms without the risks. These "designer estrogens," or selective estrogen receptor modulators, appear to improve bone density and reduce levels of low density lipoprotein (LDL) (bad) cholesterol while increasing the levels of high density lipoprotein (HDL) (good) cholesterol, but do not have the adverse effects associated with HRT. Other researchers are exploring the effects of parathyroid hormone on advanced osteoporosis.

CALCIUM AND EXERCISE TO PREVENT OSTEOPOROSIS
Certain dietary and exercise habits may help prevent osteoporosis, especially increasing the amount of calcium after age 50. The National Institutes of Health (NIA, 2001) recommends that women over age 50 should consume:

- 1500 mg of calcium daily, if they are not on HRT (and for both men and women over age 65)
- 1000 mg per day, if they are on HRT

This is higher than previously recommended; 1500 mg of calcium is equivalent to five 8-ounce glasses of milk daily, far more than most women are accustomed to consuming. In fact, some studies have recommended doses as high as 2000 mg/day in older postmenopausal women. Given the difficulty of obtaining this much calcium from dietary sources, calcium supplements may be the most effective way to get high levels. Despite concerns about side effects, such as kidney stones, related to high calcium intake, there is little evidence that such supplementation harms older women (Chiu, 1999).

Calcium is absorbed better when combined with Vitamin D. For this reason, milk in the United States is fortified with Vitamin D. Unfortunately, many older women do not consume enough milk or milk products to obtain Vitamin D in that manner. It is also produced by the human body after 15 to 20 minutes of exposure to sunlight each day, but many older women avoid the sun or are unable to get outside every day, especially in the winter. For this reason, older women who do not obtain an adequate intake of fortified milk or exposure to sunshine should take daily multivitamins with at least 400 IUs of Vitamin D (600 IUs for those over age 70) (NIA, 2001).

Although increased calcium appears to be an important preventive measure, low dietary calcium may be only partly responsible for osteoporosis. Therefore, increasing calcium intake may not prevent fracturing after bone loss has occurred. One reason is that an estimated 40 percent of osteoporotic women have a deficiency of the enzyme that is needed to metabolize calcium (lactose), thus making it difficult for them to absorb calcium. An additional problem is that once one fracture is present, the individual has a 70 to 80 percent chance of developing another.

A SUMMARY OF PREVENTIVE STRATEGIES AGAINST OSTEOPOROSIS

- increased intake of calcium daily
- increased intake of vitamin D
- moderate weight-bearing exercise such as vigorous walking and strength training
- possibly fluoride
- possibly natural estrogens (phytoestrogens)

A combination of calcium and exercise (twice-weekly brisk walks and once-weekly aerobics) appears to reduce bone loss over a 2-year period more than exercise alone. Longitudinal research has shown that high-intensity strength training using exercise machines for one year can significantly *increase* bone mineral density (BMD) in postmenopausal women (Nelson et al., 1994). The strength-training program was combined with estrogen therapy in the former study, but not in the latter. Another study documented that simple, vigorous walking on a daily basis reduced hip fractures by 30 percent in older women (Cummings et al., 1995). These clinical experiments demonstrate that high-intensity (i.e., twice weekly) strenuous exercise not only maintains, but also *increases,* BMD in older women (up to age 70 in both studies). The strength-training program implemented by Nelson and colleagues also resulted in increased muscle mass, muscle strength, balance, and spontaneous physical activity. Other researchers have compared the BMD of postmenopausal women who have been running regularly (at least 5 years, more than 10 miles per week) in conjunction with hormone replacement therapy or without. Bone mass does not seem to be protected with exercise alone, but in this study the *combination of HRT and running* increased total BMD and BMD in the spine. However, this combination did not significantly improve hip BMD, which is the critical issue for preventing hip fractures (Hawkins et al., 1999).

Because of the increased attention to osteoporosis today, many entrepreneurial clinics are offering bone density testing to postmenopausal women. These tests show the obvious results; that most women over 50 have less bone mass than younger women. However, they do not provide a comparison with any baseline data for a specific individual. Women should have a baseline bone density test before they undergo menopause, then have new tests when they are in their 60s, 70s, and 80s.

Chronic Obstructive Pulmonary Disease or Respiratory Problems

Chronic *bronchitis, fibrosis, asthma,* and *emphysema* are manifestations of chronic obstructive pulmonary diseases (COPD) that damage lung tissue. They increase with age, develop slowly and insidiously, and are progressive and debilitating, often resulting in frequent hospitalizations, major lifestyle changes, and death. In fact, by age 90, most people are likely to have some signs of emphysema, with shortness of breath and prolonged and difficult exhalation. Getting through daily activities can be extremely exhausting under such conditions. Causes of COPD are both genetic and environmental, especially prolonged exposure to various dusts, fumes, or cigarette smoke. Three to four times as many men as women have these diseases, probably due to a combination of normal age changes in the lung and a greater likelihood of smoking and exposure to airborne pollutants. This is especially true in older cohorts; men in the old-est-old group are three times more likely to die of COPD than their female counterparts. Treatment is usually continuous, and includes:

- drugs
- respiratory therapy
- breathing exercises to compensate for damage
- avoidance of respiratory infections, smoking, pollution, and other irritants

Allergic reactions to bacterial products, drugs, and pollutants also increase with age. The greater incidence of drug allergies may be a function of both decreases in physiological capacities and the in-creased use of many drugs, such as sedatives, tranquilizers, antidepressants, and antibiotics.

Diabetes

Compared with other systems of the body, the endocrine glands do not show consistent and predictable age-related changes, other than the gradual slowing of functioning. However, insufficient insulin, produced and secreted by the pancreas, can lead to *diabetes mellitus*. Diabetes mellitus is characterized by above-normal amounts of glucose (sugar) in the blood and urine, resulting from an inability to use carbohydrates. Diabetics may go into a coma when their blood glucose levels get very high. Low blood glucose (hypoglycemia) can also lead to unconsciousness.

Older diabetics include people who:

- have had the disease since youth (Type I);
- develop it in middle age, most often between 40 and 50, and incur related cardiovascular problems (Type II)
- develop it late in life and generally show mild pathologic conditions (Type II)

Type II diabetes is most common in older persons, and can often be managed without medication. Although diabetes can occur at any age, diabetic problems related to the body's lessened capability to metabolize carbohydrates can be particularly severe in older adults. Many cases are

---

SYMPTOMS OF DIABETES

- excessive thirst
- increased appetite
- increased urination
- fatigue
- weakness
- loss of weight
- slower wound healing
- blurred vision
- irritability

associated with being overweight, especially due to changes in fat/muscle ratio and slower metabolism with aging. This is particularly true among older African American and Latina women, who have a higher rate of obesity and diabetes than do older white women. Latinos are 3.5 times more likely than other adults to develop Type II diabetes (NCHS, 1995). Glucose tolerance and the action of insulin are often compromised by poor diet, physical inactivity, and coexistent diseases.

The Centers for Disease Control and Prevention reports a doubling in the prevalence of diabetes, from just under 6 million in 1980 to 12 million in 2000. A recent survey of 150,000 American households found that the rate of Type II diabetes increased between 1990 and 1998 from 4.9 percent to 6.5 percent (a change of 33 percent) of the adult population (Mokdad, et al., 2000). It is particularly disturbing that the increase is greatest among 30- to 39-year-olds. When rates were compared across ethnic minority groups, Latinos showed the greatest increase (38 percent), followed by whites (29 percent) and African Americans (26 percent). The researchers attributed these increased rates of diabetes to a rise in obesity during this same interval, from 12 percent to 20 percent. These changes raise concerns about health risks for future cohorts of elders.

The symptoms of diabetes shown in the box on page 130 may not be present in older people, however. Instead, diabetes among the older population is generally detected incidentally through eye examinations, hospitalization, and testing for other disorders. Older people may experience fatigue, a sign of this disease, but attribute it to a presumed slowing down that some assume is normal with aging. Since blood glucose may be temporarily elevated under the stress of illnesses such as stroke, myocardial infarction, or infection, people should not be labeled as diabetic unless the high glucose level persists under conditions of reduced stress.

The cumulative effect of high blood glucose levels can lead to complications in advanced stages of diabetes. These include:

- hypertension
- infections
- nerve damage
- blindness
- kidney failure
- stroke
- cognitive dysfunction
- harm to the coronary arteries
- skin problems
- poor circulation in the extremities, leading to gangrene and amputations

The interaction of diabetes with ordinary age-related physical problems such as hypertension can result in serious health difficulties and consequent limitations in ADL. Atherosclerosis and coronary heart disease, for example, are more common in diabetics than in nondiabetics. On average, life expectancy among diabetics is 15 years less than in the population without diabetes (Juvenile Diabetes Foundation, 1998). Diabetes cannot be cured, but it can generally be managed at home in many ways. These include:

- a diet of reduced carbohydrates and calories
- regular exercise
- proper care of feet, skin, teeth, and gums
- monitored insulin intake for those who require it

To minimize forgetfulness and treatment errors, older people, especially those who acquire diabetes late in life, may need reminders from health care providers and family members regarding:

- the importance of diet
- daily examination of their skin
- urine testing
- the correct dosage of insulin or other drugs

Problems with the Kidneys and Urinary Tract

The various diseases and disorders of the urinary system characteristic of old age tend to be either acute infections or chronic problems resulting from the gradual deterioration of the structure and function of the excretory system with age. As seen in Chapter 3, the kidneys shrink in size, and their capacity to perform basic filtration tasks declines, leading to a higher probability of disease or infection. One of the most common age-related problems for women is the inability of the bladder to empty completely. This often results in cystitis, an acute inflammatory state accompanied by pain and irritation that can generally be treated with antibiotics.

Older men face an increased risk of diseases of the prostate gland, with cancer of the prostate being the most frequent malignancy. For this reason, the American Cancer Society and the American Urological Association recommend annual prostatic evaluations for men aged 50 and older by both a digital rectal exam and a new test to determine levels of prostate-specific antigen (PSA) in the blood. Cancer of the prostate frequently spreads to the bones, but surgery is rarely recommended for men over age 70 because the disease usually progresses slowly in this age group. Instead, more conservative treatment and more frequent monitoring are usually the treatment of choice. Treatment of prostate cancer and its effects on men's sexual functioning are described more fully in Chapter 7.

INCONTINENCE   A more difficult, noninfectious, and chronic urinary problem is **incontinence** (i.e., inability to control urine or feces). It has been estimated to occur in at least 19 percent of men and more than 38 percent of women over age 65 and living in the community (Thom and Brown, 1998). Since older people and their families often consider incontinence a taboo topic, they tend to be unaware of methods to treat it. Most older adults do not discuss the problem with their doctors, and only a small percentage use any protective devices. Many health care providers, in turn, do not ask their older patients about incontinence. This widespread reluctance to acknowledge incontinence as a problem can have serious

---

MANAGEMENT OF INCONTINENCE

- medications to increase bladder capacity
- surgery
- dietary changes
- Kegel exercises (at least 100 times per day)
- behavioral management techniques, such as reducing fluid intake when bathroom access is limited
- reduction in the intake of caffeine (e.g., coffee, tea, cola, even chocolate) can prevent the stimulation of the kidneys to excrete fluids
- weight loss can also help, as obesity has been found to cause urine leakage

---

psychological and social implications, particularly on the decision to institutionalize an older person. Accordingly, about 50 percent of the older population living in nursing homes experience at least one episode of incontinence daily.

There are two primary types of incontinence:

- *urge incontinence,* where the person has a strong urge to urinate, due to irregular bladder contractions, and is unable to hold urine long enough to reach a toilet
- *stress incontinence,* where leakage occurs during physical exertion or when sneezing or coughing because of weakened pelvic floor muscles. This phenomenon can also occur among younger women.

Many cases of incontinence represent a combination of these two types, referred to as *mixed incontinence.* Incontinence sometimes results from a specific precipitating factor, such as acute illness, infection, or even a change in residence. It can be treated if the cause is known. For example, temporary incontinence can be caused by bladder or urinary tract infections, which may be treated with antibiotics. Prescribed medications can also cause urgent and frequent urination. If informed of the detrimental effects of medication, a physician may reduce the drug dosage. With age, the bladder and urethra in women commonly descend, resulting in stress incontinence; leaking then occurs with the increased abdominal pressure brought on by coughing, sneezing, laughing, lifting, or physical exercise. Another type of incontinence, known as *functional incontinence,* often results from neurological changes and accompanies other problems, such as Parkinson's disease and organic brain syndrome. Other physical causes that should be investigated medically are prostate problems, pernicious anemia, diabetic neuropathy, and various cancers.

Since the types and causes of incontinence vary widely, thorough diagnosis and individualized treatment programs are critical. Even habitual incontinence should not be assumed to be irreversible.

Although some physicians prescribe medications to increase bladder capacity or reduce urine production, these often have unpleasant side effects such as blurred vision and dry mouth. Noninvasive behavioral management techniques, such as frequent access to toilet facilities, restriction of fluid intake before bedtime, and systematic exercise of the pelvic muscle, are often just as effective. Even incurable problems can be managed through protective products (e.g., absorbent pads) and catheters (tubes draining the bladder) to reduce complications, anxiety, and embarrassment. Only a small proportion of older persons with incontinence, however, are so severely disabled that they are unlikely to regain continence and require a catheter or other external appliances to cope with the conditions. Physical exercise, known as Kegels, designed to promote and maintain sphincter muscle tone, can also prevent or reduce age-related incontinence, particularly among older women. All possible treatments, especially behavioral techniques, exercise, and biofeedback, should be explored, since older people's embarrassment and humiliation may result in their avoiding social gatherings out of fear of having their incontinence detected. Support groups, such as *Help for Incontinent People (HIP),* have chapters nationwide.

Problems with the Intestinal System

Many older people experience problems in digestion and continuing gastrointestinal distress, due particularly to age-related slowing down of the digestive process. Most intestinal problems are, in fact, related to unbalanced diets or diets with limited fiber content. **Diverticulitis** is one of the most common difficulties, affecting up to 50 percent of persons aged 80 and over, especially women (Greenwald and Brandt, 1996). It is a condition in which pouches or sacs (diverticula) in the intestines (especially in the colon) result from weakness of the intestinal wall; these sacs become inflamed and infected, leading to symptoms of nausea, abdominal discomfort, bleeding, and changes in bowel function. Management includes a high-fiber diet and antibiotic therapy. Diverticulitis, which is increasing in industrialized nations, may be associated with a highly refined diet lacking in fiber.

Many older people worry about constipation, but this is not an inevitable outcome of aging, as noted in Chapter 3. It is more prevalent among elders in long-term care facilities but is also reported by 26 percent of women and 16 percent of men living in the community (Talley, Fleming, and Evans, 1996). Constipation may be a symptom of an underlying disease or obstruction. If this is not the case, treatment commonly includes:

- physical activity
- dietary modification
- increased fluid intake

Because many older people are overly concerned about having regular bowel movements, they may become dependent on laxatives. Data from more than 5000 white and African American elders found that 10.2 percent of both groups used laxatives, with higher use among women, those using four or more prescriptions, those with four or more physician visits per year, and those with problems with ADL (Ruby et al., 2003). Over

---

CAUSES OF CONSTIPATION

- overuse of cathartics
- lack of exercise
- psychological stress
- gastrointestinal disease
- an unbalanced diet with respect to bulk

---

time, laxatives can cause problems, such as irritating the colon and decreasing the absorption of certain vitamins.

Hiatus hernia appears to be increasing in incidence, especially among obese women; this occurs when a small portion of the stomach slides up through the diaphragm. Symptoms include indigestion, difficulty in swallowing, and chest pain that may be confused with a heart attack. Medical management includes weight reduction, elevation of the upper body when sleeping, changes in the size and frequency of meals, and medication. Although hiatus hernia in itself is not especially severe, it may mask the symptoms of more serious intestinal disorders, such as cancer of the stomach.

The incidence of gallbladder disease, especially gallstones, also increases with age and is indicated by pain, nausea, and vomiting, with attacks increasing in number and severity. Most cases in older adults are asymptomatic, and physicians debate whether to perform surgery or follow a more conservative course of medical management. Medical treatment usually involves a combination of weight loss, avoiding high-fat foods, and using antacids as needed.

Oral Diseases

Because of developments in preventive dentistry, newer cohorts of older people have better oral health than any preceding cohort. According to the most recent National Health and Nutrition Exam Survey (NHANES III), only 30 percent over age 65 today are completely **edentulous** (i.e., no natural teeth remaining). As one might expect, edentulism increases with age:

- 25 percent of the young-old are edentulous
- 42 percent of the old-old are edentulous

This change is due entirely to historical differences in dental care delivery, not because of the aging process. Ethnic and racial differences in tooth loss are minimal in the young-old, but increase in the oldest-old, such that by age 75 the NHANES III survey (U.S. Dept. of Health and Human Services, 2000) found that all natural teeth were missing in:

- 43 percent of whites
- 44 percent of Latinos
- 53 percent of African Americans

The common problems of tooth decay and periodontal diseases also appear to increase with age, although the evidence is limited and less clear. In NHANES III, the rate of root caries (cavities that develop on exposed root surfaces) was found to be more than three times greater among people over age 65 than in those under age 45. Rates of decay on the enamel surfaces of teeth, however, are not much higher among 65- to 74-year-olds compared with 35- to 44-year-olds. Differences are much greater when the older group is compared with people aged 18 to 24, who have only about 10 percent of their tooth surfaces decayed or filled, compared with 31 percent of people aged 65 to 74 (NCHS, 1999). These differences reflect changes over time in preventive dental care, such as the widespread use of water fluoridation. NHANES III also found an age-related increase in the incidence of periodontitis or gum disease, especially after age 45 (U.S. Dept. of Health and Human Services, 2000).

In contrast, cancers of the lip, tongue, mouth, gum, pharynx, and salivary glands increase with advanced age, regardless of ethnic minority status or sex. In North America and Western Europe, cancer of the lip is the most frequent type of oral cancer and has the highest survival rates among those listed previously (between 65 and 90 percent over a five-year period) (U.S. Dept. of Health and Human Services, 2000). Smoking and heavy alcohol use are strongly linked to oral cancer.

HIV/AIDS in the Older Population

While it cannot be classified as a chronic disease in the same way as diabetes or chronic obstructive pulmonary disease, the growing number of older adults with AIDS (acquired immune deficiency syndrome) and the increasing time between infection, diagnosis, and death make this an important public health issue in gerontology. Over the next few years, AIDS will place greater demands on long-term care, especially home-based services. Since it is mandatory to report AIDS cases, the Centers for Disease Control and Prevention (CDC) receive reports from all state and territorial health departments on all diagnosed cases of AIDS. Because of stereotypes that older people are not sexually active, many physicians and HIV-testing programs do not routinely test older adults for AIDS. Often, cases go undiagnosed because older people do not report symptoms.

A report by the World Health Organization in late 2003 showed that the AIDS epidemic has not abated, with about 34 million people around the world infected with the human immunodeficiency virus (HIV) or full-blown AIDS (WHO, 2003). Most of these cases are in sub-Saharan Africa (25–28 million), although the disease has spread more recently to eastern Europe, Russia, and India. There are no reliable estimates by age, but the majority of cases are young adults in most of these countries.

Almost one million Americans are living with HIV/AIDS. Although it is difficult to guess the actual prevalence of cases without a diagnosis, it is estimated that 5 to 10 percent of HIV/AIDS cases, and almost 11 percent of AIDS cases are people age 50 and older (considered "older adults" by the Centers for Disease Control and Prevention). Men are at far higher risk than women, ranging from 86 percent of diagnosed AIDS cases at age 50 to 54 to 79 percent among those 65 and older. More than half of all cases among the population

50 and older are African Americans and Latinos (52 percent). Women of color are at greater risk than their white counterparts in this age group, representing 70 percent of women living with AIDS. The number of new AIDS cases in older women has risen sharply in the past 5 years. This increase of 40 percent is due primarily to women becoming infected through unprotected sex with infected male partners. A notable minority obtained the virus by sharing needles for drug use (CDC, 2001; HRSA, 2001; NIA, 1999b; Vosvick et al., 2003).

Many older people do not seek medical attention during the early stages of this disease because they assume many of the symptoms are merely signs of normal aging or chronic diseases that they are already managing. These include:

- general aches and pains
- headache
- chronic cough
- lack of energy
- loss of appetite and weight
- problems with short-term memory

Because of such misunderstandings, older people who become infected with the AIDS virus often are unaware that they are at risk and may not suspect their sexual partners. One reason for the significant rise of this disease among older women is that, after the menopause, they may assume that they do not need to have their male partner use a condom and practice safe sex because they need not fear pregnancy. Menopause can also cause vaginal dryness and thinning of the vaginal lining. This may result in small abrasions and tears in the vaginal walls where the virus can penetrate. Older men may be at risk because of unprotected sex with male partners and paid sex workers. The latter may be male or female, and some may use injected heroin or crack cocaine with shared needles (HRSA, 2001; NIA, 1999b; Radda et al., 2003).

Older adults may also be at greater risk because already low levels of T-cells, part of the immune system, are lost more rapidly in older people with this infection. In elders with compromised immune systems, the HIV virus is more likely to attack than in younger people or in other older people who have a fully functioning immune system. This may also explain why the incubation period for HIV is shorter in older adults, an average of 5.7 years versus 7.3 years in people under age 50. Poorer immune reactions may also explain the shorter time between diagnosis and death for people over age 50 (CDC, 1998; Emlet and Farkas, 2002).

Researchers have questioned whether older adults with AIDS are more or less likely than younger people to use health services. An analysis of 571 cases in California compared 63 AIDS patients who were age 60 and older, with 190 age 50 to 59 and 318 age 30 to 49. In addition to age, functional status and diagnosis were hypothesized to be predictors of inpatient and outpatient medical care, in-home services, and mental health services. Age was not associated with functional health or service utilization. Both younger and older patients were more likely to use all types of services as their ADL limitations increased. Among all types of health care, mental health services were least likely to be used by all age groups (Emlet and Farkas, 2002). These findings demonstrate that older adults with AIDS do not seek health services at a higher rate than younger patients unless their functional health has deteriorated significantly. However, another study found age differences in perceptions of the importance of community-based services. In this case, adults age 50 and over who were living with HIV/AIDS were compared with their 20- to 39-year-old counterparts regarding the perceived importance of other types of health and social services. Older patients rated home-delivered meals, adult day care, home chore services, and physical therapy as more important than did their younger counterparts. Both groups rated drug programs to treat AIDS plus dental and primary medical care as most important. These results suggest that supplemental services to improve their quality of life are highly valued by older HIV/AIDS patients (Emlet and Berghuis, 2002).

Recent budget cuts, however, are limiting the availability of community-based and home care services. Unfortunately, many older persons with HIV/AIDS do not have an adequate social safety net to replace these needed community services. A recent survey of adults aged 50 to 68 living with HIV/AIDS in New York City found that 42 percent perceived a lack of emotional support and 27 percent reported inadequate practical assistance. Those with a more advanced stage of the disease, who should have had *more* support, actually reported *less* emotional and practical help in coping with their activities of daily living (Schrimshaw and Siegel, 2003).

For all the reasons just described, it is important to educate older adults about *their* risk for AIDS. Even those who know something about this disease may feel that it cannot affect them if they are not engaging in homosexual activity or intravenous drug use. Many older people have relied on the media for their knowledge in this area. Unfortunately, the media rarely reports on *older* adults contracting AIDS through heterosexual intercourse or through blood transfusions. It is therefore not surprising that many older people are unaware that they may be infected. They are also less willing to be tested for the virus, and once diagnosed, are less likely to seek out AIDS support groups or other forms of emotional support. At the same time, ageist attitudes may prevent health providers from encouraging sexually active elders to be tested for this virus or even asking questions about their sexual history as part of a routine health screening.

Accidents among Older People

Although mortality statistics suggest that older people are less likely than the young to die of accidents (only 7 per 10,000 deaths compared with 10 per 10,000 among people 21 and younger), these numbers mask the true incidence of deaths due to accident-related injuries. For example, if an older person breaks a hip after falling down a flight of stairs or breaks a leg in an auto accident, she enters a hospital, often is discharged to a nursing home, and soon after may die from pneumonia. Pneumonia is then listed as the cause of death, when in fact this acute condition was brought on by the patient's problems in recovering from the accident.

Despite this underestimate, the risk of death from physical injuries is about four times greater for 80-year-olds than for 20-year-olds. Those aged 60 and older are twice as likely as younger adults to be killed in a car crash. For drivers aged 65 to 74, motor vehicle accidents are the leading cause of injury-related deaths. For those aged 74 to 84, this is the second-leading cause of injury-related deaths after falls. Older drivers and passengers are three times more likely to die than younger people following an auto crash. This is most likely due to older adults' greater physical vulnerability. Given these statistics, it is not surprising that AARP's driver education classes are one of their most widely used services.

Older Drivers

Currently 27.5 million drivers in the United States are age 65 and older. These numbers will grow as baby boomers age and more people live into their 80s and 90s, wanting to continue driving. Older people, both drivers and passengers, made up 10

> **DESIGN CHANGES THAT COULD HELP OLDER DRIVERS**
>
> - right sideview mirrors
> - wider rearview mirrors
> - pedal extensions
> - less complicated and legible instrument panels
> - better protection on doors
> - a booster cushion for shorter-stature drivers

percent of all auto fatalities in 1975, 17 percent in 1998, and are projected to represent 27 percent of auto fatalities in 2015, as more baby boomers reach old age. Between 2000 and 2020, the proportion of older persons who continue to drive will double (NHTSA, 2001).

Many older people view driving as an important part of maintaining their independence and active aging. However, a tragic accident in July 2003 attracted national attention to the issues raised by older drivers. In that accident, an 86-year-old driver in California mistakenly stepped on the accelerator instead of the brake, causing the death of 10 people and many injuries in a crowded market area. This unfortunate event raised many questions about the need for mandatory tests and restrictions on driving after a certain age. Only 21 states currently have special license requirements for older drivers. Some include:

> **RETRAINING OLDER DRIVERS**
>
> It may be useful for state licensing departments to test all adults annually on some of the relevant physiological and cognitive abilities, and to retrain older drivers who are experiencing significant declines in these areas. The AARP, National Safety Council, and the Automobile Association of America (AAA) have developed such courses. For example, AARP estimates that some 500,000 older drivers enroll in their "Mature Driver Safety" program each year. This 8-hour course is offered through retirement homes, senior centers, shopping malls, libraries, and churches throughout the United States. Older persons can obtain discounts of 5 to 10 percent on their auto insurance in many states after completing such courses.

1. Cannot renew licenses by mail after age 70: Alaska, California, and Louisiana
2. More frequent renewals (hence, more regular testing) required for older people than for younger drivers: Arizona, Colorado, Hawaii, Idaho, Illinois, Indiana, Iowa, Kansas, Maine, Missouri, Montana, New Mexico, and Rhode Island
3. More frequent vision tests for older drivers: Arizona, Florida, Maine, Oregon, and Utah
4. More frequent road tests for older drivers: Illinois and New Hampshire
5. Medical report required for drivers 70 and older: Nevada

Older drivers are less likely to drive in bad weather, at night, in freeway traffic, or in rush hour. They are less likely to drive while drunk or to speed. They generally select familiar routes of travel. They drive fewer miles per year than younger drivers. Nevertheless, they have more accidents per mile driven. A U-shaped pattern of fatal crashes has been observed, from a high rate among 17-year-olds, to a low at ages 30 to 64, to a new high rate among 75-year-olds (Bédard et al., 2001; Insurance Institute for Highway Safety, 2001). This higher rate of accidents in older drivers may be attributed to:

- changes in eye-hand coordination
- slower reaction time
- impaired vision (especially diminished night vision, sensitivity to glare, and poor peripheral vision)
- hearing impairments
- slower information processing and declining attention skills, especially divided attention
- problems with visual-spatial skills
- declines in physical strength

Even though most accidents by older drivers occur at low speeds, age-related declines in organ systems and brittle bones make the older person more vulnerable to injuries and even death as a result of accidents. Older drivers are more likely to sustain rib and pelvic fractures, and thoracic injuries, but fewer head and brain injuries in an auto accident. Regardless of their injuries, older adults, especially those 75 and older, have longer hospital stays, more pulmonary, cardiovascular, and renal complications, and greater need for rehabilitation services following trauma (Li, Braver & Chen, 2003; Salen et al., 2003). Some medications, especially those given for insomnia or anxiety, that have a long half-life in the bloodstream, are found to increase the risk of motor vehicle crashes in older adults by as much as 45 percent. This is a major risk, since many older people are prescribed these medications (Hemmelgarn et al., 1997).

Although older adults diagnosed with Alzheimer's disease or other dementias generally stop driving, researchers have found that almost 4 percent of American men aged 75 and older who drive have dementia (Foley et al., 2000). Many older adults restrict their driving to the community where they reside and avoid long highway trips. However, city driving may actually pose more hazards than highways, because of multiple intersections, traffic congestion, and other driving demands that require rapid information processing and reaction time. A national survey of more than 5000 older men and women revealed that the majority of women with cognitive impairment do not drive (75.6 percent), compared to 43 percent of their male counterparts. Men with mild and severe cognitive impairments apparently cope by avoiding long-distance driving. As one might expect, both men and women with dementia who have another driver in their household are more likely to stop driving themselves. In this same survey, elders with impaired vision and limitations in their ADL were less likely to drive, but having heart disease, diabetes, or arthritis did not cause them to restrict their driving (Freund and Szinovacz, 2002).

Better environmental design can help some older drivers. For example, older people have more accidents while making left turns; these could be avoided by designing better left-turn intersections with special lanes and left arrow lights. Road signs that are clearer and well lighted could reduce the high number of violations received by older drivers for improperly changing lanes or entering and exiting highways. Other design options are summarized in the box at the top of page 137.

Another approach to reducing person–environment discrepancies for older drivers is to install air bags that have lower power in cars; of 68 adults killed by air bags between 1991 and 2000, 26 (40 percent) were age 70 or older. Already, the Ford Motor Company has installed "force limiters" in some models. These are part of a personal safety system to use sensors to adjust air bags and seatbelts according to the weight of the driver and passenger, and how close the driver is to the steering wheel.

Falls and Their Prevention

As noted earlier, older people are at a greater risk of falls than the young. Falls are the leading cause of injuries for people over age 65 in United States, and account for 90 percent of all hip fractures. Up to 30 percent of older adults in the community, and even more in long-term care settings, experience a fall in a given year. Many older people who fall become more fearful of falling and therefore restrict their activity levels. They may also become more rigid or overly cautious in walking. This may, in turn, increase the likelihood of subsequent falls. Therefore it is important to identify risk factors for falls and try to prevent them (Lord, Sherrington, and Menz, 2001).

Despite many national and local public health efforts to prevent falls among older people, fall-related deaths and hip fractures due to falls have not declined dramatically. In 1998, 163 deaths per 100,000 people aged 85 and older were attributable to falls, much higher than the target of 105 per 100,000 in *Healthy People*

INTERVENTIONS TO PREVENT FALLS

- Environmental modifications of the homes of older people who have experienced multiple falls in the past can significantly decrease falls.
- An investment of $2000 in home modifications and assistive devices saved $17,000 in health care costs for an older person over 18 months (Mann et al., 1999).
- In a large study of 14 nursing homes, 50 percent of the homes (the experimental group) made major modifications to their physical environment, in wheelchair safety, and in the use of psychotropic medications. No changes were made in the other seven homes (control group). A significant decline in recurrent falls occurred among older residents of the experimental homes compared with the control group. Rates of falls dropped to 19 percent among those with environmental modifications versus 54 percent in the control group in the following 2 years (Ray et al., 1997).
- Training older women how to control their balance can prevent falls (Ray et al., 1997; Tinetti et al., 1994).

2000. Similarly, the target of 607 hip fractures per 100,000 older adults was exceeded in 1998, with 863 fractures per 100,000 among the age 65 and older population. In fact, both hip fractures and fall-related deaths have actually increased since 1990, in contrast to other health problems that have shown a gradual decline (Merck Institute, 2002). Fall-related injuries account for $20.2 billion in health care costs per year (CDC, 2003b).

Education and exercise training of older adults and their caregivers are needed to reduce the risk of falls, as well as preventive medications and environmental interventions (see examples of intervention recommendations in the box above). New drugs have been developed to prevent fractures by strengthening bone. Researchers in the United States and Japan have found alendronate (brand name, Fosamax) to be effective in

---

RISK FACTORS FOR FALLS

- inactivity that weakens muscles
- visual impairment
- multiple diseases
- medications (e.g., cardiac conditions and medications that cause postural hypotension)
- gait disorders that are common among older persons
- poor balance when standing
- low lighting levels
- hazards in the environment such as slippery floors, loose area rugs, poorly demarcated stairs, and slippery surfaces in showers and tubs
- unfamiliar environments

reducing fractures of the spine and femoral neck by 50 percent in one study and 44 percent in another. Other effective medications are risedronate (brand name, Actonel) and raloxifene (brand name, Evista); the latter drug has been particularly useful in preventing spinal fractures (Cranney et al., 2002). Recent findings from a study in the Netherlands suggest that thiazide diuretics used to treat hypertension may indirectly prevent bone loss. These drugs draw water from the blood but reduce calcium loss in the urine. Older adults using any one of many brands of thiazide diuretics for their hypertension for more than 1 year also lowered their risk for hip fractures by 50 percent, but the benefits diminished within 4 months of discontinuing the drug (Schoofs et al., 2003).

Use of Physician Services by Older People

The increased incidence of many chronic and acute diseases among the older population would seem to predict a striking growth with age in the use of health care services. There is some support for a differential pattern of utilization among different age groups. The probability of seeing a doctor at least once in the previous year increases slightly with age. However, the major difference across age groups is in *frequency* of use:

- 1.3 physician visits per person among those aged 25–44
- 7.3 visits for people aged 45–64
- 11.4 visits for people aged 65–84
- 15.0 visits for those 85 and older (Merck Institute, 2002).

When they visit physicians, both younger and older people do so primarily for acute symptoms and to receive similar diagnostic and therapeutic services. However, the larger number of yearly visits by older persons may indicate that they are seeking care for chronic conditions as well. It is noteworthy that only a small proportion of older adults are high users of all health services. In a longitudinal study of over 2000 older adults, only 3 percent were consistently high users of physician services over a 6-year period, while 40.5 percent were consistently low to medium users, that is, six or fewer annual physician visits (Stump, Johnson, and Wolinsky, 1995). Low use, however, does not necessarily mean that all health needs are being met. For example, low-income older adults, regardless of ethnic minority status, report more unmet health needs than middle- or high-income elders (NCHS, 2000a). Among all races:

- Among low-income elders, 22 percent report unmet health needs.
- Among middle- and upper-income elders, 2.5 percent have unmet health needs.

There is less difference between socioeconomic groups within the Latino population:

- Among low-income Latino elders, 18 percent have unmet health needs.
- Among middle- and upper-income Latino elders, 8 percent have such needs.

These differences in meeting health needs suggest that other factors, such as cost and cultural barriers, result in higher rates of unmet needs among certain groups.

Use of Other Health Services

HOSPITALS Hospital utilization apparently reflects older people's need for health care more accurately than do elective visits to physicians' offices. Older people are more frequently hospitalized and for longer periods of time than younger populations, accounting for about 30 percent of all short-stay hospital days of care (NCHS, 1995). However, the average length of stay has been reduced since the introduction of **diagnosis related groupings (DRGs)** for Medicare patients in 1983 (see Chapter 17). While DRGs prompted a transfer of care from inpatient hospital settings to outpatient settings, home-based care after a hospitalization by older people has decreased overall. This reflects more stringent eligibility and reimbursement criteria rather than a diminishing need for care. Hospital emergency rooms (ER) are used for medical care more often among low-income populations. Research with low-income African Americans shows that ER users are mostly people without a regular physician, and who have an external locus of control regarding their health (i.e., the belief that others have more control than they do over their well-being) (Bazargan, Bazargan, and Baker, 1998).

MEDICATION USE   The use of prescription and nonprescription medications, including vitamins and mineral supplements, may also be an indication of the older person's need for health care. In a national survey of 2590 adults, 94 percent of older women and 90 percent of older men reported taking at least one medication; 57 percent of the former took five or more. Prescription drugs represented 25 percent of all these drugs. Older women, especially white women, were most likely to report using both prescription and nonprescription drugs, Asians and Pacific Islanders were least likely. The most common prescription medications used by older and middle-aged respondents were antihypertensives, heart medications, and diuretics (reflecting the high prevalence of hypertension and heart disease that these drugs are intended to treat). Aspirin was the most commonly used over-the-counter (OTC) drug, reported by 58 percent of older men and 51 percent of older women who took it to prevent heart attacks. Older men and older women were second only to middle-aged adults in their use of multivitamins and specific nutritional supplements (Kaufman et al., 2002). Some older people take as many as 12 to 15 different medications simultaneously, at an average annual cost of $450. More than 2.3 million older persons spend over 10 percent of their income on prescription drugs. The burden falls especially hard on older women, who are most likely to experience chronic diseases

---

CONCERNS ABOUT COSTS OF PRESCRIPTION DRUGS

Older people with chronic diseases spend more of their health care dollar on prescriptions. For example, those who have hypertension use 39 cents of every health care dollar for prescription drugs, compared to 20 percent without hypertension (National Academy, 2000d). The growing number of people who are managing chronic conditions with medications, combined with the increasing costs of prescription drugs in the United States, have made this a volatile health care issue for many Americans (see Chapter 17). It is especially difficult for older people whose primary source of income is Social Security—who spend as much as one-third of their annual income on medications. The improvements in drug therapies for many conditions affecting older people come at a cost. The research, development, and FDA approval costs incurred by pharmaceutical companies for a single drug can exceed millions of dollars. This results in increasingly high costs to the consumer: $37.38 for an average prescription in 1998 compared with $23.68 in 1991 (Noonan, 2000).

(Noonan, 2000; Sambamoorthi, Shea, and Crystal, 2003). Coverage for high prescription drug costs may be affected by the recent prescription drug changes in Medicare, which are expected to go into effect in 2006 and described more fully in Chapter 17. Not surprisingly, because of the higher likelihood of their having many chronic conditions, nursing home residents take more prescription drugs than do community-dwelling elders.

Many older people may be taking either too many medications or inappropriate drugs, making overmedication a concern. This is because the less efficient excretion of drugs by the kidney and liver, and the changing proportions of fat and muscle tissue, as discussed in Chapter 3, may prolong the effects of some drugs. Furthermore, combinations of medications can cause adverse drug reactions. Many hospital admissions of older people result from such adverse reactions, and many falls and sudden impairments in cognitive function may be due to inappropriate medication or overmedication. Older people who are discharged from hospitals with a large number of medications are more likely to be rehospitalized because of complications from these drugs. This is especially true if they are using seven or more medications, both prescription and nonprescription. This pattern occurs independent of the elder's diagnosis and type of medication. The higher rate of medication use among older adults also may result in reporting errors and incorrect use. Older people admitted to a hospital often give inconsistent medication reports. For these reasons, health and social service providers must exercise caution in obtaining self-reports of medication use from older adults (Flaherty et al., 2000).

DENTAL SERVICES   An area of elective health care, ignored even more than routine medical care, is the use of professional dental services. Although

the rate of preventive dental service utilization has risen significantly over the past 20 years among younger cohorts, the use of dental services by older adults has increased only slightly. In the latest national survey, older persons continued to be the lowest utilizers of professional dental care; 57 percent had not seen a dentist in the past year, and 33 percent had not obtained care in the past five years (U.S. Dept. of Health and Human Services, 2000). This rate is incongruent with the level of oral diseases that require professional attention in older persons. Yet, once older adults enter the dental care system, their average number of visits is similar to that of younger people. The current state of Medicare reimbursement, whereby physician visits are covered but dental care is not, plays an important role in this differential pattern of utilization.

Health Promotion with Older People

Health promotion is defined as a combination of health education and related organizational, political, and economic changes aimed at enhancing an individual's capacities for living, including moving toward greater health, not just less disease. It contrasts with disease prevention, which is focused on avoiding diseases that can result in impairment and disability. Health promotion emphasizes a variety of interventions in recognition of the complex social, biological, cultural, and economic factors that influence health and health behavior. Accordingly, this definition includes altering individual health practices, such as diet and exercise, as well as creating healthier environments and changing cultural attitudes and expectations toward health. Health promotion represents a shift from a biomedical model that emphasizes the physician's responsibility to treat disease, to a model that emphasizes control over one's health in an effort to improve physical well-being and quality of life. Disease prevention is also important at all stages of

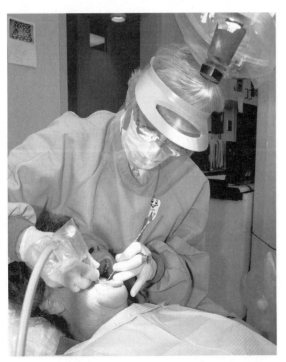

Preventive health care includes regular dental check-ups.

a disease. It includes "primary prevention" (e.g., water fluoridation to prevent the onset of tooth decay; "secondary prevention" (e.g., screening for early detection of cancer), and "tertiary prevention" to manage a disease (e.g., using antihypertensive medications appropriately in order to maintain a healthy blood pressure while preventing side effects associated with the drugs). Preventive health behaviors can save the individual and society significant amounts of money for treating more advanced disease. For example, influenza vaccines can save $118 in treatment costs per $1.50 spent on the vaccine itself (Rotherberg, Ballantonio, and Rose, 2003). Health promotion thus makes explicit the importance of people's *environments* and *lifestyles* as determinants of good health (Breslow, 1999).

Longitudinal studies have found several unhealthy behaviors that increase chances of dying at a younger age than statistically expected. The Alameda County Study (Breslow and Breslow, 1993) followed community-dwelling adults for 35 years. Mortality rates were higher among people who did not participate in regular physical activity, were obese, smoked, had high alcohol intake, did not eat breakfast, or slept less than or more than 7 to 8 hours per night. Similar results have been reported in another longitudinal study (Scott et al., 1997), although it emphasized that functional abilities as reflected by independence in IADL and PADL (physical activities of daily living) are the best predictors of survival into advanced old age.

The primary rationale for health promotion programs for older adults is to reduce the incidence of *disabling chronic diseases*. This can enhance the older person's functional independence and overall quality of life, not merely prolong life. Health promotion is also a recognition that chronic conditions cannot be cured but can be prevented from causing disability. As suggested in our earlier discussion of disease, as many as 80 percent of the chronic illnesses that afflict older individuals may be related to social, environmental, and behavioral factors, particularly poor

---

HEALTHY PEOPLE 2010

Health and Human Services Secretary Donna Shalala released a draft of *Healthy People 2010,* in 2000, proposing 500 health objectives for Americans to achieve by 2010. This was a follow-up to a document released in 1990, entitled *Healthy People 2000,* which contained 319 health objectives. Two major goals of the recent publication are:

- to increase quality and years of healthy life for all Americans
- to eliminate health disparities among segments of the U.S. population

Although the 26 focus areas of *Healthy People 2010* do not specifically address elders or any particular age group, the health topics are relevant for current cohorts of older adults, as well as younger and middle-aged people today, who could improve their quality of life as they reach age 65 and beyond. For example, by promoting healthy behaviors such as increasing levels of physical activity and fitness, improving nutrition and reducing tobacco use (focus areas #1–3), future cohorts will not only increase their life expectancy, but will improve the quality of those years (www.health.gov, 2000).

SOURCE: *Healthy People 2010* (Washington, DC: GPO, 2000).

---

health habits. In addition, 90 percent of fatal and near-fatal episodes of strokes and heart attacks are believed to be preventable.

A viable health care goal, as noted in Chapter 1, is compression of morbidity—delaying the age at which chronic illness and the infirm period of life begin (Berg and Cassells, 1992; Fries, 1980, 1984). This goal of improvement in chronic disease rates seems feasible. Evidence is provided by studies of male master athletes in their 60s. These athletes experience very little decline in their cardiovascular functions, including maximum heart rate and maximum volume of oxygen used during exercise, especially when compared with age-matched sedentary men. Furthermore, HDL cholesterol levels are higher and their triglycerides are lower than in age-matched sedentary men, and are comparable to those of healthy young men (Yataco et al., 1997).

Only a small percentage of the national health care dollar is spent on prevention and early detection services. Medicare and most private health insurance plans do not typically pay for prevention services, although the 2003 changes in Medicare will result in more coverage of preventive services than in the past. An encouraging sign is the growing number of health maintenance organizations, health care clinics, universities, and work sites that are offering health promotion programs. Some of these programs have been carried into senior centers and assisted living, retirement, and nursing homes.

Improving the Success of Health Promotion Programs

The Surgeon General's report, *Healthy People 2000,* was written in the early 1990s and laid out about 200 health targets for Americans of all ages. By the target year, 2000, only 15 percent of these goals had been achieved. Among the targets for older adults, only 4 of the 10 have been met so far; these include an increase in the proportion of women who have a mammogram (68 percent vs. the target of 60 percent), those who obtain a colorectal screening (48.5 percent vs. the target of 40 percent), annual flu vaccinations (64 percent vs. the target of 60 percent), and a reduction in smoking (down to 11.1 percent vs. a goal of 15 percent). Smoking rates among older white and African American women have declined to less than 10 percent, and for white men to slightly more than 10 percent. However, older African American men still exceed the target set, with more than 20 percent who report smoking (NCHS, 2003).

In contrast to improvements in smoking and other health behaviors, nutritional and exercise habits have not improved to levels envisioned by *Healthy People 2000.* Although obesity is less common among older Americans than in other age groups, many chronic diseases such as heart

> **CHANGES IN HEALTH HABITS TO REDUCE RISKS**
> - controlling blood pressure and weight
> - stopping cigarette smoking
> - reducing cholesterol levels
> - engaging in regular, moderate exercise
> - practicing stress-management techniques such as meditation

disease and diabetes are associated with obesity. The target of no more than 20 percent overweight elders was exceeded in the most recent national survey, with 37 percent of older adults being considered overweight in 1999 (Merck Institute, 2002). Elders of color and low-income older persons are at greatest risk for obesity. Nevertheless, improving nutritional patterns are reflected in decreased consumption of saturated fats and increased intake of vegetables, fruits, and complex carbohydrates during the past decade. Surveys have revealed that 32 percent of older adults have improved their nutritional intake, considerably lower than the target of 50 percent set by *Healthy People 2000* (Butler, 2000).

Some of the most successful health promotion interventions have occurred with older adults who have some chronic health conditions. For example, a dietary self-management program using interactive computer technology and individualized health messages for people with Type II diabetes resulted in significant improvements in nutritional habits and health care costs (Glasgow et al., 1997). Another study focused on exercise therapy for older adults with osteoarthritis in their knees. Aerobic exercise performed regularly over 15 months was more effective than health education alone in reducing arthritis pain and functional disability in this population (Ettinger et al., 1997). Long-term success in these programs appears to be related to improvements in health conditions for older adults who are coping with specific chronic diseases. Other factors that can improve the likelihood of success for health promotion programs include:

- utilizing social support, such as exercise groups or pairs
- opportunities for intergenerational activities (e.g., healthy eating programs for grandparents and grandchildren)
- utilizing available resources such as outdoor paths or malls for walking programs
- culturally sensitive nutritional and exercise interventions with written and oral materials in the elders' native language

In summary, health promotion programs must be designed to fit the lifestyle, preferences, and cultural values of older adults who are the targets of such efforts. Older adults can benefit from health promotion activities that take such factors into account.

The Relationship of Health Practices to Health Outcomes

Considerable research demonstrates the relationship of personal health habits to active aging or aging well. Factors that are related to good health outcomes include:

- not smoking
- limiting alcohol consumption
- maintaining one's weight in the ideal range
- sleeping seven to eight hours per night
- maintaining moderate levels of aerobic exercise

These relationships appear to be cumulative and independent of age, sex, and economic status. Additional epidemiological evidence demonstrates links between specific health habits and decreased longevity and/or increased health risks. These specific lifestyle factors, discussed briefly below, include alcohol consumption, cigarette smoking, diet, and exercise.

The relationship between drinking alcohol and physical health in old age is U-shaped, with the least healthy tending to be those who drink heavily and those who abstain, although abstain-

> **POINTS TO PONDER**
>
> Identify healthy and unhealthy behaviors in your lifestyle. Have you ever tried to modify these behaviors? If so, what techniques worked for you? To what extent can lifestyle changes after age 65 overcome the effects of poor health habits acquired during youth and middle age?

ers may include former heavy drinkers who have damaged their systems. Light drinking may have some cardiovascular benefits, as discussed later in this chapter. Excessive drinking (five or more drinks at a single sitting) contributes to poor physical health, more frequent hospitalizations, decreased cognitive function, poorer metabolism of prescription medications, and premature death.

The effects of cigarette smoking, especially in interaction with other risk factors, on heart disease, emphysema, and lung cancer have been extensively documented. Smokers who use oral contraceptives, are exposed to asbestos, have excessive alcohol consumption, or are at risk for hypertension have a greater chance of experiencing a nonfatal myocardial infarction and are at significant risk for cancers of the oral cavity and lung. Smoking can reduce bone density and musculoskeletal strength and interfere with the absorption of some medications. The longer one is exposed to tobacco, the greater these risks. However, quitting smoking can gradually reduce some of these health risks. For example, people who quit smoking 5 or more years ago have been shown to reduce their risk of stroke to the same level as those who never smoked (Doll, 1999).

Poor diet is related to obesity, cancer, and heart disease. Obesity carries an increased risk of cardiovascular and pulmonary difficulties, aggravates other conditions such as hypertension, arthritis, and diabetes, and adds risk to surgery. Interpretation of the relationship between obesity and morbidity and mortality is difficult, however. This is because obesity is correlated with other risk factors, such as high blood pressure.

Recent clinical studies have identified the effects of specific dietary behaviors on health outcomes. A moderate reduction in dietary fat consumption, to 26 percent of total calories, may be more beneficial than a severe reduction (18 percent fat) in reducing cholesterol levels. Indeed, among men with high levels of LDL (bad cholesterol) and triglycerides (a type of fat found in blood), those who reduced their fat intake to 26 percent showed the greatest reduction in LDL and triglycerides, while maintaining their HDL (good cholesterol) levels. When fat intake decreased to 18 percent, HDL levels also declined (Knopp et al., 1997). More recent research with 50- to 89-year-old adults who modified their fat intake to include two-thirds from vegetable sources and only one-third from animal fats demonstrated a decrease in cholesterol levels for adults whose baseline level was 233 mg/dL or higher, and a reduction in risk of death from coronary heart disease (Chernoff, 2001).

Another nutritional problem of older adults is insufficient intake of certain nutrients. As many as 40 percent of older people may have diets that are deficient in three or more nutrients. Up to 15 percent may have vitamin B_{12} deficiency, which is necessary for the production of blood cells and healthy functioning of the nervous system. These deficiencies are in part due to inadequate intake of milk, eggs, vegetables, fruit, and other sources of these nutrients. They may also result from poorer absorption of nutrients by the gastrointestinal (GI) system in older adults, especially those on multiple medications that affect GI absorption. Antioxidants were described in Chapter 3 and include vitamins A, C, E, zinc, and selenium. Some middle-aged and older adults read claims in the media of a relationship between antioxidant intake and slowing of the aging process, prevention of cancer, and cognitive decline. Although many of these claims have not been verified by research, they have led many people to use supplements of these nutrients in large doses. There is some evidence that use of supplemental antioxidants can indeed reduce the risk of developing some can-

cers, but it is better to obtain the necessary nutrients through a well-balanced diet of foods rich in these antioxidants. By following the National Cancer Institute's "Five-a-Day" campaign to consume at least five servings of fruits and vegetables per day, older adults can reduce their chances of developing colon and other types of cancer (Chernoff, 2001; Gray et al., 2003).

Excessive alcohol use by older adults can cause significant health problems, as discussed in Chapter 6. However, moderate use is shown to have beneficial effects. Consuming one to two servings of red wine with dinner, 2 to 4 times per week, appears to increase levels of HDL, the "good" cholesterol, in the blood while preventing oxidation of LDL. Polyphenols found in abundance in red wine (and less so in white wine) also reduce blood clotting and may reduce the incidence of heart attacks, as demonstrated by the "French paradox," that is, the lower rates of heart attacks among the French, who consume more red wine than Americans. It is important to note that all these benefits derive from *moderate,* not excessive consumption of wine (Frankl, 2003).

Exercise as Part of Health Promotion

There is considerable evidence of the relationship between regular, vigorous exercise and reduction in a person's chances of dying from heart disease and cancer, as well as hospital admissions for serious illness (DiPietro, 2001; Fried, Kronmal, and Newman, 1998; LaCroix et al., 1996). Physical activity is also important for older adults who have chronic heart disease. People who have been diagnosed with heart disease and participate in a regular, moderate exercise program can reduce their risk of cardiac death by 20 to 25 percent, as well as the possibility of disability. Both low- and high-intensity exercise programs can improve aerobic capacity and physical strength among the old-old. It can alleviate the problem of "stiff joints" and lower back pain reported by many older people by improving their flexibility and range of motion. Aerobic exercise and strength

> ### BENEFITS OF A DAILY, BRISK 30-MINUTE WALK FOR OLDER ADULTS
>
> - lowers blood pressure
> - boosts HDL cholesterol in blood
> - reduces risk of blood clots
> - reduces risk of heart attacks
> - reduces risk of strokes
> - boosts metabolic rate
> - reduces body fat, improves lean muscle mass
> - helps manage Type II diabetes
> - reduces risk of osteoporosis
> - improves long-term recovery from depression

training are also shown to improve the functional health of older adults with Type II diabetes. Physical activity can even reduce the risk of falls among older people, thereby preventing disability and the high costs of treatment and long-term care associated with falls (Evans, 1999; Merz and Forrester, 1997; U.S. Preventive Services Task Force, 1996; Vincent et al., 2002; WHO, 1998).

Regular exercise is found to reduce the risk of breast cancer. A large study of almost 75,000 women aged 50 to 79 who were enrolled in the Women's Health Initiative (described earlier) compared women who walked at least 10 hours per week with their counterparts who were sedentary. The former lowered their risk of developing breast cancer by 30 percent over the sedentary group. The greatest benefit was obtained by lighter-weight women, followed by women of normal weight and those who were slightly overweight. No racial or age differences emerged in the benefits of exercise. No additional benefits were accrued from more vigorous exercise such as jogging or tennis, suggesting that a simple but regular routine of walking daily can play an important role in preventing breast cancer (McTiernan et al., 2003). The box above summarizes some of the health benefits of a regular walking regimen, but it should be noted that the benefits are greatest if people begin this exercise habit during young adulthood or middle age and not wait until their 60s or 70s.

Up to 50 percent of physical changes in older people that are mistakenly attributed to aging may be due to being physically unfit. Physically inactive people age faster and look older than physically fit persons of the same age, in part because of what has been termed **hypokinesia,** a disease of "disuse," or the degeneration and functional loss of muscle and bone tissue. **Sarcopenia** is analogous to **osteopenia,** described earlier, where aging bone loses its mineral content and places the older person at increased risk for falls and fractures. Sarcopenia refers to the atrophy of muscle and can affect all muscle groups, weakening the upper body and arms. It can impair balance and cause difficulties in rising from a chair, bathtub or toilet and in maintaining elders' functional independence. Both men and women are at increasing risk for sarcopenia after age 75 (Foldvari et al., 2000).

Exercise can slow this loss of muscle mass or lean body mass. Older people who participate in higher-intensity resistance training 30 minutes per day can improve muscle mass and strength. Strength-training programs have been successful after just 8 to 12 weeks with institutionalized elders, improving their muscular strength, gait velocity (walking speed), and stair-climbing ability (Di Pietro, 2001, Evans, 1999; Hewitt, 2003).

Older people with all levels of ability can benefit from outdoor activities.

POINTS TO PONDER

Think about people you know who are between ages 75 to 85. What makes some of them look older, while others look younger than their chronological age? Compare their diets, smoking history, and exercise habits. Are there differences in their diets? Are any of them currently smokers or have they smoked in the past? What physical activities are they participating in, and what did they do in the past?

Despite the known benefits of exercise, less than 30 percent of older Americans participate in *regular* physical activity. In the 1994–1996 National Health Interview Survey, 70 percent of people aged 65 and older who had no disabilities reported doing some form of exercise at least once in the past week. However, only about 33 percent of these respondents achieved recommended levels of activity and intensity in their exercise (NCHS, 2000a). National recommendations to increase physical activity have made only a modest impact on older people, as demonstrated by a comparison of four cohorts of older men and three cohorts of older women enrolled in the Baltimore Longitudinal Study of Aging (described in Chapters 1 and 3). When leisure-time activity trends of cohorts who were age 65 and older in 1958 through 1998 were compared, the proportion of men performing high-intensity physical activities doubled over the four decades. However, in this sample of older adults who are generally more health-conscious than the general population, older women in 1998 were no more likely to engage in moderate or high-intensity physical activities than their counterparts in 1978 and 1988 (Talbot, Fleg, and Metter, 2003).

Exercise needs to occur regularly, not just once a week or less. For example, in the Physicians' Health Study with 21,481 men, those who exercised less than once a week were 74 times more likely to die during exertion than men who exercised five or more times per week. This study concluded that exercise should be vigorous and last at least 30 to 60 minutes each time (Albert et al., 2000). New national objectives have been established for regular exercise, stating that adults and children over age 6 should engage in moderate physical activity at least 30 minutes each day (*Healthy People 2010*). But current activity levels among most older adults are so low that meeting objectives for *Healthy People 2010* will require significant behavioral changes among at least one-half of people aged 65 and older. Successful strategies to increase physical activity include goal-setting, self-monitoring, group support, and regular telephone supervision of home-based activity programs. Older adults tend to adhere better to individualized home-based exercise programs than to classes with other elders (Di Pietro, 2001; King, 2001).

Nevertheless, there are indications of improvements in Americans' other health behaviors over the past decade. For example, the National Survey of Self-Care and Aging asked older adults to describe the type and frequency of their personal health care behaviors. Researchers then examined the association between these behaviors and subsequent hospitalization rates and Medicare reimbursements. They found lower likelihood of hospitalization and lower Medicare expenses among older adults who:

- maintained a healthy weight
- never smoked
- participated in regular physical exercise
- worked in their garden
- regularly checked their pulse and blood pressure
- modified their homes to prevent falls (e.g., removing throw rugs, installing extra lighting on stairs) (Stearns et al., 1997)

Increasing physical activity levels from sedentary to participation in 30 minutes of exercise even for 2 days per week can significantly reduce health care costs. In a study of more than 2000 adults whose average age was 63, comparisons in activity levels over 1 year revealed significant savings in both inpatient and outpatient health care costs. The greatest decline ($2200) was found for elders who increased from 0 to 1 day to 3 or more days per week of physical activity, a relatively minor change. These savings compensated in part for the health care costs of people with multiple chronic conditions who increased their exercise levels (Martinson et al., 2003).

The dramatic impact of self-care behaviors on health care costs, and hospital and physician use is an important indicator of the benefits for both individuals and society of a healthy lifestyle in the later years. Psychosocial conditions, particularly a loss of control, excessive stress, and the absence of social supports, are also linked to decreased longevity and/or poor health. As discussed in Chapter 9, epidemiologic studies also indicate that lower morbidity and greater longevity are found among people who:

- are married
- have close contacts with friends and relatives
- share common religious, ethnic, or cultural interests with others

Health Promotion Guidelines

Given the growing evidence about the relation of health practices to health status, most health promotion programs include components on injury prevention, nutrition, exercise, and stress management. Oral health promotion is also implemented in geriatric dentistry. An underlying theme is taking greater responsibility for one's own health, rather than relying on medical professionals. Health contracts, some as simple as making a calendar with health promotion goals one achieves each day, can help older adults maintain healthy habits. Elders who record specific behaviors (e.g., brisk walking for 30 minutes, eating five servings of vegetables) on a daily basis can increase their perceived competence and self-efficacy regarding their own health (Haber and Looney, 2000). Some health promotion programs

for older adults focus on this type of individual action. Others educate participants to change the larger social environment through collective action. Several components of health promotion programs are briefly summarized.

1. NUTRITION   Although information on older people's dietary needs is incomplete and often contradictory, the basic principles are:

- Consume a wide variety of foods, especially fruits, vegetables, and protein.
- Increase consumption of unprocessed foods containing complex carbohydrates (starch and fiber), such as whole grains and legumes.
- Restrict intake of sugar, fat, and cholesterol-containing foods.
- Increase consumption of calcium, especially for postmenopausal women.

Unfortunately, there are a number of physiological, social, and emotional barriers to adequate nutrition. Any nutritional assessment of an older person must take account of such factors that can affect the amount and type of food consumed:

- inability to chew and swallow due to no teeth, missing teeth, or loose-fitting dentures
- problems with taste or smell
- poor digestion of certain foods
- social isolation that deprives the older person from mealtime socialization
- the cost of some healthy foods
- difficulty obtaining healthy foods

2. EXERCISE   Exercise programs need to be tailored to take account of variability in physical function and fitness levels. Past exercise programs for older people often have been overly cautious. Instead, older adults need to be challenged to obtain the full benefits of an appropriately designed exercise program (National Institute on Aging, 1999a). Beyond the benefits of aerobic fitness, a

variety of physical activities, including weight training, are important for:

- maintaining overall muscle strength and endurance
- joint mobility, balance
- upright posture
- managing specific chronic diseases
- improving immune function

Prior to beginning a regular exercise program, older people should have a thorough medical examination, including a treadmill or other exercise tolerance test, to determine their baselines for physical fitness. Brisk walking is one of the safest and best exercises. Most ambulatory older persons, even those at a lower level of fitness, can build up their walking to one or more miles daily, and at a speed of three or four miles per hour. Indeed, even older adults with multiple chronic conditions have shown significant improvements in their speed of walking, gait, balance, and grip strength following a year of low-intensity exercise and weight training (Sharpe et al., 1997). There is evidence that greater physiological benefits, such as fat loss and cardiovascular change, require more intense and vigorous exercise, such as jogging or bicycling, which can be safely undertaken by healthy older people. Exercise can also reduce symptoms of depression in older adults who

A SUCCESSFUL GROUP EXERCISE PROGRAM

Senior centers may be ideal settings for health promotion programs that emphasize exercise. At the Northshore Senior Center in Bothell, Washington, the Senior Wellness Program was established between the center and researchers at the University of Washington. A six-month exercise intervention was completed by 85 percent of participants, with at least 90 percent attending any one session. These rates are much higher than individually focused interventions, perhaps because of group support for continuing with the activity program. Not only did functional health improve, but participants showed fewer symptoms of depression after the intervention than a matched sample in the same center that did not participate in the exercise program (Wallace et al., 1998).

participate in a 20-week structured exercise program compared with depressed elders who attend lectures on health care (Singh, Clements, and Fiatarone-Singh, 2001).

Oral Health Promotion

Preventive dentistry is included in only a few health promotion programs. One reason for this is that dental disease and tooth loss are frequently assumed to be natural concomitants of aging.

With increased preventive dentistry earlier in life, more people are retaining their natural teeth into old age (DHHS, 2000). Those with teeth remaining should perform regular oral health care, including brushing, flossing, and appropriate visits to a dentist or hygienist. Older people, however, are not only less inclined to use professional dental services, but also to know and value preventive dentistry techniques. Therefore, prevention must be defined differently by age. In younger persons, the initiation of dental disease and tooth loss can be prevented; in older adults, the goals are to prevent *further* tooth loss and diseases that are secondary to other medical condi-

AN IDEAL EXERCISE PROGRAM

- begins with a low level of activity
- includes an initial warm-up, with stretching, light calisthenics
- proceeds to leisurely walking
- consists of more strenuous exercise for 20 minutes or more
- ends with a relaxing cool-down period of 5 to 10 minutes of light exercise
- this pattern should be repeated at least three times each week

tions and/or medications (e.g., dry mouth caused by some medications that are used to treat hypertension and depression).

Limitations of Health Promotion

Health promotion programs are sometimes criticized for their emphasis on individual responsibility for change, which minimizes the societal health and economic disparities that underlie individual health practices such as poverty. Likewise, some educational efforts ignore the roles of policy makers, health care providers, food manufacturers, and the mass media in creating social and economic environments that may counter health promotion interventions. In addition to educating individuals to adopt healthy habits, the broader social environment must be changed.

In general, organized health promotion programs have difficulty recruiting more than 50 percent of the target population. This is true even for programs focused on people diagnosed with a potentially deadly condition such as post–myocardial infarct patients and those with high blood pressure. Attrition is also high, with rates of 30 to 60 percent. Older people most likely to participate in organized health promotion are those with a preventive attitude (e.g., regular users of physicians and dentists for checkups, nonsmokers, exercisers, and users of seat belts and smoke alarms) and those with higher participation rates in community services generally.

Another limitation is that, although the value of health promotion is widely publicized, individuals often do not act on this information. Think about the number of people who continue to smoke despite the empirical evidence linking smoking to lung cancer, or the small proportion of women over age 45 who have a Pap smear and breast exam on a regular basis even though such tests are important in detecting cancer. The gap between health knowledge and health practices can be large. On the other hand, older people are more likely to change their health behaviors after

> ### HEALTH PROMOTION ON A LARGER SCALE
>
> Health promotion efforts at a community and even a national level have demonstrated dramatic effects. In the early 1970s, the government of Finland responded to high rates of cardiovascular disease in its southeastern region with the North Karelia Project. Local communities passed bans on smoking in public zones. Dairy farms were converted to growing berries that reduced residents' intake of fatty milk while simultaneously increasing their intake of berries high in vitamin C. By 1997, death rates from both lung cancer and heart disease had declined by 70 percent. On the other hand, just a few miles away, in northwestern Russia, the health of the local population has declined; death rates from heart disease, cancer, and emphysema have increased because of worsening environmental and economic conditions with the collapse of the Soviet Union (*New York Times,* 2000).

learning new self-care topics than are younger people (Yusuf et al., 1996).

Even when individual behavior change is a legitimate goal, sustaining health practices over time is difficult in the face of years of habit. Longitudinal research is needed to assess the long-range (ten years or more) consequences of health promotion interventions for individuals and for health care costs, especially since programs may initially be very costly before they achieve long-run savings.

Nevertheless, it is encouraging that short-term educational programs that improve older participants' knowledge and preventive health behaviors in the areas of cancer, heart disease, and oral diseases have shown continued benefits at their termination (Kiyak, 1996). The most effective prevention appears to come from two approaches: eliminating iatrogenic disease that is induced in the patient by medical care, especially with regard to the side effects of medications, and preventing the transformation from disease to disability. Health promotion is clearly a growing

POINTS TO PONDER

Think about a health habit that you have tried to change, such as increasing your daily exercise and intake of fruits and vegetables. What difficulties did you face in making the desired changes? What are some strategies that worked for you? Could these same methods be used to help older adults change lifelong habits?

area, especially in light of pressure from Medicare, health maintenance organizations (HMOs), and private insurers to reduce rising health care costs for older adults.

Implications for the Future

As baby boomers age, several trends may emerge. First, this cohort includes more informed, health-conscious consumers than their predecessors. As a result, they will make more demands from the health care system, not just for themselves but for those for whom they are caregivers. A greater proportion than among previous cohorts will continue their self-care and wellness focus. Many will achieve *Healthy People 2010* objectives that their parents have not been able to achieve. At the same time, however, a significant minority of baby boomers, particularly smokers and those who have lived a lifetime in poverty with little access to preventive services, will cope with multiple chronic diseases as their life span increases.

Changes in the health care system will also influence future cohorts' access to and use of health services. For example, because of increased cost containment efforts (described in Chapter 17), more adults are enrolled in health maintenance organizations (HMOs) for their health care. In 1998, 78 million Americans were enrolled in HMOs; the numbers are expected to rise to 102 million by 2005 and 125 million by 2010. Of the 102 million in 2005, 25 percent are expected to be elders and people with disabilities who are enrolled in

Medicare (RWJF, 2003). To the extent that these health care systems are truly focused on health *maintenance,* elders will have opportunities to participate in health promotion activities. However, if services are limited and preventive programs such as exercise, smoking cessation, and nutritional counseling are not offered, future cohorts of elders will not have ready access to health promotion. The growth of health technology, including telemedicine and home-based medication dispensers that prevent under- or overmedication, can help future elders manage their own health. The impact of these technologies on older adults' ability to live independently and to age in place in their own homes is discussed in Chapter 11.

As demonstrated by the numerous indicators of improving health status and survival with multiple chronic diseases among the older population, there is a growing need for health care providers trained in gerontology and clinical geriatrics. There will be a need not only for gerontologically knowledgeable physicians, but also for dentists, pharmacists, nurses and nurse practitioners, social workers, as well as health educators, physical therapists, and occupational therapists who help future cohorts of elders manage their chronic conditions and maximize their functional abilities. The shortage of physicians and pharmacists trained in geriatrics is one reason why older Americans experience adverse reactions to medications and high rates of emergency room and inpatient hospital visits. These preventable conditions are blamed for about $20 billion in hospital stays among older adults (GAO, 1995). Health care providers who are trained in geriatrics are more likely to encourage exercise programs, smoking cessation, and dietary interventions for older people and less likely to endorse stereotypes of aging as a time of decline. Indeed, there is evidence for better health outcomes for older adults who receive specialized geriatric nursing and physician care (Kovner, Mezey, and Harrington, 2002).

The increasing need for geriatric nurse specialists comes at a time when the nursing profession is experiencing a shortage in all specialties and the median age of nurses today, 45, is higher than all other health professions. These trends do not bode well for the field of geriatric nursing care. Today only about 10,000 of the 2.56 million registered nurses are certified in gerontological nursing, while only 3 percent of the 111,000 advanced practice nurses are geriatric nurse practitioners. Likewise, the number of physicians specializing in geriatrics is far from adequate. In 2000, about 9000 geriatricians were available to treat a population of 35 million elders. This is less than half the projected need for the current patient pool, and only one-fourth of the number needed by 2030. The situation in pharmacy is especially dire, with only 720 of 200,000 pharmacists who have received certification in geriatrics (Alliance for Aging Research, 2002; Scharlach, Simon, and Dal Santo, 2002). Social workers, who are key members of interdisciplinary health care teams, are not yet prepared to meet the growing demand for geriatric social work. The National Institute on Aging has projected a need for 60,000 to 70,000 geriatric social workers by 2020; yet less than 10 percent of that projected need is currently available. In fact, only about 4 percent of social workers with Masters degrees work in services targeted at older adults. Unless health professional schools become more proactive in recruiting faculty to develop geriatric curricula, the current situation will grow into a crisis. The federal government has taken an important first step by passing the Geriatric Care Act in 2001, aimed at improving Medicare reimbursement for geriatric care and offering incentives for health professionals to obtain training in this field. In addition, the John A. Hartford Foundation remains the primary source of funding for professional development and mentoring in geriatrics in many health care disciplines.

Summary

Although older adults are at risk of more diseases than younger people, most older people rate their own health as satisfactory. Health status refers not only to an individual's physical condition, but also to her or his functional level in various social and psychological domains. It is affected by a person's social surroundings, especially the degree of environmental stress and social support available. Although stress has been found to increase the risk of certain illnesses, such as cardiovascular disease, older people are generally less negatively affected by it; this may reflect maturity, self-control, or a lifetime of developing coping skills.

Older people are more likely to suffer from chronic or long-term diseases than from temporary or acute illnesses. The majority of older persons, however, are not limited in their daily activities by chronic conditions. The impact of such conditions apparently varies with the physiological changes that occur with age, the individual's adaptive resources, and his or her mental and emotional perspective. The type and incidence of chronic conditions also vary by gender.

The leading causes of death among persons over age 65 are heart disease, cancer, accidents, and stroke. Diseases of the heart and blood vessels are the most prevalent. Since hypertension or high blood pressure is a major risk in the development of cardiovascular problems, preventive actions are critical, especially weight control, dietary changes, appropriate exercise, and avoidance of cigarette smoking. Cancers, especially lung, bowel, and colon cancers, are the second most frequent cause of death among older persons; the risk of cancer increases with age. Cerebrovascular disease, or stroke, is the third leading cause of death among older persons. It may be caused by cerebral thrombosis, or blood clots, and by cerebral hemorrhage. Healthy lifestyle practices are important in preventing these deaths.

Arthritis, although not fatal, is a major cause of limited daily activity and is extremely common among older persons. Osteoporosis, or loss of bone mass and the resultant increased brittleness of the bones, is most common among older women, and may result in fractures of the hip, spine, and wrist. New research supports the benefits of physical exercise for preventing fractures and managing arthritis. Chronic respiratory problems, particularly emphysema, increase with age, especially among men. Diabetes mellitus is a frequent problem in old age, and is particularly troubling because of the many related illnesses that may result. Problems with the intestinal tract include diverticulitis, constipation, and hiatus hernia. Cystitis and incontinence are frequently occurring problems of the kidneys and urinary system. Although the majority of older persons have some type of incontinence, many kinds can be treated and controlled.

The growth of the older population, combined with the increase in major chronic illnesses, has placed greater demands on the health care system. Nevertheless, older people seek outpatient medical, dental, and mental health services at a slightly lower rate than their incidence of chronic illnesses would predict. Like younger people, the older population is most likely to seek health services for acute problems, not for checkups on chronic conditions or for preventive care. Beliefs that physicians, dentists, and mental health professionals cannot cure their chronic problems may deter many older people from seeking needed care. The problem may be compounded by the beliefs of some health care providers who have not been trained in geriatrics that older people are poor candidates for health services. More training in geriatrics and gerontology is needed for health care providers and skills to address their attitudes toward working with older people.

Health promotion is shown to be effective in improving the well-being and enhancing the quality of life of older people. The elimination or postponement of the chronic diseases that are associated with old age is a major goal for health promotion specialists and biomedical researchers. Treatment methods for all these diseases are changing rapidly with the growth in medical technology and the increasing recognition given to such environmental factors as stress, nutrition, and exercise in disease prevention. If health promotion efforts to modify lifestyles are successful, and if aging research progresses substantially, the chronic illnesses that we have discussed will undoubtedly be postponed, and disability or loss of functional status will be delayed until advanced old age.

GLOSSARY

acute condition   short-term disease or infection, often debilitating to older persons

acute myocardial infarction   loss of blood flow to a specific region of the heart, resulting in damage of the myocardium

ADL   activities of daily living summarizes an individual's performance in personal care tasks such as bathing or dressing, as well as such home-management activities as shopping, meal preparation, and taking medications

arteriosclerosis   loss of elasticity of the arterial walls

benign hypertrophy of the prostate   enlargement of the prostate gland in older men, without signs of cancer or other serious disease; may cause discomfort

chronic condition   long-term (more than three months), often permanent, and leaving a residual disability that may require long-term management or care rather than cure

comorbidity   simultaneously experiencing multiple health problems, both acute and chronic

contracture   the loss of flexibility or freezing of a joint due to lack of use

diagnosis related groups (DRGs)   a system of classifying medical cases for payment on the basis of diagnoses; used under Medicare's prospective payment system (PPS) for inpatient hospital services

disability   an impairment in the ability to complete multiple daily tasks

diverticulitis   a condition in which pouches or sacs (diverticula) in the intestinal wall become inflamed and infected

edentulous   the absence of natural teeth

frailty   severe limitations in ADL

good health   more than the mere absence of infirmity, a state of complete physical, mental, and social well-being

health promotion   a model in which individuals are responsible for and in control of their own health, including a combination of health education and related organizational, political, and economic changes conducive to health

health status   the presence or absence of disease as well as the degree of disability in an individual's level of functioning

hiatus hernia   a condition in which a small portion of the stomach slides up through the diaphragm

hypokinesia   the degeneration and functional loss of muscle and bone due to physical inactivity

IADL (Instrumental Activities of Daily Living)   Daily activities involving use of the environment.

immunity   resistance to environmental carcinogens, viruses, and bacteria

incontinence   the inability to control urine and feces—of two types: urge incontinence, where a person is not able to hold urine long enough to reach a toilet, and stress incontinence, where leakage occurs during physical exertion, laughing, sneezing, or coughing

osteopenia   a significant loss of calcium and reduced bone density not associated with increased risk of fractures

quality of life   going beyond health status alone, this concept considers the individual's sense of competence, ability to perform activities of daily living, and satisfaction with social interactions, in addition to functional health

rheumatoid arthritis   a chronic inflammation of the membranes lining joints and tendons, characterized by pain, swelling, bone dislocation, and limited range of motion; can occur at any age

sarcopenia   atrophy of skeletal muscle mass, generally resulting from a sedentary lifestyle and some chronic diseases

stress   the gamut of social-psychological stimuli that produce physiological responses of shallow, rapid breathing, muscle tension, increased blood pressure, and accelerated heart rate

REFERENCES

AARP. Beyond 50. *A report to the nation on independent living and disability.* Washington, DC: AARP Public Policy Institute, 2003.

Albert, C. M., Mittleman, M. A., Chae, C. U., Lee, I. M., Hennekens, C. H., and Manson, J. E. Triggering of sudden death from cardiac causes by vigorous exertion. *New England Journal of Medicine,* 2000, *343,* 1355–1361.

Alliance for Aging Research. *Medical never-never land: Ten reasons why America is not ready for the coming age boom.* Washington, DC: Alliance for Aging Research, 2002.

American Cancer Society. *Breast cancer questions and answers; Cancer facts for men.* ACS, 2001.

Baker, C. W., Whisman, M. A., and Brownell, K. D. (2000). Studying intergenerational transmission of eating attitudes and behaviors. Methodological and conceptual questions. *Health Psychology, 19*(4), 376–381.

Bazargan, M., Bazargan, S., and Baker, R. S. Emergency department utilization, hospital admissions, and physician visits among elderly African American persons. *The Gerontologist,* 1998, *38,* 25–36.

Bédard, M., Stones, M. J., Guyatt, G. H., and Hirdes, J. P. Traffic-related fatalities among older drivers and passengers: Past and future trends. *The Gerontologist,* 2001, *41,* 751–756.

Berg, R. L., and Cassells, J. S. (Eds.). *The second fifty years: Promoting health and preventing disability.* Washington, DC: Institute of Medicine, National Academy Press, 1992.

Bernard, S. L., Kincade, J. E., Konrad, T. R., Arcury, T. A., and Rabiner, D. Predicting mortality from community surveys of older adults: The importance of self-rated functional ability. *Journals of Gerontology: Social Sciences,* 1997, *52,* S155–S163.

Breslow, L. From disease prevention to health promotion. *Journal of the American Medical Association,* 1999, *281,* 1030–1033.

Breslow, L., and Breslow, N. Health practices and disability: Some evidence from Alameda County. *Preventive Medicine,* 1993, *22,* 86–95.

Butler, R. N., *Maintaining healthy lifestyles.* Workshop report of the International Longevity Center, 2000.

Centers for Disease Control and Prevention (CDC). AIDS among persons aged ≥50 years—United States, 1991–1996. *Morbidity and Mortality Weekly Report,* 1998, *47,* 21–27.

Centers for Disease Control and Prevention (CDC). *HIV/AIDS Surveillance Report—Mid-Year Edition,* 2001, *13,* 14.

Centers for Disease Control and Prevention (CDC). Hospitalizations for stroke among adults aged ≥65 years: U.S., 2000. *MMWR Public Health Report,* 2003a, *52,* 586–589.

Centers for Disease Control and Prevention (CDC). National Center for Chronic Disease Prevention and Health Promotion. http://www.cdc.gov/brfss, 2003b.

Centers for Disease Control and Prevention (CDC). Percentage of persons aged >65 who reported receiving influenza or pneumococcal vaccine. http://www.cdc.gov/mmwr/preview/mmwrhtml/figures/m025a2tl.gif, 2003c.

Centers for Disease Control and Prevention (CDC). Pneumonia and influenza death rates: United States 1979–1994. *Morbidity and Mortality Weekly Reports,* 1995, *44,* 535–537.

Chernoff, R. Nutrition and health promotion in older adults. *Journals of Gerontology,* 2001, *56A*(Special Issue II), 47–53.

Chiu, K. M. Efficacy of calcium supplements on bone mass in postmenopausal women. *Journals of Gerontology: Medical Sciences,* 1999, 54A, M275–M280.

Clancey, C. M., and Bierman, A. S. Quality and outcomes of care for older women with chronic disease. *Women's Health Issues,* 2000, *10,* 178–192.

Compston, J. E., and Rosen, C. J. *Fast facts: Osteoporosis.* Oxford, U.K.: Health Press, 1997.

Cramer, N. Promoting continence: Strategies for success. *Perspectives in Health Promotion and Aging,* 1993, *1,* 1–3.

Cranney, A., Tugwell, P., Wells, G., and Guyatt, G.; Osteoporosis Methodology Group and the Osteoporosis Research Advisory Group. Meta-analyses of therapies for postmenopausal osteoporosis. I. Systematic reviews of randomized trials in osteoporosis: Introduction and methodology. *Endocrine Reviews,* 2002, *23,* 496–507.

Crimmins, E. M., and Saito, Y. Trends in healthy life expectancy in the United States: Gender, racial and educational differences. *Social Science and Medicine,* 2001, *52,* 1629–1641.

Cummings, S. R., Nevitt, M. C., Browner, W. S., Stone, K., Fox, K. M., and Ensrud, K. E. Risk factors for hip fractures in white women. *New England Journal of Medicine,* 1995, *332,* 767–773.

Di Pietro, L. Physical activity in aging: Changes in patterns and their relationship to health and function. *Journals of Gerontology,* 2001, *56A*(Special Issue II), 13–22.

Dignam, J. J. Differences in breast cancer prognosis among African American and Caucasian women. *CA—A Cancer Journal for Clinicians,* 2000, *50,* 50–64.

Doll, R. Risk from tobacco and potentials for health gain. *International Journal of Tuberculosis and Lung Disease,* 1999, *3,* 90–99.

Emlet, C. A., and Berghuis, J. P. Service priorities, use and needs: Views of older and younger consumers living with HIV/AIDS. *Journal of Mental Health and Aging,* 2002, *8,* 307–318.

Emlet, C. A., and Farcas, K. J. Correlates of service utilization among midlife and older adults with HIV/AIDS. *Journal of Aging and Health,* 2002, *14,* 315–335.

Ettinger, W. H., Burns, R., Messier, S. P., Applegate, W., Rejeski, W. J., et al. The fitness arthritis and seniors trial. *JAMA,* 1997, *277,* 25–31.

Evans, W. J. Exercise training guidelines for the elderly. *Medical Science and Sports Exercise,* 1999, *31,* 12–17.

Ferrucci, L., Kittner, S. J., Corti, M. C., and Guralnik, J. M. Neurological conditions. In J. M. Guralnick, L. P. Fried, E. M. Simonsick, J. D., Kaspar, and M. E. Lafferty (Eds.), *The women's health and aging study.* Bethesda, MD: NIH/NIA, 1995.

Flaherty, J. H., Perry, H. M., Lynchard, G. S., and Morley, J. E. Polypharmacy and hospitalization among older home care patients. *Journals of Gerontology: Medical Sciences,* 2000, *55A,* M554–M559.

Foldvari, M., Clark, M., Laviolette, L., Bernstein, M., Kaliton, D., Castaneda, C., et al. Association of muscle power with functional status in community-dwelling elderly women. *Journals of Gerontology Series A: Biological Sciences and Medical Sciences,* 2000, *55,* M192–M199.

Foley, D. J., Masak, K. H., Ross, G. W., and White, L. R. Driving cessation in older men with incident dementia. *Journal of the American Geriatric Society,* 2000, *48,* 928–930.

Frankl, W. S. Is alcohol good or bad for the heart? *Gerontology News,* 2003, *31,* 2.

Freund, B., and Szinovacz, M. Effects of cognition on driving involvement among the oldest old. *The Gerontologist,* 2002, *42,* 621–633.

Fried, L. P., Kronmal, R. A., and Newman, A. B. Risk factors for 5-year mortality in older adults: The Cardiovascular Health Study. *Journal of the American Medical Association,* 1998, *279,* 585–592.

Fried, L. P., Tangen, C. M., Walston, J., Newman, A. B., Hirsch, C., Seeman, T., Tracy, R., Kop, W. J., Burke, G., and McBurnie, M. A. Frailty in older adults: Evidence for a phenotype. *Journals of Gerontology Series A: Biological Sciences and Medical Sciences,* 2001, *56,* M146–M156.

Fries, J. F. Aging, natural death, and the compression of morbidity. *New England Journal of Medicine,* 1980, *303,* 130–135.

Fries, J. F. The compression of morbidity: Miscellaneous comments about a theme. *The Gerontologist,* 1984, *24,* 354–359.

Glasgow, R. E., LaChance, P. A., Toobert, D. J., Brown, J., Hampson, S. E., and Riddle, M. C. Long term effects and costs of a brief behavioral dietary intervention for patients with diabetes delivered from the medical office. *Patient Education and Counseling,* 1997, *32,* 175–184.

Gorelick, P. B., Shanmugam, V., and Pajeau, A. K. Stroke. In J. E. Birren (Ed.), *Encyclopedia of gerontology,* Vol. 2. San Diego: Academy Press, 1996.

Gray, S. L., Hanlon, J. T., Landerman, L. R., Artz, M., Schmeder, K. E., and Fillenbaum, G. G. Is antioxidant use protective of cognitive function in community-dwelling elderly? *American Journal of Geriatric Pharmacotherapy,* 2003, *1,* 3–10.

Greenwald, D. A., and Brandt, L. J. Gastrointestinal system: Function and dysfunction. In J. E. Birren (Ed.), *Encyclopedia of gerontology,* Vol. 1. San Diego: Academy Press, 1996.

Gresham, G. E., Duncan, P. W., and Stason, W. B. *Poststroke rehabilitation: Assessment, referral, and patient management.* Rockville, MD: USDHHS, Agency for Health Care Policy and Research, 1995.

Haber, D., and Looney, C. Health contract calendars: A tool for health professionals with older adults. *The Gerontologist,* 2000, *40,* 235–239.

Hawkins, S. A., Wiswell, R. A., Jaque, S. V., Constantino, N., Marcell, T. J., Tarpenning, K. M., Schroeder, E. T., and Hyslop, D. M. The inability of hormone replacement therapy or chronic running to maintain bone mass in master athletes. *Journals of Gerontology: Medical Sciences,* 1999, *54A,* M451–M455.

Hayflick, L. *How and why we age.* New York: Ballantine Books, 1996.

Health Resources and Services Administration (HRSA). HIV disease in individuals ages 50 and above. *HRSA Care Action,* February 2001, 1–3.

Healthy People 2010. Understanding and Improving Health. U.S. Government Printing Office. No. 017-001-00547-9, 2000.

Hemmelgarn, B., Suissa, S., Huang, A., Boirin, J. F., and Pinard, G. Benzodiazepine use and the risk of motor vehicle crash in the elderly. *Journal of the American Medical Association,* 1997, *278,* 27–31.

Hewitt, M. J. *Growing older, staying strong: Preventing sarcopenia through strength training.* New York: International Longevity Center, 2003.

Insurance Institute for Highway Safety (IIHS). *Fatality facts, elderly.* Arlington, VA: IIHS. http://www.hwysafety.org/safety%5Ffacts/fatality%5facts/elderly.htm.

Jacob, T., and Johnson, S. L. (2001). Sequential interactions in the parent-child communications of depressed fathers and depressed mothers. *Journal of Family Psychology, 15,* 38–52.

Juvenile Diabetes Foundation. *Diabetes Facts.* http://www.jdfcure.org, 1998.

Kalache, A., and Kickbusch, I. A global strategy for healthy aging. *World Health,* 1997, *4,* 4–5.

Kaufman, D. W., Kelly, J. P., Rosenberg, L., Anderson, T. E., and Mitchell, A. A. Recent patterns of medication use in the ambulatory adult population of the United States. *Journal of the American Medical Association,* 2002, *287,* 337–344.

King, A. C. Interventions to promote physical activity by older adults. *Journals of Gerontology,* 2001, *56A* (Special Issue II), 36–46.

Kiyak, H. A. Measuring psychosocial variables that predict older persons' oral health behavior. *Gerodontology,* 1996, *13,* 69–75.

Knopp, R. H., Walden, C. E., Retzlaff, B. M., McCann, B. S., Dowdy, A. A., Albers, J. J., Gey, G. O., and Cooper, M. N. Long-term cholesterol-lowering effects of 4 fat-restricted diets in hypercholesterolemic and combined hyperlipidemic men. The dietary alternatives study. *Journal of the American Medical Association,* 1997, *278,* 1509–1515.

Kovner, C. T., Mezey, M., and Harrington, C. Who cares for older adults? *Health Affairs,* 2002, *21,* 78–89.

LaCroix, A. Z. *Health promotion for older adults: Osteoporosis.* NWGEC Curriculum Modules, University of Washington, 1997.

LaCroix, A. Z., Leveille, S., Hecht, J., Grothaus, L., and Wagner, E. Does walking reduce the risk of cardiovascular disease and death in older adults? *Journal* of the American Geriatrics Society, 1996, 44, 113–120.

Lau, E. M. C., Suriwongpaisal, P., Lee, J. K., Das De, S., Festin, M. R., Saw, S. M., Khir, A., Torralba, T., Sham, A., and Sambrook, P. Risk factors for hip fracture in Asian men and women: The Asian Osteoporosis Study. Journal of Bone and Mineral Research, 2001, 16, 572–580.

Lawson, D. M., and Brossart, D. F. (2001). Intergenerational transmission: Individuation and intimacy across three generations. Family Process, 40, 429–442.

Leeb, B. F., Schweitzer, H., Montag, K., and Smolen, J. S. A meta-analysis of chondroitin sulfate in the treatment of osteoarthritis. Journal of Rheumatology, 2000, 27, 205–211.

Li, G., Braver, E. R., and Chen, L. H. Fragility versus excessive crash involvement as determinants of high death rates per vehicle-mile of travel among older drivers. Accident Analysis and Prevention, 2003, 35, 227–235.

Lin, E. H. B., Katon, W., VonKorff, M., et al. Effect of improving depression on pain and functional outcomes among older adults with arthritis. Journal of the American Medical Association, 2003, 290, 2428–2434.

Lord, S. R., Sherrington, C., and Menz, H. B. Falls in older people: Risk factors and strategies for prevention. New York: Cambridge University Press, 2001.

Lynch, J. W., Smith, G. D., Kaplan, G. A., and House, J. S. (2000). Income inequality and mortality: Importance to health of individual income, psychosocial environment and material conditions. British Medical Journal, 320, 1200–1204.

Mann, W. C., Ottenbacher, K. J., Fraas, L., Tomita, M. and Granger, C. V. Effectiveness of assistive technology and environmental interventions in maintaining independence and reducing home care costs for the frail elderly. Archives of Family Medicine, 1999, 8, 210–217.

Martinson, B. C., Crain, A. L., Pronk, N. P., O'Conner, P. J., and Maciosek, M. V. Changes in physical activity and short-term changes in health care. Preventive Medicine, 2003, 37, 319–326.

McTiernan, A., Kooperberg, C., White, E., Wilcox, S., Coates, R., Adams-Campbell, L., Woods, N., and Ockene, J. Recreational physical activity and the risk of breast cancer in postmenopausal women:

The Women's Health Initiative Cohort Study. Journal of the American Medical Association, 2003, 290, 1331–1336.

Merz, C. N., and Forrester, J. S. The secondary prevention of coronary heart disease. American Journal of Medicine, 1997, 102, 573–580.

Merck Institute of Aging and Health. The state of aging and health in America. Washington, DC: Merck Institute, 2002.

Mokdad, A. H., Ford, E. S., Bowman, B. A., Nelson, D. E., Engelgau, M. M., Vinicor, F., and Marks, J. S. Diabetes trends in the U.S.: 1990–1998. Diabetes Care, 2000, 23, 1278–1283.

National Academy on an Aging Society. Arthritis: A leading cause of disability. Chronic and Disabling Conditions, No. 5, 2000a.

National Academy on an Aging Society. Hypertension: A common condition for older Americans. Chronic and Disabling Conditions, No. 12, 2000b.

National Center for Health Statistics. Adults' health status and health care. NCHS Website: http://www.cdc.gov/nchs, 2000a.

National Center for Health Statistics (NCHS). Current estimates from the National Health Interview Survey: U.S. 1994. Vital and Health Statistics, Series 10, #193, 1995.

National Center for Health Statistics (NCHS). Death rates and age-adjusted death rates: United States 1979, 1997 and 1998. Vital and Health Statistics, #48, 2000b.

National Center for Health Statistics (NCHS). Health, United States. Hyattsville, MD: NCHS, 1999.

National Center for Health Statistics (NCHS). Health, United States, 2002. Hyattsville, MD: NCHS, 2003a, Tables 37–39.

National Center for Health Statistics (NCHS). Trends in health and aging. http://www.cdc.gov/nchs/about/otheract/aging/trendsoverview.htm, 2003b.

National Heart, Lung, and Blood Institute. Sixth report of the Joint National Committee on Prevention, Detection, Evaluation and Treatment of High Blood Pressure. NIH/NHLBI Publications, Nov. 1997.

National Highway Traffic Safety Administration (NHTSA). U.S. Department of Transportation. Traffic safety facts 2000: Older population. Washington, DC: NHTSA, 2001.

National Institute on Aging. Exercise: A guide from the National Institute on Aging. Bethesda, MD: NIH/NIA Publication No. 99-4258, 1999a.

National Institute on Aging (NIA). *Is HIV/AIDS different in older people?* Bethesda, MD: NIH/NIA, 1999b.

National Institute on Aging (NIA). *Menopause: A resource for making healthy choices.* Bethesda, MD: NIH/NIA, 2001.

National Institutes of Health (NIH). NIH asks participants in Women's Health Initiative estrogen-alone study to stop taking pills. http://www.nhlbi.nih.gov/new/press/04-03-02/htm, March 2004.

National Institutes of Health (NIH). Osteoporosis and Related Bone Diseases—National Resource Center. Fast facts on osteoporosis. http://www.osteo.org/fast+facts+on+osteoporosis&docty, 2003.

Nelson, M. E., Fiatarone, M. A., Morganti, C. M., Trice, I., Greenberg, R. A., and Evans, W. J. Effects of high intensity strength training on multiple risk factors for osteoporotic fractures. *Journal of the American Medical Association,* 1994, *272,* 1909–1914.

New York Times. An ailing Russian lives a tough life that's getting shorter. Dec. 3, 2000, pp. 1–19.

Noonan, D. Prescription drugs: Why they cost so much. *Newsweek,* Sept. 25, 2000, pp. 53–57.

Phillips, R. S. Preventing depression: A program for African American elders with chronic pain. *Family and Community Health,* 2000, *22,* 57–65.

Quinn, M. E., Johnson, M. A., Poon, L. W., and Martin, P. Psychosocial correlates of subjective mental health in sexagenarians, octogenarians, and centenarians. *Issues in Mental Health Nursing,* 1999, *20,* 151–171.

Radda, K. E., Schensul, J. J., Disch, W. B., Levy, J. A., and Reyes, C. Y. Assessing human immunodeficiency virus (HIV) risk among older urban adults. *Family and Community Health,* 2003, *26,* 203–213.

Ray, W. A., Taylor, J. A., Meador, K. G., Thapa, P. B., and Brown, A. K. A randomized trial of a consultation service to reduce falls in nursing homes. *Journal of the American Medical Association,* 1997, *278,* 595–596.

Robert Wood Johnson Foundation (RWJF). *Health and Health Care 2003* (2nd ed.). Washington, DC: RWJF, 2003.

Rosen, C. J. *Osteoporosis: Diagnostic and therapeutic principles.* Totowa, NJ: Humana Press, 1996.

Rothberg, M. B., Bellantonio, S., and Rose, D. N. Management of influenza in adults older than 65 years of age: Cost-effectiveness of rapid testing and an-

tiviral therapy. *Annals of Internal Medicine,* 2003, *139,* 321–329.

Ruby, C. M., Fillenbaum, G. G., Kuchibhatla, M. N., and Hanlon, J. T. Laxative use in the community-dwelling elderly. *American Journal of Geriatric Pharmacotherapy,* 2003, *1,* 11–17.

Salen, P. N., Kellwell, K., Baumgratz, W., Eberhardt, M., and Reed, J. How does octogenarian status affect mobility, mortality, and functional outcomes of elderly drivers in motor vehicle crashes in Pennsylvania? *Academy of Emergency Medicine,* 2003, *10,* 477–478.

Sambamoorthi, U., Shea, D., and Crystal, S. Total and out-of-pocket expenditures for prescription drugs among older persons. *The Gerontologist,* 2003, *43,* 345–359.

Scharlach, A., Simon, J., and Dal Santo, T. Who is providing social services to today's older adults? *Journal of Gerontological Social Work,* 2002, *38,* 5–17.

Schoofs, M., van der Klift, M., Hofman, A., de Laet, C., Herings, R., Stijnen, T., Pols, H., and Striker, B. Thiazide diuretics and the risk for hip fracture. *Annals of Internal Medicine,* 2003, *139,* 476–482.

Schrimshaw, E. W., and Siegel, K. Perceived barriers to social support from family and friends among older adults with HIV/AIDS. *Journal of Health Psychology,* 2003, *8,* 738–752.

Scott, W. K., Macera, C. A., Cornman, C. B. and Sharpe, P. A. Functional health status as a predictor of mortality in men and women over 65. *Journal of Clinical Epidemiology,* 1997, *50,* 291–296.

Sharpe, P. A., Jackson, K. L., White, C., Vaca, V. L., Hickey, T., Gu, J., and Otterness, C. Effects of a one year physical activity intervention for older adults at congregate nutrition sites. *The Gerontologist,* 1997, *37,* 208–215.

Singh, N. A., Clements, K. M., and Fiatarone-Singh, M. A. The efficacy of exercise as a long-term antidepressant in elderly subjects. *Journals of Gerontology,* 2001, *56A,* M497–M504.

Smith, J. P., and Kingston, R. S. Race, socioeconomic status, and health in late life. In L. G. Martin and B. J. Soldo (Eds.), *Racial and ethnic differences in the health of older Americans.* Washington, DC: National Academy Press, 1997.

Stearns, S. C., Bernard, S. L., Konrad, T. R., Schwartz, R. J., and Defriese, G. H. *Medicare use and costs in relation to self-care practices.* Poster presented at annual meetings of the Association for Health Services Research, 1997.

Stump, T. E., Johnson, R. J., and Wolinsky, F. D. Changes in physician utilization over time among older adults. *Journals of Gerontology,* 1995, *50B,* S45–S58.

Talbot, L. A., Fleg, J. L., and Metter, E. J. Secular trends in leisure-time physical activity in men and women across four decades. *Preventive Medicine,* 2003, *37,* 52–60.

Talley, N. J., Fleming, K. C., and Evans, J. M. Constipation in an elderly community: A study of prevalence and potential risk factors. *American Journal of Gastroenterology,* 1996, *91,* 19–25.

Thom, D. H., and Brown, J. S. Reproductive and hormonal risk factors for urinary incontinence in later life: A review of the clinical and epidemiological literature. *Journal of the American Geriatrics Society,* 1998, *46.* 1411–1417.

Tinetti, M. E., Baker, D. I., McAvay, C., Claus, E. B., Garret, P., and Gottschalk, M. A multifactorial intervention to reduce the risk of falling among elderly people living in the community. *New England Journal of Medicine,* 1994, *331,* 821–827.

U.S. Administration on Aging Webpage. http://www.aoa.dhhs.gov//aoa/stats, 2000.

U.S. Department of Health and Human Services (DHHS). *Oral Health in America: A Report of the Surgeon General.* Bethesda, MD: NIDCR/NIH, 2000.

U.S. General Accounting Office (GAO). *Prescription drugs and the elderly.* Washington, DC: GAO, 1995.

U.S. Preventive Services Task Force. *Guide to clinical preventive services.* (2nd ed.). Baltimore: Williams & Wilkins, 1996.

Vincent, K. R., Braith, R. W., Feldman, R. A., and Lowenthal, D. T. Improved cardiorespiratory endurance following 6 months of resistance exercise in elderly men and women. *Archives of Internal Medicine,* 2002, *162,* 673–678.

Vosvick, M., Koopman, C., Gore-Felton, C., Thoresen, C., Krumboltz, J., and Spiegel, D. Relationship of functional quality of life to strategies for coping with the stress of living with HIV/AIDS. *Psychoso-*

matics: Journal of Consultation Liaison Psychiatry, 2003, *44,* 51–58.

Wallace, J. I., Buchner, D. M., Grothaus, L., Leveille, S., Tyll, L., LaCroix, A. Z., and Wagner, E. H. Implementation and effectiveness of a community-based health promotion program for older adults. *Journals of Gerontology: Medical Sciences,* 1998, *53A,* M301–M306.

Warner, D. F., and Hayward, M. D. (2002). *Race disparities in men's mortality: The role of childhood social conditions in a process of cumulative disadvantage.* University of Pennsylvania, Unpublished manuscript.

Wickrama, K. A. S., Conger, R. D., Wallace, L. E., and Elder, G. H. (1999). The intergenerational transmission of health-risk behaviors: Adolescent lifestyles and gender moderating effects. *Journal of Health and Social Behavior,* 40(3), 258–272.

Women's Health Initiative Investigators (WHI). Risks and benefits of estrogen plus progestin in healthy postmenopausal women. *Journal of the American Medical Association,* 2002, *288,* 321–333.

Woolam, G. L. Cancer statistics 2000: A benchmark for a new century. *CA—A Cancer Journal for Clinicians,* 2000, *50,* 6–7.

World Health Organization (WHO). (2002). *Active aging: A policy framework.* Paper presented at the Second United Nations World Assembly on Aging, Madrid, Spain.

World Health Organization (WHO). *Growing older, staying well, aging and physical activity in everyday life.* Geneva, Switzerland: WHO, 1998.

World Health Organization (UNAIDS/WHO). AIDS epidemic update. http://www.who.int/hiv/pub/epidemiology/epi2003/en.

Yataco, A. R., Busby-Whitehead, J., Drinkwater, D. T., and Katzel, L. I. Relationship of body composition and cardiovascular fitness to lipoprotein lipid profiles in master athletes and sedentary men. *Aging,* 1997, *9,* 88–94.

Yusuf, H. R., Croft, J. B., Giles, W. H., Anda, R. F., Casper, M. L., and Casperson, C. J. Leisure-time physical activity among older adults. *Archives of Internal Medicine,* 1996, *156,* 1321–1326.

part three

The Psychological Context of Social Aging

The dynamic interactions between people and their environments as they age, the population trends that made gerontology such an important concern in the late twentieth century, and the historical background of social gerontology were discussed in Part One. Part Two focused on the normal biological and physiological changes that take place with aging, and our growing understanding of how biological aging may be altered. The types of chronic health problems that afflict older people and influence their social functioning were presented. The older population's use of the health care system was reviewed. Part Two concluded with a discussion of the growing field of health promotion, and how improved health behaviors can help people experience active aging.

In this section, the focus is on psychological changes with aging—both normal and abnormal—that influence older people's social behavior and dynamic relationships with their physical and social environments. As we have already seen, many changes take place in the aging organism that make it more difficult to perform activities of daily living and to respond as quickly and easily to external demands as in youth. Many older people have chronic health problems, such as arthritis, diabetes, or heart disease, that compound the normal changes that cause people to slow down. In a similar manner, some changes in cognitive functioning, personality, and sexuality are a function of normal aging. Other psychological changes may be due to the secondary effects of diseases.

Many researchers have examined changes in intelligence, learning, and memory with aging.

The literature in this area, reviewed in Chapter 5, suggests that normal aging does not result in significant declines. Although older subjects in the studies described do not perform as well as younger subjects, their scores are not so poor as to indicate significant impairments in social functioning. Laboratory tests also may be less than ideal as indicators of cognitive function in older people. Research on ways to improve memory in the later years are discussed. The chapter concludes with a discussion of wisdom and creativity in old age, and whether these abilities improve or decline with aging.

Chapter 6 describes personality development in the later years, the expression and regulation of basic and complex emotions, the importance of maintaining self-esteem, and threats to self-esteem that result from age-associated changes. This chapter also focuses on coping and successful adaptation to such changes. Given the normal age-related alterations in physiological, sensory, and cognitive functions, personality styles, and older individuals' social networks, some gerontologists argue that older people experience more stress in a given time period than young adults. Furthermore, there has been considerable debate about whether aging results in the use of different types of coping strategies. However, longitudinal research in this area is insufficient to conclude with any certainty that aging is associated with more stressful life events than young adulthood. The concept of successful aging and its similarity to active aging is discussed. It is a concept that has drawn considerable research attention and debate. It requires both high levels of physical and functional health and remaining active in cognitive and social functions.

Some forms of psychopathology, such as schizophrenia, are more common in young adults than in old age. However, as described in Chapter 6, some older people are at high risk for major depression, paranoia, and some forms of dementia. In the case of dementia, such as Alzheimer's disease, memory and problem-solving abilities decline quite dramatically, sometimes within a few years, other times over many years. Older individuals with a diagnosis of dementia experience significant impairments in their ability to interact with other people and to control their physical and social environments. To the extent that older people do not seek mental health services for treatable disorders such as depression or paranoia, their social interactions will deteriorate. Some may become reclusive and, in the case of severely depressed older persons, at greater risk of suicide. Despite the growing number of studies that document the benefits of therapeutic interventions for older adults, the older population underutilizes mental health services. This is particularly true among elders of color. Most of the mental health care provided to older adults takes place in hospitals, not in community mental health centers or in private practice. Furthermore, most therapy is provided by family doctors who generally do not have special expertise in geriatric medicine or psychiatry.

An important aspect of personality is sexuality, the individual's ability to express intimate feelings through a wide range of loving and pleasurable experiences. Chapter 7 addresses the influence of social attitudes and beliefs, normal physiological changes, and diseases on older adults' sexuality. Contrary to popular belief, aging need not reduce sexual pleasure and capacity. More often, older people withdraw from sexual activity because of societal expectations and stereotypes. As people become better informed about aging and sexuality, and as sexual taboos are reduced, older people will express their sexuality more easily. New research on maintaining sexual activity in old age is discussed.

As with physical aging, the material in Part Three suggests that aging does not affect all people's psychological functions in the same way. Normal cognitive changes, such as mild forgetfulness, generally are not so dramatic as to impair older people's social functions. A relatively small segment of the older population experiences Alzheimer's disease or other types of dementia, but the incidence increases with age. Personality and patterns of coping also do not change so dramatically as to impair social functioning, although some gender-based behaviors become less pronounced with age. Coping and adaptation skills do not become impaired with normal aging; styles of coping vary widely among older people. Indeed, aging results in increasing differences in psychological functioning among people, not greater similarity. Some older people age successfully despite chronic diseases and deterioration in cognitive function, while others experience poor adaptation to these normal and secondary changes of aging. The following vignettes illustrate some contrasts in psychological aging.

AN OLDER PERSON WITH INTACT COGNITIVE ABILITIES

Mr. Wallace, age 85, is a retired professor in a midwestern community. He retired 20 years ago, after teaching history in a large state university for 40 years. He remains active by doing volunteer work in the local historical society, teaching part-time at the university, and traveling to Europe with his wife for three months every summer, occasionally leading groups of other retirees in tours of medieval European towns. Mr. Wallace's major project that he wishes to complete before he dies is an historical novel about Charlemagne. This is a topic about which he has lectured and read extensively, and one he enjoys investigating in detail during his trips to Europe. Mrs. Wallace often remarks that he is busier these days than he was before his retirement. During the first few months after retirement, Professor Wallace experienced a mild bout of depression, but he found some relief through group therapy with other retirees. Mr. Wallace enjoys intellectual challenges today as much as he did when he was employed, in fact, more so, because he is pursuing these activities without the pressures of a day-to-day job. He vows to keep up his level of activity until he "runs out of energy." Mr. Wallace is an excellent model of active aging.

AN OLDER PERSON WITH GOOD COPING SKILLS

Mrs. Johnson, age 83, has suffered numerous tragedies throughout her life. Born to a poor farming family in Mississippi, she moved north with her mother and eight older sisters and brothers as a child, after her father died and the family farm was lost. The family supported itself through hard work in the factories. Mrs. Johnson married young; she and her husband struggled through the years to own their home and raise their three children. Her husband died 20 years ago, leaving her with a small pension. She worked at a manual labor job until she was 70 years old, when her arthritis made it painful for her to do the heavy work needed on the job. During the past three years, Mrs. Johnson has experienced a series of losses: her son and daughter-in-law died in an auto accident; her last surviving sister died; and her oldest granddaughter, the one on whom she could most depend, moved west to attend medical school. Mrs. Johnson admits these losses are painful, but that it is "God's will" that she experience them. Her strong faith in God helps her

accept these changes in her life and her deteriorating health as part of a "master plan." When she becomes too distraught, she turns to the Bible, and looks forward to visits from her grandchildren and great-grandchildren to keep her busy.

AN OLDER PERSON WITH DEMENTIA

Mr. Adams is age 64. Several years ago he started showing signs of confusion and disorientation. He was diagnosed as having Alzheimer's disease at age 60, five years before his planned retirement. He and his wife had made plans to travel around the world during retirement; now all their plans have completely changed. While there have been some brief periods during the past four years where he has seemed to be better, Mr. Adams now is extremely agitated and disoriented, wanders during the night, and is occasionally abusive to people near him. He often does not know who his wife and children are. The slightest change in routine will upset him. In his lucid moments, Mr. Adams cries and wonders what has happened to his life; at some points, he can also carry on short conversations. His wife is determined to keep him at home, even though he often verbally abuses her and does not recognize or appreciate all that she does for him. She is able to take him to an adult day-care center during the day, where the staff try to keep him active and stimulated. Mrs. Adams also attends meetings of a support group for family caregivers of Alzheimer's disease patients. She enjoys these meetings because she can express her feelings about how hard things are and then be supported for her efforts by other caregivers. Mr. Adams expresses great fear at the thought of a nursing home, but his wife worries about how long she can manage him at home.

The next three chapters describe how the aging process influences cognitive abilities, personality styles, mental health, and intimacy and sexuality, as well as responses to major life events. They emphasize the wide variations in these processes with aging. The vastly different psychological states of Mr. Wallace, Mrs. Johnson, and Mr. Adams result in significant variations in the social aspects of their lives.

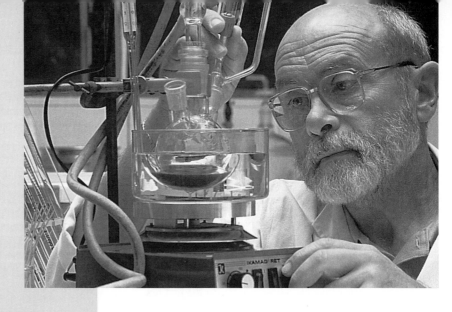

chapter

5

Cognitive Changes
with Aging

This chapter discusses

- Research on cognitive functions with normal aging
- Measuring components of intelligence in older adults
- Individual and environmental factors that influence intelligence
- How we learn, and how aging affects the learning process
- Attention and its importance for learning
- Environmental factors that affect how older people learn
- How aging affects the ability to retrieve information from secondary memory
- Tip-of-the-tongue states as an example of difficulty in retrieval
- The current understanding of wisdom and creativity in old age
- Cognitive retraining and other ways to help older adults improve their learning and memory skills

One of the most important and most studied aspects of aging is cognitive functioning; that is, intelligence, learning, and memory. These are critical to an individual's performance in every aspect of life, including work and leisure activities, social relationships, and productive roles. Older people who have problems in cognitive functioning will eventually experience stress in these other areas as well, along with an increasing incongruence between their competence levels and the demands of their environments. Researchers have attempted to determine whether normal aging is associated with a decline in the three areas of cognitive functioning and, if so, to what extent such a decline is due to age-related physiological changes. Much of the research on these issues has evolved from studies of cognitive development across the life span. Other studies have been undertaken in response to concerns expressed by older persons or their families that they cannot learn as easily as they used to, or that they have more trouble remembering names, dates, and places than previously.

Intelligence and Aging

Intelligence is difficult both to define and to measure. Of all the elements of cognition, it is the least verifiable. We can only infer its existence and can only indirectly measure individual levels. **Intelligence** is generally defined as the "theoretical limit of an individual's performance" (Jones, 1959, p. 700). The limit is determined by biological and genetic factors; however, the ability to achieve the limit is influenced by environmental opportunities, such as challenging educational experiences, as well as by environmental constraints, such as the absence of books or other intellectual stimulation. Intelligence encompasses a range of abilities, including the ability to deal with symbols and abstractions, acquire and comprehend new information, adapt to new situations, and understand and create new ideas. Alfred Binet, who developed the first test of intelligence, emphasized the operational aspects of intelligence: "to judge well, to comprehend well, to reason well, these are the essentials of intelligence" (Binet and Simon, 1905,

p. 106). **Intelligence quotient** (or IQ) refers to an individual's relative abilities in some of these areas compared to others of the same chronological age.

Most theorists agree that intelligence is composed of many different components. Guilford's (1967, 1966) three-dimensional structure of intellect is perhaps the most complete model (see Figure 5.1). The three dimensions represent:

- the content of knowledge (e.g., figures, symbols, and words)
- the operations that an individual must perform with this knowledge (e.g., memorize, evaluate, and come up with single or multiple solutions)
- the products that are derived from these operations (e.g., relations, systems, and implications)

This model yields 120 separate components, but it is difficult to test. Nevertheless, a multidimensional structure of intelligence, although not identical to Guilford's, is assumed by most contemporary tests of intelligence. Most tests of intelligence today measure a subset of intellectual abilities known as **primary mental abilities (PMAs),** which consist of seven abilities:

- number or mathematical reasoning
- word fluency or the ability to use appropriate words to describe the world
- verbal meaning or vocabulary level
- inductive reasoning or the ability to generalize from specific facts to concepts
- spatial relations or the ability to orient oneself in a three-dimensional space
- memory
- perceptual speed

A useful distinction is made between **fluid intelligence** and **crystallized intelligence** (Cattell, 1963; Horn, 1970, 1982; Horn and Donaldson, 1980). These two types of intelligence include some of the primary mental abilities described above. Fluid intelligence consists of skills that are

---

MEASURES OF FLUID INTELLIGENCE

- spatial orientation
- abstract reasoning
- word fluency
- inductive reasoning

MEASURES OF CRYSTALLIZED INTELLIGENCE

- verbal meaning
- word association
- social judgment
- number skills

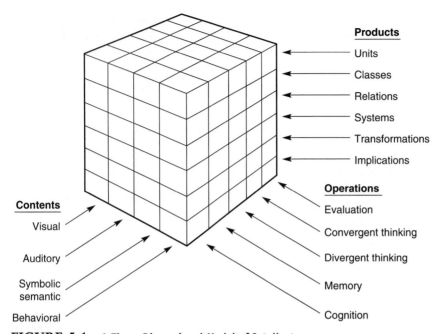

FIGURE 5.1 **A Three-Dimensional Model of Intellect**
SOURCE: J. P. Guilford, *The nature of human intelligence* (New York: McGraw-Hill, 1967) and J. P. Guilford, *Way beyond the IQ* (Buffalo, NY: Creative Education Foundation, 1977). Reprinted by permission of the author, McGraw-Hill, and the Creative Education Foundation.

biologically determined, independent of experience or learning, and may be similar to what is popularly called "native intelligence." It involves processing information that is not embedded in a context of existing information for the individual. It requires flexibility in thinking. Crystallized intelligence refers to the knowledge and abilities that the individual acquires through education and lifelong experiences. These two types of intelligence show different patterns with aging, as discussed in the next section.

There has been considerable controversy regarding intelligence in the later years. Many researchers have found significant differences between young and old persons on intelligence tests in cross-sectional studies, with older persons performing at a much lower level. Even when the same cohort is followed longitudinally, there is a decline in some intelligence tests that is indepen-

dent of generational differences (Schaie, 1996a). Others conclude that aging is not really associated with a decline in intelligence. However, standardized IQ tests and the time pressures on test-takers may be more detrimental to older persons than to the young. Still others point to methodological problems in conducting research in this area. Unfortunately, these mixed research findings serve to perpetuate the stereotype that older people are less intelligent than the young.

Many older persons are concerned that their intelligence has declined. This concern may loom so large for them that merely taking part in a study intended to "test their intelligence" may provoke sufficient anxiety to affect their test performance. Such anxieties may also influence the older person's daily functioning. Older people who are told by friends, family, test-givers or society in general that they should not expect to perform as well on intellectual tasks because aging causes a decline in intelligence may, in fact, perform more poorly.

The most widely used measure of adult intelligence is the Wechsler Adult Intelligence Scale (WAIS). It consists of 11 subtests, 6 of which are described as Verbal Scales (which measure, to some extent, crystallized intelligence), and 5 as Performance Scales (providing some measure of fluid intelligence). The performance tests on the WAIS are generally timed; the verbal tests are not.

Verbal scores are obtained by measuring an individual's ability to:

- define the meaning of words
- interpret proverbs
- explain similarities between words and concepts

In this way, accumulated knowledge and abstract reasoning can be tested.

Performance tests focus on an individual's ability to manipulate unfamiliar objects and words, often in unusual ways:

- tests of spatial relations
- abstract reasoning
- putting puzzles together to match a picture
- matching pictures with symbols or numbers
- arranging pictures in a particular pattern

Both psychomotor and perceptual skills are needed in performing these tasks.

A consistent pattern of scores on these two components of the WAIS has emerged in numerous studies; it has been labeled the **Classic Aging Pattern.** People beyond the age of 65 in some studies, and even earlier in others, perform significantly worse on Performance Scales (i.e., fluid intelligence), but their scores on Verbal Scales (i.e., crystallized intelligence) remain stable. This tendency to do worse on performance tasks may reflect age-related changes in noncognitive functions, such as sensory and perceptual abilities, and in psychomotor skills. As we have seen in Chap-

ters 3 and 4, aging results in a slowing down of the neural pathways and of the visual and auditory functions. This slower reaction time, and the delay in receiving and transmitting messages through the sense organs, explains poorer performance on subtests requiring such capabilities. Some researchers therefore argue for the elimination of time constraints in performance tasks. Studies that have not measured speed of performance have still found significant age differences in these subtests, however (Salthouse, 1996a). There appears to be a decline in performance-related aspects of intellectual function, independent of psychomotor or sensory factors. Speed of cognitive processing, such as the time to perform simple math problems, also declines with age and, in turn, slows an individual's responses on tests of performance.

Turning to verbal skills, the Classic Aging Pattern suggests that the ability to recall stored verbal information and to use abstract reasoning tends to remain constant throughout life. Declines, where they exist, typically do not show up until advanced old age, or, in the case of cognitive impairment such as the dementias, they tend to begin early in the course of the disease.

When given logically inconsistent statements in cognitive studies, older subjects analyze these inconsistencies on the basis of their own knowledge, whereas younger adults tend to ignore the logic and attempt to reach conclusions quickly. Older subjects also reject simplified solutions and prefer a complex analysis of the problem. This finding from laboratory-based research is supported by surveys of attitudes and beliefs among respondents of varying ages. Younger respondents are more willing to provide a direct response, whereas many older persons attempt to analyze the questions and give more contingency responses; that is, analyzing the question and stating that the answer could be x in one situation and y in another, rather than an all-encompassing response. For example, on a measure of environmental preference, the respondent may be asked, "How much privacy do you generally prefer?" A younger respondent is more likely to focus on the "general" situation, whereas the older respondent is more likely to consider situations both in which privacy is preferred and where it is not. It thus appears important to review older persons' responses to tests of problem solving and abstract reasoning from other perspectives beyond the traditional approaches that are grounded in cognitive theories developed with younger populations. Most tests of intelligence do not reward test-takers who provide the more analytical or complex responses typical of some older adults.

Problems in the Measurement of Cognitive Function

A major shortcoming of many studies of intelligence in aging is their use of cross-sectional research designs rather than longitudinal approaches. Age differences that are obtained in cross-sectional studies may be a reflection of cohort or generational differences rather than actual age changes. In particular, changes in educational systems and the development of television, computers, the Internet, and high-speed travel have profoundly influenced the experiences of today's youth when compared with those of people who grew up in the early twentieth century. These historical factors may then have a greater effect on intelligence scores than age per se.

Subject attrition, or dropout from longitudinal studies of intelligence, is another problem. There is a pattern of *selective attrition,* whereby the people who drop out tend to be those who have performed less well, who perceive their performance to be poor, or whose health status and ambulatory abilities are worse than average. The people who remain in the study (i.e., "the survivors") performed better in the initial tests than did dropouts. This is consistent with our earlier observation that older persons often become unduly anxious about poor performance on tests of intellectual function. Hence, the results become biased in favor of the superior performers, indicating stability or improvement over time. They

do not represent the wider population of older adults, whose performance might have shown a decline in intelligence (Schaie, 1996b).

Longitudinal Studies of Intelligence

Several major classic longitudinal studies have examined changes in intellectual function from youth to old age (Schaie, 1996a, 1983). The Iowa State Study tested a sample of college freshmen in 1919 and retested them in 1950 and 1961 (Cunningham and Owens, 1983; Owens, 1953, 1966). The researchers found general stability in intellectual functioning through middle age, with a peak in their late 40s and 50s. Declines were observed after age 60 in many men, but the degree of change varied widely among the men and across variables. The New York State Study of Aging Twins began in 1946 and followed this group through 1973 (Kallmann and Sander, 1949). Average performance declined significantly on timed tests, but, as with the Iowa State Study, individual differences were pronounced. Among the individuals who were healthy enough to complete the final follow-up, performance on nonspeed intelligence tests remained stable until they reached their ninth decade. The greatest declines were observed in the

Intellectual stimulation can help sustain higher-level cognitive skills.

test of hand-eye coordination and in fluid intelligence. Both studies had less than 25 percent of the original sample available at the final follow-up, which raises questions whether survivors are representative of their cohort in cognitive functioning.

The Seattle Longitudinal Study began in 1956 and collected data on Thurstone's primary mental abilities every 7 years over 28 years (Schaie, 1996a). At each follow-up assessment, individuals who were still available from the original sample were retested, along with a new, randomly selected sample from the same population. The 1984 cycle included a test of some older people who had previously participated in a cognitive retraining program (Willis and Schaie, 1986). This study has provided the basis for the development of sequential research models, described in Chapter 1. Peak performance varied across tests and between men and women, ranging from age 32 on the test of Numbers for men and age 39 on the test of Reasoning for women, to age 53 for Educational Aptitude. A review of age changes for the 128 people who were observed over 28 years reveals age decrements after age 60 on tests of word fluency, numbers, and spatial orientation that became progressively worse in later years. Tests of spatial abilities and inductive reasoning, both indicators of fluid intelligence, showed greater decline with age. However, other primary mental abilities, such as verbal meaning and inductive reasoning, showed no declines until the mid-70s. These results are consistent with cross-sectional results using the WAIS, as we have seen earlier. They are supported by other, shorter longitudinal studies that have found little change over three years (Christensen et al., 1999; Zelinski, Gilewski, and Schaie, 1993). The findings suggest that the Classic Aging Pattern holds up in both cross-sectional and longitudinal studies, and that some performance aspects of intelligence may begin to deteriorate after age 60, although major changes are generally rare until the mid-70s.

In all these studies, most of the significant declines occur in intellectual abilities that are less practiced. Schaie (1996b) concludes that the changes observed in the Seattle Longitudinal Study indicate a normative developmental transition from stability in general intelligence in the middle years, to a gradual decline that begins around age 60. Most people maintained their abilities in one or more areas well into their advanced years, as shown in Figure 5.2. However, Schaie found no linear decline in all five primary mental abilities for any participants as old as age 88 (Schaie, 1996a, 1996b).

The Duke Longitudinal Studies, described in Chapter 1, assessed intelligence and memory, in addition to many health variables. This series of three longitudinal samples, each measured several times, provides useful information about the relationship between intellectual function and health status, especially cardiovascular disease (Palmore, 1974, 1985; Siegler, 1983). The findings regarding age changes generally are consistent with the other longitudinal studies described in this section. That is, declines in cognitive function were not observed until individuals reached their 70s. Scores on performance tests were found to decline earlier than scores on verbal measures. Another longitudinal study in Sweden examined cognitive functioning among the oldest-old (ages 84–90 in this study). A 2-year follow-up revealed that participants who had scored high on tests of memory, attention, orientation, and ability to

---

SUMMARY OF AGE-RELATED CHANGES IN INTELLIGENCE

- Peak performance varies by test, usually between ages 30 and 55.
- Performance on timed tests declines.
- Performance on nontimed tests remains stable until the 80s.
- People rarely decline in all five PMAs.
- High scorers continue to do well even among oldest-old.
- Declines in tests of fluid intelligence begin earlier than in crystallized intelligence ("Classic Aging Pattern").

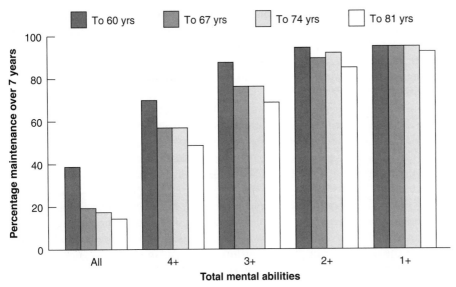

FIGURE 5.2 **Proportion of Individuals Who Maintain Scores on Multiple Abilities**
SOURCE: Schaie, K. W., The hazards of cognitive aging. *The Gerontologist,* 1989, 29, 484–493. Reprinted with permission.

follow instructions continued to perform well at follow-up. However, average performance declined slightly on all these tests (Johansson, Zarit, and Berg, 1992).

Factors that May Influence Intelligence in Adulthood

Researchers who have compared intelligence test scores of older and younger persons found wide variations in scores of both groups. Older test-takers generally have obtained poorer scores, but age per se is only one factor in explaining intellectual functioning.

As mentioned earlier, there is also a biological factor in intelligence, such that some people are innately more intelligent than others. However, it is difficult to determine the relative influence of biological factors, because it is impossible to measure the specific mechanisms of the brain that account for intelligence. Structural changes in the

brain and in neural pathways occur with aging, as seen in Chapter 3. These changes, however, are generally diffuse and not focused in a particular region of the brain. It is therefore impossible to determine what specific changes in the brain and its pathways may account for the age-related deterioration that is observed.

Other variables that have been examined are educational attainment, involvement in complex versus mechanistic work, cardiovascular disease, hypertension, and sensory deficits. Some studies have found cohort differences on tests of intelligence, with newer cohorts of older people performing better than previous cohorts who took the same test at about the same age. These differences emerge on tests of crystallized *and* fluid intelligence (represented by verbal meaning and inductive reasoning tests), even when comparing adult children and their parents (Schaie et al., 1992; Schaie and Willis, 1995). The advantage of newer cohorts has been attributed to higher educational attainment. Therefore, it is important to control statistically for educational differences

INTELLECTUALLY ACTIVE ELDERS

Increasingly, more older adults continue to participate in intellectually challenging jobs well beyond their 60s and 70s. For example, college campuses are full of retired faculty who retain emeritus status and who continue to teach or conduct research well into their 80s. One of the Poet Laureates of the United States was Stanley Kunitz, appointed at age 95. Another active octogenarian is Dr. Hilary Koprowski, whose research in 1948 led to the widespread adoption of a live vaccine to immunize children against polio. Koprowski, now aged 86, continues to conduct medical research at Thomas Jefferson University in Philadelphia. Meanwhile, James Wiggins continued to edit a weekly newspaper in Ellsworth, Maine well into his 90s.

when analyzing the relationship between age and intelligence. Significant positive effects of education have been found on all tests of cognitive function when comparing healthy independent adults aged 70 to 79 with different educational levels. In particular, participants with the highest level of education (12+ years) did three times better on a test of abstract thinking than did people with 7 or fewer years of education (Inouye et al., 1993; Steen, Berg, and Steen, 1998).

Occupational level, which is generally correlated with educational level, also influences intelligence test scores. Older people who still use their cognitive abilities in jobs or activities that require thinking and problem-solving (such as Mr. Wallace in the introductory vignette) show less decline on cognitive tests than those who do not use these skills. This is because most of the observed declines in intellectual abilities occur in highly challenging, complex tasks. In addition, people whose occupations demand more verbal skills (e.g., lawyers and teachers) may continue to perform very well on these apects of intelligence tests. Those who use more abstract and fluid skills in their occupations (e.g., architects and engineers) are more likely to do well on the performance tests of the WAIS, even into their 70s and 80s. In

general, older people who do not participate in any intellectual pursuits perform worse on intelligence tests than do their peers who are "cognitively engaged." The nature of intellectual activities is also important; those who participate in complex leisure activities (e.g., chess, complex crossword puzzles) show consistently higher scores, even among the old-old (Baltes, 1993; Gold et al., 1995; Inouye et al., 1993; Schooler and Mulatu, 2001).

The effects of declining physical health and sensory losses on intelligence become more severe in the later years, and these factors may displace any positive influence due to education and occupation for people who are 75 years and older. Several studies identified poorer performance on intelligence tests by older people in poor health.

Older adults with cardiovascular problems tend to do worse on intelligence tests than those without such disorders, particularly in tests that demand psychomotor speed (Hultsch, Hammer, and Small, 1993). In the Seattle Longitudinal Study, participants with cardiovascular disease declined at younger ages on all tests of mental abilities than did people with no disease; people who had hypertension in middle age performed worse on most tests after age 70 (Gruber-Baldini, 1991; Launer et al., 1995).

Nutritional deficits may also impair an older person's cognitive functioning. One study of community dwelling, healthy older persons (ages 66–90) examined their performance on multiple tests of cognitive functioning and nutritional status longitudinally. Older people with low intake of vitamins E, A, B_6, and B_{12} at baseline performed

HEALTH IMPAIRMENTS THAT AFFECT PERFORMANCE

- cardiovascular disease
- hypertension
- nutritional deficits
- depression
- hearing loss
- terminal drop

worse on visuospatial and abstraction tasks 6 years later; those who used vitamin supplements did better (Larue et al., 1997). These findings reinforce the results of research on the impact of nutritional deficiencies on physical performance, described in Chapter 4.

Depression, or even mild dysphoria (i.e., feeling "blue" or "down in the dumps," but not clinically depressed), is a psychological variable that can influence cognitive function. Indeed, in a large study of people aged 50 to 93 that controlled for the effects of age, education, and occupation, older people with worse scores on a measure of depression had significantly lower scores on tests of both crystallized and fluid intelligence (Rabbitt et al., 1995). In another study that measured changes in memory, spatial functioning, and perceptual speed, older adults with symptoms of depression showed the most decline over 4 years (Christensen et al., 1999). Given the prevalence of depression in the older population, it is important to consider this as a cause of poorer cognitive performance rather than aging per se.

As noted in Chapter 3, hearing loss is common in older persons, especially moderate levels of loss that affect their ability to comprehend speech. Visual deficits become more severe in advanced old age. Poorer performance by some test-takers who are very old may be due primarily to these sensory losses, not to a central cognitive decline. Older persons with hearing or vision loss do especially poorly on tests of verbal meaning and spatial relations (Lindenberger and Baltes, 1994).

An apparent and rapid decline in cognitive function within 5 years of death is another physical health factor that appears to be related to intelligence test scores. This phenomenon is known as the *terminal drop* or **terminal decline hypothesis,** first tested by Kleemeier (1962). In longitudinal studies of intelligence, older subjects whose test scores are in the lower range to start with, and who decline more sharply, are found to die sooner than good performers. This has been observed on many different tests, especially in verbal meaning, spatial and reasoning ability, and word fluency (Berg, 1996; Bosworth, Schaie, and Willis, 1999). This suggests that time since birth (i.e., age) is not as significant in intellectual decline as is proximity to death.

Finally, anxiety may negatively affect older people's intelligence test scores. As shown in the following section, older people in laboratory tests of learning and memory are more likely than the young to express high test anxiety and cautiousness in responding. These same reactions may occur in older people taking intelligence tests, especially if they think that the test really measures how "intelligent" they are. Anxieties about cognitive decline and concerns about becoming cognitively impaired may make older people even more cautious, and hence result in poorer performance on intelligence tests.

The Process of Learning and Memory

Learning and *memory* are two cognitive processes that must be considered together. That is, learning is assumed to occurr when an individual is able to retrieve information accurately from his or her memory store. Conversely, if an individual cannot retrieve information from memory, it is presumed that learning has not adequately taken place. Thus, *learning* is the process by which new information (verbal or nonverbal) or skills are encoded, or put into one's memory. The specific parts of the brain involved in this process are the hippocampus, which first receives and processess new stimuli, and the cerebral cortex, where memories are stored. Some of the most exciting research in this field is focused on the process of neuronal development as learning occurs. *Memory* is the process of retrieving or recalling the information that was once learned. Memory also refers to a part of the brain that retains what has been learned throughout a person's lifetime. Researchers have at-

RETRIEVING OLD MEMORIES

A person may have learned many years ago how to ride a bicycle. If this skill has been encoded well through practice, the person can retrieve it many years later from his or her memory store, even if he or she has not ridden a bicycle in years. This applies to many other skills learned early in life, from remembering childhood prayers to diapering a baby.

tempted to distinguish three separate types of memory: sensory, primary or short-term, and secondary or long-term.

Sensory memory, as its name implies, is the first step in receiving information through the sense organs and passing it on to primary or secondary memory. It is stored for only a few tenths of a second, although there is some evidence that it lasts longer in older persons because of slower reaction times of the senses. Sensory memory has been further subdivided into **iconic** (or visual) and **echoic** (or auditory) **memory.** Examples of iconic memory are:

- words or letters that we see
- faces of people with whom we have contact
- landscapes that we experience through our eyes

Of course, words can be received through echoic memory as well, such as when we hear others say a specific word, or when we repeat words aloud to ourselves. A landscape can also enter our sensory memory through our ears (e.g., the sound of the ocean), our skin (e.g., the feel of a cold spray from the ocean), and our nose (e.g., the smell of salt water). To the extent that we focus on or rehearse information that we receive from our sense organs, it is more likely to be passed into our primary and secondary memories.

Despite significant changes in the visual system with aging (as described in Chapter 3), studies of iconic memory find only small age differences in the ability to identify stimuli presented briefly. Such modest declines in iconic memory would not be expected to influence observed decrements in secondary or long-term memory. However, some researchers suggest that even small declines in sensory memory may result in a large decline in long-term memory (Craik and Jennings, 1994). Although research on iconic memory is limited, there has been even less with echoic memory and less still that has compared older persons with younger. We have all experienced the long-term storage of memories gained through touch, taste, or smell. For example, the odor of freshly baked bread evokes memories of early childhood in many older people. However, these sensory memories are more difficult to test. As a result, very little is known about any changes experienced with these other modes of sensory memory.

Primary or **working memory** is a temporary stage of holding and organizing information, and does not necessarily refer to a storage area in the brain. Despite its temporary nature, working memory is critical for our ability to process new information. We all experience situations where we hear or read a bit of information such as a phone number or someone's name, use that name or number immediately, then forget it. In fact, most adults can recall seven, plus or minus two, pieces of information (e.g., digits, letters, or words) for 60 seconds or less. It is not surprising, therefore, that local phone numbers in most countries are seven digits or less, although the addition of area codes for local dialing makes it more difficult to retain this information in our permanent memory store (**secondary** or **long-term memory**), it must be rehearsed or "processed" actively. This is why primary memory is described as a form of "working memory" that decides what information should be attended to or ignored, which is most important, and how best to store it. If we are distracted while trying to retain the information for the 60 seconds that it is stored in short-term memory, we immediately forget it, even if it consists of

AIDS TO WORKING MEMORY

The popularity of phones with digital memory for storing multiple phone numbers attests to the problem that people of all ages have with primary memory. Rather than looking up important phone numbers or attempting to memorize them, we can store these in the phone and retrieve them with the push of one or two buttons. Another technological development that can help reduce the information we must store in our minds is the Palm Pilot or other handheld computers. These are useful for storing phone numbers, addresses, memos and even reminders to oneself. As older adults become more comfortable with these new technologies, they may experience less stress about retaining newly acquired information.

only two or three bits of information. This happens because the rehearsal of such material is interrupted by the reception of newer information in our sensory memory. Most studies of primary memory have found minimal age differences in its storage capacity, which may be due to slower reaction time in older persons. It may also be that the encoding process which takes place in primary memory requires some organization or elaboration of the information received. Older persons are less likely than young people to process new information in this manner. Indeed, some argue that aging leads to a decline in "attentional resources," or mental energy, to organize and elaborate newly acquired information in order to retain it in secondary memory (Craik, 1994; Craik and Jennings, 1994; Smith, 1996). In fact, many of the age-related changes observed in different components of attention may explain these problems with working memory.

Another explanation for this slowing process is that **perceptual speed**—the time required to react to a stimulus and respond to it—deteriorates with aging. According to this theory, older people have more problems holding information in their working memory while receiving new stimuli

through sensory memory ("simultaneity"). This is compounded by the possibility that it takes longer for older people to ignore irrelevant stimuli and complete working memory tasks (Salthouse, 1996b). For example, if an older driver is trying to locate a street address that was just given, but is also listening to news on the radio, the driver is less likely to remember the street address and drive directly to it than would a younger driver.

True learning implies that the material we acquire through our sensory and primary memories has been stored in "secondary memory." Thus, for example, looking up a telephone number and immediately dialing it does not guarantee that the number will be learned. In fact, only with considerable rehearsal can information from primary memory be passed into secondary memory. This is the part of the memory store in which everything we have learned throughout our lives is kept; unlike primary memory, it has an unlimited capacity. The different components of secondary memory are described in the box on page 175. Researchers have demonstrated significant declines in some components, but very little or no change in others.

Older people consistently recall less information than younger people in paired associates tests with retention intervals as brief as one hour or as long as eight months. Age differences in secondary memory appear to be more pronounced than in sensory or primary memory and are often frustrating to older people and their families. Indeed, middle-aged and older people are often concerned that they cannot remember and retrieve information from secondary memory (Verhaeghen, Geraerts, and Marcoen, 2000). This perception that one has poor memory can seriously harm older adults' self-concept, as well as their performance on many tasks, and may even result in depression. Such concern, growing out of a fear of dementia, is generally out of proportion to the actual level of decline. Older individuals can benefit significantly from methods to help organize their learning, such as imagery and the use of mnemonics. Examples of such techniques to improve learning and memory are discussed later in this chapter.

The Information Processing Model

The **information processing model** of memory is presented in Figure 5.3. This is a conceptual model; that is, it provides a framework for understanding how the processes of learning and memory take place. It is not necessarily what goes on in the neural pathways between the sense organs and the secondary memory store. Having described each of the components in this model, let us review the steps involved in processing some information that we want to retain. One example is the experience of learning new names at a social gathering. Sensory memory aids in hearing the name spoken, preferably several times by other people, and seeing the face that is associated with that name. Primary memory is used to store that information temporarily, so that a person can speak to others and address them by name (an excellent method of rehearsing this information), or manipulate the information in order to pass it on to secondary memory. This may include repeating the name several times to oneself, trying to isolate some aspect of the person's physical features and relating it to the name, and associating the name with other people one has known in the past who have similar names. In the last type of mental manipulation, information from secondary memory (i.e., names of other people) is linked with the new information. This is a useful method because the material in secondary memory is permanent, and associating the new information with well-learned information aids in its storage and subsequent recall.

During any stage of this cognitive processing, the newly obtained information can be lost. This may occur if the sensory memory is flooded with similar information; in this case, if a person is being introduced to multiple new names and faces at a party, it is almost impossible to distinguish the names or to associate each name with a face. Information may also be lost during the primary memory stage. In our example, if a person is trying to use the newly heard name and is distracted by other names and faces, or receives unrelated but relevant information (e.g., a telephone call) while rehearsing the new name, the name has not been sufficiently processed to pass into secondary memory.

The learning process may also be disrupted because of inability to retrieve information efficiently from secondary memory. For example, a person may associate the newly heard name with someone known in the past; if he or she has difficulty retrieving the stored name from secondary

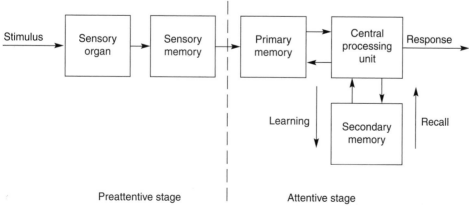

FIGURE 5.3   Schematic Representation of the Information Processing Model

TYPES OF MEMORY

It is important to recognize that secondary memory is not unilateral but has several components. The types of memory listed here (and many others) appear to be influenced differently by the aging process:

- Episodic memory — Consciously recalling events or episodes.

- Explicit memory — Consciously attempting to keep a stimulus in one's mind, in a specific order (e.g., a poem, a mental "to do" list).

- Flashbulb memory — Remembering specific events that have personal relevance, and the emotions triggered by the events (e.g., remembering where one was and how one reacted to the September 11, 2001 terrorist attacks on the World Trade Center).

- Implicit memory — Unintentionally remembering stimuli that were acquired without paying attention (e.g., words or music to an old song that one did not even know one knew).

- Procedural memory — Often nonverbal, this type of memory relies on motor functions, such as riding a bike or playing a piece on the piano without reading the music.

- Semantic memory — The storehouse of words and facts that have accumulated over one's lifetime.

- Source memory — Remembering where one saw or heard a new piece of information (e.g., source of an article read on healthy aging).

Not surprisingly, semantic memory shows the least decline with aging because it is stimulated by words and concepts learned throughout one's lifetime. Procedural memory is also retained into advanced old age; even people who have not ridden a bike in 50 years can get on and start pedaling, albeit perhaps somewhat wobbly at first. On the other hand, it appears that aging causes a noticeable decline in episodic, flashbulb, and source memory.

memory, however, this may be so frustrating as to redirect the individual's attention from the new name to the old name. How often have you ignored everything around you to concentrate on remembering a name that is "on the tip of the tongue" (i.e., in secondary memory) but not easily retrievable? As noted above, aging appears to reduce the efficiency of *processing* information in sensory and primary memory, as well as retrieval from secondary memory (i.e., working memory). It does *not* influence the storage capacity of primary or secondary memories. That is, contrary to popular opinion, these memory stores are not physical spaces that become overloaded with information as we age.

Factors That Affect Learning in Old Age

The Importance of Attention

A critical component of cognition, especially in the learning process, is attention. Researchers have addressed three components of attention as central for people's ability to perform many different functions, including learning new skills and facts. These include selection, vigilance (or sustained attention), and attentional control (Parasuraman, 1998).

Selective attention requires both conscious and unconscious skills; the learner must be able to select information relevant to a task while ignoring irrelevant information. Researchers who have tested age differences in selective attention have used visual search tasks, in which subjects must search for a target item in an array of items shown under different conditions. Older people do somewhat worse than young research subjects in such studies, but only under more complex conditions. **Vigilance,** or **sustained attention,** requires the individual to look out for a specific stimulus over time. This is the type of attention that air traffic controllers must use when watching for blips (each one representing an airplane) on their radar screen. In complex tasks in which each signal requires some decision (e.g., directing a plane to change its flight course upon seeing the blip), older people do worse than young adults. However, few differences between young and old are found when the task is simple, the person has had practice with that type of vigilance, or the task does not place significant demands on memory. Age effects emerge if an event to be attended to shows up in an unpredictable pattern (Mouloua and Parasuraman, 1995; Rogers and Fisk, 2001).

Attentional control is the individual's ability to determine how much attention should be directed at specific stimuli, and when to shift focus to other stimuli. Examples include listening to the radio or conversing on a cell phone while driving, or speaking on the phone in the kitchen while cooking a multicourse dinner. Experiments with divided attention tasks have used stimuli in the same sensory mode (e.g., listening to two channels of music or words simultaneously) or different sensory systems (e.g., listening to spoken words while reading a different set of words). As with the other two components of attention, age differences are not as dramatic as once thought. If the older person has had practice with managing multiple tasks (e.g., an experienced cook who can prepare multiple dishes simultaneously), it is just as easy for old and young subjects to shift their attention. To the extent that a task becomes practiced or "automatic," even if these skills were developed many years ago, an older person can perform them without any more attentional control than a young person.

Practical Implications of Attention Changes with Aging

A better understanding of what causes age-related changes in attention and the nature of such changes can improve the person–environment (P–E) interface for older people, and their responses for maintaining active aging and P–E competence. For example, by examining each step of the task of driving under different conditions,

---

IMPROVING WEB PAGES FOR OLDER USERS

- Avoid using a patterned background behind text material.
- Use dark type or graphics against a light background.
- Avoid excess graphics and animation.
- Avoid pop-up menus that can confuse the main text.
- Use a consistent layout in different sections of the Website.
- Limit how much information is presented on each page.
- Distinctly identify all links with a specific convention, such as underlining or a unique graphic.
- Identify clearly the content that is included under each heading.
- If animation or video is used, select short segments to reduce download time.
- Provide a telephone number and e-mail for users who want direct contact.

SOURCES: Adapted from Mead, Lamson, and Rogers, 2002, and National Library of Medicine, 2002.

---

researchers can focus on specific elements of selective attention, vigilance, and attentional control. Drivers must attend to important cues such as changes in traffic signals, traffic flow, and the speed of other cars. Vigilance plays an important role in long-distance driving, especially on monotonous stretches of interstate highways. By breaking down each component of driving and determining which conditions help or hinder older drivers, designers of traffic systems can place warning signs or traffic lights in the most complex locations in order to prevent accidents. Concurrently, classes aimed at older drivers can take advantage of this knowledge to improve their selective attention and vigilance skills under diverse driving conditions.

The design of computers and Web pages is another area in which knowledge of age-related changes in attention can improve older persons' ability to maintain active aging. Given the significant growth in the number of older adults learning to use the computer, primarily for accessing the World Wide Web, it behooves Web designers to consider older users' special needs (Morrell, Mayhorn, and Bennett, 2000; Mead, Lamson, and Rogers, 2002). In addition to the changes in attention processes just described, Web and software designers must recognize that many older people experience problems with language comprehension, fine motor movement, and reading small print. Some suggestions for Web designers are presented on page 177.

Environmental Factors

One problem with assessing learning ability is that it is not possible to measure the process that occurs in the brain while an individual is acquiring new information. Instead, we must rely on an individual's performance on tests that presumably measure what was learned. This may be particularly disadvantageous to older persons, whose performance on a test of learning may be poor because of inadequate or inappropriate conditions for expressing what was learned (Botwinick, 1984). For example, an older person may in fact have learned many new concepts in reading a passage from a novel, but not necessarily the specific concepts that are called for on a test of learning. Certain physical conditions may affect performance and thus lead to underestimates of what the older person has actually learned. These include:

- lighting levels
- size of font
- tone and loudness of the test-giver's voice in an oral exam
- time constraints placed on the test-taker

The learning environment can be improved, however. Some ways to do this include:

- glare-free and direct lighting
- lettering of good quality
- larger fonts
- color contrast

Computers use can benefit even the oldest-old.

- a comfortable test-taking situation with minimal background noise
- a relaxed and articulate test-giver

Time constraints are particularly detrimental to older people. Although the ability to encode new information quickly is a sign of learning ability, it is difficult to measure. Instead, response time is generally measured. As we have already seen, psychomotor and sensory slowing with age has a significant impact on the older person's response speed. One of the first researchers to test the effect of these conditions on learning was Canestrari (1963), who used a common test of learning, the paired associates task (i.e., linking two unrelated words, letters, digits, or symbols, such as *cat* and *82*, and asking subjects to respond with the second when the first is mentioned). He presented the paired associates at varying rates, or allowed individuals to pace the task by controlling the visual apparatus themselves. In comparing people aged 60 to 69 with those aged 17 to 35, he found striking differences between old and young individuals' performance when the task was paced fast, fewer differences in moderate pacing, and the fewest differences in self-paced conditions. Young persons did well in all conditions, but older adults in this study benefited the most from self-pacing.

Decline in perceptual speed, which can be measured separately from memory skills per se, may be a major reason why older people do worse on memory tests. Research by Salthouse (1993, 1994a, 1996b) has shown that perceptual speed accounts for a significant part of the observed age-related variance in memory performance. Even when older research subjects are given more time to complete tests of memory, their perceptual speed still plays a significant role in their performance.

The general slowing hypothesis proposed by Salthouse (1996a) suggests that processing of information slows down in the nervous system with aging. This results in more problems with responding to complex tasks, so that older subjects do worse on tests with more decisions than do younger people. This hypothesis also implies that older people do worse under multitasking conditions (e.g., working on a computer while speaking on the phone and listening to the radio) than do younger people. Research on paired associates tasks has demonstrated that older persons make more *errors of omission* than *errors of commission*. That is, older persons are more likely not to give an answer than to guess and risk being wrong. This phenomenon was first recognized in middle-aged and older adults in tests of psychomotor functioning. The older the respondent, the more likely he or she was to work for accuracy at the expense of speed. This occurs even when the older learner is encouraged to guess and is told that it is acceptable to give wrong answers (i.e., commission errors). Conditions of uncertainty and high risk are particularly difficult for older persons; here they are far more cautious than the young. Low-risk situations elicit less caution from older adults and greater willingness to give responses in a learning task. The aging process may create an increased need to review multiple aspects of a problem, probably because of past experiences with similar dilemmas. Errors of omission may be reduced somewhat by giving rewards for both right and wrong answers.

Verbal ability and educational level are important factors in learning verbal information.

Studies that entail learning prose passages show age deficits among those with average vocabulary abilities and minimal or no college education. In contrast, older persons with high verbal ability and a college education perform as well as younger subjects in such experiments. This may be due to greater practice and facility with such tasks on the part of more educated persons and those with good vocabulary skills. It may also reflect differences in the ability to organize new information, a skill that is honed through years of education and one that assists in the learning of large quantities of new material.

Stability in performing familiar perceptual-motor tasks may also occur because the accomplished performer of a specific task makes more efficient moves in completing a task than does a less skilled person. Such differences are evident in many areas demanding skill, from typing and driving to playing a musical instrument or operating a lathe. Therefore, aging workers can overcome the effects of slower psychomotor speed and declines in learning skills by their greater experience in most occupations (Salthouse, 1993, 1994a).

The conditions under which learning takes place affect older persons more than the young, just as test conditions are more critical. Older persons respond differently to varied testing situations; people tested under challenging conditions ("this is a test of your intelligence") are likely to do worse than those in supportive conditions ("the researcher needs your help"). Positive feedback appears to be a valuable tool for eliciting responses from older adults in both learning and test situations.

Pacing information presents it at a rate suitable to learners of any age and gives them opportunities to practice the new information (e.g., writing down or spelling aloud newly learned words). Another condition that supports learning is the presentation of familiar and relevant material compared to material perceived by the older learner to be unimportant. Older people do worse in recalling recently acquired information than do younger people when the new information is unfamiliar or confusing. Age differences also emerge when the material to be learned is low in meaning and personal significance to the learner. Laboratory studies of cognitive functioning often seem artificial and meaningless to older adults who are unaccustomed to such research methods, and even more so to those with little academic experience. Many people will complain that such tests are trivial, nonsense, or that these tasks have no connection to the "real world." Indeed, it may appear odd to anyone to be learning meaningless words and symbols in a lab study. But for those older people who are unfamiliar with test-taking situations, it may appear particularly foolish and not worth the effort required. This may also serve a useful ego-defensive function for individuals who feel uncomfortable or threatened by a test-taking situation. It is generally easier for people to blame the environment or the test situation for their poor performance than to accept it as a sign of a decline in their intelligence or their ability to learn.

Spatial memory, that is, the ability to recall where objects are in relationship to each other in space (e.g., when finding one's way around a community or using a map), also appears to decline with aging. It is unclear, however, if older people do worse than the young because they have difficulty encoding and processing the information, or if the problem is in retrieval. It appears that there is an age-related decline in encoding ability for spatial information. Spatial recall was tested in one study following the presentation of a two-dimensional black-and-white map versus a colored map or a three-dimensional model. Older subjects in this study recalled fewer items than the young did under the condition of no visual cues, but no age differences were found when color or 3-D representations were used (Sharps and Gollin, 1988). Similarly, older people have more difficulty than younger persons in reading maps that are misaligned relative to the user. For example, when older people stand in front of a "You are here" map that is aligned 180° away from themselves, they take up to 50 percent more time

and make 30 percent more errors than younger persons in the same condition. However, when the map is aligned directly with the user, no age differences are observed. This may be attributable to increased problems with mental rotation of external images and with perspective-taking as we age (Aubrey, Li, and Dobbs, 1994).

Age-Related Changes in Memory

As we have seen, learning involves encoding information and storing it into secondary or long-term memory, so that it can be retrieved and used later. Studies of this process have focused on two types of retrieval: recall and recognition. **Recall** is the process of searching through the vast store of information in secondary memory, perhaps with a cue or a specific, orienting question. **Recognition** requires less search. The information in secondary memory must be matched with the stimulus information in the environment. Recall is demanded in essay exams, recognition in multiple-choice tests.

Not surprisingly, most researchers have found age-related deficiencies in recall, but few differences in recognition. This may be due to the context in which multiple stimuli are presented, triggering cues for the test-taker (Smith, 1996; Sharps and Martin, 1998). Recall tasks have been further divided into **free recall** and **cued recall** situations. In the former, no aids or hints are provided for retrieving information from secondary memory. In the latter case, the individual is given some information to aid in the search (e.g., category labels and first letter of a word). Older people tend to do much worse than the young in tests of free recall, but are aided significantly by cueing. In particular, use of category labels (semantic cues) at the learning stage is found to be more helpful to older persons than the use of structural cues—for example, giving the respondent the first letter of a word to be recalled (Smith, 1996). However, cued recall tests are not as helpful as recognition tests for older learners.

EXAMPLES OF RETRIEVAL

Recall

Free recall "List the capitals of each state." "Describe how to repair a bicycle tire."

Cued recall "The capital of New York begins with the letter 'A'; what is it?"

Recognition

"Which of these three cities is the capital of New York?"

"All but one of the following is a type of memory. Select the one that is not."

Of considerable controversy in aging and memory function is the question of whether older people have better recall of events that occurred in the distant past than recent situations. Many events are firmly embedded in secondary memory because they are unique or so important that subsequent experiences do not interfere with the ability to recall them. The birth of a child, one's wedding ceremony, or the death of a parent, spouse, or sibling are events that most people can recall in detail 40 to 50 years later. This may be because the situation had great private significance or—in the case of world events, such as the bombing of Hiroshima or President Kennedy's assassination—had a profound impact on world history. Some distant events may be better recalled because they have greater personal relevance for the individual's social development than recent experiences, or because they have been rehearsed or thought about more. Another possibility is that cues that helped the older person recall events in the past are less effective with recalling recent occasions because of "cue-overload." That is, the same cues that were once helpful in remembering certain information are also used to recall many recent events. But the cues are so strongly associated with one's earlier life experiences that the newer information becomes more difficult to retrieve. For example, older people may have difficulty memo-

rizing new phone numbers because the cues that helped them recall phone numbers in the past may be so closely associated with previous ones that they confuse recent phone numbers with old ones.

One problem in determining whether recall of distant situations is really better than recall of recent events is the difficulty in validating an older person's memories. In many cases, there are no sources that can be checked to determine the accuracy of such recollections. We can all identify with this process of asking an old friend or family member, "Do you remember the time when . . . ?" If others have no recollection of the event, it may make us wonder if the situation really took place, or it may mean that the event was so obscure that it made no impact on other people. Hence, such memories are difficult to measure accurately.

Several theories have been offered to explain *why* older people may have problems with retrieving information from secondary memory. One explanation is that not using the information results in its loss (the **disuse theory**). This theory suggests that information can fade away or decay unless it is exercised, as in the adage, "Use it or lose it." However, this explanation fails to account for the many facts that are deeply embedded in a person's memory store and that can be retrieved even after years of disuse.

A more widely accepted explanation is that new information interferes with the material that has been stored over a period of many years. As we have noted earlier, interference is a problem in the learning or encoding stage. When the older person is distracted while trying to learn new information, this information does not become stored in memory. Poor retrieval may be due to a combination of such distraction during the learning stage and interference by similar or new information with the material being searched in the retrieval stage. Although researchers in this area have not conclusively agreed on any of these explanations, the **interference theory** appears to hold more promise than others for explaining observed problems with retrieval.

Tip-of-the-Tongue States

Tip-of-the-tongue states (TOTs) represent a specific type of difficulty in retrieval. We have all experienced situations when we know the name of a place or person but cannot immediately recall it. This might be the name of a favorite restaurant or park, or a famous actor or character in a story, or an acquaintance we have not seen in many years. Features of TOTs are that the target word is familiar and will be recalled by searching through one's memory, drawing associations from similar names, or mentally focusing on an image of the place or person. TOTs are also distinguished by a feeling of *imminence*, the sense that one can "almost" remember it, or that it is on the "tip of one's tongue" (Schwartz, 2002).

Although all people experience TOTs, both anecdotal evidence and cross-sectional studies show that older adults have more problems with these situations. Two different theories have been offered to explain the increase with TOTs as we age. The first of these is the *decrement model*, which suggests that memory networks deteriorate with aging, and TOTs are a manifestation of these impaired networks (Brown and Nix, 1996). The second model focuses on *incremental knowledge gain* with aging, whereby the cumulative knowledge and vocabulary of older adults can cause more names in secondary memory to interfere with the name to be recalled (Dahlgren, 1998).

When we experience a TOT, we can rely on:

1. spontaneous retrieval of the name (i.e., letting it pop into our primary memory later, when we are removed from the immediate pressure to remember the words),
2. using specific search strategies such as cues (e.g., listing similar names or going through the alphabet), or
3. using other sources to aid recall, such as asking another person or looking in a dictionary or thesaurus.

Older people seem to use spontaneous recall more often, and search strategies of any type less often

---

LIFELONG LEARNING

Continuing education is an excellent way to maintain intellectual skills in old age. Elderhostel is a popular international program that offers older adults learning options based on college campuses and through tours to educational and historic sites. "Summer College for Seniors" is a program offered by Shoreline Community College in Seattle. Each summer, more than 100 elders participate in weeklong college classes on topics as wide-ranging as constitutional law and classical music. College faculty who teach these older students enjoy the perspectives they bring, and praise their maturity both intellectually and emotionally. As one 65-year-old Summer College student noted, "The people here may be gray on top but they're not dull between the ears." Another participant, age 75, added, "I think, as a senior, mental stimulation is as important as physical exercise."

Seattle Times, July 25, 2000, p. B1 (F. Vinluan, staff reporter).

---

than young adults. These differences may be explained by the decrement model and incremental knowledge model. The former would posit that aging causes deterioration in one's efficient use of cues; the latter would attribute it to a larger bank of names in one's memory that make it difficult to search for a specific word (Schwartz, 2002).

Improving Cognitive Abilities in Old Age

Cognitive Retraining

In the Seattle Longitudinal Study described earlier in this chapter, the researchers tested the effects of **cognitive retraining**—teaching research participants how to use various techniques to keep their minds active and maintain good memory skills. This cognitive retraining is based on the premise of maximizing one's remaining potential, a widely accepted concept in physical aging but only recently applied to cognitive aging. Intellectual activities that involve problem-solving and creativity, such as Scrabble and crossword puzzles, are described by Schaie and colleagues as effective ways for older people to maximize their intellectual abilities (Schaie and Hertzog, 1986; Willis and Nesselroade, 1990; Willis and Schaie, 1988, 1986). Cognitive performance improved in about 65 percent of participants, and 40 percent who had declined in the preceding 14 years showed a return to their predecline levels. Cognitive retraining was most effective when it focused on the specific primary mental abilities that each elder had lost. However, the oldest participants benefited least from training, even with booster sessions to assist in the retraining.

There has been considerable experimentation with techniques for improving memory. Some of the most exciting research focuses on developing drugs that enhance the chemical messengers in neurons or improve the function of neural receptors. Within the next few years there may be some approved memory-enhancing drugs for older adults. Ginkgo biloba, a natural extract derived from leaves of the maidenhair tree, has received attention because it seems to improve memory by improving circulation in the brain. Systematic research on the effects of ginkgo biloba for mild memory loss, as well as for people with Alzheimer's disease, has begun (Van Dongen et al., 2000). Vitamin E is an antioxidant (described in Chapter 3) that may help enhance memory by reducing oxidative damage resulting from normal aging. No long-term human studies are yet available to support these claims for the benefits of vitamin E or other possible supplements such as lecithin, vitamin B_{12}, and folic acid.

It is also important to recognize that therapeutic doses of these and other supplements (i.e., levels that are high enough to show improved memory function) may be high enough to cause harmful side effects such as internal bleeding. Other researchers have examined practical methods such as cognitive aids. Although useful at any age, cognitive aids may be particularly helpful for an older person who is experiencing increased problems with real-world cognitive abilities, such as recalling names, words, phone numbers, and daily chores. Older persons are more likely to use external aids such as notes and lists than they are to use cognitive aids. That is, they are more likely to reduce environmental press than to enhance their competence in learning as a means of improving P–E congruence. Older adults who are most concerned about declining memory use external and cognitive aids as a way of coping with the problem. This is particularly true for elders with a strong internal locus of control—that is, a belief that they have control over their well-being rather than attributing their problems to external forces (Verhaeghen et al., 2000). Recognizing that low self-efficacy can affect older people's learning ability, researchers have used cognitive restructuring techniques to convince older learners to changes their views of aging and memory. By focusing on their strengths and believing that they could control how much they retained of newly acquired information, elders in one study improved their scores on memory tests more than their counterparts who did not focus on self-efficacy training (Caprio-Prevette and Fry, 1996).

Memory Mediators

Most memory improvement techniques are based on the concept of mediators, that is, the use of visual and verbal links between information to be encoded and information that is already in secondary memory. Mediators may be visual (e.g., the method of locations) or verbal (i.e., the use of mnemonics). **Visual mediators**—the method of locations (or loci)—are useful for learning a list of new words, names, or concepts. Each word is associated with a specific location in a familiar environment. For example, the individual is instructed to "walk through" his or her own home mentally. As the person walks through the rooms in succession, each item on the list is associated with a particular space along the way.

LOOK, SNAP, AND CONNECT

A practical method for retaining information efficiently in order to recall it later is the "Look, Snap and Connect" technique, recommended by Small (2002), who suggests that we can improve our memory at every age by using an encoding and retrieval system that is personally meaningful. The components of this method are:

Look: Actively focus on what you want to learn in order to take in the information, and record the information received through multiple senses.

Snap: Create a mental snapshot or image of the object or person or word(s) to be remembered; the more bizarre or unusual the image, the better it will be recalled (e.g., remembering Mr. Brown's name by visualizing him covered with brown paint).

Connect: Visualize a link to associate the images created through mental snapshots, thereby retaining the information through its link with existing memories (e.g., remembering a grocery list by connecting items together, such as *flour* poured over *apples* that are swimming in a bowl of *milk*).

SOURCE: From G. Small, *The memory bible* (New York: Hyperion, 2002).

Older persons using this technique are found to recall more words on a list than when they use no mediators. One advantage of the method of loci is that learners can visualize the new information within a familiar setting, and can decide for themselves what new concept should be linked with what specific part of the environment. Imaging is a useful technique in everyday recall situations as well. For example, an older person can remember what he or she needs to buy at the grocery story by visualizing using these items in preparing dinner.

Another way of organizing material to be learned and to ensure its storage in secondary memory is to use **mnemonics,** or verbal riddles, rhymes, and codes associated with the new information. Many teachers use such rhymes to teach their students multiplication, spelling (e.g., "*i* before *e* except after *c*"), and the calendar ("30 days hath September, April, June, and November/all the rest have 31, except February alone, and that has 28 days clear/except every leap year"). Many other mnemonics are acquired through experience as well as our own efforts to devise ways to learn a new concept (e.g., making up a word to remember the three components of cognition: intelligence, learning, memory might become "IntLeMe"). These can assist older people, particularly the young-old, to learn more efficiently, especially if the mnemonics are specific to the memory task at hand (Verhaeghen, Marcoen, and Goossens, 1992). Older people with mild or moderate dementia can also benefit from visual methods of recall (e.g., method of loci), but less from list-making (Yesavage et al., 1990). Whatever method is used, however, it is important to train the older adult in the use of a specific mnemonic and to provide easy strategies to help the person apply these techniques to everyday learning events. In one study, researchers provided half the sample with a "memory handbook" and 30 minutes of practical instruction; the other half were given just a pamphlet that gave examples of useful mnemonics (but no face-to-face instruction in their use). The former group demonstrated significant improvements in two subsequent memory tests; the pamphlet group did not (Andrewes, Kinsella, and Murphy, 1996).

Other mediators to aid memory include:

1. using the new word or concept in a sentence,
2. associating the digits in a phone number with symbols or putting them into a mathematical formula (e.g., "the first digit is 4, the second and third are multiplied to produce the first"),
3. placing the information into categories,
4. using multiple sensory memories, and
5. combining sensory with motor function.

In this last technique, one may write the word (iconic memory), repeat it aloud to oneself (echoic memory), or "feel" the letters or digits by outlining them with one's hand. Unfortunately, many older persons do not practice the use of newly learned memory techniques. They may not be motivated to use the techniques, which often seem awkward, or they may forget and need to be reminded. Perhaps the major problem is that these are unfamiliar approaches to the current generation of older people. As future cohorts become more practiced in these memory techniques through their educational experiences, the use of such strategies in old age may increase.

The most important aspect of memory enhancement may be the ability to relax and to avoid feeling anxious or stressed during the learning stage. As noted earlier, many older people become overly concerned about occasional memory lapses, viewing them as a sign of deterioration and possible onset of senile dementia. Thus, a young person may be annoyed when a familiar name is forgotten, but will probably not interpret the memory lapse as loss of cognitive function, as an older person is likely to do. Unfortunately, society reinforces this belief. How often are we told that we are "getting old" when we forget a trivial matter? How often do adult children become concerned that their parent sometimes forgets to turn off the stove, when in fact they may frequently do this themselves? Chronic stress can also impair older people's memory performance. Research with animals and humans has shown that some hormones released under high stress conditions (e.g., cortisol and corticosterone) cause the subject to make more errors in memory tests (McGaugh, 2000).

In addition to mediators, **external aids** or **devices** are often used by older people to keep track of the time or dates, or to remember to turn the stove on or off. Simple methods such as list-making can significantly improve an older person's recall and recognition memory, even if the list is not used subsequently. A list that is organized by topic

---

A MEMORY EXERCISE

Use the method of loci to help you remember *seven* items that you need to buy at the grocery store. Go to the store without a list, but imagine yourself walking through the kitchen at home after your trip to the grocery store, placing each of the seven items in a specific location.

---

or type of item (e.g., a chronological "to-do" list or a grocery list that groups produce, meats, dry-goods together) also is found to aid older people's memory significantly. However, older adults with higher educational attainment and better vocabulary skills benefit even more from list-making methods (Burack and Lackman, 1996). Older people can develop the habit of associating medication regimens with specific activities of daily living, such as using marked pill boxes and taking the first pill in the morning before their daily shower, or just before or after breakfast, taking the second pill with lunch or before their noontime walk, and so on. These behaviors need to be associated with activities that occur every day at a particular time, in order that the pill-taking becomes linked with that routine. Charts listing an individual's daily or weekly routine can be posted throughout the house. Alarm clocks and kitchen timers also can be placed near an older person while the oven or stove is in operation. This will help in remembering that the appliance is on without the person's needing to stay in the kitchen. With the increased availability of home computers, daily activities and prescription reminders could be programmed into an older person's computer. A fire alarm or smoke detector is essential for every older person's home, preferably one for every floor or wing of the house. Finally, for older people who have serious memory problems and a tendency to get lost while walking outdoors, a bracelet or necklace imprinted with the person's name, address, phone number, and relevant medical information can be a lifesaver.

Wisdom and Creativity

Wisdom and creativity are more difficult to define and measure. Most people have an image of what it means to be wise or creative, but it is impossible to quantify an individual's level of wisdom or creativity. It is suggested that *wisdom* requires the cognitive development and self-knowledge that come with age (Levitt, 1999). Wisdom is a combination of experience, introspection, reflection, intuition, and empathy; these are qualities that are honed over many years and that can be integrated in people's interactions with their environments. Thus, younger people may have any one of these skills individually, but their integration requires more maturity. Based on research with older adults who had been nominated as "wise" by other people, the following five criteria are recommended to assess if the individual demonstrates wise behavior (Baltes and Staudinger, 2000; Staudinger, 1999):

- *Factual knowledge*—possessing both general and specific information about life conditions and relevant issues.
- *Procedural knowledge*—using decision-making strategies, planning, interpretation of life experiences to a given situation.
- *Lifespan contextualism*—considering the context in which events are occurring and the relationship among them.
- *Value relativism*—considering and respecting values and priorities brought to the situation by other participants.
- *Managing uncertainty*—developing back-up plans or alternative strategies if one's performance is hampered by external factors.

Wisdom is achieved by transcending the limitations of basic needs such as health, income, and housing. The individual must have continued opportunities for growth and creativity in order to develop wisdom (Ardelt, 1997; Orwoll and Achenbaum, 1993). Wisdom implies that the individual does not act on impulse and can reflect on all aspects of a given situation objectively.

Younger generations can benefit from the wisdom of elder scholars.

In many cultures, older persons are respected for their years of experience, and the role of "wise elder" is a desired status. But not all older people have achieved wisdom. Wisdom suggests the ability to interpret knowledge, or to understand the world in a deeper and more profound manner. Such reflectiveness and the reduced self-centeredness that this requires allow older people to take charge of their lives and become more accepting of their own and others' weaknesses. Indeed, among older men and women in the Berkeley Guidance Study, those who scored high on the three components of wisdom (cognitive, reflective, affective thinking) also scored high on a measure of life satisfaction. This suggests that active or "successful aging" (described in Chapter 1 and 6) is enhanced when wisdom has been attained (Ardelt, 1997). Older people who have achieved this level of wisdom could play useful roles in many businesses, government and voluntary agencies, where their years of experience and ability to move beyond the constraints presumed by others could help such organizations succeed. The **balance theory of wisdom** suggests that a wise individual is one who can balance different components of intelligence—practical, analytical, and creative—and use them to solve problems that will benefit society, rather than focusing on using one's intelligence for personal gain (Sternberg, 1998; Sternberg and Lubart, 2001).

Creativity refers to the ability to apply unique and feasible solutions to new situations, to come up with original ideas or material products. A person may be creative in science, the arts, or technology. Although we can point to creative people in each of these areas (e.g., Albert Einstein in science, Wolfgang Amadeus Mozart and Georgia O'Keeffe in the arts, and Thomas Edison in technology), it is difficult to determine the specific characteristics that make such persons creative. As with intelligence in general, creativity is inferred from the individual's output, but cannot really be quantified or predicted. One measure of creativity is a test of *divergent thinking,* which is part of Guilford's (1967) structural model of intelligence. This is measured by asking a person to devise multiple solutions to an unfamiliar mental task (e.g., name some different uses for a flower). Later still, Torrance (1988) developed a test of creativity that also measures divergent thinking. Children who scored high on this test were found to be creative achievers as young adults (i.e., the test has good predictive and construct validity), but the test has not been used to predict changes in creativity across the life span.

Divergent thinking may be only one component of creativity, however. A creative person must also know much about a particular body of knowledge such as music or art before he or she can make creative contributions to it. However, this neglects the contributions to scientific problem-solving or the arts by people who may have expertise in one area and bring a fresh perspective to a different field. To date, there have been no systematic studies of divergent thinking among people who are generally considered to be creative. Much of the research on creativity has been performed as analyses of the *products* of artists and writers, not on their creative *process* directly. Indeed, no studies have been conducted to compare the cognitive functioning of artists, scientists, technologists, and others who are widely regarded as creative with that of persons not similarly endowed. Researchers who have examined the *quantity* of creative output by artists, poets, and scientists have found that the average rate of output at age 70 to 80 drops to approximately half that of age 30 to 40. However, a secondary peak of productivity often occurs in the 60s, although not as high as the first peak (Simonton, 1989, 1991, 1999). Indeed, Simonton's analysis of the last works of 172 classical composers in their final years revealed compositions that were judged highly by musicologists in terms of aesthetics, melody, and comprehensibility (Simonton, 1989). Mathematicians and theoretical physicists produce their major works in their late 20s and 30s, whereas novelists, historians, and philosophers reach their peak in their late 40s and 50s.

Implications for the Future

Advances in neuroscience will eventually uncover the specific changes in the brain that account for age-related changes in memory, attention, and learning ability. New techniques of brain research are evolving with the use of magnetic resonance imaging (MRI) and positron emission tomography (PET) that can determine which areas of the brain are responsible for different types of attention and learning. These noninvasive techniques adopted from the medical diagnostic field are already being used to study differences in attention tasks between young and old subjects, and between older persons with different types of dementia. PET scans can reveal differences in brain activity among people with varying educational levels, and in the early stages of Alzheimer's disease (Greenwood and Parasuraman, 1999; Parasuraman and Greenwood, 1998; Silverman, Small, and Chang, 2001; Small, 1999).

Unfortunately, however, these high-tech methods of early detection may not be accessible to all people as they age because of their high cost. Unless Medicare and private insurers recognize the benefits of screening for dementia, as they do with cancer, these techniques will be limited to older adults who can afford to pay for them. This is true for other computer-assisted devices and systems that can be used in older adults' homes to help them maintain person–environment competence, as will be described in Chapter 11.

Summary

This chapter presented an overview of the major studies on cognitive functioning in the later years. Researchers have examined age-related changes in intelligence, learning, and memory, and what factors in the individual and the environment affect the degree of change in these three areas of cognitive functioning.

Of all the cognitive functions in aging, intelligence has received the greatest attention and controversy. It is also the area of most concern for many older persons. One problem with this area of research is the difficulty of defining and measuring what is generally agreed to be intelligence. In examining the components of intelligence measured by the Wechsler Adult Intelligence Scale (WAIS), fluid intelligence (as measured by performance scales) has been shown to decline more with aging than verbal, or crystallized, intelligence. This may be due partly to the fact that the former tests are generally timed, while the latter are not. However, age differences emerge even when tests are not timed, and when variations in motor and sensory function are taken into account. This decline in fluid intelligence and maintenance of verbal intelligence is known as the Classic Aging Pattern. To the extent that older persons practice their fluid intelligence by using their problem-solving skills, they will experience less decline in this area. In contrast, aging does not appear to impair the ability for remembering word and symbol meanings. This does not imply that the ability to recall words is unimpaired, but when asked for definitions of words, older people can remember their meanings quite readily.

One problem with studying intelligence in aging is that of distinguishing age *changes* from age *differences*. To determine changes with age, people must be examined longitudinally. The problems of selective attrition and terminal drop make it difficult to interpret the findings of longitudinal studies of intelligence. These factors may result in an underestimate of the decline in intelligence with aging. The problem of cross-sectional studies of intelligence is primarily that of cohort differences. Even if subjects are matched on educational level, older persons have not had the exposure to computers and early childhood learning opportunities that have become available to recent cohorts. Other factors, such as occupation, sensory decline, poor physical health, and severe hypertension, are found to have a significant impact on intelligence test scores.

Learning and memory are cognitive functions that are usually examined because tests of memory are actually tests of what a person has learned. According to the information processing model, learning begins when information reaches sensory memory, and then is directed via one or more sensory stores to primary memory. It is in primary memory that information must be organized and processed if it is to be retained and passed into secondary memory. Information is permanently stored in this latter region. Studies of recall and recognition provide evidence that aging does not affect the capacity of either primary or secondary memory. Instead, it appears that the aging process makes us less efficient in "reaching into" our secondary memory and retrieving material that was stored years ago. Tip-of-the-tongue states are an exmaple of problems in remembering familiar names and words, and the role of stress in the retrieval process. Recognition tasks, in which a person is provided with a cue to associate with an item in secondary memory, are easier than pure recall for most people, but especially for older individuals. Some types of memory, such as semantic and procedural memory, are retained into advanced old age. Others, like source memory, show age-related decrements.

The learning process can be enhanced for older people by reducing time constraints, making the learning task more relevant for them, improving the physical conditions by using bright but glare-free lights and large letters, and providing visual and verbal mediators for learning new information. Helping the older learner to relax and not feel threatened by the learning task also ensures better learning. Such modifications are consistent with the goal of achieving greater congruence between older people and their environment.

Significant age-related declines in intelligence, learning, and memory appear not to be inevitable. Older people who continue to perform well on tests of intelligence, learning, and memory are characterized by: higher levels of education, good sensory functioning, good nutrition, employment that required complex problem-solving skills, and continued use of such skills in their later years. People who do not have serious cardiovascular disease or severe hypertension also perform well, although there is some slowing of cognitive processing and response speed. Even such slowing is not a problem for older people whose crystallized knowledge in the targeted area is high. Natural products and vitamins that may improve memory in older people are just now receiving research attention.

Although there is some agreement that wisdom is enhanced by age and that creativity reaches a second peak for some people in old age, there has been less research emphasis in these areas. Indeed, these concepts are more difficult to measure in young and old persons. These and other issues in cognition must be studied more fully with measures that have good construct validity before gerontologists can describe with certainty cognitive changes that are attributable to normal aging.

GLOSSARY

attentional control   ability to allocate one's attention among multiple stimuli simultaneously

Classic Aging Pattern   the decline observed with aging on some performance scales of intelligence tests vs. consistency on verbal scales of the same tests

cognitive retraining   teaching research participants how to use various techniques to keep their minds active and maintain good memory skills

crystallized intelligence   knowledge and abilities one gains through education and experience

disuse theory   the view that memory fades or is lost because one fails to use the information

echoic memory   auditory memory, a brief period when new information received through the ears is stored

external aids   simple devices used by older people to keep track of the time or dates, etc., such as list-making

fluid intelligence   skills that are biologically determined, independent of experience or learning, similar to "native intelligence," requiring flexibility in thinking

general slowing hypothesis   physiological changes that cause slower transmission of information through the nervous system with aging

iconic memory   visual memory, a brief period when new information received through the eyes is stored

information processing model   a conceptual model of how learning and memory take place

intelligence   the theoretical limit of an individual's performance

intelligence quotient (IQ)   an individual's relative abilities in making judgments, in comprehension, and in reasoning

interference theory   the view that memory fades or is lost because of distractions experienced during learning or interference from similar or new information to the memory sought

mediators   visual and verbal links between information to be memorized and information that is already in secondary memory

mnemonics   the method of using verbal cues such as riddles or rhymes as aids to memory

primary mental abilities   the basic set of intellectual skills, including mathematical reasoning, word fluency, verbal meaning, inductive reasoning, and spatial orientation

recall   the process of searching through secondary memory in response to a specific external cue

recognition   matching information in secondary memory with the stimulus information

secondary (long-term) memory   permanent memory store; requires processing of new information to be stored and cues to retrieve stored information

selective attention   being able to focus on information relevant to a task while ignoring irrelevant information

sustained attention (vigilance)   keeping alert to focus on a specific stimulus over time

spatial memory   the ability to recall where objects are in relationship to each other in space

terminal decline hypothesis   the hypothesis that persons who are close to death decline in their cognitive abilities

tip-of-the-tongue states   difficulty retrieving names from secondary memory but often spontaneously recalled later

visual mediators   the method of locations; memorizing by linking each item with a specific location in space

working (primary) memory   the active process of holding newly acquired information in storage; a maximum of 7±2 stimuli before they are processed into secondary memory or discarded

REFERENCES

Andrewes, D. G., Kinsella, G., and Murphy, M. Using a memory handbook to improve everyday memory in community-dwelling older adults with memory complaints. *Experimental Aging Research*, 1996, *22*, 305–322.

Ardelt, M. Wisdom and life satisfaction in old age. *Journals of Gerontology*, 1997, *52B*, P15–P27.

Aubrey, J. B., Li, K. Z. H., and Dobbs, A. R. Age and sex differences in the interpretation of misaligned "You-are-Here" maps. *Journals of Gerontology*, 1994, *49*, P29–P31.

Baltes, P. B. The aging mind: Potential and limits. *The Gerontologist*, 1993, *33*, 580–594.

Baltes, P. B., and Staudinger, U. M. Wisdom: A meta-heuristic to orchestrate mind and virtue toward excellence. *American Psychologist*, 2000, *55*, 122–126.

Berg, S. Aging, behavior, and terminal decline. In J. E. Birren and K. W. Schaie (Eds.), *Handbook of the psychology of aging* (4th ed.). San Diego: Academic Press, 1996.

Binet, A., and Simon, T. Méthodes nouvelles pour le diagnostique du niveau intellectuel des anormaux. *Année Psychologique*, 1905, *11*, 102–191.

Bosworth, H. B., Schaie, K. W., and Willis, S. L. Cognitive and sociodemographic risk factors for mortality in the Seattle Longitudinal Study. *Journal of Gerontology B: Psychological and Social Sciences*, 1999, *54*, 273–282.

Botwinick, J. *Aging and behavior: A comprehensive integration of research findings* (3rd ed.). New York: Springer, 1984.

Brown, A. S., and Nix, L. A. Age-related changes in the tip-of-the-tongue experience. *American Journal of Psychology*, 1996, *109*, 79–91.

Bruce, P. R., and Herman, J. F. Adult age differences in spatial memory. *Journal of Gerontology*, 1986, *41*, 774–777.

Burack, O. R., and Lackman, M. E. The effects of list-making on recall in young and elderly adults. *Journals of Gerontology*, 1996, *51B*, P226–P233.

Canestrari, R. E. Paced and self-paced learning in young and elderly adults. *Journal of Gerontology*, 1963, *18*, 165–168.

Caprio-Prevette, M. D., and Fry, P. S. Memory enhancement program for community-based older adults: Development and evaluation. *Experimental Aging Research*, 1996, *22*, 281–303.

Cattell, R. B. Theory of fluid and crystallized intelligence: A critical experiment. *Journal of Educational Psychology*, 1963, *54*, 1–22.

Christensen, H., Mackinnon, A. J., Korten, A. E., Jorm, A. F., Henderson, A. S., Jacomb, P., and Rodgers, B. An analysis of cognitive performance of elderly community dwellers: Individual differences in change scores as a function of age. *Psychology and Aging*, 1999, *14*, 365–379.

Craik, F. I. M. Memory changes in normal aging. *Current directions in psychological science*, 1994, *5*, 155–158.

Craik, F. I. M., and Jennings, J. M. Human memory. In F. I. M. Craik and T. A. Salthouse (Eds.), *The handbook of aging and cognition*. Hillsdale, NJ: Erlbaum, 1994.

Cunningham, W. R., and Owens, W. A. The Iowa State study of the adult development of intellectual abilities. In K. W. Schaie (Ed.), *Longitudinal studies of adult psychological development.* New York: Guilford Press, 1983.

Dahlgren, D. J. Impact of knowledge and age on tip-of-the-tongue rates. *Experimental Aging Research,* 1998, *24,* 139–153.

Gold, D. P., Andres, D., Etezadi, J., Arbuckle, T., Schwartzman, A., and Chaikelson, J. Structural equation model of intellectual change and continuity and predictors of intelligence in older men. *Psychology and Aging,* 1995, *10,* 294–303.

Greenwood, P. M., and Parasuraman, R. Scale of attention focus in visual search. *Perception and Psychophysics,* 1999, *1,* 837–859.

Gruber-Baldini, A. L. *The impact of health and disease on cognitive ability in adulthood and old age in the Seattle Longitudinal Study.* Unpublished doctoral dissertation. Pennsylvania State University, 1991.

Guilford, J. P. Intelligence: 1965 model. *American Psychologist,* 1966, *21,* 20–26.

Guilford, J. P. *The nature of human intelligence.* New York: McGraw-Hill, 1967.

Horn, J. L. The aging of human abilities. In B. B. Wolman (Ed.), *Handbook of developmental psychology.* Englewood Cliffs, NJ: Prentice-Hall, 1982.

Horn, J. L. Organization of data on life-span development of human abilities. In L. R. Goulet and P. B. Baltes (Eds.), *Life-span developmental psychology: Research and theory.* New York: Academic Press, 1970.

Horn, J. L., and Donaldson, G. Cognitive development in adulthood. In O. G. Brim and J. Kagan (Eds.), *Constancy and change in human development.* Cambridge, MA: Harvard University Press, 1980.

Hultsch, D. F., Hammer, M., and Small, B. J. Age differences in cognitive performance in later life: Relationships to self-reported health and activity lifestyle. *Journals of Gerontology,* 1993, *48,* P1–P11.

Inouye, S. K., Albert, M. S., Mohs, R., and Sun-Kolie, R. Cognitive performance in a high-functioning, community-dwelling elderly population. *Journals of Gerontology,* 1993, *48,* M146–M151.

Johansson, B., Zarit, S. H., and Berg, S. Changes in cognitive functioning of the oldest old. *Journals of Gerontology,* 1992, *47,* P75–P80.

Jones, H. E. Intelligence and problem-solving. In J. E. Birren (Ed.), *Handbook of aging and the individual: Psychological and biological aspects.* Chicago: University of Chicago Press, 1959.

Kallmann, F. J., and Sander, G. Twin studies on senescence. *American Journal of Psychiatry,* 1949, *106,* 29–36.

Kleemeier, R. W. Intellectual change in the senium. *Proceedings of the Social Science Statistics Section of the American Statistical Association,* 1962, *1,* 290–295.

Larue, A., Koehler, K. M., Wayne, S. J., Chiulli, S. J., Haaland, K. Y., and Garry, P. J. Nutritional status and cognitive functioning in a normally aging sample: A 6-year reassessment. *American Journal of Clinical Nutrition,* 1997, *65,* 20–29.

Launer, L. J., Masaki, K., Petrovitch, H., Foley, D., and Havlik, R. J. The association between midlife blood pressure levels and late-life cognitive function. *Journal of the American Medical Association,* 1995, *274,* 1846–1851.

Levitt, H. M. The development of wisdom: An analysis of Tibetan Buddhist experience. *Journal of Humanistic Psychology,* 1999, *39,* 86–105.

Lindenberger, U., and Baltes, P. B. Sensory functioning and intelligence in old age. *Psychology and Aging.* 1994, *9,* 339–355.

McGaugh, J. L. Memory: A century of consolidation. *Science,* 2000, *287,* 248–251.

Mead, S. E., Lamson, N., and Rogers, W. A. Human factors guidelines for web site usability: Health-oriented web sites for older adults. In R. W. Morrell (Ed.), *Older adults, health information, and the World Wide Web.* Mahwah, NJ: Erlbaum, 2002.

Morrell, R. W., Mayhorn, C. B., and Bennett, J. A survey of World Wide Web use in middle-aged and older adults. *Human Factors,* 2000, *42,* 175–182.

Mouloua, M., and Parasuraman, R. Aging and cognitive vigilance: Effects of spatial uncertainty and event rate. *Experimental Aging Research,* 1995, *21,* 17–32.

National Library of Medicine. *Making your web site senior friendly: A checklist.* Bethesda, MD: NIH/NLM, 2002.

Orwoll, L., and Achenbaum, W. A. Gender and the development of wisdom. *Human Development,* 1993, *36,* 274–296.

Owens, W. A. Age and mental abilities: A longitudinal study. *Genetic Psychology Monographs,* 1953, *48,* 3–54.

Owens, W. A. Age and mental ability: A second adult follow-up. *Journal of Educational Psychology,* 1966, *57,* 311–325.

Palmore, E. (Ed.). *Normal aging II: Reports from the Duke Longitudinal Study.* Durham, NC: Duke University Press, 1974.

Palmore, E. (Ed.). *Normal aging III: Reports from the Duke Longitudinal Study.* Durham, NC: Duke University Press, 1985.

Parasuraman, R. The attentive brain: Issues and prospects. In R. Parasuraman (Ed.), *The attentive brain.* Cambridge, MA: MIT Press, 1998.

Parasuraman, R., and Greenwood, P. M. Selective attention in aging and dementia. In R. Parasuraman (Ed.), *The attentive brain.* Cambridge, MA: MIT Press, 1998.

Poon, L. W. Differences in human memory with aging: Nature, causes, and clinical implications. In J. E. Birren and K. W. Schaie (Eds.), *Handbook of the psychology of aging* (2nd ed.). New York: Van Nostrand Reinhold, 1985.

Rabbitt, P., Donlan, C., Watson, P., McInnes, L., and Bent, N. Unique and interactive effects of depression, age, socioeconomic advantage, and gender on cognitive performance of normal healthy older people. *Psychology and Aging,* 1995, *10,* 307–313.

Rogers, W. A., and Fisk, A. D. Attention in cognitive aging research. In J. E. Birren and K. W. Schaie (Eds.), *Handbook of the psychology of aging* (5th ed.). San Diego: Academic Press, 2001.

Salthouse, T. A. Age-related differences in basic cognitive processes: Implications for work. *Experimental Aging Research,* 1994a, *20,* 249–255.

Salthouse, T. A. General and specific speed mediation of adult age differences in memory. *Journals of Gerontology,* 1996a, *51B,* P30–P42.

Salthouse, T. A. The processing speed theory of adult age differences in cognition. *Psychological Review,* 1996b, *103,* 403–428.

Salthouse, T. A. Speed and knowledge as determinants of adult age differences in verbal tasks. *Journals of Gerontology,* 1993, *48,* P29–P36.

Schaie, K. W. Intellectual development in adulthood. In J. E. Birren and K. W. Schaie (Eds.), *Handbook of the psychology of aging* (4th ed.). San Diego: Academic Press, 1996b.

Schaie, K. W. *Intellectual development in adulthood: The Seattle Longitudinal Study.* Cambridge: Cambridge University Press, 1996a.

Schaie, K. W. The primary mental abilities in adulthood: An exploration in the development of psychometric intelligence. In P. B. Baltes and O. G. Brim, Jr. (Eds.), *Life-span development and behavior* (Vol. 2). New York: Academic Press, 1979.

Schaie, K. W. The Seattle Longitudinal Study: A 21-year exploration of psychometric intelligence in adulthood. In K. W. Schaie (Ed.), *Longitudinal studies of adult psychological development.* New York: Guilford Press, 1983.

Schaie, K. W., and Hertzog, C. Toward a comprehensive model of adult intellectual development: Contributions of the Seattle Longitudinal Study. In R. J. Sternberg (Ed.), *Advances in human intelligence* (Vol. 3). Hillsdale, NJ: Erlbaum, 1986.

Schaie, K. W., Plomin, R., Willis, S. L., Gruber-Baldini, A., and Dutta, R. Natural cohorts: Family similarity in adult cognition. In T. Sonderegger (Ed.), *Psychology and aging: Nebraska symposium on motivation.* Lincoln: University of Nebraska Press, 1992.

Schaie, K. W., and Willis, S. L. Perceived family environments across generations. In V. L. Bengston, K. W. Schaie, and L. Burton (Eds.), *Societal impact on aging: Intergenerational perspectives.* New York: Springer, 1995.

Schooler, C., and Mulatu, M. S. The reciprocal effects of leisure time activities and intellectual functioning in older people: A longitudinal analysis. *Psychology and Aging,* 2001, *16,* 466–482.

Schwartz, B. L. *Tip-of-the-tongue states.* Mahwah, NJ: Lawrence Erlbaum Associates, 2002.

Sharps, M. J., and Gollin, E. S. Aging and free recall for objects located in space. *Journals of Gerontology,* 1988, *43,* P8–P11.

Sharps, M. J., and Martin, S. S. Spatial memory in young and older adults: Environmental support and contextual influences at encoding and retrieval. *Journal of Genetic Psychology,* 1998, *159,* 5–12.

Siegler, I. C. Psychological aspects of the Duke Longitudinal Studies. In K. W. Schaie (Ed.), *Longitudinal studies of adult psychological development.* New York: Guilford Press, 1983.

Silverman, D. H. S., Small, G. W., and Chang, C. Y. Evaluation of dementia with positron emission tomography: Regional brain metabolism and long-term outcome. *Journal of the American Medical Association,* 2001, *286,* 2120–2127.

Simonton, D. K. Career landmarks in science: Individual differences and interdisciplinary contrasts. *Developmental Psychology,* 1991, *27,* 119–127.

Simonton, D. K. Creativity from a historiometric perspective. In R. J. Sternberg (Ed.), *Handbook of creativity.* New York: Cambridge University Press, 1999.

Simonton, D. K. The swan-song phenomenon: Last works effects for 172 classical composers. *Psychology and Aging,* 1989, *4,* 42–47.

Small, G. W. *The memory bible.* New York: Hyperion, 2002.

Small, G. W. Positron emission tomography scanning for the early diagnosis of dementia. *Western Journal of Medicine,* 1999, *171,* 293–294.

Smith, A. D. Memory. In J. E. Birren and K. W. Schaie (Eds.), *Handbook of the psychology of aging* (4th ed.). San Diego: Academic Press, 1996.

Staudinger, U. M. Older and wiser? Integrating results on the relationship between age and wisdom-related performance. *International Journal of Behavioral Development,* 1999, *23,* 641–664.

Sternberg, R. J. A balance theory of wisdom. *Review of General Psychology,* 1998, *3,* 347–365.

Sternberg, R. J., and Lubert, T. I. Wisdom and creativity. In J. E. Birren and K. W. Schaie (Eds.), *Handbook of the psychology of aging* (5th ed.). San Diego: Academic Press, 2001.

Torrance, E. P. The nature of creativity as manifest in its testing. In R. J. Sternberg (Ed.), *The nature of creativity: Contemporary psychological perspectives.* Cambridge: Cambridge University Press, 1988.

Van Dongen, M. C. J. M., van Rossum, E., Kessels, A. G. H., Sielhorst, H. J. G., and Knipscheld, P. G. The efficacy of ginkgo for elderly people with dementia and age-associated memory impairments. *Journal of the American Geriatrics Society,* 2000, 1183–1194.

Verhaeghen, P., Geraerts, N., and Marcoen, A. Memory complaints, coping and well-being in old age: A systematic approach. *The Gerontologist,* 2000, *40,* 540–548.

Verhaeghen, P., Marcoen, A., and Goossens, L. Improving memory performance in the aged through mnemonic training: A meta-analytic study. *Psychology and Aging,* 1992, *7,* 242–251.

Willis, S. L., and Nesselroade, C. S. Long-term effects of fluid ability training in old-old age. *Developmental Psychology,* 1990, *26,* 905–910.

Willis, S. L., and Schaie, K. W. Gender differences in spatial ability in old age: Longitudinal and intervention findings. *Sex Roles,* 1988, *18,* 189–203.

Willis, S. L., and Schaie, K. W. Training the elderly on the ability factors of spatial orientation and inductive reasoning. *Psychology and Aging,* 1986, *2,* 239–247.

Yesavage, J. A., Sheikh, J. I., Friedman, L., and Tanke, E. Learning mnemonics: Roles of aging and subtle cognitive impairment. *Psychology and Aging,* 1990, *5,* 133–137.

Zelinski, E. M., Gilewski, J. J., and Schaie, K. W. Individual differences in cross-sectional and 3-year longitudinal memory performance across the adult life span. *Psychology and Aging,* 1993, *8,* 176–186.

c h a p t e r

6

Personality and Mental Health in Old Age

This chapter examines

- Normal developmental changes and stability in personality across the life span
- Theories of personality that support change or stability
- Person–environment interactions that affect personality development
- Emotional expression and regulation with personality development
- Stability versus change in self-concept and self-esteem with aging
- Older people's responses to life events and stressors
- Predictors and critiques of successful aging
- Active aging/resilience
- Major psychological disorders and dementias in old age
- The extent to which older people use mental health services

We have all had the experience of watching different people respond to the same event in different ways. For example, you probably know some students who are extremely anxious about test-taking while others are calm, and some students who express their opinions strongly and confidently while others rarely speak in class at all. All these characteristics are part of an individual's personality.

Defining Personality

Personality can be defined as a unique pattern of innate and learned behaviors, thoughts and emotions that influence how each person responds and interacts with the environment. An individual may be described in terms of several personality traits, such as passive or aggressive, introverted or extroverted, independent or dependent. Personality can be evaluated with regard to particular

194

standards of behavior; for example, an individual may be described as being adapted or maladapted, adjusted or maladjusted. Personality styles influence how we cope with and adapt to the changes when we age. The process of aging involves numerous stressful life experiences. How an older person attempts to alleviate such stress has an influence on that individual's long-term well-being. The person–environment congruence model presented in Chapter 1 suggests that our behavior is influenced and modified by the environment, and that we shape the environment around us. An individual's behavior is often quite different from one situation to another, and depends both on each situation's social norms and expectations and on that person's needs and motives.

Although personality remains relatively stable with normal aging, some older people who showed no signs of psychopathology earlier in their lives may experience some types of mental disorders in late life. For other older people, psychiatric disorders experienced in their younger years may continue or may reemerge. In some individuals the stresses of old age may compound any existing predisposition to psychopathology. These stresses may be internal, resulting from the physiological and cognitive changes, or external, that is, a function of role losses and the deaths of partners, friends, and especially one's children. Such conditions may significantly impair older people's competence, so that they become more vulnerable to environmental press and less able to function at an optimal level.

Stage Theories of Personality

Erikson's Psychosocial Model

Most theories of personality emphasize the developmental **stages** or phases of personality and imply that the social environment influences development. As we focus on stages of adult development, however, it is important to avoid the image of rigid, immutable stages and transitions that are inevitable, with no room for individual differences. In fact, people *do* make choices regarding their specific responses to common life changes. This results in numerous expressions of behavior under similar life experiences such as adolescence, parenting, retirement, and even the management of chronic diseases. There has been disagreement about whether this pattern of development continues through adulthood. Sigmund Freud's focus on psychosexual stages of development through adolescence has had a major influence on developmental psychology. In most of his writings, Freud suggests that personality achieves stability by adolescence. Accordingly, adult behavior is a reflection of unconscious motives and unsuccessful resolution of early childhood stages.

In contrast, Erik Erikson, who was trained in psychoanalytic theory, moved away from this approach and focused on psychosocial development throughout the life cycle. According to his model (Erikson, 1963, 1968, 1982; Erikson, Erickson, and Kivnick, 1986), the individual undergoes eight stages of development of the ego. One's unconscious goal is to achieve *ego identity*. Three of these stages are beyond adolescence, with the final one occurring in mature adulthood. At each stage the individual experiences a major task to be accomplished and a conflict; the conflicts of each stage of development are the foundations of successive stages. Depending on the outcome of the crisis associated with a particular stage, the individual proceeds to the next stage of development in alternative ways. Erikson also emphasized the interactions between genetics and the environment in determining personality development. His concept of the *epigenetic principle* assumed an innate plan of development in which people proceed through stages as they become cognitively and emotionally more capable of interacting within a wider social radius. Hence, each subsequent stage requires additional cognitive and emotional development before it can be experienced.

The individual in the last stage of life is confronted with the task of **ego integrity versus despair.** According to Erikson, the individual at this

ERIKSON'S PSYCHOSOCIAL STAGES

Stage	Goal
I: Basic trust vs. mistrust	To establish basic trust in the world through trust in the parent.
II: Autonomy vs. shame and doubt	To establish a sense of autonomy and self as distinct from the parent; to establish self-control vs. doubt in one's abilities.
III: Initiative vs. guilt	To establish a sense of initiative within parental limits without feeling guilty about emotional needs.
IV: Industry vs. inferiority	To establish a sense of industry within the school setting; to learn necessary skills without feelings of inferiority or fear of failure.
V: Ego identity vs. role diffusion	To establish identity, self-concept, and role within the larger community, without confusion about the self and about social roles.
VI: Intimacy vs. isolation	To establish intimacy and affiliation with one or more others, without fearing loss of identity in the process that may result in isolation.
VII: Generativity vs. stagnation	To establish a sense of care and concern for the well-being of future generations; to look toward the future and not stagnate in the past.
VIII: Ego integrity vs. despair	To establish a sense of meaning in one's life, rather than feeling despair or bitterness that life was wasted; to accept oneself and one's life without despair.

stage accepts the inevitability of mortality, achieves wisdom and perspective, or despairs because he or she has not come to grips with death and lacks ego integrity. A major task associated with this last stage is to integrate the experiences of earlier stages and to realize that one's life has had meaning, whether or not it was "successful" in a socially defined sense. Older people who achieve ego integrity feel a sense of connectedness with younger generations, and share their experiences and wisdom with them. This may take the form of:

- informal visiting
- counseling
- mentoring
- sponsoring an individual or group of younger people
- writing memoirs or letters
- assuming a leadership role in one's community

The process of shaping one's memories and experiences with others (orally or written) is described as **life review,** and is a useful mode of therapy with older adults, as described later in this chapter. Life satisfaction, or the feeling that life is worth living, may be achieved through these tasks of adopting a wider historical perspective upon one's life, accepting one's mortality, sharing experiences with the young, and leaving a legacy to future generations. Erikson's theory provides a

POINTS TO PONDER

Think about an older person you know who appears to have achieved the stage of ego integrity. What adjectives would you use to describe this individual? How would you describe your interactions with this person?

framework for studying personality in late life because it suggests that personality is dynamic throughout the life cycle. Indeed, this theory fits the person–environment model; we interact with a variety of other people in different settings, and our personality is affected accordingly. Both longitudinal and sequential research methods support the developmental stages postulated by Erikson. Standardized measures of personality demonstrate developmental changes in self-confidence, dependability, identity, and generativity (Ryff, Kwan, and Singer, 2001).

Jung's Psychoanalytic Perspective

Carl Jung's model of personality also assumes changes throughout life, as expressed in the following statement from one of his early writings:

> We cannot live the afternoon of life according to the program of life's morning, for what was great in the morning will be little at evening, and what in the morning was true will at evening have become a lie. (1933, p. 108).

Jung's model emphasizes stages in the development of consciousness and the ego, from the narrow focus of the child to the otherworldliness of the older person. Jung suggests that the ego moves from *extraversion,* or a focus on the external world in youth and middle age when the individual progresses through school, work, and marriage, to *introversion,* or to a focus on one's inner world in old age. Like Erikson, Jung examined the individual's confrontation with death in the last stage of life. He suggested that life for the aging person must naturally contract, and that the individual in this stage must find meaning in inner exploration and in an afterlife.

Jung (1959) also focused on changes in **archetypes** with age. That is, according to Jung, all humans have both a feminine and a masculine side. An archetype is the feminine side of a man's personality (the anima) and the masculine side of a woman's personality (the animus). As they age,

people begin to adopt psychological traits more commonly associated with the opposite sex. For example, older men may show more signs of passivity and nurturance while women may become more assertive as they age.

Empirical Testing of These Perspectives

In testing the validity of these theories, subsequent research has contributed to our understanding of personality development in late adulthood. Many of these studies are cross-sectional; that is, they derive information on age *differences,* not age changes. There are notable exceptions to this approach, including the Baltimore Longitudinal Studies (described in Chapter 1) and the Kansas City Studies, which examined changes in physiological, cognitive, and personality functions in the same individuals over a period of several years. Research by Costa and McCrae (1986, 1994) in the Baltimore Longitudinal Studies is related to Erikson's work, since it identifies changes in *adjustment,* with age, but stability in specific *traits* (described later in this chapter). Cross-sectional studies by De St. Aubin and McAdams (1995), and by Peterson and Klohnen (1995) examined age differences in **generativity,** Erikson's seventh stage. These researchers consistently found that middle-aged and older adults express more generative concerns (i.e., attributing more importance to the care of younger generations than to self-development) than young adults. "Generative adults" exhibit concerns not just toward their own children, but toward the younger population in general.

JUNG'S PERSPECTIVE ON INTROVERSION WITH AGING

In contrast to the young, older persons have:

a duty and a necessity to devote serious attention to (themselves). After having lavished its light upon the world, the sun withdraws its rays in order to illuminate itself (Jung, 1933, p. 109).

AGE CHANGES IN MASTERY

Young men tend to:

- be more achievement-oriented
- take more risks
- be more competitive
- be more concerned with controlling their environments

Compared to young men, older men:

- are more expressive
- are more nurturant
- have greater need for affiliation and accommodation

Young women tend to:

- be more affiliative
- be more expressive

Compared to young women, older women:

- are more instrumental
- express more achievement-oriented responses

SOURCE: Gutmann, 1992.

Other researchers have found empirical support for Jung's observations regarding decreased sex-typed behavior in old age. David Gutmann (1977, 1980, 1992), who examined personality across the life span in diverse cultures from a psychoanalytic perspective, identified a shift from **active mastery** to **passive mastery** as men age. In contrast, women appear to move from passive to active mastery. The increased passivity of older men may allow them to explore their inner worlds and move beyond the external orientation of their younger years.

The Grant Study of Harvard University Graduates longitudinal study has identified support for stage theories of personality (Vaillant, 1977, 1994; Vaillant and Vaillant, 1990). This study followed 268 men, beginning in 1938 when they were students, through age 65 when 173 of the men were still available to take part in these life reviews and qualitative interviews. These men were observed to follow a common pattern of stages:

- establishment of a professional identity in their 20s and 30s
- career consolidation in their 40s
- exploration of their inner worlds in midlife (a major transition similar to the stage of ego integrity versus despair that Erikson described as occurring in late life).

Men who were most emotionally stable and well adjusted in their 50s and 60s were characterized by:

- greater generativity (i.e., responsibility for and care of coworkers, children, charity)
- less sex-stereotyped in their social interactions
- more nurturant and expressive

These changes observed in men as they moved from youth to middle to old age have implications for contemporary family roles and responsibilities, as discussed in Chapters 9 and 10.

The Kansas City Studies

Bernice Neugarten and her associates conducted one of the first longitudinal studies of personality in middle and old age in the 1950s and 1960s. The "Kansas City Studies of Aging" have contributed to our understanding of many age-related changes in personality and coping. These researchers found that older men became more accepting of their affiliative, nurturant, and sensual side, while women learned to display the egocentric and aggressive impulses that they had always possessed but had not displayed earlier. Neugarten, similar to Jung and Gutmann, suggests that these characteristics always exist in both sexes, but social pressure and societal values encourage the expression of more gender-typed traits in youth.

The Kansas City Studies also provided the empirical basis for activity and disengagement theories described in Chapter 8. Changes in such personality characteristics as nurturance, introversion, and aggressiveness were identified in older adults. Contrary to popular stereotypes, aging was also associated with greater differences (individuation) among individuals; as people aged, they developed more unique styles of interaction. Neugarten and colleagues (1968, 1973) suggested that people do not resemble each other more in old age, but in fact become more differentiated because they grow less concerned about societal expectations. Other age-related changes observed in the Kansas City Studies included shifts toward greater cautiousness and interiority; that is, a preoccupation with one's inner life and less extroversion, as suggested by Jung. This may represent a growing concern with the meaning of life and death as one ages, to expand one's scope beyond the day-to-day details of living.

The Kansas City researchers also observed decreased impulsiveness and a movement toward using more sophisticated ego defense mechanisms with age. For example, older persons tended to use less denial and more sublimation. Attitudes toward the world were also likely to change, but these were found to relate closely to personal experiences. For instance, people do not necessarily become more conservative as they age. Based on generational (cohort) differences and personal experiences, some persons become more liberal while others adopt a more conservative social perspective during the later years. These age-related changes in impulsiveness, types of defense mechanisms used, and attitudes have been supported in studies of personality by later researchers examining a range of cultural and ethnic minority groups. Many of the changes attributed to personality in old age, such as preference for solitude or slower paced activities, are not personality traits per se, but lifestyle preferences that are influenced by life experiences, social opportunities or discrimination, and functional health status.

Dialectical Models of Adult Personality

Another model of adult personality development has been proposed by Levinson (1977, 1986) and his colleagues (Levinson et al., 1978). This model is based on secondary analyses of American men

> ### SUMMARY OF THE KANSAS CITY STUDIES
> - Older men become more affiliative, nurturant and sensual.
> - Older women accept their egocentric and assertive side.
> - There is greater individuation with aging.
> - There is increased preoccupation with one's inner life.
> - Increased cautiousness is normal with aging.
> - People become less impulsive with age.

described in published biographies and in interviews with working-class men. In a subsequent study, this model was also found to apply to women (Levinson, 1996). In contrast to Erikson, who focused on stages of ego development, Levinson and colleagues have examined developmental stages in terms of **life structures,** or the underlying characteristics of a person's life at a particular period of time. Of all stage theories of adult development, this model is the most explicit in linking each stage with a specific range of chronological age. Each period in the life structure (defined as "eras" by Levinson) represents developmental stages. Levinson defines four eras, each one lasting about 20 years. These are separated by *transitions* of about 5 years, each of which generally occurs as the individual perceives changes in the self, or as external events such as childbirth and retirement create new demands on one's relationships with others (see the box on page 200).

Levinson's model represents an example of a *dialectical approach* to personality development; it proposes that change occurs because of interactions between a dynamic person (one who is biologically *and* psychologically changing) and a dynamic environment. To the extent that an individual is sensitive to the changing self, he or she can respond to changing environmental or societal conditions by altering something within the self or by modifying environmental expectations. This process thereby reestablishes equilibrium with the environment. For example, older people

LEVINSON'S "SEASONS" OF LIFE

Era I Preadulthood (Age 0–22)

(An era when the family provides protection, socialization, and support of personal growth)

Early Adult Transition (Age 17–22)*

Era II Early Adulthood (Age 17–45)

(An era of peak biological functioning, development of adult identity)

Entering the adult world, entry life structure for early adulthood

Age 30 transition*

Settling down, culminating life structure for early adulthood

Mid-Life Transition (Age 40–45)*

Era III Middle Adulthood (Age 40–65)

(Goals become more other-oriented, compassionate roles, mentor roles assumed; peak effectiveness as a leader)

Entering life structure for middle adulthood

Age 50 transition*

Culmination of middle adulthood

Late Adulthood Transition (Age 60–65)*

Era IV Late Adulthood (Age 60+)

(An era when declining capacities are recognized; anxieties about aging, loss of power and status begin)

Acceptance of death's inevitability

*Indicates major transitions to a new developmental era.

SOURCE: D. Levinson, C. M. Darrow, E. B. Klein, M. H. Levinson, and B. McKee, *The seasons of a man's life* (New York: Alfred A. Knopf, 1978). Reprinted with permission of the author and publisher.

who deny the normal biological and physiological changes they are experiencing may have difficulty in modifying their lifestyles and environment, as illustrated by Mrs. Garcia on page 201.

Trait Theories of Personality

Another perspective on personality is to examine characteristic behaviors specific within individuals that reflect **trait theories.** Traits are relatively stable personality dispositions; together they make up a constellation that distinguishes each individual. For example, we can describe people along a continuum of personality attributes such as extroverted to introverted, passive to aggressive, and optimistic to pessimistic, as well as high or low on need for achievement and affiliation. Most personality theorists agree that traits do not change unless the individual makes a conscious effort to do so—for example, undergoing psychological counseling to become more nurturant.

This assumption of stability has led trait researchers to examine personality traits longitudinally in the middle and later years. Proponents of this approach are McCrae and Costa (1990, 1996, 1997), who measured specific traits of participants in the Baltimore Longitudinal Studies (described in Chapter 1). They propose a *five-factor model of personality traits*, consisting of five primary, independent components:

- neuroticism
- extroversion
- openness to experience
- agreeableness
- conscientiousness

Within each component are six facets or subcategories of traits. For example, neuroticism consists of anxiety, impulsiveness, self-consciousness, hostility, depression, and vulnerability. People with high neurotic tendencies would also score high on these components.

AN OLDER PERSON IN DYNAMIC INTERACTION WITH THE ENVIRONMENT

Mrs. Garcia has lived in the same house for 40 years, having raised three children there and re-modeling it as her family's needs changed over the years. Now that her husband has died and her children have their own homes, the four-bedroom house on two floors is too big for her. Her severe arthritis and heart problems make it difficult to go up and down stairs, and to maintain her house. However, Mrs. Garcia refuses to sell it, assuring everyone that she has always been able to take care of the house herself.

Standardized tests such as the Guilford-Zimmerman Temperament Survey (GZTS) are used to compare individuals with population norms on these traits. By administering the GZTS to subjects in the Baltimore Longitudinal Studies, researchers found stability in the five traits described above, independent of environmental influences. Using a cross-sectional approach, they also identified consistency in these traits in middle-aged and older adults. Both groups differed from young adults on some personality factors, especially in neuroticism, extroversion, and openness to experience (Costa and McCrae, 1994, 1995). Their research supports the idea of lifelong stability, and even heritability of some personality traits. Recent studies by McCrae and Costa, with collaborators from diverse countries, demonstrate universal patterns of stability in some personality factors and declines in others. Using their test of the five personality factors described previously (a test they have labeled the NEO-PI-R), McCrae and Costa first confirmed the cross-cultural validity of this instrument. They then worked with colleagues in Germany, Italy, Portugal, Croatia, and South Korea to compare four age cohorts (18–21 vs. 22–29 vs. 30–49 vs. 50+). Despite significant differences in cultural and historical experiences across these countries, the researchers found similar patterns of linear declines with age

in neuroticism, extroversion, and openness, and an increase in agreeableness and conscientiousness in all five countries. Although not all age differences were significant, the greatest difference was consistently between the youngest and oldest cohorts (McCrae et al., 1999).

In another cross-national comparison, the NEO-PI-R was translated to and validated in four other languages: German, Spanish, Czech, and Turkish. McCrae and Costa worked with colleagues in Germany, Spain, the Czech Republic, Turkey, and the United Kingdom to test the five-factor personality model with the same age cohorts as in their previous international study. In this sample, they also tested adolescents aged 14 to 17. They found identical patterns of significant declines with age in neuroticism and extroversion in all five countries to those identified in the earlier study. Although openness to experience was lowest in the oldest cohort, it did not show a linear, age-related decline in these countries. Agreeableness and conscientiousness also increased with age in all countries, although not necessarily in a linear pattern. Differences between the youngest and oldest cohorts were most dramatic. It should be noted that the oldest group in both of these international studies was age 50 and older, so differences after age 65 or 75 in the five personality factors cannot be distinguished from those at age 50 (McCrae et al., 2000).

Cohort and cultural influences on some personality traits have also been identified. Using a cross-sequential research design (described in Chapter 1), Schaie and Willis (1991) found few changes in specific traits of the same individuals over 7 years in the Seattle Longitudinal Study, but they did find cohort differences. That is, the oldest participants in the first wave were less flexible and adaptable than were the same older persons in the second wave of testing 7 years later. Cultural factors may also play a role in the development of certain traits. For example, traditional societies, including the United States before the women's liberation movement of the 1960s, reinforced "agreeableness" as a trait in women; the

Maintaining an active lifestyle can enhance an older person's self-confidence.

associated cluster of personality factors such as altruism, compliance, modesty, and tender-mindedness are viewed in traditional societies as important "feminine" traits. However, as women move into more diverse roles and enter occupations that were once considered "masculine," there is less gender stereotyping of traits.

Emotional Expression and Regulation

Basic emotions such as fear, anger, happiness, and shame are hardwired, or part of the core personality of every human being. However, as the individual develops and ages, feelings may become more cognitively complex and expressed differently. For example, a child often expresses every emotion under any circumstance, but with socialization and a lifetime of interpersonal experiences, older adults know how to modulate their expressive behavior, including not expressing certain emotions like anger or fear. Experiences throughout life also help adults anticipate others' emotional responses. Part of the development process is to achieve control over one's environment by expressing emotions (primary control), as well as controlling one's expressiveness through secondary control (Schulz and Heckhausen, 1998). Other personality theorists have suggested that emotion regulation serves the goal of achieving fulfilling interpersonal relations and minimizing interpersonal conflict (while at the same time maintaining a positive emotional state) in the later years (Carstensen et al., 1996; Carstensen, Pasupathi, and Mayr, 2000).

The role of family and culture on emotional expression and regulation has also been examined. People in the same age cohort may differ in their ability to express or deny emotions, based on the social conditioning they received from their parents and the cultural milieu regarding how, when, and where emotions can be expressed. Parents who discourage their children from crying in public or verbally expressing anger often set the stage for a lifetime of controlling one's emotions. Thus, emotional development depends not just on physiological and cognitive maturation, but also on familial and cultural influences (Magai, 2001; Magai et al., 2001). These early familial and cultural expectations can influence emotional expression across the life span and remain powerful messages in old age.

Self-Concept and Self-Esteem

A major adjustment required in old age is the ability to redefine one's **self-concept** or one's cognitive image of the self as social roles shift and as new roles are assumed. Our self-concept emerges from our interactions with the social environment, our social roles, and accomplishments. Through continuous interactions with the environment, people can confirm or revise these self-images. They do so either by:

- *assimilating* new experiences into their self-concept, or
- *accommodating* or adjusting their self-concept to fit the new reality.

Accommodation is more difficult and requires greater adaptive skills (Whitbourne and Primus, 1996). For example, how does a retired teacher identify himself or herself upon giving up the work that has been that individual's central focus for the past 40 or 50 years? How does a woman whose self-concept is closely associated with her role as a wife express her identity after her husband dies?

Many older persons continue to identify with the role that they have lost (think of those who continue to introduce themselves as a "teacher" or "doctor" long after retiring from those careers). This would represent a type of *identity assimilation*. Others experience *role confusion,* particularly in the early stages of retirement, when cues from other people are inconsistent with an individual's self-concept. This may require *identity accommodation*. Still others may undergo a period of depression and major readjustment to the changes associated with role loss. To the extent that a person's self-concept is defined independently of particular social roles, one adapts more readily to the role losses that may accompany old age. Both assimilation of new social roles to a stable self-concept, and some accommodation to changing realities, are indicators of successful adaptation of one's self-concept. Indeed, research with the oldest-old demonstrates that self-concept remains essentially unchanged. Even with declining health and loss of significant others, those who survive to advanced old age maintain their identity (Troll and Skaff, 1997).

For an older person whose self-concept is based on social roles and others' expectations, role losses have a particularly significant impact on that individual's **self-esteem**—defined as an evaluation or feeling about his or her identity relative to some ideal or standard.

- *Self-concept* is the cognitive definition of one's identity.
- *Self-esteem* is based on an emotional assessment of the self.

The affective quality of self-esteem makes it more dynamic and more easily influenced by such external forces as retirement, widowhood, health status, and reinforcements (both positive and negative) from others (e.g., respect, deference, or ostracism). Social roles integrate the individual to society and add meaning to one's life. As a result, alterations in social roles and the loss of status that accompanies some of these changes often have a negative impact on an older person's self-esteem. Think, for example, of an older woman whose social roles have emphasized that of caregiver to her family. If she herself becomes dependent on others for care because of a major debilitating illness such as a stroke or dementia, she is unwittingly robbed of this "ideal self," and her self-esteem may suffer.

An individual who experiences multiple role losses must not only adapt to the lifestyle changes associated with aging (e.g., financial insecurity or shrinking social networks), but must also integrate the new roles with his or her "ideal self" or learn to modify this definition of "ideal." Older persons who are experiencing major physical and cognitive disabilities simultaneously with role losses, or worse yet, whose role losses are precipitated by an illness (e.g., early retirement due to stroke or institutionalization because of Alzheimer's disease), must cope with multiple challenges at a time in their lives when they have the fewest resources to resolve them successfully. Grief and depression are common reactions in these cases.

Some studies have shown a generalized decrease in self-esteem from age 50 to 80, although many others have found improvement from adolescence through the young-old period. These varied findings may be attributed to the cross-sectional nature of research on self-esteem and age (Giarrusso and Bengtson, 1996). An analysis of 50 published studies of self-esteem among people ranging in age from 6 to 83 found a common pattern of stability in self-esteem between midlife and old age. This pattern resembles the stability of personality traits described earlier in this chapter (Trzesniewski, Donallen, and Robins, 2003). Stressful life events and disabilities such as severe hearing loss can impair older adults' self-esteem. For example, older people who are socially isolated and have significant physical disabilities are found to have the poorest self-esteem (Pinquart, 1991). On the other hand, volunteering can enhance the older person's self-esteem because it contributes to the elder's sense of personal competence. However, the long-term impact of volunteering on self-esteem is greater for people from upper socioeconomic classes than for elders from lower socioeconomic status (Herzog et al., 1998; Krause and Shaw, 2000).

Stress, Coping, and Adaptation

The process of aging entails numerous life changes, as noted in this and previous chapters. These changes, both positive and negative, place demands on the aging person's abilities to cope with new life situations. Together with health and cognitive functioning, personality characteristics influence coping responses. Self-concept and self-esteem are two important elements that play a role in coping styles, and may help explain why some older people adjust readily to major life changes, while others have difficulty. Indeed, self-esteem, health, and cognitive skills all contribute to an individual's sense of competence. Major life events and situations represent environmental stressors that place demands on an individual's competence.

Some Useful Definitions

The concept of **life events** (or *life experiences*) forms the basis for this section. These terms refer to *internal or external stimuli* that cause some change in our daily lives. They may be positive or negative, gains or losses, discrete or continuous.

Improvement in one's own health or in a family member's health are examples of *positive life events*, whereas deteriorating health and death are *negative events*. Some life experiences may have both positive *and* negative aspects. For example, older workers may view their pending retirement with great joy and make numerous plans for the post-retirement years. However, they may also ex-

> ### PERSONALITY FACTORS IMPORTANT FOR MAINTAINING SELF-ESTEEM
>
> - Reinterpretation of the meaning of self, such that an individual's self-concept and self-worth are independent of any roles he or she has played ("I am a unique individual" rather than "I am a doctor/teacher/wife").
> - Acceptance of the aging process, its limitations, and possibilities. That is, individuals who realize that they have less energy and respond more slowly than in the past, but that they can still participate in life, will adapt more readily to the social and health losses of old age.
> - Reevaluation of one's goals and expectations throughout life. Too often people establish life goals at an early age and are constantly disappointed as circumstances change. The ability to respond to internal and external pressures by modifying life goals appropriately reflects flexibility and harmony with one's environment.
> - The ability to look back objectively on one's past and to review one's failures and successes. *Life review* entails an objective review and evaluation of one's life. An older person who has this ability to reminisce about past experiences and how these have influenced subsequent personality development, behavior, and interpersonal relationships can call upon coping strategies that have been most effective in the past and adapt them to changed circumstances. Life review can also help the older person come to terms with unresolved conflicts from one's past, resulting in greater ego integrity.

perience some negative consequences as well, such as reduced income, unstructured time, and loss of the worker role.

Another distinction is made between *on-time* and *off-time* events. This concept distinguishes life experiences that a person can anticipate because of one's stage in the life cycle (on-time) from those that are unexpected at a given stage (off-time). Other researchers have used the terms *normative* and *non-normative* events, suggesting that an individual anticipates some life experiences because they are the norm for most people of a given age. For example, a man married to a 75-year-old woman is more likely to expect the death of his wife than is the husband of a 35-year-old woman. As shown later in this chapter, researchers have found differences in how people respond to on-time and off-time events.

The concept of *stress,* as defined in Chapter 4, is also important for this chapter. Since Selye's (1946) introduction of this term, many researchers have explored the antecedents, components, and consequences of stress. In fact, Selye (1970) defined aging as the sum of stresses experienced across one's lifetime. Not everyone perceives the same events to be stressful, however. Lazarus and DeLongis (1983) have introduced the concept of *cognitive appraisal*—the way in which a person perceives the significance of an encounter for his or her well-being. Cognitive appraisal serves to minimize or magnify the importance or stressfulness of an event by attaching some meaning to it. If a situation is construed as benign or irrelevant by an individual, it does not elicit coping responses. On the other hand, if a person appraises a situation as challenging, harmful, or threatening, it becomes a stressor, and calls upon the individual's adaptation responses.

Aging and Life Events

Life events are identifiable, discrete life changes or transitions that demand adaptation by the indi-

vidual, because they disrupt one's person–environment balance or homeostasis. Some researchers distinguish between life events and chronic stressors, such as poor health and financial difficulties. Both types of stressors require adaptive or coping skills (McLeod, 1996). There has been considerable discussion among researchers about the nature of life events in the later years, the older person's ability to cope with them, and whether old age is associated with more or fewer life events than youth. Significant life events that are more likely to occur in old age include widowhood, retirement, and relocation to a nursing home or assisted living facility. The nature of such roles and the novelty associated with assuming a social role for the first time result in major changes in an individual's daily functioning and demand adaptation to the new situation. Few studies have compared the relative stressfulness of role losses, role gains or replacements, and role extensions in old age, although research on life stress among younger populations is extensive. Chapter 12 examines losses and gains in both paid and nonpaid productive roles in the later years in greater detail.

The first systematic studies of the physiological and psychological impact of increased sources and amounts of stress on humans were undertaken by Holmes and colleagues (Holmes and Masuda, 1974; Holmes and Rahe, 1967; Rahe, 1972). They introduced the concept of *life change units,* a numerical score indicating the typical level of change or stress that a particular event produces in an individual's day-to-day life. It appears that the life change units assigned to some events by young respondents may not reflect the degree of stress actually produced by events that they have not yet experienced (e.g., a partner's death). Research comparing older and younger people's ratings of life events reveals:

- Some items such as "death of spouse" are perceived to be equally stressful by all ages.
- Younger people view "death of a close friend" and "marital reconciliation" as more stressful than do older people.

EXAMPLES OF INTERNALLY AND EXTERNALLY CREATED EVENTS

Internal
- changes in eating or sleeping habits
- effects of a chronic disease such as arthritis or diabetes

External
- starting a new job
- losing one's job, or retirement
- widowhood

- Older people who have experienced a life event such as "retirement" and "death of spouse" assign lower readjustment scores than people who have not experienced them.

These findings suggest that the anticipation of an event is more stressful than the actual experience, and that previous experience with a life event can help the person cope better when a similar event occurs. In addition, older people have developed greater resilience and maturity through their previous coping experiences; they may be the most adaptive members of their cohort if they have survived beyond the life expectancy predicted for them (McLeod, 1996). A more recent conceptualization suggests that it is not the major, catastrophic life events that demand effective coping responses. Instead, it is "daily hassles" such as problems related to work, family, or financial stability that create stress. Conversely, the "daily uplifts" of life, such as a friendly phone call from a grandchild who lives across the country, can help us tolerate these stressful hassles (Lazarus, 2000).

Life events such as retirement parties can have both positive and negative aspects.

What Determines Stress Responses in Old Age?

Both social and personal factors affect the process of coping with stressful events. The former encompasses friendships and family support, while the latter includes the individual's functional health, cognitive status, and self-esteem, as well as aspirations, values, vulnerabilities, and needs that mediate between a particular stressful situation and its outcomes. The individual's cognitive appraisal of a situation as being stressful or not is important. The relative desirability or undesirability of an event, whether or not it is anticipated, and previous experiences with similar events also determine how an individual responds to the situation. The availability of social supports is significant too. A person who must face a crisis alone may use different coping strategies than one who has family and friends.

Personality styles also may affect responses to stress. For example, a person with a passive style may not feel powerful enough to directly influence his or her fate, whereas one with an active style may rely more on personal abilities and less on others. Differences in responses to stress by older people with these different styles would be expected; however, research has not provided sufficient evidence for such hypothesized variations.

THE IMPORTANCE OF COGNITIVE APPRAISAL

Life events can represent a positive or negative stressor for the individual. Cognitive appraisal means that different people can view the same situation differently. One may see it as a challenge (i.e., a positive stressor), while another views it as a threat (i.e., a negative stressor). This evokes different coping responses in the two people. For example, an older woman who moves voluntarily to a retirement apartment may view it as an exciting and desirable change in her lifestyle, or she may resent the change as too demanding and disruptive. In the former case, she will adapt more readily and will experience less negative stress than in the latter. On the other hand, if this person views the move as totally benign and does not expect it to place any demands on her, she will probably be unpleasantly surprised by the level of stress that she eventually encounters, no matter how minimal.

POINTS TO PONDER

Think about some life experiences that you personally have undergone. These should include both positive and negative life events. What made each
event stressful to you? Did your cognitive appraisal
of the situations make them easier or more difficult
for you to cope with them? What specific coping
techniques did you use with each event?

Locus of control is another personality characteristic that may influence responses to stress.
This is the belief by an individual that events in his
or her life result from personal actions (internal
locus), or are determined by fate or powerful others (external locus). Internal locus of control and
a sense of mastery appear to be related to successful coping in both young and old. For example, they can help the individual maintain
functional ability in old age and improve adjustment to widowhood (Kemper, van Sonderen, and
Ormel, 1999).

Adaptation in the Later Years

As noted earlier in this chapter, a critical personality feature in the later years is an individual's
ability to adapt to major changes in life circumstances, health and social status, and social and
physical environments. **Adaptation** includes a
range of behaviors such as coping, goal-setting,
problem-solving, and other attempts to maintain
psychological homeostasis (Ruth and Coleman,
1996). Given older people's numerous experiences
with life events, role loss, and environmental
changes, it would appear that adaptation in old
age should occur with relative ease. Indeed, in one
sense, an individual who has reached age 75 or 80
has proved to be the most adaptable of his or her
generation, since the ultimate proof of adaptation
is survival. As we have seen thus far, older people
continue to face challenges to their well-being in
the form of personal and family illness, age-related

declines in sensory and physiological functions,
and changes in their social and physical environments. To the extent that older people are capable
of using coping skills that were effective in youth
and middle age, they will continue to adapt to
change successfully.

Does coping change with age? Before answering, we must first define and consider the
functions of **coping.** Coping is the manner in
which a person responds to stress. It includes cognitive, emotional, and behavioral responses made
in the face of internally and externally created
events. It differs from defense mechanisms in that
people are generally conscious of how they have
coped in a particular situation and, if asked, can
describe specific coping responses to a given stressor. Coping strategies may be described as "planful behavior" in response to a stressful situation.

These contrast with ego **defense mechanisms,**
unconscious reactions that an individual adopts to
defend or protect the self from impulses and memories that threaten one's identity. Defense mechanisms also have an underlying evaluative quality;
some defenses are more primitive or less mature
than others (see the box on page 208). As people
mature, so do the defense mechanisms that they
use. The Grant Study of Harvard Graduates found
that the men in this sample used fewer primitive
mechanisms (e.g., distortion and projection) as
they reached middle-age, and more mature mechanisms, such as sublimation, suppression, altruism, and humor (Vaillant, 1994, 2002).

Unlike defense mechanisms, coping styles cannot easily be categorized as primitive or mature.
Some forms of coping, however, are aimed not at
resolving the problem, but at providing psychological escape, as illustrated by the categories of
coping defined by some researchers (see the box on
page 209). For example, an older woman who
learns that her closest friend has a terminal illness
may cry and sympathize with her friend. This can
alleviate the stress that both are feeling, but unless
she takes some action such as searching the Internet for some newer therapies for the disease, she
has not coped with the problem itself.

MAJOR EGO DEFENSE MECHANISMS

Defense Mechanism	Example
1. Denial (a premature defense mechanism)	Denying what one really feels to avoid punishment by the super-ego and rejection by others.
2. Projection	Feeling that others are untrustworthy when one feels unsure about one's own trustworthiness.
3. Repression	Forgetting an event that could disturb the feeling of well-being if brought into consciousness.
4. Reaction formation	Extreme display of love and affection toward someone who is actually hated.
5. Regression and fixation	Returning to a comfortable stage of life and/or way of behaving under conditions of anxiety and stress.
6. Displacement	Taking out one's anger and hostility on family because one is afraid of expressing anger toward one's supervisor at work who has humiliated the individual.

This example and our earlier discussion of coping responses to life events and chronic stressors suggest that coping reactions generally serve two functions:

- *problem-focused* coping to solve a problem that has produced stress for the individual
- *emotion-focused* coping to reduce the emotional and physiological discomfort that accompanies the stressful situation (Lazarus, 1999; Lazarus and Folkman, 1984).

In some cases, an individual may focus only on solving the problem *or* on dealing with the emotional distress that it creates. Such reactions tend to be incomplete and do not resolve both the emotional and functional impact of the situation. Coping must fulfill both emotion-regulating and problem-solving functions in order to alleviate stress.

The question of whether coping styles change with age has been explored by researchers focused on specific challenges such as caregiving for a frail spouse or parent, or on different types of problems (e.g., relocation vs. death of a loved one), or on general styles of appraising coping with diverse challenges (Ryff et al., 2001). As an example of the latter type of general coping strategies, one study compared men and women across age groups. Older adults were found to use more impulse control and positive appraisal, while adolescents and young adults tended to rely on more aggressive strategies. Gender differences emerged in the use of internalizing versus outwardly expressing emotions in stressful conditions; women preferred the former and men the latter (Diehl, Coyle, and Labouvie-Vief, 1996). The extent to which life events are generated by the individual (e.g., deciding to retire) or are externally created with no choice by the person who experiences the event (e.g., being forced to take early retirement) can disrupt the individual's coping style, regardless of age. Nevertheless, uncontrollable events can propel the older person toward further growth and development (Diehl, 1999).

Religious coping is found to be an important coping strategy, especially among African American elders (Mattis and Jagers, 2001; Musick,

CLASSIFICATION OF COPING RESPONSES

General Strategies of Coping	Coping Responses to Terminal Illness	Dimensions of Coping
(Lazarus, 1975a, 1975b; Lazarus and Launier, 1978; Lazarus and Folkman, 1984)	(Moos, 1977)	(Kahana and Kahana, 1982)
• Information search in an attempt to understand the situation • Direct action to change the situation • Inhibition of action • Psychological responses to the emotional arousal created by the situation	• Searching for information • Setting goals • Denying or minimizing the problem • Seeking emotional support • Rehearsing alternative outcomes	• Instrumental (taking action, alone or with the assistance of others) • Intrapsychic (cognitive approaches, acceptance of the situation) • Affective (releasing tensions, expressing emotions) • Escape (avoiding or denying the problem, displacement activities such as increased exercise, eating, and smoking) • Resigned helplessness (feeling impotent, unable to cope)

2000; McFadden, 1996). Indeed, in the Duke Longitudinal Study, 45 percent of the respondents aged 55 to 80 mentioned trust and faith in God, prayer, and seeking help from God as a coping strategy for at least one of three major life events. Over 70 percent of adults have been found to use religion in coping with major life events. Religious coping among churchgoing adults has been identified to be associated with positive mental health (e.g., lower rates of depression) and better perceived general health (e.g., lower blood pressure and coronary artery disease risk, and improved survival rates after heart surgery) (George, 2002; Idler, 2002; Koenig and Brooks, 2002; Miller and Thoresen, 2003; Wong and Ujimoto, 1998). Social supports and a sense of belonging to a larger group are components of religious coping that influence well-being in older adults (Reiss, 2000).

Studies of coping among the old-old indicate that acceptance of change in one's life (e.g., institutionalization, divorce of children or grandchildren) may be the most adaptive coping response. Control over external events may become less important than the need to make uncontrollable events more acceptable to one's values and beliefs. In most cases, the coping styles chosen by an older person are appropriate for the problem at hand and result in successful adaptation. When cognitive deterioration is significant, however, there is a restriction in the range of an individual's coping responses and a tendency to resort to more primitive reactions, such as denying or ignoring the problem. The majority of older people appear capable of using a wide repertoire of coping responses and can call upon the most effective ones for a given situation. In sum, most people maintain their coping styles into old age, and use appropriate responses.

Successful Aging

Researchers and clinicians are increasingly interested in the concept of **successful aging** (Rowe and Kahn, 1987, 1997, 1998; Seeman et al., 1994). This interest has been sparked by the growing number of older people who have avoided the more disabling chronic health problems and declining cognitive skills that afflict other older adults and have managed to cope effectively in their daily lives. What are the characteristics of such elders who age successfully that distinguish them from their less hardy peers? Successful aging is defined as a combination of:

- physical and functional health
- high cognitive functioning
- active involvement with society

This definition implies that the successful older person has low risk of disease and disability (i.e., healthy lifestyle factors such as diet, not smoking, physical activity), is actively using problem-solving, conceptualization, and language skills, is maintaining social contacts, and is participating in productive activities (e.g., volunteering; paid or unpaid work). A model of successful aging proposed by Rowe and Kahn (1997), shown in Figure 6.1, integrates these components.

The MacArthur Studies of Successful Aging examined longitudinally a cohort of men and women (aged 70–79 at baseline) in three East Coast U.S. communities. These people were selected because they represented the top third of their age group in cognitive and physical function. Within this selective group of "robust" older persons, more specific tests of cognitive and physical

abilities, as well as physiological parameters, were conducted in 1988 and 1991. Those with the highest performance scores in this group at follow-up and those who survived three years later had fewer chronic conditions (especially cardiovascular diseases), better self-rated health, and higher educational and income levels. The majority of these robust older adults reported no problems with daily physical activities such as walking, crouching, and stooping without help. Three-year follow-ups revealed that the majority (55 percent) maintained their baseline performance levels. Another 23 percent showed a decline on the performance tests, while 22 percent actually *improved* on these tests. Those who declined or died in the interim had greater weekly variability in their physical performance, blood pressure, balance, and gait, and had entered the study with some chronic diseases (Nesselroade et al., 1996; Seeman et al., 1994). Participants in the MacArthur Studies were also assessed on their physical functioning over 7 years. Those with more social ties and a strong support system showed less decline in their functional health than elders without strong ties. Such social supports were particularly valuable for men and those who had poorer physical health at baseline (Unger et al., 1999).

As noted above, successful aging also implies maintenance of cognitive functioning. In the MacArthur Studies, *educational level* was the best predictor of continued high levels of cognitive ability (Albert et al., 1995). Rather than innate intelligence, higher educational achievement in those who aged successfully was most likely due to lifelong interest in intellectual activities such as reading and solving crossword puzzles, as well as a beneficial effect of education on the development of complex networks in the brain. Other predictors of maintaining cognitive abilities were *involvement in strenuous physical activity.* A higher level of **self-efficacy,** that is, a feeling of competence in one's ability to deal with new situations, was also a significant predictor of high physical and cognitive function at follow-up (Seeman et al., 1999).

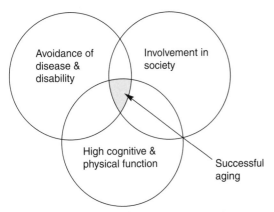

FIGURE 6.1   **A model of successful aging. This model assumes that all three components must exist for successful aging to occur.**
SOURCE: Reprinted with permission, Rowe and Kahn, 1997.

The Oregon Brain Aging Study, a longitudinal assessment of a smaller number of optimally healthy persons aged 65 to 74 and 84 to 100, measured multiple physical, cognitive, neurologic, and sensory functions as indicators of healthy aging (Howieson et al., 1993). This group of older adults was selected because they had no history of diseases affecting brain function, no psychiatric disorders, or medications that could impair cognition. Very few areas of decline were found; the oldest-old differed from the youngest-old only on tests requiring visual perception and constructional skills, *not* on tests of memory or reasoning.

The concept of "robust aging" represents a broader perspective on successful aging, one that considers exceptional functioning on measures of physical health, cognitive abilities, and emotional well-being (Garfein and Herzog, 1995; Suzman et al., 1992). Others have labeled this "optimal aging," an ideal state that is theoretically but not practically possible for most people (Schulz and Heckhausen, 1996). Four important characteristics appear to distinguish robust older adults from their less robust peers:

- productive involvement (defined as 1500 hours or more of paid or unpaid work, home maintenance, or volunteer activity in the past year)
- absence of depressive symptoms (i.e., high affective well-being)
- high physical functioning
- no cognitive impairment (Garfein and Herzog, 1995)

In the survey by Garfein and Herzog, the robust group included many in the oldest-old age range. Robust elders reported more social contacts, better physical health and vision, and fewer significant life events (e.g., death of partner, child, close friend) in the past 3 years than did poorly functioning elders. For the oldest-old, robust or successful aging also implies the ability to perform independently both basic activities of daily living and higher-level work, as well as leisure and social activities (Horgas, Wilms, and Baltes, 1998). A related concept is *resilience,* or the ability to thrive under adversity or multiple challenges by taking life's ups and downs in stride. For example, people who have strong interpersonal relationships can enhance their resilience even in the face of chronic health problems and economic adversity (Ryff et al., 2001). A recent comparison of three large longitudinal studies supports these conclusions and provides insights into personality and coping styles that result in "positive aging" (i.e., actively responding to changes in one's health and interpersonal relations). The Grant Study of Harvard Graduates studied a cohort of men born in the 1920s from their student days through old age. The Glueck Study of Inner City Adolescent Boys followed a cohort born in the 1930s, while the Terman Study of Gifted Children examined both males and females starting in 1922. Vaillant continued to interview survivors of these three groups during their middle and older years, starting with the Grant sample in 1967, the Glueck men in 1970, and only the surviving 90 women in the Terman study after 1987 (Vaillant, 1977, 1994, 2002). Vaillant found important commonalities across these diverse samples of men and women, despite their different childhood and family experiences and socioeconomic status during their youth and middle years. He concluded from these studies that:

- personality and coping strategies in youth and during college years predict adaptive ability in old age if the person does not have a psychological disorder
- childhood social class and parental problems had little impact on outcomes during these participants' old age
- self-confidence and preferences evolve with age

Vaillant observed that those who had aged "positively" shared in common the quality of resilience, which he defined as adaptability and taking life in stride. This trait was expressed by one of the Grant study subjects whose closest friends and relatives had died: "Life is like a book filled with many chapters. When one chapter is finished, you must go on to the next chapter" (Vaillant, 2002, p. 9).

Based on his analysis of the early childhood and young adulthood experiences of surviving elders in these three studies, Vaillant summarized qualities that predicted positive aging:

1. long-term "healing relationships" in which elders helped others and accepted help from these close friends and family members
2. a supportive marriage or long-term partnership
3. continued involvement with life, making new friends to replace those lost through death or relocation, as well as the ability to accept the inevitability of death
4. mature defense mechanisms and active coping responses rather than passive acceptance when faced with crises in health and interpersonal relations (Vaillant, 2002)

These conclusions support the concepts of resilience and active aging, which were first introduced in Chapter 1.

Other researchers emphasize that a *sense of purpose or contribution to society* is a critical element of successful aging. This sense of purpose requires more than reflection, acceptance, and ego integrity as Erikson describes in the eighth stage of adult development. It requires that older persons continue their active involvement with society that is the hallmark of the seventh stage—generativity. For example, research with participants in the Foster Grandparents Program reveals that those who have aged successfully believe they have achieved higher-order needs, such as helping children, making a difference in others' lives, and feeling that one's life has purpose (Fisher, 1995). These are elements of both generativity and ego integrity, and support the importance of both types of developmental tasks for successful aging. As noted in Chapter 12, older adults who volunteer generally experience greater life satisfaction than their peers who do no volunteer work. Even those who do not volunteer but maintain social ties with family and friends can increase their chances of life satisfaction in old age. A 12-year follow-up of almost 3,000 community-dwelling elders showed that people who were socially disengaged (i.e., no social contacts with friends or family) were 2.4 times more likely to experience cognitive impairment over that time period than elders of the same age, gender, ethnicity and health status who had 5 or 6 close social ties (Bassuk, Glass, and Berkman, 1999).

A Critique of the Successful Aging Paradigm

The concept of successful aging has been criticized, especially by social constructionists, for conveying a middle-age, middle-class norm of remaining active as a way to show that one is "not really old, not aging." "The unspecified but clearly preferred method of successful aging is, by most accounts, not to age at all, or at least to minimize the extent to which it is apparent that one is ageing, both internally and externally" (Andrews, 1999, p. 305). Since normal physical changes do occur with age, an implicit message of successful aging is to develop strategies to preserve "youthfulness" in order not to be seen as old. The focus on physical and mental activity is reinforced by mass marketing and advertising of "active" retirement communities (Calasanti and Slevin, 2001; Katz, 2000; McHugh, 2000). Such options may not be available to low-income and historically disadvantaged elders who cannot engage in the lifestyle habits identified for successful aging. This may have the unintended consequence of neglecting or blaming older adults who have not had such lifestyle and genetic advantages. This model may also neglect the role of structural opportunities; that is, the extent to which the physical and social environment encourages or prevents the individual's attempts to age in an active and healthy manner (Masoro, 2001; Riley, 1998; Tufts University Health and Nutrition Newsletter, 2001).

When successful aging is equated with the values of activity and productivity characteristic of mainstream Western culture, it overlooks elders who are contemplative and engage in spiritual or existential activities and may experience a high degree of subjective well-being. A narrow definition of successful aging can also be stigmatizing to older adults with chronic disabilities who develop strategies to compensate for their disabilities and are able to experience a high degree of life satisfaction. In fact, environmental and policy changes may enhance the quality of life of a person with disabilities, even though they may not appear to have aged "successfully" according to the Rowe and Kahn criteria (Minkler and Fadem, 2002). In effect, the concept of successful aging is an ambiguous one; as such, it raises questions about whose standards define "success," and overlooks the fact that older adults may rate themselves as aging successfully, even though they would not be classified as such by the theoretical models of successful aging. Indeed, in a study of 867 community-dwelling elders, 50.3 percent rated themselves as aging successfully, but when objectively assessed with Rowe and Kahn's three criteria, only 18.8 percent were classified in this manner (Strawbridge, Wallhagen, and Cohen, 2002).

It is important to note that "success" in the Rowe and Kahn model should not be viewed as a dichotomous state, but a continuous variable where elders may be more successful in one of the three criteria than in others, and still be viewed as having aged well (Kahn, 2002). Nevertheless, because of some of the class, race, and gender biases implicit within successful aging, the concept of active aging or *resilience* may be more applicable to historically disadvantaged populations that display remarkable strengths despite adversities in their lives. Their strengths may derive from internal resources (e.g., spirituality, religiosity, self-concept and sense of mastery) and from social and cultural resources (e.g., social supports, community resources and cultural values). Resilience was described earlier as adaptability in the review of longitudinal studies of personality and adaptation across the life span (Vaillant, 2002), and is discussed in Chapters 14 and 15 in the context of aging among elders of color and women.

Psychological Disorders among Older Persons

As shown in Chapter 5 and in the earlier sections of this chapter, normal psychological development with aging includes some changes in cognitive processes such as attention, memory, and learning, as well as maturation of coping responses, stability in personality traits, and a natural progression through different stages of personality development. The majority of older adults experience these changes without major disruptions in their behavior or mental health. However, some older people experience more severe problems in cognitive functions, coping ability, emotional stability, or interpersonal behavior. *Psychological disorders* consist of conditions that impair the individual's interpersonal and self-care behaviors, and often result in feelings of distress and loss of independence. These conditions are not unique to older adults and are found across the life span. However, they may be more difficult to diagnose among older people due to co-morbidities, such as chronic systemic diseases and impaired sensory function.

The major forms of psychological disorders in older adults include mood disorders, anxiety disorders (including phobias and panic disorders), schizophrenia, and substance-related disorders. Depression is the primary mood disorder of old age, and accounts for a significant number of suicides, especially among older men. Alzheimer's disease and other dementias are cognitive disorders that are more likely to affect the old than the young. Alcoholism and drug abuse are less common in older individuals, although their effect on older people's physical health and cognitive functioning is more detrimental than on younger persons. Paranoid disorders and schizophrenia are conditions that are first diagnosed in youth or middle age. Each of these conditions is reviewed in the following sections.

The prevalence of psychological disorders among older persons who are living in the community ranges from 15 to 25 percent, depending on the population studied and the categories of disorders examined. Even higher rates can occur in the institutionalized older population, with estimates of 10 to 40 percent of older patients with mild to moderate impairments, and another 5 to 10 percent with significant impairments. Twenty percent of all first admissions to psychiatric hospitals are persons over age 65. Older psychiatric patients are more likely to have chronic conditions and to require longer periods of inpatient treatment than are younger patients, as evidenced by the fact that 25 percent of all beds in these hospitals are occupied by older persons. Note the discrepancy between this proportion and that over age 65 in the U.S. population—just under 13 percent in 2000. Approximately 100,000 older chronic psychiatric patients live in state mental hospitals, 500,000 in nursing homes, and the remainder (over 1 million) in the community, where they often receive inadequate treatment for their psychiatric conditions. At the same time, however, older persons are less likely than the young to use community mental health services. Older patients comprise only 4 percent of the load of psychiatric outpatient clinics and less than 2 percent of those served by private practitioners (Gatz and Smyer, 2001; Jeste et al., 1999).

One problem with describing the prevalence of mental disorders of older people is the lack of criteria distinguishing conditions that emerge in old age from those that continue throughout adulthood. In fact, the major classification system for psychiatric disorders, the *Diagnostic and Statistical Manual of Mental Disorders*, fourth edition with text revisions (DSM-IV-TR), of the American Psychiatric Association (2000), makes such a distinction only for dementias that begin in late life. No other mental disorders are differentiated for old age, although other diagnostic categories are described specifically for adulthood as separate

from childhood or adolescence. The problem of inadequate criteria for late-life **psychopathology** (or psychological disorders) is compounded by the lack of age-appropriate psychological tests for diagnosing these conditions. An increasing number of tests are being developed, especially for diagnosing depression and dementia in older people.

Depression

Depression, dementia, and paranoia are the three most prevalent forms of late-life psychopathology. Of these, depression is the most common. It is important to distinguish *unipolar* depression from *bipolar* disorders (that is, ranging from a depressed to a manic state), as well as severe conditions such as sadness, grief reactions, and other affective disorders. Most of the depressions of old age are unipolar; bipolar disorders are rare. Still other cases in late life are *secondary* or *reactive* depressions, which arise in response to a significant life event with which the individual cannot cope. For example, physical illness and the loss of loved ones through death and relocation may trigger depressive reactions in older people. The vegetative signs, suicidal thoughts, weight loss, and mood variations from morning to night that are observed in major depression are not found in reactive depression. Studies of older individuals in community settings and in nursing homes suggest that the prevalence of major depression is generally lower than the rates of minor or reactive depression. **Dysthymic disorder** is a less acute type of depression but with symptoms that last longer than major depression.

Estimates of depression for community-dwelling elders are:

- 8–20 percent for minor depression
- 1 percent for major depression
- 2 percent for dysthymia
- 0.1 percent for bipolar disorder

These rates are about the same for whites and African Americans, although depression in nurs-

Untreated depression in older men is a risk factor for suicide.

ing home residents if often misdiagnosed. However, depression is more likely to be undetected or misdiagnosed in ethnic minority elders, in part because of cultural barriers to diagnosis and treatment (Lincoln, 2003). Asian American elders, for example, attach a strong stigma to mental illness, which can result in an underdiagnosis of depression (Surgeon General, 2001). Rates of depression among Latinos tend to be higher than among whites, especially among Mexican American females and males (25.6 percent). This is explained partially by the following sociodemographic and health-related correlates of depression: female gender, lack of insurance, financial strain, low locus of control regarding health, chronic health conditions, and functional disability. In addition, cultural factors, such as immigrant status, recency of immigration, and low levels of acculturation are all associated with increased risk of depressive symptomatology (Aranda, Lee, and Wilson, 2001; Black, Markides, and Miller, 1998). Health care

providers need to recognize such risk factors and must be sensitive to cultural differences in order to diagnose accurately and treat depression effectively. Rates as high as 20 to 30 percent have been found among institutionalized older adults (Blazer, 1999; Blazer et al., 1998; Gallo and Lebowitz, 1999; Harralson et al., 2002; Jones, Marcantonio, Rabinowitz, 2003).

As noted earlier in this chapter, most role *gains* (e.g., worker, driver, voter, partner, or parent) occur in the earlier years, whereas many role *losses* may multiply in the later years. As we have seen, loss of roles may be compounded by decrements in sensory abilities, physical strength, and health. These role losses often result in grief, which may be misdiagnosed as depression. Although depression usually does not result from any one of these losses alone, the combination of several losses in close sequence may trigger a reactive depressive episode. This may be due to changes in the brain caused by multiple stressors that affect the production of mood-regulating chemicals in the brain. It appears that acute life events can lead to a recurrence of major depression, but do not necessarily trigger its first onset (Kessler, 1997). Older people with major physical conditions such as stroke, cancer, or chronic pain and those who do not have a supportive social network are at greatest risk. Among elders hospitalized for physical health problems, 10 percent have been found to have major depression, and 30 percent minor depression (Koenig and Blazer, 1996; NIH, 1994). In addition, older people who have experienced depression in the past are at risk for a recurrence, especially if it is triggered by a major life event. Risk factors for depression in older adults include:

- female gender
- unmarried
- co-morbidity (i.e., multiple chronic diseases)
- chronic financial strain
- family history of depressive illness
- lack of social support (Aranda et al., 2001; Garrard et al., 1998)

Psychiatric symptoms that persist beyond six months in these patients may indicate the development of a major depressive episode. Consistent with the approach of a better fit between the older person and the environment, environmental and social interventions as well as psychotherapy are more effective than antidepressant medications for minor depression. However, medications and sometimes electroconvulsive therapy are necessary to treat major depression and prevent suicide, as described later in this chapter.

Death rates appear to be greater among older persons with a diagnosis of depression, almost twice that for nondepressed people within 1 year. Depressed older adults, especially if they have cognitive impairment, have a significantly higher mortality risk. The more severe a patient's depressive symptoms, the more likely he or she is to die sooner (Blazer, Hybels, and Pieper, 2001; Schulz et al., 2000). Medical hospital stays are often twice as long and health care costs in general are higher for those with depression. In addition, depressed older adults take longer to recover from a hip fracture or stroke (Chiles, Lambert and Hatch, 1999; Koenig and Blazer, 1996). This may be because older persons with depression are more apathetic, less motivated to improve their health, and more likely to entertain thoughts of suicide than younger depressives. The American Psychiatric Association lists the following criteria for major depression:

1. Depressed mood most of day, nearly every day
2. Markedly diminished interest or pleasure in activities, apathy
3. Significant weight loss or weight gain, or appetite change
4. Sleep disturbance (insomnia or hypersomnia) nearly every day
5. Agitation or retardation of activity nearly every day
6. Low energy level or fatigue nearly every day
7. Self-blame, guilt, worthlessness
8. Poor concentration, indecisiveness
9. Recurrent thoughts of death, suicide

At least five of these symptoms are present during the same 2-week period and represent a change from previous function. Among the number 1 or 2 should be at least one of the symptoms.*

Below are some symptoms of depression that may be confused with normal aging:

- reports or evidence of sadness
- feelings of emptiness or detachment with no precipitating major life event such as bereavement
- expressions of anxiety or panic for no apparent cause
- loss of interest in the environment
- neglect of self-care
- changes in eating and sleeping patterns

The depressed person may complain of vague aches and pains, either generally or in a specific part of the body. Occasional symptoms or symptoms associated with a specific medication, physical illness, or alcoholism need to be distinguished from the somatic complaints associated with depression. Only when multiple symptoms appear together and persist *for at least 2 weeks* should an individual and his or her family suspect major depression, especially if an older person speaks frequently of death or suicide.

One problem with detecting depression in older people is that they may be more successful than their younger counterparts at masking or hiding symptoms. In fact, many cases of depression in older persons are not diagnosed because the individual either does not express changes in mood or denies them in the clinical interview. A *masked depression* is one in which few mood changes are reported. Instead, the patient complains of a vague pain, bodily discomfort, and sleep disturbance; reports problems with memory; is apathetic; and withdraws from others (Gallo and Lebowitz, 1999; Lichtenberg et al., 1995). This is a common

Adapted with permission from the *Diagnostic and statistical manual of mental disorders,* 4th ed. Copyright 1994 American Psychiatric Association, Washington, D.C., p. 327.

condition in older generations because many of these people were raised in environments that discouraged open expression of feelings.

Health care professionals and family members need to distinguish depression from medical conditions and changes due to normal aging or from grief. For example, an older woman with arthritis who complains of increasing pain may actually be seeking a reason for vague physical discomfort that is related to a depressive episode. People with masked depression are more likely to complain of problems with memory or problem-solving. Their denial or masking of symptoms may lead the physician to assume that the individual is experiencing **dementia,** a condition that is generally irreversible. It is for this reason that depression in older persons is often labeled *pseudodementia*.

Because of such likelihood of denial, a physician's first goal with an older patient who has vague somatic and memory complaints should be to conduct a thorough physical exam and lab tests. This is important in order to determine if an individual is depressed or has a physical disorder or symptoms of dementia. If the cognitive dysfunction is due to depression, it will improve when the depression is treated. On the other hand, some medical conditions may produce depressive symptoms. These include:

- Parkinson's disease
- rheumatoid arthritis
- thyroid dysfunction
- diseases of the adrenal glands

In some cases, depression can coexist with medical conditions such as heart disease, stroke, arthritis, cancer, chronic lung disease, and Alzheimer's disease, compounding the dysfunction associated with these medical problems and delaying the recovery process. Certain medications may also produce feelings of depression. In fact, any medication that has a depressant effect on the central nervous system can produce depressive symptoms, specifically lethargy and loss of interest in the environment. For these reasons, older adults with depressive symptoms should be examined thoroughly for underlying physical illness, hypothyroidism, vitamin deficiencies, chronic infections, and reactions to medications. Physicians must frequently conduct medication reviews to determine if their older patients begin to show side effects to a drug, even after using it for several months or years. Late-life depression is costly not just for the individual's physical and psychological well-being, but it exacts a large economic toll. The interaction of symptoms of depression with many somatic conditions results in more visits to primary care physicians and emergency rooms as well as longer hospital stays for older adults (Surgeon General, 1999a).

THERAPEUTIC INTERVENTIONS   It is important to treat both major and secondary depressions upon diagnosis, because the older depressed patient is at higher risk of self-destructive behavior and suicide. Older adults are more likely to seek help for depressive symptoms from their family doctor than from mental health professionals. For this reason, primary care physicians must be aware and sensitized to subtle symptoms of depression. Health professionals who diagnose depression in an older person must provide psychological support for acute symptoms, including empathy, attentive listening, and encouragement of active coping skills. For patients with minor depression, this may be all they need to show a decrease in symptoms. For more severely depressed elders, alternative therapies may be required. There is some

---

MEDICATIONS THAT MAY PRODUCE SYMPTOMS OF DEPRESSION

- antihypertensives
- digoxin (used for some heart conditions)
- corticosteroids (used for preventing joint inflammation)
- estrogen
- some antipsychotic drugs
- anti-Parkinsonism drugs such as L-dopa

disagreement, however, about the efficacy of such therapies. Although short-term improvements may be achieved through treatment, the long-range prognosis is not always successful, and some older people will experience a relapse. If the onset of depression occurs before age 70, psychotherapy or counseling is generally more successful.

The most common therapeutic intervention with depressed older individuals is pharmacological, which is particularly useful for those experiencing a major depression or bipolar depression (Surgeon General, 1999a). Therapy with antidepressants is generally long-term. Although antidepressants work well for some older persons, many others cannot use these drugs because of other medications they are taking, such as antihypertensives, or because the side effects are more detrimental than the depression itself. These effects include postural hypotension (i.e., a sudden drop in blood pressure when rising from a prone position), increased vulnerability to falls and fractures, cardiac arrhythmias, urinary retention, constipation, disorientation, skin rash, and dry mouth. Because of these potentially dangerous reactions, it is important to start antidepressant therapy at a much lower dose (perhaps 50 percent lower) in older than in younger patients. Many older persons who turn to a general practitioner for treatment of depression often receive antidepressants as a first line of attack rather than psychotherapy, which may be more appropriate. There is increased evidence that a combination of well-monitored pharmacotherapy and counseling can reduce symptoms in up to 80 percent of chronically depressed older adults, even in the oldest-old (Reynolds and Kupfer, 1999). This combination was found to reduce symptoms of bereavement-related depression in 69 percent of elders in a 16-week treatment program, compared with 45 percent for drugs alone, and 29 percent for psychotherapy alone (Reynolds et al., 1999). Therapy lasting at least one year has also been shown to stabilize bouts of mania and depression in adults with bipolar disorder. This suggests that

patients with this type of depression need consistency in their therapeutic interventions (Frank et al., 1999; Keller et al., 2000).

Older people are just as likely as younger persons to benefit from the insight and empathy provided by a therapist trained in geriatric psychotherapy. In particular, secondary depression responds well to supportive therapy that allows the patient to review and come to terms with the stresses of late life. Supportive psychotherapy is useful because it allows older patients to reestablish control and emotional stability. Older depressed persons appear to benefit from short-term, client-centered, directive therapy more than from therapy that is nondirective or uses free association to uncover long-standing personality conflicts. Reminiscence therapy allows older people with depression to work through difficult memories and process their grief and loss (Cully, LaVoie, and Gfeller, 2001). Cognitive-behavioral interventions, such as self-monitoring of negative thoughts about

---

COMBINED THERAPIES MAY BE MOST EFFECTIVE WITH OLDER ADULTS

In the six months since the death of his wife of 52 years, Mr. Simon has lost interest in all the activities that he and his wife enjoyed together. He has lost weight and sleeps irregularly. His complaints of poor memory and loss of energy have alarmed his adult children, who insisted he see his family physician. The doctor prescribed an antidepressant upon recognizing the symptoms of depression. However, Mr. Simon stopped taking these medications after two weeks because they made him feel dizzy and caused dry mouth. The physician spent time discussing the immediate benefits from medications, but also arranged for Mr. Simon to participate in one-on-one psychotherapy sessions with an expert in geriatric psychotherapy. After 2 months, Mr. Simon has already seen the benefits of combining these two therapies for his condition. He now attends a local senior center daily, and has begun a regular exercise program of walking for one hour every day.

> ### SUMMARY OF THERAPEUTIC INTERVENTIONS FOR DEPRESSED OLDER ADULTS
>
> Pharmacotherapy (antidepressants)
>
> Electroconvulsive therapy
>
> Psychotherapy
> - supportive
> - directive
> - cognitive-behavioral
>
> Combination of therapies

oneself, daily monitoring of moods, and increased participation in pleasant events may be especially effective for depressed elders who are caring for a frail spouse or partner (Goisman, 1999; DeVries, 1996; Teri et al., 1997).

As noted above, psychotherapy must be accompanied by **pharmacotherapy** or electroconvulsive therapy in severely depressed elders. Despite past controversy about its use, **electroconvulsive** or **electroshock therapy (ECT)** is sometimes used in cases of severe depression. ECT is a quick and effective method for treating major depression in patients who:

- have not responded to medications
- have a higher risk of suicide
- refuse to eat
- are severely agitated
- show vegetative symptoms
- express feelings of hopelessness, helplessness, or worthlessness
- have experienced delusions
- cannot tolerate or are unresponsive to medication

Unilateral nondominant hemisphere ECT is often preferred because it is capable of alleviating depression without impairing cognitive functioning. However, older adults with a recent history of a myocardial infarct, irregular heartbeat, or other heart conditions must be treated with caution because ECT can place a significant load on the cardiovascular system. Maintenance treatment with ECT may be necessary for older depressed persons (as often as once a month). In some cases, antidepressants are used after a course of ECT to prevent relapse (Koenig and Blazer, 1996; Rudorfer, Henry, and Sackheim, 1997).

Suicide among Older People

Older people are at greater risk of suicide than any other age group. It has been estimated that 17 to 25 percent of all *completed* suicides occur in persons aged 65 and older. In 1997, the national rate was 11.4 suicides per 100,000 population. The rate for persons over age 65 was over 18 per 100,000, ranging from 13.2 for those aged 65 to 70, to 21 per 100,000 among those over age 85 (CDC, 1999). The highest suicide rates in the United States are found among older white males. The prevalence of suicide in this group, 43.3 per 100,000, is more than:

- twice the rate for nonwhite males (17.5 per 100,000)
- seven times the rate for older white women (5.8)
- 15 times the rate for older nonwhite women (2.8)

White men aged 85 and older are at greatest risk, at 65 per 100,000, or almost three times the rate for the second highest group, white men aged 15 to 24 (24.1 per 100,000) (CDC, 1999; NCHS,

> ### RISK FACTORS FOR SUICIDE IN OLDER ADULTS
> - a serious physical illness with severe pain
> - the sudden death of a loved one
> - a major loss of independence or financial inadequacy
> - statements that indicate frustration with life and a desire to end it
> - a sudden decision to give away one's most important possessions
> - a general loss of interest in one's social and physical environment

2000). Both white and nonwhite older men account for 83 percent of all suicides among the population aged 65 and older. Note that these statistics reflect direct or clearly identifiable suicides. There are probably a significant number of indirect suicides that appear to be accidents or natural deaths (e.g., starvation or gas poisoning), and cases where family members and physicians do not list suicide as the cause of death; therefore these rates may underrepresent the actual incidence of the problem.

One explanation for the higher rates of suicide among older white males is that they generally experience the greatest incongruence between their ideal self-image (that of worker, decision maker, or holder of relatively high status in society) and the realities of advancing age. With age, the role of paid worker is generally lost, chronic illness may diminish one's sense of control, and an individual may feel a loss of status. Social isolation also appears to be important; suicide rates among older widowed men are more than five times greater than for married men, but no differences have been found between married and widowed women (Li, 1995). This is because older widowed men are most likely to lack strong social support networks. Older men in many populations of color such as African American and Chinese are less likely to commit suicide because of more extensive family support systems. Suicide risk is greatest among white males who are widowed, aged 85 and older, with recurrent major depression, and with chronic pain, cardiopulmonary diseases, or cancer (Blazer and Koenig, 1996). However, contrary to popular belief, older suicide victims are no more likely than other older people to have been diagnosed with a terminal illness prior to the suicide.

There are fewer nonfatal suicide attempts in older men compared to their younger counterparts. That is, the rate of completed suicides is far greater among older men—one for every eight attempts, compared with one completed suicide for every 100 to 200 attempts by the young. This difference may be due to the use of more lethal methods of suicide such as shotguns. In 1996 firearms were involved in:

- 78 percent of suicides among older men
- 36 percent among older women (McIntosh, 1997; Surgeon General, 1999b).

Because attempts at suicide are more likely to end in death for older men, family members and health care providers need to be sensitive to clues of an impending suicide. The NIMH estimates that 70 percent of older persons who commit suicide had seen a primary care physician in the preceding month, but their psychological disturbances had not been detected or were inadequately treated. In most cases, these older persons had not sought psychiatric care. For this reason, the Surgeon General in 1999 issued a "Call to Action to Prevent Suicide." This effort, aimed at mental health providers and the older population directly, focused on increasing awareness of depression, its symptoms, and potential outcomes. However, it is crucial for primary care physicians to recognize symptoms of depression in their older patients and know how to refer them to mental health professionals *before* the older person demonstrates suicidal intentions (Surgeon General, 1999b).

Watching for subtle cues is also important, since older people are less likely to make threats or to announce their intentions to commit suicide than are young people. Clearly, not all older people displaying such symptoms will attempt suicide, but the recognition of changes in an older family member's or client's behavior and moods can alleviate a potential disaster.

Dementia

Normal aging does not result in significant declines in intelligence, memory, and learning ability, as described in Chapter 5. Mild impairments do not necessarily signal a major loss but often represent a mild form of memory dysfunction known as **benign senescent forgetfulness.** Only in the case of the diseases known collectively as the dementias does cognitive function show marked deterioration. Dementia includes a variety of conditions that are caused by or associated with damage of brain tissue, resulting in impaired cognitive func-

> ### CARE FOR DEMENTIA PATIENTS WITH ACUTE ILLNESS
>
> In the late stages of many irreversible dementias such as Alzheimer's disease, the patient is often physically frail and unable to survive an acute condition such as pneumonia or a hip fracture. A recent study followed people aged 70 or older who were hospitalized for one of these conditions, and *also* had a late-stage dementing illness. Six months later, mortality rates were much higher for elders with pneumonia and dementia than for those with no dementia (53 percent vs. 13 percent). Those with hip fractures and dementia also died at higher rates than elders without dementia (55 percent vs. 12 percent). Both patients with and without dementia received as many life-saving procedures. Only 7 percent of the former had written documents to forgo such treatment and only 24 percent had requested analgesics. These findings point to the need to establish guidelines for palliative treatment for an older person with dementia who is dying of an acute illness (Morrison and Siu, 2000).

tion and, in more advanced stages, impaired behavior and personality. Such changes in the brain result in progressive deterioration of an individual's ability to learn and recall items from the past. Previously, it was assumed that all these syndromes were associated with cerebral arteriosclerosis ("hardening of the arteries"). In fact, we now know that a number of these conditions occur independently of arteriosclerosis.

Some features are unique to each type of dementia, but all dementias have the following characteristics:

- a change in an individual's ability to recall events in recent memory
- problems with comprehension, attention span, judgment
- disorientation to time, place, and person

The individual with dementia may have problems in understanding abstract thought or symbolic language (e.g., be unable to interpret a proverb), particularly in the later stages of the disease. Although

not part of normal aging, the likelihood of experiencing dementia does increase with advancing age. Depending on the criteria used, estimates range from two to three million people over age 65 having some type of dementia; almost 2 million have severe dementia, and up to 5 million are mildly to moderately impaired (Hendrie, 1997; Teri, McCurry, and Logsdon, 1997). Because of problems in differentially diagnosing dementia, and variations in the criteria used by available tests and classification systems, prevalence rates range from 3 to 36 percent of the older population (Erkinjuntti et al., 1997). Nevertheless, there is general agreement among epidemiological studies that the incidence of dementias increases with age, especially between ages 75 and 90. For example, it is estimated that:

- 12 percent of the 75 to 79 age group have some dementia
- 54 percent of 85- to 89-year-olds have signs of dementia
- 84 percent of people over age 90 have some symptoms (Kukull et al., 2002).

However, as noted in Chapter 1, rates of dementia among "hardy" centenarians may actually be lower than among 85- to 90-year-olds because of genetic advantages experienced by those who live to age 100 and beyond.

The major types of dementias are shown below. Note the distinction between *reversible* and *irreversible* dementias.

REVERSIBLE	IRREVERSIBLE
Drugs	Alzheimer's
Alcohol	Vascular
Nutritional deficiencies	Huntington's
Normal pressure hydrocephalus	Pick's disease
Brain tumors	Creutzfeldt-Jacob
Hypothyroidism/ Hyperthyroidism	Kuru
Neurosyphilis	Korsakoff
Depression (pseudodementia)	

The first refers to cognitive decline that may be caused by drug toxicity, hormonal or nutritional disorders, and other diseases that may be reversible. Sources of potentially reversible dementias include tumors in and trauma to the brain, toxins, metabolic disorders such as hypo- or hyperthyroidism, diabetes, hypo- or hypercalcemia, infections, vascular lesions, and hydrocephalus. Severe depression may produce confusion and memory problems in some older people. Some medications may also cause dementia-like symptoms. This problem is aggravated if the individual is taking multiple medications or is on a dosage that is higher than can be metabolized by the older kidney or liver. An individual who appears to be suffering from such reactions should be referred promptly for medical screening.

Irreversible dementias are those that have no discernible environmental cause and cannot yet be cured. Although there is considerable research on the causes and treatments for these conditions, they must be labeled irreversible at the present time. Some of these are more common than others; some have identifiable causes while others do not. Pick's disease is one of the rarest; in this type, the frontal and temporal lobes of the brain atrophy. Of all the dementias, it is most likely to occur in younger persons (age of onset is usually 40–50), and to result in significant personality changes. Creutzfeldt-Jacob and Kuru diseases have been traced to a slow-acting virus that can strike at any age. In the former type of dementia, decline in cognitive abilities occurs quite rapidly, as seen in the recent epidemics of "mad cow disease" that have been attributed to consuming tainted beef in Great Britain, Europe, and now the United States. Kuru disease is quite rare. Huntington's disease is a genetically transmitted condition that usually appears in people in their 30s and 40s. It results in more neuromuscular changes than do the other dementias. Korsakoff syndrome is associated with long-term alcoholism and a deficiency of vitamin B1. This form of dementia results in severe loss of memory.

Vascular dementia is estimated to represent 15 to 20 percent of all nonreversible dementias. This form of dementia was labeled "senility" in the past. In this type, blood vessels leading to the brain become occluded, with the result that several areas of the brain show infarcts or small strokes. The primary risk factor for vascular dementia is the same as for strokes, that is, hypertension. Because of this, vascular dementia may be prevented by controlling hypertension. Nevertheless, once it occurs, this type of dementia is irreversible (Lis and Gaviria, 1997). Recent research suggests that the onset of vascular dementia may be predicted by abnormal walking patterns or gaits. In fact, elders with one of three types of abnormal gaits were 3.5 times more likely to develop vascular dementia (but no other type of dementia) in one study. Older people who walked with their legs swinging outward in a semicircle, or took short steps with minimal lifting of their feet, or had an unsteady, swaying gait and no physical condition that would have caused this problem were eventually found to have vascular dementia. These movement patterns may reflect changes in the brain that trigger this condition (Verghese et al., 2002).

Delirium

Delirium is a reversible dementia that has a more rapid onset than other types of dementia. Signs of delirium are:

- abrupt changes in behavior
- fluctuations in behavior throughout the day
- inability to focus attention on a task
- hallucinations
- speech that makes no sense or is irrational

Delirium is usually caused by some external variables such as a reaction to an injury (especially head injury) or infection, malnutrition, reaction to alcohol or prescription medications, high fever, or even a fecal impaction or urinary problems. A thorough medical assessment can help diagnose and reverse delirium and its symptoms (Logsdon and Teri, 2000).

Alzheimer's Disease

Senile dementia of the Alzheimer's type (Alzheimer's disease or AD) is the most common irreversible dementia in late life, accounting for 50 to 70 percent of all dementias. Prevalence rates are difficult to obtain, but it is estimated that about 2.3 million Americans or 7 percent of all persons age 65 and over, and 29 percent of those age 85 and older have clinical symptoms of AD (Brookmeyer and Kawas, 1998; Zarit and Zarit, 1998). However, because of selective survival, it appears that men who survive into their 90s become less likely to develop AD after this age (Perls, 1995).

Although a distinction was made in the past between pre-senile (i.e., before age 65) and senile

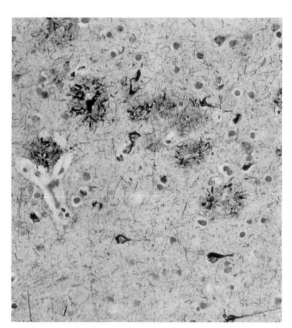

The dark patches in this brain section are neuritic plaques with a core of amyloid protein, characteristic of Alzheimer's disease.

ALZHEIMER'S DISEASE VERSUS NORMAL CHANGES IN MEMORY

Many people in middle and old age become alarmed that they may have Alzheimer's disease at the first signs of forgetting. Here are some distinctions between *normal*, age-related changes in memory (as described in Chapter 5) and AD:

Normal Aging
- Forgetting to set the alarm clock
- Forgetting someone's name and remembering it later
- Forgetting where you left your keys and finding them after searching
- Having to retrace steps to remember a task
- Forgetting where you parked your car

Possible AD
- Forgetting *how* to set the alarm clock
- Forgetting a name and never remembering it, even when told
- Forgetting places where you might find your keys
- Forgetting how you came to be at a particular location

dementia, there is now agreement that these are the same disease. Researchers do, however, make a distinction between the more common, late-onset form of AD and a rarer form that appears in multiple generations of the same family, usually when the individual is in middle age (40s, even 30s). This is known as "familial AD."

POTENTIAL CAUSES OF AND RISK FACTORS FOR ALZHEIMER'S DISEASE   Several hypotheses are proposed to explain the causes of Alzheimer's disease. Case control studies that focused on the incidence or development of AD have not found support for environmental hypotheses, such as a previous head injury, thyroid disease, exposure to therapeutic radiation, anesthesia, or the accumulation of heavy metals (e.g., aluminum) in the brain (Kokmen et al., 1996). Even though the abnormal tangles (a web of dead brain cells) found in the neurons of the brains of Alzheimer's victims contain more aluminum than is found in brains of normal controls, there is no evidence that such an accumulation *causes* AD.

Although it is difficult to assess with great accuracy an older person's childhood development, two verifiable early-life characteristics may increase one's risk of AD. In a community-based case-control study comparing 393 people diagnosed with AD and 377 controls, researchers examined the effects of mother's age at patient's birth, birth order, number of siblings, and area of residence before age 18. They found only the last two variables associated with AD risk. The more children in one's family, the greater one's AD risk. Similarly, patients were half as likely as nondemented controls to have grown up in the suburbs (Moceri et al., 2000). These results suggest that receiving more attention as a child and living in a more secluded environment may serve as a protective factor against AD in old age.

In another case-control study, information was obtained about activity patterns during ages 20–60 among 193 older persons with AD and 358 healthy controls who were currently in their 60s and 70s. These activities included nonoccupational pastimes that could be classified as intellectual, physical or passive. Elders with no signs of dementia had participated in more intellectual and physical nonoccupational activities during their middle years than did those in the control group. The greatest effect was for intellectual pastimes; the more such activities an individual participated in, the lower the probability of AD. This was true regardless of educational level, gender, and current age. Although the findings must be interpreted with some caution, the dramatic differences observed suggest that participation in intellectual activities may have a protective effect against AD (Friedland et al., 2000).

The Nun Study offers insights into the association between education, lifestyle, and cognitive and physical aging without the bias of diverse socioeconomic status, diet, and health care that is a problem with many other studies of aging among

the general population. The School Sisters of Notre Dame who have participated in this longitudinal study, including the analysis of their brains at autopsy, shared an adulthood of identical lifestyles. Therefore the differences seen among the nuns are attributable primarily to their educational levels and intellectual and physical activities throughout their lives. By analyzing the autobiographies these nuns had written at age 22, researchers found an association between linguistic skills in youth and the risk of dementia 50 to 70 years later. More plaques and tangles were found in the brains of women whose writings during their youth had fewer complex ideas and a simpler vocabulary (Snowdon, Greiner, and Markesbery, 2000). The researchers also examined the emotional content of these early autobiographies for their positive, negative, or neutral tone. By adjusting statistically for age and education, the researchers found a significant link between positive emotions and mortality; those in the highest quartile of positive emotional content in their early writings decreased their risk of death in old age by a factor of 2.5 compared with nuns whose writings lacked much positive expression. This may be because positive emotions triggered a lifetime of positive behaviors in the survivors (Danner, Snowdon, and Friesen, 2001).

This study also demonstrated that clinical manifestations of dementia may not always parallel the neuropathological changes experienced in these conditions. That is, many of the nuns at autopsy had the hallmarks of advanced dementia in their brain samples (e.g., neurofibrillary tangles in the neocortex), but they did not demonstrate any clinical symptoms of dementia before their death (e.g., disorientation to time, place, person) (Snowdon, 2001, 2003).

Besides intellectual activities, physical activity throughout life can delay the onset of AD or prevent it altogether. A recent study points to obesity as a risk factor for AD in women but not in men. Women who were overweight at age 70, 75, and 79 were more likely to develop dementia by age 88. The researchers suggest that being overweight may raise blood pressure and restrict blood flow to the brain, thereby indirectly increasing women's risk for AD, although a parallel effect was not observed in men (Gustafson et al., 2003).

Lack of estrogen is another potential risk factor that has drawn research interest. As estrogen secretion declines with aging, proteins associated with neuronal growth decrease, resulting in the synaptic impairments typical of AD. Just as estrogen replacement therapy (ERT) may prevent bone loss and cardiovascular disease in postmenopausal women, animal and human studies suggest that it can restore the brain proteins necessary for neuronal growth, and increase neuronal activity in the hippocampus (Brinton et al., 2000; Sramek and Cutler, 1999). These findings must be interpreted with caution, in light of recent research evidence for a link between ERT and cancer. Recent findings from the Women's Health Initiative Memory Study (ancillary to the WHI Study described in Chapter 4) showed that, among more than 4500 women who were placed on a combination of estrogen and progestin, or placebo for 5 years, there was no difference in the rates of developing mild cognitive impairment. In fact, twice as many women using the combination hormone developed dementia—40 versus 21 in this large sample (Shumaker et al., 2003).

The brains of AD patients experience a reduction in the number of cholinergic nerve cells (up to 80 percent loss in some key areas). These brain cells are important for learning and memory because they release an important chemical "messenger," *acetylcholine,* that transfers information from one cell to another (i.e., neurotransmitters). Their loss reduces the acetylcholine available for this important function. The noradrenergic system is another chemical messenger system that becomes impaired with Alzheimer's disease, further complicating our understanding of why and how these neurochemical systems appear to break down in this disease.

Still another neurochemical change observed in Alzheimer brains is the accumulation of *amyloid,* a protein. It appears that there may be a ge-

netic defect in one of the normal proteins located in brain regions responsible for memory, emotions, and thinking. Amyloid is actually a group of proteins found in the neurofibrillary tangles that characterize an Alzheimer's brain. The precursor protein to amyloid, *Beta-amyloid,* is coded by a gene located in chromosome 21, which is also the chromosome responsible for Down syndrome. This may explain why AD appears with greater frequency in families with a member who has Down syndrome. Deposits of amyloid or its precursor Beta-amyloid have been found in the brains of Down patients as young as age 8, and in those who die later with Alzheimer's disease. Beta-amyloid may be responsible for the death of brain cells in these patients. In fact, many Down patients have the characteristic brain changes of AD, but not the clinical symptoms. As with other changes observed in the brains of AD patients, it is not yet clear whether these Beta-amyloid deposits are the *cause* of AD or secondary to other structural or biochemical changes (Carr et al., 1997).

Genes on at least four different chromosomes may be involved in the development of AD. In addition to mutations of the gene encoding amyloid precursor protein on chromosome 21, presenilin 1 on chromosome 14, presenilin 2 on chromosome 1, and the apolipoprotein E gene on chromosome 19 have been implicated in this disease. While the mutations on chromosomes 1, 14, and 21 are associated with familial or early-onset AD, the more common late-onset form of AD appears to be linked to a genetic mutation on chromosome 19. Researchers have focused on a protein called *apolipoprotein* or *APOE* on this chromosome. APOE is responsible for transporting cholesterol in the blood, and Beta-amyloid in the brain.

Of the three common allelic variations of APOE proteins, *E2, E3, E4,* those who inherit an *E4* gene from one parent have three times the risk of developing AD than people with no *E4* variant, while those who inherit the gene from *both* parents have eight times the risk. Furthermore, they deteriorate more rapidly than AD patients who do not have the *E4* allele. In addition, AD patients with one or more *E4* alleles have an increased risk of death due to ischemic heart disease (Carr et al., 1997; Olichney et al., 1997). Those who acquire an E3 gene from each parent also have a greater risk of developing AD, but at a later age than those with two E4 genes (at an average age of 75 versus 68).

Characteristics of Alzheimer's Disease

As illustrated by Mr. Adams in the introductory vignette, Alzheimer's disease is characterized by deficits in attention, learning, memory, and language skills and, in some instances, problems in judgment, abstraction, and orientation. These changes in cognitive function appear to be related to structural changes in the brain. They include:

- a premature loss of nerve cells in some areas of the brain
- a loss of synapses
- deterioration of the free radical metabolism process described in Chapter 3
- impaired neurotransmitter function such as the cholinergic system, resulting in plaques and tangles throughout these areas

The *hippocampus* is a region in the limbic system deep inside the brain that is involved in learning new information and retrieving old information (see Chapter 5). It is one of the first regions where plaques and tangles occur, so it is not surprising that patients in the earlier stages of the disease often have difficulties with verbal memory, attention span, and orientation to the environment, as well as increased anxiety, restlessness, and unpredictable changes in mood. Family members may complain that the older person has become more aggressive or, in some cases, more passive than in the past. Depression may set in as the individual realizes that he or she is experiencing these problems. In the more advanced stages of the disease, as it spreads to the *neocortex,* which con-

trols higher-level brain functions, and links new stimuli with information stored in the brain, the elder may experience problems recalling appropriate words and labels, perseveration (i.e., continual repeating of the same phrase and thoughts), apathy, and problems with comprehension. Alzheimer's victims at this stage may not recognize their partners, children, and long-time friends. However, some patients in the moderate stages of AD may describe quite articulately and vividly events that took place many years ago. In the advanced phases, as the neurons in the motor cortex die, the patient may need assistance with bodily functions such as eating and toileting. At autopsy, there is a generalized deterioration of cortical tissue, which appears to be tangled and covered with plaque. These plaques and tangles appear first in a region near the base of the skull (**entorhinal cortex**), and move higher and deeper to the hippocampus and eventually to the neocortex as the disease advances (Snowdon, 2001).

ARE THERE STAGES OF ALZHEIMER'S DISEASE? There have been some attempts to determine if AD proceeds through a series of stages, such that symptoms become more prevalent and severe over time. This is a difficult task because the course of AD varies so widely. Some patients may experience a rapid decline in memory, while their orientation to time, place, and people may remain relatively intact. Other patients may experience mood and personality changes early, whereas still others maintain their pre-morbid personality for many years after the symptoms first appear.

A broad distinction is often made among early, middle, and advanced stages of AD. These categories are based on the patient's levels of decline in memory, orientation, and activities of daily living. Assessment tools such as the Mini-Mental Status Exam and the Dementia Rating Scale can help in categorizing levels of decline (Folstein, Folstein, and McHugh, 1975; Mattis, 1976). These give clues to the patients' levels of deterioration on the basis of their test scores. Perhaps the most extensive research to determine the

---

GLOBAL DETERIORATION SCALE

Stage 1: No cognitive or functional decrements

Stage 2: Complaints of very mild forgetfulness and some work difficulties

Stage 3: Mild cognitive impairment on cognitive battery; concentration problems; some difficulty at work and in traveling alone

Stage 4: Late confusional stage; increased problems in planning, handling finances; increased denial of symptoms; withdrawal

Stage 5: Poor recall of recent events; may need to be reminded about proper clothing and bathing

Stage 6: More advanced memory orientation problems; needs assistance with activities of daily living; more personality changes

Stage 7: Late dementia with loss of verbal abilities; incontinent; loss of ability to walk; may become comatose

SOURCE: Reisberg, B., Ferris, S. H., De Leon, M. J., and Crook, T., The Global Deterioration Scale for assessment of primary degenerative dementia. *American Journal of Psychiatry, 139*, pp. 1136–1139, 1982. Copyright 1982, the American Psychiatric Association. Reprinted by permission.

---

stages of AD has been conducted by Reisberg et al. (1982), who developed a Global Deterioration Scale that delineates seven stages of the disease, as shown in the accompanying box.

Because of attention by the media and by researchers on Alzheimer's disease, there is some tendency to overestimate its occurrence and to assume that it is the cause of all dementias. It has even created what one neurologist called "Alzheimer's phobia" (Fox, 1991). In many ways, it has replaced vascular dementia as a label given without a thorough diagnosis. The most confirmatory diagnosis of Alzheimer's disease today can still be made only at autopsy, when the areas and nature of damaged brain tissue can be identified. However, several psychological measures of cognitive functioning and a thorough physical exam

can provide clues to its existence in the earlier stages. Or they may indicate that the observed changes in behavior and/or personality are due to a reversible condition. Early diagnosis can be made with some certainty with an extensive patient workup. In fact, it is primarily through a process of elimination of other conditions that some dementias such as AD may be diagnosed. In such diagnoses, it is particularly important to detect depression, prolonged grief, drug toxicity, and nutritional deficiencies because, as stated earlier, these conditions may be reversed.

THERAPY FOR PATIENTS WITH ALZHEIMER'S DISEASE
Unfortunately, no completely successful treatment for AD is yet available. If the evidence for high levels of certain abnormal proteins in Alzheimer brains proves correct, future treatment might involve the use of drugs that interrupt the production of those proteins and their precursors so they cannot accumulate in brain tissue. Some researchers have focused on nerve growth factor, a naturally occurring protein that replenishes and maintains the health of nerve cells. Animal studies show remarkable success in repairing damaged brain cells.

Currently, only a few drugs have been approved for treating AD. Other medications in the testing phase include some drugs that restore the activity of neurotransmitters in the brain and

---

DIAGNOSING ALZHEIMER'S DISEASE

- a medical and nutritional history
- laboratory tests of blood, urine, and stool
- tests for thyroid function
- a thorough physical and psychological examination
- in some cases, a CT (computerized tomography) scan, a PET (positron emission tomography) scan, or MRI (magnetic resonance imaging) in order to detect any tumors, strokes, blood clots, or hydrocephalus, and to test the response of specific areas of the brain

some that even replace lost neurochemicals. In the last several years, one drug has been found to slow the decline of memory loss by about 5 percent, but only in the early stages of AD. This medication, donepezil (marketed as Aricept[R]), appears to slow the loss of acetylcholine in the brains of AD patients. More recently, rivastigmine (marketed as Exelon) was approved in 2000 and galantamine (Reminyl) in 2001; these drugs also prevent the breakdown of acetylcholine. However, none of these drugs reverses the destruction of brain tissue by plaques and tangles. In late 2003, the Food and Drug Administration (FDA) approved the first drug that has been tested with late-stage AD. Sold as "memantine" in Europe, it will be marketed as Namenda in the United States. This drug also does not reverse the destuction of brain tissue, but it appears to slow the rate of decline in moderate to advanced stages of AD.

Some researchers have begun to explore the possibility that AD may be related to inflammation of brain tissue. This has led to the hypothesis that nonsteroidal anti-inflammatory drugs (NSAIDs), such as ibuprofen, can prevent or delay the onset of AD. Although many older people currently use low doses of NSAIDs to prevent heart attacks, few controlled clinical trials have tested whether NSAIDs have similar benefits for AD. There is, however, some correlational evidence from the Baltimore Longitudinal Studies of Aging. Older people in this study who reported that they used NSAIDs regularly for 2 or more years had less than half the risk of AD as nonusers (Stewart et al., 1997). More recent animal studies demonstrate that a daily dose of ibuprofen reduced inflammation in the brain, and resulted in about half the number of plaques and half the amyloid deposits as in the mice that were not given NSAIDs (Lim et al., 2000). The drug may act as a preventive by improving the production of chemicals that control amyloid build-up or by clearing amyloid more efficiently. Until clinical trials with humans are conducted, it will be impossible to determine if ibuprofen and other NSAIDs can really prevent AD.

Another promising pharmacotherapy for AD may be a combination of vitamin E (described in Chapter 3 as an antioxidant that appears to prevent or reduce the symptoms of other chronic diseases) and selegiline hydrochloride (marketed as Eldepryl[R] and generally prescribed for Parkinson's disease). In one clinical trial, patients in the moderate stage of AD who were given this combination did not decline as rapidly as those given a placebo (Sano et al., 1997). Vitamin E may also be effective in reducing the risk of AD. In one study that examined almost 5000 older adults for

---

CARING FOR AD PATIENTS AT EACH STAGE OF THE DISEASE

Depending on the stage of the disease, caregivers of elders with AD can help them in different ways. Using the Global Deterioration Scale described in the accompanying box, families can try the following ways of helping the patient:

Stages 1–3 (Mild dementia)

- Set up an orientation area in the home where the patient's critical items (e.g., wallet, keys, glasses) can always be found.
- Watch for signs of driving problems.
- Encourage physical and social activities.

Stages 4–5 (Moderate dementia)

- Make changes in home environment to assure safety and independence, but maintain familiarity (e.g., improved, constant light levels).
- Put labels on important doors (e.g., patient's bedroom, bathroom) and drawers.
- Keep in visible areas photos of family and close friends taken with patient, names clearly written on photos.

Stages 6–7 (Advanced dementia)

- Visit alternative long-term care facilities that fit P–E needs of the particular patient.
- Simplify daily routines but still encourage some physical activity (e.g., walks in fenced-in yard).
- Try alternative means of communication (e.g., touch, sharing old family photos).

five years, the incidence of AD was lower among elders who used vitamin E supplements in combination with vitamin C than among those who did not use any vitamin supplements or only one of these vitamins alone (Zandi et al., 2004). However, it is important to review AD patients' medications with their physicians to confirm that Vitamin E will not interact with their other medications, in particular with blood thinners. Ginkgo biloba is an extract from the dried leaves of the maidenhair tree. Some families report that regular use of this product improves the memory of an AD patient in the early to intermediate stages. However, a study in the Netherlands casts some doubt on the benefits of this treatment. Researchers studied 214 nursing home residents with mild to moderate AD or vascular dementia. Each person was given a usual dose of ginkgo biloba (84 elders) or an elevated dose (82 elders), and compared with a group (48 elders) that used a placebo over 24 weeks. No effects were observed on tests of memory or depression, but those using ginkgo performed slightly better on self-reported ADLs (van Dongen et al., 2000).

Researchers have made dramatic strides toward understanding the neurochemical basis of this disease and are rapidly moving toward its treatment. There is even some promise of a vaccine that can help the immune system produce antibodies against amyloid proteins and clear amyloid deposits from the brain. Successful research with mice gives scientists hope that such a vaccine may be effective with humans (Schenk et al., 1999)

Medications are often prescribed to manage behavioral problems in some AD patients, including agitation, hallucinations, physical aggressiveness, and wandering. In particular, risperidone, a drug used to treat psychotic symptoms in schizophrenic patients, appears to calm aggressive, delusional behaviors in a significant segment of this population (Goldberg and Goldberg, 1997). Because of their potential side effects, however, it is important to weigh the harm caused by these patient behaviors against the possible side effects of medications. Furthermore, the prescribing physi-

cian must regularly reevaluate the need to continue or reduce the dosage of any drugs used for behavior management, perhaps as frequently as every 3 to 4 months.

Behavioral Therapies and Environmental Interventions

As noted earlier, new medications that are being approved by the FDA show some promise of slowing down the rate of decline with AD. To date, however, neither these medications nor psychotherapy can restore the cognitive functions lost with most irreversible forms of dementia. Nevertheless, many older persons can benefit from behavioral therapies such as memory retraining and from some environmental modifications.

Individual competence can be enhanced somewhat and the social and home environments simplified considerably in an effort to maintain P–E congruence and maintain some independent functioning. Simple changes, such as removing sources of glare and making lighting levels consistent throughout the house, can prevent confusion and "sundowning," a condition that affects some AD patients as natural light levels change and they become more fatigued later in the day. It is important to maintain a regular schedule, to keep the patient active, and to prevent withdrawal from daily interactions. Written schedules of activities, simplified routes from room to room, and written directions for cooking, bathing, and taking medications can aid a person in finding his or her way around and prevent the frustration of getting lost or not recognizing once-familiar people and places. AD patients can be encouraged to perform more ADLs if their grooming supplies (e.g., toothbrush, toothpaste, comb) are kept visible and in a familiar sequence of use. These items can also help AD patients recognize their own bathroom or bedroom as the disease progresses. A useful device for patients in the intermediate stages of Alzheimer's is a "memory box" that contains photos from the individual's past on the outside and mementoes on the inside, placed on his or her door to identify the bedroom. Physical activity during the day can also help the patient sleep better through the night. Productive activities such as setting the table, folding laundry, and raking leaves in a secure backyard can also help patients maintain a sense of continuity with their past lives and use their excess energy. However, the frequency and intensity of such activities should not overwhelm or confuse the patient.

Wandering is another problem that can be prevented with some environmental changes. These can be as punitive as locking all exterior doors, or more protective, such as providing a safe backyard or garden area for the AD patient to explore, within easy sight of the home's windows and doors to orient the patient. ID bracelets with silent or audible alarms that can help locate the AD patient are becoming more common for use in the home, given their demonstrated benefits in nursing homes. One company has even developed a model where family or close friends can record a message on a tape attached to the bracelet to guide the wandering person back home. Some local chapters of the Alzheimer's Association offer the "safe return" program, which provides ID bracelets for AD patients, maintains records, and assists emergency teams in locating, identifying, and returning home the AD patient who becomes lost in the community (Alzheimer's Association, 1997). Agitation may also accompany AD; elders may display irritable behavior, pacing, restlessness, and general expressions of distress. These behaviors are not a normal outcome of AD but are triggered by environmental changes, fear, fatigue, loss of control, or medical conditions such as infections or adverse reactions to medications. The patient displaying signs of agitation should first be evaluated and treated for possible underlying medical conditions. If no systemic conditions are found, behavioral and environmental interventions can be used, such as adapting the home environment to the older person's needs and providing stability in daily activities.

Ultimately, the goal of managing these dementias is to slow the rate of deterioration and to

NEW WAYS OF HELPING AD PATIENTS

Until a few years ago, reality orientation was a popular therapeutic method that was used in nursing homes and by many families caring for AD patients. The emphasis was on reorienting confused older adults to the present and correcting them when they referred to a dead spouse as being alive now, or talking about getting to work despite being retired for over 20 years. However, these techniques can frustrate and agitate the patient. Most experts today agree that it is better to acknowledge the patient's memories of the past and not argue with them about the accuracy of these memories.

prevent institutionalization for as long as possible. For the AD patient who does enter a nursing home, it is important to find a facility that can maximize the individual's remaining abilities as the disease progresses (i.e., environments that can maintain the patient's P–E congruence). In recent years, the number of special care units (SCUs) in nursing homes has grown. These units are generally designed for residents with advanced dementia, especially AD, and staffed by nurses and therapists with special training in this field. Many provide a higher staff-to-resident ratio, a safe environment where patients can wander without getting lost, and special services aimed at maintaining the patients' remaining cognitive capacities. They are less likely to use chemical and physical restraints with disruptive residents. However, because there are no national licensing regulations for SCUs, the nature of services and quality of care provided vary widely. That is, the designation of a nursing home unit as a SCU does not necessarily imply richer or more tailored services than non-SCU units that also house AD and other dementia patients (Day, Carreon, and Stump, 2000; Sloane et al., 1995). Newer options include assisted living facilities, adult family homes, and adult day care (described in Chapter 11). However, like SCUs, families must determine if these alternative housing options can provide a safe and supportive environment for AD patients, especially as the disease progresses.

CAREGIVER NEEDS   One of the most important considerations with Alzheimer's disease and other dementias is to provide social and emotional support to the family as well as the patient. It is estimated that 60 to 80 percent of all people with Alzheimer's disease remain in the community, cared for by family. In fact, about 19 million family caregivers provide an aggregate of billions of dollars in home care for their relatives with AD (Bloom, de Pouvourville, and Straus, 2003; Czaja, Eisdorfer, and Schulz, 2000). Yet most of these costs are not reimbursed through Medicare or private health insurance, Medicaid, or through tax breaks. The typical caregiver of an AD patient is a 46-year-old woman, working full-time, caring for a 77-year-old mother with AD. On average they provide care for 4.5 years. As described more fully in Chapter 10, these caregivers must balance the challenges of providing daily care to their loved ones with the need to maintain their jobs, family, and personal life (Riggs, 2000).

The stress of caring for this population often results in deterioration of family members' physical and psychological health. Many caregivers feel they must shoulder this responsibility alone, resulting in increasing levels of depression, burden, and declining physical health (Mittelman, 2002; Schulz and Beach, 1999; Vitaliano et al., 1996). As family caregivers assume more responsibility for an AD patient whose functional abilities decline, perceived burden increases. This condition is aggravated and depression becomes more likely if the AD patient also displays more disruptive behaviors such as aggressiveness, frequent wakings during the night, and wandering. Caregivers who experience the most depressive symptoms also report being most disturbed by such behaviors. Depression and physiological and physical health outcomes of stress are most severe among spousal caregivers. Problems include higher insulin and glucose levels than age-matched controls, higher levels of lipids in blood,

and cardiovascular disease (Mittelman, 2002, 2004; Vitaliano, Russo, and Niaura, 1995; Vitaliano et al., 1996).

Support groups aid their members in coping with the inevitable losses faced by the victims of AD. These groups, typically coordinated by local chapters of the national Alzheimer's Association, also provide caregivers with emotional support and respite. Depression, chronic fatigue, and anger are all common caregiver reactions. Support groups can alleviate these stress responses for caregivers who begin participating early in the course of the disease so they are able to anticipate problems. Not surprisingly, those who attend sessions regularly benefit the most. A longitudinal study that tested the effects of a year-long weekly support-group program on depression also included individual and family counseling sessions during the first 4 months of the program. Combined individual, family, and support-group intervention was the key to significant declines in depression scores among this experimental group. Spouse caregivers in the control group, who received counseling or referrals only if they requested them (which occurred infrequently), became more depressed during this same period. The multipronged intervention was also effective in reducing the number of AD patients who were placed in nursing homes and delaying institutionalization by almost one year (Mittelman et al., 1996, 2004). The results of a recently completed multisite, multipronged caregiver intervention program (known as "Resources for Enhancing Alzheimer's Caregiver Health" or REACH) suggest that the most effective therapeutic interventions are comprehensive and address multiple needs of caregivers, including behavioral skills training, problem-solving, and coping skills enhancement through in-person groups, computer, and telephone support (Burgio et al., 2001).

The Internet has emerged in the last few years as a way for caregivers to share their experiences with others facing similar burdens and frustrations. Some of these Websites include advice and updated information from experts, such as the

Alzheimer's Association, while others encourage caregivers to offer support and suggestions to their peers who have recently become caregivers. The opportunity to log on to a chat room on the Internet also avoids the need to find alternative care for the AD patient at home while attending live support groups. The growth of adult day centers is another response to the need to maintain persons with dementia in the community, to help them remain active and retain learned skills, and to provide respite for caregivers. Caregivers who regularly take their AD patients to such centers have shown lower levels of anger, depression, and stress than those who do not (Zarit, Stephens, Townsend, and Greene, 1998). The need for publicly funded adult day-centers, respite, and support groups, however, is greater than the availability of services.

Parkinson's Disease

Parkinson's is a neurodegenerative disorder that begins as a loss of muscle control, with tremors in the feet and hands, gradually progressing to slow and limited movements. Speech can become impaired, muscles become rigid, and the person moves more slowly and with a shuffling gait. In its later stages, Parkinson's can manifest dementia-like symptoms. Today about one million Americans have this condition. It usually strikes people over age 60, although some people—such as the actor Michael J. Fox—are first diagnosed in their 30s.

Parkinson's differs from AD in many ways. First, the degeneration and loss of cells in the brain occurs mostly in the *substantia nigra*, located in the center of the brain. This is the region where dopamine is produced, the brain chemical responsible for initiating voluntary movement. This is why Levodopa (L-dopa) is the drug of choice for most people with Parkinson's, as a way of replacing dopamine. However, in some people L-dopa can cause such side effects as hallucinations, agitation, and uncontrollable movement. Newer drugs known as dopamine agonists have

been developed as an alternative for such patients. One of the most exciting research developments in this area is the possibility of implanting stem cells (described in Chapter 3) into the brain of Parkinson's patients. These cells appear to revitalize damaged regions and resume production of dopamine in the substantia nigra. Another promising development is new surgical methods in the brain to stop tremors and involuntary movement. Behavioral techniques such as meditation, biofeedback, and dietary modification are also recommended. The Internet is increasing the accessibility of information about Parkinson's disease for both family caregivers and professionals. For example, the Parkinson's Association, in collaboration with "TotalLivingChoices.com," provides tutorials on characteristics and stages, treatment basics, mobility and safety, digestion and bladder problems, communication and sleep, and mood and thinking problems.

Alcoholism

For most older people, alcohol use is associated with socializing and occurs in moderation (i.e., less than once a week, and no more than two drinks each time). However, those who consume four or more drinks per occasion and do so frequently (defined as alcoholism) are more likely to use alcohol as a way to cope with some life events and to help them relax (Krause, 1995; Mockenhaupt and Beck, 1997). Obtaining accurate statistics on the prevalence of alcoholism in older adults is difficult, because of the stigma associated with this condition among older cohorts. Estimates vary from 1 to 5 percent of all older people living in the community. A national survey in 1998 revealed that 80 percent of people over age 65 reported at least one alcoholic drink once a month or more frequently. Of this group, 10 percent reported consuming five drinks in one sitting, at least once a month. Another 5 percent have that many every time they drink (Reid et al., 1999). Alcoholism in older adults is accompanied by depression in 30 percent of cases, and by dementia in 20 percent, although the direction of causality is not always clear (Koenig and Blazer, 1996; Osgood, Wood, and Parham, 1995). Those at greatest risk are widowers and well-educated white men who have never married. Older men are four times more likely to have alcohol problems than are older women. Women at greatest risk of alcohol abuse are those who are smokers, not married, not religious, and with little social support. Prevalence rates are higher for African American elders than for Caucasians. The lowest rates for alcohol abuse are found in older Latina women (Graham, Carver, and Brett, 1995; Holroyd et al., 1997; Surgeon General, 1999a).

It is important to distinguish lifelong abusers of alcohol from those who began drinking later in life. Alcoholics are less likely to be found among the ranks of persons over age 60 because of higher death rates at a young age among alcoholics. Those who continue to drink in old age tend to decrease their consumption. Surveys of alcoholism rates among older persons have revealed approximately equal proportions of those who began to drink heavily before age 40 and those who began in old age (Miller, Belkin, and Gold, 1991).

Some older persons who are diagnosed as alcoholics have had this problem since middle age, but increasing age may exacerbate the condition for two reasons:

- The central nervous system (CNS), liver, and kidneys become less tolerant of alcohol with age because of the physiological changes described in Chapter 3 (e.g., loss of muscle tissue, reduction in body mass, and reduced efficiency of liver and kidney functions). For this reason, a smaller dose of alcohol can be more deleterious in the later years. In fact, current thinking is that people age 60 and older who drink should consume about half the amount acceptable for younger persons; that is, about one 4-oz glass per day for men and somewhat less for women.
- An individual who has been drinking heavily for many years has already produced irreversible damage to the CNS, liver, and kidneys, creating more problems than those due to normal aging alone.

Perhaps because of the damage to their CNSs, men who began drinking heavily before the age of 35 are more likely to experience depression, restlessness, sleeplessness, and tension than those who started later. It is difficult to determine the incidence of alcoholism among older persons who have no previous history of this disease. Physiological evidence is lacking, and drinking is often hidden from friends, relatives, and physicians. The older person may justify overconsumption of alcohol on the grounds that it relieves sadness and isolation. Even when family members are aware of the situation, they may rationalize that alcohol is one of the older person's few remaining pleasures. Denial is a common problem among older alcoholics who are influenced by beliefs of the prohibition era that alcoholism is a moral weakness and not a disease. In addition, many older people may feel that they should be able to cope with their alcoholism on their own and not have to rely on health professionals or even on support groups such as Alcoholics Anonymous.

Physicians may overlook the possibility that alcohol is creating a health problem because the adverse effects of alcohol resemble some physical diseases or psychiatric and cognitive disorders that are associated with old age. For example, older alcoholics may complain of confusion, disorientation, irritability, insomnia or restless sleep patterns, heart palpitations, weight loss, depression, or a dry cough. Beliefs held by health care providers that alcoholism does not occur in older people may also prevent its detection. Because of the problems caused by heavy alcohol use in old age, primary-care physicians must screen their older patients by asking questions about the quantity, frequency, and context of drinking. This can help in the diagnosis and referral of older alcoholics to treatment programs, which currently are underutilized by older adults. This can also reduce the emotional, physical, and cognitive deterioration caused by alcoholism in older people and the subsequent hospitalizations and use of emergency medical services for conditions that are secondary to heavy alcohol consumption (Adams, Barry, and Fleming, 1996; Holroyd et al., 1997).

Therapy for older alcoholics has not been differentiated from that for younger alcoholics. However, it is probably more important to focus on older alcoholics' medical conditions because of physical declines that make them more vulnerable to the secondary effects of alcohol. As with younger alcoholics, counseling and occupational and recreational therapy are important for treating older people experiencing alcoholism. Recovery rates for older alcoholics are as high as for younger alcoholics.

Drug Abuse

As noted in Chapter 4, older persons use a disproportionately large number of prescription and over-the-counter (OTC) drugs, representing approximately 36 percent of outpatient prescription drug expenditures (Cook, 1999). In particular, older people are more likely than the young to use tranquilizers, sedatives, and hypnotics, all of which have potentially dangerous side effects. They also are more likely to abuse aspirin compounds, laxatives, and sleeping pills, often because of misinformation about the adverse effects of too high a dosage or too many pills. It is not unusual to hear older patients state that they took twice or three times as much aspirin as they were prescribed because they did not feel that their pain was being alleviated with the lower dose. Yet, changes in body composition and renal and liver functions that occur with age, combined with the use of multiple medications, make older persons more likely to experience adverse drug reactions. Noncompliance with therapeutic drug regimens is often unintentional; older patients may take too much or too little of a drug because of nonspecific or complicated instructions by the physician, and they may use OTC drugs without reading warning labels about their side effects and interactions with

> **MEDICATION MANAGEMENT CAN THREATEN ELDERS' INDEPENDENCE**
>
> Their inability to manage their medications can be a threat to older people's independence. Families often cannot be present at every medication administration, and neighbors may help only intermittently. Even assisted living facilities cannot provide the daily help with medications that is needed, unless the older adult pays an additional fee. Some elders use plastic pillboxes with the days of the week printed on each section, or egg cartons or other small cups that the family has labeled with instructions. However, these devices cannot help an older person remember the time of day he or she must take the medication, and are not effective at all for someone with dementia.

other drugs they are using. Intentional noncompliance generally takes the form of older patients' deciding that they no longer need the medication or that it is not working for them. Such noncompliance is found to be a factor in hospital admissions among the older population.

Both health care providers and older people themselves are more aware of the effects of "polypharmacy" today. Older persons do not abuse drugs to the extent that younger populations do, nor use illicit drugs such as heroin, cocaine, and marijuana. Nor do they use hallucinogens, amphetamines, or mood-enhancing inhalants in noticeable numbers.

Paranoid Disorders and Schizophrenia

Paranoia, defined as an irrational suspiciousness of other people, takes several forms. It may result from:

- social isolation
- a sense of powerlessness
- progressive sensory decline
- problems with the normal "checks and balances" of daily life

Still other changes in the aging individual, such as memory loss, may result in paranoid reactions. Some suspicious attitudes of older persons, however, represent accurate readings of their experiences. For example, an older person's children may in fact be trying to institutionalize him or her in order to take over an estate; a nurse's aide may really be stealing from an older patient; and neighborhood children may be making fun of the older adult. It is therefore important to distinguish actual threats to the individual from unfounded suspicions. To the extent that the individual has some control over his or her environment, the older person's perception of a threatening situation is reduced. This is consistent with the P–E competence model. The diagnosis of paranoid disorders in older people is similar to that in younger patients; the symptoms should have a duration of at least one week, with no signs of schizophrenia, no prominent hallucinations, and no association to an organic mental disorder (APA, 2000).

As with depression, counseling can be useful for paranoid older persons. In particular, cognitive behavioral approaches, in which an individual focuses on changing negative, self-defeating beliefs or misconceptions, may be useful in treating paranoid older adults who often attribute causality to external factors (e.g., the belief that someone took their pocketbook, that they themselves did not misplace it). Therapy with paranoid older persons may be effective in redirecting beliefs about causality to the individuals themselves.

Schizophrenia is considerably less prevalent than depression or dementia in old age. Its peak prevalence is about 1.5 percent at age 30 to 44, declining to 0.2% in people aged 65 and older (Meeks, 2000). Most older persons with this condition were first diagnosed in adolescence or in middle age and continue to display behavior symptomatic of schizophrenia. However, the severity of symptoms appears to decrease and to change with age; older schizophrenics are less likely to manifest thought disorders and loss of emotional expression, and more likely than younger schizophrenics to experience depression,

cognitive impairments, and social isolation (Meeks and Murrell, 1997). Late-onset schizophrenia with paranoid features has been labeled *paraphrenia* by some psychiatrists, especially in Europe and Great Britain.

Schizophrenics of any age, but especially older patients, need monitoring of their medication regimens and structured living arrangements. This is because pharmacotherapy with antipsychotic medications has been found to be the most effective treatment for older schizophrenic patients. However, many of the current cohort of older chronic schizophrenics residing in the community were deinstitutionalized in the 1960s as part of the national Community Mental Health Services Act of 1963. After spending much of their youth and middle age in state hospitals, these patients were released with the anticipation that they could function independently in the community, with medications to control their hallucinations and psychotic behavior. Although this approach has proved effective for many former schizophrenic inpatients, some have not adjusted well to deinstitutionalization, as witnessed by the number of homeless older schizophrenics on the streets in most major cities.

Anxiety

Anxiety disorders are another type of functional disorder or emotional problem with no obvious organic cause. The most common forms of anxiety disorders in the older population are:

- generalized anxiety disorders
- phobias
- panic disorders

Although more common than schizophrenia and paranoid disorders, anxiety disorders are not diagnosed as frequently in older populations as they are in the young. This may be because the older person develops more tolerance and better ability to manage stressful events. More likely, however, it may be that clinicians cannot diagnose anxiety disorders as accurately in older adults because they are often masked by physical health complaints (Scogin, Floyd, and Forde, 2000). A recent study among 182 people aged 60 and older who had been diagnosed with depression found that 35 percent had also been diagnosed with an anxiety disorder at some point in their lives. A significant number (23 percent) had a current diagnosis of panic disorder or specific phobias (Lenze et al., 2000). As with other psychiatric disorders that can be masked by physical symptoms, primary care physicians must probe further when older patients complain of diffuse pain, fast or irregular heart rate, fatigue, sleep disturbance, and restlessness. Although estimates are that 2 to 5 percent of older adults have some form of anxiety disorder, as many as 20 percent have symptoms of generalized anxiety disorder. Once the condition is diagnosed, older people can benefit from cognitive-behavioral therapy, psychosocial support, and in some cases, pharmacotherapy (Banazak, 1997).

Older Adults Who Are Chronically Mentally Ill

The plight of older persons who are chronically mentally ill has not been addressed widely by mental health providers and advocates. This population is defined as people who suffer mental or emotional disorders that erode or prevent the development of their functional capacities in ADL, self-direction, interpersonal relations, social transactions, learning, or recreation. Many chronically mentally ill older persons were institutionalized in their young adult years and released into the community after the deinstitutionalization movement began in 1963. Since then, they have been in and out of hospitals as their conditions have become exacerbated. These people have survived major upheavals and social neglect in their lives under marginally functional conditions.

The social disruption and years of treatment with psychotropic drugs take their toll on many of these people, who are physiologically old in their 50s and 60s. Obtaining medical care for purely physical symptoms may be difficult because health care providers may dismiss a complaint as hypochondriasis and/or attribute it to the patient's psychiatric disorder. Health professionals in this situation need to perform a thorough exam to exclude conditions caused by the mental disorder or by aging per se, and to treat any systemic diseases that are diagnosed.

Psychotherapy with Older Persons

Despite early doubts by Freud (1924) and others about the value of psychotherapy for older patients, many researchers and therapists have developed and tested psychotherapeutic interventions specifically for this population, or have modified existing approaches. One challenge in working with older individuals is to overcome some older persons' misconceptions about psychotherapy. For this reason, short-term, goal-oriented therapies may be more effective with older patients because they can begin to experience benefits immediately. On the other hand, older patients who are reluctant and unwilling to open up to a therapist may benefit more from long-term treatment in which rapport and trust between the therapist and the client can be established gradually. Several different types of therapy have been explored with this population.

As noted earlier, *life review* is one therapeutic approach that has been successfully used with older adults. Such therapy encourages introspection through active reminiscence of past achievements and failures, and may reestablish ego integrity in depressed older persons. This method may also be used effectively by social service providers who are not extensively trained in psychotherapy but have the opportunity to work one-on-one with older clients. It has been found to reduce symptoms of depression, and to increase life satisfaction and self-esteem in nursing home residents up to 3 years after completion of life review therapy (Haight, Michel, and Hendrix, 2000). An alternative form of life review, known as **reminiscence therapy,** has been compared with a more focused, problem-solving therapy. Although it has short-term benefits for depressed older people, it is less effective in long-term (i.e., greater than 3 months) reduction of depressive symptoms (Arean et al., 1993; Cully et al., 2001).

Group therapy is often advocated for older patients experiencing mental disorders, especially depression. Groups offer the opportunity for peer support, social interaction, and role modeling. Life review may be used effectively as part of group therapy. The opportunity to share life experiences and to learn that others have had similar stresses in their lives seems to enhance insight, self-esteem, and a feeling of catharsis. Group reminiscence therapy appears to reduce symptoms of depression immediately after the sessions have been completed, but its long-term benefits are unclear. Groups are also established for improving memory and enhancing cognitive skills. They are an ideal setting for teaching memory skills with the use of games and puzzles as well as reminiscence exercises (Gatz et al., 1998).

Empirical studies have been conducted to compare the efficacy of alternative therapeutic interventions. For example, *cognitive-behavioral* (i.e., active, structured, and time-limited therapy) and *brief psychodynamic therapy* (i.e., helping the patient to develop ego strength and feelings of control) both appear to be equally effective in alleviating minor depression, even up to 12 months following treatment. Psychodynamic therapy uses psychoanalytic concepts such as insight, transference, and the unconscious to relieve symptoms of depression and to prevent its recurrence by attempting to understand why the individual behaves in self-defeating ways. Each type of therapy may be appropriate for different types of older patients. For example, cognitive–behavioral therapy has been compared with brief psychodynamic

therapy among depressed caregivers of Alzheimer's disease patients. Longer-term caregivers are found to improve more with cognitive–behavioral methods, while shorter-term caregivers benefit more from psychodynamic therapy (Gallagher-Thompson and Steffan, 1994).

The therapeutic interventions just described are more frequently used in community settings than in nursing homes. The latter setting lends itself to more intense, long-term therapies: behavior-change programs, milieu therapy, and *remotivation therapy.* Behavior-change techniques using operant reinforcement and token economies have been successfully used in long-term care settings with psychiatrically impaired young and old patients. These methods are found to increase self-feeding and self-care and to reduce dependency. *Milieu therapy* is consistent with Lawton and Nahemow's competence model described earlier. This approach focuses on improving the therapeutic environment of the nursing home or enhancing an individual's sense of control over some important aspects of life. All staff members are encouraged to work as a team to improve the therapeutic environment of the facility.

Remotivation therapy has been used successfully with less confused elders. Groups of older persons with some cognitive impairment and who are withdrawn from social activities meet together under the guidance of a trained group leader. The purpose is to discuss events and experiences by bringing all group members into the discussion, emphasizing the event's relevance for each member, and encouraging them to share what they have gained from the session. This approach is found to be effective in psychiatric hospitals and nursing homes as well as in adult day centers.

Despite these positive reports about the benefits of psychotherapy with older adults, mental health professionals must recognize some differences in effectiveness between older and younger adults. Patients older than age 70 are more likely to experience relapse if treatment is discontinued or no booster sessions are offered. Relapse, or at least fading of treatment effects, are observed 6 to 12 months after these therapeutic interventions are discontinued (Reynolds et al., 1999).

Use of Mental Health Services

As noted in Chapter 4, older persons use physician services somewhat more than the young do, and are hospitalized at a much higher rate. In contrast, mental health services are significantly underutilized by older people, especially ethnic minority and low-income elders. Community-based care is used by older people at a far lower rate than inpatient hospital treatment, far below their representation in the U.S. population and less than the estimated prevalence of mental disorders in this group.

Older persons may be more likely to seek help from their primary physicians and to be hospitalized for mental disorders than to seek community mental health services. This may be because medical care does not carry the stigma of mental health services, especially for older ethnic minorities. For example, Asians and Pacific Islanders view psychiatric disorders with shame. A disproportionate number of older persons represent the population of patients in state mental hospitals that house the chronically mentally ill. Despite the deinstitutionalization movement of the 1960s, the great majority of all psychiatric services to older people are in hospital settings.

BARRIERS TO OLDER PERSONS' USE OF MENTAL HEALTH SERVICES   Older adults are generally unwilling to interpret their problems as psychological, preferring instead to attribute them to physical or social conditions or to normal aging. In addition, the current cohort of older persons may be less oriented to the use of mental health services because of societal stigmas, limited knowledge about mental disorders, and a lack of confidence in mental health workers. This requires a good "psychological ear" on the part of the older person's primary-care physician. As noted earlier, older patients may complain of physical symptoms rather than focus on psychological concerns. Therefore the physician must be attuned to the underlying emotional distress presented by the older patient.

Accessibility is perhaps the greatest barrier to older individuals' obtaining mental health services. In addition to the physical access issues of transportation and architectural barriers, there are significant problems of fragmented services and older people's lack of knowledge about seeking mental health services on their own or obtaining appropriate referrals from physicians and social service providers. Cultural barriers, including communication problems, underlie the low utilization rates of mental health services by elders of color. These barriers are discussed in greater detail in Chapter 14. Fortunately, many new and

---

OVERCOMING BARRIERS TO USING MENTAL HEALTH SERVICES

• Home visits by a psychiatrist, social worker, and a nurse are made to low-income, isolated older people in Baltimore through the "Psychogeriatric Assessment and Treatment in City Housing" (or PATCH) program.

• Rural elders in Iowa are served by mental health professionals through the Elderly Outreach Program (or EOP) of the community mental health system.

• The Family Services Program of greater Boston offers a community mental health program aimed especially at ethnic minority elders, entitled Services for Older People (or SOP).

• In Seattle, a mental health team from the community mental health network provides on-site evaluation and therapy to area nursing homes on a regular basis.

• In many communities, "gatekeepers" (nontraditional referral sources such as meter readers, postal carriers, and apartment and mobile home managers who have contact with isolated older people in the community) are trained to identify older persons who may require psychiatric care. These isolated older adults are typically chronically mentally ill.

innovative programs have arisen to overcome these barriers and respond to the mental health needs of older adults, as highlighted in the box on page 238. Many senior centers employ social workers trained in geriatrics to conduct support groups, education programs, and individualized sessions on coping with grief, loss, and loneliness, and on methods to improve memory. Such programs reduce the stigma of psychotherapy by their informal structure in a familiar environment.

Reimbursement for psychological services is also a problem. For example, Medicare Part A pays for no outpatient mental health expenditures, but pays for a limited number of days for inpatient treatment. Furthermore, copayment by the subscriber for mental health services is greater than for physical health services. It should be noted that this discrepancy occurs in many health insurance programs used by younger persons as well. Because of attitudes held by older patients toward mental disorders and by therapists toward older clients, however, these reimbursement issues are greater barriers to older persons' use of mental health services than they are for the young. Future cohorts of older people may be more likely to seek such services in community mental health centers, because of increased awareness of mental disorders and treatment modalities.

Implications for the Future

During the past 20 years, there has been more research emphasis on normal, age-related changes in personality, as well as psychological disorders such as depression and dementia. Larger, cross-national and longitudinal studies are providing insights into the universality of stability in some personality traits and change in others. The inclusion of larger samples of women and ethnic minorities in more recent studies offers valuable information on gender and ethnic differences in psychological processes with aging. Researchers have identified differences in rates and symptoms of some psychological disorders across ethnic groups. This in-

formation can help health and social service providers who work with older adults recognize signs of depression, dementia, anxiety disorders, and other conditions in their clients and help them obtain the treatment they need.

With the growth of the older population and increased numbers of elders who live into their 80s and 90s, the sheer numbers of people with psychological disorders will expand over the next 30 years. More emphasis will be placed on alternatives to medications to treat these conditions, as well as culturally competent methods of psychotherapy and communication with older adults and their families. Support groups for elders and their families who are coping with psychological disorders will continue to grow. New research on the biochemistry of Alzheimer's disease and Parkinson's may offer hope for victims of these diseases, including early diagnosis and stem cell transplants to repair affected areas of the brain. The Internet has already proven to be a valuable resource for older adults and their families as a means of learning more about their medical diagnoses, and even offers possibilities for group support and psychotherapy by mental health professionals. Gerontology will continue to grow as baby boomers become senior boomers.

The discussion of normal personality development with aging and psychological disorders in this chapter should encourage students interested in research and clinical careers. There is a great need for psychologists, social workers, psychiatrists, and nurses to work in direct mental health services with older adults and, in the case of elders with dementia, to provide therapeutic services to their caregivers. Geriatricians are needed who can understand the difference between normal and abnormal psychological functioning in older adults, and who can distinguish dementia and depression from adverse reactions to medications, and from grief responses to losses associated with aging. Even nurses and physicians who elect to go into primary care should develop these skills; as seen from the research described in this chapter, many older people with mood disorders and dementia seek a diagnosis and treatment from their primary care provider, not from a mental health specialist.

There is also a need for more researchers in gerontology who can advance the field of basic personality development and psychological disorders with aging. Whether you are interested in social or behavioral sciences, biological sciences, pharmacology or technology, there are many opportunities to test interventions to improve older persons' quality of life, both those who are healthy and those experiencing psychological disorders. In an era of limited resources for mental health services, it is essential to know what interventions are most effective with different groups of older adults.

Summary

Personality development in adulthood and old age has received increasing attention over the past 30 years. Earlier theories of personality suggested that development takes place only during childhood and adolescence, and stabilizes by early adulthood. Beginning with Erik Erikson, however, several theorists have suggested that personality continues to change and evolve into old age. According to Erikson's theory of psychosocial development, the individual experiences stages of development, with crises or conflicts at each stage, and the outcome of each has an impact on ego development in the next stage. The seventh stage, generativity versus stagnation, takes place mostly during the middle years, but increasingly researchers find that continued generativity in old age is important for successful aging. Programs such as foster grandparents encourage older people to experience ongoing generativity by working with young children. The eighth and last stage of personality development occurs in old age and poses the conflict of ego integrity versus despair in dealing with one's impending death. Both cross-sectional and longitudinal studies have found evidence for these last two stages of development.

The work of Carl Jung also emphasizes the growth of personality across the life span, but does not specify stages of development. Jung's model, like Erikson's, focuses on the individual's confrontation with death in this last stage. In addition, Jung described a decrease in sex-typed behavior with aging. This has been supported in cross-cultural studies by Gutmann (1977, 1980, 1992) and in the longitudinal Kansas City Studies. These investigators found that men become more accepting of their nurturant and affiliative characteristics as they age, whereas women learn to accept their egocentric and aggressive impulses. Levinson's life structures model also examines personality from a developmental stage perspective. This model is consistent with the person–environment approach in emphasizing the interaction between the individual and his or her environment as the impetus for change.

Trait theories of personality have been tested systematically in the Baltimore Longitudinal Studies of Aging (Costa and McCrae, 1986, 1994, 1995; McCrae and Costa, 1996, 1997). These researchers have tested a five-factor model of personality consisting of five primary traits (neuroticism, extroversion, openness to experience, agreeableness, and conscientiousness), and several subcategories of traits. They have found considerable stability in these traits from middle age to old age when tested longitudinally, and age differences between young and old when tested cross-sectionally. More recent studies by these researchers demonstrate the universality of age difference in the five factors of personality (McCrae et al., 1999, 2000). Emotional expression also undergoes some change with aging, although early social conditioning establishes lifelong patterns of emotion regulation. The development of self-concept and self-esteem in old age has been researched even less. It is recognized that older persons' self-concepts must be redefined as they move from traditional roles of worker, partner, and parent to less well-differentiated roles such as retiree or widow. But the process by which such changes take place and, more important, how they influence life satisfaction and self-esteem in old age is unclear.

Somewhat more research has been devoted to age-related changes in the nature of life events and the stress associated with them. Cognitive appraisal is an important consideration in understanding people's reactions to life events. To the extent that people perceive a situation as a threat, or as a negative stressor, the response may be avoidance or ineffective coping. If a particular life event is viewed as benign or unimportant, coping responses will not be activated. If an event proves to be more stressful than anticipated, an older person will be unprepared to cope with these demands.

Adaptation is influenced by an individual's access to a support network, cognitive skills, and personality traits such as active versus passive "mastery style" and "locus of control." Although ego defense mechanisms have been observed to become more mature in middle and old age, it is difficult to describe coping styles in a similar manner. Age differences in the use of coping styles have been observed in cross-sectional studies, but longitudinal comparisons reveal considerable stability in coping.

Successful or active aging may be defined as the ability to avoid disease and disability, to function at a high level cognitively, to remain involved in society, and to cope effectively with life events and chronic hassles. An individual who has survived to the age of 75 or older has proved to be adaptable to new situations. Hence, older people who remain physically, cognitively, and socially active are the most resilient of their cohort.

The prevalence of mental disorders in old age is difficult to determine, although estimates range from 5 to 45 percent of the older population. Research in acute and long-term care institutional settings provides higher estimates than epidemiological studies conducted in the community. This is because many older persons with mental disorders are treated in institutional settings rather than through community mental health services.

Depression is the most common mental disorder in late life, although estimates of its prevalence also vary widely, depending on the criteria used to diagnose it. Bipolar disorders are rare in old age; major depression is more common. Reactive or minor depression that is secondary to major life changes is found frequently in older persons. This condition responds well to environmental and social interventions, whereas antidepressant medications combined with psychotherapy are more effective for major depression. It is important that older adults continue treatment for several months in order to improve their condition. Electroconvulsive therapy works well for severe depression in older people who do not respond to other forms of therapy. Diagnosing depression in older people is often difficult. Many deny it and accept "feeling blue" as a normal part of growing old, while others attribute it to medical conditions. On the other hand, it is important to screen for medical conditions and medications that may produce depressive symptoms as a side effect.

Depression is a risk factor for suicide in older people, particularly for white men over age 85. Life changes that result in a loss of social status and increased isolation may explain why this group is more likely to commit suicide than other segments of the population. The increased risk of suicide in older adults highlights the need for family members and service providers to be sensitized to clues of an impending suicide.

Dementia includes numerous reversible and irreversible conditions that result in impaired cognitive function, especially recall of recent events, comprehension, learning, attention, and orientation to time, place, and person. It is essential to perform a complete diagnostic workup of older people who have symptoms of dementia. A medical history, physical examination, assessment of medications, lab tests, psychological and cognitive testing, as well as neurological testing will aid in distinguishing "reversible" dementias that can be treated from the "irreversible" dementias such as Alzheimer's disease that currently can be managed but not cured. The biological basis of Alzheimer's disease is receiving much more research attention today. Future treatments may involve medications that replace or prevent the loss of brain chemicals, as well as vaccines and even gene therapy. Family members and service providers should be aware of changes in the older person's cognitive functioning and behavior that may signal dementia, and must avoid labeling such changes as normal aging or as—the catchall phrase—"senility." The Nun Study is providing useful insights into early life experiences and activities that may prevent or delay the onset of dementia.

Although cognitive functioning cannot be restored in irreversible dementias, older persons in the early stages of these conditions often benefit from some medications, memory retraining, education, and counseling or psychotherapy to cope with the changes they are experiencing. Environmental modifications that simplify tasks and aid in orienting the patient may slow the rate of deterioration and postpone institutionalization. It is also important to provide emotional and social support to family caregivers of elders with Alzheimer's disease and other dementias. Support groups, education, adult day care, and other such respite programs are valuable for partners and other caregivers who assume full-time care for these patients at home, although they are limited by funding constraints.

Alcoholism and drug abuse are less common in older persons than in the young, although accurate estimates of prevalence are difficult to obtain. Physical health and cognitive function are significantly impaired in older alcoholics. Older men with a history of alcohol abuse also have a greater risk of suicide than do younger men or young and old women who are alcoholics. Drug abuse in older persons is rarely associated with illicit drugs, but often takes the form of inappropriate use or overuse of some prescription and over-the-counter drugs. Adverse reactions are more likely to occur in older persons because of age-related physiological changes that impair the ability to metabolize many medications and because of the greater likelihood of polypharmacy.

Paranoia and schizophrenia are far less common than depression and dementia in older persons. Most people with these conditions first developed them in middle age; life changes such as relocation and confusion that result from dementia may trigger paranoid reactions in old age, and may aggravate preexisting schizophrenic symptoms. Psychotherapy, especially using cognitive behavior strategies, may be effective in treating paranoia, although it is important first to determine and to verify the underlying causes of the condition.

Many researchers have explored the feasibility of psychotherapy with older patients. Both short-term, goal-oriented therapy and long-term approaches have been advocated. Specific modes of therapy with older patients include life review, reminiscence, brief psychodynamic, and cognitive-behavioral techniques. These interventions have been particularly effective with depressed older people in community settings. Nursing homes are ideal settings for long-term, intense therapies using groups, but staff may not have the time or training to implement them. Behavior change and milieu therapy have resulted in significant improvements in short-term experimental interventions.

Despite the demonstrated efficacy of many forms of therapy with older persons, they significantly underutilize mental health services. Most treatments for mental disorders in this population take place in hospitals. Many older people prefer to seek treatment for depression and other mental disorders from a general physician. This may result in an overuse of pharmacological treatment and an underutilization of psychotherapy in cases where the latter may be more effective. Such behavior may be attributed to reluctance among the current cohort of elders to admit they have a psychological problem, a lack of knowledge about such conditions and their treatment, as well as problems with accessibility. Attitudes of mental health providers and social service providers about the value of psychotherapy for older persons and, perhaps most important, the lack of effective links between mental health and social services to the older population, have been barriers in the past. As discussed in Chapter 14, cultural competence among mental health providers is needed to improve access for historically disadvantaged groups. As more programs evolve that integrate services, and as future cohorts become aware of mental disorders and their treatment, there will be greater acceptance and use of mental health services by older people.

GLOSSARY

active and passive mastery   interactions with one's social environment that are more controlling and competitive, versus more affiliative and docile

adaptation   ability to change personal needs, motivations, behaviors, and expectations to fit changing environmental demands or conditions

anxiety disorder   functional psychological disorder often triggered by external stress; accompanied by physiological reactivity such as increased heart rate and sleep disorders

archetypes   masculine and feminine aspects of personality, present in both men and women

benign senescent forgetfulness   mild age-related decline in memory and learning ability; not progressive as in dementia

cognitive appraisal   the individual's interpretation of an event as stressful, benign, or pleasant; determines individual's response to situation

coping (problem-focused versus emotion-focused)   conscious responses to stress, determined by nature of stressor, personality, social support, and health

defense mechanisms   unconscious responses to stress, in order to defend the ego from impulses, memories, and external threats

delirium   a reversible dementia characterized by sudden onset, generally caused by environmental factors.

dementia   progressive, marked decline in cognitive functions associated with damage to brain tissue; may affect personality and behavior; may be reversible or irreversible type

depression (major versus minor or reactive)   the most common psychiatric disorder in old age, diagnosed if several behavioral and affective symptoms (e.g., sleep and disturbances) are present for at least two weeks; bipolar disorders are less common in older people than reactive (or minor) and major depression

dysthymic disorder   a less acute type of depression, but lasting longer than major depression

ego integrity versus despair   the eighth and last stage of psychosocial development in Erikson's model; aging individual achieves wisdom and perspective, or despairs because he or she views one's life as lacking meaning

electroconvulsive or electroshock therapy (ECT)   a form of therapy for severely depressed patients in which a mild electrical current is applied to one or both sides of brain

generativity   the seventh stage of psychosocial development in Erikson's model; goal of middle-aged and older persons is to care for and mentor younger generations, look toward future, and not stagnate in past

life events   identifiable, discrete life changes or transitions that require some adaptation to reestablish homeostasis

life review   a form of psychotherapy that encourages discussion of past successes and failures

life structures   in Levinson's model, specific developmental stages consisting of eras and transitions

paranoia   a psychiatric disorder characterized by irrational suspiciousness of other people

pharmacotherapy   use of medications to treat symptoms of physical or psychiatric disorders

psychopathology   abnormal changes in personality and behavior that may be caused or triggered by a genetic predisposition, environmental stress, and/or systemic diseases

reminiscence therapy   a type of psychotherapy used with depressed, anxious, sometimes confused older adults, stimulating the older person's memory of successful coping experiences and positive events in the past

schizophrenia   a psychiatric disorder characterized by thought disorders and hallucinations, psychotic behavior, loss of emotional expression.

self-concept   cognitive representation of the self; emerges from interactions with social environment, social roles, accomplishments

self-efficacy   perceived confidence in one's own ability to know how to cope with a stressor and to resolve it

self-esteem   evaluation or feeling about one's identity relative to an "ideal self"; differs from self-concept in being more of an emotional, not cognitive, assessment of self

stage theories of personality development of individual through various levels, each one necessary for adaptation and for psychological adjustment

successful aging achievement of good physical and functional health, cognitive and emotional well-being in old age, often accompanied by strong social support and productive activity

trait theories personality theories that describe individuals in terms of characteristic or "typical" attributes that remain relatively stable with age

RESOURCES

See the companion Website for this text at <www .ablongman.com/hooyman> for information about the following:

- Alzheimer's Disease Education and Referral Center (ADEAR)
- Alzheimer's Disease and Related Disorders Association Inc. (ADRDA)
- Alzheimer's Research Forum
- American Association for Geriatric Psychiatry
- Eldercare Web
- Elder Care Locator
- National Family Caregivers Association
- National Institute of Neurological Disorders and Stroke

REFERENCES

Adams, W. L., Barry, K. K., and Fleming, M. F. Screening for problem drinking in older primary care patients. *Journal of the American Medical Association,* 1996, *276,* 1964–1967.

Albert, M. S., Savage, C. R., Jones, K., Berkman, L., Seeman, T., Blazer, D., and Rowe, J. W. Predictors of cognitive change in older persons: MacArthur studies of successful aging. *Psychology and Aging,* 1995, *10,* 578–589.

Alzheimer's Association. *Action series: Modifying the environment.* Chicago: Alzheimer's Association, 1997.

American Psychiatric Association (APA) Task Force on DSM-IV-TR. *Diagnostic and statistical manual of mental disorders* (4th ed., Text Revision). Washington, DC: APA, 2000.

Andrews, M. The seductiveness of agelessness. *Ageing and society,* 1999, *19,* 301–318.

Aranda, M. P., Lee, P-J., and Wilson, S. Correlates of depression in older Latinos. *Home Health Care Services Quarterly,* 2001, *20,* 1–20.

Arean, P. A., Perri, M. G., Nezu, A. M., Schein, R. L., Christopher, F., and Joseph, T. X. Comparative effectiveness of social problem-solving therapy and reminiscence therapy as treatments for depression in older adults. *Journal of Consulting and Clinical Psychology,* 1993, *61,* 1003–1010.

Banazak, D. A. Anxiety disorders in elderly patients. *Journal of the American Board of Family Practice,* 1997, *10,* 280–289.

Bassuk, S. S., Glass, T. A., and Berkman, L. F. Social disengagement and incident cognitive decline in community-dwelling elderly persons. *Annals of Internal Medicine,* 1999, *131,* 165–173.

Black, S. A., Markides, K. S., and Miller, T. Q. Correlates of depressive symptomatology among older community-dwelling Mexican Americans: The Hispanic EPESE. *Journals of Gerontology,* 1998, *53B,* S198–208.

Blazer, D. G. Depression. In W. R. Hazzard, J. P. Blass, J. W. H. Ettinger, D. B. Halter, and J. G. Ouslander (Eds.), *Principles of geriatric medicine and gerontology* (4th ed.). New York: McGraw-Hill, 1999.

Blazer, D. G., Hybels, C. F., and Pieper, C. F. The association of depression and mortality in elderly persons: A case for multiple independent pathways. *Journal of Gerontology: Medical Sciences,* 2001, *56A,* M505–M509.

Blazer, D. G., and Koenig, H. G. Suicide. In J. E. Birren (Ed.), *Encyclopedia of gerontology.* San Diego: Academic Press, 1996.

Blazer, D. G., Landerman, L. R., Hays, J. C., Simonsick, E. M., and Saunders, W. B. Symptoms of depression among community-dwelling elderly African American and white older adults. *Psychological Medicine,* 1998, *28,* 1311–1320.

Bloom, B. S., de Pouvourville, N., and Straus, W. L. Cost of illness of Alzheimer's disease: How useful are current estimates? *The Gerontologist,* 2003, *43,* 158–164.

Brinton, R. D., Chen, S., Montoya, M., Hsieh, D. and Minaya, J. Estrogen replacement therapy of the Women's Health Initiative promotes the cellular mechanisms of memory and neuronal survival in neurons vulnerable to Alzheimer's disease. *Maturitas,* 2000, *34,* S35–S52.

Brookmeyer, R., and Kawas, C. Projections of Alzheimer's disease in the United States and the public health impact of delaying disease onset. *American Journal of Public Health*, 1998, *88*, 1337–1342.

Burgio, L., Corcoran, M., Lichstein, K. L., Nichols, L., Czaja, S. J., Gallagher-Thompson, D., et al. Judging outcomes in psychosocial interventions for dementia caregivers: The problems of treatment implementation. *The Gerontologist*, 2001, *41*, 481–489.

Butler, R. N., Lewis, M., and Sunderland, T. *Aging and mental health* (4th ed.). New York: Macmillan, 1991.

Calasanti, T. M., and Slevin, K. F. *Gender, social inequalities and aging*. Walnut Creek, CA: Altimira Press, 2001.

Carr, D. B., Goate, A., Phil, D., and Morris, J. C. Current concepts in the pathogenesis of Alzheimer's disease. *American Journal of Medicine*, 1997, *103*, 3S–10S.

Carstensen, L. I., Graff, J., Levenson, R. W., and Gottman, J. M. Affect in intimate relationships. In C. Magai and S. H. McFadden (Eds.), *Handbook of emotion, adult development and aging*. San Diego: Academic Press, 1996.

Carstensen, L. I., Pasupathi, M., and Mayr, U. Emotional experience in everyday life across the adult life span. *Journal of Personality and Social Psychology*, 2000, *79*, 644–655.

Centers for Disease Control and Prevention (CDC). *Suicide deaths and rates per 100,000*, 1999. www.cdc.gov/ncipc/data/us9794/suic.htm.

Chiles, J. A., Lambert, M. J., and Hatch, A. L. The impact of psychological interventions on medical cost offset: A meta-analytic review. *Clinical Psychology: Science and Practice*, 1999, *6*, 204–220.

Col, N., Fanale, J. E., and Kronholm, P. The role of medication noncompliance and adverse drug reactions in hospitalizations of the elderly. *Archives of Internal Medicine*, 1990, *150*, 841–845.

Cook, A. E. Strategies for containing drug costs: Implications for a Medicare benefit. *Health Care Financing Review*, 1999, *20*, 29–38.

Costa, P. T., and McCrae, R. R. Cross-sectional studies of personality in a national sample. Development and validation of survey measures. *Psychology and Aging*, 1986, *1*, 140–143.

Costa, P. T., and McCrae, R. R. Solid ground in the wetlands of personality: A reply to Block. *Psychological Bulletin*, 1995, *117*, 216–220.

Costa, P. T., and McCrae, R. R. Stability and change in personality from adolescence through adulthood. In C. F. Halverson, G. A. Kohnstamm, and R. P. Martin (Eds.), *The developing structure of temperament and personality from infancy to adulthood*. Hillsdale, NJ: Erlbaum, 1994.

Cully, J. A., LaVoie, D., and Gfeller, J. D. Reminiscence, personality, and psychological functioning in older adults. *The Gerontologist*, 2001, *41*, 89–95.

Czaja, S. J., Eisdorfer, C., and Schulz, R. Future directions in caregiving: Implications for intervention research. In R. Schulz (Ed.), *Handbook of dementia caregiving intervention research*. New York: Springer, 2000.

Danner, D. D., Snowdon, D. A., and Friesen, W. V. Positive emotions in early life and longevity: Findings from the Nun Study. *Journal of Personality and Social Psychology*, 2001, *80*, 804–813.

Day, K., Carreon, D. and Stump, C. The therapeutic design of environments for people with dementia: A review of the empirical research. *The Gerontologist*. 2000, *40*, 397–406.

DeVries, H. M. Cognitive-behavioral interventions. In J. E. Birren (Ed.), *Encyclopedia of gerontology*, San Diego: Academic Press, 1996.

De St. Aubin, E., and McAdams, D. P. The relations of generative concern and generative action to personality traits, satisfaction/happiness with life, and ego development. *Journal of Adult Development*. 1995, *2*, 99–112.

Diehl, M. Self-development in adulthood and aging: The role of critical life events. In C. D. Ryff and V. W. Marshall (Eds.), *The self and society in aging processes*. New York: Springer, 1999.

Diehl, M., Coyne, N., and Labouvie-Vief, G. Age and sex differences in strategies of coping and defense across the life span. *Psychology and Aging*, 1996, *11*, 127–139.

Erikson, E. H. *Childhood and society* (2nd ed.). New York: Norton, 1963.

Erikson, E. H. *Identity, youth and crisis*. New York: Norton, 1968.

Erikson, E. H. *The life cycle completed: A review*. New York: Norton, 1982.

Erikson, E. H., Erikson, J. M., and Kivnick, H. Q. *Vital involvement in old age*. New York: Norton, 1986.

Erkinjuntti, T., Ostbye, T., Steenhuis, R., and Hachinski, V. The effect of different diagnostic criteria on the prevalence of dementia. *New England Journal of Medicine*, 1997, *337*, 1667–1674.

Fisher, B. J. Successful aging, life satisfaction, and generativity in later life. *International Journal of Aging and Human Development*, 1995, *41*, 239–250.

Folstein, M., Folstein, S., and McHugh, P. R. Minimental state: A practical method for grading the cognitive state of patients for the clinician. *Journal of Psychiatric Research,* 1975, *12,* 189–198.

Fox, J. Broken connections, missing memories. Interviewed in *Time,* April 15, 1991, 10–12.

Frank, E., Swartz, H. A., Mallinger, A. G., Thase, M. E., Weaver, E. V., and Kupfer, D. J. Adjunctive psychotherapy for bipolar disorder: Effects of changing treatment modality. *Journal of Abnormal Psychology,* 1999, *108,* 579–587.

Freud, S. *Collected papers, Volume I.* London: Hogarth Press, 1924.

Friedland, R. P., Fritsch, T., Smyth, K., Koss, E., Lerner, A. J., Chen, C. H., Petot, G., and Debanne, S. M. Participation in nonoccupational activities in midlife is protective against the development of Alzheimer's disease: Results from a case-control study. *Neurology,* 2000, *54,* Abstract #P05.076.

Gallagher-Thompson, D., and Steffan, A. Comparative effectiveness of cognitive-behavioral and brief psychodynamic psychotherapy for treatment of depression in family caregivers. *Journal of Consulting and Clinical Psychology,* 1994, *62,* 543–549.

Gallo, J. J., and Lebowitz, B. D. The epidemiology of common late-life mental disorders in the community: Themes for the new century. *Psychiatric Services,* 1999, *50,* 1158–1166.

Garfein, A. J., and Herzog, A. R. Robust aging among the young-old, old-old, and oldest-old. *Journals of Gerontology,* 1995, *50B,* S77–S87.

Garrard, J., Rolnick, S. J., Nitz, N. M., Luepke, L., Jackson, J., Fischer, L. R., Leibson, C., Bland, P. C., Heinrich, R., and Waller, L. A. Clinical detection of depression among community-based elderly people with self-reported symptoms of depression. *Journals of Gerontology Series A: Biological Sciences and Medical Sciences,* 1998, *53,* M92–M101.

Gatz, M., Fiske, A., Fox, L. S., Kaskie, B., Kasl-Godley, J. E., McCallum, T. J., and Wetherell, J. L. Empirically validated treatments for older adults. *Journal of Mental Health and Aging,* 1998, *4,* 9–26.

Gatz, M., and Smyer, M. A. Mental health and aging at the outset of the 21st century. In J. E. Birren and K. W. Schaie (Eds.), *Handbook of the psychology of aging* (5th ed.). San Diego: Academic Press, 2001.

George, L. K. The links between religion and health: Are they real? *Public Policy and Aging Report,* 2002, *12,* 4, 3–6.

Giarrusso, R., and Bengtson, V. L. Self-esteem. In J. E. Birren (Ed.), *Encyclopedia of gerontology,* Vol. 2. San Diego: Academic Press, 1996.

Goisman, R. M. Cognitive-behavioral therapy, personality disorders, and the elderly. In E. Rosowsky, R. C. Abrams, and R. A. Zweig (Eds.), *Personality disorders in older adults.* Mahwah, NJ: Lawrence Erlbaum Associates, 1999.

Goldberg, R. J., and Goldberg, J. Risperidone for dementia-related disturbed behavior in nursing home residents. *International Psychogeriatrics,* 1997, *9,* 65–68.

Graham, K., Carver, V., and Brett, P. J. Alcohol and drug use by older women: Results of a national survey. *Canadian Journal on Aging,* 1995, *14,* 769–791.

Gustafson, D., Rothenberg, E., Blennow, K. Steen, B., and Skoog, I. An 18-year follow-up of overweight and risk of Alzheimer's disease. *Archives of Internal Medicine,* 2003, *163,* 1524–1528.

Gutmann, D. L. The cross-cultural perspective: Notes toward a comparative psychology of aging. In J. E. Birren and K. W. Schaie (Eds.), *Handbook of the psychology of aging.* New York: Van Nostrand Reinhold, 1977.

Gutmann, D. L. Culture and mental health in later life. In J. E. Birren, R. B. Sloane, and G. D. Cohen (Eds.), *Handbook of mental health and aging* (2nd ed.). New York: Academic Press, 1992.

Gutmann, D. L. Psychoanalysis and aging: A developmental view. In S. I. Greenspan and G. H. Pollock (Eds.), *The course of life: Psychoanalytic contributions toward understanding personality development. Vol. 3: Adulthood and the aging process.* Washington, DC: U.S. Government Printing Office, 1980.

Haight, B. K., Michel, Y., and Hendrix, S. The extended effects of the life review in nursing home residents. *International Journal of Aging and Human Development,* 2000, *50,* 151–168.

Harralson, T. L., White, T. M. Regenberg, A. C., Kallan, M. J., and Have, T. T. Similarities and differences in depression among black and white nursing home residents. *American Journal of Geriatric Psychiatry,* 2002, *10,* 175–184.

Hendrie, H. C. Epidemiology of Alzheimer's disease. *Geriatrics,* 1997, *52,* S4–S8.

Herzog, A. R., Franks, M. M., Markus, H. R., and Holmberg, D. Activities and well-being in old age: Effects of self-concept and educational attainment. *Psychology and Aging,* 1998, *13,* 179–185.

Holmes, T. H., and Masuda, M. Life change and illness susceptibility. In B. S. Dohrenwend and B. P. Dohrenwend (Eds.), *Stressful life events: Their nature and effects.* New York: Wiley, 1974.

Holmes, T. H., and Rahe, R. The social readjustment rating scale. *Journal of Psychosomatic Research,* 1967, *11,* 213–218.

Holroyd, S., Currie, L., Thompson-Heisterman, A., and Abraham, I. A descriptive study of elderly community-dwelling alcoholic patients in the rural south. *American Journal of Geriatric Psychiatry,* 1997, *5,* 221–228.

Horgas, A. L., Wilms, H. U. and Baltes, M. M. Daily life in very old age: Everyday activities as an expression of successful living. *The Gerontologist,* 1998, *38,* 556–568.

Howieson, D. B., Holm, L. A., Kaye, J. A., Oken, B. S., and Howieson, J. Neurological function in the optimally healthy oldest old. *Neurology,* 1993, *43,* 1882–1886.

Idler, E. L. The many causal pathways linking religion to health. *Public Policy and Aging Report,* 2002, *12,* 7–12.

Jeste, D. V., Alexopoulos, G. S., Bartels, S. J., Cummings, J. L., Gallo, J. J., Gottlieb, G. L., et al. Consensus statement on the upcoming crisis in geriatric mental health: Research agenda for the next two decades. *Archives of General Psychiatry.* 1999, *56,* 848–853.

Jones, R. N., Marcantonio, E. R., and Rabinowitz, T. Prevalence and correlates of recognized depression in U.S. nursing homes. *Journal of the American Geriatrics Society,* 2003, *51,* 1404–1409.

Jung, C. G. Concerning the archetypes, with special reference to the anima concept. In *C. G. Jung, Collected works,* Vol. 9, Part I. Princeton, NJ: Princeton University Press, 1959.

Jung, C. G. *Modern man in search of a soul.* San Diego: Harcourt Brace and World, 1933.

Kahana, E. F., and Kahana, B. Environmental continuity, discontinuity, futurity, and adaptation of the aged. In G. Rowles and R. Ohta (Eds.), *Aging and milieu: Environmental perspectives on growing old.* New York: Academic Press, 1982.

Kahn, R. L. Guest editorial: On "successful aging and well-being" self-rated compared with Rowe and Kahn. *The Gerontologist,* 2002, *42,* 725–726.

Katz, S. (2000). Busy bodies: Activity, aging and the management of everyday life. *Journal of Aging Studies,* 2000, *14,* 135–152.

Keller, M. B., McCullough, J. P., Klein, D. N., Arnow, B., Dunner, D. L, Gelenberg, A. J., et al. A comparison of nefazodone, the cognitive-behavioral analysis system of psychotherapy, and their combination for the treatment of chronic depression. *New England Journal of Medicine,* 2000, *342,* 1462–1470.

Kempen, G. I., van Sonderen, E., and Ormel, J. The impact of psychological attributes on changes in disability among low-functioning older persons. *Journals of Gerontology: Psychological Sciences,* 1999, *54B,* 23–29.

Kessler, R. C. The effects of stressful life events on depression. *Annual Review of Psychology,* 1997, *48,* 191–214.

Koenig, H. G., and Blazer, D. G. Depression. In J. E. Birren (Ed.), *Encyclopedia of gerontology,* San Diego: Academic Press, 1996.

Koenig, H. G., and Brooks, R. G. Religion, health, and aging: Implications for practice and public policy. *Public Policy and Aging Report,* 2002, *12,* 13–19.

Kokmen, E., Beard, C. M., O'Brien, P. C., and Kurland, L. T. Epidemiology of dementia in Rochester, Minnesota. *Mayo Clinic Proceedings,* 1996, *71,* 275–282.

Krause, N. Stress, alcohol use, and depressive symptoms in later life. *The Gerontologist,* 1995, *35,* 296–307.

Krause, N., and Shaw, B. A. Giving social support to others, socioeconomic status, and changes in self-esteem in later life. *Journals of Gerontology: Social Sciences,* 2000, *55B,* S323–S333.

Kukull, W. A., Higdon, R., Bowen, J. D., McCormick, W. C., Teri, L., Schellenberg, G., van Belle, G., Jolley, L., and Larson, E. B. Dementia and Alzheimer disease incidence: A prospective cohort study. *Archives of Neurology,* 2002, *59,* 1737–1746.

Lazarus, R. S. *Stress and emotion: A new synthesis.* New York: Springer, 1999.

Lazarus, R. S. Toward better research on stress and coping. *American Psychologist,* 2000, *55,* 665–673.

Lazarus, R. S. *Psychological stress and coping in adaptation and illness.* In S. M. Weiss (Ed.), Proceedings of the National Heart and Lung Institute working conference on health behavior. DHEW Publication #NIH 76-868, 1975a, 199–214.

Lazarus, R. S. The self-regulation of emotions. In L. Levi (Ed.), *Emotions: Their parameters and measurement.* New York: Raven Press, 1975b.

Lazarus, R. S., and DeLongis, A. Psychological stress and coping in aging. *American Psychologist,* 1983, *38,* 245–254.

Lazarus, R. S., and Folkman, S. *Stress, appraisal and coping.* New York: Springer, 1984.

Lazarus, R. S., and Launier, S. Stress-related transactions between person and environment. In L. A. Pervin and M. Lewis (Eds.), *Perspectives on interactional psychology.* New York: Plenum, 1978.

Lenze, E. J., Mulsant, B. H., Shear, M. K., Schulberg, H. C., Dew, M. A., Begley, A. E., Pollock, B. G. and Reynolds, C. F. Comormid anxiety disorders in depressed elderly patients. *American Journal of Psychiatry,* 2000, *157,* 722–728.

Levinson, D. J. A conception of adult development. *American Psychologist,* 1986, *41,* 3–13.

Levinson, D. J. Middle adulthood in modern society: A sociopsychological view. In G. DiRenzo (Ed.). *We the people: Social change and social character.* Westport, CT: Greenwood Press, 1977.

Levinson, D. J. *Seasons of a woman's life.* New York: Knopf, 1996.

Levinson, D. J., Darrow, C. M., Klein, E. B., Levinson, M. H., and McKee, B. *The seasons of a man's life.* New York: Knopf, 1978.

Li, G. The interaction effect of bereavement and sex on the risk of suicide in the elderly. *Social Science and Medicine,* 1995, *40,* 825–828.

Lichtenberg, P. A., Ross, T., Millis, S. R., and Manning, C. A. The relationship between depression and cognition in older adults: A cross-validation study. *Journals of Gerontology,* 1995, *50B,* P25–P32.

Lim, G. P., Yang, F., Chu, T., Chen, P., Beech, W., et al. Ibuprofen suppresses plaque pathology and inflammation in a mouse model for Alzheimer's disease. *Journal of Neuroscience,* 2000, *20,* 5709–5714.

Lincoln, K. *Race differences in social relations and depression among older adults.* Paper presented at the Hartford Foundation Scholars Orientation, Washington, DC, 2003.

Lis, C. G., and Gaviria, M. Vascular dementia, hypertension, and the brain. *Neurological Research,* 1997, *19,* 471–480.

Logsdon, R. G. and Teri, L. *Evaluating and treating behavioral disturbances in dementia.* University of Washington: NW Geriatric Education Center Curriculum Modules, 2000.

Magai, C. Emotions over the life span. In J. E. Birren and K. W. Schaie (Eds.), *Handbook of the psychology of aging* (5th ed.). San Diego: Academic Press, 2001.

Magai, C., Cohen, C., Milburn, N., Thorpe, B., McPherson, R., and Peralta, D. Attachment styles in European American and African American adults. *Journals of Gerontology: Psychological Sciences,* 2001, *46B,* S1-S8.

Masoro, E. J. "Successful aging"—Useful or misleading concept? *The Gerontologist,* 2001, *41,* 415–418.

Mattis, J. S., and Jagers, R. J. A relational framework for the study of religiosity and spirituality in the lives of African Americans. *Journal of Community Psychology,* 2001, *29,* 519–539.

Mattis, S. Mental status examination for organic mental syndrome in the elderly patient. In R. Bellack and B. Karasu (Eds.), *Geriatric psychiatry.* New York: Grune and Stratton, 1976.

McCrae, R. R., and Costa, P. T. *Personality in adulthood.* New York: Guilford, 1990.

McCrae, R. R., and Costa, P. T. Personality trait structure as a human universal. *American Psychologist,* 1997, *52,* 509–516.

McCrae, R. R., and Costa, P. T. Toward a new generation of personality theories: Theoretical contexts for the five-factor model. In J. S. Wiggins (Ed.), *The five-factor model of personality: Theoretical perspectives.* New York: Guilford Press, 1996.

McCrae, R. R., Costa, P. T., deLima, M. P., Simoes, A., Ostendorf, F., Angleitner, A., et al. Age differences in personality across the adult life span: Parallels in five cultures. *Developmental Psychology,* 1999, *35,* 466–477.

McCrae, R. R., Costa, P. T., Ostendorf, F., Angleitner, A., Hrebickova, M., Avia, M. D., et al. Nature over nurture: Temperament, personality and life span development. *Journal of Personality and Social Psychology,* 2000, *78,* 173–186.

McFadden, S. H. Religion, spirituality, and aging. In J. E. Birren and K. W. Schaie (Eds.), *Handbook of the psychology of aging* (4th ed.). San Diego: Academic Press, 1996.

McHugh, K. (2000). The "ageless self": Emplacement of identities in Sun Belt retirement communities. *Journal of Aging Studies,* 2000, *14,* 103–115.

McIntosh, J. L. *U.S.A. suicide: 1994 official final statistics.* 1997. http://oit.iusb.edu/~jmcintos/suicidestats. html.

McLeod, J. D. Life events. In J. E. Birren (Ed.), *Encyclopedia of gerontology,* San Diego: Academic Press, 1996.

Meeks, S. Schizophrenia and related disorders. In S. K. Whitbourne (Ed.), *Psychopathology in later life.* New York: Wiley, 2000.

Meeks, S., and Murrell, S. A. Mental illness in late life: Socioeconomic conditions, psychiatric symptoms, and adjustment of long-term sufferers. *Psychology and Aging,* 1997, *12,* 296–308.

Miller, N. S., Belkin, B. M., and Gold, M. S. Alcohol and drug dependence among the elderly. *Comprehensive Psychiatry,* 1991, *32,* 153–165.

Miller, W. R., and Thoresen, C. E. Spirituality, religion and health: An emerging research field. *American Psychologist*, 2003, *58*, 3–16.

Minkler, M., and Fadem, P. Successful aging: A disability perspective. *Journal of Disability Policy Studies*, 2002, *12*, 229.

Mittelman, M. S. Family caregiving for people with Alzheimer's disease: Results of the NYU Spouse Caregiver Intervention Study. *Generations*, 2002, *3*, 104–106.

Mittelman, M. S., Roth, D. L., Haley, W. E., and Zarit, S. H. Effects of a caregiver intervention on negative caregiver appraisals of behavior problems in patients with Alzheimer's disease. *Journals of Gerontology Series B: Psychological Sciences and Social Sciences*, 2004, *59*, P27–P34.

Mittelman, M. S., Ferris, S. H., Shulman, E., Steinberg, G., and Levin, B. A family intervention to delay nursing home placement of patients with Alzheimer's disease. *Journal of the American Medical Association*, 1996, *276*, 1725–1731.

Moceri, V. M., Kukull, W. A., Emanuel, I., van Belle, G., and Larson, E. B. Early-life risk factors and the development of Alzheimer's disease. *Neurology*, 2000, *54*, 415–420.

Mockenhaupt, R. E., and Beck, K. H. The social context of drinking in mid-life and older persons. Paper presented at annual meeting of the Gerontological Society of America, 1997.

Moos, R. *Coping with physical illness*. New York: Plenum Press, 1977.

Morrison, R. S., and Siu A. L. Survival in end-stage dementia following acute illness. *Journal of the American Medical Association*, 2000, *284*, 47–52.

Musick, M. A. Theodicy and life satisfaction among black and white Americans. *Sociology of Religion*, 2000, *61*, 267–287.

National Center for Health Statistics (NCHS). Death rates and age-adjusted death rates: United States, 1998. *National Vital Statistics Report*, 2000, *486*, 68–73. 2000

National Institutes of Health (NIH) Consensus Development Conference. *Diagnosis and treatment of depression*. Washington, DC: 1994.

Nesselroade, J. R., Featherman, D. L., Agen, S. H., and Rowe, J. W. *Short-term variability in physical performance and physiological attributes in older adults: MacArthur successful aging studies*. Unpublished manuscript, University of Virginia, 1996.

Neugarten, B. L., Personality change in late life: A developmental perspective. In C. Eisdorfer and M. P. Lawton (eds.) *The psychology of adult developmental aging*, 1973, Washington DC: American Psychiatric Association.

Neugarten, B. L., Havighurst, R. J., and Tobin, S. S. Personality and patterns of aging. In B. L. Neugarten (Ed.), *Middle age and aging*. Chicago: University of Chicago Press, 1968.

Olichney, J. M., Sabbagh, M. N., Hofstetter, C. R., Galasko, D., Grundman, M., Katzman, R., and Thal, L. J. The impact of apolipoprotein E4 on cause of death in Alzheimer's disease. *Neurology*, 1997, *49*, 76–81.

Osgood, N. J., Wood, H. E., and Parham, I. A. *Alcoholism and aging: An annotated bibliography and review*. Westport, CT: Greenwood Press, 1995.

Pargament, K. I. *The psychology of religion and coping: Theory, research, and practice*. New York: The Guilford Press, 1997.

Perls, T. T. The oldest-old. *Scientific American*, 1995, *272*, 70–75.

Peterson, B. E., and Klohnen E. C. Realization of generativity in two samples of women at midlife. *Psychology and Aging*, 1995, *10*, 20–29.

Pinquart, M. Analysis of the self-concept of independently living senior citizens. *Zeitschrift für Gerontologie*, 1991, *24*, 98–104.

Rahe, R. H. Subjects' recent life changes and their near future illness reports: A review. *Annals of Clinical Research*, 1972, *4*, 393.

Reid, M. C., Concato, J., Towle, V. R., Williams, C. S., and Tennetti, M. E. Alcohol use and functional disability among cognitively impaired adults. *Journal of the American Geriatrics Society*, 1999, *47*, 854–859.

Reisberg, B., Ferris, S. H., De Leon, M. J., and Crook, T. The Global Deterioration Scale for assessment of primary degenerative dementia. *American Journal of Psychiatry*, 1982, *139*, 1136–1139.

Reiss, S. Why people turn to religion: A motivational analysis. *The Journal for the Scientific Study of Religion*, 2000, *39*, 47–52.

Reynolds, C. F., Frank, E., Dew, M. A., Houck, P. R., Miller, M., Mazumdar, S., et al. The challenge of treatment in 70+-year olds with major depression. *American Journal of Geriatric Psychiatry*, 1999, *7*, 64–69.

Reynolds, C. F., and Kupfer, D. J. Depression and aging: A look to the future. *Psychiatry Services*, 1999, *50*, 1167–1172.

Reynolds, C. F., Miller, M. D., Pasaternak, R. E., Frank, E., Perel, J. M., et al. Treatment of bereavement-related major depressive episodes in later life. *American Journal of Psychiatry,* 1999, *156,* 202–208.

Riggs, J. Capitol Hill Forum on Family Caregivers. *Older Americans Report,* Sept. 22, 2000.

Riley, M. W. Letter to the editor. *The Gerontologist,* 1998, *38, 51.*

Rowe, J. W., and Kahn, R. L. Human aging: Usual and successful. *Science,* 1987, *237,* 143–149.

Rowe, J. W., and Kahn, R. L. Successful aging. *The Gerontologist,* 1997, *37,* 433–440.

Rowe, J. W., and Kahn, R. L. *Successful aging,* New York: Pantheon Books, 1998.

Rudorfer, M. V., Henry, M. E., and Sackheim, H. A. Electroconvulsive therapy. In A. Tasman, J. Kay, and J. A. Lieberman (Eds.), *Psychiatry.* Philadelphia: Saunders, 1997.

Ruth, J. E., and Coleman, P. Personality and aging: Coping and management of the self in later life. In J. E. Birren and K. W. Schaie (Eds.), *Handbook of the psychology of aging* (4th ed.). San Diego: Academic Press, 1996.

Ryff, C. D., Kwan, C. M. L., and Singer, B. H. Personality and aging: Flourishing agendas and future challenges. In J. E. Birren and K. W. Schaie (Eds.), *Handbook of the psychology of aging* (5th ed.). San Diego: Academic Press, 2001.

Sano, M., Ernesto, C., Thomas, R. G., Klauber, M. R., Schafer, K., and Grundman, M. A controlled clinical trial of selegiline, alpha-tocopherol or both as treatment for Alzheimer's disease. *New England Journal of Medicine,* 1997, *336,* 1216–1222.

Schaie, K. W., and Willis, S. L. Adult personality and psychomotor performance. *Journals of Gerontology,* 1991, *46,* P275–P284.

Schenk, D., Barbour, R., Dunn, W., Gordon, G., Grajeda, H., Guido, T., Hu, K., Huang, J., et al. Immunization with amyloid-B attenuates Alzheimer-disease-like pathology in the PDAPP mouse. *Nature,* 1999, *400,* 173–177.

Schulz, R., and Beach, S. Caregiving as a risk factor for mortality: The caregiver health effects study. *Journal of the American Medical Association,* 1999, *282,* 2215–2219.

Schulz, R., Beach, S. R., Ives, D. G., Martire, L. M., Ariyo, A. A., and Kop, W. J. Association between depression and mortality in older adults. *Archives of International Medicine,* 2000, *160,* 1761–1768.

Schulz, R., and Heckhausen, J. Emotion and control: A life-span perspective. In K. W. Schaie and M. P. Lawton (Eds.), *Annual Review of Gerontology and Geriatrics* (Vol. 17). New York: Springer, 1998.

Schulz, R., and Heckhausen, J. A life span model of successful aging. *American Psychologist,* 1996, *51,* 702–714.

Scogin, F., Floyd, M., and Forde, J. Anxiety in older adults. In S. K. Whitbourne (Ed.), *Psychopathology in later life.* New York: Wiley, 2000.

Seeman, T. A., Charpentier, P. A., Berkman, L. F., Tinetti, M. E., Guralnick, J. M., Albert, M., Blazer, D., and Rowe, J. W. Predicting changes in physical performance in a high functioning elderly cohort: MacArthur Studies of Successful Aging. *Journals of Gerontology,* 1994, *49,* M97–M108.

Seeman, T. E., Unger, J. B., McAvay, G., and Mendes de Leon, D. Self-efficacy beliefs and perceived declines in functional ability. *Journals of Gerontology,* 1999, *54,* 214–222.

Selye, H. The general adaptation syndrome and the diseases of adaptation. *Journal of Clinical Endocrinology,* 1946, *6,* 117–230.

Selye, H. Stress and aging. *Journal of the American Geriatrics Society,* 1970, *18,* 660–681.

Shumaker, S. A., Legault, C., Rapp, S. R., et al. Estrogen plus progestin and the incidence of dementia and mild cognitive impairment in postmenopausal women. *Journal of the American Medical Association,* 2003, *289,* 2651–2662.

Sloane, P. D., Lindeman, D. A., Phillips, C., Moritz, D. J., and Koch, G. Evaluating Alzheimer's disease special care units: Reviewing the evidence and identifying potential sources of study bias. *The Gerontologist,* 1995, *35,* 103–111.

Small, G. W., Liston, E. H., and Jarvik, L. F. Diagnosis and treatment of dementia in the aged. *Western Journal of Medicine,* 1981, *135,* 469–481.

Snowdon, D. *Aging with grace: What the Nun Study teaches us about leading longer, healthier, and more meaningful lives.* New York: Bantam, 2001.

Snowdon, D. Healthy aging and dementia: Findings from the Nun Study. *Annals of Internal Medicine,* 2003, *139,* 450–454.

Snowdon, D., Greiner, L. H., and Markesbery, W. R. Linquistic ability in early life and the neuropathology of Alzheimer's disease: Findings from the Nun Study. In R. N. Kalaria and P. Ince (Eds.), *Annals of New York Academy of Sciences,* N.Y.: New York Academy of Sciences, 2000.

Sramek, J. J., and Cutler, N. R. Recent developments in the drug treatment of Alzheimer's disease. *Drugs and Aging,* 1999, *14,* 359–373.

Stewart, W. F., Kawas, C., Corrada, M., Metter, E. J., Risk of Alzheimer's disease and duration of NSAID use. *Neurology,* 1997, *48,* 626–632.

Strawbridge, W., Wallhagen, M., and Cohen, R. D. Successful aging and well-being: Self-rated compared with Rowe and Kahn. *The Gerontologist,* 2002, *42,* 727–733.

Surgeon General. *Mental health: A report of the surgeon general,* 1999a. http://www.surgeongeneral.gov/library/mentalhealth/home.htm.

Surgeon General. *The Surgeon General's Call to Action to Prevent Suicide,* 1999b. http://www.surgeongeneral.gov/library/calltoaction/fact2.htm.

Surgeon General. Mental health: Culture, race, ethnicity supplement to "Mental health: Report of the surgeon general," 2001. http://www.mentalhealth.org/cre.

Suzman, R. M., Harris, T., Hadley, E. C., Kovar, M. G., and Weindruch, R. The robust oldest old: Optimistic perspectives for increasing healthy life expectancy. In R. M. Suzman, D. P. Willis, and K. G. Manton (Eds.), *The oldest old.* New York: Oxford Press, 1992.

Teri, L., Logsdon, R. G., Uomoto, J., and McCurry, S. M. Behavioral treatment of depression in dementia patients: A controlled clinical trial. *Journals of Gerontology,* 1997, *52,* P159–P166.

Teri, L., McCurry, S. M., and Logsdon, R. G. Memory, thinking, and aging: What we know about what we know. *Western Journal of Medicine,* 1997, *167,* 269–275.

Troll, L. E., and Skaff, M. M. Perceived continuity of self in very old age. *Psychology and Aging,* 1997, *12,* 162–169.

Trzesniewski, K. H., Donellan, M. B., and Robins, R. W. Stability of self-esteem across the life span. *Journal of Personality and Social Psychology,* 2003, *84,* 205–206.

Tufts University Health and Nutrition Letter. Anti-aging or successful aging? April 2001, *19,* 1–2.

Unger, J. B., McAvay, G., Bruce, M. L., Berkman, L. and Seman, T. Variation in the impact of social network characteristics on physical functioning in elderly persons. *Journals of Gerontology,* 1999, *54,* S245–S251.

Vaillant, G. E. *Adaptation to life.* Boston: Little, Brown, 1977.

Vaillant, G. E. *Aging well.* Boston: Little Brown, 2002.

Vaillant, G. E. Ego mechanisms of defense and personality psychopathology. *Journal of Abnormal Psychology,* 1994, *103,* 44–50.

Vaillant, G. E., and Vaillant, C. O. Natural history of male psychological health: A 45-year study of predictors of successful aging. *American Journal of Psychiatry,* 1990, *147,* 31–37.

Van Dongen, M. C., van Rossum, E., Kessels, A. G. H., Sielhorst, H. J. G., and Knipschild, P. G. The efficacy of ginkgo for elderly people with dementia and age-associated memory impairment: New results of a randomized clinical trial. *Journal of the American Geriatrics Society,* 2000, *48,* 1183–1194.

Verghese, J., Lipton, R. B., Hall, C. B., Kuslansky, G., Katz, M. J., and Buschke, H. Abnormality of gait as a predictor of non-Alzheimer's dementia. *New England Journal of Medicine,* 2002, *347,* 1761–1768.

Vitaliano, P. P., Russo, J., and Niaura, R. Plasma lipids and their relationship to psychosocial factors in older adults. *Journals of Gerontology,* 1995, *50,* P18–P24.

Vitaliano, P. P., Scanlan, J. M., Krenz, C., Schwartz, R. S., and Marcovina, S. M. Psychological distress, caregiving, and metabolic variables. *Journals of Gerontology,* 1996, *51,* P290–P299.

Whitbourne, S. K., and Primus, L. A. Physical identity. In J. E. Birren (Ed.), *Encyclopedia of gerontology,* San Diego: Academic Press, 1996.

Wong, P., and Ujimoto, V. The elderly: Their stress, coping and mental health. In C. L. Lee and W. Zane (Eds.), *Handbook of Asian American psychology.* Thousand Oaks, CA: Sage, 1998.

Zandi, P. P., Anthony, J. C., Khachaturian, A. S., Stone, S. V., Gustafson, D., Tschantz, J. T., Norton, N. C., Welsh-Bohmer, K. A., and Breitner, J. C. Reduced risk of Alzheimer's disease in users of antioxidant vitamin supplements. *Archives of Neurology,* 2004, *61,* 82–88.

Zarit, S. H., Stephens, M. A. P., Townsend, A. and Greene, R. Stress reduction for family caregivers: Effect of adult day care use. *Journals of Gerontology,* 1998, *53,* S267–S277.

Zarit, S. H., and Zarit, J. M. *Mental disorders in older adults: Fundamentals of assessment and treatment.* New York: Guilford, 1998.

7

Love, Intimacy, and Sexuality in Old Age

This chapter reviews the following

- The prevalent attitudes and beliefs about sex and love in old age that frequently affect an older person's sexuality
- Age-related physiological changes that may alter the nature of older men's and women's sexual response and performance, but do not necessarily interfere with their overall experience of sexuality
- Chronic illness and sexuality
- Gay and lesbian relationships
- Importance of late-life affection, love, and intimacy
- Implications for families and professionals who work with older people, including in institutional settings

The previous chapter focused on personality: who one is and how one feels about oneself. An important aspect of one's personality is sexuality. In fact, **sexuality** encompasses many aspects of one's being as a man or a woman, including one's self-concept, identity, and relationships. **Sex** is not just a biological function involving genital intercourse or orgasm; it also includes the expression of feelings—loyalty, passion, affection, esteem, and affirmation of one's body and its functioning, which are part of one's intimate self. A person's speech and movement, vitality, and ability to enjoy life are all parts of sexuality. As with other aspects of aging discussed throughout this text, sexuality is thus comprised of biological, emotional, intellectual, spiritual, behavioral, and sociocultural components (Kingsberg, 2000).

Older people, family members, and professionals need to understand the normal physiological changes that may affect sexual functioning and intimacy across the life span. To understand and treat the effects of aging on sexuality, the three components of sexual desire need to be addressed: drive, beliefs/values, and motivation as well as the sexual equilibrium within the primary relationship (Kingsberg, 2000). Since our sexual nature goes far beyond whether we are sexually active at any particular point in life, older individuals need to be comfortable with whatever decisions they make regarding their sexuality. Accordingly, professionals need to respect older adults' choices and values regarding the expression of their sexuality. Although most older individuals can and do engage in intercourse, some genuinely have no desire to engage in the physical aspects of sexual behavior—just as varying patterns of sexual expression occur at all ages.

Nonphysiological factors affect sexual activity—self-esteem, chronic illness, psychosocial conditions, and professionals' attitudes. In many instances, these dynamic contextual factors may exert greater influence than physiological changes as such. Sexual behavior, because of the powerful role it plays in the lives of most people, is especially likely to be affected by:

- the interactions of physiological changes
- the physical and social environment, especially the availability of sexual partners.
- the individual's personal sexual history, self-concept, and self-esteem
- the psychological meaning attached to one's experiences
- the degree of physical fitness (Bortz and Wallace, 1999; Zeiss and Kasl-Godley, 2001)

Attitudes and Beliefs about Sexuality in Later Life

It is striking that at a time when our society is increasingly tolerant of safe sex for nearly every segment of our population, outdated ideas persist in our approach toward sex and aging (Calasanti and Slevin, 2001). Sexuality remains one of the least understood aspects of active aging, largely invisible in society (Henry and McNab, 2003; Pangman and Seguire, 2000). Widespread stereotypes, mis-

conceptions, and jokes about old age and sexuality can powerfully and negatively affect older people's sexual experience. Jokes often center on performance "He can't get it up any more," because of our society's emphasis on performance and physical appearance. Many of these attitudes and beliefs stem from ageism generally, such as the perceptions of older people, especially older women, as physically unattractive and therefore asexual. Another example of ageism is the stereotype that older people lack energy and are devoid of sexual feeling, and therefore are not interested in sex. Since sexuality in our society tends to be equated with youthful standards of attractiveness, definitions of older people as asexual are heightened for older women and for individuals with chronic illness and disability.

Other attitudes and beliefs may stem from misinformation, such as the perception that sexual activity and drive do and should decline with old age. Accordingly, older people who speak of enjoying sexuality may be viewed as sinful, exaggerating, or deviant—for example, the stereotype of the "dirty old man." Alternatively, older people who express caring and physical affection for one another may be infantilized, defined as "cute" and teased by professionals, their age peers, and family members. Such public scrutiny and ridicule frequently occur among residents and staff of long-term care facilities. The oldest-old grew up in periods of restrictive guidelines regarding appropriate sexual behavior and taboos against other forms of sexual activity, such as masturbation. Many of these attitudes and beliefs of both older people and their families may reflect a Victorian morality that views sex only as intercourse and intercourse as appropriate only for conception. Sex for communication, intimacy, or pleasure may be considered unnecessary and immoral.

Unfortunately, the widely held attitude in our society that sexual interaction between older persons is socially unacceptable and even physically harmful may have negative consequences for older people (DeLamater and Friedrich, 2002; Pangman and Seguire, 2000; Zeiss and Kasl-Godley, 2001). Surrounded by those with such

POINTS TO PONDER

Reflect upon jokes or stories you have heard about older adults and sexuality. What have they conveyed? How did they affect your understanding of sexuality and aging?

beliefs and fearing ridicule or censure, many older people may unnecessarily withdraw from all forms of sexual expression long before they need to, thereby depriving themselves and often their partners of the energy and vitality inherent in sexuality. For many older adults, sexual activity, in the broadest sense of encompassing both physical and emotional interaction, is necessary for them to feel alive, to reaffirm their identity, and to communicate with their partners. As a source of reinforcement and pleasure, sexual relations broadly defined can enhance well being (Trudd, Turgeon, and Piche, 2000). Successful sexuality involves adaptation to and compensation for life changes (Henry and McNab, 2003).

Yet, by accepting society's stereoStypes, some older individuals may bar themselves from sexual and intimate experiences that could benefit their overall physical and mental well-being. Understanding the natural physiological alterations in sexual response associated with the aging process is an essential first step toward dispelling such myths. In future years, those myths may change, as the media, gerontologists, and other professionals convey the message that sex is permissible and desirable in old age and as the baby boomers age. In fact, one sign of change is that current cohorts of older people, especially the young-old, appear more accepting of and permissive in their attitudes toward sexuality and aging than in the past (Johnson, 1997).

Myths and Reality about Physiological Changes and Frequency of Sexual Activity

One of the most prevalent societal myths is that age-related physiological changes detrimentally af-

fect sexual functioning. Such misconceptions have been created by the early research on sexuality. In part because of assumptions that older people do not engage in sex or are embarrassed to talk about it, many early surveys of sexual attitudes did not even question older people about their sexuality. Such avoidance of the topic fostered further misinformation and misperceptions.

Other early studies included questions about sexuality, but focused on changes only in the frequency of sexual intercourse. These researchers overlooked the subjective experience or more qualitative aspects of sexuality in old age. For example, from 1938 to 1948, Kinsey and his colleagues studied primarily 16- to 55-year-olds, and their discussion of respondents over age 60 focused on the frequency of sexual intercourse, not on the meaning of sexuality to older people. In fact, the 735-page report devoted only three pages to the topic of sex and aging (Schiavi, 1996). Using the number of **orgasms** or ejaculations as the

Sexuality and intimacy are important throughout the later years.

measure of good sex, they found that by age 70, 25 percent of men experienced sexual dysfunction. Women were portrayed as reaching the peak of their sexual activity in their late twenties or thirties, then remaining on that plateau through their sixties, after which they showed a slight decline in sexual response capability (Kinsey, Pomeroy, and Martin, 1948, 1953). Because Kinsey and colleagues overlooked the broader psychological aspects of sexuality, they failed to address the subjective experience, meaning, and importance of sex at different ages. Older individuals may have sexual intercourse less often, but it is not necessarily less meaningful than at a younger age. In fact, few age-related physiological changes prevent continued sexual enjoyment and activity in old age.

In addition to the small sample size and the emphasis on frequency of sexual intercourse, early research on sexuality was limited by the nonrandom and therefore nonrepresentative nature of the sample, and by comparing younger and older cohorts at one point in time. For example, the Duke Longitudinal Study, which in 1954 examined the incidence of sexual intercourse and interest in sex, found gradual age-related declines in frequencies of sexual activity for older adults compared to their young and middle-aged counterparts, especially for women and unmarried individuals. The median age for stopping intercourse was 68 in men and 60 in women (Pfeiffer and Davis, 1972). This study had several limitations, however. The definition of sexual activity was confined to heterosexual intercourse, and the respondents constituted a cohort of individuals raised during a period of strict sexual conservatism. As discussed in Chapter 1, we now know that such cross-sectional data fail to give a lifetime picture of an individual's sexual behavior. Because the cohort effect was not identified, the low levels of sexual activity reported may relate to the attitudes, values, and reluctance to report on sexual behavior among a cohort of elders who grew up in the Victorian era rather than any age-related physiological changes in sexual functioning (Schiavi and Rehman, 1995).

THE INVISIBILITY OF OLDER ADULTS IN EARLY SEXUALITY RESEARCH

- Kinsey, 1948, 1953: 126 men and 56 women over age 60; 4 men over age 80
- Masters and Johnson, 1966, 1970: 20 older males
- Hite Report on Female Sexuality, 1976: 19 women out of a total of 1844 were age 60 or older
- Janus Report on Sexual Behavior, 1993: 34 percent were age 51 and over
- National Health and Social Life Survey, 1994: excluded those age 60 and over

A subsequent reanalysis of the 1954 Duke Longitudinal Study data to control for a possible cohort effect and the second Duke Longitudinal Study over a six-year period revealed stability of sexual activity patterns from mid- to late life (George and Weiler, 1981). In other words, those who were sexually conservative and inactive in young adulthood and mid-life, perhaps because of their social upbringing, carried that pattern through their later years. Similarly, those who were more sexually involved in young adulthood and middle age continued to remain active in old age. A later analysis of the Duke data also found older women to be more interested in sex than older men; however, the rate of sexual activity among older women declined, partly because of the absence of partners and because the husband tended to curtail or discontinue sexual activities. In fact, marital status and relationship issues appear to be more important in influencing women's sexual behavior than it is for men's (AARP, 1999; Matthias et al., 1997). In the Baltimore Longitudinal Studies of Aging, sexual dysfunction or impotence was found to be the main barrier to men's sexual activity. Yet the men did not report feeling sexually deprived or lacking in self-esteem (Schiavi, 1999).

Since most of the early studies focused on sexual performance, sexual satisfaction was neglected as an independent measure that is theoretically and clinically relevant (Schiavi, 1999). One of the first large-scale studies that provided evidence for continued sexual satisfaction in old age was the work of Masters and Johnson (1981).

In their classic study of sexual responsiveness across the life span, Masters and Johnson determined that, while physiological changes occur with age, the capacity for both functioning and fulfillment does not disappear. They concluded that there are no known limits to sexual behavior. Later studies, with predominantly white samples, have identified that most older adults, especially men, and even among those over age 80, remain sexually active. As with most behaviors, there is a wide range; some individuals even experience an increase in sexual activity with increasing age, perhaps because of the absence of children in the home (Matthias et al., 1997; Schiavi and Rehman, 1995; Weg, 1996). For others, their sexual activity in old age may represent a continuation of activity earlier in life (Willert and Semans, 2000). Sexual inactivity appears to depend upon life circumstances, not lack of interest or desire.

In sum, many of the issues that affect research designs in gerontology that were described in Chapter 1 are reflected in the area of sexuality in old age. Other methodological limits are summarized in the box below.

METHODOLOGICAL LIMITS OF RESEARCH ON SEXUALITY AND OLDER ADULTS

- Small sample size in large-scale national studies of sexuality.
- Studies generally do not include elders of color.
- Because of taboo nature of sexuality, respondents may not be entirely honest; may over- or underestimate sexual activity, or provide "socially acceptable" responses.
- Cohort influence: The current cohort is likely to be less honest than the baby boom cohort because of socialization not to discuss private issues such as sex.
- Researchers' discomfort or biases about sex and aging influence the nature of their questions and interactions with respondents.
- Rely primarily on self-reports.

TABLE 7.1 Percent of Older Adults Who Report Having Sexual Intercourse Once a Week or More

AGE	MALE	FEMALE
45–59	62%	61%
60–74	30%	24%
75+	26%	24%

SOURCE: American Association of Retired Persons, 1999.

The following is a summary of general findings about older people and sexuality:

- Older people who remain sexually active do not differ significantly in the frequency of sexual relations compared with their younger selves (longitudinal data). Rather, sexual activity appears to decrease significantly when older people are compared with younger persons at the same point in time (cross-sectional data). Table 7.1 illustrates this decline with a cross-sectional survey.
- When a partner is available, the rate of sexual behavior is fairly stable throughout life. And sexually active older people perceive their sex lives as remaining much the same as they grow older.
- Although good physical and mental health are predictors of sexual activity and satisfaction, even older people with chronic health problems, depression, and cognitive dysfunction can achieve sexual satisfaction (Matthias et al., 1997; Schiavi, 1999; Willert and Semans, 2000).
- Relationships are more important than sexual activity per se. Regardless of the length or nature of a late-life relationship, its quality is enhanced by emotional intimacy, autonomy without too much distance, an ability to manage stress and external distractions, and achieving a satisfying sexual equilibrium (AARP, 1999; Kingsberg, 2000).

When sexual activity is defined more broadly than intercourse to encompass touching and caressing, rates of activity increase to over 80 percent for men and over 60 percent for women (Schiavi,

Mandali, and Schreiner-Engel, 1999; Wiley and Bortz, 1996). Studies that include open-ended questions identify the excitement, enjoyment, and pleasure—the passion and romance—of late-life sexuality and the value older adults place on the quality and meaning of intimate relationships. Accordingly, sexual activity and satisfaction are found to be related to older people's sense of self-worth and competence (Weg, 1996).

To review, as our biological clocks change with age, it is not necessarily for the better or worse in terms of the frequency or the nature of the sexual experience. Individuals who have been sexually responsive all their lives will still enjoy sexual satisfaction in their later years, although their experience may differ subjectively from their earlier years (DeLamater and Friedrich, 2002; Zeiss and Kasl-Godley, 2001). Yet, this difference can be positive. For example, 75 percent of the respondents in the classic Starr-Weiner study (1981) said that sex is the same or better than when they were younger. This was one of the first studies to move away from a narrow focus on frequency of intercourse to explore the meaning and significance of sexuality for aging individuals. Although the majority of female respondents considered orgasm essential to a good sexual experience, they also

POINTS TO PONDER

When you were growing up, how did you perceive your parents' and grandparents' sexuality? What were your sources of information about older adults and sexuality? How did these affect your thinking? Then and now?

emphasized mutuality, love, and caring as central to an enjoyable sexual relationship and willingly varied their sexual practices to achieve satisfaction. Male respondents emphasized that not only is the physical stimulation of sex important, but also that sex is necessary for them to feel alive, to reaffirm their identity, and to communicate with a person they care about. In sum, the actual level of activity may be less important than one's satisfaction with it (Matthias et al., 1997). Nevertheless, a number of physiological, age-related changes can affect the nature of the sexual response.

Women and Age-Related Physiological Changes

With the growing numbers of women in the 45- to 54-year-old age group, increasing attention is being given to **menopause.** As noted in Chapter 4, the major changes for women as they grow older are associated with the *reduction in estrogen and progesterone,* the predominant hormones produced by the ovaries, during menopause. The **climacteric**—loss of reproductive ability—takes place in three phases: **perimenopause,** menopause, and postmenopause, and may extend over many years.

Perimenopause is marked by a decline in ovarian function in which a woman's ovaries stop producing eggs and significantly decrease their monthly production of estrogen, resulting in widely fluctuating estrogen levels and unpredictable menstrual cycles. It can occur as long as 10 years before menopause, starting as young as age 35. Only recently have researchers and health

SEEKING NEW LOVE

Contrary to stereotypes of lack of intimacy and sexuality among older adults, a recent AARP survey found that many adults over age 50 are eager to date and form new relationships. The most common ways for meeting new people are religious organizations, outdoor clubs, speed dating (e.g., organized events where adults spend three or so minutes talking with each other, then indicate whom they would like to see again), the Internet, personal ads, special interest services (meet others with similar interests), and matchmakers. And for many older adults, informal networks or just being in the right place at the right time are key to forming new and intimate relationships (Mahoney, 2003).

HOME REMEDIES FOR MENOPAUSAL SYMPTOMS

Sharon "Missy" Peat described herself as a 51-year-old woman on the verge of a nervous breakdown 3 years ago. After her sleep was continuously interrupted by hot flashes, one night she opened her freezer, grabbed a box of frozen peas, and applied it to the back of her neck. After a few minutes, she felt better. The sweating subsided, the panic was gone and she went back to bed in 5 minutes' time. During the night, she experienced no more perspiration or clamminess. Since then, she has manufactured a cold, flexible gel pack sold for the relief of hot flashes. The success of her cold pack suggests the growing market for menopause products (Jacobson, 2000).

---

care providers recognized that perimenopause brings hot flashes around the head and upper body, concentration gaps and memory lapses, mood swings, sleep troubles, irritability, and migraines associated with menopause. Unfortunately, however, perimenopause often is not included in medical school curricula, and some physicians still dismiss a woman's early symptoms as "all in her head" (Bagley, 1999).

Menopause, in the strictest sense as one event during the climacteric, is a period in a woman's life when there is a gradual cessation of the menstrual cycle, including irregular cycles and menses, which are related to the loss of ovarian function. Menopause is considered to have occurred when 12 consecutive months have passed without a menstrual period (**postmenopause**). The average age of menopause is 52 years, although it can begin as early as age 40 and as late as age 58. Surgical removal of the uterus—**hysterectomy**—also brings an end to menstruation.

Physiological changes related to the decrease in estrogen in menopause and postmenopause include:

- hot flashes
- urogenital atrophy
- urinary tract changes
- bone changes (osteoporosis) (NIA, 2003a)

Hot flashes are caused by vasomotor instability, when the nerves overrespond to decreases in hormone levels. This affects the hypothalamus (the part of the brain that regulates body temperature), causing the blood vessels to dilate or constrict. When the blood vessels dilate, blood rushes to the skin surface, causing perspiration, flushing, and increased pulse rate and temperature. Hot flashes are characterized by a sudden sensation of heat in the upper body, often accompanied by a drenching sweat and sometimes followed by chills. Gradually diminishing in frequency, hot flashes generally disappear within a year or two.

Sleep disturbances can also result from hormonal changes, with sleep deprivation leading to irritability and moodiness often associated with menopause. Although 80 percent of women aged 45 through 55 experience some discomfort such as hot flashes and sweats during menopause, most find that these physiological changes do not interfere with their daily activities or sexual functioning. They also do not cause psychological difficulties, although vasomotor instability does disrupt and reduce sleep (Kaiser, 1996; Weg, 1996).

Estrogen loss combined with the normal biological changes of aging leads to **urogenital atrophy**—a reduction in the elasticity and lubricating abilities of the vagina approximately 5 years after menopause. As the vagina becomes drier and the layer of cell walls thinner, the amount of lubricants secreted during sexual arousal is reduced. Although vaginal lubrication takes longer, these changes have little impact on the quality of or-

---

RELIEF OF HOT FLASHES DURING MENOPAUSE

- avoid spicy foods, caffeine, and alcohol
- drink cold water or juice as a hot flash comes on
- wear breathable clothing (e.g., cotton), not synthetics
- dress in layers of clothing that can be gradually removed
- sleep in a cool room

gasms and do not result in an appreciable loss in sensation or feeling (Zeiss and Kasl-Godley, 2001). Nevertheless, discomfort associated with urogenital atrophy is an important contributor to decline in sexual activity with menopause. Artificial lubricants such as KY jellies and vaginal creams can help minimize discomfort. In addition, regular and consistent sexual activity, including **masturbation,** maintains vaginal lubricating ability and muscle tone, thereby reducing discomfort during intercourse (Gelfand, 2000).

Because of thinning vaginal walls, which results from estrogen degeneration and which offers less protection to the bladder and the urethra, *lower urinary tract infections* such as cystitis and burning urination may occur more frequently. These problems can be treated and often reversed with hormone replacement therapy, most often estrogen combined with progesterone. (The risks of HRT, however, are discussed more fully below.) Incontinence has been found to inhibit sexual desire and response; unfortunately, many older women are reluctant to discuss incontinence with others, which precludes their finding ways to prevent its negative impact upon sexual activity (Kaiser, 1996). Loss of estrogen during menopause also affects the absorption of calcium in the bones, resulting in osteoporosis (see Chapters 4 and 15).

Contrary to stereotypes and taboos regarding menopause, approximately 30 to 90 percent of women have no intense symptoms such as hot flashes or night sweats during menopause, while only 15 percent experience symptoms sufficiently severe to warrant treatment. The majority—65 percent—experience only mild symptoms that do not require any medical intervention. Among Caucasian women, approximately 75 percent report symptoms, but this rate is much lower among Asian American and Latina women. Although they report symptoms such as hot flashes and insomnia, African American women are generally more positive than other ethnic groups about this period in their lives. This wide variability in symptoms and responses suggests that there is not an inevitable "menopausal syndrome" (Gonyea, 1998; NIA, 2003b). Nor is there any scientific explanation for why symptoms such as hot flashes occur in some women and not in others.

The primary medical response to the symptoms of hot flashes and vaginal atrophy has been hormone replacement therapy (HRT), using estrogen alone (ERT) or in combination with progestin (EPT), which restores women's hormones to levels similar to those before menopause. As noted in Chapter 4, estrogen does alleviate hot flashes and vaginal changes, including atrophy, dryness, itching, pain during intercourse, urinary tract problems, and frequent urination (NIA, 2003b). However, recent studies suggest that the risk of breast cancer, blood clots, and strokes with long-term use may be substantially greater and the benefits in terms of risk reduction for osteoporosis less than previous research indicated. The most recent data from a well-designed study with a large sample size and good controls for competing variables, the Women's Health Initiative (described in Chapter 4), raises some questions about the safety of hormone replacement therapy. In one arm of this large, national study with participants from many different ethnic groups, some women were placed on a pill that included both estrogen and progestin (EPT), and others used a placebo. Although the study was designed to last 8.5 years, it was stopped in July 2002 after only 5 years. This was because women using EPT developed some diseases at unacceptably higher rates; there was a greater incidence of breast cancer, heart attacks, blood clots, and strokes than among women on the placebo pills. At the same time, however, women using EPT had fewer cases of colon cancer and fewer bone fractures (NIA, 2003b). A recent report from the Women's Health Initiative on the group using estrogen-only also showed no benefits for heart disease, and slightly higher incidence of stroke (NIH, 2004).

The benefits and risks of HRT are described in greater detail in Chapter 4, and must be carefully weighed by women as they attempt to assess their risks of bone loss, heart disease, and breast cancer. At the same time, women need to be cautious

**ALTERNATIVES TO ESTROGEN
REPLACEMENT THERAPY**

- herbal remedies, including soy, wild yams, beans, and black cohosh, a folk medicine made from a shrub root (known as phytoestrogens)
- drugs already proved for other conditions that may have beneficial effects on hot flashes (e.g., some antihypertensives; certain antidepressants; Neurontin, an antiseizure drug)
- combination of fluoride and calcium, but may have gastrointestinal side effects

about the use of alternative therapies not yet proved to be effective. Some therapies have been found to help moderate the symptoms of menopause and perimenopause; these include eating more foods that are high in calcium and fiber and lower in fat; more weight-bearing exercise; biofeedback; and herbal or naturopathic treatments, as shown in the box above (NIA, 2003a).

In many non-Western cultures, menopause is viewed as a time of respect and status for women. Our cultural view is that women are expected to have difficulty at this period of life. However, the incidence of insomnia, depression, and anxiety may be traced to the meaning or psychosocial significance that individuals attach to menopause, as well as the cultural value placed on body image and on women's roles as mothers. Other symptoms reported by menopausal women, such as headaches, dizziness, palpitations, and weight increase, are not necessarily caused by menopause itself, but may be due to underlying psychosocial reasons. Many women view menopause as a potentially positive transition rather than as a loss of fertility or as a cause of depression. It can be a new and fulfilling time of opportunities, self-accomplishment (Brice, 2003), meaning, and greater autonomy in lifestyle (Defey et al., 1996; Jones, 1997). Sixty percent of respondents in a recent Gallup Poll did not associate menopause with feeling less attractive, and 80 percent expressed relief with the end of their menstrual periods. The major quandary appears to be whether to use HRT (Gonyea, 1998). In sum, menopause, like other transitions experienced by women, is affected by physiological and health factors, personality, self-esteem, culture and lifestyle.

Despite some uncomfortable symptoms, menopause does not impede full sexual activity from a physiological point of view. In fact, many women, freed of worries about pregnancy and birth control, report greater sexual satisfaction postmenopause, including after a hysterectomy (NIA, 2003b). Generally, an older woman's sexual response cycle has all the dimensions of her younger response, but the time it takes for her to respond to sexual stimulation gradually increases. The subjective levels of sexual tension initiated or elaborated by clitoral stimulation do not differ for older and younger women. The preorgasmic plateau phase, during which sexual tension is at its height, is extended in duration. Contrary to stereotypes, most older women enjoy orgasm; an older woman's capacity for orgasms may be slowed, but not impaired. The orgasm is experienced more rapidly, somewhat less intensely, and more spasmodically. The resolution phase, during which the body returns to its baseline prearousal state, occurs more rapidly than in younger women (Blonna and Levitan, 2000; Zeiss and Kasl-Godley, 2001).

From a physiological point of view, no impediment exists to full sexual activity for postmenopausal women. Changes such as the thinning of vaginal walls and loss of vaginal elasticity may render intercourse somewhat less pleasurable, but these effects can be minimized by sexual regularity. Instead, older women's sexuality tends to be influenced more by sociocultural expectations than by physiological changes—by the limited number of available male partners, persistent stigma about lesbian relations in old age, and common cultural definitions of older women as asexual and unattractive, which can negatively affect women's self-image. These psychosocial barriers are discussed more fully later in this chapter.

Men and Age-Related Physiological Changes

Relatively little attention has been given to men's hormonal rhythms compared to women's. One reason for less attention is that men maintain their fertility and generally do not lose their capacity to father children, making hormonal and sexual changes less abrupt and visible. There is, however, increasing evidence that **male menopause** or "viropause" occurs and can affect the psychological, interpersonal, social, and spiritual dimensions of a man's life. However, the male climacteric differs from women's in two significant ways: it comes 8 to 10 years later (typically between ages 45 and 54), and progresses at a more gradual rate. This is because the loss of testosterone (approximately 1 percent a year on average), while varying widely among men, is not as dramatic nor as abrupt as the estrogen depletion for menopausal women.

Some of the effects of this loss of testosterone are summarized as follows:

- reduced muscle size and strength
- increased calcium loss in the bones
- declines in response by the immune system
- lessened sexual response and interest
- fatigue, irritability, indecisiveness, depression, loss of self-confidence, listlessness, poor appetite, and problems of concentration (Diamond, 1997; Weg, 1996)
- reduced interest in sex, anxiety and fear about sexual changes
- increased relationship problems and arguments with partners over sex, love, and intimacy
- loss of **erection** during sexual activity.
- changes in secondary sexual characteristics such as a man's voice becoming higher pitched, his facial hair growing more slowly, and muscularity giving way to flabbiness

Combined with the loss of muscle tissue and weight in the later years discussed in Chapter 3, it is not unusual for men to become thinner and less muscular by their seventies. The changes that men experience, which occur in varying degrees, require adaptation, but in themselves do not necessarily result in reduced sexual enjoyment and desire.

The normal physiological changes that characterize men's aging alter the nature of the sexual response, but do not interfere with sexual performance. The **preorgasmic plateau phase,** or excitement stage, increases in length, so that response to sexual stimulation is slower. An erection may take longer to achieve and may require more direct stimulation. For example, in 18-year-old males, full erection is achieved on stimulation for an average of 3 seconds; at age 45, the average time is 18 to 20 seconds, while a 75-year-old man requires 5 minutes or more. Erections tend to be less full with age and the erect penis may be less firm. But these erectile changes do not necessarily alter a man's sexual satisfaction. The frequency and degree of erections can be studied while a man is sleeping. The recording of nocturnal penile tumescence—(sleep-related erections)—offers an opportunity to evaluate objectively sexual functioning under relatively controlled conditions. Such studies have found that the volume and force of the ejaculation are decreased in older men as they sleep. The two-stage orgasm—the sense of ejaculation inevitably followed by actual semen expulsion that is experienced by younger males—often blurs into a one-stage ejaculation for older men (Blonna and Levitan, 2000; DeLamater and Friedrich, 2002; Masters and Johnson, 1981; Schiavi, 1999).

Accordingly, orgasm is experienced less intensely, and more spasmodically and rapidly, occurring every second or third act of intercourse rather than every time. The length of time between orgasm and subsequent erections increases (i.e., the **refractory period** after ejaculation, before a second ejaculation is possible, is longer). However, although these changes may alter the nature of the sexual experience, none of them causes sexual inactivity or impotence. As a result, the subjectively appreciated levels of sensual pleasure may not diminish (Bortz, Wallace, and Wiley, 1999; Masters and Johnson, 1981). In recent years, as noted in Chapter 1, there has been increasing attention to hormones such as DHEA, which are produced by the adrenal glands, the brain, and the skin, to revive men's sexual interest.

Although not an inevitable consequence of aging, erectile dysfunction or **impotence** (i.e., an inability to get and sustain an erection) is the chief cause of older men's withdrawing from sexual activity. (Note that erectile dysfunction is a more accurate medical term than impotence). By age 64, 15 to 25 percent of men experience impotence at least one out of every four times that they have sex (NIA, 2002). Most dysfunction is caused by diseases affecting the blood vessels or by age-induced deterioration of the blood vessels. Other problems are low testosterone levels and excessive use of tobacco or alcohol (American Prostate Society, 2003). Older men and their partners need to be informed that erectile dysfunctions are both common and treatable. Although impotence and lowered testosterone levels are not significantly correlated, declines in DHEA levels with aging are found to be associated with impotence (Diamond, 1997).

Despite the underlying pathologies frequently associated with impotence, it tends to be underdiagnosed because of the embarrassment and reluctance of older men and their health care providers to discuss sexual matters candidly. Since medical treatments can be effective in altering erectile dysfunction, health care providers must be sure to rule out the physiological basis of impotence, which tends to be more important than psychosocial factors (NIA, 2002). Physical risk factors include cardiovascular disease, the effects of drugs (especially antihypertensives, antidepressants, and tranquilizers), diabetes, hypertension, endocrine or metabolic disorders, neurological disorders, depression, alcohol, or prostate disorders. Most types of prostate surgery do not cause impotence, as discussed in the next section, "Chronic Illness and Sexual Activity." In recent years, new ways to treat impotence have drawn increased attention. The marketing of a wide

VIAGRA

Viagra has been touted as a wonder drug for men, with flashy ads typically featuring a romantic man and woman. The benefits described by the ads have been empirically supported, however. For example, a 1998 study of over 500 men, reported in the *New England Journal of Medicine,* confirmed Viagra's effectiveness. The most common side effects were headache, flushing, and disturbed digestion. For men and their partners who have been frustrated by impotence, the side effects are undoubtedly viewed as minor irritants (American Federation for Aging Research, 2000). About 20 percent of men, however, do not experience any benefits from taking Viagra. New pills are being developed—Levitra R and Cialis R—that are advertised to be more vigorous and longer-lasting than Viagra. Viagra is also prescribed for women, and has resulted in marked improvement in arousal, orgasm, and sexual enjoyment. Improving circulation, however, does not alter women's sexual desire, which is a key factor in older women's sexuality and sexual satisfaction.

range of products reflects, in part, drug companies' awareness of baby boomers' buying power.

Clinical trials of oral medications, such as Sildenafil or Viagra, have found that 60 to 80 percent of the men who have participated and who have varying degrees of impotence have benefited in terms of increased sexual satisfaction and improved relationships with their partners. However, among the current cohort, only 10 percent of men and 7 percent of women report that they have taken any medicine, hormone, or other treatment to enhance sexual performance (AARP, 1999; Leland, 1997). This suggests that continued attention needs to be given to the psychological factors related to intimacy and sexual enjoyment in old age, not just to chemical solutions. As noted above, the concept of sexuality in old age needs to be expanded to include more than erection and ejaculation during intercourse. For example, health care providers and counselors must encourage couples to communicate their fears about

Imagine the appeal of a recent Internet ad to some older men:

> Internet Advertising of Herbal Viagra—No prescription, no doctor, less than $1 a pill

> Welcome to the new sexual revolution. It's the all-natural male potency and pleasure pill that men everywhere are buzzing about. Herbal V is safe, natural and specifically formulated to help support male sexual function and pleasure. You just take two easy-to-swallow tablets one hour before sexual activity. . . . Herbal V—Bringing back the magic.

impotence and suggest ways that they can openly enjoy fulfilling sexual experiences and intimacy without an erection. Medical treatments for impotence should be carefully explored, including:

- oral medications that cause erections
- pellets inserted into the urethra with an applicator that dilate the arteries and relax the erectile tissues, thereby triggering involuntary erections
- injection therapy
- vacuum pumps
- penile implants
- vascular surgery

The box below summarizes the physiological changes that affect sexual activities in both older men and women, but do not necessarily alter sexual satisfaction.

Chronic Illness and Sexual Activity

Although normal physiological changes do not inevitably reduce sexual satisfaction, sexuality is associated with physical and mental well-being, including being physically active and fit. Since sexual response requires the coordination of multiple systems of the body—hormonal, circulatory, and nervous systems—if any of these are disrupted, sexual functioning can be affected. As a result, chronic illness can play a major role in the decline of sexual function, and is often cited as a reason for refraining from sexual activity. Even when an illness does not directly affect the sexual organs themselves, systemic diseases can affect sexual functioning because of the following factors:

- their effects on mediating physiological mechanisms resulting in physical decline
- chronic pain
- complications of medication, especially from antihypertensive drugs

AGE-RELATED PHYSIOLOGICAL CHANGES IN SEXUAL FUNCTION

Normal Changes in Aging Women	**Normal Changes in Aging Men**
• There is reduction in vaginal elasticity and lubrication. • Thinning of vaginal walls occurs. • There is slower response to sexual stimulation. • Preorgasmic plateau phase is longer. • There are fewer and less intense orgasmic contractions. • After orgasm, there is rapid return to prearousal state.	• Erection may require more direct stimulation. • Erection is slower, less full, and disappears quickly after orgasm. • Orgasm is experienced more rapidly, less intensely, and more spasmodically; there is decreased volume and force of ejaculation. • There is increased length of time between orgasm and subsequent erections (longer refractory period). • There is occasional lack of orgasm during intercourse. • More seepage or retrograde ejaculation is experienced.

- negative effects on well-being and self-perceptions
- the all-consuming distraction of the illness may deplete the psychic energy needed for sexual interest and responsiveness (NIA, 2002)

Given these factors, it is not surprising that 30 percent of men and 16 percent of women cite better health as something that would improve their satisfaction with their sex lives (AARP, 1999). As is true across the life span, an older adult's personal characteristics combined with the specific challenges imposed by an illness influence how they adjust to disease and respond to treatment. Accordingly, how individuals appraise threats to sexual identity, sexual intimacy, body image, and control over bodily functions determines the nature of their adaptive responses (Shiavi, 1999). The way in which older people approach losses in sexual activities entailed by chronic illness probably reflects how they have coped with other types of losses throughout their lives. Fortunately, health care providers now know more about how adults can compensate for disease to have satisfying sex lives, as shown in the box on the right on psychological treatment of sexual problems. There is also greater recognition that sexual activity can be a major component of treatment following a major illness or surgery and is a minimal risk to a person's health (Kaiser, 1996). In this section, the chronic illnesses that commonly affect sexual functioning—diseases of the prostate, diabetes, heart disease and strokes, degenerative and rheumatoid arthritis, depression and dementia—are briefly discussed.

More than 50 percent of men age 65 and over have some degree of **prostate enlargement,** known as *benign prostatic hypertrophy* or BPH. One out of every three men over age 65 will experience prostate difficulties, usually inflammation or enlargement of the prostate gland, pain in the urogenital area, and urinary flow dysfunction (Bostwick, MacLennan, and Larson, 1996; Diamond, 1997). Infections may be successfully treated with antibiotics, and new drugs are avail-

---

> ### PSYCHOLOGICAL TREATMENT OF SEXUAL PROBLEMS ASSOCIATED WITH CHRONIC ILLNESS: SUGGESTIONS FOR HEALTH CARE PROVIDERS
>
> - provision of information about normal sexual responses and the impact of the illness on sexual function
> - change of attitudes, from exclusive emphasis on intercourse to acceptance of behaviors that enhance mutual pleasure and erotic arousal
> - development of coping skills that contribute to sexual satisfaction
> - increased mutual communication about sexual preferences and needs
> - reduction of psychological factors that inhibit sexual response
> - facilitation of acceptance and adjustment to the limitations imposed by the chronic illness
>
> SOURCE: Schiavi, 1999.

---

able to shrink the prostate. Some prostate problems can be reduced through simple treatments such as warm baths and gentle massage or through antibiotics. However, when urination is severely restricted or painful, surgery is necessary. After surgery, semen is no longer ejaculated through the penis, but is pushed back into the bladder and later discharged in the urine. After healing occurs, the capacity to ejaculate and fertility may return in some men. The feeling of orgasm or climax can still be present, and sexual pleasure is not inevitably lessened.

The rate at which prostate cancer kills men is similar to that of breast cancer in women. About 80 percent of all prostate cancers are found in men age 65 and older. Men who have a family history of prostate cancer and African American men have an increased risk of developing it, and should have more frequent screening exams. A major problem in diagnosis is that prostate cancer may have no symptoms in its early and middle stages—while it is confined to the prostate gland and more likely to be amenable to treatment. After it spreads, symptoms include pain or stiffness in the lower back, hips or upper thighs. Because the early symptoms are often masked, the American Cancer Society recommends that all men 40 years of age and older have an annual rectal exam, and that men age 50 and older receive an annual prostate specific antigen (PSA) test (American Federation for Aging Research, 2000).

The most extreme treatment for prostate cancer is radical perineal prostatectomy, when nerves are cut. Although most forms of prostate surgery do not cause impotence, irreversible impotence and incontinence can result from radical prostatectomy. Fortunately, there is an increasing number of alternatives for early prostate cancer, such as radioactive pellet implantation, other forms of radiation therapy, or transperineal placement of microwave antennas (Trachtenberg et al., 1999). Nerve-sparing surgery also has been developed, and may reduce the incidence of impotence among some men who undergo radical prostatectomy. Of course, the urologist's priority is to rid the patient of cancer tissue, and nerves very close to the prostate gland must often be severed. Nevertheless, even in these cases, men who have lost their normal physiologic response can achieve orgasm. Treatments or refinements of treatments, such as penile implants, vacuum pumps, new chemotherapeutic agents, vaccines, and smooth muscle relaxants that are injected into the penis have recently been developed, but research on their effectiveness and complications is incomplete (Afrin and Ergul, 2000). A promising development is the clinical testing of a variety of vaccinations (McNeel and Disis, 2000). Health care providers must be sensitive to providing older patients with as much information as possible about the implications of surgery for sexual functioning.

Although prostate surgery does not cause impotence in the majority of cases, between 5 and 40 percent of men who have undergone such surgery can no longer achieve an erection. In addition, since treatment of prostate cancer often involves methods that lower testosterone levels or block the effects of testosterone, a large percent of men undergoing such treatment feel loss of sexual desire, and up to 40 percent actually experience hot flashes (Diamond, 1997). In such instances, psychological factors need to be addressed through counseling, and couples need to be encouraged to try alternate methods of sexual satisfaction until the man can achieve an erection. In some instances, a man's postoperative "impotence" may be a convenient excuse for not engaging in sexual activity, or may represent fears of additional illness. When impotence is irreversible, partners need to be encouraged to pursue alternate means of sexual pleasure or consider a penile implant. Masturbation, more leisurely precoital stimulation, and use of artificial lubricants can all provide satisfying sexual experiences.

While most older men fear that prostate surgery will interfere with their sexual functioning and satisfaction, women may fear that a hysterectomy (surgical removal of the uterus), an ovariectomy (surgical removal of both ovaries), or a mastectomy (surgical removal of one or both breasts) will negatively affect their sexual functioning. In most instances, however, women's sexual satisfaction and long-term functioning are not affected by these surgeries, particularly if their partners are sensitive and supportive. On the other hand, some hormonal changes associated with a complete hysterectomy may affect sex drive. When women experience menopause as a result of a hysterectomy, perhaps earlier than the average age of onset for menopause, hormone replacement therapy is advisable except when the hysterectomy was due to cancer.

More common medical causes of male impotence than prostate surgery are *arteriosclerosis*—the vascular hardening that leads to heart attacks and strokes—and *diabetes*, particularly for those who have been diabetic most of their lives. Anything that damages the circulatory system—smoking, inactivity, poor diet—can cause erectile dysfunction. Older people who have experienced a heart attack or heart surgery may assume that sexual activity will endanger their lives and give it up. Unfortunately, many health care providers are not sensitive to such fears and fail to reassure individuals that sexual activity can be resumed after they undergo a stress test without pain or arrhythmia (Kaiser, 1996). Another precaution for post–heart attack patients who have been prescribed nitroglycerin is to take their usual dose 15 to 30 minutes before engaging in sexual activity (Schiavi, 1999). Stroke patients may also feel compelled to abstain from sexual activity because of an unfounded fear that sex could cause another occurrence. Generally, strokes do not harm the physiology of sexual functioning or the ability to experience arousal. However, some antihypertensive drugs can cause impotence or inhibit ejaculation. Fortunately, a new class of antihypertensive drugs, called ACE inhibitors, has been reported to cause fewer side effects on sexual function.

Impotence in life-long diabetics occurs because diabetes interferes with the circulatory and neurologic mechanisms responsible for the supply of blood flowing to the penis for erection. In such instances, a penile implant may be an option. With late-onset diabetes, impotence may be the first observable symptom. When the diabetes is under control, however, potency generally returns. The sexual functioning of women diabetics appears to be relatively unimpaired. When diabetes is controlled through balanced blood chemistry, sexual problems other than impotence that are attributable to the disease should disappear or become less severe. Other less common diseases that may cause impotence are illnesses that affect the vascular and endocrine systems, kidney diseases, and neurological lesions in the brain or spinal cord (Schiavi, 1999).

Arthritis does not directly interfere with sexual functioning, but can make sexual activity painful. Some medications used to control arthritic pain may also affect sexual desire and performance. Yet sexual behavior can serve to maintain some range of motion of the limbs and joints and thereby help sore joints; it can also stimulate the body's production of cortisone, which is one of the substances used to treat the symptoms of rheumatoid arthritis (Cochrane, 1989). Experimenting with alternative positions can minimize pain during sexual intercourse. A warm bath, massage of painful joints, and timing the use of pain-killing medications approximately 30 minutes prior to intercourse may also help to control some of the pain associated with arthritis. As with most chronic diseases, communication with the partner about what is comfortable and pleasurable is essential. Unfortunately, the majority of older adults with arthritis do not receive treatment that could minimize its effects on sexual activity (AARP, 1999).

Depression may also affect sexual functioning, especially erectile dysfunction in men. Depression may have differential effects on sexual interest, activity, and satisfaction. On the other hand, it is not clear that depression *causes* erectile dysfunction; it may be that the depression is a *reaction* to difficulties in sexual functioning (Schiavi, 1999). The deleterious effects of chronic illness in general and of depression in particular on sexual functioning need to take into account psychological and relationship issues and the disruptive effects of hospitalization and drug treatments.

Despite the high prevalence of *Alzheimer's disease* and other dementias, along with concerns expressed by partners and caregivers, there is limited empirical information about the impact of these disorders on sexual function. Erectile problems commonly occur among male patients with Alzheimer's. Changes in functional capacity and sexual expression can be extremely distressing to partners. Common sources of distress are awkward sequencing of sexual activity, requests for activities outside of the couple's sexual repertoire, and lack of regard for the sexual satisfaction of the healthy partner. Healthy partners are often troubled by the change in the perceived nature of the marital relationship and their own loss of sexual desire as the disease progresses and they find themselves full-time caregivers.

Issues of competency arise when a patient with dementia attempts to initiate a relationship with a new sexual partner, which may occur in long-term care facilities. Although such behavior may be disturbing to heath care providers and families, it raises concerns about individuals' rights as well as the difficult task of determining a person's capacity to make informed judgments regarding new relationships. Staff in such facilities often express fears about inappropriate sexual behavior by patients with dementia. However, the incidence of sexually aggressive behaviors toward staff or other patients is actually quite low. This suggests that the same degree of skill needed by health care staff to manage other symptoms of Alzheimer's disease is required for addressing inappropriate or ambiguous sexual behaviors when they occur. Training in sexual matters may assist health care providers to assist family members as well as patients themselves in dealing with this often ignored aspect of Alzheimer's disease (Schiavi, 1999).

Closely related to the effects of chronic illness upon sexuality are those of *drugs,* including alcohol. Diagnosing drug effects on sexuality may be particularly difficult, since drugs affect individuals differently, and drug interactions frequently occur. Drugs that inhibit the performance of any one of the systems of the body can alter sexual response. For men, some medications that are prescribed for chronic conditions may cause impotence, decrease sexual drive, delay ejaculation, or result in an inability to ejaculate. Psychotropic medications used to treat depression and psychosis are particularly likely to impair erectile functioning (Corbett, 1987). Of patients taking thioridazine, 49 percent will experience impaired ejaculation, and 44 percent impotence. Yet this is one of the first drugs that a physician will prescribe for an older person who is agitated, depressed, schizophrenic, or anxious. Similarly, in 40 percent of the cases involving the drug amoxapine for treatment of depression, impotence occurs. As noted above, other types of drugs likely to affect sexual functioning are antihypertensive medications used to treat high blood pressure, drugs to control diabetes, and steroids. As a whole, medication use and the rate of adverse effects of drug therapy are consistently higher in female than in male older patients (Gelfand, 2000; Schiavi, 1999).

For women, drugs may be associated with decreased vaginal lubrication, reduced sexual drive, and a delay or inability to achieve orgasm. Fortunately, physicians as well as older people are becoming more aware of potential negative effects of drug regimes on sexual functioning. Likewise, more drugs are now available that do not have negative side effects on sexual desire and/or ability. These include ACE inhibitors among the antihypertensives; fluoxetine, trazodone, and maprotiline among the antidepressants; desipramine among the tricyclic antidepressants; and lorazepam, alprazolam, and buspirone among antianxiety agents (Lewis, 1989).

Alcohol, when used excessively, can act as a depressant on sexual ability and desire. Alcohol consumption affects male sexual performance by making both erection and ejaculation difficult to attain; consequently, a man's anxiety about performance may increase and result in temporary impotence. Prolonged alcoholism may lead to impotence as a result of irreversible damage to the nervous system. Although the effects of alcohol on women's sexual performance have not been well researched, some women who abuse alcohol appear to experience less sexual desire and no orgasms. More research is needed to differentiate the extent to which alcohol may be a means to cope with sexual problems or whether concerns about sexual performance are a consequence of alcohol abuse and contribute to sustaining the addiction (Schiavi, 1999).

Gay and Lesbian Partners in Old Age

Although most examples of sexual activity in this chapter are presented in terms of heterosexual marital relationships, this should not be assumed to always be the case. Although there are no reliable data, gay men and lesbians are estimated to comprise between 6 and 10 percent of the total

Many lesbian and gay couples maintain long-term commitments to each other.

population (Wojciechowski, 1998). Older people, their family members, and health and social service professionals need to be sensitive to heterosexual relationships outside of marriage as well as to same-gender, or **homosexual** relationships. Such sensitivity includes the discarding of stereotypical views of the nature of *gay* and *lesbian* relationships. Contrary to commonly held images, the varieties of gay and lesbian bonding are similar to those within heterosexual communities—ranging from monogamous life partners and non-monogamous primary relationships to serial monogamy and episodic liaisons. Gay and lesbian life partners face many of the issues that confront long-term heterosexual spouses, such as fears about the loss of sexual attractiveness, the death or illness of a sexual partner, or diminished interest or capacity for sex because of chronic disease. On the other hand, after a lifetime of discrimination or ostracism from family members, coworkers, or society generally, homosexual couples face additional issues related to intimacy and sexuality, which are discussed in this chapter and in Chapter 9.

Although sexual activity for gay and lesbian older people differs as much as for heterosexuals, there is also a consistent pattern of relatively high

life satisfaction with being gay, good adjustment to old age, and ongoing sexual interest and activity. Older gay individuals who define the meaning of homosexuality in terms of positive self-identity and acceptance have been found to have the fewest psychosomatic complaints (Schiavi, 1999). Both lesbians and gays are more likely to report a high level of life satisfaction if they are happily partnered and communicating effectively with one another. Satisfaction is also high if they have a strong social support system, and have reconstituted what it means to be gay and lesbian into something positive (Wojciechowski, 1998).

Older lesbians, often closeted about their sexual orientation, have been labeled the "invisible minority." They have generally practiced serial monogamy throughout their lives. The hiding of one's sexual orientation has been a survival strategy for some lesbians because maintaining employment was paramount to being self-sufficient. Nevertheless, most usually report a positive self-image and feelings about being identified as a lesbian (Jones and Nystrom, 2002; Martin and Lyon, 2001; Wojciechowski, 1998). Older lesbians generally do not fear changes in physical appearance, loneliness, or isolation in old age as

---

REDEFINING SEXUAL ORIENTATION IN LATER LIFE

After her husband left her for a younger woman, a bout with breast cancer, and the death of her 26-year-old daughter, Isabel found herself increasingly drawn to spending time only with women: in a mothers' support group, in a group of midlife women coping with divorce, and through her work. She started attending workshops and lectures through the local college's Women's Information Center. At one of those courses, she met Carla, also recovering from a bitter divorce. They began to spend nearly all their free time together, enjoying the equality and closeness in their relationship. Within a year, Carla moved in with Isabel. Although their adult children were initially shocked by their mothers' behavior, they soon saw the value of the loving support and intimacy that their mothers experienced for the next 26 years.

much as some heterosexual women do. This may be because of the strong friendship networks that characterize many lesbian relationships or flexibility in gender roles that allows them to adjust more effectively to the socially constructed beliefs of aging and being older. Most lesbians remain sexually active, although sexual frequency generally declines. The extent to which sexual activity is considered to be an integral part of a lesbian relationship varies, although sexuality in a broader sense continues to play an important role in their lives. For some, lesbianism is a wider female interdependence and sense of positive self-identity rather than a sexual relationship as such (Dorfman et al., 1995; Jones and Nystrom, 2002).

The number of gay men with partners increases with age and peaks among those 46 to 55 years old. After age 60, the percent of gay couples decreases because of death, illness, cautiousness, or rejection of the notion of having a single, life-long partner. Older gay men are more likely to be in long-term relationships (with an average length of 10 years) or none at all rather than in short-term relationships of a year or less. Similar to their heterosexual peers, gay men are devalued in their own community for the natural features of aging: graying hair, wrinkles, added weight (Yoakam, 1999). Looking fit and youthful—that is, "not your age"—tends to increase a gay man's acceptability as a partner (Adam, 2000). Nevertheless, they generally maintain positive feelings about themselves and their appearance in old age (Berger and Kelley, 2001). Compared with their younger counterparts, older gay men have been found to be just as involved in the homosexual network, satisfied with their social lives and sexual orientation, and confident in their popularity with other gays.

Consistent with the continuity theory of aging, sex appears to be equally important at all phases of a gay man's life. Contrary to the myth of lonely, rejected, depressed older gay men, most report that they are generally sexually active, although frequency does decline with age. They typically are satisfied with their partners and their sex lives; they report a positive sense of self-esteem,

well-being, and contentment, and adapt fairly well to the aging process. Despite fears of loneliness and social isolation, most gay men have closer friendships in old age than do heterosexual men, and these friends and confidants may serve to resolve some existing fears of aging (Dorfman et al., 1995; Murray and Adam, 2001; Yoakam, 1999). For many gay men, friendships may replace family ties disrupted by declaration of their homosexuality.

On the other hand, compared with their younger counterparts, *older gay men* tend to:

- fear exposure of their homosexuality
- hide their sexual orientation
- view their relatives, friends, and employers as less accepting of their homosexuality
- see their sexual orientation as outside of their personal control

However, these differences largely reflect cohort effects, rather than the aging process per se. The social support function of gay and lesbian relationships as "families of choice" is discussed further in Chapter 9.

As noted in Chapter 4, there is growing concern about the increase in AIDS among the older population. Despite the risks, most older gay men remain sexually active, although they engage less frequently in one-night encounters and are more knowledgeable about safe sex than comparably aged heterosexual males. With the growing public awareness about the importance of safe sex, future cohorts of gay men may be less likely to engage in high-risk sexual behavior. Of concern, however, is the increase in high-risk sexual behavior among younger gay men. Ongoing, accessible, and culturally relevant public education about safe sex is essential. Older persons with AIDS have been found to be less likely to use emotional support and mental health services than the younger population. Such services may need to be reconfigured and presented differently in order to meet the emotional needs of elders diagnosed with AIDS. All preventive and support interventions need also to be culturally relevant (Emlet, 1996).

Psychosocial Factors and Late-Life Affection, Love, and Intimacy

In addition to the effects of normal physiological changes and chronic disease upon sexual activity and enjoyment, a number of psychosocial factors affect the ways in which older people express their sexuality. These include:

- Past history of sexual activity and availability of a partner. Those who were most sexually active in middle age generally remain so in old age.
- Negative attitudes toward sexual activities and intimate behavior other than intercourse such as kissing, petting, holding and being held, dancing, massage, and masturbation interfere with the openness to try new ways of expressing intimacy.
- Reactions to physiological changes and to illness-induced or doctor-induced changes.
- Reactions to the attitudes of others, including the societal norm that one is "too old" for sex. Societal misconceptions regarding sexuality in later life can have a powerful effect on one's self-concept and perception of oneself as still being sexually attractive and interesting.
- Living arrangements. For example, older adults in long-term care facilities may face barriers to sexual expression, including lack of privacy and of partners, staff and family attitudes, and chronic illness.

A primary psychosocial factor, especially for women, is the availability of a partner. Although the nature of sexual relationships is becoming increasingly varied, most sexual activity for the current cohort of older people occurs within the context of a marital relationship. For women in heterosexual relationships, a central problem is differential life expectancy and the fact that most women have married men older than themselves. Because of older women's lower marriage and remarriage rates, the opportunity for sexual activity within heterosexual relationships is dramatically reduced with age, but the capacity for sexual enjoyment is not altered.

The current cohort of older women, for whom sexual activity was generally tied to marriage, have relatively few options for sexual relationships. Unfortunately, these options are made more difficult because of the lack of socially approved models of sexuality for older women. For many women, their only models for sexuality may be the young. In addition, the pairing of older women with younger men is still rare, largely because of the double standard of aging in which older men are often viewed as distinguished while older women are perceived as unattractive and asexual. Women are also more likely than men to face socioeconomic barriers to meeting new partners, given the higher incidence of poverty among women compared to men. If a woman is preoccupied with financial or health worries, sexual activity may be a low priority.

Gender differences in sexual interest and participation may also be a barrier to finding satisfying intimate heterosexual relationships. Women report that the relational aspects of sexual activities—sitting and talking, making oneself more attractive, and saying loving words—are more important to them than to men. Men, however, view sexual activities such as erotic readings and movies, sexual daydreams, and physically intimate activities, such as body caressing, intercourse, and masturbation, as more important than do women (Johnson, 1997).

As noted earlier, the presence of a partner is a primary factor affecting sexuality in both men and women. Accordingly, a man who has not had sexual intercourse for a long time following the loss or illness of a partner may experience what has been called **widower's syndrome.** He may have both the desire and new opportunities for sexual activity, but his physiological system may not respond and he may be unable to maintain an erection. If he subscribes to the myth that in sex, performance counts (how many orgasms, how long an erection), rather than focusing on pleasuring and closeness, he is likely to experience performance anxiety and fear. Since anxiety tends to block sexual interest and response, he may be caught in a bind. The more he is concerned about performing well, the harder he tries and the more difficult it becomes. In such instances, older men need to be reminded that there is no right way. Rather, sex can be whatever they and their partners find satisfying at the moment. Unhurried, nondemanding sexual interaction with an understanding partner can help resolve anxieties associated with widower's syndrome.

Similarly, women may face **widow's syndrome.** After a year or more of sexual inactivity, women are likely to experience a reduction in the elasticity of the vaginal walls. With the woman less likely to respond to sexual excitement, vaginal lubrication is slowed and reduced. Although these are all symptoms that arise from estrogen deficiency, they become more severe when there is a long period of no sexual contact. For men and women, frequent contact is important to ensure sexual responsiveness and comfort. Both men and women who are grieving the loss of a partner are initially unlikely to have the energy or interest in someone beyond themselves—both essential features of successful sexual activity.

Another critical factor in the physical and social environment is whether *living arrangements* provide opportunities for privacy. Such opportunities are most likely to be limited for those in long-term care facilities. Lack of privacy, negative staff attitudes, administrative rules, and the unromantic atmosphere of institutional environments all reduce the opportunities for residents to be sexually interested or involved. On the other hand, when conjugal rooms are set aside, residents may be too embarrassed to use them (Schiavi, 1999).

Staff attitudes, which tend to reflect those of the larger society, may be the greatest barrier. Staff tend to assume that frail residents no longer need sexual intimacy. If older residents express a desire for sexual activity, staff may ignore, infantilize, tease, or ridicule them, or report it to administrators, thereby adding to a sense of embarrassment. Other staff may believe that chronic illness makes sexual activities impossible or harmful. Despite such obstacles, some residents in such settings

are sexually active, and others would be if the opportunity allowed. The institutionalization of older persons does not necessarily mean the end of their sexual interest. Even older people with dementia in nursing homes may maintain the competency to initiate sexual relationships. Long-term care facilities are beginning to develop policies regarding residents' sexual rights to ensure privacy, establish conjugal rooms or home visits, evaluate patients' concerns about sexual functioning, encourage varied forms of sexual expression, and educate both staff and residents about sexuality and aging (Kuhn, 1999). As illustrated in the box on page 272, there is a growing recognition of sexuality among staff in long-term care facilities.

The psychological and social factors that may affect sexual activity among older people include:

- past history of sexual activity
- attitudes toward sexual activities other than intercourse
- reactions to physiological changes or to illness-induced changes
- reactions to attitudes of others
- availability of a partner, especially for women
- performance anxiety; widower's/widow's syndrome
- opportunities for privacy
- staff attitudes toward those in institutional settings, including homophobia

As noted throughout this chapter, sex encompasses more than intercourse. It is also important to recognize and to convey to older individuals that sexuality and affection may be expressed in a wide variety of ways other than through sex (Willert and Semans, 2000). In fact, older people are more experienced at loving than any other age group, but this experience is often discounted. As stated above, **intimacy**—defined as the freedom to respond to and express human closeness—love, attachment, and friendship are cherished aspects of life, vital to an older person's sense of well-being. When older persons are experiencing assaults on their self-esteem, the need for affection may become even more intense. Without such affection, older individuals may feel lonely, even though they may be surrounded by other people and not physically alone.

There are many avenues for expressing intimacy: sensory, sensual, sexual. Intimacy can involve flirting, laughing, smiling, communicating love through words, singing, touching, holding, as well as genital expression (Genevay, 1999). With age, long-term relationships frequently move toward deeper levels of intimacy expressed in terms of loyalty, commitment, sharing, and mutual emotional response. This is not the case, however, in relationships characterized by conflict, emotional distance, and emotional or physical abuse throughout the years. In addition, many older people dealing with the feelings of loss and loneliness occasioned by the divorce or death of a spouse may find it difficult to reinvest the energy needed to develop intimate relationships.

An important aspect of most intimate relationships is *touch*. The need to be touched is lifelong; physical contact through touching and caressing is as powerful in old age as in infancy,

childhood, and early adulthood. Since the sense of touch is the most basic sense, older individuals may rely upon it to a greater extent in their social interactions than other age groups (Weg, 1996). Just beneath an older person's expression of loneliness or of missing a former partner may lie the desire for someone to touch him or her. A handclasp or hand laid gently on the shoulder or arm, a child's hug, or a massage can all be vital to addressing older persons' needs for affection and can increase their responsiveness. Staff in long-term care facilities especially need to be sensitive to the life-affirming role of touch for most older people, including those with dementia and those who are withdrawn or disoriented. On the other hand, health and human service professionals must recognize cultural differences regarding the meaning and appropriateness of touch. They need to be aware that, in some cultures, differential social status, gender, age, and the setting may influence the older person's acceptance of a friendly touch.

Friends are often important sources of intimacy, especially after a major role transition such as death of a spouse, divorce, or retirement. For example, an intimate friendship with a confidant can help prevent the demoralization often produced by widowhood. The presence of a close

Staff in long-term care facilities can provide emotional support through touch.

confidant also appears to be related to life satisfaction and a sense of belonging, worth, and identity. In any senior center or congregate meal site, gatherings of highly valued same-sex companions are frequent. Among women especially, same-sex companions frequently greet each other warmly with a hug and kiss, may join arms while walking, and spend valued time together. These contacts are nonsexual in the narrow definitions of the term, but can be important to sexual health and to a person's psychological adaptation to aging. The importance of friendship in old age is discussed further in Chapter 9.

Facilitating Older Adults' Sexual Functioning

Given the importance of sexuality and sexual satisfaction, the individual's sexuality and intimacy should be part of the clinical evaluation of older persons. Concerns about sexuality surface if health care professionals initiate discussion of multiple losses and loneliness, what older people miss most in terms of intimacy, their history of loving relationships, and the extent of and their interest in repairing old relationships and establishing new ones. Treatment plans should address issues relative to past, present, and potential sources of intimacy, the meaning of past intimacies, grief work

over losses of intimacy, and permission to explore and repair intimate relationships. Unfortunately, many health care providers have been taught little or nothing about sexuality and intimacy in late adulthood. Professionals may be uncomfortable or intimidated when asked to respond to the lifelong intimacy needs of people as old as their own parents or grandparents. Physicians are often in a central position to respond to concerns about sexuality and intimacy, yet they may be more likely to prescribe treatment for physical symptoms, such as vaginal dryness, than to respond to the older person's emotional concerns or need for information. It is important for physicians to recognize that the loss of intimacy may underlie other disorders that are being treated, such as depression. This can help the physician provide treatment of the underlying cause of the problem, not just its symptoms (Genevay, 1999).

When an older person raises concerns about sexual functioning, such as impotence, it is important that the physician first differentiate potential physical causes, including medications, from psychological ones. This can be done through a careful medical and social history, a thorough physical assessment, and basic hormone tests (Kingsberg, 1998). Such an approach can help to distinguish short-term problems that many individuals experience at various times, such as transitory impotence, from problems that persist under all circumstances with different sexual partners over a prolonged time period.

Increased knowledge of sexuality and aging tends to be associated with more accepting attitudes and improved sexual activity (Willert and Semans, 2000: Zeiss and Kasl-Godley, 2001). Health care providers can encourage and assure continuity of sexual expression for those for whom this has been an important part of their lives. One of the first health professionals to address this issue, Comfort (1980) noted that sexual responsiveness should be fostered but not preached. In an AARP survey of older adults and sexual functioning, older respondents suggested guidelines for health care providers (Johnson,

1997, 1999). These included using clear and easy-to-understand terms; being open-minded, respectful, and nonjudgmental; and encouraging discussion. What an older person may want most when he or she raises sexual concerns is support, acceptance, and listening. Older people who are concerned about their sexual functioning should be encouraged to focus on giving and receiving pleasure rather than on genital sex. As noted earlier, professionals should convey that intercourse is only one way of relating sexually and that there is no prescribed way for sex to proceed. Rather, many choices can be made regarding sexuality. When a partner is not available, masturbation can be viewed as an acceptable release of sexual tension. Explicit discussion of masturbation with older people may relieve anxiety caused by earlier prohibitions during adolescence and young adulthood. Alternatively, professionals need to be sensitive to the fact that some older people do not want to engage in any sexual activity and must not put undue pressure upon them to be sexually active or ever to discuss sexuality. It is important for practitioners to take account of an older person's values, culture, religious beliefs, life experiences, and right to autonomy, and support them in making their own choices about sexual behavior and sexuality.

Many older people need to be encouraged to develop alternative definitions of sexual activity that are not performance-oriented (i.e., broader than genital intercourse) in order to gain intimacy, joy, and fulfillment through a broad spectrum of sensual interactions. Sex education and opportunities for group discussion and support can increase their sexual awareness, knowledge, interest, enjoyment, and range of activities. As noted above, sex education is also important for staff who work with older people. They need to be careful not to impose their values or assumptions on older people. For example, nursing home employees need to recognize that the desire for intimacy and closeness continues throughout life among heterosexual and gay and lesbian adults. With older people who are experiencing memory loss or disorientation, staff need to evaluate the competencies of the older person to engage in intimate relationships. These include assessing the older person's awareness of the relationship, ability to avoid exploitation, and awareness of potential risks as well as family members' attitudes (Kuhn, 1999).

In the past, sex therapists have focused on working with younger people. Fortunately, this bias is changing, and various therapies for older people who report sexual difficulties have been found to be effective.

SEX THERAPY WITH OLDER PERSONS

- First, eliminate or control medical problems, including drug interference, that may directly impair genital functions or indirectly affect sexual functioning.
- Psychotherapy and sexual therapy with older adults should include practical behavioral techniques in the form of specifically structured sexual interactions that the couple can conduct in the privacy of their home (Kingsberg, 1998).
- Emphasize activities that encompass intimacy, giving pleasure, communicating with the partner, and letting the partner know when pleasure is experienced.
- Provide opportunities to discuss problems encountered as well as concerns about performance.
- Employ a holistic approach that includes exercise, nutrition, and interventions to build self-esteem.

Implications for the Future

Compared to other areas, research on sexuality and aging remains relatively limited, suggesting that myths of older adult asexuality may still persist. However, the baby boomers are likely to impact these attitudes as they age, just as they are affecting nearly every aspect of aging. The senior boomers are likely to be more comfortable expressing their sexuality than prior cohorts that were influenced by Victorian era values and norms (Henry and McNab, 2003; Kingsberg, 2000). The boomers' attitudes toward sexuality were strongly colored by the open, permissive atmosphere of the 1960s. The "sexual revolution" along with increased options for birth control, especially influenced women, giving them permission to express their sexual needs and desires and to be more assertive in relationships. Baby boomers' focus on physical fitness, antiaging treatments, and physical appearance will also affect how sexuality in old age is viewed. The boomers may also press for more research on sexual dysfunction and ways to manage the negative effects of chronic illness on sexuality. They will view sexuality as a quality of life issue and central to health promotion or wellness (Henry and McNab, 2003). Recognizing the wide range of ways in which sexuality and intimacy can be expressed, they will probably expect health care providers to consider their sexual needs when prescribing medications or other treatments. They are also likely to ask for medications such as Viagra that can improve their sexual function and be less hesitant to buy products to enhance their sexual pleasure. Gay, lesbian, and bisexual/transgender sexual needs will also probably be out in the open, although the risks of HIV and AIDS are unlikely to diminish in the near future. Educating health care providers in the community and in long-term care facilities about the importance of sexuality across the life span is also helping to improve societal attitudes toward sexual expression in old age. Overall, senior boomers are likely to dramatically alter our images of sexuality in old age, push for more opportunities to form intimate relationships, and accept sexuality as a continuation of normal lifelong pleasures.

These trends suggest the need for mental health counselors, medical personnel and social workers to acquire basic knowledge and skills regarding older adults' sexuality. Such training will need to encompass attitudes and values as well so that professionals are more comfortable and sensitive in discussing sexual issues with older persons. Increased knowledge and understanding are essential because older adults, like younger adults, may be less likely to be seen by a specialist such as a sex therapist and more likely to be treated by health care providers in a wide range of settings.

Summary

As discussed throughout this chapter, sexuality is affected by physical, psychological, and disease-related changes. The normal physiological changes that men and women experience in their sexual organs as they age do not necessarily affect their sexual pleasure or lead to sexual incapacity. Even chronic disease does not necessarily eliminate sexual capacity. For example, many older persons, after adequate medical consultation, can resume sexual activity following a heart attack or stroke. Contrary to the myths about sexuality in old age, many people in their 70s and 80s participate in and enjoy sexual activities.

Older couples can adapt to age-related changes in sexual functioning in a variety of ways. Simply knowing that such changes are normal may help older people maintain their sexual self-esteem. For both older men and women, long leisurely foreplay can enhance sexual response. Avoiding alcohol use prior to sexual activity can be helpful, since alcohol increases desire, but decreases sexual ability. Health professionals need to be alert to medications that adversely affect sexual functioning, such as antihypertensives, tranquilizers, and antidepressants.

This chapter emphasizes how psychosocial factors also can influence an older person's sexual behavior. Myths, stereotypes, and jokes pervade the area of sexuality in old age. Unfortunately, societal expectations about reduced sexual interest may mean that older people stop sexual activity long before they need to. In future years, these myths may change as the media, gerontologists, and other professionals convey the message that sex is not only permissible but desirable in old age.

In professional work with older partners, definitions of sexuality need to be broadened beyond sexual intercourse. A variety of behaviors, such as touching, kissing, hugging, massage, and lying side by side, can contribute to sexual intimacy and satisfaction, even for institutionalized older persons. Touching older people—a handclasp or back rub, for example—is especially important in home-bound and institutional settings.

Practitioners need to be sensitive to their clients' values and life experiences and to support them in making their own choices about sexual behavior and sexuality. Many of the current cohort of older persons grew up with taboos relating not only to intercourse but also to other forms of sexual activity, such as masturbation. Hence, older individuals may need encouragement from professional counselors or others if they are to be free to affirm their sexuality and to experience intimacy with others.

GLOSSARY

climacteric   in women, the decline in estrogen production and the loss of reproductive ability; in men, the decline in testosterone

erection   the swelling of the penis or clitoris in sexual excitement

heterosexuality   sexual orientation toward the opposite gender

homosexuality   sexual orientation toward the same gender

hot flashes   a sudden sensation of heat in the upper body caused by vasomotor instability as nerves over-respond to decreases in hormone level during menopause

impotence   the inability to have or maintain an erection

intimacy   feelings of deep mutual regard, affection, and trust, usually developed through long association

male menopause   a term that suggests a significant change experienced by men as their production of testosterone decreases in later life; although male fertility is maintained, some men experience both psychological and physiological changes

masturbation   erotic stimulation of the genital organs achieved by manual contact exclusive of sexual intercourse

menopause   cessation of the menstrual cycle

orgasm   climax of sexual excitement

penile implant   a device surgically implanted in the penis to reverse impotence and allow an erection

perimenopause   unpredictable menstrual cycles—up to 10 years before menopause

postmenopause   when 12 months have passed without a menstrual cycle

preorgasmic plateau phase   in men and women, the phase of lovemaking prior to orgasm and in which sexual tension is at its height

prostate enlargement   growth of the prostate, due to changes in prostatic cells with age, which can result in pain and difficult urination

refractory period   in men, the time between ejaculation and another erection

sex   in the most narrow sense, a biological function involving genital intercourse or orgasm; in a broader sense, expressing oneself in an intimate way through a wide-ranging language of love and pleasure in relationships

sexuality   feelings of sexual desire, sexual expression, sexual activity

urogenital atrophy   reductions in the elasticity and lubricating abilities of the vagina approximately 5 years after menopause

widow(er)'s syndrome   a term coined by Masters and Johnson describing sexual dysfunction following a long period of abstinence due to a spouse's illness and/or death

REFERENCES

Adam, B. Age preferences among gay and bisexual men. *GLQ: A Journal of Lesbian and Gay Studies*, 2000, 6, 413–433.

Afrin, L. B., and Ergul, S. M. Medical therapy of prostrate cancer. *Journal of South Carolina Medical Association*, 2000, 26, 77–84.

American Association of Retired Persons (AARP). *Modern Maturity sexuality survey*. Washington, DC: American Association of Retired Persons, 1999.

American Federation for Aging Research. Research news on older men's health. *Lifelong Briefs*, 2000.

American Prostate Society. *Impotence*. Washington, DC: American Prostate Society, 2003.

Bagley, S. Understanding perimenopause. *Newsweek*. Special edition on women's health. Spring/Summer, 1999, 30–34.

Berger, R., and Kelly, J. J. The older gay man. In B. Berzon (Ed.), *Positively gay: New approaches to gay and lesbian life.* Berkeley, CA: Celestial Arts, 2001.

Blonna, R., and Levitan, J. *Healthy sexuality.* Colorado: Morton, 2000.

Bortz, W. M., and Wallace, D. H. Physical fitness, aging and sexuality. *Western Journal of Medicine,* 1999, *170,* 167–169.

Bortz, W. M., and Wallace, D. H. Sexual function in 1202 aging males: Differentiating aspects. *Journals of Gerontology,* 1999, *54,* M237–M241.

Bostwick, D. G., MacLennan, G. T., and Larson, T. *Prostate cancer: What every man—and his family—needs to know.* New York: Villard, 1996.

Brice, C. *Age ain't nothing but a number: Black women explore midlife.* Boston: Beacon Press, 2003.

Calasanti, T. M., and Slevin, K. F. *Gender, social inequalities and aging.* Walnut Creek, CA: Altamira Press, 2001.

Cochrane, M. Immaculate infection. *Nursing Times,* 1989, *26,* 31–32.

Comfort, A. Sexuality in later life. In J. E. Birren and R. B. Sloane (Eds.), *Handbook of mental health and aging.* New York: Van Nostrand Reinhold, 1980.

Corbett, L. The last sexual taboo: Sex in old age. *Medical Aspects of Human Sexuality,* 1987, *15,* 117–131.

Defey, D., Storch, E., Cardozo, S., and Diaz, O. The menopause: Women's psychology and health care. *Social Science and Medicine,* 1996, *42,* 1447–1456.

DeLamater, J., and Friedrich, W. N. Human sexual development. *Journal of Sex Research,* 2002, *39,* 10–14.

Diamond, J. *Male menopause.* Naperville, IL: Sourcebooks, 1997.

Dorfman, R., Walters, K., Burke, P., Hardin, L., Karanik, T., Raphael, J., and Silverstein, E. Old, sad and alone: The myth of the aging homosexual. *Journal of Gerontological Social Work,* 1995, *24,* 29–44.

Emlet, C. A. Case managing older people with AIDS: Bridging systems—recognizing diversity. *Journal of Gerontological Social Work,* 1996, 27, 55–71.

Gelfand, M. M. Sexuality among older women. *Journal of Women's Health and Gender-based Medicine,* 2000, *9,* S15–20.

Genevay, B. Intimacy and older people: Much more than sex. *Dimensions.* San Francisco: ASA: Mental Health and Aging Network, 1999, pp. 1, 7.

George, L. K., and Weiler, S. J. Sexuality in middle and late life: The effects of age, cohort and gender. *Archives of General Psychiatry,* 1981, *38,* 919–923.

Gonyea, J. Midlife and menopause: Uncharted territories for baby boomer women. *Generations,* Spring 1998, 87–89.

Henry, J., and McNab, W. Forever young: A health promotion focus on sexuality and aging. *Gerontology and Geriatrics Education,* 2003, *23,* 57–74.

Hite, Shere. *The Hite report: A nationwide study on female sexuality.* New York: Macmillan, 1976.

Jacobson, S., Menopause, *The Seattle Times,* November 2000.

Janus, S. S., and Janus, C. L. *The Janus Report on sexual behavior.* New York: John Wiley and Sons, 1993.

Johnson, B. Older adults' suggestions for health care providers regarding discussions of sex. *Geriatric Nursing,* 1997, *18,* 65–66.

Johnson, B. Sexuality and aging. In M. Stanley and P. G. Beare (Eds.), *Gerontological nursing: A health promotion/prevention approach.* Philadelphia: FA Davis, 1999.

Jones, J. B. Representations of menopause and their health care implications: A qualitative study. *American Journal of Preventive Medicine,* 1997, *13,* 58–65.

Jones. T., and Nystrom, N. Looking back . . . looking forward: Addressing the lives of lesbians 55 and older. *Journal of Women and Aging,* 2002, *14,* 59–73.

Kaiser, F. E. Sexuality in the elderly. *Urologic Clinics of North America,* 1996, *23,* 99.

Kingsberg, S. A. Postmenopausal sexual functioning: A case study. *International Journal of Fertility and Women's Medicine,* 1998, *43,* 122–128.

Kingsberg, S. A. The psychological impact of aging on sexuality and relationships. *Journal of Women's Health and Gender-based Medicine,* 2000, *9,* S33–38.

Kinsey, A., Pomeroy, B., and Martin E. *Sexual behavior in the human female.* Philadelphia: W. B. Saunders, 1953.

Kinsey, A. C., Pomeroy, B., and Martin, E. *Sexual behavior in the human male.* Philadelphia: W. B. Saunders, 1948.

Kuhn, D. Nursing home residents with Alzheimers: Addressing the need for intimacy. *Dimensions,* San Francisco: ASA: Mental Health and Aging Network, 1999, pp. 4–5.

Leland, J. A pill for impotence. *Newsweek,* November 17, 1997, 62–68.

Lewis, M. Sexual problems in the elderly: Men's vs. women's: A geriatric panel discussion. *Geriatrics,* 1989, 44, 76–86.

Mahoney, S. Seeking love. *AARP Magazine,* Nov./Dec., 2003, 59–67, 85.

Martin, D., and Lyon, P. Positively gay: New approaches to gay and lesbian life. In B. Berzon (Ed.), *Positively gay: New approaches to gay and lesbian life.* Berkeley, CA: Celestial Arts, 2001.

Masters, W., and Johnson, V. *Human sexual response.* Boston: Little Brown, 1966.

Masters, W., and Johnson, V. *Human sexual inadequacy.* Boston: Little Brown, 1970.

Masters, W. H., and Johnson, V. E. Sex and the aging process. *Journal of the American Geriatrics Society,* 1981, 29, 385–390.

Matthias, R. E., Lubben, J. E., Atcheson, K. B., and Schweitzer, S. O. Sexual activity and satisfaction among very old adults: Results from a community-dwelling Medicare population survey. *The Gerontologist,* 1997, 37, 6–14.

McNeel, D. G., and Disis, M. L. Tumor vaccines for the management of prostate cancer. *Archives,* 2000, 48, 85–93.

Murray, J., and Adam, B. D. Aging, sexuality and HIV issues among older gay men. *The Canadian Journal of Human Sexuality,* 2001, 10, 75–90.

National Health and Social Life Survey. *The social organization of sexuality.* Chicago: The National Organization for Research, 1994.

National Institute on Aging (NIA). *Age page: Menopause.* Washington, DC: NIA, 2003a.

National Institute on Aging. *Menopause: One woman's story, every woman's story: A companion guide 2003.* NIH Publication No. 03-5383. Washington, DC: NIA, 2003b.

National Institute on Aging. *Sexuality in later life.* Washington, DC: National Institute on Aging, 2002.

National Institutes of Health (NIH). NIH asks participants in Women's Health Initiative estrogen-alone study to stop taking pills. http://www.nhlbi.nih.gov/new/press/04-03-02/htm.

Pangman, V., and Seguire, M. Sexuality and the chronically ill older adult: A social justice issue. *Sexuality and Disability,* 2000, 18, 49–59.

Pfeiffer, E., and Davis, G. C. Determinants of sexual behavior in middle and old age. *Journal of the American Geriatrics Society,* 1972, 20, 151–158.

Schiavi, R. C. *Aging and male sexuality.* Cambridge, UK: Cambridge University Press, 1999.

Schiavi, R. C. Sexuality and male aging: From performance to satisfaction. *Journal of Sex and Marital Therapy,* 1996, 11, 9–13.

Schiavi, R. C., Mandeli, J., and Schreiner-Engel, P. Sexual satisfaction in healthy aging men. *Journal of Sex and Marital Therapy,* 1994, 20, 3–13.

Schiavi, R. C., and Rehman, J. Sexuality and aging. *Urologic Clinics of North America,* 1995, 22, 711–726.

Starr, B. D., and Weiner, M. B. *The Star-Weiner report on sex and sexuality in the mature years.* New York: Stein and Day, 1981.

Trachtenberg, J., Chen, J., Kucharczyk, W., Toi, A., and Lancaster, C. Microwave thermoablation for localized prostate cancer after failed radiation therapy: Role of neoadjuvant hormonal therapy. *Molecular Urology,* 1999, 3, 247–250.

Trudel, G., Turgeon, L., and Piche, L. Marital and sexual aspects of old age. *Sexual and Relationship Therapy,* 2000, 15, 381–406.

Weg, R. B. Sexuality, sensuality, and intimacy. *Encyclopedia of gerontology: Age, aging, and the aged,* 1996, 2(L–Z Index), 479–488.

Wiley, D., and Bortz, W. M. Sexuality and aging—Usual and successful. *Journals of Gerontology,* 1996, 51A, M142–M146.

Willert, A., and Semans, M. Knowledge and attitudes about later life sexuality: What clinicians need to know about helping the elderly. *Contemporary Family Therapy,* 2000, 22, 415–435.

Wojciechowski, C. Issues in caring for older lesbians. *Journal of Gerontological Nursing,* July 1998, 24, 28–33.

Yoakam, J. R. Beyond the wrinkle room: Challenging ageism in gay male culture. *Dimensions,* San Francisco: ASA, Mental health and Aging Network, 1999, pp. 3, 7.

Zeiss, A. M. Sexuality and aging: Normal changes and clinical problems. *Topics in Geriatric Rehabilitation,* 1997, 12, 11–27.

Zeiss, A. M., and Kasl-Godley, J. Sexuality in older adult's relationships. *Generations,* 2001, 25, 18–25.

part four

The Social Context of Aging

Throughout the previous three sections, we have identified how changes in the physical and psychological aspects of aging have diverse consequences for older people's cognitive and personality functioning, sexuality, and mental health. We have also seen how social factors (e.g., the presence of strong family and friendship ties) can affect physical changes (e.g., being at risk for certain chronic illnesses) as well as psychological experiences (e.g., the likelihood of depression and suicide). Within this framework of the dynamic interactions among physical, psychological, and social factors, we turn now to a more detailed discussion of the social environment of aging and its congruence with older people's level of functioning.

We begin with a review in Chapter 8 of the major social theories of aging—explanations of changes in social relationships that occur in late adulthood. Congruent with the person–environment perspective throughout the text, these theories address optimal ways for people to relate to their changing social and physical environments as they age. The early social gerontological theories, such as role, activity, and disengagement, were concerned with adaptation to age-related changes. These differ substantially from later theories, including continuity, age stratification, and exchange theory, which recognized the diverse and dynamic nature of the aging experience. The most recent theories are described as taking a "qualitative leap" over prior theories; these include social phenomenology, social constructionism, and critical and feminist theory, all of which raise fundamental questions about positivist or empirical approaches to studying aging and emphasize the highly subjective nature of the aging experience. These social gerontological theories, then, provide the basis for examining the primary dimensions of older people's social environments: family, friends, and other social supports; housing and community; paid and nonpaid productive roles and activities; and changes in one's social network through death and loss. These later theoretical approaches, in particular, recognize how older people's experiences along with their social environments can vary by ethnic minority status and gender.

Chapter 9 begins by examining the importance of informal social supports, particularly family and friends, to quality of life. Chapter 1 identified how longer life expectancies, combined with earlier marriages and childbearing, have reduced the average span in years between generations. This has also increased the number of three- and four- and sometimes five-generation families. The growth of the multigenerational family has numerous ramifications for relationships between spouses, between grandparents and grandchildren, between adult children and older relatives, and among siblings and other extended family members. Generally, these relationships are characterized by reciprocity, with older family members providing resources to younger generations and trying to remain as independent as possible. The normal physical and psychological changes of aging usually are not detrimental to family relationships, although caring for an older relative with a long-term illness can burden family members. Compared to the earlier years, late-life family relationships are more often characterized by losses that demand role shifts and adjustments. A widower may cope with the loss of his wife by remarrying, whereas a widow tends to turn to adult children and friends.

Although some older people live alone—including a growing number who are homeless—friends, neighbors, and even acquaintances often perform family-like functions for them. More conducive to reciprocal exchanges, friends and neighbors may be an even more important source of emotional support for an older person than one's family. As gerontologists have recognized the importance of informal social networks for older people's well-being, programmatic interventions, including intergenerational programming, have been developed specifically to strengthen these ties, which are described briefly in Chapter 9.

An important function of families and friends is social support. In the case of frail older adults, informal caregiving is provided by spouses, partners, children, and sometimes by more distant relatives and friends. The impact of caregiving on both the care receiver and the caregiver is examined in Chapter 10. Both the benefits and stresses of caregiving are explored. Elder mistreatment, although rare, can result in some cases when caregivers feel extremely stressed and lacking in social supports. Generally, however, mistreatment occurs because of the abuser's behavioral difficulties, such as substance abuse.

Where people live—the type of housing, urban–suburban location, and safety of the community—affects their social interactions. Chapter 11 illustrates the importance of achieving congruence between older people's social, psychological, and physical needs and their physical environments. Relocation is an example of a disruption of this congruence or fit between the environment and the older person. Another illustration of a physical environment that no longer fits a person's social needs occurs when older residents become so fearful of victimization that they dare not leave their homes. Characteristics of the neighborhood can enhance older persons' social interactions and, in some instances, their feelings of safety. Planned housing, home-sharing, congregate housing, assisted living facilities with multiple levels of care, adult family homes, home health care, and nursing homes are ways to modify the physical environment to support older people's changing and diverse needs. Chapter 11 also includes a discussion of housing policies and social and health services that affect older people, as well as an analysis of the problem of homelessness among older adults.

Throughout our discussion of the social context for aging, the effects of socioeconomic status on types of interactions and activities are readily apparent. Socioeconomic status is largely determined by past and current employment patterns and by the resulting retirement benefits. Chapter 12 shows overall declining rates of labor-force participation among both men and women age 65 and over, due largely to the trend toward early retirement. Most people choose to retire early, provided their public or private pensions will enable them to enjoy economic security. Although most older adults apparently do not want to work full-time, many would like the option of flexible part-time jobs, increasingly for economic reasons. For most people, retirement is not a crisis, although for those without good health, adequate finances, or prior planning, retirement can be a difficult transition. Accordingly, women, ethnic minorities, and low-status workers are most vulnerable to experiencing poverty or near-poverty in old age.

Chapter 12 also examines how people's interactions change with age in terms of their nonpaid productive roles, including involvement in community, organizational, religious, and political activities. The extent and type of participation are influenced not only by age, but also by gender, ethnic minority status, health, socioeconomic class, and educational level. Therefore, declines in participation may not necessarily be caused by age-related changes but instead represent the influence of other variables. Generally, involvement tends to be fairly stable across the life course; leisure, volunteer and community activities, and roles formed in early and middle adulthood are maintained into later life. This does not mean, however, that older people do not develop new interests and skills. Many people initiate new forms of productivity through senior centers, volunteering, civic organizations, political activism, and education programs. Or think about the reports of older athletes who complete their first marathon or mountain ascent in their sixties. Given older adults' extensive knowledge and skills, there are numerous ways in which they contribute to families, communities, and society, even when they are not compensated. These are all ways in which people can maintain active aging.

Chapter 13 examines attitudes toward death and dying, the process of dying, and the importance of palliative or end-of-life care. The impacts of social and cultural values, as well as individual factors such as the relationship between the dying person and caregivers, are discussed in reviewing grief and mourning. Recent trends in an individual's right to die, the legal and ethical debates about active and passive eu-

thanasia and the role of advance directives also are reviewed in this chapter. It concludes by examining the process of widowhood and how adults cope with this major life event.

Because of the predominance of social problems faced by older women and ethnic minorities, their special needs and relevant practice and policy interventions are discussed in Chapters 14 and 15. Economic difficulties experienced in young and middle adulthood by these groups tend to be perpetuated across the life span and into old age. These are not isolated problems, but rather of increasing concern to gerontologists and policy makers, since women over age 65 form the majority of older people, and the number of older persons of color, although a small percentage of the total older population today, is growing rapidly. These populations nevertheless display considerable strength and resilience in the face of social problems.

The following vignettes illustrate the diversity of social interactions experienced by older people and set the stage for our discussion of the social context of aging.

AN OLDER PERSON WITH LIMITED SOCIAL RESOURCES

Mr. Valdres, age 73, has been separated from his wife for 20 years. He lives in a small room in an inner-city hotel. Since he worked odd jobs all his life, often performing migrant farm labor, he collects only the minimum amount of Social Security. Some months he finds it very hard to get by and has only one meal a day. Although he is not in contact with his former wife or his six children, he does have a group of buddies in the area who watch out for one another and who get together at night to have a beer and watch TV in the hotel lobby. Although he has smoked all his life and suffers from emphysema, he refuses to see a doctor or any other staff at the downtown medical clinic. He also will not apply for any public assistance, such as SSI or food stamps, in part because he does not understand what these programs are, but also because he does not want government "handouts." The hotel manager keeps track of his activities and will occasionally slip him some extra money or food.

AN OLDER PERSON
WITH EXTENSIVE SOCIAL RESOURCES

Mrs. Howard, age 78, lives with her husband in a small town. Most of her relatives, including three of her children and eight grandchildren, live in the area, and there are large family gatherings on Sundays and holidays. She is a retired teacher; her husband was a successful local realtor until he retired. Both retired in their early seventies. They have considerable savings; in addition, they always lived simply and frugally, saving for their retirement. They have lived in the same house for the past 42 years, and their home is well maintained and recently modernized. Mrs. Howard enjoys gardening, doing housework, reading, and visiting. In addition, she is very active in her church, serves on the Advisory Board to the Area Agency on Aging, and is involved in the town's politics. She also tutors children with learning disabilities. Her days are filled with housework, talking to friends, neighbors, or relatives, or helping someone out, whether a grandchild or neighbor. Despite all her activity, she occasionally complains of being lonely and useless.

AN OLDER PERSON COPING WITH MULTIPLE LOSSES

Mr. Mansfield is 87 years old. He and his wife had six children. After having been a successful businessman in the Chicago area, he retired to the South when he turned 66. Mr. Mansfield and his wife were active in their church, and enjoyed going to plays and keeping up with their children, who had interesting careers all over the United States. He enjoyed his retirement until his wife of 50 years died when he was 80. Mr. Mansfield was heartbroken and thought that his life had ended. He then became involved in a support group offered through his church and started teaching adult education classes. Through that experience, he became involved in the ecumenical life of the small southern town and was very active in putting on an annual conference. Although he still speaks with tears when talking about his relationship with his deceased wife, it has become clear that his life has found new meaning and purpose in his church work, and in becoming a volunteer for the Area Agency on Aging. However, Mr. Mansfield recently faced a new challenge. His youngest and his oldest children have both died. The oldest died in her early fifties of a drug overdose of pills she was taking for chronic pain. The youngest, a son, died 6 months later after a long battle with AIDS. Although these were wrenching experiences for him, he is now facing these losses with a supportive network. The pain is still there, but he is able to share it with others. And he continues to be an active volunteer. His own health is beginning to deteriorate, however, and he has started to talk about his own death. He is concerned about his ability to drive, as his eyesight is diminished. His faith and belief system are integral to his dealing with these concerns about death and dying.

These vignettes show the importance of informal social support networks, whether for an apparently isolated person in a low-income hotel such as Mr. Valdres, or for an older person, such as Mr. Mansfield, coping with multiple social losses. We turn now to a review of some of the social theories that address successful and satisfying aging.

chapter

8

Social Theories of Aging

This chapter discusses

- The theoretical question of what is the optimal way for older people to relate to their environments
- The major social theories of aging
- Some important factors related to aging or age-related issues that serve as a guide for further inquiry and possible intervention in the aging process
- Different lenses through which to view and explain the phenomenon of aging, with an emphasis on feminism and social constructionism
- A framework for discussions of the social aspects of aging in later chapters: social supports, caregiving, living arrangements, socioeconomic status, and changing employment and retirement roles

The Importance of Social Theories of Aging

All of us develop interpretive frameworks or lenses, based on our experiences, by which we attempt to explain the aging process and answer questions we all wonder about:

- What makes for successful, active, or vital aging?
- Who defines what is successful aging?
- What is our society/government's role and responsibility toward older people?
- What enhances older people's life satisfaction and well-being?

We observe older people in our families and communities and make generalizations about them. For example, some of our stereotypes of older people may be the result of unconscious theorizing about the meaning of growing old. Or we may

283

devise our own recommendations for policies or programs based on our informal and implicit theories. In effect, we are developing theories based on our own experiences.

In contrast to our personal observations about age changes, the scientific approach to theory development is a systematic attempt to explain *why* an age change or event occurs. Theory-building—the cumulative development of explanation and understanding about observations and findings—represents the core of the foundation of scientific inquiry and knowledge (Bengtson, Burgess, and Parrott, 1997). By using scientific methods, researchers seek to understand phenomena in a manner that is reliable and valid across observations, and then to account for what they have observed in the context of previous knowledge in the field. Scientists never entirely prove or disprove a theory. Instead, through empirical research, they gather evidence that may strengthen their confidence in it or move them closer to rejecting the theory by demonstrating that parts of it are untrue. Scientific theories not only lead to the accumulation of knowledge, but point to unanswered questions for further research and suggest directions for practical interventions. In fact, a good theory is practical! For example, some of the biological theories of aging discussed in Chapter 3 are useful in guiding people's health behaviors. If the theory is inadequate, the research, intervention, or public policy may fail by not achieving its intended goals (Bengtson et al., 1997).

This chapter focuses on social theories of aging—explanations of changes in social relationships that occur in late adulthood. No one grand, all-encompassing social gerontological theory has emerged. Most of these theories have been developed only since the 1950s and 1960s, and some have not been adequately tested. This is because early research in the field of gerontology tended to be applied rather than theoretical, attempting to solve problems facing older people. Researchers were concerned with individual life satisfaction and older people's adjustment to the presumably "natural" conditions of old age—retirement, ill health, or poverty. Despite their relative recency, theories of aging can be classified into first, second, and third generations (Bengtson et al., 1997; Hendricks, 1992), or first and second *transformations of theoretical development* or evolution of new modes of consciousness (Lynott and Lynott, 1996). The order in which they are presented in this chapter basically reflects the temporal dimensions of this intellectual history. Although there is some overlap of the central theoretical concepts across time, these theories are distinguished by a shift from:

- a focus on the individual to structural factors to interactive processes, and
- largely quantitative methods in the positivist scientific tradition to a range of more qualitative methodologies that seek to understand the meaning of age-related changes among those experiencing them.

Social Gerontological Theory before 1961: Role and Activity

Much of the early social gerontological research was organized around the concept of adjustment, with the term "theory" largely absent from the literature (Lynott and Lynott, 1996). The perspectives on roles and activities, however, later came to be called *theories*. Some theories of adjustment have focused on the individual and his or her personal characteristics (health, personality, needs), while others have emphasized society's demands on and expectations of the individual as he or she ages. Growing old was conceptualized as the individual encountering problems of adjustment due to role changes in later life.

Role Theory

One of the earliest attempts to explain how individuals adjust to aging involved an application of **role theory** (Cottrell, 1942). In fact, this theory has endured, partially because of its applicable and self-evident nature. Individuals play a variety of social roles in their lifetimes, such as student, mother, wife, daughter, businesswoman, grandmother, and so on. Such roles identify and describe a person as a social being and are the basis of self-concept. They are typically organized sequentially, so that each role is associated with a certain age or stage of life. In most societies, especially Western ones, chronological age is used to determine eligibility for various positions, to evaluate the suitability of different roles, and to shape expectations of people in social situations. Some roles have a reasonable biological basis related to age (e.g., the role of mother), but many can be filled by individuals of a wider age range (e.g., the role of volunteer). Age alters not only the roles expected of people, but also the manner in which they are expected to play them. For example, a family's expectations of a 32-year-old mother are quite different from their expectations of her at age 72. How well individuals adjust to aging is assumed to depend on how well they accept the role changes typical of the later years.

Age norms serve to open up or close off the roles that people of a given chronological age can play. Age norms are assumptions of age-related capacities and limitations—beliefs that a person of a given age can and ought to do certain things. As an illustration, a 76-year-old widow who starts dating a younger man may be told by family members that she should "act her age." Her behavior is viewed as not *age appropriate*. Norms may be formally expressed through social policies and laws (e.g., mandatory retirement policies that existed prior to 1987). Typically, however, they operate informally. For example, even though employers cannot legally refuse to hire an older woman because of her age, they can assume that she is too old to train for a new position. Individuals also hold norms about the appropriateness of their own behavior at any particular age, so that social clocks become internalized and age norms operate to keep people on the time track (Hagestad and Neugarten, 1985). Most people in our society, for example, have *age-normative expectations* about the appropriate age at which to graduate from school, start working, marry, have a family, reach the peak of their career, and retire. These expectations have been shifting among younger cohorts, however, with more persons marrying later, and in middle age entering second or third careers.

Every society conveys age norms through *socialization*, a lifelong process by which individuals learn to perform new roles, adjust to changing

---

AGE-NORMATIVE EXPECTATIONS

Within a 5-year age range, how would you respond to the following questions *for most people, for your parents, and for yourself?* If your responses differ across these three groups, reflect upon why there are disparities:

	For Most People	For Your Parents	For Yourself
Best age for a man to marry	_____	_____	_____
Best age for a woman to marry	_____	_____	_____
When most people should become grandparents	_____	_____	_____
When most men should be settled on a career	_____	_____	_____
When most women should be settled on a career	_____	_____	_____
When most people should be ready to retire	_____	_____	_____
When a man accomplishes the most	_____	_____	_____
When a woman accomplishes the most	_____	_____	_____

roles, relinquish old ones, learn a "social clock" of what is age appropriate, and thereby become integrated into society. Older adults become socialized to new roles that accompany old age. In addition, they must learn to deal with *role losses,* such as the loss of the spouse role with widowhood or the worker role with retirement. These losses can lead to an erosion of social identity and self-esteem (Rosow, 1985). Older people may also experience *role discontinuity,* whereby what is learned at one age may be useless or may conflict with a subsequent period in one's life. For example, learning to be highly productive in the workplace may be antithetical to adjusting to leisure time in retirement. Although institutions or social situations that help older people prepare for such role changes are limited, older adults often display a considerable degree of flexibility in creating or substituting roles in the face of major changes in life circumstances. In fact, a process of *role exit* has been identified, whereby individuals disengage from roles to which they have been committed and which have been central to their identity, such as the employee role. Interventions such as retirement planning can encourage a process of gradually ceasing to identify with the worker role and its demands, slowly adapting to leisure roles (Ekerdt and DeViney, 1993).

With age, roles also tend to become more ambiguous. Guidelines or expectations about the requirements of roles, such as that of nurturing parent, become less clear (Rosow, 1985). Older people have often lacked desirable role options. Until recently, few role models existed; those in the media and the public realm have tended to be youthful in appearance and behavior, maintaining middle-age standards that can hinder socialization to old age. In addition, some groups, such as women and ethnic minorities, may lack the resources to move into new roles or to emulate younger, physically attractive models. Fortunately, with the growth and visibility of the older population, there are more models of role gains and successful aging as well as alternative roles for older people to play than in the past. There is also increasing recognition that the role of "dependent person" is not inevitable with age. Rather, the life course is characterized by varying periods of greater or lesser dependency in social relationships, with most people being emotionally dependent on others regardless of age. Even a physically impaired older person may still continue to support others and may be able to devise creative adaptations to ensure competence at home. For example, older people who volunteer as "phone pals" in a telephone reassurance program for latchkey children provide valuable emotional support.

GIVING UP THE CAR KEYS

A major role loss for many older people, especially older men, is that of driver. Families often worry about an older relative's driving, especially if he or she has had a minor accident or some near-collisions. Or families fear that their older relative will cause an accident as a result of slow driving or abrupt shifting of lanes without first checking and signaling. Yet the older driver refuses to stop driving, blaming close calls on other drivers, poor brakes, or road conditions. The driver may deny the problem and resist giving up the keys, because the loss of role of driver carries many consequences: loss of independence, identity, personal satisfaction, the ability to carry out daily tasks, and the sense of personal power and control. For most older people, losing one's ability to drive is a major role transition, symbolizing moving from independence to dependence. Any efforts to convince an older driver to give up the car keys must take account of what this role loss means to the older person.

Activity Theory

Activity theory was also an attempt to answer how individuals adjust to age-related changes, such as retirement, poor health, and role loss. It views aging to a large degree as an extension of middle age in which older people seek to maintain their status in later life. Based upon Robert Havighurst's analyses of the Kansas City Studies of Adult Life

(1963, 1968), it was believed that the well-adjusted older person takes on a larger number and variety of **productive roles** and age-appropriate replacements through activities in voluntary associations, churches, and leisure organizations. The more active the older person, the greater his or her life satisfaction, positive self-concept, and adjustment (Bengtson, 1969). Accordingly, age-based policies and programs were conceptualized as ways to develop new roles and activities, often consistent with middle-age behavior, and to encourage social integration. To a large extent, activity theory is consistent with our society's value system, which emphasizes paid work, wealth, and productivity. Losing any of these is viewed as evidence of decline. Many older people themselves have adopted this perspective and believe it helps them to maintain life satisfaction, as illustrated by the vignettes in the boxes.

Activity theory, however, fails to take account of how personality, socioeconomic status, and lifestyle variables may be more important than maturational ones in the associations found between activity and life satisfaction, health, and well-being (Covey, 1981). The value placed by older people on being active probably varies with their life experiences, personality, and economic and social resources. Activity theory defined aging

---

KEEPING ACTIVE

Bob lives in the Northwest region of the United States. He retired at age 62 after 30 years of work in a management position for an aerospace company. He and his wife of 40 years carefully saved money so that they could be very active in their retirement. They now spend their winters as "snowbirds," traveling in their mobile home to the "sun belt." Now at age 69, they have spent 7 years in the same community in Arizona where they are well-known and have made many friends. In the summer, they usually take one extended trip to the mountains. They enjoy good health and believe that keeping active is the key to their zest for life.

Rose was a nurse for 30 years. In her career in direct patient care and teaching, she has held positions of authority. She has always liked learning new things. Now 74 and retired, she is very active in her church and directs the adult education program. She has participated in Elderhostel four times, and has had the opportunity to visit several foreign countries. She has taken two trips with her teenage grandchildren as well. Staying active means learning to her, and she has shared slide shows of her journeys with her retired friends and the women's group at her church.

ROLE MODELS FOR OLDER PEOPLE

Flip through a popular magazine or newspaper, noting how older adults are portrayed in both the ads and in the news articles. What roles are older people playing in the print media? Are the roles largely positive or negative images? To what extent is diversity in terms of race/ethnicity, gender, age, social class, sexual orientation, or disability portrayed? Are the images largely homogeneous? Reflect on how these images fit with or contradict your own perspectives on others' aging as well as your own aging. We encourage you to develop a critical eye with regard to the role models portrayed for older adults in the media.

---

as an individual social problem that can be addressed by trying to retain status, roles and activities similar to those of earlier life stages. A challenge to this perspective was formulated in 1961 as **disengagement theory,** which shifted attention away from the individual to the social system as an explanation for successful adjustment to aging.

The First Transformation of Theory

Disengagement Theory

The development of disengagement theory represents a critical juncture—as the first public statement wherein social aging theory is treated as a form of scientific activity in its own right, separate from policy and practice applications and information-gathering (Lynott and Lynott, 1996). In fact, disengagement theory was the first comprehensive, explicit, and multidisciplinary theory advanced in social gerontology (Achenbaum and Bengtson, 1994). Cumming and Henry, in their book *Growing Old* (1961), argue that aging cannot be understood separate from the characteristics of the social system in which it is experienced. All societies need orderly ways to transfer power from older to younger generations. Therefore, the social system deals with the problem of aging or "slowing down" by institutionalizing mechanisms of disengagement or separation from society. Accordingly, older people decrease their activity levels, seek more passive roles, interact less frequently with others, and become preoccupied with their inner lives. *Disengagement* is thus viewed as adaptive behavior, allowing older people to maintain a

sense of self-worth while adjusting through withdrawal to the loss of prior roles, such as occupational or parenting roles. Since disengagement is presumed to have positive consequences for both society and the individual, this theory challenges the assumption of activity theory that older people have to be "busy" and engaged in order to be well-adjusted. In contrast to activity theory, it views old age as a separate period of life, not as an extension of middle age.

Disengagement theory has been widely discounted by most gerontologists. While attempting to explain both system- and individual-level change with one grand theory, it has generally not been supported by empirical research (Achenbaum and Bengtson, 1994). Older people, especially in other cultures, may move into new roles of prestige and power. Likewise, not everyone in our culture disengages, as evidenced by the growing numbers of older people who remain employed, healthy, and politically and socially active. As demonstrated by the MacArthur Studies, described in Chapter 6, successful aging is more likely to be achieved by people who remain involved in society. Disengagement theory also fails to account for variability in individual preferences, personality, and differences in the sociocultural setting and environmental opportunities within the aging population (Achenbaum and Bengtson, 1994; Estes and Associates, 2000; Marshall, 1994). Likewise, it cannot be assumed that older people's withdrawal from useful roles is necessarily good for society. For example, policies to encourage retirement have resulted in the loss of older workers' skills and knowledge in the workplace, especially during employee shortages. Although disengagement theory has largely disappeared from the empirical literature, as the first attempt to define an explicit multidisciplinary theory of aging, it had a profound impact on the field.

Continuity Theory

While challenging both activity and disengagement theory, **continuity theory** maintained the focus on

---

DISENGAGEMENT AND ADAPTATION

Inga was an administrative assistant to a highly successful businessman. She has never married. When she retired at age 62, she took a creative writing class, something she had dreamed of all her life but had not had the time to pursue. At 75 she is very content to sit in her rent-controlled apartment, which overlooks a park. She has lived there for 15 years. She finds much inspiration in watching life pass before her in the park. Writing poetry and short stories gives her an outlet for her thoughts. She feels that her writing has developed greater depth as she has achieved wisdom and contemplated the meaning of her life.

John worked for 40 years on the assembly line at a factory, making cars. He believed that it was a good job that supported his family well, but he had worked many overtime hours and had had little time for leisure. Now 70, he sits in the chair in his living room and watches TV and reads the paper. This has been his pattern since his retirement 5 years ago. Occasionally, he and his wife of 45 years will go out to dinner. John is glad not to have to go to the "rat race" of work every day.

Religious leadership can be continued across the life span.

social-psychological theories of adaptation that were developed from the Kansas City Studies. According to continuity theory, individuals tend to maintain a *consistent* pattern of behavior as they age, substituting similar types of roles for lost ones and maintaining typical ways of adapting to the environment. In other words, individuals do not change dramatically as they age, and their personalities remain similar throughout their adult lives. Life satisfaction is determined by how consistent current activities or lifestyles are with one's lifetime experiences (Atchley, 1972; Neugarten, Havighurst, and Tobin, 1968). Basically, this perspective states that, with age, we become more of what we already were when younger. Central personality characteristics become even more pronounced, and core values even more salient with age. For example, people who have always been passive or withdrawn are unlikely to become active upon retirement. In contrast, people who were involved in many organizations, sports, or religious groups are likely to continue these activities or to substitute new ones for those that are lost with retirement or relocation. An individual ages successfully and "normally" if she or he maintains a mature, integrated personality while growing old.

Continuity theory has some face validity because it seems reasonable. However, it is difficult to test empirically, since an individual's reaction to

aging is explained through the interrelationships among biological and psychological changes and the continuation of lifelong patterns. Another limitation is that, by focusing on the individual as a unit of analysis, it overlooks the role of external social factors in modifying the aging process. It thus could rationalize a laissez-faire or "live and let live" approach to solving the problems facing older people.

Alternative Theoretical Perspectives

Activity, disengagement, and continuity theories have often been framed as directly challenging one another, even though they differ in the extent to which they focus on individual behavior or social systems/social structure (Hochschild, 1975, 1976;

Lynott and Lynott, 1996; Marshall, 1996). None fully explains successful aging nor adequately addresses the social structure or the cultural or historical contexts in which the aging process occurs. During this early period of theory development, the factors found to be associated with optimal aging were, for the most part, individualistic—keeping active, withdrawing, "settling" into old age. When macro-level phenomena were considered, they were not conceptualized as structurally linked between the individual and society. Nor were race, ethnicity, and class explicitly identified as social structural variables. A number of alternative theoretical viewpoints have emerged since the 1960s, each attempting to explain "the facts" of aging better than another (Estes and Associates, 2000; Lynott and Lynott, 1996). Many of these viewpoints place greater emphasis on a macro-level of structural analysis and include symbolic interactionism or subcultures of aging, age stratification, social exchange, and political economy.

Symbolic Interactionism and Subculture of Aging

Consistent with the person–environment perspective outlined in Chapter 1, these **interactionist theories** focus on the person–environment transaction process, emphasizing the dynamic interaction between older individuals and their social world. It is assumed that older people must adjust to ongoing societal requirements. When confronted with change, whether relocation to a nursing home or learning to use a computer, older individuals are expected to try to master the changing situation while extracting from the larger environment what they need to retain a positive self-concept.

Attempting to bridge the gap between the activity and disengagement points of view, the **symbolic interactionist** perspective of aging argues that the interactions of such factors as the environment, individuals, and their encounters in it can significantly affect the kind of aging process people experience (Gubrium, 1973). This per-

spective emphasizes the importance of considering the meaning of the activity, such as disengagement, for the individuals concerned. Gubrium argued that activity may be valued in some environments, while in others it is devalued. Depending upon a person's resources (health, socioeconomic status, social support) along with the environmental norms for interpreting them, there are either positive or negative consequences for life satisfaction (Lynott and Lynott, 1996). Symbolic interactionists view both the self and society as able to create new alternatives. Therefore, low morale and withdrawal from social involvement are not inevitable with aging, but are one possible outcome of an individual's interactions that can be altered. Policies and programs based on the symbolic interactionist framework optimistically assume that both environmental constraints and individual needs can be changed.

Labeling theory, derived from symbolic interaction theory, states that people derive their self-concepts from interacting with others in their social milieu. In other words, we all tend to think of ourselves in terms of how others define us and react to others. Once others have defined us into distinct categories, they react to us on the basis of these categorizations. As a result, our self-concept and behavior change. For example, an older person who forgets where she or he parked the car is likely to be defined by relatives as showing signs

SUBCULTURE OF AGING

Roy, 63, has resided in a downtown SRO hotel in the Pacific Northwest for the past 4 years. A logger for many years, he never married, living alone in the woods for most of his work life and coming into town only when he needed supplies. When logging was curtailed, he "retired" early. Now he lives with many other older men downtown, having only a nodding acquaintance with them. He is able to make use of a low-income clinic for health care, and goes once a week to a downtown church where they serve lunch to older adults in the area.

Age stratification theory and the subculture of aging suggest that older people prefer socializing within their own cohorts.

of dementia, while younger people who do so are viewed as busy and distracted.

Proponents of a **subculture of aging theory** believe that older people maintain their self-concepts and social identities through their membership in a subculture (Rose, 1965). Behavior, whether of older persons or others, cannot be evaluated in terms of some overall social standard or norm. Rather, it is appreciated or devalued against the background of its members' expectations. Older people are presumed to interact with each other more than they do with others, because they have developed an affinity for each other through shared backgrounds, problems, and interests. At the same time, they may be excluded from fully interacting with other segments of the population, either because of self-segregation in retirement communities or "involuntary" segregation, such as younger people leaving inner city or rural areas and thereby isolating older residents. The formation of an aging subculture is viewed as having two significant consequences for older people:

- an identification of themselves as old, and thus socially and culturally distant from the rest of our youth-oriented society
- a growing group consciousness that may create the possibility of political influence and social action

Although the interactionist and subculture perspectives have implications for how to restructure environments, the focus is primarily on how individuals react to aging rather than on the broader sociostructural factors that shape the experience and meaning of aging in our society. The subculture theory of aging, however, fails to recognize that most older adults have important intergenerational roles and relationships, as grandparent, parent, friend, mentor, or employer. Instead, most people move into and out of a succession of different roles and statuses as they age, which is congruent with age stratification theory.

Age Stratification Theory

Just as societies are stratified in terms of socioeconomic class, gender, and race, every society divides people into categories or strata according to age— "young," "middle-aged," and "old." Age stratification is defined in terms of differential age cohorts. This means that individuals' experiences of aging, and therefore of roles, vary with their age strata. An older person's evaluation of life cannot be understood simply as a matter of being active or disengaged. Instead, changes in the system of age stratification influence how a person's experiences affect life satisfaction (Lynott and Lynott, 1996).

The **age stratification** approach challenges activity and disengagement theories, directing attention away from individual adjustment to that of the age structure of society (Marshall, 1996). It adds a structured time component in which cohorts pass through an age structure viewed as an age-graded system of expectations and rewards

(Riley, Johnson, and Foner, 1972). This recognizes that the members of one strata differ from each other in both their stage of life (young, middle-aged, or old) and in the historical periods they have experienced. Both the life course and the historical dimensions explain differences in how people behave, think, and, in turn, contribute to society. Differences due to the historical dimension are referred to as **cohort flow.** As we saw in our discussion of research designs (Chapter 1), people born at the same time period (**cohort**) share a common historical and environmental past, present, and future. They have been exposed to similar events, conditions, and changes, and therefore come to see the world in a like fashion (Riley, 1971). For example, older people who were at the early stage of their occupational and childrearing careers during the Depression tend to value economic self-sufficiency and "saving for a rainy day," compared to younger cohorts who have experienced periods of economic prosperity during early adulthood. This may create difficulties across generations in understanding each other's behavior with regard to finances or lifestyle.

Because of their particular relationship to historical events, people in the old-age stratum today are very different from older persons in the past or in the future, and they experience the aging process differently. This also means that cohorts as they age collectively influence age stratification. When there is a lack of fit in terms of available roles, cohort members may challenge the existing patterns of age stratification. For example, as successive cohorts in this century have experienced increased longevity and formal educational levels, this has changed the nature of how they age, how they view aging, and the age stratification system itself.

Consider how the cohort retiring in the first decade of the twenty-first century may differ from the cohort that retired in the 1950s: Although heterogeneous, this later cohort will tend to:

- view retirement and leisure more positively
- be physically active and healthier

- more likely challenge restrictions on their roles as workers and community participants through age discrimination lawsuits, legislative action, and political organization than previous cohorts
- expect to be grandparents and great-grandparents
- be more planful and proactive about the aging and dying processes

These variations, in turn, will affect the experiences and expectations of future cohorts as they age. In other words, as successive cohorts move through the age strata, they alter conditions to such a degree that later groups never encounter the world in exactly the same way, and therefore age in different ways.

Age stratification theory, with its focus on structural, demographic, and historical characteristics, can help us understand the ways in which society uses age to fit people into structural niches in the social world, and how this age structure changes with the passage of time. By viewing aging groups as members of status groups within a social system, as well as active participants in a changing society, stratification theory can provide useful sociological explanations of age differences related to time, period, and cohort.

More recently, the concept of **structural lag** has emerged from the age and society perspective (Riley, Kahn, and Foner, 1994; Riley and Riley, 1994). Structural lag occurs when social structures cannot keep pace with the changes in population and individual lives (Riley and Loscocco, 1994). For example, with the increases in life expectancy, societal structures are inadequate to accommodate and utilize postretirement elders. In some cases, the workplace, religious institutions, and voluntary associations may fail to recognize the resources that older people could contribute. Proponents argue that an age-integrated society would compensate for structural lag by developing policies, such as extended time off for education or family across the life span, to bring social

FOSTER GRANDPARENT PROGRAMS

Ten-year-old Ann lives with her mother and older brother in a public housing high-rise apartment. Her mother has to work two jobs in order to make ends meet. This means that Ann is often left at home alone after school. Through the Foster Grandparent Program administered by the local senior services and available in Ann's school, Ann has someone to call after school if she is lonely or needs help with homework. And twice a week, her foster grandmother comes to visit her, taking her on neighborhood outings, making clothes for her favorite doll, buying a special treat, or tutoring her. Ann benefits from her foster grandmother's attention and love. And her foster grandmother, a widow in her mid-seventies, feels a sense of satisfaction, accomplishment, and responsibility in her relationship with Ann. She looks forward to her time with Ann and speaks with pride to her friends about Ann's accomplishments. Most of all, the young girl and the older woman love each other—an emotional component of exchange relationships that makes analysis of relationships in strictly economic terms less appropriate.

structures into balance with individuals' lives (Estes and Associates, 2000).

Social Exchange Theory

Social exchange theory also challenged activity and disengagement theory. Drawing upon economic cost-benefit models of social participation, Dowd (1980) attempts to answer why social interaction and activity often decrease with age. He maintains that withdrawal and social isolation are not the result of system needs or individual choice, but rather of an unequal exchange process of "investments and returns" between older persons and other members of society. The balance of interactions existing between older people and others determines personal satisfaction. Accordingly, individual adjustment depends on the immediate costs and benefits/rewards between persons, al-

though exchange may also be driven by emotional needs and resources, such as social support (Bengtson et al., 1997). Because of the shift in **opportunity structures,** roles, and skills that accompanies advancing aging, older people typically have fewer resources with which to exert power in their social relationships, and their status declines accordingly (Hendricks, 1995). Society is at an advantage in such power relationships, reflected in the economic and social dependency of older people who have outmoded skills. With fewer opportunity structures and little to exchange in value, some older people are forced to accept the retirement role and to turn to deference and withdrawal in order to balance the exchange equation (Lynott and Lynott, 1996).

Despite their limited resources, most older adults seek to maintain some degree of reciprocity, and to be active, independent agents in the management of their lives. In this model, adaptability is a dual process of influencing one's environment as well as adjusting to it. Although older individuals may have fewer economic and material resources to bring to the interaction or exchange, they often have nonmaterial resources such as respect, approval, love, wisdom, and time for voluntary activities. Similarly, policies and services that are developed for older people might aim to maximize their nonmaterial resources that

Both young and old can benefit from the Foster Grandparents program.

are valued by our society as well as to increase opportunity structures for older people. For example, the growing number of intergenerational programs recognizes the volume of social exchange between generations. Exchange theory is relevant to contemporary debates about intergenerational social support and transfer across generations through public policies such as Social Security and within families through caregiving relationships.

Political Economy of Aging

The focus of exchange theory on power and opportunity structures is related to the **political economy of aging,** a macro-analysis of structural characteristics that determine how people adapt in old age and how social resources are allocated. According to the political economy perspective, social class is a structural barrier to older people's access to valued social resources, with dominant groups within society trying to sustain their own interests by perpetuating class inequities (Estes, 2000; Minkler and Estes, 1984; Olson, 1982; Overbo and Minkler, 1993). Socioeconomic and political constraints, not individual factors, thereby shape the experience of aging, and are patterned not only by age but also by class, gender, race, and ethnicity. These structural factors, often institutionalized and reinforced by economic and public policy, limit opportunities, choices, and experiences of later life (Bengtson et al., 1997). This means that the process of aging and how individuals adapt are not the problem. Rather, the major problems faced by older people are socially constructed in a capitalist society as a result of societal conceptions of aging. In fact, policy solutions, such as Social Security, Medicare, and Medicaid, are viewed as a means of social control that perpetuates the "private" troubles of older people while meeting the dominant needs of the economy (Estes and Associates, 2000; Estes, Linkins, and Binney, 1996; Olson, 1982). Estes and colleagues (1996) argue that the marginal-

ization of the older population is furthered by the development of the "Aging Enterprise," a service industry of agencies, providers, and planners funded largely by the Administration on Aging that reaffirms the out-group status of older adults in order to maintain their own jobs. Policy solutions have tended to focus on integrating and socializing older people to adapt to their status, rather than efforts to fundamentally alter social and economic structures and inequities that underlie the problems facing older people.

Life Course Perspective

The **life course perspective** is not necessarily a theory, but a framework pointing to a set of problems requiring explanation (George, 1996). It attempts to bridge sociological and psychological thinking about processes at both the macro (population) and micro (individual) levels of analysis by incorporating the effects of history, social structure, and individual meaning into theoretical models (Bengtson et al., 1997; Marshall, 1996). This approach takes account of the diversity of roles and role changes across the life span, since it suggests that development is not restricted to any one part of the life span, but rather is a lifelong and highly dynamic process. Human development cannot be solely equated with steady incremental growth or change but instead is an interactive, nonlinear process characterized by the simultaneous appearance of role gains and losses, continuity, and discontinuity. Accordingly, development is multidirectional, with stability in some functions, decline in others, and improvement in others. For example, an older person may experience some decrement in short-term memory but still be very creative. In addition, these patterns of development are not the same in all individuals, as reflected by the considerable heterogeneity of life trajectories and transitions among older individuals. The life course perspective can provide a critical analysis of how caregiving is now a standardized part of the life course, "on-time" for increasing numbers of middle-aged adult children, because more older people are living longer and requiring care by family members (Elder, George, and Shanahan, 1996). As another example, the life course perspective has been used to examine the concept of cumulative disadvantage for women across life, because of their limited opportunities to aggregate savings and private pensions as compared to men (O'Rand, 1996).

In contrast with the more individualistic approach of role theory, the life course perspective attempts to explain:

- how aging is related to and shaped by social contexts, history, cultural meanings, and location in the social structure
- how time, period, and cohort shape the aging process for individuals and social groups (Bengtson and Allen, 1993; Elder, 1992; George, 1993)

More recently, researchers have focused on how gender, race and social class structure the life course and result in cumulative disadvantage in old age (Dressler, Minkler, and Yen, 1998; Estes, 2001; O'Rand, 1996).

This approach is also multidisciplinary in content and methods, bringing together seemingly disparate approaches to the life course (Bengtson et al., 1997). Although the life course perspective is not explicitly articulated throughout this text, our multidisciplinary person-in-environment approach, which encompasses biological, psychological, physiological, and social changes, draws upon many of the concepts of intraindividual change, interindividual variability, and historical, social, and cultural contexts or environments.

Life Course Capital

Life course capital is a more recent approach to life course research that recognizes both the exchange of resources across the life course (social exchange theory) and persistent inequalities in our society. Human capital encompasses the idea of "stock"—or the accumulation of resources, such as skills and productive knowledge—as capital that can be allocated to satisfy basic human needs and wants. Capital can be social (e.g., informal social relationships), psychological and physical well-being, or biological (e.g., genetic or developmental). Environmental factors, including community capital, institutional capital and collectively held moral capital, in turn, affect the extent to which individuals possess such human capital. Over the life course, the accumulation of human capital, by acquiring valued skills and knowledge and participation in the paid labor force, is a primary mechanism of social inequality within cohorts. This differential increase in income sources and health benefits affects individual well-being. The interactions among these forms of life course capital thus have implications for outcomes in wealth, morbidity, and mortality over the life span. Whatever the formative causal sequence in early life among these different forms of capital, the subsequent developmental course is one of interdependent exchange of capital. *Life course research* aims to uncover the patterns of relationship among forms of capital (both individual and structural) and their effects on different groups within the aging population (O'Rand, 2001; Rosen, 1998).

Recent Developments in Social Gerontological Theory: The Second Transformation

Social Phenomenologists and Social Constructionists

The "second transformation" in theoretical development, occurring since the early 1980s, is described as a qualitative leap in gerontological thought (Lynott and Lynott, 1996). Phenomenological theorists have taken issue with the presumed "facts of aging," questioning the nature of age and how it is described and whose interests are served by thinking of aging in particular ways. **Social phenomenologists** and **social constructionists** claim that the approach, orientation, and other subjective features of researchers and their world are significantly connected to the nature of the data as such. Therefore, the data or facts of aging cannot be separated from the researcher's perceptions about time, space, and self—or those of the individuals being studied. People actively participate in their everyday lives, creating and maintaining social meanings for themselves and those around them. No one, including researchers, directly or objectively sees a fixed reality. Rather, each of us actively constructs meanings that influence what we each call reality (Ray, 1996). For phenomenologists and social constructionists, it is not the objects or facts but rather the assumptions and interpretations of them that are critical (Lynott and Lynott, 1996). For example, this theoretical perspective would attempt to understand how legislators and other policy makers assume relatively homogeneous characteristics about the older population in deciding whether to increase or decrease Medicare or Social Security benefits (Estes and Associates, 2000).

The emphasis of phenomenologists is on understanding, not explaining, individual processes of aging as influenced by social definitions and social structures (Bengtson et al., 1997). Instead of asking how factors such as age cohorts, life stages, or system needs organize and determine one's experience, they reverse the question and ask how individuals, whether professionals or laypersons, draw upon age-related explanations and justifications in how they relate to and interact with one another. Individual behavior produces a "reality," which in turn structures individual lives. This means that social reality shifts over time, reflecting the differing life situations and social roles that occur with maturation (Dannefer and Perlmutter, 1990).

Not only do theories construct versions of reality, but people do so in their everyday lives; and in the everyday world, people often use or critique the constructions of theories (Marshall, 1996). Gubrium (1993a) used life narratives to discern the subjective meanings of quality of care and quality of life for nursing home residents—meanings that cannot be measured by predefined measurement scales such as those used by most survey researchers. Similarly, Diamond (1992) utilized participant observation techniques as a nursing assistant to learn about the social world of nursing homes. He described the social construction of his job, how the meanings of care are constantly negotiated as the invisible work of caring for older residents' emotional needs clashes with the daily tasks of a nursing assistant. The realities of age and age-related concepts are thus socially constructed. For example, labeling older people as dependent, asexual, frail or marginal is defined socially. However, the focus is on how these definitions emerge through social interactions rather than taking account of social structure and power (Kaufman, 1994).

Social constructionists and phenomenologists, such as Gubrium and Diamond, because of their focus on individual interactions, tend to use ethnographic or more qualitative methods to obtain multifaceted views of the aging experience. For example, Diamond (1992), as a participant observer as a nursing assistant, described both the social construction of the job and the negotiation of the position of patient in a nursing home. This contrasts with the **positivist** (or *quantitative*) approach of many of the earlier theories. In order to gather extensive verbal or observational data, their samples of informants are relatively small compared to the more traditional quantitative methods typically used. To positivists, however, phenomenological and social constructionist theories may seem impossible to test, and closer to assumptions about meaning than propositions that can be proved or disproved (Bengtson et al., 1997).

From the social constructionist perspective, what is considered to be old age varies with the economic, cultural, historical, and societal context in which aging occurs. As noted in Chapter 1, chronological age is a poor predictor of social,

POINTS TO PONDER

A debate before Congress in 2003 was whether to differentially allocate Medicare drug benefits according to income. What assumptions are being made about the older population as a whole? About upper income elders? What is your position on differential allocation of such prescription drug benefits? What theoretical perspective guides your thinking?

physical, and mental abilities. Yet most of us, even gerontological scholars, may make positive or negative assumptions about someone simply on the basis of chronological age (Schaie, 1993). Most current depictions of old age in the United States present it as a negative experience, something to be avoided, a disease to be dealt with by medical interventions or what Estes refers to as the biomedicalization of old age (Estes and Associates, 2000). In fact, a recent survey by AARP found that both young and old respondents defined "old" as negative (e.g., decline and loss of roles or abilities). Older adults may shun the label "old," reserving it for those with obvious physical or mental decline (e.g., "I don't want anything to do with those old people"). Even the current preoccupation with healthy, successful aging and turning to exercise or beauty products still portrays aging as something to be forestalled for as long as possible. In addition, the visual images associated with many of these antiaging activities are unattainable by the majority of Americans.

The negative ways in which age is socially constructed has numerous consequences for social policy, employer practices, public perception, and self-concept. To a certain extent, the problems related to aging and long-term care are socially constructed (Olson, 2003). Consider how public resources are disproportionately allocated toward skilled nursing care rather than toward supplementing the personal assistance provided by families and low-wage workers. Accordingly, the majority of public funds are allocated for medical or long-term care, not psychosocial services that

might enhance elders' quality of life and active aging. Similarly, the general public tends to think of old age as homogenizing, overlooking the tremendous diversity (by genetic makeup, history, personal experiences) that exists across at least one third of our lifetimes. From a social constructionist perspective, we need to deconstruct the concept *old*, and recognize how one's position or location (gender, race/ethnicity, social class, sexual orientation, degree of ability) shapes the experiences of old age. This also suggests that gerontologists focus not only on the problems facing the old, but also on their strengths, resilience, how they overcome barriers, and ways in which cumulative disadvantage can nevertheless serve as an advantage in certain contexts (Calasanti and Slevin, 2001; Estes, 2000; Olson, 2003).

Critical Theory and Feminist Perspectives

Social constructionist theories have influenced other contemporary social gerontology theories, especially critical and feminist theories. **Critical theorists** critique the transformation of the relationships between subjects and objects from being genuine to being alienated, not the research procedures or the objective state of objects per se. With respect to age conceptualizations and theories of aging, critical theorists are concerned with how they represent a language serving to reify experiences as something separate from those doing the experiencing (Lynott and Lynott, 1996). For example, Tornstam (1996, 1992) argues that conventional gerontology draws on a limited positivist notion of knowledge and science that produces a model of aging based only on social problems. By contrast, a more critical and humane approach would allow older people themselves to define the research questions. Arguing for humanistic discourse in gerontology, Moody (1988, 2002) identifies four goals of a critical gerontology approach:

1. to theorize subjective and interpretive dimensions of aging

2. to focus not on technical advancement but on "praxis," defined as active involvement in practical change, such as public policy

3. to link academics and practitioners through praxis

4. to produce "emancipatory knowledge," which is a positive vision of how things might be different or what a rationally defensible vision of a "good old age" might be (Mandy, 2003, p. xvii)

To achieve this knowledge requires moving beyond the conventional confines of gerontology to explore contributions toward theory development from more reflective modes of thought derived from the humanities (Cole et al., 1993). Dannefer (1994) suggests that critical gerontology should not merely critique existing theory but create positive models of aging that emphasize strengths and diversity. For example, Atchley (1993) maintains that critical gerontology must question traditional positivistic assumptions and measures to try to understand the multiple dimensions of retirement, including retirement as a freeing stage in the life course. What is yet unknown is what "a good old age" means, as well as how it will be attained and what type of "emancipatory knowledge" is possible. Nevertheless, critical thinking has the potential to expand the field of social gerontology. It can do so by providing insight into, and critical self-reflection on, the continuing effort to understand the aging experience (Lynott and Lynott, 1996).

Because most gerontologists have been trained in the positivist tradition, critical theory, with its abstraction, is often not cited nor yet well understood. Nevertheless, it has become a topic of considerable theoretical discourse in contemporary social gerontology (Cole et al., 1993; Minkler, 1996; Moody, 2002; Phillipson, 1996). By questioning traditions in mainstream social gerontology, critical theory calls attention to other perspectives relevant to understanding aging, especially the humanistic dimension (Gubrium,

1993b), and has influenced feminist theories of aging. In addition, the self-reflexive nature of critical theory constantly challenges gerontologists to understand the impact of social research and policy on older individuals (Tornstam, 1992). With growing attention to ethnographic and other qualitative methodologies, the interpretive approach of critical theory will increasingly be brought to bear on empirical observations of aging, with researchers attempting to integrate critical theory with the strengths of positivist approaches.

From a critical theory perspective, current theories and models of aging are viewed as insufficient because they fail to include gender relations and the experiences of women in the context of aging (Cruikshank, 2003; Calasanti and Slevin, 2001; Estes, 2000; Olson, 2003). For example, women have traditionally been ignored in retirement research, often because paid employment is assumed to be unimportant to them (Calasanti and Slevin, 2001). Or women were not included in health studies because males were defined as the norm. **Feminist theories** draw upon a number of other theories discussed thus far:

- political economy by focusing on the economic and power relations between older men and women
- symbolic interactionism, phenomenology, and social constructionism in the belief that gender must be examined in the context of social structural arrangements

Feminist theories attempt to integrate micro- and macro-approaches to aging through the links between individuals and social structures, or between personal problems and public responses. In particular, they focus on power relations across the life course and the utilization of both quantitative and qualitative methodologies (Estes and Associates, 2000; Lynott and Lynott, 1996; Moody, 2000; Ray, 1996).

From a feminist perspective, gender should be a primary consideration in attempts to understand aging and older people, especially since women form the majority of the older population. Because gender is an organizing principle for social interactions across the life span, men and women experience the aging process differently. The intersections of gender with race, social class, sexual orientation, and disability are also examined by feminist theorists (Bengtson et al., 1997; Ginn and Arber, 1995; Moen, 2001; Calasanti and Slevin, 2001). Although feminism encompasses a wide range of intellectual paradigms and political/ideological positions, most feminist theories in aging have drawn on "socialist feminism." This model argues that women occupy an inferior status in old age as a result of living in a capitalist and patriarchal society (Arber and Ginn, 1995, 1991).

Socialist feminists point to inequities in the gender-based division of labor and argue for major changes in how society defines, distributes, and rewards "work." They attempt to understand women's aging experiences in light of macro-level social, economic, and political forces rather than as isolated results of individual choices. Caregiving, women's retirement, health, and poverty across the life course are examined by feminist theorists in light of women's differential access to power in the paid labor force, childrearing, and unpaid housework throughout their lives. Such unequal access leaves women without economic resources and necessary social support for managing problems in later life (Arber and Ginn, 1995; Bleiszner, 1993; Browne, 1998; Calasanti, 1999; Garner, 1999; Hooyman and Gonyea, 1995; Stoller, 1993). Social policy is criticized for defining the problems facing women as private responsibilities, rather than taking account of how existing structural arrangements create women's dependency and limited choices in old age. For example, the lack of public and private pensions for a lifelong career as homemaker and caregiver leaves older women vulnerable to society's whims in identifying social benefits to older adults. The need for feminist theory is also visible when considering the failure to take domestic labor seri-

A FEMINIST PERSPECTIVE ON CAREGIVING

Mrs. Reid grew up with the expectation that she would marry, have children, and take care of her family. She fulfilled this expectation, raising four children, caring for her husband when he suffered a heart attack in his early sixties, and then later caring for both her mother and her mother-in-law. She never held a full-time job, instead working occasionally and part-time in order to supplement her husband's income. When he died at age 65, she was left with only his Social Security. All her years of caregiving work, that had contributed to her family's well-being and to the economy, were not compensated in any way. If her caregiving work were valued by our society, Social Security would be altered to view such in-home care as legitimate work that contributes to society. Accordingly, caregivers such as Mrs. Reid would receive Social Security benefits in their own right in old age.

ously in life course analyses of work (Marshall, 1996). From a feminist view, work in the home is integral to economic productivity, but is undervalued or devalued. As another example of a feminist approach, the consequences of caregiving should not be evaluated on the basis of individual characteristics such as caregiver burden. Instead, the underlying problem for women of all ages is inadequate and gender-based policies, not their own individual stress level; the long-range solution is reorganizing work, including the work of caregiving, as a societal rather than an individual responsibility. Feminists argue that unpaid caring by families and underpaid work by chronic care workers must be reorganized to be more equitable and humane both for the givers and the recipients (Hooyman and Gonyea, 1995; Meyer, 1997).

More recently, there are efforts to integrate **postmodern theory** into gerontology and feminism, although postmodernism is itself antitheoretical. Postmodernism theory views knowledge as socially constructed and social life as highly improvisational. Theoretically, modernism challenges positivistic science (Marshall, 1996; Ray, 1996). Postmodernists view the primary task to be the critique of language, discourse, and research practices that constrict knowledge about older women. For example, they approach caregiving not as the result of "natural" tendencies in women toward nurturing, but as the outcome of socialization processes and polices that reify gendered patterns of caring by depending on the unpaid labor of women as efficient and cost-effective (Browne, 1998; Calasanti and Slevin, 2001; Hooyman and Gonyea, 1995; Stoller, 1993). A postmodern feminist approach in gerontology draws upon a variety of methodologies to understand women's experiences. Researchers acknowledge how their assumptions, values, and beliefs influence the research process. Accordingly, postmodernist research, oriented to changing conditions that face women, is conducted to benefit women, and includes women as active participants.

New to the field, and often ideologically based, feminist gerontological theories are less frequently cited than established models of explanation, such as social constructionism, life course, and exchange theories. Nevertheless, they can make significant contributions to gerontology and to the development of feminist theory generally. Not only are they focusing on the needs of the majority of older adults, but they also take account of diversity by race, ethnicity, social class, education, and mental/physical status. Addressing issues that are relevant to women's lives, they draw explicit linkages to practice. In addition, they provide models for integrating micro and macro-levels of analysis. They thus encompass both structural and individual levels of theory and change in order to improve the social and economic positions of women as they age. Lastly, they challenge "mainstream" feminist theories, which typically have focused on issues pertaining to younger women, to take account of age, since gender shapes everyday experiences throughout the life course (Bengtson et al., 1997; Meyer, 1997; Moen, 2000). The merger of feminist and aging scholarship has the potential

for formulating politically sustainable solutions that permit women and men, young and old, to balance the burdens and satisfactions of caregiving work and paid work (Meyer, 1997).

Summary and Implications for the Future

This review of theoretical perspectives has highlighted the multiplicity of lenses through which to view and explain the aging process. Although we have emphasized the importance of utilizing explicit theoretical perspectives to build, revise, and interpret how and why phenomena occur, it is apparent that no single theory can explain all aging phenomena (Marshall, 1994). Instead, these theories or conceptual frameworks vary widely in their emphasis on individual adjustment to age-related changes, their attention to social structure, power, and economic conditions, the methodologies utilized, and their reflective nature on the meaning of the aging experience. As noted early in the chapter, they represent different times or historical periods in the development of social theories. Some, such as disengagement theory, have been largely rejected by empirical data, while others, such as critical theory and feminist theory, are only now evolving and capturing the attention of a new generation of gerontological researchers. Other earlier perspectives, such as social exchange and symbolic interactionism, still influence research questions and social policy. As a whole, these theoretical perspectives point to new ways of seeing aging phenomena and new modes of analysis, laying the framework for future research directions (Hendricks, 1992). As the social, economic, and political conditions affecting older people change, new theoretical perspectives must develop or former ones must be revised through the gathering of information from diverse cultures, contexts, and circumstances. Given the growing heterogeneity of the aging process, interdisciplinary research is essential. Such research must take account of both individual and macro-level changes. It must encompass the role of gender, race, and class, and allow for the dynamic nature and meaning of the aging experience. We turn now to the social context and relationships addressed by many of the social theories of aging: the vital role of social supports in old age; how physical living arrangements can affect social interactions; the concept of productive aging, which encompasses both paid and nonpaid roles and activities; and coping with loss in dying, bereavement, and widowhood.

GLOSSARY

activity theory a theory of aging based on the hypothesis that (1) active older people are more satisfied and better adjusted than those who are not active, and (2) an older person's self-concept is validated through participation in roles characteristic of middle age, and older people should therefore replace lost roles with new ones to maintain their place in society

age stratification theory a theoretical perspective based on the belief that the societal age structure affects roles, self-concept, and life satisfaction

continuity theory a theory based on the hypothesis that central personality characteristics become more pronounced with age or are retained through life with little change; people age successfully if they maintain their preferred roles and adaptation techniques throughout life

critical theory the perspective that genuine knowledge is based on the involvement of the "objects" of study in its definition and results in a positive vision of how things might be better rather than an understanding of how things are

disengagement theory a theory of aging based on the hypothesis that older people, because of inevitable decline with age, become decreasingly active with the outer world and increasingly preoccupied with their inner lives; disengagement is useful for society because it fosters an orderly transfer of power from older to younger people

feminist theory the view that the experiences of women are often ignored in understanding the human condition together with efforts to attend critically to those experiences

interactionist theory a perspective that emphasizes the reciprocal actions of persons and their social world in shaping perceptions, attitudes, behavior, etc., including person–environment, symbolic interaction, labeling, and social breakdown perspectives

labeling theory a theoretical perspective derived from symbolic interactionism, premised on the belief that people derive their self-concepts from interacting with others in their social milieu, in how others define us and react to us

life course capital an expansion of the life course perspective that addresses the impact of differential acquisition of resources among different members of a cohort

life course perspective the multidisciplinary view of human development that focuses on changes with age and life experiences

opportunity structures social arrangements, formal and informal, that limit or advance options available to people based on such features as social class, age, ethnicity, and sex

political economy of aging a theory based on the hypothesis that social class determines a person's access to resources and that dominant groups within society try to sustain their own interests by perpetuating class inequities

positivism the perspective that knowledge is based solely upon observable facts and their relation to one another (cause and effect or correlation); the search for ultimate origins is rejected

postmodern theory the critique of language, discourse, and research practices that constrict knowledge

productive roles a concept central to activity theory; activities in volunteer associations, churches, employment, and politics

role theory a theory based on the belief that roles define us and our self-concept, and shape our behavior

social construction of age what is considered to be old varies with the economic, cultural, historical, and societal context

social exchange theory a theory based on the hypothesis that personal status is defined by the balance between people's contributions to society and the costs of supporting them

social phenomenology and constructionism   a point of view in studying social life that places an emphasis on the assumptions and meanings of experience rather than the "objective" facts, with a focus on understanding rather than explaining

structural lag   the inability of social structures (patterns of behavior, attitude, ideas, policies, etc.) to adapt to changes in population and individual lives

subculture of aging theory   a theoretical perspective based on the belief that people maintain their self-concepts and social identities through their membership in a defined group (subculture)

symbolic interactionism   a theoretical perspective based on the belief that the interactions of such factors as the environment, individuals, and their encounters in it can significantly affect one's behavior and thoughts, including the aging process

REFERENCES

Achenbaum, W. A., and Bengtson, V. C. Re-engaging the disengagement theory of aging: Or the history and assessment of theory development in gerontology. *The Gerontologist,* 1994, *34,* 756–763.

Arber, S., and Ginn, J. (Ed.). *Connecting gender and aging: A sociological approach.* Philadelphia: Open University Press, 1995.

Arber, S., and Ginn, J. *Gender and later life: A sociological analysis of constraints.* Newbury Park, CA: Sage, 1991.

Atchley, R. C. Critical perspectives on retirement. In T. R. Cole, W. A. Achenbaum, P. L. Jakobi, and R. Kastenbaum (Eds.), *Voices and visions: Toward a critical gerontology.* New York: Springer, 1993.

Atchley, R. C. *The social forces in later life.* Belmont, CA: Wadsworth, 1972.

Bengtson, V. L. Cultural and occupational differences in level of present role activity in retirement. In R. J. Havighurst, J. M. A. Munnicks, B. C. Neugarten, and H. Thomas (Eds.), *Adjustments to retirement: A cross-national study.* Assen, The Netherlands: Van Gorkum, 1969.

Bengtson, V. L., and Allen, K. R. The life course perspective applied to families over time. In P. G. Boss, W. J. Doherty, R. LaRossa, W. R. Schumm, and S. K. Steinmetz (Eds.), *Sourcebook of family theories and methods: A conceptual approach.* New York: Plenum Press, 1993.

Bengtson, V. L., Burgess, E. O., and Parrott, T. M. Theory, explanation and a third generation of theoretical development in social gerontology. *Journals of Gerontology,* 1997, *52B,* S72–S88.

Browne, C. *Women, feminism, and aging.* New York, NY: Springer Publishing, 1998.

Calasanti, T. M. Feminism and gerontology: Not just for women. *Hallym International Journal on Aging* 1999, *1,* 44–55.

Calasanti, T. M., and Slevin, K. F. *Gender, social inequalities and aging.* Walnut Creek, CA: Altamira Press, 2001.

Cole, T. R., Achenbaum, W. A., Jacobi, P. L., and Kastenbaum, R. *Voices and visions of aging: Toward a critical gerontology.* New York: Springer, 1993.

Cottrell, L. The adjustment of the individual to his age and sex roles. *American Sociological Review,* 1942, *7,* 617–620.

Covey, H. A reconceptualization of continuity theory: Some preliminary thoughts. *The Gerontologist,* 1981, *21,* 628–633.

Cruikshank, M. *Learning to be old.* Lanham, MD: Rowman & Littlefield, 2003.

Cumming, E., and Henry, W. E. *Growing old.* New York: Basic Books, 1961.

Dannefer, W. D. *Reciprocal co-optation: Some reflections on the relationship of critical theory and social gerontology.* Revised version of paper presented at the International Sociological Association, Bieleveld, Germany, July 1994.

Dannefer, W. D., and Perlmutter, M. Development as a multidimensional process: Individual and social constituents. *Human Development,* 1990, *33,* 108–137.

Diamond, T. *Making grey gold: Narratives of nursing home care.* Chicago: University of Chicago Press, 1992.

Dowd, J. J. *Stratification among the aged.* Monterey, CA: Brooks Cole, 1980.

Dressel, P., Minkler, M., and Yen, I. Gender, race, class and aging: Advances and opportunities. *International Journal of Health Services,* 1987, *27,* 579–600.

Ekerdt, D. J., and DeViney, S. Evidence for a preretirement process among older male workers. *Journals of Gerontology,* 1993, *48,* S35–S43.

Elder, G. H., Jr. Models of the life course. *Contemporary Sociology: A Journal of Reviews*, 1992, *21,* 632–635.

Elder, G. H., Jr., George, L. K., and Shanahan, M. J. Psychosocial stress over the life course. In H. Kaplan (Ed.), *Psychosocial stress: Perspectives on structure, theory, life-course, and methods.* San Diego: Academic Press, 1996.

Estes, C. L. From gender to the political economy of ageing. *European Journal of Social Quality*, 2001, 2, 28–46.

Estes, C. L., and Associates. *Social policy and aging: A critical perspective.* Thousand Oaks: Sage, 2000.

Estes, C. L., Linkins, K. W., and Binney, E. A. The political economy of aging. In R. H. Binstock and L. K. George (Eds.), *Handbook of aging and the social sciences* (4th ed.). San Diego: Academic Press, 1996.

Garner, J. D. Feminism and feminist gerontology. *Fundamentals of feminist gerontology*, 1999, 3–13.

George, L. K. Missing links: The case for a social psychology of the life course. *The Gerontologist*, 1996, *36,* 248–255.

George, L. K. Sociological perspectives on life transitions. *Annual Review of Sociology,* 1993, *19,* 353–373.

Ginn, J., and Arber, S. Only connect: Gender relations and aging. In S. Arber and J. Ginn (Eds.), *Connecting gender and aging: A sociological approach.* Philadelphia: Open University Press, 1995.

Gubrium, J. F. *The myth of the golden years.* Springfield, IL: Charles C. Thomas, 1973.

Gubrium, J. F. *Speaking of life: Horizons of meaning for nursing home residents.* New York: Aldine de Gruyter, 1993a.

Gubrium, J. F. Voice and context in a new gerontology. In T. R. Cole, W. A. Achenbaum, P. C. Jakobi, and R. Kastenbaum (Eds.), *Voices and visions of aging: Toward a critical gerontology.* New York: Springer, 1993b.

Hagestad, G., and Neugarten, B. Age and the life course. In R. H. Binstock and E. Shanas (Eds.), *Handbook of aging and the social sciences* (2nd ed.). New York: Van Nostrand, 1985.

Havighurst, R. J. Personality and patterns of aging. *The Gerontologist*, 1968, *38,* 20–23.

Havighurst, R. J. Successful aging. In R. Williams, C. Tibbits, and W. Donahue (Eds.), *Processes of aging,* Vol. 1. New York: Atherton Press, 1963.

Hendricks, J. Exchange theory in aging. In G. Maddox (Ed.), *The encyclopedia of aging* (2nd ed.). New York: Springer, 1995.

Hendricks, J. Generations and the generation of theory in social gerontology. *International Journal of Aging and Human Development*, 1992, *38,* 31–47.

Hochschild, A. R. Disengagement theory: A critique and proposal. *American Sociological Review,* 1975, *40,* 553–569.

Hochschild, A. R. Disengagement theory: A logical, empirical, and phenomenological critique. In J. F. Gubrium (Ed.), *Time, roles and self in old age.* New York: Human Services Press, 1976.

Hooyman, N. R., Brown, C., Raye, R., and Richardson, V. Feminist gerontology and the life course: Policy, research and teaching issues. *Gerontology and Geriatrics Education*, 2002, *22,* 3–26.

Hooyman, N. R., and Gonyea, J. A feminist model of family care: Practice and policy directions. In J. D. Garner (Ed.), *Fundamentals of Feminist Gerontology,* New York: Haworth Press, 1999.

Hooyman, N. R., and Gonyea, J. *Feminist perspectives on family care: Policies for gender justice.* Thousand Oaks, CA: Sage, 1995.

Kaufman, S. R. The social construction of frailty: An anthropological perspective. *Journal of Aging Studies,* 1994, *8,* 45–58.

Lynott, R. J., and Lynott, P. P. Tracing the course of theoretical development in the sociology of aging. *The Gerontologist*, 1996, *36,* 749–760.

Marshall, V. W. Sociology and psychology in the theoretical legacy of the Kansas City Studies. *The Gerontologist*, 1994, *34,* 768–774.

Marshall, V. W. The state of theory in aging and the social sciences. In R. H. Binstock and L. K. George, (Eds.), *Handbook of aging and the social sciences* (4th ed.). San Diego: Academic Press, 1996.

Meyer, M. H. Toward a structural life course agenda for reducing insecurity among women as they age. Book review. *The Gerontologist,* 1997, *37,* 833–834.

Minkler, M. Critical perspectives on aging: New challenges for gerontology. *Aging and Society,* 1996, *16,* 467–487.

Minkler, M., and Estes, C. *Readings in the political economy of aging.* Farmingdale, NY: Baywood, 1984.

Moen, P. The gendered life course. In R. Binstock and L. K. George (Eds.), *Handbook of aging and the social sciences* (5th ed.). San Diego: Academic Press, 2001.

Moody, H. R. *Aging: Concepts and controversies* (4th ed.). Thousand Oaks, CA: Sage, 2002.

Moody, H. R. Toward a critical gerontology: The contribution of the humanities to theories of aging. In J. E. Birren and V. L. Bengtson (Eds.), *Emergent theories of aging.* New York: Springer, 1988.

Neugarten, B., Havighurst, R. J., and Tobin, S. S. Personality and patterns of aging. In B. L. Neugarten (Ed.), *Middle age and aging.* Chicago: University of Chicago Press, 1968.

Olson, L. K. *The not so golden years: Caregiving, the frail elderly and the long-term care establishment.* Lanham, MD: Rowman & Littlefield Publishers, 2003.

Olson, L. K. *The political economy of aging.* New York: Columbia University Press, 1982.

O'Rand, A. M. The precious and the precocious: Understanding cumulative disadvantage and cumulative advantage over the life course. *The Gerontologist,* 1996, *36,* 230–238.

O'Rand, A. M. Stratification and the life course: The forms of life course capital and their interrelationships. In R. Binstock and L. K. George (Eds.), *Handbook of aging and the social sciences* (5th ed.). San Diego: Academic Press, 2001.

Overbo, B., and Minkler, M. The lives of older women: Perspectives from political economy and the humanities. In T. R. Cole, W. A. Achenbaum, P. L. Jakobi, and R. Kastenbaum (Eds.), *Voices and visions of aging: Toward a critical gerontology.* New York: Springer, 1993.

Phillipson, C. Interpretations of aging: Perspectives from humanistic gerontology. *Aging and Society,* 1996, 16, 359–369.

Ray, R. E. A post modern perspective on feminist gerontology. *The Gerontologist,* 1996, *36,* 674–680.

Riley, M. W. Social gerontology and the age stratification of society. *The Gerontologist,* 1971, *11,* 79–87.

Riley, M. W., Johnson, J., and Foner, A. *Aging and society: A sociology of age stratification,* vol. 3. New York: Russell Sage Foundation, 1972.

Riley, M. W., Kahn, R. L., and Foner, A. (Eds.). *Age and structural lag: Society's failure to provide meaningful opportunities in work, family and leisure.* New York: John Wiley, 1994.

Riley, M. W., and Loscocco, K. A. The changing structure of work opportunities: Toward an age-integrated society. In R. P. Abeles, H. C. Gift, and M. G. Ory (Eds.), *Aging and quality of life.* New York: Springer, 1994.

Riley, M. W., and Riley, J. W. Age integration and the lives of older people. *The Gerontologist,* 1994, *34,* 110–115.

Rose, A. M. A current theoretical issue in social gerontology. In A. M. Rose and W. A. Peterson (Eds.), *Older people and their social worlds.* Philadelphia: F. A. Davis, 1965.

Rosen, S. Human capital. In P. Newman (Ed.), *The new Palgrave dictionary of economics and the law* (vol. 2). London: Macmillan, 1998.

Rosow, J. Status and role change through the life cycle. In R. H. Binstock and E. Shanas (Eds.), *Handbook of aging and the social sciences* (2nd ed.). New York: Van Nostrand, 1985.

Schaie, K. W. Ageist language in psychological research. *American Psychologist,* 1993, *48,* 49–51.

Stoller, E. P. Gender and the organization of lay health care: A socialist-feminist perspective. *Journal of Aging Studies,* 1993, *7,* 151–170.

Stoller, E. P., and Gibson, R. Advantages of using the life course framework in studying aging. In E. P. Stoller and R. Gibson (Eds.), *World of difference: Inequality in the aging experience.* Thousand, Oaks, CA: Pine Forge Press, 2000.

Tornstam, L. Gerotranscendence: A theory about maturing in old age. *Journal of aging and identity,* 1996, *1,* 37–50.

Tornstam, L. The Quo Vadis of gerontology: On the scientific paradigm of gerontology. *The Gerontologist,* 1992, *32,* 318–326.

9

The Importance of Social Supports: Family, Friends, Neighbors, and Communities

Consistent with the life course perspective and the person–environment model, this chapter focuses on informal social support systems:

- Social supports, social engagement, and older adults' well-being
- Multigenerational families
- Different types of family relationships
  - Gay and lesbian families
  - Grandparents and grandchildren
  - Grandparents as primary caregivers
- Friends, neighbors and acquaintances as social supports
- Social support interventions
- Intergenerational programming
- Pets as social support

As people age, their social roles and relationships change. Earlier chapters have noted and the introductory vignettes have illustrated that the way older people interact with others is affected by physiological, social, and psychological changes. For example, with children typically gone from the home and without daily contacts with coworkers, older people may lose a critical context for social involvement. At the same time, their need for social support may increase because of changes in health, cognitive, and emotional status. Such incongruence between needs and environmental opportunities can result in stress for some older people.

The Nature and Function of Informal Supports

A common myth is that many older adults are lonely and isolated from family and friends. Even older people who appear isolated generally are able to turn to an informal network for information, financial advice, emotional reassurance, or concrete services. Families, friends, neighbors, and acquaintances, such as postal carriers and grocery clerks, can be powerful antidotes to some of the negative consequences of the aging process, as in the description of Mr. Mansfield on page 282. Older adults first use informal supports and move to formal relationships only when necessary, typically when they live alone. As suggested by the person–environment model, elders draw upon their informal networks as a way to enhance their competence.

Social integration, which encompasses both social networks and support, refers to the degree to which an individual is involved with others in his or her environment. This concept captures the degree of emotional closeness, the availability of support when needed, and the perception of oneself as an individual actively engaged in social exchanges. (Antonucci, Sherman, and Akimaya, 1996; Berkman, 2000; Grann, 2000). Both concepts of social support and social integration take account of (1) the specific types of assistance exchanged (e.g., emotional, instrumental help with

daily activities and information); (2) the frequency of contact with others; (3) how a person assesses the adequacy of supportive exchanges; and (4) anticipated support or the belief that help is available if needed (Rook, 1990). Social integration, however, tends to emphasize the giving as well as the receiving of support and assistance.

Consistent with social exchange theory described in Chapter 8, most older adults try to maintain **reciprocity**—being able to help others—in their interactions with others. Even frail elders who require personal care from their families may still contribute through financial assistance or child care. Helping others also benefits the helper and is associated with positive affect, life satisfaction, and physical and mental health. As is true across the life span, older adults give support to others because of a sense of purpose, altruism, social norms, or maintenance of a lifelong pattern of helping (Boaz, Hu, and Ye, 1999; Keyes, 2002; Kincade, 1996; Krause and Shaw, 2000; Morrow-Howell et al., 2001; Kawachi and Berkman, 2001; Seeman and Berkman, 1998).

The Impact of Social Supports on Well-Being

The importance of informal supports in older people's lives has been extensively documented over the past three decades (Berkman, 2002; Cassel, 1976; Krause and Borawski-Clark, 1995; Uchino, Cacioppo, and Kiecolt-Glaser, 1996; Lubben and Gironda, 2003). Informal reciprocal relationships, especially giving support to others, are a crucial concomitant of an older person's physical and mental well-being, feelings of personal control, morale, and even reduced mortality risk. Provision of support, like its receipt, contributes to elders' perceptions of support availability, which is in turn generally linked with good mental health (Cohen, Gottlieb, and Underwood, 2000; Eng et al., 2002; Liang, Krause, and Bennett, 2001; Seeman, 2000; Wenger, 1997). Social support can also mediate the effects of other negative life circumstances, such as retirement,

---

POTENTIAL OUTCOMES OF SOCIAL SUPPORTS

- Physical and mental well-being (morale, self-confidence)
- Feelings of personal control, autonomy, and competence
- Active aging and resilience
- Reduced negative effects of stressful life events (bereavement, widowhood)
- Reduced mortality risk

widowhood, illness, or relocation (DuPertuis, Aldwin, and Bosse, 2001; Everard et al., 2000; Oxman and Hull, 1997). It is unclear, however, whether such supports act as buffers against the negative impact of life events on health, or whether they have a more direct effect, independent of the presence or absence of major life events (Mor-Barak, Miller, and Syme, 1991).

Alternatively, loss of social support through divorce or widowhood can contribute to health problems. For example, older adults who live alone and are not tied into informal networks are more likely to use formal services and to become institutionalized. Their self-reported well-being tends to be lower. In fact, several longitudinal studies have found an association between social support structures and reduced mortality risk. Similarly, extreme social isolation may be conducive to a higher mortality rate (Bowling and Grundy, 1998; LaVeist et al., 1997).

Aging does not necessarily result in losses in social networks, but it changes network composition (e.g., less contact with couples) or functioning (e.g., increased need for instrumental support (Cantor, 1994; Van Tilburg, 1998). In fact, elders active in retirement communities and voluntary associations may actually expand and diversify their networks. A process of **social selection** may occur whereby healthy people are more likely to have supportive social relationships precisely because they are healthy. Conversely, poor health status may hinder them from initiating or sustaining social relationships (Ren et al., 1999; Wethington et al., 2000). In some instances, interaction with informal networks can be negative, if they are inconsistent with an older person's needs and competence level, such as disappointment that one's children are not doing enough to help after their parent's hospitalization (Silverstein, Chen, and Heller, 1996).

The family—the basic unit of social relationships—is the first topic considered here. We examine the rapid growth of the multigenerational family and how relationships with spouses, adult children, parents, grandparents, siblings, and gay and lesbian partners change with age.

Changing Family Structure

Contrary to past conceptualizations of elders as separate from families or families who "happen" to have an older relative, the lives of young and old, even at a geographic distance, are intertwined through cross-generational support. The family is the primary source of social support for older adults, with nearly 94 percent of elders having living family members—adult children, grandchildren or great-grandchildren, and siblings. Approximately 80 percent of adults over age 65 have children; in fact, nearly 90 percent of mothers age 80 and older have a surviving son, and 90 percent of mothers over age 90 have a surviving daughter (Uhlenberg, 1996).

About 66 percent of older adults live in a family setting—with a partner, child, or sibling—although not necessarily in a multigenerational household (Figure 9.1). Given the higher rates of widowhood among women than men, older men are more likely to live in a family setting, typically with a partner, than are women (80 and 58 percent, respectively). Only about 13 percent of elders (7 percent of men, 17 percent of women) are living with children, siblings or other relatives, not with a spouse (AOA, 1999b). While the majority of older parents do not live with their adult children, they have at least one child living close by: about 75 percent live within a 35-minute drive of their nearest child (Lin and Rogerson, 1995). Most parents see their children on a regular basis, with approximately 80 percent reporting weekly contact with at least one of their children. Factors associated with greatest geographic proximity to the nearest child are:

- family size
- health of the parent; as health declines, parents tend to move closer to an adult child

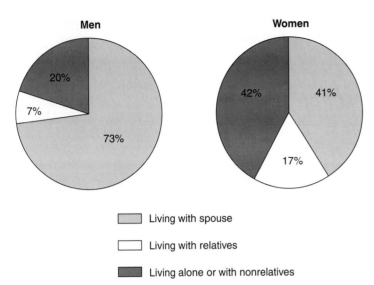

Living with spouse

Living with relatives

Living alone or with nonrelatives

FIGURE 9.1 **Living Arrangements of Persons 65+**

SOURCE: U.S. Bureau of the Census, 2002.

- age of parents: parents over age 80 live closer to adult children
- parents' socioeconomic status (higher socioeconomic class tends to be associated with greater geographic distance)
- marital status; widowed mothers live closest to daughters; remarried parents tend to live at a greater geographic distance than parents who remain married to each other (Lin and Rogerson, 1995).

Geographic distance in itself does not impair the quality of parent-adult children relationships. In fact, as described in Chapter 10, adult children often provide care at a geographic distance.

Older adults typically do not want to live with their adult children. However, declining health, loss of a former caregiver or partner, desire for companionship, and lower income often precipitate the move to a shared residence (Wilmouth, 2000). Widowed mothers are more likely to live with a child than are divorced, single, or married mothers (Riley and Roan, 1996). In a growing number of households, adult children are moving back into the family home, typically for financial reasons or following a divorce.

The Growth of the Multigenerational Family

The term *multigenerational family* encompasses the growing reciprocity across generations, both in the United States and globally. Families composed of four to five generations are more common now than ever in the past. Among Americans over age 35, 80 percent report being members of a three-generation family, and 16 percent are in families of four generations. Similarly, for individuals born in 1900, the chances of both parents dying before the child reached age 18 were 18 percent; by age 30, only 21 percent had any grandparents alive. By contrast, 68 percent of individuals born in 2000 will have four grandparents alive when they reach age 18; by age 30, 76 percent will have a grandparent alive—almost four times that of the cohort born in 1900. In fact, 20-year-olds today are more likely to have a grandmother living (92 percent) than 20-year-olds in 1900 had their mother alive (83 percent) (Bengston, 2001; Szinovacz, 1998; Uhlenberg, 1996; Uhlenberg and Kirby, 1998). Another indicator of changing multigenerational dynamics is that a growing number of people over age 65 have a child who is also over 65, who may then be both a child and a grandparent at the same time. In sum, persons at all stages of life are more likely to have kin relationships involving older people and thus more likely to be part of a modified extended family than in the past. This has resulted in parents and children now sharing 5 decades of life, siblings perhaps sharing 8 decades and the grandparent-grandchild bond lasting 3 or more decades (Gonyea, 2003).

Increased life expectancy may create multigenerational kinship networks to provide family continuity and stability across time along with instrumental or emotional support when needed. Yet increased longevity also means extended years of family differences and caring for relatives with chronic disabilities (Gonyea, 2003; Bengston, 2001). Although families are experiencing more cross-generational relationships, paradoxically, fewer people within each generation may be available to provide multigenerational care for older family members. Demographic and societal trends that underlie this paradox include a decrease in overall fertility that has reduced family size, an increase in family dissolutions, and a shift in economic roles within the family. As the birthrate has declined, delaying the age of childbearing has become more common, and life expectancy has increased, the age structure for most families has shifted from a "pyramid" to a "beanpole." (Bengston, Rosenthal, and Burton, 1990). This means that American families are smaller today than ever before, with 20 percent of American women not having the first child until after age 35 (Fields and Casper, 2001).

At the same time, the number of women entering the paid workforce has increased dramatically in the past 50 years (66 percent compared to 33 percent of women in the 1950s). The distribution of women in the paid workforce across the life span is also striking, with women in their childbearing years most likely to be employed. These women may also face multiple care responsibilities across the life span: for children and young adults with disabilities or chronic illness, parents or grandparents in middle age, a partner in old age, or an adult child with developmental disabilities. As women move in and out of the la-

bor force to be unpaid caregivers, socioeconomic and health inequities in old age often result. These caregiving patterns and life span inequities by gender, age, and race are discussed more fully in Chapters 10 and 15.

Other societal trends are increasing the heterogeneity of the American family structure: an increase in divorce and blended families, the number of people living alone, single-parent households, and never-married individuals living together in other nontraditional family arrangements (e.g., grandparents raising grandchildren, gay and lesbian families, and single parents choosing to raise children on their own). For example, the number of children living in two-parent households fell from 85 percent in 1950 to about 70 percent by the mid 1990s. In fact, the majority of African American children live with only one parent, typically their mother. As a result, the "first married nuclear family" no longer predominates, but is instead one of numerous family structures (Scharlach and Fredriksen-Goldsen, 2001; Minkler, 1999).

Defining Multigenerational Families

Consistent with social constructionist theory described in Chapter 8, definitions of families are socially constructed, and vary by culture and socioeconomic class. Family is broadly defined by interactional quality, not necessarily by members' living together or blood ties. Kinship is a matter of social definition, particularly within ethnic minority families, as reflected in the role of fictive kin, grandparents as primary caregivers to grandchildren, "play relatives," godparents, and friends. Among gay men and lesbians, chosen or "friendship" families are common. Gerontological practitioners need to be sensitive to the ways in which elders and their networks define family in order to work effectively with family members.

Multigenerational families are also characterized by cross-generational reciprocity and interdependence rather than dependence or independence. None of us, no matter what our age, is ever totally dependent; we are embedded in networks of reciprocal interactions. Generations are interdependent across the life span—each contributes to the other, through families and nontraditional informal supports (e.g., friends, neighbors, "community gatekeepers," gay and lesbian partners). Contrary to stereotypes of egocentric older adults, most exchanges are from the older to younger generations. In fact, older adults' unacknowledged functions within families encompass role models for socialization, economic transfers, bearers of family history and continuity, and daily assistance to young single mothers and divorced parents. As described more fully in Chapter 12, older adults typically remain productive in the broadest sense of the term, contributing to their communities through both paid and unpaid work—volunteers, as leaders in community institutions or government, or supporting and encouraging younger family members. They are able to devote time, financial resources, and skills and experience to strengthening families and communities.

Regardless of the particular family structure, family relationships inevitably involve both solidarity and conflict. Cohesion or consensus ap-

Family gatherings help maintain multigenerational ties.

pears to be based on sharing across generations along a variety of dimensions, including the extent to which they share activities, the degree of positive sentiment, and the exchange of assistance. Less is known about tensions, disagreements, or conflicts across generations over the life course (Bengtson, Rosenthal, and Burton, 1996).

Gerontological practitioners increasingly assess and work with families, not just with the older person, since family dynamics inevitably affect the well-being and quality of life of its oldest members. They also can encourage families to value their elder relatives' history and the sharing of stories across the generations.

Cultural Variations in Multigenerational Families

Due to the significant aging of the global population, world regions are also experiencing an increase in the number of generations within families. In contrast to the United States, three- and four-generation families are more likely to live together in countries such as Japan, Korea, India, and Mexico (NIA, 2001). Within the United States, multigenerational families living together are more common among ethnic minorities than Caucasian populations and have been a source of strength historically. For example, older African American women, especially widows, are more

---

THE STRENGTH OF MULTIGENERATIONAL TIES

During the summer of 2000, the governments of North and South Korea agreed to an unprecedented reunion of families that had been torn apart during the Korean War. Siblings who had not seen each other since their teens, parents now in their eighties and nineties were reunited with their children who were themselves in their sixties. The fortunate 100 families were selected by lottery from the citizens of North Korea and flown to South Korea for a brief visit. This bittersweet reunion lasted only one week, when those from North Korea were required to return home. Nevertheless, the stories shared by these families provided a dramatic illustration of the endurance of family bonds.

FAMILY HISTORIES: PRESERVING THE LEGACY OF AN OLDER RELATIVE

Along with the growth of multiple generations within families, younger family members are encouraging their older relatives to write or record on DVD, VHS, or CD-ROM their family history. Life stories are typically not just about one older person, but that individual in the context of the whole family history. In fact, Websites to assist with writing personal histories advertise journalistic or service professionals to assist with this age-old task. While families have always passed stories across generations, the baby boomers are "professionalizing" storytelling, sometimes paying up to $30,000 for a written record of their ancestry. Multimedia legacies can include mementos, photos, and music and provide archived materials from the relevant historical period. Such storytelling not only leaves a legacy for younger generations, but the process of life review can have psychological and physical health benefits for older adults. Perhaps most important to families who are often separated by geographic and psychological distance, "capturing the richness of mature lives can at least ensure that yesterday will keep providing gifts to tomorrow."

SOURCE: S. S. Stitch, Stories to keep. *Newsweek,* November 11, 2002, p. A3.

likely to live in extended or multigenerational family households than are older white women. Grandparents or other "fictive kin" among African American households have traditionally played a central role in caring for children, and multigenerational exchanges are often necessary for economic survival (Dilworth-Anderson, Williams, and Gibson, 2002). Even when controlling for need, ethnic minority families are more likely to live in multigenerational families or to depend on nonkin (e.g., friends and neighbors), who provide both social and instrumental support, especially for unmarried children and parents (National Academy, 2000).

This greater incidence of cross-generational households in communities of color may underlie the higher levels of assistance to elders and the generally positive parent-adult child relationships reported by African American, Latino, and Asian American families compared to their Caucasian counterparts (Dilworth-Anderson et al., 2002). On the other hand, the existence of extended family arrangements and fictive kin may carry financial and emotional costs and divert elders from the need for formal supports. These patterns may shift over time with increased economic and geographic mobility and levels of assimilation of younger generations.

By contrast, American culture and economic pressures often weaken multigenerational support networks within immigrant and refugee populations. Among Asian American immigrants, grandparents frequently provide child care to enable both parents to work outside the home, but younger generations' sense of filial responsibility may be eroded by their upward mobility. Latino immigrant families typically have strong cross-generational cohesion, but smaller family size, increased employment of women, and economic pressures may compromise such supportive interactions (Beyene, Becker, and Mayen, 2002). Although Cuban elders place a high value on extended family relationships, Cuban elders in Florida tend to live alone, in part because of declining family size related to their immigration history. They make up for the lack of large family networks, however, by engagement in large social networks and involvement in social activities through church or senior centers (Martinez, 2003). As another example of how generational influences are affected by both socioeconomic status and educational achievement, in Singapore and Taiwan, age and declining health along with socioeconomic variables, such as home-ownership, employment status, and education, are becoming more important than cultural values in whether elders are consulted in family decisions (Williams, Mehta, and Lin, 2000).

Despite pressures for assimilation and rapid economic and social changes, cultural variations remain salient in how generations and multigenerational relations are defined and experienced. Even when behaviors such as dress, appearance, and material goods differ markedly across generations, some cultural values may nevertheless be shared. For example, generation X, despite their dramatic efforts to separate from their parents, share similar values, achievement orientation, and family solidarity of their mid-1950s parents (Bengtson, 2001). Cultural notions of "family" are strong, but are reinterpreted in rapidly changing economic and social conditions; as a result, living arrangements for elders often represent a balance of cultural convictions, ability, and actual choices. What is most important to the elder, however, is not the structural makeup of family exchanges, but the subjective quality of the relationships (Martinez, 2003). Regardless of the particular family structure or nature of relationships, practitioners must be sensitive to cultural variants when working with diverse multigenerational families.

Older Partners*

The marital or partnered relationship plays a crucial support function in most older people's lives, especially men's. Of all family members, partners are most likely to serve as confidants, provide support, facilitate social interaction, foster emotional well-being, and guard against loneliness (Dykstra, 1995). Nearly 60 percent of the population aged 65 to 74 is married and lives with a spouse in an independent household. Significant differences exist, however, in living arrangements by gender and age. Because of women's longer life expectancy, higher rates of widowhood, and fewer options for remarriage, only +3 percent aged 65 and older are married and living with a spouse, as compared to 75 percent of men (NIA, 2001; U.S. Census Bureau, 2003) (see Figure 9.2). Marital status affects living arrangements and the

*Less research has been conducted on gay and lesbian partners, but is discussed on pages 315–318. Although we use the term *partner* where relevant, in some instances data are only available on married heterosexual couples.

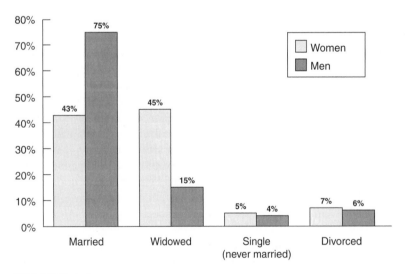

FIGURE 9.2 **Marital Status of Persons 65+**
SOURCE: AOA, 2002.

nature of caregiving that is readily available in case of illness. Accordingly, women represent 80 percent of the older individuals who live alone. Among noninstitutionalized older men, only about 17 percent are living without a partner, compared to 41 percent of their female counterparts. The percentages living with a spouse decline with age and among African Americans and Latinos, as illustrated in Figure 9.2 (AOA, 1999b). Those living alone typically have higher levels of depression, loneliness, and social isolation, and are more likely to use formal social services compared with those living with a partner (Mui and Burnette, 1994). Married people, especially men, are found to be healthier and to live longer than their nonmarried counterparts. They seem to benefit from the health promoters of social support, health monitoring, economic resources, and stress reduction. In fact, marital status appears to be related to physical and psychological health, life satisfaction, happiness, and well-being, although we can all think of exceptions to these associations (Connidis, 2001; Kulik, 1999; Miller, Hemesath, and Nelson, 1997; NIA, 2001).

Couples are faced with learning to adapt to changing roles and expectations throughout their relationship. Family life is characterized by a continual tension between maintaining individual autonomy and negotiating issues of equitable exchange, dependence, and safety. Such tensions are heightened in old age. As partners change roles through retirement, postparenthood, or illness, they face the strain of relinquishing previous roles, adapting to new ones, and experiencing accumulative losses. Failure to negotiate role expectations, such as the division of household tasks after retirement, can result in disagreements and divergent paths. Other challenges that aging partners face are connecting the past with the present, anticipatory mourning, coping with illness, and renegotiating relationships with their adult children (Mohr, 2000). Retirement can be an especially difficult transition, especially when partners

do not retire at the same time, or where marital satisfaction was already low before retirement. Couples typically experience changes in the emotional quality of their relationship, along with conflict over too much time together and the loss of personal space (Hilbourne, 1999; Smith and Moen, 1998). On the other hand, increased time together in shared activities and with friends during retirement can have favorable effects on marital satisfaction (Mohr, 2000).

Strains may be heightened by the fact that long-lived relationships are a contemporary phenomenon. At the end of the nineteenth century, the average length of marriage at the time one's spouse died was about 28 years; now it is over 45 years. Never before in history have the lives of so many couples remained interwoven long enough to encounter the variety of life-changing events that later stages of marriage now bring. Yet most older couples are more likely than younger cohorts to view marriage as a lifetime commitment governed by obligation.

Marital Satisfaction

Despite the challenges inherent in long-lived relationships, most older partners appear satisfied, with men tending to be more pleased with marriage and the degree to which their emotional needs are fulfilled than are women (Bogard and Spilka, 1996). Marital satisfaction has been found to be high among those recently married, lower among those in the childrearing period—especially in middle age—and higher in the later stages. In fact, the strongest predictor of marital satisfaction in later life tends to be the couple's level of satisfaction in the early stages of marriage. Older spouses, especially men, are more likely to report improvement in their marriages over time than younger couples. Although emotional intensity declines, positive interactions with less conflict and less negative sentiment such as sarcasm, disagreement, and criticism tend to increase (Goodman, 1999; Miller et al., 1997).

Increases in marital satisfaction among the young-old may be partially due to children leaving home. Contrary to stereotypes, most women are not depressed when their children leave home, but rather view the **empty nest** as an opportunity for new activities, although both fathers and mothers may initially be unhappy with the change. As noted in Chapter 6, sex-role expectations and behaviors are often relaxed in old age. Men tend to become more affectionate and less career-oriented, and women more achievement-oriented. Successful negotiation of such role changes appears to be related to marital satisfaction. Happy marriages are characterized by more equality and joint decision making through a gradual relaxation of boundaries between sex roles and a decreasing division of household labor based on traditional male/female sex roles (Bogard and Spilka, 1996). Nevertheless, some areas (e.g., dependent care and family finances) typically remain gender-differentiated (Miller and Cafasso, 1992). Freed from the demands of work and parental responsibilities, and with more opportunities for companionship, partners may discover or develop common interests and interdependence. As a consequence, expressive aspects of the marriage—affection and companionship— may emerge more fully (House, Mero, and Webster, 1996).

Older partners' ability to negotiate these role transitions depends, in large part, on their prior adaptability and satisfaction in their marital relationship. Studies of marital longevity have found that couples celebrating golden anniversaries (approximately 3 percent of all marriages) are characterized by intimacy, avoidance of hostile control, commitment, congruence of values, religious faith, communication, and an ability to accommodate one another (Goodman, 1999; Robinson and Blanton, 1993). Overall, the perceived rewards from being married appear to strongly influence marital satisfaction (Reynolds, 1995). For happily married older couples, their relationship is central to a "good life." As noted earlier, married persons appear to be happier and healthier, experience higher levels of self-esteem, make fewer demands on the health care system, and live longer than widowed or divorced persons of the same age (Goldman, Korenman, and Weinstein, 1995). In fact, marital satisfaction may be more important than age, health, life expectancy, education, or retirement in predicting life satisfaction and quality of life. These positive effects appear to emanate from three major functions that marriage performs for older couples: intimacy, interdependence, and a sense of belonging. Not surprisingly, unhappy marriages tend to affect health negatively, especially for women (Levenson, Cartensen, and Gottman, 1993).

Although most older couples have been together since young adulthood, a small proportion remarry after widowhood or divorce later in life. Women have fewer options to remarry, since they generally outlive their male peers, and men tend to marry women younger than themselves. The likelihood that widowed men will remarry is seven times greater than for widowed women (Connidis, 2001). Moreover, divorced people are more likely to remarry than are the widowed. Desire for companionship and having sufficient economic resources are central considerations in remarriage. A relationship with a partner appears to be of greater importance to men's well-being than to women's (Connidis, 2001). Most older people who remarry choose someone they have previously known, with similar backgrounds and interests. Factors that appear to be related to successful late-life remarriages are long prior friendship, family and friends' approval, adequate pooled financial resources, and personal adaptability to life changes. Some older couples choose to live together but not to marry, generally for economic and inheritance reasons.

Divorce in Old Age

Even though the majority of older marriages are reasonably happy, a small percentage is not, and an increasing proportion of older couples are choosing to divorce. The estimated 9 percent of

DATING IN OLD AGE

Divorce, widowhood, and increased life expectancy of adults who chose to remain single earlier in life have created growing numbers of single older adults engaged in a "dating game." As being single in later life is becoming the norm, the stigma of looking for a new partner is diminishing, although women still face more barriers than men. In fact, baby boomers, accustomed to dating services, personal ads, and Club Med singles vacations, are redefining dating and turning to creative ways to finding a partner. Already accustomed to the Internet for a range of services, they are comfortable with Internet dating services tailored to specific interests (adventure travel, hiking, science and nature, religious affiliation, environmental issues, vegetarianism, to name a few). Aware of the higher rate of divorce among remarried partners, older singles are often more interested in companionship—someone to do things with—than in marriage, especially when their children may be critical of potential partners.

SOURCE: AARP, 2003.

older adults who are divorced is almost double that of 1970 and demonstrates the growing acceptance of divorce as an option among all age groups. Rates are higher among ethnic minority older adults. The fact that the percentage divorced is higher for all age groups under age 65 than for those over age 65 indicates that more individuals in future cohorts will be divorced. Given the growing divorce rate in the baby boom cohort (age 45–54), as they reach age 65, the implications for the types of services provided by families and government are profound. The increase in the divorce rate affects all ages, both directly and indirectly in terms of the repercussions across generations (Connidis, 2001; NIA, 2001).

For both men and women, increasing age decreases the likelihood of remarriage following divorce, making rates of remarriage in old age relatively low (Cohen, 1999; Wu, 1998). As noted earlier, rates of remarriage are higher for men of all ages than for women. Socioeconomic status affects the chances of remarriage among divorced women but not divorced men. Women who remain divorced as they age are more likely to experience financial difficulties. The smaller pool of potential partners partially explains gender differences in remarriage; on the other hand, the desire to remarry tends to be lower among divorced women than those who are widowed. Such reluctance is probably related to past negative experiences with marriage (Choi, 1995, 1996). Being divorced in old age typically means economic hardships and diminished interactions with adult children for women; men tend to lose the "kin keeping" and intimacy functions performed by their wives and have less contact than women with their children and grandchildren. In fact, older divorced fathers typically do not consider their children as likely sources of support should they be in need. Generally, divorced mothers receive more advice, financial help, emotional support, and service provisions from their adult children than do divorced fathers. Among the estimated 75 percent of men and 60 percent of women who remarry across all ages, more than 40 percent are estimated to divorce again, creating complex stepfamily relationships among divorced adults in old age (Barrett and Lynch, 1999; Connidis, 2001).

Lesbian and Gay Partners

Although gerontological family research has traditionally focused on spouses in heterosexual couples, the concept of families in old age needs to be broadened to include gay men, lesbians, and transsexuals. The general invisibility of the old is heightened for those who are old and gay or lesbian. In fact, research on lesbian and gay aging is relatively new, and studies of aging transsexuals are rare. In addition, little attention has been given to the intersections of race, ethnicity, culture, and social class with sexual orientation in old age. Older lesbians also tend be ignored in research on women's health and younger lesbian health care.

Some studies suggest that the aging experience of gay men and lesbians is qualitatively different as a result of their sexual orientation and identity, in part because of a double stigma from the intersections of age and sexual orientation (Connidis, 2001; Gabbay and Wahler, 2002; Wojciechowski, 1998).

The majority of gay men and lesbians are part of a live-in couple at any one time (O'Brian and Goldberg). Whether lesbians and gay men are more concerned with age-associated changes in physical appearance is unclear (Adam, 1999, 2000; Bergeron and Senn, 1998; Calasanti and Slevin, 2001). Physical appearance among gay men is generally highly valued, with gay men often expressing dissatisfaction with the physical changes associated with the aging process. Lesbians who conform to cultural stereotypes of beauty for women may be at risk for more difficult transition to old age since they already bear an internal cultural stigma (Gabbay and Wahler, 2002; McDonald, 2001; Siever, 1994). On the other hand, intimate relationships may not be as strongly predicated on youth or youthful physical appearance as for heterosexual women. In such instances, older lesbians appear to demonstrate greater flexibility with regard to the age of potential intimates, thereby increasing the pool of possible partners (Wahler and Gabbay, 1997).

Older gay men and lesbians share concerns similar to other older adults—health, income, caregiving of older relatives, living arrangements—but what is unique is that they have lived the majority of their lives through historical periods actively hostile and oppressive toward homosexuality. Some older gay men and lesbians are concerned with "passing" or "being invisible" in a heterosexual society and only marginally accept their homosexuality. Coming out to family may be more difficult for members of ethnic minorities and for men who are working-class (Chapple, Kippas, and Smith, 1998; Connidis, 2001; Manalanson, 1996).

When the social and historical context is considered, the choice of some older lesbians and gay men to remain silent about their sexual orientation

More options are available today for gay men and lesbians who want to raise children.

is understandable. For example, older lesbians grew up in an era in which women were not supposed to be overtly sexual, much less coming out as a lesbian (Calasanti and Slevin, 2001). Both lesbians and gay men lived through historical periods where homosexuality was a reason to be placed in an institution for the mentally ill. For example, until 1973, homosexuality was classified as a mental illness by the American Psychiatric Association and was not removed from the *Diagnostic and Statistical Manual of Mental Disorders* (DSM) until 1986. In addition, they also lived through the McCarthy era, where subversion and homosexuality were linked (Fassinger, 1997). Unlike younger counterparts, older lesbians and gay men may not have benefited from antidiscrimination laws and supports for same-sex partners. In fact, they may even encounter ageism among younger lesbians and gay men and feel like outcasts, unwelcome to participate in the primarily youth-oriented gay community (Boxer, 1997; Calasanti and Slevin, 2001; Wojciechowski, 1998).

In addition, if gay men or lesbians reveal their sexual orientation later in life, they must integrate their past lives of children, friends, and other partners into the coming-out process. Yet they may be ostracized from children and family of origin at the stage when they most need support (Fullmer, 1995). They may also encounter insensitivity and, in some cases, hostility from health care providers. For example, the partners of those who are hospitalized or in a skilled nursing or assisted-living facility may be denied access to intensive care units and to medical records; staff may limit their visits and discourage expressions of affection (Cahill, South, and Spade, 2000) They also face legal and policy barriers. To illustrate, domestic partners do not qualify for benefits under the 1993 Family and Medical Leave Act. When a partner is hospitalized or institutionalized, if a durable power of attorney for health care is not in place, blood relatives, who may be unaware of or opposed to the relationship, can control visitation, treatment options, and discharge planning; they can completely exclude partners from decision-making and right to an inheritance (Wojciechowski, 1998). Fortunately, families are more accepting of gay and lesbian partners, as illustrated by groups such as Parents and Friends of Lesbians and Gays, which support families in the process of coming to terms with a family member's sexual orientation. In addition, same-sex partners' legislation in some states is gradually addressing some of the legal and health care barriers faced by earlier cohorts of gay men and lesbians.

On the other hand, lifelong marginalization because of sexual orientation may stimulate adaptive strategies to meet the challenges of aging, even while older gays and lesbians typically are constrained by social constructions of gender, sexual orientation, and age. A successful transition to one stigmatized status—being a lesbian or gay man—may contribute to future successful transition to another stigmatized status—being old (Gabbay and Wahler, 2002; Sharp, 1997). This may occur because old gay men and lesbians have learned psychological skills throughout their lives in managing their sexual orientation and dealing on a daily basis with their nontraditional roles.

Through the painful process of "coming out," or confronting legal, religious, and familial barriers, older lesbians and gay men often become stronger and more competent in adjusting to age-related changes, thereby buffering other normative age changes, such as friends and family moving away or dying. Throughout their lives they are less likely to have adhered to a traditional male-female division of labor of tasks; this increases their role flexibility in retirement and lays the foundation for greater financial security since both partners are likely to have been employed. Experiencing greater freedom and differentiation in gender-role definitions throughout their lives, gay men and lesbians tend to be more independent, nontraditional, and self-affirming and to adapt more readily to the role changes associated with aging than their heterosexual peers (Berger and Kelly, 1996; Connidis, 2001). On the other hand, carrying two stigmatized statuses (being lesbian or gay and old) may make old age more challenging (Connidis, 2001; Grossman, 1997). Nevertheless, older gay men and lesbians, especially among the young-old, generally emphasize positive aspects about aging, experience self-acceptance and self-esteem, and have satisfying long-term relationships (Wojciechowski, 1998; Fullmer, 1995).

By having confronted real or imagined loss of family support earlier in life, gays and lesbians are also less likely to assume that biological families, including their adult children, will provide for them in old age and more likely to plan for their own future security and care arrangements. Having learned self-reliance and other skills that serve them well in old age, they may more readily adjust to care tasks. Most gay men now approach old age having experienced multiple losses through deaths of friends and lovers to AIDS; their accumulated grief may paradoxically enhance their acceptance of other losses associated with age, including the loss of friends to help care for them.

Even though many older gay men and lesbians have children, they typically build a "surrogate family" through a strong mixed-age network of friends and significant others, which either complements or replaces family of origin supports (Calasanti and Slevin, 2001; Dorfman et al., 1995; Kimmel, 1995). In effect, they create "friendship families or a family of choice (Dorfman et al., 1995; Berger and Kelly, 1996). In fact, lesbians connected to at least one significant friendship/relationship generally experience an adaptive response to aging (Gabbay and Wahler, 2002; Sharp, 1997). Some gay men and lesbians share innovative housing arrangements and are surrounded by empowering communities that include social support and advocacy organizations. These include Senior Action in a Gay Environment (SAGE) based in New York City, The Lavender Panthers, and the National Association of Lesbian and Gay Gerontologists organized by the American Society on Aging. SAGE, for example, has chapters nationwide that sponsors intergenerational friendly visitors' service, housing and legal advocacy, professional counseling, as well as SAGE Net, a consortium of groups offering similar services around the nation (Yoakam, 1997). Those who have such support through informal networks, social organizations, and housing alternatives tend to be characterized by high self-esteem and life satisfaction, less fear of aging, and greater effectiveness in managing the societal aspects of aging (Slusher, Mayer, and Dunkle, 1996).

CARE NETWORKS OF OLDER LESBIANS

A group of seven lesbians with varying backgrounds took turns taking care of an 84-year-old, terminally ill, single lesbian, providing transport to medical appointments and leisure activities, coordinating the access to needed services, and talking with her about her life, politics, and dying. The primary physician, a woman with a specialty in geriatrics, became part of the network by responding to calls from the group, making home visits, and supporting their role as caregivers. As death neared, one year later than expected, the woman made arrangements to die where and how she wanted.

Health care providers need to be sensitive and avoid assumptions that all older adults are heterosexual. Assessment, psychosocial histories, and care planning practices all need to recognize that older partners may have distinctive needs related to their sexual orientation. Staff committed to enhancing the quality of life in long-term care settings also need to advocate for nonhomophobic policies and practices that allow older gay and lesbian partners to be together and to participate in critical end of life decisions.

Sibling Relationships

Sibling relationships represent the one family bond with the potential to last a lifetime. Under contemporary mortality conditions, most persons will not experience the death of a sibling until they are past 70 years of age (Uhlenberg, 1996). About 80 percent of older people have at least one sibling, and about 33 percent see a sibling monthly, although yearly visits are most typical. The likelihood of having a sibling in old age has increased most dramatically over the past 100 years (Uhlenberg, 1996). As with other kin-keeping responsibilities, sisters are more likely than brothers to maintain frequent contact with same-sex siblings, generally by phone or face-to-face interaction rather than by letter writing (Cicirelli, 1995; Connidis, 2001; Connidis and Campbell, 1995).

The sibling relationship in old age is characterized by a shared history, egalitarianism, and increasing closeness, particularly among sisters. Studies based on the criterion of feelings of closeness and affection suggest that siblings often renew past ties as they age, forgive past conflict and rivalry, and become closer, frequently through shared reminiscence (Adams and Blieszner, 1995; Bengtson et al., 1996; Cicirelli, 1995). Siblings are particularly important sources of psychological support in the lives of never-married older persons and those without children, although their ability to provide support declines with age (Barrett and Lynch, 1999). Given these ties, it is not surprising

POINTS TO PONDER

If you have a brother or sister, try to imagine what your relationship will be like in old age. If you are an only child, have you created other networks that might support you as you grow older?

that some studies have found that bereaved siblings were more impaired and rated their overall health as worse than bereaved spouses or friends who were similarly impaired (Hays, Gold, and Peiper, 1997). Assistance generally increases after a spouse's death; such arrangements help enhance the widowed person's psychological well-being. Although siblings are less frequently caregivers to each other than are spouses and adult children (with the exception of caring for the never-married), they do supplement the efforts of others during times of crisis or special need. The very existence of siblings as a possible source of help may be important, even if such assistance is rarely used (Cicirelli, 1995).

The steadily increasing rate of divorce and remarriage will undoubtedly affect sibling relationships. With the increase in blended families through remarriage, there will be more half-siblings and step-siblings. For divorced older people who do not remarry, interactions with siblings may become more important than when they were married (Goldscheider, 1994). The sibling relationship is also important to gay men and lesbians in old age, presuming their siblings have accepted differences in sexual orientation (Connidis, 2001).

Never-Married Older People

Approximately 4 percent of the older population has never married (Connidis, 2001). Contrary to a commonly held image of loneliness and isolation, the majority of never-married older persons typically develop reciprocal relationships with other kin, especially siblings, and with friends and neighbors. While living alone in old age has sometimes been interpreted as a risk factor, it may instead indicate good health, emotional well-being, and social integration. Accustomed to living independently, they are not necessarily lonely or isolated in old age. Similarly, co-residence with younger generations in itself tells little about the quality of interhousehold relationships and life satisfaction, suggesting the need to be cautious in assumptions made about preferable living arrangements in old age (Connidis, 2001; Dykstra, 1995; NIA, 2001).

Because never-married adults typically have had lifelong employment, they tend to enjoy greater financial security in old age. In addition, they may be more socially active and resourceful, with more diversity in their social networks—especially more interactions with younger person, friends, neighbors, and siblings—than their married counterparts. This pattern of greater social and economic resilience tends to differentiate never-married women from their married, divorced or widowed counterparts. Compared with widowed peers, they tend to be more satisfied with their lives, self-reliant, and focused on the present. When they do need assistance from others, they are more likely to turn to siblings, friends, neighbors, and paid helpers than are their married peers (Barrett and Lynch, 1999; Dykstra, 1995; Tennstedt, 1999).

Organizations specifically for single people are growing, although many of these are for younger singles. Alternative living arrangements, such as cross-generational home-sharing programs and assisted living facilities, may appeal to single older adults who choose not to live alone. The proportion of single older adults is likely to increase in the future, because singlehood is increasingly common at earlier life stages, especially among African Americans (Connidis, 2001).

Childless Older Adults

Although the vast majority of older people have living children, approximately 20 percent, who married in the Depression and post-Depression

THE REALITIES OF AGING FAMILIES

- The family is the primary source of support for older people.
- Most older people have family members.
- Most older people, especially elders of color, live in a community-based family setting.
- Multigenerational (4 and 5 generations) families are growing.
- The number of blended families is increasing.
- The range of alternative family structures is expanding, broadening our definition of family.
- Spouses/partners are the most important family relationship.
- Spouses are the primary family caregivers, followed by adult children.
- Sibling relationships increase in importance with age.
- Never-married and childless older adults are not necessarily lonely, unhappy, or dissatisfied.
- Intergenerational relationships tend to be reciprocal.

years, are childless. As a result, they lack the natural support system of children and grandchildren. For childless elders, relatives are most important for performing instrumental tasks, while friends typically give emotional support. When faced with health problems, childless elders turn first to their partners/spouses (if available) for support, then to siblings, then nieces and nephews. They also have a higher probability of illness, living alone, and limited emotional support. Given these factors, it is not surprising that unmarried childless elders utilize services and nursing homes more than do married childless persons (Connidis, 2001; Wu and Pollard, 1998).

On the other hand, some childless unmarried older people, particularly women, develop kin-like or "sisterly" nonkin relations and may be quite satisfied with their lives. Yet they may not want these relationships to be a source of care, fearing the change of voluntary mutuality into dependency (Wu and Pollard, 1998). The number of childless and unmarried older individuals is likely to grow, which may affect the proportion of older people who will seek both formal and informal supports in the future.

Other Kin

Interaction with secondary kin—cousins, aunts, uncles, nieces, and nephews—appears to depend on geographic proximity, availability of closer relatives, and preference. Extended kin can replace or substitute for missing or lost relatives, especially during family rituals and holidays. For example, compared to their white counterparts, African American childless elders often turn to nieces and nephews when siblings are not available. Personal or historical connections that allow for remembering pleasurable events may be more important than closeness of kinship in determining interactions.

Intergenerational Relationships: Adult Children

After spouses, adult children are the most important source of informal support and social contact in old age. Typically, the flow of support is not unidirectional from adult child to older parent, but rather exchanges are reciprocal (Silverstein, Conroy, Wang, and Giarrusso, 2002; Velkoff and Lawson, 1998). Over 80 percent of persons age 65 and over have surviving children, although the number of children in a family has decreased—a trend expected to continue. The majority of older adults live near at least one adult child, sharing a social life but not a home (Connidis, 2001). Most older people state that they prefer not to live with their children, generally for reasons of privacy and a sense of autonomy. Although less than 20 percent of older persons live in their children's households, this percentage increases with advancing age and extent of functional disability, and for widowed, separated, and divorced older adults. Approximately 33 percent of all men and 50 percent of all women age 65 and over who are widowed, separated, or divorced share a home with their children or other family members. Some research identifies that most older adults prefer to live with their children to avoid a nursing home, although children are less willing than their parents to share a residence. When older parents do live with their children, they usually live with a daughter (Boaz et al., 1999). However, less than 14 percent of those age 65 to 75 and 4 percent of those age 85 and older live in multigenerational households composed of parents, children, and grandchildren (Connidis, 2001). These percentages are higher, however, among some families of color, especially African Americans (Dilworth-Anderson et al., 2002).

Although most older parents and adult children do not live together, they nevertheless see each other frequently. Studies over the past two decades indicate the following:

- Approximately 50 percent of older people have daily contact with adult children.
- Nearly 80 percent see an adult child at least once a week.
- More than 75 percent talk on the phone at least weekly with an adult child (AOA, 2002; Bengtson et al., 1996).

Older children, especially daughters, are more likely to maintain contact with their parents. However, gender and age are less important than proximity and socioeconomic status, with more frequent contact among higher-income families (Greenwald and Bengtson, 1995). Less is known about the quality than about the frequency of interactions between older parents and their adult children. Nevertheless, most intergenerational relationships involve some types of conflict, with parents concerned about their children's habits and lifestyle choices, and children noting differences in communication and interaction styles. Despite such widely occurring conflicts, most intergenerational families report affection and mutual support and a desire for more satisfying relationships with each other. This reflects the paradoxical nature of family relationships over the life course in which solidarity and conflict fluctuate (Clarke et al., 1999).

Geographic separation of family members is generally due to mobility of the adult children, not of the older relatives. Future cohorts of older persons may have an increasing proportion of distant children because of the growing trend toward greater residential separation between adult children and older parents. For many families, holidays may be the only times adult children return home; and these special occasions often have to be distributed among in-laws, step-in-laws and other complex family arrangements. Older parents who live closer to their children have more contact with them, greater affection for them, and are more involved with grandchildren, although geographic separation does not necessarily weaken socioemotional bonds and "intimacy at a distance" can occur (Silverstein and Angelelli, 1998). Older parents expect to move closer to an adult child out of need (poor health, living alone, adult child who is financially better-off than they are) and tend to select the child with the greatest potential to provide support (most often the oldest daughter). Mental health professionals and health care providers need to recognize how each generation faces its own developmental transitions as well as complex cross-generational issues (Hargrave and Hanna, 1997).

Patterns of Intergenerational Assistance

Generally, families establish a pattern of reciprocal support between older and younger members that continues throughout an individual's lifetime. Consistent with social exchange theory discussed in Chapter 8, those with more valued resources (e.g., money or good health) assist those with less. Not only concrete assistance is exchanged, but also emotional and **social support.** At various points, older parents provide substantial support, especially financial assistance, to their children and grandchildren, oftentimes at a geographic distance. Regardless of socioeconomic status, most **intergenerational transfers** of resources, especially of knowledge and financial support, go from parent to child (Silverstein et al., 2002). On the other hand, adult children who are not married and generally have fewer financial resources than married peers are more likely to transfer resources to parents (Boaz et al., 1999). Contrary to stereotypes, however, most adult children are not motivated by the expectation of an inheritance when they assist their older parents (Sloan, Picone, and Hoerger, 1997).

In some instances, parents continue to provide care to adult children beyond normative expectations of "launching" one's adult children to be more independent. For example, parental care remains a central role late in life for parents of adult children who are developmentally disabled or chronically mentally ill. Yet many parents who are caregivers of adult children with disabilities are facing their own age-related limits in functional ability, energy, and financial resources, which can affect their ability to provide care. The history of and the cumulative nature of care demands can make their situation particularly stressful (Kelly and Kropf, 1995; Smith, Tobin, and Fullmer, 1995). A major worry is how their child will be cared for after their own deaths or if they themselves develop a debilitating illness. Despite their worry, most such caregiving parents do not make concrete long-term plans about where their children will eventually live (Freedman, Krauss, and Seltzer, 1997). Not surprisingly, when parental caregivers die, their adult children with mental disorders often experience housing disruptions and potentially traumatic transitions (Lefley and Hatfield, 1999). As the population of adults with chronic illness or developmental disabilities grows, both the aging and developmentally disabled service networks are initiating new support systems. These include respite care, more residential alternatives, and assistance with permanency planning (e.g., developing plans for permanent housing in the community) (Kelly and Kropf, 1995). Fortunately, the Planned Lifetime Assistance Network (PLAN) is now available in

some states through the National Alliance for the Mentally Ill. PLAN provides lifetime assistance to individuals with disabilities whose parents or other family members are deceased or can no longer provide care (Lefley and Hatfield, 1999).

Grandparenthood and Great-Grandparenthood

At the turn of the twentieth century, three-generation families were rare. Now, with increased life expectancy, more older people are experiencing the role of grandparenthood and, increasingly, of great-grandparenthood, although they have proportionately fewer grandchildren than preceding generations. Of the 80 percent of older parents, 94 percent are grandparents and nearly 50 percent are great-grandparents. Women may experience grandmotherhood for more than 40 years (Giarrusso, Silverstein, and Bengtson, 1996). This is because the transition to grandparenthood typically occurs in middle age, not old age, with about 50 percent of all grandparents under the age of 60 (Szinovacz, 1998). As a result, there is wide diversity among grandparents, who vary in age from their late 30s to over 100 years old, with grandchildren ranging from newborns to retirees.

The grandchild experience is another way of grasping the significance of increased life expectancy and years spent in grandparenting. It is estimated that 96 percent of all persons have at least one grandparent alive when they reach age 20. Similarly, over 66 percent of adult children began their lives with all grandparents living, and more than 75 percent have at least one grandparent alive when they reach age 30 (Uhlenberg and Kirby, 1998). Contrary to common images, the grandparent-grandchild emotional and social interaction in later life is typically with adolescents and young adults, not with young children. Young adults who are busy with their own families and careers, however, are typically not major sources of instrumental support for the oldest-old, such as help with activities of daily living (ADL).

The vast majority of grandparents do not live with grandchildren, but 80 percent see an adult grandchild at least monthly and nearly 50 percent see a grandchild weekly. Geographic proximity is the major factor determining frequency of visits. On the other hand, geographic distance does not affect the quality of the grandchild-grandparent relationship, and many grandparents travel considerable distances for frequent visits to see their grandchildren (Davies and Williams, 2002). Parents primarily determine the degree of interaction when grandchildren are young. Frequency of contact and expectation of closeness tend to decline as grandchildren become older, especially if disrupted by divorce of either the grandparents or parents. However, some young adult grandchildren, especially granddaughters, express more affection toward their grandparents as they age. Relationships tend to be closest between grandmothers and granddaughters, particularly when the two generations are geographically near (Dubas, 2001).

Given the wide diversity among a phase of the life span that can encompass more than 40 years, there are multiple grandparenting roles and meanings. Age of the grandparent/grandchild and life course position, frequency of contact, and parental influences all affect the extent of satisfaction that grandparents derive from the role (Peterson, 1999). Early research found the role to be peripheral, and not a primary source of identity, meaning, or satisfaction (Neugarten, 1964; Wood and Robertson, 1976). The prime significance of grandparenthood was reported to be biological renewal and/or continuity (e.g., seeing oneself extended into the future) and emotional self-fulfillment, especially the opportunity to be a better grandparent than parent. In terms of style, older grandparents were more apt to be formal and distant, whereas younger ones emphasized mutuality, informality, and playfulness. Surprisingly, about 30 percent did not derive satisfaction

from the role, describing it as difficult, disappointing, and unpleasant. Satisfaction tended to be higher among grandmothers than grandfathers, however (Neugarten, 1964; Neugarten and Weinstein, 1964).

More recent research concludes that grandparents derive great emotional satisfaction from frequent interaction with their grandchildren and from the opportunity to observe their grandchildren's development and share in their activities. They want to have an influence on their grandchildren, typically to encourage high moral standards, integrity, a commitment to succeed, and religious beliefs and values (Davies and Williams, 2002; Silverstein and Marenco, 2001). Age influences the types of grandparent-grandchild interactions, with younger grandparents generally living closer and having frequent contact through child care and shared recreational activities; while older grandparents provide financial assistance and more strongly identify with the role (Silverstein and Marenco, 2001). These age differences may shift, however, as baby boom grandparents remain employed longer or choose to travel more during retirement than past cohorts. These emerging trends influence the number of older adults who learn to use the Internet so they can communicate electronically when they cannot do so in person. Overall, grandparenthood provides opportunities for older adults to experience feelings of immortality, relive their lives through their grandchildren, indulge them with unconditional love, and develop an increased sense of well-being and morale (Peterson, 1999; Strom, Buki, and Strom, 1997). The box on page 324 illustrates the diversity of grandparenting styles.

The **intergenerational stake hypothesis** refers to a pattern whereby the older generation tends to be more invested in imbuing future generations with the values they hold dear, and therefore are more committed to relationships with younger generations. In contrast, younger generations, as a whole, place a higher value on establishing autonomy from older generations and thus report lower

STYLES OF GRANDPARENTING

Companionate, Friend, or Apportionate Style

Grandparent feels close and affectionate to grand-children without taking on a particular role; gives advice informally, talks about family history, serves as confidant and occasionally indulges the grandchild.

Remote Style

Grandparent is less involved, often because of geographic distance.

Involved Style

Grandparent is geographically close; often assumes parent-like responsibilities in response to a family crisis (e.g., separation or divorce).

Individualized Style

This grandparent is emotionally closer than the remote grandparent, but does not contribute substantially to the lives of grandchildren.

Authoritative or Influential

Grandparents, typically grandmothers, provide extensive support, sometimes assuming parental responsibilities; tends to characterize African American families.

SOURCE: Adapted from Davies and Williams, 2002; Cherlin and Furstenberg, 1986; Roberto and Stroes, 1995.

levels of intergenerational solidarity (Giarrusso, Stallings, and Bengtson, 1995). Congruent with exchange theory described in Chapter 8, this differential stake may reflect the greater investment by older generations in raising younger generations and the fact that grandparents view their relationship with their grandchildren as closer and more positive than do the grandchildren. On the other hand, grandchildren may perceive the relationship as an active, supportive one and less authoritative than their relation with their parents. For the most part, young adult children, whose relationship with their grandparents is no longer mediated by their parents, perceive their grandparents as "help-

ing them out" and a sign of their emotional investment in and support of their relationship (Harwood, 2001). When young adults develop open communication patterns with their grandparents—telling stories, mutual self-disclosure, chatting on the phone—both grandparents and grandchildren recognize the mutual benefits of their relationship.

Gender also influences grandparenting. Typically, grandfathers are most closely linked to sons of sons, and grandmothers to daughters of daughters. Grandmothers and grandfathers both report aiding and being interested in grandchildren, but grandmothers generally emphasize closeness, open communication, interpersonal issues, warmth and fun (e.g., an expressive approach), while grandfathers place greater emphasis on their role as advisors (e.g., an instrumental approach). Maternal grandparents tend to have closer relations with their grandchildren than paternal grandparents, reflecting the greater bond of mothers than fathers to their parents. Grandparents, in turn, are generally closer to their granddaughters than to their grandsons (Chan and Elder, 2000; Connidis, 2001; Silverstein and Long, 1998).

Some studies suggest greater interactions though an extended kin network and more grandparent responsibility for childrearing among ethnic minorities. The authoritative or influential style found among some African American families is described above. In Asian immigrant families, grandparents who provide child care help support the family's economic success. Mexican American families tend to be characterized by strong grandparent-grandchild ties, with the flow of financial assistance generally from the older to young generations (Dietz, 1995). Regardless of ethnic minority status, more grandparents are becoming involved in childrearing as a consequence of poverty, teen pregnancy, substance abuse, AIDS, incarceration, emotional problems, and parental death. Historically, grandparent-grandchildren relationships were characterized by norms of non-interference, with grandparents as-

Grandparents as primary caregivers for grandchildren is a growing phenomenon.

suming only occasional or short term responsibility in responding to emergencies. The dramatic increase in the number of grandparents as primary caregivers to grandchildren reflects a profound shift in this pattern (Davies and Williams, 2002).

Grandparents as Custodial Caregivers of Grandchildren

Grandparents and other extended family members have traditionally provided care for grandchildren across families of color and in many other counties (Cox, 2002; Pruchno, 1999). Such care provided by fictive kin in three-generation households was often in addition to parental care or to support the young parents while they worked outside the home. What has changed in the past two decades is the rapid growth of grandparents (or great-grandparents) who are the primary or sole caregivers for grandchildren because their adult sons or daughters are unable or unwilling to provide care. In fact, such **skipped-generation households**

are currently the fastest growing type in the United States (Force et al., 2000; Kelley et al., 2000; Wallace, 2001). Skipped generation refers to the absence of the parental generation; this structure is also referred to as "downward extended households." At the same time, the number of children living in a home with both a parent and grandparent present has declined (Casper and Bianchi, 2002; Szinovacz, 1998).

Approximately 5 percent of all children live in grandparent-headed households; of these, an estimated 30 percent are in such households without either of their parents for more than 6 months at a time and where grandparents have assumed sole care responsibility. Although this phenomenon crosscuts social class, race, and ethnicity, African American children are six times more likely to live in a skipped-generation household than their white counterparts. Approximately 4 percent of Caucasian children, 6.5 percent of Latino, and 13.5 percent of African American children lived with grandparents or other relatives in 1997 (Lugaila, 1998).

Being an unmarried older woman and African American are risk factors for being a primary caregiver. More than 10 percent of grandparents raise a grandchild for at least 6 months, but typically for far longer periods, in some cases for more than a decade. Of these, about 30 percent of African American grandparents assume primary care responsibility at some point in their lives (Bryson and Casper, 1999; Casper and Bryson, 1998; Fuller-Thomson, Minkler, and Driver, 1997; Minkler, 1999). Although national studies indicate that the majority of sole grandparent caregivers are white, Latinos and African Americans are disproportionately represented, given their percentage of the total population. Other relatives (aunts, siblings), who provide similar amounts of care as do grandparents, distinguish Latino households from other ethnic groups. Latino caregivers also face the additional burden of anti-immigration sentiments and their legal manifestations, making them less likely to seek help with their care tasks even if they are legal immigrants (Burnette, 1999a; Harden, Clarke, and Maguire, 1997; Minkler, 1999).

FACTORS ASSOCIATED WITH THE INCREASE IN GRAND-PARENT CAREGIVING   One factor underlying the dramatic increase in grandparent caregivers is a 2003 Supreme Court decision which upheld a lower court's decision that federal foster care benefits could not be denied to relatives who were otherwise eligible. This resulted in the practice of **kinship care**—the formal (as opposed to the widespread occurrence of informal) placement of children with relatives. The majority of states now require that preference be given to relatives for placement of foster children. Federal and state laws and policies, however, promoting kinship care do not explain the concomitant growth in the number of informal arrangements of children living with grandparents (Harden et al., 1997; Minkler, 1999). In fact, a primary reason that grandparents assume the care role, typically well before any custody relationship is established, is their fear that a grandchild will be placed in foster care; this pattern suggests that the liberalization of benefits for formal relative caregivers through foster care does not explain the dramatic increase occurring in informal placements with relatives. Contrary to conservative arguments that grandparent caregivers are taking in grandchildren for financial gain, it appears that caring for grandchildren typically exacerbates already difficult economic circumstances. Even if grandparents do qualify for foster kinship care payments, they may experience delay, eligibility problems, and other difficulties trying to access it (Jendrek, 1994; Minkler, 1999).

Rather than any financial motivation, the predominant factors underlying increased grandparent caregiving are the parents' drug and alcohol abuse, especially the cocaine epidemic, the AIDS epidemic, unemployment, divorce, incarceration, teen pregnancy, and the rise in single-parent households. It is important to note that all of these factors are tied in fundamental ways to the continued problem of poverty in our nation. Policy changes to address the factors contributing to the rise in skipped-generation households cannot be made without a commitment to confronting the underlying causes of poverty (Haglund, 2000; Minkler, 1999).

THE GAINS AND COSTS OF CARE   As with care responsibility across the life span, women predominate in the primary caring role, and experience both gains and costs. Although some grandparents enjoy emotional closeness with grandchildren as well as pride and empowerment from assisting their grandchildren in crisis and feelings of being needed from caregiving (e.g., keeping the "family together and out of foster care"), they also experience significant costs (Baydar and Brooks-Gunn, 1998; Casper and Bryson, 1998; Haglund, 2000; Pruchno, 1999).

The economic costs are greatest. As many as 50 percent of grandparent caregivers are living on a limited income and are not employed, even though the majority are young-old or even middle aged (45–64 years of age) and therefore not the typical retirement age (Casper and Bryson, 1998; Minkler, 1999; Szinovacz, 1998; Woodworth, 1996). Those who are employed may need to reduce their hours or quit their jobs in order to care for their grandchild. Others may not suffer a decline in income caused by caregiving, but nevertheless perceive a need for a higher income to cover basic costs entailed in raising a child, such as day care, clothing, food, sports, and special occasions. Such financial stress can exacerbate other types of distress, including depression. Grandparents who are sole caregivers are found to have higher levels of psychological distress compared with those who provide only supplemental care to grandchildren, and this distress, including depression, increases when they are caring for grandchildren with behavior or emotional problems. They also tend to rate their health poorly, experience multiple chronic health problems, and avoid seeking care for themselves, especially for mental or emotional health problems (Bowers and

Myers, 1999; Burnette, 1999a, 1999b, 2000; Hayslip et al., 1998; Minkler and Fuller-Thomson, 1997; Musil, 2000; Roe, Minkler, Sauners, and Thomson, 1996). These problems tend to be magnified for grandparents who are raising a chronically ill or "special needs" child, who comprise a high percentage given the past traumatic circumstances faced by many grandchildren in skipped-generation households (Trute, 2003).

INFORMAL AND FORMAL SUPPORTS Grandparent caregivers are often lonely and lacking informal networks. About 30 percent of grandmother caregivers are not married and therefore lack a confidant's support. The non-normative nature of grandparent caregiving coupled with embarrassment and shame about their adult children's inability to care for their own children can intensify feelings of loneliness and loss (Casper and Bryston, 1998; Bryshon and Casper, 1999; Burnette, 1999b; Emick and Hayslip, 1996; Giarrusso, Silverstein, and Feng, 2000; Kelley et al., 2000). When adult children are incarcerated, drug addicted, or mentally ill, this is described as being "present but not present." Grandparents may grieve the loss of the adult children whom they knew (Morrow-Kondos et al., 1997; Waldrop and Weber, 2000). Regardless of the reasons for this placement, most grandparents experience disappointment, shame, resentment, and guilt over their failure as parents who produced an adult child who could relinquish their children. In this manner, grandparents may experience loss of identity and self-esteem as "good parents." Society may reinforce this negative self-judgment because of common misconceptions of grandmothers as nondeserving poor, especially among those who hold grandmothers responsible for their adult children's problems; (e.g., "they could not have been good parents or their children would not have turned out the way they did" (Minkler, 1999).

Despite these losses, most grandparents assume the role willingly, often acting out of a deep sense of duty and obligation (Jendrek, 1994; Testa and Slack, 2002). Their grandchildren, however,

may be embarrassed by having an older relative caring for them, and may repeatedly long for their parents, further intensifying the grandparent's sense of loss. Grandparents may try to appear to be the parent in public settings, such as schools, as a way to increase the probability of support from others, typically younger parents. What can be especially painful is when other family members and peers pull away and fail to help out, intensifying feelings of alienation, isolation, and loneliness (Minkler and Roe, 1993; Szolnoki and Cahn, 2003). Such feelings are often worse among those who assumed the care role because of their adult child's substance abuse, incarceration, or AIDS. Losses are exacerbated by the lack of rewards or public recognition for the hard work of caregiving. In fact, some grandmothers seek to hide their important work by pretending that they are the child's mother, asking the child and others to call them "mother."

Other losses that intensify grandparent distress encompass the loss of retirement time or income anticipated in the child-free time of old age, dreams about their family and their life as an older adult, and envying friends who pursue their leisure instead of being constrained by child care responsibilities. Providing care may interfere with their need to achieve their own developmental tasks associated with age-related losses (Burnette, 1999b).

Some grandparents may experience the cumulative effects of lifelong structural inequities due to race, gender, or disability, exacerbating the challenges they face as primary caregivers, as illustrated in the box on page 328. To outsiders, grandparent caregivers may be invisible, largely because of their age and gender (e.g., most are women), even though they may be the primary caregivers for the majority of their grandchild's life. Service systems, such as public child welfare, community mental health, and the public schools, are not prepared to work effectively with grandparents or to recognize the losses faced by the grandchild (Wallace, 2001). The Temporary Assistance for Needy Families Program (TANF),

CHALLENGES FACING GRANDPARENT CAREGIVERS

In Washington state, a 56-year-old woman who is blind cares for her severely disabled 13-year-old grandson, who was violently shaken, struck, and thrown as a baby, suffering brain damage that left him with cerebral palsy and unable to walk, talk, drink, or eat solid food. Blind since age 16, she relies on Braille, a guide dog, and a few close friends to try to provide as full a life as possible for him. A case aid provides some daily assistance and can drive the teenager to school and other activities, but has an old, unreliable car. She survives on disability for both herself and her grandson, which does not cover additional costs entailed by the intensity of level of care that she must provide. Both grandmother and grandson dreamed of owning a van so that friends could drive him to sports events, church, and other activities that bring some joy into both his grandmother and his lives. Fortunately, after her moving story ran in the *Seattle Times,* local contributors helped them realize their dream of an accessible van.

under the 1996 Personal Responsibility Act that replaced Aid to Families with Dependent Children (AFDC), requires that teen mothers can only receive benefits by living with their parents and being in school and/or having a job. An unintended consequence of this policy change is an increase in grandparents becoming primary caregivers for their grandchildren born to teenage parents. The employment requirements and 5-year lifetime benefit limits of TANF create obstacles for grandparents in accessing services and financial support through the welfare system. (Minkler, Berrick, and Needell, 1999). Most grandparents do not qualify for TANF benefits. Although foster care payments are higher than welfare benefits, grandparents can qualify for such payments only by transferring custody of the children to the state. In other words, they cede their own parental authority and become "foster parents" to their own grandchildren. When kinship caregivers receive a foster payment, it tends to be less than what licensed fos-

ter parents who are biologically unrelated receive. Some studies suggest that the state's reliance on kinship caregivers for low- or no-cost out-of-home placements results in an inequitable burden on informal support systems (Burnette, 1999a; Smith, 2000).

Fortunately, child welfare policy makers are now recognizing the need to develop services to support grandparent sole caregivers outside the traditional foster care or TANF programs. Education and support groups as well as Internet resources have proliferated, but the major need is economic. Advocates for kinship care providers

GRANDPARENTS AS CAREGIVERS

Mary long ago earned her stripes as a mom. She raised five children alone, in a tough Los Angeles neighborhood, and managed to put them through college or vocational training. She had looked forward to retirement and being a loving grandmother, to spoiling her grandchildren on visits and then sending them home. But her life has not turned out as expected. Instead, she's raising her 8-year-old grandson, James, alone, since the incarceration of her daughter and the boy's father for selling drugs.

When Mary's daughter was charged for possession of drugs, Mary could not bear the thought of her grandson being raised by strangers in the foster care system. She petitioned the courts to become his guardian. Her daughter has only contacted her son twice in the past four years. This has made the adjustment difficult for Mary and James, who often lashes out at his grandmother. Mary tries to provide as much love and stability for him as possible, helping him with his homework, assisting with his Cub Scout troop, and attending all his school events. She derives some emotional rewards from these activities with James, but misses activities with her peers. Many of her friends have dropped away, as they have more freedom to "take off and do things." She also struggles with guilt about her daughter and her situation. She has turned her anger and grief into organizing local support groups for others like herself and pressuring legislators to recognize caregiving grandparents' needs.

> ### CHALLENGES FOR GRANDPARENTS IN RAISING THEIR GRANDCHILDREN
>
> **Legal**
>
> - Guardianship and custody, which provide parental authority to grandparents, but allow parental visitation rights
> - Adoption, which gives grandparents all authority
> - Foster parenthood
>
> **Financial**
>
> - Temporary Assistance for Needy Families (TANF)
> - Food stamps
> - Supplemental Security Income (SSI)
> - Public housing/age-segregated retirement communities
> - Foster care payment
> - Adoption assistance
>
> **Child Care (day care, preschool, babysitters)**
>
> **Medical insurance**
>
> - Medicaid but not Medicare
> - Private insurance
>
> **Schooling**
>
> - Public schooling
> - Testing evaluation
> - Remedial education
>
> **Psychological/emotional challenges for the child (grief, loss, confusion, anger)**
>
> **Psychological/emotional challenges for the grandparent**
>
> - Grief and loss
> - Stress
> - Parent education and support groups

maintain that, at a minimum, grandparents should receive full foster care rates as well as other benefits accorded to unrelated foster parents, and should have the possibility of kinship adoption with federal subsidies for low-income families (Berrick and Needell, 1998; Berrick, Needell, and Barth, 1998). As noted by Weinberg (1998), "It may be true that it takes a village to raise a child, but if children, the poor and the elderly are not to be confined to the ghettoes of that village, the community as a unit needs to recognize the value of caregiving" (p. 270). An area for further multigenerational research and practice is to understand the needs of the "invisible" middle generation of parents who are unwilling or unable to raise their offspring and how this affects cross-generational exchanges across a family's life cycle. The lack of attention to this middle generation reflects in part our societal values on who.is "deserving" of public benefits (Minkler, 1999). Social workers in child welfare settings, schools, and senior centers can play pivotal roles in providing education and support to grandparental caregivers as well as advocating on their behalf for economic resources.

Great-Grandparents

More recently, the role of great-grandparent has emerged with increasing frequency. There appear to be two predominant styles of performing this role. The most common, which tends to characterize generations separated by physical distance, is remote, involving only occasional and somewhat ritualistic contact on special occasions such as holidays and birthdays. Despite the remote nature of contacts, however, great-grandparents derive considerable emotional satisfaction and a sense of personal and familial renewal from seeing a fourth generation as representing family continuity. Living long enough to be a great-grandparent is viewed as a positive sign of successful aging or longevity. The other common great-grandparenting style occurs when great-grandparents are geographically close (within 25 miles) to the fourth generation, and thus have frequent opportunities for emotional closeness to great-grandchildren as well. Even great-grandparents who are in their seventies and eighties may serve as babysitters, go shopping, and take trips with their great-grandchildren. These activities provide diversions in their lives and can lead to renewed zeal. Such positive interactions will undoubtedly be more common in the future, when great-grandparenthood is the norm and the oldest-old generations are healthier than current cohorts. Consistent with the reciprocal nature of most intergenerational relationships, growing numbers of grandchildren care for great-grandparents (Roberto, 1990).

The Effects of Divorce on Grandparenthood

The growing divorce rate, discussed earlier, is a social trend that is affecting the meaning of grandparenthood. As noted above, at least 50 percent of all persons marrying today will face divorce. The consequences of this for younger generations—over 30 percent of children living in one-parent families or with neither parent—clearly influence the nature of the grandchild-grandparent relationship (U.S. Bureau of the Census, 2000). Since the tie between young grandchildren and their grandparents is mediated by the grandchildren's parents, divorce disrupts these links, changes the balance of resources within the extended family, and requires a renegotiation of existing bonds. Who is awarded custody primarily affects the frequency of interaction with grandchildren; the grandparents whose child, typically the mother, is awarded custody have more contact (Connidis, 2001; Cooney and Smith, 1996). Generally, grandmothers maintain more contact with their grandchildren than do grandfathers after an adult child's divorce (Hilton and Macari, 1997). Controversies regarding **grandparents' rights** for visiting and proposed state legislation to ensure such rights highlight the issues faced by grandparents when the in-law is awarded custody and reduces the amount of grandchild-grandparent interactions. Groups such as Grandparents Anonymous, the Foundation for Grandparenting, and Grandparents'-Children's Rights are pressing for grandparents' visitation rights legislation in several states (Hilton and Macari, 1997; Kruk, 1996).

During the past two decades, most states have passed laws granting grandparents the right to petition a court to legally obtain visitation privileges with their grandchildren. In 1983, a uniform nationwide statute was passed that ensures grand-

GRANDPARENTING AND LEGAL ISSUES

Laura and David's son was killed in an auto accident. He left behind two girls, 3 and 5 and their biological mother, who was his girlfriend. They had always been close to the grandchildren, and involved in taking care of them. After his death, his girlfriend returned to assume responsibility for the girls. In her grief and anger, the girlfriend claimed the grandparents had no legal right to visit the two girls and refused to allow contact. She later married, and her new husband felt even more strongly that Laura and David should not be allowed to visit the girls. The grandparents took their case to court, but the court ruled in favor of the biological mother.

parents visitation rights even if parents object. However, in June 2000, the U.S. Supreme Court ruled by a 6–3 vote that the right of responsible parents to raise their children as they see fit takes precedence over state laws that give grandparents wide visitation rights. Any state law must respect parents' wishes. These rulings raise complex issues for the involved generations and may place children in intergenerational conflicts. The long-term effects for grandchildren from visiting noncustodial grandparents over the objections of a parent are as yet unclear. What is apparent is that factors outside the family, such as the courts, are playing a larger role in how some families resolve conflicts and thus in children's development.

Conversely, complex issues have also emerged concerning the liability of grandparents and step-grandparents for support of grandchildren in the absence of responsible parents. When divorce in the parent generation occurs, the norm of noninterference by grandparents generally disappears. Instead, grandparents, especially those related to the custodial parent, provide substantial assistance to their grandchildren, function as surrogate parents, and mediate tensions. Grandparents have been referred to as "the family watchdogs," who are in the background during tranquil times, but are ready to step in during an emergency (Roberto, 1990).

Despite the dramatic growth of blended families, little is known about step-grandparenting relationships. From a grandparent's perspective, the growing phenomenon of divorce-remarriage means sharing grandchildren with their newly acquired relatives under conditions in which grandchildren will be scarcer because of declining birthrates. Grandchildren, in turn, may find themselves with four or more sets of grandparents. Kinship systems are further complicated by the fact that, with the increased divorce rate after 20 plus years of marriage, grandparents may no longer be married to one another.

Divorce among grandparents is found to have negative repercussions on the grandparent-grandchild relationship; divorced elders, especially grandfathers, have less interaction with their grandchildren because of weaker ties with their adult children (King, 2003).

Friends and Neighbors as Social Supports

Although the majority of older people live with others, approximately 30 percent of those over 65 and 46 percent of those over 85 live alone. In fact, the rate of older persons living alone increased by 1.5 times the growth rate for older people in general since 1970. Those living alone are most likely to be women, people of color, the oldest-old, adults of low socioeconomic status and those in rural areas.

Among those living alone, the most vulnerable are the homeless. While 27 percent of the homeless are estimated to be age 50 and over (including those who live in missions on skid row), their absolute numbers are increasing, especially among women. Characterized by higher rates of chronic stress, physical or mental disorders, economic deprivation, and alcohol misuse than the older population in general, homeless elders typ-

Intergenerational work activities can benefit all participants.

ically have fewer social supports (DeMallie et al., 1997).

After the homeless, the segments of the older population generally that are most vulnerable to lack of social supports are men, the widowed, and the childless. Lack of supports can exacerbate health problems and increase the risk of institutionalization. Gender differences in informal supports are more pronounced than life course differences, with men showing greater declines than women in the number of new friends, their desire for close friendships, the intimate nature of friendships, and involvement in activities beyond the family (Field, 1999). Although time with friends may decline, the majority of older adults have at least one close friend with whom they are in frequent contact and to whom they can turn in emergencies. In fact, some studies identify the average network size from 5 to 10 pesons, which typically declines after age 85 when the need for assistance with personal care may increase (Litwin, 2003; Van Tilburg, 1998). Older adults who refuse to leave their own communities to live with or near adult children may recognize the importance of friends as companions essential to their well-being and know that replacing friends can be difficult in old age (Bleiszner and Adams, 1998). On the other hand, older people steadily make new friends, and close relationships generally get closer with age, particularly among women. Some friendship networks may even expand with moves to retirement communities or volunteering (Van Tilburg, 1998).

According to **socioemotional selectivity theory,** individuals over the life course are surrounded by a convoy or group of people engaged in exchanges of social support. With age, however, they may choose deliberately to narrow their social networks to devote more emotional resources to fewer relationships with close friends and family (Antonucci and Akiyama, 1987; Lansford, Sherman, and Antonucci, 1998). Such selective engagement is not the same as disengagement or withdrawal from a wide range of social relationships. Instead, older adults may prefer to derive emotional comfort and meaning from familiar or intimate social interactions rather than expending the effort required to create and maintain a wide network of acquaintances that may provide less meaning to their lives. Careful selection of social network members is viewed as adaptive since it determines the degree to which individuals have access to social resources that can satisfy their socioemotional needs. In fact, older adults who have kin may nevertheless turn first to friends and neighbors for assistance, partially because friendship involves more voluntary and reciprocal exchanges between equals, consistent with social exchange theory (Hatch and Bulcroft, 1992; Lang and Carstensen, 1994; Wilmouth, 2000).

Whether family, friends, or neighbors become involved appears to vary with the type of task to be performed, as well as the helper's characteristics, such as proximity, extent of long-term commitment, and degree of interaction. Friends and neighbors are well-suited to provide emotional support and to assist occasionally, such as providing transportation and running errands, while

families are best equipped for long-term personal care (Dykstra, 1995; Lennautsson, 1999). Even friends facing chronic health problems may still be able to assist others, such as by listening and offering advice and support. Among populations of color, friends often link older persons to needed community services. In fact, African American peers have been found more likely than whites to provide and receive both instrumental and emotional support, often through church membership (Porter, Ganong, and Armer, 2000; Taylor and Chatters, 1991). Nonkin helpers also often link older people, particularly minority elders, to needed community services.

Friends are often important sources of intimacy and exchange confidences, especially when compared to relatives other than marital partners (MacRae, 1996; Wright, 1994). This is especially true after major role transitions such as widowhood or retirement; for example, an older widow generally prefers help from confidantes because relatives may reinforce her loss of identity as "wife." To the extent that friendships are reciprocal and satisfy social and material needs, they can compensate for the absence of a partner and can help mitigate loneliness (Adams and Blieszner, 1995; Dykstra, 1995; Field, 1999). The role of friend can be maintained long after the role of worker, organization member, or spouse is lost. The extent of reciprocity and quality of interaction, not the quantity, appear to be the critical factors in the maintenance of friendship networks. For instance, an intimate friendship with a confidant was found to be as effective as several less intimate ones in preventing the demoralization often produced by widowhood and retirement (Lowenthal and Haven, 1968). Friendship quality, including reciprocity among friends, is often related to psychological well-being and happiness (Adams and Blieszner, 1995, 2001). Given the general importance of friendships, professionals need to understand and encourage older adults to sustain these relationships.

Gender differences in informal supports are more pronounced than life course differences,

FRIENDSHIPS AMONG OLDER WOMEN

Five women had gone to high school together, married their high school sweethearts, and remained in the same Midwest town, raising their children, volunteering, and working part-time. They met occasionally to play bridge, helped watch each other's children, and shared in the joys and sadness of family life. Within an eight-year time period, all became widows. They began to meet more often than when their husbands were alive—joining each other for meals, shopping trips, and bridge. When one of the women, Marge, suffered a stroke, the other four became her primary caregivers—bringing her food, accompanying her to the doctor, visiting with her daily, and helping to clean her home. This friendship network greatly relieved the caregiving burden for Marge's daughter.

with men showing greater declines than women in the number of new friends, their desire for close friendships, the intimate nature of friendships, and involvement in activities beyond the family (Field, 1999). Women in general, such as Mrs. Howard in the introductory vignette to Part Four, have more emotionally intimate, diverse, and intensive friendships than men (Moen, Erickson, and Dempster-McClain, 2000). For many men, their wives are their only confidants, a circumstance that may make widowhood devastating for them. In contrast, women tend to satisfy their needs for intimacy throughout their lives by establishing close friendships with other women and therefore are less dependent emotionally on the marital relationship. When faced with widowhood, divorce, or separation, they can turn to these friends. Accordingly, widowed older women tend to receive more help and emotional support from friends than married older women. The resilience of some older women, in fact, may be rooted in their ability to form close reciprocal friendships (Riley and Riley, 1994).

Both men and women tend to select friends from among people they consider their social peers—those who are similar in age, sex, marital status, sexual orientation, and socioeconomic class. Most choose age peers as their friends, even though common sense would suggest that age-integrated friendship networks can reduce their vulnerability to losses as they age. A person's adult children are not likely to be chosen as confidants, primarily because they are from different cohorts who are at different places in the life cycle and more likely to produce an inequality of exchange. Age homogeneity plays a strong role in facilitating friendships in later life, in part because of shared life transitions, reduced cross-generational ties with children and work associates, and possible parity of exchange. Although friends are important resources when children are unavailable, their helping efforts usually do not approach those of family members in duration or intensity, and do not fully compensate for the loss of spouse or children, especially for low-income elders with chronic health problems (DeMallie et al., 1997; Litwin, 2003). Friendships can also be characterized by negative interactions, such as unwanted advice or assistance, and may become strained by excessive demands for assistance (Hansson and Carpenter, 1994).

Interventions to Strengthen or Build Social Supports

Because of the importance of peer-group interactions for well-being, there have been increased efforts to strengthen existing community ties or to create new ones if networks are nonexistent. Consistent with the person–environment model, such interventions are ways to alter the environment to be supportive of the older person. They can be categorized as personal network building, volunteer linking, mutual help networks, and neighborhood and community development. They aim to build upon the strengths and resources of local communities, including communities of color. Increasingly, these interventions include an intergenerational component.

Personal network building aims to strengthen existing ties, often through **natural helpers**—people turned to because of their concern, interest, and innate understanding. Such natural helpers can provide emotional support, assist with problem-solving, offer concrete services, and act as advocates. Neighbors often perform natural helping roles, and may strengthen these activities through organized block programs and block watches. Even people in service positions, often referred to as **gatekeepers,** can fulfill natural helping functions, because of the visibility of their positions and the regularity of their interactions with the older person. For example, postal alert systems, whereby postal carriers observe whether an older person is taking in the mail each day, build upon routine everyday interactions. Pharmacists, ministers, bus drivers, local merchants, beauticians, and managers of housing for older people, as in the case of Mr. Valdres in the introductory vignette, are frequently in situations to provide companionship, advice, and referrals. In high-crime areas, local businesses, bars, and restaurants may have a "safehouse" decal in their windows, indicating where residents of all ages can go in times of danger or medical emergencies. These community-based supports are further described in Chapter 11.

Churches may also serve to strengthen and build personal networks, in some cases providing a surrogate family for older people. Through intergenerational programs, church members can provide help with housework, home repair, transportation, and meal preparation, as well as psychological assurance. At the same time, older members may take on many leadership and teaching roles within the church, thereby enhancing their sense of belonging and self-worth, as in the example of Mr. Mansfield on page 282. In many private and public programs, *volunteers* are commonly used to develop new networks or expand existing ones for older persons. For example, volunteers provide chore services in older people's homes, offer peer counseling and senior center outreach activities, and serve as Friendly Visitors.

The Internet, e-mail, the Web, and interactive television also provide new opportunities for network building with peers and across generations for those with access to such information technology (Furlong, 1997).

Another approach aims to create or promote the supportive capacities of *mutual help networks,* especially through joint problem-solving and reciprocal exchange of resources. Mutual help efforts may occur spontaneously, as neighbors watch out for each other, or may be facilitated by professionals. They may also be formed on the basis of neighborhood ties or around shared problems, such as widow-to-widow programs, and support groups for caregivers of family members with chronic impairments. Interacting with peers who share experiences may reduce stress and expand problem-solving capacities (Pillemer and Suitor, 1996).

Neighborhood and community development is another approach that attempts to strengthen a community's self-help and problem-solving capabilities and may involve social action through lobbying and legislative activities. The Tenderloin Project, in a low-income area of single-room occupants in San Francisco, is an example of neighborhood development. Nearby residents acted on the immediate problem of crime and victimization of older people and then moved on to deal with issues such as nutrition and health promotion. In the process, social networks were strengthened and weekly support groups formed. Neighbor-

---

INFORMATION TECHNOLOGY AND COMMUNITY BUILDING

When the public library in a small Massachusetts town began to offer computer training, they expected the classes to be filled with teenagers and young adults. Instead, the classes were filled with adults over age 55, eager to learn how to e-mail their friends and families spread around the country, and to use the Internet to search for information related to their town's history, medical care, and Internet classes.

hood-based intergenerational helping networks are used to connect the formal service system to provide personal care services to frail elders. More recently, Internet Websites, such as Third Age, have emerged as a means to build community connections and reduce social isolation. Chat rooms, for example, are modeled upon community members' interests and needs; they can be altered by the changing will of the community. As noted by Hagel and Armstrong (1997), "people are drawn to virtual communities because they provide an engaging environment in which to connect with other people" (p. 18). Creating an electronic community, however, is obviously limited to those older people who have finances to access computers and the Internet (Furlong, 1997). Nevertheless, with the growing availability of networked computers at local libraries, senior centers, and community centers, many elders who cannot afford their own computer or online service can benefit from such services at no cost.

Intergenerational Programming

Intergenerational programs, linking older people with schoolchildren, high-risk youth, children with special needs, and young families, are a rapidly growing type of mutual help. This can also be extended to address cross-generational neighborhood and community problems, such as safety and the environment. The most common type of intergenerational programming involves older adults serving children and youth. For example, afterschool telephone support, tutoring, and assistance at day-care programs are provided through Retired Senior Volunteer Programs (RSVP). Kinder Korps and the Foster Grandparent Program both provide tutoring and mentoring, generally to low-income youth. The Computer Pals Program fosters youth and elder e-mail partnerships, with adolescents often teaching computer skills to older adults. Some programs involve elders and youth in social action projects, such as Caring Communities, that seek to improve the environment through

> ### AN INTERGENERATIONAL GRAN PAL PROJECT
>
> A second-grade school public school teacher involves his class in visiting regularly with their "Gran Pals" in a nearby skilled nursing care facility. In preparation for their visits, he first has them participate in a simulation of what it feels like to be "old and frail" wearing glasses with Vaseline on the lens, being pushed in a wheelchair, wearing gloves while opening a bottle, learning to speak clearly and directly to someone while wearing earplugs, and so on. Such simulations are frequently created for undergraduate students, but this program involves 6- and 7-year-olds, who then write and talk about what they experience when their usual activities are restricted. Each visit to the skilled care facility begins with the teacher talking with the children about what they might experience, and is then followed by the children's writing and discussing what they learned. The teacher is motivated not only by the social benefits for the older residents, but also by the recognition that by the time his second graders enter the job market, 20 percent of the population will be older adults.

music, gardening, and art. Older adults can also assist young families, especially immigrant families, related to issues of parenting, literacy training, social support and job hunting, and in creating supportive communities for foster-adoptive families or other families with high-risk children. Adolescents can in turn assist older neighbors with yardwork, home maintenance, and friendly visiting (Eheart, Power, and Hoping, 2003; Hamilton et al., 1999; Kincade, 1996; Skilton-Sylvester and Garcia, 1998).

Sharing physical space can also encourage intergenerational contact, such as child care programs housed in nursing homes or assisted living facilities, or offering senior service activities within public schools. In such instances, however, it is important that the needs of both elders and children be respected; for example, some older adults in nursing homes may not want to interact with children and may resent an environment that is too child-centered. Careful planning is necessary to ensure that interactions are age and developmentally appropriate (Hayes, 2003; Salari, 2002). Successful programs are characterized by reciprocity of benefits for both young and old and understanding of both human development and differences in communication styles. They typically enhance the self-esteem and social engagement of both young and old.

Consistent with the broad concept of productivity discussed in Chapter 11, intergenerational programs are likely to grow in the future as a way to match elders' resources with the needs of younger generations. Such a development is also congruent with the federal government's emphasis on cost-effective, private solutions to social problems. Practitioners in schools, senior centers, long-term care facilities, and other community-based settings can play pivotal roles in fostering cross-generational exchanges that benefit young and old.

Relationships with Pets

Many older adults talk to and confide in their pets and believe that animals are sensitive to their moods and feelings. Outcomes of owning a pet or participating in pet therapy are relatively unclear, and findings are mixed. Currently, anecdotal accounts of the benefits of pets are more common than rigorous empirical studies (Banks and Banks, 2002; Saito et al., 2001). What is clear, however, is that having a pet to feed, groom, or walk can provide structure and a sense of purpose to the day and can provide an anchor in days that might otherwise lack meaning. Older adults who care for pets, rather than being dependent on others, may experience meaning, purpose, and sense of control over their environment. In some instances, older participants in pet therapy programs were found to be less depressed and more communicative (National Institutes of Health, 1988). Even tropical fish and wild birds attracted to feeders were found to evoke responses such as care and stroking from previously unresponsive patients. In some in-

stances, pets may substitute for family members (Zasloff and Kidd, 1994). In some studies, pet owners score higher on measures of happiness, self-confidence, self-care, alertness, responsiveness, and dependability compared with their peers who do not own pets. At the same time, these benefits may be partially due to pet owners tending to be younger, physically active, and married or living with someone compared with non–pet owners (Dembicki and Anderson, 1996; Raina et al., 1999). On the other hand, the loss of a pet can result in intense grief; when this grief is minimized by others, elders' feelings of loss tend to be further intensified (Doka, 2001).

Perceptions of the benefits of pets have led to an increase in pet-facilitated programs for older adults in long-term care settings, as well as loan-a-pet or pet day-care programs for those elders in their own homes. Some long-term care facilities, particularly those using the Eden Alternative, create a more homelike setting by having pets living in the facility (Coleman et al., 2002). A pet should not be viewed as a substitute for human relationships (some cases of self-neglect involve homes filled with pets, but lacking food, hygiene, and other social interaction). Nevertheless, pet ownership can enhance well-being and enrich elders' quality of life. Differentiating pet ownership from occasional interaction with a pet in long-term care settings is important in future research on pets and elders.

Implications for the Future

Increases in life expectancy and declining family size will continue to result in more diverse and complex family structures. The vertical or "beanpole" family structure will grow—that is, an increasing number of living generations in a family, accompanied by decreasing numbers of family members within the same generation due to declining fertility rates. These trends, combined with an increase in the number of unmarried persons and childless partners, will mean that future cohorts of adult children will have a greater number of aging parents and grandparents to care for but fewer siblings to assist them. Top-heavy kin networks will raise caregiving challenges for both families and society, along with questions of intergenerational equity and reciprocity.

Delayed childbearing and smaller family size also will result in larger than average age differences between each generation and blurring of demarcations between generations, especially among Caucasian families. Active involvement in the daily demands of raising children will be fully completed by the time women are grandmothers, although some grandmothers will then become primary caregivers of grandchildren. Some women will simultaneously be both grandmothers and granddaughters. Growing proportions of parents, children, and grandchildren will share such critical adulthood experiences as school, work, parenthood, retirement, and widowhood. On the other hand, generational differences of 30 years, along with geographic mobility, may contribute to difficulties in building affective bonds across multiple generations due to different values or lifestyles. The increasing divorce rate, including divorce after remarriage, may mean that multiple generations will invest time in building reconstituted or blended families, which later may be dissolved. How these changes translate into new forms of family structure in the future remains unclear, since the extent to which acculturation and economic conditions will modify more traditional family arrangements is unknown. For both Caucasians and ethnic minority families, life course variations will grow as longer-lived men and women move in and out of various relationships, caregiving arrangements, living and employment situations, and communities.

All of these changes highlight the need for gerontological practitioners in a wide range of settings to be skillful at assessing and intervening with families, not only with the older person. Providers need to be sensitive to the wide variation of family forms, including grandparents as caregivers, gay and lesbian partners, mothers who have delayed childbearing and are simultaneously caring for a toddler and a frail elder, single or never-married older adults with extensive friendship networks, and elders of color with extensive fictive kin networks.

Health and human service providers in schools, community clinics, public child welfare, hospitals and mental health centers, regardless of their area of expertise, will increasingly encounter multigenerational families; this trend suggests the need for all such professionals to have basic knowledge and skills in working effectively with older adults and their increasingly complex families. In times of shrinking resources, professional creativity regarding intergenerational and multigenerational programs is needed to build on the resources and contributions of multiple generations to addressing social problems. Such problems are ways for both younger and older adults to engage in meaningful roles. In addition, service systems may shift from categorical, age-based services to ones that meet human needs across the lifespan. For example, the Lifespan Respite Bill currently before Congress and programs such as the National Family Caregiver Support Program and the federal Family and Medical Leave Act address care, giving demands accross the life course, not just for a particular age group. Given the dramatic growth in multigenerational families and the complexity of family forms, professionals will be challenged to think outside traditional boxes and models of service delivery and develop new ways to utilize older adults as a civic resource across generations.

Summary

The importance of informal social relationships for older people's physical and mental well-being has been widely documented. Contrary to stereotypes, very few older people are socially isolated. The majority have family members with whom they are in contact, although they are unlikely to live with them. Their families serve as a critical source of support, especially when older members become impaired by chronic illness. The marital relationship is most important, with more than half of all persons age 65 and over married and living with a partner in independent households. Most older couples are satisfied with their marriages, which influences their life satisfaction generally. The older couple, freed from childrearing demands, has more opportunities to pursue new roles and types of relationships.

Less is known about sibling, grandparent, and other types of family interactions in old age, although the importance of their support is likely to increase in the future. Also, comparatively little research has been conducted on lesbian and gay relationships in old age and on never-married older persons who may rely primarily on friendship networks to cope. Siblings can be crucial in providing emotional support, physical care, and a home. Interaction with secondary kin tends to depend on geographic proximity and whether more immediate family members are available.

Contrary to the myth that adult children are alienated from their parents, the majority of older persons are in frequent contact with their children, either face-to-face or by phone or letter. Filial relationships are characterized by patterns of reciprocal aid throughout the life course, until the older generation becomes physically or mentally disabled. At that point, adult children—generally women—are faced with providing financial, emotional, and physical assistance to older relatives, oftentimes with little support from others for their caregiving responsibilities. In ethnic minority and lower-income families, older relatives are most likely to receive daily care from younger relatives and to be involved themselves in caring for grandchildren.

Most families, regardless of socioeconomic class or ethnic minority status, attempt to provide care for their older members for as long as possible, and seek institutionalization only when they have exhausted other resources. Such caregiving responsibilities are affected by a number of social trends, most notable among them the increasing percentage of middle-aged women—traditionally the caregivers—who are more likely to be employed, and the number of reconstituted families resulting from divorce and remarriage. The needs of caregivers are clearly a growing concern for social and health care providers and policy makers.

With the growth of three- and four-generation families, more older persons are experiencing the status of grandparenthood and great-grandparenthood. Most grandparents are in relatively frequent contact with their grandchildren, and most derive considerable satisfaction from the grandparent role. The demands of grandparenthood are changing, however, as a result of divorce and remarriages. Perhaps the most dramatic change in the past decade has been the increase in the number of grandparents who are the primary caregivers to young grandchildren.

For many older persons, friends and neighbors can be even more critical than family members to maintaining morale and a quality of life. Generally, women interact more with friends than do men. Age-segregated settings appear to facilitate friendships rather than isolate older persons. In recognition of the importance of informal interaction to physical and mental well-being, an increasing number of neighborhood and community-based interventions have been developed to strengthen friendship and neighborhood ties. In recent years, many of these programs have attempted to foster intergenerational contacts and relationships. In sum, the majority of older persons continue to play a variety of social roles—partner, parent, grandparent, friend, and neighbor—and to derive feelings of satisfaction and self-worth from these interactions.

GLOSSARY

blended family   a family whose membership is comprised of blood and nonblood relationships through divorce or remarriage

cluttered nest   delayed departure or return of adult children to parents' home

empty nest   normative for middle-aged parents when adult children leave home for college or employment

filial responsibility   norms or expectations of what younger offspring owe older relatives

gatekeepers   people in formal (e.g., physicians, nurses) or informal (e.g., friends and neighbors) service who, because of regular interactions with older adults, can watch for signs indicating a need for assistance and mobilize help accordingly

grandparents as the custodial caregivers   grandparents who are the primary caregivers for grandchildren, when adult children are unable to provide adequate care

grandparents' rights   legal rights of grandparents to interact with grandchildren following divorce of the grandchildren's parents; liabilities of grandparent and step-grandparents as custodians of grandchildren in the absence of responsible parents

intergenerational living   families spanning two or more generations living in the same household

intergenerational programs   services that facilitate the interaction of people across generations; typically young and old

intergenerational stake hypothesis   pattern whereby the older generation tends to be more invested in future generations around transmission of values

intergenerational transfers   exchange of knowledge, finances, and other resources among family members of different generations

intimacy at a distance   strong emotional ties among family members even though they do not live near each other

kinship care   the formal placement of children with extended family members

multigenerational family   a family with three or more generations alive at the same time

natural helpers   people who assist others because of their concern, interest, and innate understanding

nontraditional families   new family structures derived through gay and lesbian partnerships, communal living, cohabitation, informal adoption, etc.

reciprocal support   sharing resources and assistance among individuals

skipped generation household   where the parent generation is absent

social support   interactions among family, friends, neighbors (informal), and programs (formal) that sustain and encourage individuals

women in the middle   women who have competing demands from older parents, spouses, children, and employment

RESOURCES

See the companion Website for this text at <www .ablongman.com/hooyman> for information about the following:

- AARP Grandparent Information Center
- Association for Gerontology in Higher Education (AGHE)
- Child Welfare League of America
- Foundation for Grandparenting
- Gatekeeper Program
- Generations Together, University of Pittsburgh
- Generations United: National Center on Grandparents and other Relatives Raising Grandchildren
- Intergenerational Innovations
- National Center for Resource Family Support, the Casey Family Program
- National Coalition of Grandparents, Inc. (NCOG)

REFERENCES

Adam, B. D. Age preferences among gay and bisexual men. *GLQ: A Journal of Lesbian and Gay Studies,* 2000, 6, 413–433.

Adams, R., and Blieszner, R. Aging well with family and friends. *American Behavioral Scientist,* 1995, 39, 209–224.

Administration on Aging (AOA). *Aging into the 21st Century.* Washington, DC: 1997.

Administration on Aging (AOA). *Family Caregiving in an Aging Society.* Washington, DC: 1999a.

Administration on Aging (AOA). *Profile of Older Americans.* Washington, DC: 1999b.

Administration on Aging (AOA). *Profile of Older Americans.* Washington, DC: 2002

Allen, S. M., Goldscheider, F., and Ciambrone, D. A. Gender roles, marital intimacy, and nomination of spouse as primary caregiver. *The Gerontologist,* 1999, 39, 150–158.

American Association of Retired Persons (AARP). *AARP's Singles Survey.* Washington, DC: Author, 2003.

Antonucci, T. C., and Akimaya, H. Social networks in adult life and a preliminary examination of the convoy model. *Journal of Gerontology,* 1987, *42,* 519–527.

Antonucci, T. C., Sherman, A. M., and Akimaya, H. Social networks, support, and integration. In I. J. Birren (Ed.), *Encyclopedia of gerontology* (vol. 2). New York: Academic Press, 1996.

Banks, M. R., and Banks, W. A. The effects of animal-assisted therapy on loneliness in an elderly population in long-term care facilities. *Journals of Gerontology,* 2002, *57,* M428–M432.

Barrett, A. E., and Lynch, S. M. Caregiving networks of elderly persons: Variation by marital status. *The Gerontologist,* 1999, 695–704.

Baydar, N., and Brooks-Gunn, J. Profiles of grandmothers who help care for their grandchildren in the United States. *Family Relations,* 1998, *47,* 385–394.

Bengston, V. C. Beyond the nuclear family: The increasing importance of multigenerational bonds. *Journal of Marriage and the Family,* 2001, *63,* 1–16.

Bengtson, V. C., Rosenthal, C. J., and Burton, L. M. Paradoxes of family and aging. In R. H. Binstock and L. K. George (Eds.), *Handbook of aging and the social sciences* (4th ed.). New York: Academic Press, 1996.

Bengtson, V. C., Rosenthal, C. J., and Burton, C. Families and aging: Diversity and heterogeneity. In R. H. Binstock and L. K. George (Eds.), *Handbook of aging and the social sciences* (3rd ed.). New York: Academic Press, 1990.

Berger, R., and Kelly, J. Gay men and lesbians grown older. In R. Cabaj, and Stein, T. S. (Eds.), *Textbook of homosexuality and mental health.* Washington, DC: American Psychiatric Press, 1996.

Bergeron, S. M., and Senn, C. Y. Body image and sociocultural norms: A comparison of heterosexual and lesbian women. *Psychology of Women Quarterly,* 1998, *22,* 385–401.

Berkman, B., and Harootyan, L. *Social work and health care in an aging society: Education, policy, practice and research.* New York: Springer, 2002.

Berkman, L. F. Social support, social networks, social cohesion, and health. *Social Work and Health Care,* 2000, *31,* 3–14.

Berrick, J., Needell, B., and Barth, R. Kin as a family and child welfare resource. In *Kinship foster care: Policy, practice and research.* Oxford Press, 1999.

Berrick, J. D., and Needel, B. Recent trends in kinship care: Public policy, payments and outcomes for children. In P. A. Curtis and D. Grady (Eds.), *The foster care crisis: Translating research into policy and practice.* Washington, DC: Child Welfare League of America and the University of Nebraska Press, 1998.

Beyene, Y., Becker, G., and Mayen, N. Perception of aging and sense of well-being among Latino elderly. *Journal of Cross-Cultural Gerontology,* 2002, *17,* 155–172.

Blieszner, R., and Adams, R. G. Problems with friends in old age. *Journal of Aging Studies,* 1998, *12,* 223–238.

Boaz, R. F., Hu, J., and Ye, Y. The Transfer of resources from middle-aged children to functionally limited elderly parents: Providing time, giving money, sharing space. *The Gerontologist,* 1999, *39,* 648–657.

Bogard, R., and Spilka, B. Self-disclosure and marital satisfaction in mid-life and late-life remarriages. *International Journal of Aging and Human Development,* 1996, *42,* 161–172.

Bowers, B. F., and Myers, B. J. Grandmothers providing care for grandchildren: Consequences of various levels of caregiving. *Family Relations,* 1999, *48*(3), 303–311.

Bowling, A., and Grundy, E. The association between social networks and mortality in later life. *Reviews in Clinical Gerontology,* November 1998, *8,* 353–361.

Boxer, A. M. Gay, lesbian, and bisexual aging into the twenty-first century: An overview and introduction. *Journal of Gay, Lesbian, and Bisexual Identity,* 1997, *1,* 187–197.

Bryson, K., and Casper, L. M. *Current populations reports: Special studies.* (P23–198). Washington, DC: U.S. Bureau of the Census, 1999.

Bryson, K., and Casper, L. M. *Coresident grandparents and grandchildren: Current populations reports: Special studies.* (P23–198). Washington, DC: U.S. Bureau of the Census, 2000.

Burnette, D. Physical and emotional well-being of custodial grandparents in Latino families. *American Journal of Orthopsychiatry,* 1999a, *69,* 305–318.

Burnette, D. Social relationships of Latino grandparent caregivers: A role theory perspective. *The Gerontologist,* 1999b, *39,* 49–58.

Burnette, D. Custodial grandparents in Latino families: Patterns of service use and predictors of unmet needs. *Social Work,* 1999a, *44,* 22–34.

Burnette, D. Latino grandparents rearing grandchildren with special needs: Effects on depressive symptomatology. *Journal of Gerontological Social Work,* 2000, *33,* 1–16.

Cahill, S., South, K., and Spade, J. *Public policy issues affecting gay, lesbian, bisexual and transgender elders.* New York: The Policy Institute of the National Gay and Lesbian Task Force, 2000.

Cantor, M. Family caregiving: Social care. In *Family caregiving: Agenda for the future.* San Francisco: American Society on Aging, 1994.

Calasanti, T., and Slevin, K. *Gender, social inequalities and aging.* Walnut Creek, CA: Altima Publishers, 2001.

Casper, L. M., and Bianchi, S. M. *Continuity and change in the American family.* Thousand Oaks, CA: Sage, 2002.

Casper, L. M., and Bryson, K. R. *Co-resident grandparents and their grandchildren.* Washington, DC. U.S. Bureau of the Census, Population Division, 1998.

Cassel, J. Contribution of the social environment to host resistance. *American Journal of Epidemiology,* 1976, *104,* 107–123.

Chan, C. G., and Elder, G. H. Matrilineal advantage in grandchild-grandparent relations. *The Gerontologist,* 2000, *40,* 179–190.

Chapple, M. J., Kippas, S., and Smith, G. "Semistraight sort of sex:" Class and gay community attachment explored within a framework of homosexually active men. *Journal of Homosexuality,* 1998, *35,* 65–83.

Cherlin, A. J., and Furstenberg, F., Jr. *The new American grandparent: A place in the family, a life apart.* New York: Basic Books, 1986.

Choi, N. G. Long-term elderly widows and divorcees: Similarities and differences. *Journal of Women and Aging,* 1995, *7,* 69–92.

Choi, N. G. The never-married and divorced elderly: Comparison of economic and health status, social support, and living arrangement. *Journal of Gerontological Social Work,* 1996, *26,* 3–25.

Cicirelli, V. G. Strengthening sibling relationships in the later years. In G. C. Smith, S. Tobin, E. A. Robertson-Tchabo, and P. Power (Eds.), *Strengthening aging families: Diversity in practice and policy.* Thousand Oaks, CA: Sage, 1995.

Clarke, E. J., Preston, M., Raskin, J., and Bengtson, V. L. Types of conflicts and tensions between older parents and adult children. *The Gerontologist,* 1999, *39,* 261–270.

Cohen, G. D. Marriage and divorce in later life (Editorial). *American Journal of Geriatric Psychiatry,* 1999, *7,* 185–187.

Cohen, S., Gottlieb, B. H., and Underwood, L. G. Social relationships and health: Challenges for measurement and intervention. *Advanced Mind Body Medicine,* 2001, *17,* 129–41.

Coleman, M. T., Looney, S., O'Brien, J., Ziegler, C., Pastorino, C. A., and Tumer, C. The "Eden Alternative" findings after one year of implementation. *Journals of Gerontology,* 2002, *57,* M419–M421.

Combs, A. Pet therapy and increased socialization among elderly clients. *Kentucky Nurse,* 2002, *50,* 15–16.

Connidis, I. A. *Family ties and aging.* Thousand Oaks, CA: Sage, 2001.

Connidis, I. A., and Campbell, L. D. Closeness, confiding and contact among siblings in middle and late adulthood. *Journal of Family Issues,* 1995, *16,* 722–745.

Cooney, T. M., and Smith, L. A. Young adults' relation with grandparents following recent parental divorce. *Journals of Gerontology,* 1996, *51B,* S91–S95.

Cox, C. Empowering African American custodial grandparents. *Social Work,* 2002, *47,* 262–267.

Davies, C., and Williams, D. *Grandparent study.* Washington, DC: American Association of Retired Persons, 2002.

DeMallie, D. A., North, C. S., and Smith, E. M. Psychiatric disorders among the homeless: A comparison of older and younger groups. *The Gerontologist,* 1997, *37,* 61–66.

Dembicki, D., and Anderson, J. Pet ownership may be a factor in improved health of the elderly. *Journal of Nutrition and the Elderly,* 1996, *15,* 15–31.

Dietz, T. L. Patterns of intergenerational assistance within the Mexican American family. *Journal of Family Issues,* 1995, *16,* 350–355.

Dilworth-Anderson, P., Williams, I. C., and Gibson, B. E. Issues of race, ethnicity, and culture in caregiving research: A 20-year review. *The Gerontologist,* 2002, *42,* 237–272.

Doka, K. J. *Caregiving and loss: Family needs, professional responses.* Washington, DC: Hospice Foundation of America, 2001.

Dorfman, R. A., Walters, K., and Burke, P. Old, sad and alone: The myth of the aging homosexual.

Journal of Gerontological Social Work, 1995, *24,* 29–44.

Dorfman, R., Walters, K., Burke, P., Hardin, L., Karanik, T., Raphael, J., and Silverstein, E. Old, sad, and alone: The myth of the aging homosexual. *Journal of Gerontological Social Work,* 1995, *24,* 29–44.

Dubas, J. S. How gender moderates the grandparent-grandchild relationship. *Journal of Family Issues,* 2001, *22,* 407.

DuPertuis, L. L., Aldwin, C. M., and Basse, R. Does the source of support matter for different health outcomes? *Journal of Aging and Health,* 2001, *13,* 494–510.

Dykstra, P. Loneliness among the never and formerly married: The importance of supportive friendships and a desire for independence. *Journals of Gerontology,* 1995, *50B,* S321–S329.

Eheart, B. K., Power, M. B., and Hopping, D. E. Intergenerational programming for foster-adoptive families: Creating community at Hope Meadows. *Intergenerational Relationships,* 2003, *1,* 17–28.

Emick, M. A., and Hayslip, B. Custodial grandparenting: New roles for middle-aged and older adults. *International Journal of Aging and Human Development,* 1996, *43,* 135–154.

Eng, P. M., Rimm, E. B., Fitzmaurice, G., and Kawachi, I. Social ties and change in social ties in relation to subsequent total and cause-specific mortality and coronary heart disease incidence in men. *American Journal of Epidemiology,* 2002, *155,* 700–709.

Everard, K. M., Lach, H. W., Fisher, E. B., and Baum, M. C. Relationship of activity and social support to the functional health of older adults. *Journals of Gerontology,* 2000, *55B,* S208–S212.

Fassinger, R., E. Issues in group work with older lesbians. *Group,* 1997, *21,* 191–210.

Field, D. Continuity and change in friendships in advanced old age: Findings from the Berkeley older generation study. *International Journal of Aging and Human Development,* 1999, *48,* 325–346.

Fields, J., and Casper, L. M. America's families and living arrangements. *Current Population Reports.* Washington, DC: U.S. Census Bureau, 2001.

Freedman, R. I., Krauss, M. W., and Seltzer, M. M. Aging parents' residential plans for adult children with mental retardation. *Mental Retardation,* 1997, *35,* 114–123.

Fuller-Thompson, E., Minkler, M., and Driver, D. A profile of grandparents raising grandchildren in the United States. *The Gerontologist,* 1997, *37,* 406–411.

Fullmer, E. M. Challenging biases against families of older gays and lesbians. In G. C. Smith, S. S. Tobin, E. A. Robertson-Tchabo, and P. W. Power (Eds.), *Strengthening aging families: Diversity in practice and policy.* Thousand Oaks, CA: Sage, 1995.

Furlong, M. Creating online communities for older adults. *Generations,* 1997, *21,* 33–35.

Gabbay, S., and Wahler, J. Lesbian aging: Review of a growing literature. *Journal of Gay and Lesbian Social Services,* 2002, *14,* 1–21.

Giarrusso, R., Silverstein, M., and Bengtson, V. L. Family complexity and the grandparent role. *Generations,* 1996, *20,* 17–23.

Giarrusso, R., Silverstein, M., and Feng, D. Psychological costs and benefits of raising grandchildren: Evidence from a National Survey of Grandparents. In C. B. Cox (Ed.), *To grandmother's house we go and stay: Perspectives on custodial grandparenting.* New York: Springer, 2000.

Giarrusso, R., Stallings, M., and Bengtson, V. L. The "intergenerational stake" hypothesis revisited: Parent-child differences in perceptions of relationships 20 years later. In V. L. Bengtson, K. W. Schaie, and L. M. Burton (Eds.), *Intergenerational issues in aging: Effects of societal change.* New York: Springer, 1995.

Goldman, N., Korenman, S., and Weinstein, R. Marital status and health among the elderly. *Social Science and Medicine,* 1995, *40,* 1717–1730.

Goldscheider, F. K. Divorce and remarriage: Effects on the elderly population. *Reviews in Clinical Gerontology,* 1994, *4,* 258–259.

Gonyea, J. Midlife, multigenerational bonds, and caregiving. In R. Talley (Ed.), *Caregiving: Science to practice.* Rosalyn Carter Institute, 2003.

Goodman, C. Intimacy and autonomy in long term marriage. *Journal of Gerontological Social Work,* 1999, *32,* 83–97.

Grann, J. D. Assessment of emotions in older adults: Mood disorders, anxiety, psychological well-being, and hope. In R. L. Kane and R. A. Kane (Eds.), *Assessing older persons: Measures, meaning, and practical applications.* New York: Oxford, 2000.

Greenwell, L., and Bengtson, V. L. Geographic distance and contact between middle-aged children and their parents; The effects of social class over 20 years. *Journals of Gerontology,* 1995, *52B,* S13–S26.

Grossman, A. H. The virtual and actual identities of older lesbians and gay men. In M. Duberman (Ed.), *A queer world: The Center for Lesbian and Gay Studies Reader.* New York: New York University Press, 1997.

Hagel, J. III, and Armstrong, A. G. *Net gain: Expanding markets through virtual communities.* Boston: Harvard Business School Press, 1997.

Haglund, K. Parenting a second time around: An ethnography of African American grandmothers parenting grandchildren due to parental cocaine abuse. *Journal of Family Nursing,* 2000, 6, 120–135.

Hamilton, G., Brown, S., Alonzo, T., Glover, M., Mersereau, Y., and Wilson, P. Building community for the long term: An intergenerational commitment. *The Gerontologist,* 1999, 39, 235–238.

Hanson, E. J., Tetley, J., and Clarke, A. A multimedia intervention to support family caregivers. *The Gerontologist,* 1999, 39, 736–741.

Hansson, R. O., and Carpenter, B. N. *Relationships in old age: Coping with the challenge of transition.* New York: The Guilford Press, 1994.

Harden, A. W., Clarke, R., and Maguire, K. *Informal and formal kinship care.* Washington, DC: Department of Health and Human Services, 1997.

Hargrave, T. D., and Hanna, S. M. (Eds.) *The aging family: New visions in theory, practice, and reality.* New York: Brunner/Mazel, Inc. 1997.

Harwood, J. Comparing grandchildren's and grandparent's stake in their relationship. *International Journal of Aging and Human Development,* 2001, 53, 195–210.

Hatch, L., and Bulcroft, K. Contact with friends in later life: Disentangling the effects of gender and marital status. *Journal of Marriage and the Family,* 1992, 54, 222–232.

Hays, J. C., Gold, D. T., and Peiper, C. F. Sibling bereavement in late life. *Journal of Death and Dying,* 1997, 35, 25–42.

Hayslip, B., Jr., Shore, G., Henderson, C. E., and Lambert, P. L. Custodial grandparenting and the impact of grandchildren with problems on role satisfaction and meaning. *Journals of Gerontology,* 1998, 53B, S164–S173.

Hilbourne, M. Living together full time? Middle class couples approaching retirement. *Aging and Society,* 1999, 19, 161–183.

Hilton, J. M., and Macari, D. P. Grandparent involvement following divorce: A comparison in single-mother and single-father families. *Journal of Divorce and Remarriage,* 1997, 28, 203–224.

Hirshorn, B. Grandparents as caregivers. In M. Szinovacz (Ed.), *Handbook on grandparenthood.* Westport, CT: Greenwood Press, 1998, 200–214.

Hobbs, F. B., and Damon, B. C. *65+ in the Unitd States.* Washington, DC: U.S. Bureau of the Census, Current Population Reports, 1996.

House, J., Mero, R., and Webster, P. Marital quality over the life course. *Social Psychology Quarterly,* 1996, 59, 162–171.

Jendrek, M. P. Grandparents who parent their grandchildren: Circumstances and decisions. *The Gerontologist,* 1994, 34(2), 206–216.

Johnson, P. Research on grandparenting: Review of current studies and future needs. *Generations,* 1996, 20, 65–70.

Kawachi, I., and Berkman, L. F. Social ties and mental health. *Journal of Urban Health: Bulletin of the New York Academy of Medicine,* 2001, 78, 458–467.

Kelley, S. J., Whitley, D. M., Sipe, T. A., and Crofts Yorker, B. Psychological distress in grandmother kinship care providers: The role of resources, social support and physical health. *Child Abuse and Neglect,* 2000, 24(3), 311–321.

Kelly, T., and Kropf, N. Stigmatized and perpetual parents: Older parents caring for adult children with lifelong disabilities. *Journal of Gerontological Social Work,* 1995.

Keyes, C. L. The exchange of emotional support with age and its relationship with emotional well-being by age. *Journal of Gerontology: Psychological Sciences,* 2002, 57B, 518–525.

Kimmel, D. C. Lesbians and gay men also grow old. In L. A. Bond, S. J. Cutler, and A. Grams (Eds.), *Promoting successful and productive aging.* Thousand Oaks, CA: Sage, 1995.

Kincade, J. Older adults as a community resource: Results from the national survey of self-care and aging. *The Gerontologist,* 1996, 36, 474–482.

Kincade, J. E., Rabiner, D. J., Bernard, S. L., Woomert, A., Konrad, T. R., DeFrisse, G. H., and Ory, M. G. Older adults as a community resource: Results from the National Survey of Self-Care and Aging. *The Gerontologist,* 1996, 36, 474–482.

King, V. The legacy of a grandparent's divorce: Consequences for ties between grandparents and grandchildren. *Journal of Marriage and the Family,* 2003, 65, 170–183.

Krause, N., and Borawski-Clark, S. Social class differences in social support among older adults. *The Gerontologist*, 1995, *35*, 498–505.

Krause, N., and Shaw, B. Giving social support to others, socioeconomic status and changes in self-esteem in late life. *Journals of Gerontology*, 2000, *55B*, S323–S333.

Kruk, E. Grandparent-grandchild contact loss: Findings from a study of "Grandparent Rights" members. *Canadian Journal on Aging*, 1995, *14*, 737–754.

Kulik, L. Continuity and discontinuity in marital life after retirement: Life orientations, gender role ideology, intimacy, and satisfaction. *Families in Society*, May–June 1999, *80*, 286–294.

Lang, F. R., and Cartensen, L. L. Close emotional relationships late in life: Further support for proactive aging in the social domain. *Psychology and Aging*, 1994, *9*, 315–324.

Lansford, J. E., Sherman, A. M., and Antonucci, T. C. Satisfaction with social networks: An examination of socioemotional selectivity theory across cohorts. *Psychology and Aging*, 1998, *13*, 544–552.

LaVeist, T. A., Sellers, R. M., Brown, K. A., and Nickerson, K. J. Extreme social isolation, use of community-based senior support services, and mortality among African American elderly women. *American Journal of Community Psychology*, October 1997, *25*, 721–732.

Lefley H. P., and Hatfield, A. B. Helping parental caregivers and mental health consumers cope with parental aging and loss. *Psychiatric Services*, March 1999, *50*, 369–375.

Lennartsson, C. Social ties and health among the very old in Sweden. *Research on Aging*, 1999, *21*, 657–681.

Levenson, R., Cartensen, L., and Gottman, J. Long-term marriage: Age, gender and satisfaction. *Psychology and Aging*, 1993, *8*, 301–313.

Liang, J., Krause, N., and Bennett, J. Is giving better than receiving? *Psychology and Aging*, 2001, *16*, 511–523.

Lin, G., and Rogerson, P. A. Elderly parents and the geographic availability of their adult children. *Research on Aging*, 1995, *17*, 303–331.

Litwin, H. The association of disability, sociodemographic background, and social network type in later life. *Journal of Aging and Health*, 2003, *15*, 391–408.

Lowenthal, M. F., and Haven, C. Interaction and adaptation. *American Sociological Review*, 1968, *33*, 20–30.

Lubben, J. E., and Gironda, M. W. *Centrality of social ties to the health and well-being of older adults*. New York: Springer, 2003.

Lugaila, T. *Marital status and living arrangements* (Series P20-506). Washington, DC: U.S. Bureau of the Census, Current Population Reports, 1998.

Macdonald, B., with C. Rich. *Look me in the eye: Old women, aging and ageism*. Denver: Spinsters Ink Books, 2001.

MacRae, H. Strong and enduring ties: Older women and their friends. *Canadian Journal on Aging*, 1996, *15*, 374–392.

Manalansan, M. F. Double minorities: Latino, Black and Asian men who have sex with men. In R. Savin-Williams and K. M. Cohen (Eds.), *The lives of lesbians, gays and bisexuals*. Fort Worth, Texas: Harcourt Brace, 1996.

Martinez, I. L. The elder in the Cuban American family: Making sense of the real and ideal. *Journal of Comparative Family Studies*, 2003, *33*, 359–370.

Metropolitan Life Insurance Company. *Met Life study of employer costs for working caregivers*. Westport, CT: Metropolitan Life Insurance, 1998.

Miller, B., and Cafasso, L. Gender differences in caregiving: Fact or artifact? *The Gerontologist*, 1992, *32*, 498–507.

Miller, B., Campbell, R., Farron, C., Kaufman, J., and Davis, L. Race, control, mastery, and caregiver distress. *Journals of Gerontology*, 1995, *50B*, S376–S382.

Miller, R. B., Hemesath, K., and Nelson, B. Marriage in middle and later life. In T. D. Hargrave and S. M. Hanna (Eds.), *The aging family: New visions in theory, practice, and reality*. New York: Brunner/Mazel, 1997.

Minkler, M. Intergenerational households headed by grandparents: Context, realities, and implications for policy. *Journal of Aging Studies*, 1999, *13*, 199–218.

Minkler, M., Berrick, J. D., and Needell, B. Impacts of welfare reform on California grandparents raising grandchildren: Reflections from the field. *Journal of Aging and Social Policy*, 1999, *10*, 45–63.

Minkler, M., and Fuller-Thomson, E. Depression in grandparents raising grandchildren. *Archives of Family Medicine*, 1997, *6*, 445–452.

Minkler, M., and Roe, K. *Grandmothers as caregivers: Raising children of the crack cocaine epidemic.* Newbury Park, CA: Sage, 1993.

Moen, P., Erickson, M. A., and Dempster-McClain, D. Social role identities among older adults in a continuing care retirement community. *Research on Aging*, 2000, *22*, 559–579.

Mohr, R. Reflections on golden pond. In P. Papp et al., (Eds.), *Couples on the fault line: New directions for therapists.* New York: The Guilford Press, 2000.

Mor-Barak, M., Miller, L., and Syme, L. Social networks, life events and the health of the poor, frail elderly: A longitudinal study of the buffering versus the direct effect. *Family Community Health*, 1991, *14*, 1–13.

Morrow-Howell, N., Sherraden, M., Hinterlong, J., and Rozario, P. A. *The productive engagement of older adults: Impact on later-life well-being.* St. Louis: Longer Life Foundation, 2001.

Morrow-Kondos, D., Weber, J. A., Cooper, K., and Hesser, J. L. Becoming parents again: Grandparents raising grandchildren. *Journal of Gerontological Social Work*, 1997, *28*, 35–46.

Mui, A. C., and Burnette, J. D. A comparative profile of frail elderly persons living alone and those living with others. *Journal of Gerontological Social Work*, 1994, *21*, 5–26.

Musil, C. M. Health of grandmothers as caregivers: A ten month follow up. *Journal of Women and Aging*, 2000, *12*, 129–145.

National Academy on an Aging Society. *Helping the elderly with activity limitations: Caregiving, 7.* Washington, DC: author, 2000.

National Institute on Aging. *An aging world.* Washington, DC: U.S. Census Bureau, 2001.

National Institutes of Health. *Health benefits of pets.* Washington, DC: U.S. Department of Health and Human Services, U.S. Government Printing Office, 1988.

Neugarten, B. *Personality in middle and late life: Empirical studies by Bernice L. Neugarten in collaboration with Howard Berkowitz and others.* New York: Atherton Press, 1964.

Neugarten, B., and Weinstein, K. The changing American grandparent. *Journal of Marriage and the Family*, 1964, *26*, 199–204.

O'Brian, C. A., and Goldberg, A. Lesbians and gay men inside and outside families. In N. Mandell and A. Duffy (Eds.), *Canadian families: Diversity, conflict and change.* Toronto: Harcourt Brace, 1999.

Oxman, T., and Hull, J. Social support, depression, and activities of daily living in older heart surgery patients. *Journals of Gerontology*, 1997, *52B*, S330–S339.

Peterson, C. C. Grandfathers' and grandmothers' satisfaction with the grandparenting role: Seeking new answers to old questions. *International Journal of Aging and Human Development*, 1999, *49*, 61–78.

Pillemer, K., and Suitor, J. J. It takes one to help one. Effects of similar others on the well-being of caretakers. *Journals of Gerontology*, 1996, *51B*, S250–S257.

Porter, E. J., Ganong, L. H., and Armer, J. M. The church, family and kin: An older rural black woman's support network and preferences for care providers. *Qualitative Health Research*, 2000, *10*, 452–470.

Pruchno, R. Raising grandchildren: The experiences of black and white grandmothers. *The Gerontologist*, 1999, *39*, 209–221.

Raina, P., Walther-Toews, D. Bennett, B., Woodworth, C., and Abernathy, T. Influence of companion animals on the physical and psychological health of older people: An analysis of a one-year longitudinal study. *Journal of American Geriatrics Society*, 1999, *47*, 323–329.

Reid, J. D. Development in late life: Older lesbian and gay lives. In A. R. D'Augelli and C. J. Patterson (Eds.), *Lesbian, gay and bisexual identities across the lifespan: Psychological perspectives.* New York: Oxford University Press, 1995.

Ren, X. S., Skinner, K., Lee, A., and Kazis, L. Social support, social selection and self-assessed health status: Results from the veteran's health study in the United States. *Social Science and Medicine*, 1999, *48*, 1721–1734.

Reynolds, W. Marital satisfaction in later life: An examination of equity, equality, and reward theories. *International Journal of Aging and Human Development*, 1995, *40*, 155–173.

Riley, M. W., and Riley, J. Structural lag: Past and future. In M. W. Riley, R. L. Kahn, and A. Foner (Eds.), *Age and structural lag: Society's failure to provide meaningful opportunities in work, family and leisure.* New York: John Wiley & Sons, 1994.

Roan, C. L., and Riley, R. Intergenerational coresidence and contact: A longitudinal analysis of adult children's response to their mother's widowhood. *Journal of Marriage and the Family,* 1996, *58,* 708–717.

Roberto, K. Grandparents and grandchild relationships. In T. Brubaker (Ed.), *Family relationships in later life.* Newbury Park, CA: Sage, 1990.

Roberto, K. A., and Stroes, S. J. Grandchildren and grandparents: Roles, influences, and relationships. In J. Hendricks (Ed.), *The ties of later life.* Amityville, NY: Baywood, 1995.

Robinson, L., and Blanton, P. Marital strengths in enduring marriages. *Family Relations,* 1993, *42,* 38–45.

Roe, K. M., Minkler, M., Sauners, F., and Thomson, G. E. Health of grandmothers raising children of the crack cocaine epidemic. *Medical Care,* 1996, *34,* 1072–1084.

Rook, K. S. *Stressful aspects of older adults' social relationships: Current theory and research.* New York: Hemisphere, 1990.

Saito, T., Okada, M., Ueji, M., Kikuchi, K., and Kano, K. Relationship between keeping a companion animal and instrumental activity of daily living: A study of Japanese elderly living at home in Satomi Village. *Nippon Koshu Eisei Zasshi,* 2001, *48,* 47–55.

Salari, S. M. Intergenerational partnerships in adult day centers: Importance of age-appropriate environments and behaviors. *The Gerontologist,* 2002, *42,* 321–333.

Scharlach, A., and Fredriksen-Goldsen, K. *Families and work: New directions in the twenty first century.* New York: Oxford University Press, 2001.

Seeman, T. E. Health promoting effects of friends and family on health outcomes in older adults. *American Journal of Health Promotion,* 2000, *14,* 362–370.

Seeman, T. E., and Berkman, L. F. Structural characteristics of social networks and their relationship with social support in the elderly: Who provides support. *Social Science and Medicine,* 1998, *49,* 737–749.

Sharp, C. E. Lesbianism and later life in an Australian sample: How does development of one affect anticipation of another. *Journal of Gay, Lesbian, and Bisexual Identity,* 1997, *2,* 247–263.

Shye, D., Mullooly, J. P., Freeborn, D. K., and Pope, C. R. Gender differences in the relationship between social network support and mortality: A longitudinal study of an elderly cohort. *Social Science and Medicine,* 1995, *41,* 935–947.

Siever, M. D. Sexual orientation and gender as factors in socioculturally acquired vulnerability to body dissatisfaction and eating disorders. *Journal of Consulting and Clinical Psychology,* 1994, *62,* 252–260.

Silverstein, M., and Angelelli, Older parents' expectations of moving closer to their children. *Journals of Gerontology,* 1998, *53B,* S153–S163.

Silverstein, M., Chen, X., and Heller, K. Too much of a good thing: Intergenerational social support and the psychological well-being of older parents. *Journal of Marriage and the Family,* 1996, *58,* 970–982.

Silverstein, M., and Marenco, A. How Americans enact the grandparent role across the family life course. *Journal of Family Issues,* 2001, *22,* 493–522.

Sloan, F. A., Picone, G., and Hoerger, T. J. The supply of children's time to disabled elderly parents. *Economic Inquiry,* 1997, *35,* 295–308.

Slusher, M. P., Mayer, C. J., and Dunkie, R. E. Gays and Lesbians Older and Wiser (GLOW): A support group for older gay people. *The Gerontologist,* 1996, *36,* 118–123.

Smith, C. J. Grandparents raising grandchildren: Emerging program and policy issues for the 21st century. *Journal of Gerontological Social Work,* 2000, *34,* 81–94.

Smith, D., and Moen, P. Spousal influence on retirement: His, her and their perceptions. *Journal of Marriage and the Family,* 1998, *60,* 734–744.

Smith, G. C., Tobin, S. S., and Fullmer, E. M. Assisting older families with lifelong disabilities. In G. C. Smith, S. Tobin, E. A. Robertson-Tchabo, and P. Power (Eds.), *Strengthening aging families: Diversity in practice and policy,* Thousand Oaks, CA: Sage, 1995.

Stephens, M. A., and Franks, M. Spillover between daughters' role as caregiver and wife: Interference or enhancement? *Journals of Gerontology,* 1995, *50B,* P9–P17.

Stitch, S. S. Stories to keep. *Newsweek,* November 11, 2002, p. A3.

Strom, R. D., Buki, L. P., and Strom, S. K. Intergenerational perceptions of English-speaking and Spanish-speaking Mexican-American grandparents. *International Journal of Aging and Human Development*, 1997, *45*, 1–21.

Stroup, A. L., and Pollock, G. E. Economic well being among white elderly divorced. *Journal of Divorce and Remarriage*, 1999, *31*, 53–68.

Szinovacz, M. Grandparents today: A demographic profile. *The Gerontologist*, 1998, *38*, 37–52.

Szinovacz, M. E., DeViney, S., and Atkinson, M. P. Effects of surrogate parenting on grandparents' well-being. *Journals of Gerontology*, 1999, *54B*, S376–S388.

Szolnoki, J., and Cahn, K. *African American kinship caregivers: Principles for developing supportive programs.* University of Washington School of Social Work: The Northwest Institute for Children and Families, 2003.

Taylor, R., and Chatters, L. Extended family networks of older black adults. *Journals of Gerontology*, 1991, *46*, S210–S218.

Tennstedt, S. *Family caregiving in an aging society.* Washington, DC: Administration on Aging 1999, Symposium.

Testa, M. F., and Slack, K. S. The gift of kinship foster care. *Children and Youth Services Review*, 2002, *24*, 79–108.

Trute, B. Grandparents of children with developmental disabilities: Intergenerational support and family well-being. *Families in Society: The Journal of Contemporary Human Services*, 2003, *84*, 119.

Tucker, J. S., Friedman, H. S., Tsai, C. M., and Martin, L. R. Playing with pets and longevity among older people. *Psychology and Aging*, 1995, *10*, 3–7.

Turvey, C. L., Carney, C., Arndt, S., Wallace, R. B. and Herzog, R. Conjugal loss and syndromal depression in a sample of elders aged 70 years and older. *American Journal of Psychiatry*, 1999, *156*, 1596–1601.

Uchino, B. N., Cacioppo, J. T., and Kiecolt-Glaser, J. K. The relationship between social support and physiological processes: A review with emphasis on underlying mechanisms and implications for health. *Psychological Bulletin*, 1996, *119*, 488–531.

Uhlenberg, P. The burden of aging: A theoretical framework for understanding the shifting balance of caregiving and care receiving vs. cohort ages. *The Gerontologist*, 1996, *36*, 761–767.

Uhlenberg, P., and Kirby, J. B. Grandparenthood over time: Historical and demographic trends. In M. E. Szinovacz (Ed.), *Handbook on grandparenthood.* Westport, CT: Greenwood Press, 1998.

U.S. Bureau of the Census. Marital status and living arrangements. *Current Population Surveys.* Washington, DC, 2003.

Van Tilburg, T. Losing and gaining in old age: Changes in personal network size and social support in a four-year longitudinal study. *Journals of Gerontology*, 1998, *53B*, S313–S323.

Velkoff, V. A., and Lawson, V. A. *Caregiving: International brief on gender and aging.* Washington, DC: Bureau of the Census, 1998, 1B/98–3, 2–7.

Wahler, J. J., and Gabbay, S. G. Gay male aging: A review of the literature. *Journal of Gay and Lesbian Social Services*, 1997, *6*, 1–20.

Waldrop, D., and Weber, J. From grandparent to caregiver: The stress and satisfaction of raising grandchildren. *Families in Society: The Journal of Contemporary Human Services*, 2001, *82*, 461–472.

Wallace, G. Grandparent caregivers: Emerging issues in elder law and social work practice. *Journal of Gerontological Social Work*, 2001, *34*, 127–134.

Weinberg, J. Caregiving, age and class in the skeleton of the welfare state: 'And Jill came tumbling after.' In M. Minkler and C. L. Estes (Eds.), *Critical gerontology: Perspectives from political and moral economy.* Amityville, NY: Baywood, 1998.

Wenger, C. Social networks and prediction of the elderly people at risk. *Aging and Mental Health*, 1997, *1*, 311–320.

Wethington, E., Moen, P., Glasgow, N., and Pillemer, K. Multiple roles, social integration, and health. In P. M. K. Pillemer, E. Wethington and N. Glasgow (Eds.), *Social integration in the second half of life* (pp. 48–71). Baltimore: Johns Hopkins University Press, 2000.

Williams, L., Mehta, K., and Lin, H. S. Intergenerational influence in Singapore and Taiwan: The role of the elderly in family decisions. *Journal of Cross Cultural Gerontology*, 1999, *14*, 291–322.

Wilmouth, J. M. Unbalanced social exchanges and living arrangement transitions among older adults. *The Gerontologist*, 2000, *40*, 64–74.

Wojciechowski, W. C. Issues in caring for older lesbians. *Journal of Gerontogical Nursing*, 1998, *24*, 28–33.

Wood, V., and Robertson, J. The significance of grandparenthood. In J. Gubruim (Ed.), *Time, roles and self in old age.* New York: Human Sciences Press, 1976.

Woodworth, R. S. You're not alone . . . you're one in a million. *Child Welfare*, 1996, *75*, 619–635.

Wright, D. L., and Aquilino, W. S. Influence of emotional support exchange on caregiving wives' burden and marital satisfaction. *Family Relations,* 1998, *47,* 195–204.

Wright, L. K. Alzheimer's disease afflicted spouses who remain at home: Can human dialectics explain the findings? *Social Science and Medicare,* 1994, *38,* 1037–1046.

Wu, Z., and Pollard, M. S. Social support among unmarried childless elderly persons. *Journals of Gerontology,* 1998, *53B,* S324–S335.

Yoakam, J. Playing bingo with the best of them: Community initiated programs for older gay and lesbian adults. *Journal of Gay and Lesbian Social Services,* 1997, *6,* 27.

Yoakam, J. R. Beyond the wrinkle room: Challenging ageism in gay male culture. *Dimensions.* San Francisco: ASA Mental Health and Aging Network, 1999, 3, 7.

Zasloff, R. C., and Kidd, A. H. Loneliness and pet ownership among single women. *Psychological Reports,* 1994, *75,* 747–752.

10

Opportunities and Stress of Informal Caregiving

This chapter addresses the central role of informal family caregiving within the long-term care system. The following issues are discussed

- Benefits and costs of caregiving
- Objective and subjective burdens
- The gendered nature of family care
  - Partners as caregivers
  - Adult children as caregivers
- Caregivers in families of color
- Caregivers of elders with dementia, expecially Alzheimer's disease
- Policies and programs to support family caregivers
- Use of formal services and informal support networks
  - For older care recipients
  - For caregivers
- Elder mistreatment
- Institutionalization
- Direct care workers in long-term care

As noted in Chapter 9, the majority of long-term care to adults age 65 and over is provided not in nursing homes, but informally and privately, at little or no public cost, within elders' homes or other community-based settings. Over 80 percent of older adults with limitations in three or more activities of daily living (ADL) are able to live in the community primarily because of informal assistance. Among elders in the community, only 5 percent rely exclusively on formal care, while over 65 percent receive care solely from family, friends, and neighbors, with about 30 percent using a combination of informal and paid assistance (Doty et al., 2001). In fact, about 50 to 60 percent of older adults outside institutional settings who need some help with ADL rely on informal networks that are not supplemented by paid caregivers (DHHS, 2003; National Academy, 2000; Ory et al., 2000; Spillman and Pezzin, 2000; Stone, 2000). The growing demand for such informal assistance is illustrated in Figure 10.1.

349

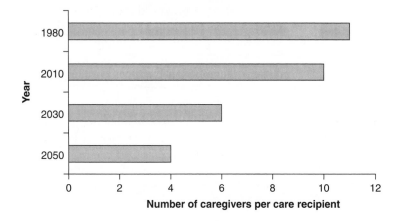

FIGURE 10.1 **The Shrinking Pool of Potential Caregivers**
SOURCE: Robert Wood Johnson Foundation, *Chronic care in America: A 21st century challenge* (Princeton, NJ: 1996).

Despite its prevalence, family care was perceived by policy makers as nonexistent and by researchers as largely invisible until the mid-1980s. Although Shanas's groundbreaking research (1979) refuted the prevailing social myth of families' alienation from their elders, policy makers and frequently the general public still assumed that many families abandoned their elders to institutional care. After three decades of caregiver research and numerous testimonials regarding care demands, the central role played by families in the lives of elders with chronic illness is now widely recognized and the term "family caregiver" is used by policy makers and the popular press (Gonyea, 2004).

Families' patterns of support are characterized by complexity and diversity in terms of geographic proximity, gender, socioeconomic class, sexual orientation, ethnic minority status, family structure, and history in addition to the nature of the relationship between caregiver and care recipient (Fredriksen-Goldsen, 2002; Karlawash et al., 2001; Martin-Matthews, 2000). Personal experiences, social class, and family context influence the nature of caregiver–care recipient interaction. For example, distance—both geographic and emotional in nature—often inhibits family members' provision of care. A recent analysis of the National Long Term Care Study found that 97 percent of primary caregivers and 93 percent of secondary

caregivers lived within an hour's distance of the elder (Spillman and Pezzin, 2000). However, emotional distance in the caregiving dyad is distinct from geographic proximity, and may occur when caring for a partner or parent after years of difficult relationships and family disruption, neglect, abuse, or separation. Changes in family relationships through divorce can negatively affect interaction with children—especially for men—and may limit adult children's availability as potential sources of support in old age (Uhlenberg, and Cooney, 1991). The effects of gender, ethnic minority status, and sexual orientation on caregiving are discussed more fully below.

The vast majority of family caregivers assist older relatives daily, with over 80 percent providing care from 1 to 5 hours per day (National Academy, 2000). The type and extent of family care is largely determined by the older adult's functional status, intensity of needed care, co-residence, and the caregiver's gender. The primary forms of care provided by families are:

- emotional support
- instrumental activities inside and outside the home (e.g., transportation, meal preparation, shopping)
- personal care (e.g., bathing, feeding, dressing)
- mediating with agencies for services

Costs and Benefits of Informal Care

For Society

Because of the many hours of care provided by family, it is not surprising that informal caregiving saves the American health care system substantial dollars; the value of such care is estimated at nearly $200 billion or nearly $7000 per patient annually. If informal supports were unavailable, total long-term care costs would more than double. Without the assistance of family and friends, the estimated costs for paid home care alone would be nearly $94 billion a year (AOA, 2003; LaPlante, Harrington, and and Kang, 2002).

While informal care is not a new phenomenon, demographic and social changes are intensifying demands on families to provide more complex care for longer periods of time and for multiple family members (Bengtson, 2001). These changes include the rapid growth of the oldest-old with chronic illness, more employed women who face multiple demands, more complex family structures (e.g., multigenerational and blended families), and increasing racial and economic inequities. These are compounded by changes in managed care and other cost-cutting health care measures, particularly Medicaid. In addition, families are increasingly expected to provide both "high-tech" and "high-touch" care, because of policies that provide incentives to discharge patients quickly from hospitals. As a result, families, who typically are unprepared for caregiving generally, may face providing medically oriented acute care along with postacute and rehabilitative care, such as intravenous drug therapy, ventilator assistance, and wound care in home and community-based settings (Stone, 2000).

For Informal Caregivers

Of greater concern to gerontologists and geriatricians are the costs and negative consequences experienced by caregivers; these are typically conceptualized as **objective and subjective burden.** *Objective burden* refers to the daily physical demands and behavioral phenomena of caregiving: the older relative's symptomatic behaviors, disruptions of family life and roles, and legal, employment, and health problems. *Subjective burden* encompasses the feelings and emotions aroused in family caregivers, such as grief, anger, guilt, worry, tension, loneliness, sadness, depression, difficulty sleeping, withdrawal, and empathic suffering. The caregiver's individual appraisal of the situation or subjective burden appears to be more salient than objective burden or the tasks performed by the caregiver (Yates, Tennstedt, and Chang, 1999; Tennstedt, 1999).

SUMMARY OF SOURCES OF CAREGIVER STRESS

Financial
- direct costs of care
- missed opportunities in career
- reduced hours (and income) at work
- work absenteeism
- job–family conflicts and disruptions
- accommodations necessary at the workplace

Physical
- health problems (headaches, stomach disturbances, and weight changes)
- use of prescription drugs and health services
- sleep disorders and exhaustion
- neglect of self and others
- increased morbidity

Emotional
- grief and loss, hopelessness, depression
- guilt, anger, resentment, and denial
- giving up of time for oneself (and family)
- strained social and family relationships
- social isolation
- worry and anxiety
- feelings of being alone and isolated
- negative attitudes or behaviors toward care recipient (anger)

Families experience costs or burdens in three primary areas:

1. *Physical and mental health outcomes:* Increases in caregiving stress are generally related to poor health outcomes over time (Beach et al., 2000). Physical health problems affect approximately 15 percent of caregivers, most often among African American, female, unemployed, and middle aged caregivers and those providing highest levels of care (National Academy, 2000; Smerglia and Deimling, 1997). Physical problems may include headaches, exhaustion, pain, depression, arthritis, back troubles, sleep disorders, intestinal disturbances, weight changes, inappropriate and greater use of prescription drugs, and self-neglect. Caregivers are found to have poorer function of their immune systems and slower healing of wounds, resulting in more colds and viral illnesses (American Association of Marriage and Family Therapy, 2002; Mittelman, 2002; Owens, 2001; Polen and Green, 2001; Strang et al., 1999). In fact, spousal caregivers are 63 percent more likely to die within 4 years compared with matched controls (Schulz and Beach, 1999). Moreover, poorer physical health or lower physical stamina is found to be associated with emotional distress and psychiatric disturbances (Loucks, 2000; Schulz et al., 1995). Not surprisingly, the physical costs of care are experienced most often by caregivers who live with the care recipient, and by those who have relatives with dementia and are providing intensive levels of care (Hughes et al., 1999; Tennstedt, 1999; Prigerson, 2003).

2. *Financial:* These encompass the direct costs of medical care, adaptive equipment, or hired help as well as indirect opportunity costs of lost income, missed promotions, or unemployment. More than 50 percent of caregiving employees report that they have made changes at work to accommodate care responsibilities. Caregivers of elders with dementia are most likely to move to part-time or less demanding work, take leave without pay, or quit work. These accommodations not only limit the caregiver financially but also reduce productivity for their employers (Metropolitan Life Insurance Company, 1998; National Alliance for Caregiving and AARP, 1997; Ory et al., 1999).

3. *Emotional:* These costs, which tend to be the greatest, encompass worry, anxiety, feeling alone, isolated, and disconnected from others; loss of time for oneself and family; "erosion of self" with one's identity completely submerged in the care role; and feeling overwhelmed, out of control, inadequate, and fearful over the unpredictability of the future (McLeod, 1999; Moen, Erickson, and Dempster-McClain, 2000; Tennstedt, 1999; Braithwaite, 2000). Caregiving is significantly associated with increased levels of psychological distress, commonly depression and anxiety (Berg-Weger, Rubio, and Tebb, 2000; Han and Haley, 1999; Polen and Green, 2001). Emotional costs tend to increase with difficult levels of care, and are experienced by women more than men (Ory et al., 1999). Among partner caregivers, levels of depression and loneliness are found to remain higher for caregivers than for noncaregivers, even after the care ends (Robinson-Whelen et al., 2001). Caregivers who feel trapped in the role are at risk of neglect, burnout, or "compassion fatigue" (National Academy, 2000; Prescop et al., 1999; Tennstedt, 1999).

Consistent with the person–environment (P–E) or ecological model, these costs or demands can be conceptualized as incongruence between the caregiver's competence (e.g., health, functional abilities, and extent of social support) and the tasks of care. Interventions to support caregivers, discussed on page 368, seek to increase the family's capacities for care (e.g., feelings of competence, self esteem and confidence; supports available) and

LOSS OF SELF IN THE CAREGIVING ROLE

"By definition, caregiving does not affect your life; it becomes your life. Outside activities disappear. In eight years, I have been to the movies three times." (McLeod, 1999: 81).

reduce the environmental press or demands of daily objective tasks through services and social supports in order to re-establish person-environment congruence (Lawton and Nahemow, 1973).

Caregiver Gains

Given the problem-focused nature of gerontological research, most caregiving studies focus on stress, burden, and the losses entailed. Recent research suggests, however, that caregiving should be regarded as a multidimensional concept that includes both negative and positive experiences (Nijboer et al., 2000). In other words, psychological well-being can coexist with distress under adverse life circumstances for both caregivers and care recipients. This means that caregivers may simultaneously experience losses of identity, privacy, and time for self along with personal enrichment. In fact, caregiving of older adults can be lonely, stressful, moving, and satisfying all at the same time. Similar to other types of difficulties and loss throughout the life span, caregivers may also experience personal benefits, such as self-gain, efficacy, confidence, self-affirmation, pride, marital satisfaction, and greater closeness with the care recipient and other family members (Beach et al., 2000; Kramer, 1997; Narayn et al., 2001; Noonan and Tennstedt, 1997).

Other caregivers on both a daily and long-term basis find personal meaning in their role, such as preservation of values and ideals and feelings of giving back to older generations. In fact, a greater sense of meaning in life is found to enhance caregiver well-being (Acton and Wright, 2000; Farran et al., 1999; Gonyea, 2004; Noonan and Tennstedt, 1997; Sherrell, Buckwalter, and Morhardt, 2001). These findings regarding caregiver gains reflect its qualitative or subjective nature and the role of individual appraisal; for example, what one caregiver experiences as stressful, another may find to be a source of satisfaction. In addition, benefits and costs vary over time, especially at points of entry and exit from the role.

These patterns also point to the need for practitioners to recognize both role gains and strains as intervening processes in understanding caregiver well-being outcomes (Gonyea, 2004; Kramer, 1997; Narayan et al., 2001; Seltzer and Li, 2000).

Based on these most recent findings, a future direction for caregiver research is further analysis of how resilience may reduce potentially negative effects of caregiver burden on well-being (Fredriksen-Goldsen, in press). More research on the caregiver–care recipient dyad is needed, given the importance of reciprocity in care relationships across the life course. Even caregivers of relatives with dementia may still experience some reciprocity in the relationship, especially when there is a family history of solidarity, deeply established attachments, and rich memories. To illustrate, a care recipient who can no longer manage daily chores can nevertheless entertain the caregiver with stories of family history (Fredriksen-Goldsen and Hooyman, 2003; Pearlin et al., 1996).

Caregivers' well-being and costs of care (and the interaction between gains and costs) are thus affected by two clusters of factors: *contextual* (e.g., level of care, care recipient's behavior and symptoms, quality of relationship with care recipient) and *dynamic* (e.g., the caregiver's internal capacities and social resources, including other supports (McDonald, Poertner, and Pierpoint, 1999). The following factors, which are more important than the elder's disability status or the amount or type of care provided, influence whether caregivers experience primarily costs or gains:

1. The nature of the relationship between caregiver and recipient (e.g., past history of conflict/neglect between them; recipient unappreciative, making unreasonable demands, adopting manipulative behavior). A good relationship prior to caregiving minimizes stress, even in the face of heavy care demands (Wolf, 1998).
2. Family support or disharmony, co-residence or geographic distance, financial resources.
3. The salience and timing in the caregiver's life course.

4. Gender (women typically experience caregiving as more stressful than men who provide similar levels of care).

5. Race and ethnicity, with ethnic minority caregivers generally using fewer services but experiencing less depression and stress.

6. Social networks (other supports and degree of reciprocity between caregiver and care recipient) (Almberg, Grafstroem, and Winblad, 2000; Kramer, 1997; Pruchno, Burant, and Peters, 1997).

Not surprisingly, when caregivers possess strong internal and social resources, they tend to be more resilient and are more likely to derive satisfaction from the role.

Who Are Informal Caregivers?

Estimates of the numbers of families actively engaged in elder care vary with the definition of "caregiving." When caregivers are broadly defined as a friend or relative age 50 or older providing care in the previous twelve months, 23.3 percent (or over 22 million) of all U.S. households are identified as caring for an elder (National Alliance for Caregiving and AARP, 1997). When family caregivers are more narrowly defined as those providing ADL or instrumental activities of daily living (IADL) for at least 3 months, slightly less than 2 percent of the U.S. population age 15 and older is actively engaged in elder care and an additional 7 percent are potential family caregivers (Gonyea, 2004; Spillman and Pezzin, 2000). However, the consequences of informal care on the well-being of both caregivers and care recipients appear to be more important than the incidence of family care per se.

The Gendered Nature of Family Care

Caregivers are primarily adult children (42 percent), followed by partners or spouses (25 percent) (National Academy, 2000). However, given high rates of widowhood among older adults, along with the sharing of care responsibilities by multiple siblings, children outnumber spouses as active carers (Spillman and Pezzin, 2000). Regardless of the type of care relationship, women form over 70 percent of family caregivers. Although gender roles are changing in our society, women are still the primary nurturers, kin keepers, and carers of family members. In fact, 50 percent of all women provide elder care at some point in the life course, whether as partners, daughters, or daughters-in-law (NASUA, 2003). Among all types of caregivers (primary and secondary), 36 percent are spouses, 29 percent are daughters, 20 percent are other females (nieces, daughters-in-law, granddaughters, etc.), and the remainder is male relatives. Among primary caregivers (e.g., one family member assumes most of the responsibility), 48 percent are spouses and 74 percent are women, with very few sons or other male relatives as primary carers (Peters-Davis, Moss, and Pruchno, 1999; Stone, 2000; Seltzer and Li, 2000; Tennstedt, 1999). The central role of gender in the hierarchy of obligation to older family members is reflected in the fact that after spouses and daughters, it is daughters-in-law and not sons who are turned to next (Quereshi and Walker, 1989). To some extent, family caregiver is a euphemism for one primary caregiver,

Growing numbers of younger women will assume both elder-care and employment responsibilities.

As noted by a daughter, "It is culturally expected to care for a parent in the home, yet it is viewed as women's work, and we don't value that very much in our society. Society thinks 'it's just an old person,' and 'it's just a woman.' So there are no benefits—no unemployment insurance, no vacations. It's insulting, and yet this is important work" (McLeod, 1999, p. 36).

typically female (Gonyea, 2004; Hooyman and Gonyea, 1995)

From the feminist theoretical perspective discussed in Chapter 8, women predominate not only because they are socialized to be carers, but also because society devalues women's unpaid pay-worthy work in the home as well as their paid work through employment. That is, because women typically earn less than men, an implicit assumption is that they can more willingly and readily give up paid employment to provide care (Calasanti and Slevin, 2001). Types of care also vary by gender and family relationship. While the participation of sons as caregivers is increasing, the gendered nature of care is reflected in the pattern that daughters are twice as likely to become the primary caregiver as are sons (Spillman and Pezzin, 2000), Women who are caregivers to older parents spend an average of 22 hours a week providing care (National Academy, 2000). Daughters predominate as the primary caregivers for older widowed women and older unmarried men, and they are the secondary caregivers in situations where the partner of an older person is still alive and able to provide care (Neal, Ingersoll-Dayton, and Starrels, 1997). Daughters are more likely than sons to be involved in *caring for* (e.g., help with daily tasks such as bathing, dressing, and eating), as well as *caring about* (e.g., relational aspects of care that involve trust, rapport, compassion, comfort, communication, and sense of psychological responsibility). Such personal care tasks are physically draining, involve daily interruptions, and entail intimate or bodily contact (Bengtson, Rosenthal, and Burton, 1996; Delgado and Tennstedt, 1997; Gonyea, 2004).

Sons tend to focus on more circumscribed, instrumental, and sporadic tasks, such as house and yard maintenance, financial management, and occasional shopping. While committed to care, they are more likely to adopt an attitude of "you do what you have to do" (Harris, 1998; Sanders and McFarland, 2002). They provide less personal care, especially to mothers, although they are more likely to perform "nontraditional" tasks (e.g., bathing, meals, dressing) when caring for a parent in the home. In addition, sons place less importance on emotional well-being and more on completing care goals. In other words, women more often feel responsible for their relative's psychological well-being and perceive greater interference between caregiving and their personal and social lives than do men. In contrast, male caregivers are more likely to obtain formal and informal assistance, relinquish the care role by withdrawing, and engage in preventive health behaviors than female caregivers (Campbell and Martin-Matthews 2000; Hughes et al., 1999; Seltzer and Li, 2000; Yee and Schulz, 2000).

Given these gender-based differences and the distinction between caring for and caring about, daughters tend to experience more stress than sons, even when both are performing similar tasks across similar time periods (Bengtson et al., 1996; Dautzenberg et al., 1999; Gerstel, 2001; Martin, 2000). Accordingly, women caregivers report

---

CHARACTERISTICS OF WOMEN AS CAREGIVERS

- form the majority of caregivers, even when male family members are available, except for spouses
- feel more psychological responsibility
- are more likely to give up or modify employment
- face multiple demands and roles from employment and/or dependent children
- caregiving is often a "career" over the life course and affects economic well-being in old age

higher levels of depression, anxiety, psychiatric symptomatology, and lower life satisfaction than their male counterparts. These gender-based patterns tend to persist across cultures. For example, although norms of filial support are weakening in Asian countries, daughters-in-law are still expected to provide care, without emotional or tangible support from other family members (Aranda and Knight, 1997; Navaie et al., 2001; Velkoff and Lawson, 1998; Yee and Schulz, 2000).

Increasingly, researchers are exploring not only how men and women differ in performing the caregiving role, but also how gender influences the meaning, social context, and consequences of caring. Women, for example, generally have more extensive social networks than do men. Although these may be useful resources, the networks themselves may also be sources of stress if they are characterized by conflict or other negative interactions (Antonucci, 1990; Gonyea, 2003). Women experience greater economic costs from the undervalued work of care across the life span than do men, which are exacerbated by policies such as Social Security. These economic in-

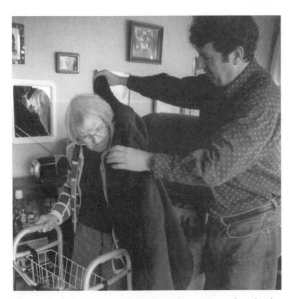

More sons today are caregivers to aging parents than in the past.

A researcher in Seoul, Korea, who studies women's labor market issues, has cared for her mother-in-law for 22 years. Although her husband and in-laws help pay for a personal assistant to care for her mother during the day, the middle-aged professional assumes all the care after her 8- to 10-hour workday and on weekends, without any assistance from her husband. She has had only one vacation during that time period, has little social life, but rarely questions her obligation to her mother-in-law.

equities for women in old age are discussed more fully in Chapter 15.

Spouses/Partners as Caregivers

The most frequent caregiving pattern is between partners, and over 12 percent of those who care for older adults are themselves age 65 and older (National Alliance for Caregiving and AARP, 1997; Matthews and Heidorn, 1998; Seltzer and Li, 2000). Since most caregiving studies have focused on heterosexual couples, the term *spouse* is used most frequently in this discussion; nevertheless, the distinctive structural challenges faced by gay and lesbian partner caregivers, who are discussed in Chapter 9, are recognized. The extent to which caring for a spouse is a normative experience—part of the marital contract and necessary for sustaining the quality of the marital relationship—affects the nature of the care experience. When the marital tie is not supportive, emotional intimacy may be more important than gender in the selection of a caregiver (Allen, Goldscheider, and Ciambrone, 1999). Spouses perform 80% of all care tasks, spending 40 to 60 hours per week on household chores and personal care. Because of differences in life expectancy, more wives than husbands over age 65 care for a partner with chronic illness. Men receive more care on average, typically from only one person—their wife. In contrast, women are more likely than men to be assisted by a larger number of caregivers, including children and grandchildren (National Academy, 2000).

Within the gender-based differences described above, husbands are more likely to provide care than are sons or sons-in-law, and they predominate among the 28% of caregivers who are male. In fact, husbands of women with chronic disabilities are more likely to provide care than are other relatives. As a result, husbands comprise nearly 40 percent of spousal caregivers and are predicted to grow in the future because of increases in male life expectancy. Husbands tend to be the first person called upon to care for their wives, to be the oldest subgroup of caregivers, and to spend the greatest number of hours in care compared with other caregivers. Caregiving husbands are found to experience more strain in the marital relationship and higher rates of depression and unhappiness than caregiving wives. Not surprisingly, the caregiver's health and the quality of the marital relationship (e.g., high levels of partner interaction and communication) affect the continuation of the care relationship (Harris, 1998; Kramer and Lambert, 1999; Tennstedt, 1999; Velkoff and Lawson, 1998).

Older spouses experience more negative consequences from caregiving than do younger adult children (Ory, Yee, Hoffmann, Tennstedt, and Schulz, 2000). Both husband and wife caregivers report considerable stress and feelings of grief and loss. These problems may be exacerbated because the caregivers are also facing their own aging-related changes, physical illnesses, or reduced finances. Emotional stress, particularly depression, tends to be highest among spouses caring for partners with cognitive impairment. The nature of the relationship also affects the consequences of care. For example, caregiving is found to be more stressful for wives than daughters, since wives more frequently experience losses in marital and family relationships and social involvement. Wives' sense of well-being, however, may increase when a husband dies (Seltzer and Li, 2000). As a whole, spousal caregivers experience more negative consequences than do younger adult children. Gay and lesbian partners' caregiving experiences are made more difficult by legal and structural barriers in most societies. For example, they may be denied visitation rights in the hospital or nursing home, overlooked by health care providers as the primary support, and excluded from decision-making roles.

Adult Children/Grandchildren as Caregivers

The importance of the parent-child bond across the life span is underscored by the fact that adult children represent the largest group of active carers for disabled elders. Parent care has become a predictable and nearly universal experience across the life course, yet many adults are not adequately prepared for it, because they are typically thrust into the role with little advance warning. Although often referred to as a "role reversal," an adult child never becomes a parent's parent. Instead, caring for parents is about letting go of outmoded patterns to meet current family needs, a process that can lead to feelings of grief and loss among adult children caregivers and that persist even after a parent's death (McLeod, 1999).

The average woman today can expect to spend more years caring for an older family member (18 years) compared to 17 years for her children. The concept of "sandwiched generation" refers to middle-aged women faced with competing responsibilities of parental and child care.

POINTS TO PONDER

Spouses/partners account for:

- 28 percent of the caregivers of Caucasian elders
- 20 percent of caregivers of Latinos
- 15 percent of African American caregivers
- What factors may account for these differences?

SANDWICH GENERATION

A woman in her mid-50s with teenage children and a full-time job, Annette had cared for both her parents. Her mother, crippled with rheumatoid arthritis, lived with Annette's family for 5 years before she died. Within a year, Annette's father suffered a stroke and lived with the family for 3 years before his death. Annette's teenagers had resented the amount of time she gave to her parents, and her husband became impatient with how little time they had alone together. They had not had a vacation in 5 years. Since family and friends were not interested in helping her with the care of her parents, Annette and her husband rarely even had a night out alone together. As an employed caregiver, Annette frequently missed work and was distracted on the job whenever she had to consult doctors or take her parents for therapy during normal business hours. She felt alone, isolated, and overwhelmed by the stress. She was physically and mentally exhausted from trying to meet too many demands, unaware that some support services were available in her community, and feeling that she had to handle these responsibilities on her own. When her mother-in-law became too frail to live alone, Annette knew her family and job would suffer once again if she tried to balance household duties, a full-time job, and the care of both older and younger relatives. She began to explore assisted living options for her mother-in-law.

Such "women in the middle" may be juggling extensive family responsibilities along with employment and their own age-related transitions (Guberman and Maheu, 1999; Ingersoll-Dayton, Neal, and Hammer, 2001; Penning, 1998). Women in the middle generation are also centrally involved in maintaining family communication and cohesion across generations. Compared to their male counterparts, they are more likely to give up employment, which can result in a loss of income (both current and retirement) and a source of identity and self-esteem (Pavalko and Artis, 1997). More recent data, however, indicate that women caring for older relatives typically do not have dependent children (under age 18) for whom they are responsible. They are more likely to face the competing demands of caring for older relatives and paid employment than the dual responsibilities of child and elder care. Nevertheless, middle-aged women may still feel psychologically and financially responsible for their young adult children, who frequently return home to the "empty nest" out of economic necessity. In fact, about 10 percent of men and 30 percent of women now remain at home (or return home) until marriage (Arnett, 2000; Goldscheider, Thornton, and Yang, 2001; Spillman and Pezzin, 2000).

Juggling multiple roles, however, may not always be a primary source of stress. In fact, women who lack any meaningful social roles may experience greater stress compared with women with multiple roles. Support for the caregiving role may be more important than the multiplicity of roles per se (Dautzenberg et al., 1999; Reid and Hardy, 1999).

WOMEN IN THE MIDDLE

A woman in her early 40s had given up a rewarding career to care for her mother-in-law with Alzheimer's disease, an 11-year-old daughter, and 8-year-old son. Her husband's siblings, who had no children, provided only occasional financial assistance, refusing to help by giving her respite or time off. Her husband worked two jobs, and although he was supportive, he was rarely present to help. Caring for her mother-in-law dominated her life, and she had little time to attend her children's special events or sports. Her son had had to give up his room for his grandmother, and her daughter complained about how her mother never spent time with her. In the 2 years of caring for her mother-in-law, she had not had a day just for herself. When she learned about the availability of respite services, she started to sob, recognizing how much she had been grieving the loss of time for herself and her children.

> **FORMAL SUPPORTS FOR CAREGIVERS**
>
> - adult day care
> - respite care
> - home health care
> - counseling in person or by phone
> - training programs/skill development
> - self-care techniques
> - support groups
> - internet resources, chat rooms

Family Caregivers of Color

Caregiving research has focused on U.S.-born whites; less is known about care in ethnic minority communities or other cultures. When race is considered, studies typically compare the experiences of African Americans and whites. African American caregivers tend to provide higher levels of care, to assist extended family members, to have higher levels of self-efficacy and gains in relation to caregiving, and to be more economically disadvantaged than their white counterparts. They also are less likely to have alternative caregivers to assist them, even though they often face more severe care situations and are less likely to use formal supports. African American caregivers' greater satisfaction and gains (e.g., pride, belief that they will be rewarded by God) may be partially due to the mediating effects of religion, prayer, and faith; to strong beliefs about filial support; and to more positive, respectful views of elders (Connell and Gibson, 1997; Cox, 1995; Dilworth-Anderson, William, and Cooper, 1999; Dilworth-Anderson, Williams, and Gibson, 2002; Foley, Tung, and Mutran, 2002; Janevic and Connell, 2001; Knight, McCallum, and Fox, 2000; Wallsten, 2000; White, Townsend, and Stephens, 2000). While several studies suggest minimal differences in depression between African American and white caregivers, other research has found that African American caregivers report lower levels of depression and stress (Dilworth-Anderson et al., 2002;

Farran et al., 1997; Janevic and Connell, 2001; Knight and McCallum, 1998; Cox 1999; White et al., 2000). On the other hand, younger African American caregivers may experience a disconnect between what they believe they do for relatives and what they are actually able to do. Accordingly, rates of nursing home placement among African American elders has increased in recent years (Clark, 1997; Groger and Mayberry, 2001). Latinos are identified as experiencing greater burden and less positive appraisals and feelings of competence than whites or African Americans, despite strong norms of filial responsibility (Clark and Huttinger, 1998; Cunio, 1999; Garcia and Oropesa, 2000; Navarre-Waliser et al., 2001). Even less is known about Asian American and Native American caregivers, although norms of filial support, extended family and other informal supports, and reluctance to use formal services are identified (Braun and Browne, 1998; McCormick, Ohata, Uomoto, Young, and Graves, 2002).

Inconsistent findings related to caregiving consequences among ethnic minorities are partially due to methodological limitations, such as using a "grouping variable" by race/ethnicity, culture, or national origin to attribute differences between groups of caregivers (Gonyea, 2004). Whether identified differences are largely due to cultural factors (e.g., language, values, beliefs, or norms) or to ethnic minority status, with the latter implying the effects of inequality and discrimination, requires further research. What is clear is that sociodemographic variables (i.e., gender, race, marital status) per se are not the causes of caregiver outcomes; rather, sociodemographic variables vary with the underlying causes. What is also known is that ethnic minorities are at higher risk of morbidity and mortality across the life span. The greater incidence of health problems does not, however, translate into higher rates of institutional care; a smaller percentage of elders of color (3 percent) than Caucasian elders (5.8 percent) live in nursing homes. Yet, as ethnogerontological research reveals, even among ethnic minorities with strong norms of filial piety and familism, economic and social forces are increasingly influencing their abilities to care for aging family members and rates of institutional care are likely to increase (Angel and Angel, 1997; Groger and Mayberry, 2001; Olson, 2001).

Caregiving for Relatives with Dementia

The demands and losses associated with caregiving tend to be intensified when caring for a relative with dementia (Prigerson, 2003). Almost 70 percent of adults with Alzheimer's disease (AD) are cared for at home by family for the entire duration of the disease (Alzheimer's Association, 2001; Kramer, 2000). This translates into families providing up to 80 percent of the care for relatives with AD for an average of 60 hours per week (Epple, 2002). Compared with other caregivers, those who care for relatives with dementia are at higher risk of strain, mental and physical health problems, and family conflicts. They have less time for leisure and for other family members, and their needs become subsumed to those of their older relative. Depression rates in studies of caregivers of relatives with dementia range from 25 to 87 percent, along with a high incidence of anger, grief, and anxiety (Adkins, 1999; Blieszner and Shifflet, 1999; Connell, Janevic, and Gallant, 2001; Meuser and

---

INTENSIFICATION OF PAST BEHAVIORS WITH ALZHEIMER'S DISEASE

In *Elder Rage: or Take my Father . . . Please!*, Marcell (2000) tells of caring for her father, who had always had a bad temper and was a controlling, dominating, explosive, and verbally abusive husband and father. Afflicted with Alzheimer's disease at age 83, he constantly raged and cursed at his daughter and his wife, threatened physical violence, and refused to take his medications.

THE "ABSENCE" OF ALZHEIMER'S PATIENTS

As described by a 36-year-old daughter, "she is not the way she used to be as my mother. Just looking in her bedroom at home, it is feeling like she is gone. Yet she's still alive. Her things are still where they have been for years, even when she was well. She sits and looks at the things that once made up her life and to her that life never existed. I ask myself daily, 'Is my mother alive or dead?'" (Sanders and Corley, 2003).

Marwit, 2001; Mittelman, 2002; Ory et al., 1999; Ory et al., 2000; Schulz et al., 2003).

The concept of "learning to bend without breaking" refers to the high level of unpredictability and continual changes to which families of AD patients must accommodate (Gwyther, 1998). For long-term partners, their roles and relationships are profoundly redefined by the pervasiveness of care responsibilities and the recognition of no end in sight (Eakes, Burke, and Hainsworth, 1998). When relatives with Alzheimer's disease are no longer psychologically present or when their personalities are markedly changed, new disruptive behaviors emerge (e.g., emotional and verbal abuse, increased aggressive or violent behavior) that increase their caregivers' sense of loss. Adult children typically grieve the loss of their relationship with their parent and of opportunities missed because of care responsibilities; older partners, on the other hand, may experience a loss of couple identity and intimacy, uncertainty, and aloneness (Meuser and Marwit 2001).

Caregivers who tolerate an ambiguous situation for long periods of time and experience anticipatory grief or "quasi-widowhood" often refer to their loved one's dying twice: first the psychological death of the person they knew and loved, and then the physical death; this can result in multiple waves of grief—denial, anger, guilt, resentment, and depression. Similarly, older adult caregivers for partners with brain injury, a stroke that has affected the loved one's personality, or

DAILY GRIEVING BY THE AD SURVIVOR

According to a 71-year-old husband, "being married to someone for over 50 years and seeing her with this disease, I am daily grieving over her loss. Upon death, you will grieve for awhile, but your life goes on. Seeing your loved one daily die for over 6 years just makes your feelings stronger. I just wish I could have killed her and myself and just got this whole thing over really quickly" (Sanders and Corley, 2003).

who are comatose experience their partner's psychological death years before the physical death. These emotional responses are similar to those felt when a loved one dies (Boss, 1999; Dupuis, 2002; Eakes, Burke, and Hainsworth, 1998; Rudd, Viney, and Preston, 1999). While health care providers need to be sensitive that caregivers of relatives with dementia often are grieving providing end-of-life care (Schulz et al., 2003).

Such instances of prolonged stress from caring for a loved one with dementia, as illustrated by the daughter and husband caregivers in the boxes, can create a sense of desperation over lacking control of a difficult situation. This chronic sorrow or "long good-bye" can negatively affect caregivers' physical and mental health and increase their risk of mortality, with grief often misdiagnosed as clinical depression. Compared with caregivers of older adults in nursing homes who experience sadness and guilt, those providing care at home tend to experience more anger (Ahmed, 2002; Mittelman, 2002; Sanders and Corley, 2003; Rudd et al., 1999; Walker and Pomeroy, 1996). Fortunately, more supports and skills training are now available to caregivers of relatives with dementia, (Bourgeois, Schulz, Burgio, and Beach, 2002).

Elder Mistreatment

In some cases, caregiving stress may become severe enough to lead to family conflict, breakdown, or mistreatment of older relatives. **Elder mistreatment**

encompasses harmful or hurtful conduct that is willfully inflicted upon an older person (Nerenberg, 2000). Our focus is on domestic abuse in the home, but elder abuse also occurs in institutional settings (e.g., nursing homes, adult family homes, group homes). Types of mistreatment range from physical, sexual, or emotional to financial exploitation and neglect (either self-imposed or by another person) that result in unnecessary suffering (Wolf, 2000). Although financial abuse and self-neglect are most common, neglect and physical abuse (e.g., slapping, hitting, bruising) are reported most frequently, with emotional mistreatment harder to document and often unreported (Quinn and Tomita, 1997; Wilber and McNeilly, 2001). Underreporting also occurs because some abusive behavior is enmeshed within complicated familial relationships (e.g., a family that has always yelled at one another) and because elders who are dependent on their abusers fear retaliation if they report mistreatment. Psychological and financial abuse is even further complicated by

TYPES AND SIGNS OF ELDER MISTREATMENT

- *Physical:* willful infliction of pain and injury, such as restraining, slapping, hitting, malnutrition
- *Emotional:* verbal assault, threats, fear, insults, humiliation, infantilization, isolation, exclusion from activities
- *Sexual:* nonconsensual sexual contact
- *Material or financial:* theft; misuse or concealment of the elder's funds, property, or estate; telemarketing fraud; investment schemes; usurious home loans; home repair scams
- *Medical:* withholding or improper administration of needed medications or aids such as dentures, glasses, or hearing aids
- *Neglect:* refusal or failure to fulfill any part of a person's obligations to an elder, withholding of food, medications, funds, or medical care
- *Violation of rights:* removal from home or into institutional setting without elder's consent
- *Abandonment:* desertion of elder by someone responsible for care

the victims' functional dependency on the abusers and the abusers' economic dependency on the victims (Wisbaum, 1997). Elder mistreatment, often invisible, has become a public issue only within the past 30 years, after the 1987 Amendments to the Older Americans Act provided guidelines for identifying abuse, and as a result of the visible advocacy of the National Center for the Prevention of Elder Abuse.

Up to 90 percent of cases of mistreatment are committed by family members (Gaugler, Kane, and Langlois, 2000). Abusers are primarily men, and approximately 60 percent are adult children or spouses/partners. Although findings on the incidence of abuse are varied because of methodological problems, an estimated 3 to 5 percent of older adults are abused by someone who lives with them, with the rate increasing among those over age 85 (AOA, 2000; U.S. Senate Special

> ### WARNING SIGNS OF ABUSE AND NEGLECT
>
> - depression, fear, or anxiety on the part of the elder
> - discrepancy in psychosocial and medical history between elder and possible abuser
> - vague, implausible explanations of illness or injuries
> - illness that does not appear to be responding to treatment; lab findings inconsistent with history provided
> - frequent visits to the emergency room; unexplained injuries or illnesses

Committee on Aging, 2003; Wilber and McNeilly, 2001; Wold, 2000). However, the National Elder Abuse Incidence Study, which was the first to estimate abuse rates nationally, found the incidence rate to be only 1.2 percent (Thomas, 1998; 2000). Since reports of abuse to Adult Protective Services appear to be only the "tip of the iceberg," large, rigorous probability samples of community-dwelling older adults' self-reports are needed along with longitudinal follow-up of the use of Adult Protective Services. Such information can help achieve greater consensus on the magnitude of the problem (Branch, 2002; Otto, 2002: Thomas, 2000).

Undue influence is an abusive behavior that is especially difficult to detect; it occurs when a person uses his or her role and power to exploit the trust, dependency, and fear of another, often isolating and creating a world controlled by the abuser. If the abuser is a family member, victims have trouble separating their feelings of care and love from the loss and trauma experienced at the hands of the abuser. The abusive situation becomes more complicated when the abuser is dependent on the victim financially, emotionally, and for housing. A web of mutual dependency is created when both the abuser and the victim rely on each other for a portion of their livelihood. Abuser dependency occurs more often than the reverse; e.g., the dependent caregiver relies on the

> ### PROSECUTING ELDER NEGLECT
>
> Neglect cases are often the most difficult to prosecute, because of the challenge of proving "failure to act." Investigating cases of elder neglect can also be complicated by the victim's underlying disease: Was the disease or neglect responsible for the person's death? When King County prosecutors in Washington State charged a daughter with killing her mother through reckless neglect, the case broke new ground. It was the first time the county medical examiner had declared a death to be homicide by elder neglect, and it sent an aggressive new message that crimes of neglect would no longer be ignored. A fire department aid crew found the mother in her garbage-littered, foul-smelling suburban home. The mother was lying in the fetal position, her head and body covered with feces. She was taken to the hospital, where she died a week later of dehydration and hypothermia. Her daughter, who had called 911 and reported that her mother had fallen, was charged with first-degree manslaughter. The daughter said she had brought her mother shampoo, assumed she was bathing, and had not noticed an unusual smell about her mother.

elder's financial resources, but the older person still prefers such exploitation to a nursing home (Blum, 2000; Quinn and Tomita, 1997; Quinn, 2000; Wilber and Nielsen, 2002).

Neglect, whether deliberate or unintentional, occurs when the caregiver does not provide goods or services necessary to avoid physical harm or mental anguish, such as abandoning the elder or denying food or health-related services.

Self-neglect occurs when the older adult engages in behavior that threatens his or her safety, even though he or she is mentally competent and understands the consequences of decisions. In some instances, the inability to perform essential self-care activities (e.g., providing for food, shelter, medical care, and general safety) may reflect a life-long lifestyle choice. Self-neglect is also associated with mental impairment such as dementia, isolation, depression, and alcohol abuse, although all of these conditions negatively affect the elder's cognitive abilities. Cases of self-neglect typically involve filthy living conditions, lack of insight that a problem exists, and hoarding behavior. Professional interventions, typically by social workers or nurses, generally focus on building trust with the elder to allow some services to reduce dangerously unhealthy living situations, while still protecting the elder's autonomy regarding his or her living situation. In some instances, professionals need to ac-

cept that there is nothing they can do to change the situation (Anetzberger et al., 2000; Otto, 2002; Quinn and Tomita, 1997; Simon et al., 1997; Wilber and Nielsen, 2002).

Whether behavior is labeled as abusive or neglectful depends on its frequency, duration, intensity, and severity and varies by each state. Lacking a national policy on elder mistreatment, states individually determine standards for what constitutes abuse, who should be protected, and how. Regardless of state statutory definitions, however, the older person's perception of the action and the sociocultural context of the mistreatment also affect its identification and consequences (Wold, 2000; Hudson and Carlson, 1999).

Cultural differences should not be used as a justification for abuse. Nevertheless, culture, degree of acculturation, and filial values and beliefs can influence the definition of abuse and the elder's response to it (Brownell, 1997; Tatara, 1997). In Korean families, for example, an elder may tolerate financial abuse because of the traditional patriarchal property transfer system, where sons enjoy exclusive family inheritance rights. This system tends to promote an adult son's financial dependence and occasional exploitation of an older parent (Moon, Tomita, and Jung-Kamei, 2001). Underreporting of abuse among ethnic minority communities may also reflect language barriers or mistrust of the legal and health care systems. The extent of elder mistreatment among gay and lesbian relationships is unknown, but may become more visible in the future with greater societal acceptance of homosexual partnerships (Cook-Daniels, 1997). With the increasing numbers of grandparents as primary caregivers for grandchildren, the hidden problem of mistreatment of grandparents by older grandchildren may also become more visible (Brownell and Berman, 2000).

The following vignette highlights the complexities of identifying abuse. As you read it, consider what you would do. What are some of the issues that you would try to assess? Who else would you involve?

SIGNS AND SYMPTOMS OF SELF-NEGLECT

- dehydration, malnutrition, untreated or improperly managed medical conditions, poor personal hygiene
- hazardous or unsafe living conditions (e.g., improper electrical wiring, no indoor plumbing, no heat, no running water)
- unsanitary or unclean living quarters (e.g., animal/insect infestation, no functioning toilet, fecal/urine smells)
- inappropriate and/or inadequate clothing, lack of necessary medical aids (e.g., eyeglasses, hearing aids, dentures)
- grossly inadequate housing or homelessness

MR. JONES'S EMERGENCY ROOM VISIT

As an intern in a regional hospital, you have been called in to the emergency room by a nurse supervisor to talk with Mr. Jones, an 80-year-old widower. The nurse, while leaving to respond to another emergency, asks you to "deal with this senile patient." Mr. Jones is sitting in a chair beside a 65-year-old man, Mr. Sloan, who brought Mr. Jones to the emergency room.

The two men have been living together for the past 16 years, after Mr. Jones became widowed. Mr. Sloan has a history of mental illness and heavy drinking, and has been unable to hold a steady job for the past 10 years. Nevertheless, the two men appear to care for one another and Mr. Sloan says that he cooks, cleans, and cares for Mr. Jones's needs. Mr. Sloan keeps repeating that he "doesn't know how much longer he can do this," and just does not understand what is wrong with Mr. Jones.

Mr. Jones is disheveled and has visible bruises on his face and arms. You learn from the nurse that he is waiting to have his broken right wrist set. You greet Mr. Jones and ask him what happened, and Mr. Sloan answers for him. He says he found Mr. Jones after he had fallen off a chair when trying to change a light bulb. As he describes this, Mr. Jones is silent and unresponsive. Mr. Sloan tells you that both the hospital intake worker and emergency room nurse admonished Mr. Jones for climbing on a chair, saying he should know better. Mr. Sloan says that he just can't control Mr. Jones every minute to prevent accidents from happening. Mr. Jones looks away. He looks confused and tells you that he couldn't find his Medicare card when the intake worker asked for it. He says he can't remember whether he took his wallet with him when he left home.

When Mr. Jones is taken into an examining room, Mr. Sloan insists on accompanying him. Mr. Jones begins an agitated monologue that does not seem to make sense. Mr. Sloan explains to you that his behavior is typical and there is no point in talking with him. Mr. Sloan says that he will answer any questions. Mr. Jones becomes increasingly agitated and starts to cry.

Although caregiver burden and the elder's functional ability may be contributing factors, caregiving stress does not in itself lead to abuse or explain its occurrence. In fact, assumptions of such stress as the cause of mistreatment can lead to inappropriate interventions for the caregiver rather than a criminal investigation (Anetzberger, 2000;

Quinn and Heisler, 2002). Consistent with the P–E model, causes are embedded in the interplay of individual characteristics of the abuser and the victim with familial, cultural, and social factors. Congruent with feminist and social exchange theories discussed in Chapter 8, power inequities appear to be more plausible explanations than family stress. There is growing recognition that elder mistreatment should be viewed largely from the perspective of power and control and thus treated as a criminal matter, whereas neglect may be a crisis in caregiving and therefore a health and social issue (Fulmer, Paveza, and Queaegno, 2002). In fact, case descriptions of abusers and victims reflect such power dynamics and marginalization of elders (especially women and the oldest-old), with the abuser exerting power and control over the vulnerable elder. Given gender inequities, it is not surprising that older women are mistreated at higher rates than men, comprising approximately 70 percent of reported victims, nor that those over age 85 are abused at two to three times their proportion of the older population (National Center on Elder Abuse, 1998). Spousal abuse may reflect lifelong patterns, with older women who are isolated and "falling between the cracks"—too old to go to domestic violence shelters designed for younger women and invisible to providers of age-based services.

Accordingly, certain behavioral characteristics of the care recipient are found to be associated with greater probability of abuse. These include being aggressive, critical, complaining, combative, and excessively dependent or unrealistic in expectations. Given these factors, it is not surprising that older adults with dementia, who may display aggressive, unpredictable behavior and who are typically less able to report abuse and access services, are highly vulnerable to abuse (Anetzberger et al., 2000; McConnell and McConnell, 2000; Wilber and Nielsen, 2002).

All 50 states have developed procedures for reporting abuse (including 24-hour toll-free numbers for receiving confidential reports of abuse), and all but 6 require such reporting to be manda-

CHARACTERISTICS OF THE ABUSER THAT REFLECT POWER INEQUITIES

- being male
- dependent on the elder for housing, finances, or other services (e.g., meals, laundry)
- mental illness, substance abuse, a history of problem behaviors, and lack of empathy for those with disabilities

tory for health care providers. In fact, 8 states require "any person" to report suspicion of mistreatment. Every state also has a long-term care ombudsman to investigate and resolve complaints about nursing homes. All states have established Adult Protective Services (APS) programs, which generally have the authority to investigate reported cases or to refer them to appropriate legal authorities such as district attorneys.

Adult Protective Services is the state or county system that investigates reports of mistreatment. They evaluate risk, assess the elder's capacity to agree to services, develop and implement case plans, and monitor ongoing service delivery (Otto, 2002). Since mandatory reporting laws require that APS accept all reports, heavy caseloads typically are filled with complex and difficult cases that other agencies are unwilling or unable to accept (Wilber and Nielsen, 2002). Another barrier is that few community-based living options and in-home supports exist for elders removed from high-risk situations. In addition, professionals are often biased toward home care and resist institutionalization, even when the latter would be safer for the abused elder than remaining at home with a suspected abuser.

Only about 16 percent of cases of mistreatment are reported; of these, over 60 percent are substantiated after investigation, but relatively few are prosecuted, often because witnesses or victims are unable or unwilling to testify (National Center on Elder Abuse, 1998; Choi and Mayer, 2000; Fulmer et al., 2002; Wilber and Nielsen, 2002; Wold, 2000). Other reasons for underreporting include

the isolation of older adults and our society's value on family privacy, which make concealment possible; lack of uniform reporting laws; and professionals' resistance to report suspected cases (Tatara, 1997). Screening measures for abuse typically assume that the alleged victim has the cognitive ability to respond to questions. In addition, the unknown consequences from reporting abuse (e.g., removal from the home, nursing home placement, abuser's anger) may be more traumatic to the abused than remaining in the negative situation. Reporting abuse may make visible to others the emotionally painful reality that a child can abuse a parent. If the abuser is arrested, restrained from the home, or abandons the elder, the older

A CASE OF FINANCIAL ABUSE

At age 85, Jean moved in with her son, her daughter-in-law and two teenage granddaughters. She brought with her assets from the sale of her home and her husband's Social Security and railroad pension. Anxious not to burden her son, who was a consultant and often unemployed, she helped him buy two cars, paid part of the family's monthly rent, and assisted with the granddaughters' private school tuition. What began as Jean's being helpful soon became financial abuse, with her son driving her to the bank to withdraw cash for him from her account and writing checks to himself. At first, Jean did not experience this as abusive since her son always had a "good reason" for "borrowing" the money. In addition, her son would often tell her that "it was going to be his money some day anyway, so what was the difference if he spent it now or later?" The lines between financial and emotional abuse began to blur; Jean was left alone all day and her son threatened that he would put her in a nursing home if she complained. When Jean had only $8000 left in her bank account, she finally stood up to her son, insisting that the remaining funds needed to be saved for a burial plot and funeral expenses. Shortly after that, her son left his wife and daughters, who were supportive and loving of Jean and invited her to continue to live with them.

adult suffers the loss of a caregiver and companion, no matter how poor the relationship may be. The elder grieves the loss of the family member who was abusive as well as the other multifaceted losses entailed by abuse (Bergeron, 2000; Wolf and Pillemer, 1989; Quinn and Tomita, 1997; Sprecher and Fehr, 1998).

Elders' rights to self-determination and autonomy, which are difficult to assess in high-risk situations, are central to any systems to prevent mistreatment. In addition, professional ethics places a high value on confidentiality and protection of clients' rights and autonomy. As result, less than 10 percent of APS clients receive services without the elder's consent (Otto, 2002). In contrast to instances of child abuse, an older person has the right to refuse assistance even if he or she is found to be incompetent. In such instances, however, APS would move to have a guardian appointed who would assume authority over the elder's personal financial and estate affairs.

In the past decade, cases of mistreatment have become criminalized under state statutes. This means that law enforcement may conduct a criminal investigation while APS supports the victim with counseling and services designed to provide safe medical and physical care. Some intervention models include teaming law enforcement professionals (e.g., police, district attorneys) with social workers and other health and human service professionals from a wide range of agencies to address the needs of both the victim and the abuser (Brownell, 2002).

Legislation to Support Family Caregivers

A barrier to the development of services for family caregivers has been policy makers' fears that service accessibility will reduce, curtail, or substitute for informal care. This concern persists, despite almost two decades of empirical documentation that formal in-home services do not appear to substitute for informal care (Binney, Estes,

and Humphers, 1993; Hooyman and Gonyea, 1995; Penning, 2002).

Despite policy makers' concerns that formal care would substitute for informal support at public expense, two federal policy initiatives aim to support families: the **Family and Medical Leave Act of 1993** (FMLA) and the **National Family Caregiver Support Program of 2000** (NFCSP). Under the FMLA, businesses with 50 or more employees are required to grant up to 12 weeks of unpaid leave annually when a child is born or adopted, when an immediate family member with a serious health condition needs care, or when the employee is unable to work because of a serious health condition. Health coverage and reinstatement of employment after the leave are guaranteed.

Because the FMLA does not apply to small employers, less than 10 percent of private sector worksites are covered. Even though this relatively small percentage of businesses employs almost 60 percent of American workers, not all workers of covered employers are eligible for FMLA benefits, because of requirements related to duration and amount of work. When these eligibility criteria are applied, less than half (46.5 percent) of private sector employees are eligible for leave. Additional barriers to using FMLA are lack of knowledge of the act and the unpaid nature of the leave. From a political economy perspective (described in Chapter 8), FMLA benefits only those who can afford

---

PRINCIPLES THAT SHAPE ADULT PROTECTIVE SERVICES PRACTICE

- the client's right to self-determination
- the use of the least restrictive alternative
- the maintenance of the family unit whenever possible
- the use of community-based services rather than institutions
- the avoidance of ascribing blame
- the presumption that inadequate or inappropriate services are worse than none (Otto, 2000)

to forgo income while on leave. Workers who cannot manage the loss of wages entailed by a family care leave are more likely to be African American, hourly wage earners who are predominantly women, and have lower levels of household income (Commission on Family and Medical Leave, 1996; Wisensale, 2001). The FMLA also does not recognize extended family members, characteristic of many ethnic minority families or gay and lesbian caregivers. Proposals to reform FMLA continue to be debated along partisan lines in the U.S. Congress (Hudson and Gonyea, 2000). The Family and Medical Leave Extension Act was introduced in 2003 for a pilot program to help states develop partially paid leave, but is unlikely to be acted upon in the near future. In contrast, some western European countries provide paid leave and special pensions for family caregivers of dependents across the life span. Attendant allowances allow older adults with disabilities to purchase and manage at least some in-home services (Linsk and Keigher, 1995). Some states are experimenting with limited amounts of money to consumer-directed and employee in-home services, including some payments to relatives (except spouses) through their Medicaid waiver programs (Tilly and Wiener, 2001).

The **National Family Caregiver Support Program** (NFCSP) was funded by the Administration on Aging in 2000. For the first time in the history of the Older Americans Act, state units on aging and area agencies on aging are required to serve not only older adults but also family caregivers. This includes family caregivers of elders and grandparents or other older kin caregivers of children/grandchildren. States are expected to partner with the local Area Agencies on Aging (AAAs) and other service providers to establish a network of services, although states have flexibility on what specific services to provide. The NFCSP gives a higher priority to services for low income older caregivers and for those caring for persons with mental retardation and developmental disabilities. In recognition of the growing phenomenon of grandparents as sole caregivers for grandchildren, each state may use up to 10 percent of the total funds to help grandparents and other family caregivers over age 60. Although NFCSP is important public policy recognition of the central role of informal care in our society, the program is modest in its impact. This is because of limited funding, the shift in thinking required by service workers to conceptualize the caregivers as clients, and the challenges of reaching caregivers when they are most likely to accept help and before they are in crisis (ASUA, 2003).

Use of Services

Most services are oriented to preventing institutionalization and thereby reducing the costs of care. As noted above, services targeted to reduce institutionalization traditionally focus on older adults, rather than the caregivers' well-being, although benefits to caregivers can help sustain better care of their older relative at home. A two-pronged service delivery approach would support

1. caregivers to enhance their ability to provide care, and
2. older persons to minimize their need for family care.

The distinction between the two levels of service delivery is blurred, however. For example, adult day health care provides socialization and health services for older adults, but also gives their caregivers a respite or break from care. The most effective models are those that provide multiple

---

SERVICES UNDER THE NATIONAL FAMILY CAREGIVER SUPPORT PROGRAM

- information and assistance
- individual counseling
- support groups and caregiver training
- respite care
- supplemental services to complement family care

(individual, group, and family) interventions of longer duration than 8 to 12 weeks and that assess the needs of caregivers as well as care recipients. (Hooyman, 2003; Mittelman et al., 1995; Whitlach et al., 1995; Zarit et al., 1998). Services targeted to older adults in general are discussed more fully in Chapters 11 and 16. This section reviews services intended for frail elders and their caregivers.

Supportive Services for Older Adults

Care or case management is typically provided to older adults and their families who wish to remain in their own homes. It involves the coordination of services to meet the older person's assessed needs, and includes outreach, screening, comprehensive assessment, care planning, service arrangements monitoring and ongoing reassessment (Naleppa, 2003). It may be provided through the local Area Agency on Aging, or by a private geriatric care manager. Although not targeted to family members, it can significantly reduce caregiver stress, depression, and burden and improve well-being, life satisfaction, and perceptions of health, albeit at a modest level. Those who receive case management also tend to access more services (Burns, Nichols, and Martindale-Adams, 2000; Chu et al., 2000; Fox et al., 2000; Newcomer et al., 1999).

More recently, service providers have focused on case management programs that strengthen older adults' competencies rather than addressing only their problems. These programs assess the older person's strengths and needs across a wide range of areas, engage them in setting goals for their care, attend to social factors in addition to medical ones, and help them mobilize and acquire resources to support their goals. The older adults' right to self-determination and participation in decision-making are central to such a strengths-based care management approach. This approach also includes frequent communication with paid and unpaid caregivers. Some case or care man-

agers focus on the family as their client, and assist caregivers with locating services and other supports for their elder (Fast and Chapin, 2000).

Supportive Services for Family Caregivers

Service Utilization

Although the Aging Network, especially through the National Family Caregiver Support Program, now provides more services for caregivers, increased service availability does not in itself enhance the caregiver or care recipient's well-being. Most family caregivers do not use services; or they do so selectively to supplement informal care for limited time periods or wait until services are absolutely necessary before contacting them. Whether reliance on informal networks is a result or cause of underutilization of formal services is unclear. To some extent, patterns of lower service use may persist because families are unaware of services, unwilling to accept them, or lack the time and resources to access them. Family caregivers typically self-select into their role, which may influence how they perceive the use of formal supports. In other instances, taking the time to partner with service providers may be perceived as more stressful (NASUA, 2003). Yet services tend to be underutilized even by caregivers who perceive a need for greater formal support (Coe and Neufeld, 1999; Davis, 1998; Dilworth-Anderson et al., 2002; Miller and Mukherjee, 1999; Tennstedt, 1999).

Gender and race also affect service utilization, with women and ethnic minority caregivers the least likely to turn to formal services. Some caregivers of color may not utilize services because of inaccessibility due to economic, religious, insurance, and other barriers, or because of discriminatory experiences that cause them to feel like unwelcome outsiders to agencies (Dilworth-Anderson et al., 1999; National Alliance for Caregiving and AARP, 1997; Wallace, Campbell, and Lei-Ting, 1999).

Even when formal services are used, the overall effects are relatively modest in terms of caregiver well-being, hours of care provided, or number of tasks performed for the care recipient. This pattern may occur because services may prolong the duration of caregiving, but not necessarily reduce subjective burden. Interventions may occur too late in the caregiving cycle after stress has already spilled over into other aspects of the caregivers' lives or problems have become too complex to solve through short-term strategies. More likely, services may not meet what caregivers perceive to be their needs (i.e., their subjective appraisal of their situation). For example, many services are oriented toward crisis intervention, short-term support, and residential care rather than in-home, long-term personal care. In many instances, families may be too poor to purchase private pay services, but not poor enough to be eligible for Medicaid-reimbursed services. Services targeted early on in caregiving and tailored to fit the care context are found to be more effective. For instance, since counseling may reduce emotional stress, telephone-based assistance is sometimes utilized to address time and geographic barriers (Davis, 1998; NASUA, 2003; Given et al., 1999; Tennstedt, 1999; Worcester and Hedrick, 1997; Yordi et al., 1997).

Support Groups for Caregivers

Although findings are somewhat contradictory, support groups for caregivers appear to be more effective than either education or counseling alone. For example, post-test measures of a support group for early-stage caregivers indicated a significant increase in preparedness for the caregiving role, competence, and use of positive coping strategies, and a decrease in their levels of perceived strain (subjective burden). This suggests that during the early phase of caregiving, families can promote their wellness and enhance their ability to face challenges through increased emotional strength and coping skills. Support group participation is also identified to be associated with de-

creased depression and increased morale; lower rates of institutionalization; greater knowledge of illness and resources; and increased informal support. In contrast to these benefits, some studies identify support groups to be less effective than individual counseling for reducing strain and improving psychological well-being. Although support groups can provide emotional assistance, they may not necessarily lower the level of caregiver stress; in fact, they may actually be perceived as an additional demand by caregivers who have to travel and arrange respite care for their elder in order to attend (Cummings et al., 1998; Gartska, McCallion, and Toseland, 2001; Mittelman, 2002; Toseland et al., 1990).

Psychoeducational Groups

Psychoeducational groups, which usually combine information and social support, are found to enhance caregiver well-being, delay institutionalization, and increase the utilization of supportive services (Bourgeois et al., 2002; Burgio, Stevens, Guy, Roth, and Haley, 2003; Oswald et al., 1999). Caregivers point to the value of understanding the nature of the illness and having knowledge of relevant resources. A limitation of some educational approaches, however, is that they may implicitly convey to the caregiver that she or he only needs to become better informed and more efficient in order to reduce stress (Hooyman and Gonyea, 1995). Some groups educate and empower caregivers to advocate for policy and programmatic changes (Morano, 2002; Schulz et al., 2002).

Respite Care

Respite care is planned for emergency short-term relief to caregivers from the demands of ongoing care. Accessible affordable respite and adult day care can provide caregivers with a break from their daily demands and be part of a multimodal approach to reducing institutionalization. Respite encompasses a range of services and may be in- or out-of-home care, for example, through adult day health (National Respite Network and Resource Center, 2002). As noted by one caregiver interviewed for an AOA study, "Respite is my number one need. I've been caring for Mom for seven years . . . in that time, I have had one vacation for three days" (AOA, 2003). Respite is one of the services offered under the National Family Caregiver Support Program. Most caregivers state that they would like respite services, but often face barriers to their use, including their own willingness to entrust their relative's care to someone else or guilt over taking a much needed break (Lustbader and Hooyman, 1996; Whitlach, Goodwin, von Eye, and Zarit, 1995).

Nationally, there is a move toward life span respite—a coordinated system of accessible, community-based respite care services for caregivers and care recipients regardless of age, ethnic minority status, special need, or situation. This recognizes the fragmentation and insufficient funding for adequate respite services based on categorical age groups (Kagan, 2003). Such an approach is also congruent with a multigenerational framework, as discussed in Chapter 9, which recognizes shared needs of caregivers across the life span.

Electronic Supports

Many Websites also provide caregivers with information on community resources, including living facilities, and an opportunity to connect with other caregivers on a 24-hour basis. Teleconferencing is being used to create virtual support groups among caregivers and can be accessed through caregiver Websites. A growing number of Websites through AARP, Assisted Living Federation of America, and Administration on Aging allow caregivers to complete an interactive assessment online to determine the services they most need. Use of the Internet for service accessibility and support is likely to increase with computer-savvy baby boomers and their adult children. Some corporations provide elder-care information, referral, education, and adult daycare through employee assistance pro-

grams. Toll-free information and referral lines are vital, with a national elder-care locator service sponsored by the Administration on Aging. However, research on the effectiveness of computer, phone, and workplace interventions is limited. Nor are these strategies generally systematic or targeted early on in caregiving, but instead are randomly used across the caregiving career (Fredriksen-Goldsen and Scharlach, 2001).

Future Service Directions

Regardless of the specific service configuration, support services should be culturally sensitive and in accessible locations, such as churches, schools, primary care clinics, the workplace, and senior and community centers. Ideally, support services are provided early in the caregiving cycle or even before it begins. This enables caregivers to plan before they may be abruptly thrust into a burdensome role. Unfortunately, it is human nature that most people do not seek out information and assistance until they need it. General information sessions about services and supports are typically

---

A MODEL FOR MULTIDISCIPLINARY COLLABORATION TO PREVENT AND PROSECUTE ABUSE

In King County in Seattle, Washington, a county-wide Elder Abuse Project sponsors an elder abuse council that includes police, prosecutors, nurses, medical examiners, and social service workers. It meets monthly to figure out how "the system" can better prevent, treat, and respond to the abuse of older and disabled adults. A criminal mistreatment review panel helps policymakers decide whether elder neglect cases can be prosecuted. The project also trains police, emergency room staff members, emergency medical technicians, and long-term care workers to detect signs of elder abuse and familiarize themselves with state laws. Recognizing that neglect is one of the most underreported and least understood crimes by police and prosecutors, the project is currently focusing on adult neglect cases.

SELF-CARE NEEDS OF THE CAREGIVER

- Learn to accept help.
- Take time for relaxing and pleasurable activities by asking others for help or utilizing respite/adult day care.
- Find ways to incorporate exercise into your daily routine.
- Take time to eat healthy food.
- Set limits on your older relative's demands.
- Attend to your spiritual needs.
- Participate in caregiver support groups.

---

not well attended. An effective early preventive strategy would engage the caregiver in planning shortly after experiencing the first acute incident or receiving the diagnosis of a chronic disease (Tennstedt, 1999).

Self-care for caregivers is also an essential component in preventing caregiver stress and institutionalization. A goal of self-care is to prevent the occurrence of signs of stress and when such signs do occur, to reduce the care demands. Learning how to accept limits, attending to one's physical and spiritual needs, and creating moments of joy are critical to both self-care and to providing effective care over the long haul (Lustbader and Hooyman, 1996).

Institutionalization

Although living alone is a major predictor of institutionalization, some 50 percent of those in nursing homes have children (Tennstedt, 1999). In most cases, families turn to institutionalization only after exhausting their own resources, although adult daughters and husbands tend to turn to out-of-home placement earlier than do other family members. The decision to seek nursing home placement is frequently precipitated by the family caregiver's illness or death, or by severe family strain. Placement is thus often the result of a breakdown in the balance between the older person's care needs and self-care abilities; the primary caregiver's internal and external resources, and the larger support network. For example, the characteristics of the caregiving context, especially perceived burden, negative family relationships, and low confidence in care, are better predictors of whether an Alzheimer's patient will be institutionalized than are the illness characteristics or symptoms of the care recipient (Fisher and Lieberman, 1999; Seltzer and Li, 2000; Tennstedt, 1999).

Most people hold negative attitudes toward nursing homes, even though the quality of care in many residential care settings is excellent. Given such attitudes, placing an older relative in a nursing home is typically a stressful family event, especially for wives who vowed to care for their husbands "in sickness and in health" (Seltzer and Li, 2000). Accordingly, the placement decision often arouses feelings of grief, loss, guilt, and fear, and may renew past family conflicts. However, some families experience improved relationships with their institutionalized relatives and continue to visit and assist with hands-on care (Pearlin et al., 1996). Although wives experience more benefits from exiting the primary care role than do daughters, the "careers of caregivers do not stop at the institution's door," partially because new stresses substitute for prior ones (Zarit and Whitlatch, 1992, p. 672). Families typically feel psychologically responsible, even though they must relinquish control over daily care decisions to staff and learn how to be "visitors" rather than primary caregivers (Schulz et al., 2003). These role changes can create family dissatisfaction with their elder's care. However, when staff–family partnerships develop, families generally experience less stress and are more satisfied with the care received by their elder (Maas, 2000).

With the growth of the oldest-old, placement in a long-term care setting may come to be viewed as a natural transition in the life cycle. Geriatric care managers can assist with the timing of this transition and with negotiating a positive role for the caregiver's continued involvement in the facility. To ease the transition to the postplacement phase, many nursing homes have developed support and educational groups for families and special training for staff. Internet-based services can now assist families with locating an appropriate long-term care facility (Tanase, 2003).

Underpaid Family Caregivers: Direct Care Workers

Although families are the primary providers of long-term care to older adults, underpaid **direct care workers** (e.g., nurses aides, personal assistants, home care workers, etc.) are also pivotal. Of the total number of direct care worker jobs in long-term care, 56 percent are in nursing and personal care facilities, 17 percent in assisted living and other residential care settings, and the remaining 27 percent in home health care services (DHHS, 2003). As the "eyes and the ears" of the long-term care system, direct care workers provide "high-touch" intimate, personal, and physically/emotionally challenging care. These hands-on providers are expected to be compassionate in their care, yet usually do not feel prepared, respected, or valued—similar to the experiences of many family caregivers. The typical paraprofessional or aide is an immigrant, single mother, with minimal education and living in poverty. Racial and gender inequities in education and employment opportunities across the life span partially explain the predominance of African American, Asian, and Latina women, many of whom are immigrants, among direct care workers. Language and cultural differences in communication may interfere with meeting older patients' needs. Our society's lack of public recognition of the socially and economically important work of caregiving is, in turn, reflected in negative working conditions. These include low pay (typically around $7 an hour), limited training, inadequate supervision, and low status (DHHS, 2003; Wichterich, 2000).

The heavy workload is often a repetition of single tasks, and the risk of personal injury from physical work is high. Workers of color may be treated disrespectfully, even verbally and physically abused, by some older patients. In addition, there are few incentives for obtaining more training or education to enhance quality of care. Not surprisingly, the turnover rate among direct care workers is high, with 90 percent replaced annually. Today, over 40 states currently face a shortage of direct care workers, and many large nursing homes and long-term care corporations recruit workers from developing countries. The demand for direct care workers will become even greater in 2030 when the baby boomers reach age 85 (DHHS, 2003). The public policy and structural factors that exacerbate this shortage along with the difficulties faced by paraprofessionals within the long-term care system are discussed further in Chapter 17.

Implications for the Future

With the aging of the baby boomers and increased longevity, family caregiving of older adults will undoubtedly encompass a longer phase of the life span, with adults devoting 40 to 50 years to caring for older relatives. Care networks will be larger and more complex because of the diversity of family structures and the effects of divorce, remarriage, blended families, and more single parents and unmarried couples raising children. Women are likely to remain the primary caregivers for elders. Even though 75 percent of married mothers with children work outside the home, women still assume primary responsibility for children. In fact, women still devote nearly as much time to household tasks as they did 50 years ago, even though the expectation and necessity for women to enter the paid workforce has grown (Coontz, 1997). The persistence of this gender-based pattern in child care and household tasks thus tempers expectations that men will soon become the primary care providers of frail elders.

The role of government in supporting family caregivers in the future is unclear, and will undoubtedly be affected by the escalating federal deficit. Current federal cutbacks and the devolution of responsibility for services to the states suggest that public funding to support informal caregivers will probably be limited. More corporations may offer elder-care services as an employee benefit, because of the effects of family caregiving on worker productivity. Other private sector initiatives, such as faith-based programs, may provide incremental supports for families, but these are unlikely to reduce substantially the burdens faced by families who may be caring for relatives with cognitive impairments for many years. For-profit geriatric care management businesses are likely to grow. However, these services will be primarily accessible to upper-middle-class adult children, often at a geographic distance, who need assistance with locating services for aging parents. Unless patterns of public funding change dramatically, low-income families will typically lack such supports.

Health care providers' assessments of older adults will increasingly include family caregivers' capacities. Nurses and social workers will be central in working to identify supportive resources for families to enhance their caregiving capability and reduce their stress. The issues of grief and loss inherent in family care, especially for an older adult with dementia, will need to be addressed by hospice workers and bereavement counselors. The professional preparation of health care providers must include more information about family dynamics, how to work effectively with families, and how to identify supportive resources for caregivers.

The use of information technology to provide family caregivers with informal and mutual support will grow. Living in a networked society, senior boomers, facile with computers and the Internet throughout their adult lives, will be comfortable accessing information and support from others, including resources for family caregivers, through computer-based technology. The Internet can already provide a wealth of information for family caregivers: These include free e-mail question-and-answer sites, bulletin board structures

for sharing concerns and joint problem-solving, digital photos of living facilities, and links to national resources. Services such as these will continue to grow. Family caregivers will increasingly turn to other caregivers for 24-hour mutual support as well as accessing medical information via the Internet. The growth of assistive technology and computerized "smart homes," as described in Chapter 11, will enable more frail elders to remain safely in their own homes, although such innovative supports will probably be more readily available to those who can privately purchase them than to low-income elders and their families. Whether computer technology can, over time, reduce inequities and barriers to services among low-income elders of color remains unknown, and will probably mirror racial and class gaps among younger generations.

Summary

Most families, regardless of socioeconomic class or ethnic minority status, attempt to provide care for their older members for as long as possible, and seek institutionalization only when they have exhausted other resources. Without informal caregiving, the costs of long-term care to society would be staggering. Adult children—generally women—are faced with providing financial, emotional, and physical assistance to older relatives, oftentimes with little support from others for their caregiving responsibilities. In ethnic minority and lower-income families, older relatives are most likely to receive daily care from younger relatives and to be involved themselves in caring for grandchildren. But there are numerous personal costs to caregiving, including financial, physical, and emotional. Elder mistreatment is one tragic outcome of a stressful caregiving situation. Responsibilities for caregiving are affected by a number of social trends, most notable among them the increasing percentage of middle-aged women—traditionally the caregivers—who are more likely to be employed, and the number of reconstituted families resulting from divorce and remarriage. The needs of caregivers are clearly a growing concern for social and health care providers and policymakers.

GLOSSARY

care or case management coordination and monitoring of services to meet older adults' assessed service needs

caregiving the act of assisting people with personal care, household chores, transportation, and other tasks associated with daily living; provided either by family members without compensation or by professionals

caregiver burden the personal energy, time restrictions, financial strains, and/or psychological frustrations associated with assisting persons with long-term care needs

direct care workers nurses aides, personal assistants, and home care workers who provide hands-on care in both private home and institutional settings

elder mistreatment maltreatment of older adults, including physical, sexual, and psychological abuse and financial exploitation

elder neglect deprivation of care necessary to maintain elders' health by those trusted to provide the care (e.g., neglect by others) or by older persons themselves (self-neglect)

empty nest a family whose adult children have left home for a job or college or marriage

Family and Medical Leave Act federal legislation passed in 1993 that provides job protection to workers requiring short-term leaves from their jobs for the care of a dependent parent or seriously ill newborn or adopted child

informal caregiving Unpaid assistance provided by family, friends, and neighbors for persons requiring help with ADL and IADL

National Family Caregiver Support Program Requires state and area agencies on aging to provide services to support family caregivers

objective burden reality demands that caregivers face (income loss, job disruption, etc.)

respite care short-term relief (rest) for caregivers; may be provided in the home or out of home (e.g., through adult day health centers)

self-neglect often the older adult engages in behavior that threatens own safety, even though mentally competent

subjective burden the caregiver's experience of caregiver burden; different caregivers appraise caregiver stress differently

women in the middle women who have competing demands from older parents, spouses, children, or employment

RESOURCES

See the companion Website for this text at <www.ablongman.com/hooyman> for information about the following:

- AARP
- Administration on Aging
- Caregiving
- Caring Concepts
- Children of Aging Parents
- Elders in Action
- Eldercare Locator
- Eldercare Web
- Family Caregiver Alliance
- The Home Care Page
- National Alliance for Caregiving
- National Center on Elder Abuse, NCEA
- National Family Caregivers Association
- National Institute on Adult Day Care
- National Institute on Aging, Family and Professional Caregiver Programs
- Total Living Choices

REFERENCES

Acton, G. J., and Wright, K. Self-transcendence and family caregivers of adults with dementia. *Journal of Holistic Nursing,* 2000, *18,* 143–58.

Adkins, V. K. Treatment of depressive disorders of spousal caregivers of persons with Alzheimer's disease: A review. *American Journal of Alzheimer's Disease and Other Dementias,* 1999, *14,* 289–293.

Administration on Aging (AOA). *National elder abuse incidence study.* Washington, DC: Department of Health and Human Services, 2000.

Allen, S., Goldscheider, F., and Ciambrone, D. A. Gender roles, marital intimacy, and nomination of spouse as primary caregiver. *The Gerontologist,* 1999, *39*(2), 150–158.

Almberg, B., Grafstroem, M., and Winblad, B. Caregivers of relatives with dementia: Experiences encompassing social support and bereavement. *Aging and Mental Health,* 2000, *4,* 82–89.

Alzheimer's Association of America. *Statistics and chapter information.* Chicago, 2001.

Amhed, I. *Coping with the burden of caregiving.* Paper presented at the National Conference on Aging and Diversity, Honolulu, Hawaii: University of Hawaii, 2003.

American Association of Marriage and Family Therapy. *Consumer update: Caregiving for the elderly.* http://aamft.org/families/Consumer_Update/Caregiving_Elderly.htm, 2002.

American Association of Retired Persons. *In the middle: A report on multicultural boomers coping with family and aging issues.* Washington, DC, 2001.

Anetzberger, G. J. Caregiving: Primary cause of elder abuse? *Generations,* Summer 2000, *24,* 46–51.

Anetzberger, G. J., Palmisano, B. R., Sanders, M., Bass, D., Dayton, C., Eckert, S., and Schimer, M. R. A model intervention for elder abuse and dementia. In E. S. McConnell (Ed.), Practice Concepts. *The Gerontologist,* 2000, *40,* 492–497.

Angel, R. J., and Angel, J. L. *Who will care for us? Aging and long term care in a multicultural America.* New York: New York University Press, 1997.

Antonucci, T. Social supports and social relationships. In R. Binstock and L. George (Eds.), *Handbook of aging and the social sciences,* 3rd ed. San Diego: Academic Press, 1990.

Aranda, M., and Knight, B. G. The influence of ethnicity and culture on the caregiver stress and coping process: A sociocultural review and analysis. *The Gerontologist,* 1997, *37,* 342–354.

Arnett, J. J. Emerging adulthood: A theory of development from the late teens through the twenties. *American Psychologist,* 2000, *55,* 469–480.

Arno, P. S., Levine, C., and Memmot, M. M. The economic value of informal caregiving. *Health Affairs,* 1999, *18,* 182–188.

Beach, S., Schulz, R., Yee, J., and Jackson, S. Negative and positive health effects of caring for a disabled spouse: Longitudinal findings from the Caregiver Health Effects Study. *Psychology and Aging,* 2000, *15, 259–271.*

Bengtson, V. L., Rosenthal, C. J., and Burton, C. Paradoxes of families and aging. In R. H. Binstock and C. K. George (Eds.), *Handbook of aging and the social sciences* (4th ed.). San Diego: Academic Press, 1996.

Bengtson, V. L. Beyond the nuclear family: The increasing importance of multigenerational bonds. *Journal of Marriage and the Family,* 2001, *63,* 1–16.

Bergeron, R. Serving the needs of elder abuse victims. *Policy and Practice of Public Human Services,* 2000, *58,* 40–45.

Bergeron, R., and Gray, B. Ethical dilemmas of reporting suspected elder abuse. *Social Work,* 2003, *48,* 96–105.

Berg-Weger, M., Rubio, D. M., and Tebb, S. S. Depression as a mediator: Viewing caregiver well being and strain in a different light. *Families in Society,* 2000, *8,* 162–173.

Binney, E. A., Estes, C., and Humphers, S. E. Informalization and community care. In C. Estes, J. H. Swan & Associates (Eds.), *Long-term care crisis: Elders trapped in the no-care zone.* Walnut Creek, CA: Sage, 1993.

Blieszner, R., and Shifflet, P. A. The effects of Alzheimer's disease on close relationships between patients and caregivers. *Family Relations,* 1999, *39,* 57–63.

Blum, B. *Elder abuse.* Paper presented at the Elder Abuse Conference, Tucson, Arizona, 2000.

Boss, P. Ambiguous loss: Living with frozen grief. *Harvard Mental Health Letter,* 1999, *16,* 4–7.

Bourgeois, M. S., Schulz, R., Burgio, L., and Beach, S. Skills training for spouses of patients with Alzheimer's disease: Outcomes of an intervention study. *Journal of Clinical Geropsychology,* 2002, *8,* 53–73.

Braithwaite, V. Making choices through caregiving appraisals. *The Gerontologist,* 2000, *40,* 706–717.

Branch, L. The epidemiology of elder abuse and neglect. *Public Policy and Aging Report,* 2002, *12,* 19–23.

Braun, K. L., and Browne, C. Cultural values and caregiving patterns among Asian and Pacific Islander Americans. In D. E. Redburn and L. P. McNamara (Eds.), *Social gerontology.* Westport, CT: Greenwood Press, 1998.

Brownell, P. The application of the culturagram in cross-cultural practice with elder abuse victims. *Journal of Elder Abuse and Neglect*, 1997, *9*, 19–33.

Brownell, P. *Project 2015: The future of aging in New York state*. New York: Department for the Aging, 2002.

Brownell, P., and Berman, J. Elder abuse and the kinship foster care system: Two generations at risk. In C. Cox (Ed.), *To grandmother's house we go and stay*. New York: Springer, 2000.

Burgio, L., Stevens, A., Guy, D., Roth, D. L., and Haley, W. E. Impact of two psychosocial interventions on white and African American family caregivers of individuals with dementia. *The Gerontologist*, 2003, *43*, 568–581.

Burns, R., Nichols, L. O., and Martindale-Adams, J. Interdisciplinary geriatric primary care evaluation and management: Two year outcomes. *Journal of the American Geriatrics Society*, 2000, *48*, 8–13.

Calasanti, T. M., and Slevin, K. F. *Gender, social inequalities and aging*. Walnut Creek, CA: Altima Press, 2001.

Campbell, L. D., and Martin-Matthews, A. Primary and proximate. *Journal of Family Issues*, 2000, *21*, 1006–1031.

Choi, N. G., and Mayer, J. Elder abuse, neglect and exploitation: Risk factors and prevention strategies. *Journal of Gerontological Social Work*, 2000, *33*, 5–25.

Chu, P., Edwards, J., Levin, R., and Thomson, J. The use of clinical case management for early stage Alzheimer's patients and their families. *American Journal of Alzheimer's disease and Other Dementias*, 2000, *15*, 284–290.

Clark, M., and Huttinger, K. Elder care among Mexican American families. *Clinical Nursing Research*, 1998, *7*, 64–81.

Coe, M., and Neufeld, A. Male caregiver's use of formal support. *Western Journal of Nursing Research*, 1999, *21*, 268–289.

Commission on Leave. *A workable balance: Report to Congress on family and medical leave policies*. Washington, DC: Women's Bureau, U.S. Department of Labor, 1996.

Connell, C. M., and Gibson, G. D. Racial, ethnic and cultural differences in dementia caregiving: Review and analysis. *The Gerontologist*, 1997, *37*, 355–364.

Connell, C. M., Janevic, M. R., and Gallant, M. P. The costs of caring: Impact of dementia on family caregivers. *Journal of Geriatric Psychiatry and Neurology*, 2001, *14*, 179–187.

Cook-Daniels, L. Lesbian, gay male, bisexual and transgendered elders: Elder abuse and neglect. *Journal of Elder Abuse and Neglect*, 1997, *9*, 35–49.

Coontz, S. *The way we really are: Coming to terms with America's changing families*. New York: Basic Books, 1997.

Cox, C. Comparing the experiences of black and white caregivers of dementia patients. *Social Work*, 1995, *40*, 343–349.

Cox, C. Race and caregiving: Patterns of service use by African American and white caregivers of persons with Alzheimer's disease. *Journal of Gerontologic Social Work*, 1999, *32*, 5–19.

Cox, C., and Monk, A. Minority caregivers of dementia victims: A comparison of black and Hispanic families. *Journal of Applied Gerontology*, 1990, *9*, 340–354.

Cummings, S. M., Long, J. K., Peterson-Hazan, S., and Harrison, J. The efficacy of a group treatment model in helping spouses meet the emotional and practical challenges of early stage caregiving. *Clinical Gerontologist*, 1998, *20*, 29–45.

Cunio, M. T. M. A cross-cultural study of Alzheimer's disease caregivers. *Dissertation Abstracts International: The Sciences and Engineering*, 1999, *59*(1/B), 5617.

Dautzenberg, M. G., Diedricks, J. P., Philipsen, H., and Tan, F. E. Multigenerational caregiving and well being: Distress of middle aged daughters providing assistance to elderly parents. *Women's Health*, 1999, *29*, 57–74.

Davis, L. L. Telephone-based interventions with family caregivers: A feasibility study. *Journal of Family Nursing*, 1998, *4*, 255–270.

Delgado, M., and Tennstedt, S. Making the case for culturally appropriate community services: Puerto /Rican elders and their caregivers. *Health and Social Work*, 1997, *22*, 246–253.

Dilworth-Anderson, P., Williams, S. W., and Cooper, T. Family caregiving to elderly African Americans: Caregiver types and structures. *Journals of Gerontology: Social Sciences*, 1999, *54B*, S237–S241.

Dilworth-Anderson, P., Williams, I. C., and Gibson, R. E. Issues of race, ethnicity, and culture in caregiving research: A 20-year review. *The Gerontologist*, 2002, 42, 237–272.

Doty, P. J., Stone, R. I., Jackson, M. E., and Drabek, J. L. Informal caregiving. In C. J. Evashiwick (Ed.), *The continuum of long-term care* (2nd ed.). Albany, NY: Delmar, 2001.

Dupuis, S. Understanding ambiguous loss in the context of dementia care: Adult children's perspective. *Journal of Gerontological Social Work*, 2002, 37, 93–114.

Eakes, G. G., Burke, M. L., and Hainsworth, M. A. Middle-range theory of chronic sorrow. *Journal of Nursing Scholarship*, 1998, 30, 179–184.

Epple, D. Senile dementia of the Alzheimer type. *Clinical Social Work Journal*, 2002, 30, 95–109.

Farran, C. J., Miller, B. H., Kaufman, J. E., and Davis, L. Race, finding meaning and caregiver distress. *Journal of Aging and Health*, 1997, 3, 316–333.

Farran, C. J., Miller, B., Kaufman, J. E., Donner, E., and Fogg, L. Finding meaning through caregiving: Development of an instrument for family caregivers of persons with Alzheimer's disease. *Journal of Clinical Geropsychology*, 1999, 55, 1107–1125.

Fast, R., and Chapin, R. *Strengths-based care management for older adults*. Baltimore: Health Professions, 2000.

Fisher, L., and Lieberman, M. A. A longitudinal study of predictors of nursing home placement for patients with dementia: The contribution of family characteristics. *The Gerontologist*, 1999, 39, 677–686.

Foley, K. L., Tung, H. J., and Mutran, E. J. Self gain and self loss among African American and white caregivers. *Journals of Gerontology*, 2002, 57, S14–S22.

Fox, P., Newcomer, R., Yordi, C., and Arnsberg, P. Lessons learned from the Medicare Alzheimer's disease demonstration. *Alzheimer's Disease and Associated Disorders*, 2000, 14, 87–93.

Fredriksen, K. I. Family caregiving among lesbians and gay men. *Social Work*, 1999, 44, 142–155.

Fredriksen-Goldsen, K. I. Caregiving and resiliency: Predictors of well being. *Journal of Family Relations*, in press.

Fredriksen-Goldsen, K. I., and Hooyman, N. *Multigenerational health, development and equality*. Seattle: University of Washington School of Social Work, Concept paper, 2003.

Fredriksen-Goldsen, K. I., and Scharlach, A. E. *Families and work: New directions in the twenty first century*. New York: Oxford University Press, 2001.

Fulmer, T., Paveza, G., and Quadagno, L. Elder abuse and neglect: Policy issues for two very different problems. *Public Policy and Aging Report*, 2002, 12, 15–18.

Garcia, E. M., and Oropesa, M. Caregiving in the context of ethnicity: Hispanic caregiver wives of stroke patients. *Dissertation Abstracts International: Humanities and Social Sciences*, 2000, 60, 4192.

Gartska, T., McCallion, P., and Toseland, R. Using support groups to improve caregiver health. In M. L. Hummert and J. F. Nussbaum (Eds.), *Aging, communication, and health*. Mahwah, NJ: Lawrence Erlbaum Associates, 2001.

Gaugler, J. E., Kane, R. A., and Langlois, J. Assessment of family caregivers of older adults. In R. L. Kane and R. A. Kane (Eds.), *Assessing older persons: Measures, meaning and practical applications*. New York: Oxford, 2000.

Gaugler, J. E., Leitsch, S. A., Zarit, S. H., and Pearlin, L. I. Caregiver involvement following institutionalization: Effects of preplacement stress. *Research on Aging*, 2000, 22, 337–360.

Gerstel, N., and Gallagher, S. Men's caregiving: Gender and the contingent character of care, *Gender and Society*, 2001, 15, 197–217.

Given, C. W., Given, B. A., Stommel, M., and Azzouz, F. The impact of new demands for assistance on caregiver depression: Tests using an inception cohort. *The Gerontologist*, 1999, 39, 76–85.

Goldschieder, F. K., Thornton, A., and Yang, L. S. The effects of childhood structure on leaving and returning home. *Journal of Marriage and the Family*, 1998, 60, 745–756.

Goldschieder, F. K., Thornton, A., and Yang, L-S. Helping out the kids: Expectations about parental support in young adulthood. *Journal of Marriage and the Family*, 2001, 63, 727–740.

Gonyea, J. Midlife, multigenerational bonds, and caregiving. In R. Talley (Ed.), *Caregiving: Science to practice*. Atlanta, Georgia: Rosalyn Carter Institute, 2004.

Groger, L., and Mayberry, P. S. Caring too much? Cultural lag in African Americans' perceptions of filial responsibilities. *Journal of Cross-Cultural Gerontology*, 2001, 16, 21–39.

Guberman, N., and Maheu, P. Combining employment and caregiving: An intricate juggling act. *Canadian Journal of Aging*, 1999, *18*, 84–106.

Gwyther, L. Social issues of the Alzheimer's patient and family. *Neurological Clinics*, 1998, *18*, 993–1010.

Han, B., and. Haley, W. E. Family caregiving for patients with stroke: Review and analysis. *Stroke*, 1999, *30*, 1478–1485.

Harris, P. Listening to caregiving sons: Misunderstood realities. *The Gerontologist*, 1998, *38*, 342–352.

Hooyman, N., and Gonyea, J. *Feminist perspectives on family care: Policies for gender justice.* Thousand Oaks, CA: Sage, 1995.

Hooyman, N. The prevention of caregiver stress in older adulthood. In T. P. Gullotta and M. Bloom (Eds.), *The encyclopedia of primary prevention and health promotion.* New York, Kluwar, 2003.

Hudson, M. F., and Carlson, J. R. Elder abuse: Its meaning to Caucasians, African Americans, and Native Americans. In T. Tattara, (Ed.), *Understanding elder abuse in minority populations.* Philadelphia: Taylor and Francis, 1999.

Hudson, R. B., and Gonyea, J. G. Time not yet money: The promise and politics of the Family and Medical Leave Act. *Journal of Social Policy and Aging*, 2000, *11*, 189–200.

Hughes, S. L., Gobbie-Hurder, A., Weaver, F. M., Kubal, J. D., and Henderson, W. Relationship between caregiver burden and health-related quality of life. *The Gerontologist*, October 1999, *39*, 534–545.

Ingersoll-Dayton, B., Neal, M. B., and Hammer, L. B. Aging parents helping adult children: The experience of the sandwiched generation. *Family Relations*, 2001, 262–271.

Janevic, M., and Connell, C. M. Racial, ethnic and cultural difference in the dementia caregiving experience: Recent findings. *The Gerontologist*, 2001, *41*, 334–337.

Kagan, J. B. *Lifespan respite. Fact sheet number 7.* Annandale, VA: National Respite Coalition, 2003.

Karlawash, J. H., Casaretti, D., Klocinski, J., and Clark, C. M. The relationships between caregivers' global ratings of Alzheimer's disease patients' quality of life, disease severity, and the caregiving experience. *Journal of the American Geriatrics Society*, 2001, *49*, 1066–1070.

Knight, B. G., and McCallum, T. J. Heart rate reactivity and depression in African American and white de-mentia caregivers: Reporting bias or positive coping? *Aging and Mental Health*, 1998, *2*, 212–221.

Knight, B. G. M., McCallum, T. J., and Fox, L. A sociocultural stress and coping model for mental health outcomes among African American caregivers in southern California. *Journals of Gerontology*, 2000, *55B*, S142–S150.

Kramer, B. J. Gain in the caregiver experience: Where are we? What next? *The Gerontologist*, 1997, *37*, 218–232.

Kramer, B. J. Husbands caring for wives with dementia: A longitudinal study of continuity and change. *Health and Social Work*, 2000, *25*, 97–107.

Kramer, B. J., and Lambert, J. D. Caregiving as a life course transition among older husbands: A prospective study. *The Gerontologist*, 1999, *39*, 658–667.

LaPlante, M. P., Harrington, C., and Kang, T. Estimated paid and unpaid hours of personal assistance services in activities of daily living provided to adults living at home. *Health Services Research*, 2002, *37*, 397–415.

Lawton, M. P., and Nahemow, L. Ecology and the aging process. In C. Eisdorfer and M. P. Lawton (Eds.), *Psychology of adult development and aging.* Washington, DC: American Psychological Association, 1973.

Linsk, N., and Keigher, S. Compensation of family care for the elderly. In P. Kane and J. Penrod (Eds.), *Family caregiving in an aging society.* Thousand Oaks, CA: Sage, 1995.

Loucks, C. *But this is my mother!* Acton, MA: Vander Wyk and Burham, 2000.

Lustbader, W., and Hooyman, N. *Taking care of aging family members: A practical guide.* New York: Free Press, 1996.

Maas, M. When elders transition, so do their caregivers: Invited Commentary. *Transitions*, Wayne State University Institute of Gerontology, 2000, *7*, 2, 8.

Marcell, J. *Elder rage or take my father . . . please!* Irvine, CA: Impressive Press, 2000.

Martin, C. D. More than the work. *Journal of Family Issues*, 2000, *21*, 986–1006.

Martin-Matthews, A. Change and diversity in aging families and intergenerational relations. In N. Mandell and A. Duffy (Eds.), *Canadian families: Diversity, conflict and change.* Toronto: Harcourt Brace, 2000.

Matthews, S. H., and Heidorn, J. Meeting filial responsibilities in brothers-only sibling groups. *Journals of Gerontology,* 1998, *53B,* S278–S286.

McConnell, B. R., and McConnell, E. S. Treating excess disability among cognitively impaired nursing home residents. *Journal of the American Geriatrics Society,* 2000, *48,* 454–455.

McCormick, W. C., Ohata, C. Y., Uomoto, J., Young, H., and Graves, A. B. Similarities and differences in attitudes toward long-term care between Japanese Americans and Caucasian Americans. *Journal of the American Geriatrics Society,* 2002, *50,* 1149–1155.

McDonald, T. P., Poertner, J., and Pierpont, J. Predicting caregiver stress: An ecological perspective, *American Journal of Orthopsychiatry,* 1999, *69,* 100–109.

McLeod, B. W. *Caregiving: The spiritual journey of love, loss and renewal.* New York: John Wiley and Sons, 1999.

Metropolitan Life Insurance Company. *Met Life study of employer costs for working caregivers.* Westport, CT: Metropolitan Life Insurance, 1998.

Meuser, T. M., and Marwit, S. J. A comprehensive stage sensitive model of grief in dementia caregiving. *The Gerontologist,* 2001, *41,* 658–670.

Meuser, T. M., and Marwit, S. J. Development and initial validation of an inventory to assess grief in caregivers of persons with Alzheimer's disease. *The Gerontologist,* 2002, *42,* 751–767.

Miller, B., and Mukherjee, S. Service use, caregiving mastery, and attitudes toward community services. *Journal of Applied Gerontology,* 1999, *18,* 162–177.

Mittelman, M. S. Family caregiving for people with Alzheimer's disease: Results of the NYU Spouse Caregiver Intervention Study. *Generations,* 2002, *3,* 104–106.

Mittelman, M. S., Ferris, S., Shalmon, E., Steinberg, G., Ambinder, A., Mackell, J., and Cohen, J. A comprehensive support program: Effect on depression in spouse caregiving of dementia patients. *The Gerontologist,* 1995, *35,* 792–802.

Moen, P. The gendered life course. In R. H. Binstock and L. K. George (Eds.), *Handbook of aging and the social sciences* (5th ed.). San Diego, CA: Academic Press, 2001.

Moen, P., Erickson, M. A., and Dempster-McClain, D. Social role identities among older adults in a continuing care retirement community. *Research on Aging,* 2000, *22,* 559–579.

Moon, A., Tomita, S. K., and Jung-Kamei, S. Elder mistreatment among four Asian-American groups: An exploratory study on tolerance, victim blaming and attitudes toward third party intervention. *Journal of Gerontological Social Work,* 2001, *36,* 153–169.

Morano, C. A psycho educational model for Hispanic Alzheimer's disease caregivers. *The Gerontologist,* 2002, *42,* 122–126.

Naleppa, M. J. Gerontological social work and case management. In B. Berkman and L. Harootyan (Eds.), *Social work in aging and health care.* New York: Springer, 2003.

Narayn, S., Lewis, M., Tornatore, J., Hepburn, K., and Corcoran-Perry, S. Subjective responses to caregiving for spouses with dementia. *Journal of Gerontological Nursing,* 2001, *27,* 19–28.

National Academy on an Aging Society. *Helping the elderly with activity limitations: Caregiving, #7:* Washington, DC: May 2000.

National Alliance for Caregiving and AARP. *Family caregiving in the U.S.: Findings from a national survey.* Washington, DC: June 1997.

National Alliance for Caregiving and the Equitable Foundation. *The caregiving boom: Baby boomer women giving care.* Bethesda, MD: September 1998.

National Association of State Units on Aging (NASUA). *The aging network implements the National Family Caregiver Support Program.* Washington, DC: Administration on Aging, 2003.

National Center on Elder Abuse, *National elder abuse incidence study: Final report,* 1998. Washington, DC: American Public Health Services Association.

National Respite Network and Resource Center. *Adult day care: One form of respite for older adults, Fact Sheet #54.* Chapel Hill, NC: Author, 2002.

Navaie-Waliser, M., Feldman, P. H., Gould, D. A., Levine, C., Kuerbis, A. N., and Donelan, K. The experiences and challenges of informal caregivers: Common themes and differences among whites, blacks and Hispanics. *The Gerontologist,* 2001, *41,* 733–741.

Neal, M. B., Ingersoll-Dayton, B., and Starrels, M. E. Gender and relationship differences in caregiving patterns and consequences among employed caregivers. *The Gerontologist,* 1997, *37,* 804–816.

Nerenberg, L. Developing a service response to elder abuse. *Generations,* 2000, *24,* 86–92.

Newcomer, R., Yordi, C., DuHan, R., Fox, P., and Wilkinson, A. Effects of Medicare Alzheimer's disease demonstration on caregiver burden and depression. *Health Services Research,* 1999, *34,* 669–689.

Nijboer, C., Triemstra, M., Tempelaar, R., Mulder, M., Sanderman, R., and van den Bos, G. A. Patterns of caregiver experiences among partners of cancer patients. *The Gerontologist,* 2000, *40,* 738–746.

Noonan, A. E., and Tennstedt, S. L. Meaning in caregiving and its contribution to caregiver well-being. *The Gerontologist,* 1997, *37,* 785–794.

Olson, L. K. *Age through ethnic lenses: Caring for elderly in a multicultural society.* Baltimore: Rowman and Littlefield, 2001.

Ory, M. G., Hoffman, R. R. III, Yee, J. L., Tennstedt, S. L., and Schulz, R. Prevalence and impact of caregiving: A detailed comparison between dementia and nondementia caregivers. *The Gerontologist,* 1999, *39,* 177–185.

Ory, M., Tennstedt, S. L., and Schulz, R. The extent and impact of dementia care: Unique challenges experienced by family caregivers. In R. Schulz (Ed.), *Handbook of dementia caregiving: Evidence-based interventions for family caregivers.* New York: Springer, 2000.

Oswald, S. K., Hepburn, K. W., Caron, W., Burns, T., and Mantell, R. Reducing caregiver burden: A randomized psychoeducational intervention for caregivers of persons with dementia. *The Gerontologist,* 1999, *39,* 299–309.

Otto, J. M. The role of adult protective services in addressing abuse. *Generations,* 2000, *24,* 33–38.

Otto, J. M. Program and administrative issues affecting adult protective services. *Public Policy and Aging Report,* 2002, *12,* 3–7.

Owens, S. D. African American female elder caregivers: An analysis of the psychosocial correlates of their stress level, alcohol use and psychological well being. *Dissertation Abstracts International: Humanities and Social Sciences,* 2001, *62,* 332A–333A.

Pavalko, E. K., and Artis, J. E. Women's caregiving and paid work: Causal relationships in late midlife. *Journals of Gerontology,* 1997, *52B,* S170–S179.

Pearlin, L. I., Aneshensel, C. S., Mullon, J. T., and Whitlatch, C. J. Caregiving and its social support. In R. H. Binstock and L. K. George (Eds.), *Handbook of aging and the social sciences* (4th ed.). San Diego: Academic Press, 1996.

Penning, M. J. Hydra revisited: Substituting formal for self- and informal in-home care among older adults with disabilities. *The Gerontologist,* 2002, *42,* 4–16.

Penning, M. J. In the middle: Parental caregiving in the context of other roles. *Journals of Gerontology,* 1998, *53B,* S188–S197.

Peters-Davis, N. D., Moss, M. S., and Pruchno, R. A. Children-in-law in caregiving families. *The Gerontologist,* 1999, *39,* 66–75.

Polen, M. R., and Green, C. A. Caregiving, alcohol use and mental health symptoms among HMO members. *Journal of Community Health,* 2001, *26,* 285–301.

Prescop, K. L., Dodge, H. H., Morycz, R. K., Schulz, R. M., and Ganguli, M. Elders with dementia living in the community with and without caregivers: An epidemiological study. *International Psychogeriatrics,* 1999, *11,* 235–250.

Prigerson, H. G. Costs to society of family caregiving for patients with end-stage Alzheimer's disease. *New England Journal of Medicine,* 2003, *20,* 1891–1892.

Pruchno, R. A. Raising grandchildren: The experiences of black and white grandmothers. *The Gerontologist,* 1999, *39,* 209–221.

Pruchno, R. A., Burant, C. J., and Peters, N. Understanding the well-being of care receivers. *The Gerontologist,* 1997, *37,* 102–109.

Quereshi, H., and Walker, A. *The caregiving relationship: Elderly people and their families.* London: MacMillan, 1989.

Quinn, M. J. Undoing undue influence. *Journal of Elder Abuse and Neglect,* 2000, *12,* 9–17.

Quinn, M. J., and Heisler, C. J. The legal system: Civil and criminal responses to elder abuse and neglect. *Public Policy and Aging Report,* 2002, *12,* 8–16.

Quinn, M. J., and Tomita, S. K. *Elder abuse and neglect: Causes, diagnosis, and intervention strategies* (2nd ed.). New York: Springer, 1997.

Reid, J., and Hardy, M. Multiple roles and well-being among midlife women: Testing role strain and role enhancement theories. *Journal of Gerontology,* 1999, *54B,* S329–S338.

Robinson-Whelen, S., Tada, Y., McCallum, R. C., McGuire, L., and Kiecolt-Glaser, J. K. Long term caregiving: What happens when it ends? *Journal of Abnormal Psychology,* 2001, *110,* 573–584.

Rudd, M. G., Viney, L. L., and Preston, C. A. The grief experienced by spousal caregivers of dementia patients: The role of place of care of patient and gender of caregiver. *International Journal of Aging and Human Development,* 1999, *48,* 217–240.

Sanders, S., and McFarland, P. Perceptions of caregiving role by son's caring for a parent with Alzheimer's disease. *Journal of Gerontological Social Work,* 2002, *37,* 61–75.

Sanders, S., and Corley, C. Are they grieving: A qualitative analysis examining grief in caregivers of individuals with Alzheimer's disease. *Health and Social Work,* 2003, *37,* 35–53.

Schulz, R., and Beach, S. R. Caregiving as a risk factor for mortality: The caregiver Health Effects Study. *Journal of the American Medical Association,* 1999, *282,* 2215–2219.

Schulz, R., Mendelsohn, A. B., Haley, W. E., Mahoney, D., Allen, R. S., Zhang, S., Thompson, L., and Belle, S. H. End of life care and the effects of bereavement on family caregivers of persons with dementia. *The New England Journal of Medicine,* 2003, *20,* 1936–1942.

Schulz, R., O'Brien, A., Bookwalla, J., and Fleissner, K. Psychiatric and physical morbidity effects of dementia caregiving: Prevalence, correlates and causes. *The Gerontologist,* 1995, *35,* 771–791.

Schulz, R., O'Brien, A., Czaja, S., Ory, M., Norris, R., Martire, L. M., Belle, S. H., Burgio, L., Gitlin, L., Coon, D., Burns, R., Gallagher-Thompson, D., and Stevens, A. Dementia caregiver intervention research: In search of clinical significance. *The Gerontologist,* 2002, *42,* 589–682.

Schulz, R., and Williamson, G. M. The measurement of caregiver outcomes in Alzheimer's disease research. *Alzheimer's Disease and Associated Disorders,* 1997, *11,* 117–124.

Seltzer, M. and Li, L. W. The dynamics of caregiving: Transitions during a three-year prospective study. *The Gerontologist,* 2000, *40,* 165–178.

Shanas, E. The family as a social support in old age. *The Gerontologist,* 1979, *19,* 169–174.

Sherrell, K., Buckwalter, K., and Morhardt, D. Negotiating family relationships: Dementia care as a midlife developmental task. *Families in Society,* 2001, *82,* 383–392.

Simon, M. L., Milligan, M., Guider, R., Puzan, L., Ellano, C., and Atkin, P. Self neglect: The revolving door. *Silent suffering: Elder abuse in America.* Long Beach, CA: Archstone Foundation, 1997.

Smerglia, V. L., and Deimling, G. T. Care-related decision-making satisfaction and caregiver well-being in families caring for older members. *The Gerontologist,* 1997, *37,* 658–665.

Spillman, B. C., and Pezzin, L. E. Potential and active family caregivers: Changing networks and the "sandwich generation." *Milbank Quarterly,* 2000, *78,* 347–374.

Sprecher, S., and Fehr, B. The dissolution of close relationships. *Perspectives on loss: A sourcebook.* Philadelphia: Bruner Mazel, 1998.

Stone, R. *Long term care for the elderly with disabilities: Current policy, emerging trends and implications for the 21st century.* New York: The Milbank Memorial Fund, 2000.

Strang, V. R., Haughey, M., Gerdner, A., Tell, C. S. Respite—a coping strategy for family caregivers/commentaries/author's response. *Western Journal of Nursing Research,* 1999, *21,* 450–471.

Tanase, T. *Alzheimer's educator.* Seattle, WA: Total Living Choices, 2003.

Tatara, T. Introduction. *Special Issue: Elder abuse in minority populations. Journal of Elder Abuse and Neglect,* 1997, *9,* 1–4.

Tatara, T. Finding the nature and scope of domestic elder abuse with state aggregate data. *Journal of Elder Abuse and Neglect,* 1993, *5,* 35–56.

Tatara, T., Thomas, C., and Cyphers, G. *The national elder abuse incidence study.* Washington, DC: The National Center on Elder Abuse, 1998.

Tennstedt, S. L. *Family caregiving in an aging society.* Administration on Aging, 1999, Symposium.

Thomas, C. The first national study of elder abuse and neglect: Contrast with results from other studies. *Journal of Elder Abuse and Neglect,* 2000, *12,* 1–14.

Tilly, J., and Wiener, J. M. Consumer-directed home and community service programs in eight states: Policy issues for older people and government. *Journal of Aging and Social Policy,* 2001, *12,* 1–26.

Toseland, R., Rossiter, C., Peak, T., and Smith, G. The comparative effectiveness of individual and group interventions to support family caregivers. *Social Work,* 1990, *35,* 256–263.

Uhlenberg, P., Cooney, T., and Boyd, R. Divorce for women after midlife. *Journal of Gerontology,* 1990, *45,* S3–S11.

Velkoff, V. A., and Lawson, V. A. *Caregiving: International brief on gender and aging.* Bureau of the Census, 1998, *IB/98-3,* 2–7.

Walker, R. J., and Pomeroy, E. C. Depression or grief? The experience of caregivers of people with dementia. *Health and Social Work,* 1996, *96,* 247–254.

Wallace, S. P., Campbell, K., and Lew-Ting, C. Structural barriers to the use of in-home services by elderly Latinos. *Journals of Gerontology,* 1994, *49,* S253–S264.

Wallsten, S. Effects of caregiving, gender and race on the health, mutuality and social supports of older couples. *Journal of Aging and Health,* 2000, *12,* 99–111.

White, T. M., Townsend, A. L., and Stephens, M. A. Comparisons of African American and white women in the parent care role. *The Gerontologist,* 2000, *40,* 718–728.

Whitlatch, C. J., Zarit, S. H., Goodwin, P. E., and von Eye, A. Influence of the success of psycho educational interventions on the course of family care. *Clinical Gerontologist,* 1995, *16,* 17–30.

Wichterich, C. *The globalized woman: Reports from a future of inequality.* New York: St. Martin's Press, 2000.

Wilber, K. H., and McNeilly, D. P. Elder abuse and victimization. In J. E. Birren and K. W. Schaie (Eds.), *Handbook of the psychology of aging* (5th ed.). San Diego: Academic Press, 2001.

Wilber, K. H., and. Nielsen, E. K. Elder abuse: New approaches to an age-old problem. *Public Policy and Aging Report,* 2002, *12,* 1, 24–26.

Wisbaum, K. Financial Abuse: A trial attorney's perspective. In *Silent suffering: Elder abuse in America.* Archstone Foundation, 1997.

Wisendale, S. Federal initiatives in family leave policy: Formulation of the FMLA. In S. Wisendale (Ed.), *Family leave policy: The political economy of work and family in America.* New York: M. E. Sharpe, 2001.

Wold, R. Introduction: The nature and scope of elder abuse. *Generations,* 2000, *24,* 6–12.

Wolf, R. S. Elder abuse: Ten years later. *The American Geriatrics Society,* 1998, *36,* 758–762.

Wolf, R. S. The nature and scope of elder abuse. *Generations,* 2000, *XXIV,* 6–12.

Wolfe, R. S., and Pillemer, K. *Helping elderly victims: The reality of elder abuse.* New York: Columbia University Press, 1989.

Worcester, M., and Hedrick, S. Dilemmas in using respite for family caregivers of frail elders. *Family and Community Health,* 1997, *19,* 31–48.

Yates, M. E., Tennstedt, S. L., and Chang, B. H. Contributors to and mediators of psychological well-being for informal caregivers. *Journals of Gerontology,* 1999, *54B,* P12–22.

Yee, J. L., and Schulz, R. Gender differences in psychiatric morbidity among family caregivers: A review and analysis. *The Gerontologist,* 2000, *40,* 147–164.

Yordi, C., DuNah, M. A., Bostrom, M. S., Fox, P., Wilkinson, A., and Newcomer, R. Caregiver's support: Outcomes from the Medicare Alzheimer's Disease Demonstration. *Health Care Financing Review,* 1997, *19,* 97–117.

Zarit, S. H., Stephens, M. P., Townsend, A., and Greene, R. Stress reduction for family caregivers: Effects of adult day care use. *Journals of Gerontology,* 1998, *53B,* S267–S277.

Zarit, S. H., and Whitlatch, C. J. Institutional placement: Phases of the transition. *The Gerontologist,* October 1992, *32,* 665–672.

11

Living Arrangements and Social Interactions

Previous chapters have examined the relationship between older persons and their social environment. In this chapter, we focus on

- P–E theories that describe adaptation to aging
- The impact of the natural and built environment on older persons' social functioning
- The influence of an aging population on community planning and housing
- New options in long-term care for frail elders
- Services to help elders remain independent in the community
- New technology to help aging in place
- Housing policy affecting older adults and the impact of federal budget cuts
- SRO housing and homelessness

As we have seen in previous chapters, active aging depends on physical and functional health, cognitive and emotional well-being, and a level of activity that is congruent with an individual's abilities and needs. Another important element in the aging process is the environment, both social and physical, that serves as the context for activities as well as the stimulus that places demands on the individual. According to person–environment (P–E) theories of aging, an individual is more likely to experience life satisfaction in an environment that is congruent with his or her physical, cognitive, and emotional needs and abilities.

Age-related changes and disease conditions make the average older person more sensitive to characteristics of the setting that may have little effect on the typical younger person. They may impair the older person's ability to adapt to and interact with complex and novel environments. On the other hand, many older people function as well as younger persons do in a wide range of

---

AN EXAMPLE OF P–E INCONGRUENCE HARMING AN OLDER PERSON

An older man who lives with his daughter and teenage grandchildren in a small home may feel overwhelmed and unable to control the high level of activity (and choice of music!) by the younger family and their friends. In contrast, an older man who lives alone in a quiet neighborhood has greater control over the level of activity in his home, even though the house may seem too quiet and unstimulating to his grandchildren when they visit.

---

physical surroundings. Observation of these differences in individual responses has led to the concept of *congruence* or *fit* between the environment and the individual. This concept is explored in other P–E theories below.

Person–Environment Theories of Aging

The impact of the environment on human behavior and well-being is widely recognized in diverse disciplines. It was in the early work of psychologist Kurt Lewin and his associates (Lewin, 1935; Lewin, Lippitt, and White, 1939) that the environment as a complex variable entered the realm of psychology. Lewin's field theory (1935, 1951) emphasizes that any event is the result of multiple factors, individual and environmental; or more simply stated, B = f(P,E) (i.e., behavior is a function of personal and environmental characteristics). Accordingly, any change in characteristics of either the person or the environment is likely to produce a change in that person's behavior.

Murray's theory of personality (1938), known as *personology,* provides the earliest framework for a P–E congruence model. This theory depicts the individual in dynamic interaction with his or her setting, the type of interaction portrayed throughout this book. The individual attempts to maintain equilibrium as the environment changes.

Murray's concepts of *need* and *press* are relevant for theories of P–E congruence. Need is viewed as a force in the individual that works to maintain equilibrium by attending and responding to, or avoiding, certain environmental demands (i.e., the concept of press in the P–E model).

According to Murray's and other theories of P–E congruence, the individual experiences optimal well-being when his or her needs are in equilibrium with characteristics of the environment. For example, an older woman who has lived on a farm will adjust more readily to a small nursing home in a rural area than to a large urban facility. In contrast, an older couple who are city-dwellers may be dissatisfied if they decide to retire to a small home on a lake far from town; adaptation may be more difficult and perhaps never fully achieved. To the extent that individual needs are not satisfied because of existing environmental characteristics and level of "press," it is hypothesized that the person will experience frustration and strain.

P–E Congruence Models in Gerontology

The environment plays a more dominant role for older than for younger people, because the older person's ability to control his or her surroundings (e.g., to leave an undesirable setting) is considerably reduced. The individual's range of adaptive behaviors to a stressful environment becomes constrained because of changes in physical, social, and psychological functioning. Therefore, this perspective may be even more useful for understanding older people's behavior than for understanding the behavior of other populations.

The *competence model,* described in Chapter 1, provides an important perspective on person–environment transactions in old age. This model assumes that the impact of the environment is mediated by the individual's level of abilities and needs. Competence is defined as "the theoretical upper limit of the individual to function in areas of biological health, sensation-perception, motives, behavior, and cognition" (Lawton, 1975, p. 7). *Environmental press* refers to the potential

---

COPING WITH DECLINING COMPETENCE

As competence in cognition, physical strength and stamina, health, and sensory functioning decline with advanced age, the individual would be expected to experience increased problems with high environmental press. Thus, for example, grocery shopping in a large supermarket on a busy Saturday morning may become an overwhelming task for an older person who is having increasing difficulty with hearing and walking. The older person might decide to shop in a smaller supermarket at nonpeak hours, or to avoid supermarkets altogether and use a neighborhood grocery store or order groceries by phone or on the Internet.

---

of a given environmental feature to influence behavior (for example, the level of stimulation, physical barriers, and lack of privacy).

For the older person with Alzheimer's disease or other forms of dementia, it can be difficult to reestablish P–E congruence or to adapt to incongruence. Severe cognitive deterioration may result in an inability to recognize the incongruence experienced between one's needs and the external world. The dementia patient may become behaviorally disturbed unless others intervene to reestablish congruence. This may be accomplished by simplifying the environment to make it fit the individual's cognitive competence; for example, by providing cues and orienting devices in the home to help the person find his or her way without becoming lost or disoriented. The ultimate goal of any modification should be to maximize the older person's ability to negotiate and control the situation, and to minimize the likelihood that the environment will overwhelm the person's competence.

Geographic Distribution of the Older Population

As the United States and other industrialized countries have become more urbanized, a smaller proportion of all population subgroups, including those age 65 and over, currently reside in rural communities. The great majority of older persons (73 percent) live in metropolitan areas (i.e., urban and suburban communities), compared with only 5 percent in communities with fewer than 2500 residents. Ethnic minority differences are particularly pronounced in the proportion of older persons who live in urban centers:

- 29 percent of non-Latino whites
- 55 percent of older African Americans
- 53 percent of Latino elders

This distribution of older ethnic minorities in central cities places them at greater risk for victimization and poor-quality housing.

There is also a "graying of the suburbs"; that is, a greater proportion of people who moved into suburban developments in the 1960s have now raised their children and have remained in these communities after retirement. Since 1977, increasing numbers of older people are living in the suburbs rather than in central cities (see Figure 11.1). Compared to their urban counterparts, elders in suburban communities tend to have higher incomes, are less likely to live alone, and report themselves to be in better functional health.

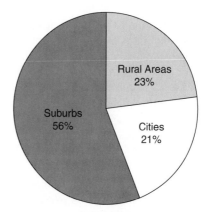

FIGURE 11.1   Population of Older Americans Living in Urban, Suburban, and Rural Areas
SOURCE: AARP, 2000.

However, the lower density of housing, greater distance to social and health services, and lack of mass transit make it difficult for older suburban dwellers to continue living independently in these suburbs if they become frail or unable to drive. Many suburban communities are responding to their changing resident needs by developing community transit (e.g., vans or special buses) programs to take older adults and persons with disabilities to social and health services, senior centers, shopping, and restaurants. Future cohorts of older adults will expect more of these services and businesses to be located in the suburbs, in the same way that shopping centers and retirement housing options have begun to be constructed in these population centers.

Older persons who live in nonmetropolitan areas have lower incomes (near the poverty level) and poorer health than those in urban areas. A greater proportion rely on Social Security benefits for their primary source of income. This is particularly true for African Americans who reside in small towns and rural areas.

Limitations in mobility and activity are greater among older people in rural communities and least among elders in suburbs. This may be a function of income and cohort differences. The greater availability of medical and social services (e.g., hospitals, clinics, senior centers, private physicians, transportation) in urban and suburban communities compared to rural settings may also explain these differences. Despite attempts to offset urban–rural differences in health and social services, significant gaps remain in terms of access and availability. Transportation remains a critical problem for older rural residents, both to transport them to medical and social services and to bring service providers to their homes. For example, public transportation is less available and, where it is provided, only 14 percent of rural elders live within a half mile of a bus stop or mass transit station. This compares with 43 percent of urban and suburban elders who live within a half-mile of public transportation (AARP, 2002).

Despite their lower income and poorer health, older persons in small communities are found to interact more with neighbors and friends of the same and younger ages than do those in urban settings. Mr. and Mrs. Howard in the introductory vignette to Part Five illustrate the positive aspects of smaller communities for older people. These include the greater proximity of neighbors, stability of residents, and shared values and lifestyles. Proportionately few rural elders live near their children and most do not receive financial and social support from them. However, friendship ties appear to be stronger and more numerous among rural older people than among those in urban settings. In sum, older persons who remain in rural areas and small towns are more disadvantaged in terms of income, health, and service availability than are those in metropolitan areas. On the other hand, P–E fit suggests that those who have a high need for social interaction and have lived most of their lives in rural areas would be most satisfied in such settings, and would experience severe adaptation problems in more anonymous urban environments.

Relocation

Relocation, or moving from one setting to another, represents a special case of P–E incongruence or discontinuity between the individual's competence and the environment's demands. Anyone who has moved from one city or one house to another has experienced the problems of adjusting to new surroundings and to different orientations, floor plans, and design features in the home. A healthy person can usually adjust quite easily. An older person who has lived in the same home for many years will require more time to adapt, even if the move is perceived as an improvement to a better, safer, more comfortable home. This is because the individual has adjusted to a particular configuration of P–E fit over a long

ADAPTING TO P–E INCONGRUENCE IN ONE'S HOME

It may seem odd to family, friends, and service providers that an older person does not wish to leave a home that is too large and too difficult to negotiate physically, especially if he or she is frail and mobility-impaired. The problem is compounded if the home needs extensive repairs that an older person cannot afford. Despite such seemingly obvious needs for relocating, it is essential to consider older people's preferences before encouraging them to sell a home that appears to be incongruent with their needs. Families should not ignore the emotional meaning of home to the older person in terms of personal identity and a treasure trove of family memories (e.g., marriage, childrearing, and grandparenting).

period of time. The greater the change (e.g., moving from a private house in the suburbs to an assisted living facility in the city), the longer it will take to adapt. Older adults who move voluntarily often feel more stress before the move than after. A relocation that entails extensive changes in lifestyle, such as a move to a retirement community or to a nursing home with its rules and policies governing the residents, requires greater adjustments. Whatever psychological and physiological distress elders experience appears to disappear within three months after the move, however (Lutgendorf et al., 2001).

Older homeowners are far more likely than younger families to have lived in their current homes for at least 30 years (50 percent vs. 4 percent). This difference also occurs among renters (16 percent vs. 1 percent, respectively), and may explain why older people are less likely to relocate. Indeed, only 4 percent of people age 65 to 85 are likely to move in a given year, compared with 34 percent of adults age 20 to 29 (HUD, 1999; U.S. Census Bureau, 2000). A national survey by the American Association of Retired Persons (AARP) revealed an overwhelming desire by people age 55 and older to remain in their own homes and community:

- 69 percent were very satisfied with their residence
- 73 percent preferred to remain in the same community

Among those who had moved in the past year, 78 percent had done so within the same state (AOA, 2000). In general, older people are less likely to move to a different community than are younger families, but are more likely to move to a different type of housing within the same community. In their life course model of retirement migration, Litwak and Longino (1987) proposed that the large migrant stream of retirees to the Sunbelt from northern states is accompanied by a smaller counterstream in the opposite direction. In their subsequent work, Litwak and Longino (1994) suggested that older people generally relocate in response to changes in life conditions, such as retirement, or disabilities that make their existing home environments incongruent with their needs. As a result, the type of housing chosen varies according to the reasons for the move. Their three-stage model of migration follows:

- Stage 1 occurs most often among the young-old and recent retirees, generally to retirement communities in the sunbelt, including Florida, California, Arizona, or Texas. This may include "snowbirds" who spend their winters in the warmer climate and the remaining months in their home states. Both patterns have resulted in a significant increase in the over age 65 population in Sunbelt states in the past 30 years.
- Stage 2 is often precipitated by chronic illness that limits the older person's abilities to perform activities of daily living (ADL). They may move to retirement communities or assisted living facilities nearby that offer some amenities (e.g., meals, housekeeping), but the older person remains relatively independent.
- Stage 3 is not experienced by most older adults, but occurs when severe or sudden disability (e.g., stroke) makes it impossible for the individual

Retirement communities offer opportunities for social interaction and support.

to live even semi-independently. In some cases the older person relocates from a Sunbelt community to a nursing home near family members. One result of this shift is that Florida has the highest population of people age 65 and older but ranks twenty-fourth in its proportion of oldest-old.

For many other elders, however, an intermediate stop may be the home of an adult child before relocating to a long-term care facility. In some cases, the older person remains in his or her own home, but receives some home care and other services. To the extent that older retirees who relocate to the Sunbelt have children and siblings living in their state of origin, and the more visits they make back home, the more likely they are to make a "counterstream migration" by moving back to their home state. However, having children who live nearby in the Sunbelt state where they have relocated and being satisfied with their new residence make it less likely that retirees will return home (Stoller and Longino, 2001).

Relocation need not be a stressful experience if the older person has some control over the decision to move and is involved in the process. However, relocation is more difficult for elders with multiple or severe physical disabilities and dementia. As we have seen in Chapter 6, these individuals have more difficulty coping with stressful life events than healthy older people. Unfortunately, they are often the very people who must relocate to hospitals and skilled nursing facilities, environments that are most incongruent with their needs. The oldest-old are most likely to relocate, often to their children's homes or near their children. Such moves are precipitated by widowhood, significant deterioration in health, or disability (Castle, 2001).

Concern about adapting to a new setting is one reason why many frail older people who can no longer maintain their own homes are reluctant to move, even though they may recognize that they "should" be in a safer environment. Indeed, the 1996 housing survey by AARP found greater support for the statement, "I'd like to stay in my home and never move," as age increased:

- 77 percent of respondents age 50–64
- 89 percent of those 65–74
- 96 percent of people age 85+ (AARP, 1996)

As anyone who has searched for a new home can attest, considerable stamina and determination are required to find housing and a neighborhood that

---

**RETIREES CAN REVITALIZE
AMERICA'S SMALL TOWNS**

New cohorts of retirees who believe in active aging have revitalized once-dying communities by relocating there, spending money for goods and services, sometimes continuing to work part-time, and creating jobs for other residents. One estimate is that a retiree who relocates to a community can have as great an economic impact as three to four factory workers because, in general, they are wealthier and have more disposable income. In 2000, new residents age 50 and older brought twice as much revenue to Florida as they cost the state in services (*Seattle Times,* 2003).

best fits one's needs and preferences. To the extent that a person is frail and unable to muster the energy to search for such housing, it becomes even more difficult to make the transition.

Some older people may live in communities that were not planned for this population (unlike a Sun City or Leisure World, for example), but have become **naturally occurring retirement communities (NORCs).** Such places have, over the years, attracted adults who have eventually "aged in place" there.

The Impact of the Neighborhood

All of us live in a neighborhood, whether a college campus, a nursing home, a retirement park, an apartment complex, or the several blocks surrounding our homes. Because of its smaller scale, the neighborhood represents a closer level of interaction and identification than does the community. Results of the American Housing Survey by the U.S. Bureau of the Census reveal:

- Seventy-six percent of older people in general are satisfied with their neighborhoods.
- Seventy-one percent in poorer neighborhoods are satisfied (HUD, 1999).

Among those who reported problems, noise and traffic concerns topped the list, followed by complaints about people and crime in the neighborhood.

Satisfaction with one's neighborhood increases if amenities such as a grocery store, laundromat, or senior center are located nearby. These services also can provide a social network. For many older people, however, special vans or other types of transportation are necessary to access such services. Older people are willing to travel farther for physician services, entertainment, family visits (although friends need to be nearby for regular visiting to occur), and club meetings, probably because these activities occur less fre-

> ### PRACTICAL HELP FROM NEIGHBORS
>
> Neighbors can provide a "security net," as partners in a "Neighborhood Watch" crime prevention program, or in informally arranged systems of signaling to each other (e.g., the older neighbor who lives alone might open her living room drapes every day by 9:00 A.M. to signal to her younger neighbors that all is well). Other neighbors might check in on the older person on a daily or weekly basis to make sure that home-delivered meals are being eaten regularly.

quently than grocery shopping and laundry. Because of the importance placed on family ties, visits to family members may occur more often, regardless of proximity. Distance is less important if family members drive older relatives to various places, including their homes.

Proximity and frequent contact with families may not be as critical if neighbors and nearby friends can provide the necessary social support. Indeed, the great majority of community-dwelling elders prefer mixed-age neighborhoods (AARP, 1996). As discussed in Chapter 9, neighbors play an important role in older people's social networks. When adult children are at a geographic distance, neighbors are more readily available to help in emergencies and on a short-term basis, such as minor home repairs or yard maintenance. It is often more convenient for neighbors than family to drive an older individual to stores and doctors' offices. This does not mean that neighbors can or should replace family support systems because of the family's central caregiving role. Nevertheless, neighbors are an important additional resource.

Victimization and Fear of Crime

A common stereotype is that crime affects the older population more than other age groups. However, national surveys by the U.S. Department of Justice's Bureau of Justice Statistics consistently show that people over age 65 have the lowest rates of all types of victimization than any age group over 12. As Table 11.1 illustrates, when compared to people age 16 to 19, those age 65 and older are:

- 30 times less likely to be victims of an assault
- 23 times less likely to experience a robbery
- 3 times less likely to be attacked by a purse snatcher or pickpocket

In fact, these rates have steadily declined since 1976 for older people. In 2000, 5 percent of all homicide victims were age 65 or older, indicating a victimization rate of 2 per 100,000 population, compared with 5.5 per 100,000 in 1976 (Bureau of Justice Statistics, 2003). Nevertheless, some segments of the older population are at greater risk for victimization:

- The young-old are more likely than those aged 75 and older to face all types of crime.
- African American elders are twice as likely as whites to experience violent and household crime.
- Older Americans with incomes less than $7500 are most likely to become victims of violent crime (twice the rate for those with incomes over $25,000).
- Not surprisingly, older people living in urban centers are 2.5 times more likely than suburban or rural elders to experience violent crime and theft.

- Urban-dwelling elders are almost twice as likely to become victims of household crime (Bureau of Justice Statistics, 2000).

Contrary to common beliefs, white women age 65 and older are at lowest risk for violent crimes:

- For aggravated assault, 0.1 per 1000 vs. 2.5 for older black women.
- For all crimes of violence, 1.7 per 1000 compared to 3.9 for their age counterparts who are white men, 4.8 for black men, and 6.2 for black women. This compares with the highest-risk group, males age 16–19, who experience 87.3 violent crimes per 1000 population (Bureau of Justice Statistics, 2000).

The conditions under which crimes are committed against older people differ from those of other age groups. For example, they tend to be victimized during the day, by strangers who more often attack alone, in or near their homes, and with less use of weapons. This suggests that perpetrators of crimes feel they can easily overtake the older victim without a struggle. The sense of helplessness against an attacker may make older persons more conscious of their need to protect themselves, and produce levels of fear that are incongruent with the statistics about their relative vulnerability to violent crimes. Such fear of crime causes many elders to take protective steps. In 1996, they reported:

TABLE 11.1   Victimization Rates per 1000 Persons or Households, 1999

AGE	VIOLENT CRIME	ROBBERY	ASSAULT	PURSE SNATCHING/ PICKPOCKETING
16–19	77.6	11.4	91.1	2.3
25–34	36.4	4.2	43.1	1.0
50–64	14.4	1.7	16.0	1.6
65+	3.9	0.5	3.0	0.8

SOURCE: Bureau of Justice Statistics, 2000.

- Ninety percent kept their doors locked.
- Sixty-five percent avoided opening doors for strangers.
- Thirty-two percent avoided going out at night.
- Twenty percent avoided using public transportation (AARP, 1996).

Such precautions are not unrealistic, given the potential negative consequences of a physical attack or theft for an older person. Even a purse snatching can be traumatic for older women, because of the possibility of an injury or hip fracture during a struggle with the thief and the resulting economic loss. It can also disrupt the victim's sense of competence and subjective well-being. Older women are particularly fearful of crime, although, as described above, they are least likely to be victims. Although seemingly irrational, such fear of crime is an important determinant of older women's behavior that requires more societal efforts to empower and strengthen their environmental competence. For example, older women can benefit from education in self-defense and from neighborhood support networks. In sum, the significance of the fear of crime is not whether it is warranted, but the effect it has on older adults' psychological well-being (Hollway and Jefferson, 1997).

Older people also are more susceptible to economically devastating crimes such as fraud and confidence games. Police departments in major cities report higher rates of victimization against older adults by con artists and high-pressure salesmen. Medical quackery and insurance fraud are also more common, perhaps because many older people feel desperate for quick cures or overwhelmed by medical care costs. They therefore become easy prey for unscrupulous people who exploit them by offering the "ultimate medical cure" or "comprehensive long-term care insurance" coverage at cheap rates. Older adults are also more vulnerable to commercial fraud by funeral homes, real estate brokers, and investment salespeople. Perhaps more devastating than the financial consequences of fraud, such salespeople

> ### NEIGHBORHOOD CRIME PREVENTION PROGRAMS
>
> In response to the problems of crime, "Neighborhood Watch" and other programs encourage neighbors to become acquainted and to look out for signs of crimes against neighbors and their homes. Such neighborhood crime prevention programs allow older people to have access to their neighbors. They break down the perception of neighbors as strangers and the fear of being isolated in a community, both of which foster fear of crime. Some large communities have established special police units to investigate and prevent crimes against older people. These units often train police to understand processes of aging, and to communicate better with older people and help them overcome the trauma of a theft or physical assault. Improvements in community design can also create a sense of security. For example, brighter and more uniform street lighting, especially above sidewalks and in alleys, can deter many would-be criminals.

prevent the older person from seeking appropriate professional services for medical conditions, insurance, and other transactions. AARP's classes on how to prevent victimization by fraud are currently their most popular educational offering.

Housing Patterns of Older People

In this section, the residential arrangements of older persons are reviewed, including independent housing, planned housing, retirement communities, community residential care, and nursing homes. We also discuss newer models of long-term care. Policies that govern such long-term care options are described in Chapter 17.

Independent Housing

Older people are more likely than any other age group to occupy housing that they own free and clear of a mortgage. In 1999, 65.4 percent of all dwelling units in which older persons resided were owned by them; 80 percent were owned free and clear of any mortgage (AOA, 2000). These include condominiums, mobile homes, and even congregate facilities that offer "life care" for retired persons; but by far the greatest proportion of owned units are single-family homes. Another way to look at this is that about 80 percent of people age 65 to 74 are homeowners, compared with 74.5 percent of those age 75 and older, and 65 percent of the total U.S. population (NCOA, 2002). As shown in Figure 11.2, home ownership varies considerably among the older population. Married couples, non-Hispanic whites, especially those with an annual income of $25,000 or more, and those residing in rural communities are most likely to own their homes. However, the cost of utilities, taxes, insurance, and repair and maintenance can be prohibitive because their homes tend to be older and poorly constructed. In addition, the older person's current level of competence may be incongruent with their physical environment, so that they require a more appropriate housing situation.

One solution is the growing number of home-sharing programs around the country. These are community-based programs that are operated out of the Area Agency on Aging or other governmental or voluntary service agencies. Their goal is to assist older persons who own their own homes and wish to rent rooms to others in exchange for rental income or services, such as housekeeping and assistance with other chores. The role of a home-sharing agency is to serve as a "matchmaker," selecting appropriate home sharers for each older person with a home. These services are popular near universities and colleges, where students find low-cost or free living arrangements and benefit from intergenerational contacts. The disadvantage is that, like any other living situation where unrelated persons share housing, differences in values and lifestyles may be too great to bridge. This is particularly true when a younger person moves into an older person's home. As a result, most intergenerational homesharing arrangements are short-lived. The success of such programs depends on appropriate matches between potential

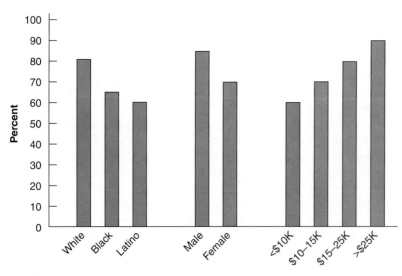

FIGURE 11.2 **Characteristics of Older Homeowners**
SOURCE: HUD, 1999.

home sharers. Generally, there are more older people with homes to share than younger people wanting rooms. In some cases, a group of older people may choose to share a home.

Another implication of prolonged homeownership is that many of these houses are old; 32 percent of homes owned by older people were built before 1949, compared with 27 percent of homes in general (NCOA, 2002). As a result, many have inadequate weatherproofing and other energy-saving features, with large indoor and outdoor spaces that are difficult to maintain. Exposed wiring, lack of sufficient outlets, and worn-out oil furnaces can be hazards. Differences exist among various subgroups; elders whose homes are in the worst physical condition include:

- 8.7 percent of the oldest old vs. 5.5 percent of the young-old
- 16.7 percent of African American elders vs. 11 percent of Latino and 4.3 percent of white elders
- 7.5 percent of women vs. 5 percent of men (Gaberlavage and Citro, 1997; HUD, 1999)

Severe problems with the quality of housing units are seen in renter-occupied dwellings at about twice the rate as for owner-occupied units (Commission on Affordable Housing, 2002).

It is not unusual to hear news stories during winter months of fires in older homes that result from faulty wiring, overloaded circuits, and the use of space heaters because of an inadequate furnace. The latter situation is particularly troublesome for older persons who have difficulties in maintaining body heat and prefer warmer ambient temperatures (see Chapter 3). Many communities attempt to prevent these problems by providing free or low-cost home repairs for low-income elders and special assistance to all older clients to make their homes more energy efficient (e.g., no-interest loans for weatherproofing and installing storm windows). Some cities that have experienced sudden increases in their electricity

and natural gas rates have also developed programs to aid low-income people of all ages, but this is becoming more difficult with current high energy costs.

Since 1989, HUD has had the authority to offer insurance for home equity conversion mortgages (HECM, or "reverse mortgages"). They are available to homeowners age 62 and older with little or no mortgage debt remaining. With insurance from HUD, numerous lenders across the country provide reverse mortgages for older persons. In addition, it is a useful option for people aged 62 and older who are "house-rich but cash-poor." It can help older people remain in their own homes and pay for needed repairs and maintenance. Lenders estimate that 83 percent of older adults have paid off their mortgages, and the average amount of equity exceeds $55,000 for these homes. This tends to be true for older individuals of all income levels (Hobbs and Damon, 1996). In effect, reverse mortgages lend the older person money via a credit line on his or her mortgage. The title is retained by the lender, or the lender puts a lien on the home. The older person receives a lump sum or monthly payment (or annuity) from the lender and still lives in the house. This can mean an additional $1000 or more each month for many older homeowners. When the older person dies or sells the house, the lender generally deducts the portion of the mortgage that has been paid, including interest, as well as a

---

REVERSE MORTGAGES ARE NOT COMMON

In its 1996 survey, AARP found that 35 percent of older homeowners had never heard of reverse mortgages. Among those who knew about this program, only 3 percent reported that they had one. Among the respondents who currently do not have one, only 27 percent would consider getting one in the future. This may change as future cohorts of elders recognize reverse mortgages as a way to retain their homes as housing prices and property taxes increase.

portion (usually about 10 percent) of the home's appreciated value or equity since the date of the reverse mortgage.

Reverse mortgages for the lender may carry long-term risks; currently, there are no guidelines for the duration of such mortgage plans. For example, what if the older homeowner outlives the home's equity? Lenders do not want to evict such a person, but at the same time they do not want to lose their investment. In addition, homeowners must consider the initial costs of such a mortgage. These include a 2 percent mandatory mortgage insurance fee, a loan origination fee, and standard closing costs. Together with interest, a borrower could pay an annualized credit-line rate of 13 to 17 percent for this loan. For older people with other assets to use as collateral, other types of loans may be more cost-effective than a reverse mortgage. HUD offers information about reverse mortgages on its Website and its toll-free phone number.

On the other hand, many people in their 50s and 60s have considerable equity in their homes because of housing prices rising so steeply since the early 1990s. As their children leave, some prefer to sell these homes and move to smaller dwellings. A growing trend, however, is represented by aging baby boomers, who prefer a large home but with many amenities that will help them remain independent and age in place. These include features such as master bedrooms and full bathrooms on the main floor, universal design in the kitchen and bathroom that allows independence for people in wheelchairs and walkers, and wiring for computer systems and "smart homes" (discussed later in this chapter). Builders and architects need to recognize that the senior boomers will expect more options in the size and amenities of homes than any previous generation.

Planned Housing

During the past 40 years, federal and local government agencies and some private organizations, such as religious groups, have developed planned housing projects specifically for older persons. These have included subsidized housing for low-income elders and age-segregated housing for middle- and upper-income older persons. Gerontologists have attempted to understand the effects of the quality and type of housing on older persons' satisfaction level and behavior following relocation to such housing environments. It appears that planned housing can indeed improve the quality of life for low-income elders, but it is difficult to generalize to other older populations, particularly those of higher income status. Where to locate planned housing projects has no simple solution. As stated earlier in the discussion of neighborhood characteristics, older adults are most likely to use services such as a senior center or laundromat if they are on site and if public transportation is easily accessible. If a particular site is not already near a bus stop, this convenience can be arranged with the local public transportation authority. Alternatively, larger developments provide van services for their older residents to obtain medical and social services, as well as planned excursions to theaters, museums, parks, and shopping centers.

Developers of planned housing for older people must also take into account such factors as whether the area is zoned for residential, commercial, or industrial use. The topography of this site, crime rates, and security of the community are important considerations, as is the need to integrate the housing project into the neighborhood. The last item is especially crucial. In a housing project that is architecturally distinct from the rest of the neighborhood, residents are likely to experience a lack of fit with their environment and to feel isolated from the larger neighborhood. Examples of this are a tall, multilevel structure in the midst of single-family homes, or a sprawling "retirement community" on the edge of an industrial area. The lack of fit may also be felt by the residents of the larger neighborhood, who often reject the presence of an entire community of older people in their midst, even if the project is architecturally consistent with other neighborhood

---

"SUMMER CAMP FOR ADULTS"

Many housing developers are expanding their markets by building active retirement communities for newer cohorts of older adults. Unlike the huge developments of the past, such as Sun Cities in California and Arizona with over 9,000 homes, recent projects have less than 1,000 units. They offer golf courses, tennis courts, and swimming pools for active adults aged 60 and older. Indeed, these developments have so many recreational amenities that they are marketed as "full-time summer camps for adults."

---

buildings. Both physical and psychological barriers are created by walls, vegetation, and architectural features that distinguish a housing project from its surroundings, adding to the older residents' sense of separation from the neighborhood. On the other hand, the increased number of elders with higher incomes has led to the growth of retirement communities with units costing $300,000 and more, offering computer access, marinas, restaurants, golf courses, hiking trails, and some communal services. These are known as "active adult communities."

Congregate Housing

Congregate housing differs from planned housing and single-family residences in its provision of some communal services, a central kitchen, and a dining room for all residents. Some congregate facilities also provide housekeeping, social, and health services. Others may have space to establish services on site, but have not done so. In 1970, when the first federally supported congregate housing act was passed, HUD programs that financed the construction could not pay for such services but could provide the space required. Developers and planners assumed that tenants would be charged for these additional services, or that the services would be subsidized by local agencies. Recent evidence suggests that such services have indeed become necessary, as the residents of congregate housing have experienced **"aging in place,"** that is, they have stayed in the same living situation for many years as their personal competence has declined. Figure 11.3 illustrates some resources needed to reduce environmental press and permit aging in place, thereby reestablishing P–E congruence. To the extent that a housing site has the space and resources by which to plan for such needs in the future, people are more likely to remain in such settings and to avoid or delay relocation to a long-term care facility. Congregate housing is a desirable option for many older persons who do not need regular help with medications or ADL, but prefer having some personal-care services available. Probably the most important feature of congregate housing is the availability of prepared meals. These not only provide a balanced and nutritional diet but also offer regular opportunities for socializing. Residents may also eat some meals in their own units, if they have units with a small kitchen (often a refrigerator, a range, and a few kitchen cabinets). The opportunity to eat in a congregate dining facility *or* to cook in their own kitchen is an important choice for many

In Home		In Community
Home care		Senior center
Home health services		Adult day health
Home-delivered meals		Transportation
Home improvement		Shopping

FIGURE 11.3 Services Needed by Elders at Home with Long-Term Care Needs

older persons. However, congregate housing differs from **assisted living**—described later in this chapter.

The growth of congregate housing is due in large part to the interest of private nonprofit and profit-making corporations. However, despite their increased numbers, congregate sites are inadequate in many regions of the country and unavailable to some segments of the aging population, particularly low income elders. Federal subsidies for constructing new congregate facilities are not as readily available today. As a result, the number of congregate housing units for middle- and upper-income older persons has increased, but low-income elders who need such housing have not benefited from this growth.

Continuous Care Retirement Communities

The number of *multilevel facilities* or **continuous care retirement communities (CCRCs)** for older persons is growing. These housing projects offer a range from independent to congregate living arrangements and intermediate to skilled care facilities; with housing for 400 to 600 elders. Such options are more widely available in housing that is purchased, less so for rental housing. The increasing number of oldest-old persons presents challenges for facilities that do not provide extensive nursing services. They realize that some of their residents will eventually need to move to other facilities; they are also more aware that potential buyers of units in these facilities would prefer to have a range of services and housing options on site. Such alternatives are often of particular concern for couples, who face the likelihood that one partner will require skilled nursing care eventually. When several levels of care are available at one site, older couples can feel assured that they will be able to remain near each other, even if one becomes institutionalized.

Many housing plans for older people that offer options in living arrangements have either *lifecare contracts* or *life lease contracts*. Under these plans, the older person must pay an initial entry

---

ADVANTAGES AND DISADVANTAGES OF CCRCs

Considering the high cost of CCRCs with lifecare contracts or founders' fees, it is important for potential buyers to consider the pros and cons of these commitments. Their greatest advantages are access to services that permit independent living and, for married respondents, the opportunity to continue to live together if one spouse needs institutionalization. A potential risk for older people who enter into a lifecare contract is that the facility will declare bankruptcy. In an attempt to avoid this, many states that license lifecare housing projects require providers to establish a trust fund for long-term care expenses.

---

fee, often quite substantial, based on projections of life expectancy and on the size of the living quarters. In the case of a *lifecare contract,* the individual who eventually needs increased care is provided nursing home care without paying more for these services. This is a form of self-insurance for small groups of older adults that provides them with institutional and home-based care as needed. With a *life lease contract,* the individual is guaranteed lifetime occupancy in the apartment. However, in the latter case, if more expensive care is required, such services are generally not provided by the facility, and the older person must give up the apartment and find a nursing home. These contracts also charge monthly fees, but the monthly costs are generally not as high as those in facilities that rely only on month-to-month payments. The advantage of lifecare contracts is that the individual is guaranteed lifetime care; this is important, given the actuarial tables of life expectancy for those who reach age 65 (another 17 years) and those who reach 70 (another 13 years). The older person who pays month-to-month may use up all of his or her life savings long before dying, if skilled care is needed. In contrast, the option of a lifecare contract may provide a sense of security for the older person who can pay a large lump sum. The individual is taking the chance that he or she will eventually need higher levels of care, so the costs are averaged out over a long period. For those who die soon after moving in, some facilities refund part of the entry fee to the family; in many cases, however, there is a policy of not refunding any portion of this fee. Obviously, the ability to purchase these contracts is limited to the small percentage of older people who have considerable cash assets. Indeed, older persons in these facilities are better educated and have greater financial resources than the general population of elders.

Long-Term Care

Nursing Homes

Many people who are unfamiliar with the residential patterns of older people mistakenly assume that the majority live in **nursing homes;** however, the actual proportion is far smaller. According to the U.S. Census Bureau (2000), 4.5 percent of the age 65 and over population occupied nursing homes in 2000. The lifetime risk of admission to

a nursing home increases with age, from 39 percent at age 65 to 49 percent at age 85 (Seperson, 2002).

As shown in Figure 11.4, there is a disproportionate use of nursing homes among the oldest-old; rates increase from 1.1 percent of the young-old, 19.8 percent of the oldest-old, to almost 50 percent of those who are age 95 and older (Seperson, 2002; U.S. Census Bureau, 1998). Each year more than 1 million older persons leave long-term care institutions, almost evenly divided among discharges to the community, transfers to other health facilities, and death. Therefore, the statistic of 4.5 percent is a cross-sectional snapshot of the population in long-term care facilities that does not take account of movement into and out of such settings.

With the increase in alternative long-term care options, such as assisted living and adult family homes, rates of nursing home admissions are changing substantially. More elders, even those with multiple physical and cognitive impairments, are selecting or are placed in long-term care facilities other than nursing homes, while

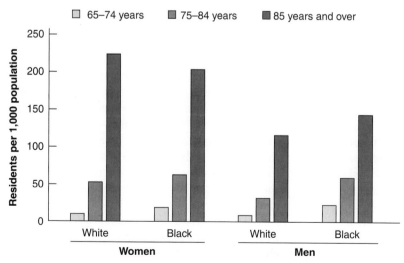

FIGURE 11.4 **Nursing Home Residents among Persons 65 Years of Age and Over, by Age, Gender, and Race: United States, 1997**
SOURCE: National Center for Health Statistics, National Nursing Home Survey, 1999.

many others receive health care in their own homes. This has resulted in a decline in the number of nursing homes in the United States from 19,100 in 1985 to 17,000 in 1997. The total number of beds and average number of beds per home have both increased, however. This reflects a decline in the number of smaller nursing homes (NCHS, 2000).

The lower rates of nursing home admissions in the United States will probably continue, despite the significant growth in the oldest-old population. Nevertheless, nursing homes are often the best choice for the oldest, most frail, and most dependent segment of the population. As a result of more options prior to choosing a nursing home, typical nursing home residents today are much sicker and require more intensive services than their counterparts 20 to 30 years ago. This greater intensity of services has raised the cost of nursing home care to an average daily rate of $158 for a semi-private room and $181 for a private room, not including specialized care such as dementia units (Met Life, 2003). The average age of nursing home residents is 81, and women are disproportionately represented. The typical nursing home includes:

- 72 percent women
- 66 percent widowed or divorced elders
- 40 percent with a diagnosis of dementia
- 82 percent requiring assistance with two or more ADL (NCHS, 2000)

The gender differential in nursing homes is due to women's longer life expectancy, their greater risk of multiple chronic illnesses, and their greater likelihood of being unmarried. The last factor is a critical one, since the absence of a partner or other caregiver is a major predictor of institutionalization. This is discussed further in Chapter 15.

In a 6-year follow-up of 634 community-dwelling persons aged 70 and over who had some disabilities at baseline, 41 percent had died and 23 percent had entered a nursing home for some time

LONG-TERM CARE IN OTHER COUNTRIES

In some countries, such as Japan and Germany, hospitals provide both long-term and acute care, so the total number of institutionalized older persons is much higher. Because hospital care is much more costly, Japanese government leaders and builders have begun to construct other types of long-term care facilities, some based on models in the United States. In Hong Kong, nonprofit groups (known as nongovernmental agencies, or NGOs) have taken the lead in developing innovative models of long-term care. These include high-rise apartment buildings with assisted living and nursing home units integrated in the building, as well as exercise and physical therapy facilities.

in those 6 years. Those whose primary caregiver was a male were more than twice as likely to enter a nursing home as elders with a female caregiver. Living with the primary caregiver reduced the risk of institutionalization by one-half. The use of formal services such as adult day care reduced the risk for cognitively impaired older persons, but increased the risk for physically frail persons by a factor of 2.5 when both formal and informal care were required. This apparent dichotomy may mean that formal services can relieve the burden of caregiving in cases of dementia (thereby postponing or preventing nursing home placement). In contrast, physically disabled older people who need both formal and informal care may have too many impairments to live in the community, even when multiple services are brought into their homes. These elders represent the segment of the population that will continue to require nursing homes in the future, even with the growth of other less restrictive and less costly long-term care alternatives (Jette et al., 1995). As noted in Chapter 10, the crucial role played by a live-in caregiver (most often a partner or adult child) in preventing or delaying institutionalization is supported by other studies where up to 25 percent of nursing home placements were precipitated by the death or serious illness of the primary caregiver (Tennstedt, Crawford, and McKinley, 1993).

Unbalanced social exchange by the elder's child who is doing caregiving can also result in placement. That is, if the adult child must help an increasingly frail parent with more ADL, and the older adult cannot reciprocate, there is greater likelihood of moving to a nursing home (Wilmoth, 2000). These health and caregiver factors also have emerged as predictors of nursing home placement in other cultures. For example, older adults in Japan are almost 7 times more likely to be admitted to a geriatric hospital (providing long-term care services similar to nursing homes) if they have dementia, 6.6 times more likely if they are moderately limited in ADL, and 6.3 times more likely if their primary caregiver is a daughter-in-law rather than a blood relative (Arai, Washio, and Kudo, 2000). Nursing home placement can be a traumatic event for some frail elders. In an analysis of 934 people aged 70 and older who moved into a nursing home, functional status declined and death rates were higher than expected within the first year (Wolinsky, Stump, and Callahan, 1997).

About 87 percent of nursing home residents are white, compared to 10.4 percent who are African American, and 3 percent who are Latino, American Indian, or Asian-Pacific Islander (NCHS, 2000; Strahan, 1997). Even at age 85 and older, when the likelihood of nursing home placement is higher, proportionately fewer African American women live in nursing homes. However, African American men are slightly more likely than their white counterparts to live in such facilities when they are 85 and older, according to the following:

- 23 percent of white women
- 20 percent of black women
- 12 percent of white men
- 14 percent of black men (NCHS, 2000)

The underrepresentation of ethnic minority groups in nursing homes appears to reflect cultural differences in the willingness to institutionalize older

---

BREAKING DOWN STEREOTYPES ABOUT NURSING HOMES

There is a small but growing trend to humanize or make nursing homes more homelike. This is a major paradigm shift from the medical or institutional model used in designing and operating these facilities. One such nursing home that underwent a dramatic physical and philosophical redesign is Mt. St. Vincent's in Seattle, Washington. Some of the changes in this facility include:

- Each floor is divided into "neighborhoods" of 20 residents per group.
- Each neighborhood has its own dining room, small enough for quiet meals.
- Residents with dementia are not housed separately but are usually mixed with healthier residents on each floor; ankle bracelets allow staff to monitor wanderers.
- Residents are not tied down in bed at night to keep them from falling out (a safety feature that some see as robbing elders of their dignity).
- Resident-directed care is practiced, with groups of elders deciding on meals and activities.
- Aides are assigned to a group of residents and are encouraged to become familiar with each resident's past and current life.
- Pets, plants, a day care center for young children, and an espresso stand for residents create a more homelike environment.

SOURCE: *New York Times,* 1998.

---

persons, greater availability of family supports, or institutionalized discrimination implicit in admission policies against elders of color. It may also reflect the dearth of facilities that address the distinctive needs of these ethnic minorities, thereby forcing them to enter nursing homes that are incongruent with their cultural needs. In some communities with large ethnic minority populations, nursing homes have been built under the auspices of nonprofit organizations or religious groups. For example, in San Francisco and Seattle, Japanese and Chinese American elders can enter nursing homes operated and staffed by people who speak their same language and serve culturally specific foods. In most of the Chinese facilities, for example, employees can communicate with residents in many dialects of Chinese (*New York Times*, 2003).

Most nursing homes (about 67 percent) are *proprietary* or *for-profit*, and thus operate as a business that aims to make a profit for the owners or investors. The number of nursing homes owned by large multifacility chains is increasing dramatically. Another 7 percent are owned by federal, state, or local governments. *Nonprofit* homes (26 percent of the total) are generally sponsored by religious or fraternal groups (NCHS, 2000). Although making a profit is not their goal, they must be self-supporting. These are governed by a board or advisory group, rather than owners or investors, as in the case of proprietary homes. Although instances of reimbursement fraud by proprietary homes are highly publicized, the terms *proprietary* and *nonprofit* do not designate type or quality of care, but rather how the home is governed and how its earnings are distributed.

Nursing homes must follow federal guidelines to become certified by Medicare and to meet regulations that are imposed by each state. Such federal regulations have improved the quality of care in nursing homes and reduced costs, although there are exceptions (Hawes et al., 1997). Most nursing homes are not certified for Medicare, however. This is because Medicare does not reimburse for long-term care or maintenance, but only for short-term care (i.e., up to 100 days of rehabilitation following hospitalization). As a result, Medicaid is the primary payer of nursing-home care. Among those who enter a nursing home after age 65:

- Twenty-seven percent start and end their time in the facility as Medicaid recipients.
- Fourteen percent who begin as private pay residents spend down their assets and become Medicaid users (Spillman and Kemper, 1995).

Many older people with incomes below a specified level (varying across states) would not be able to afford nursing home care without Medicaid assistance. Under this program, nursing homes are reimbursed according to the level of care required by each resident, although at a rate less than private pay. For example, residents who need more hands-on care by diverse staff are billed at a higher rate. Nursing personnel within the facility determine the level of care required on the basis of the older person's abilities to perform various ADL and his or her mental status. Not all nursing homes accept clients who are Medicaid recipients, although many will allow elders who later become Medicaid eligible to remain in the home. In order to guard against large numbers of residents depending on Medicaid to pay for their long-term care needs and having to accept a lower reimbursement than private-pay residents are charged, some facilities have a policy that residents must demonstrate they have resources to pay for at least 2 to 3 years of care before they will require assistance from Medicaid.

Because of stereotypes and media stories about poor-quality facilities, few older people willingly choose to live in a nursing home. Most enter after receiving informal care from family members, formal home care services, and, in some cases, following a stay in facilities such as assisted living or adult family homes. African Americans are more likely than other groups to enter directly from a hospital and therefore have less control over the placement decision. Nevertheless, nursing home life offers some advantages over other types of long-term care. These include:

- increased social contact
- accessible social activities
- intensive rehabilitation services not provided by other long-term care alternatives
- relief from the stress of caregiving on family

Although the media report instances of abuse and violation of regulations, there are many excellent nursing homes. Increased efforts to improve nursing homes and the development of innovative options signal an important change in skilled nursing

THE EDEN ALTERNATIVE

A new approach to nursing home management focuses on enhancing residents' quality of life by encouraging them to care for plants and pets in the home; to volunteer in an attached child care center if available; and generally to have more control over the home's activities. Labeled "the Eden Alternative" by its founder, Dr. William Thomas, this philosophy posits nursing homes as habitats for elders who can continue to grow, rather than institutions where frail people come to die. According to this paradigm, residents who are surrounded by and encouraged to care for pets, plants, and children in the nursing home, and facilities that deemphasize scheduled activities, avoid the use of restraints, and practice decentralized management can improve the quality of both residents' and staff's lives (Thomas, 1999; Thomas and Stermer, 1999).

facilities. Such options include subacute care for post-hospital discharge residents, palliative and hospice care for terminally ill persons, and special care units (SCUs) for residents with cognitive or severe physical impairments (Teresi, Holmes, and Ory, 2000).

Increasingly, residents of nursing homes and their families are having more influence over their lives, through resident councils, patients' bills of rights, nursing home ombudsmen, and the advocacy of groups such as the National Citizens Coalition for Nursing Home Reform (NCC-NHR). In its resident surveys, this organization has found that a major concern of cognitively intact older people is to be involved in decisions about their daily lives in the facility. Through such efforts, along with increased gerontological training, nursing home staff are also becoming more sensitive about ways to involve family, friends, and members from the larger community in their policies, procedures, and activities.

Congress enacted provisions in nursing home regulations in December 1987 that were intended to recognize and respect residents' rights. This law requires every nursing home that participates in Medicare or Medicaid to respect the dignity, choice, and right of self-determination of its residents. Most states have a nursing home ombudsman or a complaint resolution unit where residents and their families can report their concerns and complaints. An important component of the Omnibus Budget Reconciliation Act of 1987 was to discourage pharmacological and physical restraints for managing behavior problems among nursing home residents with dementia. Staff training in behavior management techniques was recommended by the Health Care Financing Administration in 1990 (now the Centers for Medicare and Medicaid Services, or CMS). These actions have resulted in research and demonstration efforts to test alternative approaches to behavior management. One successful strategy has been to train nurse aides in effective nonverbal and communication skills, as well as specific staff behaviors that can prevent the onset of problematic resident behaviors. Such training reduced agitation in residents and resulted in improved communication skills up to 6 months after the intervention (Burgio et al., 2002).

New paradigms of nursing home design, as reflected in the Eden Alternative and Mt. St. Vincent's Home, previously described in the boxes, can also help to humanize nursing home care. By adopting such a philosophy in the physical design and in staff caregiving practices, nursing homes can improve the quality of care provided for frail elders (Day, Carreon, and Stump, 2000).

One of the concerns of nursing home administrators and families whose elders live in nursing homes is the problem of recruiting and retaining staff, especially professional staff. The shortage of nurses in all fields, discussed in Chapter 4, has hurt the long-term care field particularly hard. The challenging work of caring for multiple frail elders in a climate of increasing budget constraints makes it difficult to hire specialists in geriatric nursing, or even LPNs and RNs who are willing to obtain the necessary training after they are hired. Some facilities, especially large proprietary homes, offer signing bonuses and generous benefits; others recruit nurses from developing countries such as the Philippines. Nevertheless, low pay and high resident-to-staff ratios deter many nurses and nurse aides from employment in nursing homes. Not only is it difficult to recruit these staff, but retaining nurses and nurse aides is a challenge for most facilities.

A report by CMS to Congress recommends a minimum staffing time of 4.1 hours of nursing care per resident per day, but the average is less than 3.5 hours of nursing time, ranging from 2.46 to 4.66 hours per day (CMS, 2002). Improved staffing ratios, staff training, and better wage and benefit packages could help this critical situation in nursing homes, but these improvements require funding that is unavailable in the current reimbursement system for long-term care (Wiener, 2003). In a survey of 100 staff members in New York City nursing homes, respondents complained of "burning out" because:

- "We do too many things."
- "I have no time to speak to the residents."
- "I am often the only nurse on the floor." (Perez-Pena, 2003)

Newer Options for Long-Term Care

Since the late 1980s, in response to perceived needs for more cost-effective long-term care options, there has been a dramatic growth in **community residential care options (CRCs).** This new model is defined as group housing with additional services such as meals, basic health care, and some personal assistance. Examples include **assisted living** and **adult family homes (or adult foster care).** This type of housing has increased in the past 10 years as state and local builders have sought ways to provide long-term care in a cost-effective manner for elders with some limitations in their ADLs. At a minimum, they provide room and board, at least one meal per day, and 24-hour security, although not as extensively as a medical model such as nursing homes (Hawes, 2001; Hawes, Rose, and Phillips, 1999; Quinn et al., 1999). Community residential care can help older people maintain

Chore workers and other home and community-based services can help older people remain in their homes.

their independence, even if they have multiple ADL limitations. They cost less to operate and have therefore attracted more individuals and organizations to invest in this type of housing. Large health care systems, insurance companies, and nonprofit and for-profit corporations have built new CRCs or added to their existing nursing home campuses new apartment or cottage units. The great majority of CRC residents are age 65 and older. Indeed, a national study found that:

- Fifty-six percent are age 80 and older.
- Forty percent have mild to moderate dementia.
- Most need help with two or more ADL (GAO, 1999).

As a result, more older people who, in the past, would have been placed in nursing homes are now entering CRCs. According to the U.S. Census Bureau, fewer older adults were living in nursing homes in 2000 than in 1990 (4.5 percent vs. 5.1 percent, respectively), reflecting a trend toward alternative long-term care options. Approximately one-third of residents of CRCs remain there until they die, compared with two-thirds of nursing home residents (Meyer, 1998). This is especially true for elders whose long-term care expenses are paid by Medicaid. The lower cost of CRCs has made them a more desirable option for states with growing numbers of frail elders who need public assistance. One reason for this is the trend toward state licensure and Medicaid reimbursement, albeit at lower levels, for these alternatives.

Assisted Living: A Growing Trend in Long-Term Care

Assisted living is seen by its advocates as a new, more humane model of housing that is aimed at elders who need assistance with personal care (e.g., bathing and taking medications) and with some ADL, but who are not so severely impaired physically or cognitively that they need 24-hour skilled medical care (Regnier, 2002). It is based on a social model of long-term care, rather than a medical model such as nursing homes. As such, it is not necessarily a specific building type but a philosophy of care. Nevertheless, residents in assisted living usually live in private apartment units, which typically include:

- a kitchen (but generally not a stove or oven)
- a full bathroom
- in some, a bedroom, sitting room, and partial bath

These features provide a more homelike, less institutional setting that encourages frail elders to maintain active aging and continuity with their previous lifestyles (Frank, 2002). Some assisted living facilities offer shared units as a lower-cost alternative. Most provide congregate meals in a common dining room, as well as housekeeping, laundry, and help with some activities of daily living. Staff often include at least one nurse, a social worker, and one or more people to provide case management services. Access to health care is

provided for specific residents as needed (often contracting the services of physicians, physical therapists, mental health specialists). As a result, staffing costs are lower than in nursing homes, thereby keeping the average cost of assisted living lower. The Assisted Living Federation of America (ALFA) defines assisted living as "a special combination of housing, supportive services, personalized assistance, and healthcare." However, an extensive analysis of such facilities throughout the United States and northern Europe led Regnier (2002) to develop nine criteria for a successful assisted living project. According to these guidelines, assisted living facilities that want to achieve excellent resident outcomes should:

1. appear residential in character
2. be perceived as small in scale
3. provide residents with privacy
4. recognize each resident's uniqueness
5. encourage independence and interdependence
6. emphasize health maintenance, mental stimulation, and physical activity
7. support involvement by residents' families
8. maintain contact with the immediate community
9. serve frail elders

Assisted living facilities often develop individual service plans, based on each resident's physical health and functional abilities. Families considering these options need to ask what the facility will provide as their older family members decline in their physical, cognitive, or mental functions. Like nursing homes, assisted living providers that offer a variety of services generally charge "tiered" rates, that is, increasingly costly fees for elders who need more services. As a result, some facilities can cost as much as a nursing home if they provide more amenities and health services.

Assisted living generally offers the resident more autonomy, privacy, and participation in care decisions than do nursing homes. The trade-off, of course, is that the individual may decide to participate in activities that are risky or that do not

THE DOWNSIDE OF CRCs

Despite its many advantages, housing for older adults that is based on a social model of long-term care can have its downside. These problems are aggravated in states that have few or no licensure requirements for assisted living or other CRCs. For example, state officials and industry representatives in Alabama recently agreed to enforcing stricter rules after reviewing complaints against 200 unlicensed facilities. Two particularly egregious examples are a 92-year-old man who climbed out of a window in the assisted living facility where he lived, walked away, and died of exposure; and another frail resident, in another facility, who became bedridden, lost 40 pounds and died when no medical attention was provided.

comply with health care regimens recommended by a professional. These may include choices such as refusing to use a walker or not following a specific diet. As a result of this conflict between assuring resident autonomy versus safety, many facilities have moved toward a policy of managed or **negotiated risk.** Under such policies, residents (and often their family or guardian) must sign a written agreement that allows the resident to accept greater risk of personal injury in exchange for autonomy in decisions about his or her own lifestyle in the facility.

It is important not to place assisted living in a "continuum of care," since this type of facility can generally serve older people with a wide range of disabilities, many of whom traditionally would be placed in nursing homes. Many states are exploring the option of **Medicaid waivers** for assisted living. Some, such as Oregon and Washington, have implemented programs that encourage the use of assisted living and other community-based long-term care options. Most people in assisted living facilities today are private-pay residents, however. Many who move out do so because they have run out of funds and must turn to nursing homes that are covered by Medicaid, even though they might benefit from the greater autonomy and self-care at assisted living facilities. As more states provide Medicaid waivers, it is anticipated that greater congruence can be achieved between needs of specific elders and available housing options. As a result of their lower costs and greater autonomy for residents, assisted living has become the fastest growing type of housing for older adults. Because of wide variations in the definition of assisted living, estimates range from 10,000 to 40,000 facilities that serve anywhere between 350,000 to 1 million elders (Hawes, 2001; Pynoos and Matsuoka, 2001).

Given these differences in long-term care philosophy between nursing homes and assisted living, are there differences in resident outcomes? In a comparison of 76 elders living in a nursing home with 82 elders in an assisted living facility within the same CCRC campus, medical records were examined and residents were interviewed 4 times over a 12-month period. At the baseline assessment, no differences in cognitive status were found, but nursing home residents had more symptoms of depression and poorer functional health than assisted living residents. During the 12-month follow-up, mortality rates and relocation to units or facilities with more assistance did not differ between the two sites. Residents' age was the best predictor of mortality, whereas their functional ability, educational level, cognitive state, and payment status (i.e., private vs. Medicaid) predicted whether or not they would relocate to higher levels of care. No differences emerged on these variables between the two types of facilities. These findings suggest that older adults who need residential long-term care may do just as well in terms of health outcomes in the less restrictive and less costly assisted living setting as they would in a nursing home (Pruchno and Rose, 2000).

Private Homes That Provide Long-Term Care

Adult foster care (AFC) or **adult family homes (AFH)** are other alternatives to nursing homes for older persons who do not need the 24-hour medical care of skilled care facilities. Like assisted living residents, older clients in AFCs can generally decide for themselves whether to take their medications and to exercise as much or as little as they want, unlike the more structured nursing home schedule. AFC is generally provided in a private home by the owners who may have some health care training but are not required to be professionals in the field. These homes are licensed to house up to five or six clients. Some specialize in caring for younger or older adults with physical disabilities or psychiatric disorders; others refuse to care for people with advanced dementia; while still others offer services to a small number of dementia patients only. More individuals are converting their homes to adult foster care. The owner and, in some cases, auxiliary staff provide housekeeping, help with some ADL, personal care, and some delegated nursing functions, such as giving injections, distributing medications, and changing dressings on wounds if they have been trained and certified by a registered nurse.

In 2000, 39 states covered services in AFH or assisted living through Medicaid (Mollica, 2001). Medicaid reimbursement rates for AFC are one-third to one-half the rates paid to nursing homes. This works well for residents who do not require heavy care (e.g., those who are not bedridden or with severe behavioral problems due to dementia). However, for more frail older clients, or for those who have "aged in place" (i.e., have become more impaired while living in that AFC), the reimbursement rates do not reflect the time and effort required of the facilities' caregivers. For this reason, a survey of 290 AFH providers in the state of Washington revealed high levels of dissatisfaction with reimbursement rates and complaints that case managers were not disclosing the severity of clients' needs when referring them to AFH (Curtis, Kiyak, and Hedrick, 2000).

This trend toward placing more impaired older persons in AFC or AFH is driven by states' efforts to control long-term care costs, as well as societal pressures toward a social rather than a medical model of care. Similar to the study described above, comparing residents' health out-

comes in nursing homes versus assisted living facilities (Pruchno and Rose, 2000), Hedrick and colleagues (2003) compared health, relocation, and mortality over a 12-month period among residents of assisted living (AL), adult family homes (AFH), and adult residential care (ARC) facilities. They followed 349 adults in 219 facilities (including AL, AFH, and ARC), from 3 months after the individual entered the facility to 12 months later.

At baseline, AFH residents were more likely than the other two groups to require help with multiple ADL (especially bathing and dressing), even though the oldest group resided in AL settings. General health status was similar across the three types of settings, and cognitive impairment was more common in AFH and AL residents than among those in ARC facilities (58, 43, and 23 percent, respectively). Despite these differences, there were no significant differences across the three types of long-term care in mortality rates, declines in health, or relocation to different settings over the 12 months of follow-up.

These results support the findings of the study comparing nursing homes and assisted living—that a less restrictive and less costly long-term care setting can accommodate frail elders as well as the more costly option. Furthermore, residents' health outcomes as measured by mortality, morbidity, and relocation are similar across these settings, in this case AL residents and AFH. Aging in place appears to be possible without relocating to the more expensive type of long-term care setting, whether that is AFH versus AL, or AL versus nursing homes. This can reduce the costs for elders and their families who pay out-of-pocket, as well as states that must allocate their Medicaid dollars for eligible elders (Chapin and Dobbs-Kepper, 2001).

Given these wide variations in the cost and range of services offered by the numerous options in residential long-term care, often resulting in similar outcomes with respect to mortality, morbidity and relocation, it is important to consider other outcomes. Improving the older person's quality of life, not just extending life, should become a primary goal for long-term care providers. The most critical elements of quality of life to be considered by such facilities should be:

- a sense of safety, security, and order
- physical comfort and freedom from pain
- enjoyment of daily life
- meaningful activities
- meaningful interpersonal relationships
- maintaining functional competence (or "active aging" within the limits of the elder's capacities)
- maintaining dignity
- a sense of privacy
- a sense of individuality, autonomy, and choice
- spiritual well-being (Kane, 2001).

Services to Aid Older People in the Community

In the past 10 years, the term **long-term care** has evolved from an emphasis on purely institutional care to a broad range of services to help older adults in their own homes, other community settings, and nursing homes. Under this broader definition, homemaker services, nutrition programs, adult day care, and home health care are all part of long-term care.

Home Care

Despite the increasing array of residential options for older people who need assistance with multiple ADL, many prefer to "age in place" (i.e., remain in their own homes even though declines in physical and/or cognitive functioning reduce their P–E congruence with the home). Surveys of older adults, even those in substandard housing, reveal that more than 90 percent want to stay in their own homes for as long as possible (AARP, 2000). This trend will increase dramatically as baby boomers age, with their strong values of independence and self-sufficiency.

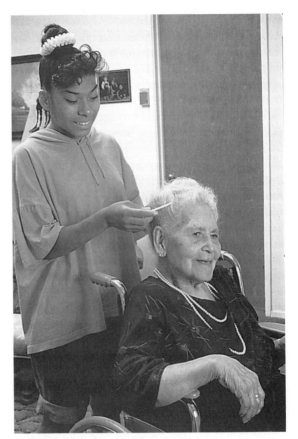

Shared housing between young and old can benefit both generations.

Over the last decades, more federal, state, and local services have become available to help older people maintain their independence in the least restrictive environment feasible. This can assist the older person to maintain P–E congruence. As shown in Figure 11.3 on page 395, some of these services (e.g., home care) are brought to the older person, whereas others (e.g., adult day health) require the individual to leave home to receive the service. As the older population has increased, newer cohorts of older adults have adopted the values of aging in place, and third-party payers (e.g., Medicare) have searched for alternatives to the escalating hospital and nursing home costs, home care services have grown dramatically.

Medicare reimburses **home health care** services, defined as skilled nursing or rehabilitation benefits that are provided in the patient's own home and prescribed by a physician. The three most widely used services, comprising 97 percent of Medicare reimbursements for home health care, are:

- skilled nursing (41 percent)
- home health aide (49 percent)
- physical therapy (7 percent) (HCFA, 1998).

Since 1989, when a class-action lawsuit resulted in a more flexible interpretation of Medicare home care regulations, agencies that provide home care expanded their visits and services to beneficiaries. Home care became the fastest-growing component of personal health care expenditures, increasing by 20 percent per year from 1991 until 1998. Starting in 1998, however, the Balanced Budget Act of 1997 limited home health coverage to 100 days maximum, thereby reducing the number of clients by 40 percent, and the number of home health visits by 30 percent (Hughes and Pittard, 2001; McCall, 2003). Not surprisingly, the average home health client is a woman aged 70 and has 1.7 ADL impairments. The oldest-old generally receive more visits on average than any other age group, about four times as many as for those aged 65–66 (Hughes, 1996; Hughes et al., 1997).

Home health care is far less expensive than acute (hospital) care, about 40 percent less than nursing homes, and comparable to adult foster care or adult family homes. However, costs become more comparable if 24-hour care is needed. Researchers have examined the costs and impact of home care on hospitalization rates among users. In one study, home health agencies that were Medicare-certified recorded the actual costs of providing an array of services (e.g., skilled nursing care, physical therapy, home dialysis, hospice). A U-shaped curve was found to be the best model of cost-efficiency; that is, a scope of 8 to 10 different services appears to be ideal for reducing the average cost of services provided by a home health agency. Those that provide either fewer or more services do so at a higher cost per visit; this suggests that these agencies can function most economically if they provide an array of services, ideally between 8 and 10 (Gonzales, 1997).

Another study examined hospital-use data among home health clients in a meta-analysis of 20 earlier studies. These studies provided a large number of home health programs and clients on which to test outcomes. When home health was defined strictly as the delivery of nursing, medical, and support services in the home of a terminally or chronically ill older person, home health users had 2.5 to 6 fewer days of hospital use, compared to similar patient populations that did not use home health care. These results support the cost-effectiveness of home health care in curtailing the use of far more expensive acute care (Hughes et al., 1997). However, it is important to assess each elder's specific health care needs when initiating home care services. In one study of more than 7000 home care recipients aged 75 and older, African American elders had few support services beyond home care. Asians and Latinos showed less improvement in their physical functioning than blacks and whites, and white elders had more depressive symptoms than the other groups. These needs were not being addressed by their home care providers (Peng, Navaie-Waliser, and Feldman, 2003).

As demand has increased, home care agencies have expanded their services beyond health care to include a broad array of "home- and community-based services" (HCBS):

- assistance such as chore services to maintain the home
- personal care to help the person perform ADL
- home-delivered meals
- automatic safety response systems

Such assistance can help older people "age in place" in their own homes. Medicaid is the primary source of funds for both home care and

PLANNING FOR AGING IN PLACE

When Mr. and Mrs. Pond bought their last home, they were in their late sixties. They chose a house on one level, installed grab bars in the bathroom, nonslip surfaces, and other safety features. When Mr. Pond was 78, he had a stroke that restricted his mobility. Mrs. Pond's vision became more impaired. However, with help from a weekly chore worker, daily meals delivered to their home, and twice-weekly visits to an adult day care facility, they were able to remain in their home until they died, he at age 82, she at 85.

nursing home care, although it pays almost three times as much for the latter. When all sources of funding are considered, home care accounted for $39 million in 1998, compared with $88 billion for nursing home care (Commission on Affordable Housing, 2002). This disparity is discussed further in Chapter 17. Other HCBS options, such as adult day care and case management, are offered in community settings. These services provide respite to family caregivers and opportunities for social interaction for isolated elders. These additional HCBS are not covered by Medicare, but by Title XX and Title III of the Older Americans Act. These funds make each state's unit on aging (SUA) responsible for their delivery. SUAs, in turn, designate Area Agencies on Aging (AAAs) to develop and administer these services at the local level, sometimes in the form of contracts to local providers.

Adult Day Care and Adult Day Health Care

Adult day care (ADC) is another long-term care option that allows the older person to remain at home and receive some health and social services. In this case, users attend a local ADC center one or more times per week, for several hours each day. ADC goes beyond senior centers in providing structured health and social services for older people with cognitive impairments such as dementia

and those with functional impairments due to stroke and multiple chronic illnesses. Some ADCs are based on a health rehabilitative model of long-term care with individualized care ("Adult Day Health Care" or ADHC), while others fit into a social psychological model ("social day care"). Although both may provide recreation, meals, transportation to and from the facility, and memory-retraining programs, ADHCs are more likely to offer nursing care, physical and speech therapy, and scheduled medication distribution (Tedesco, 1996). The greatest advantage of ADHCs over home health care is to bring together older people for social interaction. Equally important, they provide respite for family caregivers. This is an important function, especially since it can reduce feelings of stress, worry, and overload among full-time family caregivers (Gaugler et al., 2003). Clearly, such services are not suitable for the most impaired or bedbound older person; but they are an invaluable resource for elders with moderate levels of dementia or with serious physical impairments and chronic illnesses who still benefit from living in the community.

Technology to Help Aging in Place

An important consideration in helping older adults to remain independent and to age in place is to design housing that is adaptable to the changing competence levels of the aging person. These include private homes where all amenities are on one level, with easy access to a bathroom and kitchen. If the home was not initially built with these design principles, some modifications can be made as needed to improve visual and physical accessibility, and to ensure independence by the aging homeowner (Taira and Carlson, 1999).

Even among middle-aged adults, new home buyers are increasingly demanding "flexible housing." Indeed, a recent annual meeting of the National Association of Home Builders focused on designing housing that can be used throughout a lifetime. This interest on the part of home builders is clearly more than academic. It reflects the trend of first-time buyers to select neighborhoods where they will want to live for many years, and the decline in relocation rates among all ages (Longino, 1998). As a result, architects and builders are already designing homes with movable walls that can expand or shrink a room as needs change, or plumbing that can convert a small room on the main floor of the house into a bathroom. This gives families the flexibility to adapt their homes as they assume caregiving roles, or if one of the current residents needs long-term care in the future. Other options that can be built into a home are modifiability in the number and size of bedrooms, using a cluster design so that multiple generations and even unrelated renters can live under the same roof while retaining their privacy.

Knowledgeable about requirements of the Americans with Disabilities Act (ADA), builders and architects are aware of the need to make main-floor hallways and doorways in private homes wide enough for wheelchair access. Even though the ADA does not require accessibility in private homes, these trends are occurring because builders recognize the growing market for such housing features. Computerized controls for heat, artificial lighting, window coverings, and music are too costly for most of today's home buyers, but will become more prevalent in homes of the future. With portable keypads, these features can help frail older persons maintain ambient temperatures, lighting, and music at levels that are comfortable and congruent with the older person's competence level.

Newer cohorts of elders are also benefiting from recent developments in **"Universal Design"** (Mace, 1998). This concept of designing the environment to allow the widest range of users possible attracts the attention of architects, landscape architects, and interior and furniture designers. What began as an attempt to make curb cuts in streets, as well as hallways and bathrooms in homes, more accessible to people in wheelchairs has grown to a movement that makes all environments—parks, wilderness areas, automo-

> **LESSONS FROM OTHER COUNTRIES**
>
> The United States can learn from developments in other countries with larger proportions of older adults in their population. For example, new homes in Sweden are required by housing codes to include a full bathroom on the main floor. Such foresight is important when one considers the high likelihood that a very old homeowner may no longer be able to go up and down stairs to use a bathroom in the traditional upstairs sleeping quarters (Riley, 1999).

biles, and computer workstations—accommodate people who are young and old, who are able-bodied, as well as those who are limited in their mobility, vision, and hearing.

Some architects are working on cost-effective means of applying new technology to home design, known as **smart homes.** For example, systems that make a room light up through sensors in the floor can help prevent accidents when an older person gets up at night to use the bathroom. Remote controls for operating thermostats, windows, and their coverings can help an older adult change the room temperature as needed, as well as open and close windows and shades to control the ambient temperature and to prevent glare. New systems can be installed for as little as $5000, but can cost much more as their components increase. Other design features that can be built into new homes to help future elders include:

- bathrooms with roll-in showers
- hands-free sensors on faucets
- nonskid flooring
- low-pile carpeting
- uniform lighting throughout the house
- elevator shafts that are built into the home and used as closets until they are needed as elevators

However, only a small proportion of elders today have made home modifications to improve safety, and many cannot afford to do so. The most popular modification is to install grab bars in bathrooms (in about 30 percent of homes owned by older adults). Other changes are far less frequent, perhaps because of cost concerns.

- Twenty-three percent added brighter lighting in their homes.
- Sixteen percent added more handrails.
- Four percent replaced doorknobs and water faucets with lever handles.
- Four percent installed ramps in place of steps or stairs (AARP, 2000).

Although these home building patterns will help future cohorts of older adults, low-cost structural modifications, communication, and transportation systems are needed now to assist current cohorts' independence. Consistent with the person–environment model, older people's home environment can be modified to reduce the level of environmental press and enhance their level of competence and quality of life. For example, currently nearly 35 percent of individuals age 75 and older use at least one assistive device or have their home modified for accessibility, a proportion that will increase dramatically. Given trends toward computerized home-based banking and shopping services, future cohorts with computer skills may not need to leave their homes to obtain many services.

More and more older adults are using computers for accessing the Web at home or in nearby libraries and senior centers. About 24 percent of older households had a computer in 2001; 75 percent of this group had Internet access. A national survey found that 15 percent of older adults use the Web, compared to 56 percent of the total population. The majority use it to obtain the latest health information, while some use it for purchasing products online (accounting for 21 percent of e-commerce spending in the United States) (NCOA, 2002).

Computer programs have also been developed to describe potential side effects of various medications and interactions among them. Cur-

rently, these software programs are aimed at physicians, pharmacists, and other health professionals. However, it will soon be possible to buy such a program written in layman's language, type in the names and doses of medications one is taking, and then obtain a printout of potential side effects and special precautions. This would be particularly useful to the many older adults who are using numerous prescriptions and over-the-counter medications. Although too costly to implement at present, it is technically possible to conduct remote monitoring between a patient's home and a local health care facility for such information as blood pressure and heart-rate measures. Indeed, as Figure 11.5 illustrates, such monitoring may someday be as simple as a wearable or implantable device that transmits health data to a centralized database in a hospital or health provider's office.

Technology also can be used to enhance options for older adults' recreation and enrichment. For example, computers are commonly used for obtaining information via the Web and for leisure (e.g., games linked by telecommunication channels or books read on microchips). Interactive television, CD-ROM and DVD, closed-caption TV programming, and open university via television can greatly expand the social worlds of homebound elders and stimulate intellectual functioning through active participation in learning. For example, Senior Net is a nationwide computer network that encourages discussion on diverse topics and offers hands-on classes in computer use. For a small membership fee, users can attend local classes on computer literacy, word processing, database management, and how to access useful sites on the Internet.

Many products and services that do not depend on "high tech" have come into the marketplace to assist older people in emergency situations, especially those who are living alone. Some of these are simply pullcords in the bathroom or bedroom that are connected to a hospital or to the local emergency medical service. Others, such as the Life Safety System and Lifeline

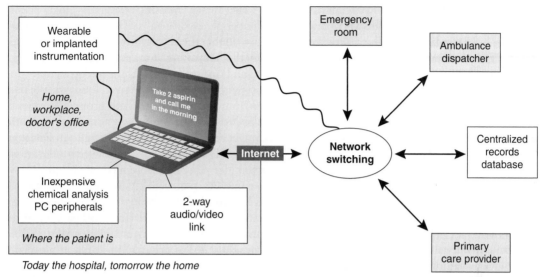

FIGURE 11.5 **Schematic Diagram of a Proposed New Model of the Interface between the Patient and the Health Care System**

SOURCE: Courtesy of Dr. Paul Yager, Department of Bioengineering, University of Washington.

Service, are more sophisticated communication systems that use a portable medical alert device or an alarm unit to transmit specific signals for a fire, a medical emergency, or "no activity" through telephone lines or computers. These systems are found to be cost-effective in enhancing the older person's sense of security about living alone.

The field of **gerontechnology,** where gerontologists and industrial and human factors engineers work together to create technology to help older adults, is growing, especially in Europe. Technology is being built into housing and products to improve P–E congruence for older adults. These new devices are not necessarily better than hands-on care by caregivers, but they may allow the elder to remain self-sufficient longer, and are often more cost-effective (Agree and Freedman, 2003; Pinto et al., 2001; Rialle et al., 2002).

Assistive technology, aimed primarily at younger people with disabilities, can also help older adults. Developments in this field include devices that aid mobility and ADL such as preparing meals, eating, and bathing. More and more of these devices are designed to help people remember tasks such as medication schedules; one product already on the market uses verbal and tone reminders, as well as flashing lights and a single red button to dispense medications on a predetermined schedule. Family members or health providers can set up a prescription routine on a specific schedule for up to 11 different drugs for 30 days. Other devices can be attached to each prescription container; a prerecorded voice announces the schedule and dose needed for that particular medication. This technique is especially useful for older people with dementia who would benefit from hearing a family member's voice reminding them what medications to take (Logue, 2002).

Assistive technology can also include home monitoiring for people with diabetes and hypertension. In this case the patient's relevant health variables (e.g., weight, blood pressure, blood glucose, and cholesterol) are transmitted to a centralized health care database, as shown in Figure 11.5. Indeed, the field of **telehealth,** where health information is transmitted electronically from the patient's home to their physician's office, or from an ambulatory care setting such as a health clinic to a specialist's office, has grown 40 percent annually since 1997. These systems are shown to increase patients' compliance with medication regimens and reduce their hospitalization rates (Lehmann, 2002, 2003).

Other developments include monitoring systems installed in the homes of elders with early-stage dementia so they can remain at home while their family caregivers are employed. The older person's activities can be tracked by the caregiver using a computer with Internet access and a password. Alarms can be added to alert family members if the frail elder has fallen, left the stove on beyond a predesignated time, or walked out of specific doors (e.g., "safe" doors may lead to a protected garden while "alarm" doors lead to the street). Sensors are available that are placed under mattresses in nursing homes to determine if the elder is sleeping, restless, or out of bed during the night. Such systems will eventually be cost-effective to install in private homes as well. Researchers and engineers at the Massachusetts Institute of Technology, Sony, Honda, and other Japanese companies are testing robots that can be used by frail elders to carry objects, open doors, and even socialize with their owners.

As the fields of gerontechnology and telehealth grow, elders and their families must be alert to the ethical issues of privacy and confidentiality, and must recognize that technology cannot substitute for personal attention and caring by a loved one. They may also be too expensive for many elders. However, these new developments can lengthen the time a frail elder can live in the community and reduce caregiver burden.

Housing Policy and Government Programs

Housing policy for older people is less well developed than in the areas of income security and health care. This is due, in part, to the influence of well-organized interest groups, such as builders and real estate developers.

The major housing programs that benefit older people involve subsidies to suppliers of housing to enable them to sell or rent housing for less than the prevailing market price. Since 1959, a special housing program for older people and those with disabilities has given loans for the construction of housing for these groups. Known as the *Section 202* program and administered by the U.S. Department of Housing and Urban Development (HUD), it provides housing for moderate-income older persons whose incomes are just above the eligibility requirements of public housing but too low to obtain housing in the private market. Rents are set by HUD, at about 30 percent of the individual's monthly income. Under Section 202, low-interest loans are made to private nonprofit organizations or to nonprofit consumer cooperatives for the financing, construction, or rehabilitation of housing for older people. In general, these buildings include:

- safety features such as grab bars and emergency systems in each unit
- no communal services such as meals and housekeeping

An emerging concern in these housing units is their lack of P–E fit with the needs of frail older adults, many of whom have "aged in place," rather than moving to a facility that meets their increasing needs for supportive services. The average age of residents in Section 202 housing has increased to 80, and continues to rise; 90 percent are women living alone (HUD, 1999). Currently 67 percent of nonprofit groups that provide supportive housing for this population utilize Section 202 funding. However, this program has slowed as the federal government has withdrawn from supporting housing production. Production of housing units under Section 202 declined from 14,000 new units in 1981 to 7000 in 2001. About 300,000 people aged 62 and older currently live in Section 202 housing. On average, nine applicants were on the waiting list for each Section 202 unit that became vacant in 1999 (AARP, 2001a, 2001b).

Section 236 and *Section 8* housing programs provide private enterprise with additional means of developing quality rental and cooperative housing for low- and moderate-income persons, regardless of age, by lowering their mortgage costs through interest-reduction payments (*Section 236*) and rent vouchers for qualifying older adults (*Section 8*). The former program is continuing with existing housing built under Section 236 funding being rented to low-income users, one-third of whom are age 62 and older. However, no new mortgages have been allowed for the past 30 years. In the latter case, landlords receive from federal and state governments the difference between the rental cost of a housing unit and 30 percent of the tenants' income available for rent. Older people make up about 40 percent of users of this rent supplement program (AARP, 2001b). However, many of these 20-year contracts with owners of low-income housing began in the 1970s and have now expired.

Federal funds have been reduced to renew the contracts, and many owners have lost interest in the low-income housing market, especially in urban centers undergoing renewal or "gentrification." Some landlords have converted their buildings into higher-rent apartments, hotels, or office spaces, or have sold the property outright to local developers. These changes in federal funding and local priorities have reduced the supply of Section 8 housing, which will continue to decline in this century. Some relief has come in the form of vouchers given directly to low-income renters to find market rate housing, although they may pay more than 30 percent of their income in rent, which is higher than the traditional form of Section 8 units. Older people make up 15 percent of low-income households with these vouchers (AARP, 2001b; Commission on Affordable Housing, 2002). Other policies that indirectly affect older homeowners are:

- Property tax relief
- Energy assistance
- Home equity conversion or reverse mortgages described earlier in this chapter. These pro-

> ### CHANGES IN SECTION 202 OBJECTIVES
>
> During the 2000 congressional session, the Senate Appropriations Committee approved an increase of $73 million for Section 202 housing for older adults. The total allocation of $783 million for fiscal year 2002 includes $50 million for converting Section 202 housing to assisted living (AL) facilities and another $50 million for hiring service coordinators to manage them.

vide long-term homeowners with some additional income that converts their homes into more liquid assets.

- Energy assistance for low-income homeowners to offset air conditioning and heating costs is provided under the federal government's allocation of block grant money to cities and states.

As a result, less than 5 percent, or 1.5 million older people, have benefited from federally funded housing assistance programs. The numbers are declining as HUD reduces its subsidies directly to older adults in the form of rent vouchers (Section 8) or indirectly through low-cost loans to builders of housing for older people (Section 202). Reasons for the decline in housing subsidies are federal cutbacks and public perceptions that older people have the financial adequacy to pay for their housing costs directly. Yet, older residents of public housing have a median income that is 35 percent of the median for all older households in the United States (HUD, 1999).

Most recent federal activity in the housing arena has maintained the programs and housing stock that currently exist, modifying programs only incrementally to serve larger numbers of older adults. The goal is to make better use of existing housing resources through homesharing, accessory apartments, and home equity conversions, rather than to increase the overall housing supply for older adults. Another major need is for more congregate housing services. As described earlier, congregate housing is an important link in the long-term care continuum enabling frail and low-income older people to remain in the community and thereby maintain P–E congruence. The best way to achieve this may be innovations that modify existing communities and neighborhoods to meet elders' changing housing needs. This may include creating "granny flats" or accessory housing as part of existing homes to accommodate older people in smaller units near family or close friends.

SRO Housing

Single-room-occupancy (SRO) hotels in urban centers have traditionally served as minimal housing for the urban poor, particularly single older men, who make up the largest group of SRO residents. Indeed, the typical SRO resident is a white older man with less than 10 years of education and an income level 20 percent lower than that of his non-SRO peers, who reports multiple chronic conditions, and who has lived in his room (often with incomplete kitchens and shared bathrooms) for at least 5 years. Increasing numbers of deinstitutionalized mental hospital patients have become SRO tenants as well. A survey in New York City found that, because of their longer tenancy, older SRO residents paid less for their SRO units than did younger tenants. Because of lower income levels, however, older residents paid a higher *proportion* of their income (44 percent) than did younger tenants (25 percent) in the same buildings (Crystal and Beck, 1992). Although overall satisfaction with SRO housing was not high, older residents liked the opportunity to have their own rooms and the physical safety afforded by such a building in an otherwise hostile city core. The lack of services such as congregate meals and counseling was not considered a disadvantage. Increasingly, however, these facilities are becoming home to younger people who are drug abusers, with psychiatric disorders, and often HIV-positive. Older SRO residents may feel threatened in such environments (Foley, 1998).

Yet, SRO housing is rapidly disappearing. As the process of "gentrification" of urban cores becomes more popular, and as more upper-income people discover the advantages of living downtown, the trend of demolishing SRO hotels and using this valuable land for upscale condominiums and office and retail space will continue. One result of this has been a dramatic increase in the number of homeless older people in urban centers over the past 20 years.

The Problems of Homelessness

Although this chapter focuses on housing and community service options for elders, a growing segment of the older population is homeless, often unable to afford basic housing and unaware of services to which they are entitled. **Homeless people** generally include those who, "for whatever reason, do not have a fixed, regular, and adequate night-time residence" (Stewart B. McKinney Homeless Assistance Act, 1987). In the mid-1960s, many homeless elders had recently been released from long-term psychiatric facilities as a result of the 1963 Community Mental Health Act. Today's homeless elders (defined as age 50 and older because physiologically they are generally 10 to 20 years older than their chronological age) are largely the chronic homeless who have lived on the streets for many years and have lost contact with their families. People over age 50 comprise between 10 and 20 percent of the homeless population. This includes an increasing number of women, although there are approximately four times more men in this population. Older homeless men are more likely to have lived this way longer than their female counterparts. Many suffer from psychiatric disorders, alcoholism, or dementia, and lack strong social support. As a result, older adults are the most vulnerable segment of the homeless population. Those who become redomiciled (i.e., find permanent housing) tend to be mostly older homeless women with some social support, who attend community facilities (presum-

Older people often offer assistance to their homeless peers.

logical and psychological processes described in earlier chapters. A life at the edge, in which the individual is constantly trying to fulfill basic human needs (food, shelter, safety from predators), does not leave much energy for these elders to maintain even a modicum of health and well-being; their problems are compounded by chronic psychiatric disorders, alcoholism, drug abuse, and cognitive impairment (often a result of long-term alcohol abuse). Homeless older persons with chronic health problems often do not have the physical, social, or psychological resources to seek regular medical care for these conditions, or even to follow the necessary medication schedules and dietary restrictions. The prevalence of chronic diseases in this group is higher than for other segments of the older population, yet their access to health services is inadequate and sporadic at best (Folsom et al., 2002). Their ability to maintain their health and medication regimens is limited by the unstable nature of their lifestyles and frequent disruptions in psychological well-being. Their health care is typically obtained through public hospital emergency rooms, and necessary clinical appointments and follow-up visits are rarely kept. Thus, they often die because of diseases that are neglected, accidents, and victimization on the streets. The number of homeless elders is estimated to double in the future, with an increase in the number of younger persons with risk factors of lifelong poverty, substance abuse, incarceration, marital disruption, and lack of family contacts (Cohen, 1999).

Implications for the Future

As we look toward the aging of baby boomers, larger numbers of older adults will reside in suburbs and few in central cities. Future cohorts will create a demand for services in the suburbs rather than traveling to city centers for their health care, social, recreational, and shopping needs. These trends are already evident as more businesses, medical and dental providers, senior centers, and shopping centers relocate to suburbs. This will

ably becoming more familiar to service providers), and who do not display psychotic symptoms (Cohen et al., 1997; Cohen, Sokolovsky, and Crane, 2001; Stergiopoulos and Herrmann, 2003). One epidemiological study interviewed 900 homeless persons using standard diagnostic criteria for psychiatric disorders. Although the rates for other psychiatric diagnoses did not differ by age or gender, alcohol abuse was significantly more prevalent among men aged 50 and older than among younger men (81 percent vs. 60 percent); the reverse was true for drug abuse (16 percent vs. 43.5 percent). No differences emerged in rates of substance abuse or other psychiatric diagnoses between younger and older homelesss women (DeMallie, North, and Smith, 1997).

Not only do homeless people have no place to live, but they also lack food, clothing, medical care, and social supports. Such a disorganized lifestyle can magnify the usual age-related declines in bio-

reduce the demand for public transportation between suburbs and city centers, which has become too costly for most municipalities to provide. Senior boomers will be more likely than their parents' generation to continue driving or to use specialized transportation such as vans provided by community agencies.

Because of earlier experiences with relocation and more travel opportunities during their youth, baby boomers will feel more confident about relocating to other parts of the United States, including less costly rural communities and small towns. Some will even choose to move to other countries, such as Mexico, where their retirement income can buy more, or as a form of reverse migration to their homeland. Instead of large, isolated retirement communities, future cohorts of elders are more likely to select independent housing in the communities where they relocate, integrating by volunteering, obtaining paid employment, and becoming active participants in these settings.

As more and more people live to age 85 and older, demand for more choices in long-term care will increase. "Aging in place" will become a more viable option than it is today, thanks to technological advances that can create smart homes and allow older people to communicate with family members, health and social service providers via the Internet and telehealth, using electronic reminders to take their medications and eat their meals as needed, to record their vital signs, and even when to exercise. This trend will be aided by the growth in "flexible housing" that is being demanded by baby boomers today. Middle-aged adults, who are building new homes or remodeling existing homes in order to accommodate their aging parents, often find that the home can benefit them as they age in place. They are finding that elder-friendly home design, including bedroom, bath, and kitchen facilities on the entry floor, easy-to-operate mechanical and electronic devices, and temperature controls for each area of the home, is practical and can be built with minimal construction costs. Such homes can create a more supportive environment for aging baby boomers, but may be limited to those who can afford it.

Middle-aged people today with adequate financial resources are more likely to purchase long-term care insurance, creating a wider range of options for those who may need such services in their later years. Some of these LTC insurance policies include home health care, adult day health care, and other non-residential services, as described in Chapter 17. Older adults who have purchased these policies in their younger years will benefit from the choices open to them, especially if they want to remain in their own homes as they become more frail.

Although future cohorts of elders will have more options open to them, these choices will depend on their financial resources. As a result, disparities between older adults with and without financial adequacy will become greater than during their youth. Those who have adequate resources will be able to travel and relocate to more desirable communities. They can purchase services and technology that can help them age in place. If they eventually need long-term care services, they can select from among multiple options in types and quality. Older adults who do not have adequate retirement income or who could not afford to purchase LTC insurance in their younger years will have to retire on the limited options available to them through Medicaid. These elders often have little choice in whether they receive home health care or institutional care, or the quality of services they obtain. Homelessness may also rise among older people in the United States, especially for those who have severed ties from their families due to divorce, alcohol, and drug abuse. These trends suggest an increasing schism between older adults who have aged with sufficient social and financial resources, and those who have faced adversity throughout their lives.

Summary

This chapter presented ways in which environmental factors affect the physical and psychological well-being of older people. Perhaps the most important lesson to be gained from this discussion is that a given environment is not inherently good or bad. Some environments are more conducive for achieving active aging among *some* people, while other older adults need an entirely different set of features. For example, an older person who has a high need for activity and stimulation and has always lived in an urban setting will be more satisfied with a large nursing home in a metropolitan center than will the individual who has always lived in a single-family dwelling in a rural community. Most P–E models point to the necessity of examining each older person's specific needs, preferences, and abilities, and designing environments that can both meet the needs of this broad cross-section and, more importantly, flexibly respond to individual differences. To the degree that environmental press can be reduced to accommodate personal abilities and needs, the aging person can function more effectively and maintain his or her level of well-being. Relocation represents a special case of P–E incongruence that can disturb the well-being of an impaired older person by raising the level of environmental press.

Differences in housing quality and services for rural older residents are of concern. Current cohorts are much less likely than previous ones to live in farm and nonfarm rural communities. However, those who do, particularly African Americans, tend to have lower incomes and poorer health, with more limitations in activities of daily living. The recognition of these disparities has led to the growth of state and federally funded services for rural elders, but more are needed. Older persons in rural communities appear to have more frequent social interactions with neighbors and friends than do urban elders, but they need more formal health and social services.

The neighborhood and neighbors play a significant role in the well-being of older adults. With retirement and declining health, the older person's physical lifespace becomes more constricted. The neighborhood takes on greater significance as a source of social interactions, health and social services, grocery shopping, banking, and postal services. Neighbors represent an important component of older people's social and emotional network, especially when family is unavailable.

Fear of crime among older persons is widespread but is incongruent with actual victimization rates. Older people experience far lower rates than younger people for violent crimes, and somewhat lower for other types of crime. African American women, however, are at greater risk for crimes than any other group of elders. The potential danger of injury and long-term disability, as well as the fear of economic loss, may contribute to this incongruence between actual victimization rates and fear of crime.

The high rate of home ownership and long-term residence in their homes make it difficult for older people to relocate to new housing, even when the new situation represents a significant improvement over the old. The poor condition of many older people's homes and the high costs of renovating and maintaining them sometimes make relocation necessary, even when an older homeowner is reluctant. Better living conditions and a safer neighborhood in which several other elders reside are found to improve older people's morale and sense of well-being, especially following a move to a planned housing project from substandard housing. The growth of planned and congregate housing for older adults raises the issue of site selection for such housing. It is especially important when designing housing that public transportation be located nearby and that facilities such as medical and social services, banks, and groceries be within easy access of the housing facility. Services need to be integrated from the beginning, as many residents who move in as young-old persons continue to live there for many years and age in place. With the increasing segment of the older population in suburbs, these services must be considered in any housing plan for this age group.

As people live longer and healthier lives beyond retirement, the need for housing that provides a range of care options will continue to grow. Several alternative methods of purchasing such housing are available—some guarantee lifetime care, others do not provide personal and health services. Considering the high likelihood of using a nursing home facility at some time in old age, many retirees prefer to select the more comprehensive options.

The proportion of older people in a nursing home at any one time is very low, but up to 50 percent will need some type of long-term care before they die. Because of the greater likelihood of physical and cognitive impairments among nursing home residents, it is critical to enhance the environmental quality of these facilities at the design stage. If the facility has already been built, features can be added that increase privacy and control and allow for the expression of territoriality and other personal needs. Aging and relocation to a nursing home do not reduce the individual's needs for identity and self-expression.

Assisted living and adult foster care or adult family homes are rapidly becoming a cost-effective option for many older people who need help with ADL. Many of these community residential care facilities provide greater autonomy, more options for privacy, and less direct supervision for their older residents. More and more states are covering these long-term care facility types under Medicaid because they generally cost less than nursing homes. This makes many of these community residential care options a viable choice for frail elders who require long-term care but who do not have adequate financial resources to choose from a variety of facilities. Home care is now the fastest-growing component of personal health care expenditures. It is partially reimbursed by Medicare and Medicaid to offer more services than other long-term care options. It allows older people to "age in place" while bringing services such as skilled nursing care, rehabilitation, and personal and household care to the person's home. Adult day care or adult day health care, both as a rehabilitative and social model, provides opportunities for social integration of frail older people who are living at home alone or with a family caregiver. The older person can attend adult day health care for several hours each day and receive nursing and rehabilitation services, while the caregiver obtains respite from caregiving tasks. Many adult day care programs also offer counseling and support groups for caregivers.

Single-room-occupancy hotels have traditionally been a low-cost housing option for older people, especially for older men living alone. However, as these buildings have been demolished or remodeled in many cities, SRO residents have become displaced; some have become homeless. Many older homeless people have chronic medical, psychiatric, and cognitive disorders that often go unattended because of lack of access to health services. As a result, these homeless elders grow physiologically old more rapidly than do their more stable peers.

GLOSSARY

adult day care (ADC)   a community facility that frail older people living at home can attend several hours each day; when based on a health rehabilitation model, it provides individualized therapy plans; those based on a social model focus on structured social and psychotherapeutic activities

adult foster care (AFC)/adult family home (AFH)   a private home facility, licensed by the state, in which the owner of the home provides housekeeping, personal care, and some delegated nursing functions for the residents

aging in place   continuing to live in a private home or apartment, even when declining competence reduces P–E congruence and more assistance with ADL is needed

assisted living   a housing model aimed at elders who need assistance with personal care, e.g., bathing and taking medication, but who are not so physically or cognitively impaired as to need 24-hour attention

assistive technology   a range of electronic and computer technologies whose goal is to assist people with disabilities to remain independent and perform as many ADL as possible without assistance from others

community residential care (CRC)   a general label for residential long-term care options other than nursing homes; includes adult foster care, adult family homes, and assisted living

congregate housing a form of group housing that provides communal services, the minimum of which is a central kitchen and dining room for residents; some facilities also provide housekeeping, social, and health services

continuous care retirement community (CCRC) a multilevel facility offering a range from independent to congregate living arrangements, including nursing home units; generally requires an initial entry fee to assure a place if long-term care is needed in the future

Eden Alternative a new paradigm for nursing home care that encourages active participation by residents in caring for plants and animals

gerontechnology a new field of research and practice, aimed at using technology to improve older adults' independence

home health care a variety of nursing, rehabilitation, and other therapy services, as well as assistance with personal care and household maintenance, that are provided to people who are homebound and have difficulty performing multiple ADL

long-term care a broad range of services geared to helping frail older adults in their own home and community settings; can include nursing homes, nutritional programs, adult day care, and visiting nurse services

Medicaid waivers exceptions to state Medicaid rules that allow use of Medicaid funds for services that are traditionally not covered by Medicaid, such as chore services and adult family homes

naturally occurring retirement community (NORC) a neighborhood or larger area occupied mostly by older people, but without having been planned specifically for this population

negotiated risk agreement between a resident, family or guardian, and facility administration that the resident in a CRC setting will maintain autonomy but will assume risks if problems such as falls and accidents result from such independence

nursing homes facilities with three or more beds staffed 24 hours per day by health professionals who provide nursing and personal-care services to residents who cannot remain in their own homes due to physical health problems, functional disabilities, and/or significant cognitive impairments

single-room-occupancy (SRO) hotels older buildings in urban centers that have been converted to low-cost apartments; often these are single rooms with no kitchen, minimal cooking and refrigeration facilities, and bathrooms shared with other units

smart homes technology built into a home that relies on computerized systems to monitor and maintain preferred lighting and heat levels, security, communication

telehealth transmitting a patient's health status and vital signs via computer or telephone lines directly to a health provider

universal design designing a product or building or landscape to make it accessible to and usable by the broadest range of users

RESOURCES

See the companion Website for this text at <www .ablongman.com/hooyman> for information about the following:

- AgeNet, LLC
- American Association of Homes and Services for the Aging
- American Association of Retired Persons (AARP)
- American College of Health Care Administrators (ACHCA)
- American Seniors Housing Association
- Assisted Living Federation of America (ALFA) [formerly Assisted Living Facilities Association of America]
- Caring Concepts
- Citizens for the Improvement of Nursing Homes (CINH)
- Gatekeeper Program
- Department of Housing and Urban Development (HUD)
- National Adult Day Services Association, NCOA
- National Association for Home Care (NAHC)
- National Association of Directors of Nursing in Long Term Care (NADONAILTC)
- National Citizens Coalition for Nursing Home Reform (NCCNHR)
- National Institute on Adult Day Care
- National Shared Housing Resource Center

REFERENCES

AARP. *Fixing to stay: A national survey on housing and home modification issues.* Washington, DC: AARP Public Policy Institute, 2000.

AARP. *The 1999 National Survey of Sector 202 Elderly Housing.* Washington, DC: AARP Public Policy Institute, 2001a.

AARP. *A summary of federal rental housing programs.* Washington, DC: AARP Public Policy Institute, 2001b.

AARP. *Transportation: The older person's interest.* Washington, DC: AARP Public Policy Institute, 2002.

AARP. *Understanding senior housing into the next century.* Washington DC, 1996.

Administration on Aging (AOA). *A profile of older Americans: 2000,* Web page: http://www.aoa.gov/stats/profile.

Agree, E. M., and Freedman, V. A. A comparison of assistive technology and personal care in alleviating disability and unmet need. *The Gerontologist,* 2003, *43,* 335–344.

American Association of Homes and Services for the Aging (AAHSA), 1997. *Senior housing,* Web page: http://www.aahsa.org/members/backgrd2/htm

Arai, Y., Washio, M., and Kudo, K. Factors associated with admission to a geriatric hospital in southern Japan. *Psychiatry and Clinical Neurosciences.* 2000, *54,* 213–216.

Ashley, M. J., Olin, J. S., Le Riche, W. H., Kornaczewski, A., and Rankin, J. G. Skid row alcoholism: A distinct sociomedical entity. *Archives of Internal Medicine,* 1976, *136,* 272–278.

Atchley, R. C. *Social forces and aging: An introduction to social gerontology.* (9th ed.). Belmont, CA: Wadsworth, 2000.

Auerbach, A. J. The elderly in rural areas. In L. H. Ginsberg (Ed.), *Social work in rural communities.* New York: Council on Social Work Education, 1976.

Barker, R. G., Dembo, T., and Lewin, K. Frustration and regression: An experiment with young children. *University of Iowa Studies in Child Welfare,* 1941, *18.*

Bazargan, M. The effects of health, environmental, and socio-psychological variables on fear of crime and its consequences among urban black elderly individuals. *International Journal of Aging and Human Development,* 1994, *38,* 99–115.

Bureau of Justice Statistics. *Criminal Victimization in the United States 1999: The National Crime Victimization Survey,* NCJ-174446, Sept. 2000.

Bureau of Justice Statistics. *Homicide trends in the United States: Eldercide.* http://www.ojp.usdoj.gov/bjs/homicide/elders.htm, December 2003.

Burgio, L. D., Stevens, A., Burgio, K. L., Roth, D. L., Paul, P., and Gerstle, J. Teaching and maintaining behavior management skills in the nursing home. *The Gerontologist,* 2002, *42,* 487–496.

Castle, N. G. Relocation of the elderly. *Medical Care Research and Review,* 2001, *58,* 291–333.

Centers for Medicare and Medicaid Services (CMS). *Appropriateness of minimum staffing ratios in nursing homes.* Report to Congress. Washington, DC: CMS, 2002.

Chapin, R., and Dobbs-Kepper, D. Aging in place in assisted living: Philosophy versus policy. *The Gerontologist,* 2001, *41,* 43–50.

Cohen, C. I. Aging and homelessness. *The Gerontologist,* 1999, *39,* 5–14.

Cohen, C. I., Ramirez, M., Teresi, J., Gallagher, M., and Sokolovsky, J. Predictors of becoming redomiciled among older homeless women. *The Gerontologist,* 1997, *37,* 67–74.

Cohen, C. I., Sokolovsky, J., and Crane, M. *International Journal of Law and Psychiatry,* 2001, *24,* 167–181.

Commission on Affordable Housing and Health Facilities Needs. *A quiet crisis in America: A report to Congress.* Washington, DC: U.S. Government Printing Office, 2002.

Crystal, S., and Beck, P. A room of one's own: The SRO and the single elderly. *The Gerontologist,* 1992, *32,* 684–692.

Curtis, M. P., Kiyak, H. A., Hedrick, S. Resident and facility characteristics of adult-family home, adult residential care, and assisted living facilities in Washington state. *Journal of Gerontological Social Work,* 2000, *34,* 25–41.

Day, K., Carreon, D., and Stump, C. The therapeutic design of environments for people with dementia: A review of the empirical research. *The Gerontologist,* 2000, *40,* 397–406.

Deatrick, D. Senior-Med: Creating a network to help manage medications. *Generations,* 1997, *21,* 59–60.

Demallie, D. A., North, C. S., and Smith, E. M. Psychiatric disorders among the homeless: A comparison of older and younger groups. *The Gerontologist,* 1997, *37,* 61–66.

Dibner, A. S., Lowry, L., and Morris, J. N. Usage and acceptance of an emergency alarm system by the frail elderly. *The Gerontologist,* 1982, *22,* 538–539.

Foley, D. Hellish conditions at single-room occupancy hotels. *Body Posit,* 1998, *11,* 18–23.

Folsom, D. P., McCahill, M., Bartels, S. J., Lindamer, L. A., Ganiats, T. G., and Jeste, D. V. Medical comorbidity and receipt of medical care by older homeless people with schizophrenia or depression. *Psychiatric Services,* 2002, *53,* 1456–1460.

Frank, J. B. *The paradox of aging in place in assisted living.* Westport, CT: Bergin and Garvey, 2002.

Gaberlavage, G., and Citro, J. *Progress in the housing of older persons.* Public Policy Institute, American Association of Retired Persons, Washington, DC: 1997.

Gaugler, J. E., Jarrott, S. E., Zarit, S. H., Stephens, M. A., Townsend, A., and Greene, R. Adult day service use and reductions in caregiving hours: Effects of stress and psychological well-being for dementia caregivers. *International Journal of Geriatric Psychiatry,* 2003, *18,* 55–62.

General Accounting Office (GAO). *Assisted living: Quality of care and consumer protection issues.* Final Report #GAO/T-HEHS-99-111), April 1999.

Gonzales, T. I. An empirical study of economies of scope in home healthcare. *Health Services Research,* 1997, *32,* 313–324.

Greene, V. L., and Ondrich, J. I. Risk factors for nursing home admissions and exits. *Journals of Gerontology,* 1990, *45,* S250–S258.

Hawes, C. Introduction. In S. Zimmerman, P. D. Sloan, and J. K. Eckert (Eds.), *Assisted living: Needs, practices and policies in residential care for the elderly.* Baltimore: Johns Hopkins University Press, 2001.

Hawes, C., Mor, V., Phillips, C. D., Fries, B. E., Morris, J. N., Steele-Friedlob, E., Greene, A. M., and Nennstiel, M. The OBRA-87 nursing home regulations and implementation of the Resident Assessment Instrument: Effects on process quality. *Journal of the American Geriatrics Society,* 1997, *45,* 977–985.

Hawes, C., Rose, M., and Phillips, C. D. *A national study of assisted living for the frail elderly executive summary: Results of a national survey of facilities.* Washington, DC: Public Policy Institute, AARP, 1999.

Hawes, C., Wildfire, J. B., and Lux, L. J. *The regulations of board and care homes: Results of a survey in the 50 states and the District of Columbia.* Washington, DC: Public Policy Institute, AARP, 1993.

Hedrick, S. C., Sales, A. E. B., Sullivan, J. H., Gray, S. L., Tornatore, J., Curtis, M., and Zhou, X. A. Resident outcomes of Medicaid-funded community residential care. *The Gerontologist,* 2003, *43,* 473–482.

Henretta, J. C. Retirement and residential moves by elderly households. *Research on Aging,* 1986, *8,* 23–37.

Hobbs, F., and Damon, B. L. *65+ in the United States.* Washington, DC: U.S. Department of Commerce, Bureau of the Census, Current Population Reports, 1996.

Hollway, W., and Jefferson, T. The risk society in an age of anxiety: Situating fear of crime. *British Journal of Sociology,* 1997, *48,* 255–266.

Hughes, S. L. Home health. In C. J. Evashwick (Ed.), *The continuum of long-term care.* Albany, NY: Delmar, 1996.

Hughes, S. L., and Pittard, M. A. Home health. In C. J. Evashwick (Ed.). *The continuum of long-term care* (2nd ed.). Albany, NY: Delmar, 2001.

Hughes, S. L., Ulasevich, A., Weaver, F. M., Henderson, W., Manheim, L., Kubal, J. D., and Bonarigo, F. Impact of home care of hospital days: A meta-analysis. *Health Services Research,* 1997, *32,* 415–432.

Jette, A. M., Tennstedt, S., and Crawford, S. How does formal and informal community care affect nursing home use? *Journals of Gerontology,* 1995, *50B,* S4–S12.

Kane, R. A. Long-term care and a good quality of life: Bringing them closer together. *The Gerontologist,* 2001, *41,* 293–304.

Kaplan, D. Access to technology: Unique challenges for people with disabilities. *Generations,* 1997, *21,* 24–27.

Lawton, M. P. Competence, environmental press, and the adaptation of older people. In P. G. Windley and G. Ernst (Eds.), *Theory development in environment and aging.* Washington, DC: Gerontological Society, 1975.

Lehmann, C. A. *Economic benefits of telehealth in managing diabetes patients in ambulatory settings.* Paper presented at SPRY Foundation Conference on Technology and Aging, Bethesda, MD, October 2003.

Lehmann, C. A. The future of home testing—Implications for traditional laboratories. *Clinica Chimica Acta,* 2002, *323,* 31–36.

Lewin, K. *Dynamic theory of personality.* New York: McGraw-Hill, 1935.

Lewin, K. *Field theory in social science.* New York: Harper and Row, 1951.

Lewin, K., Lippitt, R., and White, R. Patterns of aggressive behavior in experimentally created social climates. *Journal of Social Psychology,* 1939, *10,* 271–299.

Litwak, E., and Longino, C. F. Migration patterns among the elderly: A developmental perspective. *The Gerontologist,* 1987, *27,* 266–272.

Litwak, E., and Longino, C. F. Migration patterns among the elderly: A developmental perspective. In R. B. Enright (Ed.), *Perspectives in social gerontology.* Boston: Allyn and Bacon, 1994.

Logue, R. M. Self-medication and the elderly: How technology can help. *American Journal of Nursing,* 2002, *102,* 51–57.

Longino, C. F. Geographic mobility and the baby boom. *Generations,* 1998, *22* (Spring), 60–64.

Lubinski, E., and Higginbotham, D. J. *Communication technologies for the elderly: Vision, hearing and speech.* San Diego: Singular Publishing Group, 1997.

Lutgendorf, S. K., Reimer, T. T., Harvey, J. H., Marks, G., Hong, S., Hillis, S. L., and Lubaroff, D. M. Effects of housing relocation on immunocompetence and psychosocial functioning in older adults. *Journals of Gerontology: Medical Sciences,* 2001, *56A,* M97–M105.

Mace, R. L. Universal Design in housing. *Assistive Technology,* 1998, *10,* 21–28.

Manton, K. G., Corder, L. S., and Stallard, E. Estimates of change in chronic disability and institutional incidence and prevalence rates in the U.S. elderly population from the 1982, 1984, and 1989 National Long-Term Care Survey. *Journals of Gerontology,* 1993, *48,* S153–S166.

McCall, N. The impact of Medicare home health policy changes on Medicare beneficiaries. *The Home Care Initiative Policy Brief,* Spring 2003.

McKinney, S. B. *Homeless Assistance Act,* P.L. 100-77 (1987).

Met Life. Market survey of nursing home and home care costs, August 2003. www.metlife.com/WPSAssets.

Meyer, H. The bottom line on assisted living. *Hospitals and Health Networks,* 1998. *72,* 22–26.

Mollica, R. L. State policy and regulations. In S. Zimmerman, P. D. Sloan, and J. K. Eckert (Eds.), *As-sisted living: Needs, practices and policies in residential care for the elderly.* Baltimore: Johns Hopkins University Press, 2001.

Murray, H. A. *Explorations in personality.* New York: Oxford University Press, 1938.

National Center for Health Statistics (NCHS). *Advance Data,* No. 28, Jan. 23, 1997.

National Center for Health Statistics (NCHS). Data from the 1997 National Nursing Home Survey. *Vital and Health Statistics,* No. 311, 2000.

National Council on the Aging (NCOA). Facts about older Americans. http://www.ncoa.org/content.cfm?sectionID, December 2002.

National Low Income Housing Information Service. *The fiscal year 1991 budget and low income housing* (SM-290). Washington, DC: National Low-Income Housing Information Service, 1990.

New York Times. Immigrants now embrace homes for elderly. October 20, 2003, pp. A1, A10.

Peng, T. R., Navaie-Waliser, M., and Feldman, P. H. Social support, home health service use, and outcomes among four racial-ethnic groups. *The Gerontologist,* 2003, *43,* 503–513.

Perez-Pena, R. Overwhelmed and understaffed, nursing home workers vent anger. *New York Times,* June 8, 2003, p. 1.

Pinto, M. R., DeMedici, S., VanSant, C., Bianchi, A., Zlotnicki, A., and Napoli, C. Ergonomics, gerontechnology, and design for the home environment. *Applied Ergonomics,* 2001, *31,* 317–322.

Pruchno, R. A., and Rose, M. S. Effect of long-term care environments on health outcomes. *The Gerontologist,* 2000, *40,* 429–436.

Pynoos, J., and Golant, S. M. Housing and living arrangements for the elderly. In R. H. Binstock and L. K. George (Eds.), *Handbook of aging and the social sciences* (4th ed.). San Diego: Academic Press, 1996.

Pynoos, J., and Matsuoka, C. A. E. Housing. In C. J. Evashwick (Ed.), *The Continuum of Long-Term Care* (2nd ed.). Albany, NY: Delmar, 2001.

Quinn, M. E., Johnson, M. A., Andress, E. L., McGinnis, P., and Ramesh, M. Health characteristics of elderly personal care home residents. *Journal of Advance Nursing,* 1999, *30,* 410–417.

Redfoot, D., and Gaberlavage, G. Housing for older Americans: Sustaining the dream. *Generations,* 1991, *15,* 35–38.

Regnier, V. *Design for assisted living.* Hoboken, NJ: John Wiley & Sons, 2002.

Rialle, V., Duchene, F., Noury, N., Bajolle, L., and Demongeot, J. Health smart homes: Information technology for patients at home. *Telemedicine Journal and e-Health*, 2002, 8, 395–409.

Riley, C. A. *High access home.* New York: Rizzoli International Publications, 1999.

Rollinson, P. A. Elderly single room occupancy (SRO) hotel tenants: Still alone. *Social Work*, 1991, 36, 303–308.

Seattle Times. Retirees gaining popularity in towns yearning for growth. May 27, 2003, p. A5.

Seperson, S. B. Demographics about aging. In S. B. Seperson and C. Hegeman (Eds.), *Elder care and service learning: A handbook.* Westport, CT: Auburn House, 2002.

Silverstein, M., and Zablotsky, D. L. Health and social precursors of later life retirement-community migration. *Journals of Gerontology,* 1996, *51B,* S150–S156.

Spillman, B. C., and Kemper, P. Lifetime patterns of payment for nursing home care. *Medical Care,* 1995, *33,* 280–296.

Stergiopoulos, V., and Herrmann, N. Old and homeless: A review and survey of older adults who use shelters in an urban setting. *Canadian Journal of Psychiatry,* 2003, *48,* 374–380.

Stoller, E. P., and Longino, C. F. "Going home" or "leaving home"? The impact of person and place ties on anticipated counterstream migration. *The Gerontologist,* 2001, *41,* 96–102.

Strahan, G. An overview of nursing homes and their current residents: Data from the 1995 National Nursing Home Survey. *Vital and Health Statistics.* No. 280. Hyattsville, MD: National Center for Health Statistics, 1997.

Taira, E. D., and Carlson, J. L. (Eds.), *Aging in place: Designing, adapting and enhancing the home environment.* Binghamton, NY: Haworth Press, 1999.

Tedesco, J. Adult day care. In C. J. Evashwick (Ed.), *The continuum of long-term care.* Albany, NY: Delmar, 1996.

Tennstedt, S. L., Crawford, S., and McKinley, J. Determining the pattern of community care: Is coresidence more important than caregiver relationship? *Journals of Gerontology,* 1993, *48,* S74–S83.

Teresi, J. A., Holmes, D., and Ory, M. G. The therapeutic design of environments for people with dementia. *The Gerontologist,* 2000, *40,* 64–74.

Thomas, W. H. *The Eden alternative handbook.* Sherburne, NY: Eden Alternative Foundation, 1999.

Thomas, W. H., and Stermer, M. Eden Alternative principles hold promise for the future of long-term care. *Balance,* 1999, *3,* 14–17.

U.S. Census Bureau. *65 and older in the U.S.* Current Population Reports, Series P25-1095. Washington DC: U.S. Government Printing Office, 1996.

U.S. Census Bureau. *Household and family characteristics.* Current Population Reports. Series P20-515. Washington, DC: U.S. Government Printing Office, 1998.

U.S. Census Bureau. *Moving rates among Americans declines.* http://www.census.gov/Press-Release/www/2000/cb00-10.html, 2000.

U.S. Dept. of Health and Human Services, Health Care Financing Administration. *Health Care Financing Review* (Medicare and Medicaid Statistical Supplement), 1998.

U.S. Department of Housing and Urban Development (HUD). Office of Policy Development and Research. *Housing our elders.* Washington, DC: 1999.

Wiener, J. M. An assessment of strategies for improving quality of care in nursing homes. *The Gerontologist,* 2003, *43* (Special Issue), 19–27.

Wilmoth, J. M. Unbalanced social exchanges and living arrangement transitions among older adults. *The Gerontologist,* 2000, *40,* 64–74.

Wolinsky, F. D., Stump, T. E., and Callahan, C. M. Does being placed in a nursing home make you sicker and more likely to die? In S. L. Willis and K. W. Schaie (Eds.), *Societal Mechanics for Maintaining Competence in Old Age.* New York: Springer Publishing, 1997.

12

Productive Aging: Paid and Nonpaid Roles and Activities

What Do We Mean by Productive Aging? Definitions and Critique

Productivity is typically thought of as paid work. In fact, disengagement and role theory focuses on the losses associated with withdrawal from the employment role. Many older adults, however, are productive without being employed or engaged in obligatory activities. Productivity is broader than paid work; it includes any paid or unpaid activity that produces goods and services for the benefit of society, such as household tasks, child care, voluntarism, and help to family and friends. We use the concept of productivity throughout this chapter because of the myriad of ways in which older adults contribute to their families, neighborhoods, communities, and society, as well as the reciprocity that elders may experience through such contributions. Older adults are viewed individually and collectively as a resource to meet their own and society's needs. Engagement in such productive activity is assumed to have a positive influence on older adults' mental and physical well-being (Hinterlong, Morrow-Howell, and Sherraden, 2001).

The concept of productivity has been subject to criticisms similar to those leveled at successful aging (see Chapter 6 for a critique of successful aging). From a feminist and political economy perspective, emphasis on productivity may lead to further marginalization and blaming of low-income women and elders of color who cannot attain middle-class standards of productive activity. If such groups are not productive enough, are they then defined as failures? Accordingly, are those who are chronically impaired or who prefer to be contemplative a problem for society (Estes and Mahakian, 2001; Holstein, 1999)? Similarly, if an individual is sitting and thinking, it is difficult to quantify the value of an idea that can lead to tremendous productivity gains in society, but may not appear to be "productive behavior." Likewise, cognitive and emotional exchanges, such as Erikson's concept of generativity, cannot be quantified (Birren, 2001). Critical gerontologists maintain that the concept of productive activity has class, race, and gender biases because of implicit middle-class norms of what is considered a "productive" way to spend time. They caution against "prescribing" active engagement for elders, and emphasize opportunity and choice. Accordingly, class, race, ethnicity, and gender inequities across the life span all affect an older adult's ability to engage in meaningful and productive aging experiences. The meaning of productive aging is shaped by the increasing inequality in society and within the aging population, which creates different life chances and opportunities for elders. Overall, critics of the concept of productive aging urge caution regarding who defines productive aging, which segments of the older population is productive aging for, and who benefits from productive aging (Calasanti and Slevin, 2001; Estes and Mahakian, 2001; Katz, 2000; Moody, 2001a).

Given this context, we use the concept of productivity in this text in the broadest sense of engagement with and contributions to others—family, neighbors, friends, and community. But the contributions need not be "goods and services" in a traditional sense. Instead, there can be

Many older people enjoy participating in productive activities.

social, psychological, and spiritual dimensions to productivity, including self-improvement through learning, personal fulfillment, searching for meaning, and spirituality. Productivity is not the same as "staying busy," since a contemplative elder may nevertheless be contributing to his or her own or others' well-being. This broad definition recognizes that even a homebound, chronically disabled elder may be productive by teaching family and friends about how to age with dignity, placing phone calls to check up on other neighbors, reading to a young child, listening to a grieving friend, or providing support, encouragement, and life lessons to a confused adolescent. The older woman who prefers to spend hours working alone in her garden may be contributing to the "common good" by creating beauty for neighbors to enjoy, even though she may not view herself as contributing directly to the community. Regardless of our life circumstances, there is a universal human need to be of use, and reaching out and giving to others is a powerful antidote to loneliness, isolation, and depression.

An assumption throughout this text is that older adults represent our society's greatest underutilized asset. They bring the resilience and hardiness of survivors, and the wisdom of life experience and lessons learned. As such, they are a civic treasure that can provide leadership in community and religious organizations, volunteer, and influence decision-making and legislative processes. What is critical is for older adults to be able to exercise choice over how they spend their time. Public resources are then needed to support such choices, including those to contribute to families, neighbors, and communities. Although the concept of productive aging may have an implicit assumption that older adults *should* be productive and exert pressures on them to engage in activities that they would prefer not to undertake, the greater danger appears to be that our society has limited opportunities for older adults to be engaged and make contributions (Freedman, 2001). Consistent with the person–environment (P–E) framework of this book, older adults need op-

portunities to choose and adjust their behavior and aspirations to maintain a sense of competence in a changing environment. Accordingly, changes are needed in public policy and societal institutions to develop ways to enhance older adults' contributions to others and to provide meaningful roles in old age (Freedman, 2001).

Race, ethnicity, gender, social class, cohort experiences, living arrangements, and neighborhoods are structural or societal factors that influence the choices available to older adults. Personal capacities, such as the normal physical and psychological changes of aging, health status, personality, attitudes, skills, and values also influence how individuals choose to spend their time in old age. Self-esteem and self-concept are powerful factors. Some older adults may believe that they are "too old" or lack the capacity to perform certain activities, even though they have the objective resources of finances and a supportive living situation. Others with limited objective resources (e.g., in poor health or poverty) may nevertheless possess the inner resources to seek out new opportunities in old age, because of their zest for living and learning new things. In other words, people's use of time and arenas of involvement all vary with the opportunities provided by the larger environment as well as with each developmental phase in the life cycle. Clearly, the meanings, options, and outcomes for productive aging vary among different populations; social class appears to be the most important structural factor in shaping whatever may be possible in aging, since class is found to be related to every measure of health and illness (Estes and Mahakian, 2001). Unfortunately, poor health, reduced income, transportation difficulties, or isolated living arrangements often disrupt and reduce choices in old age. Nevertheless, many individuals pursue new activities, including art, music, running, hiking, meditating, or teaching for the first time in old age. Even with decreased competence in health and physical functioning, older people can actively maintain optimal quality of life by modifying their activities in order to establish congruence between their needs and abilities and environmental demands. It also appears that older adults generally become more selective about how they invest their time and energy than in the past.

This chapter reviews both the choices and opportunities as well as the constraints that older adults face related to productivity: retirement, employment, pursuit of leisure, membership in community associations and voluntarism, education, religious participation and spirituality, and political involvement. It concludes by recognizing how societal institutions need to change to provide options for older adults to choose how they wish to remain engaged and contributing to others, whether through lifelong learning, voluntarism, contemplative activities, or religious involvement. Community and societal responsibility, including policy changes and resource commitments, are essential elements of any program to promote productive aging to reduce inequities in opportunities for productive engagement.

We turn now to retirement, which removes older adults from paid forms of productivity and shapes opportunities for their engagement in non-paid activities.

Retirement

With increased longevity and changing work patterns, retirement is as much an expected part of the life course as having a family, completing school, or working. Men in particular, but increasingly women among younger cohorts, develop age-related expectations about the rhythm of their careers—when to start working, when to be at the peak of their careers, and when to retire; and they assess whether they are "on time" according to these socially defined schedules.

In U.S. society, the value placed on work and paid productivity shapes how individuals approach employment and retirement. Those over age 65 were socialized to a traditional view of hard work, job loyalty, and occupational stability. Current demographic trends and social policies mean that values and expectations about work

POINTS TO PONDER

How does your view of work and retirement differ from that of your parents and/or grandparents? What does retirement mean to you? At what age do you see yourself retired, and what type of planning should you do to achieve that goal?

and retirement are changing, as many of the young-old exit and re-enter the workforce through partial employment or new careers. Since more years are now spent in retirement, nearly all adults are aware that they will need to make retirement decisions, with most people in their 50s actively anticipating it (Ekerdt, DeViney, and Kosloski, 1996). As individuals live longer, a smaller proportion of their lifetime is devoted to paid employment, even though the number of years worked is longer. For example, a man born in 1900 could expect to live about 47 years. He would work for 32 years (70 percent of his lifetime) and be retired for about one year (2 percent of his lifetime). In contrast, a man born today can anticipate living about 75 years, working for about 55 percent of his life, and being retired for over 26 percent. Women, too, are living longer past the age of retirement and are devoting a smaller portion of their lives to childbearing and childrearing. A woman born in 1900 could expect that 6 years of her 48-year life span (or 12 percent) would be spent in the labor force. The comparable figure for a woman born in 1987 is nearly 40 percent of her 78-year life span (National Academy, 2000).

The institutionalization of retirement is a relatively recent phenomenon in Western society. Retirement developed as a twentieth-century social institution, along with industrialization, surplus labor, and a rising standard of living. Social Security legislation, passed in 1935, established the right to financial protection in old age and thus served to institutionalize retirement. Based on income deferred during years of employment, Social Security was viewed as a reward for past economic contributions to society and a way to support people physically unable to work. At the same time, Social Security served to create jobs by removing adults 65 and over from the labor market. From the perspective of critical gerontology, discussed in Chapter 8, retirement serves a variety of institutional functions in our society. It can stimulate and reward worker loyalty. In addition, it is a way to remove older, presumably more expensive, workers and replace them with younger employees, assumed to be more productive.

Some societal and individual consequences are negative, however. Earlier retirement, combined with longer life expectancies, has created prolonged dependency on Social Security and other retirement benefits as well as a loss of older workers' skills. This shift from "near-universal" work to near-universal retirement has raised concerns about Social Security's viability for future generations. Since retirement is associated in the public mind with the chronological age of 65 (the current age of eligibility for full Social Security and Medicare benefits), it also carries the connotation of being old, and no longer physically or mentally capable of full-time employment. In fact, society has come to associate aging with decreased employment capacity, with little regard for the older population's heterogeneity and limited knowledge of new work arrangements and retraining opportunities.

The Timing of Retirement

Retirement involves more than a decision to stop working full-time. The arbitrary nature of any particular age for retirement is shown by the fact that most people retire between the ages of 60 and 64, and very few continue to work past age 70. In fact, it can hardly be said that age 65 is the "normal" retirement age. Instead, 61.5 years is the average age for retirement compared to 74 years in 1910 (National Academy, 2000). Almost 25 percent of those 51 to 59 years of age do not work. Seventy-five percent of all new Social Security beneficiaries each year retire before their 65th birthday, and

POINTS TO PONDER

You may have some questions about retirement, such as what do retired adults do all day? How can one be sure to have enough money to retire, especially if a person lives a long time? How can I ensure a successful retirement for myself? Will Social Security still be around when I want to retire? Will I even want to retire?

most begin collecting reduced benefits at age 62.5. The average retirement age in heavy industries, such as steel and auto manufacturing, is even lower because of private pension inducements. Those who retire from the military in their early 40s after the minimum required 20 years often move on to other careers that enable them to draw two pensions after age 65. Even though the 1983 amendments to the Social Security Act delayed the age of eligibility for full benefits and increased the financial penalty for retiring at age 62, this has not altered the overall trend toward early retirement. It is not yet clear whether the scheduled increase in the age for receipt of full Social Security benefits (age 67 by 2022), reductions in early retirement benefits of private pensions, and the partial elimination of the Social Security earnings test will result in more older adults employed longer (Reitzes et al., 1998). However, there has been a slight increase in the number of older adults employed, as discussed later in this chapter.

Retirement policies, labor market conditions, and individual characteristics all converge on the decision to retire and affect the timing of retirement. Prior to 1986, mandatory retirement may have influenced the retirement age. Even so, this factor was not as salient as financial incentives, since less than 10 percent of employees were forced to retire because of legal requirements (Quinn and Burkhauser, 1993). The limited effect of mandatory retirement is also shown by the fact that federal workers retire at the average age of 61, even though they have never had a mandatory retirement age (see the box on page 429).

FACTORS THAT AFFECT THE TIMING OF RETIREMENT
This section discusses five P–E characteristics that
affect retirement decisions:

1. an adequate retirement income and/or economic incentives to retire
2. health status, functional limitations, and access to health insurance
3. the nature of the job, employee morale, and
   organizational commitment
4. gender and race
5. family and gender roles (whether a partner is
   working, degree of marital satisfaction).

An *adequate income,* through Social Security,
a private pension, or interest income, is a major

factor affecting retirement timing. Despite our
society's work-oriented values and the importance
of income, employment and retirement/pension
policies since the 1900s have encouraged early
retirement. Nine out of ten U.S. pension plans, particularly for white-collar workers, provide financial incentives for early retirement. Even employees
who are not planning on retirement may be offered
benefits too attractive to turn down. In a national
American Association of Retired Persons (AARP)
survey of more than 1000 elders in 2000, over 70
percent reported that their savings and Social Security benefits were sufficient for them to retire
(Cutler, Whitelaw, and Beattie, 2002). Economic
factors thus directly affect decisions about the feasibility of retirement and indirectly contribute to
worker health and job satisfaction. When given a
choice and assuming financial security and adequate health insurance, most people elect to retire
as soon as they can (Taylor and Shore, 1995).
Workers accumulate a significant proportion of
the wealth that will finance their retirement in the
decade preceding retirement (Mitchell and Moore,
1998). Employment experiences in the years immediately prior to retirement may be indicative of
well-being throughout old age (Flippen and
Tienda, 2000).

*Functional limitations, health impairments,
and access to health insurance* are also important
factors in the retirement decision, especially
among those for whom retirement is least attractive (Mutchler et al., 1999). Two categories of
people who retire early have been identified:
(1) those with good health and adequate financial
resources who desire additional leisure time and
(2) those with health problems that make their
work burdensome. Poor health, when combined
with an adequate retirement income, usually results in early retirement. In contrast, poor health
and an inadequate income generally delay retirement by reason of necessity, as is often the case
with low-income workers. Health problems are a
greater motivation for retirement from physically
demanding and stressful jobs for workers of color,
for men with employed wives, and for men with

RETIREMENT OF PUBLIC SERVICE WORKERS

The federal government is facing the retirement of a
large proportion of its Civil Service workforce by
2006. Many of these mature workers joined the call
to public service during the Cold War in the 1960s.
The average retirement age in the federal government
is 61; today 38 percent are 50 and older. Agencies
that will be particularly hard hit are FEMA, where 36
percent of its workers will soon become eligible for
retirement, and the FBI, Defense, and State Departments, with 30 percent each. Of course, not all eligible workers will retire; about one-half of them are
expected to do so within the next few years.

Without a large influx of new workers, these
agencies will experience a shortage of specialists in
many areas. Replacement workers will not be easy to
find, for two major reasons: (1) the birth cohort after the baby boomers is too small to fill all these
anticipated positions; (2) interest in public service
jobs has waned as young workers' preference for private companies and self-employment increases.

The problem of an aging workforce faces city and
state governments as well. For example, in Anaheim,
California, 64 percent of management level workers
will be eligible for retirement in 2004. In the state
of Maine, 32 percent of public service employees
will be eligible by 2007.

SOURCES: Spors and Fialka, 2002; Young, 2003.

limited, nonwork financial resources (Cutler et al., 2002; Mutchler et al., 1999; Richardson, 1999). In fact, 55 percent of retirees age 51 to 59 say that a health condition or impairment limits the amount or type of paid work they can do. And retirees are three times more likely to be in fair to poor health than their employed counterparts (National Academy, 2000). What remains unclear, however, is whether those in poorer health are more likely to lose their jobs, or conversely, whether job loss itself leads to poorer health, or both (Kasl and Jones, 2000). Once a person is in nonworking status, poor health acts as a barrier to labor force reentry (Mutchler et al., 1999).

A third factor affecting timing is the *nature of one's job,* including job satisfaction, employee morale, and organizational commitment. Some workers retire to escape boring, repetitive jobs such as assembly line and office work. Workers who have a positive attitude toward retirement and leisure but a negative view of their jobs, often because of undesirable and stressful working conditions, are likely to retire early. Employees with a high school education or less tend to retire earlier than well-educated employees, as illustrated by Mr. and Mrs. Howard in the Part Four introductory vignette (Fudge, 1998). In contrast, older women who are well educated and in professional jobs are the most likely to continue to be employed (Moen, 2001).

While the effects of *gender and ethnic minority status* on the timing of retirement are not clear-cut, they do affect economic inequities in old age. Although both men and women overall choose early retirement, women of retirement age are less likely to be fully retired than their male counterparts. Their retirement decisions may also be determined by different variables, such as marital status and years devoted to childrearing (Szinovacz and DeViney, 1999). Nevertheless, current income and receipt of a pension other than Social Security are primary factors in women's retirement decisions (McLaughlin and Jensen, 2000). In addition, women at any age are more likely to exit the labor market to assume family care obligations (Cutler et al., 2002; Moen, 2001; Reitzes et al., 1998).

Women who entered the labor force in middle age or later, after performing family caregiving roles, may need to work for economic reasons. African American women are more likely to have worked steadily most of their adult lives, but to retire later than their white counterparts, largely for economic reasons (Flippen and Tienda, 2000).

Employment histories that fit the expectation of lifelong work with few disruptions tend to be associated with a smoother transition to retirement (Szinovacz and DeViney, 1999). In contrast, the timing of retirement for persons of color, particularly African Americans and Latinos, differs from the traditional pattern for white males. Ethnic minorities' lifetime employment patterns often yield an unclear line between work and nonwork; they tend to have lengthy periods of nonwork at an early age and lack access to pensions, in part because of diminished opportunities that "pushed" them into retirement (Flippen and Tienda, 2000; Hogan and Perucci, 1998). Black men up to age 61 have higher rates of retirement than Caucasian men, after which African American males have lower rates. One factor may be that moderately disabled African Americans are more likely to identify themselves as partly or fully retired. Self-identification with the retiree role has more psychological benefits and social legitimacy than identfying with a sick role. Furthermore, their greater likelihood of multiple chronic illnesses (discussed in Chapters 4 and 14) makes declining health a more important reason for retirement among African Americans than among whites; 59 percent of the former and 36 percent of the latter reported this in the 2000 AARP Survey (Cutler et al., 2002; Szinovacz and DeViney, 1999). White males with a desire for leisure, low-income African Americans, and Latinos experiencing involuntary market exits are most likely to retire (Flippen and Tienda, 2000).

Satisfaction with Retirement

For most U.S. workers, retirement is desired, and their decision is not whether to retire but when. Not surprisingly, similar factors (e.g., financial security and health status) influence the degree of satisfaction with retirement. It is useful to examine retirement as a *process* or *transition* that affects people's life satisfaction and self-identity in multiple ways. This concept encompasses not only the timing and type of retirement situation as a life stage, but also the phases and the development of a retiree identity after the event of retirement. Similarly, an individual's degree of satisfaction with the outcome depends to some extent on how the retirement process is experienced, especially the extent of choice or autonomy, the amount of preparation and planning, and the degree of congruence with prior employment roles (Szinovacz and DeViney, 1999). In his classic description of a "typical progression of processes" in the retirement transition, Atchley (1983) suggested that an initial euphoric, busy honeymoon phase is followed by a letdown or disenchantment phase due to loss of status, income, or purpose. This, in turn, is followed by a reorientation to the realities of retired life. This sequence leads to a subsequent stable phase, when the retiree has settled into a predictable routine. Whether individuals adopt a retiree identity (e.g., what they make of the retiree role) depends upon their prior employment status, amount of retirement income, and extent of disability (Szinovacz and DeViney, 1999). Of course, not every individual will experience all the phases or in the order described. Another conceptualization of retirement as a *process of role-exit* found that as individuals approach retirement, they express increasing feelings of burden, discontent, and fatigue with the job as a way of withdrawing from their current role commitments (Ekerdt and DeViney, 1993).

Early gerontological studies emphasized the negative impacts of retirement as a life crisis due to loss (Atchley, 1976; Streib and Schneider, 1971). Later research has identified the positive effects of retirement on life satisfaction and health, especially during the first year postretirement. Although measures of physical and psychological health may decline slightly after 6 to 7 years of retirement, most retirees still report good health and overall life satisfaction (Gall, Evans,

and Howard, 1995). Although retirement is a major transition, it is often blurred, with the majority of retirees experiencing minimal stress and being relatively satisfied with their life circumstances (Witt, 1998). Activities other than work that provide autonomy, some sense of control, and the chance to learn new things are all related to retirement satisfaction (Moen, 1999; Ross and Drentea, 1998). On the other hand, activities that involve less problem-solving, are less complex and less fulfilling, have been associated with distress and depression in retirement (Drentea, 1999).

In general, control over the timing of retirement, financial security, and health appear to be the major determinants of retirees' satisfaction with life, rather than retirement status per se. Not surprisingly, retirees with higher incomes or at least adequate finances report being more satisfied and having a more positive retirement identity than those with lower incomes (Quick and Moen, 1998; Moen, 2001; Szinovacz and DeViney, 1999). Higher economic status is also associated with more positive health status in old age (Juster et al., 1996). In fact, there appears to be a dual relationship between positive health status and earned income. This suggests that programs that improve health status during the working years can, in turn, increase earned income in retirement (Okada, 1997).

Retirement does not *cause* poor physical or mental health, as is commonly assumed (Moen, 2001; Moen, Fields, Quick, and Hofmeister, 2001). Although some people's functional health does deteriorate after retirement, for others it improves because they are no longer subject to stressful, unhealthy, or dangerous work conditions. Contrary to stereotypes about the negative health effects of retirement, people who die shortly after retiring were probably in poor health before they retired. In fact, deteriorating health is more likely to cause retirement than vice versa. Accordingly, retirement, in some instances, has improved mental health (Ross and Drentea, 1998). The misconception that people become ill and die as a consequence of retirement undoubtedly persists on the basis of findings from cross-sectional data, as well

Many older adults derive satisfaction from reading.

as reports of isolated instances of such deaths. In addition, the traditional American ideology that life's meaning is derived from paid work may reinforce the stereotype that retirement has primarily negative consequences. Retirees may also be motivated to exaggerate their health limitations to justify their retirement. In fact, health status is interconnected with other factors, such as the normative acceptability of not working and the desire for a retirement lifestyle (Mutchler et al., 1999).

Personal and social characteristics that contribute to satisfaction in retirement include:

- perceptions of daily activities as useful
- internal locus of control
- a sense of having chosen the timing of retirement
- living in a suitable environment
- access to an adequate social support system of friends and neighbors (Drentea, 1999; National Academy, 2000)

Consistent with continuity theory, *preretirement self-esteem and identity* influence postretirement

self-esteem (Reitzes, Mutran, and Fernandez, 1996). Individuals whose primary source of meaning was not employment and who have weaker work values adjust to a satisfying routine more readily than do those with strong work ethics who did not develop leisure activities when employed. Conversely, retirees who do not adjust well have been found to have poor health, inadequate family finances, marital problems, and difficulties making transitions throughout the life span. Those who retire early because of poor health or lack of job opportunities or who are experiencing other stressful events in their life are less satisfied with being retired. But they are also dissatisfied with other aspects of their lives, such as their housing, standard of living, and leisure (Bossé et al., 1991).

Occupational status, which is frequently associated with educational level, is also an important predictor of retirement satisfaction; lower-status workers have more health and financial problems and therefore less satisfaction than higher-level white-collar workers. The more meaningful work characteristics of higher-status occupations may "spill over" to a greater variety

---

SUMMARY OF FACTORS AFFECTING RETIREMENT SATISFACTION

- retirement process that involves choice, autonomy, adequate preparation and planning, and congruence with prior job roles
- retirement activities that provide autonomy, sense of control, chance to learn and to feel useful
- financial security
- good health
- a suitable living environment
- strong social support system of reciprocal relationships
- higher-status occupation prior to retirement
- gender and race
- individual personality traits (e.g., personal resources, positive outlook)

of satisfying nonwork pursuits throughout life. These are conducive to more social contacts and more structured opportunities during retirement. For example, a college professor may have a work and social routine that is more readily transferable to retirement than that of a construction worker. Differences between retirees in upper- and lower-status occupations do not develop with retirement, but rather reflect variations in social and personal resources throughout the life course. This view of retirement as a long-term process that presents continual challenges as retirees adapt is consistent with continuity theory.

Less is known about how gender or race influences retirement satisfaction. Women's retirement plans and well-being, like men's, are influenced by their health and their own pension and Social Security eligibility, not by their husbands'. The slightly lower levels of retirement satisfaction among women seem to be due to their lower retirement incomes, typically because of the lack of a private pension. In addition, adjusting to a full-time stay-at-home role during retirement can be difficult for women accustomed to the routine, rewards, and sociability of paid employment. In such instances, women's role transition may not be in synchrony with their husband's. Women are less likely than men to take on other paid work after retirement from their primary "career" jobs (Johnson, Sambamoorthi, and Crystal, 1999; Moen et al., 2000; Moen, Kim and Hofmeister, 2001).

African Americans and Latinos with a lifetime of discontinuous work patterns and ongoing need are unlikely to define themselves as retired. As "unretired-retired," they spend a greater percentage of their lives both working and disabled, employed intermittently beyond retirement because of their low wage base. Older nonwhites are both more vulnerable to job displacement and more adversely affected by it; they experience lower reemployment rates, lower personal and household income, and lower rates of health insurance coverage following displacement than

white workers (Reitzes et al., 1998). For these workers retirement is not a single, irreversible event that represents the culmination of career employment. Instead, it is a blurred transition from employment to unemployment, partial retirement, or partial employment that may be temporary. In addition, African American males tend to have higher rates of disability and mortality across the life span and especially in the years preceding retirement, which result in retirement inequities (Flippen and Tienda, 2000).

More recent literature portrays retirement not as a single transition in a person's life course but as a dynamic process with several stages where the retired/nonretired roles may overlap, and individuals move in and out of the workforce through **serial retirement.** Instead of a "crisp" or unidirectional one-step movement from work to retirement, transitions are "blurred," involving complex patterns such as returning to employment, "unretirements," and later, second or third partial or full retirements. The exit and then reentry into the workforce reflect the increasing numbers of older people who want to return to employment, typically on a part-time or part-year basis, because they lack pensions and other types of nonwage resources. The propensity to work part-time for economic reasons appears to be generalized, not specific to a particular job. Those who change jobs shortly before retirement are the most likely to work afterward, suggesting that "unretirement" is part of a repertoire of adaptive behavior in the later years. In sum, consistent with the life-course perspective discussed in Chapter 8, there is growing diversity regarding the timing and flexibility of retirement, with changing norms about the timing and sequencing of paid and nonpaid roles or repeated work exits and reentry (Henretta, 1997; Mutchler et al., 1997; Settersten, 1998).

The Importance of Planning

Since retirement is a process, preparation and planning for productive roles in old age are important for transitioning to retirement. In fact, preparation, an orientation toward the future, and a belief in one's ability to adapt to change are associated with a more positive retirement experience (Ekerdt, Kosloski, and DeViney, 2000; Quick and Moen, 1998; Moen, 2001). Retirement affects identity, self-esteem, and feelings of competence to the extent that it influences opportunities for new nonpaid roles and activities. In addition, occupations that demand more complex thinking, decision making, and intellectual challenge (e.g., professional and highly paid positions) may better prepare people for retirement decision-making and planning (McLaughlin and Jensen, 2000). If nonwork interests and skills are not developed prior to retirement, cultivating them afterward is difficult (Drentea, 1999).

Comprehensive *retirement planning programs* that address social activities, financial well-being, health promotion, and family relationships are one way of encouraging a positive transition. Unfortunately, such programs are not widespread. Government employees and older men with more years of education, higher occupational status, and private pensions have greater access to these programs. Accordingly, older workers who especially need retirement preparation—single people, women, and those facing the probability of lower

---

PHASED RETIREMENT PROGRAMS GROW

The *New York Times* featured a story on the growth of phased retirement programs. Early retirement packages have been offered for many years to university professors. However, many large companies such as Lockheed Martin and PepsiCo have begun phased retirement packages that offer workers in their fifties a chance to work shorter hours and receive some pension income. This approach allows employers to retain skilled employees at a lower cost than full-time work, while older workers benefit from the flexibility of part-time employment with an adequate income.

SOURCE: *New York Times*, April 15, 2001, pp. 1, 17.

---

retirement incomes—are the least likely to have access to or utilize such services (Walker, 1998).

Another approach to retirement preparation is for employers to *restructure work patterns* during the preretirement years, gradually allowing longer vacations, shorter work days, job-sharing, and more opportunities for community involvement, thereby easing the transition to more leisure time. Most retirees seem not to want the constraints inherent in full-time employment. Instead, 75 percent of workers prefer to retire gradually, phasing down from full-time to part-time work. This preference is contingent upon whether their employers will retrain them for a new job, make pension contributions after age 65, or transfer them to jobs with less responsibility, fewer hours, and less pay as a transition to full retirement (Juster et al., 1996). Until recently, relatively few firms offered opportunities to transfer to jobs with reduced pay and responsibility, or for phased retirement through a gradual decrease in hours worked. Fortunately, more companies are now recognizing that older workers are eager for new career directions or for part-time and other flexible work.

In fact, options for increasing flexibility in work schedules are offered by only about 33 percent of companies. These include part-time work, job sharing, flextime, and incremental retirement through reduced work weeks or "gliding out" plans of staged retirement that permit a gradual shift to a part-time schedule. Such options tend to be more available to higher income employees, however.

Employment Status

As noted above, some older adults never fully retire, and employment remains the primary means by which they are productive. Among those over age 65, approximately 18 percent of men and 10 percent of women are in the labor force (U.S. Census Bureau, 2003a). As illustrated in Figure 12.1, these percentages represent a decline from 1950,

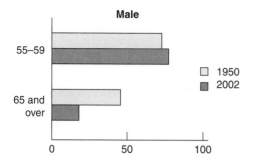

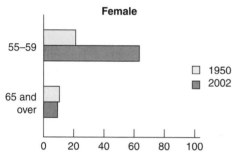

FIGURE 12.1 **Percentage of Civilian Noninstitutional Population in the Labor Force, by Age and Sex: 1950–2002**
SOURCE: U.S. Census Bureau, 2002.

older workers are less likely to be in physically demanding or high-tech jobs (National Academy, 2000).

While full-time employment has declined, part-time work among older women has expanded to 62 percent of those age 65 and over, but declined among their male counterparts, as illustrated in Figure 12.2. As noted above, part-time work that allows gradual retirement is perceived by the working public of all ages as a desirable alternative, especially when a flexible work schedule is combined with the ability to draw partial pensions (Simon-Rusinowitz et al., 1998). Although the number of older people working part-time is smaller than the number who report they would like to do so, the proportion of part-time workers increases with age. The 1997 Longitudinal Survey of Mature Women found that, among all women surveyed in 1967 who had been employed full-time, 37 percent of women under age 65 had retired and 13.5 percent had converted to part-time work, compared with 62 percent and 12 percent, respectively among

when nearly 46 percent of older men and 11 percent of older women were employed. In fact, the pattern of more men retiring early and more middle-aged and young-old women entering the labor force means that older Americans' labor force experiences are becoming similar for men and women. Since April 2000, when the Social Security "earnings test" was eliminated, there has been a gradual increase in the proportion of older adults employed. For example, 17.5 percent of women aged 65 to 69 worked full- or part-time in 1995, increasing to 19.1 percent in 2002. Composing less than 3 percent of the total labor force, older workers are concentrated in service-oriented jobs and in positions that initially require considerable education and a long training process (e.g., managerial and professional positions or self-employment), or those with flexible retirement policies (AOA, 1999). Compared with their younger counterparts,

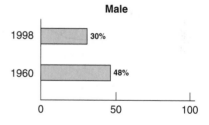

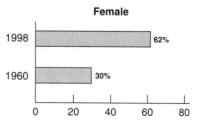

FIGURE 12.2 **Persons 65 Years and Over Who Work Part-Time**
SOURCE: AOA, 1999.

RETIREES WHO DON'T

The number of employees age 75 and older has increased more than 80 percent in the past 20 years. Marge, who is 79, is one such employee. She still works 2 days a week as a waitress in a family restaurant. She states that she would rather work than go to a social club or senior center. Marge brings a strong work ethic and commitment to the job. A younger co-worker maintains that "sometimes she runs us under the table" (Hollingsworth, 2002).

---

women aged 65 to 69, and 75 percent and 8.6 percent, respectively, among those aged 70 and older. Those who continued to work full-time made up almost 8 percent of the youngest group, 5 percent of 65- to 69-year-olds and 3 percent of the 70 plus group (Hill, 2002). Similarly, more older workers (23 percent) are self-employed compared to younger workers (7 percent). The elimination of the Social Security earnings test in 2000 also makes employment more attractive to older workers (Hill, 2002; National Academy, 2000). Depending upon one's definition of career, 25 to 50 percent of all Americans, especially those who are self-employed, remain in the labor force in some capacity after they leave their primary career jobs. It is unclear whether part-time work represents underemployment of adults whose hours of work have been reduced because of slack work, company downsizing or feeling pressured to leave full-time work, or who cannot find full-time employment (Quadagno and Hardy, 1996).

These employment rates are much higher than in European countries such as Germany and Belgium, where the mandatory retirement age is 65 and only 10 percent and 5 percent of men, respectively, remain in the labor force after this age. In contrast, 60 percent of older men in Japan continue working after age 65. For many developed countries, a sharp decline in labor force participation occurs after age 60, to less than 50 percent in France, Denmark, Australia, and New Zea-

land. The pattern for women is somewhat different, with increases over the past 30 years in labor force participation by women older than age 60 in the United States, Canada, and Denmark, compared with sharp declines in Sweden, France, and Germany. These cross-national differences are attributable primarily to more generous public pension and social insurance plans in some countries such as Sweden, France, Germany, and Belgium, as opposed to employer-provided plans being more dominant in the United States, Japan, and Canada (National Research Council, 2001).

Challenges Faced by Older Workers

A 2002 AARP survey of more than 2500 mature and older workers (ages 45–74) found that many were concerned with balancing work and family life, and obtaining flexible job opportunities and employment benefits. A surprisingly large proportion were caring for an aging partner or parent, a disabled child or a grandchild; this included 29 percent of whites, 36 percent of African Americans, and 51 percent of Latinos. Despite these stressors in their personal and work lives, these older workers expressed great loyalty to their employer and co-workers.

When asked what they expected to do after "retirement age," 69 percent said they wanted to continue working, mostly part-time or in a new career. This preference for "bridge jobs" emerges because of financial, health insurance, and social needs, as well as a desire for creative and challenging opportunities after many years in a traditional worker role. Only 28 percent said they had no desire to continue employment after retiring from their current jobs.

The majority of survey respondents (67 percent) perceived age discrimination in the workplace, although only 9 percent reported having been passed up for a promotion because of their age and 5 percent said they had not received a raise because of their age. These perceptions are supported by data from the Equal Employment

Opportunity Commission (EEOC), which has reported that the fastest growing category of complaints to the EEOC is age discrimination (AARP, 2002).

More Older People Seek Employment

About 13.2 percent of older adults are seeking employment; this rate increases for older persons of color (U.S. Census Bureau, 2002). Several factors partially explain why more older people, especially among the young-old, seek employment, despite the trend toward early retirement, as follows:

• *Financial need:* A primary factor is that many people choose to retire and then find it harder to live on their retirement income than they had anticipated. In fact, some studies found that over 52 percent of retired workers return to work within 4 years, largely for economic reasons. They move back and forth from full or partial retirement into nonretirement, or accept jobs in the service sector and in smaller firms at substantially lower pay in order to get by financially (Quadagno and Hardy, 1996). This movement in and out of the labor force is a common pattern with negative economic and health consequences in old age for African Americans and Latinos. The problem has been exacerbated in the past few years as more large companies have gone into bankruptcy and their pension plans have collapsed or shrunk. The stock-market plunge after 2000 has also reduced the value of employer-provided (defined benefit) pensions, leaving retirees with a much smaller income than they had anticipated.

• *Desire to feel productive:* Others work after retirement in order to feel productive, share expertise, and reduce boredom. In such instances, retirees are often more willing to work in lower-status positions (Quadagno and Hardy, 1996). Continued employment into old age has been found to be associated with higher morale, happiness, adjustment, and longevity, in part because of the friendship networks with coworkers (Mor-Barak

and Tynan, 1993). For some older people, a job can be a new career, a continuation of earlier work, or a way to learn new skills and form friendships.

• *Job restructuring and contingent, temporary service jobs:* Older workers seeking to reenter the workforce are more likely than younger workers to be forced out of work because of company closures, technological change, downsizing, mergers, or reorganization. When older workers feel pushed out of their jobs by workplace changes, retirement is not "voluntary," may border on age discrimination, and can be associated with poorer physical and mental health (Cascio, 1998; Couch, 1998; Gallo et al., 2000). In the past decade, more employers have tried to reduce costs and increase productivity by creating labor force structures that can be readily altered at management discretion. This has resulted in the growth of a contingent or temporary workforce, even for highly skilled professional positions, that does not provide security and benefits based on workers' seniority or skills. Contingent employees work less than 34 hours a week and may be on-call workers or independent contractors. Workers displaced by these market changes may be too old to have good job prospects, but may nevertheless need to work and accept temporary employment just to make ends meet. Those who do find jobs, often in the service industry, typically experience downward mobility to low wages and to temporary or part-time work in smaller firms with fewer benefits. This trend disproportionately affects women and older adults of color (Cascio, 1998; Dodson, 1996).

Even though the unemployment rate is lower among older workers than younger, they stay out of work longer, suffer a greater loss of earnings in subsequent jobs, experience longer periods of unemployment, and are more likely to become discouraged and stop looking for work. For older adults needing to work for economic reasons or wanting to stay active, unemployment is associated with life dissatisfaction and higher rates of morbidity (Gallo et al., 2000).

Barriers to Employment

Why do unemployed older workers have a difficult time with their job search?

- They may have been in one occupation for many years and therefore lack experience in job-hunting techniques.
- They are more vulnerable to skill obsolescence with changes in the economy, including the shift away from product manufacturing and medium-wage jobs in manufacturing toward low-wage positions in the service industries and high-wage positions in high-tech fields (National Academy, 2000).
- Until recently, many businesses did not alter the work environment to prepare older workers for rapid changes.
- Only a few programs, such as the federal Senior Community Service Employment Program, specifically target low-income older adults through retraining and subsidized employment.
- Age-based employment discrimination persists, even though mandatory retirement policies are illegal. Despite federal legislation, age discrimination alleged as the basis for loss of employment is the fastest-growing form of unfair dismissal litigation. The Age Discrimination in Employment Act has been somewhat ineffective in promoting the hiring of older workers, although it has reduced blatant forms of age discrimination (e.g., advertisements that restrict jobs to younger people).
- More subtle forms of discrimination endure, such as expectations of attractiveness in dress, makeup, and hairstyle or making a job undesirable to older workers by downgrading it.
- Negative stereotypes about aging and productivity persist. Some employers assume that older workers will not perform as well as younger ones because of poor health, declining energy, diminished intellectual ability, or different work styles.
- Others perceive older workers as less cost-effective, given their proximity to retirement; less

> ### IS THIS AGE DISCRIMINATION?
>
> A bank announces that it is opening a new branch and advertises for tellers. Jane Feld, age 53 with 22 years of banking experience, applies. The employment application includes an optional category for age. Rather than pausing to think about whether to indicate her age, she answers the question voluntarily and truthfully. The next week, Ms. Feld receives a polite letter from the bank, complimenting her on her qualities, but turning her down because she is overqualified. She later finds out that a 32-year-old woman with only 4 years' experience is hired.
>
> Sarah Nelson, age 55, is a manager with a large advertising company. For the past 5 years, she has received outstanding performance reviews. Two months after a strong review and pay increase, she was abruptly fired for "poor performance." Her replacement, age 35, started a week after she was fired.

flexible in a changing workplace; uncomfortable with new technology; and expensive to train. Despite such concerns, however, most employers rate older workers highly on loyalty, dependability, emotional stability, and ability to get along with co-workers.

In addition to these general barriers to employment, *obstacles exist to part-time work:*

- Older persons may not be able to find part-time work at a wage level similar to full-time employment.
- Employer policies against part-time workers drawing partial pensions (e.g., defined-benefit pension plans do not permit a worker to stay on the job and collect a pension).
- Employer resistance about the additional administrative work and higher health insurance costs entailed in hiring part-time or temporary older workers, (e.g., it is more costly to insure older than younger workers). Those costs, however, may be tempered by the advantage of fewer

employer-paid benefits for dependents among older workers (Quadagno and Hardy, 1996).

Creating New Employment Opportunities

Advocacy organizations for older people maintain that judging a person's job qualifications solely on the basis of age, without regard to job suitability, is inequitable, and that chronological age alone is a poor predictor of job performance. Not hiring older workers deprives society of their skills and capacities. To address future labor shortages, changes in government and corporate policies and pensions are needed to extend employment opportunities for older workers and modify the financial incentives for work. For example, tax incentives could be given to employers who hire older workers. With willing supportive employers, work environments can be modified and job-

> **WHAT IS UNLAWFUL UNDER THE AGE DISCRIMINATION IN EMPLOYMENT ACT (1967)?**
>
> Employers with 20 or more employees, including state and local governments, may not:
>
> - Discriminate against workers age 40 and older in hiring, firing, compensation, benefits, terms, conditions, or any other aspect of employment because of age.
> - Indicate age preferences in notices or advertisements for employment.
> - Retaliate against any individual for complaining about age discrimination or for helping the government investigate an age discrimination charge.

referral, training, and counseling programs provided to link older adults and potential employers.

The strong economy of the late 1990s created labor market shortages, especially in service and temporary jobs. This resulted in more job opportunities for older people who wanted to work. A decreasing pool of younger workers, a healthier and better educated cohort of older persons who are oriented toward lifelong careers, economic expectations to continue a similar lifestyle, and increasing health and long-term care expenses also have contributed to the desire of more people to continue working beyond age 65. Already, older people are moving into jobs traditionally filled by youth (e.g., providing service at fast-food restaurants), in part because of the decline among young people available to work in such positions.

> **LAWS TO PREVENT OR ADDRESS DISCRIMINATION BASED ON AGE**
>
> - The Age Discrimination in Employment Act (ADEA), passed in 1967, protects workers age 45 and over from denial of employment strictly because of age.
> - This act was amended in 1978 to prohibit the use of pension plans as justification for not hiring older workers and to raise the mandatory retirement age to 70. In 1986, mandatory retirement was eliminated.
> - In 1990, the Older Workers Benefit Protection Act prohibited employers from treating older workers differently from younger workers during a reduction in workforce.
> - The Americans with Disabilities Act of 1990 also offers protection to older adults. Employers are expected to make work-related adjustments and redesign jobs for workers with disabilities, including impairments in sensory, manual, or speaking skills.

> **POINTS TO PONDER**
>
> Next time you are talking to an employer, ask whether the firm has older workers. How are their skills utilized? Are there opportunities for training and development? What have the firm's experiences been with older workers in terms of absenteeism, productivity, and morale?

Economic Status: Sources of Income in Retirement

Economic status in old age is largely influenced by environmental conditions in the larger society, especially past and current employment patterns and resultant retirement income and benefits. Although economic resources in themselves do not guarantee satisfaction, they do affect older people's daily opportunities and competence level that can enable them to lead satisfying and productive lives—their health, social relationships, living arrangements, community activities, and political participation. For most people, economic status is consistent across the life course. For example, workers of color in low-paying jobs in young and middle adulthood generally face a continuation of poverty in old age. Other older people, including widowed or divorced women who depended on their husbands' income, or retirees with only Social Security as income, may face poverty or near-poverty for the first time in their lives. Alternatively, those in higher-paying careers with private pensions and assets continue to enjoy economic advantages in old age, reflecting a pattern of cumulative advantage across the life course (Park and Gilbert, 1999).

The median household income of people age 65 and over in 1999 was around $17,000, compared to a median figure of approximately $35,000 for all households (AOA, 2000). Median net worth increases with extent of education. Most striking is the disparity in net worth between older black and white households in 1999: $13,000 compared with $181,000 (Federal Interagency Forum, 2002). Older adults are estimated to need 65 to 80 percent of their preretirement income to maintain their living standard in retirement. Since retirement can reduce individual incomes by one-third to one-half, retirees who do not fall into upper-income brackets must markedly adjust their standard of living downward—while their out-of-pocket spending for items such as health care typically increases.

BUILDING ON OLDER ADULTS' SKILLS

Experienced older workers and retirees can provide leadership and mentoring in many workplaces. For example, the Kansas Department of Aging places retired businesspeople in workplaces to solve problems of worker productivity and turnover. This program, "Mentoring Works," has demonstrated significant reductions in turnover and improved orientation for new workers by these part-time, highly skilled mentors. The wages paid to these "unretired retirees" is easily justified by their role in reducing the cost of employee turnover in large companies (Stafford, 2001).

Sources of income for the older population include Social Security earnings, savings, assets, investments, and private pensions. The percent of aggregate income for persons over age 65 from these sources is illustrated in Figure 12.3.

The distribution of income sources varies widely, however, with women, elders of color, and the oldest-old most likely to rely on Social Security. The incremental privatization of retirement

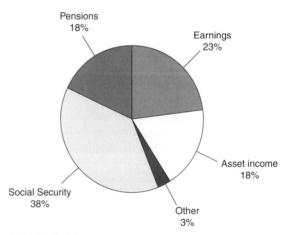

FIGURE 12.3   **Percentage of Aggregate Income of the Population 65+**
SOURCE: Social Security Administration, *Income of the Aged Chartbook*, 2000. Washington, DC: April 2002.

income (i.e., a slow decline in the proportion of retirement income from Social Security relative to that derived from employer-provided pensions and Individual Retirement Accounts) has affected income distribution. For example, older people in the bottom 40 percent of the income distribution have experienced a minimal increase in private sources of pension, while the upper ranges have shown steady gains in private benefits (Park and Gilbert, 1999). Those at the bottom of the income range rely largely on Social Security and/or Supplemental Security Income (SSI), as described below.

Social Security

Older people depend most on **Social Security** for their retirement income.

- Nearly 40 percent of all income received by older units (i.e., a married couple with one or both members aged 65 or older and living together, or a person aged 65 or older not living with a spouse) is from Social Security.
- The average Social Security benefit in 2003 was $895 per month or $9,204 per year.
- Approximately 95 percent of all older people receive Social Security.
- Of those age 65 and over, 64 percent received at least 50 percent of their income and 18 percent all their income from Social Security (see Figure 12.4).
- Among low-income households and the oldest-old, 85 percent of their income is from Social Security.
- In contrast, only 18 percent of those in the highest income categories receive Social Security (Binstock, 2000; Kingson and Williamson, 2001; Gramlish, 2000; National Center for Policy Analysis, 2003).

Social Security was never intended to provide an adequate retirement income, but only a floor of protection or the first tier of support. It was as-

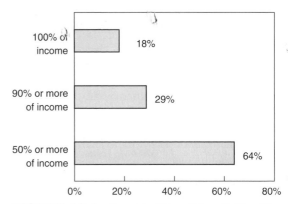

FIGURE 12.4   Percent of Beneficiary Units with Social Security Benefits as a Major Source of Income, 2003
SOURCE: National Center for Policy Analysis, 2003.

sumed that additional pensions and individual savings would help support people in their later years. This assumption has not been borne out, as reflected in the proportionately lower income received by retirees from savings and private pensions. Without Social Security, poverty rates among the older population would increase from 10 percent to nearly 55 percent (Moody, 2002). Not surprisingly, older individuals with the lowest total income have Social Security as their *sole* income source.

The Social Security system is a public trust into which all pay and from which all are guaranteed an income floor in old age or disability. In order to be insured, a worker retiring now must be age 62.5 or older and must have been employed at least 10 years in covered employment. The level of benefits received is based on a percentage of the retired worker's average monthly earnings that were subject to Social Security tax. Insured persons are eligible for full benefits at age 65 (note that the age is rising from 65 to 67 by 2027 at a rate of two months each year, beginning with workers and spouses born in 1938—who must be 65 years and two months for a full benefit). If workers choose to retire at age 62.5, their monthly benefits are permanently reduced and are not increased when

---

GENDER INEQUITIES AND SOCIAL SECURITY

• A widow may start to collect surviving dependents' benefits when she reaches age 60; however, she will lose about 28 percent of what she would have received if she had waited until age 65. But for each additional year after age 60, a widow receives a larger percentage of Social Security benefits. And after age 65, she receives full benefits even if she has been getting only 72 percent for the past 4 years.

• Widows and divorcees under age 60 who are not disabled and who do not have children under age 18 entitled to Social Security, or who are not responsible for disabled persons, cannot receive Social Security benefits. This group of women, who generally do not have a paid work history and do not qualify for any public benefits, are often referred to as **displaced homemakers.** Since the average age at widowhood is 66 years, many women face this "widow's gap."

• A woman who is divorced after at least 10 years of marriage and who reaches retirement age may collect up to 50 percent of her ex-husband's retirement benefits, but only when he turns 62 and if she remains single. Because many widows or divorced women do not meet these criteria, a large percentage of single older women live in poverty or near-poverty conditions (Older Women's League, 2002).

---

they reach age 65. Most recipients currently receive reduced benefits because they retired before the age of 62. Since 1975, Social Security benefits are automatically increased annually whenever the Consumer Price Index increases by 3 percent or more. This is known as the cost-of-living adjustment, or COLA, which protects benefits from inflation. Since benefits are related to a worker's wage and employment history, women and people of color, with patterns of intermittent or part-time work, tend to receive less than the average monthly benefit. Some of the oldest-old persons never qualify for Social Security, because they were employed in occupations such as domestic work not covered by the system.

The Social Security payroll tax is regressive (i.e., requiring the same rate of 12.4 percent for both the rich and the poor). This means that low-income workers, often women and people of color, pay a larger proportion of their monthly salary for the Social Security tax compared to higher-income workers. On the other hand, proportionately, lower-income workers benefit more from Social Security when they retire, receiving benefits equal to 56 percent of their working wages, while high-income workers' benefits on average are only 28 percent of their prior salary. In addition, higher income workers must now pay income tax on 50 percent of their Social Security benefits (Moody, 2002). Unfortunately, most low- and middle-income adults do not plan sufficiently for their retirement income, because they presume that Social Security will be adequate and fail to assess the impact of inflation and reduced income levels. Some are able to supplement their Social Security income with assets, pensions, or job earnings.

Asset Income

Income from assets (e.g., savings, home equity, and personal property), the next most important source of income, is received by about 66 percent of older adults. Assets comprise about 18 percent of the total income of older people. Not surprisingly, the median income of those with asset income is more than twice the median income of those without it (Social Security Administration, 1998). Asset income is unevenly distributed, with larger income disparities intensified by race and gender. Over a third of the older households—typically the oldest-old, women, and persons of color—report no asset income (Social Security Administration, 2002).

Older people's assets consist primarily of home equity, representing about 50 percent of their net worth. Approximately 75 percent of older people own their homes, although this percentage declines among elders of color. Yet 50 percent of older homeowners spend almost half of their incomes on property taxes, utilities, and maintenance (Social

Security Administration, 2002). Home equity therefore does not represent liquid wealth or cash and cannot be relied on to cover daily expenses. Reverse mortgages, described in Chapter 11, are one way to convert the accumulated value of a home into regular monthly income, but relatively few older people participate. Other assets are primarily interest-bearing savings and checking accounts, although today most of these accounts generate less than 2 percent interest.

Even though most older adults with fixed incomes cannot depend on assets to meet current expenses, their net worth tends to be greater than for those under age 35. In fact, the median net worth (assets minus liabilities) of older households is $86,300, well above the U.S. average. As an indicator of vast income differences among older people, net worth is below $10,000 for nearly 20 percent of older households (largely households of color), but above $250,000 for 17 percent (mostly white households) (AOA, 1999).

Pensions

Although most jobholders are covered by Social Security as a general public pension, some also have *job-specific pensions*. Most such pensions are intended to supplement Social Security, not to be the sole source of income. They are available only through a specific employment position and are administered by a place of employment, union, or private insurance company. Job-specific pensions include public employee pensions (for those who work for federal, state, or local governments) and private pensions. Since 1950, pension plans have increased from 25 to 50 percent among private sector workers and from 60 to 90 percent among civilian government workers. Overall, 45 percent of older units receive some income from public and/or private pension benefits, other than Social Security. However, only 50 percent of those eligible for benefits have had enough years of service to be fully vested in a plan and thus entitled to future benefits. Relatively few workers are enrolled in private pension programs that provide the replacement rate

---

PENSIONS AND GENDER INEQUITIES

• Women are half as likely as men to receive a pension and when they do, the benefit is only about 50 percent of what men receive.

• Women are more likely than men to be "in and out" of the labor force and therefore less likely to achieve the required length of service and level of seniority for vesting.

• Women's earnings in their longest career job, used as the base for calculating a pension, tend to be relatively low.

• Nonemployed women face an additional problem: Most pension plans reduce benefits for those who elect to protect their spouses through survivors' benefits. In the past, many men chose higher monthly benefits rather than survivors' benefits; when they died, their wives were left without adequate financial protection. As married women's employment experiences increasingly resemble those of men, the gender gap in pensions is expected to narrow (Burnes and Schulz, 2000).

---

of income necessary for retirement. Instead, job-specific pensions comprise approximately 18 percent of the older population's aggregate income, with the average annual private pension income less than $5,000. Only about 3 percent of pension plans provide for cost-of-living increases, with most such plans adversely affected by inflation. Economic recessions, escalating health care costs, and inflation have reduced pension assets. In recent years, employee pension coverage, especially among persons of color, has declined, which is a problematic trend for older adults' future well-being (Gramlish, 2000; Johnson et al., 1999; Social Security Administration, 2002).

Pension benefits are generally based on earnings or a combination of earnings and years of service. Eligibility is usually between ages 60 and 65, with a range from ages 50 to 70. Federal policies support private pension programs by postponing taxation of pension benefits, as well as allowing benefits to be invested to generate earnings that are not taxed. Tax is paid only when the pension is drawn, after the money has produced many years of earnings.

Private pensions go to workers with long, continuous service in jobs that have such coverage. In general, these are higher-income, relatively skilled positions of 30 or more years concentrated among large, unionized firms or service and financial sectors. As a result, retirees who benefit from private pensions tend to be white, well-educated males in the middle- and upper-income brackets, with the lowest-income older persons receiving, on average, only 3 percent of their income from pensions (Johnson et al., 1999). Pension coverage varies dramatically by class, race, gender, and age. It is relatively low for women, workers of color, and lower-income workers in small nonunion plants and low-wage industries such as retail sales and services, and for retirees currently over age 65. In particular, African Americans and whites with the lowest wages are ten times less likely to have a pension compared to those with the highest wages (Juster et al., 1996).

The **Employment Retirement Income Security Act (ERISA)**, enacted in 1974 to strengthen private pension systems, was the first comprehensive effort to regulate them. As a result, private pension plans must vest benefits (*vesting of pension benefits*

TYPES OF PENSION PLANS

- *Defined benefit:* guarantees a specific or defined amount of pension income for the remainder of a worker's life (e.g., a lifetime annuity). The company must set aside funds to cover the benefits promised
- *Defined contribution:* Employers, employees, or both contribute to the fund, such as 401K plans, over the years; success of the fund depends on the nature of investments. Growing in use, they create greater risks for the economic security of future retirees.
- *Cash balance plans:* Combine elements of both defined benefit and defined contribution plans. Likely to erode the value of what defined benefit plans have promised.

---

refers to the amount of time a person must work on a job in order to acquire rights to the pension). When vested, all covered workers are guaranteed a full pension upon retirement after 10 or 15 years with the company, regardless of whether they remain with that organization until retirement. This means that a person could work for one firm for 12 years, move to a second company until retirement at age 65, and then receive pensions from both based on years of service. Although vesting options increased under ERISA, *portability* (whereby pension contributions and rights with one organization can be transferred to another) remains low. This policy has been criticized for penalizing worker mobility and career changes. For example, an individual who serves 40 years with one company will receive a higher pension than one who spent 20 years with one firm and 20 with another.

ERISA also strengthened standards for financing, administering, and protecting pension plans. Tax-exempt individual retirement accounts (IRAs) were made available to all workers in 1981, in an effort to increase personal savings for retirement. Under the 1986 tax reform plan, employees with other private pensions are no longer able to use an IRA as a tax deduction. Yet IRAs are not an option for most workers; instead, they are used primarily by those earning $50,000 or more who have disposable income, and thus disproportionately benefits persons with higher incomes (Burnes and Schulz, 2000). Lower-income workers generally cannot spare the money, and the tax benefit is considerably less for them. Ironically, then, the people who need retirement income the most generally cannot take advantage of IRAs. As with employer pension plans, the tax deferral of IRAs provides the equivalent of a long-term interest-free loan (e.g., tax shelter) to the predominantly high-income taxpayers who use IRAs.

Earnings

Overall, current job *earnings* form approximately 20 percent of the income of older units, and earnings are reported by about 20 percent of older adults (AOA, 1999). This low percentage is consistent with the declining labor force participation generally among people age 65 and over. Although earnings are an important income source to the young-old and to those with the highest income from assets and pensions, they decline in importance with age. For example, over 40 percent of young-old individuals receive income from earnings, compared with only 3 percent for those 80 years and older (Social Security Administration, 2002).

In sum, the equity goals of Social Security are outweighed by private pensions, asset income, IRAs, and other preferential tax treatment for a small percentage of wealthy older adults. This creates greater economic inequality among the older population over time. The basic facts about older American household wealth are: modest wealth holdings by the typical older household, large inequities in wealth, and little evidence of prior savings by poor and even middle-class households (1997b).

Poverty among Old and Young

The economic status of older adults has improved dramatically since the 1960s. In 1969, 35 percent of those age 65 and over fell below the official poverty line. Today, 10.4 percent of older people are poor, compared with 10.1 percent of those under age 65, 16.7 percent of children under age 18, and 18.5 percent of children under age 6 (U.S. Census Bureau, 2002).

The overall improvement in older adults' economic status is due to the following factors:

- the strong performance of the economy in the 1950s and 1960s
- accumulation of home equity
- existence of Medicare
- expansion of Social Security and other pension protection
- improved and longer coverage by pensions
- the 1972 increases in Social Security benefits

- the 1975 automatic annual cost of living adjustments (COLAs) in Social Security
- implementation of the Supplemental Security Income program

When all sources of income are considered (including tax and in-kind benefits), fewer older families have subpoverty resources than younger families. In addition, the majority of poverty "spells" among older adults are 3 years or less (Rank and Hirschl, 1999). As a result of such gains, a widely held public perception is that *all* older persons are financially better off than other age groups. This perception is also fueled by the increase of poverty among children under age 6, who are the poorest age group. However, this decline in the income status of children is largely structural, caused by economic, political, and demographic forces, not by the older population itself (Ozawa, 1996).

Poverty Differentials over Time

When looked at over time, many older people are not financially comfortable, despite the overall improved income status. Forty percent of Americans between the ages of 60 and 90 experience at least one year below the poverty line, and 48 percent at least a year in which their income falls below 125 percent of the poverty line (Rank and

---

WHO ARE THE OLDER POOR?
- 8–9 percent of older whites
- 16 percent of older Asians and Pacific Islanders
- 26 percent of older African Americans
- 21 percent of older Latinos
- 20 percent of older people living alone
- 29 percent of older American Indians
- 14 percent of those over age 85
- 17 percent of nonmarried elders
- 14 percent of those who live in central cities
- 12.5 percent of those in rural areas (Federal Interagency Forum, 2002).

Hirschl, 1999). A larger proportion (6.3 percent) of older people than younger (4.5 percent) fall just above the poverty line and thus are "near poor" and at risk for poverty; approximately 17 percent are poor or near poor (AOA, 1999). These "tweeners" are caught between upper-income and poor older people—not well enough off to be financially secure but not poor enough to qualify for the means-tested safety net of Medicaid and Supplemental Security Income. Paradoxically, the only way that they can improve their economic well-being is to qualify for Medicaid and Supplemental Security Income by spending down (using up their assets). As noted earlier, the poverty rate for older adults would be about 50 percent without Social Security (Abramoritz, Grossinger, and Sachs, 2000). The percentage of subgroups who are poor, even with Social Security, and the percentage kept out of poverty by Social Security are illustrated in Figure 12.5.

These figures also do not reflect that the federal poverty standard for a single adult younger than age 65 is higher than for an older individual, $9359 and $8628, respectively (U.S. Census Bureau, 2002). The U.S. Bureau of the Census assumes that the costs of food and other necessities are lower for older people, even though they spend proportionately more on housing, transportation, and health care than do younger groups. If the same standard were applied to the older population as to the other age groups, the poverty rate for older people would increase to over 15 percent (AOA, 1999). Older adults are also less likely to have reserve funds to cover emergencies such as catastrophic medical expenses. As a result, low-income elders are at risk of malnutrition, poorly heated and inadequate housing, homelessness, and neglect of medical needs.

Contrary to the static nature of poverty that is suggested by cross-sectional data, many older

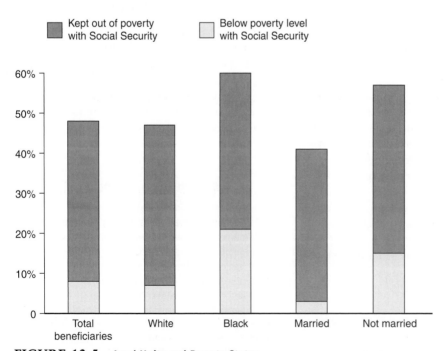

FIGURE 12.5 **Aged Units and Poverty Status**
SOURCE: Social Security Administration, Social Security Bulletin Annual Statistical Supplement, 2000.

people move in and out of poverty over time. When such individual movements are identified, the risk of falling below the poverty line at some time during a specified period is more than double the highest average risk for older couples, and is raised by almost 30 percent for widows. For example, many women become poor for the first time in their lives after depleting their assets while caring for a dying partner. Once an older person moves into poverty, she or he is less likely to exit than are younger age groups. Many "hidden poor" among the older population are either institutionalized or living with relatives and thus not counted in official census statistics. In sum, more older people are at marginal levels of income and at greater risk of poverty than the population 18 to 64 years; they are also more likely to be trapped in long-term poverty (AOA, 1999). In addition, wide socioeconomic diversity exists within the older population, with economic marginality most pronounced among older women, those who live alone, those outside metropolitan areas, ethnic minorities, and the oldest-old.

Poverty Differentials by Gender

Older women comprise one of the poorest groups in our society. In fact, the risk of poverty among couples and single men has sharply fallen, leaving poverty in old age a characteristic primarily of single frail women over age 85, especially women of color, in nonmetropolitan areas, who have outlived their husbands (McLaughlin and Jensen, 2000). Although women account for approximately 50 percent of the older population, they compose nearly 75 percent of the older poor. Nearly 13 percent of older women are poor, compared to approximately 7 percent of older men (U.S. Census Bureau, 2003).

Widows account for over 50 percent of all older poor, reflecting the loss of pension income and earned income often associated with the death of a wage-earner spouse (AOA, 1999; Simon-Rusinowitz et al., 1998). In contrast, the wife's death reduces the risk of poverty for wid-

---

POVERTY DIFFERENTIALS AMONG OLDER WOMEN

- Of women age 85 and over living in metropolitan areas, 19.7 percent are poor.
- Of widowed women, 21 percent are poor.
- Of women living alone, 23 percent are poor.
- Of those divorced or separated, 26 percent are poor.
- Fifty percent of older African American women not living with family have incomes below the poverty line.
- Almost 70 percent of rural African American women live in poverty, making them the most economically deprived group in our society.

---

owers (McLaughlin and Jensen, 2000). As implied above, the primary reasons for women's lower retirement income are:

- their interrupted employment histories related to family responsibilities
- the greater likelihood of being divorced, widowed, and unmarried
- their lower wages and resultant lower Social Security benefits
- less likelihood of their having private pensions to supplement Social Security
- the gradual erosion of assets and interest income
- their lower likelihood of having worked in higher-level or professional occupations that demand complex decision making and therefore better prepare them to plan for retirement (McLaughlin and Jensen, 2000).

These factors that lead to higher proportions of poor older women are referred to as the **feminization of poverty.**

Poverty Differentials by Race

African American and Latino elders of both sexes have substantially lower incomes than their white counterparts, as described earlier. Over 26 percent of older African Americans and over 21 percent of older Latinos are poor, compared with 8.2 percent of older whites (NIH, 2000). The median income of older African American and Latino men living alone is about 33 percent lower than older white men living alone. Although the differences are less pronounced among women, the median incomes of older African American and Latino women are generally 25 to 33 percent lower than those of white women. Minority women's slight economic advantage relative to that of their male peers stems from the higher rates of unemployment and unsteady work histories among their male counterparts. Not only are median incomes lower, but the average black or Latino households have no financial or liquid assets (Smith, 1997b). Within each population of color, poverty is more common for women, especially divorced women, than for men (Federal Interagency Forum, 2002). These higher rates of poverty among populations of color compared with whites are discussed more fully in Chapter 14.

Poverty Differentials by Age and Living Status

The poverty rates among the young-old are lower, in part due to continued employment or the greater likelihood of retirement with good pension plans. In contrast, older cohorts continue to experience income loss as they age, and therefore economic deprivation relative to younger cohorts. The poverty rate for those 65 to 74 years is over 10 percent; for those over age 85, nearly 20 percent. The fact that median income declines with age is due in part to the disproportionate number of nonmarried women among the oldest-old. The economic hardships of older cohorts are often compounded by a lifetime of discrimination, by historical factors such as working at jobs with no pension or inadequate health insurance, and by recent stressful events such as loss of spouse or declining health. Accordingly, older cohorts are more likely to live alone, which is associated with poverty. Of all older people living alone, 20 percent are poor, compared with 6 percent of those

living with others. When the poor and the near-poor are grouped together, 45 percent of older adults living alone fall into this category. In every successively older age group, nonmarried women have a lower median income than nonmarried men or married couples. Since the poverty rate increases with age, nearly 50 percent of those age 85 and over are either poor or near-poor (AOA, 1999; Social Security Administration, 1998). To illustrate from the introductory vignettes, Mr. Valdres worked as a migrant farm laborer and therefore relies on the minimum Social Security level for his income.

In sum, despite the overall improved financial situation of the older population, large pockets of poverty and near-poverty exist, particularly among women, groups of color, those over age 75, those who live alone, and those who live in rural areas. As a result, economic inequities are actually greater among older people than among other age groups. Aging advocates maintain that strategies to alleviate poverty among today's older Americans cannot rely on the labor market. Instead, they must be immediate, such as increasing levels of Social Security for those with low lifetime earnings and ensuring that women and men have full access to benefits accrued by their spouses (Smith, 1997b).

Public Assistance

Only about 5 percent of the older population receives some type of public assistance, primarily in the form of *Supplemental Security Income* (**SSI**) (Social Security Administration, 1998). This percentage increases among persons of color and women. SSI was established in 1974 to provide a minimum income for elders living on the margin of poverty. The basic federal payment in 2003 was $552 a month for a single person and $829 for a couple. These payments change each year to reflect cost-of-living increases (National Committee to Preserve Social Security and Medicare, 2003).

In contrast to Social Security, SSI does not require a history of covered employment contributions. Instead, eligibility is determined by a categorical requirement that the recipient be 65 years of age, blind, or disabled, with limits on amount of monthly income and assets determining eligibility. Nevertheless, many eligible older poor do not participate in SSI. For those who do so, the federal SSI benefits fall substantially below the poverty line. Even when states supplement federal benefits, levels remain low, so that SSI supplies only 14 percent of the income of poor older people (Social Security Administration, 1998). Those who receive SSI may also qualify for Medicaid and food stamps. The amount of SSI benefits depends upon income, assets, and gifts or contributions from family members for food, clothing, or housing. These gifts may be counted as income and may result in a reduction in benefits. Becoming eligible for SSI is a time-consuming and often demeaning process, requiring extensive documentation and the ability to deal with conflicting criteria for benefits from SSI, Medicaid, and food stamps. Despite these barriers, increasing numbers of "poor" or "near-poor" older adults rely on public assistance, through either SSI, Medicaid, or food stamps.

As noted earlier, economic status, along with health, living arrangements, and marital status, influences the nonpaid roles and activities in old age—particularly voluntary association membership, voluntarism, religious participation and spirituality, and political involvement. We turn now to discuss these other forms of productive aging.

Patterns and Functions of Nonpaid Roles and Activities

Leisure

The term **leisure** evokes different reactions in people. For some, it signifies wasting time. For others, it is only the frenzied pursuit of "leisure activities" on the weekends that sustains them through the work week. Leisure can be defined as any activity characterized by the absence of obligation that is inherently satisfying. Free time alone is not necessarily leisure. Instead, the critical variable is how a person defines tasks and situations to bring intrinsic meaning. Accordingly, leisure implies feeling free and satisfied. Individuals who do not experience such feelings may still be at "work" rather than at "leisure." People's reactions to the concept of leisure are clearly influenced by cultural values attached to paid work and a mistrust of nonwork time. Because of American values of productivity and hard work—especially among the current generation of older persons—many older adults have not experienced satisfying nonwork activities at earlier phases in their lives. Societal values are changing, however, with more legitimacy given to nonwork activities throughout the life cycle, as evidenced by the growing number of classes and businesses that specialize in leisure. For low-income or ethnic minority elders or for older people in developing countries, however, leisure may be a meaningless concept if they have to continue working to survive or lack resources for satisfying recreational time.

Disagreement regarding the value of leisure pursuits for older people is reflected in the gerontological literature. An early perspective was that leisure roles cannot substitute for employment because they are not legitimated by societal norms. Since work is a dominant value in U.S. society, it was argued that individuals cannot derive self-respect from leisure. A closely related perspective is that retirement is legitimated in our society by an ethic that esteems leisure that is earnest, occupied, and filled with activity—a "busy" ethic, which is consistent with the activity theory of aging (Ekerdt, 1986). For those with strong work values, worklike activities are probably important for achieving satisfaction in retirement. The prevalence of the "busy" ethic is reflected in a question commonly asked of retirees: What do you do to keep busy? "Keeping busy" and engaging in productive activities analogous to work are presumed to ease the adjustment to retirement by adapting retired life to prevailing societal norms, although the "busy" ethic is contrary to the definition of leisure as intrinsically satisfying. A counterargument is that leisure can replace the employment role and provide personal satisfaction in later life, especially when the retired person has good health and an adequate income, and their activities build upon preretirement skills and interests.

Although wide variations exist, *patterns of meaningful nonpaid activity* among older individuals are identified.

- Most activity changes are gradual, reflecting a consistency and a narrowing of the repertoire of activities as individuals age.
- Compared to younger people, older adults are more likely to engage in solitary and sedentary pursuits, such as watching television, visiting with family and friends, and reading.
- The time spent on personal care, sleep and rest, hobbies, and shopping composes a larger fraction of older adults' days than among younger and middle-aged individuals (Verbrugge, Gruber-Baldini, and Fozard, 1996).

When judged by younger persons or by middle-class standards, these essential and universal activities may be viewed as "boring and nonproductive." Yet, the ability to perform these more mundane activities—personal care, cooking, doing errands, puttering around the house or garden, or sitting in quiet reflection—can be critical to maintaining older people's competence, self-esteem, and life satisfaction, especially among the oldest-old. Furthermore, these routines may represent realis-

tic adjustments to declining energy levels and incomes. Such routine leisure pursuits, consistent with the broader concept of productive aging, may thus reflect rational choices about ways to cope congruent with environmental changes and may also enhance quality of life.

Leisure activities also vary by gender and socioeconomic status. Older men tend to do more household and yard maintenance and paid work outside the home, while older women perform more housework, child care, and volunteer work, and participate in more voluntary associations. Not surprisingly, higher-income older people, especially those living in planned retirement communities, tend to be more active in leisure pursuits than low-income elders (Verbrugge et al., 1996). Such differences in activities are attributable primarily to the costs of pursuing them, not necessarily to inherent differences by socioeconomic status. Several benefit programs are designed to reduce financial barriers to leisure. For instance, Golden Passports give older people reduced admission fees to national parks. Similar programs at the local or state level, including AARP membership, provide free admission to parks, museums, and cultural activities, and reduced prices from businesses and transportation. Not surprisingly, a wide range of leisure-oriented businesses, including group travel programs, are marketing services to higher-income older adults.

The *psychological benefits of leisure* perceived by older participants include:

- companionship (e.g., playing cards or going dancing)
- compensation for past activities (e.g., picnicking instead of hiking)
- temporary disengagement (e.g., watching TV)
- comfortable solitude (e.g., reading)
- expressive solitude (e.g., knitting and crocheting)
- expressive service (e.g., volunteer service, attending meetings of social groups) (Tinsley et al., 1985)

The major benefits of nonpaid activities may be maintaining ties with others and providing new sources of personal meaning and competence. Not surprisingly, leisure activities are associated with a positive identity and self-concept among older people. Accordingly, activities that result in a sense of being valued and contributing to society are found to be positively related to life satisfaction and mental well-being in retirement (Riddick and Stewart, 1994). This relationship does not mean, however, that leisure activity itself creates well-being, since older people who are active also tend to be healthier and of higher socioeconomic status. The quality of interactions with others in nonwork activities may be more salient for well-being than the number or frequency of interactions.

Membership in Voluntary Associations

Given our societal emphasis on being active and productive, voluntary association membership is often presumed to be a "good" leisure activity. Based on such assumptions, association members often go to considerable lengths to recruit older

Older adults leisure time often involves teaching younger generations.

people. Overall, older people tend to be more involved in voluntary organizations than are younger people. Membership is most closely tied to social class and varies among cultures. When socioeconomic status is taken into account, older adults show considerable stability in their general level of voluntary association participation from middle age until their 60s (Cutler and Hendricks, 2000).

Similar to most retirement activities, characteristics that influence voluntary association membership include age, gender, ethnic minority status, prior activities and memberships, health, and socioeconomic status.

The kinds of organizations in which older people participate vary by gender and ethnic minority status. Older women are more active in voluntary associations than older men. Women's multiple roles at earlier phases of the life span, such as volunteer work, are found to be positively related to health and occupying multiple roles in old age (Caro and Bass, 1997). Older African Americans have higher rates of organizational membership than do older whites or members of other groups of color; although for both blacks and whites, membership is most frequent among those with better health and higher income and education levels. Some ethnic minority differences exist in the types of associations joined. Older African Americans are especially likely to belong to church-related groups and social and recreational clubs; older whites frequently are members of nationality organizations and senior citizen groups. Latinos participate in fraternal and service-oriented organizations, mutual aid societies, and "hometown" clubs.

Senior centers encourage voluntary association activities. These vary greatly in the type of services offered, ranging from purely recreational events to social action, or the delivery of social and health services, including nutrition programs, health screening, health promotion, and support groups for caregivers and grandparents. In fact, the Older Americans Act identifies senior centers as preferred focal points for comprehensive, coordinated service delivery. Despite the range of activities, only about 15 percent of older persons participate in senior centers.

Furthermore, centers typically draw from a relatively narrow population, reaching primarily healthy, lower- to middle-class individuals under age 85 with a "lifetime of joining clubs." Nationwide, individuals who are generally less advantaged, but not the least advantaged, are most likely to participate in senior center activities. Those who participate tend to do so out of a desire for social interaction or because they were invited by friends (Wagner, 1995).

Senior centers face programmatic challenges. Their membership has become "older" as their users have "aged in place," and the young-old are less inclined to attend at the same time that the oldest-old are too frail to participate. Centers are criticized for not doing more to reach elders of color and older people who are frail, low-income, or disabled. Although African American elders are slightly more likely than whites to attend centers, most programs need to become more accessible to diverse elders. Some senior centers, established in neighborhoods of color, have successfully attracted elders who would not otherwise participate. In contrast, some observers contend that such targeting of services runs counter to the universal nature of the Older Americans Act and may reduce the participation of those relatively more-advantaged older people who currently attend centers.

Older persons who are active in community organizations such as senior centers derive a variety of benefits. Socializing appears to be the primary reward, and aids in achieving active aging,

as described in Chapters 1 and 6. Because these organizations are typically age-graded, people interact with others who are similar in age and interests. These interactions often result in friendships, support, a sense of belonging, mutual exchanges of resources, and collective activity. Consistent with the broader concept of productivity, voluntary associations can also serve to maintain the social integration of older people, countering losses in roles and in interactions with others. Older people in voluntary organizations are found to have a sense of well-being and higher morale, although this may be attributed to their higher levels of health, income, and education. When these other characteristics are taken into account, organizational membership is apparently unrelated to overall life satisfaction (Cutler and Hendricks, 2000). The most satisfied members of organizations are those who become involved in order to have new experiences, achieve something, be creative, and help others. Such members, in turn, participate actively through planning and leadership. Opportunities for more active participation are found in senior advocacy groups such as the Older Women's League and AARP or in organizations such as advisory boards to Area Agencies on Aging where older people must, by charter, be in leadership roles. Overall, voluntary association membership appears to be more satisfying when it provides opportunities for active, intense involvement and significant leadership roles.

Volunteer Work

With cutbacks in public funding, nonprofit, service, educational, and religious organizations increasingly rely upon volunteers to accomplish their missions and provide services. Because current retirees are younger, in better health, and better educated than earlier cohorts, they tend to have the time, energy, and skills to contribute to society through volunteer work. Such activity is consistent with the concept of productive aging, whereby older people, even though unpaid, produce valued

---

REASONS FOR LOW LEVELS OF PARTICIPATION IN SENIOR CENTERS BY OLDER ADULTS

- lack of interest in the center's activities
- poor health
- inadequate transportation
- desire not to be with only old people
- the low proportion of men in many centers

AN ACTIVE VOLUNTEER AT AGE 80

Edna was an elementary school librarian, forced to retire in 1986, when mandatory retirement still existed. After a few months at home, she was back in the local school, working four or five days a week as a substitute librarian. She is widely loved by the kids, and the parents and teachers respect her ability to relate to a wide range of children, managing to hook them into "listening to reading."

goods and services (Morrow-Howell, Hinterlong, and Sherraden, 2001; Hendricks, Hatch, and Cutler, 1999). Similar to participation in voluntary associations, volunteering is more characteristic of U.S. society than others.

Estimates of older adults who volunteer range from 37 to 57 percent, a rate that is lower than adults as a whole (70 percent). Those who do volunteer invest more hours into their volunteer work (approximately 72 hours a year) than do younger volunteers, in part because of having more uncommitted time (Independent Sector, 2002; Peter D. Hart Research Associates, 2002). Among the older population, *rates of community involvement and volunteerism* are highest among adults with the following characteristics:

- higher income and education
- more leisure time
- better health
- a history of volunteering throughout their lives
- a broad range of interests
- a belief that they can make valuable contributions

The primary type of volunteer work is through religious organizations, followed by direct service such as tutoring, handiwork, raising money, serving on a board or committee, or assisting in an office; most volunteers serve in only one organization. The majority volunteer only a few hours a week, but for some, volunteer work is equivalent to a full-time job (Chatfield, 1999; Cut-

ler and Hendricks, 2000; Warburton, LeBrocque, and Rosenman, 1998).

GENDER DIFFERENCES IN VOLUNTARISM   As is the case generally in voluntary activities, women (especially widows) are more likely to volunteer than men. This may shift, however, as more women enter the paid workforce. Although women generally view volunteering as a way to help others, men more frequently define it as a substitute for the worker role (Moen, 2001).

ETHNIC MINORITY DIFFERENCES IN VOLUNTARISM   Volunteering as a way to help others through informal networks is frequent in communities of color, such as through African American churches. It may represent a history of self-reliance and incorporation of a lifetime of hard work into leisure experiences and services to others (Calasanti and Slevin, 2001). Mutual aid (e.g., providing food and lodging to older persons) is common in American Indian communities. Volunteer activities among Asian and Pacific Islander elders reinforce the continuation of their value systems. Older Chinese, for example, often work through family associations or benevolent societies. Some Japanese elders participate in clubs that are an extension of the "family helping itself" concept rooted in traditional Japanese culture. The Latino community emphasizes self-help, mutual aid, and neighborhood assistance for their older members.

PROGRAMS TO EXPAND VOLUNTARISM   Within the past 30 years, a number of public and private initiatives have been designed to expand community service by older persons, as summarized in the box on page 454.

BENEFITS OF VOLUNTARISM   Volunteer programs serve *two major social benefits:* 1) provide individuals with meaningful social roles; and 2) furnish organizations with experienced, reliable workers at minimal cost (Hendricks et al., 1999).

Older volunteers appear to experience greater psychological and health benefits than do younger

---

VOLUNTEER OPPORTUNITIES FOR OLDER ADULTS

- Older Americans Act programs: assisting at meal sites, escort and transportation services, home repair, counseling, legal aid
- Senior Medicare patrol: retired professionals assist Medicare and Medicaid beneficiaries
- Family Friends: advocates and mentors to young children
- Experience Corps: in schools and youth-focused organizations
- National Senior Service Corps: Foster Grandparents offer support to children with special needs; Senior Companions program provides assistance to elders living independently; Retired and Senior Volunteer Program (RSVP) provides a wide range of community services
- Service Corps of Retired Executives (SCORE): retired executives and small business owners assist small businesses and first-time entrepreneurs
- Volunteers in Parks: volunteer programs with the National Parks Services
- Environmental Alliance for Senior Involvement: environmental protection activities
- Ask a Friend Campaign: aims to increase the number of volunteers benefiting local communities

---

volunteers. These benefits include greater life satisfaction, physical and mental well-being, self-rated health, and sense of accomplishment and feelings of usefulness. The difference may be due in part to the greater meaning that older volunteers attach to this role (Moen, 2001; Van Willigen, 2000). In fact, volunteering has been found to have a protective effect on mortality among those who volunteered for one organization or for 40 hours or more over the past year. These protective effects appear to be strongest for those who report low levels of informal social interaction and who do not live alone. This curvilinear relationship between volunteering and mortality is undoubtedly due to other factors, such as self-identity, role strain and meaningfulness (Musick, Herzog, and House, 1999).

Contrary to the assumptions of activity theory, the desire to replace lost roles (e.g., employee or spouse) is not a primary motivator. Instead, older people are more likely to volunteer if they are married, well educated, involved in other organizations, and employed part-time (Morrow-Howell et al., 2003; Wilson, 2000). For most retirees, volunteering is apparently not a work substitute, although it may protect them from any negative effects of retirement, physical decline, and inactivity. Most want roles that fully engage their capacities and interests and in ways that are meaningful to them or matter to their communities (Freedman, 1999; 2001). Consistent with the continuity theory of aging, most older volunteers have volunteered earlier in their lives and have a sense of responsibility. Volunteerism is part of an overall productive lifestyle that unfolds in the formal arenas of employment, education, and organized activities, with volunteers' long-standing involvement either remaining constant or expanding as they age. Nevertheless, it is still possible to recruit new volunteers in old age, especially by targeting those who are about to leave or have recently left their jobs (Caro and Bass, 1997). From the perspective of social exchange theory, volunteering may ensure valued social resources as a basis of exchange, primarily by assisting others and contributing to society rather than being perceived as dependent.

VOLUNTEERING AS A SUBSTITUTE FOR PAST ROLES

Ted was a teacher of sixth-grade science in an inner-city public school for 35 years. When he retired at age 57, he began a successful second career selling real estate. Now at age 72, he continues to work on average 2 days per week. He enjoys the contact with people and finds his work very different from teaching. Because he believes it is important to give back to his community, he also volunteers as a tutor in an after-school program run by his church for neighborhood "latchkey" children.

VOLUNTEERING AS A SOURCE OF SUPPORT

Mary, a homemaker and mother of four children, spent her early years being involved with Scouts and PTA and teaching Sunday school. Her last child left home when Mary was 52, and she felt "lost" because there was no one to "need" her in the same ways the children had. At 53, she began volunteering, answering the phone for a community center that served children and elders, and found a new role. When she was widowed at age 70, she increased the hours of volunteering to fill the lonely hours when she especially missed her husband. Since she has never driven, she takes the bus one day a week to the community center. Now at age 80, she was recently honored by the city at a special reception for her 8000 hours of volunteer service.

The experience of Edna and Ted (see the boxes) illustrates how some older adults achieve life satisfaction by substituting volunteering for previous professions as teachers and mentors. Mary's activities, described in the box above, illustrate how volunteering can support older adults in helping roles. A number of trends will influence the meaning and functions of volunteerism for older persons. If government service cutbacks continue, volunteers are essential to meeting the service needs of a wide range of disadvantaged groups (Musick et al., 1999; Wheeler, Gorey, and Greenblatt, 1998). Simultaneously, with the growing emphasis nationally on self-help and mutual aid, some people may choose to become more active in cross-generational neighborhood and community advocacy groups. These volunteer and advocacy efforts will continue to face the challenge of how to involve older people who are low-income, persons of color, living alone, frail and disabled, or from areas with inadequate public transportation. Regardless of the type of voluntarism, the documented benefits suggest that efforts to encourage volunteering among older persons should continue (Freedman, 2001; Van Willigen, 2000).

Educational Programs

Many educational programs have been oriented toward enrichment or practical personal assistance in such areas as health and finances, and therefore have not necessarily supported the movement of older people into new productive roles. A primary reason for the limited role of education in productive aging is that most higher education institutions have not viewed older learners as a priority, nor have they fully recognized the market potential for education among senior boomers. Even though 80 percent of state universities offer tuition-free, space-available enrollment in college classes for older people, state legislatures typically have provided little funding for older adult programs.

Fortunately, some creative late-life learning initiatives have developed in higher education that are constructed around images of productive aging, not of decline or need. One of the best known is **Elderhostel,** where older learners attend special seminars or institutes on campuses and affiliated locations throughout the country and the world. Each one of these has an educational component and is associated with a college or university, whether the group is studying architecture in London, seals in Antarctica, monkeys in Belize, antiquities in Greece, or art in the Southwest. Elderhostel involves over 250,000 participants a year at over 1500 different academic institutions.

INTERGENERATIONAL SERVICE LEARNING IN GERONTOLOGY

The Association for Gerontology in Higher Education sponsored service-learning courses at ten universities. Coursework affiliated with over 100 community agencies attracted students ranging in age from 18 to the mid-seventies. The students, in turn, had a significant impact on local communities and agencies serving older adults. Learners of all ages, within the classroom and in community settings, benefited (McCrea, Nichols, and Newman, 1998).

Elderhostel can include active learning experiences such as sailing.

To cater to the young-old and boomers, Elderhostel now offers private rooms and baths rather than dormitory accommodations.

Some gerontology certificate programs are committed to preparing significant numbers of older people for roles as advocates and service providers. Community colleges, because of their accessibility, are ideal settings in which to develop educational programs that offer older adults ways to be productive. A few states recognize the market for lifelong learning and are funding a range of programs, including liberal arts education, peer learning groups, health promotion, training of older volunteers, and intergenerational service learning programs, such as seniors' mentoring of younger undergraduates for career guidance. With the growth of distance learning and Web-based instruction, baby boomers will be a growing market for educational programs. Even for the current cohort, programs such as Senior Net teach computer skills and how to communicate on-line.

As suggested in Chapter 5, educational programs need to take account of older learners' particular needs, such as flexibility, avoidance of time pressures, self-paced learning, and sensitivity to hearing and vision problems. Senior learning programs represent an area in need of further development and funding, especially with the increase in healthy, active older people, including Baby Boomers, who seek new opportunities to contribute to society after retirement.

Religious Participation, Religiosity, and Spirituality

Of the various options for organizational participation, the most common choice for older persons is through their *religious affiliation*. After family and government, religious groups are an important source of instrumental and emotional support for older people (Cutler and Hendricks, 2000). Across the life span, church and synagogue attendance is lowest among those in their 30s, peaks in the late 50s to early 60s (with approximately 60 percent of this age group attending), and begins to decline in the late 60s or early 70s. Despite this slight decline, the level of organizational religious involvement for older adults exceeds that of other age groups, with 50 percent of persons over age 65 attending church or synagogue in an average week, and many more attending less frequently. Aside from participation in organized religion, the meaning and importance of religion are stronger in old age than in earlier phases of life (Wink and Dillon, 2001). In a 2001 Gallup Poll, 67 percent of those age 65 to 74, and 75 percent of those over age 75 indicated that religion was "very important" to them (Gallup, 2002a). Furthermore, people age 65 and over are the most likely of any age group to belong to church-affiliated groups that can provide a loving, supportive community and a

> **POINTS TO PONDER**
>
> Think about the kinds of educational or learning experiences that you would like to pursue when you are retired. What qualities characterize them?

way to contribute. In contrast to other types of voluntary organizations, leadership positions in churches and synagogues tend to be concentrated among older people.

Religiosity can be examined in terms of three factors:

1. Participation in religious organizations
2. The personal meaning of religion and private devotional activities within the home
3. The contribution of religion to individuals' adjustment to the aging process and their confrontation with death and dying

Slight declines in rates of religious participation after age 70 may reflect health and transportation difficulties and functional limitations more than lack of religiousness and spirituality per se (Barusch, 1999). In fact, while attendance at formal services declines slightly with age, older individuals apparently compensate by an increase in internal religious practices—reading the Bible or other religious books, listening to religious broadcasts, praying, or studying religion. Older adults pray, asking help from God, more often than other age groups. The emotions of hope, gratitude, and forgiveness may represent significant components by which prayer exerts a salutary influence on mental health. For many elders, **spirituality**—defined broadly as encompassing trust and faith in a power greater than oneself, prayer, and strength from a greater being—is an effective way to cope (Barusch, 1999; Koenig et al., 1998; Levin and Taylor, 1997). Religious beliefs, as contrasted with church attendance, appear to be relatively stable from the late teens until age 60 and to increase thereafter. Thus, some older people who appear to be disengaged from religious organizations may be fully engaged nonorganizationally, experiencing a sense of spirituality and strong and meaningful subjective ties to religion (Barusch, 1999).

Most surveys on religiosity are limited by cross-sectional research, as discussed in Chapter 1. That is, they do not attempt to measure adults' past religious values and behaviors. The few available longitudinal studies suggest that cohort differences may be more important than the effects of age, although one 16-year study found increased participation in religious services as people entered their 60s and early 70s, then declined by age 75 (Atchley, 1995). Thus, although religious convictions appear to become more salient over the years, this may be a generational phenomenon captured by the cross-sectional nature

> ## DO WE BECOME MORE RELIGIOUS WITH AGE?
>
> It remains unclear whether people become more religious with age, or whether the increased religiosity among older adults is a cohort or period effect. Although no definitive data support either of these perspectives, some recent Gallup Poll data tend to support the view that religiosity increases with age:
>
> - In 1975, 45 percent of persons aged 18–29 indicated their religious beliefs were "very important" to them compared with 63 percent of those age 50 and older.
> - In 2001, 58–60 percent of that same cohort (age 44–55) indicated their religious beliefs were "very important" to them, compared with 65–75 percent of those age 65 and older.
> - In 1966, 38 percent of persons aged 18–29 attended religious services in a typical week, compared to 51 percent of those age 50 and older.
> - In 2001, 44 percent of persons in that cohort (now age 54–65) attended religious services in a typical week, compared with 32 percent of 18–29-year-olds and 60 percent of those older than age 75.
>
> These data suggest that the young in the previous generation also tend to be less religious than the old; now that they have become older, they too have become more religious. On the other hand, if religiousness is related to better health, those who are less religious may be more likely to die at a younger age, leaving those who are more religious alive at a later age (e.g., a selection effect).
>
> SOURCES: Gallup Poll, 2002; Koenig, 2002; Koenig and Brooks, 2002b.

of most of the research. The current cohort of older persons, raised during a time of more widespread religious involvement, had their peak rates of attendance in the 1950s, when this country experienced a church revival. All cohorts, not only older people, have shown a decline in church or synagogue attendance since 1965, although this is now changing. Younger families are increasingly turning to organized religion.

Studies of religious activity identify both gender and racial differences. Consistent with patterns of involvement in other organizations, women, particularly African American women, have higher rates of religious involvement than men (Levin, Taylor, and Chatters, 1994). Religion appears to be central to the lives of most older African Americans of both sexes and to be related to their sense of meaning, life satisfaction, feelings of self-worth, personal well-being, and sense of resilience and integration in the larger community (Krause, 2003). The high esteem afforded African American elders in the church may partially underlie these positive associations. Historically, African Americans have had more autonomy in their religious lives than in their economic and political lives. The negative effects of life stress for older African Americans are found to be offset by increased religious involvement through prayer, other private religious activities, and a cognitive reframing of the situation in positive terms (e.g., "I have been through a lot before and I'll get through this too") (Black, 1999; Kessler, Mickelson, and Williams, 1999; Levin and Taylor, 1997; Mattis and Jagers, 2001).

FUNCTIONS SERVED BY RELIGION IN AFRICAN AMERICAN COMMUNITIES

- identity, self-esteem, and meaning
- social services
- political participation
- social support
- sense of community and belonging

For some African American caregivers, the church and God are considered part of their informal system of support and respite (Dilworth-Andersen, Williams, and Cooper, 1999). The church also provides social services such as in-home visitation, counseling, meals, household help, and transportation for African American elders, and links them with formal agencies. Such instrumental support reflects the African American church's historical responsibility for improving its parishioners' socioeconomic and political conditions.

Benefits of Religious Participation and Religiosity

The association between religion or spirituality and health is receiving growing attention by gerontological researchers, educators, and practitioners—along with increased visibility in the popular press. A primary reason for this greater attention is that the benefits of religion for physical and mental well-being appear to be significant and consistent. Perhaps the most compelling finding is that religious participation appears to reduce the risk of mortality and is associated with lower prevalence of physical illness For example, religious participation has been shown to reduce the risk of death and decrease time until recovery among patients undergoing cardiac surgery. Religious activity in later life is also associated with better immune functioning, lower blood pressure, and greater longevity overall (Koenig, 2002).

What is unclear is the extent to which religion has protective effects on health, and therapeutic effects on the course and outcomes of illness. It does appear that religious participation (e.g., attending religious services) is associated with lower incidence (and prevalence) of the onset of disability, and for those who experience functional limitations, increased likelihood of improving their physical functions. Although service attendance decreases with the onset of disability, it is typically temporary, with attendance levels later returning to almost the level observed before the disability occurred. Accordingly, individuals who report that they turn to their religious beliefs to cope with their problems exhibit better outcomes. Because religion provides a worldview that infuses the present with meaning and the future with hope, it may help people cope with health problems that are restricting, limiting, and disempowering (Ellison and Levin, 1998; Hudson, 2002; Koenig, 2002; McCullough et al., 2000; Miller and Thoresen, 2003).

Religion also has benefits for mental well-being, self-esteem, life satisfaction, a sense of usefulness, and morale. Religious participation is associated with decreased prevalence of mental illnesses, such as major depression, anxiety disorders, and substance abuse. In instances of depression, religious involvement is linked with both greater likelihood of recovery from depression and shorter time until recovery. In fact, level of service attendance is a significant predictor of better and quicker recovery. As is the case with recovery from physical illness, religious coping is the facet of religious experience most strongly related to recovery from depression (Binstock, 2002; Idler, 2002; Koenig, 1997; Koenig, George, and Peterson, 1998a). Across all religions, the more devout members are usually less afraid at death and less prone to depression and loneliness than the less devout. Accordingly, individuals for whom faith provides meaning experience greater feelings of internal control and a more positive self-concept (Krause, 1995; Leifer, 1996). Among African American women in particular, spirituality is found to engender self-esteem and positive interpretations of life circumstances (Black, 1999).

The strong association between religion and physical and mental well-being does not imply that religious factors are the only or the primary factors causing good health. Religion has beneficial effects on health because there are so many different pathways for it, through the modification of known risk factors, the provision of social support, and the availability of belief systems for coping with adverse circumstances and reducing depression in late life. Regardless of the particu-

lar pathway, a growing body of evidence shows that religious participation has protective effects on health and helps older adults cope more effectively with their health problems. In fact, the strength of these relationships between religious involvement and well-being increases over time (Levin, Chatters, and Taylor, 1995; Musick, 2000).

Although religiousness itself is beneficial, the sense of belonging and social support derived from the organizational aspects are also determinants of well-being (Idler and Kasl, 1997). Across the life span, religious groups provide support and reduce stress in people's lives. Older people list among its benefits both the meaning religion gives to life and the social interaction, support, and security that it affords. Congruent with the broad concept of productivity, religious institutions also provide innumerable opportunities to care for and serve others in need. The connection between religious activity and health appears to be especially strong among those who volunteer within religious settings; volunteers, who typically are externally oriented, are happier, healthier, live longer, and use fewer health services (Krause et al., 1999; Oman, Thoresen, and McMahon, 1999). Religious institutions are also distinctive for having memberships that cut across the entire life course, providing opportunities for intergenerational interaction and reciprocity. Given the importance of the social networks within religious settings, practitioners need to consider how social support through churches and synagogues complements and interacts with religious beliefs and activities. In addition, as public social services continue to be reduced, religious institutions are expected to play a greater role in providing counseling, referral to services, and illness prevention/health promotion. The role of faith-based services is, however, raising complex issues regarding the role of church and state that require ongoing dialogue among religious leaders, ethicists, constitutional scholars, and gerontological practitioners (Brooks and Koenig, 2002).

The Value of Spiritual Well-Being

Spirituality is a broader concept, defined in a wide variety of ways:

- a transcendent relationship with that which is sacred in life
- self-determined wisdom in which the individual tries to achieve balance in life
- self-transcendence or crossing a boundary beyond the self, being supported by some power greater than oneself
- achievement of meaning and purpose for one's continued existence
- sense of the wholeness of life and connectedness to the universe
- awe or unconditional joy
- intuitive nonverbal understanding of how to cope with life's circumstances

Spirituality—or belief in a relationship with a higher power—can be differentiated from organized religion, but not necessarily from religiousness, which can be separate from formal religious participation. Although small proportions of the population in national studies describe themselves as "spiritual but not religious," the majority of people describe themselves as both religious and spiritual, which makes it difficult to determine estimates of their unique effects on physical and mental well-being. Those who view themselves as spiritual but not religious appear to be rejecting participation in organized religion, but emphasizing personal spiritual practices such as praying or meditating, appreciating nature, applying spiritual principles to everyday life, and practicing positive emotions such as gratitude and forgiveness. For example, 85 percent of Americans pray frequently, but only 40 percent attend religious services regularly (George, 2002; Pargament et al., 1998; Zinnbauer et al., 1997). Accordingly, spirituality can be expressed in trying to find the meaning and purpose of life, looking at the significance of past events, and wondering what will happen after death.

High levels of spirituality, as measured by closeness to a supreme power, are found to be associated with mental health indicators such as purpose and meaning in life, self-esteem, and positive perception of quality of life (Burke, 1999; Kavanaugh, 1997). Similarly, spiritual beliefs influence definitions of health, the prevention of illness, health promotion, and coping with illness. For example, a study of older women diagnosed with breast cancer found that spirituality was an effective coping strategy that provided mental and social support and the ability to make meaning during their everyday lives (Feher and Maly, 1999; Koenig, 1995). Such findings are consistent with the relationships between religiousness and health, since many of the private forms of religious participation (e.g., prayer, meditation, personal rituals) are similar whether people define themselves as religious or spiritual (George, 2002).

Spiritual well-being is related not only to the quality of life but also to the will to live. Some gerontologists and theologians maintain that the person who aims to enhance spiritual well-being and to find meaning in life will have a reason to live despite losses and challenges associated with aging (Fallon, 1998). When death is near, spirituality is important for coping with disease, disability, and pain (Burke, 1999). Mr. Mansfield, in the introduction to Part Four, illustrates the role of spirituality in helping older persons cope with tragic losses in their lives.

SPIRITUALITY AND QUALITY OF LIFE

A key theme in narratives from a small sample of African American women is that their relationship with God, perceived as personal, reciprocal, and empowering, allows them to take an active and positive stance in viewing and interpreting the circumstances of their lives. Their spirituality imbues their hardship with meaning, engenders self-esteem, and gives hope for rewards in both this life and the next (Black, 1999).

MEDITATION AS A FORM OF SPIRITUALITY

Carl, age 68, is an active volunteer and employed part-time. No matter how busy he is, however, he always manages to set aside a half hour in the morning to meditate. Since he started meditating at age 62, his blood pressure has decreased; he has fewer health problems, and he has a calm, positive outlook on life. He describes his meditation to his friends as the center of his spiritual journey.

Aging can be characterized as a spiritual journey in which the person aims to achieve integration across a number of areas of life—biological, psychological, social, and spiritual. An ageless self, that is, a person who is not preoccupied or discouraged by his or her aging, has an identity that maintains continuity and is on a spiritual journey in time, despite age-related physical and social changes. For such an individual, being old per se is neither a central feature of the self nor the source of its meaning. Confronting negative images of aging, loss, and death is believed to be essential for psychological-spiritual growth and successful aging. In fact, dealing with loss can be one of aging's greatest spiritual challenges. Autobiographical storytelling, journal keeping, and empathic interactions with others are useful in supporting older persons' spiritual integration.

The central role of spirituality in many older adults' lives has numerous implications for professionals working with them. Spirituality is a quality that can be acknowledged in any situation, including professional practice with older adults. Many faith traditions emphasize the importance of silence in creating space to experience spirituality, with the silence of meditation or prayer as a way to nourish our spirituality. In hospice programs, for instance, patients, workers, and families can experience profound togetherness out of shared silence. In nursing homes, staff and families may find that silence when they are together has value. Spiritual deepening can also come from con-

fronting and working through doubt and uncertainty. For others, spirituality is a state of being rather than of doing, of approaching each other with kindness and openness to their unique way of manifesting their spirituality. It is a way to experience others authentically with little tendency to judge or evaluate them. Spiritual reflections and experiences can also be a source of insight for both practitioners and older clients. Contemplative understanding includes feelings and thoughts, and can counterbalance overly rational decision-making processes. In some instances, spirituality can provide a more balanced understanding of what is compared to what is needed. When practitioners learn to focus on experiences of spirituality with older adults, they can create common experiential ground that can transcend the confines of specific faith traditions and open opportunities for incorporating spirituality into all aspects of everyday life (Atchley, 1999).

Historically, the medical profession has taken a predominantly biological perspective toward aging, overlooking psychological, emotional, and spiritual factors. Fortunately, more health care providers are attending to the spiritual dimensions of health care and dying (Nordquist, 1999). Health care practitioners who view spiritual well-being as important to older people's physical and mental health have developed instruments to measure an individual's spiritual interests and resources, such as personal values, philosophy, and sense of purpose. Some health-promotion screening tools include questions on the individual's spiritual or philosophic values, life goal-setting, and approach to answering questions, such as: What is the meaning of my life? How can I

POINTS TO PONDER

Ask an older person—a relative, neighbor, close friend—whether he or she perceives himself or herself as spiritual. What does spirituality mean to the individual? How has that meaning developed over time?

increase the quality of my life? Increasingly, health providers are encouraged to be sensitive to, and to ask questions about, religion and spiritual well-being that may guide health care choices. Similarly, they may encourage patients to seek religious support or to reconnect with a spiritual community (Feher and Maly, 1999).

Political Participation

Another major arena of participation is political life. Political acts range from voting, to participation in a political party or a political action group, to running for or holding elective office. In an examination of older people's political behavior, three factors make any interpretation of the relationship between age and political behavior complex:

1. stages in the life cycle,
2. cohort effects, and
3. historical or period effects, as discussed in Chapter 1.

Historical effects influence interpretations of older people's political behavior, particularly analyses of the extent of conservatism. Some early studies found older people to be more conservative than younger people, as measured by preference for the Republican party and voting behavior (Campbell, 1962; Dobson, 1983). Older people's apparent conservatism partially reflects the fact that people born and raised in different historical periods tend to have perspectives reflecting those times—in this instance, the historical effect of party realignments in the late 1920s and 1930s. Before the New Deal of the 1930s and 1940s, people entering the electorate identified with the Republican party to a disproportionate extent; they have voted Republican ever since, and form the majority of the oldest-old population. This apparent association of Republicanism with age thus reflects cohort differences, not the effects of aging per se. Conclusions about older people's political behavior and attitudes are thus limited by the cross-sectional nature of most research, which has not taken account of historical and cohort effects.

In short, how a person thinks and acts politically can be traced largely to environmental and historical factors, not to that person's age.

Age differences in conservatism/liberalism are less a matter of people becoming more conservative or liberal than of their maintaining these values throughout life (Binstock and Day, 1996). Successive generations entering the electorate since World War II have become comparatively more liberal, with more older people identifying with the Democratic party since the mid-1980s. This shift may be due in part to increases in low-income and retired blue-collar people who are opposed to the stance of the Republican party on issues such as Social Security and health care. In fact, older adults are more likely to favor major health care reforms than are younger people, in part because of escalating costs not covered by Medicare. At the same time, increasing numbers of young people, including many among the baby boom generation, have identified with the conservative Republicans and with independent candidates since the 1980s (Binstock, 2000; Alwin, 1998).

Overall, various cohorts of older adults during the past 50 years have tended to distribute their votes among presidential candidates in roughly the same proportions as other age groups. In other words, voting differences are greater within than between age groups (Binstock and Quadragno, 2001). Individuals of all ages are not ideologically consistent in their issue-specific preferences, such as Medicare, Social Security, or taxes. Furthermore, both older and younger people may hold beliefs on specific issues that contradict their views on more general principles. Given the older population's heterogeneity, differences of opinion on any political issue are likely to equal or exceed variations among age groups and are more likely to be due to economic status and partisanship than age (Binstock, 2000).

Voting Behavior

Older Americans are more likely than younger adults to vote in national elections, although rates of electoral participation are low for all age groups in our society. They currently compose 20 percent of all votes, though only 17 percent of the general electorate. The participation rate of older people in the last three presidential elections has averaged 68 percent, almost three times the rate of 18- to 20-year-olds. Although voting participation declines for those age 75 and older, the 75-plus group was still more likely to vote in the last six presidential elections prior to 2004 than people younger than age 35 (Binstock, 2000; Binstock and Quadagno, 2001). The most important reason for the increase in the portion of votes cast by older people is that turnout rates of younger age groups have declined overall. Several reasons underlie the older population's higher rate of registration and voting:

- Older people are more likely to pay attention to the news and to be more knowledgeable about politics and public affairs generally, demonstrating higher levels of "civic competence" (Binstock, 2000; Binstock and Quadagno, 2001).
- Strong partisans are more likely to vote, and older people identify with the major political parties more strongly than younger persons, who are more likely to identify with independent parties (Binstock, 2000; McManus and Tenpas, 1998).

In instances where voter turnout is declining among older adults, factors other than aging are probably the cause, including gender, ethnic minority status, education, and generational variables as well as access to the polls. For example, the voter turnout of populations of color is lower than that of whites. The political acculturation of Latinos appears to influence their relatively low rates of participation; for example, Mexican American elders, historically fearful of deportation, have a more cautious, conservative approach to political involvement. On the other hand, older African Americans who are active in their communities, with a strong sense of citizen duty, an identity as Democrats, and higher levels of education, are

more likely to vote. These and earlier findings suggest that differences in the rates of political participation among older people of color do not reflect age or ethnic minority identity per se, but rather lower educational levels, feelings of powerlessness, cohort experiences, and real or perceived barriers to voting and other political activities. To public officials and the media, the older electorate is viewed as exerting substantial political influence beyond what their numbers might suggest.

Senior Power

Research on "senior power" reflects an ongoing debate about whether age serves as a catalyst for a viable political movement.

PROPONENTS OF THE "SENIOR POWER" MODEL OF POLITICS   Older people can be a powerful political constituency in the policy-making process because legislators and appointed officials are influenced by public opinion—especially by those who vote and are political party leaders, as is the case with older people. This perspective of senior power is consistent with the subculture theory of aging, discussed in Chapter 8. This theory suggests that older people, because of common values and

Many older people advocate for their rights.

experiences, develop a shared political consciousness that is translated into collective action on old-age-related issues (Rix, 1999; Street, 1999). Since future cohorts of older adults will be better educated and healthier and may retire earlier with higher incomes, it is argued that they will have more resources essential to political power. It also assumes that older people in the future will experience increasing pride, dignity, and shared consciousness about old age and thus define problems collectively. From this perspective, age is viewed as becoming a more salient aspect of politics, even if all older persons and their organizations do not speak (or vote) with a unified political voice. Heterogeneity among the older population does not preclude age—as with gender and ethnic minority status—from exerting political influence (Binstock and Day, 1996).

Although there is little evidence of old-age voting blocs, mass membership old-age interest groups that cast themselves as "representatives" of older voters (e.g., AARP) generally have significant political influence. This occurs because policy makers find it useful and incumbent to invite them to participate in policy activities, and thus to be in touch symbolically with older adults. The symbolic legitimacy that old-age organizations have for participation in interest group politics gives them power in the following ways:

- They have easy informal access to public officials, members of Congress and their staffs, and administrative officials.
- Their legitimacy enables them to obtain public platforms in the national media, congressional hearings, national conferences, and commissions dealing with issues affecting older adults.
- Mass membership groups can mobilize their members in large numbers to contact policy makers and register displeasure (Binstock and Quadagno, 2001).

"Senior citizens" have traditionally been one of the prime targets of campaign efforts focused on crit-

ical states with large blocs of electoral votes, as vividly illustrated in the 2000 Presidential election in Florida. As perceived by a Democratic pollster, "It's virtually impossible to take back the House or win the Presidency without taking back seniors; . . . that makes them the key battleground, and both parties know it" (Toner, 1999). This is because of their aggregate numerical importance and the relative ease with which they can be accessed through age-segregated housing and existing programs such as senior centers, AARP chapters, and congregate meal sites. In fact, an important form of power available to old-age interest groups is "the electoral bluff": the perception of being powerful is, in itself, a source of political influence, even though old-age organizations have been unable to swing a decisive bloc of older voters (Binstock and Quadagno, 2001).

COUNTERARGUMENT: OLDER PEOPLE DO NOT CONSTITUTE A SIGNIFICANT AGE-BASED POLITICAL FORCE
Early critics of the subculture theory argue that the diversity of the older population precludes their having shared interests around which to coalesce. Most older people, especially the young-old, do not identify themselves as "aged," nor do they perceive their problems as stemming from their age. In addition, they are not captives of any single political philosophy, party, or mass organization. In fact, some argue that "the Elderly" is really a category created by policy analysts, pension officials, and outdated models of interest group politics and not a sound basis for political mobilization (Walker, 1999). Since age is only one of many personal characteristics, age alone cannot predict political behavior or age-group consciousness based on differential access to resources. Nor are these self-interests or old-age policy issues the most important factors in their electoral decisions (Binstock, 2000; Binstock and Quadagno, 2001).

Instead, differences by socioeconomic class, ethnic minority status, gender, and religion increasingly influence older people's political interests. For example, contrary to widely held perceptions, older people are rarely unified about issues affecting the young, such as school levies, and do not vote as a bloc against increasing property taxes to support public schools (Binstock and Day, 1996). Instead, they generally recognize the importance of education for economic productivity. This example suggests that old-age–related issues are not necessarily more important to them than other issues, partisan attachments, or the characteristics of specific candidates. In fact, it appears that older and younger people are more likely to form alliances along economic, racial, ethnic, and ideological lines than to unite horizontally on the basis of age (Binstock and Day, 1996). **Generations United** is a national organization composed of over 120 organizations of different age groups, represents one such vertical cross-age coalition.

As an example of a cross-age, cross-class alliance, poor older people may work with younger welfare beneficiaries for better health insurance for all ages, while upper-income older adults may be more interested in long-term care. In the face of federal cuts, future subgroups of older people may become more politically organized, with political agendas different from most of today's senior organizations, especially around issues of means-testing and higher eligibility ages for benefits such as Social Security. For example, lower-income older people have a greater stake in the maintenance and enhancement of Social Security, since it accounts for a larger proportion of their income (Binstock, 1993). Accordingly, the failure of the 1988 Medicare Catastrophic Coverage Act illustrates the fragility of interest-group politics when upper-middle-class older adults were asked to sustain a program that benefited primarily low-income older people.

HISTORICAL DEVELOPMENT OF AGE-BASED GROUPS
At first glance, the number, variety, and strength of age-based national organizations appear to support the perspective that older people are a powerful political force. Age-based organizations are able to build memberships, conduct policy analyses, marshal grassroots support, and utilize direct mail and

political action. Conscious organizing of older individuals is not without historical precedent. The first age-based politically oriented interest group grew out of the social and economic dislocations of the Depression. The Townsend Movement proposed a tax on all business transactions to finance a $200/month pension for every pensioner over age 60. However, passage of the Social Security Act in 1935, in which groups of older people played a supporting but not a leading role, took away the Townsend Movement's momentum, and the organization died out in the 1940s. Most political divisions during the turbulent period of the Depression were class- and labor-based rather than age-based. The Townsend Movement did demonstrate, however, that old age could be a short-term basis for organizing (Binstock and Day, 1996). The McClain Movement, another early age-based organization, aimed to establish financial benefits for older persons through a referendum in the 1938 California elections, but lost followers after economic conditions improved in the 1940s. These early groups did furnish older people with a collective voice and identity, however (Torres-Gil, 1993).

Organized interest groups representing older people did not reemerge until the 1950s and 1960s. Currently, over 1000 separately organized groups for older adults exist at the local, state, and national levels, with at least 100 major national organizations involved in political action on behalf of older persons. In many ways, the diversity of the older population is reflected in the variety of organizations themselves, ranging from mass membership groups to nonmembership staff organizations and associations of professionals or service providers. Yet, the very diversity of these groups reduces their potential to act together as a unified bloc. For example, the National Caucus for the Black Aged, the National Hispanic Council on Aging, and the National Indian Council on Aging were created to address political inequities facing elders of color. They may not act in concert with organizations such as the American Association of Retired Persons (AARP) that represent primarily a white, middle-class constituency.

Three of the largest *mass-membership organizations* are the **National Council of Senior Citizens (NCSC)**, the **National Association of Retired Federal Employees (NARFE)**, and the **American Association of Retired Persons (AARP)**, together with the National Retired Teachers' Association (NRTA). The National Council of Senior Citizens (NCSC) was developed by organized labor in the early 1960s with the objective of passing Medicare. Although anyone may join, most members of NCSC are former blue-collar workers who receive insurance and other tangible membership benefits. The National Association of Retired Federal Employees (NARFE) was also formed for a specific political purpose—the passage of the Federal Employees Pension Act in the 1920s. It has since concentrated on bread-and-butter issues for federal employees, such as labor/management relations, rather than broader political issues affecting older persons generally.

The best known and largest of these organizations is the American Association of Retired Persons (AARP), which began in 1958 with a small number of older adults working to provide a special group health policy. It now has grown to a membership of 35 million, which encompasses nearly half of the nation's population over age 50 and over 13 percent of the population generally. Now using only its acronym rather than its full name, AARP seeks to recruit the young-old and baby boomers. In fact, the minimum age of membership has been lowered from 55 to 50. It has merged its two magazines—*My Generation* for adults ages 50 to 59 and *Modern Maturity* for those older than 60 into *The Magazine*. An as-

---

SERVICES OFFERED BY AARP

- AARP Tax-Aide: free tax preparation services
- peer grief and loss counseling
- legal council for older adults
- driver safety course
- money management program
- noncancel home and auto insurance
- mobile home insurance
- grandparent Information Center
- life insurance
- AARP Health Care Options (supplemental insurance)
- legal services network

---

sumption of this merger is that the retiree population has become so large that generational differences are blurred; instead it is assumed that both the young-old and the old-old (who may be their parents) share interests related to health, financial, security and travel. Nevertheless, AARP continues to publish three slightly different versions of *The Magazine* to appeal to cohorts in their 50s, 60s, and beyond. In 2001, *The Magazine* also began to be published in Spanish to reach out to the rapidly growing young-old Spanish-speaking population. In addition, AARP spends millions to advertise in popular magazines such as *Time* and *Newsweek* with ads of healthy, robust, and often physically attractive older adults. In a similar spirit, they now sponsor 10-K runs, marathons, and a wide range of fitness activities. Such ads and "repackaging" reflect AARP's recognition of the huge market for their products with the baby boomers. In fact, by 2010, over 50 percent of all AARP members will be boomers.

Members are attracted by the benefits of lower-cost health insurance, credit cards, travel, rental car discounts, discount prescriptions by mail, and a myriad of other retirement planning programs. The additional services listed in the box capture merely a portion of the benefits available to members for the current membership fee of only $12.50 a year. Most recently, its support

---

A NEW IMAGE FOR AARP

AARP ads feature themes such as "Age is just a number, and life is what you make it" or "You're ready to make this the time of your life. We help make it happen." A cover of AARP's magazine promised "Great Sex," and carried a picture of actress Susan Sarandon wearing a deep V-necked sweater.

of the 2003 Prescription Drug Coverage Bill, AARP has had a substantial impact on policies and practices that benefit older adults. However, it has been criticized for moving away from advocacy on behalf of the older population and becoming a big business, driven to market products. The box below captures only a portion of the legislation that AARP has influenced since 1958. In addition, AARP is now joining with nonaging organizations, such as the Child Welfare League and Generations United, to address issues related to grandparenting and kinship care. They are committed to intergenerational programming as well, most visibly evidenced by their national partnership with Big Brothers/Big Sisters.

A wide range of trade associations, professional societies, and coalitions concerned with aging issues also exists. *Trade associations* include:

- the American Association of Homes and Services for the Aged
- the American Nursing Home Association
- the National Council of Health Care Services (consisting of commercial enterprises in the long-term care business, such as the nursing home subsidiary of major hotel chains)
- the National Association of State Units in Aging (NASUA), which is composed of administrators of state area agencies on aging

---

LEGISLATION INFLUENCED BY AARP

- Age Discrimination and Employment Act
- older worker pension contributions
- Federal Nursing Home Reform Act
- Nutrition Labeling and Education Act
- Medigap reform legislation
- Family and Medical Leave Act
- Social Security cost of living adjustment
- Health Insurance Portability and Accountability Act (HIPAA)
- reauthorization of the Older Americans' Act
- Social Security earnings limit
- Bipartisan Campaign Reform Act

The emphasis of trade associations is to obtain federal funds and influence the development of regulations for long-term care facilities and the delivery of public services. Two *professional associations* active in aging policy issues, the Gerontological Society of America (GSA) (which now also includes the Association for Gerontology in Higher Education) and the American Society on Aging (ASA), are composed primarily of gerontological researchers, educators, and practitioners from many disciplines. The major confederation of social welfare agencies concerned with aging is the National Council on the Aging (NCOA), which encompasses over 2000 organized affiliates, including public and private health, social work, and community action agencies.

Several organizations that began at the grassroots level now have nationwide membership and recognition. The **Older Women's League (OWL),** founded in 1981, brings together people concerned about issues affecting older women, especially health care and insurance, Social Security, pensions, and caregiving. It advocates for older women both in the federal policy-making process and within the programs of national associations such as the Gerontological Society of America. Women activists within OWL represent a trend away from the comparatively lower rates of past political participation among older women. The **Gray Panthers,** founded by the late Maggie Kuhn, aimed to form grassroots intergenerational alliances around issues affecting all ages. Since Maggie Kuhn's death, the Gray Panthers' visibility has declined, but they are still involved in change efforts around cross-generational issues.

On certain issues such as health care reform, the influence of organizations of older people has been limited relative to powerful interest groups such as the insurance, medical, and pharmaceutical industries. For example, none of President Clinton's 1997 appointments to the National Bipartisan Commission on the Future of Medicare was representative of organized old-age interests (Binstock, 2000). Accordingly, despite the involvement of AARP, pharmaceutical and insurance companies

---

POLITICAL ACTIVISM AND OLDER WOMEN

Tish Sommers is an example of the increasing political activism of older women. Sommers, a long-time homemaker, learned about the vulnerability of older women when she was divorced at age 57. She found that newly single homemakers her age had a hard time getting benefits that people who have been employed take for granted. She coined the term *displaced homemaker* and built a force of women. They successfully lobbied for centers where displaced homemakers had job training during the late 1970s. In 1980, she and Laurie Shields founded the Older Women's League, a national organization that has grown to over 14,000 members and over 100 chapters. Her maxim always was "Don't agonize, organize." During the 6 years of organizing OWL, Sommers also fought a battle with cancer. Even at her death in 1986, she was still fighting, organizing groups nationally around the right to maintain control over the conditions of one's death.

---

and private managed care organizations exerted more influence on the 2003 Medicare Prescription Drug Bill than did older adults. Nevertheless, until recently, most politicians did not want to offend age-based organizations and constituencies. After higher-income older people organized to influence Congress to repeal the 1988 Medicare Catastrophic Coverage Act, no proposals concerning older adults got out of committees in the next Congressional election year.

Whether older people act as a unified bloc, many policy makers act as if there were a "politics of age" founded on cohort-based interest groups, and politicians continue to count the votes of older persons. Presidential candidates in the 2000 election actively courted the senior vote, advocating widely different proposals for Social Security and prescription drug coverage. Even if older people cannot effect the passage of legislation, they are seen as blocking changes in existing policies, especially when programs such as Social Security and Medicare are threatened. Perceptions of such influence then affect whether major changes in policies on aging are viewed as feasi-

ble, even though the political legitimacy of old-age interest groups has eroded over the past decade (Binstock, 2000; Binstock and Day, 1996).

Some national age-based organizations are criticized for being biased toward the interests of middle- and upper-working-class older people. AARP, for example, is criticized for advancing only the interests of its primarily middle-class membership, for recruiting members largely on the basis of selective incentives and direct member services (e.g., insurance, drug discounts, and travel), and for imposing its policy agenda on its members (Pear, 1995). In recent years, however, age-based organizations have not only reached out to lower-income older persons, but also collaborated with other groups. This is reflected by the cross-age coalitions that have formed around health and long-term care. In addition to national associations, a wide range of organizations at the local and state levels have mobilized around intergenerational and cross-class issues such as affordable public transportation, environmental issues, safe streets, and low-cost health care (Binstock and Day, 1996).

In sum, despite the growth of age-based organizations, the senior power model appears to have little validity with respect to older adults' voting behavior and political attitudes. Old age per se is currently not a primary basis for political mobilization, despite images of homogenous senior groups put forth by politicians, the media, and age-based organizations. With regard to the future, it can be predicted that the senior boomers will cast a higher total vote in national elections than occurs today; on the other hand, the heterogeneity of the baby boom cohort suggests that age will not form the primary basis for political behavior (Binstock, 2000). Cross-generational alliances are likely to be most important in influencing policies and programs, as further discussed in Chapter 16.

Implications for the Future

The senior boomers, who are likely to enter old age in better economic positions than prior cohorts, will shape new paradigms of work, productivity, and retirement. Baby boomers' ability to earn more during their lifetimes results from economic and demographic shifts, such as deferred marriage, reduced and later childbearing, increased labor force participation of women, higher levels of educational attainment, and greater pension coverage. More people over age 70 are likely to choose to continue to be employed, preferably on a part-time basis, or may pursue second or third careers. This will reflect a relatively new concept of "bridge jobs" that sustain older workers, offer them new experiences and provide work life flexibility between careers or before they leave the working world for good (AARP, 2002). Senior boomers will also benefit from the full lifting of the Social Security cap on outside earnings, which will allow them to be employed without financial penalty. Their continued employment may reflect their limited confidence about their financial futures and concerns about outliving their retirement savings, in part because they typically borrowed more and saved less than their parents. Despite their greater lifetime earnings than prior cohorts, baby boomers generally are not actively preparing for financial security in retirement that will allow them to maintain their current standard of living.

The numbers of economically vulnerable elders will not diminish dramatically. Instead, a permanent underclass of boomers is projected, with disproportionate representation of African Americans and Latinos, those with a sporadic employment history, single women, and the poorly educated. This pattern is unlikely to change without interventions earlier in the life cycle to prevent poverty and ensure educational and employment opportunities in young adulthood and middle age.

Retirement will generally not be a single irreversible event. Instead, more adults will change careers two or three times throughout their lives and move in and out of the workforce. The retirement transition will be eased by businesses that provide sabbaticals, extended vacations and leaves, retraining programs, and career development alternatives. Educational opportunities will become more accessible through distance learning formats that use information-based technology. Such educational options benefit employees by allowing them to explore new careers and volunteer and leisure interests; in turn, this can serve to prevent job burnout or boredom, so that early retirement is not perceived as the only viable option. Incentives to encourage people to work longer are a pragmatic response to the projected labor shortage among youth, especially in the service sector. Although more companies are beginning to modify the workplace in order to retain older workers longer, such workplace modifications do not adequately meet the growing interest in part-time employment. The economic downturn and high unemployment of the early part of this century has also adversely affected efforts to retrain and retain older workers, especially when it is more cost-efficient to encourage their early retirement and hire lower-paid younger workers.

From a societal perspective, a work-retirement continuum for a population with a longer life span requires changes in our expectations regarding lifelong education and training. Changing societal values about the "appropriate age" for education, employment, retirement, and leisure demand a reexamination of employment policies and norms. The traditional linear life cycle of education for the young, employment for the middle aged, and retirement for the old is already undergoing major changes. This is occurring as more middle-aged and older persons enter college for the first time, move into new careers, or begin their studies for graduate or professional degrees. Other countries provide models for reconceptualizing work and retirement. A "gliding out" plan of phased retirement in Japan and some European countries permits a gradual shift into a part-time schedule. Some Scandinavian countries give workers year-long sabbaticals every 10 years as a time to reevaluate their careers or to take a break instead of working straight through to retirement. Jobs can also be restructured, gradually allowing longer vacations, shorter workdays, and more opportunities for community involvement during the preretirement working years. Barriers to such changes in our society, however, include the fact that Americans have fewer vacation days than any other Western industrialized society and tend to work more days per week. On the other hand, movement in and out of the workforce and new retirement options may come to be viewed as legitimate alternatives for both men and women because of the following factors:

- increasing numbers of career-oriented women who are committed to an ideology of shared family responsibilities, with a modest increase in the fathers who share or assume primary responsibility for child care
- growing awareness of the possibility of two or three careers over the life course
- younger generations who are less likely to compartmentalize employment and leisure and who are more open to modified work schedules, job sharing, and phased retirement.
- increasing numbers of retirees who work part-time and also volunteer
- growing corporate awareness of employee needs, such as on-the-job exercise and fitness programs, child care, and staff training and counseling.

To some extent, these factors reflect a shift from the traditional 40-plus-hours a week work ethic to a more balanced view of employment and leisure. Future cohorts of older adults may view leisure in retirement merely as a continuation of prior non-work activities and not regard it as a new stage in life. Integration of leisure and other nonpaid activities across the life span will undoubtedly smooth the transition to retirement for those who have had the economic resources to enjoy leisure throughout their lives.

Whether the economy will create such work and leisure alternatives is unclear. Many new jobs are in the service sector (e.g., health and social services, food, and recreation) rather than in manufacturing. Such jobs are unlikely to provide older workers with financial security. Whether technological advances will produce new jobs or result in net job losses is also unknown. What is certain is greater labor market diversity among the older population and greater variations in the reasons for retirement, unemployment, and economic well-being. Definitions of the nature of work, family, careers, and retirement will gradually reshape cultural and organizational expectations.

The concept of the "Third Age" moves beyond focusing only on employment roles; instead, it denotes the stage in life that occurs after middle age but before the final stage, and is conceptualized as a time of continued involvement and development in areas of life beyond employment and family. This concept is congruent with the broad perspective of productivity, discussed throughout this chapter, which seeks new ways to develop and use our human potential in old age. The vitality of the older population must be recognized as a way to involve their skills and wisdom through both paid and unpaid positions for the benefit of society and of older adults themselves. Increasingly, questions will be raised about how "work" should be defined and "contributions" measured. Advocates of a productive aging society point to the need to place a real value on unpaid volunteer and caregiving activities. Volunteer effort may be perceived as contributing more to the common good than paid work and therefore as deserving greater rewards than currently exist. However, flexible options for productive activity by older adults are unevenly distributed across all sectors of society. Therefore, initiatives to encourage voluntarism and other types of unpaid productive contributions must occur within a broader framework that seeks to eliminate economic inequities across the life span and in old age.

These changes in work, retirement, and productivity will require new skills and knowledge among social and health care providers and planners of services for older adults. Preretirement counseling, lifelong distance learning opportunities, career development and retraining programs, and expanded volunteer programs all pose new roles for gerontological practitioners and researchers. Professionals and laypersons alike will be challenged to reconceptualize the use of time and human resources, given reduced rates of disability and increased longevity.

Summary

Paid employment is typically associated with productivity in our society. Increasingly, however, Americans are retiring in their early 60s and looking forward to two to three decades of leisure time in relatively good health. Health status, income, and attitudes toward the job influence the decision about when to retire. Most retirees adjust well to this important transition and are satisfied with the quality of their lives. Those with good health, higher-status jobs, adequate income, and existing social networks and leisure interests are most likely to be satisfied. Not all retirement is desired, however; many older people would prefer the opportunity for part-time work, but are unable to find suitable and flexible options. Preparation for the retirement transition is beneficial, but planning assistance is generally not available to those who need it most—workers who have less education, lower job status, and lower retirement incomes. Retirement by itself does not cause poor health or loss of identity and self-esteem. Dissatisfaction in this stage of life is more often due to poor health and low income.

Although a smaller percentage of older people have incomes below the poverty line than was true in the past, more older than younger people live at marginal economic levels. Social Security is the major source of retirement income for a large proportion of the older population; those who depend on Social Security alone are the poorest older group. Private pensions tend to be small in relation to previous earnings, be subject to attrition through inflation, and go primarily to workers in large, unionized, or industrialized settings. Income from assets is distributed unequally among the older population, with a small number of older persons receiving sizable amounts from savings and investments, whereas the most common asset of older people is their home, which provides no immediate income. In addition to those older adults who are officially counted as living below the poverty line, many others live near this level, and many are "hidden" poor who live in nursing homes or with their families. Frail, unmarried women—ethnic minority women, especially—are the most likely to live in or near poverty. Public assistance programs such as SSI have not removed the very serious financial problems of the older poor.

As earlier chapters have documented, changes in employment and parenting roles, income, and physical and sensory capacities often have detrimental social consequences for older adults. Nevertheless, there are arenas in which older people may still experience meaningful involvement and develop new opportunities and skills, consistent with the broader definition of productive aging that includes nonpaid contributions to society. This chapter has considered six of these arenas: leisure pursuits, voluntary association membership, volunteering, education, religious involvement, and political activity. The meaning and functions of participation in these arenas are obviously highly individualized. Participation may be a means to strengthen and build informal social networks, influence wider social policies, serve other persons, and substitute for role changes. The extent of involvement is influenced not by age alone, but also by a variety of other salient factors including gender, ethnic minority status, health, socioeconomic status, and educational level.

Because of the number of interacting variables, age-related patterns in participation are not clearly defined. There are some general age-related differences in types of leisure pursuits; with increasing age, people tend to engage in more sedentary, inner-directed, and routine pursuits in their homes than social activities or obligations outside the home. Changes in organizational participation and volunteering are less clearly age-related. Participation in voluntary associations stabilizes or declines only slightly with old age; declines that do occur are likely to be associated with poor health, inadequate income, and transportation problems. Volunteering, which is higher among the older population than other age groups, tends to represent a lifelong pattern of community service.

Past research on religious and political participation has pointed inaccurately to declines in old age. Although formal religious participation such as church or synagogue attendance appears to diminish slightly, other activities such as reading religious texts or listening to religious broadcasts increase. Religiosity appears to be an effective way of coping, particularly among ethnic minority elders. Spirituality is differentiated from religion as a positive factor in older people's physical and mental well-being and their quality of life.

Voting by older people has increased since the 1980s. Declines in voting and political participation in the past may have been a function of low educational status or physical limitations, not of age per se. In fact, older persons' skills and experiences may be more valued in the political arena than in other spheres. The extent to which older people form a unified political bloc that can influence politicians and public policy is debatable. Some argue that older adults form a subculture with a strong collective consciousness; others point to their increasing diversity and political inequity, as apparent in reactions to the Medicare Catastrophic Health Care legislation.

Most forms of organizational involvement appear to represent stability across the life course; the knowledge and skills necessary for a varied set of activities in old age are generally developed in early or middle adulthood and maintained into later life. On the other hand, preretirement patterns of productivity are not fixed; individuals can develop new interests and activities in later life, often with the assistance of senior centers, continuing education programs, or community or special interest organizations.

GLOSSARY

Age Discrimination in Employment Act (ADEA) federal law that protects workers age 45 and over from denial of employment strictly because of age

American Association of Retired Persons (AARP) national organization open to all adults age 50 and over, offering a wide range of informational materials, discounted services and products, and a powerful lobby

American Society on Aging (ASA) association of practitioners and researchers interested in gerontology

assets an individual's savings, home equity, and personal property

displaced homemakers widowed or divorced women under age 60 who do not yet qualify for Social Security benefits but may lack the skills for employment

Elderhostel program in which older adults can take inexpensive, short-term academic courses associated with colleges and universities around the world

Employment Retirement Income Security Act (ERISA) 1974 legislation to regulate pensions

feminization of poverty variety of factors that lead to higher proportions of poverty among women than men

Foster Grandparents Program volunteer program pairing seniors with children with special needs

Generations United a national intergenerational coalition

Gerontological Society of America (GSA) an association of researchers, educators, and practitioners interested in gerontology and geriatrics

Gray Panthers a national organization, founded by Maggie Kuhn, that encourages intergenerational alliances around social issues

leisure time (not devoted to "work") when one has options in selecting activities

National Association of Retired Federal Employees (NARFE) national organization of adults retired from the federal government, primarily involved in political and social issues

National Council of Senior Citizens (NCSC) mass-membership organization involved in political action for older adults

National Council on the Aging (NCOA) national organization of over 2000 social welfare agencies concerned with aging that provides technical consultation and is involved in federal legislative activities

Older American Volunteer Program federally sponsored volunteer program that recruits older people to work with disadvantaged groups

Older Women's League (OWL) a national organization, formed by Tish Sommers and Laurie Shields, concerned about issues affecting older women

Retired Senior Volunteer Program (RSVP) federally sponsored program in which older adults volunteer in schools, hospitals, and other social agencies

retirement the period of life, usually starting between age 60 and 65, during which an individual stops working in the paid labor force

Senior Community Services Employment Program (SCSEP) programs sponsored by government or business that encourage the employment of older workers

Senior Companion Program a volunteer program in which seniors assist other seniors

senior learning programs academic programs specially designed for older adults, or programs of tuition waivers that allow older adults to take college courses at no cost

Senior Net national educational program that teaches older adults computer skills and provides opportunities for on-line communication

serial retirement term to describe individuals who move in and out of the workforce

Service Corps of Retired Executives (SCORE) a program that links executives as technical and financial consultants with companies in the United States and abroad asking for assistance

Social Security federal program into which workers contribute a portion of their income during adulthood and then, beginning sometime between age 62 and 65, receive a monthly check based on the amount they have earned/contributed

spirituality believing in one's relationship with a higher power without being religious in the sense of organized religion

Supplemental Security Income (SSI) federal program to provide a minimal income for low-income older people (and other age groups with disabilities)

vesting of pension benefits amount of time a person must work on a job in order to acquire rights to a pension

RESOURCES

See the companion Website for this text at <www.ablongman.com/hooyman> for information about the following:

- Action
- American Association of Retired Persons (AARP)
- Elderhostel
- Federal Council on Aging
- Generations United
- Grey Panthers
- National Association of Retired Federal Employees
- National Council on the Aging Inc. (NCOA)
- National Council of Senior Citizens (NCSC)
- National Senior Citizens Education and Research Center (NSCERC)
- Service Corps of Retired Executives (SCORE)
- The Leadership Council of Aging Organizations

REFERENCES

Administration on Aging. *Profile of Older Americans: 1999.* Washington, DC: 1999.

Alwin, D. The political impact on the baby boom: Are there persistent generational differences in political beliefs and behaviors? *Generations,* Spring 1998, 22, 46–54.

American Association of Retired Persons (AARP). *Staying ahead of the curve: The AARP work and career study.* Washington DC: AARP, September 2002.

Atchley, R. C. *Aging: Continuity or change.* Belmont, CA: Wadsworth, 1983.

Atchley, R. C. Continuity of the spiritual self. In M. A. Kimble (Ed.), *Aging, spirituality, and religion: A handbook.* Minneapolis, MN: Fortress Press, 1995.

Atchley, R. C. Incorporating spirituality into professional work in aging. *Aging Today,* July/August 1999, 17.

Atchley, R. C. *The sociology of retirement.* New York: Wiley/Schenkman, 1976.

Barusch, A. S. Religion, adversity and age: Religious experiences of low income elderly women. *Journal of Sociology and Social Welfare,* March 1999, 26, 125–142.

Binstock, R. H. Some thoughts on a faith-based initiative in long-term care. *Public Policy and Aging Report,* 2002, *12,* 20–22.

Binstock, R. H. The 1996 election: Older voters and implications for policies on aging. *The Gerontologist,* 1997, *37,* 15–19.

Binstock, R. H. Older people and voting participation: past and future. *The Gerontologist,* 2000, *40,* 18–31.

Binstock, R. H. Older voters and the 1992 Presidential election. *The Gerontologist,* 1993, *32,* 601–606.

Binstock, R. H., and Day, C. L. Aging and politics. In R. H. Binstock and L. K. George (Eds.), *Handbook of aging and the social sciences.* San Diego, CA: Academic Press, 1996.

Binstock, R. H., and Quadagno, J. Aging and politics. In R. H. Binstock and L. K. George, *Aging and the social sciences* (pp. 333–350). San Diego: Academic Press, 2001.

Birren, J. Psychological implications of productive aging. In N. Morrow-Howell, J. Hinterlong, and M. Sherraden (Eds.), *Productive aging: Concepts and challenges* (5th ed.). Baltimore: Johns Hopkins University Press, 2001.

Black, H. K. Life as gift: Spiritual narratives of elderly African-American women living in poverty. *Journal of Aging Studies,* Winter 1999, *13,* 441–455.

Bossé, R., Aldwin, C. M., Levenson, M. R., and Workman-Daniel, D. How stressful is retirement? Findings from the normative aging study. *Journals of Gerontology,* 1991, *46,* 9–15.

Brooks, R. G., and Koenig, H. G. Having faith in an aging health system: Policy perspectives. *Public Policy and Aging Report,* 2002, *12,* 23–26.

Burke, K. J. *Health, mental health, and spirituality in chronically ill elders.* Dissertation Abstract, University of Chicago, 1999.

Burnes, J., and Schulz, J. H. *Older women and private pensions in the United States.* Waltham, MA: National Center on Women and Aging, 2000.

Calasanti, T. M., and Slevin, K. F. A gender lens on old age. In *Gender, social inequalities and aging.* Walnut Creek, CA: Altamira Press, 2001.

Campbell, A. Social and psychological determinants of voting behavior. In W. Donohue and C. Tibbits (Eds.), *Politics of age.* Ann Arbor: University of Michigan, 1962.

Caro, F. G., and Bass, S. A. Receptivity to volunteering in the immediate postretirement period. *Journal of Applied Gerontology,* 1997, *16,* 427–441.

Caro, F. G., Bass, S. A., and Chen, Y-P. Introduction: Achieving a productive aging society. In S. A. Bass, F. G. Caro, and Y-P Chen (Eds.), *Achieving a productive aging society.* Westport, CT: Auburn House, 1993.

Cascio, W. F. Learning from outcomes: Financial experiences of 300 firms that have downsized. In M. Growling, J. Kraft, and J. C. Quick (Eds.), *The new organizational reality: Downsizing, restructuring and revitalization.* Washington, DC: American Psychological Association, 1998.

Chatfield, D. L. Expectations of civic intrastructure in an age-restricted retirement community: Implications for community development. *Dissertation Abstracts International, A: The Humanities and Social Sciences,* 1999, *60,* 2250A–2251A.

Chatters, L. M., and Taylor, L. J. Religious involvement among older African-Americans. In J. S. Levin (Ed.), *Religion in aging and health: Theoretical foundations and methodological frontiers.* Thousand Oaks, CA: Sage, 1994.

Couch, K. A. Late life job displacement. *The Gerontologist,* 1998, *38,* 7–17.

Cutler, N. E., Whitelaw, N. A., and Beattie, B. L. *American perceptions of aging in the 21st century.* Washington DC: National Council on the Aging, Publication No. APA100, December 2002.

Cutler, S. J., and Hendricks, J. Age differences in voluntary association memberships: Fact or artifact. *Journal of Gerontology,* 2000, *55B,* S98–S107.

Danigelis, N. C., and McIntosh, B. R. Resources and the productive activity of elders: Race and gender as contexts. *Journals of Gerontology,* 1993, *48B,* S192–S203.

Day, C. L. The organized elderly: Perilous, powerless, or progressive. *The Gerontologist,* 1993, *33,* 426–427.

Dilworth-Anderson, P., Williams, S. W., and Cooper, T. Family caregiving to elderly African Americans: Caregiver types and structures. *Journals of Gerontology,* 1999, *54B,* S237–S241.

Dodson, D. The contingent workforce: Implications for today's and tomorrow's midlife and older women. *AARP Women's Initiative Fact Sheet,* 1996, D14561.

Drentea, P. The best or worst years of our lives? The effects of retirement and activity characteristics on well-being. *Dissertation Abstracts International, A: The Humanities and Social Sciences,* 1999, *60,* 1771A.

Ekerdt, D. J. The busy ethic: Moral continuity between work and retirement. *The Gerontologist,* 1986, *26,* 239–244.

Ekerdt, D. J., and DeViney, S. Evidence for a pre-retirement process among older male workers. *Journals of Gerontology,* 1993, *48B,* S35–S43.

Ekerdt, D. J., DeViney, S. S., and Kosloski, K. Profiling plans for retirement. *Journals of Gerontology,* 1996, *51B,* S140–S149.

Ekerdt, D. J., Kosloski, K., and DeViney, S. The normative anticipation of retirement by older workers. *Research on Aging,* 2000, *22,* 3–22.

Ellison, C. G., and Levin, J. S. The religion-health connection. Evidence, theory and future directions. *Health Education and Behavior,* 1998, *25,* 700–720.

Estes, C., and Mahakian, J. L. The political economy of productive aging. In N. Morrow-Howell, J. Hinterlong, and M. Sherraden (Eds.), *Productive aging: Concepts and challenges.* Baltimore: Johns Hopkins University Press, 2001.

Fallon, P. E. An ethnographic study: Personal meaning and successful aging of individuals 85 years and older. *Dissertation Abstracts International: Section B: The Sciences and Engineering,* Feb. 1998, *58.*

Federal Interagency Forum on Aging-related Statistics. *Older Americans 2000: Key indicators of well-being.* Washington, DC: Federal Interagency Forum, 2002.

Feher, S., and Maly, R. C. Coping with breast cancer in later life: The role of religious faith. *Psycho-Oncology,* Sept.-Oct. 1999, *8,* 408–416.

Fischer, L. R., and Schaffer, K. B. *Older Volunteers: A guide to research and practice.* Newbury Park, CA: Sage Publications, 1993.

Flippen, C., and Tienda, M. Pathways to retirement: Patterns of labor force participation and labor market exit among the pre-retirement population by race, Hispanic origin, and sex. *Journals of Gerontology,* 2000, *55B,* S14–S27.

Freedman, M. *Prime time: How baby boomers will revolutionize retirement and transform America.* New York: Public Affairs, 1999.

Freedman, M. Structural lead: Building new institutions for an aging America. In N. Morrow-Howell, J. Hinterlong, and M. Sherraden (Eds.), *Productive aging: Concepts and challenges.* Baltimore: Johns Hopkins University Press, 2001.

Gall, T. L., Evans, D. R., and Howard, J. The retirement adjustment process: Changes in the well-being of male retirees across time. *Journals of Gerontology,* 1995, *52B,* P110–P117.

Gallo, W. T., Bradley, E. H., Siegel, M., and Kasl, S. V. Health effects of involuntary job loss among older workers: Findings from the health and retirement survey. *Journals of Gerontology,* 2000, *55B,* S131–S140.

Gallup, G. J. The religiosity cycle. In *Gallup Tuesday briefing.* Retrieved July 1, 2002, from http://www.gallup.com/poll/tb/religValue/20020604.asp. June 2., 2002a.

Gallup, G. J., and Jones, J. *One hundred questions and answers: Religion in America.* Princeton, NJ: Princeton Research Center, 1989.

Gallup Poll. *Poll topics and trends: Religion.* Retrieved July 1, 2002, from http://www.gallup.com/poll/topics/religion2.asp. 2002, March 18–20, 2002b.

General Accounting Office (GAO). *Demographic trends pose challenges for employers and workers.* Publication No. GAO-02-85. Washington DC: GAO Office, November, 2001.

George, L. K. The links between religion and health: Are they real? *Public Policy and Aging Report,* 2002, *12,* 1, 3–6.

George, L. K., Larson, D. B., Koenig, H. G., and McCullough, M. E. Spirituality and health: What we know, what we need to know. *Journal of Social and Clinical Psychology,* 2000, *19,* 102–116.

Glass, J. C., Jr., and Kilpatrick, B. B. Financial planning for retirement: An imperative for baby boomer women. *Educational Gerontology,* Sept. 1998, *24,* 595–617.

Goyer, A. Intergenerational shared-site programs. *Generations,* Winter 1998–99, 79–80.

Gramlish, E. M. *Social Security in the 21st century.* The Nineteenth Leon and Josephine Winkelman Lecture Presentation, University of Michigan, 2000.

Hendricks, J., Hatch, L. R., and Cutler, S. J. Entitlements, social compacts, and the trend toward retrenchment in U.S. old-age programs. *Hallym International Journal of Aging,* 1999, *1,* 14–32.

Henretta, J. C. Changing perspectives on retirement. *Journals of Gerontology,* 1997, *52B,* S1–S3.

Herzog, A. R., and Morgan, J. N. Formal volunteer work among older Americans. In S. A. Bass, F. G. Caro, and Y-P. Chen (Eds.), *Achieving a productive aging society.* Westport, CT: Auburn House, 1993.

Hill, E. T. The labor force participation of older women: Retired? Working? Both? *Monthly Labor Review,* 2002 (September), 39–50.

Hinterlong, J., Morrow-Howell, N., and Sherraden, M. Productive aging: Principles and perspectives. In N. Morrow-Howell, J. Hinterlong, and M. Sherraden (Eds.), *Productive aging: Concepts and challenges.* Baltimore: Johns Hopkins University Press, 2001.

Hogan, R., and Perrucci, C. C. Producing and reproducing class and status differences: Racial and gender gaps in U.S. employment and retirement income. *Social Problems,* 1998, *45,* 528–549.

Hollingsworth, B. Retirees who don't. *Seattle Times,* November 10, 2002, p. H1.

Holstein, M. Women and productive aging: Troubling implications. In M. Minkler and C. L. Estes (Eds.), *Critical gerontology: Perspective from political and moral economy.* Amityville, NY: Baywood Publishers, 1999.

Hudson, R. B. Religion and health: Legal and policy implications. *Public Policy and Aging Report,* 2002, *12,* 2.

Idler, E. L. The many causal pathways linking religion to health. *Public Policy and Aging Report,* 2002, *12,* 7–12.

Idler, E. L., and Kasl, S. V. Religion among disabled and non-disabled persons in cross-sectional patterns in health practices, social activities, and well-being. *Journals of Gerontology: Social Sciences,* 1997, *52B,* S294–S305.

Idler, E. L., and Kasl, S. V. Religion among disabled and nondisabled persons: Attendance at religious services as a predictor of the course of disability. *Journals of Gerontology,* 1997, *52B,* S306–S316.

Independent Sector. *Giving and volunteering in the United States, 2001.* Washington, DC: Independent Sector, 2002.

Johnson, R. W., Sambamoorthi, U., and Crystal, S. Gender differences in pension wealth: Estimates using provider data. *The Gerontologist,* 1999, *39,* 320–333.

Juster, F. T., Soldo, B., Kingson, R. S., and Mitchell, O. *Aging well: Health, wealth, and retirement.* Washington, DC: Consertium of Social Science Associations, 1996.

Kasl, S. V., and Jones, B. A. The impact of job loss and retirement on health. In L. F. Berkman and I. Kawachi (Eds.), *Social epidemiology.* New York: Oxford University Press, 2000.

Katz, S. Busy bodies. Activity, aging and the management of every day life. *Journal of Aging Studies,* 2000, *14,* 135–52.

Kavanaugh, K. M. The importance of spirituality. *Journal of Long-Term Care Administration,* 1997, *24,* 29–31.

Kessler, R. C., Mickelson, K. D., and Williams, D. R. The prevalence, distribution, and mental health correlates of perceived discrimination in the United States. *Journal of Health and Social Behavior,* 1999, *40,* 208–230.

Kingson, E. R., and Williamson, J. B. Economic security policies. *Handbook of aging and the social sciences* (5th ed.). San Diego: Academic Press, 2001.

Koenig, H. G. *Aging and God: Spiritual pathways to mental health in midlife and later years.* New York: Haworth Pastoral Press, 1995.

Koenig, H. G. *Is religion good for your health? Effects of religion on mental and physical health.* New York: Haworth Press, 1997.

Koenig, H. G. An 83-year-old woman with chronic illness and strong religious beliefs. *Journal of the American Medical Association,* 2002, *288,* 487–493.

Koenig, H. G., and Brooks, R. G. Religion, health, and aging: Implications for practice and public policy. *Public Policy and Aging Report,* 2002, *12,* 13–19.

Koenig, H. G., George, L. K., and Peterson, B. L. Religiosity and remission of depression in medically ill older patients. *American Journal of Psychiatry,* 1998, *155,* 536–542.

Koenig, H. G., McCullough, M. E., and Larson, D. B. *Handbook of religion and health.* New York: Oxford University Press, 2001.

Koenig, H. G., Pargament, K. I., and Nielsen, J. Religious coping and health status in medically ill hospitalized older adults. *Journal of Nervous and Mental Disease,* Sept. 1998b, *186,* 513–521.

Krause, N. Religiosity and self-esteem among older adults. *Journals of Gerontology,* 1995, *50B,* P236–P246.

Krause, N. Religious meaning and subjective well-being in late life. *Journals of Gerontology,* 2003, *58B,* 3, S160–S170.

Krause, N., Ingersoll-Dayton, B., Liang, J., and Sugisawa, H. Religion, social support and health among Japanese elderly. *Journal of Health and Human Behavior,* 1999, *40,* 405–421.

Levin, J. S., Chatters, L. M., and Taylor, R. J. Religious effects on health status and life satisfaction among Black Americans. *Journals of Gerontology,* 1995, *50B,* S154–S169.

Levin, J. S., and Taylor, R. J. Age differences in patterns and correlates of the frequency of prayer. *The Gerontologist,* 1997, *37,* 75–88.

Levin, J. S., Taylor, R. J., and Chatters, L. M. Race and gender differences in religiosity among older adults: Findings from four national surveys. *Journals of Gerontology,* 1994, *49,* S137–S145.

Mattis, J. S., and Jagers, R. J. A relational framework for the study of religiosity and spirituality in the lives of African Americans. *Journal of Community Psychology,* 2001, *29,* 519–539.

McCrea, J. M., Nichols, A., and Newman, S. (Eds.). *Intergenerational service-learning in gerontology: A compendium.* The Corporation for National Service, Generations Together, University Center for Social and Urban Research, University of Pittsburgh, 1998.

McCullough, M. E., Hoyt, W. T., Larson, D. B., Koenig, H. G., and Thoresen, C. Religious involvement and morality: A meta-analytic review. *Health Psychology,* 2001, *20,* 228–229.

McLaughlin, D. K., and Jensen, L. Work history and U.S. elders' transitions into poverty. *The Gerontologist,* 2000, *40,* 469–479.

McManus, S. A., and Tenpas, K. D. The changing political activism patterns of older Americans: "Don't throw dirt over us yet." In J. S. Steckenrider and T. M. Parrott (Eds.), *New directions in old-age policies.* Albany: State University of New York Press, 1998.

Miller, W. R., and Thoresen, C. E. Spirituality, religion, and health: An emerging research field. *American Psychologist,* 2003, *58,* 3–66.

Mitchell, O. S., and Moore, J. F. Can Americans afford to retire? New evidence on retirement saving adequacy. *The Journal of Risk and Insurance,* 1998, *65,* 371–400.

Moen, P. The gendered life course. In R. Binstock and L. K. George, *Aging and the social sciences.* San Diego: Academic Press, 2001.

Moen, P. *Retirement and well-being: Does community participation replace paid work?* American Sociological Association, 1999.

Moen, P., Fields, V., Quick, H. E., and Hofmeister, H. A life course approach to retirement and social integration. In K. Pillemer, P. Moen, N. Glasgow, and E. Wethington (Eds.), *Social Integration in the Second Half of Life.* Baltimore, MD: Johns Hopkins University Press, 2000.

Moen, P., Kim, J., and Hofmeister, H. Couple's work status transitions and marriage quality in late midlife. *Social Psychology Quarterly,* 2001, *64,* 55–71.

Moody, H. R. Productive aging and the ideology of old age. In N. Morrow-Howell, J. Hinterlong, and M. Sherraden (Eds.), *Productive aging: Concepts and challenges.* Baltimore: Johns Hopkins University Press, 2001a.

Moody, H. R. What is the future for Social Security? In H. R. Moody, *Aging concepts and controversies.* Thousand Oaks, CA: Pine Forge Press, 2001b.

Mor-Barak, M., and Tynson, M. Older workers and the workplace: A new challenge for occupational social work. *Social Work,* 1993, *38,* 45–55.

Morrow-Howell, N., Hinterlong, J., Rozario, P., and Tang, F. The effects of volunteering on the well-being of older adults. *Journal of Gerontology,* 2003, *58B,* S137–S146.

Morrow Howell, N., Hinterlong, J., and Sherraden, M. W. *Productive Aging: Concepts and Challenges.* Baltimore, MD: Johns Hopkins University Press, 2001.

Musick, M. A. Theodicy and life satisfaction among Black and White Americans. *Sociology of Religion,* 2000, *61,* 267–287.

Musick, M. A., Herzog, A. R., and House, J. S. Volunteering and mortality among older adults: Findings from a national sample. *Journals of Gerontology,* 1999, *54B,* S173–S180.

Mutchler, J. E., Burr, J. A., Massagli, M. P., and Pienta, A. Work transitions and health in later life. *Journals of Gerontology,* 1999, *54B,* S252–S261.

Mutchler, J. E., Burr, J. A., Pienta, A. M., and Massagli, M. P. Pathways to labor force exit: Work transitions and work instability. *Journals of Gerontology,* 1997, *52B,* S4–S12.

National Academy on an Aging Society. *Who are young retirees and older workers?* Data Profile. Washington, DC, June 2000.

National Center for Policy Analysis. *2003 Annual report of the Board of Trustees of the Federal Old-age and Survivors Insurance Trust Funds.* Washington, DC, 2003.

National Committee to Preserve Social Security and Medicare. *Facts on SSI.* Washington, DC, 2003.

National Research Council. *Preparing for an aging world: The case for cross-national research.* Washington DC: National Academy Press, 2001.

Nordquist, G. 1999. American health care and the medicalization of dying. *Journal of Applied Social Sciences*, 1999, *23*, 31–42.

Okada, S. Health and earned income: Recursive and non-recursive models. *Dissertation Abstracts International, Section A: Humanities and Social Sciences*, 1997, *58(3-A)*, 1095.

Older Women's League. *Social Security privatization: A false promise for women*. Washington, DC: Older Women's League, 2002.

Oman, D., and Thoresen, C. E. Does religion cause health? Different interpretations and diverse meanings. *Journal of Health Psychology*, 2002, *4*, 301–326.

Oman, D., Thoresen, C. E., and McMahon, K. Volunteerism and mortality among the community-dwelling elderly. *Journal of Health Psychology*, 1999, *4*, 301–316.

Ozawa, M. N. *The economic well-being of the elderly in a changing society*. The Seventeenth Annual Leon and Josephine Winkelman Lecture, Ann Arbor: University of Michigan, School of Social Work, December 2, 1996.

Pargament, K. I., Smith, B. W., Koenig, H. G., and Perez, L. Patterns of positive and negative religious coping with major life stressors. *Journal for the Scientific Study of Religion*, 1998, *37*, 710–724.

Park, N. H., and Gilbert, N. Social Security and the incremental privatization of retirement income. *Journal of Sociology and Social Welfare*, 1999, *26*, 187–202.

Pear, R. Senator challenges the practices of a retirees association. *New York Times*, p. A14, June 14, 1995.

Peter D. Hart Research Associates. *Older Americans and volunteerism*. New York: Peter D. Hart Research Associates, 2002.

Quadagno, J., and Hardy, M. Work and retirement. In R. H. Binstock and L. K. George (Eds.), *Handbook of aging and the social sciences* (4th ed.). San Diego, CA: Academic Press, 1996.

Quick, H., and Moen, P. Gender, employment and retirement quality: A life course approach to the differential experiences of men and women. *Journal of Occupational Health Psychology*, 1998, *3*, 44–64.

Quinn, J. F., and Burkhauser, R. V. Labor market obstacles to aging productively. In S. A. Bass, F. G. Caro, and Y-P Chen (Eds.), *Achieving a productive aging society*. Westport, CT: Auburn House, 1993.

Rank, M. R., and Hirschl, T. A. Estimating the proportion of Americans ever experiencing poverty during their elderly years. *Journals of Gerontology*, 1999, *54B*, S184–S193.

Reitzes, D. C., Mutran, E. J., and Fernandez, M. E. The decision to retire: A career perspective. *Social Science Quarterly*, 1998, *79*, 607–619.

Reitzes, D.C., Mutran, E. J., and Fernandez, E. Pretirement influences on post-retirement self-esteem. *Journals of Gerontology*, 1996, *51B*, S242–S249.

Richardson, V. E. How circumstances of widowhood and retirement affect adjustment among older men. *Journal of Mental Health and Aging*, Summer 1999, *5*, 165–174.

Riddick, C., and Stewart, D. An examination of the life satisfaction and importance of leisure in the lives of older female retirees: A comparison of blacks to whites. *Journal of Leisure Research*, 1994, *26*, 75–87.

Rix, S. E. The politics of old age in the United States. In A. Walker and G. Naegele (Eds.), *The politics of old age in Europe*. Buckingham, PA: Open University Press, 1999.

Ross, C. E., and Drentea, P. Consequences of retirement activities for distress and the sense of personal control. *Journal of Health and Social Behavior*, Dec. 1998, *39*, 317–334.

Settersten, R. A., Jr. Time, age, and the transition to retirement: New evidence on life course flexibility? *International Journal of Aging and Human Development*, 1998, *47*, 177–203.

Sherraden, M., Morrow-Howell, N., Hinterlong, J., and Rozario, P. Productive aging: Theoretical choices and directions. In N. Morrow-Howell, J. Hinterlong, and M. Sherraden (Eds.), *Productive aging: Concepts and challenges*. Baltimore: Johns Hopkins University Press, 2001.

Simon-Rusinowitz, L., Wilson, L., Marks, L., Kroch, C., and Welch, C. Future work and retirement needs: Policy experts and baby boomers express their views. *Generations*, Spring 1998, *22*, 34–40.

Smith, J. P. *The changing economic circumstances of the elderly: Income wealth and Social Security*. Syracuse, NY: Maxwell School Center for Policy Research, 1997b.

Smith, J. P. Wealth inequality among older Americans. *Journals of Gerontology*, Special Issue, 1997a, *52B*, S74–81.

Social Security Administration. *Income of the population 55 or older*. Washington, DC: Social Security Administration Office of Research and Statistics, 1998.

Spors, K. K., and Fialka, J. J. Federal work force faces retirement bubble, personnel shortfall. *Wall Street Journal*, September, 19, 2002, p. A4.

Stafford, D. Aging employee pool posing challenges. *Terre Haute Tribune-Star*, September 3, 2001, p. E10.

Street, D. Special interests or citizens' rights? Senior power, Social Security, and Medicare. In M. Minkler and C. L. Estes (Eds.), *Critical gerontology: Perspectives from political and moral economy*. Amityville, NY: Baywood Publishing Company, 1999.

Streib, G., and Schneider, C. J. *Retirement in American society. Impact and process*. Ithaca, NY: Cornell University Press, 1971.

Szinovacz, M. E., and DeViney, S. The retiree identity: Gender and race differences. *Journals of Gerontology*, 1999, *54B*, S207–S218.

Taylor, M., and Shore, L. M. Predictors of planned retirement age: An application of Baehr's model. *Psychology and Aging*, 1995, *10*, 76–83.

Thomson, D. Generations, justice and the future of collective action. In P. Laslett and J. Fishkin (Eds.), *Philosophy, politics and society, Relations between age groups and generations*. New Haven, CT: Yale University Press, *Vol. VI*: 1993.

Tinsley, H., Teaff, J., Colbs, S., and Kaufman, N. A system of classifying leisure activities in terms of the psychological benefits of participation reported by older persons. *Journals of Gerontology*, 1985, *40*, 172–178.

Toner, R. Parties see older Americans as a critical swing vote in 2000. National Politics, *New York Times*, May 31, 1999, http://members.cox.netfweil/NYT053199.html.

Torres-Gil, F. M. Interest group politics: Generational changes in the politics of aging. In V. L. Bengtson and W. A. Achenbaum (Eds.), *The changing contract across generations*. New York: Aldine de Gruyter.

U.S. Census Bureau. *Annual demographic supplement. Current Population Survey*. Washington, DC: U.S. Government Printing Office, March 2002.

U.S. Census Bureau. *The older population in the United States: March 2002. Current Population Reports*, No. P20-546: Washington, DC: U.S. Government Printing Office, April 2003.

U.S. Census Bureau. *Poverty in the United States, 1999*. Washington, DC: September 2000.

U.S. Census Bureau. *Poverty in the United States, 2002. Current Population Reports*. Washington, DC: U.S. Government Printing Office, 2003b.

Van Willigen, M. Differential benefits of volunteering across the life course. *The Journals of Gerontology*, 2000, *55B*, No. 5. pp. S308–S319.

Verbrugge, L., Gruber-Baldini, A. C., and Fozard, J. L. Age differences and age changes in activities: Baltimore Longitudinal Study of Aging. *Journals of Gerontology*, 1996, S30–S41.

Wagner, D. L. Senior center research in America: An overview of what we know. In D. Shollenberger, *Senior centers in America*. Washington, DC: The National Council on the Aging, 1995.

Walker, A. Age and employment. *Australian Journal on Ageing*, 1998, *17*, 99–103.

Walker, A. Political participation and representation of older people. In A. Walker and G. Naegel (Eds.), *The politics of old age in Europe*. Philadelphia: Open University Press, 1999.

Warburton, J., LeBrocque, R., and Rosenman, L. Older people—The reserve army of volunteers?: An analysis of volunteerism among older Australians. *International Journal of Aging and Human Development*, 1998, *46*, 229–245.

Wheeler, J. A., Gorey, K. M., and Greenblatt, B. The beneficial effects of volunteering for older volunteers and the people they serve: A metaanalysis. *International Journal of Aging and Human Development*, 1998, *47*, 69–79.

Wilson, J. Volunteering. *Annual Review of Sociology*, 2000, *26*, 215–240.

Wink, P., and Dillon, M. Religious involvement and health outcomes in late adulthood: Findings from a longitudinal study of women and men. In T. G. Plante and A. C. Sherman (Eds.), *Faith and health: Psychological perspectives*. New York: Guildford Press, 2001.

Young, M. B. *The aging and retiring government workforce: How serious is the challenge?* Lexington, MA: Linkage, Inc. Center for Organizational Research, 2003.

Zinnbauer, B. J., Pargament, K. I., Cowell, B. J., Rye, M., and Scott, A. B. Religion and spirituality: Unfuzzing the fuzzy. *Journal for the Scientific Study of Religion*, 1997, *38*, 412–423.

13

Death, Dying, Bereavement, and Widowhood

You have probably heard of people who "lost their will to live" or "died when they were ready." Such ideas are not simply superstitions. Similar to other topics addressed throughout this book, death involves an interaction of physiological, social, and psychological factors. The social context is illustrated by the fact that all cultures develop beliefs and practices regarding death in order to minimize its disruptive effects on the social structure. These cultural practices influence how members of a particular society react to their own death and that of others. Although measures of death are physical, such as the absence of heartbeat or brain waves, psychosocial factors, such as the will to live, can influence the biological event. For instance, terminally ill people have been found to die shortly after an important engagement, such as a child's wedding, a family reunion, or a holiday, suggesting that their social support systems, enthusiasm for life, and "will to live" prolonged life to that point (McCue, 1995). How people approach their own death and that of others is closely related to personality styles, sense of competence, coping skills, and social supports, as discussed in Chapter 6.

The Changing Context of Dying

In our culture, dying is associated primarily with old age. Although we all know that aging does not cause death, and younger people also die, there are a number of reasons for this association. The major factors are medical advances and increased life expectancy. In pre-industrial societies, death rates were high in childhood and youth, and parents could expect that one-third to one-half of their children would die before the age of 10. Most deaths now arise from chronic disease. This means that it is increasingly the old who die, making death predictable as a function of age. Death has thus come to be viewed as a timely event, the completion of the life cycle in old age.

Others view death not only as the province of the old, but also as an unnatural event that is to be fought off as long as medically possible. In this sense, death has become medicalized, distorted from a natural event into the end point of untreatable or inadequately treated disease or injury. Prior to the 1900s, the period of time spent dying was relatively short, due to infectious diseases and catastrophic events. With improved diagnostic techniques and early detection, individuals are living for longer periods of time with terminal illnesses. At the end of a prolonged illness, when medicine may care for but not cure the patient, dying may seem more unnatural than if the person had been allowed to die earlier in the progression of the disease. With expanded technological mastery over the conditions of dying, chronically ill people have often been kept alive long beyond the point at which they might have died naturally in the past. As noted by Callahan (1993), achieving a peaceful death is difficult because of the complexity in drawing a clear line between living and dying—which is partially a result of technology and of societal and professional ambivalence about whether to fight or accept death.

The surroundings in which death occurs have also changed with increased medical interventions. In preindustrial societies, most people died at home, with the entire community often involved in rituals surrounding the death. Now approximately 75 percent of all deaths occur in institutions where aggressive treatment is common, generally in hospitals and nursing homes, and with only a few relatives and friends present. The majority of dying patients, regardless of age, experience severe, undertreated pain, and nearly 40 percent spend at least 10 days in an intensive care unit. This is the case even though most people express a preference to die at home, without pain, surrounded by friends and family (Preston, 2000; Wilkinson and Lynn, 2001).

Attitudes toward Death

More insulated from death than in the past, most people are uncomfortable with talking about it, especially the prospect of their own death. This discomfort is shown even in the euphemisms people use—"sleep, pass away, rest"—instead of the word "death" itself. Freud, in fact, recognized that although death was natural, undeniable, and unavoidable, people behaved as though it would occur only to others; that is, "they" will die, but not "me." Fear of death is an ongoing anxiety in everyday life, in contrast to a more acute fear stimulated by an immediate threat to one's life (Cicirelli, 1999). Fear and denial are natural and comforting responses to our inability to comprehend our own death and lack of physical existence. Such fear tends to make death a taboo topic in our society. Although in recent years death has become a more legitimate topic for scientific and social discussion, most people talk about it on a rational, intellectual level rather than discuss and prepare for their own deaths or those of loved ones. When diagnosed with a terminal illness, nearly 30 percent of patients remain in denial, and 15 percent in fear (Butler, 2000).

POINTS TO PONDER

Do you talk about death, your own or others, with someone else? If so, whom do you talk with? What kinds of concerns, fears, hopes, or questions do you express? How comfortable are you in talking about death? What might increase your feelings of comfort?

Whether people's fear of death is natural or learned is unclear. When asked what they fear most about death, respondents mention suffering and pain, loss of their body and personality, loss of self-control, concern over an afterlife and the unknown, loneliness, and the effect on survivors. In general, people fear the inability to predict what the future might bring (e.g., fear of the unknown afterlife, of nonexistence) and the process of dying, particularly of a painful death, more than death itself (Cicirelli, 1999). Generally, older patients tend to choose *quality* of life in their end-of-life decision-making, while younger patients tend to select *quantity* of life. Older African Americans, however, are the least likely to employ advanced directives and more likely to want life-saving technology (Fauser, 1999). When questioned directly, people typically are more concerned with the death of close friends and family than with their own, and generally express an acceptance of their own death. Although the validity of responses to questions about one's own death is difficult to ascertain, it appears that most people both deny and accept the reality of dying. These ambivalent views reflect the basic paradox surrounding death, in which we recognize its universality, but cannot comprehend or imagine our own dying. Dying is one of the few events in life certain to occur, but not one for which we plan.

Variation by Age and Gender

Multiple factors, particularly age, previous experience with the death of a loved one, and gender but not health status, influence socioemotional responses to death and dying. Younger women tend to express significantly greater fear than older women regarding both their own death and the death of others. Older women more often report anxiety and fear of dying, but less fear of the unknown than their male counterparts, although this may reflect gender differences in religiosity and socialization, and greater ability to express emotions such as fear (Wilkinson and Lynn, 2001). Findings are mixed regarding fear of death among older adults compared with younger persons (Cicirelli, 1999; Wilkinson and Lynn, 2001). In general, older people think and talk more about death and appear to be less afraid of their own death than are younger people; they are concerned about a painful death, loss of control, and the uncertainty of an afterlife. When they face "unfinished business," however, they are more likely to fear death (Thorson, Powell, and Samuel, 1998a, 1998b). Regardless of age, the most universal fear is concern over an afterlife—the possibility of either no afterlife or a threatening one (Cicirelli, 1999).

A number of factors may explain this apparent paradox of a lessened fear of death in the face of its proximity. Having internalized society's views, older people may see their lives as having ever-decreasing social value, thereby lowering their own positive expectation of the future. If they have lived past the age they expected to, they may view themselves as living on "borrowed time." A painless death tends to be viewed as preferable to deteriorating physically and mentally and being socially useless or a burden on family. In addition, dealing with their friends' deaths, especially in age-segregated retirement communities or nursing homes, can help socialize older people toward an acceptance of their own. Experiencing death and other losses more fre-

POINTS TO PONDER

We spend more time planning for a 2-week vacation than we will for our last 2 weeks of life. What factors might explain this?

Spirituality is a source of strength for many older adults.

quently, they are more likely to think and talk in a matter-of-fact way about death on a regular basis and to develop realistic and effective means of coping, including humor, than are younger people (Ingebretsen and Solem, 1998; Lamberg, 2002). Many older people are already experiencing "bereavement overload" through the increased frequency of family and friends' deaths, and thus worry less about the impact of their death on others (Thorson, Powell, and Samuel, 1998a, 1998b). On the other hand, sustained family contacts tend to create a greater desire to prolong life (Mutran et al., 1997). Elders who achieve the developmental stage of ego integrity, as described in our discussion of Erikson in Chapter 6, and engage in life review are generally able to resolve conflicts and relieve anxiety, becoming more accepting of death as fair and a release.

Older adults confronting death often turn inward to contemplation, reminiscence, reading, or spiritual activities. The awareness of one's mortality can stimulate a need for the "legitimization of biography," to find meaning in one's life and death. People who successfully achieve such legitimization experience a new freedom and relaxation about the future and tend to hold favorable attitudes toward death. Many older people consider a sudden death to be more tragic than a slow one, desiring time to see loved ones, say good-bye, settle their affairs, and reminisce. Older people generally can accept the inevitability of their own death, even though they tend to be concerned about the death of relatives.

It is unclear whether variability in the acceptance of death is due to age or to cohort differences. For example, the current cohort of older people has fewer years of formal schooling than younger generations, a factor that affects attitudes toward death. The interactive effects of other variables with age need to be further probed. For instance, in all age groups the most religious persons who hold the greatest belief in an afterlife have less anxiety about dying (Sullivan et al., 1998). For the religious, they have less fear of the unknown and view death as the doorway to a better state of being. Those most fearful about death are irregular participants in formal religious activities, or those intermediate in their religiosity whose belief systems may be confused and uncertain or those whose religious motivation is extrinsically rather than intrinsically motivated (Cicirelli, 1999; Clements, 1998). Religion apparently can either comfort or create anxiety about an afterlife, but it provides some individuals with one way to try to make sense of death. The age of the person who died is also a factor in

---

POINTS TO PONDER

What thoughts, feelings, or images do you experience when you hear that a baby has died? What about the death of a young adult just graduating from college? A 50-year-old mother just starting her new career? An 80-year-old who has advanced dementia? A 79-year-old who is hit by a car while crossing the street? What variables or factors might explain differences in your reactions?

how survivors react to death. Because the death of older people is often anticipated, it may be viewed as a "blessing" for someone whose "time has come" rather than as a tragic experience.

The Dying Process

As noted earlier, most older people do not fear being dead as much as the painful process of dying. The **stages of dying,** one of the most widely known and classic frameworks for understanding the dying process, was advanced by Kübler-Ross (1969, 1981). Each stage represents a form of coping with the process of death.

The five stages of grief are a widely known and debated classic framework applied to both the dying and their survivors. Kübler-Ross (1969, 1981) identified the stages of:

1. shock and denial
2. anger ("why me?", resentment, and guilt)
3. bargaining, such as trying to make a deal with God
4. depression and withdrawal from others
5. adjustment/acceptance

Although Kübler-Ross cautioned that these stages were not invariant, immutable, or universal, she nevertheless implied that dying persons need to complete each stage before moving onto the next. She encouraged health care providers to help their patients to advance through them to achieve the final stage. This perspective, sometimes misused with the dying and the bereaved and widely debated, has been empirically rejected. Family members and health care providers must be cautious about implying that the dying person must move through these stages, and thus creating an illusion of control or what one "should do." Grief is more "messy" than sequential stages. Grieving does not proceed in a linear fashion but reappears again and again to be reworked, and the emotional reactions to dying vary greatly (Neimeyer, 1998; Walter, 2003). In fact, sequencing may not occur at all; rather, feelings of guilt, protest, anger, fearfulness, and despair can intermesh with humor, hope, acceptance, and gratitude, with the dying person moving back and forth between them. Alternatively, some people remain at one of the first stages of denial or anger, while others move readily into acceptance (Buckman, 1999; Weiss, 2001). What is most important is that family and health care providers create choices and supports for the dying person, without making judgments about "the right way to die." In all instances, cross-cultural variations in how dying is experienced and grief expressed need to be attended to.

Other models conceptualize dying and grief as *tasks* (Worden, 2002), *phases,* or *processes* (Rando, 1993). A process perspective recognizes the alternating currents of emotion, thought, and behavior, which individuals move through at varying rates, oscillating through some emotions multiple times. Phases of the grieving process are conceptualized as:

1. *Avoidance:* shock, numbness, disbelief, and denial, all of which can function as buffers from the painful reality, especially when first learning that one is dying; fear, anxiety and dread; feelings of unreality, disorganization, and not being able to comprehend the situation; trying to gain some control and understanding by gathering facts of what happened. Some dying individuals surround themselves with as many people as possible, while others isolate themselves.
2. *Confrontation:* guilt; blaming self or others; rage; feelings of being overwhelmed and losing control; helplessness, panic, confusion, and powerlessness; the diffused energy of unfocused anger and despair, loss of faith, sense of injustice, or disillusionment; intense sadness.
3. *Accommodation:* acceptance of the reality of death, saying good-byes, and gradually letting go of the physical world.

Although agreement now exists that there is no "typical," unidirectional way to die through pro-

"Once you learn how to die, you learn how to live" (Moyers and Moyers, 2000).

gressive stages, Kübler-Ross's controversial work was a pioneering catalyst; it increased public and professional awareness of death and the needs of the dying and their caregivers. Her framework can be a helpful cognitive grid or guideline, not a fixed sequence that determines a "good death." Another contribution was her emphasis on dying as a time of growth and profound spirituality. By accepting death's inevitability, dying persons can use life meaningfully and productively and come to terms with who they really are. Since the dying are "our best teachers," those who work with them can learn from them and emerge with fewer anxieties about their own death (Kübler-Ross, 1969, 1975).

Consistent with the framework of dynamic interactions discussed throughout this book, the process of dying is shaped by:

- an individual's own personality, resilience, and philosophy of life
- the specific illness
- the social context (e.g., whether at home surrounded by family who encourage the expression of feelings, or isolated in a hospital)
- the cultural context: values, beliefs, shared meanings, and rituals

End-of-Life Care

The concept of the dying process highlights the importance of the ways in which end-of-life care is provided. As noted earlier, although most dying people prefer to be at home, the common practice has been to hospitalize them, with most deaths occurring in hospital intensive care units or, in the case of older people, nursing homes (Butler, 2000; Last Acts, 2002). Rather than death as sudden from accident or infection, it is now the culmination of years with chronic illness, such as dementia, congestive heart failure, or cancer. The

majority of older people die of chronic disease, and often suffer debilitating symptoms such as nausea, delirium, or severe pain. Since medicine focuses on treating the disease, physicians and families may see death as a defeat, not an inevitable culmination. The traditional problem-oriented model of health care that emphasizes life-enhancing therapies falls short in guiding end-of-life care. What is necessary is for more people to abandon rescue medicine, when the hope of a cure is miniscule, and to seek comfort care.

Because of traditional medicine's emphasis on cure, most patients and families find that care provided at the end of life is inappropriate or unwanted. SUPPORT (Study to Understand Prognoses and Preferences for Outcomes and Risks of Treatment), funded by the Robert Wood Johnson Foundation, was the largest study ever to examine the care of seriously ill and dying patients. It found that patients and their physicians did not routinely make plans for end-of-life care or for how to address predictable complications, nor did they discuss the overall course and aims of care. Patients most often died in pain and in intensive care for long time periods, with their families financially devastated by efforts to keep their loved one alive. Even in illnesses with a predictable course, physicians often considered an order to forgo resuscitation only in the patients' last few days (Christopher, 2003; Kaufmann, 2002).

POINTS TO PONDER

If you have experienced the dying process of someone close to you or for whom you provided care, what phases did you observe? Did you observe the dying process as flowing, alternating between different stages, or rather unidirectional? Did the person ever reach the stage of acceptance? How did you know?

Medical experts agree that at least 90 percent of all serious pain can be effectively treated, yet at least 50 percent of dying patients report being in pain (Last Acts, 2002). The pain of dying is intensified by the fact that terminal patients often experience clinical depression, delirium, anxiety, despair, helplessness, hopelessness, anticipatory grief, and guilt. Both depression and delirium are underdiagnosed in older patients, yet they are treatable causes of suffering at the end of life. The prevalence of clinical depression increases with the severity of the illness, active disease, inpatient status, physical discomfort, and limitations related to symptoms or treatment (Vachon, 1999). Yet depression is often dismissed as a natural reaction of sadness and grief from knowing that one's life is ending. When left untreated, depression causes significant emotional harm and suffering, reduces patients' ability to fully participate in life and comply with medical treatments, and can contribute to other medical problems (Wilkinson and Lynn, 2001). The incidence of depression is perhaps not surprising, given findings that older patients with cancer, for example, have less symptom management than other age groups. One study found that 25 percent of nursing home cancer patients who reported daily pain received no analgesia; in addition, patients age 85 and over, and ethnic minority patients were more likely to receive no analgesia (Bern et al., 1998). Although older patients have higher levels of untreated symptoms, there is limited information on pain and drug therapy among this group, and elders are often excluded from research trials and studies on pain management (Wilkinson and Lynn, 2001).

The **Dying Person's Bill of Rights,** developed over 20 years ago, states that individuals have the right to personal dignity and privacy; informed participation, including to have their end-of-life choices respected by health care professionals; and considerate, respectful service and competent care. As highlighted below, the **right to die** with dignity and without pain, rather than to endure

> ### A "GOOD" DEATH
>
> The Institute of Medicine Committee on Care at End of Life defined a "good death" as one that is:
>
> - free from avoidable distress and suffering for patients, families, and caregivers
> - in general accord with patients' and families' wishes
> - reasonably consistent with clinical, cultural, and ethical standards (Field and Cassel, 1997)

prolonged suffering through life extension, is currently emphasized more than it was at the time the Dying Person's Bill of Rights was first introduced. Although controversy surrounds the use of life-sustaining technology, both sides agree that the dying person's self-determination and right to be free from physical pain are essential to humane care. As articulated by the Ethics Committee of the American Geriatrics Society (1996), dying persons should be provided with opportunities to make the circumstances of their dying consistent with their preferences and lifestyles.

The U.S. Supreme Court ruled in 1997 that Americans have a constitutional right to palliative care. **Palliative care** focuses not on lifesaving measures, but on relief of pain and other physical symptoms by addressing the patient's emotional, social, and spiritual needs. Physicians, nurses, and social workers use both pharmacological and psychosocial approaches to cope with symptoms and needs. The box on page 487 differentiates pain management, hospice care, and formalized palliative care. Pain management is a major component of such care.

With palliative care, both the patient and health care providers recognize that, although the disease cannot be cured, quality of life can be enhanced. It does not treat the terminally ill patient as on the brink of death. And it neither hastens nor postpones death. Instead, it simply recognizes that life can be meaningful and rewarding even with a diagnosis of a terminal illness (Payne, 2000). Listening to music, art therapy, and reminiscence through photos and mementos may all be encouraged as a way to add enjoyment and meaning at the end-of-life. Such care is characterized by respect for the patient's own values and choices about privacy and end-of-life care, candid and sensitive communication, encouragement to express feelings, and a multidisciplinary team approach. The social support of friends and family can be a major source of strength and enhance the quality of the dying process. Improved tools for

---

FACING DEATH ON YOUR OWN TERMS

Ruth, age 85, was diagnosed with incurable cancer. She told her family and doctor that she wanted to live long enough (5 months) to see her first grand-daughter married. Her doctor arranged for low-dose chemotherapy that did not cause much discomfort, and she experienced a remission. After her grand-daughter's wedding, the doctors found that the cancer had returned and spread. Her response was that she was now ready to die. She received excellent palliative care, lived three months without pain through morphine, and was alert almost to the end, sharing memories and saying good-bye to her family.

TYPES OF PAIN AND PALLIATIVE CARE SERVICES AS DEFINED BY THE AMERICAN HOSPITAL ASSOCIATION

- **Pain management:** a formal program that educates staff about how to manage chronic and acute pain based on accepted academic guidelines.
- **Hospice:** a program providing palliative care and supportive services that address the emotional, social, financial, and legal needs of terminally ill patients and their families.
- **Palliative care program:** a program providing specialized medical care, drugs, or therapies to manage acute or chronic pain and to control other symptoms. The program, run by specially trained physicians and other clinicians, also provides services such as counseling about advance directives, spiritual care, and social services to seriously ill patients and their families.

Although the number of organized palliative care programs in hospitals is increasing beyond the 14 percent identified in 2002, they still are far from the norm and do not easily fit into the coverage and payment policies of Medicare and other insurers. Funding for these programs often depends on piecing together resources from different funding streams, including short-term grants. This funding pattern thus jeopardizes existing formal palliative care programs (Last Acts, 2002).

---

prognosis and to measure quality of life at its last stages are needed to document the effectiveness of palliative care and to enhance such care, however (Teno, 1999).

Medical professionals are more open in talking about death with their patients and families than in the past. Most now believe that dying persons have the right to know their condition and prognosis and to have some control over their death, although they also acknowledge they are not adequately prepared to minimize the suffering of the dying (Christ and Sormanti, 1999). Increasingly, the pursuit of a peaceful, pain-free death is viewed as the proper goal of medicine, even though less agreement exists on how this is to be achieved (e.g., how aggressively pain-killing narcotics should be used). This breaking of "professional silence" is in part a reaction to external pressures, including growing public support for physicians to provide aggressive pain control and palliative care along with patients who insist on having some control over their dying.

Some physicians still wrongly assume that they will be censured or prosecuted for giving controlled substances to the terminally ill, even when the controlled drug is the approved treatment. In fact, the Supreme Court has cited two legal methods for more aggressive pain management:

1. the "morphine drip," a continuous administration of morphine at a dose that will abolish pain, and if that is not effective,
2. physician-prescribed "terminal sedation" with barbiturates and other drugs providing continuous anesthesia.

Despite the growth of Websites for "pain control" or "death and dying," many patients and their families are unaware that pain-killing narcotics are legally available. However, both professional and public awareness of these options is growing.

A 1997 report by the Institute of Medicine criticized health care providers for failing to pro-vide competent palliative and supportive care and recommended ways to improve care, as summarized in the box on page 489 (Field and Cassel, 1997). Although certification in palliative care is now available for physicians and nurses, few providers who offer this care have specialty training. For example, as of 2002, only 917 physicians nationwide had passed the certifying exam of the American Board of Hospice and Palliative Medicine. Although accreditation standards for medical schools now include the mandate to cover end-of-life care, the requirement contains no clear standards for that instruction (Last Acts, 2002). Nevertheless, there are many encouraging signs among the professional associations of medicine, nursing, and social work, including the following:

- American Medical Association and the American College of Physicians: guidelines for quality pain-management technologies
- American Medical Association: profession-wide educational program on how to provide quality advance care planning and comprehensive palliative care
- American Geriatrics Society: fosters the development and study of instruments that measure quality of care at the end of life, including physical and emotional symptoms, advance care planning, and aggressive care near death
- American Board of Internal Medicine: educational resource documents to promote physician competency during internal medicine residency and subspecialty training
- American Association of Colleges of Nursing: national education program to improve training in end-of-life care in nursing curricula
- National Association of Social Workers: standards for social work practice in palliative and end-of-life care
- Social Work Leaders in End-of-life Care: proposal for a Council on Social Work in Palliative and End-of-life Care as a result of the Priority Agenda set at the Social Work Summit on End-of-Life and Palliative Care

---

AN INTEGRATED HOSPITAL-BASED PALLIATIVE CARE PROGRAM

One of the nation's premier hospital-based palliative care programs functions at Mount Sinai Hospital in New York City: the Lilian and Benjamin Hertzberg Palliative Care Institute. A consultation team is composed of a nurse, 10 physicians, some rotating fellows, and a few medical residents in training. This team advises hospital physicians who care for seriously ill patients in topics such as when to use comfort care, how to talk about treatment choices with patients and families, and pain and symptom management.

A four-bed inpatient unit is available for patients with difficult emotional and physical symptoms and for those who need assistance planning a course of care for their terminal illness. Nurses, social workers, interns, and residents staff this unit, which works closely with the consultation team. Home care is available for those seriously ill patients who are able to return home. All efforts are made to allow patients to go home, usually with hospice care, or to a nursing home, rather than die in a hospital.

To ensure that palliative care is available to all patients in the hospital, new physicians are trained in palliative care through bedside teaching, clinical rotations, and lectures. In fact, all oncology and geriatric fellows are required to complete a one-month clinical palliative care rotation.

RECOMMENDATIONS OF THE INSTITUTE OF MEDICINE FOR IMPROVING END-OF-LIFE CARE

People with advanced, potentially fatal illnesses and those close to them should be able to expect and receive reliable, skillful, and supportive care.

Health care providers should commit themselves to improving care for dying patients and to use existing knowledge effectively to prevent and relieve pain and other symptoms.

Policy makers, consumer groups, and purchasers of health care should work with health care practitioners, organizations, and researchers to:

- strengthen methods for measuring quality of life and other outcomes of care for dying patients and those close to them

- develop better tools and strategies for improving the quality of care and holding health care organizations accountable for care at the end of life

- revise mechanisms for funding care so that they encourage rather than impede good end-of-life care

- reform drug prescription laws, burdensome regulations, and state medical board policies and practices that impede effective use of opioids to relieve pain and suffering

Educators should initiate changes in undergraduate, graduate, and continuing education to ensure that practitioners develop empathy, knowledge, and skills to care well for dying patients. Palliative care should become a defined area of expertise, education, and research.

The nation's research establishment should define and implement priorities for strengthening the knowledge base for end-of-life care.

Public discussion on end-of-life issues is needed to improve understanding of the experience of dying, the options available to patients and families, and the obligations of communities to those approaching death (Field and Cassel, 1997).

- Institute for Health Care Improvement: breakthrough collaborative in quality improvement for end-of-life care, for advanced heart and lung disease, and for pain

- The accrediting body for hospitals: requirement for hospitals to implement pain management plans for terminally ill patients

- Department of Veterans Affairs: innovations aimed at better care of advanced illnesses; pain as a fifth vital sign; quality measures in advance care planning and pain management and faculty development

- National Consensus Project on Palliative Care sponsored by five national palliative care/hospice associations

- The Soros Foundation's Death in America Project: fellowships in end-of-life care awarded to physicians and social workers

- Last Acts: a coalition of 72 organizations launched by the Robert Wood Johnson Foundation, to enhance communication and decision-making among health care providers, insurers, hospitals, nursing homes, and consumers

We turn next to discussing the primary delivery system for end-of-life care, hospice.

Hospice Care

Another trend toward being more responsive to dying patients and their families is the expansion of the **hospice** model of caring for the terminally ill. Hospice is not a "place" but a philosophy of, and approach to, care that is offered primarily in the home but also in hospital and nursing home settings. It is a central component of palliative care by providing physical, medical, emotional, and spiritual care not only to the patient but also to his or her support system. As one type of end-of-life care, hospice is dedicated to helping individuals who are beyond medicine's curative power to remain in familiar surroundings where pain is reduced and personal dignity and control over the dying process maintained. Ensuring the patient's quality of life, and assessment and coordination of the physical, psychosocial, and spiritual needs of patient and family, are fundamental to the hospice approach. In recent years, more nursing homes, responsive to a changing market, are providing

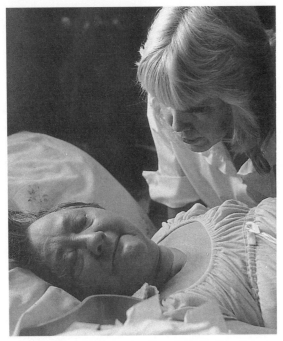

Hospice care can enhance quality of life for the dying person.

hospice care and pain management programs, although the percentage of nursing home residents who participate is relatively small (Castle, 1998; Miller and Mor, 2001).

Most hospice programs share the following characteristics:

- focus on quality of life
- service availability 24-hours per day, 7-days per week, as needed
- respite care for the family
- management of physical symptoms, including pain management through medications
- psychological, social, and spiritual counseling for the patient and the family
- coordination of skilled and homemaker home care services and collaboration among providers (home health care, hospitals, nursing homes)
- physician direction of services by a multidisciplinary team

- use of volunteers as central to the team
- inpatient care when needed
- bereavement counseling for family and friends for up to 1 year after the death

St. Christopher's Hospice, started in Great Britain in 1967, was the first formal hospice in the world, although TB asylums for younger people had informally performed similar functions. The first hospice in the United States was developed in 1974 in New Haven, Connecticut, and now nearly 3,200 hospices exist nationwide (Wilkinson and Lynn, 2001). The majority of these provide in-home services for cancer and HIV/AIDS patients with a prognosis of 6 months or less to live. In 1986, Congress passed legislation making hospice a permanent Medicare benefit, including reimbursement for prescriptions, and granting a modest increase in reimbursement rates. Medicare's hospice benefit includes services that are not generally covered under Medicare, such as home nursing care without homebound or skilled service requirements, on-call availability of providers for crises 24 hours a day and 7 days a week, interdisciplinary team management for comprehensiveness and continuity, spiritual counseling, family support, treatment for pain/symptoms, medications, emergency acute medical care, bereavement care for survivors, and inpatient care when needed (e.g., for respite or symptom management). Medicare pays a capitated, all-inclusive, prospectively set per day payment for four categories of service; of these, routine home care accounts for almost 90 percent of all care delivered (Wilkinson and Lynn, 2001).

Although most research on end-of-life care focuses on Medicare utilization, Medicaid also plays a major role in funding end-of-life care, including hospice care, in the last 6 months of life. While Medicaid funding for hospice varies widely by states, Medicaid accounts for about 5 percent of total hospice revenues. Most of Medicaid's funding for long-term care for the dually eligible (those eligible for both Medicaid and Medicare), however, goes to nursing home care at the end of life. Although about 35 percent of older people who die use nursing home care during the last year of life, few nursing home residents receive hospice services per se. Unfortunately, this means that nearly 15 percent of nursing home residents are in daily pain, and receive inadequate pain treatment or none at all (Last Acts, 2002). On Lok, a community-based program for nursing home eligible elders, and Ever Care, a managed care plan that emphasizes nurse practitioner and physician teams for preventive and primary care to nursing home residents, have both used Medicaid funds in innovative ways to care for dying Medicaid beneficiaries (Tilly and Wiener, 2003).

Even though hospice patients tend to receive at least 3 hours a day more attention than nursing home residents, only about 20 percent of dying Americans of all ages participate in hospice, the majority of whom are age 65 and older (Wilkinson and Lynn, 2001). On the other hand, the oldest-old generally do not have access to hospice, because they are more likely to die from chronic illnesses such as heart or lung disease or dementia, rather than cancer. Unlike the treatment of cancer, where a more definable process of decline can be projected, most deaths result from the accumulation of conditions that actually may be more imminently terminal yet more difficult to recognize and do not qualify such terminally ill elders for hospice (Waldrop, 2003). Because of the difficulties of predicting length of life, less than 40 percent of terminal patients receive an accurate diagnosis. In such instances, they are less likely to be informed about or qualify for hospice. Another barrier to hospice is the Medicare reimbursement requirement that 80 percent of care days be at home, which often makes hospice unavailable to those who lack informal supports for remaining at home. In addition to these prognostic and home care requirements, there are psychological barriers. Many people do not know about hospice and its benefits, including pain relief. Among those who do, a substantial percent resist hospice because it requires abandoning hope of full recovery and acknowledging that one is dying (Last

Acts, 2002; Tilly and Wiener, 2003). As a result, the average length of stay in a hospice for Medicare patients tends to be around 36 days. This suggests that most patients are not utilizing the services as early or fully in the dying process as they might (Last Acts, 2002; Morrison and Siu, 2000).

Low-income individuals and persons of color also appear to be underserved by hospice, even though groups such as African Americans have a higher overall incidence of death from cancer, and presumably a greater likelihood of inadequate treatment of pain from cancer (Freeman and Payne, 2000). Culturally specific end-of-life care programs are needed. African Americans and Latinos are less likely than other groups to prepare a living will, to talk to their doctors about end-of-life care, or to participate in a palliative hospice program. When death is inevitable and imminent, blacks are twice as likely as whites to request life-sustaining treatments and to then die in hospital. In some cases, this may occur because African Americans perceive advance directives and palliative care as "giving up hope," or not respecting their cultural and personal values. Some may fear hospice or palliative care is being prescribed as a way to limit care or "trying to get rid of them" rather than a vehicle for increasing control or self-determination (Berger et al., 2002; Owen, Goode, and Haley, 2001; Payne, 2000). Aggressive medical treatment is viewed as a sign of respect, even if it means feeding tubes, pain, and losing life savings. Providers need to be sensitive to cultural differences in the ways the patient chooses to die and be able to discuss alternatives to life-sustaining treatments in order to give African Americans the gift of a "good death." Despite the different definitions of "death with dignity" among culturally diverse groups, underutilization of hospice may also be due to inadequate knowledge of this service and the lack of providers who are trained to discuss end-of-life care with persons of color. Working through African American ministers and community centers may be a way to provide hospice information

THE COMFORT PROVIDED BY HOSPICE CARE

Three months of chemotherapy followed by 6 weeks of radiation was not working for Mr. Frank. His last hope was a stem cell transplant, but those prospects were dimming each day, as he became weaker and weaker. Mr. Frank decided that he did not want to spend his final days in a losing battle with his rapidly advancing and painful lymphoma. He preferred to be as comfortable as possible and to leave the hospital and return home.

Mr. Frank and his wife Jean contacted a local hospice that helped them set up a range of services that would assist both of them through the final months of his life. A nurse and physician were assigned to his care. The hospice staff also trained Jean, friends, and family in how to administer Mr. Frank's pain medications and to use tiny ice chips to help him deal with his extremely dry throat and mouth. The staff also taught Jean how to tell when Mr. Frank's pain was increasing, so that he could be given a high dose of morphine to relieve the pain.

Mr. Frank also received visits from the hospice team social worker who talked with him about how to resolve some issues with his daughter, who held considerable anger toward her father. When the hospice team estimated that Mr. Frank would probably die in about 3 days, they encouraged Jean to contact family and friends who lived at a distance so that they would have time to visit and say good-bye. In those last 3 days, Mr. Frank was lucid and able to talk, laugh, and cry with those who loved him, including his daughter.

His family and friends all commented later that they felt Mr. Frank had a "good death." They appreciated being able to be part of his peaceful death in the comfort and familiar surroundings of his home. The hospice social worker kept in touch with Jean for a year after her husband's death, encouraging her to express her grief and learn new coping skills. Mr. Frank's daughter was especially grateful for the opportunity to reconcile with her father before he died.

a range of culturally diverse communities may be the locus for discussion about death, dying, and end-of-life care, even though religious leaders are not necessarily comfortable with initiating such topics (Braun, Pietsch, and Blanchette, 2000).

Hospice professionals and volunteers, working as an interdisciplinary team, advocate for giving dying persons full and accurate information about their condition. They also try to develop supportive environments in which people can tell their life stories (e.g., life review), attain resolution and reconciliation in relationships, and find meaning in their deaths. Listening, touching the dying person, music and art, family involvement, and ritual celebration of special events such as birthdays and weddings are all emphasized by the staff. For those who value spirituality, staff support them in their quest for meaning and the intrinsic quality of dignity in the last stage of life. In addition, hospice staff work directly with family and friends to help them resolve their feelings, clarify expectations, relate effectively to the dying patient, and provide bereavement counseling after the death. Hospice programs also offer counseling and support to staff members to help prevent "burnout." There is increasing evidence that hospice provides better quality of life for both end-of-life patients and their caregivers than hospitals. Savings to families and to Medicare are also associated with hospice care relative to conventional care (Last Acts, 2002).

One of the barriers to a "good death," however, is that doctors often refer patients to hospice too late. Currently, 33 percent of all hospice patients (82 percent of whom are over age 65) die within a week of admission (National Hospice and Palliative Care Organization, 2003).

A primary reason for this is that doctors are no better at predicting length of survival of terminally ill patients than they were 30 years ago. In addition, some physicians remain uncomfortable with telling a person that he or she is dying. In fact, physicians tend to convey an optimistic bias when discussing prognoses with each other and sharing

to African American communities (Kurent, 2000). In addition, medications for managing pain must be affordable and accessible in pharmacies in minority neighborhoods. Religious organizations in

A GOOD DEATH

Anne was a 68-year-old retiree who had battled breast cancer for over 4 years. She had received radiation and chemotherapy, but the cancer had metastasized and spread to other organs in her body. She had lost more than 40 pounds, had no appetite, and had difficulty breathing, even with the aid of an oxygen tank. She had decided to end her suffering and wanted to die.

Her husband contacted the local office of Compassion in Dying. The case management staff arranged for a visit and included medical staff to verify the primary physician's diagnosis. Mentally alert, Anne assured the staff that she understood and met the requirements outlined in Compassion's Guidelines and Safeguards. She indicated that her physician had already prescribed half the necessary medications needed to hasten her death; the rest would be obtained within 2 weeks. The physician carefully reviewed with Anne the procedures to follow to self-administer the required medications. She hoped for a hastened death within the next 6 weeks. Her husband, Ed, confirmed that he supported Anne's decision to choose when the end would come rather than watch her continue to suffer.

A month later, Ed phoned the Compassion staff and indicated that Anne was ready. Upon their arrival, the staff reminded Anne that she need only tell them if she had changed her mind. She was clear and adamant in her decision to proceed: "Today is the day." According to Compassion's protocol, she ate some food to be certain she had something in her stomach before taking the first dose of medications. Anne began to take the pills with a glass of orange juice, according to Compassion's guidelines that patients must be able to ingest all of the medications by themselves. As suggested in the protocol, Anne asked for some vodka to speed the effect of the drugs. She expressed her appreciation to the Compassion staff for their assistance, kissed her husband and two sons, laid her head back on the pillow, and looked as if she were going into a peaceful sleep. In about 15 minutes, she stopped breathing. She had died what Compassion calls a good death.

them with patients and families. They are likely to overestimate survival and future quality of life, in part because they may fear that a short prognosis will be self-fulfilling. Most patients come to hospice during a period of rapid physical change and often in crisis. At such times, the immediate management of symptoms and relieving the family overshadows the need to address the emotional and spiritual issues of remembering, forgiving, and bringing closure to a person's life. When more time is available, the dying person can participate in the process of validating the past and planning for the future, and this gives the family the chance to enjoy or repair family relationships. On the other hand, some families and patients may have been unlikely to use hospice earlier. For them, 2 to 3 weeks may be just right (Waldop, 2003). The National Hospice Organization tries to educate physicians on how to predict appropriate entry points to hospice for various conditions.

The Right to Die or Hastened Death

Along with increased attention to the ways in which people choose to die and the meanings they assign to their deaths, the right-to-die movement is growing; this has given rise to new ethical and legal debates regarding the right to a "good death." Advocates of the right to die increasingly use the term *hastened death* rather than **euthanasia,** because it hastens the inevitable (Compassion in Dying, 2000). Whether others have a right to help people die, and under what conditions, has been discussed throughout history (see the box on page 495 summarizing the history of major events in the right to die movement). But recent debates about the ethical, social, and legal issues raised by euthanasia or hastened death have intensified with increased medical advances used to prolong life. These issues revolve around three different types of patients:

1. the terminally ill who are conscious
2. the irreversibly comatose

"The good death: We only get one time to get it right."

3. the brain-damaged or severely debilitated who have good chances for survival but have limited quality of life (e.g., Alzheimer's patients, patients with Lou Gehrig's disease)

Central to these debates is the doctrine of **informed consent,** which establishes a competent patient's right to accept or refuse medical treatment based on his or her understanding of the benefits and harms of that treatment. Standard informed-consent procedures work best in the acute-care setting, where they involve treatment choices that lead to cure, significant improvement, or death. Decision making for older people with chronic illness, often in long-term care settings, is much more ambiguous than in acute-care environments, and long-term care providers tend to disagree about patients' rights to end their lives (McClain, Tindell, and Hall, 1999). Findings are mixed regarding the acceptability of a range of end-of-life decision options among older people. Some research has found that the majority of elders want to live for as long as possible, undergoing whatever treatments might extend their lives (Cicirelli, 1997; Walker, 1997). Other studies have reported that increased age is associated with preferring quality over quantity of life (Fauser, 1999).

The value of autonomy, articulated in informed consent and advance directives, may conflict with cultures that are more collectivist than individualist in nature. For example, decisions about end-of-life care in Asian and Pacific Islander cultures are influenced by the value placed on shared or deferred decision making within families; filial piety; silent communication, whereby it is improper to discuss issues of death and dying with parents; and preservation of harmony, whereby families may be unwilling to share bad news if it disrupts the group's harmony. When patients have difficulty making independent health care decisions and defer to the family or doctor, they may unfortunately be labeled noncompliant by traditional Western medicine. To take account of such cultural variations, family-centered, shared, or negotiated models of medical decision-making recognize the legitimacy of multiple points of view (McLaughlin and Braun, 1998).

Passive Euthanasia (Voluntary Elective Death)

Euthanasia can be passive (allowing death) or active (causing death). In **passive euthanasia,** treatment is withdrawn, and nothing is done to prolong the patient's life artificially, such as use of a feeding tube or ventilator. Suspension of medical interventions or physician aid in dying allows the natural dying process to occur, but no active steps are taken to bring about death. In order to relieve pain, medications are sometimes given that may hasten death, but the object is to relieve suffering,

POINTS TO PONDER

DEFINING END OF LIFE

How the end of life is defined has implications for quality of care and quality of life, when decisions need to be made about life-sustaining care, and eligibility for hospice. One definition of the end of life is the beginning of an illness that is characterized by any of the three dimensions of severity:

- Diagnosis of a potentially fatal illness
- The beginning of a functional limitation in one's ability to perform any of the basic physical activities of daily living, or
- The advent of pain or physical symptoms that are either or both (a) a major distress to the patient and (b) precursors to and resulting in death (Lawton, 2001).

What would you consider to be end of life? What kind of care would you want? Would you want any measures taken to sustain life, even if you were in a coma or had dementia?

HISTORY OF MAJOR EVENTS RELATED TO THE RIGHT TO DIE MOVEMENT IN THE UNITED STATES

1937 The Euthanasia Society of America is founded.

1967 The first living will is written.

1968 The first living will legislation is introduced in Florida.

1973 The American Hospital Association creates the Patient Bill of Rights, which includes informed consent and the right to refuse treatment.

1974 The first U.S. hospice opens in Connecticut.

1975 The New Jersey Supreme Court allows Karen Ann Quinlan's parents to disconnect the respirator that was keeping her alive.

The California Natural Death Act is passed, which is the first aid-in-dying statute, which gives legal standing to living wills and protects physicians from being sued for failing to treat incurable illnesses.

1980 The Hemlock Society is founded, distributing how-to-die information.

1987 The California State Bar Conference passes a resolution to become the first public body to approve of physician aid-in-dying.

1990 The American Medical Association adopts the position that, with informed consent, a physician can withhold or withdraw treatment from a patient who is close to death, and may also discontinue life support of a patient in a permanent coma.

The Supreme Court decision in the Nancy Cruzan case rules that competent adults have a constitutionally protected right to refuse medical treatment and allows a state to impose procedural safeguards.

Congress passes the Patient Self-Determination Act; hospitals that receive federal funds are required to tell patients about their state's legal options.

1991 Washington State voters reject Ballot Initiative 119 (54 to 46 percent), which would have legalized physician aid-in-dying.

The Federal Patient Self-Determination Act requires health care facilities that receive Medicare or Medicaid funds to inform patients of their right to refuse medical treatment and to sign advance directives.

1992 California voters defeated Proposition 161. a law similar to the Washington State initiative, and at a similar proportion 54 to 46 percent.

1993 Compassion in Dying is founded in Washington State.

1994 The Death with Dignity Education Center is founded in California.

Compassion in Dying files a lawsuit challenging the constitutionality of laws banning assisted dying in Washington State and New York. They win in the District Court in Washington State, but not in New York.

Oregon voters approve (51 to 49 percent) Measure 16, the Oregon Death with Dignity Act, which permits terminally ill patients, under proper safeguards, to obtain a physician's prescription to end life in a humane and dignified manner.

1995 Both Washington State's Compassion ruling and Oregon's Death with Dignity Act are ruled unconstitutional at the district court level.

1996 The Ninth Circuit Court of Appeals issues a landmark decision in Compassion vs. Washington State, which upholds that assisted dying is protected by the liberty and privacy provisions of the U.S. Constitution.

1997 The U.S. Supreme Court reverses the Circuit Court decisions in Washington State and rules that state laws against assisted suicide are not unconstitutional. The Court also finds that patients have a right to aggressive treatment of pain and other symptoms, even if the treatment hastens death.

Oregon citizens vote by a margin of 60 to 40 percent to retain the Oregon Death with Dignity Act.

1998 Congressman Hyde introduces the Lethal Drug Abuse Prevention Act of 1998 to prohibit the dispensing or distribution of drugs for the purpose of causing the suicide or euthanasia of any individual. His intent is to overturn the Oregon law.

Jack Kevorkian videotapes himself administering a lethal medication to a terminally ill man, which is broadcast on *60 Minutes*. He is charged with first-degree premeditated murder.

2001 U.S. Attorney General John Ashcroft reinterprets the federal Controlled Substance Act in a way to nullify Oregon's Death with Dignity law. A U.S. district judge rules against this interpretation.

2002 The Hawaii Senate narrowly fails to pass legislation legalizing physician-assisted suicide, even though the measure had overwhelming support of the House and the governor.

2003 Oregon issues its fifth year report on the implementation of the Death with Dignity Act: 58 people received legal prescriptions for lethal medications, and 38 of them used the medication.

not to bring about death. Withholding or withdrawing useless or unwanted medical treatments, or providing adequate pain relief, even if it hastens death, has been determined to be legal and ethical. The legal context for this is the 1990 U.S. Supreme Court case of *Cruzan v. Director, Missouri Department of Health,* which recognized the right of a competent patient to refuse unwanted medical care, including artificial nutrition and hydration, as a "liberty" interest, and therefore as constitutionally protected. The Supreme Court later delegated regulation of this constitutional right to the states.

Another indicator of changing legal interpretations is the position of the American Medical Association (AMA). Their 1984 statement on euthanasia presented two fundamental guidelines:

- The patient's role in decision making is paramount.
- A decrease in aggressive treatment of the hopelessly ill patient is advisable when treatment would only prolong a difficult and uncomfortable process of dying.

In 1989, the American Medical Association adopted the position that, with informed consent, physicians could withhold or withdraw treatment from patients who are close to death. Most physicians agree that withholding and withdrawing nutrition and hydration are permissible in certain circumstances and that it is the physician's duty to initiate discussion of these issues with patients and their families.

In contrast to passive euthanasia, where deliberate decisions are made about withholding or withdrawing treatment, there is also a form of hastened death whereby older people may voluntarily make decisions that are equivalent to choosing to die. For example, an older person may refuse extra help at home or insist on hospital discharge directly to the home, in spite of the need for skilled nursing care. When an older person commits suicide through the process of **self-ne-**

glect, the effects of his or her decisions are subtle and gradual. If older people neglect their care needs or choose an inappropriate living situation because of impaired judgment, involuntary treatment laws can sometimes be used to move them to protected settings. If their "failure to care," however, is not immediately life-threatening, they usually have to be allowed to deteriorate to that point before being legally compelled to comply with treatment.

Active Euthanasia

Active euthanasia refers to positive steps taken to bring about someone else's death, by administering a lethal injection or by some other means. Sometimes called *mercy killing,* the legality of active euthanasia has been tested by several highly controversial court cases, voter initiatives, and state legislation. As noted above, a subject of intense controversy is *physician-assisted suicide* or *assisted suicide;* this occurs when someone else provides the means by which an individual ends his or her life. For example, a physician may prescribe medication, typically barbiturates, knowing that the individual intends to use it to commit suicide, but it is the individual who decides when and whether to take it.

COMPASSION IN DYING

Compassion in Dying is a nonprofit national organization with local chapters created to support the right of terminally ill patients to choose to die without pain, without suffering, and with personal assistance, if necessary, to intentionally hasten death. Its mission is to provide counseling and support about end-of-life choices to individuals who have been diagnosed by their physicians with either a terminal illness or an incurable illness that will lead to a terminal diagnosis. Through education and advocacy, Compassion will uphold the individual's right to aid in dying.

THE CONTROVERSIAL DR. KEVORKIAN

One of the states in which the legality of assisted suicide has been the focus of public attention is Michigan, where Dr. Jack Kevorkian has assisted over 100 people to commit suicide. In the first case, involving a woman with Alzheimer's disease, the court dismissed the murder charges on the grounds that no law in Michigan prohibited assisting in a suicide. Subsequently, the legislature passed a bill to stop Dr. Kevorkian's activities. Some cases have been dismissed on the grounds that the law is unconstitutional; others are pending. Although controversial, Kevorkian's crusade to legalize active euthanasia has served to push the debate on physician-assisted suicide to the forefront of the American political scene.

Those who argue against the legalization of assisted suicide fear a "slippery slope," that a "right to die" could become a "duty to die" and be inappropriately applied to older adults and other dependent members of society. They fear that a law made to convey permission could come to be seen as prescriptive, with assisted suicide viewed as a solution to solve societal problems faced by the poor, persons of color, or individuals with disabilities. The American Medical Association, based on the historical role of physicians as advocates for healing, officially oppose physicians' directly assisting their patients in committing suicide by prescribing lethal medications, although about 44 percent of rank-and-file doctors support physician-assisted suicide (Death with Dignity, 2001). There is greater agreement that whatever decision is made should be as part of the physician-patient relationship, and not determined by law.

Citizen initiatives and recent legislation in several states reflect increasing public support for physician-assisted suicide. In fact, by approximately 2 to 1, most adults in national polls believe that doctors should be allowed to help terminally ill patients in severe pain take their own lives

(Harris Poll, 2002). The degree of support, however, diminishes among those with conservative religious affiliations. Most believe that forcing people to endure prolonged suffering is inhumane and cruel. *Compassion et al. v. Washington State* was the first case to challenge in a federal court the constitutionality of a state law on assisted suicide insofar as it applies to mentally competent, terminally ill patients seeking prescribed medications with which to hasten death. An initiative in Washington State to permit physician aid in dying was only narrowly defeated in 1991. Patients could request such assistance in writing at the time they wanted to die, as long as two witnesses would certify that the request is voluntary and two doctors would state that the patient would die within 6 months. However, 4 months after the

---

OREGON: THE ONLY STATE TO LEGALIZE PHYSICIAN-ASSISTED SUICIDE

The Death with Dignity Act, passed by Oregon voters in 1994 and again in 1997, allows doctors to write a prescription of lethal drug doses for an aware, terminally ill adult who asks for it, orally and in writing. Nevertheless, doctors are not compelled to comply with this request, and there are numerous safeguards. A 15-day waiting period is required for the first oral request, and two witnesses are necessary for the written request, along with agreement of a second doctor. The doctor must inform the patient about options, including pain control, and make sure that the request really is voluntary. At the end of this elaborate process, only the patient can decide whether and when to take fatal drugs and must do so him- or herself. This citizen initiative made Oregon the second entity (after the Netherlands) to legalize physician-assisted suicide. Since the second passage of the law in 1997, 38 patients, most of whom were suffering from cancer, have taken their lives with barbiturates; their average age was 69. At the same time, there are ongoing threats to overturn the Oregon Death with Dignity Act.

initiative was defeated at the polls, the legislature passed a bill giving comatose and dying people the right to have food and water withdrawn (*Seattle Times*, 1992). In 1994, the federal district court ruled that the Washington State ban on physician-assisted suicide violates the patient's constitutional right to liberty, but this ruling did not protect physicians from prosecution if they assisted in a terminally ill patient's suicide (Hudson, 1994). In 1996, a federal appeals court struck down both Washington and New York statutes banning physician-assisted suicide. The plaintiffs (near-death patients and physicians) argued that no public interest is served by prolonging pain in truly hopeless situations and that to do so is to subject patients to potential abuse. The courts linked the right to facilitate death with the right to refuse medical treatment. They argued that the Fourteenth Amendment protects the individual's decision to hasten death with physician-prescribed medication and that statutes prohibiting physician-assisted suicide deny equal protection guaranteed by the Fourteenth Amendment to competent terminally ill adults who are not on life supports (Tucker, 1999).

These conflicting state rulings and pressure from advocacy organizations such as Compassion in Dying brought the issue of assisted suicide to the U.S. Supreme Court. In June 1997, the Court ruled that there is no constitutional or fundamental "right to die." They thus upheld the Washington and New York laws that make it a crime for doctors to help patients kill themselves, although several justices indicated that they are willing to revisit the issue in specific cases. This ruling by the Supreme Court, however, does not preclude states from deciding on their own to pass laws allowing doctor-assisted suicide. By returning the debate to the states, the justices apparently opened the way for other jurisdictions to follow Oregon, the only state to legalize the physician-assisted suicide choice for patients who are diagnosed by two doctors as having less than 6 months to live. Several states—Maine, California, Alaska, and Hawaii—have considered legalization of physician-assisted suicide. The Supreme Court ruling also left open the possibility that the court might extend federal constitutional protection in the future.

Nor will the Supreme Court ruling stop patients from seeking physicians to prescribe lethal medications or stop doctors from providing them illegally. The court ruled that prescribing medication with the intent to relieve suffering is legal and acceptable, but presenting drugs with the intent to cause death is not. Since "intent" is difficult to determine, the Court does give significant discretion and latitude to physicians to use adequate pain medication and explicitly endorses "terminal sedation." Nevertheless, many physicians incorrectly assume that they can be censured or prosecuted for giving patients controlled substances. A dying patient who is suffering and is in pain, wrote Justice Sandra Day O'Connor, "has no legal barriers to obtaining medication from qualified physicians to alleviate that suffering, even to the point of causing unconsciousness and hastening death" (Ostrom, 1998). In many ways, this solution, known as the "double effect," is an old one. In the Supreme Court's definition, this occurs when a physician, intending to relieve pain or suffering, gives a terminally ill patient medication that has the unintended—but foreseeable—side effect of hastening death. Often, this medication is morphine.

In spite of individual physicians' assistance with suicide, the American Medical Association continues to oppose such actions. Instead, the AMA advocates compassionate, high-quality palliative care and assistance in addressing fears as a way to reduce the expressed need for physician-assisted suicide (Compassion in Dying, 2000). Some critics of physician-assisted suicide fear that it will be used to the detriment of the oldest-old and persons with disabilities, some of whom could be pressured to feel that it's "their duty to die" (Callahan, 1996). Some health care providers believe that if patients are afforded compassionate care and assistance in addressing fears, the need for assisted suicide would diminish (Hornik,

ingly, Oregon leads the country in lowest in-hospital death rates, better attention to advance planning, more referrals to hospice, fewer barriers to prescribing narcotics, and a smaller percentage of dying patients in pain (34% compared to 50% nationally) (Ostrom, 2000).

Recent actions taken by Attorney General John Ashcroft to reinterpret the federal Controlled Substances Act so as to nullify Oregon's Death with Dignity Act are another sign of ongoing legal debates regarding assisted suicide and pain management. This makes using a controlled substance to "assist suicide" per se "illegitimate," thereby subjecting any physician or pharmacist who acts under the Oregon act to the revocation of his or her prescribing license (and criminal penalties under drug laws). The U.S. District Court for Oregon has ruled against Ashcroft's reinterpretation, allowing Oregon's law to remain in effect during the appeals process. Others have opposed Ashcroft's action as an unwarranted expansion of federal

1998). Others argue that a health care system driven by both profits and cost containment poses a greater risk to frail elders than does physician-assisted suicide (Olson, 1998).

Oregon voters' support of a law allowing doctors to prescribe lethal medications to terminally ill patients also conveyed the public's lack of confidence in physicians' pain management. As a result, Oregon leads the nation in aggressive pain management through a 1995 Intractable Pain Act, which set new rules to ease doctors' fears about prescribing controlled substances for pain control. In fact, the state's medical board shocked professionals around the country by disciplining a doctor for not prescribing enough pain medication! California now has a similar law in which physicians who undertreat pain can be charged with unprofessional conduct (see box). Not surpris-

authority over states' rights to self-determination. In contrast, the American Civil Liberties Union put forth the "End of Life Care Act of 1998"; this would remove legal liability from physicians who offer patients a full range of end-of-life care choices, including palliative sedation. The ACLU argues that if a patient is uncomfortable, then it is appropriate to offer stronger pain medication. These debates are likely to intensify in the near future.

Legal Options Regarding End-of-Life Care

While active euthanasia continues to be debated in courtrooms and the ballot box, all 50 states have laws authorizing the use of some type of **advance directive** to avoid artificially prolonged death. This refers to patients' oral and written instructions about end-of-life care and someone to speak on their behalf if they become incompetent; it may include proxy directives (see medical power of attorney, on page 502). The most common type of advance directive is a **living will.** An individual's wishes about medical treatment are put into writing in the case of irreversible terminal illness or the prognosis of a permanent vegetative (unconscious) state. Under such conditions, living wills can direct physicians to withhold life-sustaining procedures and can assist family members in making decisions when they are unable to consult a comatose or medically incompetent relative.

Both federal and state laws govern the use of advance directives. The federal law, the **Patient Self-Determination Act,** requires health care facilities (hospitals, skilled nursing facilities, hospice, home health care agencies, and health maintenance organizations) that receive Medicaid and Medicare funds to inform patients in writing of their rights to execute advance directives regarding how they want to live or die; state regulations vary widely. State-specific advance directives can be ordered

from the national organization, Choices in Dying, or downloaded from their Website. However, these facilities do not require that the patient make an advanced directive; the law specifies only that people must be informed of their right to do so.

This act assumes that increased awareness of advance directives will generate discussion between patients and their health care providers and result in more completed advance directives (Galambos, 1998). Despite this act, few patients have advance directives, and those who do tend to be white and middle to upper class. Only 15 to 20 percent of the general population has an advance directive, such as a living will, and only 35 percent of those over age 75 do so. Ethnic minorities are least likely to have living wills or to have discussed end-of-life care with their families and doctors. Among nursing home residents, only 20 percent have living wills and 40 percent have "do not resuscitate" orders (Butler, 2000; Last Acts, 2002; Compassion in Dying Federation, 2000). The box on page 501 summarizes the relatively limited impact of advance directives on end-of-life decision-making (Butler, 2000).

In an attempt to resolve some of the problems with implementing the Patient Self-Determination Act, the **Uniform Health Care Decision Act** was passed in 1993 to provide uniformity and a minimum level of standards in statutes across state lines. This act promotes autonomous decision making by acknowledging individuals' rights to make health care decisions in all circumstances, including the right to decline or discontinue health care. Given people's preference for informal methods, oral directives as well as written are honored. To safeguard the patient's end-of-life autonomy, providers, agents, surrogates, and guardians are mandated to comply with an individual's instructions. Even with such safeguards, compliance is not guaranteed, and, as noted above, a health care provider may decline to honor an advance directive (1) for reasons of conscience if a directive conflicts with institution policy or values, and (2) if the instruction is contrary

ADVANCE DIRECTIVES

To what extent do patients participate in determining their care? Research conducted by the Agency for Healthcare Research and Quality (AHRQ) indicates:

- Less than 50 percent of the severely or terminally ill patients studied had an advance directive in their medical record.
- Only 12 percent of patients with an advance directive had received input from their physician in its development.
- Between 65 and 76 percent of physicians whose patients had an advance directive were not aware that it existed.
- Advance directives helped make end-of-life decision in less than 50 percent of those cases where a directive existed.
- Providers and patient surrogates had difficulty knowing when to stop treatment and often waited until the patient had crossed a threshold over to actively dying before the advance directive was invoked.
- Physicians were only about 65 percent accurate in predicting patient preferences and tended to make errors of undertreatment, even after reviewing the patient's advance directive.
- Surrogates who were family members tended to make prediction errors of overtreatment, even if they had reviewed the advance directive with the patient or assisted in its development.
- Overall, care at the end of life appears at times to be inconsistent with patients' preferences to forgo life-sustaining treatment, and many patients received life-sustaining care that they did not want.

SOURCE: Kass-Bartelmes and Hughes, 2003.

vance directive mandates with the Uniform Health Care Decisions Act. Without federal mandates, the number of states that have done so is limited.

Although it is human nature to delay discussions about aging and dying, in many instances, families and patients may be confused about both their prognosis and the choices that they need to make. Communication difficulties with health care providers are another common barrier. Ironically, 33 percent of dying patients in an AHRQ study would discuss advance care planning if the physician brought up the subject, but 25 percent thought that such planning was only for people who were very ill or very old. Contrary to family and health care providers' perceptions that older people do not want to discuss their dying, only 5 percent of patients stated that they found the discussions about advance planning too difficult (Kass-Bartelmes and Hughes, 2003).

When advance care planning is discussed with both family members and physicians, however, it tends to increase patient satisfaction, their sense of ability to influence and direct their care, their belief that their physicians understand their wishes, and reduces their fear and anxiety about dying.

STEPS TO TAKE TO AVOID AN ARTIFICIALLY PROLONGED DEATH

- Download state-specific, advance-directive documents from Partnershipforcaring.org.
- Issue an advance directive, witnessed or notarized according to state laws.
- Give copies to your personal physician and family members.
- While healthy, make sure that your family understands your wishes.
- Be sure that your desires are also noted in your medical record.
- Begin this process while you are still healthy, your thought processes are clear, you are not in crisis, and time is available.

to accepted health care standards. However, according to the act, reasonable efforts must be made to transfer the patient to a facility that can honor the directive. In such situations, the act provides for court mechanisms for dispute resolution. A major limitation of this act is that each state may choose whether to replace its own ad-

Such discussions usually help families, physicians, and patients to reconcile their differences about end-of-life care. These findings suggest the importance of physicians conducting advance care planning discussions with patients during routine outpatient office visits and hospitalization, and reviewing documents on a regular basis and updating documentation (Kass-Bartelmes and Hughes, 2003). The American Medical Association's **Advanced Care Planning Process** is an ongoing series of discussions among the patient, physician, social worker, and family to clarify values and goals, and to have principles to guide decisions (Gossert, Forbes, and Bern-Klug, 2001).

Even when advance directives exist, other problems with implementation may arise. Older adults may fail to tell their doctors about the directive, instead trusting that their families know what to do. Or the advance directive may be in a safe deposit box, unavailable to either family or health care providers. Of those who designate someone to make medical decisions if they are unable, 30 percent of those designees do not know they have been selected (Cloud, 2000). Family members, when faced with the impending death of their loved one, may later change their minds about adhering to an advance directive. In such instances, physicians are more likely to comply with the family's preference than the written directive (Galambos, 1998). In addition, federal law does not require that the health care provider follow such directives, only that the provider follows state laws or court decisions that deal with advance directives. This means that in some instances, the physician's decision may override both patient and family preferences. Thus, health care providers may not necessarily follow living wills unless family members are advocating for the patients' wishes.

Patients and their families can access their state's particular law and forms through national organizations, such as **Partnership for Caring** and **Compassion in Dying,** local hospitals, state attorney general offices, or the Internet through Web sites (PartnershipforCaring.org) (see Figure 13.1,

Florida State Health Care Directive or Living Will).

In situations where there is no living will, the family of an incompetent patient must go to court to obtain legal authority if they wish to refuse life support on the patient's behalf. This expensive and time-consuming process is viewed as necessary where doctors and health care facilities are unwilling to make decisions to remove life-sustaining treatment because of the perceived risk of liability. To obviate this court process, 24 states and the District of Columbia have passed statutes governing a **surrogate decision maker.** The surrogate has a duty to act according to the known wishes of the patient; if those wishes are not known, the surrogate must act according to the patient's "best interest." Such laws support the concept that the people closest to the patient are in the best position to know his or her wishes or to act in the patient's best interest. Each state's law includes a prioritized list of people connected to the patient who are potential surrogates. The doctor must approach these individuals, in order of priority, to find someone who is willing to make decisions about life support (Choice in Dying, 1994).

Durable power of attorney is another type of written advance directive, usually in addition to a living will. This authorizes someone to act on an individual's behalf with regard to property and financial matters. The individual does not relinquish control with a power of attorney since it is granted only for the financial matters specifically set forth in the relevant document. An advantage of durable power of attorney is that a living will cannot anticipate what might be wanted in all possible circumstances.

A **medical power of attorney** (or durable power of attorney for health care) specifically allows for a health care surrogate to make decisions about medical care if the patient is unable to make them for him- or herself. A durable power of attorney for healthcare may be used instead of, or in addition to, a living will because it is more broadly applicable to nearly any type of health care during periods of incapacitation. *Durable* means that the arrangement continues even when the person is incapacitated and unable to make his or her own medical decisions. A durable power of attorney agreement may be written either to go into effect upon its signing or only when the disability occurs. At that point, bills can continue to be paid and revenues be collected while other more permanent arrangements are being made, such as the appointment of a conservator or guardian.

Conservatorship generally relates to control of financial matters. In this instance, probate court appoints a person as a **conservator** to care for an individual's property and finances because that person is unable to do so due to advanced age, mental weakness, or physical incapacity. Such a condition must be attested to by a physician. Once appointed, the conservator will be required to file an inventory of all the assets and to report annually all income and expenses. The individual, however, loses control over his or her property and finances.

Guardianship is a legal tool that establishes control over a person's body as well as financial affairs. In a guardianship, a probate court appoints someone to care for the individual's person, property, and finances because of the individual's mental inability to care for him- or herself. The **guardian** has a responsibility for directing the individual's medical treatment, housing, personal needs, finances, and property. To establish guardianship, a medical certificate from a physician must state that the individual is mentally incapable of caring for him- or herself. As with conservatorships, the medical certificate by the physician must be made not more than 10 days before the probate court hearing, so in this sense, guardianship cannot be arranged in advance of need. However, through a medical power of attorney, an individual may nominate someone he or she would like to act as guardian if such a need develops. Since the guardian manages all the individual's affairs, guardianship is generally considered a last resort. This is because the process

essentially eliminates an individual's legal rights, since consent is not required, and it is costly and rarely reversible.

Family members who are concerned about finances may move too quickly through these options. However, families and service providers should try, as long as possible, to respect the older person's wishes with regard to living arrangements, legal will, and other financial decisions. In other words, the older person should be encouraged to exercise as much control as possible, to the extent that his or her cognitive status allows. In general, less restrictive approaches than guardianship, which balance the need for protection with self-determination, are needed.

Some nursing homes include a statement with their admissions packet that, unless otherwise noted in writing, there will be "no code" for the patient. This type of advance directive means that if the patient quits breathing or his or her heart stops, the staff will not "call a code" to initiate cardiopulmonary resuscitation (CPR). In other nursing homes or hospitals, this type of statement must be written in the patient's chart and signed by the patient and witnesses.

A wide range of organizations exist to educate the public, health care providers, and lawmakers regarding right-to-die issues and advance directive options. The largest of these is **Partnership in Caring,** formerly known as Choice in Dying, a national not-for-profit organization that was created in 1991 by a merger of the nation's two oldest organizations advocating the rights of dying patients, Concern for Dying and Society for the Right to Die. These two organizations pioneered patients' rights to refuse unwanted life support and developed the first living will document in 1967. Partnership for Caring has provided national leadership on living wills, guided the enactment of advance directives in all states, and lobbied for the passage of the Patient Self-Determination Act. Its goal is to achieve full societal and legal support for the right of all individuals to make decisions regarding the nature and extent of life-sustaining measures as well as the conditions

INSTRUCTIONS

FLORIDA Living Will

PRINT THE DATE

Declaration made this __________ day of ____________________, ________.
(*day*) (*month*) (*year*)

PRINT YOUR NAME

I, ____, willfully and voluntarily make known my desire that my dying not be artificially prolonged under the circumstances set forth below, and I do hereby declare that:

PLEASE INITIAL EACH THAT APPLIES

If at any time I am incapacitated and

_____ I have a terminal condition, or
_____ I have an end-stage condition, or
_____ I am in a persistent vegetative state

and if my attending or treating physician and another consulting physician have determined that there is no reasonable medical probability of my recovery from such condition, I direct that life-prolonging procedures be withheld or withdrawn when the application of such procedures would serve only to prolong artificially the process of dying, and that I be permitted to die naturally with only the administration of medication or the performance of any medical procedure deemed necessary to provide me with comfort care or to alleviate pain.

It is my intention that this declaration be honored by my family and physician as the final expression of my legal right to refuse medical or surgical treatment and to accept the consequences for such refusal.

In the event that I have been determined to be unable to provide express and informed consent regarding the withholding, withdrawal, or continuation of life-prolonging procedures, I wish to designate, as my surrogate to carry out the provisions of this declaration:

PRINT THE NAME, HOME ADDRESS AND TELEPHONE NUMBER OF YOUR SURROGATE

Name: ____

Address: ____

____ Zip Code: __________

Phone: ____

FIGURE 13.1 Florida Living Will
SOURCE: Partnership for Caring, 2000.

PRINT NAME, HOME ADDRESS AND TELEPHONE NUMBER OF YOUR ALTERNATE SURROGATE	**FLORIDA Living Will—PAGE 2 OF 2**

FLORIDA Living Will—PAGE 2 OF 2

I wish to designate the following person as my alternate surrogate, to carry out the provisions of this declaration should my surrogate be unwilling or unable to act on my behalf:

Name: _____

Address: _____

_____ Zip Code: _____

Phone: _____

ADD PERSONAL INSRUCTIONS (IF ANY)

Additional instructions (optional):

SIGN THE DOCUMENT

I understand the full import of this declaration, and I am emotionally and mentally competent to make this declaration.

Signed: _____

WITNESSING PROCEDURE

Witness 1:

Signed: _____

TWO WITNESSES MUST SIGN AND PRINT THEIR ADDRESSES

Address: _____

Witness 2:

Signed: _____

Address: _____

© 2000
PARTNERSHIP FOR CARING, INC.

Courtesy of **Partnership for Caring, Inc.**   6/00
1620 Eye Street, NW, Suite 202, Washington, DC 20006 800-989-9455

FIGURE 13.1 continued

under which dying occurs, and to have those decisions recognized and honored. Another national patient advocacy group that promotes legal strategies for death with dignity is the **Compassion in Dying Federation.** It also established a Center for End-of-Life Law and Policy that assists in the development of challenges to state laws that bar patients from requesting aid in dying from their physicians. Compassion in Dying aims to provide a safe, respectful environment for the consideration of end-of-life choices, as well as the personal presence of case management volunteers who form relationships with terminally ill individuals as they explore end-of-life possibilities.

An organization that has actively attempted to change the law in order to legalize assisted suicide for the terminally ill is the **Hemlock Society.** The society's popular publication, *Final Exit,* by its founder, Derek Humphry, is a manual on nonviolent methods to commit suicide with prescription barbiturates to assure a gentle, peaceful death. The Hemlock Society distinguishes between "rational or responsible suicide" (i.e., the option of ending one's life for good and valid reasons) and suicide that is caused by a rejection of life because of emotional disturbance. In response to prohibitions against physician-assisted suicide, the society also advocates nonfelonious methods, such as gas masks and paper bags. It views the right to request assistance in dying as merely an extension of the individual's right to control the kind of treatment he or she receives when dying. Rejecting remote chances of recovery as a basis to justify prolonging life, the society also discards the notion of any ethical distinction between stopping treatment and assisting someone to die.

POINTS TO PONDER

Have you and your family members ever discussed how to die, your preferences and fears? If not, how could you initiate such a discussion, either with your parents, your partner, or your adult children?

ETHICAL DILEMMAS

"With the use of our moral imagination, we can reshape the way we behave toward people with any kind of disability. It goes back to Aristotle's question, How does one live a good life? How does ethical thinking help older people live a good life? Ethics is part of what we do every day. It's so much more than making a decision about putting in a feeding tube. . . ." (Holstein, 1998, p. 4). On a personal and practical level, many dying people find that the medical technology that prolongs their lives may financially ruin their families. It is important that families discuss in advance such issues as who should assume medical care decision making on the patient's behalf, if necessary, or under what circumstances one would prefer or not prefer life support. However, most families find it emotionally difficult to do such planning, especially if the older adult refuses to do so or cannot make a rational decision because of dementia.

Societal cost-benefit criteria inevitably come into play in discussions of active and passive euthanasia. Admittedly, a significant proportion of the money spent on medical care in a person's lifetime goes to services received during the last years and months of life. In spite of that, even if such end-of-life care were eliminated, the nation's health care expenditures would be reduced by only one-half of one percent—or even less (Butler 2000). Nevertheless, the public often perceives that the costs to keep alive a comparatively small number of people are prohibitively high (Cole and Holstein, 1996).

Rapid improvements in medical technology are not matched by refinements in the law and the ethics of using those therapies. This is the case even though the field of **bioethics** or medical ethics, which focuses on procedural approaches to questions about death, dying, and medical decision making, has grown in the past 30 years. Hastened death raises not only complex ethical and legal dilemmas, but also resource-allocation issues. Both policy makers and service providers face the issue of how to balance an individual client's needs for personal autonomy with the community's demand to conserve resources. A fundamental question is whether the doctrine of personal privacy under the U.S. Constitution and related state laws extends to individuals' decisions about their physical care, even when those decisions involve life or death choices for themselves or others. Alternatively, as older people seek to remain at home to die, what are equitable ways to allocate community services such as home care in the face of a growing public distrust of broad-based "entitlements" and perceptions of shrinking resources (Weinberg, 1998)? As noted by Holstein (1998), providers, policy makers and families are taking ethics beyond autonomy and decision making into the broader realm of how we treat the terminally ill—how we look at them, what we expect of them, and how we talk to them.

Bereavement, Grief, and Mourning Rituals

Death affects the social structure through the dying person's survivors, especially spouses and partners, who have social and emotional needs resulting from that death. How these needs are expressed and met varies across place, time, groups, and culture. This is because grief is a highly individualized phenomenon with a complexity and wide range of what is considered "normal" within different social and cultural environments.

Bereavement is defined as the objective situation of having lost someone significant (e.g., being deprived) and the overall adaptation to loss (Stroebe et al., 2001). It usually refers to loss through death, although individuals can be bereaved through other types of losses such as divorce or relocation.

The Grief Process

The **grief process** is the complex emotional response to bereavement and can include shock and disbelief, guilt, psychological numbness, depression, loneliness, fatigue, loss of appetite, sleeplessness, and anxiety about one's ability to carry on with life. **Mourning** signifies culturally patterned expectations about the expression of grief. What is believed about the meaning of death, how it should be faced, and what happens after physical death vary widely by culture and its associated religions (Braun, Pietsch, and Blanchett, 2000). Cultural variations are particularly marked with regard to how loss through death is understood and beliefs about death, including the possibility of future reunion with the dead, the meaning of various forms of emotions following the death, and what to say to oneself and others following a death (Rosenblatt, 2001). With the increasing diversity of American society and globalization, professionals working with older people and their families need to be sensitive to the influences of multiple cultures and to the patient's generation and acculturation level. For example, among Asian Americans, there tends to be reluctance to talk about death; grief is kept within the family, and the body is not to be moved nor organs removed for donation until the soul has had time to travel from it (Braun and Nichols, 1997).

Although there are clusters or phases of grief reactions, the progression is more like a roller coaster—with overlapping responses and wide individual variability—rather than orderly stages

> Bereaved persons are like ducks: Above the surface . . . looking composed and unruffled.
> Below the surface, paddling like crazy!
>
> SOURCE: Northwest Geriatric Education Center, 2000.

Photos of a deceased loved one can provide solace in the grieving process.

or a fixed or universal sequence. To expect grieving individuals to progress in some specified fashion is inappropriate, and can be harmful to them. The highs and lows within broad phases can occur within minutes, days, months, or years, with grieving individuals moving back and forth among them. Even within the individual, there can be mixed reactions, with a person simultaneously experiencing anger, guilt, helplessness, loneliness, and uncontrolled crying—along with personal strength and pride in their coping—all within a matter of hours. Emotions change rapidly, beginning with shock, numbness, and disbelief, followed by an all-encompassing sorrow. Early months following the loss are the most difficult, with early indicators often serving as predictors of longer-term adjustment (Lund, 1993; Lund, Caserta, and Dimond, 1993). However, even when a grieving person has tried to work through early phases and move toward integrating the loss into his or her life, a picture, a favorite song of the deceased, or a personal object may evoke more intense grief.

An intermediate phase of grief often involves an idealization and searching for the presence of the deceased person, as well as an obsessive review to find meaning for the death and to answer the inexplicable "why"? Anger toward the deceased, God, and caregivers may also be experienced, as well as guilt and regrets for what survivors did not do or say. When the permanence of the loss is acknowledged and yearning ceases, anguish, disorganization, and despair often result. The grieving person tends to experience a sense of confusion; a feeling of aimlessness; a loss of motivation, confidence, and interest; and an inability to make decisions. Simply getting out of bed in the morning can require intense effort. These feelings may be exacerbated if the grieving person tries to live according to others' expectations, including those of the deceased. Instead, successful adjustments require active coping strategies in which the bereaved individual finds his or her own best way to live with grief (Lund, 1993).

The final phase—reorganization—is marked by a resumption of routine activities and social relationships, while still remembering and identifying with the deceased, and recognition by the bereaved individual that life will never be the same. The ability to communicate effectively one's

---

STRATEGIES FOR GRIEVING

- Remember that grief is an emotion and needs to be felt; it cannot be worked out in the head.
- Tears are not a sign of weakness; they are an emotional first aid.
- Only the individual can decide what's right for him or her during this time.
- Grief is a life-changing experience; it takes time and patience to adjust.
- Be kind to oneself and lower expectations of what one can do. Grief takes up a lot of emotional and physical energy.
- Lack of concentration, difficulty sleeping, forgetfulness, confusion, and anger toward others and the deceased are normal.
- It can be comforting to carry or wear something that belonged to the person who has died.

SOURCE: Northwest Geriatric Education Center, 2000.

thoughts and feelings to others, form new relationships, and learn new skills and competencies enhances the adjustment process (Lund, 1993). *Integration of the loss into one's life* might be a more appropriate description than the term *recovery* to describe changes in the person's identity and emotional reorganization to ordinary levels of functioning (Weiss, 1993).

Process of Mourning

A "six-R process of mourning" appears to integrate much of what has been written about grief stages, phases, and tasks, and can provide guidelines for family members and professionals:

- Recognize and accept the reality of the loss.
- React to, experience, and express the pain of separation or active confrontation with the loss, including deep weeping and expressing feelings of guilt.
- Reminisce: tell and retell memories, writing, dreaming.
- Relinquish old attachments. More recently, grief theorists have identified the importance of maintaining connections with the person who has died, but in a way different than in the past, while being able to form new relationships.
- Readjust to an environment in which the dead person is missing, adapt to new roles, and form a new identity.
- Reinvest in new personal relationships and acts of meaning rather than remaining tied to the past, while recognizing that the pain of the loss may continue throughout life. (Rando, 1988; Stroebe et al., 2001; Weiss, 2001)

The classical paradigm of grief, derived from Freud's psychoanalytical perspective, assumed that grieving individuals needed to let go of their relationship to the deceased in order to complete their "grief work." Individuals who did not engage in grief work were assumed to be at risk of pathological grief and increased risk of physical and mental illness. Later postmodern and constructionist theoretical perspectives make no assumptions about the universality of how individuals respond to death. Instead, they acknowledge the tremendous diversity of healthy grieving, and that the "grief work" model of actively confronting negative emotions is not always the best approach. Instead, some degree of denial, distraction, and humor can be effective ways to grieve. From the postmodern perspective, the process of vacillation between avoiding and engaging in grief work is fundamental to reconstructing meaning and a basic sense of self. Later theorists also emphasized that the goal of grieving is not to disengage completely from memories and bonds with the deceased. Instead, bereaved individuals redefine their connection to the deceased (Klass, Silverman, and Nickerson, 1996; Lindenstrom, 2002; Walter, 2003; Wortman and Silver, 2001). It is important to acknowledge that conflicting views about healthy grieving exist, and that we have too little knowledge to claim that we know the best way for older adults to grieve.

Some people never fully resolve their loss or cease grieving, but learn to live with the pain of loss for a lifetime (Martin-Matthews, 1996; Thompson et al., 1998). Older adults' experiences with grief may be even more complex than other age groups' for several reasons. As noted in Chapter 6, they are more likely to experience unrelated, multiple losses over relatively brief periods, at a time when their coping capacities and environmental resources are often diminished. The cumulative effects of losses may be greater, especially if the older person has not resolved earlier losses, such as a child's death, or interprets current losses as evidence of an inevitable continuing decline. Health care providers must be careful not to misdiagnose grief symptoms as physical illness, dementia, or hypochondria. On the other hand, prior losses can facilitate accommodation to a partner's death. Whether other losses have been interpreted as positive (i.e., leading to personal growth) appears to be a critical factor (van den Hoonaard, 2001).

Whether grieving is more difficult when death is sudden or unexpected is unclear. In comparison to the young, older people may be less affected by a sudden death because they have rehearsed and planned for widowhood as a life-stage task. They have also experienced it vicariously through the deaths of their friends or spouses of friends. An expected death can allow survivors to prepare for the changes through **anticipatory grief,** but it does not necessarily minimize the grief and emotional strain following the death. In fact, some studies indicate that a longer period of anticipatory grief, through caring for an individual with chronic illness, can actually create barriers to successful adaptation and increase the risk of depression and other psychiatric disorders (Raveis, 1999). Family members who experience the death as a relief from long-term demands of care may feel premature detachment, ambivalent and hostile feelings, guilt, depression, and a reduced ability to mourn publicly. Other researchers have concluded that the overall grief process is similar whether the loss is expected or unexpected, although suddenness may make a difference early in the process of bereavement (Randolph, 1997). Some preventive predeath psychosocial interventions have been developed to minimize postdeath complications. These include facilitating communication with the ill partner, preparing the survivor for the practical aspects of life without one's spouse, and enabling the surviving partner to deal with his or her own illness-related demands and losses.

Factors that are found to facilitate the grieving process are whether the death is viewed as natural, the degree to which relationships seem complete, and the presence of surviving confidants to provide emotional support. A central dynamic in caregiver bereavement is the support experienced while providing care, as well as the possibility of continued support (Almberg, Grafstroem, and Winblad, 2000). To deal with grief successfully requires facing the pain and fully expressing the related feelings. Fortunately, understanding is growing about how grief and loss affect the bereaved individual's life and how to respond appropriately. Health care providers now recognize the importance of grief counseling, and view grieving as a natural healing process. Assistance in grieving, perhaps through life review and encouragement of new risk-taking, is especially important for older adults.

Unfortunately, most research of bereavement consists of case studies or retrospective studies

---

HOW PROFESSIONALS AND FAMILIES CAN SUPPORT THE GRIEVING PROCESS

- Listen, without judgment or giving advice, to the bereaved individual's expression of feelings including guilt, anger, and anxiety, rather than suggesting what he or she *should* feel.
- Realize that the grieving process can be a lengthy and emotional roller-coaster, not a fixed progression in which one learns to live with grief.
- Be careful to avoid endless chatter or simplistic statements ("I know just how you feel." "She is happier now." "God loved him more than you did." "You should feel better in six months." "You can marry again/you'll meet someone else").
- Resist telling your own stories.
- Listen carefully to the silences, to what is not said as well as said.
- Encourage sharing of memories.
- Sometimes the most helpful response is simply "to be there" for the bereaved.
- Time itself does not heal. Healing most frequently takes place through dealing with grief, which can be painful and exhausting. But some mourners never engage in "grief work."
- Recognize that one never completely gets over a loss but one can learn to live with grief.
- Do not tell the bereaved to stop crying or not be sad; provide time and space to cry; sometimes hugging or patting the crying person's hand actually shuts down the crying.
- Identify concrete tasks by which to help, such as organizing meals, child care, and house cleaning, so the bereaved has time and space to grieve.
- Recognize gender and cultural differences in grieving.
- Encourage meditation and deep breathing.

during the early phase of grief. There are few well-controlled longitudinal studies of the bereavement process. An additional limitation is that few researchers have controlled for the effects of variables such as gender, race, age, social class, and education. Our understanding of the emotional components of bereavement is based largely on middle-aged, middle-class Caucasians, thereby limiting the cultural relevance of interventions to address the emotional aspects of grieving.

Mourning involves cultural assumptions about appropriate behavior during bereavement. Mourning rituals develop in every culture as a way to channel the normal expression of grief, define the appropriate timing of bereavement, and encourage support for the bereaved among family and friends. Professionals need to be sensitive to cultural and ethnic differences regarding the form and meaning of death and the burial or cremation of the dead. Grief rituals, such as sorting and disposing of personal effects and visiting the grave site, are important in working through the grief process.

The funeral, for example, serves as a rite of passage for the deceased and a focal point for the expression of the survivors' grief. Funerals also allow the family to demonstrate cohesion through sharing rituals, food, and drink, and thus to minimize the disruptive effects of the death. Funerals and associated customs are more important in societies with a high mortality throughout the life cycle than in societies where death is predominantly confined to the old. Money donations instead of flowers, memorial services and celebrations of the deceased person's life instead of funerals, and cremations instead of land burial signal the development of new kinds of death rituals. Traditional funeral ceremonies are criticized for being costly, for exploiting people at a time when they are vulnerable, and for elaborate cosmetic restorations of the body. Legislation has been enacted to control some of the excesses of the funeral industry; organizations such as the People Memorial Association ensure lower funeral costs to its members. Despite criticisms of the funeral industry, however, most people approve of some type of ceremony to make the death more real to the survivors and to offer a meaningful way to cope with the initial grief.

Widowhood

A spouse's death (or that of a partner, in the case of gay and lesbian couples or unmarried heterosexual couples) may be the most catastrophic and stressful event experienced by older adults, altering one's self-concept to an "uncoupled identity" (Cicirelli, 2002; Raveis, 1999). Widowhood for both men and women not only represents the obvious loss, but numerous other dramatic changes in the survivor's life: loss of a shared past and a future; loss of the role or status of married; lack of a sexual partner; loss of companionship, social networks, and a confidant; and especially for women, loss of economic security (Benedict and Zhang, 1999; Cicirelli, 2002).

Death of a partner tends to trigger "cascading effects," with one's grief interacting with or exacerbating other changes, such as chronic illness, disability, or involuntary relocation (O'Bryant and Hansson, 1995). Both widows and widowers mention loneliness as the primary consequence of widowhood. In fact, the terms *widow* and *alone* are almost synonymous, at least during the early phases of widowhood (van den Hoonaard, 2001).

As discussed in Chapter 15, among women age 65 and over, up to 70 percent are widowed, more than three times the rate among their male peers (Federal Interagency Forum, 2000). The average age of widowhood is 66 years for women and 69 years for men; when combined with women's greater life expectancy, this means that the average duration of widowhood for women is 15 years compared with 6 years for men. Among the oldest-old, widows outnumber widowers 5 to 1; among people of color, the proportion of widows is twice that among whites; women of color are also widowed earlier (Martin-Matthews,

Older widows generally have more extensive peer support than widowers.

1996). This is a reflection of the shorter life expectancy of men of color in our society.

Findings are mixed about the impact of a partner's death on physical and mental health and mortality. Health status and perceived health have been found to decrease, and mortality and suicide rates increase, but only in the short term following a partner's death. Bereaved individuals (especially men) generally show higher levels of physical illness, somatic complaints (e.g., headaches, dizziness, muscular aches, weight changes, sleep disturbances), appetite loss, and utilization of health services, in addition to lower well-being and morale, especially for the first 2 years after a partner's death. However, such negative effects on physical health tend not to persist beyond 2 years (Nieboer, Lindenberg, and Siegwart Ormel, 1999; Raveis, 1999). Similarly, rates of depression, anxiety, substance abuse, mood alterations, obsessive thoughts of the deceased, disorientation, memory problems, and difficulties concentrating are found to be nearly 9 times as high among the newly bereaved, especially men, as among married individuals. The first 6 months of widowhood appear to be the most stressful, especially when partners

face multiple losses and have limitations due to chronic illness or disability. Over the long term (e.g., more than 2 years), the effects on physical and mental health are greatly diminished (Rosenzweig et al., 1997; Turvey et al., 1999). Despite the stress, the course of spousal bereavement is often characterized by resilience and effective coping, which allows feelings of self-confidence, self-efficacy, and personal growth to follow short-term depression and sadness. Nevertheless, the greatest problem faced by widows and widowers is loneliness—and being alone (Utz et al., 2002; Worden, 2002).

The negative effects of widowhood can be attenuated through a number of psychosocial variables (Bennett, 1997). Quality of the prior relationship affects how partners experience the death of a spouse. Grief tends to be less for those whose relationship was marked by conflict (Carr et al., 2000). By contrast, short-term grieving is more difficult for those whose marriage was characterized by warmth and emotional dependence, but over time, these qualities may bring solace and foster personal growth. In addition, harmonious marriages appear to have a protective effect in terms of health service use and health care costs, until immediately after widowhood, when health costs are higher than for survivors of discordant marriages (Prigerson et al., 2000).

Other variables that affect the long-term effects of widowhood are the adequacy of the social support network, including professional support and closeness to children and intimate friends; the individual's characteristic ways of coping with stress; religious commitment and cultural values and beliefs. Although family plays an important role following widowhood, 20 percent of widowed persons report not having a single living relative to whom they feel particularly close. Older widows are more likely to use social supports as a coping strategy when their social networks are characterized by reciprocity and reliability, but men generally do not. At the same time, friendships developed on the basis of marital relationships may not survive widowhood. In fact, the

---

THE EXPERIENCE OF WIDOWHOOD

Darlene became a widow at age 56. Although she was too young to qualify for her husband's Social Security, her dependent children at home received a monthly benefit of approximately $1000 per child. A successful career woman, Darlene sought refuge in her work, her friends, and her children. She learned skills that she had not mastered during her marriage, such as home and car repairs, and appeared to be self-sufficient and "moving on" to her friends and children. During the day, she did function well. It was only at the end of the day, when other family members were asleep and she was climbing into the bed she had shared with her husband for many years, that she would be overcome by feelings of intense loneliness, hopelessness, and regret. At times, she felt overwhelmed by all the years ahead when she would bear both responsibilities and pleasure alone, without an intimate with whom to share. For more than two years, she cried every night before she fell asleep.

ability to make new friends may be an important indicator of how an individual is coping with the loss of a spouse (Ducharme and Corin, 1997). Age, gender, and health status of the widowed person also affect the degree of stress of widowhood. Age by itself, however, is found to have little effect on bereavement outcomes. Differences between younger and older widows can be explained by the relationship of age to employment status and income. Age is associated, however, with a greater need to learn new life skills, such as an older woman's mastering of financial-management tasks after the death of her husband.

Whether the stress of bereavement is greater for the young than for the old is unclear. The intensity of psychological distress tends to be greater for younger widows than older ones, since the death of one's spouse is more likely to be unanticipated and few of their peers are experiencing similar loss. Although younger spouses are found initially to manifest more intense grief, a reverse trend is noted after 18 months, with the

grieving process lasting longer for older partners who have lost a lifelong relationship (Moss, Moss, and Hansson, 2001). As noted earlier, older people are more likely to experience other losses simultaneously, or "bereavement overload" (Kastenbaum, 1991), which may intensify and prolong their grief. On the other hand, spousal bereavement in later life is an "on-time" or normative event, especially for older women, who typically have had other opportunities to develop appropriate coping strategies for a variety of losses. In such instances, widowhood may be less stressful, even among the oldest-old, and different death circumstances do not appear to have a significant impact on long-term adjustment (Lund, 1993).

Preventive psychoeducational interventions initiated predeath, such as through hospice, have been found to prevent or minimize problems in mourning as opposed to interventions postdeath, after problems have surfaced. Interventions postdeath focus on assisting the surviving spouse review and reflect on the loss, providing support for grieving, and helping the surviving spouse to withdraw emotionally from his or her dead partner (Raveis, 1999). Since bereaved partners who have extensive contacts with friends and family and belong to church groups and other voluntary associations are less likely to die soon after the death of a spouse, interventions need to encourage network building and affiliations. Community mental health centers, primary care clinics, and senior centers are suitable venues for such cost-effective interventions.

Gender Differences in Widowhood

Whether widowhood is more difficult for women or men is unclear. Certainly, coping or adaptation to widowhood is related to income for both men and women. Adequate financial resources are necessary to maintain a sense of self-sufficiency and to continue participation in meaningful activities. Older widows are generally worse off than widowers in terms of finances, years of education, legal problems, and prospects for remarriage.

Women who have been economically dependent on their husbands often find their incomes drastically reduced, especially if they do not yet qualify for Social Security or if their husbands had not chosen survivors' pension benefits. Financial hardships may be especially great for women who have been caring for a spouse during a long chronic illness or who have depleted their joint resources during the spouse's institutionalization. Furthermore, older widows generally have few opportunities to augment their income through paid employment. Insurance benefits, when they exist, tend to be exhausted within 2 years of the husband's death. Not surprisingly, higher income has been found to be associated with better bereavement outcomes. Accordingly, more years of schooling are related to higher levels of personal functioning, since education tends to provide the ability to clarify problems, identify resources, and take action toward solutions (Lopata, 1993). Gender has fairly consistent effects on personal functioning; women tend to exhibit lower levels of completing plans, lower self-efficacy, and higher levels of depression, and to express greater fatalism and more vulnerability than their male counterparts (Arbuckle and deVries, 1995).

Some women, however, do not depend on a man for economic or social support. Because women generally have more diverse, extensive friendship networks than men do, and because widowhood is a more typical component of the life cycle for women, older women often form strong support networks with other widows. These friendship groups can compensate for the loss of a husband's companionship and ease the adjustment to living alone. Friends are of greatest support, in some instances more so than children. This is especially true when friends accept the widow's emotional ambivalence, do not offer advice, and respond to what she defines as her needs. Adjusting to the loss of a spouse is likely to be most difficult for women who are in poor health, have had few economic and social resources throughout their lives, and perceive themselves as dependent (Raveis, 1999). It is also problematic for women whose identity as a wife is lost without the substitution of other viable roles and lifestyles. A closely related factor appears to be whether a gap exists between how a woman was socialized to be dependent upon a man and how she must now live more independently as a widow (Lopata, 1987). For example, in a classic study, Lopata (1973) found that widows who did not have their own friends or who had only couple-based friendships before the husband's death generally had difficulty forming new friendships and developing satisfying roles. They also tended not to access social services. In our couples-oriented society, such women were lonely and isolated, and turned primarily to their children for emotional support. Friendships were thus the least frequent and the least deeply involving among the most disadvantaged and uneducated of the urban widows studied by Lopata. However, because more women have entered the workforce in the past 30 years, future cohorts of older women may be better prepared to live independently than the women in Lopata's early studies.

Among women over age 70, two-thirds of whom are widowed, the married person is the unusual case, but she may still have an extensive helping network (Barrett and Lynch, 1999). Whether widows have strong friendship networks appears to vary with socioeconomic class and

---

DEVELOPING NEW ROLES IN WIDOWHOOD

Martha had always seen her role as wife and mother and left the paying of the bills and "business" aspects of family life to her husband. Her "job" was to keep the home a comfortable place for him and their daughter. When he died 5 years ago, she was 63. She felt ill-prepared to take on paying the bills and managing other financial matters. She sought the advice of her banker on the best way to set up a bookkeeping system. After paying the bills, ordering some appliances for the house, and taking care of the Medicare paperwork for the past few years, she now sees herself as being in the role of "manager" for herself, and is pleased with what she has learned.

race, whether they had a social network and satisfying roles before their husbands' deaths, and the prevalence of widowhood among a person's own age, sex, and class peers. Latina and Asian American widows are more likely to live with others and thus to have more active support systems than do Caucasian widows or those from other ethnic minority groups (Moen, 1996).

While older widowed men are seven times more likely than older widows to remarry (Cohen, 1999), many widows have no interest in remarriage. Even among Lopata's (1973) study of widows described above, 36 percent said they would not marry again. Although many persons feel great loss following a spouse's death, for some who have been restricted in their marriage or who faced long-term caregiving responsibilities, widowhood can bring relief and opportunities to develop new interests. Although a husband's death is devastating, personal growth can be a positive result of the loss. Some widows recognize how they have changed and redefined themselves, calling themselves "new women" (van den Hoonaard, 2001).

A woman's change in status inevitably affects her relationship with her children and other relatives. Most widows move in with their children only as a "last resort," although their children may view them as "helpless" and urge them to make the move. Older widows tend to grow closer to their daughters through patterns of mutual assistance, but sons may provide instrumental support (home repairs, yardwork) for mothers in their own homes. Nevertheless, although children provide both socioeconomic support and assistance with tasks, this may not necessarily reduce their widowed parent's loneliness. For example, interactions with an adult child are less reciprocal, while friends and neighbors are better suited for sharing leisure activities and providing companionship. Such reciprocity tends to be associated with higher morale. What is clear is the importance of diverse social networks that include age-generational peers, whether family or nonfamily (McCandless and Conner, 1997).

Research on widowhood has focused on women, since there are five widows to every widower in our society. Less is known about the effects of widowhood on older men, for whom their wife's death tends to be unexpected (think about how many widowers will say "I always thought I was the one who would go first"). Men more often complain of loneliness and appear to make slower emotional recoveries than do women. Accordingly, they are more likely to experience declines in mental health, morale, and social functioning (Bennett, 1998). They may have more difficulty expressing their grief and adjusting to the loss than women do. This is because of their lower degree of involvement in family and friendship roles throughout life, their lifelong patterns of restraining emotions, their limited prior housekeeping and cooking, and the greater likelihood of a double role loss of worker and spouse (Patterson, 1996). For men who focused largely on work, their wife's death may raise issues of self-identity separate from their partner (Carverhill, 1997). On the other hand, some men experience pride and enhanced self-esteem from mastering new housekeeping skills (Lund et al., 1993). Many older men depended on their wives for emotional support, household maintenance, and social planning. Given these factors, men appear

MEN AND WIDOWHOOD

George's first wife died in childbirth; his second wife, who suffered a long bout of cancer, when he was 79, and his third wife, when he was 85. After the deaths of his first two wives, he quickly sought out someone else who could help fill the void left by their deaths. Each time, he looked for someone who would attend to his needs, listen to his stories, and join him on short outings and trips. He was seeking a companion, not a lover. After the death of his third wife, he became socially isolated and depressed. She had been the one who kept their social life going. Without her, friends seemed to drop away.

to "need" remarriage more than women do, and perhaps have been socialized to move more quickly into restructuring their lives through remarriage. Men, however, experience more medical problems (as measured by increased physicians' visits and use of medications, and higher rates of depression) and are at greater risk of dying during the 6 months following their wife's death (Nolen-Hoeksema and Larson, 1999). Higher rates of illness may result from hormonal responses to the stress of loss, which can lead to suppression of the body's immune system. Although the death of their wives may significantly impair older men's emotional and medical well-being, it is less likely to place men at an economic disadvantage. More research is needed on how men cope with the loss of their wives. Even less is known about how older men's experience of widowhood varies by social class or ethnic minority status.

As noted above, widowhood generally increases social isolation for both men and women, with loneliness perceived as a major problem. Alternatively, social support can reduce the risk of illness and mortality (Thorson and Powell, 2000). In order to provide such support for persons coping with loneliness and isolation, mutual help groups and bereavement centers are developed by both mental health professionals and lay organizations. Women are the most frequent participants. These widow-to-widow groups are based on the principle of bringing together people who have the common experience of widowhood and who can help each other identify solutions to shared concerns. They recognize that a widowed person generally accepts help from other widowed people more readily than from professionals or family members. Support groups thus can provide widows with effective role models and can help integrate them into a social network and enhance their sense of competence toward their environment. Similar groups also need to be developed for gay men and lesbian women who are coping with the loss of a partner. Some studies, however, have suggested that a widowed person's sense of self-esteem, competence, and life satisfaction may be as important

resources as the self-help intervention—or more so. One implication is that group interventions should focus upon ways for the bereaved to draw upon and enhance their internal resources, to experience increased confidence, and to learn new skills, not just serve as a forum to address the disruptive effects of the loss (Caserta, Lund, and Rice, 1999). Clearly, more research is needed on how support-group dynamics and structure relate to specific adjustment outcomes.

Implications for the Future

The right-to-die movement, death with dignity, palliative care, pain management, and use of advance directives all raise ethical dilemmas related to the prolongation and termination of life. These dilemmas are framed within the context of escalating health care costs and use of expensive technology to prolong life. Many older adults are now saved, often at considerable cost, from diseases that previously would have killed them, only to be guaranteed death from another disease at equally high or even higher cost. Physicians have traditionally been taught to spare no effort in keeping a patient alive. Nevertheless, health professionals and laypersons are increasingly questioning whether dying should be prolonged when there is no possibility of recovery.

The timing, place, and conditions of death are increasingly under medical control. For almost any life-threatening condition, some interventions can now delay the moment of death, but not its inevitability. Doctors and nurses have always dealt with dying, but not until the present technical advances have they had so much power and responsibility to control the end of life and to determine when treatment is medically futile. These new medical capacities demand a new set of ethics and practices. The field of bioethics was born out of the dilemmas surrounding the introduction and withdrawal of invasive treatments, the patients' decision-making capacity to participate in treatment decisions, and the quality of the patient's life. Health care facilities are now required to have the capacity to address such bioethical issues, typically through ethics committees. Bioethics is a field that will continue to grow in this century, encompassing a wider range of professionals in debates about end-of-life care.

Concerns about when and whether treatment should be withheld frame the debates regarding the right to die and to assisted suicide. Proponents of the right to die and active euthanasia maintain that prolonging excruciating pain and threatening a person's dignity in a hopeless situation serve no public interests. These decisions become even more complex when the elder is mentally incompetent or comatose. Cross-cultural differences also affect how life-sustaining treatment and palliative care are interpreted and the value and respect accorded elders' lives.

The increased visibility of right-to-die legislation, court rulings, and individual cases means that more people know about their legal rights and have thought about what they might choose for themselves or other family members when faced with a terminal illness. In most cases, there is agreement that individuals should have the right to control how they die, but disagreement persists about what is meant by terminal and medical finality and under what circumstances decisions to cease life-sustaining treatment should be made. The 1997 Supreme Court decision put at the forefront the issue of aggressive pain management and how well health care providers are trained in end-of-life care. More and more professional organizations are seeking to ensure that providers are prepared to provide palliative care.

Public support is relatively widespread for individual determination regarding life-sustaining treatment through advance directives, including living wills. Baby boomers, who will be better educated and accustomed to having control over their lives, are more likely to complete advance directives than the current cohort of elders. Even though all 50 states have laws authorizing the use of advance directives, variability across states in their interpretation and implementation will probably continue.

Divided votes on state legislation to legalize assisted suicide will probably persist, especially given the conservative political climate and current federal efforts to undermine laws such as Oregon's Death with Dignity Act. Regardless of the laws, however, it is likely that individuals and their families will continue to make decisions to hasten death, especially for terminal patients with pain or for those with neurological disorders, such as Lou Gehrig's disease. Internet resources on dying, including those that provide information on how to hasten death, foster the debates taking place at the grassroots level and allow families and patients to take matters into their own hands. For example, Death NET, founded by Derek Humphrey of the Hemlock Society, offers the largest collection of "right to die" materials and services on the Internet. The Website of Partners in Caring is a comprehensive resource for those wanting to understand the right-to-die movement and to download advance directive packages geared to the laws and regulations of a particular state. Such Internet resources, which once were unimaginable, will increase in number and detail in the future. Not surprisingly, the number of antieuthanasia websites are also growing, such as Life WEB of the International Anti-Euthanasia Task Force. Such Internet resources articulating the pros and cons of the right to die and assisted suicide will undoubtedly proliferate. These legal and ethical debates—whether in courtrooms, ethics committees, or cyberspace—translate into daily practice and hard choices for those who are caring for chronically ill and dying elders. The questions of who should control decisions about life and death will continue to be argued philosophically and legally, but doctors, nurses, social workers, and families will be faced with the hard decisions for timely practical solutions for their older patients and relatives. As noted throughout this chapter, the professional preparation of a wide range of health care providers in the future must address such legal and ethical issues as well as how to deliver culturally competent end-of-life care.

Summary

Although death and dying have been taboo topics for many people in our society, they have become more legitimate issues for scientific and social discussion in recent years. At the same time, there is a growing emphasis on how professionals should work with the dying and their families, as well as a movement to permit death with dignity. A major framework advanced for understanding the dying process is the concept of stages of dying. However, the stage model is only an inventory of possible sequences, not fixed steps.

Most people appear both to deny and to accept death, being better able to discuss others' deaths than their own, and fearing a painful dying process more than the event of death itself. Different attitudes toward dying exist among the old and the young. Older people are less fearful and anxious about their death than younger people and would prefer a slow death that allows them time to prepare. Likewise, survivors tend to view an older person's death as less tragic than a younger individual's.

Professionals and family members can address the dying person's fears, minimize the pain of the dying process, and help the individual to attain a "good death." One of the major developments in this regard is hospice, a philosophy of caring that can be implemented in both home and institutional settings, and which provides people with more control over how they die and the quality of their remaining days.

The movement for a right to a dignified death has prompted new debates about euthanasia. Both passive and active euthanasia raise complex moral and legal questions that have been only partially addressed by the passage of living will legislation and a growing number of judicial decisions, including the June 1997 Supreme Court decision that ruled that there is no constitutional "right to die." Economic issues are also at stake; as costs for health care escalate, questions about how much public money should be spent on maintaining chronically ill people are likely to intensify. Bioethics, with its emphasis on informed consent, patient rights, and autonomy, addresses the moral issues raised by the health care of older people.

Regardless of how individuals die, their survivors experience grief and mourning. The intensity and duration of grief appear to vary by age and sex, although more research is needed regarding gender differences in reaction to loss of spouse and adjustment to widowhood.

By age 70, the majority of older women are widows. A much smaller number of older men become widowers, generally not until after age 85. The status of widowhood has negative consequences for many women in terms of increased legal difficulties, reduced finances, and few remarriage prospects. Although men are less economically disadvantaged by widowhood, they may be lonelier and have more difficulty adjusting than women do. For both men and women, social supports, particularly close friends or confidants, are important to physical and mental well-being during widowhood. In addition to mourning rituals to help widows and widowers cope with their grief, services such as widows' support groups are also needed. Comprehensive and diverse service formats are essential, given the variety of grief responses, and interventions should be available early in the bereavement process and continue over relatively long periods of time to ensure maximum effectiveness. Health and social service professionals can play a crucial role in developing services for the dying and their survivors that are sensitive to cultural, ethnic minority, sexual orientation, and gender differences.

GLOSSARY

active euthanasia   positive steps to hasten someone else's death, such as administering a lethal injection; assisted suicide, perhaps by a physician

advance directive documents such as living wills, wills, and durable power of attorney for health care decisions that outline actions to be taken when an individual is no longer able to do so, often because of irreversible terminal illness

anticipatory grief grief for a loved one prior to his or her death, usually occurring during the time that the loved one has a terminal illness that may allow survivors to prepare; may be a barrier to adaptation

bereavement state of being deprived of a loved one by death

bereavement overload an experience of older adults who are exposed to the increased frequency of family and friends' deaths and become desensitized to the impact of death

bioethics discipline dealing with procedural approaches to questions about death, dying, and medical decision making

Compassion in Dying Federation national organization supporting the right to die and working to educate health care providers about aggressive pain management

conservator person designated by a court to manage the affairs, either personal or fiscal or both, of persons unable to do so for themselves

death crisis an unanticipated change in the amount of time remaining to live

death with dignity dying when one still has some independence and control over decisions about life

durable power of attorney legal document that conveys to another person designated by the person signing the document the right to make decisions regarding either health and personal care or assets and income, or both, of the person giving the power; it is a durable power that does not expire, as a power of attorney normally does, when a person becomes incompetent

Dying Person's Bill of Rights affirms dying person's right to dignity, privacy, informed participation, and competent care

dying process stages as advanced by Kübler-Ross; five stages experienced by the dying person: (1) denial and isolation, (2) anger and resentment, (3) bargaining and an attempt to postpone, (4) depression and sense of loss, and (5) acceptance

euthanasia the act or practice of killing (active euthanasia) or permitting the death of (passive euthana-sia) hopelessly sick or injured individuals in a relatively painless way; mercy killing

grief process intense emotional suffering caused by loss, disaster, misfortune, etc.; acute sorrow; deep sadness

grief reaction emotional and cognitive process following the death of a loved one or other major loss

guardian person who establishes legal control over another person's body as well as finances

Hemlock Society national organization that promotes the right to die for terminally ill persons, calls for legalizing assistance for those who decide to take their own lives, and publishes information on nonviolent painless methods to commit suicide

hospice a place or a program of care for dying persons that gives emphasis to personal dignity of the dying person, reducing pain, sources of anxiety, and family reconciliation when indicated

informed consent written or oral document that states indications/reasons for treatment, its benefits, risks, and alternatives

living will legal document in which an individual's wishes about medical treatment are put in writing should he or she be unable to communicate at the end of life, directing physicians and hospitals to withhold life-sustaining procedures, take all measures to sustain life, or whatever seems appropriate to the person executing the document

medical power of attorney similar to "durable power of attorney," but focuses on a health care surrogate to make decisions about *medical* care

mourning culturally patterned expressions of grief at someone's death

palliative care treatment designed to relieve pain provided to a person with a terminal illness for whom death is imminent

Partnership for Caring national organization supporting passive euthanasia and providing information on advance directives (formerly known as Choice in Dying)

passive euthanasia voluntary elective death through the withdrawal of life-sustaining treatments or failure to treat life-threatening conditions

Patient Self-Determination Act federal law requiring that health care facilities inform their patients about their rights to decide how they want to live or die; for example, by providing them information on refusing treatment and on filing advance directives

right to die   the belief that persons have a right to take their own lives, especially if they experience untreatable pain, often accompanied by the belief that persons have a right to physician assistance in the dying process

self-neglect   a process by which a person voluntarily makes decisions that are equivalent to choosing to die (e.g., refusing help, not eating)

surrogate decision maker   person legally designated to act according to patient's known wishes or "best interest"

RESOURCES

Web Resources on Grief and Loss   Web pages dedicated to grief and loss are increasing in both quantity and quality. Sites offer information on the grief process and provide opportunities to share feelings, questions, and concerns with others. Below is a small sampling of some of these sites. See the companion Website for this text at <www.ablongman.com/hooyman> for information about the following:

- Compassion in Dying
- Griefnet
- Death with Dignity National Center
- Hemlock Society
- Hospice Association of America
- National Alliance for Caregiving
- National Hospice Organization (NHO)
- AARP Grief and Loss Programs
- National Hospice and Palliative Care Organization
- Partnership for Caring
- www.caregivertips.com
- www.griefworks.com
- www.petloss.com

REFERENCES

Almberg, B. E., Grafstroem, M., and Winblad, B. Caregivers of relatives with dementia: Experiences en-

compassing social support and bereavement. *Aging and Mental Health*, 2000 4, 82–89.

American Geriatrics Society. *Measuring quality of care at the end of life.* Washington, DC: Author, 1996.

Arbuckle, N. W., and deVries, B. The long-term effects of later life spousal and parental bereavement on personal functioning. *The Gerontologist*, 1995, *35*, 637–645.

Barrett, A. E., and Lynch, S. M. Caregiving networks of elderly persons: Variation by marital status. *The Gerontologist*, 1999, *39*, 695–700.

Benedict, A., and Zhang, X. Reactions to loss among aged men and women: A comparison. *Activities, Adaptation and Aging*, 1999, *24*, 29–39.

Bennett, K. M. A longitudinal study of well-being in widowed women. *International Journal of Psychiatry*, 1997, *12*, 61–66.

Berger, A., Pereira, D., Baker, K., and O'Mara, A. A commentary: Social and cultural determinants of end-of-life care for elderly persons. *The Gerontologist*, 2002, *42*, 49–53.

Bern-Klug, M., Gessert, C., and Forbes, S. The need to revise assumptions about the end of life: Implications for social work practice. *Health and Social Work*, 2001, *26*, 38–43.

Braun, K. L., Look, M., Yang, H., Onaka, A., and Horiuchi, B. Native Hawaiian mortality in 1980 and 1990 in the State of Hawaii. *American Journal of Public Health*, 1996, *86*, 888–889.

Braun, K. L., and Nichols, R. Death and dying in four Asian American cultures: A descriptive study. *Death Studies*, 1997, *21*, 327–359.

Braun, K. L., Pietsch, J. H., and Blanchette, P. L. (Eds.). An introduction to culture and its influence on end-of-life decision making. In *Cultural Issues in end-of-life decision making,* Thousand Oaks, CA: Sage, 2000.

Braun, K. L., Tanji, V. M., and Heck, R. Support for physician-assisted suicide: Exploring the impact of ethnicity and attitudes toward planning for death. *The Gerontologist*, 2001, *41*, 51–60.

Bretscher, M., Rummans, T., Sloan, J., Kaur, J., Bartlett, A., Borkenhagen, L., and Loprinzi, C. Quality of life in hospice patients: A pilot study. *Psychosomatics*, July–August 1999, *40*, 309–313.

Buckman, R. Communication in palliative care: A practice guide. In D. Doyle, G. W. Hanks, and N. McDonald (Eds.), *Oxford textbook of palliative medicine* (2nd ed.). New York: Oxford University Press, 1999.

Butler, R. Keynote Address, Presented at the Open Society Institute. *Project on Death in America,* Lake Tahoe, CA: July 17–22, 2000.

Callahan, D. *The troubled dream of life: Living with mortality.* New York: Simon and Schuster, 1993.

Callahan, S. A feminist case against euthanasia: Women should be especially wary of arguments for "the freedom to die." *Health Progress,* 1996, 21–29.

Carr, D., House, J. S., Kessler, R. C., Nesse, R. M., Sonnega, J., and Wortman, C. Marital quality and psychological adjustment to widowhood among older adults: A longitudinal analysis. *Journals of Gerontology,* 2000, *55B,* S197–S205.

Carverhill, P. Bereaved men: How therapists can help. *Psychotherapy in Private Practice,* 1997, *16,* 1–20.

Caserta, M. S., Lund, D. A., and Rice, S. J. Pathfinders: A self-care and health education program for older widows and widowers. *The Gerontologist,* 1999, *39,* 615–620.

Castle, N. G. Innovations in dying in the nursing home: The impact of market characteristics. *Journal of Death and Dying,* 1998, *36,* 227–240.

Choice in Dying, *Fact Sheets: National Advance Directive Campaign.* New York: Choice in Dying, 1994.

Christ, G. H., and Sormanti, M. Advancing social work practice in end-of-life care. *Social Work in Health Care,* 1999, *30,* 81–98.

Christopher, M. J. The new place of end-of-life issues on the policy agenda. *Public Policy and Aging Report,* 2003, *13,* 23–26.

Cicirelli, V. G. *Older adults' views on death.* New York: Springer Publishing, 2002.

Cicirelli, V. G. Personality and demographic factors in older adults' fear of death. *The Gerontologist,* 1999, *39,* 569–579.

Cicirelli, V. G. Relationship of psychosocial and background variables to older adults' end-of-life decisions. *Psychology and Aging,* March 1997, *12,* 72–83.

Clements, R. Intrinsic religious motivation and attitudes toward death among the elderly. *Current Psychology: Developmental, Learning, Personality, Social,* 1998, *17,* 237–248.

Cloud, J. A kinder, gentler death. *Time,* 2000, *156,* 60–67.

Cohen, G. D. Marriage and divorce in later life (Editorial). *American Journal of Geriatric Psychiatry,* 1999, *7,* 185–187.

Cole, T. R., and Holstein, M. Ethics and aging. In R. H. Binstock and L. K. George (Eds.), *Handbook of aging and the social sciences* (4th ed.). San Diego, CA: Academic Press, 1996.

Compassion in Dying. Senate bill threatens Oregon's death with dignity act and pain care nationwide. *Compassion in Dying,* 2000, 13.

Death with Dignity. *Physicians: Leave assisted suicide to doctors, patients.* www.Deathwithdignity.org/fss/opinion/amn62001.

Ducharme, F., and Corin, E. Widowed men and women—An exploratory study of the significance of widowhood and coping strategies. *Canadian Journal on Aging,* 1997, *16,* 112–141.

Fauser, M. C. Hospice patient perspectives regarding the implementation of advanced directives. *Dissertation Abstracts International: Section B: The Sciences and Engineering,* 1999, *60,* 0410.

Federal Interagency Forum on Aging. *Aging-related statistics. Older Americans 2000: Key indicators of well-being.* Washington, DC: U.S. Government Printing Office, 2000.

Field, M. J., and Cassel, C. K. *Approaching death: Improving care at the end of life.* Washington, DC: National Academy Press, 1997.

Freeman, H., and Payne, R. Racial injustice in health care: An editorial. *The Washington Post,* March 2000, 1–2.

Galambos, C. M. Preserving end-of-life autonomy: The Patient Self-Determination Act and the Uniform Health Care Decisions Act. *Health and Social Work,* 1998, *23,* 275–281.

Gossert, C. E., Forbes, S., and Bern-Klug, M. Planning end-of-life care for patients with dementia: Roles of families and health professionals. *Omega,* 2001, *42,* 273–291.

Harris Poll, *2–1 Majorities continue to support rights to both euthanasia and doctor-assisted suicide.* Washington, DC: The Harris poll, 2002.

Holstein, M. Ethics and aging: Bringing the issues home. *Generations,* 1998, *22,* 4.

Hornik, M. Physician-assisted suicide and euthanasia's impact on the frail elderly: A social worker's response. *Journal of Long Term Home Health Care: The Pride Institute Journal,* 1998, *17,* 34–41.

Hudson, T. Court strikes down assisted suicide ban in Washington State. *Hospitals and Health Networks,* August 5, 1994, *68,* 180.

Ingebretsen, R., and Solem, P. E. Death, dying, and bereavement. In I. H. Nordhus and G. R. VandenBos et al., *Clinical geropsychology.* Washington, DC: American Psychological Association, 1998.

Johnston, S. C., Pfeifer, M. P., and McNutt, R. The discussion about advance directives: Patient and physician opinions regarding when and how it should be conducted. *Archives of Internal Medicine,* 1995, *155,* 1025–1030.

Kass-Bartelmes, B., and Hughes, R. *Advance care planning: Preferences for care at the end of life. Research in action.* Washington, DC: Agency for Healthcare Research and Quality, 2003.

Kastenbaum, R. *Death, society and human experience* (4th ed.). New York: Macmillan/Merrill, 1991.

Kaufman, S. R. A commentary: Hospital experience and meaning at the end-of-life. *The Gerontologist,* 2002, *42,* 34–39.

Klass, D. S., Silverman, P. R., and Nickonson, S. L. (Eds.). *Continuing bonds: New understandings of grief.* Washington, DC: Taylor and Francis, 1996.

Kübler-Ross, E. *On death and dying.* New York: Macmillan, 1969.

Kübler-Ross, E. (Ed.). *Death: The final stage of growth.* Englewood Cliffs, NJ: Prentice-Hall, 1975.

Kübler-Ross, E. *Living with dying.* New York: Macmillan, 1981.

Kurent, J. E. *The Institute for Community and Professional Education in End-of-Life Care.* Presented at the Open Society Institute, Project on Death in America, Lake Tahoe, CA: July 17–22, 2000.

Lamberg, L. "Palliative care" means "active care": It aims to improve quality of life. *Journal of the American Medical Association,* 2002, *288,* 943–944.

Last Acts. *Means to a better end: A report on dying in America today.* Washington, DC: Author, 2002.

Lawton, M. P. Quality of life and the end of life. In J. Barren and K. W. Schaie (Eds.), *Handbook of the psychology of aging* (5th ed.). San Diego: Academic Press, 2001.

Lee, G. R., Willetts, M. C., and Seccombe, K. Widowhood and depression: Gender differences. *Research on Aging,* 1998, *20,* 611–630.

Lindenstrom, T. It ain't necessarily so: Challenging mainstream thinking about bereavement. *Family and Community Health,* 2002, *25,* 11–21.

Lopata, H. Z. The support systems of American urban widows. In M. Stroebe, W. Stroebe, and R. Hanson (Eds.), *Handbook of bereavement: Theory, research and intervention.* New York: Cambridge University Press, 1993.

Lopata, H. Z. *Widowhood in an American city.* Cambridge, MA: Schenkman, 1973.

Lopata, H. Z. *Widows.* Durham, NC: Duke University Press, 1987.

Lund, D. A. Widowhood: The coping response. In R. Kastenbaum (Ed.), *Encyclopedia of adult development.* Phoenix, AZ: Onyx Press, 1993.

Lund, D. A., Caserta, M., and Dimond, M. The course of spousal bereavement in later life. In M. Stroebe, W. Stroebe, and R. Hanson (Eds.), *Handbook of bereavement: Theory, research and intervention.* New York: Cambridge University Press, 1993.

Maro, R. Victory through the courts. *Compassion in Dying,* Spring 1996, 1.

Martin-Matthews, A. Widowhood and widowerhood. *Encyclopedia of Gerontology,* 1996, *2,* 621–625.

McCandless, N. J., and Conner, F. P. Older women and grief: A new direction for research. *Journal of Women and Aging,* 1997, *9,* 85–91.

McClain, V. R., Tindell, S., and Hall, S. H. Ethical dilemmas in right to die issues. *American Journal of Forensic Psychology,* 1999, *17,* 77–88.

McCue, J. D. The naturalness of dying. *Journal of the American Medical Association,* 1995, *273,* 1039–43.

McLaughlin, L. A., and Braun, K. L. Asian and Pacific Islander cultural values: Considerations for health care decision making. *Health and Social Work,* 1998, *23,* 116–126.

Miller, S. C., and Mor, V. The emergence of Medicare hospice care in U.S. nursing homes. *Journal of Palliative Medicine,* 2001, *15,* 471–480.

Moen, P. Gender, age and the life course. In R. H. Binstock and L. K. George, *Handbook of aging and the social sciences* (4th ed.). San Diego, CA: Academic Press, 1996.

Morrison, R. S., and Siu, A. L. Survival in end-stage dementia following acute illness. *Journal of the American Medical Association,* 2000, *284,* 47–52.

Moss, M., Moss, S., and Hansson, R. Bereavement in old age. In M. Stroebe, R. Hansson, W. Stroebe, and H. Schut (Eds.), *Handbook of bereavement research.* Washington, DC: American Psychological Association, 2001.

Moyers, B., and Moyers, J. *On our own terms: Moyers on dying.* Public Affairs Television, September 2000.

Muir, J. C. No title. Presented at the Open Society Institute, *Project on Death in America,* Lake Tahoe, CA: July 17–22, 2000.

Mutran, E. J., Danis, M., Bratton, K., Sudha, S., and Hanson, L. Attitudes of the critically ill toward prolonging life: The role of social support. *The Gerontologist,* 1997, *37,* 192–199.

National Hospice and Palliative Care Organization Research Department. *NHPCO facts and figures.* http//:www.hnpco.org. Accessed December 11, 2003.

Neimeyer, R. (1998). Can there be a psychology of loss? In J. H. Harvey (Ed.), *Perspectives on loss.* Philadelphia: Taylor and Francis, 1998.

Nieboer, A. P., Lindenberg, S. M., and Siegwart Ormel, J. Conjugal bereavement and well-being of elderly men and women: A preliminary study. *Journal of Death and Dying,* 1999, *38,* 113–141.

Nolen-Hoeksema, S., and Larson, J. *Coping with loss.* Mahwah, NJ: Erlbaum, 1999.

Northwest Geriatric Education Center, Dealing with grief and loss, *NWGEC Viewpoint,* Winter 2000, *9,* 1–3.

O'Bryant, S. L., and Hansson, R. O. Widowhood. In R. Blieszner and V. H. Bedford (Eds.), *Handbook of aging and the family.* Westport, CT: Greenwood Press, 1995.

Olson, E. Physician-assisted suicide and euthanasia's impact on the frail elderly: A physician's reply. *Journal of Long Term Home Health Care: The Pride Institute Journal,* Summer 1998, *17,* 28–33.

Ostrom, C. New focus on debate on assisted suicide. *The Seattle Times,* January 1998, *1,* A18.

Ostrom, C. The war on pain. *The Seattle Times,* May 14, 2000, pp. 1, A15, A17.

Ostrom, C., and Westnext, D. Next target of assisted suicide efforts: State laws. *The Seattle Times,* June 27, 1997, A2.

Owen, J. E., Goode, K. T., and Haley, W. E. End-of-life care and reactions to death in African American and white family caregivers of relatives with Alzheimer's disease. *Omega,* 2001, *43,* 349–361.

Patterson, J. Participation in leisure activities by older adults after a stressful life event: The loss of a spouse. *International Journal of Aging and Human Development,* 1996, *42,* 123–142.

Payne, R. At the end of life: Color still divides. *The Washington Post,* February 15, 2000.

Preston, T. A. Facing death on your own terms. *Newsweek,* May 22, 2000, 82.

Prigerson, H. G., Maciejewski, P. K., and Rosenheck, R. A. Preliminary explorations of the harmful interactive effects of widowhood and marital harmony on health, health service use, and health care costs. *The Gerontologist,* 2000, *40,* 349–357.

Rando, T. A. *Grieving: How to go on living when someone you love dies.* Lexington, MA: Lexington books, 1988.

Rando, T. A. *Treatment of complicated mourning.* Champaign, IL: Research Press, 1993.

Randolph, J. D. Timing of conjugal loss in late life and successful outcome: A life-span perspective. *Dissertation Abstracts International: Section B: The Sciences and Engineering,* February 1997, *57,* 5366.

Rao, R., Deming, T., Brayne, C., and Huppert, F. A. Attitudes toward death: A community study of octogenarians and nonagenarians. *International Psychogeriatrics,* June 1997, *9,* 213–221.

Raveis, V. H. Facilitating older spouses' adjustment to widowhood: A preventive intervention program. *Social Work in Health Care,* 1999, *29,* 13–32.

Rosenblatt, P. C. A social constructionist perspective in grief. Introduction to M. Stroebe, R. Hansson, W. Stroebe, and H. Schut (Eds.), *Handbook of bereavement research: Consequences, coping and care.* Washington, DC: American Psychological Association, 2001.

Rozenzweig, A., Prigerson, H., Miller, M. D., and Reynolds, C. F., 3rd. Bereavement and late-life depression: Grief and its complications in the elderly. *Annual Review of Medicine,* 1997, *48,* 421–428.

Seattle Times. "Death with dignity" bill approved by Senate, March 6, 1992, 1-B2.

Seattle Times. "No right to die, say justices." June 26, 1997, 1, 23A.

Stroebe, M. Hanson, R., Stroebe, W., and Schut, H. In M. Stroebe, R. Hansson, W. Stroebe, and H. Schut, *Handbook of bereavement research: Consequences, coping and care.* Washington, DC: American Psychological Association, 2001.

Stroebe, M., and Schut, H. The social context of grief and grieving. In *Proceedings of the Social Context of Death, Dying and Disposal.* Glasgow: Glasgow Caledonian University, 1998.

Stroebe, M., Schut, H., and Stroebe, W. Trauma and grief: A comparative analysis. In J. H. Harvey (Ed.), *Perspectives on loss.* Philadelphia: Taylor and Francis, 1998.

Sullivan, M., Ormel, J., Kemper, G. I. J. M., and Tymstra, T. Beliefs concerning death, dying, and hastening death among older, functionally impaired Dutch adults: A one-year longitudinal study. *Journal of the American Geriatrics Society,* 1998, *46,* 1251–1257.

Teno, J. M. Putting patient and family voice back into measuring quality of care for the dying. *Hospice Journal,* 1999, *14,* 167–176.

Thompson, L. W., Gallagher-Thompson, D., Futterman, A., Gilewski, M. J., and Peterson, J. The effects of late-life spousal bereavement over a thirty-month interval. In M. P. Lawton and T. A. Salthouse et al. (Eds.), *Essential papers on the psychology of aging. Essential papers in psychoanalysis.* New York: New York University Press, 1998.

Thorson, J., and Powell, F. C. Death anxiety in younger and older adults. In A. Tomer (Ed.), *Death attitudes and the older adult: Theories, concepts and applications.* Philadelphia: Taylor and Francis, 2000.

Thorson, J. A., Powell, F. C., and Samuel, V. T. Age differences in death anxiety among African American women. *Psychological Reports,* 1998a, *83,* 1173–1174.

Thorson, J. A., Powell, F. C., and Samuel, V. T. African and Euro-American samples differ little in scores on death anxiety. *Psychological Reports,* 1998b, *83,* 623–626.

Tilly, J. A., and Wiener, J. M. End of life care for the Medicaid population. *Public Policy and Aging Report,* 2003, *13,* 17–22.

Tucker, K. L. Physician-assisted dying: A constitutionally protected form of "rational suicide." In J. L. Werth et al. (Eds.), *Contemporary perspectives on rational suicide. Series in death, dying, and bereavement.* Philadelphia: Brunner/Mazel, Inc., 1999.

Turvey, C. L., Carney, C., Arndt, R. B., and Herzog, R. Conjugal loss and syndromal depression in a sample of elders aged 70 or older. *American Journal of Psychiatry,* 1999, *156,* 1596–601.

Utz, R., Carr, D., Nesse, R., and Wortman, C. The effect of widowhood on older adults' social participation: An evaluation of activity, disengagement, and continuity theories. *The Gerontologist,* 2002, *42,* 522–533.

Vachon, M. The emotional problems of the patient. In D. Doyle, G. W. C. Hanks, and N. MacDonald (Eds.), *Oxford textbook of palliative medicine* (2nd ed.) New York: Oxford University Press, 1999.

van den Hoonaard, D. *The widowed self: Older women's journey through widowhood.* Waterloo, Ontario: Wilfred Laurier University Press, 2001.

Waldrop, D. P. *At the eleventh hour: Psychosocial factors that contribute to delayed hospice care for older adults.* John A. Hartford Foundation Scholars meeting, Washington, DC: October 18, 2003.

Walker, G. C. The right to die: Healthcare workers' attitudes compared with a national public poll. *Journal of Death and Dying,* 1997, *35,* 339–345.

Walter, T. *The loss of a life partner: Narratives of the bereaved.* New York: Columbia University Press, 2003.

Weiss, R. S. Grief, bonds and relationships. In M. Stroebe, R. Hansson, W. Stroebe, and H. Schut, (Eds.), *Handbook of bereavement research: Consequences, coping and care.* Washington, DC: American Psychological Association, 2001.

Wilkinson, A. M., and Lynn, J. The end of life. In R. H. Binstock and L. K. George, *Handing of aging and the social sciences* (5th ed.). San Diego: Academic Press, 2001.

Worden J. W. *Grief counseling and grief therapy: A Handbook for the mental health practitioner.* New York: Springer Publishing, 2002.

Wortman, C., and Silver, R. C. The myths of coping with loss revisited. In M. Stroebe, R. Hansson, W. Stroebe, and H. Schut (Eds.), *Handbook of bereavement research: Consequences, coping and caring.* Washington, DC: American Psychological Association, 2001.

14

The Resilience
of Elders of Color

When discussing the physiological, psychological, and social changes experienced by older adults, there is a tendency to speak about them as if they were a homogeneous group. Yet, as illustrated throughout this book, the older population is more heterogeneous than any other. Two primary variables in this heterogeneity are gender and ethnic minority status; both influence an individual's position in the social structure and experiences. To be an older person of color, or an older woman, is to experience environments substantially different from those of a white male across the life span. For example, both older women and African American elders are more likely to live alone, which places them at greater risk of poverty, poorer health status, and social isolation.

The interaction of gender, ethnic minority status, living arrangements, and social class (or socioeconomic status) is illustrated by the following facts:

- The poverty rate for women who live alone is five times greater than that for their peers who live with a spouse.
- The mean income of older African American households is about half that of older white households.
- Older women of color are more likely to obtain health care from hospital outpatient units, emergency rooms, and neighborhood centers than from private physicians.
- Older women of color who live alone form the poorest group in our society (AOA, 2003).

Consistent with the *life course perspective* outlined in Chapter 8, such economic and health disparities in old age are typically related not only to current living arrangements, but also to early experiences in education, labor force participation, health status and access to health care, and cultural beliefs and practices. Elders of color bring to well-being in old age the cumulative effects of a lifetime of disadvantage because of their race. Inequities from earlier in life are usually intensified in old age.

Relevant differences among older people arising from their gender and their ethnic minority status are noted throughout this text. This Chapter and Chapter 15, however, focus specifically on these factors because of their interactive effects with age and the resulting higher incidence of poverty, poor health, barriers to health care, and inadequate living arrangements. In this sense, both older women in general and persons of color of both genders are affected by environmental changes that are not always congruent with their needs as they age. Socioeconomic status (SES), along with race and gender, create inequities across the life course. SES also influences variation within groups, not only between groups. Despite the greater problems facing both women and people of color, both groups display strengths and resilience in old age.

The concept of resilience or "hardiness," which was introduced in Chapter 6, encompasses the behavioral patterns, functional competence, and cultural capacities that individuals, families,

and communities utilize under adverse circumstances, and the ability to integrate adversity as a catalyst for growth and development (Fredriksen-Goldsen, in press; McCubbin et al., 1998; Staudinger and Marsiske, 1993). Populations of color, despite experiencing high levels of adversity, often have extensive personal (e.g., spirituality, sense of mastery, faith), cultural (e.g., beliefs and values), and social (e.g., friends, extended family) resources that help them solve problems and cope with negative life conditions and experience well-being. By emphasizing resilience, we do not intend to minimize the growing economic and health inequities faced by populations of color within our society. However, a focus on resilience and strengths among populations of color recognizes their strengths in the face of such adversity. As such, it moves beyond individual characteristics to include contextual or environmental factors and contrasts with earlier research that emphasized deficits among minority populations.

Defining Ethnicity and Culture

Ethnicity involves three components:

1. sense of peoplehood based on a distinctive social and cultural heritage
2. social status
3. social support systems (Barresi and Stull, 1993)

These components—the way people feel about themselves and how they interact with their environments—result in particular patterns of adaptation to aging. Ethnicity serves the following functions:

- an integrating force in passing through significant life changes and transitions
- a buffer to stresses of old age, especially when the environment supports the expression of ethnicity and culture
- a filter to the aging process, influencing beliefs, behaviors, and interactions with informal and formal supports

Given these various functions, social and health care providers need to understand ethnicity and how it influences cultural values and behaviors such as help-seeking, family obligation, and mutual support.

Ethnicity encompasses *culture*, which is defined as a complex system and process of shared knowledge, beliefs, traditions, symbols, language, art, and social organization. Culture is a lens through which individuals perceive and interpret the world, and create meaning in their everyday lives and their world (Helman, 2000). Of interest to gerontologists is how culture influences the definition and conceptualization of problems as well as the meaning, values, and experiences of aging, health, and healing. Based on its unique history and culture, each ethnic minority population develops its own methods of managing the inevitable conflicts between traditional and westernized ways of life, leading to both vulnerabilities and strengths.

For most immigrants from non-European countries—78 percent from 1960 to 1989—values of cooperation and interdependence contrast with Western values of competition and independence. For example, many Chinese American elders emigrated from small farming villages where ancestor worship was practiced, reflecting the respect traditionally accorded elders. They have grown old in a country where youth and material success are more highly valued than age, and thus may experience conflicts between their views and those of their children and grandchildren. By identifying cultural values in an older person's heritage, gerontologists can gain a better understanding of attitudes and behaviors that influence both their experience of aging and utilization of social and health services. A study of how three ethnic minority groups manage their chronic illnesses highlights the central role of cultural values. Filipino Americans, for example, felt a strong sense of responsibility for maintaining good health, but this was to their family and social group, rather than individual responsibility as an end in itself. In contrast, the notion of individual responsibility for taking care of illness in Western culture was foreign to Latino elders, who did not perceive themselves as responsible for making changes in their lifestyle, such as exercise and diet, nor for developing self-care practices to enhance their health. They believed that medication alone would control their illness, although some also used alternative healing (e.g., herbal teas and roots) as adjuncts to biomedical treatment (Becker et al., 1998). Since people's cultural lens profoundly affects actions, social and health care providers need to understand the ethnic, cultural, and racial differences that affect well-being and utilization of services by diverse elders.

Defining Minority and People of Color

For purposes of this chapter, *ethnic minority elders* include older people of color belonging to groups whose language and/or physical and cultural characteristics make them visible and identifiable, who have experienced differential and unequal treatment, who share a distinctive history and bonds of attachment among group members, and who regard themselves as objects of collective discrimination and oppression *by reason of their race*. Specifically, this chapter examines the life conditions and adaptation to aging among people of color who are defined by the federal government as protected groups—African Americans, Latinos* (including Mexican Americans/Chicanos, Puerto Ricans, Cubans, and Latin Americans), American Indians, and Asian/Pacific Islanders. We

---

*Twenty-eight years after the federal government agreed on the use of the term *Hispanic* to identify persons with mixed Spanish heritage, debate regarding whether to use "Hispanic" or "Latino" continues. *Latino* refers to the Latin-based Romance languages of Spain, France, Italy, and Portugal. *Hispanic* is an American derivative from "Hispana," the Spanish-language term for the cultural diaspora created by Spain. People who are disturbed because the diaspora is the result of a bygone age of conquest prefer the term Latino. A recent survey found that a majority of Hispanics and Latinos—53 percent—have no preference for either term, instead identifying themselves by national origin (e.g., Cuban, Mexican, Puerto Rican). Students, intellectuals, and scholars tend to use the term Latino. Throughout this textbook, we are using the term Latino because of the negative association of Hispanic with colonialism and because it appears to be most widely used in scholarly circles. Nevertheless, we recognize that both terms have limitations (Fears, 2003).

recognize how ethnicity or cultural homogeneity in general influences the aging process, and the importance of ethnic identity for white populations, such as Jewish Americans. Our focus, however, is on people of color who have experienced economic and racial discrimination, and thus often face greater problems.

Two distinct issues should be kept in mind in this discussion of ethnic minority elders:

1. the unique historical and cultural calendar of life events and their impact on aging, many of which are positive and sources of strength and resilience
2. the consequences of racism, ageism, discrimination, and prolonged poverty, most of which are negative and perpetuate inequities across the life span

For people of color, race is a social status that shapes an individual's values, behaviors, and distribution of resources. In fact, race may interact with individual conditions (e.g., functional impairment) and social structural factors (e.g., socioeconomic status) to influence the receipt of help, including the use of informal and formal care (Norgard and Rodgers, 1997). It is not only their

ethnic and cultural traditions that influence their socialization process, but also their experience of being a racial minority within a white majority culture. Accordingly, the aging process and quality of life of elders of color are inevitably affected by the experiences of a lifetime of racial discrimination and disadvantage.

The use of the term "people of color" recognizes, however, that in most instances, by the middle of the twenty-first century, groups that are currently numerical minorities will become the numerical majority in many areas. They may, however, continue to face oppression and discrimination. For example, Latinos are already the numerical majority in California but continue to be poorer and less healthy than their Caucasian counterparts.

Today, ethnic minorities comprise over 16 percent of the population over age 65, as shown in Table 14.1 (AOA, 2003). They include a smaller proportion of older adults and a larger percent of younger adults than the white population. This differential results primarily from patterns of immigration and higher fertility rates among the young and higher mortality rates among ethnic minorities over age 65 compared with their white counterparts. Populations of

TABLE 14.1   Ethnic Minority Distribution of the Older Population

	% OF TOTAL POPULATION, 65+	% OF THE ETHNIC MINORITY POPULATION, 65+	PROJECTED PERCENTS IN 2050
Whites	84.3*	—	
African Americans	8.1*	8.4	12.2
Asian/Pacific Islanders	2.4*	7.5	6.5
American Indians	0.4*	7.2	0.6
Latino	5.6*	5.8	16.4

*The sum of the specific percentages reported here will never round off to approximately 100 percent if a Hispanic percentage is included. The reason for this anomaly is that the U.S. Census Bureau does not treat the Hispanic category (which includes Mexicans, Venezuelans, and Latinos who self-designate themselves as being white) as one that is mutually exclusive from the racial categories. Thus, the Hispanic data are also included within each of the racial categories. Persons of Hispanic origins may be of any race, and represent 3 percent of the older population.

SOURCE: AOA, 1999.

color are of increasing concern to gerontologists because of:

- the disproportionately higher number of social problems that they face relative to whites. For example, as noted in Figure 14.1, rates of poverty and near-poverty are highest among elders of color, which negatively affects health status, living arrangements, and access to health care.
- the disproportionately higher rate of increase compared with the white population, with older ethnic minorities projected to increase by 219 percent as compared to an 81 percent increase among older Caucasians between 1999 and 2030. In fact, elders of color are predicted to form more than 33 percent of the total older population by 2030 (NIH, 2000).

As noted in Chapter 1, this dramatic growth is occurring partially because of the large proportion of children among populations of color who, unlike their parents and especially their grandparents, are expected to reach old age.

The greatest growth among elders of color will occur in those age 85 and over: from 1 in 10 today to 1 in 5 by the year 2050, with the largest increase among Latino oldest-old. Although immigrants tend to be largely younger persons, many have bought the passage fare or sent for their older parents and other relatives, especially from countries with political oppression. Accordingly, it is predicted that immigrant groups—Latinos and Asian/Pacific Islanders—will redefine American culture in the twenty-first century (Angel and Hogan, 1994).

There are recurring themes in analyses of ethnic minority status and older people, such as conflicts of traditional cultural values with those of mainstream American society and barriers to use as well as underutilization of social and health services. Nevertheless, variations *within* as well as *among* these groups must be understood. Differences in immigration patterns, birthrates, region, social class, rural or urban location, gender, and

acculturation level add to the intragroup variations. Latinos, for example, who are defined by the U.S. Census Bureau as Spanish-speaking persons, include people from many different cultures and a high percentage of recent immigrants. Accordingly, no one term for persons of Spanish heritage is accepted by all. They can be from any of the following racial groups: Caucasians, Native American, Indian/African. Mexican Americans are generally of Spanish Caucasian/Indian descent, while Cubans/Puerto Ricans are of Spanish Caucasian/African descent. American Indian refers to the indigenous peoples of North America, including Indians, Eskimos, and Aleuts and over 500 recognized tribes, bands, or Alaskan Native villages. African Americans differ from one another in terms of cultural background, socioeconomic status, and geographic location—especially recent immigrants from Africa, Haiti, or the Caribbean Islands. Recent immigrants from Laos, Cambodia, and Vietnam have a higher proportion of elders than do other Asian/Pacific Islander groups. Given this within-group diversity, generalizations about ethnic minority elders' health, economic, and social status are limited, and numerous exceptions to the norm exist.

Research History

Ethnogerontology, a growing field of social gerontology, is the study of the causes, processes, and consequences of race, national origin, and culture on individual and population aging. From 1940 to 1970, when both scholarly and political concern with older adults grew, little was written about the special circumstances of ethnic minority elders; this was, in part, because of their relatively small size compared to Caucasian older adults (Markides and Black, 1996). In 1956, Tally and Kaplan first raised the **double jeopardy hypothesis:** Does being both minority and old result in a double disadvantage to health and well-being in old age? That is, do lifetime factors of economic and racial discrimination make the aging experience more difficult for African Americans (and other minorities) than for whites? Debates about double jeopardy—whether it exists and is related to socioeconomic status or to race per se—have been central in research and policy discussions in ethnogerontology.

A second but related position asserts that patterns of racial inequality are changing, and that minorities' opportunities throughout their lives are related more to their economic class position than to their race. Social class, not minority status, jeopardizes them. The **multiple hierarchy stratification** perspective encompasses both views, defining race as one source of inequality along with class, gender, and age itself (Bengtson, 1979). Some ethnogerontologists argue that double jeopardy should not be a central concept because cross-sectional studies have rarely produced useful information about age changes as opposed to age differences (Markides, Liang, and Jackson, 1990). They suggest that double jeopardy may be time-bound, resulting largely from major social and political changes in the status of minorities, not from racial differences. Therefore, in an effort to separate these factors, these authors have suggested that more longitudinal studies are required to determine the effects of ethnic minority group status on age changes.

A counterargument to the double jeopardy hypothesis is that age is a leveler of differences in life expectancy. This mortality **crossover effect** refers to the fact that people of color experience poorer health and higher death rates than whites at all ages until very old age. After age 75, the death rates for African Americans, Asian/Pacific Islanders, and American Indians are actually lower than for whites. Accordingly, life expectancy after age 75 for these survivors is greater, due to a combination of biological vigor, psychological strength, and resources for coping with stress, such as religious practices that link individuals to the community. Thus, the oldest-old segment of the ethnic minority population may represent selective survival of the biologically more robust or "hardy" individuals. In fact, although people of

color may experience increasing income and health disparities with age, they nevertheless display considerable strengths and may experience higher levels of psychological well-being and emotional support than do Caucasian elders (Markides and Block, 1996; Wykle and Kaskel, 1994). It is unclear, however, if the apparent racial crossover and selective survival are due to enumerative errors, such as misreporting of age, and reliance on cross-sectional data to compare advantaged and disadvantaged populations, rather than to health differences per se. The apparent racial crossover effect also raises questions about the usefulness of chronological age as a measure of aging. Given these issues, the relative status and mortality risks of whites and nonwhites in old age are still debated. What is clear is that tremendous variation occurs both across and within ethnic minority categories and that inequities in childhood and adulthood often persist throughout the life span (Ferraro and Farmer, 1996).

The concept of **health disparities**—socioeconomic and racial/ethnic inequalities in health, mortality, and other adverse conditions across the life span—is a growing area of study among health care and gerontological researchers. Increasing concerns with such disparities have led the National Institutes of Health (NIH) to fund research centers that will address the reasons for and test interventions to reduce such disparities. **Health care disparities** are defined as differences in the access, quality, or use of health care services, where ethnic minorities have a substantively lower rate of usage. Such differences in utilization rates appear to be a function of both a failure within the health care system (e.g., overexposure to medical errors, missed diagnoses, and inappropriate treatments) and the patient's underutilization of existing services (LaVeist, 2003). It appears that the effects of social inequality on health within ethnic minority populations may be compounded with aging, leading to growing gaps in health status of individuals within and across families (Burton and Whitfield, 2003). The concept of health disparities is congruent with the concept of cumulative disadvantage due to economic inequities across the life span, which was discussed in Chapter 8.

Ethnic Minorities in Gerontology

The year 1971 marked a turning point in the recognition of ethnic minority elders as an area of gerontological study. In that year, the National Caucus on the Black Aged was formed (later becoming the National Center and Caucus on the Black Aged), and a session on "Aging and the Aged Black" was held at the White House Conference on Aging. This conference, especially important from a policy perspective, highlighted the need for income and health care supports. Since 1971, the National Association for Spanish-Speaking Elderly, the National Indian Council on Aging, and the National Asian Pacific Center on Aging have been established. These associations function as advocacy groups for elders of color and as research and academic centers.

The census is the primary source of information for organizations planning services for ethnic minority elders. Census data, however, are criticized for undercounting minority subgroups, misclassifying individuals, or merging data about various nonwhite groups. For example, the Census Bureau traditionally grouped people by race as "white," "black," or "other." However, the 2000 Census was the first to include multiracial categories. Another data source that is problematical is the use of birth certificates and self-reports of age. Racial and ethnic classifications that are based on self-reports often fail to take account of the growing interracial/interethnic heterogeneity of individuals (Whitfield and Baker, 1999). In addition, the use of major racial and ethnic categories to define groups masks substantial within-group heterogeneity pertaining to cultural beliefs. Immigration dynamics (movements in and out of the country) and settlement patterns pose additional challenges for determining the morbidity and mortality experiences of diverse populations.

In addition to the limitations of census data, high-quality population-level mortality and disease data are lacking. Most national estimates are

---

THE CHARACTERISTICS OR PATTERNS SHARED ACROSS POPULATIONS OF COLOR

Cumulative disadvantages from being people of color:

- limited resources throughout their lives to meet health care needs
- influence of socioeconomic status on health differences between people/populations of color and whites
- women outnumbering men, and more likely to be widowed than their male peers

Centrality of family/kin values affecting long-term care:

- preference for in-home services
- reluctance to use out-of-home services, especially nursing homes
- more likely to turn to informal supports

Lower rates of insurance coverage and health care utilization, especially preventive services:

- lower rates of Medicare coverage, especially among immigrant populations
- sociocultural and political barriers to health care (e.g., different communication styles, history of racism and discrimination, language barriers)
- preference for non-Western methods of healing (especially among Asian/Pacific Islanders and American Indian elders)

Chronic illness:

- major causes of death: diabetes and hypertension
- greater number of functional disabilities (e.g., restricted activity and bed-disability days)
- may be recognized as old prior to chronological age
- more likely to experience psychosocial distress, erroneous diagnoses of mental health problems, and culturally inappropriate treatment

limited to comparison of blacks and whites and thus exclude other populations of color (Whitfield and Hayward, 2003). Research on ethnic minorities generally does not break down data by gender, and studies on older women do not cross-classify data by minority status. From the feminist perspective discussed in Chapter 8, it is difficult to determine how racism and sexism interact to produce "gender-specific race effects and race-specific gender effects" (Gould, 1989). Studies in the 1970s and 1980s were limited by small, nonrepresentative samples. Fortunately, research methodology in recent years has improved, especially in the areas of cross-cultural measurement and sampling.

Because of census data limitations and the wide diversity of cultural patterns, few other generalizations are valid for ethnic minority older populations as a whole. Using race per se as a variable may not lead to straightforward interpretations, because cultural values (e.g., the meaning attached to caregiving or to spirituality) and socioeconomic status are interdependent and difficult to separate. Within the overall context of these limitations, we next briefly review the life conditions of each of the four major ethnic minority groups in the United States.

Older African Americans

Although African Americans are the largest population of color in the United States, only about 8 percent of them are over 65 years of age, compared to 14 percent of the white population. The young outnumber the old, due primarily to the higher fertility of African American women and blacks' higher mortality, including homicide, in their younger years. The median age of African Americans (29.5 years) is 5 years younger than the median age for whites (34.6). The life expectancy for African American men and women is 64.9 and 74 years, respectively, compared with the life expectancy of 74.1 years for white men and 79.5

years for white women (National Women's Health Information Center, 2003). Comparisons of white–black differences in life expectancy need to take account of socioeconomic status, since high-income white males and high-income black males both live longer than their lower-income counterparts (William and Wilson, 2001).

Although these disparities in life expectancy reflect differences in childhood and youth mortality rates and socioeconomic status, differences in life expectancy after age 75 are less dramatic. African American men who live to age 65 can expect to live another 14 years; African American women, 18 years. This is only slightly less than for their white counterparts (15.5 and 19 years, respectively). This narrowing of difference in life expectancy after age 75 (the crossover effect discussed earlier) may be explained by the fact that African Americans who survive to this age tend to be the most robust of their cohort.

Although they are a relatively small percentage of the total African American population,

Older African American men can inspire their grandchildren.

adults over age 65 form the fastest-growing segment of that group. While the overall African American population is expected to grow by 45.6 percent by 2020, the proportion of older people generally will likely increase by 90 percent, from 8 percent to 15.3 percent in the year 2020, and to 21.3 percent by 2050. The greatest proportion (nearly 60 percent) are young-old, although as with other groups, the oldest-old is the fastest-growing segment of African American elders. The ratio of men to women is slightly lower than among whites, 62 males for every 100 females, compared to 67 per 100 among the Caucasian population. Oldest-old women are the most rapidly growing group of African American elders, and they have the longest average remaining life expectancy (NIH, 2000).

Economic Status

Over three times the proportion of older African Americans live below the poverty line compared to older whites: 26.4 percent versus 8.2 percent, respectively (AOA, 2003). The poverty rate across groups is shown in Figure 14.1. The incidence of poverty increases dramatically among households composed of unrelated black individuals, especially females age 65 and over. The median income of African American males over 65 is approximately 60 percent of white men; that of black women about 66 percent that of white women, with the proportion of older African American female-headed families in poverty increasing in the past 20 years. Poverty rates are highest among women living alone and the oldest-old, with the rate of oldest-old black women ten times that of young-old (65–74) white women (Hudson, 2002; Williams and Wilson, 2001). Differences in education do not explain the gaps in socioeconomic status, which have persisted since 1985. In fact, these inequities are increasing, due to general economic conditions, such as increased unemployment and underemployment, the lack of growth in real wages, decline in pension coverage, and re-

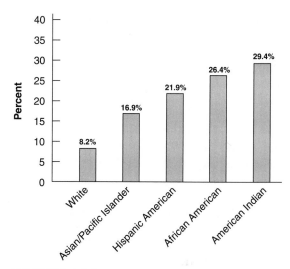

FIGURE 14.1 **Poverty Rates across Elders of Color**
SOURCE: AOA, 2003.

ductions in public supports such as Supplemental Security Income (SSI).

The primary reasons for the lower socioeconomic status of older African Americans are:

- limited access to educational opportunities earlier in the life span
- limited employment opportunities and periods of unemployment or underemployment throughout their lives
- concentration in low-paying, sporadic service jobs, especially in nursing homes and hospitals
- greater likelihood of leaving the workforce earlier, frequently because of health problems
- decreased likelihood of receiving pension income
- greater likelihood of depending on Social Security benefits, as their only income source
- greater dependence on Supplemental Security Income

Some studies point to African Americans returning to work after retirement because of economic necessity, creating the phenomenon of "unretired/retired." In such instances, blacks spend a greater proportion of their lives working, with fewer years in retirement compared with their age peers (Hayward, Friedman, and Chen, 1996). Other studies suggest that older African Americans face more difficulties in securing and maintaining employment than whites and are often forced out of the labor market because of unemployment. This means that they are more likely to exit the labor market through pathways other than retirement (Flippen and Tienda, 2002). If they are employed, they are less able to retire because of inadequate savings and pension benefits (Hudson, 2002). Lifetime patterns of unemployment and underemployment in low-paying jobs mean that not only can they not retire, but they also experience problems in securing employment across the life span (Williams and Wilson, 2001).

Given this pattern, analyses of older African Americans' economic status need to consider not only their income but also their total net worth, including assets. Compared with whites, blacks not only have lower earnings at equivalent levels of education, but also less wealth at the same levels of income and less purchasing power due to racial differences in residential environments. The following statistics highlight the dramatic differences in overall economic status

- Financial assets of white households are 11 times that of African American households.
- African American households on average have only 26 cents of wealth for every dollar in net worth of white households (Williams and Wilson, 2001).

Health

By most measures, the health of African American adults is worse than that of their white counterparts, which is oftentimes a continuation from middle age and an outcome from cumulative effects of poverty, racism, and genetics. Being either black or poor is a powerful predictor of higher rates of disability, illness, and mortality. The socioeconomic disadvantages experienced by African Americans explain much of the variance in:

- their lower utilization of health services
- reduced access to health care
- longer reported delays in obtaining health care due to cost
- poorer health status and self-reports of health
- higher rates of mortality

Gaps in mortality are reduced to some extent when social class is controlled for. In fact, marginal increases in socioeconomic status and education generally have larger positive effects on the health of blacks than on whites (National Center for Health Statistics, 2001; Schoenbaum and Waidman, 1997).

The prevalence of chronic diseases is estimated to be twice as high among African Americans as among whites, and the former more often perceive themselves as being in poor health than do their white counterparts. Older African Americans experience hypertension, cancer, heart disease, stroke, and diabetes more frequently than do their white peers, although these differences are greatest at age 45 and decline with age, especially after age 85 (Freeman and Payne, 2000; NIH, 2000). In addition, they have more undetected diseases such as depression. The stresses of constantly struggling to make ends meet may translate into higher rates of depression, especially among women. Obesity is a frequent health problem among African American women, which can lead to complications of hypertension and diabetes. The rate of diabetes mellitus among black women is twice that among white women, and has been described as an epidemic (NIH, 2000). Kidney failure, which may result from hypertension and diabetes, is more common in older African Americans. They also experience more rapid declines in functional ability, more days of functional disability (i.e., substantially reduced ability to complete daily activities) and bed disability (i.e., being confined to bed for at least half of the day), and at earlier ages than whites. Proportionately more African American older people are completely incapacitated and unable to carry on any major activity (e.g., paid employment, keeping house), although still residing in community-based households.

African American elders also appear to have less access to health care than their white counterparts, and delayed access due to cost is highest among African Americans (Federal Interagency Forum, 2000). They are more likely to use hospital emergency rooms as a way to enter the health care system. An important predictor of health service utilization is the availability of health insurance. Older blacks are more often dependent on Medicaid, less likely to have private supplemental health insurance than their white counterparts, and therefore less likely to receive adequate medical care (Kahn, Pearson, and Harrison, 1994). Alternatively, they may turn to kin and friends for information and use self-care health practices, such as home remedies, lay consultations, and folk medicines (Becker et al., 1998).

African American elders face a wide range of social and political barriers to health care:

- With the legacy of history of discrimination within health care systems, especially in the South, health care providers may be perceived as unwelcoming.
- Individuals are reluctant to report poor care for fear of being ignored or retaliation.
- Indirect communication styles used to function in a racist society may interfere with the sharing of information needed for diagnosis, and make it difficult for health providers to understand health concerns in misdiagnosis of conditions.
- Providers may be unaware of how skin color can affect the presentation or manifestation of a disease.
- Potentially significant conditions may not be detected until advanced stages, or benign conditions may be misdiagnosed as more serious than they are.

The early onset of chronic disease and premature death substantially reduces the number of African Americans who live to age 65 and beyond. Although heart disease, stroke, and cancer are the leading causes of death for both African Americans and whites at age 65 and older, rates for African Americans are higher for each of these conditions and occur earlier in the life span. For example, the rates of heart disease and stroke experienced at ages 45 to 54 among blacks are higher than those reported for all other groups at ages 55 to 64. This pattern, which is described as premature or accelerated aging among African Americans, means that other groups do not reach the level of mortality experienced by this group at ages 45 to 54 until many years later. African Americans not only have a shorter life expectancy but a protracted period of dependent life expectancy, managing chronic disabling conditions, and a higher likelihood of multiple fatal conditions than whites (Whitfield and Hayward, 2003). Deaths in late life due to lifestyle and environmental hazards, including accidents and homicides among men, are also much higher among African Americans than whites, except for those who survive into their 80s. This is consistent with the crossover phenomenon when, after age 75, both African American men and women begin to have a lower incidence of death from all causes than their white counterparts.

Differentials in mortality rates are a function not only of the number of persons with specific illnesses but also of the severity and progression of each disease. They also reflect differences in access to medical care and racial disparities in the quality of care. To illustrate, African Americans' higher death rates from certain cancers (e.g., lung, prostate, and cervix) are an outcome of greater risk factors, health practices, and quality of health care. They have many of the risk factors for cancer: higher occupational and residential exposure to cancer-causing substances, higher rates of obesity, higher prevalence of smoking, and less knowledge about cancer and its prevention. This greater vulnerability is compounded by their disparities in access to health care and higher rates of undetected diseases, so that many cancers are not detected early enough to prevent metastasis. Blacks have also been found to receive curative surgery for early-stage lung, colon, and breast cancer less often than whites, and to be inadequately treated for pain from cancer (Freeman and Payne, 2000; NIH, 2000; Williams and Wilson, 2001).

A complication in understanding ethnic minority differences in life expectancy and chronic illness is how minority status, through its association with socioeconomic status, influences health. Socioeconomic status can modify the degree to which black–white disparities in chronic disease are observed in middle and old age. The power of socioeconomic status to shape differences in health for both whites and blacks is vividly apparent when low-income whites are compared with high-income African Americans. High-income black males have a life expectancy at age 65 that is almost 3 years longer than that of white men in the lowest income groups (Williams and Wilson, 2001). Similarly, education can be protective against years of life lost. Nevertheless, the incidence of chronic disease is often higher or roughly equivalent for African Americans with 16 years of education than for whites with 8 years of education. This suggests that education does not appear to overcome the disadvantages of being black in our society. These disadvantages include chronic everyday experiences of discrimination or unfair treatment based on race (Kessler, Mickelson, and Williams, 1999). Such experiences have been linked to poorer physical and mental health, not only for African Americans but also for Asian/Pacific Islanders and Latinos (Noh et al., 1999; Williams, 2000; Williams and Wilson, 2001). In addition, some research suggests that ethnic minorities' perceptions of discrimination make an incremental contribution to racial disparities in health beyond that of SES (Williams et al., 1997).

Social Supports and Living Situations

Living arrangements affect blacks' health and socioeconomic status. The proportion of married African Americans is lower than that of any other population. This is because of lower life expectancy for black men in particular and high rates of widowhood among black women (48% are widowed compared to 19% among their male peers). Among African Americans over age 65, 54 percent of men and 25 percent of women are married. This compares with 80 percent and 41 percent, respectively, among whites (NIH, 2000). Almost 50 percent of African American women live alone, a higher proportion than that of their white counterparts or older black males. Those who live alone are more likely to be impoverished, marginally housed, and even homeless (Killon, 2000). In addition, rates of remarriage are lower than in other groups. One reason for these differences is that widowhood, separation, and divorce are more prevalent among older African Americans and more likely to have occurred at an earlier age compared to other groups (NIH, 2000).

Even though most older African Americans do not live in extended families, approximately 20 percent, compared to 12 percent of their white counterparts, live with a family member other than their spouse. Comparative studies have found that older African Americans have larger, more extended families than do whites, a higher frequency of family-based households, and higher levels of social support from their extended families, including friends, neighbors, and coworkers. Accordingly, older African American women are more likely than white women to have family living with them in their homes. Most often, these are three-generation households, with older women at the top of the family's power hierarchy, playing an active role in the management of the family (Dilworth-Anderson, Williams, and Cooper, 1999; Smith, 1997). As noted in Chapter 9, older African American women often provide financial assistance and care for grandchildren, as well as children of other family members and friends.

Similar to whites, adult children remain a primary source of assistance and support for older African Americans. For childless older adults, siblings are the most important kin tie (Johnson, 1999). The family has flexible definitions of membership and more elastic boundaries that can potentially expand the numbers to include **fictive kin.** Creation of fictive kin is another source of loving support. This includes foster parents or children who function in the absence of blood relatives or when family relationships are unsatisfactory. As an illustration, African American women active in church may turn to nonrelatives in times of need than to their children, but these nonkin may be considered part of an extended family network. Similarly, they are more likely than whites to have larger, looser social networks that include nonimmediate family members among their pool of unpaid caregivers (Johnson, 1999). By redefining distant kin and friends as primary kin, they increase the number of close relationships. The process of enlarging their extended family beyond lineal ties thus expands their pool of supportive resources.

Although many African American elders live alone, they generally tend to draw from a more varied pool of friends, fellow church members, and other associated contacts, and are more likely to use them interchangeably than are whites (Johnson, 1999). While blacks are more likely to receive help from children and grandchildren, and to take children into their homes, intergenerational assistance is a function not just of race, but of age, marital and socioeconomic status, and level of functional disability. In some instances, such multigenerational households may be an adaptation to poverty or other problems rather than an indicator of a supportive extended family. Some social supports may be characterized by negative social interactions that can adversely affect elders' well-being (Swindle, Heller, and Frank, 2000). Indeed, an increasing number of older blacks are affected by stressors influencing members of their social networks, such as crime and substance abuse by children and grandchildren, and face caregiving responsibilities as a result. On the other hand, intergenerational households that develop out of financial necessity illustrate the resourcefulness of black families whose domestic networks expand and contract according to economic resources. Even though so-

cioeconomic factors partially explain race differences in intergenerational exchanges, there is strong adherence to norms of filial support and attitudes of respect toward elders among African Americans across social classes (Smith, 1997).

Overall, African American elders appear to have a broader range—not just a larger number—of informal instrumental and emotional supports than is characteristic of Caucasian older people. Norms of reciprocity are strong and have evolved from a cooperative lifestyle that served as a survival mechanism in earlier times and which continues to be a source of support. Such informal helpers often function as critical links to social services (Dreeban, 2001). On the other hand, health and social service providers need to be cautious not to assume the existence of strong social supports, especially at the point of discharge to home care settings. For example, in a recent study of home health service use among four ethnic minority groups, black elders were more likely than any other group to be left to self-care without any support, despite the expression by black families of the importance of filial support. Patterns of familial support vary within the African American population and are undoubtedly affected by increased economic pressures on younger family members. Such patterns need to be carefully assessed because of their implications for greater isolation, home confinement, and need for additional health care services (Peng, Navaie-Waliser, and Feldman, 2003).

Studies of psychological and general well-being among African American elders illustrate the benefits of social support. Despite significant economic hardships, the majority of older blacks, especially those age 75 and older, report high life satisfaction and happiness compared to their white counterparts, regardless of living conditions. This may reflect the decreasing demands of family and employment responsibilities in this oldest group, and the associated perception of few significant stressors affecting them. At the same time, however, older African Americans are more likely to report high levels of life satisfaction and happiness if they perceive their physical health to be good; this is consistent with other evidence of the link between physical and psychological health generally among the older population. Black elders who survive to age 75, are in good health, and are relieved of the burdens of family caregiving are most likely to experience life satisfaction.

African Americans elders' life satisfaction is also explained in terms of their spiritual orientation and their religious participation. As noted in Chapter 12, spirituality and religion, which are important in the lives of many black elders for adaptation and support, are related to feelings of well-being, self-esteem, and personal control. The church also provides a support network of spiritual help, companionship, advice, encouragement, and financial aid. Faith in God is one way that older African American women living in poverty cope with hardship and enhance self-esteem. For example, qualitative interviews with 50 women identified their belief that they enjoy a partnership with God in which God responds to their faith with reciprocal blessings, both in this life and the next. They believe that their hardship is part of a divine plan that will eventuate in rewards both in this life and the next; the women are thereby released from despair. God is regarded as a personal friend who knows each woman intimately and cares for her (Black, 1999).

In general, African Americans prefer formal services in the home rather than institutional care, which is considered a last resort, and are less likely to enter a nursing home than whites. Only 3 percent of all African Americans age 65 and older and only 12 percent of those over age 85 are institutionalized, compared to 5 and 23 percent of their white counterparts, respectively. Low rates of nursing home placement may reflect the following factors:

- lack of nursing homes in African American communities
- inadequate income to pay for private nursing home care
- perceptions that nursing home services are not culturally compatible

- greater probability that an African American elder, dependent upon Medicaid, has fewer institutional options
- current or historical racist practices among medical providers and nursing home staff
- preference for traditional folk medicine and/or informal supports (NIH, 2000)

African Americans residing in nursing homes are found to be more limited in their ability to carry out activities of daily living and less often receiving the appropriate level of care than are whites. Once admitted to a nursing home, older blacks are less likely to be discharged, largely because they are too impaired to live in the community and their informal resources have been exhausted.

Older Latinos

Latinos are the largest ethnic minority population and the fastest growing group in the United States, due to high rates of fertility and immigration. They are highly diverse and include many groups, each with its own distinct national/cultural heritage and their racial designation by the majority. The predominant groups are:

Mexican American	49%
Central and South Americans	24%
Cubans	15%
Puerto Ricans	12%

(Angel, Angel, and Markides, 2000)

The greatest proportion of Latinos—and also the poorest—are Mexican Americans or Chicanos, who are concentrated in five, primarily rural, southwestern states. The history of some Mexican Americans predates settlement by English-speaking groups, while other Mexican Americans who have migrated since 1942 were recruited primarily to fill the need for low-paid agricultural workers. More recent immigrants face barriers to obtaining citizenship. Immigration remains a significant component of population growth among Mexican

Family celebrations are an important part of Latino culture.

Americans, and can have negative health consequences for those who immigrated in middle and late life (Angel et al., 2000). In contrast, Cubans who were political refugees have created "Little Havana" in Miami, where they rapidly achieved economic success, and represent the wealthiest and most educated of Latinos. Puerto Rican elders are distinguished by their citizenship that provides full access to U.S. government services and their ability to travel back and forth between the mainland and Puerto Rico. Yet they have not achieved the degree of economic success that Cubans have. Among Central and South Americans, the Dominican population is growing rapidly. Their elders, whose strong sense of spirituality affects their coping with the stress of immigration, face pressing needs for housing, assistance with the naturalization process, and obtaining basic medical and social services (NIH, 2000; Paulino, 1998).

Latinos thus encompass native-born, legal, and undocumented immigrants with varying lengths of residence in the United States. Although bonded by common language, each group differs substantially by geographic location, income, education, cultural heritage, history, and dialect—all differences that pose challenges in providing culturally competent services to Latino elders.

Another complicating factor is that Latino elders' needs may be underestimated, since many studies include Latinos in either black or white categories. Those that have an Hispanic classification often fail to differentiate among the diverse subgroups. The Latino older population is projected to grow much faster than their white or black counterparts. In fact, the percentage of oldest-old among the Latino population will triple by 2050. Compared to other ethnic groups, the Spanish-speaking population is youthful, with a median age of 26 years, 8 years younger than the norm in the United States (NIH, 2000). A number of factors underlie their relative youthfulness. One variable is lower average life expectancy, which may be partially explained by poor economic and health status among Mexican Americans and Puerto Ricans. The most important contributing factor, however, is their generally high fertility rate. The number of children born and the average family size among Latinos exceed the national average. High levels of net immigration and repatriation patterns are secondary factors, with the youngest (and often poorest) people most likely to move to a new country, and some middle-aged and older Mexican Americans moving back to Mexico. Despite its current relative youthfulness, the Latino population experienced the greatest increase in median age of all ethnic groups from 1960 to the late 1990s. As noted above, this suggests that the percentage of older Latinos will rise steeply in the future, as younger cohorts reach old age. Accordingly, the parent support rate is expected to triple by 2030, with more middle-aged and young-old adults faced with family care responsibilities (NIH, 2000).

Within the overall Latino population, the sex ratio varies because of the gender imbalance in previous immigration streams and women's survival rates. As a whole, there are proportionately more Latino men to women over age 65 than among the white older population, but this is due to the higher mortality rate of Latino women than white women at earlier ages, not to increases in longevity among Latino men. Nevertheless, the overall gender patterns of this population are similar to those of other older people. Women live longer and outnumber men, comprising over 60 percent of the population age 65 and over, and 62 percent of the oldest-old (NIH, 2000). They more often remain widowed and live alone than men do. Older Latino men marry or remarry more often than men in other groups: over 80 percent of older Latino males are married, compared with 33 percent of older Latinas (AARP, 2000; AOA, 2003). Those female-headed households are most likely to be poor.

Economic Status

Sociocultural conditions underlie Latinos' poor educational and economic status. More than any other group, they have retained their native language, partially because of geographic proximity to their home countries, combined with the availability of mass communication. In fact, approximately 33 percent of older Latinos speak only Spanish (NIH, 2000). Although serving to preserve their cultural identity, their inability to speak English is a major barrier to their education, employment, and utilization of health services. Mexican Americans and Puerto Ricans are also the most educationally deprived group, with approximately 60 percent having less than a ninth-grade education (Munet-Vilaro, 2004).

Another barrier encountered by those who entered the country illegally is the inability to apply for Social Security, Medicare, or Medicaid. All these factors partly explain why such large numbers of Mexican American and Puerto Rican elders have minimal education and have worked in unskilled, low-paying jobs with few benefits. Nearly 20 percent receive neither Social Security nor pension income, and nearly 10 percent have no public or private medical insurance, although Social Security and SSI are the primary sources of retirement income for other Latinos (AOA, 2003). Such patterns have been intensified by the 1996 Welfare Reform Act, which restricts benefits for immigrants.

These employment and educational conditions contribute to the high rate of poverty among older Latinos. An estimated 22 percent live below the poverty level, compared to approximately 18 percent of older whites. Another 33 percent, compared to 18 percent of older whites, hover just above the "near poverty" threshold at incomes below 125 percent of the poverty line. The median personal income of Latino men age 65 and over is about 65 percent of white males; for Latinas, older women the median income is 68 percent of white females (AOA, 2003).

Health

Low socioeconomic status is typically associated with poorer health across the life span, which then reduces chances for employment, education, and accumulation of income. However, despite their high rates of poverty, Latinos in general have lower mortality rates from both acute and chronic diseases than that of the white population (Markides et al., 1997; Williams and Wilson, 2001). In part, this is a function of the tremendous diversity within the Latino population, with Cuban Americans having higher life expectancy and enjoying better health than their Mexican American or Puerto Rican counterparts. In other words, some Latinos are quite healthy while others suffer from several chronic diseases and rarely see a doctor during the course of a year. As a result, when we examine mortality and morbidity rates for the Latino population as a whole, these intragroup differences "balance" each other out.

The relatively good overall health profile of Latinos also reflects the impact of immigration, with a large percent of the population foreign-born. In fact, across all racial and ethnic groups in the United States, immigrants tend to enjoy better health than the native-born, even when those immigrants are lower in socioeconomic status (Hummer et al., 1999). The discrepancy between their socioeconomic risk profile and their group's favorable health outcomes has been termed an "epidemiological paradox." Recent immigrants appear to bring some protective aspects of their culture of origin with them and experience better health throughout their lives. As they become more culturally and behaviorally American, their morbidity and mortality profiles more closely resemble those of native-born Americans (Angel and Angel, 2003). Studies of Mexican Americans, for example, find that disease rates increase progressively with degree of acculturation to the United States. As length of stay increases, fiber consumption and breast feeding decline, but the use of cigarettes, alcohol, and illicit drugs increases. Rates of infant mortality, low birthweight, cancer, high blood pressure, adolescent pregnancy and psychiatric disorders increase with length of residence in the United States (Cantero et al., 1999; Vega and Amaro, 1994; Williams and Wilson, 2001). This suggests that increasing length of stay and greater acculturation of the Latino population will lead to future trends in worsening health for those who came to the United States as youths and grew old here.

Despite their lower mortality rates, Mexican Americans, Puerto Ricans, and Dominicans, especially among those who are female and living alone, do suffer considerable chronic and disabling illness earlier in life, and experience worse physical functioning in old age than others. As a result, physiological aging tends to precede chronological aging, with those in their early 50s experiencing health disabilities typical of 65-year-old whites. Their primary health problems in old age include adult-onset (Type II) diabetes, obesity, and arthritis. Diabetes mortality is higher for Latinos than for African Americans, and Latino elders experience more diabetes-related complications, such as blindness and kidney disease, than do whites (Otiniano et al., 2003). Compared with older adults in general, they are more likely to experience depression, which tends to be associated with female gender, lack of insurance, financial strain, chronic health conditions, and functional disability (Aranda, Lee, and Wilson, 2001). They are also more likely than the general population to require assistance with personal care and to have greater

limitations in carrying out daily activities such as preparing meals, shopping, and doing housework (Angel and Angel, 2003; Munet-Vilaro, 2004). Women are more likely than men to experience multiple chronic disorders. Compared with their white counterparts, Latina women have higher mortality rates from cervical cancer and cancer of the uterus. This may be due to inadequate access to health care and preventive services, resulting in cancer detection occurring too late for successful treatment (Munet-Vilaro, 2004; NIH, 2000).

Early studies suggested that Latino elders were the least likely among all groups of older adults to utilize formal health services (Miranda, 1990). As with differences in mortality and morbidity, use of health care services appears to vary within the Latino population. More recent research found that Puerto Ricans and Cuban Americans made more physician visits than whites, but this may be an outcome of a higher likelihood of insurance coverage (Angel and Angel, 2003; Burnette and Mui, 1999; Lum, Chang, and Ozawa, 1999). Immigrants, especially those who have not attained legal status, lack access to health care insurance tied to employment. If they are dependent upon emergency room care, they typically deal with a new doctor on each visit and do not have the chance to build rapport and a trusting relationship with one physician. In addition, Latinos who speak primarily Spanish face communication difficulties, which can negatively influence their perceptions of health care providers (Becker et al., 1998; Derose and Baker, 1999). Language and trust barriers combined with a greater reliance on home remedies, folk medicine, and religious healing result in patterns of delayed diagnosis, which can negatively affect their health status (Becker et al., 1998; Doty, 2003; Munet-Vilaro, 2004). These examples highlight the fact that that the wide heterogeneity in immigration experiences and socioeconomic status affect how Latinos perceive both their health and their service utilization.

Only about 3 percent of Latinos are in nursing homes, with 10 percent of those over age 85 institutionalized, compared to 23 percent of oldest-old whites. Since families attempt to provide support as long as possible, when older Latinos do enter nursing homes, they tend to be more physically and functionally impaired than their Caucasian counterparts (NIH, 2000).

Social Supports and Living Situations

Historically, the extended family has been a major source of emotional support to older Latinos. Older Latinos are more likely than whites to turn to family than to friends and to believe that elders should be cared for by family in the community (Williams and Wilson, 2001). They are more than four times as likely as Anglos between the ages of 65 and 74, and more than twice as likely as those 74 years of age and older, to live with their adult children. Widowed women over 75 are the most likely to live in extended-family households. Latino older couples are more likely to head households containing relatives, and Latino older singles more likely to live as dependents in someone else's household than are other ethnic minority groups (Choi, 1999).

Family caregiving among Latinos is influenced by the cultural values and beliefs of:

- *familism* (family as central to the life of the individual)
- *marianismo* (female superiority and the expectation that women are capable of enduring all suffering)
- *machismo* (socially learned and reinforced set of behaviors that guides male behavior)
- *respeto* (respect for people by virtue of age, experience, or service)

As a whole, Latinos highly value family relations, believing that the needs of the family or its individual members should take precedence over one's own. Although patterns of intergenerational assistance are strong compared to Caucasian populations, the percentage of Latinos living in multigenerational households has declined recently.

With their urbanization and greater acculturation, some younger Latinos are unable to meet their older parents' expectations to support an extended family in one location. Those who live alone are often inadequately housed, with substandard housing rates substantially greater among Latinos than among whites (NIH, 2000). Nevertheless, despite cultural, economic, and lifestyle changes, the extended family continues to be the most important institution for Latinos regardless of their country of origin, length of U.S. residence, or social class (Beyene, Becker, and Mayer, 2002).

When families are living apart, elders often still perform parental roles; assist with child care, advising, and decision making; and serve as role models (Garcia et al., 1999; Martinez, 2003). So-

---

EL PORTO LATINO ALZHEIMER'S PROJECT: A MODEL FOR CULTURALLY COMPETENT PRACTICE

The El Porto Latino Alzheimer's Project in Los Angeles aims to increase the community's capacity to provide culturally and linguistically competent educational, medical, social, and supportive services for Latino elders with dementia and their caregivers. Services include outreach and education, support groups, day-care services, legal services, purchase of services, and case management. The program assumes that public awareness of the diseases and services is limited in the general Latino public. Emphasis has been placed on outreach and access, beginning with the project name, meaning the "doorway" or entrance. Outreach efforts include the use of Spanish and English helplines, bilingual print and electronic media advertising (Spanish-language television and radio stations are the official project sponsors), community fairs, and informal referrals. Access has also been enhanced through two agencies serving as points of entry for services; this also ensures a single fixed point of responsibility for assessing clients' needs. A full-time social work care advocate ("servidora") coordinates case management services, leads support groups, conducts family and community education, and provides informal services and referral (Aranda et al., 2003).

cioemotional help and advice are typically sought across generations. Although families remain the most important support for their older members, a division of labor is emerging. This takes place between the family, which provides emotional support and personal care, and public agencies, which give financial assistance and medical care, along with churches and mutual-aid, fraternal, and self-help groups. These community-based groups provide outreach, advocacy, and information about resources, socialization opportunities, financial credit for services, and folk medicine. The supportive social and cultural context of neighborhood and community is congruent with Latinos' strong sense of cultural identity. Being part of "La Raza" encompasses a shared experience, history, and sense of one's place in the world that can be a powerful base for community and political mobilization (Torres-Gil and Kuo, 1998).

American Indian elders play a central role in their tribes' cultural activities.

Older American Indians

American Indian refers to indigenous people of the United States, including Eskimos and Aleuts (i.e., Alaskan Natives). Their median age is 27 years (approximately half of all Indians are under the age of 27.6 years), compared to 34 years for the general population. Only 6 percent of this population is 65 years of age and older. Their current life expectancy at birth is 67 years, approximately 8 years less than for the white population, although women tend to live longer than men. Life expectancy is generally lower in nonreservation areas. Not surprisingly, with a gender ratio of approximately 64.5 men to every 100 women age 65 and over, women comprise almost 60 percent of American Indian elders (NIH, 2000). More than 75 percent of American Indian men, but less than 50 percent of their female counterparts, are married. Although only 13 percent of the American Indian population will enter the 65-plus age category, compared to 19.5 percent of the U.S. population, by the end of this century the number of American Indians who are in the oldest-old cat-

egory will at least double. In fact, between 1940 and 1980, life expectancy for American Indians at birth increased by 20 years, from 50 to 71.1 years, compared to a 10-year increase for whites to 74.4 years (AOA, 1997; NIH, 2000). This increase is due, in large part, to efforts of the **Indian Health Service** (IHS) to eliminate infectious diseases and meet acute-care needs earlier in life. The greatest reductions have occurred in death rates due to tuberculosis, gastrointestinal disease, and maternal and infant mortality. Nevertheless, mortality rates for the major killers of older people—heart disease, cancer, and stroke—have not been reduced in the American Indian population.

Less systematic data are available for American Indians than for other populations. The two federal agencies responsible for collecting data, the Bureau of Indian Affairs (BIA) and the Census Bureau, frequently have different estimates, making it difficult to generalize about American Indian older people. An additional complication in generalizing findings is that there are nearly 535 federally recognized tribes, an estimated 100 non-recognized tribes, and approximately 300 federally recognized reservations (NIH, 2000). Also, 60 percent live in urban areas rather than on reservations, and therefore their conditions and needs are less visible. A further complication is that approximately 20 percent of American Indian elders who live in federally recognized areas are not enrolled in a tribe, and thus would not be seen by providers within the Bureau of Indian Affairs (BIA) or the Indian Health Service (IHS) (Baldridge, 2002). Among this highly diverse population, nearly 300 native languages are spoken, and cultural traditions vary widely. More American Indian elders live in rural areas than do other older populations of color, with nearly 25 percent on reservations or in Alaskan Native villages. On the other hand, most do not return to their reservations as they age, instead preferring to age in place, similar to many elders. Relatively high levels of residential stability characterize the older American Indian population. Over 50 percent are concentrated in southwestern states, with the remainder mostly in states along the Canadian border (Williams and Wilson, 2001).

Economic Status

Over 20 to 30 percent of older American Indians are estimated to be poor, with per capita incomes approximately half that of whites. The median income is barely above the poverty threshold. Although about 50 percent of older urban American Indians live with family members, their families are also more likely to be poor than their white counterparts (AARP, 2000; Redford, 2001). Similar to other ethnic minority populations, the poverty of older American Indians tends to reflect lifelong patterns of unemployment, employment in jobs not covered by Social Security, especially on reservations, and poor working conditions. Of all populations, American Indian elders are the most likely to have never been employed. By age 45, incomes have usually peaked among men in this group, and decline thereafter. In addition, historical circumstances and federal policies toward tribes have intensified the pattern of economic underdevelopment and impoverishment in "Indian country," which has led to a steady net migration to urban areas (Baldridge, 2002).

American Indian women are generally less educated than their male counterparts, and seldom earn even half the income of the men, putting them in a severely disadvantaged position. Another factor that negatively affects their socioeconomic and living conditions is that nearly 50 percent of women age 60 and over are widowed. Compared with their male counterparts, older American Indian women are at greater risk of social isolation and economic hardship with health-related consequences as they age (Baldridge, 2002). High unemployment and low income levels tend to necessitate larger households of intergenerational living arrangements, with the elders often the sole provider of the family through their Social Security or Supplemental Security Income. A surprisingly high 50 percent of American Indian elders do not receive Social Security and Medicare benefits, even though such public supports appear to be essential to their survival. A substantial percentage also do not receive Medicaid.

Health

American Indians may have the poorest health of all Americans, due in part to inadequate housing conditions and the isolation of many of their communities. Their elders have a higher incidence than their white counterparts of diabetes, hypertension, accidents, tuberculosis, heart disease, liver and kidney disease, strokes, pneumonia, influenza, hearing and visual impairments, and problems stemming from obesity, gallbladder, or arthritis. In fact, nearly 75 percent suffer limitations in their ability to perform activities of daily living. Cancer survival rates are the lowest among all U.S. populations (NIH, 2000). Diabetes has reached nearly epidemic proportions in this population, which places heavy demands on families to help manage elders' diet, exercise, and insulin (Baldridge, 2002). The primary risk factors for diseases among American Indians are smoking and diet, especially consumption of alcohol. The death rate from alcoholism is seven times higher than that of the United States generally. Alcoholism, however,

Characteristics of American Indians/Alaska Natives that influence their use of health services:

- strong values favoring tribal autonomy
- nonlinear thinking, especially about time
- use of indirect communication and styles
- historical suspicion of authority

usually takes its toll before old age. Alcohol-related deaths drop sharply among American Indians who have reached age 55. Automobile accidents also take a disproportionately heavy toll on American Indian men. In addition, poverty has combined with the historical suppression of indigenous religions and medical practices to place American Indians/Alaska Natives at higher health risks due to environmental degradation. These risks result from living in poor-quality housing, which may lack electricity and running water; being exposed to local toxins; and lacking safe water supplies and sewage disposal systems.

For traditional American Indians, medicine is holistic and wellness-oriented. It focuses on behaviors and lifestyles through which harmony can be achieved in the physical, mental, spiritual, and personal aspects of one's role in the family, community, and environment. The loss of access to traditional environments and the suppression of religious and medical practices also threaten traditional knowledge derived from the use of plants and herbs. Fortunately, the IHS is allowing medicine men and other traditional healers to treat patients in some of their clinics. This may help foster and preserve their heritage and enhance IHS professionals' learning of nonwestern healing practices. Unfortunately, most procedures that focus on treating specific diseases rather than the whole person have typically not incorporated healing elements, such as the medicine wheel. This then reduces the effectiveness of such programs with American Indian elders.

Given these health problems, it is not surprising that people on reservations appear to be physiologically old by 45 years of age, and in urban areas, by age 55. In fact, three times as many American Indian persons die before reaching the age of 45 than non-Indians (NIH, 2000). American Indians have higher death rates than whites up through age 65. Between the ages of 65 and 94, the rates are comparable. After age 75, however, there is evidence of mortality crossover, where the mortality rates for American Indians are lower than for whites (Williams and Wilson, 2001).

American Indians are less likely than non-Indians to define aging chronologically. Social functioning and decline in physical activities are generally used to identify an elder. As a result, a significant barrier to using publicly funded health services is that eligibility is typically based on chronological, not functional, age.

Because of the importance of tribal sovereignty, many American Indians believe that health and social services are owed to them as a result of the transfer of land and that these services derive from solemn agreements between sovereign nations. Despite this attitude, the majority of elders rarely see a physician, often because of living in isolated areas, lacking transportation, and mistrusting non-Indian health professionals. Accordingly, the prevailing life circumstances for many elders—of poverty, low self-esteem, alcoholism, and substance abuse—may interfere with their ability to seek preventive health care. In addition, language remains a barrier. For example, some of the languages of indigenous elders contain no words for *cancer*. Many feel that talking about the disease will bring it on; they may hold fatalistic views, or believe that their culture stigmatizes cancer survivors. In addition, many prefer traditional health care from their tribal medicine people and resist using non-Indian medical resources.

To understand their health care patterns, a life course perspective is necessary that considers their experiences with racism and discrimination. The urbanization of the American Indian population during and after World War II created two worlds of aging. For American Indian elders who are dispersed among the general urban population, there is no tribal community or government concerned with their welfare. Nor do they have special government institutions, such as the Indian Health Service or the Bureau of Indian Affairs, responsible for the well-being of American Indians on reservations.

In contrast, those on reservations have access to the *Indian Health Service* for health care. As noted earlier, the IHS is effective in controlling infectious diseases and providing acute care earlier in life, thereby extending life expectancy. The IHS, however, tends to emphasize services to youth and families and acute care, rather than addressing elders' needs or providing long-term care either in the community or in institutional settings (Baldridge, 2002; NIH, 2000). As a result, the majority of American Indian elders receive social and medical services from the BIA and IHS only periodically. For example, the IHS operates only 10 nursing homes on reservations, as compared to 49 hospitals. This means that older American Indians who need nursing home care may find themselves in long-term care facilities that are at a geographic distance and not oriented to Indian peoples. Such cultural and geographic barriers have resulted in a pattern of repeated short-term stays or revolving-door admissions for chronic conditions. Accordingly, among those over 85 years of age, only 13 percent of American Indians are in nursing homes, compared to 24.5 percent of whites (Manson, 1993).

The sociocultural and political barriers to health care among American Indians encompass the following:

- They ascribe ill health and debility to the normal aging process and are therefore less likely to seek care for conditions that are treatable and curable.
- They distrust medical care that is not native.
- They encounter professionals' lack of sensitivity to ritual folk healing and cultural definitions of disease.
- They have experienced racism, discrimination, and stereotyping, and have been turned away from public clinics where staff insist

that IHS is the sole agency responsible for them.
- They anticipate adverse contacts and being treated unfairly by non-Indian health professionals.
- They are unwilling to sit through long waits at non-native clinics.
- They perceive health care providers as rude because of such behaviors as getting right down to business, addressing strangers in a loud voice, confident tones, and frequent interruptions of the patient.

American Indian elders perceive their physical and mental health to be poorer than do white older adults. Some studies document a higher incidence of suicide, but findings are mixed. Depression appears to be a major mental health problem but is difficult to diagnose because of cultural factors. American Indians' low utilization of mental health services is not necessarily a reflection of fewer emotional problems, but may represent barriers to treatment and lack of information about available psychological services from their health care providers (Markides and Black, 1996). On the other hand, maintaining a tribal identity may serve to buffer various stresses. With age, American Indians appear to shift to a more passive relationship with their world, accepting age-related changes as a natural part of life and utilizing passive forbearance to cope. This movement from active mastery to passive accommodative styles is consistent with Gutmann's findings for diverse cultures, described in Chapter 6. It is also an adaptation to the decreasing person–environment congruence experienced by many ethnic minority elders as they age.

Emotional problems may be intensified by the degree to which older American Indians' lives are dictated by government bureaucratic policies. Unlike any other group, various tribes are sovereign nations that have a distinct and special relationship with the U.S. government, based largely, but not exclusively, on treaties agreed to by the two parties. Congress and the BIA, not the individual states, largely determine daily practices on the reservations. Although the Bureau's regulations are intended to ensure basic support, it is criticized for expending the majority of its budget on maintaining the bureaucracy, with only a small percentage actually going to services. It is also criticized for denying traditional cultural values. As an example, land-grazing privileges were historically extended to all tribal members for as long as they desired. Today, older American Indians must transfer their grazing rights to their heirs before they qualify for supplemental financial assistance. Although extra income may be welcome, the program serves to deprive the old of their traditional position within the tribal structure. In 2000, the head of the BIA apologized to tribal leaders for the agency's "legacy of racism and inhumanity," including attempts to eliminate Indian languages and cultures, but this apology was not made on behalf of the federal government as a whole (Kelly, 2000). The history of American Indian elders and the federal government's mistreatment of them must be considered in developing culturally appropriate social and health services (Ferraro, 2001).

Social Supports and Living Situations

Historical and cultural factors also strongly influence family and community relationships. Family is the central institution; "honoring" and giving respect to elders and sharing family resources are an integral part of their ethos. American Indians' deep reverence for nature and belief in a supreme force, the importance of the clan, and a sense of individual autonomy as a key to noncompetitive group cohesion all underlie their practices toward their elders. Historically, as described in Chapter 2, the old were accorded respect and fulfilled specified useful tribal roles, including that of the "wise elder" who instructs the young and assists with child care, especially for foster children and grandchildren. They also maintained responsibility for remembering and relating tribal philosophies, myths, and traditions, and served as religious and political advisors to tribal leaders. These relationships have changed, however, with the restructur-

> **SHARED EXPERIENCES AMONG THE HIGHLY DIVERSE AMERICAN INDIAN/ALASKA NATIVE ELDERS**
>
> - the rapid and forced change from a cooperative, clan-based society to a capitalistic and nuclear family–based system
> - the outlawing of language and spiritual practices
> - the death of generations of elders to infectious disease or war
> - the loss of the ability to use the land walked by their ancestors for thousands of years

ing of American Indian life by the BIA and by the increasing urbanization and assimilation of native populations fostered by federal policies.

Despite these changes, many American Indian older people, particularly in rural settings, continue to live with an extended family, often as its head. Approximately 66 percent of all American Indian elders live with family members (e.g., spouse, children, grandchildren, and foster children), and over 40 percent of these households are headed by an older woman. Some 25 percent of Indian elders, typically the grandmother, care for at least one grandchild, and 67 percent live within 5 miles of relatives. Given cultural values and norms of intergenerational assistance, family caregivers may accept such care as reciprocity for the help they and their children have received from now-aging relatives, even though their care responsibilities adversely affect their own health. As noted above, this pattern of helping family members, combined with mistrust of government programs and the lack of long-term care services, may underlie American Indians' low utilization rates. In turn, these factors put undue pressure on families to keep their elders at home, even when they lack sufficient resources to do so (Baldridge, 2002). Unintentional neglect has been found to be common due to the caregiver's poverty, lack of access to resources, and uncertainty about how to provide health care (Brown, 1999; Carson and Hand, 1999).

Older Asian/Pacific Islanders*

Asian/Pacific Islander elders encompass at least 30 distinct cultural groups who speak more than 100 different languages:

1. Asian Americans include Burmese, Cambodian, Chinese, East Indian, Filipino, Indonesian, Japanese, Korean, Laotian, Malaysian, Thai, and Vietnamese.
2. Pacific Islanders encompass Fijian, Guamanian, Hawaiian, Micronesian, Samoan, and Tongan populations.

Some classifications include Native Hawaiians and other Pacific Islanders under Native Americans. Each group represents a culture with its own history, religion, language, values, socioeconomic status, lifestyle, and patterns of immigration and adaptation. Adding to this diversity is the timing of immigration, with two distinct groupings: (1) those who arrived during the late nineteenth and early twentieth century and their children, and (2) older migrants, primarily from Southeast Asia, who entered the United States after the 1970s with their families. These two waves differ widely in terms of ethnic and class composition from those who immigrated before 1965. Siegel (1999) lists the percent of Asian/Pacific Islander elders by country of origin:

Chinese	30%
Japanese	24%
Filipino	24%
Korean	8%
Asian Indians	5%
Other	5%

*Although Asian/Pacific Islanders is the term used to describe Asian Americans *and* Pacific Islanders, most research has been conducted on Asian Americans. The fact that relatively little information is available about Pacific Islander elders is why our discussion largely focuses on Asian American elders' health, economic, and social status. Therefore, we refer primarily to Asian Americans in this chapter.

Multigenerational family activities are highly valued in Asian American culture.

The first wave of immigrants shares the experience of discrimination and isolation. Laws discriminating against Asians are numerous:

- the Chinese Exclusion Act of 1882
- the Japanese Alien Land Law of 1913
- denial of citizenship to first-generation Asians in 1922
- the antimiscegenation statute of 1935
- the Executive Order of 1942 for the internment of 110,000 persons of Japanese ancestry during World War II
- more recently, Public Law 95-507 excluding Asians as a protected minority under the definition of "socially and economically disadvantaged"

Such legislation, combined with a history of racism, contributes to feelings of mistrust, injustice, powerlessness, and fear of government—and thus to a reluctance to utilize services among many Asian/Pacific Islander elders.

In 1965, immigration quotas based on race and nationality were repealed. These changes resulted in a rapid growth of Southeast Asian immigrants, primarily after 1975, as the conflicts in Cambodia, Laos, and Vietnam were winding down. The majority of refugees were Vietnamese, (60 percent), followed by Cambodians and Laotians (20 percent each). However, there is tremendous diversity by education, socioeconomic status, language, and refugee experiences among Indochinese refugees, depending on the time of their immigration. The first wave, shortly after 1975, was largely the highly educated, wealthier Vietnamese, who had worked with the American military. The second, more recent wave of Vietnamese, ethnic Chinese, Lao, Hmong, and Cambodian refugees included illiterate farmers and merchants from lower socioeconomic backgrounds that had experienced the ravages of war and revolution in their homeland. These conditions, combined with the trauma of dislocation and resettlement, adversely affected their health and economic status. For both waves, however, the normal aging process is complicated by cultural differences.

The diversity of Asians/Pacific Islanders is also increased by the direct immigration in recent years of Asian American elders, often the parents or grandparents of younger immigrants, primarily from India, China, Korea, and Vietnam (Siegel, 1999). For example, 70 percent of Chinese elders in the United States are foreign-born. They typically do not speak English and have deeply rooted Eastern traditional values that differ from the dominant culture, as described in Chapter 2; these differences intensify their difficulties in accessing services. In addition, the 1996 welfare reform legislation poses new barriers, since legal alien and immigrant older adults are restricted from receiving government assistance for their first 5 years in the United States.

Approximately 6 percent of the Asian/Pacific Islander population is 65 years of age and over. They are the fastest-growing ethnic minority group over age 65, due mostly to immigration rates. As with other groups, the oldest-old are the most rapidly growing segment (NIH, 2000). As the largely young immigrant population of Asian/Pacific Islanders ages over the next 50 years, the number who are old is expected to increase by

1,000 percent (Tanjasiri et al., 1995). Within the Asian/Pacific Islander population, the percentage of foreign-born varies widely.

Economic Status

A widely held perception is that Asian/Pacific Islanders are a "successful" minority because, as a whole, they are better educated and better off financially than other ethnic minority groups (Braun and Browne, 1998). The model minority epithet tends to trivialize the health problems of Asian Americans, suggesting that they can take care of these on their own. It overlooks the socioeconomic and educational diversity among Asian/Pacific Islanders and the problems faced by the newest refugees. In other words, the success of some mask the severe problems of others (Chen and Hawks, 1995). Asians who immigrated prior to 1924, especially Japanese and Chinese, generally differ substantially in their occupational and educational backgrounds from those who came later. As a result of denial of property rights and discrimination against them for public jobs, most older Asians who immigrated earlier are less educated and more economically deprived than their white counterparts. In addition, subgroups of poverty exist among recent immigrants; for example, Vietnamese-Americans tend to have incomes below the poverty level and high rates of no education. Older Asian Americans have, on average, 6 years of school, with the exception of Japanese Americans, who average 8.5 years, which is less than their white counterparts. Many still speak only their native language. In fact, 30 percent of all Asian/Pacific Islanders who are age 65 and over live in households where no adults speak English. This reduces their ability to interact with most public services (Tanjasiri et al., 1995). Their social worlds may be limited to ethnic enclaves, such as Chinatown and Koreatown where they have developed small retail and service businesses, mutual-aid or benevolent societies, and recreational clubs, and where they have access to traditional health care. Although segregated from the general society, these ethnic enclaves are a center for social interaction and the delivery of services to elders.

These social functions, however, may not exist for future generations of Asian/Pacific Islanders, who will be more geographically and socially mobile and more socioeconomically and linguistically diverse (NIH, 2000). Differences between foreign-born and American-born, urban residents and suburbanites, old timers and newcomers, northerners and southerners, Christians and Buddhists, professionals and laborers, and rich and poor frequently override a common ethnic identity, making unity at times an elusive goal.

Although U.S.-born Chinese American and Japanese American older people tend to be economically better off than other groups, approximately 13 percent of Asian/Pacific Islander elders live below the poverty level. As noted above, poverty rates increase dramatically among recent immigrants as follows (Federal Interagency Forum, 2000):

Hmong	64%
Cambodian	43%
Laotian	35%
Vietnamese	21%

Poverty rates may be even higher than reflected in official statistics, since the number of employed adults, often self-employed as farmers or in small businesses, is greater than in other groups, thereby inflating "family" income. Many older Chinese and Filipinos have experienced a lifetime of low-paying jobs, often in self-employment, garment factories, and service or farming work not covered by Social Security or other pensions. Filipino males, in particular, were concentrated in live-in domestic, migrant agricultural, or other unsettled work, often living in homogeneous male camps. This prevented them from gaining an insured work history as well as from developing close ties with family and neighbors.

As is the case with older Latinos, many older Asian/Pacific Islanders who qualify for public financial supports, such as Supplemental Security Income, often do not apply. After years of living under discrimination and fear of deportation, they resist seeking help from a government bureaucracy that they distrust. Their reluctance to seek nonfamilial assistance is also influenced by cultural and linguistic traditions emphasizing hierarchical relationships, personal social status, and self-restraint. When unsure of others' social status, some older Asian/Pacific Islanders avoid interacting with them. In the past, they turned to their families and the benevolent societies and clubs in their tightly knit communities. Now many are caught between their cultural traditions of group and familial honor and the values of their adopted culture that stress independence and self-sufficiency, making them loath to seek support from others (Braun and Browne, 1998).

The cultural values of Asian/Pacific Islanders also underlie their expectation to rely on family as their only source of support and their reluctance to utilize services (Thomas, 1999). Filipino Americans, for example, are guided by values of both respect and shame. Respect includes listening to others, self-imposed restraints, loyalty to family, and unquestioning obedience to authority; shame involves fear of being left exposed, unprotected, and unaccepted. Filipino Americans are also very concerned with good relations or the avoidance of disagreement or conflict. The high value they place on personal relationships may impede their accepting formal assistance, including institutional care. For first-generation Japanese, or Issei, a value that transcends that of family is group conscience, characterized by cohesiveness, strong pride, and identity through a devotion to and sense of mutuality among peer-group members. This value has been preserved through the residential and occupational isolation of older Japanese American cohorts from mainstream American culture. Even among the second generation (Nissei), the Japanese vision of Buddhism endures in the cherishing of filial devotion and the loving indulgence of the old toward young children. Such interdependence with and respect for elders who have greater life experience, knowledge, and wisdom are widely accepted values. Accordingly, Japanese American older people tend to value social interaction, hierarchical relationships, interdependency, and empathy—all values that may not characterize formal services. These situations illustrate a lack of person–environment fit between a group's cultural values and the service system's insensitivity to cultural differences (Browne, Fong, and Mokuau, 1994).

Health

Information on the health of Asian/Pacific Islanders is limited. Less comparative research has been conducted on their health status and behaviors because of difficulties in collecting epidemiological data on the relatively small Asian groups. Given the wide variability within population groupings, their overall health status compared to the general population is unclear. Nevertheless, immigrants appear to be healthier than native-born Americans, and some studies have defined the Asian/Pacific Islander population as a whole as healthier than the general U.S. population (Braun et al., 2000; Markides and Black, 1996). As noted earlier, in terms of socioeconomic and health status, there appears to be a bimodal distribution. Some Asian/Pacific Islanders (e.g., Japanese and Chinese Americans) fare quite well, while others have very low income and poor health status (e.g., Vietnamese and native Hawaiians) (Braun et al., 2000). For example, when health data are disaggregated, native Hawaiian mortality rates are generally higher than other groups for heart disease and all causes of death (Braun et al., 2000). Asian/Pacific Islanders tend to face higher rates of hypertension, cholesterol, osteoporosis, and cancer, especially among low-income subgroupings. A higher incidence of osteoporosis among Asian American women may be due to inadequate exercise (NIH, 2000). The incidence of strokes in Chinese Americans and Japanese Americans is actually lower than among their counterparts in China and Japan. The relatively better health status of these two Pacific Asian groups may be due to their diet, with lower fat and higher carbohydrate intakes compared with whites, and lower

obesity rates compared with other groups. On the other hand, the rates of digestive system cancers, diabetes, and suicide are higher in Japanese Americans than among their white counterparts (Wright and Mindel, 1993). Asian/Pacific Islanders report greater emergency room use and longer hospitalizations than other groups, suggesting that they are less likely to have a regular source of care or that they wait too long to use it (Braun and Browne, 1998). With respect to health status and health service utilization for this highly diverse group, the relative impact of socioeconomic status and other variables that confound race and ethnicity needs to be tested.

There is even less research on the mental health of Asian/Pacific Islanders. The rate of clinically diagnosable depression is slightly higher than that for whites, with the highest rate among Koreans, which may be attributed to their recent immigration status and difficulties in adjusting to American society (Markides and Black, 1996; Stokes et al., 2002). The suicide rate among Korean American women is higher than for whites. Suicides are often explained by perceived incongruities between the elders' values and the reality of their relatively isolated lives in an alien culture (NIH, 2000). Older Japanese males in California have been hospitalized for schizophrenia more frequently than their white counterparts. However, since cultural factors influence the diagnosis of mental health problems, these findings may not necessarily reflect the actual mental health status of this highly diverse population. For example, some groups somaticize mental distress, in part because of the shame and stigma attached to mental illness and to seeking help from formal services (Braun and Browne, 1998).

Use of mainstream health services by immigrant elders is influenced by their status as a subordinate group and their degree of acculturation. The greater their acculturation, the higher their use of services (Tabora and Flaskerud, 1997). Overall, Asian/Pacific Islanders tend to underutilize most social and health services, including Medicare and Medicaid. In some instances, they may be excluded from Medicare because they do

Health-Seeking Behaviors	Belief Systems	Structural and Linguistic Barriers
• lack of knowledge of risk factors or preventive behaviors • lower likelihood than whites or African Americans of checkups or blood pressure tests • lack of knowledge of what blood pressure is, and what can be done to prevent heart disease • low rates of breast self-exams or screening for breast or cervical cancer • limited familiarity with cancer risk factors • perceptions that illness always involves symptoms of pain, weakness, dizziness, or nausea; thus not seeking treatment for diseases that cannot be seen (e.g., cancer, hypertension, diabetes mellitus) • increased difficulty in accepting their diagnoses as real or accepting western treatment regimens for them • holding themselves and their families responsible for their health status rather than turning to providers	• belief in the supernatural powers of ancestral and natural spirits • viewing hospitals as places to die, not a place to get well • defining the use of public services as shameful and an indicator of dependency and inability to care for oneself • belief that cancer is inevitably fatal and carries a stigma • use of over-the-counter or traditional home remedies rather than going to physicians • discomfort with male physicians among women • reverence for authority may result in not questioning a physician's diagnosis and treatment and indicating agreement when there is none • stigma associated with mental illness and the desire to "keep up appearances" result in low utilization of mental health and addiction treatment services	• culturally accepted medical models (e.g., acupuncture and herbal medicines) are not covered by insurance • high noncompliance with western prescription medications • fear of communication problems • difficulties in translating English medical/health terminology into Southeast Asian languages and translating Asian health concerns to English (e.g., cancer is not mentioned as a disease in texts on Chinese medicine) • perception of health care providers as "impatient, disrespectful" of their culture • if residing in this country illegally, fear that seeking medical care will result in deportation

not have the minimal work history and/or the payroll contributions to be eligible for enrollment. Not surprisingly, they are more likely to seek help from family and friends and to use nonwestern medicine. It is estimated that 33 percent of Asian/Pacific Islander elders have never seen a western doctor or a dentist, and only about 2 percent are in nursing homes (Braun and Browne, 1998; Federal Interagency Forum, 2000). This low utilization of western health services is due to a combination of the following factors:

• fewer chronic diseases compared with their majority group peers

• sociocultural and structural barriers to health care

• traditional values such as endurance and "looking the other way"

• reluctance to use formal western health services

• greater likelihood of turning to traditional healers (Ma, 1999; Pourat et al., 1999)

The health problems of Asian/Pacific Islanders are exacerbated by a complex and wide set of cultural, linguistic, structural, and financial barriers to care, as summarized in the box above.

On the other hand, cultural values can provide a source of mutual support and pride. For example, *Bayanihan* is the Filipino concept of a community working together, doing heroic deeds and lending helping hands for community betterment. As Filipino immigrants encountered the individualistic spirit of the United States, the *Bayanihan* spirit faded. The economic value placed on time hampered volunteerism and devalued unpaid community work. However, in some communities, advocates are seeking to resurrect the spirit of *Bayanihan* to promote the health and well-being of Filipino elders. The concept of this spirit is also promoted as a culturally significant health advocacy tool (Bagtas, 2000). Similarly, traditional healers provide broader social benefits for Native Hawaiian and Korean elders compared to Western medicine. For example, healers typically spend a longer time with older patients, discuss personal situations thoroughly, are more accessible after hours and on weekends, and have personal contact with family members and friends (Hurdle, 2002; Pourat et al., 1999).

Social Supports and Living Situations

Although Asian/Pacific Islanders represent tremendous diversity in terms of country of origin, degree of acculturation, and values and religion, they all share the erosion of the **law of primogeniture.** This refers to the relationship between aged parents and the oldest son who provides care for them (typically through his wife) and, in turn, inherits their wealth. Today all children, not just the eldest son, are expected to display filial piety and to repay their parents for sacrifices made for them (Braun and Browne, 1998). Nevertheless, this value of filial piety is being eroded due to smaller family size, family mobility, more daughters and daughters-in-law working outside the home, and acculturation of younger generations into the larger society. As a result, intergenerational living arrangements have declined, with increasing numbers of elders living by themselves or with a spouse, not with children (Chow, 2001; Thomas, 1998). A strain faced by many families is the duality of cultures and the inevitable clashes when generations have different languages, values, and ethos. Erosion of the traditional family network in some instances has resulted in intergenerational conflict and family disunity. For example, Chinese American elders no longer can offer financial support, land, or other material goods as they would have in their homeland and fear being a burden to their children. They generally live with their children only in cases of extreme poverty or poor health, or when dependent upon them for language translation. In contrast, Korean American elders often accept separation from their upwardly mobile children as a way to promote their children's happiness and success. Nevertheless, compared with the majority culture, Asian Americans place a higher value on reciprocal exchanges between young and old and the prestige of being old. Accordingly, compared to the national average, Asian Americans show higher proportions of extended-family arrangements and reliance on families as their only source of support. For these reasons, any discussion of family living arrangements and caregiving needs to take account of differences in culture, social class, timing of immigration, and generations among Asian/Pacific Islanders (Braun, Takamara, and Mougeot, 1996; Hikoyeda and Wallace, 2001).

In contrast to other ethnic minorities and to white older persons, men living alone constitute a larger percent of the older Asian/Pacific Islanders population. This reflects the continuing influence of disproportionate male immigration in the early part of the century and past restrictions on female immigration, rather than a higher life expectancy for men. In contrast to other subgroups of older adults, the ratio of men to women among Asian/Pacific Islanders increases with age, controlling for gender, social class, and levels of functional ability. On the other hand, women in this group are much more likely to be married than their white counterparts, with a smaller proportion remaining single in their later years (Angel and Hogan, 1994).

Advancing age increases the probability of living alone, although the rate of institutionalization among older Asian Americans is significantly lower than for their white counterparts (Manson, 1993). Some 2 percent over age 65, and 10 percent over age 85, are in nursing homes, compared to 23 percent of whites.

This chapter highlights only a few characteristics of Asian/Pacific Islander elders, because of the large inter- and intragroup differences that exist. Because of population and political pressures in Asia, the high rate of immigration is likely to continue, and the diversity under the label of Asian/Pacific Islander to increase. A major challenge for researchers and service providers is to recognize this diversity of history and cultural values when developing culturally sensitive research and practice models (Braun and Browne, 1998).

Implications for Services

Because it is important that services are responsive to ethnic minority elders, we consider further the implications of sociocultural factors for service delivery. As noted above, findings are mixed regarding whether elders of color underutilize social and health care services. For example, some studies have found that Medicaid is not fully used by potentially eligible minority elders. Such underutilization is attributed to lack of knowledge about the program, difficulties in applying, and an aversion to accepting publicly funded benefits (Wykle and Kaskel, 1994). Nevertheless, an analysis of three national data sets found that living arrangements, health status, number of functional limitations, region, and insurance/income status affect use of services more than race or ethnicity (Markides and Black, 1996; Miller et al., 1996). On the other hand, service use by minority elders may vary more in the cultural contexts of local and regional levels than at the national level.

Although some service providers rationalize that elders of color do not utilize formal services because of their families' assistance, patterns of underutilization cannot fully be explained in this way. Underutilization of in-home services, for example, may result more from perceptions of culturally inappropriate alternatives within long-term care than to the existence of family supports. In fact, when medical and psychosocial interventions are culturally sensitive, ethnic minority ser-

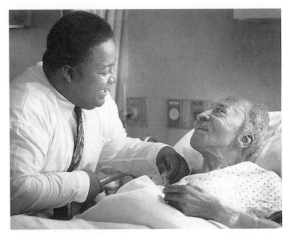

Shared cultural backgrounds can enhance communication between health care providers and older patients.

vice utilization is increased (Miller et al., 1996). Barriers to service utilization can be conceptualized at the level of service recipients and the delivery system, as illustrated in the box on the next page.

Gerontologists generally agree that services need to be designed to take account of inter- and intra-cultural and geographic differences within and across groups. From this perspective, preferential consideration is needed to reduce social inequities between the elders of dominant and minority groups, to respond to the diversity of needs, and to increase the participation of various groups. Accordingly, service providers need to be trained to be culturally competent, and the importance of cross-cultural care or **ethnogeriatrics** is increasingly recognized (Yeo, 1996–97). There has been a shift from only cultural sensitivity (awareness of cultural differences) to **cultural competence** or specific knowledge and skills to work effectively with ethnic minorities.

Fortunately, many health providers recognize and respect older ethnic minorities' adherence to traditional paradigms of health and illness, as well as to associated folk beliefs and behaviors that diverge from mainstream Western scientific medical concepts. Some elders combine these with ortho-

BARRIERS TO UTILIZATION

I. Cultural and Economic Barriers

- Cultural isolation, including language differences.
- Perceived stigma of utilizing services, especially mental health, and embarrassment and fear in attempting to describe symptoms.
- Confusion, anger at, and fear of health care providers and hospitals, which may be related to present or historical acts of racism by medical providers.
- Lack of trust and faith in the efficacy of service professionals within a Western biomedical health care system, which may be intensified by cohorts' experiences. For example, segregated health care and explicit policies, such as the Tuskegee experiment with African Americans and the internment of Japanese Americans on the West Coast, underlie a distrust of the health care system.
- Lack of knowledge of services, including how to make appointments, how to negotiate a clinic visit, and how to describe symptoms.

II. Structural Barriers within the Service System

- The 1996 Welfare Reform Bill that eliminated some public benefits to legal immigrants.
- Lack of services that are specifically oriented toward and operated by members of respective ethnic minority groups.
- Real or perceived discrimination by service providers.
- Assessment instruments whose meaning is altered in translation.
- Geographic distance of services from ethnic minority neighborhoods.
- Lack of transportation to services.
- Nonminority staff who are not bilingual, are insensitive to ethnic and cultural differences, and serve meals that conflict with customary dietary preferences.

---

dox or scientific treatments. As noted earlier, such folk treatments can enhance psychological well-being (Braun and Nichols, 1997; Cheng, 1997). Accordingly, current health promotion efforts aimed at older whites may not be appropriate for populations of color. For example, social entities that play a key role in older African Americans' lives, such as the church and religious leaders, are more likely to influence health beliefs and behaviors than are traditional approaches to health promotion. The involvement of health-promotion experts from the same culture may also help bridge the gap between cultural values and scientific knowledge about the causes and treatment of disease. This is particularly true for American Indian and Asian/Pacific Islander cultures, where traditional ways of treating disease are still widely practiced among older cohorts. Health-promotion efforts that ignore traditional beliefs about harmony between the individual, nature, and the universe are unlikely to be effective in these cultures. To illustrate, the Chinese believe

that health represents a balance between Yin and Yang energy forces; certain foods are assumed to bring about this balance. Believing that the aging process predisposes people to Yin (or cold forces), Chinese elders avoid eating many cold foods such as leafy green vegetables (Yee and Weaver, 1994). Health-promotion facilitators must recognize the basis for such avoidance if they are to encourage healthier diets among older Asians. Accordingly, western assessment measures may not be appropriate for elders of color. For example, most research on caregiving among populations of color has described lower levels of burden. However, caregivers of color may express their burden in different ways than Caucasian caregivers, and available measures of caregiver burden may not adequately measure the impact of caregiving on them. In fact, some qualitative studies have found that African American and Puerto Rican caregivers express anger, frustration, loneliness, and resignation similar to their white counterparts, despite their appearance of coping effectively

GUIDELINES FOR CULTURALLY APPROPRIATE ASSESSMENT

- With the growth of immigrant populations, it is very important to be sensitive to issues of acculturation and language when administering assessment measures and interpreting test results.
- Both the content of the test as well as the language in which it is administered affects a test's multicultural applicability.
- To enable accurate translations, test instructions should be written in simple, concise terminology.
- Use "back translation" to obtain an equivalent fair battery for any language: Material produced in one language is translated into another language by a bilingual translator, then translated back into English by a second individual, and then the original and back-translated English versions are compared.
- Bilingual staff should be required to administer the measures in the client's native language.
- All staff assessing the cognitive and functional status of the older adult must be trained to deal appropriately with the client's cultural background and be closely monitored for any class, race, and other biases, of which they may be unaware, that could imperil the assessment.

SOURCE: Adapted from Arguelles and Lowenstein, 1999.

through religion (Calderon et al., 2002; Delgado and Tennstedt, 1997).

Service use by elders of color is increased by the following conditions:

- Services should be located in ethnic minority communities, easily accessible, and near complementary supports; transportation should be easily available.
- Services should adhere to the cultural integrity of the elders' lifestyles; for example, nutrition programs should include appropriate ethnic foods, and nursing homes should offer culturally appropriate recreation.
- The organizational climate should be informal and personalized.

- Staff should include bilingual, bicultural, and/or indigenous workers, or translators who are culturally competent, who convey respect and who use personalized outreach methods to establish trust and rapport. Medical and insurance forms, newsletters, and descriptions of services should be bilingual.
- Ethnic minorities should be involved in both the planning and the delivery of services to be accountable to the community served.
- Services should be advertised in ways to reach ethnic minorities, such as through minority-oriented television, radio programs and newspapers, and announcements made through churches, neighborhood organizations, civic and social clubs, natural support systems, and advocates. For example, black churches, linked with other agencies, can recruit more African American elders to use social and health care services.
- Given major differences in the epidemiology and risk factors of certain diseases (such as diabetes), screening, prevention, and education are essential.

Overall, rather than a deficits model, in which interventions are developed to ameliorate personal or social problems, service providers should identify community strengths to supplement and augment existing services. This also suggests the value of utilizing existing organizational structures, such as churches, to provide services and to link informal and formal sources of help. Underlying such strategies are assumptions that the needs of elders of color are best understood by members of their own groups, that these elders should be treated as distinct populations, and that research and training programs should give special attention to them. It is also important to employ ethnic minority practitioners as service providers, and to state explicitly minority-specific statutes in federal regulations for aging programs.

Due to increasing longevity and recent waves of immigration, growth rates of minority elders are expected to far exceed those of same-aged whites in the twenty-first century. To advance research on populations of color and thus provide an empirical basis for service interventions, clear and consistent terminology is needed to define and target populations. Issues related to design, data collection, and measurement for and across different groups must be resolved (Burnette and Mui, 1999). The National Institute on Aging's strategic plan for fiscal years 2001–2005 proposes ways to eliminate health disparities among populations of color over time (NIH, 2000). Such a focus will provide a better basis for review and evaluation of proposed future directions in minority aging research and practice.

Implications for the Future

The recent trend that the older population among ethnic minorities is growing faster than among whites is expected to continue. Nevertheless, white elders will continue to outnumber their ethnic minority peers. The socioeconomic status of ethnic minority elders is unlikely to improve greatly in the immediate future. This negative forecast is due largely to the growing income inequality in our society, with a worsening of economic conditions for a substantial portion of the population, many of whom are people of color. Accordingly, poor people of all ages face an increased risk of health problems and disabilities. Widening health disparities often parallel growing economic inequities (Lynch et al., 2000; Williams and Collins, 1995; Williams and Wilson, 2001). Since elders of color are overrepresented among lower-income groups, declining health status linked to economic inequities is likely to affect ethnic minority elders disproportionately. In addition, increasing length of residence in the U.S. and greater acculturation of the Latino and Asian populations will lead to worsening health, as they adopt less healthy western diets and are exposed to unhealthy environments. The intractability of racism also suggests that the disparities in ethnic minority health, mortality, and well-being are likely to persist in the foreseeable future.

Growing rates of childhood poverty will profoundly affect the well-being of elders of color in the future. Among all children in the United States, less than 20 percent are living in poverty; this rate increases to 40 percent for African American and Latino children. Health status of adults is affected not only by current socioeconomic status but also by exposure to economic deprivation over the life course. Early economic and health conditions appear to have long-term adverse consequences for adult health.

Although the likelihood of chronic illness increases with age, research increasingly shows that the origins of risk for chronic health conditions begin in early childhood or earlier (WHO, 2002; Takeuchi and Gage, 2003). Furthermore, risk continues to be impacted by factors such as socioeconomic status and life experiences across the life span. For example, childhood conditions explain a substantial portion of the difference in men's mortality by race, operating indirectly through adult socioeconomic achievement, not lifestyle factors (Warner and Hayward, 2002). This pattern particularly affects African Americans, who have faced the greatest barriers to socioeconomic mobility (Williams and Wilson, 2001). Increasingly, the importance of improving the economic and health status of groups earlier in life is being recognized as critical to well-being in old age. In fact, this life span intergenerational perspective is illustrated by the theme of the 2003 annual meeting of the Gerontological Society of America: *Our Future Selves: Research, Education, and Services for Early Development and Childhood in an Aging Society.* Longitudinal research is needed to capture such lifetime disparities and influences on well-being.

New research paradigms are needed to capture the unique and culturally bound features of the aging process among ethnic minorities and to determine interventions that are effective in reducing racial and socioeconomic disparities in health status and health services (Jackson, 2002). Future research also needs to give greater attention to characteristics presumably linked to race, such as socioeconomic status, acculturation, and discrimination. Regardless of the nature of the research, recruiting and retaining older ethnic minorities as research participants presents complex challenges. Empirically tested strategies, trust and connection with the community of ethnic minority elders, and involvement of minority researchers at all levels are vital (Curry and Jackson, 2003). In addition, as noted in the discussion of service implications, social and health providers need to become more culturally competent.

Summary

Although age is sometimes called the great equalizer, today's elders are highly diverse. As we have seen throughout this book, differences in income, health, and social supports significantly affect older adults' quality of life. An important source of this diversity is ethnic minority status. Ethnogerontology is the study of the causes, processes, and consequences of race, national origin, and culture on individual and population aging. One of the earliest debates in that field continues: whether ethnic minorities experience double jeopardy because of their race or whether age is a leveler of differences in income and life expectancy. Recent studies indicate a narrowing of differences in health status and life expectancy after age 75, or a crossover effect.

This chapter reviewed the social, demographic, economic, and health status of African Americans, Latinos, American Indians, and Asian/Pacific Islander elders. Although there are variations among these groups, several common themes also emerge. For most ethnic minority older adults, their resources and status reflect social, economic, and educational discrimination experienced earlier in life. Those who immigrated to the United States especially experience cultural and language differences. As a whole, they face shorter life expectancy and increased risks of poverty, malnutrition, substandard housing, and poor health, although within-group variations

exist. Nevertheless, many ethnic minority elders, especially among the oldest-old, display considerable strengths and resilience. Social and health care assistance is of particular concern. Cultural and language difficulties, physical isolation, and lower income, along with structural barriers to service accessibility, contribute to their underutilization of health and social services. Efforts must continue to modify services to be more responsive to the particular needs of ethnic minority older adults and to train social and health care providers to be culturally competent.

GLOSSARY

crossover effect the lower death rates among African Americans, Asian Americans, and American Indians after age 75

cultural competence having the knowledge and skills to work effectively with ethnic minorities

double jeopardy hypothesis the hypothesis that aging persons of color are in jeopardy in our society due to both growing old and being part of an ethnic minority

ethnogeriatrics cross-cultural geriatric care that recognizes cultural differences in response to health and disease

ethnogerontology study of causes, processes, and consequences of race, national origin, and culture on individual and population aging

fictive kin foster parents of children, close friends, or neighbors who function in the absence of blood relatives or when family relationships are unsatisfactory

health disparities socioeconomic and racial/ethnic inequalities in health, mortality, and other adverse conditions across the life span

health care disparities differences in access, quality, or rate of utilization of a health care service, where ethnic minorities have a substantially lower utilization rate

Indian Health Service federal program that provides health care for Native Americans and Alaskans of all ages through hospitals and community clinics

multiple hierarchy stratification the theory that social class, in addition to ethnic minority status, can jeopardize older minorities

primogeniture, law of   the exclusive right of the eldest son to inherit his father's estate that was traditional among Asian families

RESOURCES

See the companion Website for the text at <www .ablongman.com/hooyman> for information about the following:

- AARP Minority Initiative
- Administration on Aging Minority Initiatives
- National Asian Pacific Center on Aging
- National Association for Hispanic Elderly
- National Caucus and Center on Black Aged
- National Indian Council on Aging
- U.S. Public Health Service
- www.4women.gov (Women of Color Health Data Book)

REFERENCES

Administration on Aging (AOA). *Facts and figures: Statistics on minority aging in the U.S.* Washington, DC: Author, 2003.

Administration on Aging. *Profile of older Americans.* Washington, DC: Administration on Aging, 1999.

American Association of Retired Persons (AARP), *A profile of older Americans 1999.* Washington, DC: Author, 2000.

Angel, J., and Angel, R. Hispanic diversity and health care coverage. *Journal of Aging and Public Policy,* 2003, *13,* 8–12.

Angel, J., Angel, R., and Markides, K. S. Stability and change in health insurance among older Mexican Americans: Longitudinal evidence from the Hispanic Established Populations for Epidemiologic Study of the Elderly, *American Journal of Public Health,* 2002, *92,* 1264–1271.

Angel, J., and Hogan, D. P. The demography of minority aging populations. In *Minority elders: Five goals toward building a public policy base* (2nd ed.). Washington, DC: The Gerontological Society of America, 1994.

Aranda, M. P., Lee, P., and Wilson, S. Correlates of depression in older Latinos. *Home Health Care Services Quarterly,* 2001, *20,* 1–20.

Aranda, M. P., Villa, V. M., Trejo, L., Ramirez, R., and Ranney, M. The El Portal Latino Alzheimer's Project: A model program for Latino caregivers of Alzheimer's disease–affected persons. *Social Work,* 2003, *48,* 259–272.

Arguelles, T., and Lowenstein, D. Making assessment culturally appropriate. *Diversity Current.* San Francisco: American Society on Aging, Multicultural Aging Network, Fall 1999, *2,* 6.

Bacon, C. *A portrait of older minorities.* Washington, DC: American Association of Retired Persons, 1995.

Bagtas, A. P. Filipino elders community promotes health with dose of bayanihan. *Asian Pacific Affairs,* 2000, *8,* 1.

Baldridge, D. Indian elders: Family traditions in crisis. In D. Infeld (Ed.), *Disciplinary approaches to aging, Vol 4: Anthropology of aging.* New York: Routledge, 2002.

Barresi, C., and Stull, D. Ethnicity and long-term care: An overview. In C. Barresi and D. Stull (Eds.), *Ethnic elderly and long-term care.* New York: Springer, 1993.

Becker, G., Yewoubdar, B., Newsome, E. M., and Rodgers, V. Knowledge and care of chronic illness in three ethnic minority groups. *Family Medicine,* 1998, *30,* 173–178.

Bengtson, V. L. Ethnicity and aging: Problems and issues in current social science inquiry. In D. E. Gelfand and A. J. Kutzik (Eds.), *Ethnicity and aging: Theory, research and policy.* New York: Springer, 1979.

Beyene, Y., Becker, G., and Mayen, N. Perception of aging and sense of well-being among Latino elderly. *Journal of Cross-Cultural Gerontology,* 2002, *17,* 155–172.

Black, H. K. Poverty and prayer: Spiritual narratives of elderly African-American women. *Review of Religious Research,* 1999, *40,* 359–374.

Braun, K. L., and Browne, C. Cultural values and caregiving patterns among Asian and Pacific Islander Americans. In D. E. Redburn and L. P. McNamara (Eds.), *Social gerontology.* Westport, CT: Greenwood Press, 1998.

Braun, K. L., and Nichols, R. Death and dying in four Asian American cultures: A descriptive study. *Death Studies,* 1997, *21,* 327–359.

Braun, K. L., Takamura, J. C., and Mougeot, T. Perceptions of dementia, caregiving, and help-seeking among recent Vietnamese immigrants. *Journal of Cross-Cultural Gerontology,* 1996, *11,* 213–228.

Braun, K. L., Yang, H., Onaka, A. T., and Horiuchi, B. Y. Asian and Pacific Islander mortality difference in Hawaii. In K. Braun, J. Pietsch, and P. Blanchette (Eds.), *Cultural issues in end-of-life decision making.* Thousand Oaks, CA: Sage Publications, 2000.

Brown, A. S. Patterns of abuse among Native American elderly. In T. Tatara (Ed.), *Understanding elder abuse in minority populations.* Philadelphia: Bruner and Mazel, 1999.

Browne, C., Fong, R., and Mokuau, N. The mental health of Asian and Pacific Island elders: Implications for research and mental health administration. *Journal of Mental Health Administration,* 1994, *21,* 52–59.

Burnette, D., and Mui, A. C. Physician utilization by Hispanic elderly persons: National Perspective. *Medical Care,* 1999, *37,* 362–374.

Burton, L. M., and. Whitfield, K. E. "Weathering" towards poorer health in later life: Comorbidity in urban low-income families. *Public Policy and Aging Report,* 2003, *13,* 13–18.

Calderon, R. V., Morrill, A., Change, B. H., and Tennstedt, S. Service utilization among disabled Puerto Rican elders and their caregivers: Does acculturation play a role? *Journal of Aging Health,* 2002, *1,* 3–23.

Cantero, P. J., Richardson, J. L., Baezconde-Garbanati, L., and Marks, G. The association between acculturation and health practices among middle aged and elderly Latinas. *Ethnicity and Disease,* 1999, *9,* 166–180.

Carson, D. K., and Hand, C. Dilemmas surrounding elder abuse and neglect in Native American communities. In T. Tatara (Ed.), *Understanding elder abuse in minority populations.* Philadelphia: Bruner and Mazel, 1999.

Chen, M. S., and Hawks, B. L. A debunking of the myth of healthy Asian Americans and Pacific Islanders. *American Journal of Health Promotion,* 1995, *9,* 261–268.

Cheng, B. K. Cultural clash between providers of majority culture and patients of Chinese culture. *Journal of Long Term Home Health Care: The Pride Institute Journal,* 1997, *16,* 39–43.

Choi, N. G. Living arrangements and household compositions of elderly couples and singles: A comparison of Hispanics and Blacks. *Journal of Gerontological Social Work,* 1999, *31,* 41–61.

Chow, N., and Chi, J. *Assessment of Asian American/Pacific Islander organizations and communities.* London: Allyn and Bacon, 2001.

Chow, N. The practice of filial piety among the Chinese in Hong Kong. In I. Chi, N. L. Chappell, and J. Lubben (Eds.), *Elderly Chinese in Pacific Rim Countries.* Hong Kong: Hong Kong University Press, 2001.

Chow, N., and Chi, I. *Twilight glory: Joy and sorrow of the elderly in Hong Kong.* Hong Kong: Cosmo Books, 2000.

Curry, L., and Jackson, J. The science of including older ethnic and racial group participants in health-related research. *The Gerontologist,* 2003, *43,* 15–17.

Delgado, K. P., and Baker, D. W. Limited English proficiency and Latinos' use of physician services. *Medical Care Research and Review,* 1999, *57,* 76–91.

Delgado, M., and Tennstedt, S. Making the case for culturally appropriate community services: Puerto Rican elders and their caregivers. *Health and Social Work,* 1997, *22,* 246–255.

Doty, M. *Hispanic patients' double burden: Lack of health insurance and limited English.* New York: The Commonwealth Fund, 2003.

Dreeban, O. Health status of African Americans. *Journal of Health and Social Policy,* 2001, *14,* 1–17.

Fears, D. A defining moment for Hispanics. *Seattle Times,* October 19, 2003, p. A10.

Federal Interagency Forum on Aging and Related Statistics. *Older Americans 2000: Key indicators of well-being.* Hyattsville, MD: Federal Interagency Forum on Aging and Related Statistics, 2000.

Ferraro, F. R. Assessment and evaluation issues regarding Native American elderly adults. *Journal of Clinical Geropsychology,* 2001, *7,* 311–318.

Ferraro, K. F., and Farmer, M. M. Double jeopardy, aging as leveler or persistent health inequality? A longitudinal analysis of white and Black Americans. *Journals of Gerontology,* 1996, *51B,* S319–S328.

Flippen, C., and Tienda, M. Workers of color and pathways to retirement. *Public Policy and Aging Report,* 2002, *12,* 3–8.

Fredriksen-Goldsen, K. (in press). Caregiving and resiliency: Predictors of well-being. *Journal of Family Relations.*

Freeman, H. T., and Payne, R. Racial injustice in health care. *New England Journal of Medicine,* March 2000, *11,* 17–20.

Garcia, J. L., Kosberg, J. I., Mangum, W. P., Henderson, J. N., and Henderson, C. C. Caregiving for and by Hispanic elders: Perceptions of four generations of women. *Journal of Sociology and Social Welfare,* 1999, *26,* 169–187.

Gould, K. H. A minority-feminist perspective on women and aging. *Journal of Women and Aging,* 1989, *1,* 195–216.

Hayward, M. D., Friedman, S., and Chen, H. Race inequities in men's retirement. *Journals of Gerontology,* 1996, *51B,* S1–S10.

Helman, C. G. *Culture, health and illness.* Oxford: Butterworth-Heinemann, 2000.

Hikoyed, N., and Wallace, S. Do ethnic-specific long-term care facilities improve resident quality of life? Findings from the Japanese American community. *Journal of Gerontological Social Work,* 2001, *36,* 83–106.

Hudson, R. Getting ready and getting credit: Populations of color and retirement security. *Public Policy and Aging Report,* 2002, *12,* 1–2.

Hummer, R. A., Rogers, R. G., Nam, C. B., and LeClere, F. B. Race/ethnicity, nativity and U.S. adult mortality. *Social Science Quarterly,* 1999, *80,* 136–153.

Hurdle, D. E. Native Hawaiian traditional healing: Cultural based interventions for social work practice. *Social Work,* 2002, *47,* 183–192.

Jackson, J. S. Conceptual and methodological linkages in cross-cultural groups and cross-national aging research. *Journal of Social Issues,* 2002, *58,* 825–835.

John, R. The state of research on American Indian elders' health, income security, and social support networks. In *Minority elders: Five goals toward building a public policy base* (2nd ed.). Washington, DC: The Gerontological Society of American, 1994.

Johnson, C. L. Fictive kin among oldest old African Americans in the San Francisco Bay area. *Journals of Gerontology,* 1999, *54B,* S368–S375.

Kahn, K., Pearson, M. L., and Harrison, E. R. Health care for black and poor hospitalized Medicare patients. *Journal of the American Medical Association,* 1994, *271,* 1169–1174.

Kelly, M. BIA head issues apology to Indians. *The Seattle Times,* September 9, 2000, p. 3A.

Kessler, R. C., Mickelson, K. D., and Williams, D. R. The prevalence, distribution and mental health correlates of perceived discrimination in the United States. *Journal of Health and Social Behavior,* 1999, *40,* 208–230.

Killon, C. M. *A broken or crystal stair? Life histories of marginally housed elderly African American women.* University of Michigan, Ann Arbor: Program for Research on Black Americans, 2000.

LaVeist, T. A. Pathways to progress in eliminating racial disparities in health. *Public Policy and Aging Report,* 2003, *13,* 19–22.

Lum, Y. S., Chang, H. J., and Ozawa, M. N. The effects of race and ethnicity on use of health services by older Americans. *Journal of Social Service Research,* 1999, *25,* 15–42.

Lynch, J. W., Davey-Smith, G., Kaplan, G. A., and House, J. S. Income inequality and mortality: Importance to health of individual income, psychosocial environment, or material conditions. *British Medical Journal,* 2000, *320,* 1200–1204.

Ma, G. X. Between two worlds: The use of traditional and western health services by Chinese immigrants. *Journal of Community Health,* 1999, *24,* 421–437.

Manson, J. Long-term care of older American Indians: Challenges in the development of institutional services. In C. Barresi and D. Stull (Eds.), *Ethnic elderly and long-term care.* New York: Springer, 1993.

Markides, K. S., and Black, S. A. Race, ethnicity and aging. In R. H. Binstock and L. K. George (Eds.), *Handbook of aging and the social sciences* (4th ed.). San Diego, CA: Academic Press, 1996.

Markides, K. S., Liang, J., and Jackson, J. Race, ethnicity and aging: Conceptual and methodological issues. In R. Binstock and L. K. George (Eds.), *Handbook of aging and the social sciences* (3rd ed.). New York: Academic Press, 1990.

Markides, K. S., Rudkin, L., Angel, R. J., and Espino, D. Health status of Hispanic elderly in the United States. In L. J. Martin, B. Soldo, and K. Foote (Eds.), *Racial and ethnic differences in health care of older Americans.* Washington, DC: National Academy Press, 1997.

Martinez, I. L. The elder in the Cuban American family: Making sense of the real and ideal. *Journal of comparative family studies,* 2003, *33,* 359–370.

McCubbin, H. I., Thompson, A. I., Thompson, E., Elver, K. M., and McCubbin, M. *Ethnicity, schema and coherence.* New York: Sage, 1998.

Miller, B., Campbell, R. T., Davis, L., Turner, S., Giachello, A., Prohaska, T., Kaufman, J. E., Li, M., and Perez, C. Minority use of community long-term care: A comparative analysis. *Journals of Gerontology,* 1996, *51B,* S70–S81.

Miranda, M. Hispanic aging: An overview of issues and policy implications. In M. S. Harper (Ed.), *Minority aging*. DHHS Publication #HRS (P-DV-90–4). Washington, DC: U.S. Government Printing Office, 1990.

Munet-Vilaro, F. *Health promotion for older adults: Latino elders*. Seattle: University of Washington, Northwest Geriatric Education Center, 2004.

National Center for Health Statistics, *Health, United States, with Urban and Rural Health Chart Book*, Washington, DC: author, 2001.

National Institutes of Health (NIH). *Women of color health data book*. Washington, DC: Office of Research on Women's Health, 2000.

National Women's Health Information Center, *Women of color health data book*, Washington, DC: U.S. Department of Health and Human Services, Office on Women's Health, 2003.

Noh, S., Beiser, M., Kaspar, V., Hou, F., and Rummens, J. Discrimination and emotional well-being: Perceived racial discrimination, depression and coping: A study of Southeast Asian refugees in Canada. *Journal of Health and Social Behavior*, 1999, 40, 193–207.

Norgard, T. M., and Rodgers, W. C. Patterns of in-home care among elderly black and white Americans. *Journals of Gerontology*, 1997, 52B, S93–S101.

Otiniano, M. E., Du, X. L., Ottenbacher, K., and Markides, K. S. The effect of diabetes combined with stroke on disability, self-rated health and mortality in older Mexican Americans: Results from the Hispanic EPESE. *Archives of Physical Medical Rehabilitation*, 2003, 84, 725–730.

Paulino, A. Dominican Immigrant elders; Social service needs, utilization patterns and challenges. *Affilia*, 1998, 18, 68–79.

Peng, T., Navaie-Waliser, M., and Feldman, P. Social support, home health use and outcomes among four racial-ethnic groups. *The Gerontologist*, 2003, 43, 503–513.

Pourat, N, Lubben, J., Wallace, S., and Moon, A. Predictors of use of traditional Korean healers among elderly Koreans in Los Angeles. *The Gerontologist*, 1999, 39, 711–719.

Rawlings, S. Household and family characteristics: March 1992. *Current Population Reports*, Series P-20, No. 463. Washington, DC: U.S. Bureau of the Census, 1993.

Redford, L. J. Long-term care in Indian country: Important considerations in developing long-term care services. Paper presented at the meeting of the American Indian and Alaska Native Round Table of Long-Term Care. Final report 2002. http://www.his.gov/PublicAffairs/PressRelease/Long_Term_Care_Report.org.

Rumbaut, R. G. Vietnamese, Laotian, and Cambodian Americans. In P. G. Min (Ed.), *Asian Americans: Contemporary issues and trends*. Newbury Park, CA: Sage Publications, 1995.

Schoenbaum, M., and Waidman, T. Race, socioeconomic states and health: Accounting for race differences in health. *Journals of Gerontology*, 1997, 52B, 61–73.

Siegel, J. S. Demographic introduction to racial/Hispanic elderly populations. In T. Miles (Ed.), *Full color aging: Facts, goals and recommendations*. Washington, DC: The Gerontological Society of America, 1999.

Smith, S. H. Now that mom's gone: African-American middle-aged daughters' experiences of bereavement. *Dissertation Abstracts International: Section A: Humanities and Social Sciences*, 1997, 57(11-A): 4933.

Spolidoro, A., and Demonteverde S. *Asian and Pacific Islander elderly in Los Angeles county: An information and resource handbook*. Los Angeles: Asian and Pacific Older Adults Task Force and Los Angeles County Area Agency on Aging, 1998.

Staudinger, U., and Marsiske, M. Resilience and levels of reserve capacity in later adulthood: Perspectives from life-span theory. *Development and Psychopathology*, 1993, 5, 541–566.

Stokes, S. D., Thompson, L., Murphy, S., and Gallagher-Thompson, D. (2002). Screening for depression in immigrant Chinese American elders: Results of a pilot study. In N. Choi (Ed.), *Social work practice with the Asian American elderly*. New York: Haworth Press.

Swindle, R., Heller, K., and Frank, M. Differentiating the effects of positive and negative social transactions in HIV illness. *Journal of Community Psychology*, 2000, 28, 35–50.

Tabora, B. L., and Flaskerud, J. H. Mental health beliefs, practices, and knowledge of Chinese American immigrant women. *Issues in Mental Health Nursing*, 1997, 18, 173–189.

Takeuchi, D., and Gage, S. What to do with race? The changing conceptions of race in the social sciences. *Culture, Medicine and Psychiatry,* 2003, *27,* 435–445.

Tanjasiri, S. P., Wallace, S. P., and Shibata, K. Picture imperfect: Hidden problems among Asian Pacific Islander elderly. *The Gerontologist, 1995, 35,* 753–760.

Thomas, M. Estranged bodies and Vietnamese identities. *The Australian Journal of Anthropology, 1998, 9,* 74–89.

Torres-Gil, F. M., and Kuo, T. Social policy and the politics of Hispanic aging. *Journal of Gerontological Social Work,* 1998, *30,* 143–158.

U.S. Census Bureau. *Population projection of the United States by age, sex, race, Hispanic origin and nativity, 1900–2100.* Washington, DC: Current Population Reports, 2000.

U.S. Census Bureau. *Statistical Abstract of the United States,* 116th edition. Washington, DC: Current Population Reports, 1996.

Vega, W. A., and Amaro, H. Latino outlook: Good health, uncertain prognosis. *Annual Review of Public Health,* 1994, *15,* 39–67.

Warner, D. F., and Hayward, M. D. *Race disparities in men's mortality: The role of childhood social conditions in a process of cumulative disadvantage.* Unpublished manuscript, Philadelphia: University of Pennsylvania, 2002.

Whitfield, K. E., and Baker, T. A. Individual differences in aging among African Americans. *International Journal of Aging and Human Development,* 1999, *48,* 73–79.

Whitfield, K. E., and Hayward, M. The landscape of health disparities among older adults. *Public Policy and Aging Report,* 2003, *13,* 1, 3–7.

Williams, A. Therapeutic landscapes in holistic medicine. *Social Science and Medicine,* 1998, *46,* 1193–1202.

Williams, D. R. Race and health: Basic questions, emerging directions. *Annals of Epidemiology,* 1997, *7,* 322–333.

Williams, D. R. Race, stress, and mental health. In C. Hogue, M. Hargraves, and K. Scott-Collins (Eds.), *Minority health in America.* Baltimore: Johns Hopkins University Press, 2000.

Williams, D. R., and Collins, C. U.S. socioeconomic and racial differences in health. *Annual Review of Sociology,* 1995, *21,* 349–386.

Williams, D. R., and Rucker, T. D. Understanding and addressing racial and ethnic disparities in health care. *Health Care Financing Review,* 2000, *21,* 75–90.

Williams, D. R., and Wilson, C. M. Race, ethnicity and aging. In R. A. Binstock, and L. K. George (Eds.), *Handbook of aging and the social sciences* (5th ed.). New York: Academic Press, 2001.

Williams, D. R., Yu, Y., Jackson, J., and Anderson, N. Racial differences in physical and mental health: socioeconomic status, stress and discrimination. *Journal of Health Psychology,* 1997, *2,* 335–351.

Wong, P., and Ujimoto, V. The elderly: Their stress, coping and mental health. In C. L. Lu and N. W. Zane (Eds.), *Handbook of Asian American psychology.* Thousand Oaks, CA: Sage, 1998.

Wood, J. B., and Wan, T. Ethnicity and minority issues in family caregiving to rural black elders. In C. Barresi and D. Stull (Eds.), *Ethnic elderly and long-term care.* New York: Springer, 1993.

World Health Organization (WHO). *Active aging: A policy framework.* Paper presented at the Second United Nations World Assembly on Aging, Madrid, Spain, 2002.

Wright, R., and Mindel, C. Economics, health and service use policies: Implications for long-term care of ethnic elderly. In C. Barresi and D. Stull (Eds.), *Ethnic elderly and long-term care.* New York: Springer, 1993.

Wykle, M., and Kaskel, B. Increasing the longevity of minority older adults through improved health status. In J. Jackson, T. P. Miles, M. R. Miranda, C. Nunez, E. P. Stanford, B. W. K. Yee, D. L. Yee, and G. Yeo (Eds.), *Minority elders: Five goals toward building a public policy base.* Washington, DC: The Gerontological Society of America, 1994.

Yee, E., Kim, K., Liu, W., and Wong, S-C. Functional abilities of Chinese and Korean elders in congregate housing. In C. Barresi and D. Stull (Eds.), *Ethnic elderly and long-term care.* New York: Springer, 1993.

Young, J. J., and Gu, N. *Demographic and socio-economic characteristics of elderly Asian and Pacific Island Americans.* Seattle: National Asian Pacific Center on Aging, 1995.

chapter

15 The Resilience of Older Women

This chapter covers

- The economic conditions faced by older women
- Their health and social status
- How these factors interact
- The strengths and resilience of older women
- Program and policy options to reduce older women's vulnerability to poverty, poor health, and social isolation

Previous chapters illustrate how women's experiences with aging differ from men's: in patterns of health and life expectancy, marital opportunities, social supports, employment, and retirement. This chapter elaborates on these gender differences, with attention to how personal and environmental factors interact vis-à-vis the particular problems facing women in old age. The impact of social factors, particularly economic ones, on physiological and psychological variables is vividly illustrated in terms of women's daily lives.

Rationale for a Focus on Older Women's Needs

A major reason for gerontological research and practice to take account of older women's needs is that they form the fastest-growing segment of our population, especially among the oldest-old, both in the United States and globally (Moen, 2001; Velkoff and Lawson, 1998). As noted in Chapter 1,

Many older women have overcome a wide range of obstacles and are remarkable survivors.

the aging society is primarily a female one. Women represent 55 percent of the population aged 65 to 74 and 71 percent of those over age 85. They outnumber men age 65 and over by three to two, men age 85 and over by five to two; and centenarians by three to one. These ratios differ among ethnic minorities, as described in Chapter 14. Chapter 1 noted that these disproportionate ratios result from a nearly 7-year difference in life expectancy at birth and a 3-year difference at age 65 between women and men. This is due to a combination of biological factors, such as the genetic theory that the female's two X chromosomes make her physiologically more robust, and to lifestyle factors, such as women's greater likelihood of consulting doctors and their lower rates of smoking, problem drinking, and other high-risk behaviors

across the life span. At age 65, women can expect to live an additional 19 years compared to 16.4 more years for male counterparts. At age 75, the comparable figures are 12 more years for women and 9 for men. Even at age 85, female life expectancy is 1.5 years more than that for males (U.S. Census Bureau, 2000). However, men who survive beyond age 85 are likely to be in better health and to have a similar life expectancy—or even more remaining years than women (Moen, 2001).

Another reason to focus on the status of older women is that gender structures opportunities across the life course, making the processes of aging and the quality of life in old age markedly different for men and women. Consistent with the feminist perspective described in Chapter 8, research on women and aging recognizes that gender and age interact to affect the distribution of power, privilege, and social well-being, and resulting in distinctive patterns for men and women throughout the life course. In other words, older women do not become poor with old age, but their long-term circumstances (e.g., patterns of employment and caregiving and access to adequate wages, pensions, and full Social Security benefits) make them more vulnerable to poverty (Chodhury and Leonesia, 1997). As noted by feminist gerontologists, as more women reach old age in our culture, age compounds a woman's already devalued status and increases her powerlessness (Browne, 1998; Garner, 1999; Holstein, 1993; Moen, 1996, 2001). Since gender and age are powerful systems for patterning inequities in roles, relationships, and resources across the life course, neither can be understood fully without reference to the other (Moen, 2001).

Given these inequities, it is not surprising that the problems of aging are increasingly women's problems. Older women are more likely than older men to be poor; to have inadequate retirement income; to be widowed, divorced, and alone; to live in assisted living or a nursing home; and to be caregivers to other relatives. Women are viewed as experiencing double jeopardy—they are discriminated against both for being old and for being female. Ethnic minority women, who are poorer and face more health problems than their Caucasian counterparts, in effect experience triple jeopardy. In addition, the emphasis on youth and beauty in our society, which traditionally values women for their physical appearance, sex appeal, and ability to bear children, is particularly difficult for older women. In fact, it is this cultural emphasis that underlies the growing popularity of expensive chemical skin peels, laser treatments, and antiwrinkle creams, available largely to upper-middle-class women.

Given the numerical predominance of older women and their greater probability of problems in old age, it is even more surprising that older women were nearly invisible in social gerontological research until the mid-1970s. To illustrate, they were only added to the Baltimore Longitudinal Study (described in Chapter 1) in 1978, since it was previously assumed that women's hormonal cycles would affect the data (Leonard, 1991). The first older women's caucus was not held until 1975 at the annual meetings of the Gerontological Society of America. And the 1981 White House Conference on Aging was the first to sponsor a special committee on older women's concerns. Research on issues specific to women, such as menopause, breast cancer, hormone replacement therapy, and osteoporosis, had been relatively limited until the 1980s. In 1991, Congress directed the National Institutes of Health to establish an Office of Research on Women's Health to redress the inadequate attention paid to women's health issues in the biomedical and behavioral research community. One positive result is the Women's Health Initiative; this is the first randomized controlled study of postmenopausal women and the impact of fat intake and hormone replacement therapy on breast cancer and heart disease. It is to be completed by the year 2008, but preliminary results, especially related to hormone replacement therapy, have already had an impact on women's health practices (as discussed in Chapter 4). Similarly, the Women's Health and Aging Study, funded in 1994 by the National In-

stitutes of Health, is focusing on the causes, prevention, management, and rehabilitation of disability among older women.

Research on aging has thus moved from (1) ignoring gender, (2) merely controlling for gender, (3) describing gender-based contracts, to (4) efforts to understand the sources of gender variations as well as their implications for individual lives. As noted in Chapter 8, a feminist gerontological perspective is emerging that analyzes the intersections among age, race, class, and gender, with the long-term goal of gender equity that will benefit both women and men. Feminist and postmodern researchers emphasize how women's unpaid and undervalued work as family caregivers, along with their employment in low-status, low-paid jobs, results in economic hardship in old age, with consequent negative effects on their health status and long-term care options. Accordingly, the women's movement has tended to ignore issues specific to older women, although some younger feminists are now aligning themselves with older women around shared concerns, especially related to caregiving across the life course. In recent years, older women's resilience and strengths, not only their greater vulnerability to problems, have been increasingly recognized, primarily as a result of the educational and advocacy efforts of such activist groups as the Older Women's league (OWL). Despite the greater visibility of older women's issues, such advocacy organizations confront major challenges, since older women's economic status as a whole still lags behind their male counterparts; this remains a major concern, given the relationship between economic status and quality of life (Weitz and Estes, 2001).

Older Women's Economic Status

Financial resources—especially older women's concerns about their financial situation—are major determinants of their life satisfaction and perceived quality of life (Choi, 2001). This is not surprising, given that women over age 65 account for nearly 75 percent of the poor older population. They thus form one of the poorest groups in our society, with nearly 13 percent of them living in poverty, compared to 7 percent of men, personifying the feminization of poverty across the life course (Weitz and Estes, 2001; Women's Institute for a Secure Retirement, 2003). With fewer older women than men who are employed, the median annual income of older women is approximately $15,000 compared to over $29,000 among their male counterparts (OWL, 2003b). Furthermore, older men are three times as likely as older women to be financially well-off, and this difference persists even among employed women (Costello and Krimgold, 1996).

Although women's wages peak, on average, at age 44 before beginning to decline, men's median earnings continue to climb until age 55. Lower lifetime earnings produce lower retirement income and higher poverty (Estes and Michel, 1999). While women among this current cohort of elders have less education and employment experience than both men and younger women, these differences do not completely account for gender-based inequities in income, which persist even among those with educational levels similar to their male peers. Structural reasons for these economic differences result from gender-biased economic systems. These include:

- the methods used to calculate Social Security (women are disadvantaged by their years spent in caregiving and out of the workforce that calculate as zero earnings);
- employment patterns that differ between men and women (e.g., men typically are employed for the 35 years required for maximum Social Security benefits, while women are employed on average about 11 years); and
- women's reduced access to other retirement income, particularly private pensions, and to retirement planning opportunities.

Women's marital status is directly tied to their income in old age. Women currently and continuously married to the same man receive more retirement income than women who have experienced widowhood or divorce, and in some instances, women who have been employed while married (Weitz and Estes, 2001). To some extent, long-lived marriages—irrespective of the extent of marital satisfaction—offer economic protection in old age. Accordingly, poverty rates are highest among the following groups of women:

- never married women (20 percent)
- divorced (22 percent)
- widows (18 percent)
- ethnic minorities (nearly 75 percent of African American and 66 percent of Latinas), and
- those age 75 and over (approximately 50 percent of Caucasian women, a rate that increases dramatically among women of color) (OWL, 2003c).

These figures may not reveal the full extent of poverty among women, especially widows, who are not counted as poor, despite their low income, because they may live in a household headed by a younger person whose income is above the poverty line. When these hidden poor are taken into account, as many as 55 percent of older women are estimated to be poor. In addition, older women are more likely than old men to be "near poor" or slightly above the poverty line (National Policy and Resource Center on Women and Aging, 1996a).

As noted in Chapters 10 and 12, the gendered nature of the life course—for example, female family roles throughout their lives— profoundly affects women's economic status in old age. Gender-based differences in employment history, child care, and other household responsibilities, career interruptions, types of occupations, earnings, and retirement circumstances all contribute to older women's higher rates of poverty and near-poverty (Calasanti and Slevin, 2001; Hooyman and Gonyea, 1999; Moen, 2001). A primary reason for their economic vulnerability is that most women of this current cohort age 65 and over did not consistently work for pay, largely because they were expected to marry, raise children, and depend on their husbands for economic support. Their labor force participation rate was only 9.7 percent in 1950, rose slightly in the 1950s, and then dropped to 7.8 percent in 1983, when many would have been near retirement age. They spent, on average, 11.5 years out of the workforce caring for children or older relatives (OWL, 2003b). When they were employed, they tended to be concentrated in low-paying clerical or service positions without adequate pensions and other benefits. Although older African American women are more likely to have been employed throughout their lives than their Caucasian counterparts, they were concentrated in low-paying jobs without benefits. Overall, most of the current cohort of older women lacked the opportunities to build up their economic security separate from their husbands' pensions and Social Security earnings for old age.

Social Security is the primary source of income for older women, and women are more likely than men to rely on it as their sole source of income (Estes and Michel, 1996). They represent 50 percent of all Social Security beneficiaries at age 65, and by age 85, 71 percent of recipients are women. Social Security provides 90 percent of income for nearly 40 percent of all older women; 25 percent, many of whom are women of color, have no other sources of income (OWL, 2003b). Marital status directly affects benefits received; the mean proportion of income that nonmarried women receive from Social Security is 72 percent, in contrast to married couples who receive about 55 percent of their income from Social Security (Estes and Michel, 1999; National Economic Council, 1998; Weitz and Estes, 2001). Women's family roles negatively impact their Social Security benefits, since benefit levels are tied to earnings and based on the earnings of the best 35 years of employment. Due to family care responsibilities across the life span, women are far more likely than men to have been employed fewer than 35 years, and thus have years of zero earnings included in the calculations of benefits. Men, on average, have only one zero year out of 35, compared to women's average of 12 zero years (Abel, 1998; Calasanti and Slevin, 2001). Even when a wife worked outside the

home, she often draws a benefit based on her husband's employment record, since his record typically reflects a higher income and more years of continuous employment.

Poverty for women is either created or exacerbated by widowhood or divorce, with 60 percent of older women living without a spouse. Being widowed, divorced, separated, or never married renders a woman much more vulnerable to poverty when compared with a married older woman. To illustrate, married older women have a four to five times lower poverty rate than nonmarried older women. Eighty percent of all widows in poverty become poorer only after their husband die, and divorced older women have higher poverty rates than widows of the same age (Estes and Michel, 1999; National Economic Council, 1998; Weitz and Estes, 2001).

Because women's economic security is so closely tied to their husbands, when they become widowed or divorced—and women are more likely to do so than their male counterparts—they frequently lose their primary source of income. When they turn to Social Security, their benefits may be less than anticipated. At age 65, widows can receive full Social Security benefits based on their husband's earnings or their own, whichever is larger. However, because most women age 60

A CATCH-22 FOR WIDOWS

A widow who enters or continues in the workforce past age 65 receives credit for her own retirement benefits for any month after age 65 that she does not receive Social Security. If her own benefits are greater than her widow's benefits, she will receive credit toward her own retirement. But if her widow's benefits are the greater amount, when she retires she will actually receive no delayed retirement credits whatsoever. Her benefits could be identical to those she would have received if she had never entered the workforce, or had retired at an earlier age.

SOURCE: OWL, 2003a.

and over are unemployed, the majority opt for benefits that are substantially less than what they would have received if their husbands had lived to retire at age 65. Widowed women receive an average of 60 percent of their income from Social Security (Costello and Krimgold, 1996). If a widowed woman becomes disabled more than 7 years after her husband's death, she is not eligible for disability benefits.

Divorced women tend to fare even less well in terms of Social Security. A divorced woman age 62 and over can receive Social Security upon divorce if:

1. she had been married at least 10 years prior to the date of divorce, and
2. her former husband is age 62 or older, and
3. he is drawing Social Security.

If her former husband is still in the workforce, she must wait until he retires. For women without other options, this waiting period can be a time of deprivation and can be experienced as imposing a penalty on women who are divorced. The gender inequity is apparent, since 60 times more women than men are dependent on their divorced husband's earnings for Social Security benefits (OWL, 2003a,b). Women who have been divorced or widowed earlier in their lives tend to have lower retirement incomes than those who have been continuously married (Calasanti and Slevin, 2001). In addition, the economic gaps between married and widowed women—and between widowed men and women—are increasing, especially among the oldest-old. For example, the median income of widowed women is approximately 75 percent that of widowed men, since men are more likely to retain pension incomes through current earnings after their wife dies (OWL, 2003a).

Women are also less likely to have private pensions and to receive lower pension income than men. For women in the oldest-old cohort, mandatory pension laws were not in effect when they were employed. The primary reason, however, is that women are concentrated in low-paying positions and have shorter employment work histories. Most pensions plans vest after 5 years; but women average a job change every 3.5 years (OWL, 2003b). Although pension coverage has increased for women of all ages, it is still less than for men. This inequity is exacerbated for women of color. As discussed in Chapter 12, pension plans reward the long-term steady worker with high earnings and job stability, a pattern more characteristic of men than of women who are more likely to interrupt their careers to marry, rear children, and perhaps care for older relatives. They are also more likely to be concentrated in low-wage, service, part-time, non-union and small firm jobs where pension coverage is less common. Only about 13 percent of women age 65 and over currently receive a pension compared to nearly 20 percent of men age 65 and over (Heinz, Lewis, and Hounsell, 2002). Those with pensions receive approximately half the benefit income of men because of salary differentials during their working years (OWL, 2003a; Waite and Estes, 2001). A woman whose family role resulted in economic dependence on her husband can benefit from his private pension only if the following conditions exist:

- He does not die before retirement age.
- He stays married to her.
- He is willing to reduce his monthly benefits in order to provide her with a survivor's monthly annuity.

Given the economic vicissitudes of aging, some older men choose higher monthly benefits rather than survivor's benefits. Such a choice can be detrimental to older women, who typically outlive their husbands. Only about 20 percent of older widows receive survivor pensions based on their husbands' benefits (Heinz et al., 2002). Fortunately, pension provisions enacted by Congress in 1984 (Retirement Equity Act) benefit older women by shortening the time it takes to earn a pension and improving coverage for lower-income workers, for those who begin work after age 60, and for those who continue to work after age 65.

Most of these provisions, however, are not effective for years worked before 1988, and thus do not affect the current cohort of older women. In addition, federal laws designed to provide protection to spouses of private pension recipients do not apply to state government plans. As a result, over half the states do not have a requirement that a wife must agree to her husband's waiving survivor benefits (e.g., **spousal consent requirement**). This means that a wife may discover only after her husband's death that she will no longer be entitled to pension benefits that were paid prior to that point (AARP, 1999). Another limitation is that policies to address women's vulnerability as nonemployed or late-entry workers focus on benefiting women at risk of impoverishment as they age, not those who have been poor throughout life.

Not surprisingly, older women who have never married and who have been employed throughout their lives tend to have a higher average annual income than their divorced or widowed counterparts. They are also far more likely to derive their income from pensions, annuities, interest, and dividends. These figures do not hold true, however, for never-married mothers who have had child care responsibilites.

Older women without private pensions and whose Social Security income falls below the poverty line may turn to Supplemental Security Income (SSI). In fact, women comprise nearly 75 percent of older SSI recipients (OWL, 2003). For women who value economic self-sufficiency, dependency on government support can be stigmatizing. On the other hand, some older low-income women cope by reducing the stigma associated with poverty. They "count their blessings," redefine poverty to exclude oneself, compare themselves to others less fortunate, and describe poverty as temporary (OWL, 1998).

Given these patterns, the historical and contemporary economic outlook for women in the future remains bleak. Poverty and insecurity will be as much a problem of older women in the middle of the twenty-first century as for women retiring today, especially since women earn only 74 percent

of what men earn (Smeeding, Estes, and Glasse, 2000; Weitz and Estes, 2001). The Social Security system was designed nearly 70 years ago at a time when women had limited employment prospects (and therefore depended upon the marriage benefit); They were widowed young, and divorce was unusual. These conditions are dramatically different today. Even though more middle-aged and older women are employed, they are more likely to hold part-time and poorly paid jobs in sales, administrative support, including clerical, and service sectors. It is predicted that by the year 2020, poverty will remain widespread among older women of color and those living alone—those who are divorced, widowed, or never married—while Social Security and pension systems will have practically eliminated poverty among older men and couples (Smeeding et al., 2000). Accordingly, fewer women will receive either spousal or survivor benefits due to their increased earnings, declines in marriage rates, and better health of older men. Poverty rates will increase among divorced women and never-married mothers.

In summary, women's traditional family roles and limited job options in the past tend to result in discontinuous employment histories. This pattern, combined with fewer pension opportunities and lower Social Security benefits, produces a double jeopardy for economic status among older women, especially women of color. These structural barriers and the interaction of gender and age (and race/ethnicity) mean that government policies (e.g., Social Security, SSI, and public pensions) are differentially effective in raising men and women and persons of color out of poverty. Accordingly, women of color remain at the lowest income levels across the life course. Since most changes in Social Security and pension laws have improved the benefits of women as dependents rather than as employees, they do not address structural inequities across the life span.

Despite the seeming intractability of these interconnections among gender, age, and socioeconomic class, a number of strategies could be taken to reduce the poverty rate among older women:

- Increasing survivor's benefits would improve the status of widowed women.
- Improving benefits for low earners would help many divorced and never-married women.
- Improving the Supplemental Security Income Program would assist the poorest older women (e.g., increase asset limits).
- Targeted benefits could be established within Social Security, such as an income-tested minimum benefit guarantee of $600 per month for beneficiaries taking home less than $400 a month.
- Regarding divorce benefit eligibility, the number of years of marriage required for qualification for spousal benefit under Social Security could be lowered.
- Earnings sharing could be instituted by combining a couple's earnings and dividing the credits.
- There could be Social Security plans that would provide a better return on earnings and better survivor's benefits.

From both a feminist and political economy perspective (discussed in Chapter 8), some of these strategies are incremental and fail to address gender inequities across the life course. For example, legislation such as the Family and Medical Leave Act of 1993, which supports women's "taking time off" for caregiving of dependents across the life course, does not promote women's long-term economic security. This is because such legislation fails to provide credit toward Social Security or access to private pensions. As long as women leave the paid workforce to provide unpaid work in the home, they remain dependent on a husband's retirement or Social Security, which is problematic for their future economic security (Weitz and Estes, 2001). Such feminist and political economy analyses recognize that women's economic status and retirement are conditioned by gendered employment patterns and by social and economic policies that link women's economic security to that of men's. An examination of the interconnections between women's family and employment roles requires so-

lutions that provide benefits for women's unpaid caregiving in the home, ensure adequate access to pensions in positions typically held by women, and work toward increasing women's salaries and wages across all positions, as illustrated in the box on the next page. Thirty years after the Fair Pay and Equal Pay legislation, women still earn only about 75 percent of what their male counterparts earn. Until those inequities are addressed, gender and racial inequities in economic status will remain in old age (Calasanti and Slevin, 2001).

OLDER WOMEN WHO CANNOT AFFORD TO RETIRE

For many older women, retirement is not an option. Instead of counting the days until retirement, some count the number of days they have worked in a row. Consider Patsy Secrest, who at age 58 rises at 3 A.M. to open up a fast food restaurant at 4 A.M., ready to serve the first drive-through customers at 5:30. She has worked in this service job for 28 years, but is paid only $8.50 an hour. She is caught in a vicious circle; employment exacerbates numerous chronic conditions, including high cholesterol and blood pressure, back pain, depression, and insomnia; the resultant rising co-payments of her frequent doctor visits ($300 a month) and prescription drugs ($3600 a year) necessitate that she remain employed to be able to cover her medical expenses. Her job has provided the health care benefits for her husband of 38 years, whose job is threatened by plant layoffs and who last year earned only $11,000. Her life consists of long hours at a physically exhausting job, surrounded by teenagers and young adults. In order to rise early, she needs to be in bed each evening by 6 P.M. This leaves her little time for a social life or leisure activities; her one indulgence of the week is a $16 shampoo and styling. At a time when more affluent couples are anticipating retirement, Mrs. Secrest sees only a future of long exhausting days, dozens of pills to manage her chronic illnesses, and Social Security as her sole source of retirement income.

SOURCE: Finkel, 2003, p. A3.

GENDER INEQUITIES IN SOCIAL SECURITY: PROPOSALS TO IMPROVE BENEFITS FOR OLDER WOMEN

Care credits that reward women's disproportionate caregiving responsibilities:

- Move away from marital status as criteria for eligibility (e.g., eliminate spousal benefits),
- Shift women onto worker benefits that are contributory in nature,
- Reflect the societal value of women's unpaid care work by moving women onto the worker benefit, while buffering their low earnings by valuing their unpaid work,
- Improve the progressive nature of benefits, and
- Contrast with earnings-sharing proposals that divide total earnings of married couple between the Social Security accounts of both spouses.

Care credits that drop zero earning years from women's benefit calculations have limitations:

- Women most likely to have zero earnings years are those who can afford not to work, primarily white upper income women.
- Women's care labor only rewarded when they do not participate in paid labor; but most women do not combine paid work and unpaid care work.

- Fewer women are going to have zero earnings years in their benefit calculations in future cohorts.
- Only 43 percent of women currently in the workforce would benefit from this proposal.

Care credits that drop low earnings years (on top of 5 currently allowed) from the benefit calculation benefit women with high earnings more than women with low earnings.

Care credits that place a value on caregiving:

- Would be a set amount of earnings, which would substitute for a certain number of years of earnings that are below this level. For example, a credit would be set at $15,000. If a woman, within her highest 35 years of earnings, had two years where she earned only $7000, she would be credited with an additional $8000 for those years.
- Rewards those who suffer significant cuts in earnings because of caregiving work.
- Would benefit low-income women and women of color (Herd, 2002).

Older Women's Health Status

Women's disadvantaged economic status increases their health risks. They may live longer than men, but they have higher rates of illness, physician visits, and prescription drug use as a result of more acute illnesses and nonfatal chronic conditions (Calasanti and Slevin, 2001). As described in Chapter 4, older people who are poor, represented primarily by women and ethnic minorities, tend to be less healthy than higher-income older adults. Their living conditions generally are not conducive to good health. Compared to their wealthier peers, low-income elders as a whole are more likely to be living alone, have inadequate diets, have less access to information about how to maintain their health, and have fewer dental visits and physician

contacts per year. Since women, especially the divorced and widowed, predominate among the older poor, women's health status is more frequently harmed by the adverse conditions associated with poverty than is men's. Older women of color, for example, are more likely to obtain health care from hospital outpatient units, emergency rooms, and neighborhood clinics than from private physicians. In turn, poor health combined with inadequate insurance can deplete the limited resources of the low-income women.

Health Insurance and Gender Inequities

Previous family and employment patterns affect older women's access to adequate health care and health promotion information. Specifically, the workplace determines such access through opportunities to enroll in group insurance plans. Most insurance systems exclude the occupation of homemaker, except as a dependent. As a result, more women than men lack health insurance. This is often because women have never been, or have sporadically been, employed or in part-time positions that do not provide health benefits. Low-income divorced and/or widowed women, unable to rely on their husbands' insurance, are especially disadvantaged. Divorced women are about twice as likely to lack health insurance as married women, and are more likely than widows to be uninsured (Costello and Krimgold, 1996). Women of color, especially Latinas, also have lower rates of insurance coverage, including Medicare, than their white counterparts (NIH, 2000).

Some uninsured women gamble on staying healthy until qualifying for Medicare coverage at age 65. Since the incidence of chronic disease is higher among older women than among men, many women do not win this gamble. They may not qualify for Medicaid at an earlier age or for Medicare at age 65. For example, if a divorced woman is diagnosed with cancer in her late fifties, she is too young to qualify for Medicare and too sick to obtain private insurance; yet she may fall just above the income limits for Medicaid; and, as a divorcee, is unable to turn to her former husband's insurance. Fortunately, groups such as Older Women's League have succeeded in advocating for **conversion laws** that require insurance companies to allow women to remain in their spouse's group insurance for up to 3 years after divorce, separation, or widowhood (Consolidated Omnibus Budget Reconciliation Act or COBRA). After age 65, women comprise the vast majority of Medicare beneficiaries, in fact, 70 percent of Medicare beneficiaries are women age 85 and over. Because women have more chronic conditions than men, their prescription drug usage is high—a cost that is not currently covered by Medicare, adding to older women's financial stress. As a result, even with health insurance, older women spend more of their annual income for out-of-pocket health care costs, typically around 20 percent, compared to their male peers (OWL, 2003a).

Because of their lower socioeconomic status, older women are more likely than men to depend on Medicaid. An insidious negative effect of this dependency is that health care providers, concerned about low reimbursement rates, may be unwilling to accept Medicaid patients. This may make it difficult for older women to obtain adequate health care. Male–female differences in longevity, marital status, and income are central in assessing the impact of recent Medicaid cuts in the majority of states. Women outnumber men two to one among frail elders, for whom health and long-term care use and costs are greatest. For example, white women living alone have the highest utilization of nursing homes and home health services and for longer periods of time than white males. As more Medicaid costs are shifted to the patient through higher copayments and deductibles, more low-income frail women will be unable to afford health care, especially for prescription drugs.

Higher Incidence of Chronic Health Problems

Limited insurance options and greater dependence on Medicaid are especially problematic since 85 percent of older women have a chronic disease or disability. Although men tend to experience fewer daily aches and pains than do women, when they do become ill, men are more likely to face life-threatening acute conditions and to require hospitalization. In contrast, women are more likely to experience the disabling effects of multiple chronic conditions (Estes and Michel, 1998). These differences in types of health problems may be one reason why women live longer than men, even though they are less healthy (National Center on Women and Aging, 1999). Since many chronic conditions can be prevented through early detection and treatment or through changes in health behavior, older female baby boomers may be healthier in the future.

Contrary to common perceptions that men are at higher risk of heart attacks and strokes than are women, cardiovascular disease is the number-one killer for both men and women, although men experience the symptoms of coronary heart disease at younger ages. In fact, cardiovascular disease kills more women than the next 16 causes of death combined. Breast cancer and stroke are numbers two and three, respectively. The primary causes are unhealthy diets and sedentary lifestyles, which affect cholesterol levels and blood pressure. The rate of heart disease triples for women age 65 and over, while remaining nearly equal for men and women between the ages of 45 and 64. In fact, five times as many women die from heart disease than from breast cancer. This is because, as noted in Chapter 4, women lose the advantage of estrogen's protection against heart disease after menopause and have a longer life expectancy than do men after age 55.

Women also increasingly face health problems specifically associated with their reproductive functions, such as breast, cervical, and uterine cancers—as well as high-risk complications from hysterectomies. Of women with breast cancer, 75 percent are over age 50 (National Policy and Resource Center on Women and Aging, 1997). In the past 25 years, the chances of a woman developing breast cancer have grown from 1 in 16 to 1 in 8, while prevention, diagnosis, and treatment have lagged. One improvement in Medicare made by Congress in 1990 was to include **mammography** screening as a biennial Medicare benefit. In addition, the 1997 changes in Medicare provided for fuller reimbursement for mammograms. Yet, physicians frequently do not refer older women for mammography, even though yearly mammograms generally are recommended after age 40 (physicians vary in whether they recommend it at age 40 or 50). Even when referred, some older women may not get a mammogram, mistakenly believing that they will not get breast cancer because of their age. In reality, the longer a woman lives, the more likely she is to develop breast cancer, although it may be slow-growing. A similar pattern can be seen where women over age 60, who are most at risk of cancers of the reproductive system, are least likely to have annual pap smears (National Policy and Resource Center on Women and Aging, 1997).

As noted above, although women suffer from more chronic health conditions, most of these are not life-threatening; they do, however, interfere with daily functioning and require frequent physician contacts. Some studies find that older women also experience more injuries and more days of restricted activity and bed disability compared to their male counterparts. These measures are generally indicators of chronic disorders, such as high blood pressure and arthritis, although they may reflect women's greater readiness to take curative action and spend more time in bed recuperating when they are ill. The Women's Health and Aging Study found that the majority of women respondents, despite high levels of disability, engage in some form of physical activity, typically related to household chores (Simonsick et al., 1995). Furthermore, women who begin an exercise program even in their 70s and 80s can improve their fitness and strength.

Among people aged 85 and over, gender differences in patterns of illness become even more striking, with 65 percent of women age 85 and over likely to enter a nursing home compared to 50 percent of men (Estes and Michel, 1998). Women comprise about 75 percent of nursing home residents, and 66 percent of home care consumers (OWL, 2003a). Among women over age 65, 52 percent will spend at least a day in a nursing home, compared to 33 percent of their male peers. Several factors besides health status may account for such differences, however. As discussed in Chapter 9, old men are more likely to be married, with wives to care for them at home instead of being placed in a nursing home. Women over age 75, on the other hand, have few available resources for home-based care, and are often unable to afford private home health services. In addition, as noted earlier, men who survive to age 75 and older are the healthiest and hardiest of their cohort.

More recent analyses of gender and health suggest that the pattern of women outliving men and experiencing more chronic health problems may not be immutable. Scholars on gender and health are urging a shift away from equating "gender" solely with "women" toward a "relatively undifferentiated model of consistent sex differences" in morbidity (Hunt, and Annandale, 1999; Calasanti and Slevin, 2001). For example, a strong association has been found between indicators of gender inequality (e.g., women's position in relation to men for employment and earnings, indicators of women's economic status) and mortality for both women *and* men. Some of these socioeconomic gradients of macroindicators show a stronger association with male rather than female mortality (Hunt and Annandale, 1999; MacIntyre and Hunt, 1997). A growing body of research seeks to question empirically whether important influences on health (e.g., working conditions, social and material circumstances) show similar associations in men and women, rather than simply assuming a difference. Some studies have discovered a "new paradox." Men are more likely than women to assess their health as being poor, despite women's higher level of functional impairment (Arber and Cooper, 1999; Hunt and Annandale, 1999; National Center on Women and Aging, 1999). In sum, the relations between gender and health are not necessarily clear-cut, and may not be in the direction commonly assumed: that women experience more health and mental health difficulties in their longer lives. This also suggests the limitations of trying to make "all things equal" in a social order where gender remains such a powerful influence on life chances. Proponents of this gender-based approach also recognize the importance of considering race, ethnicity and social class along with gender in terms of health status (Calasanti and Slevin, 2001).

Osteoporosis

As noted in Chapter 4, the majority of older people with osteoporosis are women. In fact, 25 per-

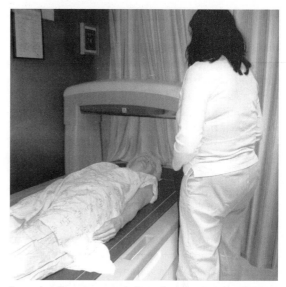

Screening for osteoporosis is an important preventive health behavior.

cent of women over age 65, but 70 percent of women in their 80s have osteoporosis in their hips or spine (Williams, 1999). One in two women will have an osteoporosis-related fracture in their lifetime (Compston and Rosen, 1997). Osteoporosis has been called the silent disease because a woman feels no pain as her bones gradually thin to the point where even a slight bump or fit of coughing can cause a fracture. The higher incidence of wrist, spinal, and hip fractures related to post-menopausal osteoporosis is one reason for the greater number of injuries and days of restricted activity among older women. Spinal fractures frequent and severe enough to cause dowager's hump (loss of up to 8 inches in height) occur in 5 to 7 percent of women. Over 50 percent of postmenopausal Caucasian women are estimated to have at least one fracture of the spine, wrist, hip, or other bones in their lifetime. The incidence of hip fractures in older women doubles every 5 years after the age of 60 (Sedlak, Doheny, and Jones, 2000). The threat of hip fractures can create numerous fears and losses among older women—and circumscribe their social world, especially since half of those affected lose the ability to walk independently. Indeed, up to 20 percent of hip fracture patients die within a year from fracture or surgery-related conditions (OWL, 2003).

The case for and against hormone replacement therapy discussed in Chapter 4 is not clear-cut. Women who do not replace their estrogen can lose 3 to 4 percent of their bone mass every year; for the first 5 years after menopause. HRT has been found to increase bone mass in the spine and hip by 3 to 5 percent in the first year; this increase is maintained as long as the individual takes hormones. It can reduce the risk of both hip and forearm fractures by 50 percent, and the risk of spinal fractures up to 75 percent. These benefits decline somewhat after age 75, the period when women are most at risk. This pattern holds even among women who start using HRT in their sixties (Williams, 1999). Because of growing concern about estrogen replacement therapy on risk of breast cancer, diet (increased calcium and vitamin D) and exercise are increasingly emphasized as a way to reduce bone loss. Low-impact aerobics and weight-bearing upper body strength training can boost bone density 3 to 5 percent a year in those who previously did not exercise. Accordingly, women with calcium supplementation have higher bone mineral densities than those without, and fewer fractures if residing in nursing homes. In addition, several drugs can halt bone loss and may re-

---

WAYS TO PREVENT OSTEOPOROSIS AND RELATED INJURIES

- Be physically active through weight-bearing and strength-training exercises (brisk walking, running, hiking, dancing, climbing stairs, dancing, lifting weights, and jumping rope).
- Don't smoke, since smoking weakens bones.
- Get enough calcium (1200–1500 mg) and vitamin D (400–800 mg) through supplements, but do not exceed recommended daily allowances for women.
- Eat yogurt, milk, cheese, sardines, dry roasted soybeans, or leafy green vegetables, which are high in calcium and vitamin D.
- Prevent falls:
  - Avoid high-heeled or loose-fitting shoes, loose throw rugs, slippery bathtubs, and wet steps.
  - Turn on lights when the room is dark; move things that one could trip on; use nonslip bathmats and bathroom grab rails.
- Talk to your health care provider about cutting down on drugs that make you more likely to fall and those that lead to bone loss (pain and sleep medications, steroids, epilepsy medicines, and thyroid hormones).

---

sult in a 2 or 3 percent yearly increase in bone mass (Meunier, 1999; Williams, 1999). Fortunately, increasing attention is directed toward both the prevention and treatment of osteoporosis. Bone density tests, including X-rays, CT scans, and ultrasound are covered by Medicare. Since 1999, the National Osteoporosis Foundation has recommended testing all women age 65 and over, as well as younger postmenopausal women who are small-boned, have low estrogen levels, or a family history of the disease. Osteoporosis education is now more widely available, but it may not increase preventive health behavior (Howard, 2001; Sedlak et al., 2000).

Menopause

The physiological changes associated with menopause were discussed in Chapters 3 and 7. Social

---

LIFE SPAN RISK FACTORS FOR OSTEOPOROSIS

- being female
- advanced age
- family history of osteoporosis
- smoker; moderate or heavy drinker
- Caucasian or Asian heritage; thin, small-boned body build
- little exercise
- cessation of menstrual periods from strenuous exercise or dieting
- anorexia or bulimia
- taking steroids, thyroid hormone, or other medicines that can cause osteoporosis

and cultural attitudes can also make menopause troublesome, since many of its associated discomforts result from our society's tendency to view menopause as a disease rather than a normal biological process. Hence, many women anticipate that depression, loss of sexual desire and sexual attractiveness, and such signs of aging as wrinkled skin and weight gain are inevitable. Contrary to such expectations, menopause is not an illness or a deficiency, and 30 to 50 percent of women have no symptoms as they pass into menopause. In fact, for most women, it can be a positive transition (Gonyea, 1998). Increasingly, women find that menopause can bring a renewed sense of living and time for oneself, or what the anthropologist Margaret Mead termed **postmenopausal zest.** Menopausal symptoms thus provide another example of the interaction of normal physiological changes with psychological conditions and societal cultural expectations.

The culturally prevalent model of menopause as a disease attributes changes to loss of estrogen.

NONMEDICAL APPROACHES TO MENOPAUSE

- Hypnosis, meditation, biofeedback, acupuncture, paced respiration, and muscle relaxation techniques
  - Exercise
  - Support groups, and use of humor
  - Herbal remedies, such as black cohosh roots to reduce hot flashes; kava to reduce mood swings, irritability, and stress; St. John's wort for depression and anxiety. Despite the growing popularity of herbal approaches, most herbs sold in health food stores (as capsules, teas, tinctures, extracts, or infusions) are not regulated by the Food and Drug Administration. Caution also needs to be exercised in terms of possible interactions with prescription drugs
  - Vitamin E to alleviate hot flashes
  - Dietary changes to reduce fats and preservatives and increase fiber, calcium, soy (through tofu, soymilk, tempeh, miso), or wheat flour (Murkies, 1998)

PLANNING PROACTIVELY FOR A POSITIVE OLD AGE

- Protect your health (diet, exercise, screening tests).
- Improve your skills (e.g., computer literacy).
- Maximize your workplace benefits (e.g., Simplified Employee Pension plan).
- Learn as much as you can about your retirement income.
- Take charge of your finances.
- Determine if you are eligible for public benefits.
- Research your housing options and alternatives.
- Learn about resources to assist with caregiving.
- Be prepared for changes in your marital status.
- Protect yourself through safety strategies.

When it is thus defined as a "deficiency disease," the treatment implication is that estrogen must be replaced. Accordingly, the primary medical response to treating symptoms such as hot flashes has been hormone replacement therapy. When menopause is viewed as a normative life transition, however, lower estrogen levels among postmenopausal women can be considered normal. Recently, many women have been using nonmedical approaches to minimize uncomfortable symptoms.

Although the disease model of menopause links depression with the endocrine changes, depression among postmenopausal women appears to be more closely associated with psychosocial variables, particularly changes in women's roles and relationships, than with physiological factors. Women who have had prior episodes of depression, especially during other periods of hormonal fluctuation (e.g. postpartum depression), those with poor social supports, and those who experience menopause at a younger age are at higher risk, but menopause alone is *not* a risk factor for depression. Health care providers have often treated the symptoms of depression with drugs, or have assumed that women were "too old" to benefit from therapeutic interventions. More recently, efforts have been made to provide women with ways of exerting control over their lives, and to develop counseling and social support interventions as a means of combating depression. Social support groups are found to reduce women's feelings of isolation and to enhance their self-esteem and self-efficacy.

Unfortunately, women do not always get useful information for coping with menopause. Doctors are unlikely to talk about the long-term health effects of decreased estrogen unless women are experiencing unpleasant menopausal reactions, such as hot flashes or mood swings. This then puts women at a disadvantage in making informed decisions about ways to reduce risks. In addition, nonmenopausal health conditions may be ignored because they are attributed to the "change of life" (National Center on Women and Aging, 1999). Not surprisingly, the National Women's Information Center, a resource center that can be accessed by phone or Internet, reports that the topic on which they receive the highest number of inquiries is menopause. Increasingly, newer cohorts of middle-aged women are proactive in seeking accurate information about what to expect, what therapies work, and what the risks and benefits are (Clinton, 1999).

Regardless of age and marital or socioeconomic status, if you are a woman, steps can be taken to ensure a positive old age.

Older Women's Social Status

Approximately 40 percent of older women (compared to 20 percent of older men) live alone for nearly one-third of their adult lives, primarily because of widowhood or divorce. When never-married older women are included, the percentage living alone increases to over 70 percent. At the turn of the century, widows lived alone for 5 to 10 years; now the average is 24 years, yet fewer adult children are available to provide care (Velkoff and Lawson, 1998). In fact, less than 50 percent of all women aged 65 and over live with their spouses, compared to 75 percent of men, and only 17 percent live with other family members, generally a

daughter. Among women aged 75 and over, the percentage living with their spouses drops to less than 25 percent compared with 70 percent of men; and the proportion living alone increases to over 54 percent, a rate at least twice that of older men. Only about 2 percent of older women live with nonrelatives, although a growing number say they would consider asking a friend for assistance if they needed help around the house or with personal care (Chalfie, 1998).

Living alone in itself does not necessarily translate into low socioeconomic status and loneliness for women nor result in deterioration in functional health (Sarwari et al., 1998). For women who were employed throughout their lives, they may enjoy more stable and secure financial circumstances than do widowed, separated, and divorced women because of their longer and continuous employment. In addition, single women often maintain social networks of friends, neighbors, and siblings established across the life course. Embedded in such support systems, they are less likely than previously married peers to be placed in an institution in old age, although this difference probably disappears among the oldest-old. It may be that the negative consequences of living alone are greatest for those who were previously married, many of whom express little interest in remarriage (Connidis, 2003).

Nevertheless, some older women's problems are intensified by the greater likelihood of their living alone. For example, those who live alone are more likely to be diagnosed as malnourished. This is not surprising when the social functions of eating are considered. The older person living alone may derive no pleasure from eating and may skip meals, subsisting instead on unhealthy snacks. The high poverty rates among older women who live alone may also account for their poor diet. Even mild nutritional deficiencies may produce disorientation, confusion, depression, and reduced ability to respond to stress. In addition, a person with few immediate social supports may be less likely to resist infections and viral diseases. Her ability to live in the community may thus be sharply curtailed. In fact, socially isolated African American women are found to have higher rates of mortality than their peers with strong social networks (LaVeist et al., 1997).

In contrast, older women of color who are divorced and widowed are more likely to live in extended family households, with children and/or grandchildren living in their home. For example, African American (36%) and Latina (34%) women live with relatives compared with only 14 percent of older white women. Women of color often extend their households to include children and grandchildren, assuming child care and housekeeping responsibilities into old age (Cochran, Brown, and McGregor, 1999). This may help them meet housing and food costs, but it may also impose additional strains.

Widowhood

As discussed in Chapter 13, the average age of widowhood for women is 66 years. Because women generally marry men older than themselves, live longer than men, and, in their later years, seldom remarry after the death of their husbands, 85 percent of all wives outlive their husbands. Some 52 percent of women aged 65 and over are widowed, in contrast to 14 percent of men in this age group; this gap increases dramatically with age. The expected years of widowhood are far more than the 8-year difference in life expectancy between women and men at these ages. At age 65 a widow can anticipate living another 18 years; at age 70, 11 years; and at age 85, another 9 years. Not surprisingly, after age 85, 66 percent of women live alone (National Policy and Resource Center, 1996a). Moreover, this increased time living alone is accompanied by shrinking family size, with fewer children available as potential caregivers (Moen, 2001). The probability of widowhood increases among older women of color; for example, 75 percent of African American women over age 75 are widows (Weir et al., 2002).

As noted previously, the primary negative consequence of widowhood is low socioeconomic sta-

Group exercise offers physical and social benefits.

tus. Women who have been widowed longest have the highest poverty rate; within this grouping, women who were widowed in their 50s are among the poorest, often having depleted their assets (Weir, Willis, and Sevak, 2002). Economic status has numerous social implications: Low-income women have fewer options for social interactions, fewer affordable and safe accommodations, and fewer resources to purchase in-home support services. The most negative consequence may be that older women's economic situation precludes continued independent living when health problems arise. In fact, widowhood has been found to result in increased health service use and costs (Prigerson, Maciejewski, and Rosenbeck, 2000). Despite these objective disadvantages of widowhood, the "lonely widow" may be a stereotype to some extent, and widowhood may not necessarily produce the major, enduring negative emotional effects typically reported. Instead, over the long term, widowhood may represent a positive shift into a new life phase (Feldman, Byles, and Beaumont, 2000).

Limited Opportunities to Remarry

Although remarriage may be viewed as a way to ensure economic security, older widowed and divorced women have fewer remarriage options than do their male peers. In addition, they may choose not to remarry either because their marriage was not a positive experience, or because they enjoy being on their own. The primary obstacles to re-marriage are the disproportionate number of women age 65 and over to men and the cultural stigma against women marrying younger men. With the ratio of 80-year-old women to men being three to one, the chances for remarriage decline drastically with age. These gender differences lead to differential needs for support in the face of failing health; most older men are cared for by their wives, whereas most older women rely on their children, usually daughters, for help and may turn later to paid assistance. Increasingly, adult daughters who assist their widowed mothers are themselves in their 60s and 70s, and are faced with their own physical limitations. One consequence of this pattern is that older women may have to depend more on public support services, even though these are not well funded. As invisible laborers, women's work is essential to the health care system and to their relatives' long-term care, but it is not adequately supported by public policies.

In addition to high rates of widowhood and increasing rates of divorce, the current cohort of older women has relatively high proportions of unmarried women throughout their lives (approximately 5 percent for those now in their 70s and 80s). Therefore, a cohort effect also may explain the large numbers of older women living without spouses. Another factor that increases the probability of being alone among this current cohort is that approximately one in five has either been childless throughout her life or has survived her offspring (Saluter, 1994). In the future, the proportion of old women living alone, including those unmarried throughout their adult lives, will increase.

As noted earlier, the absence of children and a spouse also increases the chance of being placed in a long-term care facility. This suggests that women may be institutionalized for social rather than medical reasons, and may be inappropriately placed in a nursing home when alternative community supports might have permitted more independent lifestyles. As noted in Chapter 11, women in nursing homes are typically widowed

---

FORMATION OF COMMUNITY AMONG OLD WOMEN IN A BEAUTY SHOP

An unintentional community of older women is formed at an old-fashioned beauty shop, based on a shared universe of meaning as Jewish mothers, housewives, and caregivers in a society that expects women to be attractive, despite the realities of aging and physical decline. Women in a beauty shop are brought together around a common concern with appearance as a source of self-worth. The face and the body are used to maintain self-respect and community status. Taking care of oneself is a moral imperative for these old women. Friendships formed in the beauty shop illustrate the diversity of women's connectedness and their varied expression of mutual supportiveness and caring. They talk about illness, aches, and pains, experiencing an outlet for subjects that they feel they cannot discuss with family. Discursive personal stories permit exchange of lived experiences and strengthen social bonds. Shows of physical and verbal affection, humor about the inevitability of wrinkles, sags and bags, and food shared further strengthen social ties. The beauty shop is a search for a good old age among women disadvantaged by age and gender. In the process of seeking beauty, the women gain a sense of belonging, affirmation, and being cared for. The beauty shop thus also acts as a community of resistance against being old and female in a gendered society.

SOURCE: Adapted from Markson, 1999.

---

or single, often dependent on Medicaid, and lacking family members to assist them either socially or financially. After age 85, 25 percent of women, especially never-married and widowed women, are in nursing homes (Adams, Nawrocki, and Coleman, 1999; NIH, 2000).

Sources of Support

In general, older women have fewer economic but more social resources and richer, more intimate relationships than do older men. Men tend to have larger nonkin networks, perhaps as a result of employment, but are less resourceful in planning social get-togethers and building networks that substitute for the sociability in marriage (Erickson et al., 2000; Moen, 2001; Wethington and Keevey, 2000). Widowed women, in particular, and women in retirement communities generally have frequent and intimate contacts with friends and social activities. One reason for this is that retirement communities provide women with peers at the same stage of life and shared similar experiences. Even when their friends die, women generally establish new relationships, exchanging affection and material support outside their families, although they may not be able to call upon such relationships to care for them. Instead, they value the mutuality of their friendships and do not want to become dependent for personal care upon friends (Roberto, 1996). Support groups for widows and family caregivers build on such reciprocal exchange relations among peers. In addition, with age, some women first become comfortable with being open about their lesbianism and their strong emotional bonds with other women. One function of the affirmation of women's competencies by the women's movement has been to encourage them to support each other rather than depend on men. This is evidenced by the growth of shared households, older women's support and advocacy groups, support groups for caregiving grandmothers, and intergenerational alliances.

Consistent with feminist theory discussed in Chapter 8, a feminist analysis of older women's social status would articulate their strengths and resilience, as well as their vulnerabilities. Growing numbers of older women are coping with age-related loss through staying active, involved, and finding meaning and spiritual resilience in their lives. Feminist research seeks to "rediscover, revalue, and bring to public view women's experiences that have been obscured, occluded or devalued because they have been seen as socially insignificant or morally irrelevant" (Furman, 1997, p. 6). Although cohort, period, historical, and gender-based life circumstances mold older

women, they are not passive. By studying gender and age power differentials, feminists seek to deepen our understanding of both women and men, their uniqueness, and their similarities in actively meeting life's challenges (Calasanti and Slevin, 2001; Markson, 1999).

Implications for the Future

Since women's socioeconomic status compounds problems they face in old age, fundamental changes are needed to remove inequities in the workplace, Social Security, and pension systems. Most such changes, however, will benefit future generations of older women, rather than the current cohort, which was socialized for work and family roles that no longer prevail. For example, efforts in some states to assure that women and men earn equal pay for jobs of comparable economic worth and to remove other salary inequities may mean that future generations of older women will have retirement benefits based on a lifetime of more adequate earnings, and will have more experience in handling finances. Some businesses and government agencies have initiated more flexible work arrangements with full benefits, which will allow men and women to share employment and family responsibilities more equitably.

When such options exist, women may have fewer years of zero earnings to be calculated into their Social Security benefits, and will be more likely to hold jobs covered by private pensions. Even so, it is predicted that 60 percent of women in the year 2030 will still have 5 or more years of zero earnings averaged into the calculation of their Social Security benefits. This will widen the current gap between older women living alone and all other groups (Crystal, 1996). This is in large part due to the fact that despite three decades of legislation, women have not achieved equality in the workforce. Women remain disproportionately in the secondary service sector, marked by low wages, few benefits, part-time employment, and little job security. Even the entrance of more women into previously male-dominated positions has not resulted in a significant restructuring of the distribution of roles within families, with women still responsible for the majority of child care and housework (Moen, 2001).

Changes in Social Security to benefit women workers have been proposed by federal studies and commissions. The current Social Security system is based on an outmoded model of lifelong marriage, in which one spouse is the paid worker and the other is the homemaker. As the prior discussion of divorce and changing work patterns suggests, this model no longer accommodates the emerging diversity of employment and family roles. Nor, for that matter, has this model ever represented the diversity of American families. One remedy is **earnings sharing,** whereby each partner in marriage is entitled to a separate Social Security account, regardless of which spouse is employed in the paid labor force. Covered earnings would be divided between the two spouses, with one-half credited to each spouse's account. Credits for homemaking and caregiving of dependents across the life span, partial benefits for widows under age 62, full benefits for widows after age 65, and the option of collecting benefits as both worker and wife have also been discussed by older adult advocacy groups and by some legislators. The likelihood of any such changes being instituted in the future is small, given the current economy and escalating military expenditures. Instead, the greater risk is that efforts to privatize Social Security will disproportionately hurt older women (see Chapter 16).

Pension reforms have also been passed on the federal level that would increase by more than 20 percent the number of women covered by private pensions, through a reduction of the amount of time required for vesting. In the long run, more fundamental changes are needed in society's view of work throughout the life cycle, so that men and women may share more equitably in caregiving and employment responsibilities. At the same time, employers must value skills gained through homemaking and voluntary activity as transfer-

---

CHANGING CONCEPTS OF BEAUTY AND AGE

The feminist Gloria Steinem, when told that she looked really good for her age, responded, "This is what 60 looks like on me." The model Lauren Hutton, who returned to modeling at age 44, remembers opening the *New York Times Magazine* and seeing a beautiful old face and realizing it was herself. She is now in her 60s and considering returning to modeling. One of her reasons: "It's good to show what beauty is—all ages, all sizes" (Sherrill, 2003). Although these women have the financial and social resources to purchase numerous antiaging products and surgeries, both are conveying a more positive image of older women—celebrating their age rather than being focused on looking younger.

---

able to the marketplace. As discussed in Chapters 9 and 12, the ways in which women contribute to society through their volunteerism, caregiving, housekeeping responsibilities, and informal helping of others need to be recognized under a broad concept of productivity, rather than equating productivity with only paid work (Holstein, 1993).

Another positive direction is that despite our societal emphasis on physical appearance, more women are becoming comfortable with their aging and accepting its visible signs, such as wrinkles and hair. They value exercise, nutrition, and meditation as pathways to better health and personal growth, not as means to avoid looking older. Freed from past roles as wife or mother, they discover the strength from learning who they are and sharing their feelings, insights, and fears about aging with each other. Some women collectively identify themselves as "Crones" or "Sages," rejecting past stereotypes and restoring images of wisdom, honor, and respect to being an old woman. Fortunately, some women who are highly visible are also helping to change concepts of physical beauty in old age.

Another important direction to enhance the quality of women's lives is that more women of all ages are increasingly supporting one another, as illustrated by the intergenerational advocacy efforts of the Older Women's League. Another promising change is the growth of social support groups among older women. Groups of older widows and women caregivers are found to be effective in reducing isolation. They encourage group members to meet their own needs and expand women's awareness of public services to which they are entitled. This function of educating and politicizing older women also helps many to see the societal causes of the difficulties that they have experienced as individuals. Awareness of external causes of their problems may serve to bring together for common action women of diverse ages, ethnicity, race, socioeconomic classes, and sexual orientation. Cross-cultural evidence shows that age permits women in a wide range of cultures to experience increased freedom and to become more dominant and powerful, with fewer restrictions on their behavior and mobility and increased opportunities to engage in roles outside the home. Rather than passivity, growing numbers of older women are aiming to resist denigration and invisibility (Markson, 1999). As women unite to work for change, they can make further progress in reducing the disadvantages of their economic and social position.

Summary

Older women are the fastest growing segment of our population, making the aging society primarily female. In addition, the problems of aging are increasingly the problems of women. Threats to Social Security, inadequate health and long-term care, and insufficient pensions are issues for women of all ages. Increasingly, older women are not only the recipients of social and health services, but also are cared for by other women, who are unpaid daughters and daughters-in-law, or staff within public social services, nursing homes, and hospitals.

Women's family caregiving roles are interconnected with their economic, social, and health status. Women who devoted their lives to attending to the needs of children, spouses, or older relatives often face years of living alone on low or poverty-level incomes, with inadequate health care, in substandard housing, and with little chance for employment to supplement their limited resources. Women face more problems in old age, not only because they live longer than their male peers, but also because, as unpaid or underpaid caregivers with discontinuous employment histories, they have not accrued adequate retirement or health care benefits. If they have depended on their husbands for economic security, divorce or widowhood increases their risks of poverty. As one of the poorest groups in our society, women account for nearly three-fourths of the older poor. The incidence of problems associated with poverty increases dramatically for older women living alone, for ethnic minority women, and for those age 75 and over. Frequently outliving their children and husbands, they have no one to care for them and are more likely than their male counterparts to be in long-term care facilities.

On the other hand, many women show remarkable resilience in the face of adversity. Fortunately, the number of exceptions to patterns of economic deprivation and social isolation is growing. With their lifelong experiences of caring for others, for example, women tend to be skilled at forming and sustaining friendships, which provide them with social support and intimacy. Recently, increasing attention has been paid to older women's capacity for change and to their strengths, largely because of efforts of national advocacy groups such as the Older Women's League. Current efforts to expand the employment and educational opportunities available to younger women will undoubtedly mean improved economic, social, and health status for future generations of women.

GLOSSARY

conversion laws legal requirement for insurance companies to allow widowed, divorced, and separated women to remain on their spouses' group insurance for up to 3 years

earnings sharing   proposed change in Social Security whereby each partner in a marriage is entitled to a separate Social Security account, regardless of employment status

gendered nature of the life course   ways in which gender, which is socially constructed, influences the nature, extent, and experience of caregiving for older relatives across the life course

mammography   an X-ray technique for the detection of breast tumors before they can be seen or felt

Older Women's League   a national educational and advocacy organization on issues affecting older women

postmenopausal zest   renewed sense of life and time for oneself that many women experience at menopause

postmenopause   in women, referring to the period of life after menopause

spousal consent requirement   federal law requiring that a spouse must consent to or agree to waiving survivor's benefits; not true of state government pension plans

RESOURCES

See the companion Website for this text at <www .ablongman.com/hooyman> for information about the following:

- AARP Women's Initiative
- National Black Women's Health Project
- National Center on Women and Aging
- National Women's Health Network
- Older Women's League
- Women's Institute for a Secure Retirement

REFERENCES

AARP. *A Woman's Guide to Pension Rights.* American Association of Retired Persons, 1999.

Abel, S. L. Social Security retirement benefits: The last insult of a sexist society. *Family and Conciliation Courts Review,* 1998, *36,* 54–64.

Adams, S., Nawrocki, H., and Coleman, B. Women and long-term care. AARP Public Policy/Institute, 1999.

Arber, S., and Cooper, H. Gender differences in health in later life: The new paradox? *Social Science and Medicine,* January 1999, *48,* 61–76.

Browne, C. V. *Women, feminism, and aging.* New York: Springer, 1998.

Calasanti, T., and Slevin, K. *Gender, social inequalities and aging.* Walnut Creek, CA: Altima Press, 2001.

Chalfie, D. Facts about older women: Housing and living arrangements. *AARP Fact Sheet* D12880, 1998.

Chodhury, S. L., and Leonesia, M. V. Life-cycle aspects of poverty among older women. *Social Security Bulletin,* 1997, *60,* 17–36.

Choi, N. G. Relationship between life satisfaction and postretirement employment among older women. *International Journal of Aging and Human Development,* 2001, *52,* 45–70.

Clinton, H. Essay: The next frontier. *Newsweek,* Special Edition on Women's Health, Spring/Summer 1999, 94–95.

Cochran, D. L., Brown, D. R., and McGregor, K. C. Racial differences in the multiple social roles of older women: Implications for depressive symptoms. *The Gerontologist,* 1999, *39,* 465–472.

Compston, J. E., and Rosen, C. J. *Fast facts—Osteoporosis.* Oxford, U.K.: Health Press, 1997.

Connidis, I. A. *Family ties and aging.* Thousand Oaks, CA: Sage, 2001.

Connidis, I. A., and McMullin, J. A. *Sociological ambivalence and family ties: A critical perspective.* Unpublished manuscript, 2000.

Costello, C., and Krimgold, B. K. (Eds.). *The American woman 1996–97: Women and work.* New York: W. W. Norton and Company, 1996.

Crystal, S. Economic status of the elderly. In R. H. Binstock and L. K. George (Eds.), *Handbook of aging and the social sciences* (4th ed.) San Diego, CA: Academic Press, 1996.

Duggleby, W., Bateman, J., and Singer, S. The aging experience of well elderly women: Initial results. *Nursing Health Science,* 2002, *4*(Suppl.), A10.

Erickson, M. A., Dempster-McClain, D, Whitlaw, C., and Moen, P. Does moving to a continuing care retirement community reduce or enhance social integration? In K. Pillemer, P. Moen, E. Wethington, and N. Glasgow (Eds.), *Social integration in the second half of the life course.* Baltimore: Johns Hopkins University Press, 2000.

Estes, C., and Michel, M. Social Security and women. In America Task Force on Women (Ed.), *Social Secu-*

rity in the 21st century. Washington, DC: Gerontological Society of America, 1999.

Estes, C. L., and Michel, M. *Fact sheet on women and Social Security,* Gerontological Society of America Task Force on Women. Washington, DC: Gerontological Society of America, 1999.

Feldman, S., Byles, J. E., and Beaumont, R. "Is anybody listening?" The experiences of widowhood for older Australian women. *Journal of Women and Aging,* 2000, *12,* 155–176.

Finkel, D. Stuck behind the counter: Retirement is an elusive dream for women. *The Seattle Times,* October 7, 2003, pp. A3.

Furman, F. K. *Facing the mirror: Older women and beauty shop culture.* New York: Rutledge Press, 1997.

Garner, J. D. *Fundamentals of feminist gerontology.* New York: Haworth Press, 1999.

Gonyea, J. G. Midlife and menopause: Uncharted territories for baby boomer women. *Generations,* Spring 1998, 87–89.

Heinz, T., Lewis, J., and Hounsell, C. *Women and pensions: An overview.* Washington, DC: Women's Institute for a Secure Retirement, 2002.

Herd, P. Care credits: Race, gender, class and Social Security reform. *Public Policy and Aging Report,* 2002, *12,* 13–18.

Holstein, M. Women's lives, women's work: Productivity, gender, and aging. In S. A. Bass, F. G. Caro, and Y-P Chen (Eds.), *Achieving a productive aging society.* Westport, CT: Auburn House, 1993.

Hooyman, N., and Gonyea, J. A feminist model of family care: Practice and policy directions. *Journal of Women and Aging,* 1999, *11,* 149–170.

Howard, W. J. A critical review of the role of targeted education for osteoporosis prevention. *Journal of Orthopedic Nursing,* 2001, *5,* 131–135.

Huckle, P. *Tish Sommers, activist and the founder of the Older Women's League.* Knoxville: The University of Tennessee Press, 1991.

Hunt, K., and Annandale, E. Relocating gender and morbidity: Examining men's and women's health in contemporary Western societies. Introduction to Special Issue on Gender and Health. *Social Science and Medicine,* 1999, *48,* 1–5.

LaVeist, T. A., Sellers, R. M., Brown, K. A., Elliott, E., and Nickerson, K. J. Extreme social isolation, use of community-based senior support services, and mortality among African American elderly women.

American Journal of Community Psychology, 1997, *25,* 721–732.

Macintyre, S., and Hunt, K. Socioeconomic position, gender and health: How do they interact? *Journal of Health Psychology,* 1997, *2,* 315–334.

Markson, B. Communities of resistance: Older women in a gendered world. Review of Frida Furman, Facing the Mirror. *The Gerontologist,* 1999, *39,* 496–497.

Meunier, P. J. Calcium, vitamin D and vitamin K in the prevention of fractures due to osteoporosis. *Clinical Pearls News,* 1999, 223.

Moen, P. Gender, age and the life course. In R. H. Binstock and L. K. George (Eds.), *Handbook of aging and the social sciences* (4th ed.). San Diego, CA: Academic Press, 1996.

Moen, P. The gendered life course. In R. H. Binstock and L. K. George (Eds.), *Handbook of aging and the social sciences* (5th ed.). San Diego, CA: Academic Press, 2001.

Murkies, A. L. Postmenopausal hot flashes decreased by dietary flour supplementation: Effects of soy and wheat. *American Journal of Clinical Nutrition,* 1998, *68,* 1533S.

National Center on Women and Aging, *Women are Aging Better,* Waltham, MA: Brandeis University, 1999.

National Economic Council. *Women and retirement security.* Paper presented at the Interagency Working Group on Social Security, Washington, DC, 1998.

National Institutes of Health (NIH). *Women of Color: Health Data Book,* Washington, DC: U.S. Department of Health and Human Services, 2000.

National Policy and Resource Center on Women and Aging. Half of America's women are not getting the mammograms they should. *The Women and Aging Letter,* Waltham, MA: Brandeis University, May 1997, 2, 8.

National Policy and Resource Center on Women and Aging. Osteoporosis. *The Women and Aging Letter,* Waltham, MA: Brandeis University, March 1996b, 1, 8.

National Policy and Resource Center on Women and Aging. *Planning for retirement security.* Waltham, MA: Brandeis University, May 1996a, *1,* 1–6.

Neill, C. M., and Kahn, A. S. The role of personal spirituality and religious social activity on the life satisfaction of older widowed women. *Sex Roles,* 1999, *40,* 319–329.

Older Women's League (OWL). Path of poverty: An analysis of women's retirement income. In C. L.

Estes and M. Minkler (Eds.), *Critical gerontology: Perspectives from political and moral economy.* Amityville, NY: Baywood, 1998.

Older Women's League (OWL). *Social Security privatization: A false promise for women.* Washington, DC: Older Women's League, 2002.

Older Women's League (OWL). *The state of older women in America.* Washington, DC: Older Women's League, 2003a.

Older Women's League (OWL). *Women and retirement income.* Washington, DC: Older Women's League, 2003b.

Older Women's League (OWL). *Retirement security and women of diverse communities.* Washington, DC: Older Women's League, 2003c.

Prigerson, H. G., Maciejewski, P. K., and Rosenbeck, R. A. Preliminary explorations of the harmful interactive effects of widowhood and marital harmony on health, health service use, and health care costs. *The Gerontologist,* 2000, *40,* 349–357.

Quadagno, J., and Hardy, M. Work and retirement. In R. H. Binstock and L. K. George (Eds.), *Handbook of aging and the social sciences* (4th ed.). San Diego, CA: Academic Press, 1996.

Richardson, V. E. Women and retirement. *Journal of Women and Aging,* 1999, *11,* 49–66.

Roberto, K. A. Friendships between older women: Interactions and reactions. In K. A. Roberto (Ed.), *Relationships between women in later life.* Binghamton, NY: The Haworth Press, 1996.

Roberto, K. A., Allen, K. R., and Blieszner, R. Older women, their children, and grandchildren: A feminist perspective. In J. D. Garner (Ed.), *Fundamentals of feminist gerontology.* Binghamton, NY: The Haworth Press, Inc., 1999.

Saluter, A. *Marital status and living arrangements: March 1994.* Washington, DC: U.S. Bureau of the Census, Current Population Reports, Population Characteristics, 1994.

Sarwari, A. R., Fredman, L., Langenberg, P., and Magaziner, J. (1998). Prospective study on the relation between living arrangement and change in functional health status of elderly women. *American Journal of Epidemiology,* 1998, *147,* 370–378.

Sedlak, C. A., Doheny, M. O., and Jones, S. L. Osteoporosis education programs: Changing knowledge and behaviors. *Public Health Nursing,* 2000, *17,* 398–402.

Sherill, M. Walk on the wild side. *AARP Magazine,* Nov.–Dec. 2003, 10–14.

Simonsick, E. M., Phillip, C. L., Skinner, E. A., David, D., and Kasper, J. D. The daily lives of disabled older women. In J. Guralnik, L. P. Fried, and E. M. Simonsick (Eds.), *The women's health and aging study: Characteristics of older women with disability.* Bethesda, MD: National Institute on Aging, NIH Publication No. 95–4009, 1995.

Smeeding, T., Estes, C., and Glasse, L. *Social Security in the 21st century: More than deficits: Strengthening security for women.* Washington, DC: Gerontological Society of America, 2000.

U.S. Census Bureau. *Statistical abstract of the United States,* (118th ed.). Washington, DC: U.S. Government Printing Office, 2000.

Velkoff, V. A., and Lawson, V. A. *Caregiving: International brief, gender and aging.* U.S. Bureau of the Census, 1998, IB/98–3, 2–7.

Weber, P. The role of vitamins in the prevention of osteoporosis—A brief status report. *Clinical Pearls News,* 1999, 222.

Weir, D. R., Willis, R. J., and Sevak, P. A. The economic consequences of widowhood. Papers wp9905, University of Michigan, Michigan Retirement Research Center, 2002.

Weitz, T., and Estes, C. L. Adding aging and gender to the women's health agenda. *Journal of Women and Aging,* 2001, *13,* 3–20.

Wethington, R., and Keevey, A. Neighborhood as a form of social integration and social support. In P. M. K. Pillemer, N. Glasgow, and E. Wethington (Eds.), *Social integration in the second half of life.* Baltimore: Johns Hopkins University Press, 2000.

Williams, S. Preventing osteoporosis. *Newsweek,* Special Edition on Women's Health, Spring/Summer 1999, 60–63.

Women's Institute for a Secure Retirement. *Special report: Long-term care: What are your options?* www.wiser.heinz.org/longtermcare_care.html, 2002.

Women's Institute for a Secure Retirement. Minority women and retirement income, *Pension Benefits,* 2003, *12,* 1–2.

part five

The Societal Context of Aging

The final section of this book examines aging and older people from a broader context. The values and beliefs that policy makers and voters hold toward a particular group or issue are often the basis for developing policies and programs. To the extent that these policies also are grounded in empirically based knowledge, they can enhance the status and resources of that group. On the other hand, policies that are based on stereotypes or generalizations may be inadequate and even harmful.

Throughout this book, the current state of knowledge about the physiological, psychological, and social aspects of aging has been reviewed. We have examined variations among older ethnic minority groups, between older men and women, and among other segments of older adults. The diversity in the aging process has been emphasized. Differences in lifestyle, health behaviors, employment and family caregiving patterns, and social interactions in earlier periods of life can significantly impact health and social functioning in old age, often reflecting health and socioeconomic disparities across the life span. As a result, variations among the older population are greater than among any other population group. As Chapter 16 points out, increasingly this diversity affects the development, implementation and effectiveness of social policies and programs.

Some age-based programs such as Social Security are directed toward all people who meet age criteria, whereas others, including Supplemental Security Income (SSI) and food stamps, are based on financial need. Eligibility criteria and services are often determined by the prevailing social values and by those of the political party and presidential administration in power. These values, in turn, reflect society's attitudes toward older people, their contributions, and their responsibilities to society. For example, attitudes and values regarding older people's rights and needs, whether chronological age is an appropriate basis for services, and whether care of the aging population is a societal or individual responsibility all influence the development of social, health, and long-term care policies. The historical development of aging policy and alterations in existing programs are also reviewed within the context of larger societal changes that influence such values. One societal change examined in this section is the growing economic well-being of a proportion of older adults. This change, in turn, has fueled an attitude that older adults are financially better off than other age groups. As noted in Chapter 12, such an attitude also stereotypes older adults as being "all alike"; it overlooks both the economic and racial/ethnic diversity among older people and the fact that younger and older generations engage in reciprocal exchanges and share resources across the life span.

Health and long-term care policies toward older people also have evolved incrementally in response to society's values and expectations of responsibility and need. Chapter 17 describes these policies; their rising expenditures; the growing need for comprehensive long-term care coordinated with acute care; obstacles to their public funding; and current cost-containment initiatives in Medicare and Medicaid, especially managed care and health maintenance organizations.

The following vignettes illustrate the impact of changing societal attitudes and policies regarding the older population on individuals who have been raised in different eras. The historical and societal context, in turn, influences the services and economic supports to older adults and the likelihood that they will be utilized.

AN OLDER PERSON BORN EARLY IN THE TWENTIETH CENTURY

Mr. O'Brien was born in 1920 in New York City. His parents had migrated to the United States from Ireland ten years earlier, in search of better employment opportunities for themselves and a better life for their children. One of Mr. O'Brien's brothers died during a flu epidemic while still in Ireland; a sister and brother who were born in New York died of measles. Mr. O'Brien and his three surviving siblings worked from the age of 12 in their parents' small grocery store. He could not continue his education beyond high school because his father's death of tuberculosis at age 45 left him in charge of the family store. Mr. O'Brien thought of signing up for the newly created Social Security program in 1945, but he was confident that he would not need any help from the government in his old age. The family grocery was supporting him and his wife quite well; he planned to work until the

day he died. And besides, his family had all died in their forties and fifties anyway. He has been a heavy smoker all his life, just as his father had been. As he approaches his 84th birthday, however, Mr. O'Brien has been having second thoughts about old age. His emphysema and arthritis make it difficult for him to manage the store. He has had two heart attacks in the past ten years, both of which could have been fatal if it had not been for the skills of the emergency medical team and their sophisticated equipment in his local hospital. Mr. O'Brien's savings, which had seemed substantial a few years ago, now are dwindling as he pays for his wife's care in a nursing home and for his medications and doctor's care for his heart condition, emphysema, and arthritis. Despite these struggles, Mr. O'Brien is reluctant to seek assistance from the government or from his children and grandchildren. They, in turn, assume that Mr. O'Brien is financially independent because he still works part-time, and never seems to require help from anybody.

AN INDIVIDUAL BORN IN THE POSTWAR BABY BOOM

Ms. Smith was born in 1949, soon after WWII ended and her father returned from his military duty. Her father took advantage of the GI bill to complete his college education and purchase a home in one of the newly emerging suburbs around Chicago. As Ms. Smith grew up, her parents gave her all the advantages they had missed as children of the Depression: regular medical and dental check-ups, education in a private school, a weekly allowance, and a college trust fund. She completed college, obtained a master's degree in business, and now holds a middle-level management position in a bank. She has already begun planning a "second career" by starting work on a master's degree in systems analysis. Recognizing the value of health promotion at all ages, she has been a member of a health club for several years, participating in aerobic exercise classes and jogging every day. She has also encouraged her parents, now in their late 70s and early 80s, to participate in health promotion activities in their assisted living facility. Her parents both receive pensions, are enrolled in Medicare Parts A and B, and have planned for the possibility of catastrophic illness by enrolling in a supplemental health insurance program. Ms. Smith has encouraged her parents to get on the waiting list of an excellent nursing home nearby, should they ever need it. She is also examining her investments and pension plan while she is in her prime earning years. She realizes that Social Security cannot be her primary source of income after retirement. She recently purchased private long-term care insurance for herself. In this way, both Ms. Smith and her parents are planning for an independent and, to the extent they can control it through prevention, a healthy old age.

These vignettes illustrate the changing social and economic status of older people today and in the future. The implications of these changes for the development of policies, programs, and services, as well as on individuals' planning for their own aging, are discussed in the remainder of this book.

16

Social Policies to Address Social Problems

A wide range of policies, established within the past 70 years, aim to improve the social, physical, and economic environments of older people. Approximately 50 major public programs are directed specifically toward older persons, with another 200 affecting them indirectly. Prior to the 1960s, however, the United States lagged behind most European countries in its development of public policy for its older citizens. For example, Social Security benefits were not awarded to retirees in the United States until 1935, whereas alternative Social Security systems were instituted in the nineteenth century in most Western European countries. The United States has slowly and cautiously accepted the concept of public responsibility, albeit only partial, for its older citizens.

Since the 1960s, however, federal spending for programs for older adults rapidly expanded, resulting in the "graying of the federal budget" and a dramatic change in the composition of expenditures. The growth in federal support for these services is vividly illustrated through budgetary figures (see Figure 16.1). In 1960, only 13 percent of federal expenditures went to general health, retirement, and disability programs benefiting older adults, compared to approximately 45 percent in 2001 (U.S. Government Budget, 2003).

Raising public concern is that approximately 66 percent of federal spending goes toward **entitlement programs**—those for which spending is determined by ongoing eligibility requirements and benefit levels rather than by annual Congressional appropriations. These programs—Social Security, Medicare, Medicaid, and civil service and military pensions—are growing so fast that they are predicted to consume nearly all the federal tax revenues by 2012. Already, Social Security represents 23 percent of the federal budget, and Medicare nearly 12 percent, compared with 15.5% and 3.2%, respectively in 1970 (Public Agenda, 2003) (see pie chart in Figure 16.2). By

2030, Social Security, Medicare, and Medicaid are expected to compose up to 70 percent of total federal outlays (Smeeding, Estes, and Glasse, 2000). The long-term increase in the share of the budget spent on older adults occurred primarily because of legislative improvements in income protection, health insurance, and services enacted in the late 1960s and early 1970s to reduce poverty and health care costs among older persons. Since then, the rapid growth of the older population raises concern about the long-term financial viability of these programs and whether older adults are benefiting at the expense of younger groups. Such concern is reflected in contemporary debates in Congress about changes in Social Security and Medicare, including increased privatization, to reduce age-based public expenditures.

It is important to recognize, however, that when Social Security and Medicare are excluded from these federal allocations, only about 4

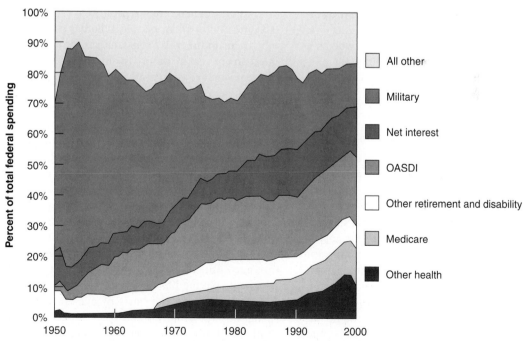

FIGURE 16.1   Change in the Composition of the Federal Budget, 1950–2000

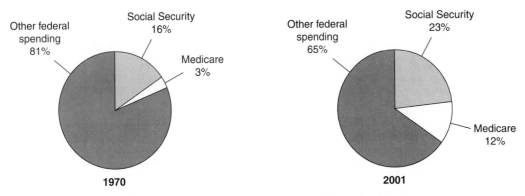

FIGURE 16.2   Social Security Spending Is a Larger Part of the Federal Budget
SOURCE: Budget of the United States Government, fiscal year 2003.

percent of the total federal budget is devoted to programs that benefit older adults. These growing expenditures also mask the fact that funded aging services are often fragmented, duplicated, and do not reach those with the greatest need, thus perpetuating health and income inequities. Despite growing allocations, the United States lacks an integrated, comprehensive, and effective public policy to enhance the well-being of all older adults, and faces complex policy challenges as well as a growing federal deficit.

Variations among Policies and Programs

The purview of **social policy** is not only to identify problems, but also to take action to ameliorate them. The development of policy thus implies a change whether in situations, systems, practices, beliefs, or behaviors. The procedures that governments develop for making such changes encompass planned interventions, bureaucratic structures for implementation, and regulations governing the distribution of public funds. Policy for the older population thus reflects society's definition of what choices to make in meeting their needs and the division of responsibilities between the public and private sectors. Each policy development serves to

determine which older persons should receive what benefits, from which sources, and on what basis.

Social programs are the visible manifestations of policies. The implementation of the 1965 Older Americans Act, for example, resulted in numerous programs—senior centers, nutrition sites, Meals-on-Wheels, homemaker and home health services, and adult day care. Some programs are designed specifically for older people, whereas others benefit them indirectly. Programs can be differentiated from each other in many ways; these dimensions are presented in Table 16.1 and described next.

1. *Eligibility Criteria for Benefits:* When **eligibility** for benefits depends on age alone (i.e., a person is entitled to Medicare benefits at age 65), **age-entitlement programs** are categorical and specifically for older adults. However, in **need-based entitlement programs**, eligibility depends on financial need, for example, Medicaid, Supplemental Security Income (SSI), food stamps, and public housing. Most programs for older adults are age entitlements, with the government automatically paying benefits to anyone who is "entitled" to them on the basis of age. In contrast, programs for children and for younger persons with disabilities are typically discretionary and **means-based,** which limits participation.

TABLE 16.1 Dimensions along Which Programs and Policies Vary

	EXAMPLES
Eligibility	
On basis of age	Medicare
On basis of financial need	Supplemental Security Income
	Medicaid
Form of benefits: Direct or indirect	
Cash	
Direct cash transfers	Social Security
Indirect cash transfers	Income tax exemption
Cash substitute	
Direct cash substitutes	Vouchers
Indirect cash substitutes	Medicare payments to service providers
Method of financing	
Contributory (earned rights)	Social Security
Noncontributory	Supplemental Security Income
Universal or selective benefits	
Universal—for all persons who belong to a particular category	Older Americans Act
Selective—determined on an individual basis	Food stamps

2. *Form of Benefits:* Another variation is the form in which benefits are given, either as **direct benefits** or as **indirect benefits** through a cash transfer or substitute. Social Security benefits are a *direct cash transfer,* and vouchers for the purchase of goods, such as food stamps and rent supplements, are a *direct cash substitute.* Tax policies that affect selected groups (e.g., personal income tax exemptions for older persons) are *indirect cash transfers* of funds from one segment of the population to another. Medicare payments to health care providers, rather than directly to beneficiaries, are *indirect cash substitutes.*

3. *Method of Financing:* Programs also vary in how they are financed. Social Security and Medicare are **contributory programs;** benefit entitlement is tied to a person's contributions to the system as a paid worker across the life span. In contrast, Supplemental Security Income (SSI) is a **noncontributory program** available to older persons and adults with disabilities who meet finan-

cial need criteria, regardless of their prior contributions through payroll taxes.

4. *Universal or Selective Benefits:* Programs differ according to whether they benefit populations on a universal or selective basis. **Universal benefits** are available as a social right to all persons belonging to a designated group. Eligibility for Medicare, the Old Age Survivors Insurance of Social Security, and the Older Americans Act is established by virtue of belonging to the older population. In contrast, **selective benefits** are determined individually. These include Supplementary Security Income, Medicaid, food stamps, and housing subsidies, which use economic need as a criterion. Whether or not aging services should be targeted to low-income elders and subsidized by higher-income older adults is debated. Public consensus on the best approach to service delivery does not exist, as reflected in the following discussion of the factors that influence social policy.

Factors Affecting the Development of Public Policies

Despite the orderliness of these dimensions, the policy-development process is not necessarily rational nor strategic. Approaches to the financing and delivery of aging services evolved in a very different time period, when life expectancy was shorter and federal revenues were of less concern. A major characteristic of our public policy process is its shortsightedness—its general inability, because of annual budgetary cycles and the frequency of national partisan elections, to deal with long-term economic, demographic, and social trends, or to anticipate future consequences of current policies to meet needs or political imperatives. As the number and diversity of older adults has grown, shortsightedness in public policy development has resulted in a fragmented array of services with separate entitlements and eligibility requirements. In fact, this complexity can be so confusing to older people and their families that it has spawned the growth of private case or care managers and Internet services to locate, access, and coordinate services for them.

The complexity of the public policy formation process is also magnified by the variety of societal factors influencing it. These factors include:

- individual and societal values and beliefs
- economic, social, and governmental structures
- the configuration of domestic and international problems
- powerful interest groups and their lobbyists

Values Affecting Social Policy

Two different sets of values have been played out in American public policies:

1. Individual welfare is essentially the *person's responsibility* within a free-market economy unfettered by government control. This belief in individual freedom and autonomy, self-determi-

nation, and privacy is deeply rooted in our history and culture, is widely embraced by many segments of our society, and underlies many public policies.

2. Individual welfare is the responsibility of *both the individual and the community* at large. Government intervention is necessary to protect its citizens and to compensate for the free market's failure to distribute goods and opportunities more equitably. Given the belief in individual productivity and competitiveness, however, some degree of income disparity is accepted as inevitable.

Our society's emphasis on individual and family responsibility has resulted in government's *residual* or "back-up" role to informal support systems. Programs are developed to respond *incrementally* to needs, not to prevent problems or to attack their underlying causes. This contrasts with the approach of many other countries, where national health and welfare polices represent a consensus that citizens are universally entitled to have certain needs met. Even when the U.S. government intervenes, it is generally justified because of the failure of the market economy, the family, or the individual to provide for themselves or their relatives. Accordingly, solutions tend to be patterned after private-sector initiatives, as illustrated by many of the proposed changes in both Social Security and Medicare (Olson, 2003).

Since the New Deal of the 1930s, policy has oscillated between these two value orientations as public mood and national administrations have shifted. American cultural values of productivity, independence, and youthfulness, public attitudes toward government programs and older citizens, and public perceptions of older people as "deserving" converged to create universal categorical programs (e.g., the Administration on Aging, Medicare) that are available only to older persons, regardless of income. In contrast, policies that use income (e.g., means-testing of Medicaid) to determine if a person is "deserving" of services reflect our cultural bias toward productivity and economic independence. Although Social Security was the first federal initiative to address older adults' income needs, it succeeded largely because it was perceived as an insurance plan for "deserving" elders who have contributed through their prior employment, not a means-tested income maintenance policy for all vulnerable citizens.

In the past, the American public tended to perceive older people as more deserving of assistance than other groups. Accordingly, Social Security and Medicare have, until recent years, been viewed as inviolate and not to be cut drastically. The passage of such otherwise unpopular programs as a national health insurance for older people (i.e., Medicare) and guaranteed income (i.e., Supplemental Security Income) can be partially explained by the fact that older persons in the past aroused public support. In addition, older adults are often viewed as a powerful, organized constituency. As a result, they are more likely than low-income or homeless families, for example, to arouse a favorable response from politicians. As noted in Chapter 12, the increasingly diverse older population is now less likely to act as a unified block to influence legislation than in the past. Nevertheless, most politicians do not want to lose the votes of older adults.

Ongoing debate about the nature and extent of public provisions versus the responsibility of individuals, families, and private philanthropy often has moral overtones. Judgments about the relative worth of vulnerable populations that compete for a share of limited resources (e.g., older persons within the prison system as undeserving) and about the proper divisions between public and private responsibilities are ultimately based on individual or group values or preferences. A major policy issue therefore revolves around the question of whose values shape policy.

Economic Context

Society's technical and financial resources and current economic conditions also significantly influence policy development. Adverse economic conditions can create a climate conducive to the passage of income-maintenance policies. For instance, Social Security was enacted in part because the Great Depression dislodged the middle class from financial security and from their belief that older adults who needed financial assistance were undeserving. A strategy to increase the number of persons retiring at age 65 was also congruent with economic pressures to reduce widespread unemployment in the 1930s. With economic constraints, program cost factors were also salient; Social Security as a public pension was assumed to cost less than reliance on local poorhouses, as had been the practice prior to the 1920s. Thus, a variety of economic and resource factors converged to create the necessary public and legislative support for a system of social insurance in the 1930s. In contrast, periods of economic growth can be conducive to new social and health care programs. Both Medicare and the Older Americans Act were passed during the 1960s and early 1970s. During economic growth and social consciousness, government resources expanded under the so-called War on Poverty on behalf of both the younger poor and older people. Funding for the National Institute on Aging increased during the economic boom of the late 1990s but is now constrained, largely because of the federal deficit.

The influence of both economic resources and cultural values is also evident in the current public emphasis on smaller government, tax cuts, voluntarism, private responsibility, program cost-effectiveness and cost containment, and targeting services to those most in need. Under the fiscal conservatism of a Republican Congress in the 1990s and currently, the concept of states' rights and prerogatives was emphasized. Because of federal budget cuts and cost-shifting strategies, states have had to assume a stronger role in the development and financing of social programs. This resulted in increased variability of eligibility criteria and benefits such as SSI and Medicaid among the states. Periods of scarcity tend to produce limited and often punitive legislative responses, as occurred in the 1980s and early 1990s.

POLITICAL ECONOMY OF AGING

1. Older individuals, not economic or social structural conditions, are defined as a "social problem."
2. Older people are seen as special and different, requiring separate programs.
3. Through categorical and age-segregated services, public policy has promoted an "aging enterprise" of bureaucracies and providers to serve older people.
4. A perception is growing that problems of older adults cannot be solved by national programs, but rather by initiatives of state and local governments, the private sector, or the individual.
5. The problems of older people are individually generated and best treated through medical services to individuals. This has resulted in the medicalization of aging and limited public funding for home- and community-based social services as alternatives to institutional care.
6. The use of costly medical services is justified by characterizing old age as a period of inevitable physical decline and deficiency (Estes et al., 1996).

---

thereby adversely influence age-based policies. These conceptions, discussed briefly as the political economy perspective in Chapter 8, are shown in the box at left. According to Estes, our society's failure to develop a comprehensive, coordinated policy framework reinforces older persons' marginality and segregates them.

In contrast to Estes, others maintain that the older population has benefited at the expense of other age groups and is "busting the budget." Benefits for older persons are viewed as a primary reason for growing federal expenditures and for the declining economic status of some younger groups. Spending for entitlement programs is perceived as "mortgaging the future" of succeeding generations. In reality, however, the actual contribution of Social Security and Medicare to the federal deficit has been nearly the same since 1980. In fact, the current reserves in the Social Security Trust Fund help fund other federal expenditures. Within this context of the factors affecting policy development, we turn now to the formulation of public policy for older persons.

As illustrations of the erosion of public support for universal age-based benefits in the 1980s and 1990s, Medicare copayments, deductibles, and Part B premiums increased; Social Security benefits for higher-income older people were taxed; and many legislators proposed cutting Medicare and Medicaid, or privatizing Social Security to reduce federal expenditures. Growing preoccupation since the 1990s with ways to limit public funding has meant that priority is often placed on the most efficient and least expensive solutions, rather than equity and the common good.

In sum, these values, economic conditions, and the consequent resource capacity underlie a *categorical, residual, and incremental* public policy approach for older adults. One of the most vocal critics of this approach, Estes (1979, 1984, 1989, 2000; Estes, Linkins, and Binney, 1996) maintains that our conceptions of aging socially construct the major problems faced by older people, and

The Development of Public Policies for Older People

1930 to 1950

Prior to 1930, the United States had few social programs for older adults. Family, community, charity organizations, and local government (e.g., county work farms) were expected to be responsible. Factors such as the lower percentage of older adults, a strong belief in individual responsibility, and the free-market economy partially explain why our government was slow to respond. Table 16.2 traces these historical policy developments. The Social Security Act of 1935, the first national public benefits program, established the federal government as a major player in the social welfare arena (Bryce and Friedland, 1997). The act is based on an implicit guarantee of social insurance—that the succeeding generation will provide

TABLE 16.2   Major Historical Developments of Policies That Benefit Older People and Their Families

1935	Social Security Act
1950	Amendments to assist states with health care costs
1959	Section 202 Direct Loan Program of the Housing Act
1960	Extension of Social Security benefits
1960	Advisory commissions on aging
1961	Senate Special Committee on Aging
1961	First White House Conference on Aging
1965	Medicare and Medicaid, Older Americans Act, establishment of Administration on Aging
1971	Second White House Conference on Aging
1972 & 1977	Social Security amendments
1974	Title XX
1974	House Select Committee on Aging
1974	Change in mandatory retirement age
1974	Establishment of the National Institute on Aging
1980	Federal measures to control health care expenditures
1981	Third White House Conference on Aging
1981	Social Services Block Grant Program
1986	Elimination of mandatory retirement
1987	Nursing Home Reform Act
1989–90	Medicare Catastrophic Health Care Legislation passed, then repealed
1995	Fourth White House Conference on Aging
1996	Family and Medical Leave Act
1999	United Nations: International Year of Older Persons
2000	National Family Caregiver Support Program
2003	Medicare Prescription Drug Bill

for its older members through their Social Security contributions as employees. The original provisions of the act were intended to be only the beginning of a universal program covering all "major hazards" in life. However, this broader concept of the program, including a nationwide program for preventing illness and ensuring security for children, was never realized.

After the passage of Social Security, national interest in policies to benefit older persons subsided. One exception was President Truman's advocacy to expand Social Security benefits to include farmers, self-employed persons, and some state and local government employees. He also proposed a national health insurance plan, but was opposed by organizations such as the American Medical Association. President Truman did succeed, however, in his push for a 1950 Social Se-

curity amendment to financially assist states that choose to pay partial health care costs for needy older persons. This amendment then became the basis for the establishment of Medicare in 1965.

Program Expansion in the 1960s and 1970s

Since the 1960s, programs for older people have rapidly evolved, including Medicare, Medicaid, the Older Americans Act, Supplemental Security Income (SSI), the Social Security Amendments of 1972 and 1977, Section 202 Housing, and Title XX social services legislation. The pervasiveness of "compassionate stereotypes"—which assumed that most older adults are deserving poor, frail, ill-housed, unable to keep up with inflation, and therefore in need of government assistance—created a "permissive consensus" for government

Politicians seek the support of older voters.

action on age-based services in the 1960s and 1970s. A negative consequence of "compassionate ageism," however, was the development of programs that obscured economic and racial diversity among the older population. A large constituency—including older adults who are not poor, frail, or inadequately housed—has benefited from the policy consensus built upon the "compassionate stereotype" in the 1960s and 1970s (Binstock and Day, 1996). Since old-age constituencies have been viewed as relatively homogeneous (white, English-speaking, and male), many older people with the greatest needs—women, ethnic minorities, the oldest-old, and those living alone—have not always benefited from program improvements relative to their needs. Some of these inequities were described in Chapters 14 and 15.

The first White House Conference on Aging and the establishment of the Senate Special Committee on Aging in 1961 highlighted older people's distinctive needs. Four years later, Medicare

and the Older Americans Act were passed, for which eligibility is determined by age, not by need. Although the Older Americans Act established the Administration on Aging at the federal level, as well as statewide area agencies and advisory boards on aging services, funding to implement these provisions has remained low. Therefore, one of the primary objectives of the 1971 White House Conference on Aging was to strengthen the Older Americans Act. In 1972, Social Security benefits were expanded 20 percent, and the system of *indexing* benefits to take account of inflation (**"cost-of-living adjustments"** or **COLA**) was established. Additional funding was provided for the Older Americans Act in 1973.

The 1970s, with its prevailing liberal ethos, propelled more developments to improve older people's economic status:

- the creation of the Supplemental Security Income (SSI) program
- protection of private pensions through the Employee Retirement Income Security Act (ERISA)

FACTORS THAT AFFECTED THE DEVELOPMENT OF SOCIAL SECURITY

Demographics

Only 5 percent of the population was age 65 and over in 1935. Therefore reserves were projected for the system, and early retirees benefited dramatically from the "pay as you go" system.

Historical and Economic Context

- the New Deal and federal response to the Great Depression; distrust of the private sector
- compassionate stereotype of older adults as "deserving"
- incentive for and institutionalization of retirement; disengagement or exit of older workers from the workforce was functional by creating more opportunities for younger workers
- influence of other Western European countries that had funded various social security systems

- formation of the House Select Committee on Aging; increases in Social Security benefit levels and taxes
- the change in mandatory retirement from age 65 to 70 (As noted in Chapter 12, mandatory retirement was later abolished for most jobs in 1986.)

As described by Hudson (forthcoming), public policy on aging begat more public policy, by creating its own constituencies. During this period of federal government expansion, more than 40 national committees and subcommittees were involved in legislative efforts affecting older adults. As a result of the expansion of age-related programs, agencies, and benefits, along with more age-based interest groups, individuals grew to expect that they were entitled to receive certain benefits such as Social Security and Medicare automatically, based on age rather than on income or need. Yet, the presumed influence of many aging advocacy organizations appears to result more from their defending existing policy rather than their affecting the development of these policies. Paradoxically, many older adults assumed that they were entitled to continued political support and public benefits, even though their needs, along with their political efficacy, had declined.

Program Reductions in the 1980s and 1990s

Although compassionate stereotypes and a "permissive consensus" underlay the growth of age-entitlement programs in the 1960s and 1970s, fiscal pressures and increasing concern about the well-being of younger age groups in the 1980s and 1990s brought into question the size and structure of these programs. In those years, a new stereotype of older people as relatively well-off resulted in their being scapegoated and blamed as "greedy geezers." In fact, older people were seen as responsible for the increasing poverty rates among younger age groups (Minkler, 2002).

The impact of tax cuts, reductions in federal programs, the huge federal deficit, and an overem-phasis on economic growth prevented consideration of any large or bold programs for domestic spending in social and health services during the Reagan Administration (1980–1988). At the same time, public perceptions of and support for aging programs varied widely. Senior advocates urged more funding, particularly for social services, and watched closely to see that Social Security not be cut. Concern over the future of Social Security was fueled by the near-term deficit facing the Social Security trust fund in the 1980s. As a result, Social Security was amended in 1983 to address short-term financing problems. As public scrutiny of the costs of Social Security, Medicare, and Medicaid grew, *cost-efficiency* measures were implemented, such as taxation on Social Security benefits and less generous cost-of-living increases.

During the 1980s, the political reality of the economic and social diversity of the aging population—that chronological age is not an accurate marker of economic status or functional ability—became more apparent. The variability in distribution of income is reflected among three different groupings of older people:

- those ineligible for Social Security, including both the lifelong underclass and the working poor who have discontinuous employment histories, hourly wages without benefits, and few personal assets, typically women and elders of color
- those who depend heavily on Social Security, with small or no private pensions and few assets except for their own home
- those with generous private pensions and personal savings investments, in addition to Social Security benefits

A number of policies passed in the 1980s recognized that the older population has differential capabilities for helping to finance public programs, so that both age and economic status began to be considered as eligibility criteria for old-age benefit programs (Binstock, 2002). For example, the Social Security Reform Act of 1983 taxed Social Security benefits for higher-income recipients. The Tax Reform Act of 1986 provided tax credits on a sliding scale to low-income older adults and eliminated a second or third exemption on federal tax income previously available. Meanwhile, programs funded under the Older Americans Act have been gradually targeted toward low-income individuals. These policy changes, combined with public perceptions that older people are better off than younger ones, reflect a transition from the legacy of a modern aging period (1930–1990) to a new period in which old age alone is not sufficient grounds for public benefits (Torres-Gil and Puccinelli, 1994).

The Politics of Diversity and Deficit Spending in the 1990s

The growing federal deficit profoundly affected public policy development in the 1990s. To reduce the deficit, there were two major options—reductions in spending through program cutbacks, or revenue enhancement through higher taxes. National groups that cut across the political spectrum, such as the Bipartisan Commission on Entitlement and Tax Reform and the Concord Coalition, maintained that entitlement programs for older people were growing so fast that they would consume nearly all the federal tax revenues by the year 2012, leaving government with little money for anything else. Increasingly such groups argued that programs such as Social Security, Medicare, and Medicaid must be drastically curtailed to balance the federal budget early in the twenty-first century. Such a perspective, for example, is reflected in the Balanced Budget Act of 1997 where Medicare and Medicaid were cut, but not Social Security. In reality, since Social Security is financed by its own dedicated payroll tax, none of the federal deficit has ever been caused by Social Security spending—a reality that is typically not portrayed by the media (NCPSSM, 2003).

In the 1996 Personal Responsibility Act, President Clinton signed restrictive welfare legislation, but vetoed the bill containing changes to alter the nature of entitlements to Medicare and Medicaid. Social Security remained basically untouched. Resistance against dramatically changing these entitlement programs for older people remained strong in the Clinton/Gore Administration. However, it is now being challenged by the Republicans in the White House and Congress who favor privatization of Social Security and other programs. The fact that such entitlement programs are "under attack" and that means testing now applies to Medicare (see Chapter 17) reflects a societal shift in attitudes toward the older population. They are less likely to be perceived as a "politically sympathetic" group compared to other populations (Binstock, 2002; Hudson and Quadagno, 2001). At the same time, disparities within the older population are more evident, with subgroups of poor, ethnic minorities, women, and persons living alone likely to join political alliances around class, race, or ethnity that compete with groups of more affluent elders. The "politics of diversity" may thus fragment the political influence of established aging organizations and affect support for universal programs. In fact, incremental changes in Social Security, the Older Americans Act, and Medicare to target benefits toward relatively poor older people reflect recognition of this diversity (Binstock, 1995).

Such diversity among the older population, combined with a focus on reducing federal expenditures, has resulted in a greater emphasis on private sector initiatives that can be supported by higher-income older adults (e.g., individual retirement accounts instead of Social Security). With more older adults able to self-finance or privately insure against the social and health costs of later life, the base of support for high-quality government programs appears to be eroding. This could result in limiting services to elders without retirement plans and health insurance and thus lead to increasing inequality among the older population. A policy challenge in the 1990s was targeting policy responses to those who risk losing a significant part of their income and who have never had economic stability, while maintaining public support for the financing of quality universal programs. These complex issues set the framework for the 1995 White House Conference on Aging. Delegates at the 1995 conference voted to maintain Social Security, the Older Americans Act, the basic features of Medicaid and Medicare, and some advocacy functions under the Older Americans Act. These directions fundamentally conflicted with the emphasis of the Republican Congress on cutting entitlement programs to reduce the federal deficit. Even though the deficit is now escalating, many Republicans seek to reduce taxes and allow more individual control over Social Security investments, while Democrats want to preserve basic programs such as Social Security and Medicare.

Era of the Market and Personal Responsibility

Issues of contemporary intergenerational equity—trading off current expenditures on older adults with other social benefits—are not articulated as frequently today as they were in the 1980s. Instead, the present emphasis on the market and individual responsibility for one's economic well-being are reflected in a range of privatization proposals: (1) to privatize Social Security in full or in part with individuals responsible for making their own market investment; (2) to encourage enrollment of Medicare beneficiaries in managed care organizations as reflected by financial incentives for managed care systems in the 2003 Prescription Drug Bill; and (3) to provide partial federal tax credits and deductibility for premiums paid for private long-term care insurance. The politics of responsibility encourages competition in private sector and voluntary enrollment in personal savings plans as a way to "save" Social Security and Medicare (White, 2003). These shifts are laying the framework for more policy approaches that combine public programs with private mechanisms of incentives for savings (Binstock, 2002).

Social Security and SSI

We next review the specific programs that account for the majority of age-based federal expenditures:

- Social Security (OASDI) and Supplemental Security Income (SSI)
- tax provisions and private pensions that provide indirect benefits
- social services through Title XX *block grants* and the **Aging Network** of the Older Americans Act

As noted earlier, Social Security (Old Age Survivors and Disability Insurance), federal employee retirement, and Medicare and Medicaid combined represent the largest and most rapidly growing federal entitlements, as was illustrated in Figure 16.2. However, many younger people also benefit from OASDI and Medicaid, as described on page 602 and shown in Figure 16.3.

Income Security Programs: Social Security and Supplemental Security Income

Social Security

As indicated earlier, the 1935 Social Security Act aimed to establish a system of income maintenance for older persons through individual insurance. A secondary purpose was to provide a basic level of protection for the most needy older adults, initially through state plans for Old Age and Survivors Insurance (OASI) and, since 1974, through the federally funded Supplemental Security Income (SSI) program. A more recent objective is to provide compensatory income to persons, regardless of age, who experience a sudden loss of income, such as widows, surviving children, and persons with disabilities.

To meet these objectives, Social Security has four separate *trust funds:*

1. Old Age and Survivors Insurance (OASI)
2. Disability Insurance (DI)
3. Hospital Insurance (HI), which is funded through Medicare
4. revenues for the supplemental insurance portion of Medicare, as described in Chapter 17

Social Security is financed through separate trust funds; revenues raised equally from the taxing of employees and employers; and income based on current tax revenues. As illustrated in Figure 16.3, out of every tax dollar from *payroll taxes* that a worker pays into Social Security and Medicare:

- Sixty-nine cents goes to a trust fund that pays monthly benefits to retirees and their families and the equivalent of a life insurance policy worth over $300,000 to surviving widows, widowers, and children of workers who have died.
- Nineteen cents goes to a trust fund that pays some of the cost of hospital and related care of Medicare beneficiaries.
- Twelve cents goes to a trust fund that pays benefits to people with severe disabilities and their families.

Figure 16.3 illustrates the beneficiaries from three of the trust funds. Every worker contributing to Social Security, regardless of age, has disability insurance worth over $200,000—a fact often overlooked by younger critics of Social Security (Social Security Administration, 2003a). This discussion focuses on the combined OASDI fund, of which programs for persons with disabilities are only 7 percent of the combined obligation. Funding for Medicare is discussed in Chapter 17.

As described in Chapter 12, the Social Security system is based first on the concept of earned rights. Initially, only 60 percent of the labor force was eligible to earn future benefits on the basis of the 1935 law. Coverage has since expanded to insure 95 percent of workers, reflecting nearly universal protection across socioeconomic classes. In addition, wage-price indexing protects recipients against economic changes over which they have

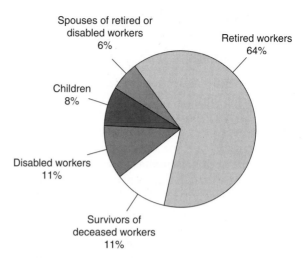

FIGURE 16.3   Recipients of Social Security Benefits
SOURCE: Social Security Administration, Fact Sheet on the Old-Age, Survivors, and Disability Insurance Program (Washington, DC: 2003).

no control. Although Social Security provides a mechanism to pool resources and share the risk, no one is excluded no matter how "bad" a risk he or she may be. This is a fundamental difference from private insurance or income maintenance programs for children and families (Williamson, Watts-Rey, and Kingson, 2002). Social Security can be described as similar to fire or collision insurance. You might not ever need to collect on your policy, but that does not mean you do not need to pay the premiums!

Contrary to public perceptions, Social Security is not an investment program or the sole source of retirement income, but rather a minimum floor of protection. Yet, it is the major source of income (providing for at least 50 percent of total income) for 66 percent of total beneficiary units, and the only source for about 20 percent. Retirees typically need 70 to 80 percent of their preretirement income to continue living comfortably. Social Security's average older recipients are paid 42 percent of their income, a figure that is projected to remain stable through the year 2040 (AARP, 2000; SSA, 2003a; Zebrowski,

2000). This average percentage varies with income, however. Social Security provides 75 percent of the aggregate income of older households with annual incomes of less than $10,000, 42 percent of the aggregate income for those earning $30,000–$40,000, and only 12 percent of income for those earning $80,000 plus. While higher-income workers receive higher benefits, lower-income workers are assured a greater rate of return for what they have paid into the system (e.g., the proportion of preretirement earnings that is replaced after retirement is higher for lower-paid workers). Social Security benefits therefore are progressive (AARP, 2000) or most helpful to those with low and moderate income who qualify.

This distribution of benefits reflects Social Security's dual goals of social adequacy and individual equity.

- *Social adequacy* refers to a shared societal responsibility to provide a basic standard of living for all potential beneficiaries, or a "safety net," regardless of the size of their economic contributions.
- *Individual equity* refers to an individual's receiving benefits that reflect that person's actual monetary contributions proportionate to what workers have paid into the system.

It is a myth that Social Security is a funded pension system in which retirees are merely paid back, with interest, the "contributions" that they made during their working years. Instead, it is a system whereby current workers support retired or disabled workers. This "pay-as-you-go" system is like a pipeline; payroll taxes from today's workers flow in, are invested in special U.S. government bonds, and then flow out to current beneficiaries. Today's retirees generally recoup their Social Security contributions within seven years. Actuaries expect that today's young workers will recoup their contributions after eleven years of retirement (NCPSSM, 2003b). In short, Social Security's nearly universal coverage and predictability of income make it the foundation of economic security for most retirees.

Payroll taxes, however, have risen enormously, from a combined 3 percent on employers and employees in 1950 to 12.4 percent. But the average return that a worker can expect has declined dramatically. An average earner born in 1915 could expect to get back at age 65 approximately $60,000 more than he or she paid into the system (adjusted for inflation and interest), while today's retirees will just about break even and recoup their contributions (Miller, 1998). By 2030, up to 50 percent of one's wages may be needed to support Social Security and Medicare.

This pay-as-you-go method of financing partially underlay the fiscal crisis in the early 1980s, when the Social Security reserves were inadequate for projected benefits. Primary factors behind threats of bankruptcy were:

1. The economic recession: High unemployment and low productivity resulted in fewer taxes collected, so that less money was available in the Social Security trust funds.
2. Increased longevity and more retired workers in proportion to younger employees, with fewer workers paying into Social Security.

The issue of privatizing Social Security generates activism among older adults.

CURRENT CONTEXT FRAMING THE SOCIAL SECURITY DEBATES

- increased life expectancy
  - when Social Security was enacted, life expectancy was 61 years, compared with 78 years today
- changed age-dependency ratio
  - 1935: 50 to 1 (passage of Social Security)
  - 1950: 16 to 1
  - 2003: 3.3 to 1
  - 2031: 2 to 1
- shift from a focus on adequacy of benefits to concerns with system financing
  - era of the market and personal responsibility
- improved economic status of older adults, which is a result, in part, of Social Security and Medicare
- older adults are healthier, better educated, able to continue to be employed
- economic pressures on young adults: high unemployment, loss of jobs, growth of contingent labor force
- government preoccupation with terrorism, war in Iraq and Afghanistan, national security, the federal deficit and cuts in domestic spending, Medicare reform, and prescription drug coverage

---

The box above summarizes the changing demographic, economic, and political context that now frames debates about the future of Social Security.

The Future of Social Security

Within this context, some policy makers and the media portray Social Security as being in crisis. They argue that "apocalyptic demography" will make it difficult for our nation to sustain all age-related benefits through the first half of this century. The "graying of the welfare state" is perceived as having catastrophic consequences for the after-tax living standards of most working-age Americans. This view, fostered by the media, is put forth by groups such as the Third Millennium, which points to a survey in which people under age 35 stated that they believed in UFOs more than in Social Security's future viability (Conte, 1997). Data such as these, however, are misrepresented as public support for "radical reform". In fact, many polls consistently show that Americans overwhelmingly support protecting Social Security, even though they lack confidence in its future and are confused about eligibility criteria (NCPSSM, 2003b; Quinn, 2000).

An alternative, more optimistic view is that projected shortfalls—approximately 35 years in the future—are a warning that can be addressed with relatively minor adjustments in the program (NCPSSM, 2000b). One incremental change, for example, is a 0.7 percent reduction in annual cost-of-living adjustments that would, over time, result in enormous cost savings. Accordingly, future benefits to older people will not depend solely on the proportion of workers to retirees. It will also depend on whether the economy generates sufficient resources to be transferred and whether the political will to transfer them to older adults exists (Binstock, 2002; Friedland, 2000).

As noted above, the short-term danger of bankruptcy was averted through remedial legislation passed in 1983, which resulted in benefit reductions and increased the age of full Social Security eligibility from 65 years to age 67, beginning in 2003 (and to be fully implemented in 2027). These reforms allowed the system to accumulate reserves, which currently exceed the benefits paid. The latest report of the Social Security actuaries predicts that a funding shortfall will not occur until at least the year 2040 (Board of Trustees, 2001). If, however, the fund continues to grow well above actuarial projections, a shortfall could be smaller or even nonexistent. Despite such solvency, a long-range concern is that the federal government debt is turning the surplus into paper savings. This concern stems from the fact that the Treasury Department borrows and then spends the Social Security reserves by investing them in Treasury bonds. In effect, it gives Social Security an IOU, so that the reserves accumulated now may be consumed by deficits in later

SHOULD A 25-YEAR-OLD WORRY ABOUT FUTURE SOCIAL SECURITY BENEFITS?

If no changes are made to Social Security, when a 25-year-old in 2003 reaches age 64 in the year 2042, benefits for all retirees could be cut by 27 percent and could be reduced every year thereafter. If this 25-year-old lived to be 100 years old (which will be more common by then), his or her scheduled benefits could be reduced by 35 percent from to-day's scheduled levels. But this future elder will still receive approximately 65 percent of scheduled bene-fits (Social Security Administration, 2003a).

years. In effect, this is akin to a family borrowing from their college trust fund to pay off their household debts (Moody, 2002c).

When and if Social Security expenditures (or the "outgo") will exceed funds collected through current taxes is unknown. At that point, Social Se-curity will be funded through a combination of payroll taxes and interest generated by the trust fund. If and when the benefit payouts are pro-jected to exceed taxes and interest, the reserves in the trust fund would be drawn down. The ex-haustion of the trust fund, however, would not mean that Social Security benefits would stop; this would happen only if Congress passed legislation ending Social Security payroll taxes. In fact, even by 2040, the benefits would not end, but the fi-nancial security of a trust fund would be lost and benefits would be lower. Congress would be able to pay only around 75 percent of its obligations promised to future retirees (e.g., 75 cents for every dollar of benefits). Most proposals for change suggest that the only way to repay the reserves in the future within the current system is for the fed-eral government to raise payroll taxes, increase the age of eligibility, use means testing, increase borrowing, reduce benefits, or rely on economic growth (Williamson et al., 2002).

Points of view vary widely about the magni-tude of the Social Security crisis, along with pro-posed solutions. Variations in Social Security

reform proposals can be attributed to differing perspectives regarding program goals, whether as:

- *social insurance* (e.g., provide benefits upon disability or death), or
- *income redistribution* (transfer resources from the wealthier to those with fewer resources, both within and between generations).

Contemporary critics of Social Security prefer to view it as a savings program that maximizes the "rate of return" to beneficiaries and fosters eco-nomic growth by encouraging savings. They argue for the privatization of Social Security by greater reliance on individual savings, and predict higher rates of return on individual contributions through investments in the stock market. *Privatization* would divert payroll taxes (or general revenue in-come tax credits) to new systems of Social Security investment accounts. The most frequently dis-cussed privatization models are:

- Workers invest a portion of their Social Secu-rity retirement funds in the stock market and set aside the remainder in individual retire-ment accounts (IRAs)
- Workers contribute to a "first-tier" minimum benefit account through Social Security; above that amount, however, contributions

POINTS TO PONDER

How much will *your* Social Security benefits be when you retire? Since 1988, the Social Security Adminis-tration has sent individual statements to every U.S. worker age 25 and older, listing their years of em-ployment, earnings, and Social Security taxes paid each year. Best of all, it lists each person's esti-mated benefits if they retire at age 62, 67, or 70, based on past contributions to the system, current age, and income. Individual workers can also esti-mate their benefits by checking SSA's Website: www.ssa.gov/planners/calculators.htm.

would be deposited in one's own personal retirement account.

- Future benefits would be prefunded through direct investments of the trust funds into the stock market.

These models assume a strong economy and stock market as well as individual knowledge and skills to make informed investment decisions. Yet these assumptions are undermined by the reality of poor stock market performance since 2000 and the pattern that most workers fail to adequately plan financially for their retirement. Even with optimistic assumptions of return rates, retirement benefits could decline by 20 percent for single wage earners and 38 percent for married couples (Bosworth, Butler, and Keys, 2003; NCPSSM, 2003b). Supporters of privatization are primarily Republican lobbyists (e.g., insurance and investment companies; corporations that would profit from privatization), and Washington DC think tanks such as the conservative Concord Coalition and the libertarian CATO Institute. They maintain that personal investment accounts, by allowing individual ownership and degree of responsibility over one's retirement investments, would lead to higher retirement benefits. Personal accounts would also allow participants to pass wealth onto their survivors in the event of a premature death. Proponents point to over 20 countries that have already established versions of personal accounts. Nevertheless, supporters acknowledge that private accounts would not "solve" all of Social Security's financing problems, and initial returns are likely to be low since workers are already committed to paying for the system's past debt (Mitchell, 2002).

Proponents of privatization maintain that the fundamental goals of any reforms should be to:

- provide insurance to prevent retirees from outliving their resources
- promote at least some redistribution of resources
- promote consumer choice

Values Reflected in Current Social Security System

- universalism
- mutual responsibility: obligation of those who can work to provide for those who cannot
- national community, not individual, bears risks
- earned right: benefits can be counted on regardless of inflation, business cycles, and market fluctuations
- maintain dignity, strengthen families and communities

Values Reflected in Privatization

- market as the most efficient and fair way to distribute resources; social insurance undermines free markets
- increase national savings, reward work effort/success
- primacy of individual responsibility and freedom of choice (and risks)
- limited role of government in market economy

- promote at least some redistribution of resources to lower-income households
- promote market efficiency
- substitute personal savings for tax-financed entitlement
- take advantage of economies of scale (Smallhout, 2002).

In contrast, a wide range of negatives or "downsides" of privatization are identified by the Social Security Administration, Presidential commissions appointed to study privatization, and even an organization of young adults, the "2030 Center," that aims to strengthen Social Security. The costs of privatization include:

- The transition costs of moving from the current system to a privatized plan, which are estimated to be more than $1 trillion over 10 years.

- Costs entailed by adding a new federal agency in addition to the Internal Revenue Service and the Social Security Administration.
- High administrative costs (13 to 20 percent of worker's annual contributions) of managing individual accounts.
- Any money directed into individual retirement accounts must be replaced or Social Security benefits must be cut dramatically.
- Funds used to pay current retirement benefits would have to be replaced, whether by a tax increase, increases in the federal deficit, or benefit costs.
- Current workers would be double taxed: they would have to pay for their own retirement through their own private accounts while continuing to pay for current beneficiaries.
- The uncertainty and vicissitudes of the stock market mean that investment income may not be sufficient to last until a person dies.
- Death and disability protection and the cost of living (COLA) increase, which are available through Social Security, would be eliminated. This would disadvantage the young worker who is disabled early in his or her career before investments yield a profit.
- Privatization would not be cost-effective because of the large numbers of very small businesses and low-income employees (Cavanaugh, 2002; Favreault and Sammartino, 2002; NCPSSM, 2003b).

One of the major costs of privatization is how it would negatively impact low-income, historically disadvantaged workers, perpetuating life span inequities by putting them at greater financial risk rather than guaranteeing a benefit based on their earnings records. The primary beneficiaries will be higher-income, unmarried workers who will not be born until 2025 and will be largely Caucasian males. Low-income women and ethnic minorities, who are the most vulnerable elders and benefit the most from Social Security, would be hurt the most by privatization, because of their limited resources

to invest privately. In addition, low-income workers who lack skills and knowledge about investment decisions will be disadvantaged, and class differences in retirement income are likely to be increased (NCPSSM, 2003b; Schulz, Rosenman, and Rix, 1999; Williamson, 2002)

In addition to privatization, a number of other proposals are currently debated as ways to address the funding of Social Security. These include:

1. *Raising the retirement age for full benefits to age 69 or 70, and for partial benefits to age 65.* However, this could negatively impact ethnic minorities, who have lower life expectancies and face greater pressure to retire early from low-paying, physically demanding jobs.
2. *Increasing the number of years needed to compute Social Security benefits from 35 to 38 to 40 years.* This would negatively impact women and other low-wage workers who are less likely to have been employed that length of time.
3. *Increasing payroll taxes from the current rate of 12.4 percent to about 13.3 percent by 2042.* Although this is an increase of only .09 percent over almost 40 years, it would be regressive in its impact. This would tax a greater share of workers' income, primarily women and ethnic minorities, than high-income workers.
4. *Reducing the cost-of-living adjustments (COLA) to the level equal to actual inflation.* This across-the-board reduction in benefits would create the greatest hardship for the poorest beneficiaries, primarily women and people of color.
5. *Reducing benefits across-the-board (3 to 5 percent).* This also is regressive, negatively impacting the lowest-income workers who depend upon Social Security for a much greater share of their retirement income than do higher-income retirees.
6. *Raising the cap on the amount of wages and salaries subject to payroll taxes.* This would

be progressive in its impact, with higher-income workers facing the burden of closing the Social Security funding gap.

7. *Affluence test by eliminating benefits for higher-income workers above an income threshold ($40,000 in 2003 dollars).* This could result in higher-income workers choosing to opt out of the Social Security system, thereby eroding its universal nature (Breyer and Kifmann, 2002; NCPSSM, 2003b).

Many of these proposals, particularly privatization, are counter to the basic philosophy of a social insurance plan with universal eligibility. This philosophy represents societal willingness to compensate those whose income has been destroyed or lowered by marketplace forces, regardless of the individual's actual contributions. These proposals then challenge the fundamental notion that the federal government should subsidize programs deemed to be in the common good. They may also undermine Social Security's role in preventing poverty in old age (Gorin, 2000). Although there are no credible plans that would replace Social Security as the foundation for the retirement of American workers, some incremental modifications to Social Security are likely, given the long-term funding scenarios. The National Committee to Preserve Social Security and Medicare maintains that full solvency can be extended beyond 2038 by expanding the number of workers participating in Social Security (e.g., requiring local and state workers to participate); raising the cap on taxable income; or allowing the government to invest the funds in equity markets. Such changes are likely to be incremental, and represent political compromises between those who favor privatization and those who view Social Security as a "sacred entitlement." Any such compromise must take account of the majority of Americans' ongoing support to protect Social Security. In fact, the majority of the public does not perceive that older people benefit at the cost of younger populations or that benefits are too costly. This support may reflect recognition of

how Social Security also benefits younger generations (Minkler, 2002; Williamson et al., 2002), as summarized in the box below. Cross-generational transfer programs may actually receive more support than typically portrayed by the media and politicians, an issue discussed below vis-à-vis the intergenerational equity framework.

Supplemental Security Income

As described in Chapter 12, about 6 percent of Social Security recipients also qualify for Supplemental Security Income (SSI). This program is financed fully by the federal general revenues (not the Social Security Trust funds) and administered by Social Security. States may supplement the federal payments through state revenues, which results in benefit variability among states. For most states, a person who receives SSI benefits is automatically eligible for Medicaid health benefits. SSI beneficiaries include older adults, persons with disabilities, and those who are visually impaired. Since its inception in 1972, the percentage of older persons re-

---

CROSS-GENERATIONAL NATURE OF SOCIAL SECURITY BENEFITS

Contrary to common perceptions, Social Security benefits individuals across the life span, not just older adults.

It provides:

- basic protection for the neediest (Supplemental Security Income), which is not tied to age
- compensatory income, regardless of age, to those who experience sudden loss of income (e.g., widows, surviving children, persons with disabilities), as illustrated by the fact that:
  - 30 percent of beneficiaries are not retirees
  - three million beneficiaries are under age 18
- survivor or disability support for a grandchild or step-grandchild based on the earnings record of a grandparent or step-grandparent

SOURCE: Generations United, 2003.

ceiving SSI benefits has declined, while those who are blind or disabled has increased. This difference is due in part to Social Security's annual cost-of-living benefits that decreased the number of older persons who fall into poverty (Beedon, 2000).

SSI is intended to be a protective system or "safety net," but it has not eliminated poverty among vulnerable elders. This is because the federal benefit level equals only about 78 percent of the poverty level for those age 65 and over. When the program was designed, it was assumed that SSI recipients would also receive benefits from other programs such as food stamps and that states would provide supplements that would bring the total benefit package up to the poverty threshold. Even with state supplements, however, SSI fails to raise needy older adults out of poverty. In addition, only about 9 percent of low-income older adults receive food stamps to supplement their income. A reason for this low participation rate is that eligible older adults think that their income or assets make them ineligible for food stamps. Congress has attempted to facilitate participation by older persons in the food stamp program by enacting special provisions that make applications and certification of need easier (Beedon, 2000; Kassner, 2001).

Private Pensions and Income Tax Provisions

Private Pensions

Some older persons receive a combination of government-supported public and/or private pensions to supplement Social Security. As described in Chapter 12, less than 50 percent of the current labor force, primarily middle- and high-income workers, is covered by an employer-sponsored pension plan. This translates into nearly 40 percent of older adults receiving some income from public or private pensions. However, only about 10 percent of these receive in private pensions an amount equivalent to that of Social Security

Older people who have multiple sources of income are generally financially secure.

(AARP, 2000). Overall, the rate of pension growth has slowed due to the changing nature of the workforce. Manufacturing jobs that historically provided pensions have declined, and service sector and part-time, temporary contingent and nonunion jobs have grown but may be only short term. In addition, with the bankruptcy of large corporations such as United Airlines and Enron, their pension plans have disappeared or shrunk to levels too low to support retirees.

As noted in Chapter 12, the pension system tends to perpetuate systematic inequities across the life span by income, ethnic minority status, and gender. Lower-income workers, often women and persons of color, are least likely to be in jobs covered by pensions and to have attained the vesting requirements (e.g., 5 years on the same job). Another inequity is that retired military veterans, civil service workers, and railroad employees also receive cash benefits in addition to Social Security. This means that cash benefits from government-supported private savings plans and favorable tax policies accrue to those who are already relatively well off, intensifying economic disparities over time. Although private pensions help upper- or middle-income workers to replace more of their income when they retire, they do not meet the value of adequacy inherent in Social Security, since lower-income workers generally do not participate (Wheeler and Kearney, 1996).

As described in Chapter 12, the Employee Retirement Income Security Act of 1974 (ERISA) established standards for participation, vesting, and minimum funding to protect workers. Since then, corporate contributions to pension plans have declined, and many businesses have instead used pension funds to pay for employee health care expenses and to increase their own profitability. Defined benefit plans beneficial to employees have been terminated and replaced by **contributory plans,** such as 401(K)s, described in Chapter 12, increasing uncertainty for the employee. This represents a shift in pension responsibility away from the company and toward the individual.

Income Tax Provisions

Pension plans are not the only "tax expenditures" related to aging. Some older individuals also enjoy extra tax deductions and pay on average a smaller percent of their income in taxes. Many older people who file tax returns benefit from not paying a tax on railroad retirement and other government pensions, for example. Higher-income older persons enjoy property-tax reductions and preferential treatment of the sale of a home (e.g., exemption from capital gains taxation for the sale of a home after age 55). The 1997 Tax Reform Act also benefits wealthy older adults who own stocks and bonds. Capital gains realized from the sale of stocks and mutual funds now are taxed at lower rates for those in the highest income brackets. Tax benefits go to the majority of the older population who have an annual income of over $20,000, and only a small percentage goes to persons with incomes less than $5,000. Tax provisions are thus another way that public benefits are inequitably distributed within the older population.

Social Services

Federal and state policies and expenditures are primarily oriented toward medical care. Less than 1 percent of the older population's share of the federal budget is spent on social service programs. From a political economy perspective, as discussed in Chapter 8, social services are underfunded because they do not fit within the dominant medical model (Estes et al., 1996).

Funding for age-based social services derives from four federal sources: Medicare, Medicaid, amendments to the Social Security Act (Title XX), and the Older Americans Act of 1965. This section will focus on Title XX (or Social Services Block Grants) and the Older Americans Act as the primary basis of social service funding.

Title XX, established in 1974, provides social services to all age groups. Entitlements are means tested, with most services to older adults going to those who receive SSI. In terms of the program classification system discussed earlier, Title XX is a universal program aimed at redressing needs. Yet it is also means tested by income as an eligibility criterion. This means older people compete with a diverse group of Title XX recipients—primarily families with dependent children and persons who are visually impaired or mentally and/or physically disabled. Title XX encompasses basic life-sustaining, self-care services to compensate for losses in health and the capacity for self-maintenance: homemaker and chore services, home-delivered meals, adult protective services, adult day care, foster care, and institutional or residential care services. These have generally ensured a minimum level of support for vulnerable older adults.

Under the federal Omnibus Budget Reconciliation Act of 1981, Title XX was converted to the Social Services Block Grant program, while federal funds allocated to the states were reduced on average by 30 percent (Estes et al., 1996). The Social Services Block Grant program was one of the initial decentralization efforts emerging from the 1980s new federalism under President Reagan.

Block grant funding increased the states' discretion in determining clients' needs and allocating Title XX funds among the diverse eligible groups. For example, national income-eligibility guidelines aimed at targeting programs to needy persons were eliminated. Accordingly, the competition for funds, along with variability in services between and within states, increased. As a result, most states allocated a greater percentage of block grant funds to children than to older adults. Decentralization decreased revenues for social services under Title XX for older people while the demand for services increased. Competition for limited funds intensified under the Bush administration, which suggests the need for cross-generational policy approaches.

The Older Americans Act (OAA) was first funded in 1965 to create a national network for the comprehensive planning, coordination, and delivery of aging services. At the federal level, the act charges the Administration on Aging (AOA), through the Assistant Secretary on Aging, to oversee and support the aging network (i.e., the system of social services for older adults) and to advocate for them nationally. The establishment of AOA as a discrete unit in the Department of Health and Human Services took more than 27 years, from before the passage of the act until 1992, and required 13 amendments. At that time, the Administration for Children and Families was also organized. This decision to create parallel organizations rather than giving special status to the AOA made a significant statement regarding equity of responses to the needs of all age groups. There are three grant programs administered by AOA.

1. Title III: community planning and services to meet older adults' needs
2. Title IV: research and development
3. Title V: training personnel to provide services to older adults

Title III is the single federal social service statute designed specifically for all older people age 60 and over, regardless of income and need. In terms of the policy criteria identified on page 593, entitlement to AOA services is therefore universal based on age. The aging network encompasses the federal, state, and area agencies on aging, along with its advisory and advocacy groups. There are 57 State Units on Aging (SUAs); each of these has a state advisory council to engage in statewide planning and advocacy on behalf of older adults' service needs. The SUAs designed local Area Agencies on Aging (AAAs) to develop and administer service plans within regional and local areas. There are nearly 700 AAAs and 222 tribal organizations with AAA functions. Each of these has an advisory board, which must include older adults (Koff and Park, 1999).

In addition to federal, state, and local agencies that are responsible for planning and coordination, a fourth tier is composed of direct service providers in local communities, summarized below. Many of

---

SERVICES PROVIDED UNDER THE OLDER AMERICANS ACT

Access Services: Information and referral; care management.

In-Home Services: Homemaker assistance, respite care, emergency response systems, home health care, friendly visiting, and telephone reassurance.

Senior Center Programs: Social, physical, educational, recreational, and cultural programs.

Nutrition Programs: Meals at senior centers or nutrition sites; in-home meals (Meals on Wheels).

Legal Assistance Advocacy: For individual seniors and on behalf of programs and legislation. The Older Americans Act is the only major federal legislation that mandates advocacy on behalf of a constituency.

Additional services provided based on local community needs and resources.

these OAA services, central to long-term care, overlap with the goals and provisions of the Social Services Block Grants. Within this wide range of programs, the relatively low level of funding requires the OAA to target services to low-income, ethnic minority, rural elders, and frail older adults at risk of institutionalization, even though it still retains its original goal of universality.

Because participation rates in many OAA services are highest among middle-income older individuals, proposals for cost sharing of services have been introduced. This raises fears among some OAA program staff and advocates that cost sharing would introduce means testing and stigmatize OAA programs as "welfare," thereby discouraging their use. However, an implicit means test is already being employed by targeting services to low-income older people. Another goal is to increase services to those in greatest social and economic need and to increase participation of elders of color through targeted outreach and increased recruitment of ethnic minority staff and board members of agencies receiving OAA funds. Such targeting, however, can result in reductions in programs that would have long-range benefits through prevention and wellness. Cost-sharing, means testing, targeting, sliding fee schedules, and private partnerships have developed as alternative approaches to provide more than can be offered with the limited funding available through the Older Americans Act. However, each of these approaches challenges the act's basic premise of entitlement and raises questions about its net effect on the quality and quantity of services for the very poor. For example, whether costly home care services should be provided to all who request or require them is consistently questioned. Advocates of aging services are concerned that the Older Americans Act may start to provide a two-tiered system, one for the poor and another for the well-to-do. The fundamental dilemma is whether the Act can meet its changing and increasing role with regard to the growing numbers of frail elders without major changes in funding. Other advocates of the Act fear that in the absence of a national long-term care policy, AOA

activities, de facto, have become the nation's provider of many chronic care services targeted to frail and homebound elders, but without the benefit of a clear national policy or appropriate funding (Koff and Park, 1999).

Policy Dilemmas

Age-Based versus Needs-Based Programs

Longtime debates about the need for age-based programs have influenced policy developments in the aging field. These debates highlight choices about whom to serve and how to restrict benefits eligibility. Advocates of age-based programs view them as an efficient way to set a minimum floor of protection, less stigmatizing than means-tested services, and supporting the values of individual dignity and interdependence. Efficiency is presumably enhanced by the fact that age-based policies exclusively or predominantly affect older people. Similarly, age-based programs are assumed to involve fewer eligibility disputes and be less administratively intrusive into applicants' lives (Holstein, 1995).

Neugarten (1982; Neugarten and Neugarten, 1986), was among the first gerontologists to argue strongly against age-based services. She maintained that they reinforce the perception of "the old" as a problem, thereby stigmatizing older people and adding to age segregation. The Older Americans Act, for example, implicitly views anyone over age 60 as vulnerable and therefore needing services. Yet, as we have seen, growing numbers of adults over age 60 are healthy, have adequate incomes, and do not need services. As a result, many universal age-based programs benefit the young-old who are relatively healthy and in the top third of the income distribution. In fact, Torres-Gil (1992) argues that with up to 25 percent of the population qualifying for age-related benefits, a purely age-based approach is politically and economically unfeasible. The use of age as a benefits criterion assumes that older people are

Many agencies funded by AOA provide free or low-cost transportation services.

homogeneous and different from other age groups; but Neugarten contends that old age in itself does not constitute a basis for differential treatment. As noted in Chapter 1, chronological age is a poor predictor of the timing of life events and of health, income, and family status—and therefore of needs. Since age is an inadequate indicator of changes within a person, it is an arbitrary criterion for service delivery.

An alternative view is that economic and health needs should be the basis for selectively targeting services, rather than age. Proposals for income eligibility, for example, means testing for Social Security and Medicare, are congruent with a needs-based approach. Some advocates for targeting services to high-risk older persons favor a combination of categorical and group eligibility mechanisms. For example, a portion of OAA service funds could be restricted for allocation to SSI and older Medicaid recipients, thereby reaching individuals with the lowest incomes and presumably the most service needs. Given the increasing economic inequality within the older population, means-testing programs that comprise the

"safety net" for the least well-off older adults, (e.g. SSI and Medicaid) are viewed as priorities for improvement.

The Politics of Productivity versus the Politics of Entitlement

Closely related to the ongoing debate about age-based versus needs-based programs is the politics of productivity versus entitlement (Moody, 2002b). As implied throughout this chapter, the **politics of entitlement** is characterized as follows:

- In a "failure model of old age," older people, solely because of their age, are defined as needy, worthy, and deserving of public support.
- Issues are defined in terms of needs and rights.
- The emphasis is on what older people deserve to receive as their right rather than what they can give.
- Resources are transferred to the older population as a categorical group.
- Other groups must pay for the benefits due the older population.

The **politics of productivity,** as discussed in Chapters 8 and 12, is characterized this way:

- The older population is increasingly diverse.
- The implementation of new policies requires an expanding economy toward which older adults can contribute.
- Older people are defined as a resource in an interdependent society and can contribute to younger populations. Old age is a time for cross-generational assistance contributing to families and communities.
- "Investing in human resources" across the life span is essential to future economic growth to benefit all ages.

As noted earlier, conservative national groups and members of Congress are questioning entitlement programs for all age groups. While they point to the increased socioeconomic diversity of the older population as a rationale for means testing, they do not agree on how much to target resources to benefit those most at risk, such as women and elders of color. In other words, most advocates for changing entitlement programs appear to be motivated by fiscal goals, not by a desire for service adequacy to reduce status inequities within the older population.

Intergenerational Inequity Framework

Closely related to the debate about both age-based entitlement programs and a politics of productivity is the argument that older persons benefit at the expense of younger age groups, who lack the political clout represented by senior organizations. The **intergenerational inequity** debate began in 1984 with Samuel Preston's classic analysis of poverty rates among the young and old and public expenditures on behalf of older people. The old were perceived to be thriving, at the expense of children, as a result of expanded Social Security benefits and inflationary increases in real estate and home equity (Preston, 1984). This generated a rather simplistic picture of generational conflict, expounded in a growing number of newspaper and magazine editorials. It also resulted in the formation of groups such as Americans for Generational Equity (AGE), which later merged with the American Association of Boomers (AAB) and the National Taxpayers Union, although these organizations are no longer active. These organizations maintain that the baby boom generation (i.e., those born between 1946 and 1964) will collectively face a disastrous retirement, and its children will, in turn, be disproportionately burdened with supporting their parents as no other generation has been historically. The Third Millennium and PAC 20/20 emerged in the 1990s and are concerned about the future of *Generation X*, young adults in their 20s.

Underlying their arguments is the assumption that our country faces significant distribution choices, especially related to Social Security and other retirement incentives, about how to pay the

---

THEMES OF THE INTERGENERATIONAL INEQUITY ARGUMENT

- America's older citizens, now better off financially than is the population as a whole, are selfish and concerned only with personal pension and income benefits and their share of the federal budget.
- Programs for older people are a major cause of current budget deficits, economic problems, inadequate schools, and increases in poverty among mothers, children, and young adults.
- Children are the most impoverished age group.
- Younger people will not receive a fair return for their Social Security and Medicare investments in the future.

---

costs of an aging society. It was in this political climate that some of the long-standing features of old-age programs began to undergo significant revision: Social Security benefits at higher-income levels were taxed for the first time; the Tax Reform Act of 1986 eliminated the extra personal exemption for all older adults, although tax credits continue for very low income older persons on a sliding scale; and the Older Americans Act began targeting services to low-income older adults.

Critique of the Intergenerational Inequity Framework

The intergenerational inequity framework that attempts to measure the relative hard times of one generation against the relative prosperity of another has been widely criticized by advocates for older adults. The major criticisms are as follows:

- Contrary to the pessimistic argument that society will not be able to provide for future generations, the economy of the future, barring unforeseen disasters, will be able to support a mix of programs for all age groups. The distribution of benefits extends far beyond the older population, with the majority of American families receiving at least one benefit from entitlements or other safety-net programs.

- Evidence of significant intergenerational conflict is limited. Younger and older generations appear to recognize their interdependence and to support benefits for each other across the life span. For example, the Children's Defense Fund argues that funding for programs for the young should be increased at the cost of military spending, not at the expense of programs for the old. The AARP concurs, and maintains that older people's well-being contributes to the welfare of all other generations. In 2003, 135 organizations, cross-cutting the interests of young and old, lobbied Congress for life span respite programs that would benefit caregivers of all ages. In addition, Generations United involves more than 100 organizations to promote the well being of children, youth, and older adults.
- The definition of fairness put forth by groups such as Americans for Generational Equity is narrow and misleading. When fairness is equated with numerical equality, this assumes that the relative needs of children and older adults for public funds are identical, and that equal expenditures are the equivalent of social justice. Even if needs and expenditures for each group were equal, this would not result in equal outcomes or social justice.
- By framing policy issues in terms of competition and conflict between generations, the intergenerational inequity perspective implies that public benefits to older individuals are a one-way flow from young to old, and that reciprocity between generations does not exist.
- The intergenerational debate is a convenient mechanism to justify shifting responsibility for all vulnerable groups from the federal level of public good to individuals, the private sector, and local governments.
- It overlooks other ways to increase public resources through economic growth, increased tax revenues, or reduced defense spending, and that future generations' economic well-being will ultimately depend on growth rates of real wages (Kingson, Hirshorn, and Cornman, 1986; Kingson, Hirshorn, and Harootyan, 1994; Kingson

and Williamson, 2001; Williamson et al., 2002; Minkler, 2002).

Nevertheless, advocates for older adults increasingly acknowledge that it is no longer realistic to proceed on the assumption that all benefits are sacrosanct. They now recognize that it is counterproductive to oppose all measures imposed on financially better-off older persons, such as treating part of Social Security as taxable income.

The Interdependence of Generations Framework

Consistent with social exchange theory described in Chapter 8, a "contract between generations" exists. Typically, this is defined as parents to children and children to aging parents. What is different today is the focus on relationships between age groups in society rather than individuals within the family. This shift from generations to age groups has increased the magnitude and complexity of the issues involved, so that it is no longer youth versus elders, but rather elders versus middle-aged adults and youth. Never before have so many individuals lived so long, and never have there been so relatively few members of the younger generation to support them.

The **interdependence of generations framework** recognizes the changing societal and political context: increases in life expectancy, decreases in fertility, and growing concerns about age-based public expenditures. Within this larger context, public and private intergenerational transfers are viewed as central to social progress. A major way in which generations assist one another is through the family; for example, through care for children and dependent adults, financial support, gifts to children and grandchildren, and inheritances. Private intergenerational transfers are essential to meeting families' needs across the life course and to transmitting legacies of the past (e.g., culture, values, and knowledge). In addition, the growing number of intergenerational programs reflects how both generations gain from these social exchanges.

Art lends itself to intergenerational interactions.

Transfers based on public policy (e.g., education, Social Security, and health care programs) also serve intergenerational goals. As noted above, Social Security benefits are distributed widely across all generations and protect against risks to families' economic well-being across the life span, such as when a younger worker becomes disabled or a middle-aged parent dies. Social Security is not simply a one-way flow of resources from young to old. Instead, younger generations gain from programs that support their older relatives' autonomy and relieve them from financial responsibilities. Grandchildren cared for by grandparents also benefit from Social Security. In addition, long-term care affects all age groups—particularly younger adults with AIDS or who are developmentally disabled or chronically mentally ill—and thus benefits all generations. Likewise, it is erroneous to think of education as a one-way flow to children that is resisted by older people. Instead, older adults have contributed to public education throughout their careers. In addition, they now enjoy access to a growing range of lifelong learning opportunities. Older adults' support for school levies reflects

recognition that they gain from education programs that increase workforce productivity (Moody, 2002a; Schorr, 1998, 1999).

Within the framework of interdependence, other paradigms are proposed as ways to conceptualize how burdens and opportunities within our society can be fairly shared among generations. One paradigm is the concept of **generational investment,** in which age-based services and other social programs, such as public education, play an integral part in the system of reciprocal contributions that generations make to one another. Programs such as Social Security and Medicare are mechanisms through which generations invest in one another and publicly administer returns to older cohorts for the investments made in the human capital of younger groups. As such, old-age benefits represent claims based on merit and social contributions and should not be subject to means testing.

Similarly, older people can be the vanguard of renewed efforts to ensure a decent standard of living for all Americans, perhaps through measures such as a universal family-allowance program and paid parental leaves that recognize the societal contributions of childrearing (Marmor, Cook, and Scher, 1997; Williamson et al., 2002). This assumes that enhancing people's opportunities earlier in their lives can reduce intergenerational

---

THE INTERGENERATIONAL COMPACT

- More than 3 million children under the age of 18 receive Social Security benefits because their parents are retired, disabled, or deceased.
- Temporary Assistance to Needy Families (TANF) assists children and their caretaker relatives (parents or grandparents).
- More than 3 million children live in households where an adult, often a grandparent, receives Social Security (Weill and Rother, 1998–99).
- A growing percentage of older Americans help children, adolescents, and young families through their volunteerism.

competition. A broadened welfare consensus also can be fostered through an understanding of the life-course experiences that lead to problems in old age. This perspective of our common human vulnerability across the life course is not a new one. In fact, President Lyndon B. Johnson's charge to the 1968 Task Force Report on Older Americans was to determine the most important things to be done for the well-being of most older Americans. Since vulnerability in old age is the product of lifetime experiences, the task force concluded that providing social and economic opportunities for young and middle-aged persons is a priority (Binstock, 1995).

Similar to the "politics of productivity" and the interdependence framework, Torres-Gil (1992; Torres-Gil and Moga, 2001; Torres-Gil and Puccinelli, 1994) argues for a paradigm of *New Aging*. The politics of the New Aging aims to identify how all generations can contribute to a new society. In contrast to the prior focus on the older population from 1930 through the 1990s, our society must alter both our view of older adults to acknowledge their growing diversity and the manner in which we provide for them. With such increased heterogeneity, intergenerational conflict of old versus young cannot be assumed. While some tensions between young and old will remain, the *politics of diversity* will become the norm, whereby some older adults have more in common with younger age groups than with their peers. Differences of political opinions among older people and between age cohorts will increase, with more linkages based on political priorities, not age per se.

In the Politics of the New Aging, advocacy and lobbying should be rechanneled from special-interest issues toward policies to benefit all future generations. Groups of older adults should shift from the horizontal alliances that characterize interest-group politics to new vertical alliances, representing common needs across aging and nonaging groups (Binstock, 1995). Previously underrepresented groups of older persons—ethnic minorities, women, and rural residents—must es-

> ### INTERGENERATIONAL POLICY AGENDA OF GENERATIONS UNITED
>
> - Prevent cuts in Title XX Social Service Program.
> - Stop efforts to change Medicaid to a block grant program.
> - Keep and expand the dependent care tax credit.
> - Forbid landlords from discriminating in housing rentals against families with children while also allowing legitimate senior housing to stay exempt.

tablish alliances with nonaging groups (Ozawa, 1999). In fact, this is already occurring. For example, the Child Welfare League of America, the National Council on the Aging, and the Children's Defense Fund helped establish *Generations United*, a coalition of consumer, labor, children, and senior groups, to reframe policy agendas around our common stake in cross-generational approaches. AARP is also forming networks with populations of color and supports policies to benefit children cared for by grandparents. The United States Student Association and the Gray Panthers have joined together to support policies that enhance quality of life for all. Not only should older adults be viewed as a resource able to contribute to the economy and their own income security, but the young should be educated to assume full adult responsibilities and prepare for their own aging. The real potential of cross-generational advocacy depends on whether the approach pioneered by Generations United is adopted by mainstream age-based and social service organizations (Weill and Rother, 1999).

For the interdependence framework to address the problems of the disadvantaged, an ideological consensus is required that government should help people in need, regardless of age. Given that such consensus does not exist, some policy analysts argue that the real issue for the future is not intergenerational interdependence but rather redefining the role of the public sector in caring for its vulnerable citizens and the relationship between the public and private sectors.

Who Is Responsible?

As noted, many of these policy debates revolve around the role, size, and purpose of the federal government, and the division of responsibility between the public and private sectors. The current public–private debate is not new, but long-standing, reflected even in the passage of Social Security. Until recently, Social Security benefits, Medicare, Medicaid, SSI, and services under the Older Americans Act settled the question of responsibility for older citizens. It was to be a collective responsibility, exercised through the national government, and a protection to which every older citizen was entitled, simply by virtue of age.

A growing view held by public officials is that the problems of older adults and other disadvantaged groups cannot be solved with federal policies and programs alone. For former President Clinton to have stated in the 1990s that the "era of big government is over" indicates a major shift in how public policy and government intervention are viewed (Hudson, 2004). Instead, solutions must come from state and local governments and from private-sector and individual initiatives, such as advocacy, self-help, family care, personal retirement planning and private investments, and faith-based organizations. Individuals are assumed to be responsible for their own problems, and federal government interventions are considered too costly and often ineffective. An antitax mentality, combined with growing public concern about the federal deficit, has resulted in legislative changes to reduce federal funds and to rely increasingly upon the states through block grants. The assumption that states can most efficiently and creatively respond to local needs is used to justify such cuts. This decentralized approach, however, is flawed by the fact that states have the fewest resources for services, especially during economic downturns such as the one that has plagued the United States since 2000. Accordingly, they are least likely to respond to the needs of the most disadvantaged. Historically, decentralization has not assured policy uniformity and equity for powerless groups across different states. We have already seen evidence for such inequality in state-funded education and nutrition programs for children and youths. National initiatives that establish stable, uniformly administered federal policies are necessary to bring the states with the lowest expenditures up to a minimum standard, but are highly unlikely in the near future.

Reductions in Government Support

What is more important than federal-state relations, however, is the level of public spending. Although public spending has increased in terms of total dollars, it has declined when measured as a percentage of the gross national product or as government expenditures per capita, corrected for inflation. Economically disadvantaged older persons have been hurt the most by the budget cuts of the past 25 years, especially under the Republican "Contract with America" and the 1996 "Personal Responsibility and Work Opportunity Legislation" (welfare reform), which was passed during the Clinton administration.

Public spending levels are being reduced at the same time that private and local spheres are being expected to be more responsible for older people with chronic disabilities. Policy makers often assume that public programs reduce family involvement and that families could do more for their older relatives. However, as discussed in Chapter 10, the family has consistently played a major role in elder care. Family members provide all the support that they are able or willing to do, although such assistance is not necessarily financial. When resources become scarce, the family should not be viewed as simply a cost-effective alternative to nursing home placement and to publicly funded social services.

Not only are families unable to carry expanded responsibilities on their own, but the private non-profit service sector, especially faith-based organizations, lack the resources to fill the gaps created by federal cuts or changed priorities. In fact, federal tax laws have reduced incentives for corporate giving. In addition, private contributions traditionally have not been concentrated on social services, so that increased private giving would not automatically flow into areas most severely cut, nor would this benefit the most disadvantaged. The challenge is that, as the older population's need for services increases, both public and private funds will be needed.

Implications for the Future

Social policies in the future will be shaped by economic, demographic, and social factors, including the following:

- the demographic bulge of the senior boomers
- increasing economic and racial inequities across the life span and in old age
- budget cuts or flat funding in federal and state programs along with the escalating federal deficit, currently the largest in U.S. history.
- the economic downturn nationally and globally along with economic pressures for older adults to be employed longer, which will gradually increase the average retirement age
- the national emphasis on security and foreign policy
- increased competition for limited public dollars, with greater emphasis on cost-effectiveness, fiscal responsibility, and devolution of federal authority to state and local levels
- privatization of public policies, such as the 2003 change in Medicare and the current administration's push toward individual savings accounts in lieu of or in addition to Social Security
- growing expectations that the private sector, including faith-based organizations, and family and other informal caregivers will meet the gaps in responding to the needs of vulnerable populations

- the influential role of AARP in national policy debates
- deep partisan divisions at the federal level, with an intense focus on party positioning

Given this context, we are unlikely to see an expansion of public policies that will benefit older adults, unless this expansion occurs through privatization. Instead, issues of income security and long-term care are likely to continue to be addressed in a piecemeal fashion, and deficit-driven budget pressures will collide with the needs of an aging population (Crystal, 2003). As suggested by Ornstein (2002) in his predictions of what type of reform can be expected in the current political context, the challenge of developing a comprehensive policy approach to the problems of an aging society is to adopt a framework larger than the current budget politics and partisan bickering. The need for compelling proposals for change is critical. One such direction is to adopt an intergenerational or multigenerational approach to policy development, as represented by the strong support from both parties for a national life span respite bill that crosscuts all ages and was proposed by Generations United. Such life span initiatives move away from age-based categorical funding and have the benefit of pooling resources across age groups. They also serve to move beyond the intergenerational competition debates that have framed policy discussion since the 1980s. Another way to frame a comprehensive policy approach would be to reconceptualize aging policy as family policy and the aging of the baby boomers as a crisis for families, rather than a crisis in Social Security (Binstock, 2002).

The probability of a comprehensive policy approach that can bring together diverse actors in the near future is extremely low. The general approach historically to addressing social issues through government intervention, with the exception of Social Security and Medicare, has been piecemeal and incremental. Another barrier is the fragmentation of political power endemic to our political system. And last remains the challenge of effective implementation that involves both private and public entities. The process of implementation often impedes fulfillment of the intent of policies. An exception to this is Social Security, which is a relatively self-implementing and therefore successful program (Binstock, 2002). On the other hand, the "crises" entailed by the aging of the baby boomers may force action, despite the lack of a forward-looking national policy.

The importance of gerontologists as advocates for programs that benefit individuals across the life span and into old age is critical. Translating gerontological research findings for policy makers and the public is inherent within effective advocacy. This means that gerontologists need to be visible at the local, state, and federal levels in presenting evidence-based testimony and offering comprehensive, creative solutions. For example, policies that benefit older adults may need to be framed in terms of the current funding emphasis on national security. Given the nature of our political system and the critical policy and funding challenges created by the senior boomers, gerontological policy, practice, and research need to be linked in the training and development of gerontological professionals.

Summary

Rapid demographic and social changes mean that U.S. society is faced with complex, difficult policy choices. It is increasingly apparent that the older population is not one constituency but several, in which race, gender, socioeconomic class, and rural/urban residence may be greater unifiers than age. A political agenda must be drafted that can unite different older constituencies—low-income, middle-class, and wealthy—as well as different racial and ethnic groupings with common needs. Limited public resources in itself is not the primary barrier to action, however. For example, the cost of eliminating poverty among both older people and children is well within our societal resources, but our society lacks the public will to do so. The greater challenge is to frame the political consensus to ensure a minimal level of economic security and health for all Americans. Progress could be made in both areas largely by improving the basic income support of SSI and expanding Medicaid eligibility. Unfortunately, such gains are unlikely to occur without major changes in our political structures and belief systems of democratic pluralism, states' rights, and individual freedom. Until then, Americans will continue to be personally generous, but reluctant to support income-maintenance programs for an entire class of needy persons or a national health care system that is perceived to threaten individual choice.

This chapter has reviewed federal programs that benefit older persons. Since 1960, age-specific spending has increased significantly, mostly through Medicare and Old Age and Survivors and Disability Insurance of Social Security. In the past, such age-entitlement programs have been based on cultural values and public beliefs that older people are deserving. However, the rapid expansion of these programs, combined with the improved economic status of the majority of older adults, has created a growing public and political sentiment that such age-based entitlement programs must be reduced, perhaps through means testing to minimize the benefits received by higher-income older adults.

The United States developed policies aimed at older populations more slowly than European countries. The Social Security Act of 1935 was the first major policy benefit for older people. Social Security was expanded slightly in 1950 to support partial health care costs through individual states. These changes led to the enactment of Medicare in 1965. Since then, the number of programs aimed at improving the welfare of older people has grown significantly: the Older Americans Act, Supplemental Security Income, the Social Security Amendments of 1972 and 1977, and Title XX social services legislation. National forums such as the 1961 and 1971 White House Conferences on

Aging strengthened these programs. During the 1980s, however, social service funding declined despite recommendations from the 1981 White House Conferences on Aging to increase funds for aging services. Allocations for homemaker, nutrition, chore services, adult day care, low-income energy assistance, respite, and volunteer programs such as Retired Senior Volunteer Programs all diminished. These cost-efficiency measures were based on a national perception that the older population has greater financial security than younger age groups. The fiscal crisis faced by the Social Security system in the early 1980s fueled this stereotype through speculations that the growing number of older persons would drain the system before future generations could benefit. However, numerous structural factors are responsible for the problems. Changes that have subsequently been made in this system assure its future viability until approximately 2040.

The debate over age-based versus needs-based programs has also led to the emergence of organizations that expound arguments about older people benefiting at the expense of younger age groups. Yet, evidence for such inequities is weak; numerous other organizations such as the Children's Defense Fund and Generations United recognize generational interdependence and the importance of seeking increased public support for all ages through other sources. This framework, known as the interdependence of generations, assumes that assistance from young to old and old to young benefits all ages and supports the role of families across the life span.

The policy agenda for older Americans early in the twenty-first century is full and complex. The current federal emphasis on fiscal austerity and decentralized government underlies all policy debates about how much the federal government should be expected to provide and for whom. Increasing public perceptions of older people as well off, combined with decreased government expenditures, will undoubtedly affect the types of future programs and policies developed to meet older adults' needs. Older adults are less likely to act as a unified bloc in support of age-based programs. Instead, their increased diversity suggests that alliances will be formed between at-risk elders and other age groups. Consistent with the frameworks of interdependence and generational investment, such alliances may foster policies that benefit both older people and future generations. Threatening such cross-age efforts, however, is the anti-tax mood of the public and the fiscal conservatism of the Bush administration. These pressures suggest that advocates for older adults will need to find new ways to address the complex needs created by their increased life expectancy and diversity. A major challenge is the development and funding of health care, especially home- and community-based forms of long-term care, the topic addressed next in Chapter 17.

GLOSSARY

age-entitlement (age-based) programs   programs only available to people of a certain age

Aging Network   the system of social services for older adults funded by the Older Americans Act

Area Agencies on Aging   offices on aging at the regional and local levels that plan and administer services to meet the needs of older adults within that area; established and partially funded through the Older Americans Act

cash substitute   a benefit given in a form other than cash, such as a voucher, which may be exchanged for food, rent, medical care, etc.

cash transfer   a benefit paid by cash or its equivalent

categorical   in this context, a manner of dealing with public problems by addressing the problems of specific groups of persons rather than attempting solutions that are comprehensive or dealing with problems as they affect the entire population

contributory plans   programs providing benefits that require the beneficiary to contribute something toward the cost of the benefit

cost-of-living adjustments (COLA) changes in benefits designed to maintain steady purchasing power of such benefits

direct benefit a benefit given directly, in the form of either a cash payment or of some commodity such as food or housing

eligibility criteria factors that determine the ability of programs to deliver benefits to people

entitlement programs government programs organized in such a way that appropriations from a legislative body are not required; rather, eligibility on the part of applicants triggers receipt of benefits regardless of the total cost of the program

generational investment investments made by one generation for the benefit of another, such as the payment of Social Security taxes by the working population for the benefit of retirees, the services provided by older persons for the care of children, and the payment of property taxes that benefit school children

indirect benefit a benefit given through tax deductions or exemptions or other indirect means

interdependence of generations framework recognition of intergenerational transfers that occur across the life span

intergenerational inequity the view that one generation or age group receives benefits that are disproportional to those received by another

need-based (or means-based) entitlement programs social programs delivered to persons who meet defined criteria of eligibility based on need or ability to pay for the benefits

noncontributory programs programs providing benefits that do not require the beneficiary to contribute toward the cost of the benefit

Older Americans Act federal legislation for a network of social services specifically for older people

politics of entitlement political preferences, especially as applied to elders, for the allocation of resources based on notions of older persons as needy, worthy, and deserving of public support

politics of productivity political preferences, especially as applied to elders, for the allocation of resources based on a recognition of the diversity of the aging population (some are well-off, others are poor; some are capable of continued productive work, while others are ill or disabled)

selective benefits benefits available on an individually determined need or means basis

social policy government policy designed to address a social problem or issue

social programs the visible manifestations of policies

Title XX or the Social Services Block Grant funding for social services (e.g., homemaking chores, adult day care) based on need, not age

universal benefits benefits available on the basis of social right to all persons belonging to a designated group.

RESOURCES

See the companion Website for this text at <www.ablongman.com/hooyman> for information about the following:

- The 2030 Center
- Administration on Aging (AOA)
- Cato Institute
- Generations United
- International Federation on Aging
- National Academy on Aging
- National Association of Area Agencies on Aging
- National Center for Policy Analysis
- National Committee to Preserve Social Security and Medicare
- National Policy and Resource Center on Women and Aging
- Social Security Administration

REFERENCES

American Association of Retired Persons (AARP). *Beyond 50: A report to the nation on economic security.* Washington, DC: AARP, 2000.

Beedon, L. *Supplemental Security Income (SSI): Yesterday, today and tomorrow.* Washington, DC: AARP, Public Policy Research Group, 2000.

Binstock, R. H. A new era in the politics of aging: How will the old-age interest groups respond? *Generations,* Fall 1995, *19,* 68–74.

Binstock, R. H. The politics and economics of aging and diversity. In S. Bass, E. Kutza, and F. M. Torres-Gil (Eds.), *Diversity in aging.* Glenview, IL: Scott, Foresman and Co., 1990.

Binstock, R. H. The politics of enacting reform. In S. H. Altman and D. I. Schatman, *Policies for an aging society.* Baltimore: Johns Hopkins University Press, 2002.

Binstock, R. H., and Day, C. L. Aging and politics. In R. H. Binstock and L. K. George (Eds.), *Handbook of aging and the social sciences* (4th ed.). San Diego, CA: Academic Press, 1996.

Board of Trustees, OASDI. *2001 Annual Report of the Board of Trustees of the Federal Old-Age and Survivors Insurance and Disability Insurance Trust Funds,* Washington, DC: Author, 2001.

Bosworth, B., Butler, G. T., and Keys, B. *Implications of the Bush Commission pension reforms for married couples.* Chestnut Hill, MA: Center for Retirement Research at Boston College, 2003.

Breyer, F., and Kifmann M. Incentives to retire later—A solution to the Social Security crisis? *Journal of Pension Economics and Finance,* 2002, *1,* 111–130.

Bryce, D. V., and Friedland, R. B. *Economic and health security: An overview of the origins of federal legislation.* Washington, DC: The National Academy on Aging, January 16, 1997.

Calhoun, G., Kingson, E., and Newman, S. Intergenerational programs and public policy: A context for growth and change. In Newman, S., Ward, C., Smith, T., Wilson, J., and McCrea, J., *Intergenerational programs: Past, present and future.* New York: Taylor and Francis, 1997.

Cavanaugh, F. X. *Feasibility of Social Security individual accounts.* Washington, DC: Public Policy Institute, AARP, 2002.

Conte, C. Executive Summary: Assessing Social Security reform alternatives. In D. Salisbury, *Assessing Social Security reform alternatives.* Washington, DC: Employee Benefit Research Institute, 1997.

Crystal, S. Groundhog day: The endless debate over Medicare "reform." *Public Policy and Aging Report,* 2003, *13,* 7–10.

Eheaert, B. K., Power, M. B., and Hopping, D. E. Intergenerational programming for foster-adoptive families: Creating Community of Hope Meadows. *Journal of Intergenerational Relationships,* 2003, *1,* 17–28.

Ekerdt, D. J., and Hackney, J. K. Workers' ignorance of retirement benefits. *The Gerontologist,* 2002, *42,* 543–551.

Estes, C. L. *The aging enterprise.* San Francisco: Jossey-Bass, 1979.

Estes, C. L. Aging, health and social policy: Crisis and crossroads. *Journal of Aging and Social Policy,* 1989, *1,* 17–32.

Estes, C. L. Austerity and aging. 1980 and beyond. In M. Minkler and C. L. Estes (Eds.), *Readings in the political economy of aging.* Farmingdale, NY: Baywood, 1984.

Estes, C. L. From gender to the political economy of aging. *European Journal of Social Equality,* 2000, *2,* 28–45.

Estes, C. L., Linkins, K. W., and Binney, E. A. The political economy of aging. In R. H. Binstock and L. K. George (Eds.), *Handbook of aging and the social sciences* (4th ed.). San Diego, CA: Academic Press, 1996.

Favreault, M. M., and Sammartino, F. J. *Impact of Social Security reform on low-income and older women.* Washington, DC: Public Policy Institute, AARP, 2002.

Friedland, R. B. *Investing in Our Future.* Washington, DC: National Academy on an Aging Society, 2000.

Generations United. *Social Security: A program that benefits all ages: Fact sheet.* Washington, DC: Author, 2003.

Gorin, S. H. Generational equity and privatization: Myth and reality. *Health and Social Work,* 2000, *25,* 219–225.

Goyer, A. Intergenerational shared-site programs. *Generations,* Winter 1998–99, 79–80.

Gran, B. Public and private pensions: Survival or retrenchment. *International Sociological Association,* 1998

Henkin, N., and Kingson, E. Advancing an intergenerational agenda for the twenty-first century. *Generations,* 1998/1999, *22,* 99–105.

Holstein, M. The normative case: Chronological age and public policy. *Generations,* Fall 1995, *19,* 11–14.

Hudson, R. H. The history and place of age-based public policy. In Hudson, R. (Ed.), *The future of age-based public policy,* forthcoming.

Hudson, R. H. The role of government in "A Society for all Ages." *Health and Social Work,* 1999, 24, 155–160.

Hudson, R. H. (Ed.). *Critical perspectives on age-based public policy.* Baltimore: Johns Hopkins University Press, 2004.

Hudson, R. H., and Quadagno, J. Aging and politics. In R. H. Binstock and L. K. George, *Handbook of aging and the social sciences.* San Diego: Academic Press, 2001.

Johnson, M. L. Dignity for the oldest old: Can we afford it? *Journal of Gerontological Social Work,* 1998, 29, 155–168.

Kassner, E. *The food stamp program and older Americans.* Washington, DC: AARP, Policy Institute Research Group, 2001.

Kingson, E. R., Hirshorn, B. A., and Cornman, J. C. *Ties that bind: the interdependence of generations.* Cabin John, MD: Seven Locks Press. 1986.

Kingson, E. R., Hirshorn, B. A., and Harootyan, L. K. *The common stake: The interdependence of generations (A policy framework for an aging society).* Washington, DC: The Gerontological Society of America. Reprinted in H. R. Moody, *Aging: Concepts and controversies.* Thousand Oaks, CA: Pine Forge Press, 1994.

Kingson, E. R., and Williamson, J. Economic security policies. In R. Binstock and L. K. George, *Handbook of aging and the social sciences* (5th ed.). San Diego: Academic Press, 2001.

Koff, T., and Park, R. The Aging network. In T. Koff and R. Park, *Aging public policy: Bonding the generations* (2nd ed.). Amityville, NY: Baywood Publishing, 1999.

Marmor, T. R., Cook, F. L., and Scher, S. Social Security politics and the conflict between generations. Are we asking the right questions? In E. R. Kingson, and J. H. Schulz, *Social Security in the 21st century.* New York: Oxford University Press, 1997.

Miller, M. Rebuilding retirement. *US News and World Report,* April 20, 1998, 20–26.

Minkler, M. "Generational equity" and the new victim blaming. In H. R. Moody, *Aging: Concepts and controversies* (4th ed.). Thousand Oaks, CA: Sage, 2002.

Mitchell, O. S. *Personal retirement accounts and Social Security reform.* Philadelphia: Pension Research Council, The Wharton School, University of Pennsylvania, 2002.

Moen, P. The gendered life course. In R. Binstock and L. K. George, *Handbook of aging and the social sciences* (5th ed.). San Diego: Academic Press, 2001.

Moody, H. R. Focus on practice: Intergenerational programs. In H. R. Moody, *Aging: Concepts and controversies* (4th ed.). Thousand Oaks, CA: Sage, 2002.

Moody, H. R. Should age or need be the basis for entitlement. In H. R. Moody, *Aging: Concepts and controversies* (4th ed., pp. 179–190). Thousand Oaks, CA: Sage, 2002.

Moody, H. R. What is the future of Social Security? In H. R. Moody, *Aging: Concepts and controversies* (4th ed.). Thousand Oaks, Sage, 2002.

Munnell, A. H., Sunden, A. E., and Lidstone, E. *How important are private pensions?* Chestnut Hill, MA: Center for Retirement Research at Boston College, 2002.

National Committee to Preserve Social Security and Medicare, letter to the U.S. Senate, June 12, 2003b.

National Committee to Preserve Social Security and Medicare (NCPSSM). *The many myths about Social Security privatization.* Washington, DC: Author, 2003a.

National Committee to Preserve Social Security and Medicare (NCPSSM). *The truth about privatization.* Washington, DC: Author, 2003b.

Neugarten, B. Policy in the 1980s: Age or need entitlement. In B. Neugarten (Ed.), *Age or need: Public policies for older people.* Beverly Hills, CA: Sage, 1982.

Neugarten, B., and Neugarten, D. Changing meanings of age in the aging society. In A. Pifer and L. Bronte (Eds.), *Our aging society: Paradox and promise.* New York: W. W. Norton, 1986.

Olson, L. K. *The not-so-golden years. Caregiving, the frail elderly and the long-term care establishment.* Lanham, UK: Rowman and Littlefield, 2003.

Ormstein, N. J. Enacting reform: What can we expect in the current political context? In S. H. Altman and D. I. Shactman, *Policies for an aging society.* Baltimore: Johns Hopkins Press, 2002.

Ozawa, M. N. The economic well-being of elderly people and children in a changing society.

Park, N. H., and Gilbert N. Social Security and the incremental privatization of retirement income. *Journal of Sociology and Social Welfare,* 1999, 26, 187–202.

Preston, S. H. Children and the elderly in the United States. *Scientific American,* 1984, *251,* 44–49.

Public Agenda Online. www.publicagenda.org/issues/ factfilesSocialSecurity.org. 2003.

Purcell, P. J. Pension sponsorship and participation: Trends and policy issues. *Social Security Bulletin,* 2001–2002, *64,* 92–102.

Quinn, J. *Entitlements and the federal budget: Securing our future.* Washington, DC: National Academy on Aging, 2000.

Schorr, A. L. Income supports across the life course. *Generations,* 1998/1999, *22,* 64–67.

Schulz, J. H., Rosenman, L., and Rix, S. E. International developments in Social Security privatization: What risk to women? *Journal of Cross Cultural Gerontology,* 1999, *14,* 25–42.

Smalhout, J. H. Benefit design choices for personal Social Security accounts. *Benefits Quarterly,* 2002, *18,* 44–64.

Smeeding, T. M., Estes, C. L., and Glasse, L. More than deficits: Strengthening security for women. *Social Security in the 21st Century.* Washington, DC: The Gerontological Society of America, 2000.

Social Security Administration. *Fast facts and figures about Social Security.* Washington, DC: Author, 2003a.

Social Security Administration. *Frequently asked questions about Social Security's future.* Washington, DC: Author, 2003b.

Torres-Gill, F. M., and Moga, K. Multiculturalism, social policy and the new aging. *Journal of Gerontological Social Work,* 2001, *36,* 12–32.

Torres-Gill, F. M. *The new aging: Politics and change in America.* New York: Auburn House, 1992.

Torres-Gill, F. M., and Puccinelli, M. Mainstreaming gerontology in the policy arena. *The Gerontologist,* 1994, *34,* 749–752.

U.S. Government. *Budget FY 2003.* Washington, DC: U.S. Government Printing Office, 2003.

Weill, J., and Rother, J. Efforts of advocacy organizations to strengthen the social compact. *Generations,* 1999, *22,* 94–98.

Wheeler, P. M., and Kearney, J. R. Income protection for the aged in the 21st century: A framework to help inform the debate. *Social Security Bulletin,* 1996, *59,* 3–19.

White, J. The Social Security and Medicare debate three years after the 2000 election. *Public Policy and Aging Report,* 2003, *13,* 15–19.

Williamson, J. B. What's next for Social Security? Partial privatization? *Generations,* 2002, *26,* 34–39.

Williamson, J. B., Watts-Ray, D. M., and Kingson, E. R. The generational equity debate. In H. R. Moody, *Aging: Concepts and controversies* (4th ed.). Thousand Oaks, CA: Sage, 2002.

Zebrowski, J. Social Security: You've been warned. *Business Monday, Seattle Times,* Monday, November 20, 2000, p. C6.

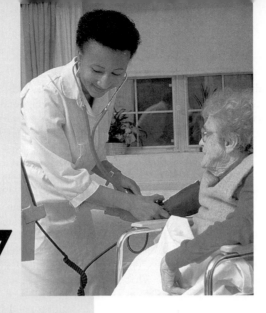

17

Health and Long-Term Care Policy and Programs

Throughout this book we have examined the interplay of social, physiological, and psychological factors in how older people relate to their environments, and how health status affects this interaction. Technological advances oriented toward cure have created the paradox that, while adults now live longer, they face serious, often debilitating or life-threatening disabilities that create the need for ongoing care. Although Chapter 4 notes that disability per se in old age does not create dependency, many older adults, especially among the oldest-old, are physically or mentally frail and depend on informal supports as well as medical and social services. This dependence is often intensified by the interaction of age, race, gender, and poverty, as well as changes in family structure described in Chapter 9. And, as we have seen, the oldest-old, persons of color, women, and those who are low-income are more likely to have chronic disabilities that affect their ability to function.

As described in Chapter 11, *long-term care* (LTC) refers to a range of supportive services and assistance provided to persons who, as a result of chronic illness or disability, are unable to function independently on a daily basis. The need for LTC does not necessarily correspond to medical conditions, but rather to problems with performing *activities of daily living (ADL)*—bathing, dressing, toileting, eating, and transferring—and *instrumental activities of daily living (IADL)*—shopping, cooking, and cleaning. In addition, adults with cognitive impairments such as Alzheimer's disease may need nearly constant supervision. Long-term care is not an integrated system nor comprehensive policy; instead, it is characterized by services to minimize, rehabilitate, or compensate for the loss of independent functioning and to enhance functional capabilities. Although largely "low-tech" assistance with basic activities, long-term care services are increasingly complicated because those with complex medical needs are being discharged home earlier than was previously the case. In effect, long-term care aims to integrate health care treatment and assistance with daily life tasks and to address social, environmental and medical needs over a prolonged period (Kane, Kane, and Ladd, 1998).

Because nursing homes are the major institutional setting for long-term care, many older people and their families first think of them when they consider such care. However, as seen in Chapter 11, the boundaries between long-term care in institutional and noninstitutional environments are far from clear. For example, long-term care services are provided in:

- nursing homes
- home and community-based care settings
- noninstitutional settings, such as congregate care and residential care (assisted living, board and care, and adult family homes)
- adult day centers

Services provided within *home and residential care settings* include:

- personal assistance (home-delivered meals, visiting nurse or social work services, chore services, homemaker/home health aides, in-home respite, friendly visiting, and telephone reassurance)
- assistive devices (canes, walkers), home modifications
- technology (computerized medication reminders and emergency alert systems)

Services delivered in *community-based settings* encompass:

- nutrition programs
- senior centers
- adult day care
- respite
- hospice
- transportation

Although long-term care also encompasses younger adults with AIDS, serious and chronic physical and mental illness, and developmental disabilities, the focus of our discussion is on the structural, funding, staffing, and regulatory aspects of long-term care that affect older people. Overall, nearly 60 percent of those who report using long-term care are age 65 or older. The need for long-term care services is growing rapidly, especially among the oldest-old. While only 5 percent of those age 65 and over are in nursing homes at any one point in time, 12 percent in the community have ADL or IADL restrictions. Among those age 85 and over, the corresponding rates increase to 21 and 49 percent, respectively. When all adults age 65 and over are considered across their lifetimes, almost 65 percent of them will be in a nursing home, if only for a short time period (for over 50 percent, less than a year) before they are discharged to community settings. This translates into 75 percent of those over age 65 requiring some degree of home health care or personal assistance (Feder, Komisar, and Niefeld, 1999; Seperson, 2002; Stone, 2000). Although the health care system has traditionally emphasized primary and acute care, the boundaries with long-term care are blurred. In fact, our "acute" health care system is increasingly devoted to chronic care by various providers in a range of settings (Stone, 2000). Given the high incidence of chronic health needs among the growing population of older adults, it is not surprising that health and long-term care costs are one of the most critical and controversial policy issues facing our nation.

Although home-based long-term care services are available in nearly all communities, family and friends are the major providers of care (see Chapter 10). As many as 80 percent of older adults in need of long-term care live in their own homes or community settings. The majority of those with severe disabilities who reside in the community rely exclusively on help from family and friends.

After informal supports, most paid providers are paraprofessionals or direct care workers such as certified nursing assistants in nursing homes or home care workers who deliver low-tech personal care and assistance with daily life tasks. Women predominate among both the unpaid and under-paid service providers, comprising up to 80 percent of family caregivers and 90 to 96 percent of paraprofessionals (Stone, 2000). In contrast to physicians who play a key role in acute-care hospital settings, nurses and ancillary therapists are the primary providers within chronic-care facilities. We turn next to examining the rising health and long-term care costs and the factors underlying these.

Health and Long-Term Care Expenditures

Policy makers, service providers, and the general public are all concerned about the "crisis in health care." This refers mostly to the costs of care, the growing numbers of uninsured individuals, and the status and future of health care systems. Peo-

CHARACTERISTICS OF LONG-TERM CARE

- It is targeted at persons of all ages who have functional disabilities.
- Disabilities may be physical or mental, transitory or permanent.
- Aim is to enhance independence in functional abilities and quality of life, including the right to die with dignity for those who are terminally ill.
- It encompasses a wide range of services, professions, and settings of care.
- Care addresses physical, mental, social, and financial aspects of a person's life.
- Care is organized around the distinctive needs of each individual and family.
- Services change over time as the patient's and family's circumstances change.
- Unlike hospital services, it is not widely insured.
- Funding sources are a patchwork of federal, state, and local governments; private foundations; and out of pocket.

ple over 65 account for over 30 percent of the nation's annual federal health care expenditures (Moody, 2002). In fact, the average expenditure for health services for adults age 65 and over is nearly four times the cost for those under age 65 and increases even more among the oldest-old. This is largely attributable to their greater chronic disease needs and use of hospital and nursing home services. Of all long-term care expenditures in the United States (e.g., nursing home, home health care), nearly 70 percent are for people age 65 and over (Evashwick, 2001). Figure 17.1 shows dramatic spending increases by 2050, with families carrying the primary burden.

Although cost-containment changes in the private health care marketplace, such as managed care, have slightly slowed the rate of medical costs, expenses are still rising faster than the national income. Medicare and Medicaid are expanding at several times the economic growth rate, adding to the pressure to change them in order to cut federal spending. Spending on Medicare

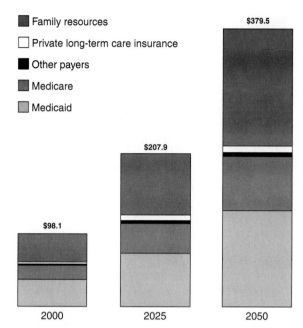

Family resources
Private long-term care insurance
Other payers
Medicare
Medicaid

$98.1

$207.9

$379.5

2000 2025 2050

FIGURE 17.1 **Billions of 1999 Dollars Projected to Be Spent on Long-Term Care**

Note: The projected expenditure increases assume reductions in mortality of 0.6 percent a year and 0.6 percent a year in disability rates in the older population, current age- and sex-specific use rates for institutional and home care services, static public policies, and a real inflation rate of 1.2 percent for long-term care services.

SOURCE: *Urban Institute, 2001.*

and Medicaid consumes approximately 26 percent of the federal budget. Nevertheless, most analysts do not fear a fiscal crisis in the Medicare trust fund in the near future. Although public expenditures for health and long-term care are increasing, older individuals and their families continue to pay more out-of-pocket for their care than do younger Americans. Only 67 percent of total personal health care costs of older people are covered by government funding (Medicare, Medicaid, and other sources such as Veterans Administration). As noted in Chapter 12, older Americans now spend a higher proportion (and more in actual dollars) of their incomes on acute health care services than they did before Medicare

and Medicaid were established three decades ago (23 percent versus 11 percent, respectively). Part of this increase is due to the costs of prescription drugs, which are discussed later under "Medicare Reform and Prescription Drug Coverage." In addition, long-term care costs are a growing proportion of total personal health care expenditures, increasing from less than 4 percent in 1960 to approximately 12 percent (Urban Institute, 2001). The distribution and source of personal health care expenditures are illustrated in Figure 17.2. In sum, the burdens of health care are expected to expand faster than the older population's ability to pay. At the same time, private health insurance costs are growing more rapidly than Medicare spending, and increases are greatest for home health and skilled nursing facility care.

Factors Underlying Growing Costs

A number of structural factors underlie escalating health care costs.

- The success of modern medical care: Costs have grown not in the overall number of visits to health care providers, but in the type and complexity of services. Although advances in medical science produce cost-saving breakthroughs, they also make possible more sophisticated and expensive medical treatments. These tend to be in addition to prior services rather than replacements for old technologies or procedures. For example, an older patient now may receive X-rays, CAT scans, and MRIs to diagnose a problem, whereas before only X-rays would have been used.
- Related to the success of medical technology in prolonging life is the conflict between the curative goals of medicine and the chronic-care needs of older adults. As a result, there is a poor fit between the medical and social service needs of the older population (e.g., long-term care needs) and the funding mechanisms, regulations, and fragmented services of the health care system.

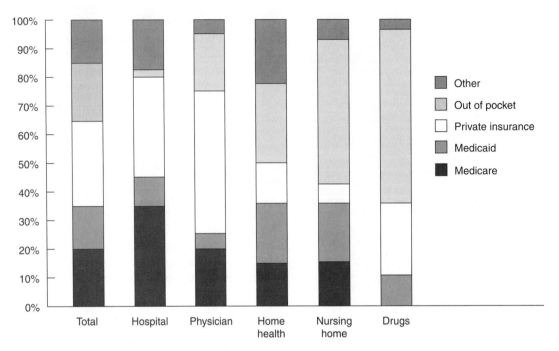

FIGURE 17.2 **Estimated Personal Health Care Expenditures, 1998**

- The system of public financing is biased toward acute care.
- Comprehensive, coordinated health and long-term care policy and programs that integrate acute and chronic care are lacking.

As seen in Chapter 16, some powerful beliefs and assumptions underlie these structural factors. These include a growing distrust of government and its ability to fund health care, and a strong belief in the private sector. These combine to produce an approach to service delivery that is determined largely by the market or who provides the best services at lowest cost. In other words, the shape of health care is largely influenced by its method of payment. The private provision of health services, without effective market control or uniform government regulation of expenditures, is emphasized. Nevertheless, most health services are financed by a mix of public programs, private insurance, and direct patient payments. Patients have been largely free to choose the health care providers they prefer. In turn, physicians have been able to charge patients whatever they choose. Only recently has Medicare, and subsequently most private health insurance companies, instituted a system of Preferred Provider Plans (PPPs) that require physicians to accept a set fee for each procedure in order to be paid by that insurer. **Managed care** also aims to control the level of resources devoted to health care and is described more fully later in this chapter.

The fundamental problem, however, is not funding per se but the fact that acute and long-term care remain largely two separate fragmented systems, with distinct providers, treatment settings, financing structures, and goals. Physicians are the primary care providers in hospitals and outpatient settings, and Medicare covers most of the costs. Nursing staff, paraprofessionals or di-

Preventive health services can reduce long-term care costs over time.

rect care workers, and family members are the principal caregivers in nursing homes and private home settings. Medicaid pays for a large percentage of institutional care and, increasingly, home-based care. In the acute-care setting, intensity of services determines costs, compared to duration of treatment in long-term care. The different purposes between Medicaid and Medicare, which are the primary sources of funding and regulation for health and long-term care for older adults, are significant barriers to the integration of these two systems.

Medicare

As a social insurance system, **Medicare,** or Title XVIII of the Social Security Act of 1965, is intended to provide financial protection against the cost of hospital and physician care for people age 65 and over. Prior to the passage of Medicare, only about 50 percent of older adults had health insur-

ance. Many could not afford insurance, or were denied coverage because of their age. In contrast, a value underlying Medicare is that older people are entitled to access to *acute medical care,* and society has an obligation to cover the costs associated with inpatient hospital care. Medicare's focus on the older population grew out of a compromise with the medical profession, which successfully opposed comprehensive health insurance for the general public. Yet Medicare was also viewed as the "first step" toward increasing access to health care for all age groups. Despite Medicare's goal of financial protection, it covers less than 50 percent of the total health expenditures of older adults (Schoen and Cooper, 2003). As noted above and illustrated in Figures 17.1 and 17.2, the remainder is paid by older people out-of-pocket, by private supplemental insurance, by Medicaid, and by other public payers such as the Veterans Administration.

Contrary to many older adults' assumptions that their acute health care costs will be covered, Medicare pays only 80 percent of the allowable charges, not the actual amount charged by health providers. The patient must pay the difference between "allowable" and "actual" charges, unless the physician accepts "assignment" and agrees to charge only what Medicare pays. Beneficiaries whose doctors do not accept Medicare assignments are responsible for the amount that their doctor charges above the Medicare-approved rate, as illustrated by the vignette about Mr. Fox on page 637.

Beneficiaries of Medicare must also pay an annual deductible and, in recent years, increasing copayments. About 90 percent of Medicare beneficiaries, such as Mr. Fox, now have supplemental insurance (**"medigap"**) coverage to help pay for additional health care costs, especially for the catastrophic costs of intensive care, numerous tests, or extended hospitalization. However, the purchase of such private coverage is not a solution to health costs. Instead, it means that the average spending on health care has increased. Since the majority of older people pay fully for this insurance, they effectively still bear the burden of health care costs (Brown, 2001).

Medicare's major limitation is its focus on acute care (e.g., inpatient hospital and physicians), as shown in Figure 17.3, and lack of coverage for chronic care expenses (e.g., nursing homes, preventive health measures, mental health services, and social support services). Instead, the majority of Medicare dollars pay for hospital care, typically for catastrophic illness and increasingly for home care. Nursing home care is restricted to 100 days of skilled nursing care or skilled rehabilitation services, with eligibility contingent on acute illness or injury after hospitalization and requiring co-payments. This automatically excludes ongoing care for chronic conditions. As a result, Medicare covers 45 percent of all health care spending for older people overall, but less for the oldest-old who require more nursing home care. In fact, less than 29 percent of the total Medicare budget covers nursing home expenditures. Accordingly, Medicare covers

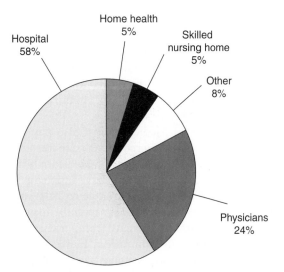

FIGURE 17.3 Medicare Personal Health Care Spending in 1998
SOURCE: Urban Institute, 2001.

the long-term care expenses of only 3 to 5 percent of the institutionalized older population. In a 2001 AARP survey, most respondents underestimated nursing home care costs, and over 33 percent mistakenly believed that Medicare covered long-term care expenses (Barrett and Roper, 2001). Believing that Medicare pays for long-term care, some older adults become aware of its lack of protection only upon their first hospitalization or admission to a nursing home (Berenson and Horvath, 2003).

Home Health Care under Medicare

A past gap in Medicare funding had been home- and community-based care, but now this is the most rapidly growing Medicare benefit (as shown in Figure 17.4) and the fastest-growing component of the United States health care sector. With over 20 percent of nursing home placements estimated to be incongruent with older persons' needs, home care is widely advocated as the lower-cost preferred alternative to inappropriate institutionalization. Even those in nursing homes or hospitals may require home care at some point, since 50 percent of those elders who stay less than 3 months are able to return to live in the community (Kane and Kane, 2001). As described in Chapter 11, home care permits earlier discharge, reduces the number of days of hospital care, and thus can cut costs. Whether home care is cost-effective varies with the person's condition and the range and duration of services. Not only do most older people require home care, but they also prefer it and tend to recover faster at home, when there is continuity of care (Kane and Kane, 2001; Stone 2000). Medicare over time has responded to the need for home care, and can now provide unlimited home health care for accredited provider agencies, but only under specific restricted conditions, as noted in the box on the next page. If these criteria are met, Medicare will fund the cost of other services, including home health aides and medical equipment and supplies. But any personal assistance must be directly re-

---

ELIGIBILITY FOR MEDICARE-REIMBURSED HOME CARE

- Older person must be homebound.
- Person must be capable of improvement.
- Person must require short-term intermittent nursing care, physical, occupational, or speech therapy.
- All services and durable medical equipment must be prescribed by a physician, who presents a plan for recovery and certifies that skilled services are medically necessary.

lated to the medical treatment of an illness or injury (Berenson and Horvath, 2002).

Given the preference for home care, it is not surprising that the number of beneficiaries and the average number of visits per user have grown dramatically; almost one in ten Medicare beneficiaries have a home health visit during a given year. This translates into Medicare financing almost 35 percent of home care compared with funding by state and local sources, including Medicaid (17%) and out-of-pocket (21%) (Figure 17.4). Home health care services are available for as long as beneficiaries remain eligible, without any burden of co-payments or deductibles.

Home care services are delivered by over 11,000 agencies nationwide, many of which are dually certified to serve the needs of both Medicare and Medicaid. The field, however, has shifted from primarily Visiting Nurses Associations and public agencies to hospital-based and private for-profit or nonprofit agencies. The data suggest that Medicare beneficiaries are using home health for longer periods and less medically intensive services (e.g., more long-term, unskilled personal care by home health aides) for a recovery period after hospital discharge. This has translated into home health aide visits that are lucrative for the agencies; this is because less skilled care is still highly compensated. Whether this shift indicates better coverage of chronic disabilities for older persons requiring unskilled care after early dis-

charge or greater provision of more discretionary services is unclear. It appears that incentives for agencies to spend as little as possible could place at greatest risk the patients who need the most skilled care (Feder et al., 2001). The checklist on page 634 summarizes factors that families should consider in selecting home health care services.

A number of factors underlie the extraordinary growth in Medicare-funded *home care services:*

1. Earlier hospital discharges as a result of the 1983 Prospective Payment Systems mean that patients require more technical care at home. Home care serves as the "safety net" for patients being discharged from acute and rehabilitation institutional settings after shorter lengths of stay (Federal Interagency Forum, 2000).

2. A 1989 class action lawsuit created a more flexible interpretation of definitions (homebound), scope of services (both management and evaluation), regulations (part-time or intermittent

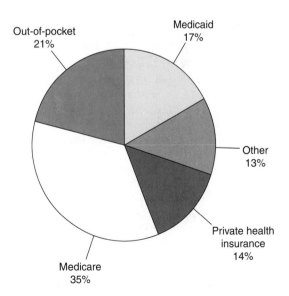

FIGURE 17.4 **Spending for Home Health Care 1998**

SOURCE: Urban Institute, 2001.

care) and skilled nursing judgment, not just skilled nursing care. In addition, some home health care remains a brief recovery "subacute" service, usually after a hospital stay. Medicare-funded home health benefits thus serve a dual purpose: caring for both the short- and long-term needs of beneficiaries (Moon, 1996).

3. The number of **proprietary** or for-profit home health agencies that are reimbursed under Medicare has increased dramatically. For-profit chains grew in response to the 1980 and 1981 Omnibus Budget Reconciliation Acts. These eliminated the requirement for state licensing as a basis for reimbursing proprietary agencies. These regulatory changes served to stimulate competition for the provision and contracting out of services to new proprietary agencies, including managed care. Such agencies, however, are less likely to concentrate on the ambulatory care of older people after hospital discharge.

4. There are isolated instances of Medicare–home health agencies not complying with federal health and safety standards, overcharging, fraud and abuse, and providing substandard care.

CHECKLIST FOR CHOOSING HOME HEALTH CARE SERVICES

- Is the agency licensed, accredited and certified to give home health care?
- Is the agency Medicare certified/approved?
- Does it have a written statement about its services, eligibility, costs, and payment procedures?
- Are homemakers and home health aides trained? For how long? By whom?
- How are employees supervised?
- Will the same person provide care on a regular basis?
- What are the hourly fees? Minimum hours required?
- How does the agency handle theft and other unacceptable behaviors?
- Will you be given a copy of the treatment/service plan?
- Does the agency have a Bill of Rights for patients?

THE COST OF PRIVATE CARE

Mrs. R., age 87, suffers from severe osteoporosis and arthritis. Although she worries about falling, she wants to stay in her home as long as possible. Since she is not eligible for any publicly funded home care program, she must pay out of pocket for daily assistance with bathing, walking, and cooking. Her daughter is employed and has a family to care for, but tries to stay with her mother on weekends and assist her with the household chores. Because the cost of home care is so much greater than her income, Mrs. R.'s savings are dwindling. She and her daughter worry that she will have to go into a nursing home as a Medicaid patient as the only way to fund her care.

---

5. High-tech home therapy, such as intravenous antibiotics, oncology therapy, and pain management, continues to grow. Such care involves expensive pharmaceuticals and equipment that require special staff expertise to use and monitor, and is costly to the patient or insurer.

The number of for-profit home health corporations that serve primarily private-pay and contract patients is also growing. They fill the demand for home care by patients who do not qualify for Medicare or Medicaid, and offer more services than Medicare-certified agencies. In contrast to the intermittent skilled visits of Medicare home care agencies, noncertified private agencies typically provide 24-hour daily care for an indefinite period, as well as specialty services. They also offer homemaker/home health aide care services, typically on an on-call basis. As with all long-term care services, there are problems of recruiting and retaining quality part-time contractual staff. A dilemma for families, however, is that many private agencies, especially those affiliated with large nationwide chains, require a minimum number of hours of care, which can become prohibitively expensive.

The 1997 Federal Balanced Budget Amendment cut funding for home health care, which

SUMMARY OF COMPONENTS OF MEDICARE

Hospital Insurance (Part A)

- Covers 99 percent of the older population.
- Financed through the Social Security payroll tax of 2.9 percent.
- Available for all older persons who are eligible for Social Security.
- Pays up to 90 days of hospital care and for a restricted amount of skilled nursing care, rehabilitation, home health services (if skilled care is needed), and hospice care.
- Recipients are responsible for their first day's hospital stay and for copayments for hospital stays exceeding 60 days.
- When the 90 days of hospital care are used up, a patient has a "lifetime reserve" of 60 days.

Supplemental Medical Insurance (Part B)

- Covers 97 percent of the older population.
- Financed through a combination of monthly premiums and general tax revenues.
- Annual $100 deductible.
- Generally pays 80 percent of physician and hospital outpatient services; home health care limited to certain types of health conditions and specific time periods; diagnostic laboratory and X-ray services, and a variety of miscellaneous services, including 50 percent of the approved amount for outpatient mental health care.

resulted in a 2-year temporary slowdown. Expanded funding in 1999–2000 reversed this. As a result, Medicare expenditures have continued to increase.

Medicare currently forms over 12 percent of the federal budget, the fourth largest expenditure following Social Security, defense, and interest on the national debt. Total Medicare spending is projected to grow by 10 percent per year over the next decade, just to provide the same level of services for a growing Medicare population (GAO, 2001). The Trustees of the Hospital Insurance Trust Fund continue to warn Congress of the need to restore the balance between income and spending in order to reduce insolvency, which is

projected to occur in 2025 (Schoen and Cooper, 2003). The threats to the trust fund are due, in part, to the fact that the number of workers paying taxes relative to the number of beneficiaries is decreasing as the population continues to age (i.e., the age-dependency ratio discussed in Chapters 1 and 16). This projected shortfall could be addressed if the combined payroll tax on employers and employees were raised from 2.9 percent to 4.11 percent (Almanac of Policy Issues, 2003). Other initiatives to cut Medicare costs, including the 1997 Balanced Budget Act, are described next.

Efforts to Reduce Medicare Costs

A number of measures attempt to reduce costs under Medicare, as follows:

1. A **prospective-payment system (PPS)** was instituted in 1983 to reduce incentives for physicians to provide more hospital-bed services under fee-for-service payment plans. Instead of reimbursing providers for each service for each patient, the Health Care Financing Administration (HCFA) (now known as the Centers for Medicare and Medicaid Services) determines payment by the diagnostic category in which each patient is placed. These categories, which classify patients by medical condition and thus establish fixed Medicare payments prior to admission, are called **diagnostic related groupings, or DRGs.** The rates for DRGs are based on the diagnosis and expected length of stay for each condition. A hospital that keeps patients longer than needed or orders unnecessary tests must absorb the differential in cost between the care provided and the amount reimbursed by Medicare. Alternatively, hospitals that provide care at a cost below the established DRG can keep the financial difference. This serves as an incentive for hospitals to release patients as soon as possible. In effect, DRGs were an early form of managed care, designed to curb skyrocketing costs (Abramson, 1998). Although findings are mixed, both lengths of stay per hospital admission and number of admissions appear to have fallen under

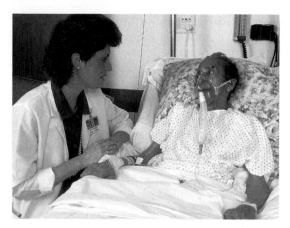

Medicare reform seeks to reduce the spiraling costs of hospitalization.

PPS and DRGs. This is partially explained by the trend toward performing simple surgical and diagnostic procedures on an outpatient rather than an inpatient basis, usually in ambulatory settings and doctors' offices. Early studies found patients being discharged on average 2 days earlier and sicker than before DRGs; these premature discharges resulted in a "revolving door pattern of more patients in and out of hospitals" (Gaumer et al., 1989; Sager et al., 1989). Later studies suggest that findings of greater need for care and higher rates of mortality may be due, in part, to differences in risk factors (e.g, the inpatient population is now older and sicker than before the PPS), not because of shorter stays or declining quality of care. Nevertheless, quality of care as a whole appears to be affected by earlier hospital discharge and restrictions on physician payment levels (Moon, 1996), as illustrated by the experience of Mr. Jones in the box at right. This is partly because DRGs discourage the extra time required to make appropriate discharge plans and the use of ancillary personnel such as social workers, except to expedite hospital discharges (Olson, 2003).

2. Congress passed the *Medicare Catastrophic Health Care Act* (MCHCA) in 1988 to reduce costs. Expanded benefits were to be financed by a mandatory supplemental premium.

This surtax affected approximately 40 percent of older adults, specifically those with incomes over $30,000 or couples with incomes over $50,000 a year. Many older adults organized rapidly against changes in the basic premise of Medicare financing—that higher-income older adults would pay a surtax for benefits serving primarily low-income elders. In 1989, Congress voted to repeal the legislation, leaving many legislators wary of making changes in Medicare until the prescription drug bill, discussed on page 639.

3. In 1992, a physician payment reform was implemented to limit Medicare spending on physician care. This established a physician fee schedule and a system of limiting payment increases when the total cost of physician services billed in a year exceeds estimated levels. The physician payment reform program also limits the amount doctors can charge above the approved Medicare rate.

4. In an effort to maintain the solvency of Medicare, the 1997 Federal Balanced Budget Agreement cut $115 billion in Medicare payments to doctors, hospitals, and HMOs, the largest reduction in the program's history. It also aimed to limit escalating home health care costs and ser-

---

THE COSTS OF EARLY DISCHARGE

Mr. Jones underwent major surgery—a radical prostatectomy for prostate cancer. Despite the pain that he was still experiencing, he was discharged after 3 days in the hospital and had to return home with a catheter in place that required careful monitoring by a physician or nurse. His wife was in her late 80s and unable to provide the skilled care that a catheter requires. He was extremely fatigued. With only his frail wife to care for him, he required the services of a visiting nurse. He continued to experience considerable pain for which his medication was inadequate; if he could have remained in the hospital, his pain could have been relieved by an anesthesiologist. Perhaps the most difficult issue was his uncertainty and anxiety about a variety of symptoms, such as loss of appetite, which could have been resolved with a somewhat longer hospital stay.

MEDICARE PAYS ONLY PARTIAL HEALTH CARE COSTS

Mr. Fox went to his physician for a sigmoidoscopy, a procedure to examine the large colon for polyps or cancer. His physician charges $300 for this procedure. Medicare determined that the going rate for the procedure in Mr. Fox's community is $180, which means that Medicare pays the physician 80 percent of that amount, or $144. If Mr. Fox's physician accepts the assignment, then Mr. Fox owes his doctor the difference between $180 and $144, or $36. Fortunately, Mr. Fox has private "medigap" insurance that covers this difference. If Mr. Fox's physician had not accepted assignment, then Mr. Fox would have been responsible for paying $300 less the amount paid by Medicare ($144) or a total of $156.

---

vices. The **Centers for Medicare and Medicaid Services (CMS)** (known as the Health Care Financing Administration prior to July 1, 2001), the federal agency that approves or denies Medicare claims, froze the licensing of new home health agencies. Another major approach to curbing health care costs was to implement new payment methods for postacute (after hospitalization) services, which substantially changed Medicare's payment for home health care. Instead of separate payments for each visit, Medicare adopted the *prospective payment system* (PPS), with fixed limited payments in advance for a general course of treatment. It operates in a manner similar to the DRG system in hospitals; home care agencies and nursing homes are reimbursed at a capitated rate per patient per episode of service. Another iteration of PPS is the *interim payment system (IPS),* which sets limits on the number of visits by home health agencies. Even though the regulations were not issued until 1998, the new IPS rates were applied retroactively to all payments after October 1, 1997. In addition, home health agencies were restricted to historical cost patterns since 1994, even if their current costs are higher.

As a result, many home health agencies, which had expanded under Medicare funding of

the early 1990s, closed and patients were dropped from care. Preliminary analysis of the IPS found it caused reductions to the overall proportion of Medicare beneficiaries who received the service; the number of home health visits per beneficiary; the average length of home health care; and—as intended—overall Medicare expenditures (McCall and Korb, 2003). Despite the dramatic reductions in home care service use, IPS does not appear to have resulted in an increase in adverse outcomes following hospital discharge.

5. The National Bipartisan Commission on the Future of Medicare was created by Congress in 1998 to study how Medicare can accommodate baby boomers in this century. Some of the commission's recommendations were controversial, including giving beneficiaries a fixed amount of money to purchase private health insurance and to raise the age of Medicare eligibility from 65 to 67. Unable to achieve sufficient unity to forward official recommendations to Congress, the commission was disbanded in 1999.

6. Because of the 1997 cuts in funding, Medicare expenses declined in 1999. In response, a massive lobbying campaign to restore and expand funding was mounted by national associations of nurses, physicians, nursing home operators, hospitals, managed care organizations, and the home care industry; these providers threatened reduced access to services, especially for older adults most in need of services, if Medicare funding was not restored to address the 1997 cuts. As a result of this intensive lobbing effort, Congress restored billions of dollars to various providers in 1999 and 2000.

As a result, Medicare expenditures continue to grow, albeit at a slower rate than might have occurred otherwise. This growth is partially because the prospective payment system has not altered Medicare's basic approach or the structural arrangements that depend upon fee-for-service financing. Nor have DRGs reduced all the incentives for applying costly technologically oriented care. In fact, there has been an increase in the use of specialists and improved procedures such as hip replacement and cataract surgery that result in higher utilization rates.

As noted earlier, with earlier hospital discharges and more medical procedures performed on an outpatient basis, families and home health agencies were not prepared to provide complex, intensive levels of care required after these procedures. Nursing homes were also affected by the PPS and DRGs. For example, nursing homes shifted to provide **subacute care,** which are intensive coordinated services to minimize or avoid hospital stays. Such services, such as rehabilitation, fell between acute hospital care and skilled nursing care.

The 2000 presidential and congressional elections set the tone, temperament, and direction of budget, tax and entitlement politics in the future, and especially in the fiscal years 2002 through 2004. Not surprisingly, Republicans and Democrats differ on the nature and size of cuts in Medicare, although both agree on the need for reforms. Republicans advocate increased application of market principles to the health care market, more HMOs, additional managed care, increased privatization, and more coverage choices. These values are reflected in the Medicare prescription drug bill, passed in late 2003 and designed to be implemented in 2006. It is discussed on page 639 and represents a shift toward privatization of Medicare.

The New Medicare

The Federal Balanced Budget Act of 1997 also established **Medicare Plus Choice** with dual goals of cost-savings and quality of care. This allows Medicare to pay for a wider range of preventive services, including mammograms, PAP smears, cervical exams, prostate screening, bone density measurement procedures, diabetes screening and self-care, and enhancement of the vaccination program. The major change, however, is that beneficiaries have more choice in where and how they obtain health care. The choices available include:

STRATEGIES TO REDUCE MEDICARE COSTS

- Limit eligibility for the next cohort of Medicare recipients by increasing the age of eligibility to 67.
- Bill enrollees $5 for home health visits.
- Ration services by age.
- Use an income test as a basis for eligibility.
- Increase the combined payroll tax from 2.9 to 4.11 percent.
- Increase coinsurance and deductibles to shift more financial risk onto the beneficiaries.
- Increase Supplemental Medical Insurance premiums (Part B) for higher-income beneficiaries.
- Reduce the coverage of services and the reimbursement given to providers.

---

1. Medicare **Health Maintenance Organizations/Preferred Provider Organizations (HMOs/PPOs):** Networks of independent hospitals, physicians, and other health care providers who contract with an insurance entity to provide care at discount rates. Medicare beneficiaries who join HMOs are given incentives to use the HMO/PPO physicians, but also may use providers outside the network at higher out-of-pocket costs. (See page 652 for more descriptions of Medicare HMOs.)

2. Purchase of *private insurance plans,* including long-term care insurance (see page 648 for a discussion of such insurance).

3. Establishment of **medical savings accounts,** which allow beneficiaries to put Medicare dollars into a tax-exempt account to pay for qualified medical expenses.

The medical savings account is combined with a high-deductible insurance policy to cover catastrophic injuries or illness. Advocates of these accounts believe that older adults will become more cost-conscious by their deciding, not their insurers, where to seek care. Critics fear that only the wealthier and healthier older adults can afford such a plan. With all the options under Medicare Choice, Medicare begins to look more like a private health care system than a publicly funded base of services for all older adults. About 14 percent of

Medicare beneficiaries initially enrolled in managed care plans (Barry and Kline, 2002). Of even greater concern, however, is the number of managed care plans that have left Medicare, severely reduced their service areas, or cut benefits, which adversely affected coverage for thousands of Medicare beneficiaries. As a result, those still enrolled have faced higher out-of-pocket costs (an average increase of 10 percent in 2003) (Cardin, 2003; Gold and Achman, 2002). In general, Medicare Plus Choice programs need to be more effective at reducing the costs of care to ensure that beneficiaries can have access to their more comprehensive services.

Other strategies to reduce Medicare costs continue to be debated at the national level, as illustrated in the box above. Contrary to these proposed changes, the majority of Americans agree that the federal government has a basic responsibility to guarantee adequate health care for older people and oppose cost-cutting. It is also noteworthy that while Medicare is the current focus of many cost-cutting debates, costs remain below those of private insurers on a per capita basis. One major reason for this is that Medicare is administratively more efficient (less than 2 percent on overhead) than most private insurers or HMOs (average of 15 percent on overhead) (Schoen and Cooper, 2003).

Medicare Reform and Prescription Drug Coverage

The most dramatic and controversial change since Medicare's passage is the prescription drug bill passed by Congress in November 2003, after the longest roll call vote in the House chamber's history. What is not disputed is the need for prescription drug coverage for older adults, which has long been identified by both Democrats and Republicans. Adults over age 65 account for over 40 percent of total spending on medications, and consistently spend more out of pocket (approximately 50 percent of all their out-of-pocket expenditures) on prescription drugs than younger adults. In fact, Medicare beneficiaries spend more, on average,

out of pocket each year on prescription drugs than on physician care, vision services, and medical supplies combined. About 40 percent of Medicare beneficiaries lack prescription drug coverage at some point each year, most for the entire year (Gross, 2002; Xu, 2003). The lack of prescription drug coverage under Medicare is a historical accident. When Medicare was enacted in 1965, drugs were less numerous and not a central part of medical treatment. Now, prescription drugs are often the primary means of treatment.

The burden of drug costs falls hardest on older women, those over age 80, those without a high school education, and those in poor health or with limitations in more than three ADL (Sambamoorthi, Shea, and Crystal, 2003). Even states with pharmacy assistance programs fall far short of closing the gap for low-income older adults. Medicare beneficiaries without drug coverage and who are in poor health average 27 prescriptions a year, while those with coverage average 42 per year. This means that elders without coverage go without needed medicine at twice the rate of those with coverage (Kaiser Family Foundation, 2002; Poisal and Murray, 2001). Those without drug coverage have been found to restrict their medications because of cost; they may skip filling prescriptions, split drug amounts (e.g., breaking pills in half), eliminate doses, or use physician samples, all of which can have adverse health outcomes and, over time, increase health care costs (Adams, Soumerai, and Ross-Degnan, 2001; Kaiser Family Foundation, 2002; Steinman, Sands, and Covinsky, 2001; Voelker, 2001). Medicare beneficiaries in 2003 are estimated, on average, to have spent $2,317 on drugs. In addition, the price of the most commonly used drugs tends to increase by three times the rate of inflation and is expected to grow by 12 percent a year through 2011 (Families USA, 2002; Gross, 2002; McCloskey, 2002).

Because there have not been restrictions on drug prices in the United States, the profit margins for drug companies surpass those of nearly every economic sector. Drug company lobbyists argue that such costs are necessary to cover research and testing of new, high-risk drugs. Admittedly, the research to produce new drugs is expensive and may yield only one or two FDA-approved drugs out of years of testing. On the other hand, critics argue what good is research and new drugs if no one can afford them? They maintain that too many dollars are spent on marketing and advertising drugs. Such costs and lack of coverage were hot issues in the 2000 presidential campaign, and the debate regarding ways to provide coverage has been long-running.

What was disputed in congressional debate over the prescription drug bill and among older adults and their advocates was government's responsibility to promote human welfare versus increased privatization, and whether entitlement to government support should be age based (e.g., universal) or needs based (e.g., means tested). A central issue being tested is whether private health care plans can deliver better care at lower cost than the traditional Medicare program that was created almost 40 years ago. The primary components of the legislation, which will go into effect in 2006, are:

- The premium for the optional prescription benefit will be $35 a month; the Medicare beneficiary would be responsible for the first $250 of drug costs, and insurance would then cover 75 percent of drug costs up to $ 2,250. Although payment of the monthly premium would continue, coverage would then stop until the beneficiary had spent $3,600 out of pocket, or about $5,100 total cost. Above $5,100, catastrophic coverage through the prescription benefit will cover 95 percent of the cost. The average drug bill is projected to be $3,160 in 2006; the standard plan would cover one-third of this bill. Medicare beneficiaries may choose not to participate in this prescription plan.

Who benefits the most from the new law?

- Low-income elders earning less than $12,123 a year and with less than $6,000 in liquid as-

sets; the premium, deductible, and coverage gap will be waived. These subsidies would end when a beneficiary has more than $13,470 in annual income.
- Elders who join a private managed care plan, which covers drugs along with doctor's services and hospital care. The government will heavily subsidize such private plans. Or a Medicare beneficiary could stay in traditional Medicare and get drug coverage by signing up and paying for a stand-alone drug insurance policy.
- Private health care companies, which will have incentives of billions of dollars to return to the Medicare HMO market.
- Affluent elders who will be the most likely to buy low-cost, high-deductible health insurance policies and then shelter income from taxes by putting money into private tax-free health savings accounts. The investment will be tax deductible and earnings can be withdrawn tax-free as long as the money is used for health expenses, and can be passed on to a surviving spouse. Such health savings accounts are expected to cost the U.S. Treasury $6.4 billion over 10 years (Crenshaw, 2003).
- More affluent elders would not benefit in other ways from the prescription drug plan, but would typically be able to absorb the additional costs. For the first time in Medicare's history, beneficiaries with incomes of more than $80,000 a year would have to pay higher premiums for the part of Medicare that covers doctors' care. The size of their premium would increase on a sliding scale, topping out at 80 percent for people with incomes greater than $200,000.
- Drug companies that will be able to maximize profits, since the government cannot negotiate lower drug prices. This means that the problem of the high cost of medications will continue.
- Employers who currently offer health care plans to their retirees will receive tens of billions of dollars in subsidies to encourage them to continue providing drug coverage to retirees.

- Doctors and hospitals that will receive increased Medicare payments.
- Elders with the resources to enroll in private plans will receive preventive health care through a comprehensive medical examination for new beneficiaries, screening exams for heart disease and diabetes, and coordinated care for those with chronic illnesses.

Arguments against this bill included:

- Using income levels to determine access to Medicare benefits is counter to the idea that all beneficiaries earn access by virtue of paying Social Security and Medicare taxes throughout their working years. This bill thus undermines Medicare's universal nature.
- It further privatizes Medicare, therefore eroding its universal and entitlement nature. For example, private health plans through HMOs will receive $12 billion in subsidies over ten years to encourage them to compete with Medicare. Private plans can change premiums and benefits after elders are enrolled.
- The gap in coverage between $2250 and $5100 (referred to as the "donut") plus the deductible and the monthly payment may make a plan too expensive or not cost-effective for many older adults. This gap means that some beneficiaries will be paying their $35 monthly premium while receiving no help until after they have incurred $3600 in drug costs. Only a small proportion of older people, however, are likely to require catastrophic care above $5100. In addition, older adults will not be able to purchase "medigap" policies to supplement these private plans in covering drug costs above $3600.
- Employers who currently provide health insurance to their retirees and employees over age 65 may drop coverage as a way to save money, "pushing" employees to depend solely on Medicare. In fact, the Congressional Budget Office estimates that 23 percent of employees now receiving drug benefits from their

employers will lose those benefits after the Medicare drug program is instituted in 2006.
- More than six million elders will lose the drug coverage they now have under Medicaid; they may have to pay higher co-payments or lose access to particular drugs not covered under Medicare. Some advocates for the poor maintain that low-income elders will actually have less drug coverage than is now available through Medicaid.
- The law restricts the importing of less expensive, more readily available prescription drugs from Canada and Mexico, which have been important sources for drugs for older adults.
- The government will be prohibited from using the size of the Medicare program as leverage to negotiate lower drug prices or discounts from drug companies, as it has done in the past (Chaddock, 2003; NCPSSM, 2003; Pear, 2003; Goldstein and Dewar, 2003; Zitner, 2003).
- The cost of implementation will be higher than initially projected.

One of the most controversial and highly visible conflicts revolved around AARP's support of the bill, which did not reflect the will of 65 percent of its members, who said they opposed the bill. By contrast, the AFL-CIO, with 13 million members, opposed the bill for its "skimpy drug coverage." Critics of the bill accused AARP, which sells insurance and prescription drugs and

---

WAYS TO DETERMINE COST SAVINGS

If you have an older relative wondering what the new legislation means for him or her, encourage the elder to determine their costs savings by using a calculator at the Kaiser Family Foundation Website: www.kff.org/medicare/rxdrugscalculator.cfm. This will help your older relative make a better-informed decision about whether to purchase one of the plans and pay a monthly premium or take the chance that his or her prescription drug bills will be under $420 a year.

receives a commission from corporations for these sales, of selling out to pharmaceutical companies, HMOs, and Republican lawmakers. In response, 85 members of Congress canceled their AARP membership and thousands of AARP members burned their membership cards and jammed the association's phone lines protesting AARP's support of the bill. AARP justified its support by acknowledging that the bill was not perfect, but better than what now exists. They also cited polls and focus groups with baby boomers, who are accustomed to employer-sponsored private health care, and indicated that they favored experimentation with private competition with Medicare. In fact, AARP's president stated "We had to change. We had the boomers coming and you didn't want to be perceived by the boomers as just being for old people" (Stolberg and Freudenheim, 2003). As discussed in Chapter 12, AARP is increasingly seeking ways to appeal to younger members. Whether there will be a backlash among its older members, especially those who lose their current employer-sponsored health and prescription drug coverage, will probably not become apparent until after the bill's implementation in 2006. Public opinion polls immediately after President Bush signed the bill into law indicated both Republican and Democrats' lack of support for the bill and the projected cost of the coverage has escalated from original estimates. Grassroots groups, such as America's Health Care Voice, are mobilizing to amend the new law to allow Medicare to negotiate drug discounts and to legalize the purchase of drugs from Canada. Such issues also surfaced in the 2004 presidential election campaign.

Medicaid

In contrast to Medicare, **Medicaid** is not a health insurance program specifically for older people, but rather a federal and state means-tested welfare program of medical assistance for the poor, re-

gardless of age (e.g., to recipients of Aid to Families with Dependent Children and Supplemental Security Income). Unlike Medicare, it covers long-term care but only for the poor or those who become poor by paying for long-term or medical care. Medicaid also differs from Medicare in that federal funds are administered by each state. As such, it is the major public program covering long-term care for older adults and for people with disabilities of all ages, as illustrated in Figure 17.5. However, the greatest proportion of Medicaid spending for long-term care, 75 percent, is for nursing home care. Ironically, when Medicaid was enacted, it was never intended to be a major payer of long-term care, especially nursing home care. Medicaid plays three essential roles related to long-term care for older adults:

1. Makes Medicare affordable for low-income beneficiaries by paying Medicare's premiums,

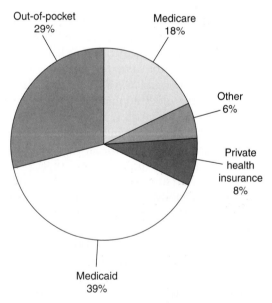

FIGURE 17.5   Sources of Long-Term Financing in 1998
SOURCE: Urban Institute, 2001.

deductibles, and other cost-sharing requirements ("dual eligibles").

2. Provides coverage of medical benefits that Medicare does not cover, such as prescription drugs and long-term care.

3. Stands alone as the only public source of financial assistance for long-term care in both institutional and community settings (Lyons and Rowland, 1996).

Older persons comprise a small percentage (approximately 12 percent) of the total users of Medicaid, yet they account for approximately 75 percent of the total expenditures nationally. The primary cause of this disproportionate rate of expenditures is that Medicaid is the primary public funding source of long-term care; institutional care dominates long-term care spending under Medicaid, with only 25 percent for in-home and community services. Nursing home expenditures, which are the fastest-growing category of Medicaid costs, are increasing at an average annual rate of 10 percent, with the average expenditure per Medicaid-funded nursing home resident at $73,000. Despite Medicaid as the primary funder of nursing home care, about 29.5 percent of nursing home care is still paid by individuals out of pocket (Barrett and Roper, 2001; Burwell, 2001; Feder et al., 2001; GAO, 2001a; NCPSSM, 2003; U.S. Senate Special Committee on Aging, 2001).

Federal regulations require that all state Medicaid programs provide the following: hospital inpatient care, physician services, skilled nursing facility care, laboratory and X-ray services, home health services, hospital outpatient care, family planning, rural health clinics, and early and periodic screening. In contrast to Medicare, home health care services are a mandatory area of coverage for Medicaid, while personal-care services and home and community-based services are optional. Although Medicare covers only skilled nursing care for patients with rehabilitative potential in nursing homes, Medicaid can cover both skilled care for rehabilitation

and intermediate nursing home care of a more custodial nature.

Although states are the major financiers of Medicaid long-term care, they vary widely in their eligibility standards; the types, amount, scope, and duration of services; and reimbursement rates. For example, states may elect to provide coverage for personal care services but are not required to do so. States differ greatly in the provision of "optional" services, such as intermediate care, prescription drugs outside the hospital, dental services, eyeglasses, and physical therapy. Similar to Medicare, coverage for mental health and social services is limited. Because of such limitations, Medicaid, like Medicare, provides only 60 to 80 percent of daily care charges. In a majority of states, Medicaid expenditures for older adults account for nearly 60 percent of the Medicaid budget (NCPSSM, 2003). As with Medicare, the growth in expenditures is due primarily to price increases by health providers and fragmented funding mechanisms, not population growth per se or expansion of care.

Older adults may qualify for Medicaid in the following ways:

1. Participation in Supplemental Security Income (SSI), which encompasses the provision of Medicaid. Although Medicaid is the principal health insurance provided for the poor and

---

POINTS TO PONDER

What is your position on Medicaid "spend down"? Do you think that it unjustly impoverishes older people and their families needing nursing home care? Or do you think that those with assets find ways to protect them and still get Medicaid to cover the cost of nursing home care? Reflect on family members or others you know who have used the Medicaid spend down to access nursing home care. What were some of their experiences?

LONG-TERM CARE OMBUDSMAN

The most successful approach to monitoring quality in nursing homes is the long-term care ombudsman. An ombudsman office in each state develops non-regulatory approaches to monitoring care in nursing homes. Their influence is constrained, however, by limited funding and reliance on volunteers.

is viewed as a "safety net program," only 33 percent of low-income elders meet these stringent categorical eligibility requirements. Those who do qualify for cash assistance under SSI are provided the broadest coverage under state Medicaid programs, including payment of Medicare cost sharing, premiums, and additional services, such as prescription drug, vision care, and dental care coverage.

2. Designated as "medically needy" under state-specific rules (e.g., ineligible for cash assistance but are in economic distress after paying medical expenses). Older adults who are "medically needy" are allowed to exclude their medical and long-term care expenses from income in determining whether they meet specific income limits, and may "**spend down**" by incurring medical bills that reduce their income and other resources to the necessary level. These income levels are established by each state and therefore differ.

3. Nursing home residents with income and assets below a state-designated cap. Depletion of almost all personal assets may occur prior to nursing home admission, but most often occurs as a result of nursing home costs. Of those who do not have Medicaid at the time of admission to a long-term care facility, 66 percent spend down their savings to Medicaid levels. Nursing home residents must contribute all of their income except a small personal-needs allowance toward cost of their nursing home care. On any given day, 60 to 70 percent of nursing home residents have Medicaid as a payment source (Grogan and Patashnik, 2003).

4. **Dual eligibility:** being eligible for both Medicare and Medicaid; typically, those whose income falls 100 percent below the poverty guidelines and have limited financial assets. These beneficiaries are often very ill, less likely to have a spouse or any living children, and more likely to live in a nursing home. Known as qualified Medicaid beneficiaries (QMB) or specified low-income Medicaid beneficiaries (SLMB), they get help from Medicaid to cover Medicare's co-payments and deductibles (e.g., out of pocket expenses) and their monthly premium for physician and outpatient coverage. In other words, even though they have too many financial resources to be eligible for full Medicaid benefits, Medicaid pays for what Medicare does not cover (Feder et al., 2001).

Medicaid-Funded Nursing Home Care

As noted above, Medicaid has been biased toward institutional care, because it covers about 50 percent of what is annually spent on nursing home care in all states (Bishop, 2003; Grogan and Patashnik, 2003). Since the federal government has reduced Medicaid funding to the states, states have focused on limiting their Medicaid expenditures (Wiener, Stevenson, and Kasten, 2000). Because states are required to pay for every Medicaid-eligible person residing in a nursing home, one of the earliest approaches was to control the supply of available openings. A majority of states in the late 1970s imposed certificate of need (CON) restrictions on additional Medicaid-certified beds and placed a moratorium on construction of new nursing home beds or facilities. This resulted in high occupancy rates, which inflated charges and bolstered nursing home profits. States also developed strict preadmission screening procedures and tightened the medical and functional eligibility requirements for nursing home admission to limit Medicaid beneficiaries' access to nursing homes. Other approaches have been to:

- set nursing home reimbursement rates (e.g., capitated payments), which lowered payments for Medicaid nursing home residents
- limit eligibility and utilization of benefits covered (e.g., eliminating prescription drug coverage);
- increase co-payments
- ration or limit services only to those that proved most cost-effective (Gregory and Gibson, 2002).

As a result, Medicaid recipients, especially those requiring high levels of care, often have more difficulty finding a nursing home bed—and wait longer to do so—than higher-paying private-pay clients. In fact, some nursing homes do not even accept Medicaid patients. This can be especially difficult for older adults who are discharged prematurely from hospitals. In addition, the mix of high occupancy rate and the comparatively low payment per bed tends to relegate Medicaid patients to the most substandard facilities; in fact, a relationship has been found between the residents' socioeconomic status and the quality of care received. Paradoxically, while nursing homes need Medicaid residents to survive, they decrease services, including staffing, in order to maintain a profit (GAO, 2202; Meyer and Storbakken, 2000).

Overall, benefit reductions fail to address rising nursing costs caused by provider price increases. In addition, efforts to control medical spending for nursing homes are difficult because of resistance by nursing home lobbyists. With the growth of the oldest-old who are most at risk for institutional care, but lack the resources to pay for it, Medicaid is faced with how to provide coverage for low-income and vulnerable populations at a time of intense pressure to limit public spending.

Medicaid-Funded Home Health Care

As noted earlier, only about 25 percent of Medicaid expenditures go to community-based home health services, even though home health services are more cost-effective (approximately $19,000 annually) and preferred by elders and their families (compared with about $73,000 annually for Medicaid-funded nursing home care) (Burwell, 2001). Given elders' preference for home and community-based care, Medicaid's bias toward institutional care is slowly shifting and funding for home and community-based services is expanding (Nauth, 2002; Redfoot and Panaya, 2002).

The *financing of home care services* under Medicaid occurs under three different coverage options:

1. Home health services, which are skilled services typically provided by a Medicaid-certified home health agency
2. Personal care services, which are semiskilled or unskilled services provided to Medicaid beneficiaries who need assistance with basic activities of daily living in their own home (typically provided by nonlicensed individuals, these constitute the majority of total spending of home care services under Medicaid)
3. Home and community-based waiver services

Eligibility for Medicaid Home Health Care

Older adults must:

- meet strict income/asset eligibility criteria
- be medically eligible for nursing home placement (e.g., placement is imminent)
- require more services than homemaker services

Home care must not cost more than nursing home care (i.e., be budget neutral)

The home and community-based waiver services were first authorized under the 1981 Omnibus Budget Reconciliation Act. This permits the waiver of Medicaid statutory requirements so that states can provide community-based options by targeting benefits to limited geographic areas

THE IMPACT OF STATE BUDGET CUTS ON LONG-TERM CARE SERVICES FOR LOW-INCOME OLDER ADULTS

- In Michigan, the state stopped taking applications from people who wanted in-home services. As participants in their home care service program died, new people were not added, reducing the numbers from 15,000 to 7,000 consumers statewide in 2003.
- In Colorado, new enrollment for a program that helps elders pay for home care services has been frozen.
- In California, home-delivered meals were cut off when the area agencies lacked the funds to pay food providers.
- In Arkansas, meal programs were reduced from 5 to 4 days.
- In Oregon, 9,000 people lost health benefits, including drug coverage, when the state eliminated its medically needy program under Medicaid. The state also tightened their eligibility criteria regarding extent of physical and mental incapacity to qualify for alternatives to nursing homes (Lieberman, 2003).

dren and young adults with mental or physical disabilities being the primary beneficiaries. Tremendous variability exists by state in the implementation of the waiver program. Some states, such as Oregon and Washington, have widely implemented waivers. Viewing nursing homes as the last resort, they have deliberately reduced the number of nursing home beds and have chosen to support in-home care, respite services, adult day care, and residential options such as assisted living, adult foster homes, and adult family homes. Several states have demonstration programs that improve the coordination of long-term care with the acute care system, as described on page 654 (Mollica, 2003). Other states augment or create their own separate home care programs with state funds; a few states fund through lottery revenues or county levies for long-term care. Nevertheless, most states spend long-term care funds on institutional facilities, largely because of the difficulty of surmounting federal eligibility restrictions. As a result, most state policy initiatives have a modest

and to specific groups and numbers of beneficiaries. The waiver program specifies seven core services that have not been traditionally considered "medical," but which allow people to remain at home—case management, homemaker, home health aide, personal care, adult day care, rehabilitation, respite care—and other services approved by the federal government as "cost-effective." The primary criterion is that states must demonstrate that the costs of such home and community-based services are less than care in institutions, and also that they serve to divert at-risk individuals from nursing home placement. Although nearly all the states have an array of waivers, the program's cost-containment goals mean that most states restrict the scope of services and the number of recipients (Branch, 2001).

In many states, there is a per diem cap on allowable services and long waiting lists, with chil-

Medicaid is the primary source of public funding for nursing home care.

impact on the allocation of resources between nursing homes and home and community-based care. In addition, older adults who have too many assets to qualify for Medicaid, but are unable to afford to purchase private home care, often lack access to home and community-based options (Kane and Kane, 2001; Olson, 2003).

Medicaid is a highly visible target for federal and state cost-cutting, because it forms a growing proportion of state budgets at the same time that federal funds allocated to states for Medicaid have declined. States attempt to limit expenditures in a wide variety of ways:

- limits on the supply of nursing home beds through certificate of need requirements for nursing homes and moratoria on construction of new nursing home beds or facilities
- preadmission screening and tightening the medical and functional eligibility requirements for nursing home admission, thereby limiting the number of people entering nursing homes
- unlinking Medicaid from welfare benefits and using managed-care models with **capitated payments** to control Medicaid expenditures
- reducing benefits covered (for example, eliminating coverage of prescription drugs), restricting eligibility and utilization, and increasing co-payments
- rationing or limiting services only to those proved most cost-effective

Medicaid Spend-Down

Another way to reduce Medicaid costs is to enforce current laws that make it more difficult to qualify. The 1993 Omnibus Budget Reconciliation legislation prohibited the sheltering of assets through trusts during the 5 years prior to an application for Medicaid benefits, and the transfer of assets during the 3 years prior to a Medicaid application. It also mandated estate recovery, forcing states to reclaim Medicaid costs from the estate or property of beneficiaries age 55 and over who lived in nursing homes or received home and community services. In addition, states could also consider jointly owned property, including homes and bank accounts, as part of the estate, recoverable after the death of the recipient or his or her spouse. However, most states have not enforced estate recovery laws and federal Medicaid officials are reluctant to impose penalties for noncompliance. This 1993 legislation, referred to as "Send Grandma to Jail," was extremely controversial; in 1997, the legal burden was shifted to the Medicaid estate planning industry.

There are ways, however, to shelter up to half of a nursing home resident's financial assets from the spend-down requirement even within the 3-year time period. An industry of Medicaid estate planners has developed to give relatively affluent older adults legal advice on how to establish trusts to preserve family estates without compromising Medicaid eligibility. Congress also passed measures to protect against spousal impoverishment, raising the amount of income the "community spouse" could keep, and retreated from plans that would enforce adult children's financial responsibility for their parents. It is apparent that through the Medicaid spend-down process, as well as the conversion and transfer of assets prior to a nursing home stay, a substantial portion of Medicaid outlays go to people from essentially middle-class backgrounds In fact, the media, politicians, and senior organizations increasingly frame Medicaid as a core social entitlement for all older adults. Yet Medicaid, unlike Medicare and Social Security, is not contributory. Program recipients do not have a legal or moral right to long-term care benefits on the basis of tax payments or a lifetime of employment (Grogan and Patashnik, 2003). Nevertheless, as long as nursing home costs and the cost of long-term care insurance continue to rise, this tension between Medicaid as an entitlement program for low-income elders and strategies that middle-income elders use to qualify for Medicaid is likely to continue.

Social Services Block Grants and the Older Americans Act (OAA)

In addition to the limited allocations of Medicare and Medicaid for community-based services, Title XX Amendments to the Social Security Act (Social Services Block Grants) and Title III of the Older Americans Act (OAA) provide some funding for nonmedical, custodial services for older people with disabilities.

As discussed in Chapter 16, most services to older persons under Title XX go to those who receive Supplemental Security Income, and are viewed as necessary to carry out basic ADLs. They include:

- homemaker and chore services
- home-delivered meals (Meals on Wheels)
- adult protective services
- adult day care
- foster care
- institutional or residential care

With federal reductions in block grant funding to the states, competition for decreasing funds at the local level has increased.

OAA services may be provided without the restrictions of Medicare and the means test of Medicaid, since the primary eligibility criterion is age 60 regardless of income. However, services must be targeted to persons with the greatest social or economic need and to frail older adults. Because of Medicaid cuts, some states are targeting their resources to only the most severely disabled.

Both Title XX and Title III are limited in their impact by the fact that funding has fallen behind inflation and by constraints on nonmedical services (e.g., homemaker, chore, and personal care). Despite the demand for aging network programs, the Administration on Aging (AOA) remains a relatively small federal government unit. Funding constraints through the Social Services Block Grant and the Older Americans Act, along with changes in Medicare and Medicaid, have reduced overall access to long-term care, especially for low-income women and elders of color. The general approach under both programs is to give a few services to as many people as possible, which does not necessarily reach the most vulnerable older persons nor remove inequities.

Private Long-Term Care Insurance

Although the U.S. health and long-term care system is based on the assumption that individuals are first responsible for paying for their care, 44 million Americans under age 65 lack insurance for hospital and physician costs. A substantially greater number—over 200 million—have no insurance for long-term care. Therefore, as noted earlier, about 30 percent of all long-term care expenditures are paid on an out-of-pocket basis (Feder et al., 2001). Those paying out of pocket use a combination of pension income, Social Security benefits, savings and investments, including reverse mortgages which allow them to tap the equity in their homes to pay for care.

Among the older population, wide disparities exist in terms of their ability to purchase private supplemental and **long-term care insurance.** For older adults who can afford more extensive coverage than Medicare, private **"medigap" supplemental insurance** is available to pay for protection that Medicare does not cover. As noted above, these basic gaps are:

1. Medicare deductible and co-payments
2. items and services not covered by Medicare (eye exams and hearing aids)
3. charges exceeding the amount approved by Medicare (in excess of Medicare's "allowable" or "reasonable" charges)

Despite the 1990 passage of the Medigap Fraud and Abuse Prevention Act, older people and their families need to be careful and explore options before purchasing Medicare supplemental insurance. About 75 percent of the older population has purchased some private supplemental insurance. Of these, about 50 percent were able to obtain coverage through their former place of employment (NCPSSM, 2003). This translates into unequal access to private health insurance for higher-income elders or those who have access through employment/unions. Eleven percent of Medicare's recipients have neither assistance from Medicaid nor supplemental health coverage to help pay for Medicare's coinsurance, deductibles, and uncovered services. Not surprisingly, this group is more likely to have low incomes and/or to be in poor health (Rowland, Feder, and Keenan, 1998). Of poor or near-poor older persons, who suffer from more chronic illness and disability, only 47 percent have private insurance, compared to 87 percent of their higher-income and healthier peers. Less than 18 percent of older persons of color have private coverage, compared to 48 percent of poor older whites. Furthermore, older women are less likely than men to have access to group health insurance through employment (Moen, 2001).

Even those who carry supplemental coverage can suffer burdensome medical expenses if they are seriously ill, since Medicare does not cover the full costs of care. Few "medigap" policies pick up physician charges in excess of Medicare's allowable fees, nor do they ordinarily cover prescriptions in full, dental care, or nursing home care—all services essential to the long-term well-being of the older population. In addition, most medigap policies lack inflation protection and initial premiums may be raised later (AARP, 2001; Mellor, 2000). Less than 6 percent of the expenditures for nursing home care and home and community-based services are paid by private insurance. Instead, nearly 45 percent of elders' health care expenditures are out of pocket; this rate increases even more for those in poor health, without Medicaid or supplemental insurance, and for low-income women who are not eligible for Medicaid (GAO, 2001c). This pattern means that many older adults admitted to nursing homes incur catastrophic financial expenses prior to admission.

As older adults become more aware of the limits of public funding, an increasing number of insurance companies are selling **private long-term care insurance plans.** Most policies are written to exclude people with certain conditions or illnesses and contain benefit restrictions that limit access to covered care. The period of coverage is usually only 4 or 5 years. The majority of policies pay a fixed amount for each qualified day in a nursing home (at a range of $40 to $120 a day). Home health and adult day-care services, which are often preferred by older adults and their families, are usually reimbursed at 50 to 80 percent of the selected nursing home benefit, although home health services have expanded in recent years (Miller and Cohen, 2001). Indeed, high-quality policies cost as much as $2,500 annually when purchased at age 67 and $7,700 for those age 79. The high premiums and copayments mean that most policies are out of the financial reach of up to 20 percent of Americans age 55 to 79. The policies are expensive for two reasons: most are sold individually and therefore carry high administrative costs, and most are bought by older people whose risk of needing long-term care is great. Given these costs, only 10 to 20 percent of older people can afford private long-term care insurance (Mellor, 2000). As with health insurance generally, women are less likely than men to be able to afford long-term care insurance, and they spend a higher proportion of their income when they do, reflecting both gaps in coverage and their lower median income (Moen, 2001). The age when a policy is first purchased is important, because the premium paid, although it remains level once the policy is purchased, rises sharply with age when it is first purchased.

The cost of private long-term care insurance can be deducted from federal income taxes, but this benefits only those with higher-income levels who can take deductions. Not surprisingly, people who are most likely to purchase and benefit from long-term care insurance are those:

- in relatively good health, that is, without serious preexisting chronic conditions
- in their 60s
- with higher income and assets

- with higher educational levels
- with a partner to protect
- and without children living nearby, although informal networks have little overall effect on whether one purchases long-term care insurance (Cohen, 2003; Cohen and Miller, 2001).

Given the restrictions and costs of such insurance and widely held misperceptions that Medicare will cover long-term care, it is not surprising that only about 6 percent of Americans of all ages have long-term care insurance (Barrett and Roper, 2001; Grogan and Patashnik, 2003). This number is likely to grow in the future, however, with the greater purchasing power of the baby boomers, states' tax incentives for the purchase of long-term care insurance and benefits for state employees, workplace education to encourage long-term care planning by employees, and younger policyholders who want to guarantee their retirement lifestyle by protecting their accumulated retirement assets (Childs, 2001). Nevertheless, private long-term care insurance is likely to remain beyond the reach of the majority of the middle class (Cohen, 2003; Yakoboski, 2002).

Resultant Inequities

Because public funding is biased toward institutional and acute care, and private policies are beyond the financial reach of most low-income elders, a *two-tier system of health care delivery* has resulted: one level for those with private health insurance or the means to pay for expensive medical treatment, and another for those forced to rely on Medicaid or Veterans' Assistance, or to do without health care altogether.

Even with Medicare recipients, there are disparities. Older people who have Medicare only, many of whom may be near-poor, tend to have fewer doctor visits and hospital stays, and buy fewer prescription medications than those who can afford cost-sharing provisions and other private insurance. In fact, low-income Medicare beneficiaries are nearly twice as likely to delay getting

> **OUT-OF-POCKET HEALTH EXPENDITURES BY SOCIOECONOMIC CLASS**
>
> - Fifty-four percent of the annual income of poor older Americans goes toward fee-for-service health care.
> - Forty-eight percent of the annual income of poor older Americans goes toward Health Maintenance (HMOs).
> - Eight percent of the annual income for those with Medicaid goes toward health care.
> - Poor older Americans spend 35 percent of their income on acute care compared to 10 percent of income for middle- and upper-class families (above 400 percent of poverty) (Rowland et al., 1998).

care than those with private or Medicaid coverage to supplement Medicare (Black and Kominski, 2001). Not surprisingly, the proportion of income spent on health care increases as income decreases.

Medicaid also perpetuates class inequities. In fact, less than 50 percent of all low-income Medicare beneficiaries benefit from Medicaid's financial protection. Inequities are intensified for elders of color who tend to underutilize services that could enhance their health. Even in programs designed for the poor, such as Medicaid, elders of color are represented far less than their reported objective needs indicate. Such low participation levels in Medicaid are attributed to lack of awareness and understanding of the assistance provided by Medicaid, complex enrollment processes, limited outreach activities by federal and state governments, and reluctance to apply for help from a welfare-linked program. Fortunately, some providers are recognizing the need for targeted outreach to underserved populations, as illustrated in the box on page 651.

Other major barriers include physicians who refuse to take Medicaid patients, especially those with a high level of need. This occurs because Medicaid reimbursement rates are generally below prevailing cost levels. Physicians who accept Medicaid patients typically limit them to a rela-

> ### EXAMPLES OF OUTREACH TO UNDERSERVED MEDICARE BENEFICIARIES
>
> - "Medicare University," funded by the National Asian Pacific Center on Aging, offers training workshops for providers and community leaders to update their knowledge of Medicare and other health benefits.
> - "Help for Health" bilingual booklets are available in Chinese, Khmer, Korean, Samoan, Tagalog, Tongan, and Vietnamese and are funded by the Centers for Medicare and Medicaid Services (CMS).
> - There are bilingual Websites with information on Medicare and Medicaid.
> - CMS funds pamphlets on "Dual Eligible Buy-in Programs."
> - "Voices of Minority Elderly" for consumers and advocates on Medicare and managed care issues is funded by the Kellogg Foundation.
> - These publications can be obtained through the National Asian Pacific Center on Aging (see resources, Chapter 16).
>
> SOURCE: Khamvongsa, 2000.

tively small percentage of their patient load. As noted above, Medicaid patients also must wait longer for nursing home placement than do private-pay patients. These burdens also fall disproportionately on older women and ethnic minorities. Another inequity is experienced by approximately 40 percent of the older population who have incomes that are too high to be eligible for Medicaid, yet they typically lack the resources to pay out of pocket for long-term care. Those "tweeners" who fall in this "Medicaid gap" often receive inadequate care or must depend solely on families (Wallace et al., 2001).

Health and Long-Term Care Reforms

Given these gaps, national reform in health and long-term care is widely debated. Such debates are often polarized between those advocating private-sector strategies and those who look to the public sector or some combination of public and private coverage. In some respects, the debates are not new, but rather more visible. In fact, since 1912, there have been efforts to create a program of access to health care for all Americans. Yet the United States remains the only industrialized power that does not provide some form of universal health coverage, regardless of ability to pay. Under the Clinton Administration, health care reform moved from academic debates to the legislative process, but ended in gridlock, without even modest changes in insurance industry practices. In spite of escalating costs, growing numbers of uninsured citizens, and restrictive insurance policies, attempts to change the health care system clash over the goals of cost containment and individual choice versus guaranteeing access to all. Although the majority of Americans support health care reform in the abstract and believe that government should guarantee adequate health care for all, they are generally satisfied with their own care. Their ambivalence is expressed further by their overall unwillingness to accept government interference and any restriction of their own choice of doctors or hospitals, even if doing so would reduce health care costs or make universal coverage possible.

What ultimately killed national health care reform was the disproportionate influence of powerful special-interest lobbies, particularly insurance companies and small businesses that sought to protect their financial interests and ways of doing business. Today, for all intents and purposes, fundamental health care reform at the national level is a "dead" issue. Nevertheless, the growing alliance between senior organizations, such as AARP, and groups serving other populations requiring long-term care has been a positive development, despite the current lack of a successful outcome.

Although major changes in long-term care have been stalled at the national level, most states have moved to plan, finance, and implement their

HISTORY AND STATUS OF NATIONAL LONG-TERM CARE LEGISLATION

- **1988:** The first comprehensive long-term care legislation was introduced by the late Florida Representative Claude Pepper, who linked an initiative to fund long-term care in the home to the ill-fated catastrophic health care legislation.
- **1990:** The Pepper Commission recommended public funding of home, community, and nursing home care for seriously disabled Americans.
- **1992:** The Democratic leadership in the House and the Senate introduced bills for long-term care known as the Long Term Care Family Security Act.
- **1992:** Bill Clinton was the first presidential candidate to call for expanded public funding for home care services provided on a non–means-tested basis.
- **1990–94:** The National Committee to Preserve Social Security and Medicare and the Leadership Council of Aging Organizations proposed universal and comprehensive long-term care plans for all people with disabilities; this encompassed institutional, home- and community-based care, and personal assistance.
- **1993:** President Clinton's National Health Security Act offered new long-term care benefits and set forth the principles of universal access, comprehensive health care benefits, and high-quality care, but was not passed.
- **2000:** Long-Term Care Security Act enables federal employees to purchase long-term care insurance at group rates.

more quickly to achieve the goals of competitiveness and reduced costs, largely through managed health care (HMOs or PPOs) that provides an established package of services for enrollees for a single monthly capitated (limited) rate.

Health Maintenance Organizations (HMOs)

As noted earlier, the 1997 Balanced Budget Act created, under Medicare Choice, managed care options for older people. Medicare managed care refers to a health plan option in which Medicare beneficiaries receive care from a network of providers employed by or under contract to an HMO. Under HMOs, coverage of health care costs and delivery of health care are provided through a prepaid premium. This means that a single payment per user covers all preapproved services, rather than fee for service. Because consumers pay on a capitated basis, HMOs are intended to overcome the access barriers of fragmented funding from the consumer's perspective for packaged services. As private plans, Medicare HMOs are able to

HMOs with a health promotion orientation offer exercise programs as a benefit.

own long-term care packages. They often did so to overcome the bias in federal funding toward institutional care, to contain costs, and to address the growing numbers of individuals who lack access to adequate care. In addition, states such as Washington and Oregon have dramatically restructured their long-term care delivery system, primarily by consolidating their financing and delivery systems into more streamlined and coordinated administrative structures (Burwell et al., 1996). At the same time, the market has moved

limit paperwork on claims forms and typically offer broader services such as prevention, education, eyeglasses, hearing aids, health promotion, and prescription drug coverage—in addition to a traditional Medicare benefits package. Most plans offer these benefits for no additional premiums and limit co-payments. However, enrollees cannot choose their own doctors, hospitals, or service providers. Financial incentives encourage providers to be efficient in getting the necessary services to patients. While HMOs have been able to negotiate lower prices from health providers, they assume the risk of providing the full range of Medicare-covered services in return for a fixed payment that approximates 95 percent of the costs for similar enrollees in fee-for-service systems. As a result, most HMOs try to avoid enrolling elders with disability conditions that are ongoing and expensive to treat and typically serve primarily younger, healthier populations (Olson, 2003; Rice, Snyder, Kominski, and Pourat, 2002).

To reduce costs, some HMOs have shortened hospital stays, set upper limits on the number of home care visits and rehabilitative services, steadily increased out-of-pocket beneficiary costs, canceled or placed caps on special benefits that initially attracted beneficiaries (e.g., coverage of prescription drugs, eyeglasses and hearing aids). This has resulted in a troubling pattern of reducing services, terminating plans, and dropping beneficiaries. In a growing number of HMOs, elders have withdrawn because of this pattern (Barry and Kline, 2002; HWM, 2001; Olson, 2003).

Because HMOs are a capitated system and thus charge a fixed payment per beneficiary, costs to Medicare are presumed to be more predictable. Findings are mixed on whether Medicare expenditures are decreased under HMOs. After controlling for factors such as health status, some studies find that the costs to Medicare associated with HMO enrollment are actually *higher* than through Medicare per se. This is because Medicare only "saves" 5 percent on each HMO participant, since the capitated rate is set at 95

percent of the expected expenditure level. HMO Medicare enrollment is associated with reduced health care utilization (e.g., hospital length of stay), but this may result from HMO beneficiaries being healthier than the average older adult. This means HMOs may selectively attract and contract with enrollees who are healthier than average, or have fewer propensities to use health services, and thus lower than expected costs. As a result, they may skim off enrollees who would never have cost Medicare the estimated expenditure level even if they had remained in the regular fee-for-service part of Medicare. When this occurs, Medicare is not saving dollars under the HMO program (Baker, 2000; Newhouse, Buntin, and Chapman, 1997). Thus, managed care does not necessarily deliver promised cost savings nor reduce the regulatory burden on government (Oberlander, 1997).

A greater concern is that chronically ill elders within HMOs may be denied benefits and access to care (Dallek, 1998; Stone and Niefeld, 1998). While the effects on quality of care are unclear, critics fear that incentives are greater to reduce costs than to improve quality (Berenson and Dowd, 2002; Escarce, Shea, and Chen, 1997; Miller and Luft, 1997). Consumers in HMOs are also less satisfied with their care than those utilizing the fee-for-service system. But these same people are more satisfied with their out-of-pocket expenses being reduced as a result of their HMO membership. Regulatory procedures to ensure quality care in HMOs are needed, especially in light of the financial incentives for managed care plans under the 2003 prescription drug bill.

Social Health Maintenance Organizations (SHMOs) and Other Model Innovative Programs

Because of growing awareness of the inadequacies of the current system, there is increasing policy interest in bringing the acute-care and long-term care sectors together into a single integrated system. Some of the best known of these initiatives are

Social Health Maintenance Organizations (SHMOs), On Lok, and The Program for All-inclusive Care for the Elderly (PACE). SHMOs are demonstration projects initiated in 1985 by the Health Care Financing Administration (HCFA). As prepaid health plans, they try to integrate acute and long-term care to voluntarily enrolled Medicare beneficiaries. They offer all Medicare benefits, as well as home and community-based care, prescription drugs, and case management to support beneficiaries' social needs. SHMOs test whether comprehensive health services with social services linking acute and chronic care under an integrated financing scheme within a managed care setting can (1) be provided at a cost that does not exceed the public costs of Medicare and Medicaid; (2) improve medical care; and (3) reduce nursing home placement. In other words, they are examining the relative cost-effectiveness of a capitated payment system that includes chronic and extended benefits and medical services. SHMOs have the following characteristics:

- A single organizational structure that provides a full range of acute and chronic care services to voluntarily enrolled Medicare beneficiaries.
- A coordinated case management system authorizes services for members who meet disability criteria.
- Designed to reach a cross-section of older people, they try to spread the risk of service use over a representative population (5000 to 10,000 at each site).
- Financing is through prepaid capitation by pooling funds from Medicare, Medicaid, and member premiums.

The Centers for Medicare and Medicaid Services (CMS) funded a second generation of SHMOs that set reimbursement rates based on an individual's impairment and illness profile at the time of enrollment and annually thereafter. By establishing geriatric health programs for all enrollees, CMS aimed to better coordinate acute care with a set of flexible, user-friendly and efficient long-term care

services. SHMOs, however, have faced ongoing difficulties in controlling and coordinating acute and chronic care (Wallace et al., 2001). In fact, a 2001 CMS report found few significant outcomes in terms of utilization, health status, and slowing of decline in functional ability. They recommended that the SHMO demonstration be phased out or transitioned, perhaps to a standard Medicare Plus Choice (Wooldridge et al., 2001).

Another model tested in a wide range of communities is San Francisco's On Lok model of social care. **On Lok** aims to integrate a full continuum of acute and chronic care into one agency, and thus to prevent institutionalization of frail elders who are certified as needing a nursing home level of care. As a capitated system, On Lok is paid a flat amount for each person served, similar to the way that HMOs are paid. A comprehensive day health program is integrated with home care, including nursing, social work, meals, transportation, personal care, homemaker, and respite care. The On Lok model is effective at serving low-income and elders of color in their communities and is widely replicated to varying degrees nationwide.

The **Program for the All-inclusive Care for the Elderly (PACE)** replicates aspects of On Lok and differs from SHMOs by its focus on only a relatively small number of frail elders (120–300 per site) who are eligible for nursing home placement. It has nearly 20 years of experience fully integrating medical, home-based, and community-based care in a small, managed-care model. "One-door access" is provided to a comprehensive care package of preventive, acute, and long-term care services. Programs must provide basic Medicare and Medicaid services, but have flexibility to use less typical interventions, including activities such as fishing trips and drama groups, as well as educational or preventive activities. Interdisciplinary teams of physicians, nurses, social workers, aides, therapists and even van drivers coordinate their care through adult day health centers and case management at predetermined reimbursement rates. In effect, PACE is built

CHARACTERISTICS OF INTEGRATED SERVICES

- broad, flexible benefits (primary, acute, and long-term care)
- far-reaching delivery systems that encompass community-based long-term care, care management, and specialty providers
- mechanisms that coordinate various services, such as care management and care planning protocols, interdisciplinary care teams, centralized records, and integrated information systems
- overarching quality control and management information systems with a single point of accountability
- flexible funding that enables pooling of funds and has incentives to integrate funding streams and minimize cost shifting (Booth, Fralich, Saucie, and Mollica, 1997)

around the day health model, which combines primary care with long-term care. To date, evaluations of both On Lok and PACE reveal cost savings to Medicare and Medicaid, as well as success in integrating the delivery of acute and long-term care across both the Medicare and Medicaid programs (Lynch et al., 2003). Despite its success, PACE has reached only about 10,000 Medicare beneficiaries. Such model programs that aim to control costs and integrate services need to be expanded across both the Medicare and Medicaid programs to a larger population.

Unfortunately, a wide range of barriers make service integration difficult to achieve:

- lack of a national policy or program on long-term care; responsibility is left to individuals and families
- fragmentation of funding sources, especially Medicare and Medicaid
- different eligibility requirements and coverage rules that impede the development of a rational plan of care
- fear of financial risk on the part of providers involved in integrating acute and long-term care

- lack of training and knowledge among providers on how to coordinate and manage an array of services
- lack of communication between acute and long-term care providers
- no recognized authority for managing care across time, place, and profession
- absence of management information systems and patient data bases that span time and place

States are also attempting to integrate acute and long-term care, especially for the population that is "dual eligible" for both Medicare and Medicaid. Some are experimenting with innovative financing and service delivery of acute and long-term care for older people on Medicaid and younger people with disabilities. However, gaps in care are unlikely to be filled by the states' share of Medicaid and by programs funded entirely by states (Stone, 2000). In addition, some providers are attempting to create integrated service systems, in part for altruistic reasons and in part for market incentives. Hospitals are integrating vertically—buying nursing homes, rehabilitation centers, and home health agencies—in an effort to become an all-purpose provider in the community. Skilled nursing facilities and, to some extent,

AN EXAMPLE OF PROVIDERS' INTEGRATED CARE PLANS

The National Chronic Care Consortium (NCCC) is an alliance of over 30 nonprofit health systems that share a vision of integrated care. Member organizations serve as laboratories for establishing chronic-care networks. It advocates the creation of integrated administration, information, financing, and care management arrangements to help providers work together to minimize costs while maximizing the long-term health of the populations being served. It has developed the Self-Assessment for Systems Integration, funded by the John A. Hartford Foundation, that identifies nine key objectives for chronic care integration.

home health agencies are integrating horizontally—building alliances with hospitals, physicians groups, assisted living developers, and other community-based providers. Some models of managed care for nursing home residents are also developing. Aiming to reduce hospitalization rates of nursing home residents, The Ever Care program enrolls residents in a risk-based HMO, with nursing home costs covered by Medicaid or private insurance. It is distinguished by a team of geriatricians and nurse practitioners that offer intensive primary care services that are coordinated with long-term care services provided by nurses and nurses' assistants. To date, savings from shorter hospital stays have been realized (Lynch et al., 2003).

A promising direction is the growth of consumer-directed care, where older adults and adults with disabilities take an active part in choosing their own care (Polivka, 2000). This model is described in the box below.

In most programs funded at a state level under Medicaid waivers, consumers take on all worker management tasks with the exception of paying the worker. Medicaid-funded programs must comply with the federal rule that prohibits Medicaid beneficiaries from receiving their benefits in cash (Tilly and Wiener, 2001). However, demonstration projects funded by the Kellogg Foundation have implemented and evaluated cash and counseling programs in three states: Arkansas, Florida, and New Jersey. Recipients of Medicaid personal care or home and community-based services receive a cash allowance based on a professional assessment, which varies by state and ranges from $400 to $1400. The cash allowances received are comparable to the value of services that would be provided through traditional agencies. However, consumers have their own budget to purchase personal care instead of receiving it from an agency. Some become employers, choosing to hire (and fire) family or friends as workers; the states provide bookkeepers to assist with the paperwork. Because they have control of their budget, they can decide whether to use funds to make their home more accessible, buy a pair of dentures, pay for over-the-counter medications, or pay a grandson to mow their lawn. Counselors or consultants are available to assist them with decision-making, but the consumer retains control over the final decision. Preliminary findings are that those who received a cash allowance were able to purchase more services to fit their needs than would be available to them under traditional programs; institutional costs were lower; Medicaid costs per recipient per month were identical for both the cash and counseling group and a control group; and being able to hire their own caregivers was the primary variable associated with satisfaction and quality of life (Cash and Counseling Demonstration and Evaluation Program, 2003; Stone, 2003). Even when consumers cannot hire their caregivers, satisfaction with consumer-directed care is high (Polivka, 2000; Wamsley, Eggert, and Sead, 2002).

Agreement is emerging about the major components of an ideal long-term care system, but, as noted above, there is not the national political will to achieve it. These components include:

- integrated administration, information, and financing
- integrated acute and long-term care
- easy access at a single point of entry

UNDERLYING VALUES AND ASSUMPTIONS OF CONSUMER-DIRECTED CARE

- Adults requiring long-term care have a right and ability to make decisions about their care.
- Consumers are experts about their service needs and are capable of managing their own affairs; they have the right to "manage their own risk."
- The dignity of the consumer who needs personal assistance is preserved.
- Choice and control can be introduced into all service delivery systems.
- Consumer-directed care should be available to all persons needing long-term care, regardless of the payer (public or private).
- It can level the playing field between institutional and home and community-based care.

- case or care management
- uniform client needs assessment
- home- and community-based care
- nonmedical social services
- supportive housing

Clearly, health care has shifted from a system oriented toward acute care, independent providers, and fee-for-service insurance to one that is focused on chronic care, disability prevention, and managed care. Because of market changes and the growth of managed care, these patterns of consolidation and cost savings will continue at the local level. This will occur even without the passage of national legislation to ensure health and long-term care as a right, regardless of income or age. As noted earlier, the current dichotomy between long-term care and acute care is not functional for either older persons or care providers, since long-term care is a health crisis for which virtually every American is uninsured. From the perspective of older people, an ideal is a national health plan that integrates preventive, acute, hospital, ambulatory, community-based, and home care to ensure continuity of care across the life span. In the short run, however, legislation at the federal level will be focused on ways to reduce Medicare and Medicaid expenditures, on delegating more financing responsibility to the state level, and on funding demonstrations that attempt to integrate acute and long-term care.

Implications for the Future

Long-term care is characterized by the lack of a comprehensive policy, resulting in fragmentation, segmentation, and often-bitter debates among advocates for various services. Past changes have focused on short-term fixes and responding to fiscal and regulatory concerns, particularly those of providers. Without dramatic changes in how long-term care is delivered, costs will continue to escalate both for the individual and for society as a whole.

Although concerns about the costs of long-term care are widespread, there are many unresolved issues regarding potential solutions. Currently, the prospects for a comprehensive health and long-term care reform bill that guarantees universal access along with cost containment are virtually nil. As noted in Chapter 16, the economy and political factors profoundly shape public policy. The sluggish economy early in this century, the federal and state emphasis on cost containment, and the Republican political dominance suggest that cost-cutting of programs, especially Medicaid, and subsidies for private market solutions to address long-term care are likely to dominate the national agenda. The 2003 prescription drug bill represents a profound shift toward privatization and means testing of what had been a universal program based on age. The reduced governmental responsibility and increasing reliance on private sector solutions could shift in the future as political parties and the economy change.

Although the future of long-term care is difficult to predict because of political and economic shifts and rapid changes in health care, we do know that the following factors will continue to shape the need for long-term care:

- the growing numbers of elders who rely on family caregivers for the majority of long-term care
- the preference of elders for home and community-based care
- senior boomers' preference for choice and having more say about health care for themselves and their older relatives
- the human tendency to avoid planning in the event of disability or frailty, thus denying the need for long-term care
- the importance of long-term care models that are culturally congruent and sensitive
- the growth of for-profit home health care, but the need for publicly funded, comprehensive, coordinated, and accessible in-home and community-based supportive services

- nursing homes becoming more like hospitals that provide rehabilitation and short-term skilled nursing
- the emphasis on ambulatory care rather than hospitalization and the growth of managed care
- the growth of information technology as a way to provide information to consumers and to provide medical care to underserved areas
- the need for more health care professionals trained in geriatrics
- the long-term care industry as a major employer of low-income people, who increasingly are immigrants who may have cultural and language differences with the elders under their care

Given these contextual factors, the need for public/private partnerships for long-term care insurance, service delivery, and accountability is critical. An ideal model might be a social insurance approach that involves lifelong, intergenerational sharing and paying for risks of frailty. However, partisan debates about the role of government versus the marketplace and private sector; the modes of service delivery; and societal responsibility toward vulnerable low-income elders suggest that incremental compromises are the most we can expect in the near future.

Summary

The growing health and long-term care expenditures by both federal and state governments and by older people and their families are a source of concern for most Americans. Escalating hospital and physician costs have placed enormous pressures on Medicare—the financing mechanism through which almost half of the funds for the older population's acute care flows. The government's primary response to these Medicare costs has been cost-containment, especially through diagnostic-related groupings (DRGs), financial incentives for shortening the hospital stays of Medicare patients, greater deductibles and copayments, and cuts in Medicare funding. Efforts have also been made to provide more choices for Medicare recipients, including managed care or HMO options. For most older adults, Medicare fails to provide adequate protection against the costs of home- and community-based care. In fact, changes in Medicare funding have affected the availability of nonprofit home care agencies. They have also meant that more older persons and their families have either had to pay privately for home care or do without. As a rapidly growing portion of the federal budget, Medicare is under intense scrutiny. The prescription drug bill that became law in 2003 attempts to address the problem of rising prescription drug costs, but does so by subsidizing private plans and altering the universal nature of Medicare.

Medicare is the major payment source of hospital and physician care for older adults, but it is almost absent from nursing home financing. The reverse applies to Medicaid, however. The largest portion of the Medicaid dollar goes to services needed by older persons, but not covered by Medicare—nursing home, home and personal care, and prescription drugs. However, as Medicaid has been increasingly subject to cost-cutting measures at the state level, benefits have been reduced. For example, copayments for health care services have increased as a way to reduce Medicaid spending, but this cost is borne disproportionately by low-income elders. Another disadvantage for Medicaid recipients is that most nursing homes and doctors limit the number of Medicaid recipients they will accept. Although waivers by the federal government have allowed state funding of some community-based alternatives to institutionalization, Medicaid remains biased toward nursing home care. Title XX and Older Americans Act programs have relatively flat funding levels and are limited in impact. Given the gaps in public funding for long-term care, private insurers are offering long-term care insurance options, but these are beyond the financial reach of most older adults.

GLOSSARY

capitated payments payments for services based on a predetermined amount per person per day rather than fees for services

Centers for Medicare and Medicaid Services (CMS) the federal agency that administers the Medicare and Medicaid programs

Health Maintenance Organizations (HMOs) health plans that combine coverage of health care costs and delivery of health care for a prepaid premium, with members typically receiving services from personnel employed by or under contract to the HMO

long-term care insurance private insurance designed to cover the costs of institutional and sometimes home-based service for people with chronic disabilities

managed care policies under which patients are provided health care services under the supervision of a single professional, usually a physician

Medicaid a federal and state means-tested welfare program of medical assistance for the categorically needy, regardless of age

medical savings accounts proposed Medicare program that will allow beneficiaries to carry private "catastrophic" insurance for serious illness and pay routine costs from a special account

Medicare the social insurance program, part of the Social Security Act of 1965, intended to provide financial protection against the cost of hospital and physician care for people age 65 and over

Medicare Choice starting in 2002, Medicare beneficiaries can choose between traditional Medicare and a Choice Plan that includes HMOs

On Lok a comprehensive program of health and social services provided to very frail older adults, first started in San Francisco, with the goal of preventing or delaying institutionalization by maintaining these adults in their homes

PACE federal demonstration program that replicated On Lok's integrated services to attempt to prevent institutionalization

Preferred Provider Organizations (PPOs) networks of independent physicians, hospitals, and other health care providers who contract with an insurance entity to provide care at discounted rates

prospective-payment system (PPS) a system of reimbursing hospitals and physicians based on the diagnostic category of the patient rather than fees for each service provided, as applied to inpatient services

Social Health Maintenance Organizations (SHMOs) prepaid health plans that provide both acute and long-term care to voluntarily enrolled Medicare beneficiaries

spend down to use up assets for personal needs, especially health care, in order to become qualified for Medicaid

subacute care intensive health services to patients after a hospital stay

RESOURCES

See the companion Website for this text at <www .ablongman.com/hooyman> for information about the following:

- American Health Care Association
- American Medical Directors Association
- American Physical and Occupational Therapy Association. (Section on Geriatrics)
- Committee to Preserve Social Security and Medicare
- Families USA
- Medical Matrix: Geriatrics
- Medicare
- National Association for Home Care (NAHC)
- National Association of Directors of Nursing in Long Term Care (NADONAILTC)
- National Association of Professional Geriatric Care Managers
- National Citizen's Coalition for Nursing Home Reform (NCCNHR)
- National Council on Aging
- Women's Institute for a Secure Retirement

REFERENCES

Abramson, K. B. Understanding the world of managed care: Opportunities and obstacles for rehabilitation teams. *Topics in Stroke Rehabilitation*, 1998, *5*, 1–10.

Adams, A. S., Soumerai, S. B., and Ross-Degnan, D. The case for a Medicare drug coverage benefit: A critical review of the empirical evidence. *Annual Review of Public Health,* 2001, *22,* 49–61.

Almanac of Policy Issues. Medicare. 2003. http://www.policyalmanac.org/health/medicare/shtml

American Association of Retired Persons (AARP). Across the states: Profiles of long-term care systems. (Bulletin 41, 10.) Washington, DC: Public Policy Institute, 2000.

American Association of Retired Persons (AARP). *Reforming the health care system: State Profiles 2001,* Washington, DC: author, 2001.

Baker, L. C. Association of managed care market share and health expenditures for fee-for-service Medicare patients. *Journal of the American Medical Association,* 1999, *281,* 432–437.

Barrett, L. L., and Roper, A. *Costs of long-term care: Public perceptions vs. reality.* Washington, DC: AARP, 2001.

Barry, C. L., and Kline, J. Medicare managed care: *Medicare+choice at five years.* New York: Commonwealth Fund, 2002.

Berenson, R. A., and Dowd, R. E. *Future of private plan contracting in Medicare.* Washington, DC: Public Policy Institute, AARP, 2002.

Berenson, R. A., and Horvath, J. Confronting the barriers to chronic care management in Medicare. *Health Affairs,* 2003, *22,* W337–W353.

Bernstein, J. *Restructuring Medicare: Values and policy options.* Washington, DC: National Academy of Social Insurance, 1997.

Bishop, C. Long-term care needs of elders and persons with disability. In D. Bluementhal, M. Moon, M. Warshawksky, and C. Boccuti (Eds.), *Long-term care and Medicare policy: Can we improve the continuity of care?* Washington, DC: National Academy of Social Insurance, 2003.

Black, G. F., and Kominski, G. F. Medicare reform. In R. Anderson, T. H. Rice, and G. F. Kominski, *Changing the U.S. health care system: Key issues in health services, policy and management.* New York: Jossey-Bass, 2001.

Booth, M., Fralich, J., Saucie, P., and Mollica, R. *Integration of acute and long-term care for dually eligible beneficiaries through managed care.* Robert Wood Johnson Foundation Medicare/Medicaid Integration Program, 1997.

Branch, L. G. Community long-term care services: What works and what doesn't? *The Gerontologist,* 2001, *41,* 305–306.

Brown, S. *Growth in Medicare and out-of-pocket spending: Impact on vulnerable beneficiaries.* New York: The Commonwealth Fund, 2001.

Bryce, D. V., and Friedland, R. B. *Economic and health security: An overview of the origins of federal legislation.* Washington, DC: The National Academy on Aging, January 16, 1997.

Burwell, B. Medicaid long-term care expenditures in fiscal year 2000. *The Gerontologist,* 2001, *41,* 687–691.

Burwell, B., Crown, W. H., O'Shaugnessy, C., and Price, R. Financing long-term care. In C. J. Evashwick (Ed.), *The continuum of long-term care: An integrated systems approach.* Albany, NY: Delmar Publishers, 1996.

Cardin, B. National policy-makers on long-term care policy. In D. Bluementhal, M. Moon, M. Warshawksky, and C. Boccuti (Eds.), *Long-term care and Medicare policy: Can we improve the continuity of care?* Washington, DC: National Academy of Social Insurance, 2003.

Cash and Counseling Demonstration and Evaluation Program. Boston: Boston College Graduate School of Social Work, 2003.

Childs, N. LTC insurance market growing younger, survey shows. *Provider,* 2001, *27,* 11.

Chaddock, G. R. New world of Medicare may be hard to navigate. *The Seattle Times,* November 23, 2003, 1, A4.

Cohen, M. A. Private long-term care insurance: A look ahead. *Journal of Aging and Health,* 2003, *15,* 74–98.

Cohen, M. A., and Miller, J. Patterns of informal and formal caregiving among elders with private long-term care insurance. *The Gerontologist,* 2001, *41,* 180–187.

Crenshaw, A. B. Medicare bill could spur changes in worker benefits. From the *Washington Post* and printed in *The Seattle Times,* November 28, 2003, D1.

Dallek, G. Shopping for managed care: The Medicare market, *Generations,* Summer 1998, *22,* 19–23.

Eng, C., Pedullo, J., Eleazer, G. P., McCann, R., and Fox, N. Program of all-inclusive care for the elderly (PACE): An innovative model of integrated geriatric care and financing. *Journal of the American Geriatrics Society,* 1997, *45,* 223–232.

Escarce, J. J., Shea J. A., and Chen, W. Segmentation of hospital markets: Where do HMO enrollees get care? *Health Affairs,* 1997, *16,* 181–192.

Evashwick, C. J. (Ed.), *The continuum of long-term care: An integrated systems approach* (2nd ed.). Albany, NY: Delmar Publishers, 2001.

Families, USA. *Bitter pill: The rising prices of prescription drugs for older Americans.* Washington, DC: 2002.

Federal Interagency Forum on Aging and Related Statistics. *Older Americans 2000: Key indicators of well-being.* Hyattsville, MD: Federal Interagency Forum on Aging and Related Statistics, 2000.

Feder, J., Komisar, H. L., and Niefeld, M. The financing and organization of health care. In R. Binstock and L. K. George (Eds.), *Handbook of aging and the social sciences.* San Diego: Academic Press, 2001.

Feder, J., Kolmisar, H. L., and Niefeld, M. *Long-term care in the United States: An overview.* Commonwealth Fund International Symposium on Health Care Policy, October 1999, Washington, DC.

Feder, J., and Moon, M. Managed care for the elderly: A threat or a promise? *Generations,* Summer 1998, 6–10.

Gage, B. The history and growth of Medicare managed care. *Generations,* Summer 1998, 11–18.

Gage, B. Medicare home health: An update. *The Public Policy and Aging Report,* 1998, Vol. 9, 12–15.

Gaumer, G. L., Poggio, E. L., Coelen, C. G., Sennett, C. S., and Schmitz, R. J. Effects of state prospective reimbursement programs on hospital mortality. *Medical Care,* 1989, *27,* 724–736.

Gold, M., and Achman, L. *Medicare + Choice 1999–2001: An analysis of managed care plan withdrawals and trends in benefits and premiums.* New York: The Commonwealth Fund, 2002.

Goldstein, A., and Dewar, H. AARP backs prescription drug plan. From the *Washington Post* and printed in the *Seattle Times,* November 18, 2003, A4.

Gregory, S. R., and Gibson, M. J. *Across the states: Profiles of long-term care* (5th ed.). Washington, DC: Public Policy Institute, 2002.

Grogan, C. M., and Patashnik, E. M. Universalism within targeting: Nursing home care, the middle class and the politics of the Medicaid program. *Social Service Review,* 2003, *77,* 51–71.

Gross, D. Medicare beneficiaries and prescription drugs: Costs and coverage. *AARP Issue Brief,* Washington, DC: AARP Public Policy, 2002.

Hing, E. Effects of the prospective payment systems on nursing homes. *Vital health statistics.* Hyattsville, MD: National Center for Health Statistics, 1989.

Hughes, S. C., Ulasevich, A., Weaver, F., Henderson, W., Manheim, L., Kubal, J., and Bonango, F. Impact of home care on hospital days: A meta analysis. *Health Services Research,* 1997, *32,* 416–431.

Kaiser Family Foundation, The Commonwealth Fund, Tufts-New England Medical Center. *Seniors and prescription drugs: Findings from a 2001 survey of seniors in eight states.* (Publication #6049). www.kff.org. Menlo Park, CA: The Kaiser Family Foundation, 2002.

Kane, R. A. Kane, R. L. and Ladd, R. C. *The heart of long-term care.* New York: Oxford University Press, 1998.

Kane, R. L., and Kane, R. A. Emerging issues in chronic care. In R. Binstock and L. K. George (Eds.), *Handbook of aging and the social sciences* (5th ed.). San Diego: Academic Press, 2001.

Khamvongsa, C. Translated Help for Health books reach thousands. *Asian Pacific Affairs Newsletter,* National Asian Pacific Center on Aging, February 2000, *1,* 10.

Komisar, H. L., and Feder, J. *The Balanced Budget Act of 1997: Effects on Medicare's home health benefit and beneficiaries who need long-term care.* New York: The Commonwealth Fund, 1998.

Komisar, H. L., and Feder, J. *Medicare Chart Book,* Washington, DC.: Institute for Health Care Research and Policy, 1997.

Landi, F., Gambassi, G., Pola, R.,, Tabaccanti, S., Cavinato, T., Carbonin, P., and Bernabei, R. Impact of integrated home care services on hospital use. *Journal of the American Geriatrics Society,* 1999, *47,* 1430–1434.

Langwell, K. M., and Moser, J. W. Strategies for Medicare health plans serving racial and ethnic minorities. *Health Care Financing Review,* 2002, *23,* 131–147.

Lieberman, T. Feeling the squeeze. *AARP Bulletin,* 2003, (October), 8–10.

Lynch, M., Estes, C., and Hernandez, M. Chronic care initiatives: What we have learned and implications for the Medicare program. In D. Bluementhal, M.

Moon, M. Warshawksky, and C. Boccuti (Eds.), *Long-term care and Medicare policy: Can we improve the continuity of care?* Washington, DC: National Academy of Social Insurance, 2003.

McCall, N., and Korb, J. *The impact of Medicare home health policy changes on Medicare beneficiaries.* Princeton, NJ: Robert Wood Johnson Foundation, Home Care Research Initiative, 2003.

McCloskey, A. High price of prescription drugs and its impact on the elderly. *Care Management Journal,* 2002, *3,* 143–153.

Mellor, J. M. Filling in the gaps in long-term care insurance. In M. H. Meyer (Ed.), *Care work: Gender, labor, and welfare states* (pp. 202–217). New York: Routledge, 2000.

Mellor, J. M. Long-term care and nursing home coverage: Are adult children substitutes for insurance policies? *Journal of Health and Economics,* 2001, *20*(4), 527–547.

Meyer, M. H., and Storbakken, M. Shifting the burden back to families? In M. H. Meyer (Ed.), *Care work: Gender, labor, and welfare states.* New York: Routledge, 2000.

Miller, J. S., and Cohen, M. A. Private LTC insurance: The home care claimant experience. *Caring,* 2001, *20,* 12–15.

Miller, R., and Luft, H. Managed care performance: Is quality of care better or worse? *Health Affairs,* 1997, *16,* 7–25.

Moen, P. The gendered life course. In R. H. Binstock and L. K. George (Eds.), *Handbook of aging and the social sciences* (5th ed.). San Diego, CA: Academic Press, 2001.

Mollica, R. Coordinating services across the continuum of health, housing, and supportive services. *Journal of Aging and Health,* 2003, *15,* 165–188.

Moody, H. Should we ration health care for older people? In H. Moody, *Aging concepts and controversies* (4th ed.). Walnut Creek, CA: Pine Forge Press, 2002.

Moon, M. *Medicare now and in the future* (2nd ed.). Washington, DC: The Urban Institute Press, 1996.

Moses, S. A. Long-term care choice: A simple, cost-free solution to the long-term care financing puzzle. *The Public Policy and Aging Report.* Washington, DC: National Academy on an Aging Society, Gerontological Society of America, 1998.

National Academy on Aging. *Facts on long-term care.* Washington, DC: The National Academy on Aging, 1997a.

National Committee to Preserve Social Security and Medicine. *Medicare Managed Care,* Washington, DC: 1999.

National Committee to Preserve Social Security and Medicare. *Passages: Planning for long-term care.* Washington, DC, February 2000.

National Committee to Preserve Social Security and Medicare. *Congress warned on changes needed to Medicare Rx Bill for support of key senior groups.* Letter submitted to the House and Senate, July 16, 2003.

Nauth, K. K. Stay-at-home subsidies. *Secure Retirement,* 2002, *11,* 12+.

Newhouse, J. P., Buntin, M. B., and Chapman, J. D. Risk adjustment and Medicare: Taking a closer look. *Health,* 1997, *16,* 26–43.

Oberlander, J. Managed care and Medicare reform, *Journal of Health Politics, Policy and Law,* 1997, *22,* 595–631.

Olson, L. K. *The not so golden years: Caregiving, the frail elderly and the long-term care establishment.* Lantham, MD: Rowman and Littlefield, 2003.

Ostrom, C. M. Lower drug prices in Canada a prescription for outrage in U.S., *The Seattle Times,* September 5, 2000, *1,* A12.

Pear, R. Medicare debate focuses on merits of private plans. *National Desk,* June 9, 2003, 1.

Pear, R. Senate backs bill: Measure provides drug benefits for millions of elderly people. *The New York Times,* November 26, 2003, A1, A18.

Pear, R., and Toner, R. Medicare overhaul gets House victory by a whisker. From *The New York Times* and printed in the *Seattle Times,* November 23, 2003, A1, A4.

Poisal, J. A., and Murray, L. A. Growing differences between Medicare beneficiaries with and without drug coverage. *Health Affairs,* 2001, *20,* 74–85.

Polivka, L. The ethical and empirical basis for consumer-directed care for the frail elderly. *Contemporary Gerontology,* 2000, *7,* 50–52.

Redfoot, D. L., and Pandya, S. M. *Before the boom: Trends in long-term supportive care for older Americans with disabilities.* Washington, DC: Public Policy Institute, AARP, 2002.

Rice, T., Snyder, R. E., Kominski, G., and Pourat, N. Who switches from medigap to Medicare HMOs? *Health Services Research,* 2002, *37,* 273–290.

Rowland, D., Feder, J., and Keenan, P. S. Managed care for low-income elderly people. *Generations,* Summer 1998, 43–50.

Sager, M. A., Easterling, D. U., Kindig, D. A., and Anderson, O. W. Changes in the location of death after passage of Medicare's prospective payment system. *New England Journal of Medicine,* 1989, *320,* 433–439.

Sambamoorthi, U, Shea, D., and Crystal, S. Total and out of pocket expenditures for prescription drugs among older persons. *The Gerontologist,* 2003, *43,* 345–359.

Schoen, C., and Cooper, B. S. *Medicare's future: Current picture, trends, and prescription drug policy debate.* New York: The Commonwealth Fund, 2003.

Seperson, S. B. Demographics about aging. In S. B. Seperson and C. Hegeman (Eds.), *Elder care and service learning: A handbook.* Westport, CT: Auburn House, 2002.

Steinman, M. A., Sands, L. P., and Covinsky, K. E. Self-restriction of medications due to cost in seniors without prescription coverage. *Journal of Generalist Intern,* 2001, *16,* 864–866.

Stolberg, S. G., and Freudenheim, M. AARP support came as group grew "younger." *The New York Times,* November 26, 2003, 1, 1A.

Stone, R. I. *Long-term care for the elderly with disabilities: Current policy, emerging trends and implications for the twenty-first century.* New York: The Milbank Memorial Fund, 2000.

Stone, R. I. *Long-term care in Japan: A window on the future?* Washington, DC: National Academy on Aging, Gerontological Society of America, Fall 1999, *10,* 1–3.

Stone, R. L., Dawson, S. L., and Harahan, S. *Why workforce development should be part of the long-term care quality debate.* Washington, DC: Institute for the Future of Aging Services, American Association of Homes and Services for the Aging, 2003.

Stone, R. L., and Niefeld, M. R. Medicare managed care: Sinking or swimming with the tide. *Journal of Long-term Home Health Care,* 1998, *17,* 7–16.

Tilly, J., Goldenson, S., and Kasten, J. *Long term care: Consumers, providers and financing: A chart book.* Washington, DC: The Urban Institute, 2001.

Tilly, J., and Wiener, J. M. *Consumer-directed home and community services: Policy issues.* From Urban Institute, http://newfederalism.urban.org/html/op44/occa44.html.

U.S. General Accounting Office (GAO). *Historical tables.* Washington, DC: U.S. Government Printing Office, 2001a.

U.S. General Accounting Office (GAO). *Long-term care: Baby boom generation increases challenge of financing needed services.* Statement of W. J. Scanlon, Director of Health Care Issues, before the Committee of Finance, U.S. Senate, March 27, 2001. Washington, DC: U.S. Government Printing Office, 2001b.

U.S. General Accounting Office (GAO). *Medicare: Cost-sharing policies problematic for beneficiaries and program.* Statement of W. J. Scanlon, Director of Health Care Issues, May 9, 2001. Washington, DC: U.S. Government Printing Office, 2001c.

U.S. General Accounting Office (GAO). Statement of W. J. Scanlon, Director of Health Care Issues, before the Subcommittee on Health, Committee on Energy and Commerce, U.S. House, June 14, 2001. Washington, DC: U.S. Government Printing Office, 2001d.

U.S. General Accounting Office (GAO). *Nursing homes: Quality of care more related to staffing than spending,* June 13, 2002. Washington, DC: U.S. Government Printing Office, 2002.

U.S. Government, Budget of the U.S. Government. *Budget, FY 2001.* Washington, DC: U.S. Government Printing Office, 2001.

U.S. House, Committee on Ways and Means (HWM), Subcommittee on Health. *Medicare reform.* Testimony of G. F. Grob, OIG, March 15, 2001. Washington, DC: U.S. Government Printing Office, 2001.

U.S. Senate, Special Commerce on Aging. *Long-term care: States grapple with increasing demands and costs.* July 18. Washington, DC: U.S. Government Printing Office, 2001.

Voelker, R. Immediate prescription coverage in doubt for Medicare recipients. *Journal of the American Medical Association,* 2001, *285,* 1144.

Wallace, S. P., Abel, E., Stefanowicz, P., and Pourat, N. Long-term care and the elderly population. In R.

Anderson, T. H. Rice and G. F. Kominski (Eds.), *Changing the U.S. health care system: Key issues in health services, policy and management.* New York: Jossey-Bass, 2001.

Wamsley, B., Eggert, G. M., and Saad, Z. *Satisfaction with consumer-directed care approaches in an older, functionally impaired population.* http://apha.confex.com/apha/130am/techprogram/paper _35988.htm., November, 2002.

Wiener, J. M. Managed care and long-term care: The integration of financing and services. *Generations,* Summer 1996, *20,* 47–51.

Wiener, J. M., and Illston, L. H. Financing and organization of health care. In R. H. Binstock and L. K. George (Eds.), *Handbook of aging and the social sciences* (4th ed.). San Diego, CA: Academic Press, 1996.

Wiener, J. M., and Illston, L. H. Health care reform in the 1990s: Where does long-term care fit in? *The Gerontologist,* 1994, *34,* 402–408.

Wiener, J. M., Stevenson, D. G., and Kasten, J. *State cost containment initiatives for long-term care services for older people.* Washington, DC: Congressional Research Service, Library of Congress, 2000.

Woolridge, J. et al. Social Health Maintenance Organizations: Transition into Medicare + Choice. Contract 500-96-005 (2), submitted to the Health Care Financing Administration. Washington, DC, 2001.

Xu, K. T. Financial disparities in prescription drug use between elderly and nonelderly Americans. *Health Affairs,* 2003, *22,* 210–221.

Yakoboski, P. J. Understanding the motivations of long-term care insurance owners: The importance of retirement planning. *Benefits Quarterly,* 2002, *18,* 16–21.

Zitner, A. Medicare prescription drug bill wins endorsement of AARP. *Los Angeles Times,* Nov. 16, 2003, 1.

Photo Credits

INDEX